EUROPE

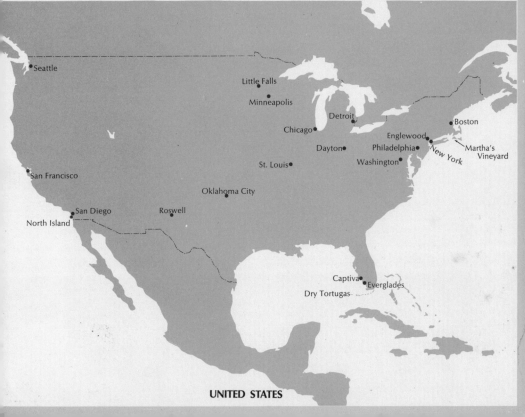

UNITED STATES

The Wartime Journals of
Charles A. Lindbergh

BOOKS BY CHARLES A. LINDBERGH

We

The Culture of Organs
(*with Alexis Carrel*)

Of Flight and Life

The Spirit of St. Louis

The Wartime Journals

The Wartime Journals of Charles A. Lindbergh

HARCOURT BRACE JOVANOVICH, INC., NEW YORK

ISBN 0-15-194625-6
Library of Congress Catalog Card Number: 78-124830
Printed in the United States of America

Contents

Illustrations

Introduction

THE quarter century that has passed since the ending of World War II has dimmed our recollection, which is reason enough for us to be interested in reading a unique record of that terrible time. But the years have also lessened our sense of certitude. The past is always compromised by the present: many of the assurances of long ago, on re-examination, turn into questions and speculations. Both the exercise of memory and the writing of history tend to make it so, however different they are in resource. The historian will attempt to read the whole record of the past so far as he is able, but since he cannot *write* the whole record, he will select those events and circumstances that accommodate his thesis or his bias or his style or whatever. Those selected items of occurrence become, as Max Weber concluded, the facts of history.

So, too, in writing of the moment, as in a diary or journal, an act of selection takes place. One must decide what was significant in the course of a day before he can keep a reasonably short record of its passing. Yet the journal becomes, in the hands of a serious and candid person, an exceptional means by which events can be depicted literally, which is to say depicted with both accuracy of account and a consistency of view. This one recognizes, casting back, in the journals of John Wesley, of Thoreau, and of General Charles ("Chinese") Gordon, among a few others. It may be seen, now, in the wartime journals of Charles A. Lindbergh, which are here published twenty-five years after the last of the entries was written.

General Lindbergh undertook to keep these journals in November of 1937 because, as he says, he recognized the portent of the time and realized, too, that he was fortunately able to speak to leaders and representatives of the world's large military powers. He kept the journals until the summer of 1945; they close with an account of his return to the broken cities of Europe. It is relevant to note that at no other extended period throughout his long career did Lindbergh maintain a daybook in this thorough manner other than during the time from 1937 to 1945.

His career as a public figure began in 1927 with the flight of the *Spirit of St. Louis,* and it continues today as he pursues his interest in international aviation and space travel, wildlife conservation, scientific research, and writing. Except for the wartime period he has never kept a daily record for more than a few weeks at a stretch—none that covered his great Atlantic flight, his exploration of air routes to South America, to the Orient and to Europe, his "discovery" and support of Dr. Robert Goddard, the space-rocket pioneer, his invention and development of an organ perfusion pump, his experiments with the phenomena of life with Dr. Alexis Carrel; or during his family's suffering from the public's fascination with their grief; or during the work of his later years, when he has helped to save wildlife in Africa, the Americas, and the Far East, when he followed the advance of man beyond the barriers of sound and atmosphere, when he has been (as he is now) compiling his reflections on the impact of science and technology upon man. The wartime journals are unusual not only in the life of Charles Lindbergh but also in the experience of contemporary history. There is a plainness of purpose, at once rigorous and bracing, in these journals, a purpose best described in the following letter from the author to the publisher:

December 18, 1969

Dear Bill:

You ask why I waited twenty-five years before publishing my World War II journals. Various reasons come to mind. In the first place, when I wrote them I had no intention of publication. They held a private record. Second, some of the data they contain were too sensitive to be published before the passage of time had exerted its buffering effect. A third factor relates to the objectivity that comes with years and the eyes of a new generation. Even now, the effects of World War II bitterness and propaganda have not entirely disappeared.

I don't recall even considering publication of the journals before you and I discussed, earlier this year, the comments I had recorded concerning numerous errors in biographies written about me. False statements about my life and activities were especially rampant during the war years. After our talks, I thought of my wartime journals and suggested to you the possibility of publication, for they contain, to the best of my ability, an accurate record.

In preparing for their publication, I have fully reread my journals for the first time since they were written. This reading has been fascinating to me. In general, I find that I still hold the beliefs I entered on the journal pages. I only wish that time and circumstance had allowed me to write more fully—so much was left unrecorded—so often items of greatest interest were omitted, or skimped over, because of sleepiness or lack of time. And, of course, there were the militarily classified items that I was not permitted to record at all.

I began writing the first journal in England late in 1937. I had kept a journal previously on several occasions, but never for more than a few weeks at a stretch. The active life I led, in and out of aviation, did not encourage keeping a journal; but this life was so interesting that I often regretted I had not kept one. I finally decided to start a journal in which I would make daily entries for at least a year.

A major reason for this decision lay in my realization that I was taking part in one of the great crises of world history. Europe was on the verge of war, a war that I felt would be catastrophic for our civilization, one that might still be prevented. Aviation constituted a new and possibly decisive element in preventing or fighting a war, and I was in a unique position to observe European aviation—especially in its military aspects. I had the full support of our American embassies, and I could travel and visit with much greater freedom than the military members of their staffs. Two years previously, an invitation from Field Marshal Goering to inspect the German Luftwaffe had given me disturbing insight into the magnitude of Hitler's intentions. Manifold developments were bound to make a journal well worth keeping.

But soon after starting the journal, Anne and I sailed for America for a visit of several weeks. Entries during this period relate almost entirely to routine and family affairs. I have therefore submitted to you, for publication, the journal beginning with our departure from America on our return voyage to Europe, in the spring of 1938.

Anne and I had been staying at her mother's home, Next Day Hill, on the outskirts of Englewood, New Jersey. During our weeks in the United States, in addition to my aviation activities, I had been working with the French biologist and surgeon Dr. Alexis Carrel on the manuscript for a jointly authored book describing new apparatus and techniques for the culture of isolated organs. Anne had been working on the manuscript for a book about one of our Atlantic-survey flights, to be published by Harcourt, Brace and Company under the title *Listen! the Wind*.

Somewhat over two years before (late in 1935), we had moved our home to Europe temporarily because of excessive newspaper publicity in America. This publicity had forced us to keep our house and grounds under armed guard as a protection from criminals, lunatics, reporters, and photographers. Federal and state authorities had made fourteen investigations and arrests as a result of threatening letters we received.

You will note a gap of about a year in the journals between November, 1942, and December, 1943. (We were living in Michigan.) This was caused by the increasing pressure of my wartime activities. During these months, the production of bombers at Willow Run had gotten under way, and, in addition to my consulting work for the Ford Motor Company, I took on a consulting position with United Aircraft Corporation, headquartered at East Hartford, Connecticut.

As a United consultant, I worked primarily with the Vought-Sikorsky Division at Stratford in connection with fighter requirements and design. Vought was producing the Navy Corsair (F4U) and studying designs for fighters with still more advanced performance. My trip into Pacific Ocean areas in 1944, described in the next section of the journal, was to study the Corsair under service conditions and to discuss with personnel of combat squadrons the characteristics desired in the next generation of fighting aircraft.

Intensive activity after returning from this Pacific Ocean mission resulted in another gap in the journals. I began the writing again in the spring of 1945, prior to a trip to Europe which immediately followed Germany's surrender. The purpose of this trip, made under the auspices of the Naval Technical Mission Europe, was to study the latest developments in German aircraft and missiles.

With the trip to postwar Europe, my journals ended by intent. I wanted to devote the equivalent thought and writing time to the manuscript I had under way for a book to be published under the title *The Spirit of St. Louis.*

I continued my activities with United Aircraft until Japan surrendered, and for more than a decade thereafter I worked actively in military fields —as a member of Army Ordnance's CHORE at the University of Chicago; as a consultant to the Secretary of the Air Force in Washington; in the reorganization of the Strategic Air Command; as a member of scientific ballistic-missile committees, first under the Air Force and then under the Department of Defense. During this period, I was commissioned a brigadier general, United States Air Force Reserve.

You ask what my conclusions are, rereading my journals and looking back on World War II from the vantage point of a quarter century in time. We won the war in a military sense; but in a broader sense it seems to me we lost it, for our Western civilization is less respected and secure than it was before.

In order to defeat Germany and Japan we supported the still greater menaces of Russia and China—which now confront us in a nuclear-weapon era. Poland was not saved. The British Empire has broken down with great suffering, bloodshed, and confusion. England is an economy-constricted secondary power. France had to give up her major colonies and turn to a mild dictatorship herself. Much of our Western culture was destroyed. We lost the genetic heredity formed through aeons in many million lives. Meanwhile, the Soviets have dropped their iron curtain to screen off Eastern Europe, and an antagonistic Chinese government threatens us in Asia.

More than a generation after the war's end, our occupying armies still must occupy, and the world has not been made safe for democracy and freedom. On the contrary, our own system of democratic government is being challenged by that greatest of dangers to any government: internal dissatisfaction and unrest.

It is alarmingly possible that World War II marks the beginning of our Western civilization's breakdown, as it already marks the breakdown of the greatest empire ever built by man. Certainly our civilization's survival depends on meeting the challenges that tower before us with unprecedented magnitude in almost every field of modern life. Most of these challenges were, at least, intensified through the waging of World War II.

Are we now headed toward a third and still more disastrous war between world nations? Or can we improve human relationships sufficiently to avoid such a holocaust? Since it is inherent in the way of life that issues will continue between men, I believe human relationships can best be improved through clarifying the issues and conditions surrounding them.

I hope my journals relating to World War II will help clarify issues and conditions of the past and thereby contribute to understanding issues and conditions of the present and the future.

Sincerely,

Charles

It is clear that Lindbergh recognized the particular importance of his role as observer. He had moved his family to England in the winter of 1935. Inevitably, the Lindberghs were soon familiar with a number of European leaders. By the summer of 1938, when they moved to the isle of Illiec, a half mile from the north coast of Brittany (and within sight of Saint-Gildas, where Alexis Carrel and his wife lived), Charles Lindbergh was convinced that a European war, and probably a world war, was imminent. He had started to write daily reports in 1937, and now these became the record of his thoughts and activities as he traveled from Illiec to London, to Paris, to Berlin—and even to Moscow, where he and his wife flew in the summer of 1938. The then Colonel Lindbergh had access to ambassadors and military attachés in most of the European capitals; moreover, he was able to move from country to country as an observer of the relative conditions of military preparedness among the European powers, and in this he was far freer than military attachés, who were, by decree, largely confined to the countries of their assignment. Lindbergh traveled constantly, yet he returned to the United States only once during the period from 1935 until 1939, when his family was settled on Long Island.

After the outbreak of war in Europe in September of 1939, Colonel Lindbergh was caught up in the political contentions between those who advocated American intervention and those who opposed it. For the first time in his career he became politically prominent. It indicates the seriousness of his political commitment that the Lindberghs thereby gave up the privacy they had so painfully secured—by leaving their home and their friends and accustomed interests—after the incredible events that occurred during the tracking and trial of the kidnaper and murderer of their first-born child. As an "isolationist" who warned against his country's entry into the war, Lindbergh eventually became a leading speaker for the American First Committee led by General Robert E. Wood. At this period the daily journal notations served beyond their original and prime purpose, for Lindbergh was subjected to intense attacks in public. He now concluded that it was essential for him to record his viewpoint and actions so that at some later time there would be available an account as free as he could possibly make it of the propaganda and the extreme bitterness that was so commonly conveyed by the prewar press and radio. The importance of the *Journals* as biography seems obvious. Indeed, because of his wariness of granting interviews—a caution that developed from his 1927 experiences and was deepened by the attacks of the press on him during his opposition to American intervention in the war—and because of his longtime search for privacy for his family, there is probably no accurate "outside" record of his life other than what appears in his first two books, in *The Spirit of St. Louis* (1953), and in *The Wartime Journals* (1970), and of course what may appear in his unpublished manuscripts and letters. (On one occasion I urged General Lindbergh to read one of the more than twenty books that have been written about him—it was a sympathetic biography that I thought to be unusually free of melodramatic revelations and conclusions. Soon afterward I received from him a document of seventy-six typewritten pages in which he listed the factual inaccuracies of the book, whose author had naturally depended mostly upon newspaper sources.)

Once war was declared by the United States and after Lindbergh had volunteered his services, his daily work left him with little time to write the journal entries on certain days. During the period he spent with Henry Ford at Willow Run on the construction of bombers and, later, when he served as an adviser and as a combatant who flew fifty missions, he was not able each day to write a full entry. Occasionally he could do no more than take notes during the course of a busy day and afterward, even so long as two or three weeks later, actually write the complete entry. By 1945 his original purpose in keeping the journals was fulfilled—the terrible time of first anticipating and then enduring the war was almost over—and he discontinued them. He was, moreover, occupied in writing *The Spirit of St. Louis:* today he recalls that he "consciously stopped" the journals in order to complete that book (it was actually begun in 1938).

The journals were all written in small leather-bound books. (A representative page is pictured on page xvii.) Subsequently, the books were transcribed by secretaries and, as two people were so engaged, it was possible for the final manuscript to be read against the originals and the accuracy of the transcription to be attested by both the typist and the reader. (See the sample manuscript page on page xviii.) It is clear that General Lindbergh took exceptional precaution to authenticate the fact that the journals were not rewritten at later times, even though he did not expect that they would be made public during his lifetime. The original handwritten record and a typewritten one were deposited in a university library, with additional copies at a college and at a historical association, all of which institutions are under instruction not to make the journals currently available for inspection by anyone under terms that apply to all of the papers of Charles and Anne Lindbergh.

In preparing the text for publication, Lindbergh was confronted with a number of personal and editorial considerations that he has, I think, admirably resolved. His main concerns were these chiefly: that the text of the entries should not be rewritten in any way; that the main alteration of the text should be a cutting that would make it more readable—and short enough to fit into a single volume. These prescriptions have been met. Not even the occasional instance of infelicitous syntax or usage has been corrected or improved, although spelling and punctuation have been put right where necessary. The redaction of the text was carried out on the principle that a great many details of day-to-day living are insignificant because they are routine—getting to and from local places, meeting people who are not again seen, confirming appointments, carrying out household or clerical chores—and are therefore of no interest to anyone but the author and, perhaps, the scholar. Moreover, some material of an intimately personal content has been deleted by the writer, as have a number of references to people who are still living and who might be offended by their publication. The text has been cut where it was clearly repetitive; there are omissions, too, where passages were finally adjudged not important enough to warrant adding to the length of the work as a whole. The original manuscript is just short of three thousand typewritten pages. This published version is in length about two-thirds of the original.

The *Journals* are presented to the general reader as the personal record of what one American, a singular and most remarkable American, thought and said and did during the seven years when tens of millions of people died violently at the hands of their fellow men. It is a record that was written because its author was himself convinced, without a trace of vanity, that it was worth keeping. It is published because it recalls an important and unique experience that is told with a steadiness of view, an openness of character, and told with the intimation that we dare not, on penalty of the living, put our lives beyond recall, beyond comprehending.

WILLIAM JOVANOVICH

May 21, 1970

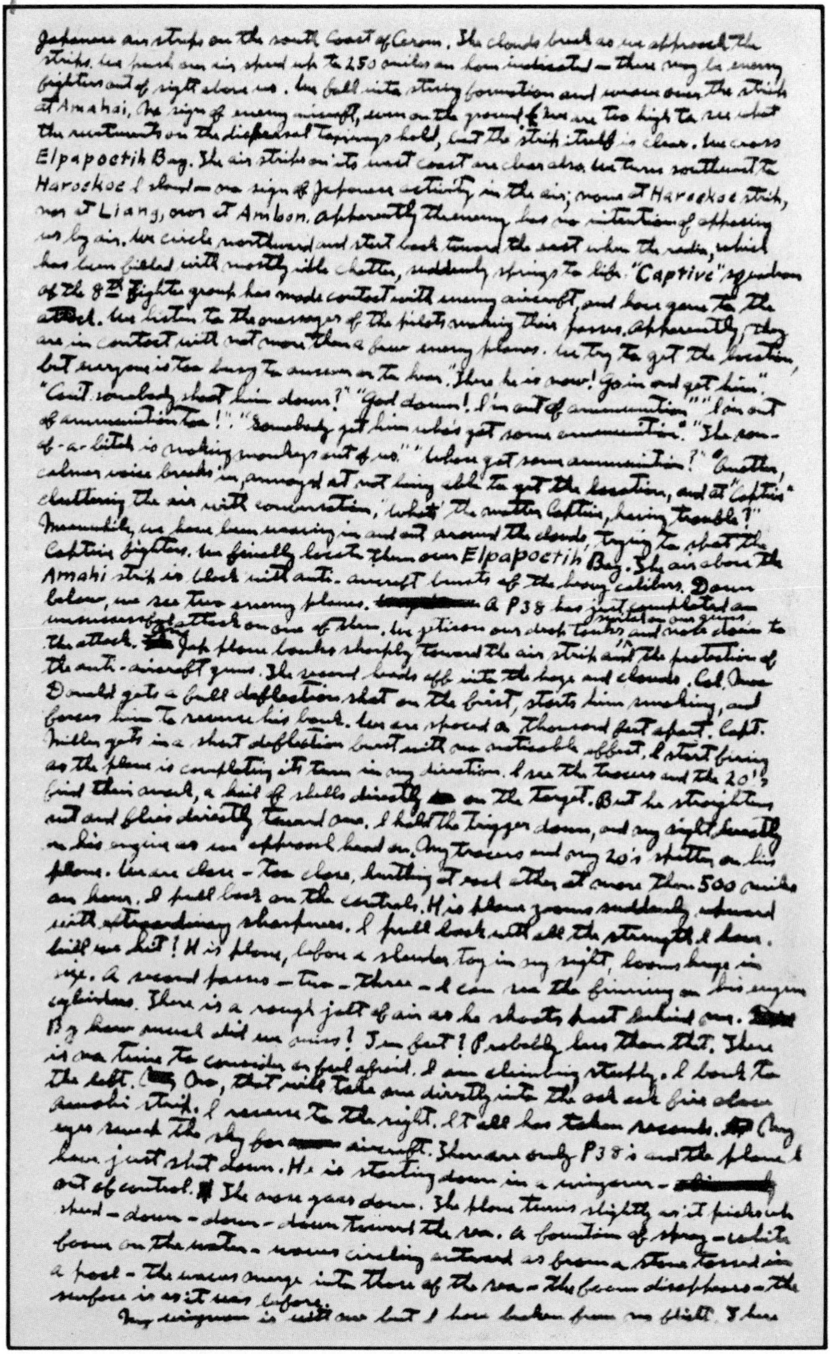

A page from Colonel Lindbergh's July 28, 1944, journal entry

about five minutes. After trying out the controls in banking and climbing, I turned my place over to Tomlinson. (Tomlinson has tested most of the recent American designs of large land transport planes). I stood at the back of the cockpit while Tomlinson flew. After making several minor tests of the controls, he put the plane into a left bank (not very steep) and kept

This is an accurate copy of
Charles A. Lindbergh's diary,
beginning Saturday, October 8, 1938,
and ending Monday, October 17, 1938.

It was copied from, and carefully
checked with, the original. Notes
which were inserted in the opposite
page in the diary are placed between
dotted lines in this copy.

Christine L. Gawne
Christine L. Gawne

Jeannette Greene
Jeannette Greene

Checked:

C. A. L.

A page from the verified copy of the journals, typed about 1940

Europe Prewar

Anne and I left the house about 10:45 [P.M.] in Burke's[1] car—Burke driving. (Everything left in good shape at Next Day Hill.[2] Important items packed and locked. All arrangements completed.) Drove to corner of Forty-sixth and one block east of West Street, where we met Mr. Von Glahn[3] and an officer of the North German Lloyd. They got in our car, and we drove in the freight entrance and boarded the *Bremen* without difficulty (via crew's gangplank). Were taken to a room in the crew's quarters where we were to wait until ship sailed before going to our own stateroom. After about fifteen minutes an officer came to tell us that the press had learned we were on board and were looking all over the ship for us.

Left dock about 12:30. An officer knocked on our door and said everyone had gone ashore. He escorted us to our room. A very well-designed stateroom. I like the appearance of this ship.

Can now really think about seeing Jon and Land[4] again.

Papers carry reports of German invasion of Austria. Headlines: GERMAN TROOPS ENTER AUSTRIA. *Stories too mixed to permit any accurate conclusions. Hope England and Germany can find some way of working together. If they could do so, there need be no major war in Europe for many years to come. If they fight again, it will be chaos.*

1. Alfred Burke, chauffeur for Mrs. Dwight W. Morrow, mother of Anne Morrow Lindbergh.

2. The Morrow home in Englewood, N.J.

3. Jack M. Von Glahn, an officer with J. P. Morgan & Co., who was helping the Lindberghs with their travel arrangements.

4. The Lindbergh sons, aged six years (Jon) and eight months (Land), who had been left in England during their parents' temporary return to the U.S.

Late breakfast in dining room with Anne. Walk on sun deck afterward; no sun and no one else on the deck. Always easy to be alone in bad weather. This is a beautifully designed boat, and well run.

Morning spent making pencil drawing of oil flask—only piece of work I have not finished for book.[5] Must send it back to publishers as soon as we land in England. Afternoon spent drawing. Also walk on top deck with Anne. Sea smooth and ship steady.

Sunday, March 13

Afternoon spent drawing. Sea has been rough all day. Makes ink drawing difficult. Finished tracing of oil flask. Started drawing of intermittent circulation tissue-culture flask.[6] Spent evening drawing.

Monday, March 14

Radio reports German troops have crossed Austria and taken position on Italian border. Am watching English policy. Believe peace or war depends on it.

Finished drawing and tracing of circulation flask. Several walks on top deck with Anne. Drawings are now done except for those to go in Anne's new book.[7] Hope to spend more time reading. Have hardly done any since we left England.

5. The oil flask was a portion of the organ-perfusion apparatus Lindbergh had designed and constructed for Dr. Alexis Carrel (who had been awarded the Nobel Prize in physiology and medicine in 1912 for his contributions to the surgery of blood vessels) at the latter's Department of Experimental Surgery in the Rockefeller Institute for Medical Research, New York City. This was the first apparatus in which living organs could be perfused without the entrance of infection. The book, written by Carrel and Lindbergh, was published as *The Culture of Organs*.

6. A glass flask Lindbergh had designed and developed in connection with tissue-culture experiments being carried on in Carrel's Department of Experimental Surgery.

7. This was published by Harcourt, Brace and Co. as *Listen! the Wind*—an account of the South Atlantic crossing on the Lindberghs' 1933 survey flight of potential transatlantic air routes and bases.

Tuesday, March 15

Woke late. Walk on top deck with Anne. [We] lay plans for her book. Discuss title. Started reading *The War in Outline* by [Basil H.] Liddell Hart.

Wednesday, March 16

This has been a pleasant voyage. A very considerate crew and almost no bother from passengers. I cannot help liking the Germans. They are like our own people. We should be working with them and not constantly crossing swords. If we fight, our countries will only lose their best men. We can gain nothing. We both know how to fight too well, although at the moment they are better equipped than we for war. It must not happen.

Captain [Adolf] Ahrens called on us this afternoon. Spent about fifteen minutes visiting. We are late and will not reach Southampton until about 6:00 P.M. tomorrow.

Thursday, March 17

Anchored at Cherbourg about 1:00. Finished *The War in Outline*. Ship's officer arrived with note from Southampton office of Hamburg-American Line, suggesting we go ashore in baggage tender to avoid trouble with press. They offer to arrange for special customs clearance.

We arrive at Southampton (really the river below Southampton) about 6:00. Chief steward takes us aboard baggage tender. Mr. Gregory[8] is waiting there for us. He has made all arrangements for baggage. A customs inspector goes on board with us. He is a pleasant and considerate fellow and will not even let us open our baggage. We give him a list of purchases made abroad, but there is no duty to pay as the items are all clothing which has been worn or articles we have had in America for several years. We had between $5.00 and $10.00 worth of new toys for Jon and Land, but he passed them without charge. One thing I like about the English is that they treat people as though they are honest. I don't

8. Walter H. Gregory, an officer of Morgan Grenfell & Co. Ltd., London, who met the Lindberghs to help them with their travel arrangements.

think they lose anything by that policy in the long run. The officials of so many countries make you feel as though they constantly suspected you of trying to do something you should not.

Gregory, the customs officer, Anne, and I talk about conditions in England and in Europe during our trip up the river to the Southampton dock. There seems to be less worry in England than in America about the German invasion of Austria. The English are more practical than we are about the problems in Europe.

Such a relief to know that what we say will not be retold to the press within an hour or two after we have left. An Englishman just doesn't do that. I wish I could say the same about our own people.

Miss Hutchison[9] is waiting on the dock with our Ford car. We pack in the suitcases, and somehow four of us get into the car also. We leave Mr. Gregory at the entrance to the main dock. Then we start toward home. Stop at Winchester long enough for an English supper of the worst type and arrive at Long Barn[10] about midnight. The moon is out, and it is very beautiful.

Friday, March 18

Breakfast at 8:00 with Anne, Jon, Miss Wesley[11] and Miss Hutchison. I made the mistake of trying to save time after breakfast by using the English telephone. It never works!

Anne and I drove Jon to school—about a fifteen-minute drive each way—to Tonbridge. He enjoys school and is getting along well.

Saturday, March 19

Took first train for London, leaving Sevenoaks about 10:45. It is a fast train, and I arrive in London before 11:30. Started reading *The Growth of Political Thought in the West* by C. H. McIlwain.

The stores in London close at 1:00 P.M. on Saturday, so I took taxi from Charing Cross Station to the Zeiss Optical Company. I was trying to find a lettering pen to use with a template—to put the numbers on the drawing of the oil flask for the book on the cultivation of organs.

9. Dorothy Hutchison, the Lindberghs' secretary.

10. A fourteenth-century house in Sevenoaks Weald, Kent. It is one of several houses in Weald where William Caxton is alleged to have been born.

11. Katherine Wesley, the Lindberghs' nurse.

The Zeiss Company said I should go to the Carl Zeiss Company around the corner. The Carl Zeiss Company said they didn't have any lettering pens, but gave me an address where they thought I could get them. And again I am on one of those endless London hunts for some item that I could get in ten minutes in New York. I tried to get a lettering pen by telephone yesterday morning without success, and now it looks as though I would waste another morning with no better result.

The last shop carried a complete list of drawing instruments, including lettering pens and templates but "not in stock," of course. "You see, there are so many sizes that we can't carry them all." So apparently they didn't carry any. How like an English store! "We can get one for you next week." I told the salesman that I had to have one today. (But how, I don't know. It was ten minutes of one. And *try* to get anything in London after 1:00 on Saturday!) "Well, I'll let you take mine. It's nearly new, and I'll get another next week." And again, how English. That's the way things are done over here. They will go far out of their way to help you if they can, but their methods are different than ours. In the United States the store would almost certainly have had the pen in stock. In fact, I would have obtained it easily by telephone. But if by any chance an American store did not have a lettering pen in stock, it is not likely that the clerk would offer you his used one.

I took the pen, ordered a smaller new one, and got to the Times Bookstore in time to purchase two books before they closed for the weekend.

Arrived Long Barn about 3:00. Jon and I started working on the house I am helping him build. We began it last fall, but nothing has been done while I was in the United States, of course. I cut the boards and put the long ones in place. Jon does all the nailing. The frame is up. Three sides are finished, and half the roof is on.

Tuesday, March 22

Day spent dictating and with Anne, working out final details in regard to her book. Decide to call it *Listen! the Wind*. Sent cover drawing and letter covering all preliminary details to Harcourt, Brace.

Wednesday, March 23

Mme. Carrel[12] cables that she will visit us, arriving next Saturday.

12. Wife of Dr. Alexis Carrel. Anne-Marie de la Motte, widow of the Marquis de

Friday, March 25

Raining all day and no sun. However, we have had unusually good weather ever since we landed. Studied Goddard's[13] last report this morning, then wrote to both Goddard and Harry Guggenheim,[14] in addition to several other shorter letters. Spent most of the afternoon and evening writing a description of the new circulating tissue-culture flask I designed last winter at the Rockefeller Institute.

Saturday, March 26

Worked on papers for a short time after breakfast, then drove to Croydon Aerodrome to meet Mme. Carrel. She arrived ten minutes late, due to head winds, in one of the new Lockheeds.

Mme. Carrel came primarily for the purpose of talking to us about the purchase of Illiec.[15] Details too complicated for her to write about. She did not want me to meet her in Paris, as she was afraid the owners of the island would suspect that she was trying to buy it for us and raise the price. The owners of Illiec want to set the price in American dollars, as they know Dr. Carrel lives in New York. They are carrying on a typically French type of bargaining. One of the sons does not want to sell, etc. It would have been very difficult for me to have gone to Paris without causing a certain amount of publicity and speculation in regard to why I went.

Afternoon spent talking to Mme. Carrel. She, Anne, Jon, and I went for an hour's walk along the wood paths south of Long Barn. Spent a

---

la Mairie, and a distinguished physician, met Dr. Carrel when they were both engaged in medical work. They were married in 1913.

13. Professor Robert H. Goddard, the great pioneer in astronautics.

14. Close friend of the Lindberghs. (Lindbergh wrote most of *We* at Guggenheim's home near Port Washington, Long Island, in 1927.) Guggenheim was president of the Daniel Guggenheim Fund for the Promotion of Aeronautics (1926–30); from 1929 to 1933 he was Ambassador to Cuba. He served in both World War I and World War II, becoming a captain in the Navy's aviation branch. Starting in 1930, at the instigation of Lindbergh, he and his father gave decisive personal and financial support to Robert H. Goddard, making possible the latter's experiments and rocket launchings at Roswell, New Mexico.

15. The largest of a number of small islands lying a short distance off the north coast of Brittany.

little time writing description of tissue-culture flask during odd moments of afternoon and evening.

Sunday, March 27

Franco continues advance toward Barcelona.

Mme. Carrel, Anne, Jon, and I went for a drive in the Ford in the afternoon. About an hour over the country roads south of Long Barn— through Chiddingstone and Penshurst.

Monday, March 28

Morning at Long Barn, talking to Mme. Carrel and working on papers. Left about 11:30 for Croydon Aerodrome. Anne stayed home to work on book. Mme. Carrel and I had lunch on aerodrome. She left for Paris at 1:15 on British Airways. I drove back to Long Barn and spent afternoon on papers. Anne went to London in afternoon. Hugo Leuteritz[16] came to spend night. He has been in Ireland to attend aviation conference and to see radio facilities there. We talked about Pan American and aircraft radio at home and in Europe.

Wednesday, March 30

Started writing preface for Anne's book. The Weald postmistress came for tea. I have never quite gotten over my "Western" feeling about tea! The whole idea seems a little effeminate to me. I don't even like it to drink. It is hard to explain why, except that I grew up with that idea. I thought tea was only for society women and "Eastern dudes."

Mr. Merkel [17] came to spend the night. We talked of Germany and of conditions in Europe. He gave us a great deal of information about taxes and economic policies under Hitler. We also talked of aviation, and especially the Focke-Wulf helicopter. He has recently joined the Nazi Party.

16. Chief communications engineer for Pan American Airways.
17. Otto Merkel, an officer with Lufthansa Airlines.

Thursday, March 31

A letter arrived from Mme. Carrel. We have Illiec! I took the 11:39 train to London to arrange to transfer money from New York to Paris for payment. Had a bad lunch near Charing Cross Station, then went to Morgan Grenfell Ltd. to make the arrangements—a cable to J. P. Morgan & Co., New York, etc.

We are all looking forward to the summer at Illiec. We now own the most beautiful island in the world; yes, in some ways it is even more beautiful than Saint-Gildas.[18] That is the only justification for buying it. I know only too well that conditions in France are bad, that they may even lead to revolution. But one summer at Illiec would almost justify buying it. The very memory of such a summer would strengthen the rest of life. I have never seen a place where I wanted to live so much. Nothing could do Anne and Jon and Land as much good.

Friday, April 1

Morning dictating and thinking. Consider plans for summer and next winter. Also try to look into future. Will there be a major war in Europe? If there is, will America become involved? What are the trends at home? In England? How much longer can this trend toward mediocrity continue? What has happened to the English? What will happen to our own people? Will Franco's probable victory prevent a revolution in France? How can the French get out of the mess they are now in? What policy should I follow for my family's future? The only sure thing is in giving them health and experience and education of the right kind. I must teach my children to know and to love the earth itself. If they can keep in contact with the land and the water and the sky, they can obtain all worth while that life holds.

My children must be taught how to fight well, to survive. Military training is both desirable and essential for them. They must be taught how to make a living among men. But they must also be taught not to measure success by any material value. I must teach them how to keep this civilization we are building from deadening their true senses.

18. An island off the north coast of Brittany, which at low tide is connected to the islands of Illiec and the mainland. Dr. and Mme. Carrel owned the island.

Jon and I drove to Page's store in Weald this morning and bought an old paintbrush and some creosote. Jon started painting (with creosote) the sides of his house.

Saturday, April 2

Breakfast at Long Barn; then drove Ford to Woodley Aerodrome, Reading. Flew Mohawk for one hour, thirty-five minutes, making a total of about twelve landings. F. G. Miles[19] showed me some of his new planes —the Monarch and the experimental Peregrine with the boundary-layer-control wings and an extra motor in the fuselage. Miles is an excellent engineer and has vision. He has apparently done well with the factory at Reading in spite of many troubles in expanding. (One of William Randolph Hearst's sons was on the flying field with his bride—a girl of seventeen.)

The contrast between an English aircraft factory and an American or German factory is ununderstandable. The English simply do not seem to have equivalent ability along those lines. God! How they will have to pay for it in the next war. This country has neither the spirit nor the ability needed for a modern war. And the worst of it is that countless Englishmen will die needlessly because of lack of training and equipment. It is not only in aviation that they are behind. I sometimes wonder if history will not eventually show that the British Empire has already passed its greatest period. I cannot see the future for this country. The value of the Channel is passing with every improvement in military aircraft. The colonies are manufacturing their own products from their own raw materials. Even the quality of British goods is frequently mediocre. And the people show little sign of changing. They need an entirely new spirit if British greatness is to endure.

Sunday, April 3

Franco advance continues. Now only twenty-five miles from the Mediterranean.

Another clear sunny day. Wonderful weather since we landed last month. Was beginning to become enthusiastic about the weather in Eng-

19. Chief engineer and designer for Phillips & Powis Aircraft, Ltd., at Reading.

land until Anne read in this morning's *Observer* that it was the warmest March for 150 years. Have started reading Tolstoy's *War and Peace*. Finished first draft of preface for Anne's book.

Monday, April 4

Telegram from Mme. Carrel from Saint-Gildas. The transaction is completed. We will fly there on Wednesday to see Illiec. We have never been on the island before—only seen it walking past at low tide.

Took Jon to Page's store in Weald after lunch to get roll of roofing paper for his house. They had the paper, but after a long, slow search, decided they were out of nails.

Tuesday, April 5

Left Long Barn about 6:15 for London to attend the Ends of the Earth Club dinner. Drove Ford instead of taking train, as I thought dinner might last too late to get train home. Have had so much correspondence with Mr. Bigelow[20] about the club that I was curious to see its members and to attend a meeting. Even so, I probably would not have gone if I had not thought it would disappoint the old man so much. I have grown to like him through his letters.

Before dinner I was talking to a group consisting of Mr. Bigelow and two Englishmen, one of whom had been in the Air Ministry. He is now retired—a man of about sixty-five. Bigelow started to talk about the Japanese bombing in China. "But," said the Englishman (Air Ministry), "of course they can't hit anything, you know. Nothing is ever hit with bombs. Why, look at the last war; they never hit what they were aiming at!" Turning to me: "Did you ever see anyone come down in a parachute?" I said I had. "They never land where they want to, you know. Too many cross currents in the air. Now, it's the same way with a bomb."

I suggested that they were not using gyroscopic bombsights during the last war, but I was not even heard. When an Englishman is stating his opinion, anything you say has about as much effect as spray on a rock. He continued until dinner was announced. Look at the war in China.

20. English traveler, lecturer, and author, Poultney Bigelow was born in 1855. President of the Ends of the Earth Club, he had made a voyage around the world in a sailing ship in 1875–76.

Why, the Chinese planes couldn't hit the Jap boats even when they bombed from *very* low altitude. And in Spain . . . But it was dinnertime.

The dinner was like all men's formal dinners—probably a little more interesting than the average. That may be because I sat between two Englishmen who were interesting—Admiral Sir W. Goodenough[21] and Sir Harry F. Batterbee.[22]

The speeches were good from the standpoint of oratory, I suppose, but very dull from all others. The speakers were asked by the chairman to "be indiscreet." This resulted in slightly less caution than if they had been speaking to national radio hookups; but, on the whole, I think it would have been almost as interesting to read a morning newspaper.

"The chairman has told me to be indiscreet," etc.

"The good feeling between the English people and the American people is bound to improve," etc.

"We know that our American cousins will always be behind us in a crisis," etc.

"The liberty-loving peoples of the world must stand against aggressor nations," etc.

While the speeches hardly seemed worth going to hear, I felt my evening well spent if for no other reason than the opportunity it gave me to see how the thought of war is weaving in and out among the minds of leading Englishmen at the present moment. It was obvious in every talk. The German acquisition of Austria and Franco's success in Spain seem to be the main reasons for this change in attitude, for it was by no means as conspicuous when we sailed for America last December.

Wednesday, April 6

Planned on flying to Brittany today, but discovered that our French visas were expired. They would have been good for months, but our passports had been renewed in December, and consequently we needed new visas. I knew that, but it slipped my mind until I made a final check of our papers. There are so many forms and regulations for flying in Europe that it is hard never to forget any of them. In consequence, we had to postpone our trip one day.

21. A retired naval officer, Admiral Sir William Goodenough had been First and Principal Naval Aide-de-Camp to King George V, 1929–30.
22. Assistant Undersecretary of State for Great Britain, 1930–38.

Thursday, April 7

We arrived at Woodley Aerodrome, Reading, at 12:00. Anne and I took off [for Illiec] at 12:20 in the Mohawk. Landed at Morlaix at 5:30. Day was good. Partly overcast most of way. Patches of fog along coast, but only local. Visibility five miles or more at all times.

Mme. Carrel and M. and Mlle. Masson[23] were waiting for us at the Morlaix flying field. A local customs officer arrived a few minutes later. Why, I don't know, because we had cleared customs at Saint Inglevert, and we never had to clear again on any of our flights last year.

Mme. Carrel, Anne, and I left the field in Mme. Carrel's Ford at 6:00 and drive to Port Blanc. The tide was well down, so we had to walk over rocks and seaweed to get in the boat—a stubby, wide motorboat, more like an oversized and very clumsy rowboat. It is completely open, except for a place in the bow where packages can be stowed, and where two or three people could crouch in case of necessity. The trip to Saint-Gildas takes about five minutes. The island is beautiful, as it always is, but we have never been here in April before. The fog is so thick that we cannot see far—only about halfway to the mainland. We arrived in time for late supper, and an evening talking to Mme. Carrel about Illiec.

Friday, April 8

After breakfast Mme. Carrel, Anne, and I went to the mainland, and I drove Mme. Carrel's car to Tréguier. Mme. Carrel had an engagement with a lawyer there in regard to Illiec. We returned to Saint-Gildas in time for an early lunch before starting for Illiec. The tide was high enough to go by boat with Pierre, Mme. Carrel's boatman. On the way we stopped at Ile de Milieu and climbed one of the rocks from which we could see all the little islands of Illiec.

There was no one on Illiec but the caretaker and his wife. The island could not be more beautiful. The sea and rocks and groves of trees combine with the changing sky and tide to make perfection which is almost unbelievable. The house[24] is well designed and built, but terribly fur-

---

23. M. Francis and Mlle. Madelaine Masson, friends of Mme. Carrel.

24. A gray-stone, three-story Breton house with a castlelike tower, built around 1865 by Ambroise Thomas, the composer, who wrote his opera *Mignon* there.

nished. All the interior will have to be changed, but that is not important. Every room has a beautiful view of the sea. Ambroise Thomas must have been a man of judgment and a lover of beauty. Only that which has been done since his death is bad, and it can all be changed.

We spent two or three hours walking over the island and making plans for the house. There is a little stone cottage near the house, where a fisherman and his wife live. They are the caretakers. We waited until the tide was low enough to walk back to Saint-Gildas. On the way we visited several of the small islands which are part of Illiec.

Mme. Carrel is an extraordinary woman. She seems never tired, and she attacks everything she does with an ability and determination that I have never seen surpassed. Except for her, I doubt very much we would have been able to buy Illiec. The owners were undecided and wavering about selling until the last minute. It was really her determination that put the transaction across. One might almost say that she forced them to sell, although she had no means of forcing them to do anything except through her own personality.

We spent the evening making plans for Illiec. A contractor will come to Saint-Gildas in the morning, and we will take him to Illiec.

Saturday, April 9

Mme. Carrel went to Tréguier after breakfast to see the lawyer. Anne and I went with Pierre and a local pilot to see Illiec from the sea. We went in the motorboat and were gone about an hour. After lunch the contractor arrived, and Mme. Carrel, Anne, and I went with him to Illiec.

(Mme. Carrel returned from Tréguier with the news that Blum[25] is out. Conditions are bad in this country and have been for a long time. Strikes are increasing again.)

Most of the rooms must be replastered. The floors are to be stained. The shutters and doors must be repaired and painted, etc. We are having a partition put in the dining room, as it is now too big. One end will be

---

Madame Adelina Patti had lived there, and also Henryk Sienkiewicz, while he was writing *Quo Vadis.*

25. Léon Blum, French socialist, statesman, and writer. Blum headed the Popular Front government from 1936 to 1937, but opposition to his fiscal measures forced his resignation in 1937. He was Vice Premier from 1937 to 1938, and briefly Premier in 1938.

15

an office or extra parlor. After an hour or so, Pierre came running to tell us that the sea was going down and we must start back. Life runs by the tide here.

(There is a strange old law in France—Mme. Carrel says still enforced—which prevents people from taking water from the sea. It is to prevent the use of sea salt and consequent escape from the salt tax. Mme. Carrel says it is illegal to take a bucket of sea water for any purpose—a strange law for the French people to have. And apparently they cannot eat the wheat they grow on French farms but must take it to the miller to be mixed with other ingredients and made into flour.)

Sunday, April 10

Went rabbit hunting with an air rifle this morning, but the air chamber leaked and the gun would not shoot straight. After an unsuccessful attempt to set the sights, using a mud flat as a target, I returned home and gave up hunting for the morning.

After lunch Mme. Carrel, Anne, and I went to Illiec again (in the motorboat with Pierre). Anne picked out the furniture she wanted to keep, and we put the rest in a pile in the parlor to be sold. Mme. Carrel arranged with the fisherman and his wife to work for us. They will have 1,000 francs a month—four times as much as they are now getting. The man is making a little money fishing at present in addition to the 3,000 francs a year he has been paid. They have had a hard time living and are happy about the arrangement Mme. Carrel made, i.e., 12,000 francs per year for man and wife, a garden for their own use, vegetables when they grow any, and the cottage to live in. We are giving them the entire cottage (it seems small enough). There are two small rooms under the roof and one large room on the ground floor. Heretofore, they have been allowed only the ground-floor room.

After we returned from Illiec I took another gun, an antiquated weapon that looked like a .40-cal. rifle but was really a shotgun. The shell fitted so loosely in the barrel that I thought I had the wrong ammunition at first. I missed my first shot at long range. Also my second, at a rabbit running through the gorse on the "Island of the Moon." My third was at a standing rabbit, so close I was ashamed to pull the trigger. I missed that, too. Then I went to a pool of water and shot at a rock in the center of it—about ten meters away. The charge hit the water two feet to the left and five feet under the rock. I gave up hunting and went back to the house. I already have a bad reputation as a hunter. The next gun must be a good one.

The moon is nearly full and the night very beautiful, but we are too tired for a walk around the island.

Monday, April 11

Breakfast at 8:30. Always good French cooking—a contrast to the indifferent and usually poor preparation of food in England.

I went hunting again this morning and managed to get two rabbits. They are very wild.

After lunch Mme. Carrel, Anne, and I took the boat to the mainland. We then drove to Tréguier. We went to three shops where old furniture is sold, but found nothing worth buying. Mme. Carrel then went to her lawyer and obtained the final papers for Illiec. The transaction is now complete. We have only to arrange a few details concerning the company which has been formed, so that our name could be kept out of the transaction. It is best for people to think we rent Illiec from the Carrels. That will save us from difficulty with the newspapers at least. The less they know about what we do the happier we find life. And, unfortunately, the newspapers are an element we have to think about in most of the plans we make—invariably a disagreeable problem for us.

We drove to Lannion from Tréguier, then back to Port Blanc in time to reach Saint-Gildas about 6:00. I shot another rabbit after supper. We needed three for a good meal.

Tuesday, April 12

Mme. Carrel had to see a lawyer in Baugé in regard to her mother's estate. I drove her there, as she wishes to return to Saint-Gildas today, and the trip would be too much for her driving alone. We were a little early for Mme. Carrel's appointment so drove to her old home, a few kilometers from Baugé. It is now owned by her son, Henri.[26] It is a huge place, an old castle which was in the family (Mme. Carrel's first husband) for many generations.

There was once a spring-fed moat around the castle, but it was filled up a generation or two ago because the wife of the owner preferred her

26. The Marquis de la Mairie.

castle moatless. The buildings are now in a dilapidated condition—windows boarded up, roof leaking, and open places here and there where the slates have fallen away, cracked and broken places in the walls, a castle in the first stage of ruin. We did not go inside. Mme. Carrel had not the keys with her, she said, but I believe she was so depressed with the condition of the place that she wanted to leave as soon as possible. Her son wishes to keep it because it has been in the family so long, but he is a rancher in Argentina and seldom comes to France.

We next [went] to Mme. Carrel's mother's home for lunch. A large house with a huge living room, two floors high. A large palm in an unpainted wooden box was in the center of this room, surrounded by complicated French furniture. Two old-fashioned phonographs with great horns emphasized the atmosphere of half a century ago, which pervaded the entire house. A small parlor, opening off one end of the large one, was still cluttered with canes, needlework, and recent magazines. The grounds were poorly kept and high with grass. Fences were fallen down, shrubs uncut.

I turned back to the large room again while Mme. Carrel was busy with the details of her mother's estate. The walls were lined with paintings of ancestors. A photo of Dr. Carrel, taken many years ago, was on one table beside other family photographs. In the little parlor at the end, where Mme. Carrel's mother obviously spent most of her downstairs time, there was a closet full of tools (used only by the old lady), a radio set she had made with them, several unknown objects she had apparently been experimenting with, and other family pictures. The place showed both character and lack of attention. Mme. Carrel said her mother refused to let anyone work on the house or grounds without her own supervision of every detail. Being ninety-one years old, many details obviously went without supervision. She must have been a grand old lady from all I could gather about her. And her pictures confirmed my belief. She held the reins firmly for nearly a hundred years. Keen and alert to her death—until a fall resulted in a broken hip bone, followed by pneumonia and death within a few days.

Wednesday, April 13

More work on Anne's book in evening. It is beautifully written. Better even than *North to the Orient*.

This is a wonderful place to work. When you are tired of sitting down, there is almost indescribable beauty at every door and window. A five-minute walk leaves you more refreshed than any amount of walking through city parks. I have never seen such perfection before I came to this island. No mortal wish could improve the beauty of this place.

Thursday, April 14

Mme. Carrel, Anne, and I left at 9:30 this morning for the mainland. The tide was receding rapidly and was barely deep enough for the motor-boat. We drove to Saint-Brieuc, where we bought some tools for Illiec (brush knives, spades, rakes, etc.). Anne bought three pieces of old furniture at an antique dealer's shop—two chests and a cupboard. We returned to Saint-Gildas in the midafternoon. Anne and I went rabbit hunting—came back with only one rabbit but had a good time. The rabbits of Saint-Gildas are well able to take care of themselves. It is very difficult to get near one.

Worked a little on book after supper.

Friday, April 15

M. Savina[27] came at 4:00 from Tréguier. He, Mme. Carrel, Anne, and I went by boat to Illiec. We went over the details to be changed in the house. Savina is to take charge. We have great confidence in his taste and judgment. He is to make a small library out of the lower floor of the tower.

Returned to Saint-Gildas for supper. There has been a strong wind today, and it is the highest tide of the month. We walked around the island after supper. We return to England tomorrow, if the weather is not too bad.

Saturday, April 16

Weather low overcast and hazy. Decided not to start today.

After lunch we went clam hunting. You take a jar of salt and a basket and go to the sand and mud patches in the tideland. You find an oblong hole and put a pinch of salt in it. Soon, there is a movement of water at

27. Joseph Savina, a young Breton sculptor, who also made and sold furniture in his shop on the mainland.

the mouth of the hole, and a few seconds later, if you are lucky, a long clam thrusts its shell out of the sand. It was a little early in the year, but we got enough for supper.

Sunday, April 17

Franco has reached the sea. The strikers in France are returning to work.

Weather bad. Decided not to start today.

In the afternoon Anne and I walked to one of the little islands of Illiec. It is strange to be able to walk over the bottom of the sea, where a few hours later you can go with a motorboat.

Monday, April 18

Anne and I took off on our return flight to England at 1:55, and, after landing at St. Inglevert and Lympne to clear customs, we arrived at Woodley Aerodrome at 7:00. Mr. and Mrs. Miles drove over to the hangar and asked us to come to their home before starting our drive to Long Barn. There were several guests there—all aviation people—and we talked aviation, as is usual under such circumstances. Miles said anti-German feeling was increasing. I told him that if England and Germany fought it would probably throw Europe into a chaotic condition for an indefinite period. The only hope for Europe is an understanding between England and Germany. We also spoke of the prospect of England buying military aircraft in the United States.

Anne and I stopped for supper at an old house along our road. We reached Long Barn about midnight.

Tuesday, April 19

Entire day spent going over galley proofs for *The Culture of Organs.* Wanted to have them ready for [the] *Queen Mary.* The galleys do not require much correcting, but must be checked very accurately. Could not finish them in time for the boat mail. They will have to wait for the S.S. *Washington.*

Saturday, April 23

After lunch Anne, Jon, and I drove to Maidstone. Anne drove the car with big red L (Learners) plates on front and rear bumpers. She must take a driving test Monday because of the regulation that a foreigner can only drive a car for one year in England without taking a test. When we first came, they gave us English driving licenses with no test because we had American licenses. My license expired before Anne's, so (not knowing the regulation) I applied for renewal and got it. Then, a few days before we took off for India (last year) I received a letter to the effect that my license had been renewed by mistake and that I would have to take the test, which I did, after returning from India. Anne was expecting Land soon after we returned, so did not take the test, and it has not been convenient for her to do so until the present time—a few weeks before we leave for Brittany. However, it will probably simplify her getting a French license. We have been away so much, and she has worked so hard when we have been at Long Barn that the driving license has seemed of secondary importance.

We spent half an hour driving through the streets of Maidstone, where she will be tested, then returned to Long Barn.

Sunday, April 24

Spent morning making drawings and on plans for drawings in *Listen! the Wind*. Most of afternoon on drawing. Anne and I went for an hour's walk with Jon through the fields. Showed Jon how to shoot the bow and arrow Anne bought him several months ago. He was too young then, but is now able to shoot as much as twenty or thirty meters.

Monday, April 25

Took the 12:46 train to London to meet an appointment with our dentist. I bought some maps covering the areas I intend to draw for *Listen! the Wind,* also some books, including Plato's *Republic.*

Anne failed her driving test!!!! After fifteen years of driving without an accident! The examiner told her she drove a little fast and not quite far enough to the left! They pass our nurse, who does not handle a car at all

21

well—reactions not quick and co-ordination bad—and fail Anne, who handles a car exceptionally well and who has driven in New York City traffic for years without difficulty. Also for over a year in England. There is something very strange about it. Either the examiner wanted to be smart, or he was so stupid that he mistook experience and ability for incompetence.

Wednesday, April 27

Took train to London for 12:00 engagement with Colonel Scanlon.[28] We talk about the condition of English military aviation and the rearmament program in general. Colonel Lee[29] comes in, and we continue the discussion. Why is this country so far behind, and what is happening to the English? Even if England buys modern aircraft in sufficient number from the United States, is there the ability to use them? We all like England and are distressed about present conditions and trends. This country seems hopelessly behind in military strength in comparison to Germany. And modern instruments of war and modern military tactics all work against the characteristics of the English people and the old geographical advantages of their island.

The impression which has been given in the English press about the strength of the country in case of war is not in keeping with the facts. There is a combination of bluff and vanity in the English that leaves them extremely vulnerable to an enemy who knows these characteristics. Personally, I believe the assets in English character lie in confidence rather than ability; tenacity rather than strength; and determination rather than intelligence. However, any conclusion one reaches in regard to the English is constantly shaken by the exceptions which arise. It is necessary to realize that England is a country composed of a great mass of slow, somewhat stupid and indifferent people, and a small group of geniuses. It is the latter to whom the empire and its reputation are due. They lead and conquer while the mass holds in a deliberate, semiappreciative manner what their leaders have gained.

But is this a sufficient explanation for the world's most far-flung empire? There must be other reasons, too. One of them is the past impor-

28. Colonel Martin F. Scanlon, assistant military attaché for air in the U.S. Embassy in London, 1936–41.

29. Colonel Raymond L. Lee, military attaché for air in the U.S. Embassy in London, 1935–38.

tance of the Channel and the time it gave the British to prepare for war. Undoubtedly the Channel is as responsible as any element for the empire. Being on an island, the English had good ships, which were useful both in protecting them from all enemies and in encouraging them to explore an unknown world. England was always a safe refuge for retreat from failure and for fresh attempts at success. A place where Englishmen could rest secure, and wait, and spring refreshed.

Then there was the superiority of British manufacture, which hardly exists today. The English colonies, and others, were only too glad to trade raw material for finished products. Now the colonies have their own factories.

But what is the future? I think the empire is passing; even now well started on its decline. Not that the English-speaking countries are all declining. They are too universal and too young. But the importance of England must decrease. In the great changes of the present era even the genius of that small group of English leaders cannot overcome the effect of aviation on the Channel, mature colonies on manufacture and trade, and the antithesis of democratic ideals to empire.

Thursday, April 28

Flew to Brooklands (solo), taxied to hangars near Hawker assembly plant, and met Burdette Wright[30] as planned. We were shown through the Hawker works. There were a number of Hurricanes under construction and assembly. Also one Henley. The design was clean and the workmanship good.

After going through the Hawker factory, we were driven to the Vickers works. They have finished an order for Wellesleys and are starting the production of Wellingtons. Both embody the geodetic type of construction. The designs are good and the workmanship excellent, but I am still doubtful about the desirability of geodetic construction for quantity production. I am also somewhat skeptical about the use of fabric covering, although the covering is beautifully done at the Vickers plant. Neither the Vickers nor the Hawker plant at Brooklands are well laid out for mass production, according to American standards.

After lunch we took off for Southampton. Wright flew in a Falcon, and I in my Mohawk. We were met at the Southampton airport and driven to the Vickers factory—the one where Anne and I landed the *Tingmis-*

30. Vice president and director of Curtiss-Wright Corp.

23

sartoq[31] in 1933, and where we left it for a week or two while we visited Aubrey and Elisabeth[32] in Wales. This factory is producing a biplane type of flying boat which looks obsolete by five years at least. They are also producing Spitfires—a very clean, low-wing monoplane, single-seat fighter. There were about sixteen jigs for the latter.

After about an hour in the factory we drove back to the airport and took off on our return flight.

Friday, April 29

Anne and I drove to Sevenoaks and took the train for London in time to meet a luncheon engagement with His Highness the Maharaja of Baroda and the Maharanee. They had sent us an invitation through Sir Francis Younghusband.[33] We had lunch at the Dorchester Hotel. Conversation a little difficult but interesting. The Maharanee is against everything British and spent a large part of the time telling me how bad the British airlines are. She knew her facts amazingly well, and none of them were any credit to the English. She simply refused to listen to anything good about them and, I think, never forgot anything bad. There were five of us at the table: the Maharaja, the Maharanee, their English secretary (poor man), Anne, and I. We talked a great deal about India, our trip there last year, etc.

31. A low-wing, single-engine, tandem-cockpit monoplane, specially designed to Lindbergh's specifications by the Lockheed Aircraft Corp. at Burbank, Calif., in 1929. This plane started the Lockheed "Sirius" series. Originally produced as a landplane (with which Charles and Anne Lindbergh in 1930 established a new transcontinental speed record), it was converted to a twin-pontoon seaplane for the Lindberghs' survey flight over the great-circle route between New York and Tokyo in 1931. It was named *Tingmissartoq* after the Eskimo cries heard on landing in Arctic areas, meaning "one who flies like a big bird." This plane was used by the Lindberghs for their 1933 survey of potential transatlantic air routes and bases.

32. Aubrey Niel Morgan, grandson of the founder of David Morgan, Ltd., a large department store in Cardiff, Wales, married Anne Morrow Lindbergh's elder sister, Elisabeth, who died in 1934. In June, 1937, he married her younger sister, Constance. Cattle rancher; later, wartime Controller of the British Information Services in New York, Counsellor of the British Embassy in Washington, and assistant to the British Ambassador, Sir Oliver Franks.

33. British soldier, explorer, and author of numerous books on India, Sir Francis made contributions to the defining of geographic border positions in India and Tibet. He traveled extensively in India, Manchuria, China, and South Africa.

Saturday, April 30

Anne, Margaret Morgan,[34] and I drove to Sissinghurst Castle for tea with Mrs. Nicolson. Harold Nicolson[35] is on the Continent. We returned to Long Barn about 6:30. Mr. and Mrs. Burdette Wright and Colonel Scanlon came for supper. We spent the evening talking about aviation in America and in Europe. Wright estimates that about twenty-five per cent to thirty per cent more workmen are required in England to equal American production. The English workman does not seem able to compete with the American in output. Our pace is probably too fast in America for our own good. On the other hand, everything seems incredibly slow in this country.

Sunday, May 1

Lady Astor[36] telephoned this morning and invited us for lunch, dinner, and the night. We (Anne, Margaret Morgan, and I) drove to Cliveden for lunch and returned after tea. There were fifteen or twenty people there, including Sir Thomas Inskip.[37] He, Lord Astor,[38] and I left the others after lunch and spent half an hour talking about military aviation in England, Germany, and the United States. Afterward, Lord Astor took us over his estate to see his dairy farm and modern milking equipment. He said he was milking over 160 cows. I sat next to Lady Astor again at tea. She is violently opposed to any commitments to

34. Sister of Aubrey Morgan.

35. English diplomat, biographer, and historian. He was an M.P. (National Labour) from West Leicester, 1935–45. Author of a biography of Anne Morrow Lindbergh's father, *Dwight Morrow* (1935). Mrs. Nicolson, under the name V. [Victoria] Sackville-West, was the author of novels, poetry, short stories, and travel books.

36. Nancy Witcher (Langhorne) Astor, wife of Waldorf Astor, 2nd Viscount, who, upon succeeding his father as Viscount, had to give up his seat for Plymouth in Parliament. Nancy Astor ran as a Conservative for Plymouth, becoming in 1919 the first woman to sit in Parliament. The Astors were old Morrow family friends. Cliveden, the Astor country house, was famous for its gatherings of the great literary and political figures of the time.

37. British Minister for the Co-ordination of Defence.

38. Waldorf Astor, 2nd Viscount. Former Parliamentary Secretary to the Prime Minister, M.P. for Plymouth, and British delegate to the League of Nations Assembly.

France. Wants better understanding with Germany. I was encouraged about the feeling of most of the people there in regard to Germany. They understood the situation better than most Englishmen do these days.

Inskip said the bombing in China and in Spain had not been as effective as many people had expected it to be. Said the bombers had not been very successful in hitting their objectives. I told him I didn't think you could judge much from the Japanese bombing, as their aviation is so poor. However, there should be some modern machines and skilled aviators in Spain from both Germany and Italy.

Inskip asked me about American planes, potential output, etc. Also about the possibility of flying large bombers across the ocean in case of necessity. I do not think the English aviation people yet fully realize the great capacity of the German aviation industry. I believe the Germans can probably produce more military aircraft than the British Empire and the United States combined, with the facilities which now exist. Of course, we could expand our output very rapidly in the United States.

Thursday, May 5

Anne and I took the train to London for a lunch engagement at Lady Astor's. In addition to Lord and Lady Astor there were Mr. and Mrs. George Bernard Shaw, Ambassador Kennedy,[39] Ambassador Bullitt,[40] an editor from the *Times* (London), and two or three others whose names I do not recall. It was one of the most interesting lunches I ever attended. Always several conversations, each of which I wanted to listen to. Not that I like several conversations at the same time, but it is so seldom that even one is absorbing at a lunch or dinner table.

Kennedy interested me greatly. He is not the usual type of politician or diplomat. His views on the European situation seem intelligent and interesting. I hope to see more of him. Jerry Land[41] told me he was well worth knowing. The conversations at the table and afterward covered too much ground to permit describing in detail. England, America, Russia, France, Germany, all were touched. Also aviation, both civil and military, present and future.

39. Joseph P. Kennedy, U.S. Ambassador to Great Britain, 1937–40.
40. William C. Bullitt, American diplomat, and Ambassador to France, 1936–41.
41. Rear Admiral Emory Scott Land, cousin of Charles Lindbergh, and chairman of the U.S. Maritime Commission.

Sunday, May 8

Anne and I drove to Hever Castle for lunch with Lord and Lady Astor.[42] After arriving, we found that Lady Astor had been called to the Continent unexpectedly, due to her sister's illness. About eight or ten people at lunch table. Usual conversation, only slightly more interesting—gardens, aviation, Germany, the history of the castle. After lunch Lord Astor took us through the rooms and around the grounds. He is a pleasant and interesting man. I enjoyed being with him and talking to him.

Hever Castle is indescribably beautiful. A moated castle, small, in excellent repair, and cared for with exceptionally good taste. It is by far the most attractive castle I have seen. In keeping with its external appearance, each room is filled with objects of great interest and historical significance. Henry VIII courted Anne Boleyn there and afterward stayed in one of the rooms. It is a pleasure to see anything so beautiful. Gives me a feeling of encouragement, like the feeling I have after a visit to Saint-Gildas, or reading a well-written book, or completing a difficult flight.

Mrs. Morrow[43] arrived about 5:30, after driving from Southampton. She and Jon are having a wonderful time.

Tuesday, May 10

Spent afternoon writing and reading the manuscript of Dr. Carrel's biography (by [Arthur] Train, Jr.),[44] which has just arrived. It contains interesting material but . . . needs much more work.

42. The Honorable John Jacob Astor and his wife, Violet. Lord Astor was the youngest son of the 1st Viscount Astor, chairman of the Times Publishing Co., and M.P., Dover Division of Kent.

43. Mrs. Dwight W. Morrow was born in Cleveland, Ohio, in 1873. A graduate of Smith College, she married Dwight W. Morrow in 1903. They had four children: Elisabeth, Anne, Dwight, and Constance. She had a lifelong interest in women's education, was chairman of the board of trustees of Smith College and, for a time, acting president. Author of *The Painted Pig; Beast, Bird and Fish; Quatrains for My Daughter; My Favorite Age* (a collection of children's stories).

44. This biography was never published.

Sunday, May 15

Day at Long Barn working on last drawing for *Listen! the Wind*. Finished about midnight.

Tuesday, May 17

Drove to London in time to change clothes at Ritz Hotel and go to American Embassy with Anne and Mrs. Morrow for dinner. Very little chance to talk except with table partners. There was a long talking picture after dinner—*Test Pilot*. Lord knows how they happened to pick that one. All guests left immediately after it was over.

I had a few minutes' conversation with Mr. Hore-Belisha[45] before dinner about English aviation, and German. He asked me if I thought England would be able to produce airplanes fast enough in the future. I told him that I was very much worried about the situation which now exists in English aviation. He suggested that it was not possible to compete with German aircraft production under the present economic system in England, that Germany was sacrificing everything to rearm, etc. The announcement of dinner broke up our conversation, and there was no opportunity to renew it later.

Sunday, May 22

After lunch Anne, Mrs. Morrow, and I drove to Sissinghurst for tea. Mr. and Mrs. Nicolson, Ben Nicolson,[46] and Mrs. St. Aubyn[47] were there. Harold Nicolson and I talked about the crisis in Czechoslovakia. He [is] greatly worried and very anti-German. I took Germany's side, possibly too ardently, as is usually the case in an argument of this kind. After all, there are many things I don't understand about the Germans myself.

45. The Right Honorable Leslie Hore-Belisha, Secretary of State for War, Great Britain, 1937–40.

46. Eldest son of Harold Nicolson.

47. Mrs. Francis St. Aubyn, sister of Harold Nicolson.

Monday, May 23

Dinner at Lady Astor's home, and ball afterward. The King and Queen[48] were there. Also the Duke and Duchess of Kent, and dozens of people we had never met before. Lord Astor was ill and could not attend.

The Queen talked to Anne for about fifteen minutes. Later on, the Queen sent word through the master of the bedchamber that she wished me to dance with her!! I said I had never danced a step in my life. He replied that she would sit out the dance and that it would be all right anyway. The Queen was talking to someone and, while I waited for her to finish, he pointed to a huge gold key he was wearing and said it was a symbol of the time when his predecessors guarded the Queen's bedchamber. "Only the Queen and her maids were allowed to enter, and, of course, the King."

I sat with the Queen for about twenty minutes. It was the second time. The first time was at Sir Philip Sassoon's[49] home about a year ago. Sassoon invited me to come there after the air display at Hendon. We had dinner (there were probably thirty people present) and later watched a fireworks display on the lawn.

The Queen is a fine woman. Very natural. Dignified, but not at all stiff. Making a tremendous effort to carry on her part as Queen of England. She did it beautifully, but it was easy to see what a strain she was under. She asked me about aviation. Said it was a relief to sit out the dance. Spoke of the troubles the world is having. Asked about the Hearst press and American newspapers. She seemed relieved whenever I talked. As though she wanted a rest from the necessity of leading the conversation constantly. I liked her very much and felt extremely sorry for her. She is making a desperate struggle to keep the character she had when her life was reasonably normal. May God help her. I think it is an almost impossible task for the Queen of England. I shall always respect and like her for what I saw in her that night.

Anne and I left about 2:00 A.M. after saying good-by to Lady Astor.

48. King George VI and Queen Elizabeth.
49. First Commissioner of Works in the British government, M.P. since 1912, and Undersecretary of State for Air, 1931–37.

Tuesday, May 24

Herschel Johnson[50] came for supper. We talked about the European situation, about my visit to Tegucigalpa[51] in 1928 (he was a member of the consulate then), about Elisabeth, and many things.

Thursday, May 26

Morning at Long Barn working on *Listen! the Wind* and making plans for leaving Long Barn. We have extended our lease for a week.

Attended the annual Wright Memorial Lecture of the Royal Aeronautical Society in London at 6:30. Also the dinner later in the evening. Sat between Mr. Short[52] and Mr. Fairey.[53] Talked of aviation most of the evening. The problems of war ran through all conversation. Short spoke of the time, about 1928, when he was in the United States and we (he, Dick Hoyt,[54] several other people, and I) were considering taking a Short boat from England to America over the northern route. Fairey said he was on the coast of England and saw me fly over in the *Spirit of St. Louis* in 1927. We discussed the problems involved in increasing the production of military aircraft in this country. He is in favor of starting production directly from the drawing board without wasting time on prototypes.

Glenn Martin[55] was there, and I talked to him for a few minutes.

Tuesday, May 31

The packers arrived at 10:30, and the day was given over to them until they left at about 6:30.

50. Foreign service officer and counselor of the U.S. Embassy in London; he had been a member of Ambassador Dwight W. Morrow's staff in Mexico City.

51. During Lindbergh's tour around the Gulf of Mexico and Caribbean Sea in 1927–28 with the *Spirit of St. Louis*.

52. Hugh Oswald Short, English aircraft designer. He designed and manufactured seaplanes and flying boats before and during World War I and supervised the design of the Short flying boat.

53. Charles R. Fairey, English aviation engineer and founder of the Fairey Aviation Co. in 1915. He was awarded the Wakefield Gold Medal by the Royal Aeronautical Society for the invention of the wing flap.

54. Richard F. Hoyt, financier, executive of Haydn, Stone and Co., and member of a syndicate that bought Orville Wright's factory and patent rights.

55. Early aircraft pioneer and president of Glenn L. Martin Co. of Baltimore.

Glenn Martin and his mother came for supper. Glenn is extremely pessimistic about conditions in the States. Expects serious trouble in about "two or two and a half years." He looks for trouble sooner than that in France. We spent the evening in front of a big wood fire in the Long Room, talking of aviation and general conditions throughout the world.

Wednesday, June 1

The sample covers for *Listen! the Wind* came this morning. Anne and I don't feel that any of them are exactly right and have sent for still more.

Anne and I took the 1:40 to London. We go to the ball at Buckingham Palace at 10:30 tonight. Knee breeches!!!

I went to the Dorchester at 4:30 to meet the Maharanee's nephew, Mr. Ghatge. She wrote, asking me to talk to him about aviation and to give him some advice.

It turned out to be a difficult problem. He is a second pilot on Imperial Airways and, of course, an Indian. He has flown for several years and has seen his juniors (English) made first pilots, while he has had difficulty in even remaining on as second pilot. It's the same old problem the airlines have been putting off from year to year and which eventually they must face—whether or not to let native pilots (Indian, Mexican, etc.) handle the transport planes of England and the United States. On the one hand there is the desire to use personnel of the operating country. Also a genuine feeling (not without foundation) that very few native pilots (again Indians, Mexicans, etc.) are competent. Whether they are or not, there is the very serious difficulty of persuading the British and American passengers that they are.

Ghatge had the idea that if I would take him up in a plane and test him, it would make it hard for Imperial to refuse to make him a first pilot. That is, if I said he could fly properly. I countered this with the argument that I, an American, could not very well do that in England, where I was living as a guest. He seemed to understand and agree to this, but I had a few difficult minutes.

Later on, the Maharanee came in, and we talked of India. She invited us to visit them.

Left for Buckingham Palace in time to arrive at 10:30. The ball was extremely interesting and not at all difficult, as I had expected it would be. Lady Astor helped to make it very enjoyable. I have never seen Anne happier. These things are done better in England than anywhere else.

31

There is a taste and dignity here that I have never seen equaled elsewhere. The King and Queen danced until 3:00 A.M. Many people had left. Anne and I drove back to Claridge's for the night.

Friday, June 3

Juan Trippe[56] telephoned from New York. Said he had been asked to get in touch with me to find out in confidence whether I would take the chairmanship of the new Civil Aviation Commission, which is being formed in the United States. I told him that I did not think it advisable to move my family back to America under present circumstances, and that, consequently, I did not see how it would be possible for me to accept the position. There was not time to tell him more, or to talk about details over the transatlantic phone. Trippe said the request came from headquarters, which means Roosevelt. I wonder what is behind it. Political gesture? Outside pressure? Knowledge that I would not be very likely to accept? I wish I could feel that the President had made the suggestion without pressure and without thinking primarily of the political effect. It would be a great honor, although one for which my temperament is not well suited.

The appointment would be for six years. They would probably be the six unhappiest years I ever spent. There are people who like that type of work and who can put the best they have into it. They are the ones to whom such an appointment should go. I might, through great effort, have been successful if I had undertaken it, but one can do his best only in the work in which he is most interested. I have never been, and never will be, well fitted for any routine office. My mind, my ability, and my life lie in other lines.

Saturday, June 4

Took early train to London. Put suitcase containing Anne's diaries in the Morgan Grenfell vaults. Signed the book at Buckingham Palace.

Sunday, June 5

Day at Long Barn packing. Read a few pages of Plato's *Republic* in between. A long day but nearly everything finished. Will save much time

56. Close friend of Lindbergh. World War I naval pilot, airline pioneer, organizer and president of Pan American Airways, later chairman of the board.

later on when we need the things I am now packing. It always saves time, to pack well, eventually.

Tuesday, June 7

Finished final arrangements. Anne and I took the 10:37 train to London, en route to Reading. Mohawk waiting in hangar, but no one was in the hangar—all workmen away for lunch; not even a guard left. We packed in our bundles and looked over the plane and engine. Finally, one man sauntered in the door and very obligingly helped us push the plane out onto the field. We warmed up the engine and took off immediately. Landed at Lympne and Saint Inglevert to clear customs. Then set course for Morlaix, detouring along the coast line. The weather was good, and we made fast time. Our new Menasco engine and controllable-pitch propeller had been installed a few days before we left England. The propeller seemed to increase our cruising speed by about ten knots.

Mme. Carrel and M. and Mlle. Masson were on the field at Morlaix waiting for us. Miss Hutchison was also there with the little Ford car and Thor and Skean.[57] We drove to Saint-Gildas for the night. The tide was quite low when we crossed to the island. It seems more beautiful every time we come.

Wednesday, June 8

Took the motorboat to Illiec—Mme. Carrel, Anne, and I. The workmen were far behind and had just finished the plastering. It was obvious that we could not move in for another week at least. Returned to Saint-Gildas.

Sunday, June 12

Up at 2:45 and at 3:50 started with both cars (Mme. Carrel's Ford and ours) to Saint-Malo to meet Jon and Land and Miss Wesley. Anne and I went ahead in the V-8 Ford. Miss Hutchison followed in ours. The boat from Southampton was about on time, and the children had stood the crossing well.

We started the return drive before 9:00 and stopped for breakfast on the way (they had had none). Reached Buguélès about 12:30. Mme. Carrel was waiting for us with the donkey and cart from Saint-Gildas.

57. A German shepherd and Scottie respectively.

She and Miss Wesley went in the cart with the children. Miss Hutchison and Anne and I drove the cars back to Port Blanc. Later, Anne and I drove our Ford to Illiec. The road is very bad (completely covered by the sea at high tide). Then we walked to Saint-Gildas.

Monday, June 20

[We] started packing for our move to Illiec.

We left Saint-Gildas in the boat about 10:30. Mme. Carrel, Pierre, Miss Wesley, Jon, Land, Anne, and I. Most of our luggage was packed in the bow. The rest was put in the little rowboat and towed.

It is about a ten-minute trip to Illiec by boat. The tide was in, and we could go right up to the little stone pier. We unpacked and began to organize the house. The rooms on the middle floor are finished, but there is painting to be done everywhere else.

We spent the rest of the day on the infinite number of details involved in moving into a new home and in going over Anne's manuscript. It must be mailed soon if it is to reach the publishers by the first of July.

Tuesday, June 21

First morning on Illiec. We could hear the waves all night, although there was almost no wind. At high tide they roll the stones up and down on the beach outside our window. A storm on the island must be wonderful.

Spent the first part of the morning on Anne's book. The manuscript is nearly ready to send to Harcourt, Brace and Company. There is nothing left to do except for Anne to look over the places I mark on this reading. I am working on the high rock beside the house. This is the most ideal place to work I have ever seen. I read two or three chapters, and then Anne comes and checks over my marks.

Mme. Carrel arrives about midmorning. She tells us she must go to Paris tomorrow. I offer to take her by plane.

Anne and I spend the rest of the morning and afternoon on *Listen! the Wind*. We finish it and seal the manuscript. Anne writes a letter of enclosure, and it is done—after about two years of work.

I walk to Saint-Gildas before supper. Thor goes over with me, but gets tired of waiting and returns alone to Illiec—and Anne. He is never happy away from her.

Wednesday, June 22

Mme. Carrel and I drive to Morlaix. I refuel and we start for Paris. We fly over Saint-Gildas and circle Illiec en route. We land at Buc Aerodrome after a flight of two hours, fifteen minutes. Take taxi to Paris. Go first to Mme. Carrel's apartment. Later, I take taxi to Hôtel Crillon, were Anne and I stayed while we were in Paris on our 1933 trip. Try to phone Détroyat[58] but no answer. Walked around the streets and in the park after eating and before returning to the hotel. Paris is getting ready to welcome the King and Queen of England. The streets are lined with grandstands and horrible plaster casts around the lampposts. People seem to be doing everything they can to make the streets look ugly when the King comes.

Thursday, June 23

A noisy night. As bad as New York, but seems worse after the peace and quiet of Saint-Gildas and Illiec.

Breakfast in room. Would rather go down to the dining room but there may be press people there, and, if not, there are almost certainly American tourists. Better to stay in my room and start the day fresh. Also, my window looks out over the Place de la Concorde, and I can watch the traffic. It is amazing to watch the motorcars and trucks sift through the crossings of Place de la Concorde. There is no regulation, and they go fast, dashing at each other from right angles and missing by inches. It is as though all the cogs in an intricate machine came off the wheels and still meshed.

I phoned Ambassador Bullitt. Went to the embassy and spent quarter of hour talking to Bullitt and about an hour talking to the military attaché. We discussed a variety of subjects, including European conditions in general and military aviation in particular. France seems to be in worse shape from an aviation standpoint than I believed, and I knew conditions were bad. There are not enough modern military planes in this country to even put up a show in case of war. In a conflict between France, England, and Russia on one side, against Germany on the other,

58. Michel Détroyat, one of the French aviators who rescued Lindbergh from the crowd at Le Bourget Aerodrome, Paris, in 1927. He was classed among the most skillful test and acrobatic pilots.

Germany would immediately have supremacy of the air. Even if the present French program is carried out during the next two years, there will be a relatively small number of planes available for service. Germany has developed a huge Air Force while England has slept and France has deluded herself with a Russian alliance.

It seems that the French Air Corps is infiltrated with Communism. Especially among the higher officers. The French Army, on the other hand (according to the people I have talked to here), is still in very good condition and contains comparatively little Communistic influence.

Left the embassy about 12:00 and had lunch with Captain [Townsend] Griffis (my commanding officer, when I was a cadet at Brooks Field; C.O. of the cadet detachment, not of the field). He had recently come back from Spain, where he has been the American air attaché. He has probably seen as much of the Spanish aviation situation as anyone not directly connected with the fight. He expects Franco to win but not without more hard fighting. Says the military aviation has not been very well used by either side in Spain and that, consequently, it is dangerous to draw conclusions from the results. The bombing has been inaccurate and the pilots not well trained. Many of them just out of training school when they are sent out on service missions. The equipment, too, has been of all types—modern and old, good and bad.

Griffis says that both sides are shooting down any pilot who jumps from his plane. About the only hope seems to be for the pilot to wait until he is nearly to the ground before pulling his rip cord. He told me of a report about a Spanish government pilot who was shot down near Bilbao some months ago and who jumped from his plane. A German Heinkel was diving on him as he hung from his parachute and was obviously about to shoot him. The government pilot drew his gun, placed it to his head, and faked a collapse as though he had shot himself. The German plane pulled off, thinking the man was dead, and flew away.

Griffis said one of the greatest dangers in the air war in Spain was to be shot down by your own ground troops. He said that the sky-blue paint on the bottom of war planes had been abandoned and every effort made to mark the plane clearly for the ground troops. The ground troops are, he said, prone to believe that their safety lies in shooting first and investigating afterward. Griffis said that all American pilots had left the government side in Spain, but that many Russian pilots were flying against Franco. He (Griffis) is a great supporter of single-seater pursuit, both for defense against bombers and for ground attack.

After lunch Griffis drove Mme. Carrel and me to Buc. We talked about Spain during the entire drive and left many subjects untouched.

Mme. Carrel and I took off for Illiec about 4:00, or a little after, and landed at Morlaix about 6:45. We flew over Illiec en route, and I dropped a note, written on my map, for Anne, telling her we would arrive for 8:15 supper. We found Anne walking with Jon and Thor between the little islands of Illiec. The message landed within a few yards of her, as we were able to fly very low. (There is, fortunately, no one at Illiec to complain about flying low.) We encountered fog between Illiec and Morlaix but were delayed only a few minutes in detouring. It was a sea fog and did not reach more than a few miles inland. Otherwise, the weather was excellent.

Friday, June 24

Anne and I spent the day on Illiec, arranging the house and making plans for the work which must be done to put the island in good condition. Savina and two of his men came to put the oak doors in the study and to set up some of the furniture.

Saturday, June 25

Savina and his men came again this morning. Anne, Jon, and I drove back to Tréguier with him to talk over plans for furnishing the house. On the way back we stopped at Port Blanc to see the old chapel there. We thought we might be able to get some ideas for reconstructing the chapel on Illiec. Everything old about the Port Blanc Chapel is quite lovely. Everything new is horrible. We decided that we might be able to copy the floor and one of the windows.

Mme. Carrel came over at high tide. The barometer is going down slowly, and there is some hope of rain. The country needs it very badly. No one around here can remember as long a drought before. We have had no rain for several months; the grass on the island is brown. Conditions on the farms are becoming serious.

Mme. Carrel leaves for Cherbourg tomorrow to meet Dr. Carrel, who will arrive on the *Normandie* Monday.

Tuesday, June 28

Spent morning with Anne, purchasing articles for Illiec. Returned home in time for late lunch. Dr. and Mme. Carrel had just walked over from Saint-Gildas and were in front of the house when we arrived. We showed them the island and talked to Dr. Carrel about the Rockefeller Institute and about conditions in the United States. He has had a very successful winter, although a difficult one in many ways.

Anne and I went to Saint-Gildas for supper (by boat with Pierre). A strong wind was blowing, and we had a rough trip. It is Dr. Carrel's sixty-fifth birthday. We walked back to Illiec just before dark.

Wednesday, June 29

Dr. and Mme. Carrel came for lunch. It has been a day spent thinking about the future and without anything very definite accomplished. However, even though there is little to show for them, these are probably among the most important days in life. Tangible results always rest on intangible foundations.

Friday, July 1

Dr. and Mme. Carrel came over twice today. First in the morning with the rector of the church at Port Blanc to look at the chapel and consider the changes to be made. Second in the evening just before sunset. We all watched the sun go down from the top of the big rock.

Saturday, July 2

Mother[59] sails today and will be here within a week now. She has never seen Land and has not seen Jon since 1936—two years ago.

I walked to Saint-Gildas to see Dr. and Mme. Carrel. Dr. Carrel is

59. Mrs. Evangeline Lodge Land Lindbergh was born in Detroit, Mich., in 1876, and was a B.S. graduate of the University of Michigan. She taught at the high school in Little Falls, Minn., where she met and in 1901 married Charles A. Lindbergh. She had one child, Charles, Jr. After her husband's death in 1924 she returned to teaching and held positions at Roberts College, Istanbul, Turkey, and at Cass Technical High School, Detroit, Mich.

starting his new book. We talked of closing his department at the Rockefeller Institute next year and of his plans for the future. A definite retirement age is a stupid regulation and one which shows the weakness of the officers and directors of an institution. Some men should be retired at thirty and others should be allowed to work until they die. How silly it is to retire a man of genius because he is sixty-five and at the same time keep fools of forty because they are young. However, there is more than that behind Carrel's retirement next year. Many of the people of the Institute dislike him and misunderstand him. Carrel has never gone out of his way to make friends and, on the other hand, has created many enemies. It is often that way with a man of strong character. Carrel wants to continue active work, and he should have the facilities to work with. I hope to find some way of helping him. I think his new book is his most important work at present, but he cannot devote the rest of his life to writing. Good writing should always be done slowly. One cannot write eight hours a day and write well.

Sunday, July 3

Morning on Illiec, thinking about plans and climbing rocks with Jon. Jon is careful and has no fear whatever—a perfect combination.

After lunch Anne, Jon, and I walk over to Saint-Gildas to hunt for "knife" clams. Mme. Carrel goes with us, and Dr. Carrel comes later. We return to Illiec about five with a half pailful of clams of various sorts, mostly "cockles." Jon is very pleased and very tired.

I spend the evening reading the second volume of *War and Peace*.

Tuesday, July 5

Dr. and Mme. Carrel came for lunch. We spent an hour on the rocks before lunchtime. There was a strong sea and high waves. Jon went with us. Dr. Carrel and I talk about experiments, past and future, new apparatus, etc., also general and political conditions in America and Europe.

Wednesday, July 6

Day on Illiec, dictating, working, and reading. And, of course, walks around the island. I never tire of it. A wonderful place to work. The greatest possible beauty outside every door and every window.

The contractor came from Port Blanc this afternoon, and we talked about various changes to be made. Also repairs to the sea walls. His men are now working on the wall on the sea side of the house, replacing the earth top with stone.

Land and Jon are both very well. I think they will have different characteristics. It will be extremely interesting to watch them develop.

Thursday, July 7

Mme. Carrel came in the middle of the morning to warn us that a boatload of reporters was en route to Illiec. They came, but started back within a half hour after being met by Kerleau and Louis.[60]

Saturday, July 9

After lunch Jon and I went to Buguélès in the sailboat with Louis and Kerleau, and drove to Plouaret to meet Mother. Her train was late, and we were too late for the tide when we reached Buguélès. We all walked to Illiec over the stone beach. Mother did not want to wait until we could drive. Anne had kept Land up so Mother could see him. Everyone very happy. Mother has the tower room, looking out over the tideland.

Tuesday, July 12

Mother, Anne, and I went to Saint-Gildas for dinner with Dr. and Mme. Carrel. Dr. Carrel says there are rumors of war starting in August (by Germany, of course). We walk across the bridge and to the top of the hill after supper. Mme. Carrel tells us that we must start back, as the tide is going out rapidly. We get to Illiec without difficulty, but the motorboat grounds while Pierre is rowing us to shore. (You can actually see the tide go out it moves so fast.) They have to leave the motorboat, and Pierre rows Dr. and Mme. Carrel back to Saint-Gildas in the small rowboat.

Tuesday, July 19

Started dictation this morning when Pierre arrived in the boat with a message from Dr. Carrel that a water diviner was coming to Saint-Gildas

60. Fishermen who worked for the Lindberghs on Illiec. Louis was the island's caretaker.

to try to locate a well. I returned with Pierre, but the man did not arrive until after lunch. Meanwhile, Dr. Carrel and I talked of possible experiments and new techniques. We also talked of plans for closing his department next year. I believe the Rockefeller Institute is making a great mistake in taking this action.

When the diviner arrived, he started working in the walled garden and later covered most of the island of Saint-Gildas. He found water frequently but usually at a depth of twenty meters (too deep for a dug well). He walks about holding a forked stick in his hands—the ends clasped so that the spring of the wood makes the position of the stick unsteady. I tried with another stick and got plenty of indications but don't feel at all sure of being able to get an indication in the same spot twice.

The diviner says he can use a bent wire as well as a forked stick. (He used to be a sailor and started divining only in the last few years.)

I have not gained very much confidence in the method, but the people around here swear by it. The local contractor (François Tinnevez) went with us and has complete confidence in the diviner. Says he has dug many wells according to the man's directions and has always found water within a foot of the depth prophesied by the diviner.

The only place on Saint-Gildas where the diviner found water near the surface was at "Saint-Gildas Fount." [61] He said it was only about four meters down at that point.

He measures the depth of water by holding a watch on a long chain as a pendulum. Every swing back and forth indicates one foot (found out by previous experiment, he says). When the pendulum begins to rotate, he stops counting. The measurements took a long time, as the pendulum usually swung sixty times before it began rotating. (Dr. Carrel asked the diviner if he had tried to find other things than water. He replied that he had once found the true father of an illegitimate child, but had gotten into so much trouble he hadn't tried again.)

Later in the afternoon I took the diviner to Illiec. I wanted Anne and Mother to see him, and I was curious to see what he would find. He got many indications of water but at about twenty meters, as at Saint-Gildas. Said the Illiec well was located in a good position and had two veins of water feeding it, but that it was not deep enough.

61. The existing well.

Sunday, July 24

Jon and I went swimming after lunch. Dr. and Mme. Carrel came for a short visit. Mother spends most of her time with Jon and Land. Gives them far too much attention, but she gets so much pleasure from them that we hate to take any of it away from her. If she only didn't want to pick up Land every time he starts to cry and to protect Jon from the little knocks essential for a child's experience.

I walked to Saint-Gildas after supper to give Dr. Carrel some American papers and magazines.

Monday, July 25

Dr. Nute[62] came in the afternoon. Anne and I drove to Lannion to meet her.

Tuesday, July 26

Talked to Dr. Nute about her work in Sweden and her plans for Father's biography.[63]

Thursday, July 28

After lunch we all went hunting abalones, as there was a very low tide. We got enough for a meal. It was the first time I had ever looked for them, and it took a little time to learn how to find them. Kerleau and Louis showed us where to look—under stones and in cracks. They can only be obtained for about an hour and only at the low tides of the month. After the tide began to come in we went shrimp and crab hunting on the other side of the island.

62. Grace Lee Nute, historian, author, and curator of manuscripts for the Minnesota Historical Society.

63. Charles A. Lindbergh, Sr., emigrated as an infant with his parents from Sweden to the Minnesota frontier about 1860. He became a lawyer and was a Progressive Republican Congressman from the Sixth District of Minnesota from 1907 to 1917. He was a candidate for governor in the Farmer-Labor primary election at the time of his death. Author of *Banking and Currency and the Money Trust; Why Is Your Country at War?; The Economic Pinch.* Dr. Nute's biography was never completed.

Saturday, July 30

Walked to Saint-Gildas and found Mme. Carrel ill. Dr. Carrel very worried. Afraid it might be serious—bad symptoms.

Anne, Dr. Nute, and I drove to Lannion where Dr. Nute took the train to Paris. She sails for America in a few days. The tide was high, and we were able to go to and from the island by boat.

Sunday, July 31

Jon has had a boil on his knee for several days. It seemed worse this morning. We went to Saint-Gildas with the old sailboat to see Mme. Carrel and took Jon with us. Mme. Carrel was very much better and was in a chair in the garden with Dr. Carrel. She insisted on bandaging Jon's knee. It is impossible to keep her still no matter how ill she is. Mme. Carrel is apparently having trouble with her heart and should remain still for a time. When she saw Jon, she refused to stay in her chair and ran into the house to get bandages, hot water, and Clonozone. Anne and I left as soon as possible so that she would rest.

We decided to take Jon to the doctor in Tréguier, so set sail for Buguélès from Saint-Gildas. The tide was against us, and there was very little wind. It took a long time to make the trip, and there was barely enough water. Kerleau had to leave the boat at Buguélès. The tide was falling too fast for him to return to Illiec.

Anne, Jon, and I drove to Tréguier to Dr. Le Guent. He advised a hot compress soaked in H_2O_2 three times a day.

Dr. Carrel had told us that Mme. Carrel might eat some peaches, so we bought a number and I took them to Saint-Gildas in the late afternoon. She was much better, had slept, and was moving about actively again.

Monday, August 1

Jon's knee much better this morning. Did some dictating and inspected work on island. Dr. and Mme. Carrel came over by boat after supper. Mme. Carrel should have been in bed, but it is impossible to keep her there.

Tuesday, August 2

Telegram came from Colonel Lee, suggesting that we go to Russia between August 10 and 20.[64] Went over flying papers, passports, etc., to make sure all in order.

Have fallen so far behind in this record recently that I have not tried to include all details of life on the island. We have gone swimming frequently, I have made numerous trips to Saint-Gildas, and we have spent many hours on the rocks, especially in the evening.

Friday, August 5

Anne and I make plans for trip to Moscow. I do not want to leave Mother so soon, but she must sail for home soon, and we will probably see her this winter in the United States. I think it is essential to see enough of Europe to be able to think intelligently about the problems which exist here. I do not want war to start without having a fairly good idea of its causes and probable consequences. I plan on seeing as much of the European situation as possible in the next few months.

Kerleau and I walked to the mainland before supper to see our boat and the engine, which has just arrived. The boat will be finished in a few days. It is small and well built, with both engine and sail.

Saturday, August 6

Day spent getting ready for trip to Russia—packing, going over equipment lists, and dictating letters. Spent as much time as possible with Mother. Made several inspection trips around Illiec. The workmen are building a sea wall in front of the two trees on the rock and are removing the plaster from the chapel walls. Walked to Saint-Gildas in the evening to tell Dr. and Mme. Carrel that we are leaving in the morning. Returned by moonlight.

64. The purpose of this trip was to study Russian aviation; it was part of a larger project to make a comparative study of air strength of the major European countries.

Sunday, August 7

Mother, Anne, Miss Hutchison, and I drove to Morlaix airport. I made one solo flight to test the plane, then took Mother for a thirty-minute flight over Illiec. Anne and I took off about 2:00 and flew over Illiec. It is only about ten minutes off our route. We landed at Le Havre because of a slight smell of hot rubber and excessive oil on the windshield, but found nothing wrong. Took off again and headed for England via Saint Inglevert. Struck rain and fog areas—long detours. Got within fifteen miles of Saint Inglevert but had to turn back. Landed at Le Bourget and took taxi to Paris—Hôtel Crillon.

Now 10:30 and too tired to write more. Always that way at end of the fullest and most interesting days. After a day filled with action it seems impossible to concentrate on writing.

My only regret about this trip is leaving Mother before I had intended to. I had counted on another week with her, at least. Feel I did not do enough for her this summer. Seems that I was always asking her not to pick up Land when he cried, or to let Jon take care of his own little problems. I wonder whether it is more important to bring up your children as you think best for them or to give the utmost happiness to their grandmothers by letting them do almost everything you refrain from doing yourself? There must be some satisfactory solution to this problem, but I have not yet been able to find it.

Monday, August 8

Rumors of Germany starting war on August 15—was August 1 a month ago.

Arrived at airport about 11:00. Weather still bad along route, although high clouds and sky showing at Le Bourget. Decided to try to get through and to land at intermediate field if too bad. Had no trouble in reaching Saint Inglevert, however, as fog was clearing. Channel was covered with low fog, but Lympne fairly clear, with only slight haze and few low clouds scattered about.

Minister of War's plane was on aerodrome. He was inspecting nearby troops. Left Lympne soon as customs formalities completed, flew over Long Barn, and landed at Reading. Train to London, taxi from Paddington to Brown's Hotel on Dover Street. Called Colonel Lee on phone and then went to American Embassy. Lee and I went to Russian Embassy to apply for permits, etc., for Moscow flight.

Thursday, August 11

People are constantly talking about war. There is a persistent rumor that Hitler will take action again about August 15 and that general European war will result. Armistice declared between Japan and Russia on Siberian border.

Went to American Embassy after breakfast for conference with Colonel Lee. Russian authorization has not arrived yet. Lee and I went to the Polish Embassy to obtain visas. Plane should be ready for flying tomorrow. Now only waiting for clearances from Moscow.

Dinner at Colonel Lee's home with Colonel and Mrs. Lee and Colonel and Mrs. Scanlon. Talk always reaches possibility of war—this month, next month, next year. There is much more talk and worry about European war than at any time since we have been living in Europe. The French Army, the English fleet, the German Air Force are the units of technical strength, and no one knows what effect the air will have on the land and sea forces. Germany has the X quantity.

Friday, August 12

Called Colonel Lee after lunch, but no word from Russia. Called Russian Embassy and suggested that we go to Warsaw and wait for Russian clearances there. Obvious that the Russian Embassy preferred not to take responsibility for our leaving here before they heard from Moscow.

Tension obvious everywhere. People expect something to happen either this weekend or next. England is in no shape for war, but it is impossible to foretell whether she can keep out if serious fighting starts in Europe. Probably not.

Saturday, August 13

Anne and I went to a Swedish restaurant for lunch, then to a news picture. Latter very cheap and boring. Discouraging to see the type of thing which holds people's interest. Life is becoming cheaper each year, it seems to me, in England as well as in America. Of course, this trend cannot go on indefinitely, but what is it leading to?

Later in the afternoon we went to see the Russian film *Last Night*. Well acted but rather disconnected. Full of shooting and the eventual supremacy of the working class. Did not give me more confidence in the Russians, but the film was much better done than the Russian films I have seen in the past.

Sunday, August 14

German plane (four-engine Focke-Wulf) landed in Berlin after nonstop return flight from New York.

Morning papers carry reports of "German maneuvers tomorrow." There are apparently very extensive military preparations going on in Germany. And England is now awake, but still very sleepy. I am afraid it will take a hard blow to make the English people aware of their true condition. Almost every sign indicates to me that the strength of England is passing. Both in war and in commerce England has been losing ground in recent years. And in the air she is at as great a disadvantage as she has advantage on the sea. London, a few minutes' flight from her coast line, too small for the development of great internal airlines, bad weather for the training of fliers. The fog, which will protect her point objectives, may make her cities more vulnerable.

The weekend has passed and no war—rather no *more* war in Europe.

Telegram from Colonel Faymonville[65]—Russian permits have been granted.

Monday, August 15

Called Russian Embassy and was informed that authorizations had arrived. Took taxi to Russian Embassy and saw the Ambassador. We discussed maps and our route. The Ambassador invited Anne and I for tea at 4:30.

European situation very tense—touch and go. Rumor that British fleet

65. Lieutenant Colonel Philip R. Faymonville, military attaché, U.S. Embassy, Moscow.

has been ordered to war stations. Colonel Scanlon called German Embassy to inquire about our route over Germany. He was told that General [Rudolf] Wenninger was on vacation in France. Another indication that the Germans may be planning a military action. Too many Germans are on "vacation" or taking part in "routine" maneuvers.

Made out maps after lunch. Went to Russian Embassy for 4:30 tea. Talked of Russia, of course, previous trips there in 1931 and 1933. Ambassador asked about aviation in various countries, and we soon found ourselves talking about Germany and Japan.

German Embassy sent a *laissez-passer* to the hotel at 6:00.

Tuesday, August 16

We took off just before 8:00. Landed at Lympne to clear English customs. Circled Saint Inglevert and headed for Hanover, detouring prohibited zones en route. Weather cloudy most of way, with local storms and haze in places. Worst in Belgium where clouds low and raining. Spent almost an hour on field at Hanover, refueling and clearing customs. Then took off for Warsaw, again detouring several prohibited zones.

Several press reporters and photographers on airport at Warsaw. As usual, they caused delay and unpleasantness. Insisted on crowding into customs room with us and had to be put out. Demanded interviews, pictures, etc. Always trouble wherever we see press people.

Anne and I drove over to the American Embassy to see the Ambassador (Drexel Biddle).[66] We talked about the Polish-Russian frontier, the European situation, etc., etc. Wish there had been more time to find out what conditions are actually like in this country.

Moscow tomorrow, if all goes well.

Wednesday, August 17

Finally took off at 9:26 G.M.T. Weather good—partly overcast and small rainstorms along the route; ceiling seldom less than 700 meters. Followed compass course to Russian border, then route laid down by Russian officials—Negoreloye, Minsk, Mogilev, Roslavl, Medyn, Moscow. Never did find Negoreloye on the maps, but followed railroad across border and know it is on the railroad. Planned on landing for fuel

66. Anthony J. Drexel Biddle, U.S. Ambassador to Poland.

at Minsk (Russian Embassy, London, gave me a paper in English, stating route to be followed and two places where we could refuel—Minsk and Mogilev). But at Minsk there was no aerodrome where we were told to land, i.e., 13.5 kilometers southwest of city. There was one, however, on the southwest edge of Minsk. Several hangars, all shut, but no planes on the field and no signs of flying activity. We circled the aerodrome and decided to go on to Mogilev.

Found aerodrome at Mogilev on southwest side of city. Military field, with several modern Russian pursuit planes lined up around the four hangars. Landed, after circling field, at 12:53 G.M.T.

Several officers in center of aerodrome. Apparently flying practice was under way, although no planes were in the air. They flagged us to the center of field. Obvious by actions and scowls that they were not pleased. One came to our plane and shouted something in Russian. I shook my head. Some confusion on part of officers. Then they motioned us to a place near a line of red flags and signaled to cut the engine. I jumped out and handed over our papers and letters from the Russian Embassy in London. While the officer in charge was examining them, the planes began to land—had been out on some mission. All low-wing fighters. Fast, and very high landing speed. Fabric wings, retracting landing gear, no flaps, radial air-cooled engines. Somewhere between ten and twenty landed while we were on the field. There were more in the hangars.

A higher officer came to examine our papers, then the commanding officer of the field. Smiles began to replace the scowls. A young soldier was produced who could speak a few words of English (very few). What did we want? Gasoline? What kind? How much? (All with great difficulty, pencil drawings, and many gestures.) One hundred liters, I answered, but I could not make them understand what kind of gasoline. "Benzine or gasoline?" I told them we wanted the same kind they used, but they could not understand. Finally, they asked the compression ratio of the engine (by drawing pictures) and said, yes, they had gasoline for an engine like that. After another wait, a fuel tank was pulled up to the plane and one hundred liters put in. I had it put in the outboard tanks, so that I had a known grade of fuel in the inboard tanks for taking off.

We knew people were waiting for us on the aerodrome at Moscow and were anxious to start as soon as the fuel was in. But the interpreter then said, "The—commander—wishes—you—to—take—something—to—eat—at—his—house." Slow speech, but good accent and words easy to understand. But he could understand almost nothing we said.

"We must start. There are people waiting for us on the aerodrome at Moscow."

"I—don't—understand—what—you—say."

"We must start quickly—soon—people are waiting at Moscow for us."

"What—is—quickly?"

And so on, with no result. Officers all standing around with perplexed and smiling faces.

Finally I said, "We must land in Moscow before night."

"Night—night—what—is—night?"

"Night—day—sunset," I said. "We must get to Moscow before sunset."

He understood. "The—sun—sets—at—Moscow—at—nine [he counted on his fingers] one—two—three—four—five—seven." I started counting on mine when he skipped six. Nine seemed to be the right number.

He went on, "You—fly—two—hundred—kilometers—each—hour. It—is—six—hundred—kilometers—to—Moscow. Takes—you—three—hours. Leave—here—at—half—past—five. Land—Moscow—before—the—sun—sets." All clearly spoken. He remembered and pronounced the words well. But he could hardly understand a word we said in return.

After another argument on our part, met by blank looks by the Russians, we got in the commander's car. We drove to a building near the hangars. A five-minute wait while the commander went inside. Then we drove across the road to a large wooden building—the restaurant. Many long tables inside. Dozen or so people eating. Some wearing coats, some in shirt sleeves. The restaurant seemed fairly clean, and the people less so. We sat down at one of the tables with several flying officers and our interpreter. Everyone was happy and laughing at our table, and the food good and the dishes clean. Milk soup. Tomatoes, steak and onions, cider, etc. We tried to leave after each course, but without any success. They thought we wanted to land in Moscow before sunset, and they would get us off in time to do that, but no more. There was plenty of time for supper.

We finally took off at 5:52. The sun set long before 9:00, but the weather was good and the twilight long in Russia. The beacon was flashing from the Moscow aerodrome when we approached the city. Landed at 17:43 G.M.T. (Several press correspondents on field but not as much trouble as usual. Gradually getting used to the fact that we are not to be interviewed.)

Mr. Kirk,[67] Colonel Faymonville, and others had been at the airport several times during the afternoon. Reports had said we would arrive at Moscow at noon, at 3:00, at 6:00, at 9:00. Finally, a message had come from Mogilev to the effect that we had landed and were staying for supper. We started to explain, but everyone seemed to understand and were extremely nice about it. Drove to American Embassy with Mr. Kirk and had very late supper (another one) with him and Colonel Faymonville.

Thursday, August 18

We got up late, had breakfast, and went for an hour's drive around Moscow with Mr. Kirk's Italian chauffeur. Great change in the city since we were last here in 1933. Much brighter in appearance. Better streets and buildings. People better dressed. Many more motorcars, trucks, and buses. The faces of the people did not seem happy and gave the impression of an underfed body. Best people seemed to be in army and in government offices.

Early lunch at embassy. Then drove to the aerodrome where the demonstration was to be held. Anne and I and Colonel Faymonville were given special tickets to the roof (of the club building), where the members of the Supreme Council of the Soviets were watching the demonstration. They were an extremely interesting study in types, coming from all parts of the Soviet Union. Some looked like Chinese, some almost Indian. Others could easily have passed as gypsies. Both men and women in all imaginable garbs and colors—the people who made up the Russian equivalent of our House and Senate. (I wondered whether the members of our own House and Senate would have made a more intelligent-looking group if they had been similarly dressed.)

The aerodrome was covered with people. Crowd estimated at 800,-000. The crowd was divided, with about half on each side of the field, and space for the planes to land and take off in between.

On the whole, the Russian air demonstration was rather slow and indicated much less aviation development than exists in the United States, Germany, or England. The flying was good but not the best in most instances. None of the planes were as good as those of the leading countries in aviation.

A long wait before the program started. Then a series of about a

67. Alexander Kirk, acting U.S. Ambassador to the U.S.S.R.

dozen balloons carrying huge pictures of political leaders below them. Next, a formation of about seventy-five training biplanes, flown by students "who work in a factory during the day and learn to fly after work." Then about twenty-five student monoplanes. Between events there was music over the radio, including an American jazz song with words in English.

The most interesting events on the program were the glider-towing and parachute-jumping demonstrations. These were the two things done better in Russia than in other countries. Nine gliders were towed behind one plane, and about seventy-five to one hundred parachutists jumped from three big four-engine bombers (old type). These events added greatly to the show but did not demonstrate much advance in aviation from a practical standpoint. Both were extremely well done, however.

There was some very good individual acrobatics and an interesting formation flight and combat by the "Red Five"—five low-wing monoplanes of the type used by the Spanish government in Spain—the ones which have caused the Germans and Italians so much trouble.

After supper at the embassy Anne and I were taken to see the open-air ballet, *The Prisoner of the Caucasus*. We were introduced to the leading actors after the performance. The ballet was beautifully done. The Russians certainly have natural ability along these lines.

Friday, August 19

Anne and I both went to the conference in the morning where plans were laid out for our visit: several days to be spent in Moscow and several more flying to other places in Russia. After the conference we had lunch at the embassy. In the afternoon we were taken to the Museum of Fine Arts and to another museum showing the last stand of the White Army. The latter was full of propaganda, especially the lecture, which was translated for us. White Army always "running away" and Red Army always "winning through great hardship," etc. It was the first real propaganda we have been subjected to on this trip. It reminded us of our previous visit to Russia in 1933. The paintings of the battles were not very inspiring and certainly not very good art. We were told that they are to be enlarged four times and put in a special building. It was all hot and uninteresting.

Between the museum and the embassy we were given a ride in Moscow's new subway, recently built and probably the best in the world today. Roomy stations and good trains. The cleanest thing I have seen in Moscow.

There was a cocktail party at the embassy at 6:00, at which we met the people connected with the American Embassy and the few other Americans living in Moscow. Operetta after supper—not very good— story about a state farm.

Saturday, August 20

Went to army experimental station in the morning. Was shown the plane types now being used by the Russian Air Corps. Was able to examine them closely and get inside. There was a two-place plane at the far end of the line that I saw only at a distance—low-wing, single-engine type.

There are two main types (apparently) of modern military planes now in general use in Russia. A single-engine fighter and a two-engine light bomber. I got inside both. The fighter has one cockpit with a sliding hatch. Low wing (fabric covering), wooden oval fuselage. It has landing flaps, although I did not see them used when the planes of a similar type landed on the field at Mogilev. It has a retracting landing gear and mounts two machine guns in the wings outside of the propeller. Both telescope and open-type sights in the cockpit. The following performance figures were volunteered to me: top speed, 500 kilometers; landing speed, 100 kilometers; fuel for two and a half to three hours. The engine was a Russian-built Cyclone. Probably 900 h.p.

The bomber was a low-wing, all-metal type. Smooth skin forward of the spar, round head rivets behind. Landing flaps and retracting wheels. Crew of three. Bomber in nose. Single-seat pilot's cockpit. Radio operator in rear. Two machine guns in nose, two in rear. One of latter shoots up and one down (under fuselage). Better machine-gun protection than I have seen in German and English bombers of similar type and size. Hispano-Suiza 950 h.p. engines (two). Following performance given by Russian officers: top speed, 450 kilometers; ceiling, 10,500 meters; range, 1,500 to 2,000 kilometers; bombload, 600 to 800 k.g.

There was a horizontal bomb bay. It was stated that this type had been built in Russian for three years. There was a gyromagnetic compass in the cockpit.

There was also a biplane type of pursuit plane, which has probably been built in some quantity. Single seat, sliding hatch, Cyclone (900 h.p.?) engine, four synchronized guns in cockpit. Said to be slower but more maneuverable than the monoplane type.

In general, these planes are not as good as the similar designs of the United States, Germany, and England. However, they are good enough to be used effectively in a modern war.

I was again impressed by the fact that the faces of the officers and soldiers on the field were far better than most we see in Russia.

After a heavy Russian meal—table piled with caviar, fruit, all kinds of wines, vodka, of course, tins of meat, sweets, and everything else one can think of—I was taken to the Aviation Academy, a large building with the usual run-down appearance. There was a long walk through rooms filled with drawing boards, lecture rooms, classrooms, etc. Most of the students were away on vacation.

Cocktail party at Colonel Faymonville's apartment at 6:00, crowded with Russians and Americans—Russian officers, fliers, diplomats. Said to be the first party attended by Russians for a long time. They don't mix much with foreigners since the recent executions, I was told.

Dinner at the American Embassy in the evening, attended by British Ambassador and some members of the Italian Embassy. Overheard argument by one of the Italians, in which he told the British Ambassador that Italy hated Anthony Eden and ended by stating that "most of the trouble in the world is caused by fanatics like Eden."

Sunday, August 21

Morning at engine factory No. 24 on outskirts of Moscow. The factory was filled with American machinery, with a few German machines here and there. It appeared that the Russians had transported bodily from the United States a completely equipped factory for the manufacture of Wright Cyclone engines, including the best types of high-production machines. I saw almost no Russian machinery in use—a few dilapidated-looking lathes.

It is difficult to estimate the production of this factory. Possibly twenty or more engines per day on American standards. The buildings were not well laid out. The machines were crowded, and there was a general lack of order, even taking into consideration the fact that a change-over was under way.

We walked over the entire factory, from foundry to test stands. It seemed to be a complete unit, with little or no necessity for parts supplied from the outside. I saw a total of about eighteen test stands. The workers did not appear to me as being of a high type. There were many women among them. It was really a case of an American factory moved to Russia and operated by Russian workers.

Another heavy lunch at the factory, lasting, it seemed, for hours. Then to the Motor Experimental Laboratories in the afternoon. Nothing very impressive here. Large facilities but mediocre equipment (nearly all the instruments and testing machines were foreign—some modern machines among them—mostly German). The building was old—said to have been used by Napoleon.

Monday, August 22

Went to a large aircraft factory in the morning. Colonel Faymonville always accompanies me on these trips. Also, the young Intourist girl from the Ukraine, who is our interpreter, tireless, not very intelligent, overweight, but a good interpreter and very willing. (No wonder she is so fat if she lives on the meals we have had here.) There is also a major from the Red Army, the flier who flew to Vladivostok a few weeks ago, and several others. In addition, we are always joined by a number of the officials of the factory we are visiting. Often there are ten or twenty people in our group.

The factory was in active production of the two-engine bombers I saw previously on the field at the Army experimental station. A few commercial transports (two-engine, low-wing, all metal) were being built. (I saw only five or six in all.) This was a large factory with good machine equipment (again American and German). There were about twenty-five bombers in the final assembly (counting from the time the engines were installed). Hispano-Suiza-type engines—stated 950 h.p. The assembly was done on tracks and seemed fairly efficient. I roughly estimated the production at between one and two per day. There were from ten to twenty jigs for the various parts. There were about seventy-five of these planes on the flying field adjoining the factory.

This was the largest and best factory I have seen since coming to Russia. Again, it seemed complete and able to produce practically all details needed for the construction of the planes. What impressed me most, though, was that it was another case of transporting an American factory to Russia. These people must order American factories as one would order groceries.

Another table piled with food before we left the factory. Then the remainder of the afternoon at the embassy. The Danish Minister had been invited and several other guests. This embassy life is deadly. Even when interesting people come (and they are few), you or they are often too tired to talk, or some stupid woman comes up and insists on taking an active part in the conversation.

After the guests left, Anne went to bed to rest before our supper. It was to be at 10:00. A fine time to start supper! I sat at the table with Mr. Kirk. No one else had been invited, so we were alone in the dining room, except for the servants. Kirk is very "anti." In fact, most of the Moscow diplomats are "anti." They have little contact with the Russians. Kirk is both an interesting and sensitive man, with far more wisdom than most people give him credit for. I thoroughly enjoy talking to him and never find his conversation boring.

Dinner at ten at the apartment home of Mr. and Mrs. [Mikhail] Vodopyanov (one of the Russian Arctic fliers, and one of those who landed at the North Pole). Only Russians present, except for Anne, Colonel Faymonville, and me. Several of the polar fliers were there. An interesting evening, but a little too late to enjoy to the utmost. We talked, of course, about Arctic flying almost entirely. The room became very hot and stuffy.

Supper ended about midnight; another elaborate Russian meal with excellent food and far too much of it. There was a good group of people there. Probably a typical Russian gathering, except for the amount of food, and the fact that no gathering is quite typical with strangers present.

Tuesday, August 23

Morning at hydroaerodynamic research laboratories. Fairly large building facilities but did not see anything very interesting. Everyone was considerate and obliging. Insisted on demonstrating in detail many well-known devices. And we were taken for *two* rides on the test basin carriage. The same wind tunnel was shown me in detail which I had been shown five years ago in almost as much detail. An iron bar was pulled apart for me to demonstrate another machine. And so on through the morning. Most of the machinery and laboratory equipment were German.

Another Russian lunch lasting till 4:00. I enjoy the food, and its preparation is excellent, but I dislike sitting around so long. The talk gets boring and silly after an hour, like too much of anything.

Wednesday, August 24

This morning (rest day in Russia) Anne and I were taken for a trip on the new canal connecting the Volga to the Moscow River. Most of our Russian acquaintances went with us, together with their wives. The trip was interesting and pleasant, despite an unusually hot, sunny day.

The canal was recently completed (about 1936), and there is still very little building along its banks. Thousands of people were in swimming, nude in some instances (both men and women). Usually, however, they wore trunks of some sort. We went through two locks and then left the boat at a sort of park. Our entire party walked about through the woods for a time. Then some of the men went in swimming. I would have gone except for the fact that there was a photographer and a reporter present. The procedure for both sexes is to walk to the river bank, remove all clothes except trunks, and jump in. (The women also wore brassières.)

We returned to Moscow by car, Anne and I with Mr. and Mrs. [I. P.] Mazuruk. He was pilot of one of the planes that landed at the Pole, and now chief of the flying service of the Northern Seaways. She is one of the most intelligent girls I have seen here in Moscow.

Dinner at the embassy with various Russians who have been connected with our visit. These dinners are not very interesting on the whole. There is the difficulty of translation in most instances, but, still more, the obvious fear of the Russians to talk freely. One must be careful in choosing the subject of conversation. The most interesting subjects must not be mentioned at all. We have about worn out polar flying and stupid jokes about drinking vodka. And I am terribly tired of searching my mind for good impressions of a general mediocrity. I have praised a few things (such as the ballet) so much that the others must stand out like deep shadows beside them.

Thursday, August 25

We are out of contact with the news here in Moscow, but war tension is still acute throughout Europe. September 15 is now the dreaded date, due to its significance in Germany. It is, of course, Germany that everyone fears.

Visited the War College this morning to see the attention given to instructing all officers in the command and operation of aircraft. The Red Army considers its aviation to be of great importance. Consequently, considerable time is devoted to training officers in its potentialities.

Visit was to end at 10:00. We left at 11:30 after a heavy "breakfast." I went to the airport and told the mechanics about servicing our plane. Had planned on servicing it myself but found the mechanics very able. The Russians have been extremely considerate about helping with such things. I like the people I meet in the majority of instances. But this system *will not* work. There has already been a great change since the Revolution, and it will continue to change for a long time to come. There would be far greater progress if they had not killed and pushed out so many of their best people.

Stopped at American Embassy on way back from airport to arrange for permission to cross Rumania and Czechoslovakia.

The American Embassy was called by a French newspaper correspondent and informed that press is carrying a report to the effect that I had a fight with a Russian policeman on the day we were on the canal. Apparently the story has already been printed abroad. No basis whatever, of course.

Large dinner at 8:30 given by VOKS (Cultural Relations Society for Foreign Nations) and the Civil Air Fleet. Almost everyone was there whom we have met during our trip. Also many others. Aviation people, polar explorers, and Russian artists. An interesting evening, somewhat spoiled by the presence of a very active photographer with a brilliant spotlight. The Russians were very nice when they saw we did not like to be constantly photographed, and we were not bothered after the first half hour. Anne danced a little, and I had a good chance to talk to several Russians. They are an open, likable people, obviously suppressed by fear of getting into trouble. They love to talk and to discuss any subject not politically dangerous. Unfortunately, "politically dangerous" covers a wide ground.

Friday, August 26

Left embassy at 10:30 after usual problem of tipping the servants. More difficult here because of exchange problem and the fact that American Embassy help are mostly Italian. Mr. Kirk brought them with him from Rome. It seems that the "official" exchange here is about five rubles to the dollar and that it is not possible for a salaried person to live on this exchange rate. In consequence, an arrangement is made unofficially for the embassy people, and in fact most permanent residents, to obtain a much more favorable "unofficial" exchange rate. The members of our embassy obtain a rate of fifteen rubles to the dollar at present.

Arrived at aerodrome shortly before 11:00. Many Russians and Americans there to see us off. Impossible to keep them from doing this, although it makes extra work for them and delays us in getting started. Took off Moscow 11:15.

We shall miss Mr. Kirk. He is considered a little eccentric by most people and is so "anti" that he can see no good whatever in the present Russian system. He is tall, thin, looks about forty, and is fifty. He has kept an interesting and original mind through all the twaddle of diplomatic life. He was at the field when we took off.

Colonel Faymonville was there, too. He has been of the utmost assistance to us on this trip. Has better contact with the Russians, probably, than anyone else in our embassy. Possibly a little blinded by his liking for them. We found him averse to discussing anything in the least unfavorable to them. In fact, everyone here seems to be either very "pro" or very "anti." It is, consequently, difficult to carry on an objective conversation.

We flew first to Tula, then to Orel, then to Kharkov, making our first landing at the latter place. After a half hour's stop at Kharkov, we flew practically direct to Rostov on Don. Our routes are laid out for us by the Russian officials, and we attempt to follow them exactly. I miss the unrestricted routes of the United States. Immediately after taking off from the Moscow aerodrome, we passed over the aircraft factory I visited several days ago. A few minutes later we passed several training fields.

The day was clear and hot. Ceiling and visibility unlimited. We passed over an aerodrome containing a small factory and several hangars on the northeast side of Kharkov. Too far away to see details, but there were a number of planes, probably low-wing, single-engine, in front of the factory. Total of nine hangars. We landed on the commercial aerodrome southeast of the city. There was a building going up on the south side of the field. Looked like a small aircraft factory.

Refueling was done quickly and efficiently. The plane which was sent ahead of us with our Intourist interpreter was waiting for us, and, after refueling, we took off for Rostov. We throttled down to allow them to get there a few minutes ahead of us. Did not want an advance plane but had no choice in the matter. It is an old biplane—500 h.p.—and very slow.

We are having high oil temperatures in this hot weather. Sometimes above 90° C. Everything else all right, except both voltmeter and ammeter are fluctuating excessively. The English mechanics don't understand this equipment, even though Phillips & Powis are the agents for our Menasco engine. In consequence, it is never properly serviced. The English regulations load you down with logbooks, licenses, and other papers, but one good American mechanic is worth all of them, ten times over, including the Air Ministry inspections. I keep up the logs only enough to get by regulations. They are of no value whatever from my standpoint, but if I should crash the plane I am sure the authorities would blame it on some omitted entry or a bit of overload, regardless of the actual cause.

The readiness to blame a dead pilot for an accident is nauseating, but it has been the tendency ever since I can remember. What pilot has not been in positions where he was in danger and where perfect judgment would have advised against going? But when a man is caught in such a position he is judged only by his error and seldom given credit for the times he has extricated himself from worse situations. Worst of all, blame is heaped upon him by other pilots, all of whom have been in parallel situations themselves, but without being caught in them. If one took no chances, one would not fly at all. Safety lies in the judgment of the chances one takes. That judgment, in turn, must rest upon one's outlook on life. Any coward can sit in his home and criticize a pilot for flying into a mountain in fog. But I would rather, by far, die on a mountainside than in bed. Why should we look for his errors when a brave man dies? Unless we can learn from his experience, there is no need to look for weakness. Rather, we should admire the courage and spirit in his life. What kind of man would live where there is no daring? And is life so dear that we should blame men for dying in adventure? Is there a better way to die?

We had a good opportunity to see the collective farms and coal mines of the Ukraine. The collective farms are unlike anything I have seen elsewhere. They consist of a row of twenty or so houses, strung out along a road, with garden patches of an acre or so behind them, and large fields outside.

Landed Rostov 7:01. There was a group of people to meet us, including the mayor and the head of the local Intourist. Also the head of the flying school we came to see. Colonel Slepnev was there, having flown from Moscow ahead of us. The Russians are doing everything possible for us. I feel embarrassed because it is so much. Dislike to cause so much trouble. Colonel Slepnev had only one hour's sleep last night. We have never seen anything to exceed Russian hospitality. Also, they have been unusually considerate in not crowding our days with too many engagements.

Saturday, August 27

Anne and I were driven to the flying school outside of the city, a civil school, but there seems to be little difference between a civil and military school for primary flying training. We were taken first to the section of the field where the "second-year" girl students were flying. The girls who were not flying were lined up at attention when we arrived. They had good faces and were obviously far above the average type. Only those between the ages of twenty and twenty-three are accepted for training. Almost all who are accepted are graduated, we were told.

From the field we went to the barracks. How strange to see sixty cadet bunks with embroidery all over the pillows. Since the room was for only one class, there must have been 180 girls in the school. They are training to be commercial pilots in most cases. However, there are a number of women pilots in the Soviet Air Force. We met one of them in Moscow. A clean-cut young girl of about twenty-five—excellent type. We are told that women fit into the Air Force just as men. They command men and are commanded by men without regard for difference in sex, are given the same missions, etc. I don't see how it can work very well. After all, there is a God-made difference between men and women that even the Soviet Union can't eradicate.

From the girls' barracks we went to that of the boys. Latter not as clean. The girls' had a much neater and snappier appearance. Next, we went to the main school building. The field has been organized for about six years as a training school, but the buildings already have the neglected, run-down look of most buildings in Russia. Floors in very bad shape. One board I stepped on sank down and seemed to almost snap with my weight.

We attended the examination of one of the cadets. I felt sorry for the boy, having to take an important examination in front of visitors, but they said he did well. It was verbal and very stiff and formal, with the answers to questions shouted rather than spoken by the cadet.

We were told that there were more boys than girls in the school, that the boys soloed in about seven hours, and the girls in from ten to eleven hours. No satisfactory answer as to why. Girls said to be better at night flying; boys best at instrument flying. I left the school without a clear answer to many of the questions I asked, and with many more questions unstated. For instance, why train girls for transport flying? I do not believe it will bring them happiness in later life. And, especially, why train them as fighting pilots? There is plenty of manpower in the Soviet Union and, unless the lessons of history are to be reversed, it would be far more effective to train men. There is no reason why women should not fly, but they should not be encouraged in entering aviation as an occupation. Their greatest contribution to life can be made in other and less material ways. How can a civilization be classified as "high" when its women are moved from home to industry, when the material efficiency of life is considered first and the bearing of children second, if not third?

From the flying school we went to the new Rostov theater, jolting back over the rough dust roads on which we had come. The theater is built in the form of a tractor. God knows why, but it is typical of a great deal of Soviet art. It was somewhat better built than most of the buildings I have seen and very much better finished inside. However, I doubt that it will last for long without becoming spotted where the plaster has peeled off. It has seating for 2,000, we were told, with a concert hall for 1,000 in addition. The stage is large, with a revolving center. We walked all over each floor of the theater and then were taken to see the ice cream factory.

This type of thing always happens when you let someone else arrange a schedule for you. Why take us to an ice cream factory? A quiet hour reading or writing would be worth much more. However, one can learn to know a place better even by walking through an ice cream factory. As a matter of fact, it confirmed my general impression of the present-day condition of Soviet Russia. Very few things here are really first class. They are good only by comparison with Russia's own past. There has been a definite improvement since we were in Russia in 1933 (judging by Moscow and the general appearance of the country we fly over), but conditions were pretty bad then. If they were worse before the Revolution, they must have been actually unbearable.

The ice cream factory was not very clean, although much more so than most places we have been. There were quite a few flies, and there was flypaper on rails and tables in various places. The machinery was not working too well and did not compare with that of an American factory. However, the products seemed first class. They had a special sweet cheese unlike anything I have seen before. It was excellent. I wish we could get it at home. The ice cream was better than the average we get in England. Of course, several times as much as we could eat was placed before us.

This is a strange country. They preach the doctrine of dividing between people according to their need. There is great poverty and at times actual starvation. Yet I have never seen a greater waste of food than at some of the lunches and dinners we have attended. The people who have, in Soviet Russia, do not seem to be greatly concerned about those who have not. I do not believe the idea of division, equality, and state ownership will last long. Given a chance, the social classes will develop much the same as in the past. The signs are in the parties, the dinners, the women's dresses, decorations, etc. Of course, there is already a great difference in the salaries and privileges of different people.

After supper we went for a half hour's walk along the streets. There are crowds of people walking on the streets all day long. It is very hot, even in the evening. We passed a parade of several hundred young men and women with gas masks over their shoulders. Earlier in the day we had seen them marching past the hotel, a band in front, all wearing the masks. It was a strange sight. Looked like a parade of creatures from a foreign planet.

Sunday, August 28

We took off for Kiev at 9:40 after the usual handshaking and good-bys. The fields of the Ukraine were similar to parts of our Middle West— Kansas and Nebraska. Met [at Kiev aerodrome] by usual group of officials of city and Intourist. Interesting drive to city and chance to see Russian life along the roadside. Another big meal, then a drive around city. We stop and go into St. Sophia Cathedral. Beautiful old building, with paintings and mosaics going back nearly 1,000 years. We have it all explained to us by one of the most objectionable women I have ever seen. She represented Soviet propaganda at its worst. Not an original thought in her head. Was born to be a temperamental and mediocre cook, and would have been much happier as such. After the cathedral we walked through the catacombs—now an antireligious museum.

Monday, August 29

Lunch on a boat on the river. Then a long wait while an old speedboat was made ready for a trip on the river—a long, narrow boat, badly in need of paint. It had to be filled with gasoline, poured sloppily from a barrel into buckets, and then into a funnel, with much waste. Something was wrong with the engine. It was started and stopped and the spark plugs taken out several times. Finally, we got in together with ten or twelve Russians. Half of us, including Anne and myself, were in the open stern. The other half were in the cabin. (I was afraid it might turn over.) The mayor of Kiev sat forward beside the pilot. Everyone outside the cabin got wet, those in the stern completely soaked. Everyone ended up inside the cabin, steaming, with wet clothes. However, the trip was great fun and much more interesting than many of the things we have done here. We went about fifteen kilometers up the river and back.

An hour's drive to a collective farm in the country. I was amazed that we were shown this farm. It was badly run, overgrown with weeds, and the crops were poor, although our interpreter said it had been a good year. The fruit trees were in bad condition, the apples of a poor type and covered with blemishes. It would be classed as a badly managed farm in the United States. The peasants, however, looked well and reasonably happy. There were about 900 hectares and between 200 and 300 families. Each family had 50/60ths of a hectare for its own garden. Each worker received about three rubles for a "labor day" normally. The farm was successfully run and therefore paid at the rate of one and a half labor days for an actual day's labor. Pay in kind could be taken instead of money. In other words, fifteen kilograms of potatoes could be obtained for a labor day instead of three rubles. (All of this from our local interpreter.)

Tuesday, August 30

Landed Odessa 10:35 G.M.T. More officials and flowers. We drive to hotel and change clothes. Then drive to Young Pioneers Camp for lunch. But the children had finished lunch and were asleep, so we drove back to the hotel again after walking through the camp. (Our local interpreter in Kiev pointed out a large building and said, "Here is the building of the Young Pioneers. It is here that all the best Soviet children are taken to be demonstrated." How truthful!) The camp was one of the best projects we have seen in Russia. Located on the shore of the Black Sea; buildings clean and quite well arranged. The children, both boys and girls, were of a good type and looked well.

Telegram from Colonel Faymonville at hotel. Rumanian permission (to cross border) had not arrived. Rather, the permission to fly had been granted but the route had not been designated, and we were told that we must fly over a prescribed route. I wired Colonel Faymonville, suggesting that if there were more delay, we get permission to cross Poland to Czechoslovakia.

Late dinner, starting about 10:00 and lasting until nearly 1:00. Toasts and speeches, and I have to answer. (How I dislike these stiff "great honor–great appreciation" speeches.) This was to be our last night in Russia, so everyone had to act accordingly. The Russians saying what an honor our visit had been, we saying how interesting it had been and how enjoyable. And so on into the night.

Wednesday, August 31

A telegram has arrived from Colonel Faymonville stating that we could cross the Rumanian border at a point near Odessa and that there were no restrictions as to the route we followed after that.

Took off at 10:05 G.M.T. and landed Cluj at 13:13. There was an air tour on the field at Cluj, and the planes were taking off when we arrived. Press and photographers on the field. People crowded around, wanted autographs, interviews, etc. We finally drove to the military side of the aerodrome, and I taxied the plane over later for refueling. Very difficult to do anything because of excitement on field, but much better on military side. Always have to be more careful when people are excited. They run past the propeller, push against the wings, and forget almost everything that it is necessary to remember in operating aircraft. Whenever people get excited, you can expect accidents and trouble. I would rather do almost anything than land on a crowded aerodrome.

Thursday, September 1

Take off at 8:35 G.M.T. Set course for Czechoslovakia. Soon after crossing the border we struck a storm area—mountains covered with clouds. Turned north and eventually landed at Cracow, Poland. Refueled and waited for weather report to Prague. Storm area over Germany moving over our route but probably still flyable. We took off and crossed the Polish-Czech border in rain and with low ceiling. Continued low ceiling in Czechoslovakia. We flew through two mountain passes with sides climbing up into the clouds. Very narrow and air rough. Unable to get through a third pass so turned back and landed on the military aerodrome at Olmütz.

Friday, September 2

Weather report good. We drive to field. Many Czech officers there. Good-looking men, up to the reputation I have heard of the Czech Army. We took off, escorted by three pursuit planes, and headed for Prague. About an hour's flight. Crowd on Prague aerodrome badly controlled. Started running for plane as we taxied toward hangars, led by press photographers, of course. Finally got into legation car with Major Riley[68] and drove to American Legation, where Minister Carr[69] had invited us to stay. Afternoon spent with Major Riley, visiting aviation factories. Two Czech officers accompanied us. We visited the Avia, Letov, and Aero plants.

Saturday, September 3

Left legation at 8:30 with Major Riley to see the military field, Kbely. They have purchased a number of the Russian two-engine bombers, and there were no other modern types on the field. The Czech pursuit bi-

68. Major Lowell M. Riley, military attaché, U.S. Legation, Prague.

69. Wilbur John Carr had been U.S. Assistant Secretary of State from 1924 to 1937; he was with the U.S. Legation in Prague in 1938.

planes are too slow to be called modern—400 kilometers per hour, they said. Some very good flying done, and an exceptionally fine demonstration of stunt flying by one of the pilots. They demonstrated the maneuverability of one of the Russian bombers for me. Seemed quite good.

Back to Prague for an 11:00 appointment with President Beneš.[70] Went to the legation first, and then with Mr. Carr to see the President. The Russian Ambassador was leaving as we arrived. Spent half an hour with the President. He asked about modern aircraft and their effectiveness. We spoke of the war in Spain, of the Russian air fleet, of Czechoslovakian aviation. Obvious that he had been, and was, under tension. He spoke excellent English.

Met Major Riley after leaving the President. We drove to the General Staff offices. Spent an hour there. Was greatly impressed by the Czech generals and thoroughly enjoyed talking to them. All had experience with the forces of the Czech legions during the Great War, and all had made the march through Russia to the Pacific.[71] An exceptionally fine and able group of men (General [Ludvik] Krejci, Chief of General Staff, General [Karel] Husarek, Director of Fortifications, General [Fravntišek] Fiala, General [Rudolf] Medek).

After General Staff offices, we went to the Walter factory, a well-organized plant, doing good work. They are making about fifteen different types of engines, mostly on license.

Sunday, September 4

After the visits I have made to aviation establishments here, I conclude that Czechoslovakia is not well equipped in the air. Her pursuit planes are too slow to be effective against the fast German bombers, and she has only a few fast bombers for counterattack. These have been obtained from Russia. They are not as good as the German types, but have a sufficiently good performance to be effective. The French and Czech types of bombers, which are being built here, are too slow for modern

70. Eduard Beneš, President of Czechoslovakia, 1935–38. After the Munich Pact Beneš resigned and went into exile.

71. At the end of World War I there were still 92,000 Czechoslovakian troops in Russia. They had control of the Volga area and the Trans-Siberian Railway, and were considered an important factor in the Allies' attempt to intervene directly in Russia against the Bolshevik regime. Forced by the French and English to continue the struggle in Siberia after the war had ended, they fought their way to safety across thousands of miles of enemy territory with great heroism.

warfare. The Czechs are starting to build the Russian bombers, but have just begun. None can be produced for use this year. They are starting to build a faster pursuit plane, I am told; but, again, only starting. It seems that the main Czech defense against air attack will rest in their machine and antiaircraft guns, which have an excellent reputation.

Anne and I drive with Major Riley to the Sudeten to have lunch with Prince and Princess Clary Aldringen in their old palace at Teplice-Šanov. They tell me they would vote for a German Anschluss if given the opportunity. Apparently dislike being under the Czechs.

One of the ladies at the table says they are "sitting on a bomb," that there are many Communists in the territory, all armed, and that there "wouldn't be enough lampposts to hang them [members of the castle] by if trouble started." Said the castle would be the first place attacked.

Shown about castle, including the oil portraits they had recently discovered. It seems that they decided to clean out an old attic in one of their buildings. It contained "refuse" which had accumulated for 150 years. Under the refuse were forty oil portraits of family ancestors, apparently hidden there for safety and forgotten.

We were told that the Czech Army in Sudeten territory had acted more as an army of occupation than protection.

Wednesday, September 7

In the afternoon Mrs. Carr, Anne, and I went with the Swiss Minister[72] and his wife to the library to see the art galleries. Afterward, I had a quarter hour's talk with the Minister (Swiss) at the legation (American). He is afraid war cannot be avoided, but does not expect it to come this year. He is an interesting and, I think, able man. Married an American girl, the sister of Secretary Wallace.[73]

Tea at 5:00 at home of Mr. and Mrs. Bruins[74] of the American Legation. Talked to a very interesting Englishman, who had been a British agent in Russia during the war. Knew the language well and passed as a Russian. Told stories of shootings, torture, etc., under the Reds after the Revolution. Said the peasants were better off under the Czar.

72. Carl Bruggmann, later minister to the Swiss Legation in the U.S., 1939–54.

73. Henry A. Wallace, Secretary of Agriculture, 1933–1940. Later Vice-President of the U.S., 1940–44.

74. John H. Bruins, consul, U.S. Legation, Prague.

Thursday, September 8

Good weather report. Mr. and Mrs. Carr drove us to the aerodrome, and we took off at 11:32. No crowd and no difficulty. Several officers of Czech Army came to see us off. Cleared customs, etc., at Stuttgart, then took off for Paris. Germans had given us special permission to fly over their country without landing; but I was afraid that if we cleared Prague directly for Paris, we would be bothered by newspapers, as they would know of our coming far enough in advance to prepare for it. By landing at Stuttgart we would give them much less notice. Unfortunately, it is necessary to give your destination flying about Europe.

Clear weather all the way to Paris. Landed at Le Bourget. Press began telephoning hotel as soon as we arrived, but have caused no other trouble as yet.

Friday, September 9

We had planned on flying to Morlaix this afternoon, but Ambassador Bullitt asked us for dinner, so we will leave tomorrow instead. Anne and I planned on going for a walk but found photographers and reporters at every entrance. Finally got into a taxi but were followed by four or five press cars, so returned to hotel. Arranged through American Embassy to change cars at Ambassador Bullitt's town residence so press will not follow to country.

Left Crillon at 6:20. Crowd of people at door and many photographers with flashlights. How I dislike to have a camera shoved in front of my face and a blinding flash in my eyes! Feel as though I had been slapped. We got into Mr. MacArthur's[75] car (third secretary of embassy) and drove to Ambassador Bullitt's town house (the same house I stayed in with Ambassador Herrick[76] in 1927). We went in the front door and out the rear door, and into another car. Then drove to Bullitt's country home. No press cars followed us, but a phone call from the embassy said that nine were outside waiting during the evening.

Ambassador Bullitt has rented one of the old houses of Chantilly and,

75. Douglas MacArthur II, foreign service officer with the U.S. Embassy in Paris in 1938 and 1944–48.

76. Myron T. Herrick, U.S. Ambassador to France when Lindbergh arrived in the *Spirit of St. Louis,* 1927.

consequently, has unlimited forests and grounds available outside his door. There are artificial lakes a few yards from the house and a water-fall in the background.

The Minister of Air, M. [Guy la] Chambre, came for dinner, and we talked of French aviation, German aviation, and that of the other countries in Europe. The French situation is desperate. Impossible to catch up to Germany for years, if at all. France is producing about forty-five or fifty warplanes per month. Germany is building from 500 to 800 per month, according to the best estimates. England is building in the vicinity of seventy per month. France hopes to have 2,600 first-line planes by April, 1940. Germany is probably building that many every three or four months. One is forced to the conclusion that the German air fleet is stronger than that of all other European countries combined.

M. la Chambre apparently realizes this fact. The French are also deficient in antiaircraft guns, and the people of Paris are not equipped with gas masks. Yet the French Army is apparently ready to attack on the old Western front if Germany invades Czechoslovakia. It is suicide. The opportunity of stopping the extension of German control to the east passed several years ago. An attempt to do so now will throw Europe into chaos. It would be much worse than the last war and would probably result in a Communist Europe.

Saturday, September 10

Anne and I walked around the grounds with Ambassador Bullitt in the morning. After lunch we drove to Le Bourget and took off en route to Morlaix. Cloudy day, but good visibility. Flew over Illiec and Saint-Gildas en route.

Louis and Petit Louis were waiting for us at Buguélès, as the tide was high. They had the new boat—*Medric*. It is rather small and we got a bit wet as there was a fairly strong wind blowing. After leaving Anne, Miss Hutchison (who had met us at Morlaix), Louis, and Petit Louis [at Illiec], I took the *Medric* to Saint-Gildas. I arrived just as Dr. and Mme. Carrel were starting for Illiec in their boat. We returned to Illiec and talked for an hour at the supper table.

Friday, September 16

The mast and sail for the *Medric* have finally been completed. Anne, Jon, and I took the boat out into the bay to try it out. We went out from anchorage with the engine, as we wished to have plenty of room when trying the sail for the first time. When we reached the bay, the wind had died. We put up the sails, but there was not a breath, so we lowered sails and returned with the engine.

Sunday, September 18

Morning at Illiec, writing and reading Plato. Mme. Carrel came in her boat and asked me to come to Saint-Gildas in the afternoon. I went over for tea and returned in time to walk back with Anne for supper on Saint-Gildas with Dr. and Mme. Carrel. We talked of plans for the winter. Dr. Carrel will sail [for the United States] about October 1. We consider the possibility of carrying on experiments with latent life and with whole-blood perfusion. Anne and I not certain of where best to take the children this winter. We speak of Berlin and discuss advantages and disadvantages. Dr. Carrel says his friends in Paris say the crisis is past and that war will not come this year. Everyone apparently more optimistic.

Monday, September 19

Urgent telegram from Ambassador Kennedy about 6:30. He asks Anne and I to come to London as soon as possible. We plan on leaving in the morning.

Supper at Saint-Gildas with Dr. and Mme. Carrel. They leave for Paris Saturday morning. We may not see them again before he sails.

Tuesday, September 20

Anne and I left Illiec about 11:30, and walked over the sillon to Buguélès. Took off at 2:21. Flew over Saint-Gildas and Illiec. Jon and Thor always very much in evidence when we fly over. Rain and low clouds in places, but reached Saint Inglevert without difficulty. Anne landed plane and made good landing. I taxied up to customs house. As I turned, I noticed a strange movement of the plane. Cut engine and jumped down to look at landing gear. Right side was broken. Lucky it did not collapse completely and break wing and propeller. Got several men to help, and we carried the right wing while several others pushed the plane into the hangar. Same trouble we had in Germany last year. Caused by a broken fitting.

Anne and I went to Boulogne and took the boat for Folkestone. Supper on boat. Officers extremely considerate and arrange all passport and customs clearances for us. The English are always courteous about matters of this kind and go far out of their way to be helpful. It always seems to me that the best Englishmen have gone either to the empire or to the sea.

Train to London.

Wednesday, September 21

Kennedy invited Anne and I for lunch at 1:15—14 Princess Gate. It is a typical fall day in London, with a misty rain falling and coal smoke in the air.

Lunch with Ambassador and Mrs. Kennedy. (Before lunch we were introduced to six of their children.) Talked with Ambassador Kennedy for an hour after lunch. We discussed the crisis and the aviation and general military situation in Europe. Everyone in embassy is extremely worried. Hitler is apparently ready to invade Czechoslovakia and has his divisions on the border. Hitler told Chamberlain [according to Kennedy] that he (Hitler) would risk a world war if necessary. Kennedy says England is ready to fight, even though not prepared. Chamberlain realizes the disastrous effects of a war with Germany at this time and is making every effort to avoid one. English opinion (Kennedy) is pushing him toward war.

It is a terrible situation. The English are in no shape for war. They do not realize what they are confronted with. They have always before had a fleet between themselves and their enemy, and they can't realize the change aviation has made. I am afraid this is the beginning of the end of England as a great power. She may be a "hornets' nest" but she is no longer a "lion's den."

Phoned Lady Astor at Sandwich. She invited us to come there this week or to Cliveden next week. Very much worried about situation.

Anne and I returned to the hotel after lunch. Later I went to the embassy to see Herschel Johnson. Spent half an hour talking to him. Then Kennedy came in and we talked together for another half hour. Chamberlain is going to meet Hitler again. If Hitler makes more demands, the feeling here is that England will declare war. God knows what the result will be. There is already great criticism of Chamberlain for making concessions to Hitler in regard to Czechoslovakia and the Sudeten territory.

Anne and I had supper alone at a Hungarian restaurant, then returned to hotel. I am writing a report for Kennedy on the military aviation situation in Europe.

Thursday, September 22

Finished draft of letter to Ambassador Kennedy. Had my letter[77] typed and left it with Herschel Johnson for Ambassador Kennedy. Conditions are becoming more and more critical. The Czech Cabinet has resigned.

Back to embassy in afternoon. Kennedy wants me to talk to some of the British officials.

Friday, September 23

English Intelligence thinks Russia might have had aircraft production up to 5,000 per year at one time, but they believe much lower now. A great drop recently, they say. They say Russian machine guns are excellent— fire up to 1,800 or 2,000 rounds per minute. English Intelligence believes speed of Russian planes is much slower than Russians claim (which is not unnatural). They say bomber probably does about 240 to 250 miles (Russians claim 270), and low-wing pursuit about 240 to 260 (Russians claim 300). English say latter has bad maneuverability.

Went to Morgan Grenfell this morning and cashed $500.00 check. It will be necessary to have an amount of ready money if trouble starts. Five hundred dollars will not go far, but it will be enough to travel on for a few days. People on streets are talking war. I hear bits of their conversation as I pass by.

There is an A.R.P. [Air Raid Precautions] gas mask station on Piccadilly, around the corner from our hotel. Makes one think, to see gas masks being fitted in the center of London.

Lunch at 1:00 at Carlton Grill with Sir Wilfrid Freeman.[78] We talk of

---

77. In essence, the letter stated that Germany's strength in military aviation was greater than that of all other European countries combined, and that the U.S. was the only country in the world capable of competing with Germany in aviation. Ambassador Kennedy cabled the substance of the report to the U.S. Secretary of State.

78. Air marshal in the R.A.F. and member of the Air Council for Research and Development.

production facilities here and on the Continent. Also about general situation. I accompany Sir Wilfrid to Adastral House and spend an hour or two talking to members of the Air Ministry. An English officer told me that their Intelligence was bad in regard to German aviation. Said it made a "chap think twice" when he knew he would have his head chopped off if he was caught.

Supper with Colonel and Mrs. Lee at their home.

During supper, Colonel Lee received a message that Chamberlain and the entire English delegation were returning from Germany in the morning and that negotiations were broken off. (Press report, so not too reliable.)

Conditions are becoming worse. The English are in no condition to fight a war, but the average Englishman does not know it. If France and England attack Germany at this time, the result will be chaotic and may easily result in the destruction of democracy. I am afraid it may result in the destruction of European civilization.

Saturday, September 24

News somewhat worse this morning. Chamberlain flying back to England. Czechs mobilizing. France taking firmer stand. What will the French do? Attack on the old Western front? Bulletins say French have called 900,000 men to colors. German ultimatum to Czechoslovakia reported.

News seems a little better tonight. The fact that the German troops have not yet entered Czechoslovakia is an encouraging sign to me. I still think there is a reasonable chance that we will not have war this year. Hitler is in a unique position. No one is going to start fighting before he does. Consequently, he can bluff about as he wishes without danger. He probably enjoys having the fate of the world in his hands, especially after the way the world treated Germany after the war. I cannot blame him too much for making France and England worry a bit, but I cannot believe he will throw Europe into a major war over the present situation. It would take a madman to do that. Hitler is a mystic and a fanatic, but his actions and results in the past do not lead me to believe he is insane.

Sunday, September 25

I walked down to Piccadilly Circus. A number of Mosley's[79] men and women were distributing antiwar handbills, and there was to be a parade.

About 5:00 Anne and I went to Hyde Park. There was the usual group of religious speakers. In addition, the Communists were holding a demonstration—red banners, speeches, and a parade headed by a band and escorted by bored and good-humored bobbies. A banner at the head carried the inscription "Stand by the Czechs."

Anne went back to the hotel, and I took a bus to Hammersmith, where Mosley was to hold a meeting at 7:00. To get to the Mosley meeting I had to pass through a Communist meeting two or three blocks away. The Mosley meeting was much larger (both were street meetings, and the speakers stood on top of light trucks containing amplifiers). The street was jammed for nearly a block. I listened to Mosley for a few minutes. He was speaking against war with Czechoslovakia, and his statements were not too intelligent. However, Mosley's meeting, and even his speech, was of a much higher quality than that of the Communists. It always seems that the Fascist group is better than the Communist group. Communism seems to draw the worst of men.

Not much definite war news today. Mostly Cabinet meetings and statements by various people in various countries. Nothing at all satisfying. Conditions look very bad. Seems to depend on Hitler. I can't believe he wants to start a general European war, but I wish I felt surer.

Monday, September 26

Czechoslovakian frontiers closed. Hitler submitted six-point proposal, which would end Czechoslovakia as a menace to Germany and open it to German military and economic invasion. Opinion is hardening in England and France. No tendency apparent for more concessions. All depends on Hitler at the moment.

Colonel Lee says trenches are being dug in Hyde Park.

Anne and I were invited to spend the night with Lord and Lady Astor at Cliveden. We packed a few of our things into a roll, and took the 6:08

79. Sir Oswald Mosley, who in 1932 organized the British Union of Fascists, modeled upon the German and Italian fascist parties, and conducted street meetings and campaigns.

from Paddington. (Sandbags are being placed around the doors and windows of a number of buildings in London.)

Arrived at Cliveden shortly before dinner. Lord and Lady Astor were there. Also Mr. Tom Jones,[80] several members of the Astor family, and two or three other guests. Everyone greatly depressed. It was as though war had already begun. Lord Astor and Mr. Jones felt it was necessary for England to fight if Germany moves into Czechoslovakia. Lady Astor against war at this time. Also her son. I argue that it is necessary to take stock of armaments before jumping into a war. There was no use talking. Sentiment was too high. Except for Lady Astor and her son, the spirit of the "Light Brigade" had taken hold. Again, the English are ready to fight for their principles, throwing all judgment to the winds and, in a sense, discarding the more important issues of European civilization itself. Again, they are ready to move too late. Argument must wait for a calmer time. Fortunately, there are a few days left. There is still some hope. I believe it is still possible to avoid a war at this time. And with more time, there is more hope. It is amazing to have seen the lack of willingness in England to make the preparations necessary for war and now to see how ready people are to enter one.

Hitler spoke at 8:00, and we all went into the parlor to hear him. Lord Astor and his son and I and two German boys who were visiting remained to hear all of the speech. The German boys took notes and translated the important points. Hitler held his audience in his hand. They were ready to cheer at the slightest opportunity and at anything he said. Hitler started slowly, but ranted and snarled at times. Huge cheering after he finished. He spoke over an hour in all. Was introduced by Goebbels. Speech seemed to leave considerable hope that war may be avoided. Many people in England expected Hitler to declare war during his speech (i.e., to say that German troops were marching into Czechoslovakia, as he did when they moved into Austria last March). Hitler has certainly "left the door open" for the time being at least.

Supper after his speech ended. The tension was somewhat relieved. There was again the willingness to consider the armament situation and possible alternatives to declaring war. Whereas before Hitler's speech there was no use talking about these things.

Anne and I slept in the "Tapestry" Room. Beautiful view from window in the morning. Night fog just clearing and bend in Thames just visible. Same room we had on last visit.

80. Confidant of Lloyd George, Ramsay MacDonald, and Stanley Baldwin, Thomas Jones was Deputy Secretary to the British Cabinet in 1938.

Tuesday, September 27

Breakfast with Lord Astor, Mr. Tom Jones, Lord Astor's son, and Anne at 9:00. More hopeful atmosphere this morning. Lord Astor wanted me to talk to some of his friends in London. He tried to make appointments by phone, but could not get through. All lines busy. So we drove to his London residence (4 St. James's Square).

Trenches were being dug in most of the parks and open places we passed. There were lines of people waiting to get into the A.R.P. centers we passed by, for a gas mask fitting. While I was waiting at 4 St. James's Square, two cars drove by with loudspeakers, telling everyone to go to the nearest A.R.P. station for a gas mask fitting. I phoned the Army & Navy store and asked if they sold gas masks. Reply was "Yes, but we are sold out and can't fill an order for at least six weeks."

Lunch with Mr. Tom Jones and a group of his friends at 16 Queen Anne's Gate. We discussed the general situation after lunch. People are being very badly misled in regard to Great Britain's military position. Baldwin[81] seems to be as much responsible for the situation as anyone.

Back to 4 St. James's Square after lunch. Leave in Lord Astor's car for a 4:30 appointment with Lloyd George[82] at his home in Surrey (Bron-y-de Churt).

Lloyd George was in the parlor and met me as I came in the door— active, very white medium-long hair. Obviously not an Englishman. He poured tea. There was a typical Welsh tea table, filled with cakes. We talked over the question of war and armament. He felt war now unavoidable. I tried to convince him that it must at least be postponed. He spoke of the weakness of the present government and the series of mistakes which had been made. In the latter discourse he went back to 1918. Lloyd George spoke several times of the "prestige of democracy" and said he doubted it could stand another retreat after Ethiopia, Spain, Austria, etc. He suggested that a war now might end by a quick victory for Germany in Czechoslovakia before France and England could really get started fighting. If that happened, he thought the English and French people would not be willing to fight to get Czechoslovakia back. His reasoning did not seem to me very clear in regard to this and several

81. Stanley Baldwin, Prime Minister of England three times: 1923–24; 1924–29; 1935–37.

82. David Lloyd George, Prime Minister of England and First Lord of the Treasury, 1916–22.

other points he made. I told him I did not see how democratic prestige would gain much from an unsuccessful war.

Lloyd George spoke of his confidence in Eden and Churchill and lack of confidence in Chamberlain.

Lloyd George said Beneš was responsible for a lot of the trouble Czechoslovakia was in. Said that the Czech borders were not drawn right in the first place. Said he was writing about this, but might not publish the book if war came. Said there was less justification for the present Hungarian border than for the Sudeten border.

Lloyd George spoke of the lack of leaders in present-day democracies. Said the Nazi system was just as bad as the Russian system. He does not seem to recognize any difference to England between an alliance with European Germany and Asiatic Russia. He apparently does not worry about the effect of Asia on European civilization.

Lloyd George mentioned several times his feeling that war could not any longer be stopped. Said Hitler was a strong man and not in any way bluffing, or even trading. Said the same of Mussolini.

Left Lloyd George's home about 6:00. Drove to Guildford, and took train to London.

Took train to Taplow and taxi to Cliveden. Everyone depressed. Seems less hope every hour. Hitler is actually mad if he starts a general war under these circumstances. No one can win anything worth having. The best blood of Europe will be dead when it is over. The last war took more than we could afford to lose.

Wednesday, September 28

Kept waking up at intervals during the night, thinking about England being bombed.

Took the 9:55 for London and went direct to American Embassy. Anne remained at Cliveden and came in later with Lady Astor.

There was a line of people in front of the embassy. Learned later that they were waiting for visas. Went to see Herschel Johnson. The shipment of United States Army gas masks had just arrived. Herschel arranged for me to get two. Ambassador Kennedy came in for a moment and said, "You may not need them. There's some good news coming in." But there was no time to talk or to find out what the "news" was.

Returned to hotel and adjusted and tested my mask. Then Anne came in and said Lady Astor was waiting downstairs, and had asked us for lunch at her son's home.

Anne and I walked to No. 4 St. James's Square and drove with Lord Astor to "Bill" Astor's[83] home (Upper Grosvenor Street). Lunch was rather hurried because of the meeting of Parliament at 3:00. The editor of the *Times* was there (Dawson).[84] Also, several members of the Astor family.

Returned to hotel after lunch. Anne and I practiced putting on and packing away the gas masks. Packing takes longest. Putting them on is quite simple after the original adjustments are made.

Headlines on press billboards say Hitler, Mussolini, and Chamberlain are to meet in Munich. If true, must have been the news Ambassador Kennedy had. Lady Astor just called Anne. It is true, and war is *probably* avoided for the time being, at least. Am not surprised, but very much relieved.

Called Mr. Tom Jones. Anne and I drove to his home and spent half an hour talking to him. We talked, of course, of the turn of events away from war. Discussed whether England would wake up after the experience she has gone through. If she does not wake up now, there is no hope. Tom Jones has worked for a better relationship between England and Germany, but has had very little support from the English government. It seems to me that Baldwin and Eden are responsible for many of the present difficulties.

Thursday, September 29

Went to see Ambassador Kennedy at 11:15. Everything is looking better, and Kennedy has taken a large part in bringing about the conference between Hitler, Chamberlain, Mussolini, and Daladier. The English like him and are saying that we have at last sent a real man to represent us. I have not heard any criticism of the fact that he is an Irish Catholic. Kennedy has been very active during the last few days. He had several American cruisers sent to England simply for effect on Germany. He went to see Chamberlain one day on business, and then went back a second time for no reason at all except to have it known that the American Ambassador went twice on the same day to see the Prime Minister about the crisis.

Just before lunch I had a phone call from the embassy asking me to

83. The Honorable William Astor, eldest son of 2nd Viscount Astor, Parliamentary Secretary to the Secretary of State for Home Affairs.

84. Geoffrey Dawson, once with the British Colonial Office, had been editor of the London *Times* since 1923.

call Ambassador Bullitt in Paris and to use a government pre-emptory call to get through (the lines have been jammed lately). Got through in about ten minutes. Bullitt asked me to be in Paris for a conference tomorrow morning. Asked us to stay in embassy with him in room I occupied in 1927. (I have not been in it since.)

Friday, September 30

Arrived Paris 10:00 A.M. Train was comfortable, but lots of starting and stopping during the night. Ambassador Bullitt's secretary met us at the station and drove with us to the American Embassy. Ambassador Bullitt was at the door when we arrived and took us to our rooms. Seems very strange to be in the room I had in 1927, when Herrick invited me to stay in the embassy, and to gradually remember some of the old surroundings —the court in front, the staircase, the corner parlor. The rooms have been changed a great deal, but there are still many familiar things. There is a brass plate on the bed I slept in eleven years ago. Agnes Herrick had it put on.

Ambassador Bullitt told me that he asked me to come to Paris to take part in a conference in regard to the establishment of factories in Canada to supply military aircraft to France. His idea is that since France is not able to build sufficient planes to supply her needs, she should purchase them from America. The Neutrality Act[85] makes it impossible for a foreign country to rely on buying planes direct from the United States. Yet the United States is the only country except Germany capable of producing first-class aircraft in large quantity. Consequently, according to Bullitt (the idea is not new), factories should be built in Canada, just across the border. These factories could be supplied with machines and tools from the United States and could manufacture aircraft of American design without hindrance from the Neutrality Act in time of war.

Bullitt has already talked to the Minister of Air, Guy la Chambre, about the idea. He wants me to take part in organizing the plan and factories. How like old times! Everyone getting wonderful ideas about aviation enterprises, which they think it would be advisable for me to spend my life carrying on. This plan is not without merit, however (unlike many). The complications are numerous; but there would be great ad-

85. Passed by the U.S. Congress and signed by President Roosevelt in August, 1935. Its purpose was to keep the U.S. out of war by banning shipments of war materials to belligerents.

vantage, from a military standpoint, to having an aircraft supply based in Canada out of range of enemy bombardment.

Bullitt had taken M. Monnet[86] into his confidence, and M. Monnet was waiting at the embassy when we arrived. Ambassador Bullitt had invited the Minister of Air for lunch. He wanted to talk the plan over with M. Monnet and me before the Minister arrived.

I listened to Bullitt and Monnet, but felt it inadvisable to state my own feeling at that time. Besides, the plan was so new that I wanted time to think about it alone. My immediate reaction was that while it is of great importance for England and France to build up their military strength, especially in the air, there are more immediate and pressing problems. These consist of, first, the need for a different spirit among the people and, second, the absolute necessity of a changed attitude toward Germany if a disastrous war is to be avoided in the future.

Strength is necessary for character and for survival, but strength cannot be bought by gold, except temporarily, and with the danger of bringing greater demoralization at a later date. Strength is an inherent quality in a people. No amount of foreign aircraft will give France the security she wishes. It is to be found only in her own people. It would be better not to spend great sums in buying aircraft in America but to use the money in France in an attempt to bring back life to a corrupt and demoralized nation. The purchase of aircraft abroad would be second only to the hiring of soldiers—the last act of a dying nation. Those who talk of buying foreign aircraft are looking only at the superficial problems of Europe. It is men we need, not machines; leaders, not factories.

Lunch with Bullitt, G. la Chambre, and M. Monnet. We discuss the plan. How is it to be financed, how organized, how is the problem of English and metric measurement to be overcome? I raised the problems of the different systems of measurement because the Minister of Air said he wanted to build a factory in France similar to the one which would be built in Canada. The question of systems of measurement sounds like a detail at first, but it is of great and fundamental importance. Machinery

86. Jean Monnet, French banker, political economist. In World War I he served with Dwight W. Morrow on the Allied Maritime Transport Council to secure war materials, foodstuffs, and shipping facilities for the Allies. From 1919 to 1923 he was Deputy Secretary General of the League of Nations; in 1939 chairman of the Franco-British Economic Co-ordination Committee. During World War II he helped to co-ordinate the Allied war effort and was a member of the British Supply Council in Washington from 1940 to 1943. He was responsible for the Monnet Plan in 1947 and in 1955 the European Common Market.

built to work in inches could not be used in France without serious difficulty.

M. Monnet and I discuss a production potential of 10,000 planes per year in Canada. Bullitt says it should be 50,000. Present American production facilities are probably in the vicinity of 2,000 planes per year. (I have made no survey and so am not sure.)

After lunch Monnet and I talk for a short time and then decide to meet again in an hour. (I suggest this so that I can be alone for a time to think.)

After lunch I began to talk to M. Monnet about the underlying problems France is facing. I told him I felt a crisis would come which would be but little affected by the production of aircraft in Canada. I told him I doubted that democracy of the present type could last much longer in France. I told him that the expenditure of large sums of money in buying arms abroad would only hasten an internal collapse, with the resulting loss of the system of government which the foreign arms were to protect. France is in a very serious political and financial condition as it is.

We met again about 4:15, and went to the Ministry of Air at 5:00 P.M., for another conference with G. la Chambre.

After the conference we returned to the embassy, and Anne, Ambassador Bullitt, and I went to M. Monnet's home for dinner. (Mrs. Monnet and Anne had been together during the afternoon.) Just before leaving the embassy, Ambassador Bullitt had a phone call from the Polish Ambassador, saying that Poland had sent an ultimatum to Czechoslovakia and was ready to march into Teschen if the Czechs did not accept. Another war in the offing, but no one seems to be able to take it seriously, except the Polish Ambassador, of course.

Bullitt looks about all in. Everyone has been under a great strain during the last few days.

Spent the night in my 1927 room and bed.

Saturday, October 1

M. Monnet arrived at 9:45, and we left for the Air Ministry. Conference all morning with la Chambre and M. Hoppenot.[87] Discuss number of planes needed, number necessary to build in Canada, types, cost of factories, etc., etc.

The French estimates of German production facilities indicate that

87. Roger Hoppenot, economist and government finance official.

Germany can build 24,000 planes per year. French Intelligence places the existing German air fleet at 6,000 modern planes, with an additional number of older models, bringing the total to possibly 8,000 or 9,000. The 6,000 modern planes include about 1,500 fighters and 2,000 bombers on the line, ready for flight; and about 1,500 planes (of both types) in reserve.

The French are now building about forty-five planes per month, of all service types (bombing, pursuit, and observation). The French officers feel that within one year the rate of production in France can be brought to 5,000 or 6,000 per year. (This seems too optimistic to me, in view of internal conditions in France.) We estimated that the production rate in England might be 10,000 per year at the end of one year. England has approximately 2,000 service planes, of which probably 700, including all types, are of modern design.

This left a deficit of approximately 10,000 planes per year, at the end of one year, comparing the combined, hoped-for production capacity of France (5,000) and England (10,000) to the estimated present production capacity of Germany (24,000). (It also leaves Italy out of the picture.) In view of this rough estimate, the talk at our conference centered on a Canadian production capacity of 10,000 planes per year.

I brought up the fact that, in the first place, it would not be possible to establish a production capacity of 10,000 planes per year in Canada within twelve months and that, in the second place, even with an eventual production capacity of 25,000 planes per year, the result would only equal Germany's present estimated capacity and took for granted the improbability that Germany (who has done the most in the past) would stand by and do nothing while all this French and English activity was going on.

The French officers also raised the question of how to obtain 1,000 foreign bombers by July 1, 1939. (They feel it necessary to have at least this number.) Obviously it would not be possible to build factories in Canada and start to produce by next July, to say nothing of producing 1,000 bombers. Therefore, if any bombers are to be obtained from the United States by July, 1939, they must be purchased from existing factories. But the total production capacity in the United States is not large, measured by present European standards.

The American Army and Navy are absorbing most of our present production capacity, and the airlines (domestic companies and Pan American) are absorbing a large part of the capacity not taken by military orders. Also, there have been many foreign orders for both military and commercial planes. The recent British order for 200 twin-engine Lockheeds and 200 North American trainers has given both companies about all they can handle for the time being. The French order for 200 (or 300?) Curtiss pursuit planes (P-36) has taken up the excess Curtiss production facilities. I understand that the French have also taken an option on about 200 additional P-36 planes. When this situation is taken into account, it is obvious that the United States cannot produce a large additional number of military aircraft between now and next July. (I learned at the Air Ministry that some time ago Italy offered to sell military aircraft to France.)

I suggested that France purchase some bombers from Germany. Of course, this astounded everyone at the table, but it was accepted with more calmness than I expected (after the first laugh, when they took the suggestion as a joke). However, the conversation soon returned to Canada.

I intend to carry this idea further. It is possible that an arrangement might be made between France and Germany for the purchase of German aircraft by France. It is also possible that many problems might be solved by such a procedure. I believe this would depend very largely upon Germany's future intentions and the attitude of France and England in regard to them. A purchase of aircraft from Germany might be to the interest of everyone concerned. It would start a little trade between the countries taking part, it would be in the direction of a limitation of armament, and it would relieve Germany from part of the cost of her air fleet. It would ease the general European problem.

On the other hand, if France and England simply continue to arm in competition with Germany, we are moving in the direction of a general war in the future. There is nothing to gain by war for either side. War is sometimes necessary, but under present conditions in Europe it would be disastrous. Europe must not be divided against itself.

(English military authorities estimate that the proper protection of England against bombing raids would require 5,000 searchlights, 12,000 antiaircraft guns, and 100,000 men. At present there is a great shortage.)

The conference ended about noon.

At 3:00 we drove to Villacoublay,[88] where I was shown the latest types of French military aircraft.

88. An aerodrome situated west of Paris and east of Versailles.

I flew the new Moran 406 fighter for about twenty minutes (860 h.p. Hispano-Suiza engine; low-wing full-cantilever monoplane; retracting wheels; wing flaps; 487 kilometers top speed at 4,000 meters; landing speed about 124 kilometers; single cockpit; sliding hatch; metal construction; fuel for two hours at cruising).

It is the first time I have flown one of the fast modern fighters. The flight was more interesting because of the difference between French and American controls and gauges. For instance, the French throttle works in the opposite direction from the American. These things make it necessary to think about every move one makes and require a more mechanical type of flying until one gets used to them.

The plane handled well in the air and was easy to land. The second time I came in for a landing, however, the wing flaps would not go down more than part way, so I went around the field again. Neither could I get them down on my next approach, although I worked the control handle several times (they work by compressed air). I climbed up a few hundred feet and found that the flaps would go down properly if pressure on the control lever was continued long enough.

The various types of planes were flown for me—both bombing and fighting models of the latest design. In addition to the Moran 406 fighter, there was a smaller Moran fighter, built around a Renault in-line, air-cooled engine of 400 to 500 h.p. It makes a top of 460 kilometers per hour, they say. (Clean plane but a little small for a modern fighter.)

There was also a twin-engine pursuit plane, which carried two cannon shooting forward (three cockpit, low-wing type). This was built by Potez.

The French designs are reasonably good, but they are hampered by the lack of engines of high horsepower. This is partly due to being behind in engine design, and partly to the fact that it seems impossible for them to get the best quality of gasoline in sufficient quantity to permit the use of the type of engines we fly in the United States.

The most modern German bombers probably make about 500 kilometers top speed. Consequently, there is little object in building pursuit planes which make less than 550 kilometers. It would be desirable to have a still greater advantage in speed.

The most amazing fact, however, is that if war had come last week, France did not have a single modern pursuit plane ready for the defense of Paris! There was not, and is not, in France one fighting plane as fast as the latest German bombers! The French air fleet is almost nonexistent from the standpoint of a modern war. And many people in France and in England were advising their governments to declare war!

From Villacoublay I returned to la Chambre's office in the Air Ministry. M. Monnet was there, and we all again discussed the Canadian plan.

Monday, October 3

French Intelligence places the English August production at 180 service-type planes.

Short walk around grounds after breakfast. Another walk with Bullitt later; then drove to Paris with him, arriving at embassy house at 9:45. We discussed the Canadian plan on the way in. As is usually the case with such projects, the last draft is for a factory, or factories, located in Canada, capable of producing 1,500 planes and 4,000 engines per year with one shift, and capable of producing about 5,000 planes and equivalent engines with three shifts in wartime. This would constitute a valuable military reserve, but is not a figure which would impress Germany greatly.

(The road from Château de Saint-Firmine passes the monument which marks the nearest German approach to Paris during the last war. It is especially impressive under present circumstances.)

M. Monnet was waiting for us at the embassy house. He had finished a paper in French, outlining the "Canadian plan."

Bullitt and Monnet want me to go to the United States almost immediately to start inquiries and negotiations. I consider the present developments in Europe to be of the utmost importance and do not want to go away at this time. I replied that I was going to Germany next week and was not sure when I could go to the United States.

Monnet and I went to see la Chambre at the Air Ministry at about 10:30. After a conference there, we all returned to the embassy house. Ambassador Bullitt arrived soon after we did, and we talked together until Daladier came. Daladier (speaking always in French) told of his meeting with Chamberlain, Hitler, and Mussolini. He also spoke of Goering. Hitler had definite personal magnetism, he said. Goering was very amusing and had definite ability, according to Daladier's impression.

We had lunch at a small table which was carried into the parlor. The discussion continued. After lunch we began talking about the Canadian plan. M. Monnet translated some of the points for me, and I could follow part of the conversation. Daladier was interested and seemed to ap-prove of the idea. He asked why it was that France, who had produced Blériot[89] and other famous fliers and designers, should have reached such a terrible condition in her aviation. Bullitt cited the fact that France has a separate Air Force and said he thought this an important factor. La Chambre spoke about the disastrous effect of the nationalization of the aviation industry, of the chaotic labor conditions which now exist in France, of the fact that the French have considered it sufficient to build a few prototypes without going into production on any of them. La Chambre is a good man, and French aviation should improve greatly under him.

The conversation turned to immediate needs and the impossibility of constructing factories quickly enough to produce aircraft for next summer. I suggested again the possibility of buying planes from Germany. This did not startle Daladier, and he apparently was entirely willing to consider the idea.

I told Daladier that the purchase of aircraft in Germany might help in the solution of other problems. It would lead to trade and an eventual arms-limitation agreement. I also told him that continued competition in building military aircraft would simply lead to the destruction of Europe at a later date. It would also lead to economic collapse.

The talk then turned to French politics, and when and how the Chamber should be dissolved. Daladier expects to call for a vote in the near future. The question of what issue to dissolve on was discussed. Should it be the necessity of a new financial policy, or the recent crisis? (Financial conditions in France are very bad, and another more serious financial crisis has been predicted for a long time. Apparently it is now close.)

Daladier left with la Chambre at about 3:00. M. Monnet, Ambassador Bullitt, and I discussed plans. Bullitt had to leave for an engagement, and Monnet and I continued the discussion. It is all very well to get an idea such as this Canadian plan, but it is a complicated problem for someone to work out and put in actual operation. Bullitt and Monnet both think it is the most important step which can be made in the direction of peace in Europe. I cannot follow them in this argument at present, and feel a little resentful of their feeling I should give up my own plans for the winter and rush off to America on the next boat in order to begin work on their idea. As a matter of fact, it is Bullitt's idea, although he has convinced Monnet of its prime importance.

Bullitt told me that he suggested months ago the possibility of building

89. Louis Blériot, French engineer and aviation pioneer, who built France's first airplane factory, and was the first to fly across the English Channel, in July, 1909.

factories across the Canadian border for the purpose of supplying France and England with military aircraft. Apparently, a few days before he telephoned to me in London, la Chambre told him that he wanted to talk to me about the condition of French aviation and what steps might be taken to improve it. La Chambre said he was anxious to talk to someone he could trust about the purchase of supplies in the United States.

I told Monnet that in addition to the personal problems involved, this project (Canadian) necessitated the greatest caution and consideration. In event of war, those who were responsible for the project would, of course, be given great credit. And, still much more important, would have made a great contribution to the French cause. Under any circumstances there would, of course, be political opposition in France, with the usual claims of graft and corruption. And, in a project involving the expenditure of between $50 million and $100 million (for factories, to say nothing of future operating costs), it would be almost impossible to avoid instances of graft, which would give strength to the charges. If there is no war, then the people who have taken part in the expenditure of large sums of French money abroad will be cursed by politicians and public alike, even though the existence of Canadian aircraft factories might be the factor which prevented war.

In other words, those who take part in the establishment of factories in Canada for the production of warplanes for France will be considered successful only in case a war is fought. Therefore, success would depend upon the destruction of European civilization.

In times of emergency, personal problems and desires must be given second consideration. However, the Canadian project involves great difficulties from my standpoint. We have no home in the United States, and if we went back there suddenly, there would be tremendous publicity with all the worry it involves. It would be extremely difficult for Anne and the children.

The children cannot very well stay on Illiec this winter. I had planned on taking them to a European city for the winter and had considered Berlin. If I went to the United States on this Canadian project, there would be no opportunity to arrange for a winter home before going. Anne could do so, but it would be difficult for her alone, and our secretary, Miss Hutchison, has not enough experience to be of much help.

Also, the study I hope to make of Europe this winter will be impossible if I start work on the Canadian project. I don't know how much I can do here; but I feel that if anything can be done to avoid European war, it must be based upon an intimate understanding of conditions in Europe.

Tuesday, October 4

Walked to Eiffel Tower and back after breakfast. M. Monnet came for a conference about 10:30. I outlined some of the problems I saw in regard to the Canadian project. Ambassador Bullitt came about 12:00, and we talked to him for half an hour.

Colonel Fuller[90] called at the embassy house about 1:00, and I went with him to his apartment for lunch. We talked mostly of Germany's ambitions and of the possibility of European war developing as a result of them. Talked to Colonel Fuller about possibility of making a trip to Spain to study effect of their use of aviation.

Returned to embassy house. M. Monnet came about 6:30. Ambassador Bullitt arrived about 7:15. Another conference. Then Monnet left. I am to meet him in Paris on Sunday, October 9. Told both Monnet and Bullitt that I wanted two or three days on the island to think over the Canadian project.

Dinner at embassy house with Ambassador Bullitt, M. Reynaud [91] (Minister of Justice), and Palewski, his Chief of Cabinet.[92] M. Blum came in after dinner. Blum and Reynaud were extremely interested in the French and European aviation situation. Bullitt talked to them in French, which I could follow only in a few parts.

I leave for Calais on the 8:20 train in the morning and plan on flying to Illiec in the afternoon. Will be glad to get back, if only for a few days.

Wednesday, October 5

Arrived Calais station 11:45. The broken sky at Paris had changed to rain and low clouds. Stopped at a café to get some sandwiches (two big buns, one filled with cheese and one with ham).

Still raining hard when I took off. Ceiling about 150 meters. The

90. Colonel Horace H. Fuller, military attaché and military attaché for air, U.S. Embassy, Paris.

91. During the 1930's Paul Reynaud served as Minister of Colonies, Justice, and Finance. He became France's Premier in March, 1940, but resigned on June 15, 1940, rather than ask Germany for an armistice.

92. Gaston Palewski was closely associated with Paul Reynaud for many years. He served as director of the Finance Minister's office when Reynaud was nominated to this post in 1938. During this period he was also a member of the French delegation to the Disarmament Conference in Geneva.

cockpit leaks badly, and water streamed in over my clothes and maps. Very strong head winds. Rain stopped at times, and clouds broke to show clear sky above first layer. Soon after Dieppe, however, the sky became completely overcast, and I entered a storm area with turbulent air and heavy rain. Ceiling lowered, and wisps of fog appeared over the forests. Had to keep cockpit hatch open to see clearly, and my legs soon became soaked where leather coat did not cover. Engine ran perfectly on both magnetos.

South of Le Havre the rain increased, visibility lowered, and turbulence shook plane violently. Clouds lowered and storm ahead looked worse. Unable to see ahead more than 300 meters, and that vaguely. Turned back and started to follow the Seine to Rouen, but storm too bad. Followed back course, but storm had blown over route and conditions much worse.

Suddenly saw wireless tower ahead and slightly to one side. Was flying about even with the top of it. Circled to make sure there was only one tower and continued on back course.

Wireless tower reminded me of time, years ago (about 1928), when I was flying east through the Alleghenies in bad weather. I was alone in the Ryan monoplane which was presented to me by the Ryan Company after I had put the *Spirit of St. Louis* in the Smithsonian. (It was a terrible plane, with a blue plush cabin for four passengers. It was overloaded and had a rotten take-off. Not at all like the *Spirit of St. Louis*.)

I was following a river through a deep and narrow valley. The mountains on each side ran up into clouds. Suddenly, I saw a high-tension-line tower well up on the side of the mountain to my right. It was one of those oversize towers which are placed at each end of a long span of cable. A glance to the left showed another tower opposite. I could not see the span of wire between. No time to turn. I dove close as possible to the water. And the cables showed clearly a few feet above the plane as I passed under them.

Finally reached Dieppe and turned south along river valley (Varennes), but storm too bad. Turned north and struck coast at mouth of Somme. Followed Somme past Abbeville about ten miles, where weather improved rapidly. Then set course 177° magnetic to Le Bourget. Ceiling and visibility good over remainder of route. Slight rain at intervals.

Landed Le Bourget about 4:30. Put plane in hangar, gave instructions to mechanic for servicing, and took taxi to embassy house. Met Douglas MacArthur II at embassy house and accepted his invitation for dinner.

Drove to his apartment at 7:00. Mrs. MacArthur in bed. We talked to her for half an hour, then dinner. MacArthur drove me to station in time to catch the 10:00 train for Plouaret. Tried to get bed, but conductor started to put me in with a woman! (Not at all attractive, either.) Decided to sit up, but found I could get second-class compartment for myself.

Thursday, October 6

Changed trains at Plouaret at 7:55. Arrived Lannion at 8:40. Miss Hutchison there to meet me with Ford. Drove to Buguélès, put car in garage, and walked across flats to Illiec (low tide). Anne and Thor met us at the pine grove.

Rest of day dictating paper and letter in regard to Canadian plan. Mme. Carrel came for a short visit in the afternoon. She had charge of evacuating a group of pregnant women from Paris at the time of the [Munich] crisis. Some of them had babies while on the train, she said.

Sixty copies of *Listen! the Wind* arrived a few days ago—the first we have seen. Anne and I signed some of them for mailing to our friends.

In between dictation I took several walks around the island and spent quarter of an hour with Anne and Jon gathering the few bits of driftwood which are washed up on the beaches. Jon and Land are looking very well. Thor is rather thin, and I am trying to get him to eat a little dog biscuit with his meat. Skean is, as usual, much too fat.

Friday, October 7

Most of day spent dictating and working on letter and outline concerning the Canadian plan. In the afternoon Anne, Jon, and I climbed the big rock on the northeast side of Illiec and sat for half an hour watching the waves dash over the rocks and shore. There has been a fairly strong wind all day. The islands are extremely beautiful when there is a storm. In fact, no weather seems disagreeable here.

This Canadian plan has taken a great deal of time. I grudge being kept away from Illiec, but conditions in Europe are so critical that it is necessary to do everything possible to try to make them better. I am hopelessly behind with letters, and can see no chance of catching up, as I must leave for Paris tomorrow night.

Jon is looking and feeling well. The last month has done him a great deal of good. Land is a sturdy, healthy baby. He walks all around the edges of his "pen."

Saturday, October 8

The nights on Illiec are wonderful. Last night the moon was nearly full, and the rocks had a weird, moonlike appearance. Our room (over the kitchen) is closest to the sea. We go to sleep and wake up with the sound of surf on the beach. The waves roll the stones around so that a harder, crunching sound is mixed in with the splash and roar of the breakers. The white spray on the distant rocks and the changing tide and light are beyond description.

Anne decided to go with me tonight instead of taking the morning train as she originally intended. The tide was low, so we walked across the flats. Low clouds covered the moon at intervals, bringing a light rain with them. Louis and Kerleau went with us to help carry the baggage, and Miss Hutchison to drive the car back from the station. I enjoy these walks over the sea bottom, wet feet and all.

We drove to Plouaret and arrived just in time to catch the train. Apparently has been some change in the schedule. Not even time to buy tickets. Large crowd of people waiting for train, and considerable excitement at station. Train also crowded. Two women and three small children, with dozens of bundles and suitcases, came into the compartment with us. I helped stow their suitcases on racks, and wondered what the night would be like. These French trains do not seem to pay much attention to accommodations or comfort. I don't mind much sitting up all night, but I wish Anne could get a night's sleep. We will probably have full days in Germany.[93] The women and children left at the next station.

Sunday, October 9

Train arrived Paris at 7:10. We took a taxi to the Crillon and engaged a room for today and tonight. M. Monnet called for us at 1:30, and we had lunch at his apartment. After lunch M. Monnet and I discussed the Canadian plan and my decision not to go to the United States or to take an active part in its organization. To my surprise he agreed with my decision and with many of the points in the letter I wrote to him.

93. Lindbergh was going to Germany to study recent developments in aviation.

Détroyat and his wife came at 5:00. We talked of French, German, and English aviation. Détroyat has flown the Spitfire. Says it is a difficult plane for an amateur. Take-off especially hard—too much torque, and plane tends to swing. Necessary to start slowly, with full opposite rudder. He says Spitfire makes 550 kilometers top speed, but only for five minutes. Normal top is 490 kilometers; about the same as the Morane (487). He says Spitfire is easy to land but, on the whole, does not handle as well as the Morane. Détroyat says he understands the new German Messerschmitt bomber (the 110) will make 600 kilometers at altitude.

Détroyat says that some of the "confidential" talks and conferences last week are already known by various people.

Détroyat drove me to M. Monnet's apartment at 6:00. M. Monnet and I went for a walk while we talked about the Canadian plan. Monnet is sailing for the United States this week and will see Bullitt and probably the President as soon as he arrives. He asked me whom in the aviation industry he could talk to in absolute confidence about the plan. It would be necessary, of course, to find someone with experience and good judgment. I suggested Guy Vaughan. Guy is completely honest and has great ability both as an executive and an engineer. He came up through Wright Aeronautical Corporation at Paterson, and is now president of Curtiss-Wright.

I suggested that Monnet also talk to Glenn Martin, whom I do not know as well but in whom I have great confidence. Martin has built some of the world's best aircraft and is one of the oldest manufacturers in the business.

M. Roger Hoppenot came at 8:00. We had dinner in the apartment (M. and Mme. Monnet, M. Hoppenot, Anne, and I). After dinner Monnet, Hoppenot, and I talked about the Canadian plan for fifteen minutes. I was again surprised by the fact that Hoppenot agreed it was best for me not to take part in the survey. I had expected strong criticism from both Monnet and Hoppenot.

Anne and I took a taxi back to the hotel. I wrote letters of introduction for Monnet to Guy Vaughan and Glenn Martin. We went to bed early due to the previous night on the train and a day's flying [to Berlin] ahead.

Monday, October 10

Raining. Called weather bureau at Le Bourget to get route report. Weather very bad between Paris and Berlin. (Anne does the telephoning about weather—in French.) Weather will be better in afternoon, about 1:00 or 2:00. The Strasbourg route is closed, with fog on all the German mountains, but we might get through by flying to Calais and along the coast to Holland, then to Berlin via Hanover.

We packed and took taxi to Le Bourget. Took off about 2:30. There is so much red tape and clearance formalities in Europe that much of the time saved in flying is lost in routine details at aerodromes. I miss the old barnstorming hayfields, where it was only necessary to take the ropes off the wings, start the engine, and take off—provided you had done a thorough job servicing the plane on the previous afternoon. At least one was not loaded down with logbooks, carnets, and rules.

At first we planned on landing at Brussels, but as we approached the city the clouds lowered, and there was a heavy haze. Turned north again and finally landed at Rotterdam for the night. Telephoned Smith[94] in Berlin. He said my telegram, sent from the Crillon at noon, did not arrive in Berlin until 5:00, and that he and a number of German officers had gone to the aerodrome to meet us. He was very good-humored about it. Said also that Colonel Faymonville was greatly worried because of a story which had come out in London, quoting me about Russia in an uncomplimentary way.

I telephoned Colonel Lee in London to find out about this. Lee told me that a "scurrilous" weekly, with only a private circulation, had come out with a statement to the effect that I had stated that 1) Russian aviation was in a chaotic condition; 2) I had been invited to be the chief of the Russian Civil Air Fleet; 3) the German air fleet could whip the Russian, French, and English air fleets combined. This may not be the exact phraseology, but Lee said it was close. He said the Russians probably wouldn't know the difference between the standing of the sheet that printed the story and the *Times*.

These statements, according to the sheet, were made by me to Lloyd George, and at Cliveden, and at Transport House. I have, of course, made none of these statements. However, I have said that I consider the weakness of Russian military aviation to lie in inefficiency and bad organization. I have also said that the German Air Force was stronger than that of all other European nations combined. These two statements are probably strong enough to annoy the Russians as much as the ones quoted. The story about my being asked to be chief of Russian civil aviation has no basis whatever.

94. Lieutenant Colonel Truman Smith, military attaché and military attaché for air with the U.S. Embassy in Berlin, 1935–39.

Lee said that Faymonville was greatly upset by the story because it had been reprinted by papers in Moscow. Lee is sending a copy of Faymonville's telegram airmail to Colonel Smith in Berlin. I shall take no action until I see it.

Tuesday, October 11

Clear sky outside. Telegrams began arriving from various press organizations asking me to comment on statements I am reported as having made about Russia. No comment, of course. Fatal to begin denying press reports.

Anne and I had breakfast in our rooms. There was a small crowd waiting for us in the hotel lobby, including reporters and photographers. As usual, refused all interviews. I phoned Truman Smith and arranged to land at Tempelhof at 2:00 G.M.T. (3:00 Central European).

Took off 10:36 G.M.T. Weather was good, with an overcast sky and light haze along most of route. Landed Tempelhof at 3:00 G.M.T. Met by Colonel and Mrs. Smith, Major and Mrs. Vanaman,[95] and various German officers. Field was well controlled. Drove to Colonel Smith's apartment. Light lunch. Drove to American Embassy (house) at 5:00 for tea with Ambassador and Mrs. Wilson.[96]

Ambassador Wilson, Colonel Smith, Major Vanaman, and I drove to Potsdam to attend the dinner at the Neue Palais at 7:00. The palace is ordinarily used as a museum. Dinner in huge room, lit by thousands of candles. Sat next to General Milch[97] and talked about Germany's plans in the air. Many people there whom I knew: Détroyat, Sikorsky,[98] Tomlinson,[99] and most of the German aviation group.

Milch is an able and intelligent officer. We talked of possible arms

95. Colonel Arthur Vanaman, military attaché for air with the U.S. Embassy in Berlin. In 1942 he became a brigadier general.

96. Hugh R. Wilson, U.S. Ambassador to Germany. In 1937 he had been Assistant Secretary of State.

97. Erhard Milch. Inspector-General of the Luftwaffe and State Secretary.

98. Igor Sikorsky, Russian-born scientist, aviation pioneer, and aeronautical engineer. He built and flew the first multiengined airplane in Russia before coming to the U.S. in 1919. He organized the Sikorsky Engineering Corp. in 1925, and thereafter developed various types of aircraft, among them multiengined amphibians, flying boats, and the first successful helicopter in the Western Hemisphere. The Sikorsky organization eventually became a branch of United Aircraft Corp.

99. Daniel W. "Tommy" Tomlinson, naval officer and test and aerobatic pilot; later vice president in charge of engineering with Trans World Airlines.

agreement in the future (Germany, England, France). He said that Germany had to settle the Sudeten question this year, because it could not have been done without war next year.

Wednesday, October 12

Went for a drive through Berlin and nearby country in the afternoon. Berlin has greatly changed since we were here a year ago. Much more activity of every kind: buildings going up, great increase in traffic, store windows more attractive. In fact, Berlin has lost the air of tenseness I noticed in 1936 and now has the appearance of a healthy, busy, modern city (if the word "healthy" can be applied to a modern city).

Dinner at Haus der Flieger. Hundreds of people. Seemed that everyone in German aviation was present. Sat between Frau von Gronau[100] and Mme. Liotta (wife of Italian air attaché).[101] Anne sat next to General Milch. After dinner Anne danced several times.

It is difficult to write during and after these long days. It seems that the best time to keep a record is during the days when there is the least to write about. On the fullest days, and the most interesting, you are too tired to write well. It would be better to wait until the next morning, but there is usually something else which must be done then. If one is to be accurate, it is necessary to put down events soon after they happen. Possibly this is an explanation of the fact that the most active people seldom are able to write well. A clear mind is essential for writing. And one's mind cannot be the clearest at the end of many hours of activity.

Thursday, October 13

Vanaman and I went to the Haus der Flieger for lunch with the officers of Lufthansa. I sat between [Carl von] Gablenz and [Martin] Wronsky. We talked of landplanes v. flying boats and the development of transatlantic airlines. Gablenz believes that the landplane will be the type eventually used for flying between Europe and America (as I do). Wronsky has been won over to landplanes, although he was originally a supporter of flying boats. He and I had an argument over this problem in Berlin in 1936. (Of course, all of us believe in the use of flying boats during the developmental stages of the transatlantic routes.)

100. Wife of Hans Wolfgang von Gronau, president of the German Aero Club, 1934–38; German air attaché in Tokyo and Manchuria, 1939–45.

101. General Liotta d'Aurelio.

Sikorsky and Tomlinson also attended the lunch. Sikorsky, of course, believes in the future of the big flying boat. He is one of the world's best aircraft designers and one of the most interesting men I have ever met. He and I talked at length about conditions in Russia. He cannot go back. He was last there in 1918.

Friday, October 14

Talked to Dr. Focke[102] about his helicopter development. Talked to C. G. Grey[103] about future transoceanic flying, etc. General Udet[104] came in for a time after lunch. We are doing comparatively little from a social standpoint, yet I am already tired of lunches, teas, and dinners. I like to see and talk to interesting people, but it is best to select carefully and to see not too many in one week. Too much contact with people dulls the edge of appreciation.

Saturday, October 15

Invited Sikorsky to lunch at Hotel Esplanade and took Anne and Kay Smith[105] to meet him. I have wanted Anne to meet Sikorsky for years. We talked first of aviation (flying boats, helicopters, transatlantic flying, etc.), then of Russia. Sikorsky expects the present system to break down, "maybe in one year, maybe in a generation." I think he is right. Conditions in Russia are too bad to continue indefinitely, and the present system cannot work. It kills ability, and that is fatal to the system which causes it. Sikorsky estimates the executions which have taken place in Russia since the war to be in the millions and claims that between 30 and 40 million people have been killed directly or indirectly as a result of the Revolution. Says he knows of one concentration camp where about one hundred people are being executed each day at the present time. He did not state the source of this information.

Anne and I attended a tea at 6:00, given by Ambassador and Mrs. Hugh Wilson at the American Embassy (house). We both dislike this

102. Henrich Focke, German aeronautical engineer, who did pioneering work with helicopters.

103. English writer and editor of aviation publications.

104. Ernst Udet, a leading World War I German ace. In 1938 he was chief of the Technical Bureau of the German Air Force. He developed the dive-bombing technique used with success by the Germans in World War II. In 1940 he was promoted to general.

105. Mrs. Truman Smith.

type of thing, but the Smiths had accepted the invitation for us before we arrived. Due to the [Munich] crisis, I was not able to make detailed arrangements for our visit by mail. However, Mrs. Wilson was extremely considerate, and the function was much less difficult than most I have attended in the past. There were probably 150 guests.

Dinner (stag) at Major Vanaman's apartment. Probably twenty men attended, including Truman Smith, Sikorsky, Tomlinson, Merkel, von Massow (Richthofen squadron), and Wendland. Talk covered everything from conditions in Russia to pursuit tactics. Von Massow told me: "I know one fellow—I won't say who—that shot down four Martin bombers in twenty minutes with a Messerschmitt 109 (fighter)."

"Martins, or copies of Martins?" I asked him.

"Copies of Martins," he replied. Copies of Martins are the Russian bombers used in Spain by the "government" side. Von Massow disappeared for two or three months recently, and it may be that he was fighting with the Franco forces in Spain. Possibly the "fellow" he referred to is himself.

Sunday, October 16

Kay and Truman Smith, Anne, and I drove to palace built for Frederick the Great by his father at Rheinsberg. Walked around the grounds, then had lunch at a small hotel in the village. We were recognized by the German people there, but they were very nice and caused us no trouble. Returned to apartment in late afternoon.

Dinner at British Embassy, at invitation of Sir Nevile Henderson.[106] About twelve or fifteen people at dinner, including Belgian and Italian Ambassadors, the British military attaché, Colonel MacFarlane,[107] one of the S.S. leaders and his wife, and several members of the British Embassy. Talked to Colonel MacFarlane about British-German relationships, military aviation, etc. Ambassador Henderson asked me about the German aviation development and said he hoped I would do all I could to make the people in England realize the quality and magnitude of the aviation program in Germany. He said they did not believe him when he described it.

106. British Ambassador to Germany.

107. Colonel F. N. MacFarlane, military attaché in the British Embassy in Berlin.

Monday, October 17

Drove to Heinkel factory at Oranienburg. Ambassador Wilson, Vanaman, Wendland, and I made up the party. The Ambassador had expressed a desire to visit one of the modern German aircraft factories.

We arrived at the factory about 10:00 A.M. and spent the rest of the morning going through the works. This is a modern factory, nicely designed and built, with great attention given to the welfare of the workmen. The factory consists of a number of separate buildings, laid out to minimize the effect of an air attack. Each building has its "bomb proof." These shelters are well built and are equipped for a gas attack.

The factory is now producing Heinkel 111 bombers. Present production is probably in the vicinity of two per day. Apparently this is with only one shift. One of the newest types was demonstrated for us, and I was permitted to get into the cockpit of one on the ground. The pilot is completely enclosed in normal flight and looks forward through the nose of the plane and *under* the instrument board. This makes the nose of the bomber an almost perfect streamline, as there is no windshield. For flying in bad weather the pilot's seat, together with the controls, can be pumped up so that he can see out over the top of the bomber. (A hatch opens above the pilot, and a small windshield folds up, giving the advantage of an open cockpit when it is desired.) This is an excellent light bomber. Undoubtedly one of the best in existence.

An interesting and important feature of the factory (and the German system) is the apprentice school, where young boys are trained to be workmen. After a course of four years these boys are said to be often better workmen than the older and more experienced men. We had lunch at the factory with the officers. Then drove to the aerodrome where a Focke-Wulf 200 (four-engine, low-wing monoplane—same type that flew to the United States a few weeks ago) was waiting to take us to Tempelhof.

"Tommy" Tomlinson went with us in the Focke-Wulf. He had been at the Heinkel factory with another party, and joined us after lunch. Tomlinson and I flew the plane for about ten minutes each, testing its stability and flying characteristics on various combinations of engines.

After landing at Tempelhof, Tomlinson, Merkel (who had been with us in the flight in the Focke-Wulf 200), Wendland, and I waited for the JU-90 to arrive from Vienna. The JU-90 is the latest and largest Junkers transport (four-engine, forty-passenger, all-metal, low-wing mono-plane). Arrangements had been made for us to fly it after it arrived. The JU-90, however, was late, and did not land until after the field lights had been turned on. By the time the passengers had disembarked and the details completed, night had set in. However, we took off anyway, and the German pilot climbed the plane over the lights of Berlin. I was in the co-pilot's seat for the take-off. After reaching an altitude of about 1,500 feet, the pilot proceeded to demonstrate the stability characteristics of the plane. Then I flew it for about five minutes. After trying out the controls in banking and climbing, I turned my place over to Tomlinson. (Tomlinson has tested most of the recent American designs of large land transport planes.)

I stood at the back of the cockpit while Tomlinson flew. After making several minor tests of the controls, he put the plane into a left bank (not very steep) and kept pulling the stick back. Suddenly, he appeared to be shaking the stick violently. I learned later that Tomlinson was trying to stop this movement of the stick, but it seemed at first as though he were doing it intentionally. After several seconds, during which the entire plane was shaking, the German pilot asked Colonel Wendland to tell Tomlinson to stop shaking the control column. It was only then we dis-covered that Tomlinson had nothing to do with the vibration. It stopped immediately, however, as soon as the German pilot throttled down the engines. Tomlinson got by far the greatest thrill from all this, because none of the rest of us realized what was happening until it was nearly over.

It seems that the vibration was caused by the design of the flettner system. This is being changed in the new JU-90's. The difficulty would not have arisen in ordinary flying, but I do not think a plane with such a dangerous characteristic should be flown with passengers. All this time we were flying about 500 meters over Berlin. There were probably ten or fifteen people in the cabin, including Mr. Merkel, who, of course, knew something was wrong. We made a few more maneuvers, with the Ger-man pilot flying, then returned to Tempelhof.

Tuesday, October 18

Drove to Junkers engine factory at Magdeburg with Détroyat, Vanaman, and Colonel Wendland. This is a large engine factory, now changing over from the manufacture of the Junkers 210 engine to the 211 engine. The factory also makes airplane propellers and many of its own machine tools, including propeller-cutting machines. We saw six of these machines in operation, each of which cuts two propellers at one time. The factory is well equipped with modern machine tools. The engines were assembled on tracks, and there were two assembly lines. One of the officers told me that the engines moved forward every sixty-five minutes (i.e., the No. 210 engines). This would make a production of nearly two Junkers 210 engines per working hour. The factory was equipped with twenty-four test stands (two groups of twelve stands each). The factory was nicely built and laid out. Like the Heinkel plant at Oranienburg, it had a well-equipped apprentice school.

After inspecting this factory, we drove to the airport and flew in a JU-52 to Dessau. (The JU-52's we have been using are Air Ministry planes, specially assigned to take us on the trips we make.)

We had lunch in the Junkers factory at Dessau with Dr. [Heinrich] Koppenberg and various officers of the company. After lunch we went through part of the factory. There were three JU-90's under construction. One of them was being fitted with twin-row Pratt & Whitney engines. I was told that this plane was going on foreign service. We spent quarter of an hour inspecting the JU-90 construction. We also saw a number of Junkers 87 dive bombers being assembled, and there were about fifteen of these planes on the field outside the factory. Also a number of JU-86 bombers. The Junkers Dessau factory, like all the others I have visited, is filled with work and is producing planes rapidly.

This was my second visit to the Junkers Dessau factory. The first was during 1936. Visited the factory museum on both occasions. It gives a wonderful history of the Junkers developments.

From Dessau we flew back to Berlin.

Attended a men's dinner at the American Embassy in the evening. Ambassador and Mrs. Wilson were at the Embassy when I arrived. Mrs. Wilson left before the dinner. The guests included Marshal Goering, General Milch, General Udet, the Italian Ambassador, the Belgian Ambassador, Dr. Heinkel,[108] Dr. Messerschmitt,[109] Colonel Smith, Major Vanaman, the American naval attachés, Minister Baeumker,[110] and var-

---

108. Ernst Heinkel, who in 1929 founded the Heinkel-Flugzeugwerke in Warnemünde, which produced bombers.

109. Dr. Willy E. Messerschmitt, chief aviation designer and director of Bayerische Flugzeugwerke, later called Messerschmitt-A.G., in Augsburg from 1927 to 1945. His Me-109 held the speed record for landplanes in 1937, and the world speed record in 1939. He designed the jet-propelled Me-262.

110. Adolf Baeumker, chief of the air research division of the German Air Ministry.

ious other German officers and members of the American Embassy. There were two tables. Ambassador Wilson sat at the head of one and I at the head of the other.

Marshal Goering, of course, was the last to arrive. I was standing in the back of the room. He shook hands with everyone. I noticed that he had a red box and some papers in his hand. When he came to me, he shook hands, handed me the box and papers, and spoke a few sentences in German. I found that he had presented me with the German Eagle, one of the highest German decorations, "by order of der Führer."

At dinner I talked to General Milch about many of the infinite subjects connected with aviation. He asked me why we did not spend the winter in Berlin. I told him that we had been considering it. (Anne and I have talked frequently about staying in Berlin this winter. It would be an excellent base—extremely interesting.)

After dinner we left the dining room and broke up into small groups. I spent most of the first half hour trying to explain to the Italian Ambassador that I could not accept an invitation he had extended for dinner because I was going on a trip arranged by the Air Ministry, which could not be canceled.

Later in the evening Goering came over and suggested that we go into the next room and talk. Ambassador Wilson went with us to interpret. Goering seems a little less stout than when I last saw him. We sat down in the corner. Goering's first question was about the trip Anne and I made to Russia in August and September. Ambassador Wilson interpreted the question and my answer, and then (wisely) jumped up and, turning to the nearest member of the embassy, who spoke German, said, "Mr. Geist[111] can interpret better than I can. Let him take my place." (Or words to this effect.) This move placed us in the center of both internal and external politics. Ambassador Wilson left, because to take part in a conversation between Goering and me about Russia would place him in an extremely embarrassing position. He asked Geist to take his place only because he (Geist) was standing nearby.

Goering asked why we had gone to Russia; what the hotels were like; whether many Russians stayed in the hotels; how the Russian cities compared to other cities; and many other questions. I talked to him frankly about what we saw in Russia and the impressions we had during our trip. I told him that Anne and I were treated with the utmost hospitality by the Russians and that we met many very likable people among them; that

111. Raymond H. Geist, diplomatic officer in the U.S. Embassy, Berlin.

we went to Russia to see what the conditions were and that we found our trip extremely interesting; that the Russian hotels were not as good as those in other countries; that the cities were hardly comparable to the cities of Germany, France, and England, because the life and atmosphere was entirely different; that I did not think the conditions now existing in Russia are at all good; and that the people did not seem to me to be well fed and happy.

After talking about Russia, Goering turned the conversation to aviation, to Germany's plans and accomplishments. He spoke of the performances of present military planes and of the quantity of production. He said the new Junkers 88 bomber (which no one we know has seen) is far ahead of anything else built, and that he would arrange that it be shown to me. Goering said the Junkers 88 did 500 kilometers per hour and that it was not "a magazine figure," but an actual speed of 500 kilometers. He said they expected to have a plane which would make 800 kilometers per hour in the near future (at critical altitude).

Goering spoke of the apprentice schools in connection with the factories in Germany and of the system of retraining workers from overcrowded industries. He spoke at length on the ability of a man to attack any problem, regardless of his previous experience. Said there was too much tendency to think a man had to be a specialist before he could understand a problem, while the actual fact was that a specialist is often the worst man to put in charge. Goering referred to his own experience in German financial problems. Said that at one time he knew so little about finance that he couldn't even keep his own pocketbook filled. Goering said he told Hitler he would be willing to take on any problem in Germany except the religious problem, but that he did not know how to solve the religious problem.

During all of this conversation Goering sat in a large armchair in the corner of the room. He spoke at length, then sat back and frequently closed his eyes while the translation was going on. Then he would speak again. He was wearing a blue Air Corps uniform which, I was told later, was of a new design. Some of the air officers (German) were laughing because they had never seen it before. Apparently, Goering has the habit of turning up unexpectedly in new uniforms. The last time I saw him, two years ago, he was wearing a uniform of white and gold.

I remained for a few minutes after Goering left, then returned with Colonel Smith to his apartment.

Wednesday, October 19

Drove to Staaken with Détroyat, Colonel Wendland, and Major Vanaman. (Staaken is a military aerodrome northwest of Berlin.) We boarded a JU-52 and took off for the Messerschmitt factory at Augsburg. Dr. Messerschmitt went with us. The sky was overcast at Berlin, but clear in southern Germany. We had a strong headwind, and the air was unusually rough. We had to keep our belts on a large part of the time. The wing tips of the plane seemed to move up and down two feet in the bumps.

We landed at Augsburg and had a "breakfast" of sausages and sandwiches, then began our inspection of the factory. Dr. Messerschmitt went with us and explained many of the details of construction. He is a young man, probably about forty, and undoubtedly one of the best designers of airplanes in the world. He has a strong face and honest eyes. An interesting and likable character.

We went through the room where the 109 and 110 wings and fuselages are being built. Messerschmitt has the ability of combining simple construction with good lines and high performance. The 109 is the standard German fighter. The 110 is a new type of long-range fighter. It may be used to accompany bombers in the future. Both planes are all-metal, full-cantilever monoplanes. The 109 carries one engine. The 110 carries two. The latest types of these planes use the Junkers 211 engine (about 1,200 h.p.).

The 109 is a single cockpit fighter with closed hatch. It mounts two synchronized machine guns in addition to two wing guns, which can be either machine guns or cannon. Messerschmitt told us that the standard 109 with a Junkers 211 engine had made a record (official) of 611 kilometers per hour, and that it was capable of making about 750 kilometers per hour at critical altitude. It has a monospar wing with a three-point connection to the fuselage. The retracting landing gear is simple.

After inspecting the factory, we walked to the flying field, where demonstration flights of the 109 and 110 were made for us. The speed and maneuverability of the 109 was, of course, most impressive. A small plane always looks much faster than a larger one and is quicker in maneuvers. On the other hand, it was amazing to see a two-engine plane do acrobatic flying almost as well as the smaller type.

After watching the demonstrations I made two flights in the Messerschmitt 108, a small, four-place, all-metal, low-wing monoplane, with slots, flaps, and retracting gear. (Both the 109 and 110 have slots and flaps.) It was originally planned that I fly a 109, but the Germans did not want Détroyat [a French military pilot] to fly this plane and did not want to let me fly it without asking him to do so. (They had no objection to his flying the 108.) Consequently, I will fly the 109 at Rechlin after this trip.

The 108 is by far the best plane of its type I have flown. It has excellent control characteristics—very light stick and rudder loading. The high speed is slightly over 300 kilometers, with an Argus 240 h.p. engine. The test pilot flew the plane on the first flight. I flew it on the second (about ten minutes each).

Détroyat told us (including the Germans with us) that some of the French pilots had tested a 109 captured in Spain. It had a 211 Junkers engine and made 465 kilometers per hour. Everyone laughed. This incident is well known to both French and German aviators. The French were apparently much impressed with the characteristics of the 109.

After a late lunch we took off in the JU-52 for Munich and drove to the hotel. Dr. Messerschmitt stayed at Augsburg.

I sent another telegram to Colonel Faymonville. Am extremely sorry he has had trouble about our visit to Russia, but I can see no advantage in taking part in a newspaper controversy. It never does any good, and usually causes much more trouble. Any statement I made to the Moscow press would almost certainly be misused. They have brought this situation on their own heads by paying attention and giving publicity to an irresponsible article in an almost unknown English publication. I said none of the things I was quoted as saying, but during the recent crisis, when it was necessary to speak frankly, I gave opinions about Russia and the Russian air fleet which (being true) probably bother the Russians even more than the statements I was quoted as making.

Thursday, October 20

Breakfast at hotel with Détroyat, Wendland and Vanaman. Afterward, we drove to the aerodrome, where the same JU-52 and crew was waiting for us, and took off for the Dornier factory at Friedrichshafen. The day was clear, except for a light haze, and the flight very beautiful.

Dr. Dornier[112] was ill, and we were met on the airport by his son and

112. Dr. Claude Dornier, pioneer in the field of metal aircraft construction. His

several officers of the company. There were a number of DO-17 bombers on the field, with various types of engines, some of which were French. We were informed that a number of DO-17's were being built for Yugoslavia, and that the Yugoslavians had specified French engines. Therefore, Hispana-Suiza and Gnome Rhone types were being installed.

A DO-17 with BMW [Bavarian Motor Works] engines was flown for us. Then we made a trip through the factory, ending at the assembly hangar for flying boats. There were a number of pontoon planes (single-engine, high-wing monoplanes) in this hangar—built for Greece.

The tandem-engine flying boat was demonstrated for us. Also, a three-engine flying boat of the type built for the Dutch government for military service in its colonies. After the demonstrations we got into a launch and went out to inspect the [flying boat]. Détroyat, Vanaman, and I made a flight in this boat with the test pilot. Détroyat and I each flew for about five minutes. The plane handled well and should be a good service type.

After lunch we went to the Zeppelin works. Dr. Eckener[113] was away. We went first to the museum, then to the hangar which sheltered the new *Graf Zeppelin* (the sister ship to the *Hindenburg*). There were very few people about, and a noticeable lack of workmen in the hangar. The great ship, shining new and clean, floated stilly at her cables. I felt depressed looking at her. She seemed so capable of life and movement, yet held quietly in that hangar by intangible forces. This airship represented the result of all the years of development of lighter-than-air. She seemed to me like a last member of a once proud and influential family.

For I can see no future for the airship. It is inherently too slow—about half the speed of a plane. There is not room for the dirigible between the steamship and the airplane. It may have a few more years of life, but then it will probably become even more extinct than the square-rigger and the tea clipper—for sailing exists as a sport, even though the seas are now crossed by steam. Still, the free balloon and the small blimp may live on to remind people of the days when the future of transoceanic air travel seemed to belong to the dirigible.

---

giant DO-X was a forerunner of later transoceanic flying boats, and his DO-17 two-engine airplanes were among the most versatile and widely used German aircraft in World War II.

113. Dr. Hugo Eckener, German pioneer pilot of Zeppelin airships and commander of the *Graf Zeppelin*. He engaged in extensive research on dirigible and related problems.

We went inside the *Graf Zeppelin,* through the passenger staterooms, along the narrow catwalk, to the control room. It seemed beautifully designed and built, with comfortable cabins and plenty of room for the forty passengers to move around in. But only forty passengers in such a huge machine? A plane a fraction the size could carry more people a greater distance, and twice as fast. True, they would not have as much room.

After a half hour spent going through the dirigible, we took off in the JU-52 for Berlin. I watched the sun set in a broken sky and the lights appear in houses and towns below us.

Friday, October 21

Colonel Wendland called for me in the morning and, together with Major Vanaman, we drove to Staaken and took off for Rechlin in a JU-52. On this trip I flew as co-pilot. We had the same crew as on the previous flights we have made around Germany, but for the flight to Rechlin we took a JU-52 equipped with bomb racks (vertical) in the cabin. There was one machine-gun mount in the tail.

After landing we were escorted to a line of four planes: the JU-88, the Messerschmitt 110, and two Messerschmitt 109's. It is probably the first time anyone but a German (or possibly an Italian) has seen the 88. It was rather a strange-looking plane with its protrusions for machine guns, but it looked capable of high performance. It was a mid-wing, all-metal monoplane, with trailing-edge flaps interconnected with the stabilizer— so that when the flaps passed 30° down they moved the stabilizer automatically. Retracting landing gear, of course. One of the most interesting external features lay in the engine nacelles. The 88 at first appeared to carry air-cooled engines, but closer examination showed them to be liquid cooled. The cowling was round, as for air-cooled engines, but the opening was filled with oil and water radiators.

The interior arrangement of this bomber was also a departure from convention. It carried a crew of three. (I was told that the next 88's built would carry a crew of four.) The crew positions were grouped so close together that each man could touch the other two without moving. The pilot and radio operator–gunner sit back to back. The bomber sits on a sliding seat beside the pilot. He also has a place where he can lie down to shoot below to the rear.

Major Vanaman and I were asked not to mention the fact that we had been shown the Junkers 88.

We next inspected the Messerschmitt 110. Then passed on to the 109 I was to fly. I got in the cockpit while one of the officers described the instruments and controls. The greatest complication lay in the necessity of adjusting the propeller pitch for take-off, cruising, and diving. Then there were the controls for the flaps, the retracting gear, for flying above 2,000 meters, for locking and unlocking the tail wheel, and for the other usual devices on a modern pursuit plane. After studying the cockpit, I got out and put on a "chute" while a mechanic started the engine. Then, after taxiing slowly down to the starting point, I took off. The plane handled beautifully. I spent quarter of an hour familiarizing myself with the instruments and controls, then spent fifteen minutes more doing maneuvers of various types (rolls, dives, Immelmanns, etc.). After half an hour I landed, took off again, circled the field, and landed a second time; then taxied back to the line. The 109 takes off and lands as easily as it flies.

We had lunch with the officers at Rechlin, then boarded the JU-52 for our return flight to Berlin. I flew the plane back to Staaken. It is an old type, but is very stable and safe for blind flying. Will probably be used for several more years, but a better plane should be designed for the purpose it serves (troop and passenger transport). Of course, the Germans have specialized in military aviation, and their commercial types have been neglected.

Anne and I have been talking about, and considering very carefully, the possibility of spending the winter in Germany. In keeping a record of the full days I have been spending, I have neglected to record the really more important plans we have been making for the future. They are always less tangible and more indefinite, and therefore harder to write about.

Saturday, October 22

In the morning I drove with Colonel Wendland to the Regiment Goering —an antiaircraft regiment stationed on the outskirts of Berlin. We were taken on a tour of inspection by the commanding officer. This regiment has by far the best quarters I have ever seen. Built among the typical Berlin pines, the offices and barracks have a homelike atmosphere about them which is almost unknown to the average American Army post. The most careful attention has been given to architecture and to planting, and the keynote is simplicity.

This "regiment" consists of two regiments of antiaircraft, one attack battalion, and a battalion of guards for Field Marshal Goering. There are now about 3,500 men. Another regiment will be added to bring the total strength to about 7,000 men.

The barracks are well equipped, although I felt that more attention could be given to decorating the individual rooms. (There are an average of about six men to a room.) The dining rooms were especially attractive. There is a large outdoor swimming pool and a smaller indoor one. The gymnasiums are adequate and well equipped. The C.O. pointed to a truck which was taking straw from one of the gymnasiums and said that the big rooms had been very convenient during the recent crisis, when they had had extra troops to care for. They had simply covered the floors of the gymnasiums with straw and let the men spread their blankets on top of it.

We visited the sheds where the guns were kept. The C.O. said [the regiment] could be on the march on two hours' notice. Said the regiment had gone from Berlin to Vienna in sixty-two hours last March, "without sleep."

The heavy batteries consist of four 88's (88-mm. antiaircraft) and two 20-mm. for the protection of the battery against air attack. The 88's have a vertical range of over 10,000 meters and fire twenty rounds per minute. The 20's fire 300 rounds per minute. I was told that the new type of 20-mm. cannon fire 500 rounds per minute. The light batteries consist of twelve 20-mm. cannon. There is also a battery of 37-mm. cannon. The attack battalion is organized for movement by air (in the JU-52's at present).

Dinner at the American Embassy (house) with Ambassador and Mrs. Wilson. I spoke to Ambassador Wilson about the possibility of our spending the winter in Berlin.

Monday, October 24

I went with Major Vanaman and Colonel Wendland to see the headquarters of the Arbeitsfront in Berlin. We were met by Professor Karl Arnhold, second in command. He talked to us for an hour about the work and objectives of the organization. They train young people for trades, retrain workers from overcrowded industries, reorganize factories, etc. At the end of an hour, the head of the organization, Dr. Ley,[114] arrived,

114. Head of the National Socialist German Workers Party in Cologne, Dr. Robert Ley was appointed by Hitler to take over German labor unions and establish the German Labor Front.

and we were conducted through the display rooms where examples of the work are shown.

I stopped at the apartment for Anne and the Smiths. We went to see plans for the new city of Berlin. They are to take from ten to fifteen years to complete, and [the planners] contemplate tearing down and rebuilding huge areas. The proposed architecture is simple and attractive. This is undoubtedly the greatest city-building project of modern times. Similar building plans are going on in Munich, Hamburg, Nürnberg, and other cities.

Later, we went to the studio of Arno Breker (sculptor). He has more work than he can do in connection with the building projects in Germany.

Tuesday, October 25

Went to see Ambassador Wilson at 3:15 at American Embassy. Talked to him about our plans for staying in Berlin this winter. Wilson said he could see no objection whatever, from his standpoint, to our living here this winter. (I asked him if it would in any way complicate his problems.)

I am anxious to learn more about this country. The Germans are a great people, and I believe their welfare is inseparable from that of Europe. The future of Europe depends upon the strength of this country. It cannot be kept down except by war, and another European war would be disastrous for everyone. We must build our future on strength and not on a balance of power through the cultivation of weakness.

Wednesday, October 26

Anne got an envelope from her mother with all the reviews of *Listen! the Wind*. They are excellent without exception—the best I have ever seen—and make us both very happy.

Thursday, October 27

Truman read a report in an afternoon German paper that the Russian government has ordered my arrest if I ever again enter Russian territory, and have designated me as an "enemy of the people of the Soviet Union."

Friday, October 28

The Russian report (about my arrest, etc.) seems to have originated in a newspaper article in Moscow.

In the afternoon Anne and I went to look at houses. First one was fairly well-, though heavily, furnished, and large enough for our needs. The most attractive feature was the garden—a large one, well planted with trees and shrubs, and running downhill to a river with swans. It would be an excellent place for Jon and Land—probably as good as we can hope to find. We plan on taking it if we can get a satisfactory lease.

Saturday, October 29

Major Vanaman had received an offer from the Air Ministry to help us locate a house. As a result, I went to see Colonel Wendland at his office in the Air Ministry. He said that Herr [Albert] Speer, the head of the city planning for Berlin, had offered to help us find a house. Mr. Speer sent word that if by any chance we wanted to build a house, we could have it at almost any location we wished in Berlin. I gave Colonel Wendland information about the place we saw yesterday, and he called the owner. There seemed to be something strange about the transaction; the man apparently wanted foreign currency and a very high price. Colonel Wendland advised us not to go any farther.

Anne and I talked the situation over and decided to take the night train to Paris. It will probably take several days to locate and inspect the houses which may be available. There is no object to our staying in Berlin during this time. Much better for us to come back again later on.

Sunday, October 30

Train arrived Paris about 10:00. As we started walking toward the station gates, I heard an almost whispered exclamation from Anne and sensed a tension in her walk that always means trouble ahead and usually means photographers. Looking up, I saw a group of men carrying press cameras. They had not yet seen us. In a few seconds I heard a shout, and I expected a very unpleasant walk to the taxi stand. Suddenly, I saw a man head one of them off and signal to them to stop. I then realized that among the crowd standing on the platform were ten or more plain-clothes men, apparently sent by the French government to see that we were not bothered. They escorted us to a taxi and kept all photographers and pressmen away. They handled the situation so skillfully that few people in the station noticed that anything unusual was happening. We drove to the Crillon and engaged a room.

Monday, October 31

Anne went out to buy supplies for Illiec. I phoned M. G. la Chambre and made appointment to see him at his home. Went out for an hour's walk around Place de la Concorde and through the gardens of the Tuileries.

Went to see Guy la Chambre at 2:45. I talked to him about Germany, taking care, of course, not to discuss anything I had been told or shown in confidence. I told la Chambre that I wished he would visit Germany and that I thought it would be a good thing for him to do. La Chambre said he would like to go and would speak to Daladier about it, but that they would have to invite Goering in return and were worried about giving him adequate protection in France. Said they would be glad to have Goering come here if it were not for the danger of some incident occurring.

This was the first opportunity I have had to talk to Guy la Chambre alone. I told him of my reservations about the advisability of spending large sums of French money in constructing aircraft factories abroad. I told him that, in my opinion, the best way to increase French strength was to straighten out her internal situation, and that anything else was superficial in comparison. I told him that no amount of money spent abroad for armament would be of much value if France were weak internally.

We then discussed the idea I advanced several weeks ago that France might purchase aircraft from Germany. La Chambre said he thought it might be possible. His main objective, he said, was to build up an air force of 2,000 or 3,000 fighting planes at the earliest possible date. He said that he would be more interested in purchasing engines than planes from Germany, as France did not have engines of sufficient power. Also, he said, it would be less difficult politically to purchase engines from Germany than to purchase planes. I told la Chambre that I would be glad to assist in any way I could, and that my interest lay in helping to avoid a European war. We talked a little of the disastrous consequences of a general war.

Tuesday, November 1

Took 10:05 train for Plouaret, the main-line station nearest Illiec. Anne wrote during most of the trip. I read *In Hazard* by Richard Hughes. An interesting book, well written.

Miss Hutchison met us at Plouaret, and we drove to the garage at Buguélès where Louis, Petit Louis, and Kerleau were waiting to help us carry our baggage to the island; the tide was low. Jon was still at supper when we arrived. Thor was eating and, for once, was not watching for us. Skean was asleep by the fire. Land was in his crib but not asleep. Anne and I walked up on the big rock and then around the island. The moon is not yet full, but it gives a good light. The island is at its best by moonlight. I think I shall never see greater beauty.

Wednesday, November 2

Inspected work done on island since we left. Everything done by Savina is excellent. Spent part of the afternoon on mail, then helped Anne and Jon put rocks around the flower beds in front of the house. It looks much better after taking away the old chicken-wire guards. Jon likes to work and does whatever job is assigned to him well.

Jon talks a different language to Kerleau and Louis. He will be talking perfectly good English to me and then turn to Louis and say, for instance, "Me no want 'em now." Miss Hutchison says that Jon speaks quite a little French with Petit Louis, mixing in English words here and there. Jon changes his language with apparent ease and without seeming to confuse one with the other. Land is just about walking now. Crawls with great speed and walks while holding on to a rail or something, but not yet alone.

It was almost night when we finished work at five. Walked to Saint-Gildas to see Mme. Carrel and spent about an hour talking to her. She has had good news from Dr. Carrel. His experiments are apparently going well, and he has worked out some plan for next year after he retires from the Institute.

Friday, November 4

Morning spent in laying out lines for the trees we expect to plant this fall. Anne and I put in stakes, and Louis and Kerleau began digging the holes. We will plant the entire west side of the island with cypress and pine. We feel grateful to Ambroise Thomas for the trees he planted. They have added greatly to the beauty of the island.

Anne and I walked to Saint-Gildas for a 12:00 lunch with Mme. Carrel. After lunch we all drove to a tree nursery and ordered the trees which are to be planted on Illiec and Saint-Gildas this fall. We ordered 500 pines and 500 cypress for Illiec. Then we drove to another nursery and ordered some fusain plants.

On the way back, we stopped to see the rector of Port Blanc and talked to him about rebuilding the chapel on Illiec.

Saturday, November 5

Spent the morning planning where to plant the trees. Anne and I laid out lines on the south side of the house and along the road curving past the chapel and back around the big rock toward the west. We also laid out imaginary lines for the fusain hedges. Jon preferred to saw wood. It is his favorite occupation. When wood runs short, he climbs the big pines to get dead branches to saw up. It is terrific work with his little hand saw, but he stays at it by the hour.

Mme. Carrel came for lunch. We talked to her about our plans for the island, including the possibility of building a walled garden on the south side of the house.

After lunch we went to Port Blanc, where the rector was waiting to go with us on a drive through the nearby country to look for old stone doorways. We want one for the chapel and possibly two or three for a walled garden. The rector knows the country well and took us to several tumbling-down ruins, where the doorways were still intact. Mme. Carrel had previously found one ruin with three doorways. We stopped to visit an old farm where one of the buildings, now practically in ruins, contained a "priest hole" (where they used to hide from persecution) and a secret room where Mass was said at night. Almost all of these places are falling to pieces. There seems to be little local interest in keeping them up. The decay of Brittany started to take place after the Napoleonic

Wars (I am told). It probably really began with the French Revolution. The decay of a country is seldom recognized until some years after it starts.

The rector took us to see a large dolman—one of a series which made a passage. Some of the others have been broken up for rock to make farm cottages. These things mean very little to the farmers in Brittany. They have broken up many of the old ruins rather than carry rock from a slightly greater distance. We stopped to see an old gate, then drove back to Port Blanc through the winding dirt roads, filled with ruts and stones. It was a beautiful and interesting drive.

Monday, November 7

Showed Kerleau where to plant the cypress trees on the east side of Illiec, along the north sea wall. Also showed him how to space the pines which are to go inside the cypress rows on the west side of the island. I make frequent trips to inspect the work of digging tree holes, to be sure they go in the right place. We have a workman from Buguélès helping Kerleau and Louis, and will have two more tomorrow.

The masons came today to start work on the sea wall north of the house. We raised half of it about two feet during the summer (the half nearest the house). We now plan on raising the entire length.

Sunday, November 13

The *Times* (English) carries a long account of the Jewish troubles in Germany. I do not understand these riots on the part of the Germans. It seems so contrary to their sense of order and their intelligence in other ways. They have undoubtedly had a difficult Jewish problem, but why is it necessary to handle it so unreasonably? My admiration for the Germans is constantly being dashed against some rock such as this. What is the object in this persecution of the Jews? Do the Germans feel that in this way they can frighten all Jews sufficiently to prevent incidents such as the Herr vom Rath[115] shooting? Or is this a countermove to the Jew-

115. On November 7, 1938, Herschel Grünspan, a young Polish Jew living in Paris, went to the German Embassy with a pistol and fired two shots at the German attaché, Ernst vom Rath, wounding him fatally. Grünspan had sought revenge for the fate of his parents, who were among 17,000 Jews of Polish origin

ish pressure on Germany? Or, by bringing up the Jewish issue and forcing German Jews into other countries, do the Germans hope to create an international anti-Jewish movement? Or is it simply an inherent German hatred of the Jews—at least on the part of members of the present government? Probably a combination of these and other factors.

Wednesday, November 16

Train arrived Paris about 7:15. Taxi to Hôtel Crillon. Bath (no baths at Illiec, except with a wet cloth, so a tub feels good for a change, especially after a night on the train). Called Jean Monnet and made appointment for 12:00. Took taxi to Monnet's apartment. We went for a walk along the Seine before lunch (Monnet and I) and discussed the results of his trip to the United States. He had talked to Roosevelt, but had done very little about enquiring into the feasibility of the Canadian plan we talked about so much with Ambassador Bullitt. Monnet told me that, as so often happens, "the reason you go somewhere develops into something else before you return" (or words to this effect). Apparently he had spent more time discussing the French financial situation than in looking into aviation. It seemed that the Canadian plan had passed out of the picture almost as rapidly as it had come in.

Taxi back to hotel. Walked alone through the streets and stopped to see a French motion picture—one of the wartime type (1914). All in French, so did not understand much. However, such things give a good idea of what French people are seeing and thinking. It is a good way to get to understand a country in one sense. Walked back as far as tomb of Unknown Soldier, where I stopped in 1927 with Détroyat and Weiss[116] on the way from Le Bourget to the American Embassy. Stopped for a few minutes. Broke rest of walk to hotel by a short ride on the subway to see how it compares with those of the United States and England. The Moscow subway, from outward appearances, is still the best I have been on.

---

taken to the German eastern border to be deported to Poland, and who, upon Warsaw's refusal to accept them, remained stranded, without shelter, in a no man's land between Germany and Poland.

116. Major Pierre Weiss of the French Air Force, whose nonstop distance record to Persia Lindbergh broke in 1927. Major Weiss was one of the three French pilots who escorted Lindbergh from Le Bourget to the American Embassy in Paris after the landing of the *Spirit of St. Louis*.

Friday, November 18

Phoned Ritz Hotel at 8:00. Mrs. Morrow and Anne had just arrived. Went to Ritz for breakfast.

Lunch with Bertrandais.[117] We talk of aviation in Europe and America. Sikorsky came at 6:00, and we spent an hour together. He is a very unusual man. Extremely interesting and likable. I always enjoy being with him. He gave me a copy of his book, *The Winged S.*

Saturday, November 19

Anne stayed with her mother at Ritz last night. I wrote until 10:45, then walked to Ritz. Anne and I drove with Mrs. Morrow to train. We left soon after putting her on the train, as a movie actress came on board surrounded by press photographers. Anne went to Détroyat's home to talk to their nurse. She knows of a good Swiss nurse who is free. Miss Wesley is leaving at the end of the month.

Monday, November 21

Nurse arrived from Switzerland for interview.[118] We decide to try her. Excellent recommendations, and apparently good disposition. Something about her face we like.

Tuesday, November 22

I had lunch with Jean Monnet and M. Hoppenot at Monnet's apartment. The meeting ended in an argument about French politics and democratic principles, which overshadowed our discussions about aviation. Monnet made a speech about the value of individual freedom. Hoppenot took the stand that it might have to be sacrificed somewhat for the security and welfare of France. Even Monnet admits that something must be done about the present instability of government in France.

117. Victor Bertrandais, an executive of Douglas Aircraft Co., 1931–42, who later became vice president. A veteran of World War I, he advanced to the rank of brigadier general in World War II.

118. Soeur Lisi, who was to stay with the Lindberghs for several years.

Spent the remaining part of the afternoon reading and writing at the Crillon, except for a trip with Anne to see an apartment she has located on the Bois (11 bis Maréchal-Maunoury).

Anne and I went to Tour d'Argent on the Seine for dinner. Americans and French at next table. The Americans were not sure whether they recognized us or not and proceeded to talk about us in loud voices. They talked as only a certain type of American can talk—about newspaper rumors, about the kidnaping of our baby, about the trial at Flemington, about all the things that discretion should have prevented their mentioning at an adjoining table—and so loudly that we could not help hearing. I felt depressed, not so much because of what they said, as because of the type of American they represented and the knowledge that there are so many more like them at home. Anne is wonderful under such circumstances, but I would have given anything not to have taken her there that night.

Wednesday, November 23

Anne and I went to Despiau's[119] studio at 10:00. She starts sitting for a head today. I planned on leaving her there, but Despiau said it would not bother him if I watched the start, so I stayed. I like Despiau and believe he is an exceptionally fine sculptor.

Thursday, November 24

Détroyat called for me at 9:45. We drove to the Block aircraft factory on the outskirts of Paris. I was shown through the factory, not a very large one, and not particularly interesting, except in the fact that it gives me an insight into the present condition of French aviation.

From the Block factory we drove to Villacoublay and went through the Block hangars there. They were assembling two- and four-engine bombers and single-engine fighters, all of the low-wing, metal-construction type. They looked like reasonably good planes, but I was not at all impressed with the appearance of the factory or the assembly hangars. They could hardly be compared to similar establishments in the United States or Germany. Détroyat told me, however, that the French factories

119. Charles Despiau, French sculptor, who worked with Rodin. His portrait busts were distinguished for their sensitive perception and restrained presentation.

were in much better condition than they had been for many months. But they still look pretty bad to me.

From the Block hangars we went to see the new Bréguet light bomber —two-engine. It looks like a good plane—very clean design. We had lunch in a nearby restaurant with the French test pilots. They have formed a sort of club and have lunch together regularly. They had some meat dish from Morocco (called something which sounded like "kus kus"), which they thought was very hot and peppery. They gave me some and watched with amusement while I tried it. Fortunately, it was quite mild compared to Mexican dishes, and I made a good showing.

We went to the Amiot factory. I was much impressed with the design and performance of the Amiot bomber. It is the most encouraging thing I have seen in French aviation. Top speed stated to be 500 kilometers per hour with two 875 h.p. Hispanos. Construction looked simple, and great attention had been given to jigs.

From the Amiot factory Détroyat and I went to the aviation exhibition, which will be opened tomorrow. It is in a huge building, and the exhibit is well arranged. Many of the most modern ships are left out, however, and therefore a rather false impression of European aviation is given. The Amiot bomber is not included, although it is probably France's best design. Germany is represented by a Dornier bomber—the only plane she sent—nothing from Messerschmitt or Heinkel. Poland had a huge exhibit in proportion to her aviation activity. England was well represented with a Supermarine Spitfire, a Hawker Hurricane, and a Blenheim bomber. The Spitfire was the best fighter at the exhibition. Its only competitor would be the Messerschmitt. The United States was represented by a Vought monoplane (for deck landings). The show was interesting, but I could not help wondering what was gained to justify the expense and effort.

Friday, November 25

Anne and I had lunch with Senator de la Grange and a number of French and English members of Parliament and several other guests. After lunch we all went to the aviation exhibit, except Anne. (She had several things to attend to in connection with our coming to Paris next month.) I went with Détroyat, who had been one of the guests at the lunch. We went around the exhibit as a group. To my surprise, there were no photographers to bother us. It was the opening day, too. Consequently, I had a good chance to look at the exhibits and thoroughly enjoyed the visit.

Dinner with la Grange and various English and French aviation people (men only). Sat next to la Chambre. The same M.P.'s were there. Probably twenty or thirty men in all. Boring speeches: good-will, hands-across-the-sea type. They took advantage of my being there to speak about friendship with the United States and democracies sticking together. It is a little annoying to see England's change in attitude toward America since Europe has gotten out of hand. The English have a tendency to be practical in policy and hypocritical in speech.

Guy la Chambre asked me if I could find out whether or not the Germans would be willing to sell aircraft engines to France.

Saturday, November 26

I have been thinking about la Chambre's request last night concerning the possibility of Germany selling engines to France. With a world full of war and hatred one must be very careful about such things. Is it a constructive move? It seems to me that a closer German-French relationship is of the utmost importance. These things, however, can be easily misunderstood. What would be the result of a change in the French government? It is by no means impossible with a general strike coming next week. I decided to make no move until after the strike. The Germans would undoubtedly be watching that, too. La Chambre said two or three weeks would be soon enough to get a reply.

Anne and I walked to an art store in the late afternoon and purchased some pictures for Illiec. We walked by Brentano's on the way. *Listen! the Wind* was in the window. It has been selling well in Paris, we are told.

Sunday, November 27

Anne and I left the Crillon about 9:40 and caught the 10:05 train [for Illiec].

It is wonderful to get back to this island after the city. The old farm at Little Falls[120] is the only other place I have loved as much.

120. The nearest town to Lindbergh's farm home in Minnesota where he spent much of the first twenty years of his life.

Monday, November 28

Morning spent inspecting the work being done on the island. The masons have done a good job on the chimney for our room. No architect could do better. They took the stones from the beach at the north end of the island. The trees are well planted, too, but many of them need retying. A few will have to be changed.

Jon has a period of school each morning, which Anne arranges for him. She always works with him herself when she is here. Jon developed a loose front tooth while we were away. I pulled it out for him with a huge pair of wire cutters. He said it did not hurt at all when I pulled it. Nevertheless, he was very good and lay still while I got hold with the cutters. I would not have pulled it except for the fact that it seemed to be interfering with the new tooth coming in and was nearly ready to fall out anyway. Jon was proud and happy afterward and carried the tooth around in a match box to show everyone.

Anne and I walked to Saint-Gildas to see Mme. Carrel. She does not look well, and we are quite worried about her. She insists that she is all right and plans on driving her car to Saint-Brieuc tomorrow morning. I offered to drive for her, but she wouldn't hear of it. Mme. Carrel had a telegram from Dr. Carrel saying that the anti-German feeling in America was very strong and suggesting that we change our plans about going to Germany this winter. I wrote him that we had changed our plans, but he has apparently not received the letter yet.

Wednesday, November 30

Took *Medric* to Saint-Gildas after breakfast. The waves were high for such a small boat, and I was covered with spray during the entire trip. It was lots of fun. I anchored the boat to the sillon with a rock anchor and went to see Mme. Carrel. She looked much better. The trip to Saint-Brieuc yesterday seems to have done her good instead of harm. We talked for an hour—about Dr. Carrel, Illiec, and Saint-Gildas. She told me she thought a man had tried to get into her house at night. She had informed the local police and was sleeping with a revolver on the table beside her bed.

Anne and I walked around Illiec before lunch. It was extremely beautiful—a broken sky, with the sun at intervals between rain, and the rocks all covered with white spray. We marked where the trees are to be put north of the house, between the sea wall and the little *maison* of Louis and Marie Yvonne. I dug small holes to show where each tree was to be put. All of the thousand trees we ordered are now planted, some of them on the little islands. We need about one hundred more to finish our plans for this year.

We started packing [for the return to Paris] in the afternoon. In the evening we read and wrote letters in our bedroom, with a coal fire burning and the sound of waves coming in through the window. I am reading Lin Yutang and Plato.

Friday, December 2

Wind all day and waves dashing over the rocks, a constant roar. The house trembles in gusts. Rainstorms at intervals. Sky mostly overcast but clear at times. Spent the entire day packing except for a few walks around the island. The men have finished the trenches for the fusain bushes and are now enlarging the garden area inside. We have bought 500 fusain bushes at one franc each. They average about three feet high. The wind is very bad for the small trees. They seem to be standing it, though.

Anne and I finished packing after supper. Anne, Land, Jon, and Miss Hutchison leave tomorrow night. I will stay one more day. Went up on the big rock, alone, before going to bed. Moonlight—not yet full.

Saturday, December 3

Anne and I walked around the island for the last time, and up on the big rock next the house. The men are planting the fusain hedge. Mme. Carrel came for a few minutes at teatime.

Bellac came with his cart at about 8:00 in the evening. We piled in the last of the suitcases. Anne, Jon, Land, and Miss Hutchison rode to Buguélès in the cart. I walked over the sillon. Keraudran drove us to Plouaret. I returned to Buguélès with him after the train left. Walked back over sillon to Illiec. Thor was waiting. He has been downcast for days, ever since the packing started. Thor knows that trunks mean a long trip. He was overjoyed to have me come back, but showed clearly that he felt it was only a temporary return. He slept on a blanket on the floor next to my bed. His very posture showed that he was resigned for the worst—quiet, tail still, head on floor, not interested in anything. When Thor knows we are going on a trip, I think he prefers to have us go quickly.

Sunday, December 4

Walk before breakfast with Thor and Skean. Thor lost his depression somewhat during the walk. Skean is always happy and loves the rabbit smells on Illiec. As usual, he is much too fat. We went around the island and up on the rock. The little trees are slightly wind burned, but otherwise look in good condition. Spent an hour with Mme. Carrel, then walked back to Illiec. Supper alone, dressed, said good-by, told Thor to stay on the island, and started over the sillon for Buguélès. Last look back at the island from the end of the sillon. I took the 10:38 train for Paris.

Monday, December 5

The train arrived at Paris at 7:15. I took a taxi to our apartment (which we have rented for December) at 11 bis Avenue Maréchal-Maunoury.

Tuesday, December 6

Went for a walk in the Bois after breakfast, around one of the lakes. Full moon in the evening. Think of Illiec in moonlight. Jon has not been happy; he misses the island. Anne has arranged to send him to a French school a few blocks from the apartment.

Wednesday, December 7

Anne to Despiau's studio for a sitting. I went for a walk in the Bois for an hour after breakfast. Anne and I went to Jean Monnet's apartment for supper. His sister and father were there. His father is a lively old man of eighty-three or eighty-four. Looks and acts less than seventy. Speaks English fairly well. He invited us to visit his home in Cognac.

Saturday, December 10

Jean Monnet phoned. He is sailing today on the *Queen Mary*. Sudden change in plans. Apparently the French government has decided to purchase more airplanes from the United States. They have (wisely, I think) given up the idea of building factories in Canada, but will set up a Canadian company on paper, so that the transactions can be carried on through Canada instead of directly between the United States and France. Less difficulty with public opinion, etc. The workings of democracy would be amusing if they were not so serious.

Tuesday, December 13

The press has finally learned that we are in Paris, although some of them are not very sure about it. One of the French papers carries front-page headlines across half the width of the sheet, announcing that we have rented a big apartment and hired a nurse. Fortunately, our address is not given. The article ends by saying that we desire peace, will find it in Paris more than any other city in the world, and that French people should let us alone, etc. As though any amount of preaching about letting us alone would counteract the effect of front-page publicity. We have learned from long experience that it is not what press articles say, but the fact that our name appears in headlines on the front page that causes trouble. In some ways a critical article is better than a favorable one. Criticism usually creates an attitude of dignity along with the curiosity it brings. People may stare at you, but they tend to keep their distance, as though you were some wild animal that would scratch or bite. But favorable articles, in addition to curiosity, create an atmosphere of sickly sentimentality. People run after you as children run after a spaniel puppy. They want to feel you and fondle you and, if they had their way, make you into something akin to a spoiled, domesticated pet.

The Paris New York *Herald Tribune* says that we are understood to be at present at Illiec, that we still have a place in Kent (we gave up the lease on Long Barn last June), and that "our friends" expect us to go back to England this winter. Almost every lie they print is attributed to our friends; friends say this and friends say that. The press seem able to pull our friends down out of the sky whenever they want to make them responsible for a new statement. Well, if there must be publicity about us, it is better for it to put us somewhere where we aren't. That at least avoids contact with the people we don't want to see and lets us walk along the streets in peace.

Anne and I had lunch with M. and Mme. Guy la Chambre at their Paris home. La Chambre still wants me to find out whether the Germans would sell a number of their new engines to France (Junkers 211 type). Says he thinks it would be a very constructive move and advantageous from France's standpoint if they would do so. He feels that such a move could be used as an important step to promote better relationships between the two countries. This is along the lines I suggested several weeks ago during our conferences, except that I suggested buying planes and engines if possible, whereas la Chambre is primarily interested in engines. He says France can produce more planes than engines and that it would be less difficult to arrange (from the French political standpoint) the purchase of engines than planes. I think he is right about this. It is democracy again; it is the obvious rather than the actual which influences the minds of the people, the name rather than the fact. La Chambre says that Daladier will back the purchase of German engines and that he (la Chambre) is ready to order several hundred if the Germans will make a reasonable proposition. We talked about conditions in France. La Chambre said he felt that the Daladier government was in a strong position and would not be replaced in the near future.

After lunch I returned to the apartment to telephone Truman Smith about going to Berlin. I shall take the train from Paris either the night of the fifteenth or the morning of the sixteenth.

We had dinner with Dr. and Mme. Du Noüy[121] at their apartment. They have just returned from the United States and a summer in the Grand Canyon area. We talked of Dr. Carrel and the necessity of closing his department in the spring.

Friday, December 16

Took the 9:05 from the Gare du Nord.

During the time I have been in Paris I have attempted to carry on

121. Pierre Lecomte du Noüy, French biophysicist, writer, and philosopher, known primarily for his *Human Destiny,* a work that unites the ideals of religion and science. He worked at Dr. Alexis Carrel's front-line hospital during World War I. From 1920 to 1927 he was an associate member of the Rockefeiler Institute in New York. In 1927 he returned to France, where he created the first European biophysics laboratory, at the Institut Pasteur.

some philosophical writing in regard to the problems we find ourselves confronted with in this modern industrial era and the need for reconsidering our viewpoint of right and justice in the relationships between men and between nations. I attempted to bring out the fact that right is a relative rather than an absolute quality, and that the "right" course is not always the one which benefits the greatest number of people. I also attempted to show that we must change our present standards of life, making the products of men secondary to the welfare of men themselves. But I am not at all satisfied with the writing I did, in its present form. It does not give the impression I want to convey in many instances. It is heavy and uninteresting.

I have put this writing away for the present and will attempt to rewrite and improve it at a later date. It is by far the most difficult type of writing I have ever attempted. I find that sometimes in trying to clarify my own mind on some subject, I end up with a written picture I do not agree with. I think this type of writing must be done over a period of years, written and rewritten again and again.

Arrived at Berlin just before midnight, after spending the day reading [H. A.] Fisher's *History of Europe,* writing (description of my grandfather's house in Detroit), and watching the countryside we passed until the early European sunset darkened all objects outside of the train.

At the German border the customs and immigration officers came on board, and a plain-clothes member of the secret police asked my destination. All were considerate. The immigration officer, a fine-looking type of young German, happened to open my passport to the Russian visa. He looked at it a long time but made no comment. Everything was orderly and efficient. There was an air of discipline and precision which was in sharp contrast to the easygoing pleasantness of Belgium and France.

I had lunch in Belgium and dinner in Germany.

Truman Smith was waiting for me at the station, and I drove with him to his apartment for the night.

Saturday, December 17

Spent half an hour talking to Major Vanaman about his trip to the States. (He has just returned from America.) He says that agitation is going on for a huge expansion of our military program—Army, Navy, and Air (as has been reported in the press)—without very careful consideration of a balanced and continuing program. His outline sounded typically Washington and Roosevelt Administration.

Sunday, December 18

Truman and I drove around the streets of Berlin, and then out to the forest for a short walk before lunch. A cold wind was blowing, and there are traces of snow—the dry snow that whirls and eddies with the wind gusts and gives a powdered whitish appearance to the frozen ground.

I went to a German picture after lunch—a news film followed by a love story with a background of skiing in the Alps. In between the news and the serial a sketch of a Jew was thrown on the screen for a few seconds. I could not read the caption. The sketch showed the typical, old-country type of Jew with a long black beard, a black gown, a caricatured Jewish nose, and a hand stretched out, obviously to receive money. There was no movement in this sketch, and the screen changed after five or ten seconds. I learned later that this was an advertisement for the anti-Jewish exhibit in Berlin.

Monday, December 19

Truman and I walked to the attachés' offices. I called the Air Ministry to find out whether Milch and Udet had returned to Berlin. Truman received a letter from the War Department ordering him to return to the States as soon as he could arrange to do so and report to Walter Reed Hospital for examination and care. He has not been well recently and has worked much too hard, especially during the time of the "crisis." It may mean retirement and the end of a brilliant Army career. It comes at a good time, if it has to come, for Truman has an excellent record here in Germany, and the recent crisis closed a chapter. He would return to the States in August under any circumstances; his tour is over then. There would hardly be time for him to finish anything new between now and August. Everything is quiet at the moment (relatively at least), and it may be the best time for him to leave. The developments which may take place during the intervening months would put an additional strain on his health, and an August departure might easily be in the midst of them. Nevertheless, it is depressing for Truman and Kay and means an immediate change in their plans and an uncertain future.

Dinner with Udet and his mother. Udet had invited me to take part in a shooting competition with him. However, it was the first chance I had had to talk to him alone, so after I arrived we postponed the shooting while I discussed with him the possibility of Germany selling aircraft engines to France. I told Udet there was nothing in any way official about my inquiry, but that I thought that if Germany would be willing to sell engines, a purchase by France might be arranged. I told him I could give no guarantee and I was making no request, that it was obvious that France would not want to make an official inquiry in such a matter unless it was known in advance that the inquiry would not be turned down by Germany. I told Udet I felt the policy was more important than the actual value of the engines and that it might be used as a step toward a closer relationship between the two countries.

Udet was immediately interested, grasped the importance of the matter, and said that obviously it was a matter which would have to go at least as far as Goering. Udet said he personally felt it was very desirable to have co-operation between Germany and France in the future. He said he would arrange for a meeting with Milch tomorrow. (I had told him that I wanted to talk to Milch about the matter.) I think it will have to go to Hitler unless a definite policy has already been laid down.

We then began the shooting competition. Udet lives in a medium-sized apartment, which he has filled with all kinds of trophies—flying, hunting —and the objects one always picks up and is given in a life of travel and activity. The walls of one room were covered with photographs of aviators and Udet's friends. There were also pieces of fabric from planes he had shot down during the war—English and French. I understand he stood second to [Manfred von] Richthofen in victories. In another place was the broken end of the stick from a plane he had crashed in a year or two ago—a Messerschmitt 109. Then there were various cups, plaques, and medals from competitions he had won. In the adjoining room, on one wall, were a number of photos of pretty girls. In the hall there was a glass cabinet containing rifles and shotguns. Over his bed hung an oil painting of a reclining nude. Another small room, a sort of second hallway, held the stuffed heads of various animals he had shot, including a rhinoceros and a panther. Also a number of stags' horns. A corner of one small room was filled with wooden figures from Africa, and others from the southwestern United States.

There was a small metal target box on a table in the first room in front of some of the photographs and trophies. If a shot missed the box, it could not miss one of the photos behind it. Udet was obviously a good shot. He picked out a handmade .22-cal. rifle from the cabinet (peep and ring sights). I made three trial shots (all in the black), and we started the competition. It is many years since I have done target shooting, but I made both pistol and rifle teams during my freshman year in the University of Wisconsin and was raised with a gun as a child, having my first rifle at the age of six—a small .22-caliber.

I shot five times, then Udet five (all standing). I won the first three rounds straight. We decided to settle the match with the best two out of three sets of fifteen shots each per set. I lost two out of the next three. Udet won, although my score total was higher. We will shoot again sometime.

Tuesday, December 20

Udet, Milch, and I had a conference for about half an hour. I outlined again the possibility of selling German engines to France. Milch said it would have to be taken up with Goering and possibly with Hitler. He asked me if I thought the French were simply trying to sound out the German attitude without any interest of really purchasing. I told him I did not think so. Milch said he would try to contact Goering immediately (I had told him that I wanted to return to Paris as soon as possible) and would phone me as soon as he had done so.

We continued talking for a time. Milch was obviously interested in the proposition. I told him I did not wish to take part in anything which would not be constructive from both the German and French standpoints, but that I felt an understanding between the two countries to be very desirable and that a war in Western Europe would be disastrous. He said he did not think there would be a war in *Western* Europe. This tended to confirm my feeling that the Germans intend to entrench themselves in the West and continue to expand their influence in the East.

Milch told me that the recent anti-Jewish demonstrations "were not done by Goering and were not done by Hitler." I suppose this means that Himmler and Goebbels were responsible. The general feeling in Berlin seems to be that Goering was very much opposed to what has happened and leads the "element of moderation" in the party. The German people seem to be definitely anti-Jewish but ashamed of the violence with which the last demonstrations were carried on.

Taxi back to apartment, but soon after I arrived Udet called up and asked if I could be back at the Air Ministry by 6:00. (We had agreed not to carry on any conversations over the phone and that everything would be done in the utmost confidence, so that there would be no embarrassment for anyone if a deal was not concluded.) I returned to Milch's office immediately. Milch said he called Goering, but that Goering had gone to see Hitler (apparently Hitler had called him unexpectedly) and that Goering could not be reached for a day or two and had left instructions with his secretary to avoid all new questions until after Christmas.

Milch said he thought it would be advisable to make no attempt to press the matter until Christmas had passed and that he had phoned me (through Udet) immediately so I could return to Paris tomorrow if I wished to do so. He suggested that after Christmas he would send me an invitation for dinner or something in Berlin, with Udet and himself, and that by then he would have been able to talk to Goering and, if necessary, get a decision from Hitler.

I immediately wondered whether this was a way of avoiding an answer, but Milch's face and eyes did not confirm that impression. I believe he was telling me facts and giving his honest opinion. In the contacts I have had up to date in Germany no officer has lied to me or attempted to mislead me. Of course, it is always necessary to consider such a possibility.

Wednesday, December 21

Vanaman's mechanic called at 9:00 with the weather report. It was bad: low clouds, ice, and bad visibility along the route. I decided to get another report in the afternoon and to take the night train if it did not seem probable that I could get through on Friday. I wanted to be with Anne and the children for Christmas, and there seemed to be a certain advantage in leaving my plane in Berlin, as that would give me an obvious reason for returning after Christmas.

Flying conditions will continue bad (impossible without radio control) for several days. I purchased passage on the train leaving Berlin at 9:32. Returned to the apartment in time to meet Major Rocamora (Spanish military attaché for Franco). He told me it had been arranged for me to visit Franco Spain whenever I wished to do so and that I could land at Vitoria, about fifty kilometers across the French border. I replied that I wanted very much to go to Spain and that, among other things, I was interested in the effects of the bombing raids which had taken place, but that in view of the developments of the last several weeks I felt it would be better to postpone my trip for the time being. We arranged that I would contact him whenever I felt the time was opportune in the future.

It would be interesting to go to both sides in Spain. The effects of bombing would be more interesting on the Red side, because Franco has had the best and most modern aircraft. Unfortunately, all the silliness which took place in Moscow after our trip to Russia last summer and the attacks on me for accepting the decoration from Hitler in October make a trip to the Red side inadvisable, if not impossible. One should really see both sides in Spain to get a reasonably accurate and comprehensive picture.

Major Rocamora told me he could not estimate how much longer the war in Spain would last. He said that if Franco could arrange another offensive this winter it might be decisive. We talked frankly and I found him extremely interesting.

I drove to the station in time for the 9:32 train.

Thursday, December 22

During the days I was in Berlin I tried to obtain a better understanding of the German mind in regard to the Jewish problem. Germans all seem to be anti-Jewish, but in varying degrees. I did not talk to a single person who I felt was not ashamed of the lawlessness and disorder of the recent demonstrations. But neither did I talk to anyone who did not want the Jews to get out of Germany, even though they disagreed with the methods now being used. The Jew, according to the German, is largely responsible for the internal collapse and revolution following the war. At the time of the inflation the Jews are said to have obtained the ownership of a large percentage of property in Berlin and other cities—lived in the best houses, drove the best automobiles, and mixed with the prettiest German girls.

Train arrived Paris about 3:30.

Friday, December 23

Called la Chambre and made an appointment for 2:15 P.M. Anne and I went for a walk in the Bois, then took taxi to buy a Christmas tree for Jon and Land.

Went to la Chambre's house at 2:15 and gave him an outline of the inquiries I had made in Berlin in regard to the sale of engines without, of course, using any names. I told him I had spoken to my "friends," but that they were unable to make the contacts they wished before Christmas and that I would not be able to get an answer for several days.

I told la Chambre that the Germans I talked to seemed to strongly favor a better understanding with France. I told him I felt there was more chance of an understanding with Germany now than there had been previously and that if it were possible for France and Germany to work together, peace could be maintained in Western Europe for an indefinite period. He seemed to agree to this but, of course, asked what the German attitude was in relation to the present Italian demands on France. I replied that I had been given no indication in this matter but that, personally, I did not think Germany was likely to enter a major war to back up these demands. I told him I thought Germany would stand behind Italy up to a point.

La Chambre is still anxious to obtain German engines, both because France is in need of them and because he feels, as I do, that the deal might be used as a step toward a better relationship. I told la Chambre that, while I had received no such intimation from the Germans, I wondered whether the French-Italian controversy might prevent the Germans from selling engines to France. La Chambre replied that the Italians themselves had just recently offered to sell France airplane engines. (How interesting and amusing it is to see the back stage of Europe. And how little the public knows about what is really taking place! Headlines in the press make one think that Italy and France are on the verge of war. Back of the curtains they offer to exchange airplane engines for phosphate.) I told la Chambre I would return to Berlin as soon as I had an indication that I could obtain an answer.

Mme. Carrel came for supper. She sails for America on the fourth of January. Has had good word from Dr. Carrel. Everything is going well apparently. He is considering doing some writing for a newspaper syndicate. I would rather see him start another book.

Saturday, December 24

Anne and I arrived at Mme. Carrel's apartment at 10:45. We all had accepted an invitation for lunch at the home of Mr. [P.] Bunau-Varilla, an old friend of Dr. Carrel. One of his sons called for us with a Stout automobile—the only one in Europe, he told us. It is a streamlined, like affair, with the engine behind and a small table inside. Doors ctrically, etc. Mr. Bunau-Varilla has a home in the hills outside

Mr. Varilla is eighty-two or eighty-three, active, keen, interesting, and does not look over seventy. He is one of those old people who make you realize how much character there can be in human life. He speaks a little English, enough for me to understand him. I enjoyed every minute of the time. We talked about Germany and France and many other subjects.

Anne and I went for a walk in the park before supper, then to a flower shop to get some flowers for Christmas. Anne wrapped presents for Jon and Land in the evening. Jon still in bed with cold.

Sunday, December 25

Jon opens presents. Still in bed with slight fever. Wants to open Land's presents for him. Anne and I go for walk in the Bois and around one of the lakes. (It is still quite cold and the lakes are frozen over.)

Anne and I went for another walk in the afternoon. Took taxi to the Seine and walked across one of the bridges to the island and to Notre Dame. It was closed, so we went home after half an hour. Very cold. Mme. Carrel came for supper.

Jon likes a globe of the world best. Next are the pieces of wood which Mr. Merkel sent him. Then a mechanical tractor. Land prefers a little music box that works by turning a handle. Anne is wonderful with her children. I have never known anyone who I think understands children as well. They cannot help developing character with such a mother.

Wednesday, December 28

Went to Gare du Nord to meet Truman, Kay, and [their daughter] Katchen Smith. Anne has rearranged the rooms so we can have them stay with us instead of at a hotel. Truman said that for a time it was doubtful whether Germany would break off relations with the United States. Consequently, he postponed coming here for a day.

Thursday, December 29

After lunch Truman, Kay, Katchen, Anne, and I went to Notre Dame, then to Sainte-Chapelle. Notre Dame and Sainte-Chapelle are beautiful but somewhat spoiled by a tourist atmosphere. I have no feeling of religion in these places. The only time I have sensed religion in one of these old places was at Mont-Saint-Michel, when Anne and I were alone in the moonlight late at night. Places of religion should not be thrown open to tourists, except, possibly, at times which are specially set aside.

Too tired to write a fuller description. It is a mistake to try to see and do so much in one day. Not that it is too hard work, but one cannot take it all in. Better to spend an hour in Notre Dame and the rest of the day thinking about it. That would leave a worthwhile and permanent impression on your memory.

Friday, December 30

Truman, Kay, Katchen, Jon, and I went to the Eiffel Tower in the morning, and [then we] set out for Versailles via subway station and train. We went through the royal apartments before lunch, spending about an hour inside the palace. Versailles gives one an idea of some of the causes of the French Revolution.

Lunch at Trianon Palace Hotel with General and Mme. Gaston Renondeau and their daughter. They are friends of the Smiths. The general was French military attaché in Berlin until a few weeks ago. After lunch the general drove us to the Grand Trianon and Petit Trianon palaces. We went through the first and walked through the grounds of the second. The grounds contained the *hameau* of Marie Antoinette.

Saturday, December 31

Mr. Kirk (Moscow) came for lunch, and we all talked of Russia and Germany. Kirk is as anti-Communist as ever. The talk touched on the continued Russian executions and "liquidations" and the constant turmoil in the country. We discussed the attacks made on me at the time of the crisis. Kirk is here to have some dental work done. Says he cannot obtain an experienced and reliable dentist in Moscow.

After Kirk left, the rest of us went to the Louvre. The light is very bad at this time of year, and most of the paintings are hard to see. I am not at all impressed with the way the Louvre is being cared for. Some of the world's most famous paintings can hardly be seen because of the lighting.

Monday, January 2

We hired a car in the afternoon and drove to Chartres (Kay, Truman, Anne, and I). This is the second time I have been to Chartres. Anne and I stopped there on one of our motor trips through France in 1936 (with the little 10-h.p. Ford). It is by far the most beautiful cathedral I have yet seen from the standpoint of architecture. But I like Mont-Saint-Michel better because of its natural setting. Even the windows and carvings of Chartres cannot make up for the shifting tides, the changing sky, and the isolated beauty of Mont-Saint-Michel.

Wednesday, January 4

We took the Smiths to the Gare du Nord in time for the 6:15 train to Berlin.

Thursday, January 5

After lunch Anne, Jon, and I took a taxi to the Eiffel Tower and went up in the elevator to the second landing. The top of the tower is closed. Jon saw seventeen trains! Seeing trains is his greatest pleasure in life. They have, at least temporarily, replaced stumps and dead branches.

Read a few pages of [Alfred North] Whitehead's *Adventure of Ideas,* an exceptionally fine book.

Saturday, January 7

Morning papers carry an article about some of the letters I have written to America about European aviation. The article in the Paris edition of the New York *Herald Tribune* is headed LINDBERGH REPORTED PROVIDING U.S. WITH DATA ON REICH AIR FORCE. It is as inaccurate as press articles usually are, but among the statements that are wrong there are enough which are correct to make it certain that the article was based on letters I wrote. Denials were issued by Roosevelt, Welles,[122] and other officials, but it is apparent that information leaked out and was picked up by some reporter. There is nothing I have written that I am in any way

122. Sumner Welles, Undersecretary of State, 1937–42.

ashamed of, but it is astounding and disturbing that confidential information is regularly obtained by the press from official sources in Washington. I have little confidence in either the State Department or the War Department as far as secrecy is concerned. And I have had experience with both. It is also a strange situation when the press of a country is free to publish secret government information regardless of the difficulties publication may cause.

I phoned Truman Smith in Berlin and told him to inform the Air Ministry that the American press was publishing false statements concerning what I had said. I told him I was very anxious to avoid any misunderstanding with the Germans. Four hours later, I received the following telegram: "Udet as requested stop they are not disturbed stop press told by Air not to notice—Smith."

As a matter of fact, I think there is no letter I have written about Germany that I would object to the Germans reading. But by the time the newspapers have stated their version of what I said, it is an entirely different matter. I think it is of vital importance to come to some understanding with Germany. In fact, I believe the future welfare of Western civilization depends largely upon the strength of Germany and the avoidance of a major war in Western Europe. In the present situation the newspapers make it appear that I have advocated and am largely responsible for the extensive air rearmament program in the United States. They also make it appear that this rearmament is against Germany.

As a matter of fact, I have for a long time believed we should have a stronger Army and Air Force, but I think a hysterical rearmament, such as is now being proposed, may easily do more damage than good. Congress is not likely to follow it up with the necessary appropriations in the future. A balanced and smaller program would lead us to a far greater eventual strength. The present ideas of expansion, which are being advocated at home, fall most heavily on the Air Corps. If we are not careful, we will have a huge number of semiobsolete planes and a "hump" in both personnel and material that will hamper us for years to come.

If we must arm, we should arm for the purpose of our own strength, just as a man trains his body to keep fit and for the purpose of health. But to arm specifically against Germany or Japan is a serious error unless we do not even desire to avoid a war. The thing that bothers me most of all is that our own northern peoples are now snarling at and arming against each other. If England and Germany enter another major war on opposite sides, Western civilization may fall as a result.

Sunday, January 8

Dr. and Mme. Lecomte du Noüy came for supper. We discussed many subjects, mostly scientific. He has written another book, which will come out in France about March. We talked at length about the Darwinian theory and the arguments for and against it, the laws of chance, etc. It was an extremely interesting evening.

Monday, January 9

Evening at home, reading and writing—and thinking. One must think constantly and clearly these days. The time may come soon when there must be action without time for thought. One must have a general and fundamental plan laid out to meet whatever emergencies arise. Life throughout the civilized world has become so complex that it is difficult to think clearly, even when time exists for thinking.

In the afternoon Anne and I took Jon to the Jardin d'Acclimatation and spent an hour among the animal cages. Jon liked the seals best and the monkeys next but enjoyed most of all the little train we rode out in—three small open cars drawn by a gasoline locomotive.

After supper Anne and I went to see a motion picture, *Suez;* better acted and more interesting than most.

Wednesday, January 11

The morning paper carries an account of what was said by Ambassadors Kennedy and Bullitt at a joint *"secret"* session of the House and Senate committees on military affairs! The article can be summed up by the headlines, KENNEDY, BULLITT HOLD GLOOMY VIEWS ON EUROPE'S FUTURE. There seems to be a sort of plot to 1) get the rearmament appropriations Roosevelt wants and, 2) give Germany the impression that the United States will enter a European war if one starts. During the crisis Kennedy and Bullitt were telling (*confidentially*) England and France that the United States would not enter a war in Europe, while [Ambassador] Wilson was telling Germany (*also confidentially*) that we probably would enter one. There is an advantage to this policy if it works, but we may find ourselves in another Abyssinian situation if it doesn't.

I have been working a little each day lately on an outline of an autobiography,[123] which I hope someday to complete. Have made a rough draft of the beginning chapters. I plan on doing this in spare time, probably taking several years to finish it.

Friday, January 13

Am reading *Can Chamberlain Save Britain?* by Collin Brooks.

René l'Hôpital [124] and his daughter came for dinner. Her husband arrived afterward. Talked of France, Germany, Italy, England, Czechoslovakia, and Russia. L'Hôpital is able, intelligent, and interesting. He is very broad-minded in regard to the European situation. We agree that war this year is improbable, but wonder what Italy is after, if she knows herself. Cannot believe that she expects to get any important French territory. We agree that Germany is facing east. Discuss possibility of a German-French agreement.

Saturday, January 14

Met Anne at Despiau studio. He has made a great improvement in the head. It is a beautiful piece of work and now looks very much like Anne, in addition to bringing out an amazing amount of her underlying character. It will now be cast in plaster, and then Despiau will put on the finishing touches.

I have been thinking a great deal these days about the future—of the world, of the various countries of Europe, and of our own personal future. It is difficult to see clearly and to steer a straight course. It is necessary to think constantly and to try to lay plans for all possible emergencies.

Sunday, January 15

Land suddenly walked out of his room this morning and is now walking all over the house, overjoyed at the discovery of his new powers.

Wrote a number of letters in the morning and afternoon. Then took a

123. This eventually resulted in *The Spirit of St. Louis.*

124. Former aide to Marshal Ferdinand Foch. Lindbergh met l'Hôpital soon after he landed the *Spirit of St. Louis* at Paris.

taxi to the Gare du Nord to buy my Pullman ticket. The station office was closed, and I was informed that I would have to buy my ticket on the train! Returned to the station about 6:00. Fortunately, the train was not crowded and I had no trouble getting a room.

Monday, January 16

Arrived at Berlin about 8:25. Truman was there waiting for me, although I had asked him not to bother. We drove to his apartment for breakfast.

I phoned Udet and put in a call for Ambassador Dieckhoff,[125] then took my bags to the Esplanade Hotel, where I took a room. Lunch at 1:30 with George and Juliet Rublee.[126] He told me that he had made some progress (Jewish situation) and was by no means discouraged. Went to see Mr. Merkel at 3:00. We talked about aviation. Also about the Jewish situation.

Met Kay Smith at her apartment at 4:45, and we drove to Ambassador Wilson's residence. Truman had just arrived in another car. Ambassador Wilson is in Washington, and no one knows whether or not he will return to Germany, but Mrs. Wilson is here. (Ambassador Dieckhoff is in Berlin, and no one knows whether or not he will return to America. Mrs. Dieckhoff is in Berlin, too. Such is diplomacy in 1939.)

After we had been there about ten minutes the phone rang—General Udet calling me. He asked if I could meet him and General Milch at the Air Ministry at 6:00. It was then 5:30. I left ten minutes later and went to Milch's office. Udet was there also. The three of us spoke first about the stories which have been carried in the American press about my activities at the time of the crisis, etc. I told Milch and Udet that I was anxious to avoid any misunderstanding because of newspaper articles and that if there was anything they had any question about in this regard, I would be glad to talk it over. They said they were not in the least worried and that they fully realized the irresponsible condition of the press.

Newspapers cause all sorts of unnecessary trouble. I am inclined to

125. Hans Heinrich Dieckhoff, German Ambassador to the U.S.

126. George Rublee, lawyer, government counselor, and old and close friend of Dwight Morrow. Chairman of the Inter-governmental Refugee Committee with headquarters in London. In 1939 he was in Berlin for talks with German government officials, seeking moderation of the German attitude to the Jewish population.

think that an irresponsible and completely unrestricted press is one of the greatest dangers of democracy, just as a completely controlled press is a danger in another direction. Udet had the front page of the *Express* (London) for last Sunday in his pocket. It had headlines across the entire width about the German air fleet. The article which followed said German planes were badly built, had an excessive number of accidents, were improperly equipped, and were inferior to those of England. What constructive value has an article of this type? It misleads the British and angers the Germans. There are few things which will cause more misunderstanding.

Milch next brought up the question of selling engines to France. I told him I did not want to press the matter and that there need be nothing more said about it unless he wished to carry on negotiations. Milch replied that, on the contrary, Germany would be willing to sell engines to France. He said they could supply Daimler-Benz 1250-h.p. motors and that the number and price could be settled in subsequent negotiations. He said their conditions were that secrecy be maintained by both the French and German governments while negotiations were taking place. He said Germany would want pay in *Devisen* (i.e., money instead of goods). Said Germany was in a position where she had to ask for money in payment for manufactured articles such as engines, whereas she could afford to trade with raw materials such as coal, accepting something in exchange which she needed herself.

Milch suggested that all communications in regard to the transaction should discuss the purchase of one Storch airplane and make no mention of engines. He said he would know that such communications actually referred to the purchase of engines. Milch mentioned the fact that the engine-sales question in this instance raised an important political issue. (Of course, that is obvious.)

After we finished discussing this subject, I told Milch and Udet that Mr. Rublee happened to be an old friend of our family and that he was an honest, conscientious, and reliable man, and as good a man as they could have to negotiate with in regard to the Jewish issue. I told them I knew nothing about Rublee's mission, but that I was anxious for the Germans to understand his character and not feel that he might go out of his way to cause them trouble after he left Germany. Milch said that he would give this information to Schacht.[127]

127. Dr. Hjalmar Schacht, president of Germany's Reichsbank, 1933–39. Schacht was a brilliant economist and helped extend German economic influence throughout central Europe in the 1930's.

Milch and I did most of the talking, all in English, of course. Udet helped in translating where we had difficulty.

Tuesday, January 17

I invited Mr. Merkel to meet Mr. Rublee. Also invited Truman Smith, making four of us, all told. We had an interesting and enjoyable time. Talked of aviation, the Jewish problem, and other subjects. I felt that in some way Merkel might be of assistance to Rublee. He [Merkel] is one of the most able men I know, and I think will appreciate Rublee's good qualities, which may not be immediately obvious to all Germans.

Checked out of the hotel after lunch and took my bundles to the Smiths' apartment. Then went to the Dieckhoffs' apartment for tea. Both Ambassador and Mrs. Dieckhoff were there. Spent an hour and a half talking to the Ambassador about the unsatisfactory conditions existing in the relationship between the United States and Germany and what might be done to bring about a better understanding.

Wednesday, January 18

Truman and I took a taxi to Tempelhof. I took off at 9:47 G.M.T. Overcast sky and heavy head wind, but ceiling and visibility satisfactory. Flew north to Hanover, because clouds reported on mountains to the south, then set course for Cologne, where I crossed the border through the authorized corridor and set course for Paris.

Became hungry about noon and had brought no lunch in the plane. However, there was a can of baked beans in the baggage compartment. I pulled the backs off both seats and let the plane fly itself while I leaned and wiggled back far enough to reach the can. When I got into position again, I saw a small German plane coming toward me, obviously to find out what was wrong, as my plane had undoubtedly been jumping around a bit in the sky. It turned away as soon as I straightened out.

The storms which had been reported were light, with only a little rain and no fog whatever. Landed at Le Bourget at 3:42 G.M.T. The head wind lasted during the entire flight. It was a beautiful trip, though, and it felt good to be flying again after three months on the ground. I love being alone over mountains and in clouds and rain, with sunshine above and moist earth below. Flying, after a long time on the ground, is like a breath of fresh air after coming out of a stuffy room.

Thursday, January 19

Met la Chambre at his residence at 9:30 and told him of the Germans' willingness to sell engines, together with the conditions they laid down. La Chambre was greatly interested. Said he had hardly dared to hope the answer would be favorable. Said he would get in touch with Daladier as soon as possible and asked me to telephone him (la Chambre) at 2:30. Said he felt sure Daladier would wish to carry on the negotiation. We discussed the question of who would be the best man to send to Germany for this purpose. La Chambre suggested that the French military attaché in Berlin was a good man, well liked by the Germans, and able to speak German fluently. Said a mission sent directly from his office might be difficult to keep secret. La Chambre feels, as I do, that this negotiation may be used as a step toward much more important things if it is intelligently handled.

La Chambre told me, incidentally, that the present type of American bomber was too slow for the French needs, but that a new type would be out in July, which would be faster, and that France would be given the opportunity of purchasing the first of these. Said Roosevelt had agreed to this and that the necessary arrangements had already been completed. Therefore, the roundabout Canadian plan, which I have always been doubtful about, has proven unnecessary. It is fortunate that it was not actually started.

I walked from la Chambre's home to the Trocadéro and spent nearly an hour in the wing which contains casts of cathedral doorways and carvings from various parts of France. Then took taxi to Despiau's studio to meet Anne. He has had the head cast in plaster and is now putting on the finishing touches.

I called la Chambre at 2:30. He said Daladier was very much pleased and wished to go ahead with the transaction. La Chambre said he had asked the French military attaché in Berlin to come to Paris immediately. I arranged to see la Chambre again at 9:15 tomorrow morning. (Of course, the phone conversation was guarded, but the meaning was obvious.)

Friday, January 20

Met la Chambre at his home at 9:15 and gave him the outline of the letter to be sent to General Milch. La Chambre asked me whether I thought it would be more advantageous for France to build the English Rolls-Royce Merlin engine or the Daimler-Benz on license (said the English had offered to sell several hundred Merlins to France). I told him I was not well enough acquainted with the two engines to be able to judge and that such a decision should be left to a careful study of the two engines by experts. I told him that in reaching a decision it was important to take into consideration the relative advantages of metric and English dimensions for manufacture in France.

La Chambre then asked what I thought the reaction in the United States would be to the purchase of German engines by France. I told him that would probably depend largely on the way it was brought out. I told him that if it were brought out as an attempt at better relationships between France and Germany and as an improvement in the prospect of peace in Europe, the reaction would probably be favorable. I told him, however, that there were a number of people in America who felt so bitter against Germany that they actually desired war and would be opposed to any relationship between France and Germany whatever. I told him that the Jewish influence would probably support the latter. But, I said, what hope is there for peace in Europe if we adopt such an attitude? If there is to be no friendly negotiation between Germany and France when the opportunity arises, then we must look forward to eventual war and the devastation it will bring to everyone. He agreed to this.

I returned to our apartment and wrote a letter to General Milch, then went for a half hour's walk in the Bois before lunch.

Sunday, January 22

Weather report indicated that route to London[128] would be flyable until at least 1:00. Anne and I left for the aerodrome immediately and, after a slight delay getting our plane out of the hangar, took off. Landed Reading 14:16 G.M.T. There has been another increase in the buildings for the Phillips & Powis factory. They have at least quadrupled in size since I first saw the aerodrome in 1936; bunched together in an ugly group on one side of the field, they are typical of industrial England at its worst.

We left our plane at the hangar and took a taxi to the station, then a train to London, and another taxi to Brown's Hotel. Phoned to several of our friends, but most of them are out of the city. I went to see Colonel

128. The Lindberghs were going to England for talks with the U.S. Embassy staff and to renew the Certificate of Airworthiness for their plane.

Scanlon and spent an hour at his home discussing aviation developments and a variety of other subjects.

Anne and I had dinner alone at the hotel. After dinner we took the elevator to our room, but by mistake got off at the floor above. We walked down the stairs and turned left. There, standing facing us in the center of the narrow hallway, directly in front of our door, was Haile Selassie! Black beard, tunic, and all, just as his pictures show him to be. If I had seen a ghost, I am sure I would have had the same reaction during the first second. I knew he was staying in the hotel. I would have thought nothing about seeing him in the lobby or in the elevator. But standing alone in front of our door, looking directly at us, in his unusual yet photographically familiar costume, he made an impression I shall never forget. As we approached, he stepped quickly back through the doorway opposite ours, and the hall was empty—just like an apparition, or some wild animal visible for a moment in a clearing, then gone like a flash.

Monday, January 23

A typical London winter's morning. Dark and hazy, a light rain and the smell of coal fires in each breath of air. We had to put the lights on, even though our room is on the street and has large windows. After breakfast Anne and I went for a half hour's walk and visited the Royal Academy's exhibit of Scottish art.

Caught the 4:15 train for Reading. F. G. Miles happened to get into the same compartment. He feels, as do other people to whom I have talked, that British aircraft production is now well under way, although there is still much inefficiency and muddling. He invited me to go through the factory, but I told him I preferred not to give anyone the opportunity to say that I was attempting to get information about the Royal Air Force, and that the press would be only too glad to find such an opportunity. We drove with Mrs. Miles (who was waiting at Reading station) to the aerodrome. I talked to George Miles (F. G.'s brother) about overhauling our plane in order to renew its Certificate of Airworthiness. We discussed the engine and landing-gear problems the plane has had, etc. I returned to London in time for an 8:00 P.M. dinner with Colonel Scanlon.

Tuesday, January 24

Lunch with Dr. Tom Jones at 16 Queen Anne's Gate—with almost the same group of men who were there at the time of the crisis. It was from that lunch that the rumors started about statements I was supposed to have made concerning the Russian Air Force. Of course, there was very little connection between what I said and what eventually came out in the British press. Jones told me it was the first time in nearly twenty years that anything said at that lunch table had reached the newspapers. He had previously told me I could speak with complete assurance, that it would be held in confidence. There were no speeches, but there was a discussion in which I took part, guardedly, of course. Jones tells me that one of the members had brought a guest who was an M.P. He apparently repeated some of what was said in front of a reporter. Either he or the reporter or someone else added to and distorted the conversations before they were eventually published. And, of course, the final product was attributed to me.

Supper at home of Colonel and Mrs. Lee; then we all went to the ballet, *Lac des Cygnes*. Very well done and well worth going to, but by no means as good as the Russian ballet. The English go through the motions, but don't put themselves into it as the Russians do. I have the feeling that the Russians dance in the ballet, while the English imitate ballet dancers.

Wednesday, January 25

It is another dark day, with a sticky snow falling and trying rather unsuccessfully to cover the streets and taxi windshields. I shall never get used to these dark winter days in London.

Mrs. Kennedy and her son Joe[129] came and spent half an hour with us. The Ambassador will not be back for some weeks.

After they left, I called the station but was told that all reservations for the night train to Paris had been taken. We decided to leave in the morning. Went to a Chinese restaurant for dinner, then to a picture theater showing *The Good Earth*. Very close to the story, interesting, and excellent acting. Well worth seeing.

129. Joseph Kennedy, Jr., eldest son of Ambassador Kennedy, who died during World War II on a dangerous mission as a Navy pilot in July, 1944.

Conditions in Europe are again becoming disturbing. Also in America!

Thursday, January 26

Checked out from hotel and took 11:00 train from Victoria (Anne and I). Press photographer tried to get photo through car window. First time this has happened in an English station, to the best of my memory. Not serious, of course, but annoying and rather depressing.

Read the *Times* and *Telegraph* on the way to Calais. Barcelona is expected to fall within the next few days. Italy and France are both calling up troops, statedly for routine training. Most people I talked to in England look for another crisis in February or shortly thereafter.

Another press photographer at the gangplank. We took a semicabin, a curtained-off affair, to be sure of privacy on the boat. We had lunch in the dining saloon without bother, but a reporter came to try to interview us just before we landed and was a considerable nuisance while we were walking from the boat to the train. The French authorities finally arrested him. Fortunately, one of the officials had met us at the boat and walked with us to the train. The reporter was English, or possibly American.

The sun came out on the way to Paris and shone in our window. How one appreciates the sun in the winter over here. I never appreciated sunlight so much before I came to Europe.

Read Whitehead most of the way to Paris. When we got off the train, I noticed immediately that we were surrounded by plain-clothes men, at least three or four of them, who walked inconspicuously beside us to a taxi. Their leader then came up, shook hands, and said good-by. The French have been extremely considerate to us in this way.

Taxi to apartment. Jon was having his supper when we arrived. Land asleep, of course. A pile of letters and papers waiting for us. The letters from the States depress me—a complete lack of understanding of the situation in Europe. I wonder what the future holds for us all.

Friday, January 27

Called la Chambre after breakfast. He has heard nothing from Berlin in regard to the engine purchase. However, his representative, the French military attaché, could hardly have made contact before Wednesday or Thursday at the earliest. We will certainly at least have a report from the attaché.

It is a bright and sunny day with a completely different feel to the atmosphere than that of London. I wonder how much the spirit of a people is affected by the climate of their country. I believe there is a relationship far greater than is generally admitted. The buoyancy of the French weather has a kinship to that of the people.

European affairs are becoming more disturbed. England is, I believe, in desperate situation. She has been asleep too long, and in the changed conditions of the modern world I am afraid her old position of leadership has gone. Aviation has largely destroyed the security of the Channel, and her superiority of manufacture is a thing of the past. The conditions which built the British Empire were far different than those of today.

Saturday, January 28

La Chambre called at 9:15. Said he had received a letter from the military attaché in Berlin saying he had sent the letter about the Storch plane to General Milch last Monday. The attaché's letter arrived through the "pouch" and there was not time for a reply from Milch when it was written.

Monday, February 6

A foggy morning, with the trees on the far side of the street hardly visible. Went for a long walk alone in the Bois, the mist giving a blue tinge to all objects and shutting out the crowd and clamor of the streets.

Anne and I went to the home of Mr. and Mrs. Harlan Miller[130] for lunch. They had invited Mr. and Mrs. Lin Yutang[131] and Jo Davidson, the artist. A very interesting time. Davidson took us to his studio after lunch and showed us his painting and sculpture.

130. Harlan Miller, writer, columnist, and aviator; with the U.S. Embassy under Ambassador Herrick when Lindbergh landed the *Spirit of St. Louis* in France, 1927.

131. Chinese-American writer. Author of *The Importance of Living; Between Tears and Laughter,* a critical view of Western relations with China; *Moment in Peking,* a novel; *The Wisdom of China and India.*

Tuesday, February 7

Took taxi to Despiau's studio to meet Anne. Despiau is still working on the plaster head. He hardly seems to make any change during a day's sitting—just paints on a little plaster in one place and scrapes it off somewhere else. But he has caught a great deal of Anne and much that is below the surface. It is a beautiful piece of sculpture, I think one of the best heads he has ever done.

Dinner at American Embassy. Saw la Chambre. He told me that his representative in Berlin (military attaché) had received a letter from the Air Ministry to the effect that nothing could be discussed until General Udet returned from Tripoli. I wonder if that means the Germans have changed their minds. Many things have happened since I was last in Berlin.

Wednesday, February 8

Lunch at home of Mr. and Mrs. Harlan Miller. They had invited Père Chardin[132]—an old friend of Dr. Carrel's—a remarkable man.

Thursday, February 9

Have spent a great deal of time recently thinking about the future. We are faced with many complicated problems, but I have not time to outline them now. However, problems are not new to us.

Friday, February 10

Anne and I went to an art gallery to see some work by Eugène Berman,[133] who is being considered, among a list of painters, by Mrs. Morrow for her portrait. I was not greatly impressed by his work, but feel it is worth while looking at more, as there were only two paintings of his in

132. Pierre Teilhard de Chardin, noted French Jesuit paleontologist and author. He lived in China for many years and played a major role in the discovery of Pekin man.

133. Russian-born painter and theatrical designer, who lived in France from 1917 to 1937, when he came to the U.S.

the gallery, neither being portraits. Anne saw an oil painting of flowers by Vlaminck,[134] which she liked, at 5,500 francs. We phoned the gallery later in the afternoon and offered 5,000 francs, and got the painting. It is to be delivered tomorrow.

Mr. Offie,[135] Ambassador Bullitt's secretary, telephoned and said some magazine writer had told Bullitt that he was assigned the task of getting an interview from me! I told him I would prefer to avoid articles about myself wherever possible. I learned long ago how unsatisfactory interviews are. You are never quoted correctly, and the fact that you gave the interview made the reader feel you were responsible for the accuracy and shading, which was usually wrong. It is best either to write an article entirely yourself or else leave it alone completely, so that all responsibility rests on the author's shoulders.

Monday, February 13

We went to get our "cards of identity" after lunch, then to the Countess de Noailles'[136] residence to see a portrait by Eugène Berman. I thought it terrible, although possibly good technique in some ways. I certainly would not want Mrs. Morrow to be done by him. The Countess also had a number of paintings by [Salvador] Dali. When I look at his work and realize that it is considered art, I feel the modern world is well on the road to insanity. Something is definitely wrong. Anne said she had to do something to get Dali's paintings out of her thoughts. We went to the Orangerie [Museum] for a half hour and walked from there to the Louvre, but were too late and found it closed.

Tuesday, February 14

Anne and I discussed the possibility of a trip home this spring.

Jon wrote a letter to Mother about three weeks ago, asking her for balloons. Reminds me of the letters I wrote to my grandmother asking for leaden soldiers. Jon received a letter from Mother this morning, con-

134. Maurice de Vlaminck, French painter, writer, and printmaker.

135. Carmel Offie, vice consul and third secretary, U.S. Embassy in Paris.

136. Vicomtesse de Noailles, patron of avant-garde art and renowned Parisian hostess, who entertained aristocrats, politicians, poets, musicians, and artists in her home.

taining fourteen balloons, and the day was made for him. Anne and I had great difficulty in persuading him to give one of them to Land. We finally compromised by Jon giving Land an old one, which had not yet burst. Balloons have now even replaced stumps, dead trees, and trains for Jon. They are the most important things in his life.

Wednesday, February 15

Afternoon spent on income tax and writing autobiography—San Diego and *Spirit of St. Louis.*

Thursday, February 16

Land is developing with great rapidity and is an exceptionally active baby. He is always after Jon's toys and causes Jon considerable worry keeping his things together. By the time Jon has retrieved his balloons, Land has Jon's ball and is running away with it. Jon handles the situation with tact and practically never makes Land cry. In fact, Jon can do things with him that no one else can. They get along splendidly together.

Friday, February 17

MacArthur (American Embassy third secretary) called up and said the president of the American Club wanted me to attend a club dinner on Tuesday evening in honor of Washington's birthday. Daladier, the Duke of Windsor, Bullitt, etc., were to be there. It is just the type of dinner I hate going to. I told MacArthur that Anne and I were going to England about that time and to give that as a reason for my not coming. I also told him, in confidence, that I practically never went to functions of that kind. (That may help hold down the invitations in the future.)

Monday, February 20

My "1927" tailor came at noon. He had written me last summer at Illiec, saying he would like to make some suits for me. I remembered him as a good type of fellow, and the suits he made me in 1927 were the best I ever had. I need more badly—all of my present ones are nearly worn out—so phoned for him to call. He looks very bad—just out of the hospital—and has lost all the money he had. I like his face and felt anxious to help him. He told me some of his troubles, but not in the usual complaining way.

I ordered four business suits and a tuxedo from him—the biggest clothes order I ever placed by far. But he needs it, and I can use the suits for years. Besides, his prices are reasonable, and I could not do better elsewhere. Gave him half the money in advance. May have made a mistake doing so, but somehow I trust him. When he was leaving, he told me that the day he received my phone call he was ready to ask for charity relief and a ticket for his wife and himself to England, where he would try to start life at the beginning again. He apparently ran one of the best tailoring businesses in Paris in 1927. Had borrowed money in pounds, he said, when the franc collapsed, his business decreased, and he had to sell everything he had. He had brought a huge suitcase full of samples. It was so heavy and he looked so weak that I carried it down to a taxi for him.

Jon and Land always have tea with us. Land eats rusks, and Jon and I drink milk. Land is in the "ball" stage, throwing them, shouting in glee, running after them, falling all over himself and bumping his head regularly and hard, but not seeming to mind much and almost never crying about it, even the hard bumps.

Tuesday, February 21

Anne and I took a taxi to Despiau's studio, arriving at 9:45. I had not seen the head for several sittings. It is a beautiful piece of work and now looks very much like Anne. He was feeling very *fatigué* as usual and said that he would only do a little work this morning. I arranged a table in one corner of the studio, well out of the way, and began to write the chapter on St. Louis and the flight to New York (1927) for my book. I kept looking at the pieces of sculpture around the studio and watching Despiau work on the head. He hardly seemed to be doing anything, just scraping a thin skin of plaster off here and brushing a bit of white powder on there. I have never seen an artist work so long on such small changes.

Despiau works in an old suit, with a vest on over his shirt, but never a coat. He always has a felt hat pulled down over his eyes to shade them. Mild-mannered, agreeable, always smiles a welcome as he shakes hands when I enter. Small, never stands erect when he works. White beard—

151

pointed—face unshaven. He has apparently changed and aged greatly in recent years, judging by the descriptions I have heard and read about him.

After leaving the studio, Anne and I took a taxi to the Galerie de l'Élysée, which handles Vlaminck's paintings. We purchased a village snow scene for 5,000 francs, then returned to apartment and walked around the big lake before lunch. On the walk Anne told me that the Vlaminck she liked best of all was the flower picture at the Zak Gallery (9,000 francs).

After lunch I had Miss Hutchison call the gallery on the phone and ask the price, using her name in making the inquiry. They said 10,000 francs. That was 1,000 francs more than they had asked us a few days before. I thought that if they had gone up 1,000, they would probably come down 1,000, so I told Miss Hutchison to call back in five minutes and offer to take it for 8,000 francs, and to hold firm. She did, and after the usual French discussion under such circumstances, our offer was accepted. The banks were closed on account of its being a holiday, but we managed to scrape together 5,000 francs by taking everything that Anne, Miss Hutchison and I had. I made up the difference in English pounds, left over from our last trip to that country. Miss Hutchison went to the gallery in a taxi to get the painting. I was afraid that if Anne or I went there to get it, we would never again be able to buy anything from them at a reasonable price. As it is, they don't know that we had anything to do with the transaction.

The painting is much more beautiful here in the apartment in daylight —more color and more subtly done than we realized when we saw it in the gallery under a rather poor light. Anne and I both feel that Vlaminck is a coming artist and that his work will someday have great value. It has strength and health and beauty and is extremely refreshing in contrast to the diseased and perverted type of work which seems to attract the most attention these days.

Wednesday, February 22

Anne and I went for lunch with Jo Davidson at his studio. He has an exceptionally beautiful marble head of his wife, which we had not seen before. (She died some time ago.) Anne left soon after lunch, but I stayed while Jo Davidson showed me various pieces of his work. When I was about to leave, he asked if I would like to see the casting works where he had all of his bronze heads done. Said he was going anyway, so I went along. Have for a long time been curious about the procedure used in casting bronze statuary. We spent half an hour at the works, while he explained the various steps in molding and casting. After that, he offered to drop me at our apartment as it was on the way to his studio, but accepted my invitation to come in for tea.

Unfortunately, Anne was out, so we took tea alone (i.e., he took tea and I milk; I will never learn to like tea). Jo Davidson was very much impressed with our Vlaminck paintings and likes his style and work. We talked of Russia, Germany, Spain, in fact, about European conditions in general and of their effect on the United States.

After he left I packed my suitcase. Anne and I had supper together at the apartment, then took a taxi to the Gare du Nord in time to catch the 9:50 boat train for London.

Thursday, February 23

The Channel was smooth, exceptionally so, but there was enough noise getting the train on and off the ferry to make up for it. We arrived at London about 9:00 and had no bother from the press at the station. The customs and immigration officers let us through without inspection and without waiting in line. I always feel a little embarrassed about going ahead of other people who are waiting in line and would usually much prefer to wait our turn. However, when I think of the trouble we are subjected to in most instances where people recognize us, when we have to stand and wait for something, I feel that going through ahead of others is no more than just compensation.

If there had been press photographers there, or if anyone had been annoying us, I would not have thought twice about it. But no one was paying any attention to us at all, and there were apparently no pressmen present. Consequently, I felt rather ashamed of not waiting in line. Anne told me afterward that she felt the same way about it. The officers had everything arranged, though, and there was nothing else to do without making a fuss; they would not have understood. They were terribly nice about it, and no one seemed to mind our going ahead of them.

From the station we took a taxi straight to No. 4 St. James's Square. Lord Astor was still at breakfast so we had ours with him. Lady Astor came in later.

Anne and I had lunch at the home of William Astor. I had an interesting time talking to a wing commander who has spent considerable time on both sides in Spain. He did not (like a loyal air officer) gather a very good opinion of the effectiveness of antiaircraft fire in the Spanish war. And, as we began to discuss aviation in the various countries of Europe, he (like a loyal Englishman) said that one English pilot was worth two German pilots any day. Still, in between his prejudices and loyalties, he was very interesting to talk to.

At the table I sat between one Englishwoman, who was very dull, and one Scotchwoman, who might have been interesting in a better environment. The Englishwoman talked a great deal about nothing of interest, and the Scotchwoman spoke very little, but what she said was intelligent. The Englishwoman—young and rather attractive when quiet—was interested in horses and hunting. These hunting and racing horses seem to do something strange to people. Both men and women who are with them a great deal seem to take on something of the personality of a horse. They even get to look a little bit like a horse eventually. At a table, sitting next to one of them, I often feel that a good whinny would not be out of place.

Half an hour before supper Lady Astor called up and asked me to come downstairs. She took me to Lord Astor's office, where Lord Astor was talking to a Scotch Quaker, who had just returned from Palestine. He was trying to organize an appeal for the orphans of the Arabs who have been killed in the fighting there. He said the British authorities estimated that there were now about 10,000 Arab orphans.

At dinner I sat next to Mr. [Geoffrey] Dawson—*Times* editor—and we discussed the trend and effect of modern journalism. He seemed to be as much concerned about it as I am.

Friday, February 24

We left for Cliveden at 4:00 in one of the cars. It is about an hour's drive, starting slowly through the crowded streets of London. Anne and I went for a walk through the grounds just before sunset. Beautiful trees, and all the peace and stability of Old England, a great contrast to London and present-day conditions.

Supper with Lord Astor and Mr. Brand.[137] Lord Astor asked me what I would do if I were the Prime Minister and had to come to some agree-

---

137. The Honorable Robert Brand, author and authority on finance, who held various government economic posts.

ment with Germany on air disarmament. He placed his question in two parts: 1) What ratio should England demand of Germany in limiting air power, and what ratio would give her safety, i.e., one to one, one to two, or what? 2) Should there be an attempt to abolish bombers completely, and if so, how could they be described? It was an extremely broad and fundamental question. I told Lord Astor that I would not think of answering it without very careful study and investigation and that what I said at this time would be only in the form of a discussion of some of the elements involved.

I told him that my observations had led me to believe that Germany was the natural air power of Europe, that her record in the design, construction, and operation of aircraft spoke for itself, and that in addition it was necessary to realize that Germany had certain geographical advantages which England lacked. I told Lord Astor that if I were a German I would demand a minimum of two to one with England in the air. I told him I would be surprised if the Germans did not demand the same superiority in the air that England has on the sea, i.e., three to one.

I said I would not attempt to suggest what ratio the Prime Minister should agree to, or what ratio would give England safety from air attack. I brought out the point that even if England had equal numbers with Germany, London was much more vulnerable to attack than Berlin because of her population, centralization of government and industry, and proximity to the border. Berlin is less centralized, and attacking aircraft would have to fly over hundreds of miles of German territory, which is thoroughly organized with listening posts, antiaircraft, and pursuit squadrons. Then there are the added difficulties of training pilots in England—worse weather and smaller area.

In answer to the second part of the question I said I was not in close contact with the problem and would like to hear arguments on both sides before coming to a definite conclusion, but that at first glance, it seemed to me it would be extremely difficult to abolish bombing completely or to describe a bomber accurately enough for effective limitation. I mentioned the fact that a commercial transport could be transformed very quickly to a bomber, especially if it had been designed with that transformation in view. Then, a two-engine pursuit plane could be turned into a fast light bomber by the simple installation of wing bomb racks. Also, factories can start the production of bombers with great rapidity if plans are laid for doing so in advance. On the whole, bombing aviation is far more difficult to define and limit than battleships, which are far different than merchantmen and which require years to build. I told Lord Astor that it seemed to me necessary to consider how far England could and would compete with Germany in military aviation before deciding what ratio she would be willing to accept in a disarmament program.

Saturday, February 25

Anne and I went for a half hour's walk through the grounds. Later, we drove with Lord and Lady Astor to an adjoining estate, which is to be sold at auction. The articles in the house were piled in rows and tagged with numbers according to their lot—all very depressing. I do not like to see an old home broken up in this way, the treasures of a lifetime broken up and sold to strangers for whom their old associations have no value. Back to Cliveden for lunch. The guests are beginning to arrive: Tom Jones, Lord Lothian.[138] The house will be full by evening. The police guards are being placed in preparation for the Prime Minister's [Neville Chamberlain] arrival.

Anne and I went for a short walk in the rain before tea. More people kept arriving: Lionel Curtis,[139] Ambassador Kennedy, and others whose names I do not know. Ambassador Kennedy read a letter from his son Joe, who is in Madrid, describing conditions in "government" Spain as being extremely bad. The Prime Minister arrived soon after the letter was finished, looking amazingly young and well. I would not have judged him to be over sixty, and one would never believe that he has been going through one of the most difficult periods in British history.

About thirty people at the dinner table. Too many to make conversation interesting, and too much noise, although much quieter than an American table of similar size. Usual English custom of women going out after dinner and men remaining around the table for nearly an hour. The party did not break up until just before midnight, yet the Prime Minister was still standing up talking when Anne and I went to our room.

138. Philip Henry Kerr, 11th Marquess of Lothian, former secretary to Prime Minister Lloyd George (1916–21), and active in the Paris Peace Conference of 1919. In 1939 he became British Ambassador to the U.S.

139. British author and diplomat.

Sunday, February 26

Anne and I were down for breakfast at 9:00, but no one else was in sight, except butlers, so we went out on the porch and down onto the walks below. The sun was shining and the sky clear except for a few low cumulus clouds. A constable, with his high blue hat and overcoat, was standing at one corner of the house, and as we turned to walk slowly back into the sun we saw another at the opposite corner. Since the recent bombings, attributed to the Irish, the Prime Minister has been kept carefully guarded. Lord Astor came down about 9:30, and Chamberlain arrived a few minutes later. Soon, the entire table was full. People always serve themselves at breakfast at Cliveden. There are side tables with fruit, cream from the estate, and hot plates for the warm dishes. It is an excellent system, and the food could not be better cooked. It is seldom one finds good cooking in England, but Cliveden is an exception to the rule. The table was full again for lunch—about thirty people in all—including several newcomers to replace those who left last night.

I talked to the Prime Minister for a few minutes after lunch. Later in the afternoon, Bill Astor, Lionel Curtis, Arnold Lawrence, Anne, and I drove to Eric Kennington's[140] studio to see the reclining figure of Lawrence,[141] which he is carving directly from a large block of rock. It is to go in Salisbury Cathedral. We were very much impressed with the design and execution. Kennington has been working on it for a number of years. He is a middle-aged, rather shy, very likable Englishman.

Chamberlain left soon after we returned to Cliveden, and with him the police guards stationed around the grounds vanished.

During tea I talked with Arnold Lawrence. He is an archaeologist and has recently returned from Syria. He is anxious to obtain some air photographs of a number of sites where the old French castles were built, so he can compare and study them in connection with those in Syria. I told him that if I was in France when he came over (he plans a trip in April), I would try to fly him over some. They are apparently located in the central part of France.

140. English sculptor and friend of T. E. Lawrence. He made the bronze head of Lawrence in St. Paul's Cathedral and was art editor for his book, *The Seven Pillars of Wisdom*.

141. T. E. Lawrence ("Lawrence of Arabia"), British adventurer, soldier, and scholar.

After supper I talked for some time with Lord Lothian. He has just come back from a trip to the United States and knows America exceptionally well for an Englishman. We discussed the possibility of war this year. It is the subject of most conversations. He feels, as I do, that a general war in 1939 is unlikely and that a lasting peace is by no means impossible provided 1) that Germany is given a reasonable opportunity for trade and influence; 2) that German leadership does not go mad with the feeling of power and destiny. I think I have a little more confidence in the sanity of German leadership than he has. What I am most afraid of is that a combination of stupid moves on both sides may make each seem mad in the eyes of the other. He agrees with me that France, England, and America are just as responsible for present conditions in Germany as the Germans are themselves.

No one goes to bed early here, and it is a struggle to get away before midnight. Everyone enjoys being in Cliveden. Both Lord and Lady Astor have the ability of making their guests feel at home and enjoy themselves. Cliveden gives one the feeling of stepping back a century into the feudal days of England. The great halls, filled with paintings, tapestries, suits of armor, and fireplaces, do not seem to belong to the modern world. The house sometimes makes me think of a dinosaur which has outlived its age, to give the people of a new era the opportunity of tasting the life of the old one. But is England herself not in the same position? I wonder if someday Jon and Land will see Cliveden open as a museum for the public, with felt-covered ropes holding curious hands away from the beds and chairs and tables we use today. Or will the pendulum swing back away from democracy and equality, away from the leveling process which is taking place today?

Monday, February 27

Breakfast at 9:00 as usual. The guests began to start home by car and train immediately afterward. Anne and I packed our suitcases and left in a car with Lionel Curtis at 10:20, arriving at No. 4 St. James's Square about 11:40. I phoned the Air Ministry and made an appointment to take my regular medical examination for renewing my pilot's license. Then went for a walk to the middle of Bond Street and back. Anne and I had lunch at the home of William Astor. After lunch I took a cab to Clement's Inn where the Central Medical Establishment is located. Passed without difficulty, as usual. Held my breath for three minutes, thirty seconds this time and understand it is a record. I apparently inherited my father's exceptionally good lungs.

Dinner with Ambassador Kennedy and one of his daughters at 14 Princess Gate. I cannot help liking Kennedy. He is an unusual combination of politician and businessman. He has, I believe, raised a good family, and he has apparently given his children an important place in his life. I admire and greatly respect this quality in his character. He has great vanity, but he also has ability. He does not seem to like the press, yet seems fascinated by it, and, I understand, keeps his own public relations representative. I am not sure whether he enjoys being in the spotlight of publicity or whether he simply considers it a necessity in present conditions. I doubt that he knows himself. However, I place him among the men who are a constructive influence in this so-called modern world.

Kennedy does not expect war this year and feels that Chamberlain has handled the situation well. He does not feel very certain what the next move will be on the part of Hitler and Mussolini. No one seems to know that. I wonder if Hitler and Mussolini do themselves. I, personally, do not see how Germany and Italy can move effectively against France or England without too high a cost (i.e., from a military standpoint). The English fleet, the Maginot Line, and the French Army form a combination which will be difficult to overcome.

Suppose Italy does demand concessions in Tunis, Jibuti, and Corsica, and suppose (which is most likely unless the demands are very reasonable) that France refuses them. Then what? Will an Italian army move against a French army? I cannot believe that will happen. But if such a move were made, where would it be? In Tunis, with the Italians moving in from Libya? They would have to control the Mediterranean before an army could be maintained in Africa, and that is a bit of a problem in itself. The Italians will hardly march into France itself from northern Italy. Their aviation is not yet in a position to operate effectively directly against France, even though it may be very effective in the Mediterranean. No, France is still strong enough to defend herself against Italian arms without great difficulty. Italy will not attack unless Germany is behind her.

Suppose Germany is behind Italy. Then what are the moves? England is practically certain to fight with France in that case. The Mediterranean might, and I believe would, be closed to English shipping, but it would also be a dangerous place for Italian shipping on the way to Africa.

What would Germany do? Send troops to Italy? Probably she would send instructors and arms, but hardly an army. Would she attack France? Through the Maginot Line and against one of the world's best armies? Not likely. Move into Holland or Belgium? The gain hardly seems to warrant the price. Would German planes bomb Paris and London? They could do this, but at what profit? Nothing would bring the United States in more quickly.

No. The only cause I can see for a general European war at this time would be if Germany desires one for retaliation for the last, and I do not think that is the case. Why should she try to move west at great expense when the Danube basin and the East are open to her desires. I look for Germany to "dig in" on the western border and continue her eastward expansion. What Italy does must conform to German policy.

I outlined this to Kennedy and asked him if he could see any other procedure which Germany would be likely to follow. He could not, he said, although Germany might be mad enough to want a European war.

Kennedy told me that most people at home were devoting ninety-nine per cent of their attention to foreign problems and one per cent to our own, which he felt (as I do) are much more serious and important from our standpoint. We talked about the young men who have been unemployed at home for many years now and the eventual effect such things are bound to have on our country.

Tuesday, February 28

Anne, Lord Lothian, and I had supper together at No. 4 St. James's. Discussed conditions in America and Europe. Lord Lothian spoke of the danger to democracy of the present European situation. Said it was essential for the United States to take part in preserving it and that England could not carry on longer alone, as the cost was too high for her to bear. He advocates some sort of organization among the democratic nations. I told him that I regarded alliances of strength as necessary in these times, but that I did not think a world-wide democracy either desirable or possible. I said that I thought any attempted organization should be confined to Western European peoples (in the sense that would include America) and that such an organization would be difficult enough to bring about. I told him I felt democracy's danger was internal and not external.

We arrived at the Queen's Theater at 8:15, just in time for the start of the first act of *Dear Octopus*. The acting was excellent and the play reasonably well written. It was not the type I enjoy very much. It left me with the impression of a rather decadent English family struggling on for one more generation. In a strange way it depressed me, for it reminded me so much of present-day English life—loss of spirit and hope and spark, nearing the end of a great era, without more than vague realization, and with a sort of dazed complacency. Everything done too late— marriage, children, the feel of life, and then that desperate attempt to catch up, to bring back lost opportunity, and the feeling that they have succeeded in bringing back true life by that gesture. A great past, a failing present, a gallant but aged attempt—England, the only hope resting in another generation, which by some Mendelian law may inherit the spark of genius which built this empire.

Wednesday, March 1

Lunch (Anne and I) with Mr. and Mrs. Geoffrey Dawson at their home. They had also invited the Trenchards,[142] so the conversation was mostly on aviation—the progress, or lack of it, since the war, etc. Extremely interesting. Trenchard said that at the end of the war they were doing long-range bombing at 20,000 feet.

We returned to No. 4 St. James's after lunch, then went to see Sir Francis and Lady Younghusband at their apartment.

To the home of Mrs. Yates Thompson,[143] where we met Dr. Tom Jones. I had spoken to him about my desire to have another portrait painted of Anne and had asked his advice about English painters. He said he knew several and offered to take us to see some of their work, suggesting that we meet at Mrs. Yates Thompson's home. She is eighty-four, confined to a wheel chair, and one of those grand old ladies who are well able to cope with life regardless of its circumstances. We had tea with her in a room filled with old books, drawings, and illuminated pages. Her husband had made a famous collection of illuminated pages and books, part of which is now owned by the British Museum. While there, we met a Miss Cazalet, M.P.,[144] who has a number of paintings by

142. Hugh Montague Trenchard, 1st Viscount of Wolfeton, Marshal of the Royal Air Force, had been Chief of the British Air Staff 1918–29, and Principal Air Aide-de-Camp to King George V, 1921–25.

143. Widow of Henry Yates Thompson, a barrister and book collector, who formed a famous collection of one hundred illuminated manuscripts.

144. Thelma Cazalet, Conservative M.P. for East Islington, 1931–45.

Augustus John.[145] She told us that John was doing excellent work again and drinking less. She invited us to stop at her home later in the evening and see the paintings.

We went to the house where Miss Cazalet and her mother live. They had two rooms full of Johns! And several more in other parts of the house. In fact, the house seemed devoted to paintings by John and sculpture by [Jacob] Epstein. The recent work by John belied the statements I have heard about his uncertainty and deterioration. There was one landscape he did last fall, and it was by far the best I have seen. I decided immediately to see if I could get him to do Anne. Miss Cazalet said she would inquire about it, and thought he would be glad to.

Thursday, March 2

Called Croydon for weather. Flying conditions reported good: clear in France, overcast in England but ceiling never less than 1,000 feet. We packed, said good-by, and took the train for Reading. Taxi from Reading station to aerodrome. Plane looked new again, shining in its coat of varnish. We took off at 12:28. I had a headache and felt a cold coming on ever since morning. Felt much worse during last part of flight. Anne flew most of way between Saint Inglevert and Paris. Landed on the Morane field at 15:44. Détroyat happened to be there. He and one of his friends drove us to Paris. I went to bed immediately on arrival at our apartment. Worst headache I have ever had and 103° fever. Probably have caught the influenza, which is going around everywhere.

Monday, March 6

In bed all day. First day I have spent in bed since I had German measles when I was five or six years old. No doubt about it being the flu now. Not even able to read.

Tuesday, March 7

Very much better, but spent the morning in bed.

I have been thinking about England and the changes which have taken place there. What does the future hold? I am not encouraged, although I

145. Welsh painter, known especially for his portraits.

admire the attempt the English are making to uphold their position and honor. I think that Chamberlain has done a good job with the material and conditions he had to work with. His acceptance of the facts and conditions which existed is, I think, one of the greatest things about him. But England is making a great effort only by her own comfortable, accepted standards of life, and that is not enough these days. Effort, like everything else, is relative. England's standard of effort should be that which is being made against her. She is, of course, being influenced by the German Reich, but she is not able to assess properly anything which is not British and, consequently, is unable even to assess properly that which is.

England is surrounded by military power, yet will not even change her ways enough in these critical times to enforce universal military training. That would benefit her people in peace as well as in war. If war comes without previous military training, it will go hard with her.

But what concerns me most about England is that I see so little sign of life and virility in this time of crisis. Her people do not seem attuned to this modern world. As I wrote to one of my friends some months ago, the English mind seems more attuned to the age of ships than to the age of aircraft. Now that action is quick and time short, it seems to me the Englishman is at a fatal disadvantage.

It is a strange fact that the country which started the industrial revolution seems singularly ill-adapted to the results of industrial life. (Or is it that being exposed to industrialization the longest, England is the first to feel its effect?) Whatever the causes, and they are many, I believe England's great period is past. I am sorry in many ways, for I am afraid that the readjustment which must result will bring great hardship. The important thing is to avoid letting this readjustment overthrow our entire civilization. One danger is that people do not yet fully realize that the balance of power has changed among nations, and their rights have changed accordingly. If these rights cannot be asserted by peaceful means, war will probably be resorted to.

Wednesday, March 8

Up for breakfast. Much better. Took a taxi to Jo Davidson's studio and began sitting at 11:00. I had an appointment with him for 10:00 last Friday but, of course, had to postpone it. He worked quickly and within half an hour the clay began to take on a definite resemblance. I had lunch with him and then continued the sittings. Jo gave me a miniature bronze head he had done of [Ambassador] Herrick—an exact copy of the one in the embassy which I think is so good.

Friday, March 10

Short walk after breakfast, then to Davidson's studio at 11:00. Feel much better, but still notice the effects of flu. Davidson worked until about 12:30 and said that tomorrow would be the last day before the plaster cast was made. I returned to the apartment for lunch and spent most of the afternoon reading *A Passage to India* by [E. M.] Forster— an excellent and subtle book which describes the character and problems of the Indian and of the Englishman better than anything I have ever read.

Saturday, March 11

Short walk in Bois after breakfast, then to Davidson's studio (Anne to Despiau's). Davidson started talking about Chamberlain and Munich —is very down on Chamberlain and cannot understand why I am not. Thinks I always see and talk to the wrong people, etc. I try to steer the conversation away from politics without insulting him or hurting his feelings. I can see that he is very bitter. I like Jo and would hate to have political differences come between us. We change from Chamberlain to Despiau. Anne told Jo that Despiau was doing her head. Since then, Jo has brought the subject up frequently. However, Despiau is better than Munich, and we talk about him and his work. Anne came in at 12:00, and that helped a lot. Jo asked me to come back at 3:00. I don't think he was able to do much during the morning. Will try to keep our conversation on less disturbing grounds this afternoon.

Back at Davidson's studio at 3:00. Could not keep him from Chamberlain and Munich. Don't know why he feels so much more strongly about it today than heretofore. He finished the head, though, and it will be cast in plaster tomorrow. Hope it does not show the effect of the "crisis." I don't blame Jo for his attitude, although I do not think it is the type which will lead us out of trouble. Still, he is far more broad-minded than most artists, and, being Jewish, he has every reason to oppose the trends taking place these days.

Thursday, March 16

Germany and Hungary take over Czechoslovakia. Hitler enters Prague. And the German expansion continues eastward.

Friday, March 17

We went to have dinner with Mr. and Mrs. Harlan Miller at their home. We were the first to arrive and found them listening to Chamberlain's speech on the radio. We were very anxious to hear it and so were they; but within five minutes four more guests arrived, and the women burst into the room, both talking loudly at the same time—as usual about nothing. Harlan Miller greeted them and introduced them to us. Then he said we had been listening to Chamberlain on the radio. That bounced right back off their ears. They had not yet reached the listening stage, still both talking rapidly to no one in particular about how nice it was of Mrs. Miller to invite them, and what a wonderful house she had —perrrfectly chhaaarming.

Harlan waited for a break and again mentioned Chamberlain. This time it caught. "Chamberlain? Oh, yes. My dear, I don't want to think any more about it." But everyone quieted down enough for us to hear once more. Not more than four or five sentences, though, when the rest of the guests arrived. It was like a stage set with the actors entering from the wings, talking in stage voices a conversation rehearsed before it began. It was obviously hopeless, and we turned off the radio. Most of the people there had been talking about war all day and thinking about it for months, but Chamberlain's speech was so unimportant to them that they would not even listen to it in a time of crisis.

I sat next to Agnes Herrick and had a very pleasant time talking to her about the Ambassador and my week at the embassy in 1927.

Sunday, March 19

Conditions in Europe are becoming critical again. Papers are full of American protests and French and English plans. I still feel that conditions are not right for a general war this year, but when people get angry and excited, almost anything can happen. The trouble is that many people want France and England to fight, without having the slightest idea of how they are going to fight. They never even think about any of the practical problems involved in waging a successful war. They just say "fight," and there all their ideas end. A few years ago, many of the same people were shouting for peace and disarmament. And their ideas ended with their shouts then, too.

Monday, March 20

Anne and I walked around the lake before lunch and talked over plans as we walked. It looks as though there may be one crisis after another this summer. If there should be a war, of course I want to be either in the States or taking an active part of some kind over here. I am undecided about whether I could accomplish enough at home to make it worth while spending the summer, and maybe longer, there. The press would, of course, make constructive work as difficult as possible with their lies and rumors. The worst part is that I am afraid—almost certain—that they would not leave Anne and the children alone. How can democracy hold its head high when there is no freedom for those who have once attracted the interest of its public and its press? For twelve years I have found little freedom in the country which is supposed to exemplify freedom. What I have found I have had to seize, and I did not find real freedom until I came to Europe. The strange thing is that of all the European countries, I found the most personal freedom in Germany, with England next, and then France. But in comparison to America we move freely in any country over here.

Yet if there is a war, it is to America that my loyalty goes—a loyalty which looks forward with both hope and misgivings to a time when there will be less crime and more freedom than exist today. But whenever I think of the future of our people, there seem almost insurmountable problems, which in our youth we have only begun to face, hardly yet realizing that they exist. What of our 10 million Negroes? What of our industrial immigration? One thing is certain: if democracy is to continue on this earth it will not be by the blood of its soldiers but only by great changes in its present practices.

Dinner in the evening at the apartment of Mr. and Mrs. Lin Yutang. Mr. and Mrs. [Harlan] Miller and Jo Davidson were the other guests. The three Lin Yutang daughters were there when we arrived—fine-looking girls, eight to sixteen. We had a dinner of Chinese food—strange dishes, but extremely good. We talked war most of the evening. It has again became the main subject of conversation at all gatherings. It seems impossible to avoid, and no one really desires to. The Lin Yutangs are among the most pleasant and interesting people I have ever met. He has a brilliant mind, full of philosophy, humor, wisdom. I like them all and hope we will see them often in the future. One is bound to be enriched by contact with such a man.

Tuesday, March 21

I went to Jo Davidson's studio. He worked on both the plaster and terra-cotta heads until lunchtime. He finished the plaster head and sent it to the foundry to have the wax head made. Anne came for lunch; also Mrs. Diego Rivera,[146] dressed in a Mexican costume.

After lunch Jo spent the rest of the afternoon finishing the terra cotta and talking about the situation in Europe. He is greatly worried and depressed. His philosophy of life is, I am afraid, going to have increasing troubles in the coming years. He has an idealism which I admire, but which, I think, is not based on a thorough understanding either of human nature or of human happiness. Why is it that Jo and Lin Yutang, and countless other fine and able men, insist on building up a sort of Platonic utopia of their own, in which people, with the nature God gave them, would never be happy? And no matter how many times such ideas are tried and fail—like Russia—other people will want to try them again in a slightly different form, confident that the changes they would make would bring success. Real wisdom is content to walk hand in hand with nature and with life.

Wednesday, March 22

Wrote for the first part of the morning, then walked twice around the lake in the Bois. Found work difficult—too many problems to think about. Have about decided to sail for America next month, but is it safe to leave Anne and the children here alone? I will be able to decide that better after the developments of the next few days. Illiec is safe enough, probably safer for our children in war than America is for them in peace under the present conditions of press and crime. But no one

146. Wife of the Mexican mural painter.

wants to live or have his family in a foreign country in war unless he is taking part in it, and moving a family by ship in wartime is not a simple problem. I went for another walk in the Bois while I thought out various plans of action and reserves for unforeseen emergencies.

Mrs. Miller phoned after supper saying that a radio broadcast had just announced that Hitler was on the way to Memel[147] in the battleship *Deutschland,* and that he had notified Estonia, Latvia, Lithuania, and Denmark that Germany would incorporate them in the Reich and that they would be bombed if they resisted.

Thursday, March 23

I wrote for an hour, went for a short walk, and then took a taxi to the bank (Morgan Cie). Ordered $500.00 in traveler's checks to have ready money on hand in case we should have to move quickly (although things seem to be momentarily less tense). We have decided to send all diaries, which we are not using, to Englewood in order to reduce to a minimum the important papers we have here. We are attempting to keep our affairs in as flexible a condition as possible. But after all, that is nothing very new for us.

Have finished about 45,000 words of the first draft[148] (since roughly the first of January), but it must all be done again. I am devoting the first draft largely to refreshing my memory.

Supper at apartment with Anne. We always have supper alone when there are no guests. Jon and Land are in bed by our suppertime, and the nurse has hers on a separate table in the room we use for an office. These evenings with Anne alone in the dining room are among the happiest times of my life. There is no pressure, no rabble of conversation— time to think, and to talk, and to enjoy living.

Monday, March 27

I have tentatively decided to sail for America during the first part of April. If I consider the situation not too difficult, Anne and the children may come over and spend the first part of the summer in Maine. This all depends on many factors we will not know about until I have spent a week or two in the States. We are both anxious not to lose contact with

147. Ceded to Germany by Lithuania, March 22, 1939.
148. *The Spirit of St. Louis.*

our country and, with the exception of a three months' trip a year ago, we have now been away for over three years. We would like very much to spend a few months at home, even though we would miss Illiec terribly. Also, I am anxious to get around the different sections of the country to see how much the outlook has changed in the light of recent developments.

Tuesday, March 28

Finished first draft of chapter on New York–Paris flight. Will stop writing for a few days now. Must concentrate on preparations for sailing, and am getting a little stale anyway, writing too much, but wanted to finish this chapter.

We went to Jo Davidson's studio at 5:00 to see the bronze statue of Walt Whitman which is to go in Bear Mountain Park. Left early to avoid the crowd. The statue is to be exhibited at the New York World's Fair.

Thursday, March 30

I went with Anne to Despiau's studio to arrange about paying him and to try to get some estimate from him in regard to when the head will be finished. He greeted me with his usual smile and handshake. I have grown to like him very much, even though we cannot talk together, and I shall miss seeing him occasionally. I wrote a few pages for my autobiography while he worked on the head. Finally, he said he had done as much as he could until he had another plaster cast made. Then he would like to have Anne come again for a few finishing touches. He said it was almost done, but you can never be sure how many more sittings that means.

Dr. Madariaga[149] came for lunch. We discussed the general European situation. He is more practical than I thought after my first acquaintance with him, but he still has ideals about some type of organization to do what he had hoped the League of Nations would do. I could never get from him an answer which satisfied me in regard to the problem of representation.

How can we measure the strength and influence of a nation and give it

149. Don Salvador de Madariaga, scholar, author, and diplomat, had been the Spanish permanent delegate to the League of Nations, 1931–36. He was Spanish Ambassador to the U.S. in 1931 and to France, 1932–34.

a peaceful means of representation equal to that it can demand and enforce by arms? Yet unless we can find some means of doing so, how can any representative body hope to run the world? I think that is the reason the League of Nations failed and the reason why such leagues have failed in the past and will continue to fail in the future—until some means of measuring human character and strength is found. Counting heads is not satisfactory. If we carried that system to its logical conclusion, India and China would rule the world. Representation in proportion to geographical area is worse and not even to be considered seriously. What then can we fall back upon? There is no tangible measure. When agreement fails in matters of vital importance among strong nations, war is likely to result. It is the method of decision we have resorted to in the past, and I see no indication that we will be able to leave it in the future. The most we can do is to reduce the frequency of wars by intelligent agreements among groups of peoples, mutually beneficial, and backed by sufficient armed strength to make war in opposition unprofitable.

Madariaga has a brilliant mind, full of ideas flavored by long experience. I like talking to him, and we are often on common ground. But when he suggests that France and England should lay their colonies on the table of the League of Nations for reapportionment, it makes me question the practicability of his other ideas. That is simply not going to be done. (I am not certain whether he refers to all colonies or only to mandated colonies. Even in the latter case, although there is more argument for it, such a procedure is not likely to be agreed to.) Even if it were done, it would not solve the problems of Europe. And when the reapportionment was going on, the same question of representation and rights would arise.

Dinner with the Duke and Duchess of Windsor at their home on Boulevard Suchet, about three blocks away from our apartment. Probably a dozen guests in all, including Ambassador Bullitt. At the table I sat between the Baroness de Rothschild and the Duchess of Polignac. The former told me that her husband was too tired to come. He had been an Austrian. Most of their property was in Czechoslovakia, she said. Now he has just taken French citizenship—all arranged in a few days, she told me.

On the whole I did not enjoy the evening very much. I am not interested in the same things those people are, and I find conversation a great effort. But such an evening is extremely interesting in other ways. Meeting these people, listening to their conversations, and watching their movements is worth the effort many times over and is an education in itself. After supper the women left the room, English fashion, and the Duke asked me to sit on his left. The entire time was spent in talking about two subjects: the flavor of wines and how much higher the Etoile is than the Place de la Concorde. The Duke started the latter discussion out of a clear sky—abruptly from an argument about the quality of 1928 v. 1929 champagne, carried on largely by Ambassador Bullitt. It startled everyone there, and estimates ran from ten to fifty meters. "We'll call S.V.P. [telephone information bureau] and find out," said the Duke. Then we all got up from the table and went upstairs to join the ladies. The Duke delegated a Frenchman to call S.V.P. about the height of the Etoile. "Tell them you are calling for the Duke of Windsor," he said. S.V.P. replied that they would call back later. S.V.P. called back later and said that they could not get the information before morning.

I was completely out of both these conversations, not knowing the taste of one wine from another, and having no idea whether the Etoile was higher or lower than the Place de la Concorde. It was a relief to sit quietly and listen.

When we arrived in the little parlor, the Duchess came over and told me about their house on the Mediterranean coast of France. Said the Duke hated the city but had to spend the winter in Paris because of the number of people who came to see him from England; their summer home was too far away. She sent for their two dogs (cairns) and for pictures of the summer house. I cannot remember most of the conversation, but I never can remember much of what is said at dinner tables and parties. It was a late evening (on our standards), and we left about midnight.

Friday, March 31

Chamberlain has announced that England would definitely support Poland in case of aggression.

This Polish situation may cause trouble. I do not like the present trends in Europe. If England and France attempt to stop the German eastward movement there will be war, a war in which England and France will have to attack. That would mean the loss of many of the best men in Europe. A general war now will be disastrous, yet it is coming closer and is considered inevitable by many people. Why in heaven's name did not

England move in 1934 if she intended to stop Germany? These last five years of indecision may well bring the end of her empire, if not of all Europe.

The more I see of modern England and the English people, the less confidence I have in them. She took part in Versailles. She stood by and watched Germany rearm and march into the Rhineland. She imposed sanctions against Italy. She advised a Czech mobilization last spring. She advised them to surrender to Germany last fall. She recognizes Franco after originally opposing him, at least unofficially. And now she wants to guarantee Polish integrity. And Lord knows what else. Where is the long-range vision, the stability, and the strength that we were brought up to believe lay in Great Britain? Her present actions seem desperate—another reversal of what might be called a lack of policy.

I feel sorry for the English. They have been a great people, and now this generation is seeing the decline of their empire, seeing the leadership of Europe move to the Continent and to their recently defeated enemy, seeing the end of their isolated position and of their great commercial advantage. It is no wonder they are desperate, yet they continue very largely in their old ways of life, not even yet adopting conscription, although by their own action they are again on the verge of war and not well prepared to enter it.

I sometimes think that the English have a natural anesthesia, that they are constituted so that they never fully realize the results of their follies, that they seldom compare themselves to others or look at facts squarely where their own measure is involved. The generation which commits an error dies without the realization that it has been committed. English life has moved too slowly for cause to be closely connected to effect. Now the events on the Continent, and a modern world working on a modern tempo, has forced itself into English consciousness, forced them to become aware of foreign progress and foreign ability, forced the judgment of England by others than Englishmen, forced the measure of her strength by that concrete scale of war.

Saturday, April 1

Papers confirm that Chamberlain has agreed to support Poland against aggression and indicate that England may make a similar pact with Rumania. This may lead quickly to war. Germany will certainly fight if she feels it necessary to gain an important objective.

I have tentatively decided to sail on the *Aquitania* on April 8, leaving Anne and the children here, if conditions are fairly quiet. After I have been in America for a few days I will decide whether to send for them or not. That will depend on what I find I may be able to do if I spend the summer there.

Sunday, April 2

Hitler's speech[150] is carried in the morning papers. On the whole, it is plausible and states the German case well—one of the best-written political speeches I have read. Yet one of the English papers (Sunday *Graphic*) headlines it over the front page as HITLER GETS THE JITTERS. The press is misleading the people as usual, giving them a completely wrong impression.

It seems to me that this man, damned almost everywhere except in his own country, called a fanatic and a madman, now holds the future of Europe in his hand. Civilization depends upon his wisdom far more than on the action of the democracies. Whether he now desires to or not, Hitler can dominate all of the Eastern Hemisphere if he uses intelligence and lays his plans well. I am more than ever depressed by the shortsightedness and vacillation of democratic statesmen. Much as I disapprove of many things Germany has done, I believe she has pursued the only consistent policy in Europe in recent years. I cannot support her broken promises, but she has only moved a little faster than other nations have in breaking promises. The question of right and wrong is one thing by law and another thing by history.

Monday, April 3

The tailor came at 6:00 to deliver the coats to two of the suits I ordered from him. I now have four of the five, but the sleeves on one don't fit. Poor fellow, he has had constant trouble fitting the suits, and I feel sure it is because he cannot afford skilled workmen. I paid him half his price in advance and eventually took a chance and gave him the entire amount before he delivered the first suit. Then I gave him an extra hundred francs per suit, because I could see he was about at the end of

150. On April 1, 1939, Hitler spoke at Wilhelmshaven at the launching of the battleship *Tirpitz*.

his rope—told him it was to pay him for coming to the apartment for the fittings.

I doubt that I ever will see the last suit, but I won't mind that, if he really can't deliver it. I am sure he is honest. He will deliver unless he goes broke. I have thought about lending him some money, but my experience has been that lending money under these conditions does more harm than good. People I have loaned money to in the past have usually failed anyway, and even though I have never asked for repayment, I have invariably lost them as friends, simply because it embarrassed them to see me. Still, if I can persuade myself that it will really help him, instead of prolonging his exhausting attempt to carry on his business, I think I will loan [him] enough to buy some cloth. He cannot borrow from banks because of his age and ill-health and lack of security. If he fails, he and his wife will go back to England to the dole. The trouble is I am doubtful that he is still in a position where his business can be saved.

Thursday, April 6

Anne and I went for a short walk in the Bois after breakfast. Then I took taxi to Morgan Cie to arrange for my boat ticket. Back to apartment in time to take Anne to lunch at the American Embassy at 1:00. Probably forty people there, including some of society's greatest bores. They will *never* get over talking about the time I landed at Le Bourget in 1927, and they all seem to have done the same thing: start to Le Bourget from Paris, get stuck in the traffic jam, see me ride by somewhere in an automobile, and meet me at a lunch at the embassy which Ambassador Herrick invited them to. And they usually want to hold my hand while they tell it all. It was really one of the most interesting times in my life, but I get so sick of having the whole conversation revolve around it that I really should not go to these Paris lunches and dinners. After all, most of these people have nothing to talk about anyway.

Agnes Herrick was there. The amazing thing is that she has led a life of these stupid social parties and yet is still interesting and full of life herself. I know of no one else who has gone to so many and been affected by them so little. But why she enjoys it I cannot understand.

Friday, April 7

Italian troops entered Albania this morning. Germany and Italy undoubtedly plan on dominating all of Eastern Europe (and what of the

August Lindbergh,
grandfather of
Charles A.
Lindbergh, Jr.,
with his family in
Minnesota
about 1873.
Left to right:
August,
Linda (*behind*),
Juno,
Charles,
Louisa,
Frank

Dr. Charles Henry Land, grandfather of Charles A. Lindbergh, Jr., in his dental laboratory at Detroit, Michigan, about 1915

Charles A. Lindbergh, Sr.,
about 1915

Evangeline Lodge Land Lindbergh
and her son, Charles, 1902

Evangeline Lodge Land Lindbergh,
about 1930

Dwight W. Morrow, about 1930

Mrs. Dwight W. Morrow, 1940

Next Day Hill, Englewood, New Jersey

Long Barn, Sevenoaks Weald, Kent, England

Anne Morrow Lindbergh and Thor in the garden of Long Barn

Viscount and Lady Astor

Cliveden, Taplow, Buckingham—the Astor estate

Colonel Lindbergh flying his Mohawk over England, 1937

The house and chapel on Illiec

Below: The tidelands of Illiec

Richard W. Brown

Zeitgeschichtliches Bildarchiv

Major Arthur Vanaman, Colonel Lindbergh,
and Field Marshal Erhard Milch

Field Marshal Erhard Milch and
General Ernst Udet

Colonel Truman Smith and Colonel Lindbergh during an inspection trip
in Germany

UPI

Colonel Lindbergh and Anne Morrow Lindbergh with Reichsmarshal Hermann Goering at his residence in Berlin

Colonel Lindbergh with Michel Détroyat, inspecting an airplane factory in Germany

Russian Ukraine?). What will France and England do? And America? Are we on the verge of the world's greatest and most catastrophic war? Possibly the end of European civilization? It could be all of those things. Human life will, of course, go on, but with what changes?

Morning spent making final preparations for sailing. Anne will make all preparations for sailing or for going to Illiec about the twentieth (April). Decision will depend on my cable from the United States.

Saturday, April 8

Breakfast at 8:15 with entire family. Most of morning spent packing the three suitcases I am taking with me and completing last details. Anne and I went out for a short walk. Then said good-by to everyone and left by taxi at 11:55. I won't see any of our staff again except Soeur Lisi. Miss Hutchison is going back to be with her father. Walked right past the newspaper people and got on board the train without being bothered. Pleasant trip to Cherbourg. Boarded the tender and an hour later the *Aquitania.* Met the Lin Yutangs on the tender and talked to them while we were waiting for passengers and baggage to come on board.

Went to the dining room early to avoid the crowd. The boat is full, including many refugees. Asked for a small table, but have been assigned to a five-place one. The steward said he would try to arrange for a different one tomorrow. The trouble is that if I talk to my table companions, they will be interviewed by the reporters at New York. This always happens. They seldom have had any experience with the press and, consequently, fall right into their traps, saying all kinds of silly things and getting their own ideas and what they think I said all mixed up. Then I am quoted in the papers as saying things I never said, never thought, and don't believe. On the other hand, if I don't talk to them at all, it is very unpleasant and impracticable when people must be together for six days at the same table. It is just one of those problems that newspapers cause in our lives.

I went in and sat down at the "temporary" table, hoping to finish before the other people came. Within five minutes, however, a young girl came in and sat down in the next chair. I expected more to follow, but they did not. The first ten minutes passed stiffly; we were sitting in adjoining chairs, with three empty places on the other side of the table, and had not spoken a word. There was no use letting the time pass that way. I asked her if she was returning to America. "No," she said in slightly accented English. "I am going there for the first time." She was obviously relieved to talk to someone, and as she talked I looked at her for the first time. She was in the vicinity of twenty and quite pretty. She said she was from Rumania and was married to an American in Dayton. I steered the conversation to the places she had been to in Europe, and to the geography and climate of Dayton, until the dinner was over.

But what an amusing and in some ways annoying situation to be in— just the two of us there at the table all during the meal. And, of course, everybody in the dining room looking and wondering. That amuses me. But, although it is the only thing to do, it will hurt her feelings when I change tables today and she will never understand it. Unfortunately, I think she is at least partly Jewish, and she will think it is on that account. But if I don't change tables, the newspapers in America will grab her, photograph her, interview her, and then throw her in the gutter according to their usual procedure.

Went for a walk on the top deck after supper. It is cold and a little windy, so I had it to myself. Spent the rest of the evening reading [W. G. Phelps's] *The Glory That Was Greece.*

Sunday, April 9

Last night was the quietest I have ever spent on the open ocean. I could hardly tell we were moving. The sea was a bit choppy, but without rollers, and this boat seems to be exceptionally steady. I can feel and hear no vibration whatever in my stateroom. Whoever built her did a good job, and they tell me she is now twenty-five years old.

Had my table changed to a small one, alone, in another part of the room. But the young lady has not turned up today, fortunately. As a matter of fact, very few passengers were there for lunch. Wrote for an hour after lunch.

Went to call on the Lin Yutangs about 4:00. Found them all sick except Yutang. He and I talked for half an hour. Then I returned to my stateroom and spent another hour writing. On deck again before supper. Very few passengers in the dining room this evening; the pitching is worse.

I have received a radiogram from "Sol Bloom,[151] acting chairman of the Foreign Affairs Committee, Washington," asking me to appear before the committee. Wonder what is behind this? Publicity for Sol Bloom? Newspapers? Intrigue of some kind? He wants me to testify in

151. Democratic Representative from New York City.

connection with the pending neutrality legislation. I shall give an indefinite answer, postponing any decision until after I land and have a chance to find out what it is all about.

Monday, April 10

Up at 6:45. Medium rough night. Pitching, but no rolling. Broken sky with sun at intervals. Spent forty-five minutes on top deck before breakfast. Have the ship almost to myself this morning. Breakfast at 8:00. Very few people down. Read ship's paper after breakfast and do not like the European situation. Germany is reported moving troops in the direction of Poland, Holland, and Switzerland. This may be just press reports, and almost certainly some of it is. But I look for German expansion to come rapidly now. In view of the present situation, I think there is at best an even chance of the year passing without a general war. It depends largely on Hitler. Germany will dominate Europe unless he makes some error. Only another miracle can save England now. And she is apparently beginning to realize the position she is in.

Had to dress (black tie) tonight as they are having some kind of a "gala" affair. Paper "clown" hats at the tables and balloons tied to strings around the room. Most of these things seem awfully stupid to me. And the people themselves don't seem to have very much real fun. What there is seems to consist of getting more or less drunk and making yourself *think* you are having fun. Nothing had started by the time I finished eating, so I went down to my stateroom to read.

Going west, we set the clock back one hour each night. I have noted that I wake at the same time each morning that I did in Paris, regardless of the changing clock and light. In other words, I am still running, subconsciously or physiologically, by the Paris clock and not by the sun. This indicates that there is a delicate time mechanism within the human body, which is independent of astronomy and mechanical clocks. It would be an interesting subject for research.

Tuesday, April 11

The sea is rough, and we are slowed down to about half speed. The deck was covered with spray, so I returned for a raincoat and to put on an old suit.

Ship paper reports that Italy has called up over 300,000 more troops and that the Dutch harbors are being mined. The English Parliament is called and meets Thursday. The situation remains critical.

Another walk on deck before lunch at 1:00. The wind has increased, the sea is very rough, and the ship is practically hove to. We were four hours behind schedule at noon.

United States
Prewar

Wednesday, April 12

The staff captain sent for me to come to his cabin to discuss a code message he had received from the Cunard Line offices in New York. My friends there suggest that I disembark via the crew's gangway. Apparently the newspapers are getting ready to cause their usual annoyance and trouble. I think, however, that I will use the regular passenger gangway and see what happens. They will be watching all of the gangways anyway.

The three Lin Yutang girls sent a copy of their new book, *Our Family*, autographed, to Anne and me. At about 5:00 I spent half an hour with Lin Yutang in his cabin. They are not good sailors, so I kept away during the days of rough sea. After supper I bought three dolls, a small one, a middle-sized one, and a large one. I shall leave them in the Lins' cabin in the morning. Adet is sixteen, Anor thirteen, and Meimei eight. I shall be interested to hear how they settle the situation, and especially how Adet reacts to receiving a doll at the age of sixteen.

Thursday, April 13

Radio from Victory[1] asking me to attend a NACA[2] meeting on April 20. Radio from General Arnold[3] asking me to telephone him as soon as

1. John Victory, secretary of the National Advisory Committee for Aeronautics.
2. The National Advisory Committee for Aeronautics had been created by an Act of Congress on March 3, 1915, for the primary purpose of aeronautical research. It was composed of two members each from the War and Navy Departments and the Civil Aeronautics Authority; one member each from the Smithsonian Institution, the National Bureau of Standards, and the Weather Bureau; six members appointed by the President; six members acquainted with the needs of aeronautical science. It was merged with the National Aeronautics and Space Administration in October, 1968.
3. General Henry H. ("Hap") Arnold, Chief of the Air Corps, 1938–40. Through-

I arrive. Radio phone call from Truman and Kay Smith. They are on the *Washington* and say they just saw the *Aquitania* a few miles away.

Friday, April 14

Spent morning reading, packing, and walking.

I tipped the waiters and stewards and went to my cabin and locked the door. The customs officials were just boarding as I got there, the press with them. After quarter of an hour there was a knock at the door, and a voice—a familiar voice—called to me. It was Mme. Carrel! She and Dr. Carrel and Jim Newton[4] had come on one of the tugs to meet me. Soon the reporters and photographers began hammering on the door. We did not answer. I had arranged with the steward to let me know when the gangplank was down after the ship was docked. As we were talking, a press photographer broke in through the door to the adjoining cabin, took a flashlight photo and ran. After that we locked the door to that cabin too. It is a ridiculous situation when one cannot return to one's own country without having to go through the roughhousing of photographers and the lies and insults of the press. It takes the sweetness from the freedom of democracy and makes one wonder where freedom ends and disorder begins.

Two New York police officers came to the cabin and asked if they could be of any assistance, and suggested that they form a cordon around me as I went out of the stateroom. I replied that I would prefer to go out alone if possible. They advised against it and told me that one of the last fellows who tried that got one of his ribs broken. I told them that I would try it anyway. They said all right, shook hands, and went out. (Said they would be there to help if necessary.) Apparently the gangway was down at that time, but the steward had forgotten to tell me about it. He had been excited by the press jam and probably didn't know we had even docked.

At 10:15 I asked Newton to go out and size up the situation. In five minutes he returned and said all of the passengers were off and the gangway clear except for press representatives. He said the boat was

---

out World War II, he was Chief of the U.S. Army Air Forces. In 1944 he was made a five-star general of the Army, and in 1949 a five-star general of the Air Force.

4. Close friend of the Lindberghs, Henry Ford, and Alexis Carrel. One of the leaders of the Moral Re-Armament movement.

jammed with them. We then left the cabin. I went first, Mme. Carrel next, and last, Dr. Carrel and Newton. Both sides of the corridor and stairs were lined with cameramen and flashing, blinding lights. They started shoving and blocking the way in front of us. The police immediately formed a wedge and pushed them out of the way. There were dozens of uniformed police in addition to many plain-clothes men. All the way along the deck the photographers ran in front of us and behind us, jamming the way, being pushed aside by the police, yelling, falling over each other on the deck. There must have been over a hundred of them, and the planks were covered with the broken glass of the flashlight bulbs they threw away. I have never seen as many at one time before, even in 1927, I think.

It was a barbaric entry to a civilized country. We went down the gangplank and finally into a big elevator. Mme. Carrel got in, and also Aubrey [Morgan], who was waiting for me at the bottom of the gangplank. But I did not see Dr. Carrel or Newton again; they had gotten lost in the jam and the shoving. Mrs. Morrow's chauffeur, Ambrose, was waiting in a small car on the lower deck. Aubrey and I got in, but there was too much jam to get Mme. Carrel. We left orders for another car to take her wherever she wished to go. Drove along the Hudson highway and across the Washington Bridge to New Jersey and Englewood. Mrs. Morrow, Con, and Margot[5] were at the house when I arrived. Phoned General Arnold and made appointment to meet him at West Point tomorrow. Bed at 1:30.

Saturday, April 15

Up at 7:15. Walk around the grounds and down to the "Little School"[6] site. It is very well placed. Exactly where I wanted it to be. The excavating is almost completed. A clear, sunny day. Spent part of morning telephoning—Jerry Land, Carrel, and others.

Left for West Point (alone) in the De Soto. Arrived at 12:00. Lunch with General and Mrs. Arnold. Discussed the general situation with

5. Constance Morrow Morgan, wife of Aubrey Niel Morgan, and sister of Anne Morrow Lindbergh; later member of the wartime staff of the British Information Services in New York, and chairman of the board of trustees, Smith College. Margot (Loines) Morrow, wife of Dwight W. Morrow, Jr.

6. A nursery and elementary school that had been started by Elisabeth Morrow some years earlier. This later became the Elisabeth Morrow School. The building and grounds were a gift of the Morrow family.

Arnold. In the afternoon he took me for a tour of West Point and introduced me to his son, who is a cadet there. Saw the cadets drilling— a fine-looking bunch. Drove back to Englewood, and then to New York for dinner with the Carrels and Newton at their apartment.

Sunday, April 16

Wrote a letter to Bloom, asking what he felt I would be able to assist by my testimony. Left in De Soto immediately after lunch for southern Maryland (Leonardtown) to meet Jerry Land.[7] A long drive, heavy traffic, and raining. Arrived at the house at 2:00 A.M.

Monday, April 17

Up at 6:30. This is a beautiful farm, with a great open view out toward the Potomac, but there is no time to walk over it as Jerry must be at his office [in Washington] before 10:00. Left with Jerry and Betty[8] in their car. Colonel Fay will bring mine tomorrow morning. We discuss many things during the hour-and-a-half drive to Washington, especially congressional committees and general conditions in America and Europe. Jerry got out at his office, and I went on to their apartment with Betty. Called Victory (NACA), and he came over for an hour in the afternoon to discuss NACA activities. General Arnold phoned later and asked me to meet him at his home after supper.

Supper with Jerry and Betty at their apartment. Then drove to Arnold's home. He wants me to go on active duty, to make a study of and attempt to increase the efficiency of American [aeronautical] research organizations. I tentatively accept and agree to give him a definite answer at 8:30 tomorrow morning.

Tuesday, April 18

Called Arnold at 8:30 and accepted active duty [as a colonel in the Army Air Corps] to begin at once. Dr. Lewis[9] (NACA) came over at

7. Admiral Land was visiting the home of a friend, Colonel W. Garland Fay.

8. Mrs. Emory S. Land.

9. Dr. George W. Lewis, aeronautical engineer, who served for twenty-three years as an executive officer of NACA. He was instrumental in establishing several laboratories for research on engines and jet propulsion.

10:30, and we spent an hour talking about the problems of research which must be carried on.

After lunch I went to a tailor to order my uniform. Went to War Department at 3:00 (Arnold's office). Spent an hour talking to him and other officers. Returned to apartment to meet Dr. Bush[10] (NACA and Carnegie) at 4:00. Spent an hour with him discussing problems of both institutions. Evening spent reading and studying NACA data.

Wednesday, April 19

S.S. Paris *burns at dock! Anne, Jon, and Land were to sail on it today.*

Attended meeting of officers of Naval Intelligence at 10:00. They asked me questions, and we discussed European aviation for about an hour. Then went to General Arnold's office. I received my appointment yesterday and begin active duty today. Lunch with General Arnold and other officers. We discussed ways of increasing the performances of Army planes. Spent afternoon to 3:30 studying various reports.

Thursday, April 20

Drove to Munitions Building in time to meet Arnold at 8:50. We drove to the War and Navy Building for a 9:00 appointment with Secretary Woodring.[11] Discussed military aviation in America and Europe. Woodring seems very anxious for me not to testify before any of the congressional committees. As a matter of fact, I prefer not to do so, but I wonder just what politics are working in his mind.

General Arnold impresses me more as I get to know him better. I think our relationship will be a very pleasant one. And I am already beginning to see ways in which I can be of help.

I returned to the Munitions Building from Woodring's office, but left immediately for Bolling Field to take the regular Army physical exami-

10. Dr. Vannevar Bush, administrator and electrical engineer, president of the Carnegie Institution in Washington (of which Lindbergh was once a trustee) from 1939 to 1955. He was chairman of the National Defense Research Committee, 1940–41. From 1941 to 1946 he was director of the Office of Scientific Research and Development and was, consequently, a leading figure in the development of the atom bomb.

11. Harry Hines Woodring, Secretary of War.

nation. Passed satisfactorily and had just time to have my parachute fitted before leaving in an Army car for the Munitions Building. On the way out from Bolling the guard stopped us at the gate. There was a phone call from Betty Land. I called her back and was informed that a cable from Englewood stated that Anne and the children were sailing on the S.S. *Champlain*. Went on to Munitions Building, and then to the White House in time for a 12:00 appointment with the President. A crowd of press photographers at the door and inane women screeching at me as I passed through—a disgraceful condition to exist on the White House steps. There would be more dignity and self-respect among African savages.

Roosevelt was behind with his appointments (as usual, I understand), so I waited for about three-quarters of an hour for mine. Meanwhile, I talked to the Congressmen who were also waiting for appointments—very political they were, but quite interesting and pleasant. I also met Early[12]—the secretary who took part in the air-mail controversy I had with the President about 1934.[13] He looked like a good-natured fighting Irish politician.

I went in to see the President about 12:45—the first time I have ever met him. He was seated at his desk at one end of a large room. There were several models of ships around the walls. He leaned forward from his chair to meet me as I entered, and it is only now that I stop to think that he is crippled. I did not notice it and had no thought of it during our meeting. He immediately asked me how Anne was and mentioned the

12. Stephen Early, secretary to President Roosevelt, 1937–45, and before that assistant secretary, 1933–37.

13. On February 9, 1934, the cancellation of domestic air-mail contracts was announced by presidential decree. This cancellation was based on the findings of a special Senate committee, headed by Senator Hugo Black of Alabama, which alleged that there were inequities and irregularities in the Post Office Department's awarding of air-mail contracts to commercial aviation companies. Without hearings or adequate preparation for continued air-mail service, President Roosevelt abruptly canceled all existing contracts. Lindbergh sent a telegram to Roosevelt on February 11, which was released to the newspapers on February 12, charging that this action condemned the airlines without fair trial and would greatly damage American aviation. Within two months the Army Air Corps, which had begun to fly the mail when the commercial contracts were canceled, suffered a series of disasters, including twelve fatalities. After competitive bidding and some politically forced superficial reorganization, the air mail was quickly returned to private lines. Years later, a district court determined that the government's cancellation of contracts was arbitrary and without due process of law since the airlines had been given no opportunity to defend themselves.

fact that she knew his daughter in school. He is an accomplished, suave, interesting conversationalist. I liked him and feel that I could get along with him well. Acquaintanceship would be pleasant and interesting.

But there was something about him I did not trust, something a little too suave, too pleasant, too easy. Still, he is our President, and there is no reason for any antagonism between us in the work I am now doing. The air-mail situation is past—one of the worst political maneuvers I know of, and unfair in the extreme, to say the least. But nothing constructive will be gained by bringing it up again at this time.

Roosevelt gave me the impression of being a very tired man, but with enough energy left to carry on for a long time. I doubt that he realizes how tired he is. His face has that gray look of an overworked businessman. And his voice has that even, routine tone that one seems to get when mind is dulled by too much and too frequent conversation. It has that dull quality that comes to any one of the senses when it is overused: taste, with too much of the same food day after day; hearing, when the music never changes; touch, when one's hand is never lifted.

Roosevelt judges his man quickly and plays him cleverly. He is mostly politician, and I think we would never get along on many fundamentals. But there are things about him I like, and why worry about the others unless and until they necessitate consideration? It is better to work together as long as we can; yet somehow I have a feeling that it may not be for long.

Returned to Munitions Building from the White House, again through the mob of pressmen and silly women. Lunch with General Arnold and one or two other officers, during which we discussed aircraft performances. Then we went to the NACA offices. The meeting room was packed with photographers—motion picture and still. They lined one entire end of the room. I told Victory I would come in after the pictures had been taken. He said the photographers had told him they wanted no pictures unless I was in them! I replied that I would not pose for press pictures there or anywhere else. They came back with the proposition that they would let me alone in the future if I would let them take one picture, that they would give *their word of honor*. Imagine a press photographer talking about his word of honor! The type of men who broke through the window of the Trenton morgue to open my baby's casket and photograph its body—they talk to me of honor.

We had them put out of the room, and the meeting started. First, the regular routine business, then a demonstration of new developments by

Dr. Lewis. Afterward, I brought up the question of research facilities. I asked how we expected to catch up with military developments abroad (in aviation research) with our present facilities. I pointed out that we had fallen behind while the foreign facilities were even less than they are today, that even with the full appropriation for the new Sunnyvale experimental station, we would be far behind a country like Germany in research facilities, and that we really needed the full Sunnyvale appropriation and much more besides. I made the point that while we could not expect to keep up with the production of European airplanes as long as we were on a peacetime basis, we should at least keep up in the quality of our aircraft.

Orville Wright[14] asked to see me after the meeting, and we discussed the old Smithsonian controversy about his Kitty Hawk plane (now in England).[15] It is a difficult situation. I believe the fault lies primarily with the Smithsonian people, but Orville Wright is not an easy man to deal with in the matter. I don't blame him too much, though, when I think of the way he was treated for a period of years. He has encountered both the narrow-mindedness of science and the dishonesty of commerce.

Returned to apartment and walked through Rock Creek Park to the zoo, to the same cages of bears and seals and coyotes Mother and I went to see when I was going to school here. It was strange, going back to them thirty years later.

Friday, April 21

Conference with General Arnold and General Brett,[16] C.O. of Wright Field, Dayton. Morning spent in conferences with various Air Corps officers. Lunch in "Trophy Room," where I have a desk. Discussed various

14. American aviation pioneer and inventor. He and his brother Wilbur designed and constructed the first airplane to achieve man-carrying, power-sustained flight. Orville piloted the first flight of this plane on December 17, 1903.

15. In 1928 the original Wright Kitty Hawk airplane was sent by Orville Wright to the Science Museum at South Kensington, London, after years of controversy between Wright and the Smithsonian Institution over the question of whether the Wright brothers or Dr. Samuel P. Langley had built the first airplane capable of man-carrying, power-sustained flight. The controversy was eventually resolved in favor of the Wright brothers, and their airplane was returned to the Smithsonian Institution. It is now on display in Washington.

16. General George H. Brett. In 1942 he was appointed Commander in Chief, Air Forces of Allied Forces in the Southwest Pacific.

Air Corps problems with three officers who had lunch with me. After lunch I drove to Bolling Field. Got in the cockpit of the P-36A which is assigned to me (just ferried up from Langley), while Captain [Charles H.] Deerwester explained the controls, radio, and instruments. It is better finished, more completely equipped, and much more complicated to operate than the European machines, but not as fast—only about 300 miles per hour. I spent plenty of time studying the cockpit, then made three practice flights. Dinner with Miss [Christine] Gawne, a friend of Jerry's and Betty's who is interested in doing secretarial work for us: a nice, intelligent, and apparently able girl about twenty-three years old. Only question in my mind is whether we need someone with more experience and whether she would stay for more than a few months.

Saturday, April 22

Drove De Soto to Bolling Field. Took off in P-36A for Wright Field at 8:10. Good weather and clear skies except overcast and local storms over mountains. Landed at Wright Field at 10:35 E.S.T. Conference with General Brett and various officers, including Major [Alfred J.] Lyon, Lieutenant [Merrill D.] Burnside, Lieutenant [Benjamin S.] Kelsey. Lunch with General Brett and officers. Was shown over field by Major Lyon. Saw the Bell P-39 fly, and inspected a number of experimental and service types, including the B-17 (four-engine bomber), the new Martin and Steerman attack bombers, the P-35 (Seversky pursuit), and others. In the later afternoon Lieutenant Burnside and I walked from Wright Field to Patterson Field—about two miles. We walked past the old Wright hangar, which lies in a dilapidated condition about a hundred yards to the right of the road we were following. We went over to it and spent five or ten minutes looking around. It is leaning over, almost ready to fall down, and there are great cracks between the boards on the roof, through which the rain has run in so long that it has formed trenches in the black earth floor. (General Brett told me later that a project was under way to repair the hangar and keep it in good condition. It is not the original Wright hangar, he said, but it is the first one used by the Wright brothers in developing airplanes for the United States Army.)

I went to General Brett's home, where I am to spend the night. We went out for supper to the home of one of the officers. There were about twenty guests in all, all officers and their wives. One of the women had taken too many cocktails and was in a disgraceful condition. She insisted on heading for me at every opportunity and made the evening rather difficult. However, she was the only one who showed the effects of over-drinking. The more I see of these parties, the more thankful I am that I do not care for liquor.

Sunday, April 23

Major Lyon and Lieutenant Burnside called for me at 10:00, and we drove to Wright Field, where I had a conference with them and other officers, primarily regarding attack bombers, their performances, engines available, plans for the future, etc. Later, we made a tour of the field and an inspection of its various types of planes (B-17, Martin Attack, and others).

Monday, April 24

Drove to Wright Field with General Brett in time to get maps and take off for Buffalo at 6:45. Clear weather and tail wind, so was far ahead of time as I approached Buffalo. I climbed to 15,000 feet and tried out the P-36 in various maneuvers—Immelmanns, wing overs, dives, stalls, etc. It rolls out beautifully on top of a loop and handles better than the European planes, even if it is not as fast. Then I climbed to 31,000 feet (using oxygen) and dove to 20,000, until my air speed reached 375 miles per hour.

Landed at Buffalo at 11:00. The press representatives were there as usual, so we put the plane in the hangar and closed the doors. (The only reason they were not on Wright and Patterson fields was that both are Army posts and the gates were closed to them. They are, of course, writing their usual incorrect, and silly articles. It is amusing to compare them from day to day to see how far our newspapers stray from fact. On the whole, though, I find life more pleasant and its values more true when I don't read them at all. I wish we had one reliable and accurate publication in the country, either daily or weekly. The New York *Times* is among our best, but one cannot by any means believe all it says. There is too much of a rush for news here, more of a premium on speed than on accuracy. It is considered more important for a press service to be one minute ahead of its competitor than to have its story correct.

Personally, I would much rather have my news a day late and feel it is reasonably accurate.)

Drove from the airport to the Curtiss factory with Burdette Wright. We made a tour of the factory and then had lunch with a number of the officers. We held a conference after lunch and discussed plane and engine types and the necessity of increasing speeds. "Temp" Joyce[17] arrived from Washington shortly after lunch and was of great help. I said we had to get pursuit types to 500 m.p.h. or above. Joyce felt that it would be possible with the flat-type engine the Wright Company is building at Paterson.

Tuesday, April 25

Called Arthur Springer[18] at Englewood and found that my letters from Washington had not arrived. Talked to him about arrangements for Anne's landing. He said indications were that the press would be very difficult and that it would be advisable to have a large police guard. (So that a woman and two children can land safely in America!)

Burdette Wright drove me to the Bell Aircraft Corporation at 10:00, and I went directly to Bell's[19] office. He and I had a half hour's discussion, during which he called in some of his engineers. After that we made a tour of the factory and then had lunch with about twelve or fifteen of his officers. Then to the airport to see the "Airacuda" fly. There was trouble with the turbosupercharger, and the flight was postponed.

Wednesday, April 26

Phoned Allison Engine Corporation in Indianapolis to arrange for visit and find out where to land. Burdette drove me to the airport at 10:30, and I took off at 11:00. Overcast and some haze en route but clear at

17. Temple Nash Joyce, aviation corporation executive and author of articles on aviation, former president and director of Berliner-Joyce Aircraft Corp. and Bellanca Aircraft Corp. In World War II he served as a naval technician attached to Fast Carrier Task Force 58.

18. Former secretary to Dwight W. Morrow, later estate manager for Mrs. Morrow.

19. Lawrence D. Bell, who in 1935 organized with associates the Bell Aircraft Corp. in Buffalo. In 1937 the company completed the Airacuda, and in 1939 the Airacobra, a cannon-carrying fighter turned out in mass production for the U.S. Army.

Indianapolis. Landed on Stout Field at 1:35. Met by Hazen[20] of Allison. He drove me to his home, where he, Mrs. Hazen, and I had lunch while we discussed the engine situation. Allison has the only large liquid-cooled engine in the United States at the present time, and they are not likely to have strong competition for two or three years at least.

After lunch we drove to the Allison factory, and Hazen showed me through it. The factory is well laid out but small. Will have to be expanded to take care of the new Army orders. Hazen and I spent an hour after the tour discussing engine performances and future possibilities.

Thursday, April 27

After breakfast Hazen drove me to Stout Field. Weather report was bad east of Dayton, so I cleared for Wright Field. Later radio reports indicated improving conditions at Bolling, so I changed course and headed toward Washington. Eventually picked up Washington beacon and found hole in clouds south of field to spiral down through.

Started for Englewood about 5:00, taking dinner en route at small roadside restaurant. Picked out one with nice appearance, as I will not patronize the type that is spoiling the appearance of all our major roads in this country. Arrived Englewood about 1:15 A.M. Expected to find Anne, but the watchman told me the *Champlain* will not dock until early morning—about 6:00 A.M.

Friday, April 28

Anne and the children arrived about 7:30. I did not go to meet them to avoid adding to difficulty because of newspapers. We arranged for a police guard, and I understand about one hundred were there. They had a good trip and all look well. Soeur Lisi is in this country on the Swiss quota, so can stay with us indefinitely. That removes the problem of getting a new nurse.

Secretary Woodring called from Washington and asked me to attend a dinner with him in Kansas City (United States Chamber of Commerce)! Kansas City is his home territory. Just what I expected: everything I try to do here will be impeded by these political requests. They would take

20. Ronald M. Hazen, director of engineering for the Allison Division, General Motors Corp.

all of my time if I accepted only a fraction of them. Imagine! The Secretary of War asking me to go to Kansas City to attend a dinner just as I am starting to concentrate on my work here.

Saturday, April 29

Thor and Skean arrived this morning, overjoyed to see us again. It has been five months since we left them on Illiec.

I drove to New York in the afternoon. Got a haircut—the first since Europe—at the Engineers Club, then drove to the Rockefeller Institute to see some "pyrex" glass cloth[21] Dr. Carrel left there for me.

Sunday, April 30

Anne and I spent more of the morning outside in the sun with the dogs. Spent most of afternoon getting ready for return to Washington. Drove to New York in the evening to meet Dr. and Mme. Carrel, who have just returned from Washington.

Monday, May 1

Breakfast at 8:00, with Anne. She takes Jon to school this morning. Packed. Went for a walk around grounds. Talked to Arthur Springer for a few minutes. He says the policeman at the gate reported 200 cars driving up to the entrance on Sunday. That is the result of newspaper publicity. We must keep a uniformed guard there until it stops. The policeman had difficulty with two or three people who demanded the right to drive in!

Drove Franklin to Pennsylvania Station in time to catch the 11:30 train for Washington. Have paid for two tickets to get a drawing room to avoid being bothered on the trip. I certainly miss the privacy and decency of Europe. Tried to get lunch on the train but too crowded. People constantly knocking on door to my room. Impossible to do anything. They want to see me, to get autographs—giggling high-school girls, silly boys, and older people who should have more consideration. Arrived Washington about 2:30.

21. For possible use in experimental apparatus.

Thursday, May 4

Met General Arnold at his office in the Munitions Building at 8:00. He must appear before a congressional Appropriations Committee on the fifteenth, and it is obvious that we must have more money for research and development if we hope to catch up on foreign countries in military aviation within the next five years.

General Arnold wants me to sit on an Army board to revise the Army development program and submit recommendations to him prior to his appearance at the Capitol on the fifteenth. I decide to go immediately to the West Coast to become acquainted with the aviation situation there. Plan on leaving in the morning tomorrow and postponing the trip I had planned on making to the eastern factories in the New York area. It will be a fast trip—only four or five days in California—but I want to have some idea of what is going on out there before I take part in the proceedings of the Army board.

Went to the Commerce Building for a conference with the CAA[22] at 10:00. Had a very pleasant and interesting meeting, but believe they were originally under the impression that I had made an extensive study of European commercial aviation, which was not the case. However, I told them that before I accepted their request to appear before them. The meeting was very informal.

Friday, May 5

Took off at 6:10 E.S.T. Straight over Alleghenies to Patterson Field (Dayton). Landed at 8:00 E.S.T. Refueled and took off at 8:23 E.S.T. Landed at Lambert Field, St. Louis, at 10:13 E.S.T. Saw Jimmy Tate, one of the mechanics and parachute packers when I was an officer in the squadron in 1926 and 1927 [110th Observation Squadron, Missouri National Guard], and several of the later members of the squadron. Took off again at 10:47 E.S.T. Flew direct to Marshall, Kansas, and landed at 12:30 E.S.T. Talked to the officers on the field while the plane was being refueled, and took off at 1:07 E.S.T. . . . Landed at Albuquerque at 7:55 E.S.T. and, since they had had plenty of warning

22. Civil Aeronautics Administration, a U.S. government agency for administering and enforcing the rules and regulations of the Civil Aeronautics Board and for operating the federal airways.

of my coming, I was met by the mayor, some other city official, and the usual group of reporters and photographers. They were not much bother. It is only in the larger cities where I have trouble that is really annoying. Country people and those who live in small cities are less artificial, closer to life, and consequently much easier to get along with. At Albuquerque, they shook hands, took their pictures, and then stood to one side while I arranged for refueling. There was none of the excitement and running around like monkeys that one finds at the large city airports. Took off from Albuquerque at 8:20 E.S.T.

Landed at Winslow at dusk, after watching the sunset, and making it rise again by climbing rapidly. (Landed at 9:33 P.M. E.S.T.). Planned on going on to March Field [California] after having supper at the Harvey House, where Anne and I stayed several years ago on our trip through. Gave refueling instructions and took a taxi to Winslow.

Sat down at a table in the dining room but was immediately joined by the manager, who sat down and began talking. I was tired and didn't want to talk. Some other people soon came up. Then two men came to ask me to attend a dinner which was being given in an adjacent room. The manager called his little daughter over to shake hands, and by that time it became obvious that I would not have much chance to eat supper. I had only started on the roast beef, but called the waitress, paid the bill, said I had no more time, and left.

I decided to walk to the field, which is only about one and a half miles from the town. The stars were all out, and I felt much better in the clear, fresh air and away from the people in the hotel. I decided to spend the night at Winslow and reach March Field in the early morning instead of pushing on. That would give me a good night's rest before I encountered the high-pressure methods of Southern California. Also, I could get supper sent to my room.

It is not the flying which is tiring on a trip like this, not the problems of weather, machinery, and navigation, but the people who flock around and want this or that, meaning well, trying to help, but always getting in the way, distracting attention, demanding consideration and turning ordinary routine work into a complicated problem of human relationships. People can be extremely interesting and pleasant to be with at times, but not when one is working hard, or very tired. Then it is much better to be alone, or with others doing the same work, who understand its problems and do not, in consequence, demand extra attention.

Saturday, May 6

Took off at 7:45 Mountain time and flew over meteor crater, which was only a few miles off course; then set compass course for March Field. Flew over beautiful desert rock formations and high, tree-covered mountains. All the beauty of the Southwest. Clear weather as far as San Bernardino Mountains; then I had to drop down close to the ground to get under the clouds which were bunched up against the mountains on the Pacific side, seemingly trying to get through the pass, but not quite able to. Very rough going through the pass. Landed at March Field at 9:45 Mountain time. Met by C.O. and other officers. Called Reuben Fleet[23] and arranged to meet him in San Diego.

Took off from March Field at 9:55 Pacific time. Landed San Diego at 10:32 Pacific time. Taxied up to National Guard hangar. Met by Fleet, Doug Kelly (Ryan Airlines pilot, 1927), T. C. Ryan,[24] and others. Went with Fleet to factory, went through it with him, and talked with him (listened to him talk, to be more exact) until lunchtime. Then he, Donald Hall [25] (designer of *Spirit of St. Louis*), and another engineer, and I, went out to Point Loma[26] for lunch at the Fleet home—in a beautiful location overlooking the harbor. We went back to the factory in the afternoon and discussed aircraft designs, production, research, etc.

Sunday, May 7

I stopped at Airtech for a few minutes to see Doug Kelly and then went on to the National Guard hangar. T. C. Ryan was there, and I went with him to his factory, where trainers are being built. Spent half an hour there, then returned to my plane and took off at 12:02 Pacific time. Tried out stalls and glides with flaps and landing gear down on way back to March. Landed at March at 12:35. Took an Army car to Los Angeles, to "Dutch" Kindelberger's[27] home.

23. One of the first men to fly mail by air, in 1918. In 1923 he organized the Consolidated Aircraft Corp., of which he was president from 1923 to 1941.

24. T. Claude Ryan began building airplanes in 1923; he was for a time president and general manager of Ryan Airlines Co. (San Diego). Later, he became president of Ryan Aeronautical Co.

25. Chief engineer and designer for the Ryan Airlines Co.

26. Where Lindbergh had done his first soaring gliding along the coast, in 1929.

27. J. H. Kindelberger, aeronautical engineer, and president of North American Aviation Co., 1935–48.

Monday, May 8

Drove with Kindelberger to the North American factory. We went through the factory together and discussed plans for future designs, production, and development. It is a very efficient establishment—in many ways the most efficient I have yet seen. They are now producing airplanes for England and France in addition to those for the United States.

We had lunch in Kindelberger's office. Then I went through the El Segundo Douglas factory, which is just a few yards away. From there I took the Army car and driver assigned to me to the Douglas factory at Santa Monica. After a fifteen-minute talk with Douglas[28] and some of his officers, we went through the factory and the experimental department. From the Douglas factory I flew to Mines Field in the DC-5 (as passenger). The DC-5 is the latest Douglas attempt at a bimotored passenger transport—high wing and tricycle gear.

At Mines Field I borrowed a single-engine plane from the Douglas Company and flew to the Vultee factory, where I spent an hour with Dick Miller, going through the factory and talking over plans. Then flew back to Mines and took Army car to Douglas home for dinner and night. Douglas had invited a dozen or so of his officers and military "attachés" for dinner. Discussion again about various phases of aviation. I spent half an hour talking to Douglas alone after they left.

Tuesday, May 9

Left in Army car at 9:00 for the Lockheed factory at Burbank. Arrived at 10:00 and spent the morning talking to Robert Gross[29] and [Richard] von Hake (chief engineer, and one of the engineers who worked on the design of our Lockheed Sirius—*Tingmissartoq*). We went through the factory, which is extremely crowded because of the British purchases. They say they are now employing 6,500 men and expect to take on another 1,000 during the next month. Lunch in Gross's office; then to Pasadena, to the California Institute of Technology, where I spent an

28. Donald Wills Douglas, aircraft manufacturer, and president of the Douglas Aircraft Co., which built the great Douglas transports of the DC class. Recipient of the Collier and Guggenheim awards for his contributions to aviation.

29. President and chairman of the board of Lockheed Aircraft Corp., Burbank, Calif.

hour talking to Drs. Robert and Clark Millikan[30] at the Guggenheim College of Aeronautics. I had a very instructive and interesting conference, and later went to see the mirror being ground for the 200-inch telescope.

Left Cal Tech for March Field in time to arrive for supper with General and Mrs. Fickel.[31] Dismissed the driver, whose expenses I have been paying myself, since there is no arrangement for the Army to do so. (I am paying everything but plane expenses myself, now, and am drawing no pay, since my active duty lasted for only two weeks. It is apparently difficult for General Arnold to arrange for an extension, so I agreed to continue working without pay. That will leave me a little freer anyway, and there will be a few advantages. I would rather have it that way as long as my income is sufficient from other sources.)

During the evening General Fickel and I talked about the old days of aviation. He started flying about 1910 and was the first to shoot a gun from an airplane, he says, making the test for the Army with a Springfield rifle while Glenn Curtiss[32] flew the plane.

Wednesday, May 10

Breakfast with General and Mrs. Fickel; then went to the operations building with General Fickel and cleared for Tucson. The ceiling was about 500 feet and the fog layer several thousand feet thick. They did not want to clear me because of the proximity of the mountains, but I managed to talk them out of that. Took off at 8:13 Pacific time and followed the radio beam west until I broke through the clouds at about 3,500 feet. Reported back to March Field and took up course for Tucson. The clouds extended only as far as the mountains, and after that I had clear weather and tail winds. I love to fly over the southwestern deserts in the early morning. The faded and changing shades of color, the weird rock formations, and the vastness and loneliness of it all give me an understanding of why religion owes so much to the desert.

Landed at Tucson at 10:05 Pacific time. I had been flying at 10,000

30. Dr. Clark Millikan was a professor of aeronautics (Guggenheim College of Aeronautics), California Institute of Technology in Pasadena, and the son of Dr. Robert Millikan, physicist, director of the Norman Bridge Laboratory of Physics, and chairman of the executive council of C.I.T. Dr. Robert Millikan was awarded the Nobel Prize for physics in 1923.

31. General Jacob E. Fickel, who in 1940 became Assistant Chief of the Air Corps.

32. Pioneer American aviator, inventor, and builder of aircraft, including the first U.S. Army dirigible in 1905.

feet and above. Coming down to land was like approaching the open door of a huge furnace, being surrounded by wave after wave of constantly increasing heat. The reservicing was done quickly, and I took off again at 10:42 Pacific time. I climbed immediately to 11,000 feet for coolness. Clear weather to El Paso, where I landed at 11:56.

I took off again at 1:13 for Roswell, New Mexico, to see Dr. Goddard.[33] A dust storm was reported over Tucumcari, moving in the direction of Roswell and due there about 6:30. I planned on talking to Goddard for half an hour and then taking off for Midland before the storm arrived.

As soon as I landed, I called Dr. Goddard. He was at the field within fifteen minutes, and it soon became apparent that there were too many things to talk over to cover in half an hour. He asked me to stay overnight. I phoned Albuquerque for a weather forecast, as it was essential for me to leave in the morning in order to be in Washington for the board meeting on the twelfth. The forecast indicated that the dust storm would not last overnight; so we put the plane in the hangar, and I drove with Dr. and Mrs. Goddard to their home—the same place where Anne and I stayed when we were last here together.

We spent the rest of the afternoon discussing rocket plans and developments—stabilization pumps, tanks, liquid oxygen, and nitrogen, etc. Dr. and Mrs. Goddard and I went for about a half hour's walk along the road before supper. Mrs. Goddard's mother is visiting her—a fine old Scandinavian lady. We all had supper together. After supper Dr. Goddard showed me the latest motion pictures of his work and flights. We spent the rest of the evening going over various papers, reports, and programs. Had planned on taking off at daybreak, but postponed it to 9:00. Goddard has done good work and had a very successful year.

Thursday, May 11

Took off at 8:57 Mountain time and set a direct course for Midland. Flew over an uninhabited country broken now and then by a dirt road and, during the latter portion of the flight, by a railroad. Civilization has spread greatly in the Southwest since I made the survey flights for the central transcontinental air route (Transcontinental Air Transport) in 1928 and '29. Somehow I feel every road and oil well is an imposition,

33. Dr. Goddard had established his laboratory at Roswell, with his launching tower on the outlying Mescalero Ranch.

an intruder on the solitude which was once mine as I flew over it. The great western plains and deserts are giving way rapidly to the marks of men. And looking down on them from the air, those marks seem like a disease—a rash spreading slowly over the earth's surface. I wonder if there will someday be a reaction sweeping it away again, if the forests will grow again like a new coat of fur in fall. Or will man and earth eventually adjust to one another, supplementing each other, the beauty and character of each gaining from the other? The dust storms and wasted farms I often fly over make me think the former will take place, while some of the older sections of Europe give me hope that civilization and nature are not irreconcilable and that time will eventually overcome the excesses of industrialization.

Landed at Midland at 9:49 Mountain time, refueled and took off (10:17) en route to Barksdale. Landed at Charlotte, North Carolina, at 17:17 Mountain time and decided to remain for night. Neither radio nor brakes working well. Radio frequency too high, and I get a shock from the transmitter button.

Friday, May 12

Up at 4:00. Cleared airport formalities, and took off at 5:18 E.S.T. The sun rose soon after I left the field—coming up through a layer of scattered clouds. Landed at Bolling at 6:57 E.S.T. Put plane in hangar and took taxi to the Land apartment, where Jerry and I had breakfast together. Phoned Anne in Englewood and found that she expected to arrive on the afternoon train.

To Munitions Building in time for the board meeting (for the revision of the Air Corps five-year program). Board consists of General Kilner,[34] Lieutenant Colonel Spaatz,[35] Lieutenant Colonel Naiden,[36] Major [Alfred J.] Lyon, and myself.[37] The discussion centered around the appro-

---

34. General Walter Glenn Kilner, a member of NACA, had served in World War I with the A.E.F. as organizer and commander of the U.S. Aviation Center at Issoudun, in charge of training flying personnel for the front.

35. Lieutenant Colonel Carl Spaatz, a pioneer Army pilot, became Chief of Air Staff in 1941.

36. Lieutenant Colonel Earl L. Naiden became a brigadier general in 1942.

37. The Kilner Board was appointed by General H. H. Arnold. On June 28, 1939, it submitted a comprehensive outline of proposed military characteristics for aircraft weapons and equipment that could be procured by 1944 and sketched an administrative plan for a major research and development program to be undertaken in the interval.

priations available for research and development, the branches which were in most need of improvement, the necessity for a larger yearly appropriation for research and development, etc.

After the meeting I took a taxi to the Land apartment for my suitcase, and was met by a car which took me to the Lee home outside of Washington. (Anne's old friend Thelma married Major [Brook] Lee.) Anne and I went for a walk along the country roads before dinner. Rest of time spent in conversation with the Lees.

Saturday, May 13

Borrowed a car from the Lees and drove to the Munitions Building for an 11:00 meeting of the board. Arrived about an hour early in order to help with preparation of the report (preliminary). Lunch with General Kilner at the Army & Navy Club. After lunch we drove to Walter Reed to see Truman Smith, and the three of us talked for an hour about conditions in Germany and the possibility of war in Europe. Afterward, I returned to the Lees' home for supper and the night.

Anne and I made plans for the summer. We will look for a house near Washington, preferably on the water, but what we are told about the summer heat and climate makes me doubt the advisability of bringing Jon and Land here for July and August—and also Anne, for I doubt she would be able to do much writing.

Tuesday, May 16

Spent first part of morning in room with Anne, talking over plans. We would like to have gone walking while we talked, but the recent publicity we have had makes that impossible. People would recognize us, ask for autographs, follow us, and run in front of us to take photographs. Often when someone in an automobile recognizes us they put on the brakes and block whatever traffic is behind them while they stare at us. It is not pleasant and often makes us wish for the privacy of France and England. We decided that in view of the uncertainty of the summer, the hot climate of Washington, the difficulty of finding a house, arranging for servants, guards, etc., and other considerations, we would take a bedroom and parlor temporarily and put off finding a more permanent home until later. It seems that we have been looking for and organizing new homes constantly during the last year. We left Long Barn in June to go to Illiec. Then we looked for a house in Berlin, took an apartment in Paris, took the children to Englewood, are now looking for a house in the vicinity of Washington, and hope to spend part of the summer in Maine.

I left the hotel for the Munitions Building at 11:00, and Anne took the early-afternoon train to New York.

Lunch at 1:00 with Harry Byrd [38] in his office in the Capitol. We discussed the general situation in America and Europe. Neither of us is optimistic about the trends in this country. Met Dr. Lewis in the NACA offices at 3:00 and talked to him about co-ordinating the research facilities in the United States. He leaves for England tomorrow. Back to the Munitions Building from the NACA offices. Conference with General Arnold. The congressional Appropriations Committee wants me to appear at 2:00 tomorrow.[39] Returned to the Hay-Adams with a suitcase filled with several thousand unopened letters which had been addressed to me at the Munitions Building.

Wednesday, May 17

Wrote and studied reports until 10:00, when Miss Gawne called to say she had been to see the Wardman Park apartment. I told her to see one at the Anchorage suggested by Betty Land. Later, we drove around the outside of both places. The Wardman Park was large but close to Rock Creek Park. The Anchorage was small and closer to the Munitions Building. I decided to take the Anchorage apartment and arranged with the manager to move in immediately. There are two rooms—bedroom and parlor—and a rather old-fashioned bathroom. They are small but plenty large enough considering the small amount of time I will be in Washington. Spent the rest of the morning moving my things over from the Hay-Adams and arranging them in drawers and shelves.

Taxi to Munitions Building after lunch to meet General Arnold at 1:40. We took an Army car to the Capitol, where I testified before the congressional Appropriations Committee for about an hour (Honorable J. B. Snyder,[40] chairman). I thought I felt a slight air of antagonism as I entered the room and shook hands with the committee members.

38. Democratic Senator from Virginia.
39. To testify about Air Force requirements for an expansion program.
40. J. Buell Snyder, Democratic Representative from Pennsylvania.

But I answered their questions honestly, frankly, and to the best of my ability, and I believe they all soon realized this fact. If there was any antagonism at the beginning, I think it was gone by the time I left. The major point I tried to make was that the strength of our Air Corps could be increased at less cost by devoting more money to research, that the total strength would be greater with fewer planes of higher quality.

Friday, May 19

Took off Bolling 11:25 E.S.T. Clear skies but very hazy over Newark–New York area. Circled Next Day Hill fifty-five minutes after taking off from Bolling. Landed Stewart Field 12:40 E.S.T. A driver was waiting for me at the hangar with my Franklin, and I took him back to Englewood with me. Went for a swim with Anne and Jon. Jon can't get enough of the pool and hates to go out even when he is cold. Glanced through the latest mail and telegrams. There is a drawer filled with unopened letters —thousands of them. Anne has gone through most of them and selected those that looked important from the writing or had a return address on the envelope that she knew. As soon as our name is carried on the front pages of the newspapers, mail begins to pour in. It is impossible to give each item attention and a letter answered usually brings two more. Most of the mail is from people who really have no reason to write.

Saturday, May 20

Pan American Clipper took off from North Beach with first air mail for Europe.

Phoned Carrel and then drove to the Institute. Spent a half hour in conference with Carrel, then made the rounds of the rooms and personnel— Dr. [Albert H.] Ebeling, Dr. Parker,[41] Dr. [Lillian E.] Baker, Miss McFaul,[42] the nurses, and everyone else. Conference with Parker after lunch about the virus-circulating flask. We decided it was time to publish the article I wrote about it last year, and that the results Parker had obtained warranted publication.

41. Dr. Raymond C. Parker, member of Dr. Carrel's staff, and author of *Methods of Tissue Culture,* one of the standard books in its field.

42. Irene McFaul (later a doctor), chief nurse in Dr. Carrel's Department of Experimental Surgery.

Tuesday, May 23

Drove to New York for lunch with Juan Trippe at the Cloud Club. There has been a reorganization in Pan American and "Sonny" Whitney[43] is now apparently in control. He has Juan Trippe's office, and Juan has moved to the other corner of the building. I do not yet fully understand all of the details and will not attempt to set down the rumors on these pages. Juan continues as president, but with much less influence. In many ways I am sorry to see this, for I like Juan and have always felt he had great ability. Spent most of the afternoon in the Pan American offices, meeting old acquaintances and talking over company affairs.

Wednesday, May 24

Drove the Franklin to Brooklyn for a 12:15 conference and lunch at the Sperry-Gyroscope factory. Made a tour of the factory after lunch. This is a field in which we still definitely lead all other countries.

Thursday, May 25

Guy Vaughan stopped for me about 9:15. We drove to the Curtiss-Wright Propeller Company, inspected the factory, and then drove to Wright Aero. Conference with the engineers and officers regarding new engine developments. Lunch with officers of company. Tour of factory with Vaughan and others. Back to Next Day Hill in late afternoon. Went for quick swim. Put on uniform and drove Franklin to Stewart Field. Left car in hangar and took off in P-36 at 7:13 Daylight and landed at Rentschler Field, Hartford, at 7:43 Daylight. Don Brown[44] and other Pratt Whitney officers were waiting for me, and we drove to Brown's home for supper with a number of the company's officers and engineers. Night at the Brown home.

43. Cornelius Vanderbilt Whitney, chairman of the board of Pan American Airways.

44. Donald L. Brown, president of United Aircraft Corp. from its organization until January, 1940, and one of the founders of Pratt & Whitney Aircraft Corp.

Friday, May 26

Breakfast at 8:15 with Brown and Deac Lyman,[45] who is now in charge of public relations for United Aircraft. Then drove with Meade[46] to their research building in the country. Spent the rest of the morning there in conference with Meade, [Igor] Sikorsky, Caldwell,[47] Hunsaker,[48] and others. Lunch at Meade's home, then to Pratt Whitney factory, where I spent half an hour in conference with Gordon Rentschler.[49] Made a tour of the engine and propeller factories, and then took off for Stewart Field at 4:28 Daylight. Climbed up through a high overcast sky en route and spent ten minutes above the clouds in sham combat, dives, and acrobatics. Landed at Stewart Field at 5:18 Daylight. Turned plane over to mechanics and drove to Next Day Hill in time for a swim and late supper.

Tuesday, May 30

Drove to Long Island with Anne to look at a house on Lloyd Neck we may take for the summer. We passed the World's Fair grounds on the way. The house (on the Colgate property) is in an exceptionally good location, nicely furnished, and about the right size. I think we will take it for the summer. It is on a hill overlooking Long Island Sound and neither too accessible nor too isolated.

45. Lauren D. Lyman, friend of Lindbergh. As a New York *Times* reporter he covered the 1927 New York–to–Paris flight. In 1938 he joined United Aircraft Corp., and became a vice president in 1946.

46. Dr. George J. Meade, aeronautical engineer. A founder and vice president of Pratt & Whitney Aircraft Co. (1925–30); subsequently with United Aircraft as vice president and member of the executive committee. Vice chairman of NACA.

47. Frank W. Caldwell, American aeronautical engineer and designer of propellers. He designed aircraft propellers used by the U.S. Army in World War I and was a pioneer in non-wood propeller development. Director of research for United Aircraft Corp. from 1940 to 1954.

48. Jerome C. Hunsaker, aeronautical engineer and designer of the NC4, the first airplane to cross the Atlantic (1919). He was in charge of Navy aircraft design from 1916 to 1923, including design of the airship *Shenandoah*. From 1933 to 1951 he was head of the Departments of Mechanical and Aeronautical Engineering at Massachusetts Institute of Technology.

49. New York banker and machinery manufacturer; brother of Frederick Rentschler, chairman of the board of United Aircraft Corp.

Thursday, June 1

Drove to Guggenheim College of Aeronautics at New York University in time to make a 10:00 appointment with Professor Klemin.[50] We discussed the problems connected with the co-ordination of aeronautical research and what the relationship should be between the various colleges and NACA. After the meeting I drove downtown for lunch with Harry Guggenheim. Met him at his office at 120 Broadway, and we lunched at the Bankers Club, higher up in the same building. We talked about the co-ordination to be brought about between research organizations, with special reference to the various colleges of aeronautics. We also spoke in detail of Goddard's project and his plans and results. Harry was enthusiastic about the last year's progress.

Went to see Jean Monnet at his New York office at 3:30. We discussed the French purchases of American aircraft and the general European situation.

Friday, June 2

Signed lease (or rather had Miss Gawne sign it, since we have used her name in leasing the property) for the Long Island house. We take it to November 1 with a verbal option for renewal ($2,000 to November 1). Spent a short time on mail, then left for a lunch appointment with Harry Davison.[51] Stopped at the American Geographic Society on the way to leave our sextant (Bausch & Lomb) and the propeller we used on our flight to the Orient in 1931. They are having a small exhibition and asked for something from our flights. Lunch with Harry Davison at 23 Wall Street[52] at 1:00. Mr. Morgan[53] was there. Also several other members of the firm. We discussed political conditions in Europe and America.

50. Alexander Klemin, aeronautical engineer. Professor at Daniel Guggenheim School of Aeronautics, New York University.

51. Family friend, banker, and J. P. Morgan & Co. partner, who had served with the U.S. Naval Air Force in World War I.

52. The bank and offices of J. P. Morgan & Co.

53. John Pierpont Morgan, Jr., banker and president of J. P. Morgan & Co.

Saturday, June 3

Drove to the Rockefeller Institute after breakfast and set up the circulating-virus-flask apparatus for an assembly photograph. Lunch with Carrel, Ebeling, and Wyckoff [54] at the Century Club. We discussed the possibility of organizing a small institute for virus and other research, to be headed (actively) by Wyckoff. Considered the possibility of using High Fields[55] for this purpose. Discussed methods of obtaining the necessary funds. Estimated $50,000 per year was minimum needed, and $100,000 was desirable. Believe the project is practicable and feasible.

Monday, June 5

Up at 6:00. Phoned Stewart Field and told them to have the plane ready. Drove there in Franklin, arriving about 9:30. Left car in hangar and took off in P-36 at 9:50. Had just pulled up the wheels and was turning toward the course to Washington when the emergency door on the cockpit hatch blew open. Someone had apparently tripped the emergency release in getting in and out of the cockpit. I could not get the door back into position so landed again. It took only a minute or two to fix on the ground. Took off again at 10:10. Clear skies to Washington; could see cities from thirty to forty miles ahead. Landed Bolling at 11:30. Army car took me to our apartment.

Taxi to Munitions Building for 1:00 meeting of board. Discussed bomber specifications and procurement methods until 5:00. Supper alone in apartment. After long discussions I prefer to spend the evening alone or with Anne and the children. That gives my mind a chance to settle down and become untangled from the day's mass of detail.

Tuesday, June 6

Arrived at the Munitions Building at 9:00. Spent the morning with officers from Wright Field going over pursuit and bomber specifications.

54. Dr. Ralph W. Wyckoff, head of the Department of Physics, Rockefeller Institute, 1927–37, and specialist in crystal physics, biophysics, and virus diseases.

55. The Lindbergh home (1931–32) and property in the Sourland Mountains near Hopewell, N.J.

Invited Guy Vaughan for lunch in our apartment. He is one of the ablest men in the industry, absolutely honest, and I always find time spent with him to be extremely enjoyable and interesting. Back to the Munitions Building for the afternoon meeting of the board at 1:00. We listened to the reports of various Wright Field officers on planes and engines. The meeting ended at 4:30.

Went to a picture theater after supper. By wearing glasses without lenses and using care, I can usually get into a theater without being recognized. It is much more difficult when Anne and I go together.

Wednesday, June 7

Arrived Munitions Building at 9:00 for board meeting. Spent the morning discussing medium-bomber specifications with Colonel Spaatz, Colonel Naiden, and Major Lyon. General Arnold asked me to have lunch with Dr. Bush and himself in order to discuss the problems of co-ordinating research facilities.

Roy Alexander[56] called just before we left for lunch. Said he had written an article about me and that it would be out in the next issue of *Time*. I told him I would rather have him write the article than anyone else I knew but that frankly all articles, good or bad, simply added to our difficulties and that we wanted to avoid them wherever it was possible to do so. I like Roy Alexander, and I understand—at least partially—his ideas. He is definitely a friend, and I do not want to lose him, but how I wish none of my friends were reporters for newspapers and magazines.

General Arnold, Bush, and I left for lunch about 12:15. We spent the entire time discussing NACA, its future, and its shortcomings. We talked also about the best method of co-ordinating Langley Field and such colleges of aeronautics as M.I.T. and C.I.T. Bush asked me if I would consider taking the chairmanship or vice-chairmanship of NACA. I told him that much as I appreciated the importance of the NACA, I did not feel I could accept such a position. I told him my greatest interests lay in other fields, and that after my present work with the Army was finished, I did not wish to devote my entire attention to aviation. I told him I felt I could live more happily and contribute more in other ways.

56. Friend of Lindbergh, whom he first met when Alexander was a reporter for the St. Louis *Post-Dispatch* and Lindbergh was an air-mail pilot on the St. Louis–Chicago route. Alexander later became managing editor of *Time* Magazine, 1949–1960.

We all drove back to the Munitions Building after lunch. Bush and I spent about ten minutes discussing possible names for the chairmanship of NACA. Dr. Ames,[57] who is still chairman in name, is not well enough to ever be active again. Bush, who is now acting chairman, has too much to do as president of the Carnegie Institution. There does not seem to be anyone else on the committee who could take the position, who would be suitable. It is an extremely difficult position to fill properly. We also discussed the possibility of creating a position of "Co-ordinator of Research" (my suggestion). This office would report directly to the main NACA committee and be completely independent of Langley Field.

Arnold asked me to come to see him as soon as Bush left. As soon as I sat down, he said, "Do you mind if I ask you a personal question?" I told him to go ahead. "Say," he said, "what are you shooting at? Have you set a goal for yourself, or do you just take life as it comes?" I replied that I was not shooting at anything and that life was sufficiently complex in these modern times without trying to foresee its future too clearly. I told him I did not want political office or any special reward for what I did, and that while I often worked toward an objective it was usually one which was not so very far in the future. I said I liked to feel my way along as I lived and let life have a hand in guiding its own direction. Arnold told me he had always followed somewhat the same policy and that he, too, had never set a definite objective as his life's work (although it seems to me that an Army career is a pretty definite objective).

Thursday, June 8

Sat on the board all morning. We are still on medium bombers. The cavalry from Fort Snelling rode by on their way to meet the King and Queen of England. Later in the morning, formations of bombers and pursuit planes flew over.

Friday, June 9

Lunch at Army & Navy Club with General Arnold and Dr. Bush. Discussed NACA and methods for improvement. We agree that NACA prestige has fallen. Probably because the committee has been without an active head since Dr. Ames has been ill. I agreed to take the chairman-

57. Dr. Joseph S. Ames, physicist, and chairman of NACA, 1927–39.

ship of a committee to be composed of General Arnold, Admiral Towers,[58] and someone from CAA, to study methods of reorganization for NACA and ways of co-ordinating Langley with other research organizations such as C.I.T. and M.I.T.

Colonel Faymonville came for supper (embassy, Moscow, when we were there last fall). We discussed Russia and the various incidents which occurred after Anne and I departed. I like Faymonville. He is idealistic and not any too practical—a good combination for the military attaché to Russia.

Saturday, June 10

Decided to fly to San Francisco and Seattle between now and the next board meeting in order to see the Boeing factory and the facilities at Washington University and around the San Francisco area.

Spent first part of the morning dictating and on phone calls to National Geographic Society in regard to the possibility of their publishing an article on Dr. Goddard's rocket experiments.

Packed and put on uniform and took taxi to Bolling Field. Started to make out maps for trip west. Phone call from General Arnold, saying that my testimony before the House Appropriations Committee was being misquoted and used against him. He asked me to return to Washington on Monday to help counteract the effects. Consequently must postpone trip west.

Took off in P-36A at 2:34 E.S.T. Encountered thunderstorms en route. Could have gone under and around them but decided to climb up through. Reached the top and sunshine at 17,000 feet, using oxygen after about 12,000. I find that I can fly comfortably at over 20,000 feet without oxygen, but I think more clearly and am more alert when I use it. Did a few rolls and after flying for a few minutes at about 20,000 feet I dove down through cloud layers and found myself over a hilly country with numerous lakes. Had not been watching my navigation and had the radio turned off. Soon discovered that I was in New York State east of the Hudson. Reset course and landed at Stewart Field at 4:25 E.S.T. The field was full of planes which had come for the graduation exercises at West Point.

Spent fifteen minutes talking with the local Air Corps officer about

58. Admiral John Henry Towers, pioneer in naval aviation; chief of the Bureau of Aeronautics.

possible improvement to the field—lengthening runways, etc., then drove to Englewood in time to have supper with Anne and Dwight.[59] A telegram had come from Arnold, asking me to be in Washington in time for a 9:00 A.M. appointment with Congressman Houston[60] at his office in the new House Office Building. Jon (from bed) says he has a surprise for me tomorrow. Anne tells me he has discovered that he can swim by himself.

Sunday, June 11

The two boxes containing the paintings we bought in France have arrived, and Anne and I unpacked them after breakfast. We put them in a semicircle in the big room, leaning them against the various chairs and tables. We went swimming before lunch, and Jon demonstrated that he could swim alone. Before we went out, he had made half the width of the pool nonstop (about fifteen or twenty feet). He has learned to swim as Land learned to walk—all of a sudden. I even persuaded him to fall into the pool in a sort of flat dive. "I didn't know I would come back up," he said on reaching the surface.

I packed my bag and then we drove to Stewart Field (Anne, Con, Aubrey, and I). I showed them the plane and cockpit and then took off for Washington in my P-36A. There were storms to the west, and the sunset colored the layers of clouds in shades of translucent pink and red, contrasted to the deadly black of the thicker areas of the storm. I wished Anne could be with me in the cockpit to see the beauty of that sky. Climbed to 20,000 feet, taking oxygen. Tried out various maneuvers.

Monday, June 12

Phoned Munitions Building at 8:00. General Arnold answered the phone. (He starts work at 8:00.) I took a taxi to Munitions and talked with him for fifteen minutes. It seems there has been the usual misquotation of my testimony before the congressional Appropriations Commit-

59. Dwight W. Morrow, Jr., brother of Anne Morrow Lindbergh. A graduate of Amherst, with a Ph.D. in history from Harvard, he taught history at Lincoln University, where he was a trustee, at Temple University, and at the Monterey Institute of Foreign Studies.

60. John M. Houston, Democratic Representative from Kansas.

tee. Arnold was anxious that I see Congressman Houston, who is friendly and who will stand with the Air Corps in any controversy. This does not surprise me at all. The unusual thing would be if it had not happened. One must first be illusioned before he can be disillusioned about congressional committees. Arrived at Houston's office at 9:00. Found the president and one of the officers of Steerman Aircraft Corporation (division of Boeing) there. Spent about an hour in conference, during which time Houston called in one of the Republican Representatives who is also on the Appropriations Committee.

Walked to the National Geographic Society for a 2:00 meeting with Dr. Grosvenor.[61] I talked to him about the possibility of the *Geographic* carrying an article on Dr. Goddard's work. He liked the idea and agreed to send a photographer to Roswell and someone to write the article if that is desired.

Returned to apartment and read and wrote until dinnertime. Then took taxi to General Arnold's home for dinner with him, Mrs. Arnold, and Colonel Spaatz. During the meal Arnold and Spaatz told me of some early Pan American Airways history with which I had not been previously acquainted.

Arnold said that in about 1925 he heard through Army Intelligence that von Bauer[62] of SCADTA (the German airline operating in Colombia) was planning on extending his airline to Panama and eventually to Miami. Arnold went to Postmaster General New[63] and asked him what steps would be necessary in order to have von Bauer refused permission to operate over the Panama Canal and into the United States. New replied that plans for the organization of an American airline must be completed. Then Arnold, together with Spaatz and Jouett,[64] worked out in detail the organization of an airline from the United States to Panama

61. Dr. Gilbert H. Grosvenor, director of the National Geographic Society and editor in chief of the *National Geographic* Magazine.

62. Dr. Peter Paul von Bauer, European representative in Colombia of SCADTA (Sociedad Colombo-Alemana de Transportes Aereos) in 1920; in 1923 he became vice president.

63. Harry S. New, Postmaster General, 1923–29. He gave great stimulus to commercial aviation by awarding mail contracts to private companies.

64. John Hamilton Jouett. In World War I he commanded balloon units in France. He was chief of Air Corps personnel from 1926 to 1928 and from 1932 to 1935 aviation adviser to the Republic of China, where he organized the Chinese Air Force aviation school. In 1936 he returned to the private aviation industry in the U.S.

and named it Pan American Airways. They very nearly left the Army in order to carry out the organization, but Arnold decided against doing so.

Saturday, June 17

Drove [from Englewood] to Engineers Club [in New York] for dinner with Dr. Wyckoff, Dr. Ebeling, and Mr. [Edward E.] Moore (a friend of Dr. Carrel's). Discussed the project of an institute to be organized around Carrel and Wyckoff. Considered the possibility of using the High Fields property. We decided to meet tomorrow morning and drive down to High Fields. (I have not been there for several years—1935 or before.)

Sunday, June 18

Met Wyckoff at Washington Bridge. We drove to Nineteenth Street, under the elevated, where me met Moore, [Jim] Newton, and Ebeling. Drove to New Jersey through the Holland Tunnel and left my car at a parking place in the first town we passed through. Went on to High Fields in Moore's car. The place has changed considerably since I last was there. The bushes have jumped upward, and there is a feeling of much heavier foliage. The house needs a new coat of whitewash, and the shutters should be painted, but everything is in good condition. I went to the back door and was met by the watchman. We went through the house from basement to attic, through the pump house and out around the grounds. We walked down to the little brook to the north.

Started back after about an hour, via Princeton and the grounds of the Rockefeller Institute. We drove through the latter without stopping—to get an idea of the layout and buildings. Stopped for a lunch of sandwiches on our way back to New York. Wyckoff was anxious for us to see his laboratory at Pearl River, New York, in order to get an idea of buildings, equipment, etc. Consequently, I decided to postpone flying to Washington until tomorrow morning. I picked up the De Soto on the way back. Newton went with me, and we followed Moore's car to Pearl River. Spent about an hour in Wyckoff's laboratory. It is simple and well equipped and shows signs of competent management. After that, I took Newton to the Nyack ferry and then drove back to Englewood for an early supper.

Tuesday, June 20

I left at 11:00 in the De Soto for Mitchel Field. Miss Gawne went with me to drive the car back. She will go to Lloyd Neck, after dropping me at Mitchel, to make the first contact with the local chief of police and to tell him of our plans to live there for the summer. It is always important for us to have a good relationship with the police.

Obtained an "instrument clearance," as the ceiling at Mitchel was only 200 or 300 feet. Washington was reported clear, however. Started the engine and then found that the radio was again out of order. Went to the Post Exchange for lunch while it was being repaired.

Took off [P-36] at 12:50 E.S.T. and climbed up through the overcast. Called Washington radio soon after passing Baltimore and requested permission to come down. Received authority to glide to 3,000 feet, but was instructed to hold that altitude if I was not clear of the clouds when I reached it. A Douglas was coming in from 2,000 feet. Began descent and came out of the clouds at 4,000. The Douglas was below me and half a mile to one side. Landed Bolling at 2:15.

Friday, June 23

Arrived Munitions Building at 9:30. Short conference with General Arnold and General Brett. We walked through the corridors to the Navy Building, to the NACA offices. All members present except Orville Wright and Dr. Ames. Dr. Lewis was just back from Europe, and he told us of his trips and impressions in England, Germany, and France. Says the English production is probably about 700 planes per month and that they expect to be producing 1,000 per month in the near future. The French production, he says, is now about 300 per month. The Italian production is reported at about 120 per month. Lewis says the Germans seem to feel they have a sufficient quantity of planes on hand and are now just "coasting" along with their production, not using their full facilities.

After Lewis's report and the routine details of the meeting were finished, the Sunnyvale project[65] was brought up. I stated that the aviation industry was not behind NACA in regard to the Sunnyvale project and that NACA seemed to have lost generally in prestige recently. I said it was essential to regain the confidence of the industry and of the col-

65. Relating to the aeronautical research laboratories at Sunnyvale, Calif.

leges of aeronautics. This brought about considerable discussion. Arnold proposed the formation of a committee to study the best method of co-ordinating American research facilities, including NACA and the various colleges of aeronautics.

"Moved: That the chair appoint a committee to examine the aeronautical research facilities now available in the country and their best interrelationship and to prepare a comprehensive plan for the future extension of such facilities, with special attention to facilities of the NACA and the universities, including the training of the necessary research personnel." The motion was passed, and I was appointed chairman of a committee consisting of General Arnold, Admiral Towers, and Mr. Hinckley.[66] Another motion was proposed by Arnold authorizing the chairman (Bush) to appoint a committee to select a co-ordinator of research for the NACA.

After the meeting broke up, I had lunch with Towers and Jerry Hunsaker at the Army & Navy Club. We discussed the steps to be taken in a sort of NACA reorganization and research co-ordination. After lunch Hunsaker and I went to my apartment and continued the discussion for another hour. After that I took a taxi to the Munitions Building and talked to General Arnold and later to General Brett about the matter. Then went to the NACA offices for a conference with Lewis and Victory. Back to apartment in time for a walk before supper. It is too hot here to do much walking. Evening reading [Antoine de Saint-Exupéry's] *Wind, Sand and Stars.*

Saturday, June 24

Breakfast; packed; taxi to Bolling Field. Clear weather to New York. Took off at 9:42 E.S.T. and began climbing at 140 m.p.h. and 25 inches manifold pressure. Began taking oxygen at 12,000 feet and reached 32,000 feet in southern New Jersey. This seemed to be the absolute ceiling of my plane (P-36A). I continued at this altitude for about quarter of an hour. All the southern part of the state was visible, even though there was a light haze. I took up the course for Mitchel Field, via Sandy Hook, and landed at 10:57 E.S.T. Took an Army car to Lloyd Neck in time for lunch with Anne, Jon, and Land, and a swim in the sound in the afternoon. Jon is becoming quite at home in the water and has no trouble

66. Robert M. Hinckley, chairman of CAA, 1939–40. In 1940 he became Assistant Secretary of Commerce.

in covering forty or fifty feet in a dog-paddling fashion. Land is still very doubtful about getting wet.

The place is quite beautiful, with its three great trees screening the house from the water. It is not Illiec, or even Maine, but it has a charm of its own, which is quite different from either. Anne has handled the moving extremely well, and Christine [Gawne] has been a great help. It will be a fine place for the summer—half an hour from Mitchel Field, a beach for the children (and for us). Best of all, I think Anne will be happy and be able to write here.

Dr. Carrel called in the afternoon and asked if I could meet him in New York before I returned to Washington. He was with Jim Newton, so I suggested we all have dinner at the Japanese restaurant on Fifty-eighth Street. There were five of us in all for dinner: Carrel, Newton, Wyckoff, Moore, and myself. We spent most of the evening discussing plans for the institute. Everyone has agreed that it should be built at High Fields and that the advantages of space and immediate availability more than outweigh the disadvantage of distance from New York. The next problem is financing the enterprise. Newton feels he can arrange this and has agreed to devote the next week to starting. We now have the men and the property. I hope the financing will not prove too difficult.

Sunday, June 25

Drove to Englewood in the afternoon to get storage bundles of Anne's old letters and other articles. Called Anne from Next Day Hill. She says the newspapers have been calling up the estate and the neighboring houses. She says a boat, apparently containing reporters, has been anchored offshore. The estate foreman has suggested posting a guard on the gate. Again, our greatest problem—the press. But someday they will need friends and find them lacking. Took a full carload back to Lloyd Neck, arriving in time for a late supper with Anne outside on the porch. The sun was just setting over the water, and the trees were taking on the silhouettes of evening.

Tuesday, June 27

Spent the first part of the morning telephoning and dictating, then packed, put on uniform, and drove to Mitchel Field. Took off at 12:35 E.S.T. Landed Bolling at 1:55. Army car to Munitions Building. Major

Lyon had just arrived from Dayton, and he, Colonel Naiden, Colonel Spaatz, and I spent the rest of the afternoon on our board report, which is now in about its third draft.

Wednesday, June 28

Taxi to Munitions Building for 9:00 board meeting, which lasted all morning. Lunch with General Arnold, Admiral Towers, and Mr. Hinckley. We discussed the research facilities in this country and the best methods for assisting and co-ordinating them. We also discussed the NACA Sunnyvale project at length. I volunteered to see a number of the heads of the colleges of aeronautics to get their ideas about how their facilities can be put to the best use and what relationship should exist between them and NACA.

Thursday, June 29

Took taxi to Munitions Building after breakfast and spent part of the morning on the board meeting and part on studying the ground-looping reports on the P-35 (Seversky pursuit). I plan on using one of these planes while my P-36 (Curtiss) is sent to the depot to have some past-due "technical orders" carried out. It seems that the Seversky has a bad ground-looping tendency, especially on a runway in a cross wind. I dislike ships that ground-loop. They take away your reserve of safety unnecessarily. Not that ground-looping is likely to result in personal injury, but it can do tremendous damage to a plane—and to your personal dignity.

Friday, June 30

Put on uniform and took taxi to Munitions Building. Had photograph taken (at General Arnold's second request) by official Army photographer. Conference with General Arnold regarding Lycoming engine and fuel injection and about a meeting of representatives of the industry he is calling for July 10. Phoned Harry Byrd and made an appointment with him at the door to the Senate Chamber at 1:30. Phoned Anne (Lloyd Neck) to tell her I was starting west; but she was in New York, so left the message for her.

The European situation is reported as extremely tense. The French are

217

predicting war within two weeks. Personally, I think the chances are we will not have a war this year, if at all. I wish I felt surer about it. By "at all," I mean arising from the present situation. I am not one of those who believe war is a thing of the past.

Taxi to Capitol for appointment with Byrd. We went into Garner's[67] office adjoining the chamber and talked for fifteen minutes about the tension which is developing in Europe and the course the United States should take if war should start over there. We are both anxious to avoid having this country pushed into a European war by British and Jewish propaganda, of which there is already too much. I can understand the feeling of both the British and the Jews, but there is far too much at stake for us to rush into a European war without the most careful and cool consideration. We over here, 3,000 miles away, have a false and immature conception of most European problems. Those problems cannot be solved by American good will and idealism; they are far deeper, and I am not sure that our participation in another European war would help the solution in the end. I think it would be more likely to throw the entire world into chaos than to "save it for democracy."

Taxi back to apartment. Packed, and put on uniform again. (I had taken it off to go to the Capitol. It is the practice not to wear uniforms in Washington. Also, my visit with Byrd was as a citizen and not as a soldier.)

Taxi to Bolling Field. Cleared for Patterson Field (Dayton) and took Army car from the operations building, which is still on "Old Bolling Field," to the hangar where my plane is kept on "New Bolling." The O.D. told me that landing-gear trouble and the buckling of wing plates back of the landing-gear struts is being experienced with the P-36 planes. We inspected mine and found it to be in good condition. Started the engine and was about to taxi out onto the field when I discovered that my radio was out of order again. Was delayed a half hour while it was being fixed.

Finally took off at 16:35 E.S.T. There were storms en route, and I flew by instrument for short periods. Then began to climb to get over the storm area. Dayton was reporting clear skies, and I would have no trouble getting down. I tested out the effect of breathing oxygen as I climbed, going without it entirely for periods and then breathing it in excess to see what the effect would be. I realized when I needed it by a feeling of discomfort and lack of alertness, coupled with a slight though apprecia-

67. John Nance Garner, Vice-President of the U.S., 1933–41. Garner opposed Roosevelt's third-term candidacy and retired from politics in 1941.

ble loss of awareness. As soon as I turned the oxygen on, I could feel the keenness of my senses return, and I began to have the exhilaration of flying once more and to appreciate the mechanical perfection of my plane and the natural beauty of the clouds and sky.

I passed through a thin layer of cirrus clouds at 30,000 feet and finally reached an indicated altitude of 32,000 feet, which seems to be the absolute ceiling of the plane. Most of the storm clouds were far below, but one great thunderhead, a few miles to the north, raised its head to my own altitude, penetrating boldly through the layer of cirrus I had passed at 30,000. As I approached Dayton and left the storm-covered Alleghenies behind, I dove and rolled the plane down to 5,000 feet and flew at that altitude for twenty minutes before landing at Patterson Field at 18:50 E.S.T.

General Brett asked me to stay at his home. I had a family dinner with him, Mrs. Brett, and their son and daughter. Conference after dinner with General Brett and one of the officers from Wright Field. Very tired after altitude flying and dives. Glad when it came time for bed. Could hardly keep awake during the conference.

Saturday, July 1

Drove to Patterson Field, cleared for St. Louis, and took off at 10:00 E.S.T. Clear weather. Practiced radio-beam flying en route (through cone of silence, etc.). Landed at Lambert Field at 11:50 E.S.T. [Major Edwin H.] Lauth (C.O.) and other officers arrived shortly after I landed. We discussed the characteristics which should be incorporated in the future designs of observation planes. Lauth and one of the other officers drove me to the Chase Hotel.

Phoned Major Lambert,[68] Mrs. Beauregard,[69] and others. Lunch with Mrs. Beauregard in the parlor adjoining my room. We discussed the possibility of engaging someone to go over my papers, which are now largely in storage boxes, in order to separate the important material and possibly publish a record of some of that which relates to the 1927 period. There have been so many erroneous articles written, and so much rumor and

68. Major Albert Bond Lambert, for whom the St. Louis airfield was named, was an aviation pioneer and one of the first to support Lindbergh's New York–to–Paris project.

69. Mrs. Marie Antoinette ("Nettie") Beauregard, archivist-curator of the Missouri Historical Society, Jefferson Memorial Building, St. Louis, whose museum contains exhibits relating to various Lindbergh flights. In 1928 she wrote a booklet called "Decorations and Trophies of Colonel Charles A. Lindbergh."

misinformation circulated about what took place at that time that I would like to have an accurate record established.

Went over to the Jefferson Memorial Building after lunch and walked through the wing containing my exhibit. The [Missouri Historical] Society is taking excellent care of it. Afterward, I went through the other wing and was especially interested in a case containing the original records of the Lewis and Clark Expedition.

Major Lambert sent his police car for me, and I went to visit him at his office. He is continuing his excellent work as police commissioner and has established an extremely efficient police organization in the city.

Major Lambert took me out to the field, where I went to see Bill Robertson,[70] Scotty,[71] and Herwig. They were all that were left of the people who were on Lambert Field when I used to fly there. Bill Robertson is now again operating the old Robertson Aircraft Corporation. Scotty is still making a living taking up passengers on short flights around the field and on an occasional cross-country trip. Herwig is still the night watchman.

Sunday, July 2

Breakfast alone in hotel room. Made out maps with courses to San Francisco, using the glass dresser top as a ruler. Lauth called for me with his car at 9:45, and I rode out to the field with him and Mrs. Lauth. There were many people at the National Guard hangar that I knew, and I was unable to avoid a delayed take-off while I talked to them. Finally in the air at 11:12 C.S.T. Set course for Sherman Field, Fort Leavenworth. The tachometer began reading high twenty minutes after I left Lambert Field. Was turning 2,500 r.p.m. when I first noticed it. (Normal cruising about 2,200.) Found that the automatic feature was not functioning. Could not change the pitch by manual control either. So throttled down to about 160 m.p.h. with the propeller in low pitch. Sky clear except for broken cumulus clouds as I approached Kansas City. Flew part of the time under and part over the clouds.

Landed at Fort Leavenworth at 12:30 C.S.T. It was a holiday, and the propeller expert was on leave. The field mechanics knew nothing

70. Major William B. Robertson was president of Robertson Aircraft Corp. (1919–28), which operated the St. Louis–Chicago air-mail route that Lindbergh inaugurated as chief pilot in 1926. He was one of the backers of Lindbergh's New York–to–Paris flight.

71. O. E. Scott, pilot and field manager of Lambert Field, St. Louis.

about my propeller—a new and complicated type. We got out the drawing of the electrical system and the maintenance instructions, which I carry in the plane. They were not very clear and after a half hour we had made no progress. I went to the PX for lunch with the major who was in command of the field, while an attempt was being made to locate the prop expert.

The general came into the PX while we were eating lunch and returned to the field with us afterward. When we arrived, we found that the mechanics had located the trouble. One of the carbon brushes was not making proper contact with its ring. The tension of the brush spring was increased, the ring cleaned, and the propeller functioned properly on ground test. I made a ten-minute test flight and found that it also functioned properly in the air. We refueled all tanks, and I took off for Denver at 15:12 C.S.T.

My course to Denver lay directly over Bird City, Kansas, where I went with my exhibition parachute in 1922 to join Lynch[72] and Rogers[73] in barnstorming and making exhibition flights. It was at Bird City that I started my "professional" career in aviation and left my status as a flying student at Lincoln. It was with Rogers and Lynch that I received pay for my work for the first time, small and irregular as it was. (What a contrast it seemed as I passed over the little group of houses, stores, and warehouses, called Bird City! Cruising at 200 miles an hour, at an altitude of 7,000 feet, flying a plane of metal, with one little wing holding it up, with its engine of more than 1,000 h.p.—over seven times as powerful as the Lincoln Standard Tourabout I flew in with Lynch. We used to cruise at about seventy miles an hour, and either wing of our biplane would have covered the wing of my Curtiss pursuit. Flying was more an art and less a science in those days. More depended on the man and less on the machine. You had more the sense of flying when you went up; it was less mechanical. Instruments were only referred to for checking your own feelings and estimates. One flew on fabric and wood and wire through sheer skill and daring.)

I flew through the edge of a local but rather violent storm after crossing the Colorado border, and landed at the Municipal Airport at Denver at 17:50 C.S.T.

The mechanics at St. Louis had noticed a bulge in the tire of my tail

72. Harold J. Lynch, pilot of the plane Lindbergh accompanied as wing-walker, parachute-jumper, and mechanic in 1922.
73. "Banty" Rogers, owner of the plane (a Lincoln Standard Tourabout). A wheat rancher near Bird City.

wheel, due to a defective casing. It seemed worse at Denver and another wheel was available, so we decided to change. Just after the work was finished, several of those violent sandstorms came up and covered us with dust. I was in the cockpit, about to start the engine, and escaped most of it by closing the hatch. Denver is noted for such storms, turbulence from the mountains. They are local and pass quickly but can cause all kinds of trouble for planes, sometimes rolling them over and over along the flying field and wrecking them completely. They cause less damage to the modern planes with their heavy wing loadings. The wind velocities in the storms this afternoon probably reached as much as fifty-five or sixty miles per hour in gusts. Took off, in between storms, at 18:52 M.T. and set my course directly across the mountains for Salt Lake City.

The high peaks are so close to Denver that I had to climb the plane almost at its maximum rate to get over them without circling. The peaks were snow-capped and clear except for an occasional rain cloud hiding one of them here and there. Above, the sky was broken, with scattered clouds at different altitudes all the way up to 20,000 feet and above. I climbed through them and rode on top like a god—the cloud-strewn sky, the white-capped peaks, the rain-filled valleys, mine. I owned the world that hour as I rode over it, cutting through my sky, laughing proudly down on my mountains, so small, so beautiful, so formidable. I could dive at a peak; I could touch a cloud; I could climb far above them all. This hour was mine, free of the earth, free of the mountains, free of the clouds—yet how inseparably I was bound to them, how void my space would be if they were gone. Everything—life, love, happiness—all depended on their being there when I returned. Everything depended on their being there to receive me when I glided back down into those valleys, to take my place among the great mountains, to be covered coolly by those mists of rain. This hour I rode the sky like a god, but after it was over, how glad I would be to go back to earth and live among men, to feel the soil under my feet and to be smaller than the mountains and the trees.

Landed at Salt Lake City at 19:40 M.T. The sun was going down and shadowing the mountains as I approached and dropped down into that great expanse of salt-filled desert. The sunset glow was bringing out all the softness of the desert colors. I had no landing lights on my plane, and the fields ahead had poor floodlights, if they had any at all. So I decided to stay in Salt Lake City for the night. The Army sergeant stationed at Salt Lake drove me to the hotel (Newhouse).

Monday, July 3

Up at 7:00, when my alarm watch began ringing. The sergeant from the field called at 8:00 and drove me to the airport. Usual press nuisance, although not quite as unpleasant as at most large cities. St. Louis is always the most considerate, and Washington next to St. Louis. I have the most trouble in New York, and Chicago and Los Angeles are the next worst.

Took off from the Salt Lake airport at 8:50. My course to San Francisco lay over Lake Tahoe in the Sierra Nevadas, where I spent several days in the summer of 1928. I circled over the empty naval dirigible hangar at Moffett Field, Sunnyvale, to see the location where the new NACA laboratories may be placed. Then turned north and landed at Hamilton Field [San Francisco] at 12:30 M.T. Had lunch with Colonel and Mrs. [John F.] Curry (C.O.) at their home on a hill overlooking the flying field. Almost as soon as I landed, the mechanics started giving my P-36 a forty-hour check.

Colonel and Mrs. Curry drove me to the University of California in the afternoon, where I had a conference with some of the professors of the College of Mechanical Engineering. It was a holiday, but I had managed to locate one of them, and he found one or two of his colleagues. The University of California does not specialize in aviation. The courses of aerodynamics, etc., are given as a part of their mechanical-engineering training. The facilities are limited, consisting primarily of a small wind tunnel two or three feet in diameter. They have a good structural laboratory, however, which could be applied to certain problems in aeronautical research.

Colonel and Mrs. Curry returned for me in about an hour, and we drove back over the bridges and through San Francisco. We passed through the dock area, deserted because of the labor troubles.

Tuesday, July 4

Packed. Drove to Operations with Colonel Curry. Laid out maps to Sunnyvale and to Seattle. Cleared for Sunnyvale (Moffett Field) and took off at 10:20 P.T. The fog was coming in through the Golden Gate and starting to fill up the bay as I flew over. It covered Treasure Island, the bridges, and the city of San Francisco. But beyond, the water was clear and the sun was shining when I landed on Moffett Field at 10:38.

Was met by Major Harper (C.O.) and by the professors from Stanford University (Guggenheim College of Aeronautics). Made a tour of Moffett Field and the big hangar with the major and then drove to Stanford University with the professors. After arriving at the Guggenheim laboratory, we held a conference about the possibility of government assistance to the universities and what the relationship should be between them and NACA.

The Guggenheim College of Aeronautics at Stanford is in a serious financial condition. They have used up the original grant from the Guggenheim Foundation—it lasted a little over ten years—and are not certain where they will obtain funds for continued operation after the next year or two. They have already curtailed their activities to the bone.

We had lunch with a number of men from the different departments of the university in the Union Club. We went back to the laboratory and spent a few minutes looking at the wind tunnel and at some of the propeller models they had tested. After that, they took me to Moffett Field.

Took off at 15:00 P.T. The sea and coastal mountains were covered with fog, but the sky over the inland valleys was broken, and farther east, over the desert, there were no clouds at all. I flew along one of the valleys with great trees climbing its sides and with tiny streams running threadlike to the long narrow lakes in the center. Ahead, the clouds were tumbled about and spread in layers, with clear blue sky in between.

It was overcast at the Oregon border and I followed the valleys with their streams and roads. Passed through several local storms and landed at Medford at 16:45 P.T. Medford is one of the Army fuel stations, with Army personnel to take care of fueling. While I was there, the field manager—it is a small place—asked me to come sometime and go fishing. He reminded me of the time I had stopped in Medford in 1928 with my Ryan monoplane in which I brought Tom Eastland[74] and one or two of his friends for a short vacation. We went to a cabin in the high timber, on the side of a trout stream.

Took off from Medford at 17:11 P.T. The rest of my flight was under overcast skies. I followed valleys and detoured the cloud-covered mountains, trying to keep high enough above the trees to be able to jump in case my motor stopped. This plane lands too fast to permit getting down safely in anything but a fairly level field. I had decided that if there were

74. California businessman, influential in organizing Transcontinental Air Transport.

not a good-sized clearing or farm field within gliding range, I would cut the switch, pull the plane up into a stall, and jump. There would be no use riding it down into those great tree tops of the northwest. At one place, shortly after I passed Portland, the clouds dropped down to less than 500 feet above the valley I was following. The mountainsides on my right and left ran steeply up into the white mist. But the ceiling soon raised again and stayed at a reasonable height until I landed at Seattle at 19:25 P.T. We put the plane in the Army hangar and Mr. Egtvedt[75] drove me to his home for the night.

Wednesday, July 5

Breakfast at 8:00 with Mr. and Mrs. Egtvedt. He drove me to the Boeing hangar where the big planes are being assembled. There was a new B-17 bomber there, and one of the "stratoliners." Major [John D.] Corkille was waiting for us at the hangar door. I saw him fly the Verville-Sperry racer at St. Louis in 1923, and he was a "check" pilot when I was a cadet at Brooks Field. He accompanied us through the rest of our tour. Next, we went to Boeing plant No. 2, and then to No. 1, where the company started its first business. They have good facilities and are constructing good aircraft—in spite of the troubles they have had.

The Boeing Company is still being held up with the delivery of their pressure-cabin transports due to the CAA's insistence on better control and stability. After the crash of the first plane, with the loss of its entire crew, the utmost caution has been used with the rest. They are trying out new designs for the fin and tail surfaces.

Back to lunch, followed by a press car, with Mr. and Mrs. Egtvedt. He drove me to Washington University after lunch, where I went through the Guggenheim laboratory and spent an hour or so with Professor Kirsten[76] and one or two others connected with the university. Then back to the Boeing factory for a conference with their engineers on supercharging and high-altitude flying, etc. Finally back to Mr. Egtvedt's house, where I spent the evening laying out my route east through Montana and North Dakota. I also laid out an alternate route farther south in case of bad weather.

75. Clairmont L. Egtvedt, aircraft manufacturer and chairman of the board of Boeing Airplane Co., Seattle.

76. Frederick K. Kirsten, pioneer aeronautical engineer. He designed the Kirsten-Boeing propeller for the dirigible *Shenandoah* in 1924.

Thursday, July 6

Breakfast at 7:00 with Mr. and Mrs. Egtvedt. He drove me to the field, and I took off at 8:20 for Missoula [Montana]. The weather report I got at Boeing field indicated contact flying all the way, but clouds were covering the Cascades when I reached them. I climbed up through the layer—1,000 feet or so thick—and found clear skies above. The clouds stopped with the mountains as though held by a great dam—almost but not quite spilling over into the ranch-filled valley beyond.

Landed at Missoula at 10:24 P.T., after dragging the field several times. It was near a mountain, and the runways were short and ill-defined. There was a long wait for fuel while I got in contact with the proper officials. Finally got off the ground again at 11:17 P.T.

Landed at Billings, Montana, at 12:35 P.T. Lynch and I based in Billings for several weeks when we were barnstorming in 1922. The present airport is on top of the "rim rocks," where I used to climb around on some of the days we did not fly. I talked to the field manager for a time. Then Bob Westover arrived. He was interested in aviation when Lynch and I stayed in Billings, had done some flying since then, but now was back at his old work—in charge of an automobile filling station. He and his brother ran a garage in Billings in 1922. I worked for them for a short time as night attendant, sitting up in the dusty garage office, playing an old phonograph to pass the time, selling gasoline to an occasional traveler in the dark. I can still remember some of the words of one of the records I played during those nights: "In the quaint old town of Richmond, of Civil Wartime fame, there lived a Southern maiden, Virginia was her name," etc., etc.

Took off Billings at 14:15 M.T. Detoured slightly to fly through the edge of a violent local storm in eastern Montana. It lay two or three miles north of my course, but flying had been so monotonous after I left Billings that I decided to fly over to it. I could see the lightning strike the ground, and the rain whipped heavily on the windshield as I flew through the edge. I could just see a little town below, almost blotted out by the rain.

Landed at Fargo at 16:44 M.T. Took off again, after refueling, at 18:24 C.T. and set my course for Little Falls. I passed over the lake region of northern Minnesota and found that, as I hoped, the Minnesota National Guard squadron was training at Camp Ripley. Their planes stood in a neat line at the edge of the field. I flew over Little Falls at 5,000 or 6,000 feet, circled the farm two or three times, and landed at Camp Ripley at 19:17 C.S.T.

Supper with the National Guard officers, then drove to Engstrom's[77] store with some of them. Martin and Mrs. Engstrom and Lottie Wood[78] were there. Lottie stayed with the store, while Martin and Mrs. Engstrom and I drove down to the farm. We found the watchman in one of the camp shelters and made a night tour with him, by flashlight. Down to the creek and over to the house and through the rooms—first floor, upstairs, and basement. They have attempted to locate and replace some of the old furniture which was stolen. I recognized a few of the pieces, but others were never in the house when we were there. The place has changed a great deal, of course, but it still retains much of its old attraction and beauty. We drove back to Little Falls, stopping on the way long enough for me to call on the Johnsons and Sandstroms.[79]

Finally, after all good-bys, I went back to Camp Ripley with the officers. We stopped to call on the general in command, and he kept us talking about National Guard problems for more than an hour before we could get back to the tents and to bed—long after midnight.

Friday, July 7

Breakfast with the general and a number of the officers at 7:30. We made an inspection of the camp, and then I took off at 9:53 C.S.T. Flew over Little Falls and circled the farm, then set my course for Chicago, but decided that the Chicago newspapers would probably cause trouble so changed it slightly for Chanute Field, Rantoul, instead. Landed at Chanute Field at 12:27 C.S.T.

Took off Chanute Field 15:05 C.S.T. and set course for Detroit. Passed over the Ford field, with its dirigible mast and early American village on the edge. Circled the house at 508 Lakepointe,[80] and landed

77. Martin Engstrom, an old friend of Lindbergh, who owned the hardware store in Little Falls, Minn., at which Lindbergh traded when he ran the family farm from 1918 to 1920.

78. An assistant in Engstrom's soft-drink parlor.

79. Farm neighbors of the Lindberghs in Minnesota. As a boy, Lindbergh played with the children of these families.

80. The house where Lindbergh's mother and her brother, Charles H. Land, Jr., a mining and mechanical engineer, lived.

at Selfridge at 16:50 C.S.T. Spent half an hour with the commanding officer, then took Army car to 508 Lakepointe. Mother and B.[81] both there. Spent the rest of the afternoon and evening with them. They had finished dinner but sat down in the dining room while I ate. Afterward, we went out into the yard, in among the trees and bushes. They have planted it beautifully and fed the birds until the trees and yard are always full of them. Even pheasants come in to eat and in the spring bring their young with them.

Saturday, July 8

Breakfast with Mother and B. The Army car arrived at 9:00, and I left for Selfridge Field, arriving about 10:00. Spent an hour in conference with the Selfridge Field officers, talking about pursuit aviation and the characteristics of pursuit airplanes. I took off as soon as possible after lunch, leaving the ground at 13:35 E.S.T.

Landed at Cleveland at 14:27 E.S.T. Refueled at the National Guard hangar and took off again at 14:57. Landed Mitchel Field at 16:50 E.S.T. I took an Army car to Lloyd Neck. Jon lifted the curtain at the head of his bed and called loudly, "Mother, Father has arrived." Supper outside with Anne, and afterward we walked down to the beach together and watched the gathering night.

Sunday, July 9

Swim in the sound before lunch—Anne, Jon, Land, and I. In the afternoon Anne and I tried oil painting for the first time. It was great fun, and we each tried our hand at painting the three big trees back of the house, with the sound and the far shore beyond. We spent most of the afternoon with the paints.

Monday, July 10

Took off from Mitchel [for Washington] at 12:47 E.S.T. Flew via Annapolis and landed at Bolling Field at 14:00. Took Army car to Muni-

---

81. When Lindbergh was a child, he told his mother he would like to have a brother like hers. She told him she would share hers with him; from then on he called his uncle "Brother," or "B."

tions Building. Found there were three conferences going on, at all of which I was supposed to be present. There was an aircraft manufacturers conference where General Arnold had gone. There was a final meeting of our research board, and there was a NACA hearing before the congressional Appropriations Committee at the Capitol. The latter was in regard to appropriations for the Sunnyvale laboratories and for university research projects.

Dr. Lewis called from the Capitol and asked me to come down there. I decided that my participation in the NACA hearing was the most important, so I took a taxi to my apartment, changed into civilian clothes, and took another taxi to the Capitol. (Congressmen do not like military uniforms; I think it is a bad sign. The uniform of a country should be welcome anywhere within it.)

After a half-hour wait outside the committee room we were called in ("we" being Dr. Abbot,[82] Dr. Lewis, and myself). Dr. Abbot read a long paper to the committee, during which most of the members apparently went to sleep. After Dr. Abbot finished, Dr. Lewis gave an excellent presentation of the NACA position. And after that I talked to the committee for ten minutes, emphasizing the necessity of keeping the performances of our aircraft abreast of those of any other country. I tried to bring out the error of making great expenditures for airplanes without carrying on a research and development program in proportion. I cited the inadequacy of our laboratory facilities compared to those of Europe. Last of all, but with the greatest emphasis, I tried to outline what could be gained by the financing (by NACA) of more university research projects. We can probably gain important results at the lowest possible cost by this method. The committee was considerate and listened attentively.

Tuesday, July 11

The galley of my "circulating flask" article arrived in this morning's mail. It is to go into the September issue of the *Journal of Experimental Medicine*. I designed the flask just over a year ago during our trip to the United States in the winter of '37–'38. I finished the article after returning to England, but did not publish at that time, because I was not sure how much value the flask really had. Since then, about thirty of them have been built and they have worked successfully in Dr. [Raymond]

82. Dr. Charles G. Abbot, astrophysicist engaged in original research on solar radiation, and secretary of the Smithsonian Institution.

Parker's experiments with virus. I really designed them for the experiments Dr. Parker was making with poliomyelitis virus. Parker was going to try to apply my "gas lift" method of circulation to the old Carrel circulating flask, which never did work satisfactorily. I designed the present type for him instead.

I started work on correcting the galley and, with the exception of a trip to the Munitions Building for a conference with General Arnold, I spent most of the day on it. The corrections did not take long, but I had to write a summary and an outline of the article. Also, I reread it carefully, going through each operation visually in my mind.

Wednesday, July 12

Left in taxi for Bolling at 8:00. Cleared for Langley and took off at 9:25 E.S.T. in P-35 No.36-409. My P-36A is to be sent to the depot for overhaul and to have some of the many "technical orders," which have accumulated, carried out. It has been due to go for some time. I am to use a P-35 until the P-36A is returned.

The P-35 was designed and built by Seversky on Long Island. Most Army pilots consider it a "tricky" plane and say that it can't be depended upon. It is unstable in the air and has a tendency to ground-loop when landing, especially in a cross wind. Many of them have lost their landing gears ground-looping. One officer told me that "every landing is a feat with the P-35." There are a few who seem to like it better than the Curtiss P-36, but they are a small minority. So it was with acute attention and with some misgivings that I climbed into the cockpit, taxied to the end of the runway, and took off for Langley Field.

The P-35 did not take long in showing off its temperament, although it was really my own fault. One could almost always say that about P-35 accidents, it seems. They would never have happened if the pilot had just done something a little differently. Therein lies my main criticism of the P-35. There is no reserve in the plane. It must all be in the pilot. If he makes a mistake, the plane doesn't help him a bit—no teamwork at all. You have to have a firm grip on the reins every second. If you let them hang loose, it's only a matter of time before there's a runaway.

I did not have a runaway, but I was forced to the realization that my plane was ready for it. No sooner had I opened the throttle than the load on the stick became excessive. I had to push forward on it with many times the normal pressure, and still the plane seemed to jump into the air. When I could spare my attention for a few seconds, I looked down at the stabilizer adjustment and found that I had set it in the center of the quadrant, whereas the neutral point was a little farther forward. I moved it slightly, and the load on the stick disappeared instantly—exceptional sensitivity. My fault, of course, but what a delicate balance that plane was designed to. How carefully she would have to be watched and coached and held in check—no margin of reserve there. The P-35 represented that old maxim in aviation that pilots used to grow up with: "You only make one bad mistake."

Langley Field was full of activity when I approached. Planes taking off and landing and others circling around in the sky, waiting to get down. I circled around several times before getting a clearance to land. Even then, a Boeing bomber (B-17) cut in front of me. I lowered the landing gear and flaps and felt as though I was balanced on a pin point, ready to fall quickly in any direction if I let myself be off guard for an instant. I thought of the captain who said, "It's a feat every time you land in a P-35." I came in with the engine idling rapidly and let the wheels touch first—a two-point landing—taking no chance. The plane landed slowly for a pursuit—more slowly than the Curtiss P-36 by quite a margin, but I did not feel at ease until I stopped rolling, had lifted the flaps, and had turned in toward the line.

Dr. Reid[83] was waiting for me, and we drove to the C.O.'s office for a short call before proceeding to the NACA laboratories—one of those military procedures so useless and yet so necessary. I am always getting into trouble by forgetting these customs. Spent several hours going through the laboratories with [Dr. George] Lewis and Reid. Lunch with the various department heads. Discussion afterward about ways of increasing the speed of the "cut-down" P-40 and many other subjects. Looked at the cowling and cooling experiments now being carried on. Inspected the new Seversky being tested in the full-scale tunnel, etc., etc. Discussed the need for additional facilities.

Finally took off at 15:03 E.S.T.

Thursday, July 13

Jim Newton came to my apartment for breakfast at 8:00. We discussed the Carrel Institute project, High Fields, "Moral Re-Armament," etc. Jim has been interested in the Oxford movement[84] for years and has been

83. Dr. Henry John Reid, aeronautical engineer, and engineer in charge of NACA laboratories at Langley Field, Va.

84. The Oxford Group (not to be confused with the Oxford Movement of the

very active in it. Personally, I have not been very much attracted by what I have heard of the Oxford movement. But it is gathering strength and has helped many people. From that standpoint, at least, it is worth watching. Also, it interests me that Jim Newton is in the movement. He is a very able and intelligent fellow. If a religious movement can attract enough of his type, it will amount to something. I shall watch this more closely in the future.

One of Jim's friends came in after breakfast—also working in the Oxford movement. Seemed a fine young fellow, and full of enthusiasm. All of the Oxford workers seem to be bubbling over with enthusiasm. I can never quite get a clear picture of what the movement really is. There seem to be no very clear objectives. They all believe in truth and good will and are against sin. They apparently feel that the problems of mankind can be settled by good will and that peace on earth will reign for evermore. But Christ hasn't been able to accomplish that in 2,000 years, and I am not sure that peace and good will would make men happier if they had to be taken in excess. At present, the Oxford people sort of believe in bigger and better babies, but they have not gone very deeply into the problems of obstetrics. Still, we lack religion in the world today. I can't believe the Oxford Group is the answer, but they may be a sign pointing in the right general direction.

Conference with Lewis in the NACA offices at 11:00. Then to the Chief of Air Corps's office for a conference with General Arnold. Lunch at the Army & Navy Club with Lieutenant Colonel [Howard C.] Davidson and Captain Luke Smith. Talked about Europe mostly. Captain Smith, during the conversation, asked how the English really felt about us in America. (Smith is a Texan and has never been abroad. Davidson was once military attaché in London—lived there four years, I believe. He is a Southerner.)

"Well, I'll tell you," said Davidson in his slow, even Southern voice. "The English feel about us just the way we feel about a prosperous nigger."

Took off in Seversky P-35 at 16:12 E.S.T. Flew off airways, via Annapolis. Landed at Mitchel Field at 17:20 E.S.T. Miss Gawne waiting for me with Franklin. Home in time for a swim with Anne before supper on the porch overlooking the sound.

1830's), so called after Frank Buchman preached "world-changing through life-changing" among the students at Oxford University. Known also as Moral Re-Armament (M.R.A.).

Saturday, July 15

Spent most of morning painting. Have become very much interested in mixing the colors and trying to put what I want in the picture. It is true that painting teaches you to see.

Tuesday, July 18

Spent the morning writing a preliminary draft of our special NACA committee report.

Wednesday, July 19

Walked down to the shore and along the beach after breakfast, then packed, and drove the De Soto to Mitchel Field. Cleared for Bolling and took off at 11:15 E.S.T. Set course via Annapolis. Broken sky all the way but hazy near Washington. Landed on Bolling at 12:22 (Seversky P-35). The plane showed a tendency to ground-loop on landing, but I was able to hold it.

Thursday, July 20

Phoned General Arnold and found that he and Admiral Towers were meeting for lunch. Phoned Mr. Hinckley and arranged for him to come, too. Taxi to Army & Navy Club. We made tentative plans during lunch for our committee report. Went to the NACA offices to get the original act setting up the committee. Walked back to the apartment. Glenn Martin phoned, and I arranged to meet him at the Baltimore airport next Thursday. Spent the rest of the afternoon writing a rough draft of the committee's report.

Major John T. Lewis of the Coast Artillery came for dinner. We discussed antiaircraft, and I arranged with him to see some practice firing early in August. We spent the evening talking about the effectiveness of different antiaircraft guns, from high-explosive bursts down to the stream of fire from a .30-cal. machine gun. We also discussed methods of increasing the co-operation between the Air Corps and Antiaircraft.

Saturday, July 22

Sent copies of rough draft of committee's report to Arnold, Towers, and Hinckley (for discussion only). Walked back to the apartment and spent the rest of the morning packing and writing. Finished packing and put on uniform. Phoned Anne to have a car waiting for me at Mitchel Field. She told me that Mother and B. had already arrived. Taxi to Bolling. The driver was one of the few who do not talk all the time.

Made two test flights around the field, testing out flap positions and landing characteristics. Took off for Mitchel at 16:55 E.S.T. Landed on Mitchel Field at 18:22 E.S.T. Mother and B. had come in the Franklin and were waiting for me. We returned to Lloyd Neck in time for a late supper.

Sunday, July 23

Family breakfast. Morning outside with Mother, B., Jon, and Land. Mother very happy. We all went down to the beach for a swim before lunch. Afternoon outdoors also. Wish Mother could be with Jon and Land oftener. We spent the evening in the parlor, discussing old times, ancestors, and past years in Detroit, among many other subjects.

Tuesday, July 25

Mother and B. left in their Ford at 9:30. They plan on driving through Canada on their way back to Detroit—possibly going as far north as Nova Scotia. I completed a few details, put on my uniform, and drove to Mitchel Field. Took off at 10:22 E.S.T. Landed on Bolling at 11:45 E.S.T. Changed to civilian clothes in the officers' locker room and took an Army car to the Army & Navy Club for a committee lunch with Arnold, Towers, and Hinckley. We discussed the first draft of our report and decided on various changes.

Taxi to General Arnold's residence for a 6:30 dinner with General Marshall.[85] Mrs. Arnold had dinner with us. Talked to Marshall about Truman Smith. Told him it would be inexcusable if the Army failed to

---

85. General George C. Marshall, Army Chief of Staff, 1939–45. Marshall became Secretary of State in 1947 and was responsible for the European Recovery Program (the Marshall Plan) for postwar economic recovery in Europe. For this he was awarded the Nobel Peace Prize in 1953.

make use of Smith's ability and knowledge and discharged him simply because he was not physically able to carry on duty with troops. I found that Marshall had a very high regard for Smith already. We discussed various subjects of a confidential nature, bearing on the Air Corps, etc., which it is inadvisable to put in writing at this time.

Thursday, July 27

Phoned Glenn Martin that I would meet him at 11:00 on the Baltimore airport. Taxi to Bolling Field. Took off at 10:36 E.S.T. in the P-35. Landed on Logan Field, Baltimore, at 10:54. Glenn Martin was waiting and drove me in his Cadillac to the factory. The old Martin factory field is torn up due to the expansion of his plant, and the new one, farther north, is not yet in condition for landings. Martin is a fast but excellent driver—only a few minutes from field to factory. We made a tour of the factory, accompanied by various officers—through the machine shops, drafting rooms, laboratories, etc. We stopped for a moment to see the work on the design for the Navy's new "giant" flying boat and at the portion of the factory where the French bombers are being built.

We went out into Chesapeake Bay on Martin's yacht for lunch. Martin and I discussed various problems, including the effect that politics is playing in our expansion program and the rumors of corrupt practices in the letting of certain contracts in Washington. As usual, our conversation turned to Europe and to Germany. Martin gained a great respect for German aviation during his trip through that country. Back to dock and factory after lunch. One of the engineers took me to the airport in his car.

Took off at 17:20 E.S.T. Landed at 18:33 E.S.T. Army car to Lloyd Neck. Everyone had finished dinner. Anne got one together for me, and we sat in the dining room and talked while I ate it. We were really fortunate in finding such a place for our summer home—comfortable, beautiful, sufficiently isolated, within driving range of New York, other children for Jon and Land to play with, a sunny beach for swimming, stars, and the outline of oaks on our lawn at night.

Sunday, July 30

Anne went down to her study in the "garage house" at 10:00. I carried down the suitcases containing her books and papers. She spends almost every morning from 10:00 to 12:00 working on her new book. We are extremely fortunate in having this room where she can work—shaded by the branches of trees, away from household noises, quiet, yet within shouting distance of the children and the house. I spent the morning painting. We all went for a swim before lunch.

Monday, July 31

Major Lewis wants me to fly him from Washington to New York so he can go with me to see the antiaircraft demonstration at Fort Hancock. I decided that the simplest procedure would be to arrange for him to come on one of the Eastern Air passenger planes to Newark Airport, where I could meet him with a car. Phoned Lewis and told him of this plan. (Did not tell him I was paying for the ticket.)

Tuesday, August 1

The box containing the head Despiau did of Anne arrived. Unpacked the head—beautifully done—a real masterpiece.

Wednesday, August 2

Left house at 9:10 in De Soto and arrived at Newark Airport just as Major Lewis's plane landed. We drove to Fort Hancock, stopping en route at a small-town hotel for a very mediocre lunch. I wore glasses, as I always do in this country on such occasions, but was recognized by people at a nearby table. As we went out, one of the men jumped up and tried to stop me by grabbing my arm—unsuccessfully, of course. What is it that makes this difference between our people and those of European countries? There is a cheapness here, a lack of respect and dignity which alarms and discourages me.

When we arrived on the post we found the Commanding Officer had been holding lunch for us. In some way, the messages they had sent Major Lewis gave him the impression that we were expected to arrive on the post after [eating] lunch. So we ate a second time with the officers and their wives. Immediately after lunch we went to see the eight-inch guns firing at a target towed several miles off the coast. I could see the shells for a second or two after they left the guns. Then, after what seemed a long interval, there would be a great column of water rising suddenly at the target—always remarkably close. The day's demonstration was for the West Point cadets who had been brought down to Fort Hancock in a truck train that morning. Later, we went to see the 37-mm. cannon fire at a burst sent up by one of the large three-inch guns. The 37-mm. fires 120 rounds per minute, and the battery of them seemed to fill the air with tracers—a stream of fire toward that puff of smoke several thousand feet up over the water. It was impressive enough, directed toward a stationary target, although all the tracers seemed to pass far below the shrapnel burst, but I could not help feeling that a plane flying 300 to 400 miles an hour would stand very little chance of being hit.

To me the three-inch antiaircraft cannon were much more impressive. They will make straight-line flying quite dangerous at altitudes of 10,000 feet and probably considerably higher. They will by no means stop bombing raids, however, and I think their percentage of effective hits will be very low. This "tow target" shooting gives a false impression and is poor training. The target is flown at a known time and altitude in a straight line and under ideal conditions. It continues to fly in a straight line and at the same altitude even after the first shells burst around it. Nothing approximating these conditions would happen in time of war.

After the antiaircraft firing we visited Battery Kingman, one of the two twelve-inch gun batteries at Fort Hancock (coast defense, New York harbor). After that we saw the .50-cal. machine gun firing at low-altitude tow targets. I tried firing one of the machine guns and found it very difficult to hold on the target. The general impression seems to be that the .50-cal. guns are not proving very satisfactory.

We returned to the house of Major and Mrs. Hennessy for dinner. At night we went out to watch the searchlight practice. A fairly strong wind was blowing, and the lights made a poor showing—did not pick up the plane a single time until the pilot brought it down to 4,000 feet and *turned on the wing lights*. The bottom surface of the plane had a special gray paint, which made it much more difficult to pick up with the beams. But it flew back and forth overhead a dozen times at only 6,000 feet, and they never found it.

Spent the night at the home of Major and Mrs. Hennessy.

Thursday, August 3

Stopped to thank the Commanding Officer of the post for his courtesy, then went to Battery Mills to see one of the twelve-inch guns fire. Watched the firing from the "safety tower"—two shots. Major Lewis

and I left the post at about 9:30. We left his suitcase at Newark
Airport, and I dropped him at the first subway station we came to in
New York. Met Anne on the road to Lloyd Neck (between Lloyd Neck
and Huntington). Changed cars, giving her the De Soto; it is newer and
in better shape than the Franklin. I went on to Lloyd Neck and found a
turtle on the road. Had brought a .50-cal. machine-gun shell for Jon
from Fort Hancock and had bought a thirty-five-cent airplane kite for
him, so I was well prepared for my arrival.

Saturday, August 5

Phoned Antoine de Saint-Exupéry[86] and invited him to spend the night
with us. Agreed to meet him at Ritz at 5:00 and drive him to Long
Island. I had already arranged to meet Dr. Nute (Minnesota Historical
Society) at the mountain cottage near Cold Spring, New York, where she
is staying with her sister. Had a difficult time finding the route through
the Bronx after I crossed the Whitestone Bridge. Lost at least half an
hour. Finally arrived very late at the cottage—about 2:30. Lunch with
Dr. Nute and her sister and her sister's husband. They had waited for
me, although Anne phoned and told them I would be late. If I stayed
long enough to talk to Dr. Nute about my father's biography, I could not
meet Saint-Exupéry at the Ritz at 5:00. There would barely be time to
get there by 5:00 if I left immediately. I phoned Anne and arranged for
her to go in and meet Saint-Exupéry—wonderful wife to do something
like that for you, and Anne always is ready to do anything in an emergency. Dr. Nute and I talked until 5:30. Then I started back to Lloyd
Neck, arriving about 9:00. Anne and Saint-Exupéry had been in the
house for only a half hour or so. We talked until midnight. He has an
exceptional mind—a real artist and all that one would expect after reading his books—*Night Flight* and *Wind, Sand and Stars;* an experienced
aviator and a skillful writer.

Sunday, August 6

We drove Saint-Exupéry to the home of one of his friends for lunch,
about twenty minutes away. Anne and I returned home for our lunch. I

86. French aviator and writer (*Night Flight, Wind, Sand and Stars, Flight to
Arras, The Little Prince*). He was lost in action (1944) in World War II.

spent the afternoon until 4:30 painting. Then Anne and I drove over to get Saint-Exupéry. We spent half an hour with his friends before starting back. We talked for an hour or two in the evening—the effect of industry and the machine on man, etc. (I asked the question, trying to clarify something I had read in his book.) Saint-Exupéry does not speak English, so I did not understand everything he said, although Anne translated all that she could.

Monday, August 7

Anne and I drove Saint-Exupéry to New York after breakfast. I was so much interested in listening to him that I forgot to get gasoline, and we ran out just before we got on the Fifty-ninth Street Bridge. Fortunately, we were on a down grade with a gas station just ahead. We left Saint-Exupéry at the Ritz and stopped for the De Soto on the way back.

Phoned Dr. Lewis and found that Congress had appropriated money for the new laboratories but had turned down our request for $250,000 for university research projects.

Friday, August 11

Phoned Dr. Hunsaker and arranged to meet him at the Lake Placid airport tomorrow at 11:30. Must see him to talk over NACA matters.

Saturday, August 12

Took off at 9:12 E.S.T. for Lake Placid. Clear weather except for haze in places. Landed at 10:36 Lake Placid airport—a medium-size field. Dragged the field twice before coming down. Had called by radio but no answer. On landing, I found that the field manager was away. His wife was running the field, carrying her small baby in her arms. Dr. Hunsaker and his wife were there to meet me. We helped push the plane in the hangar—a small wooden one—and drove to the Hunsaker cottage in the Ausable Club reserve. It is a beautiful location, on the steep bank of a mountain brook. Hunsaker and I held a conference after lunch on NACA matters: the duties of a co-ordinator, the relationship of NACA to the universities, extension of research facilities, etc. Later on, we took a bus over the reservation road to the "lower lake," a mile or two into the mountains. We walked back over the trail at the side of the same brook that passes the Hunsaker cottage.

Sunday, August 13

Slept on the open porch overlooking the brook. Woke at daybreak. Sky stormy and completely overcast. Slept for another hour or so, then dressed and went for a forty-five-minute walk along the brook with the Hunsakers' dog. By the time I returned for breakfast the sky was broken, but with storm areas on all sides. Hunsaker and I spent the first part of the morning discussing NACA matters. Lunch at 12:30. Heavy rainstorm afterward. Drove to clubhouse and phoned Lloyd Neck. Weather clear on Long Island. Left word to have car meet me at Mitchel Field at 5:00. Dr. and Mrs. Hunsaker drove me to the field. Small crowd waiting. One man was hit by the wing as we pushed the plane out of the hangar. He was taking a picture and, as so often happens, forgot to get out of the way. Fortunately not serious. I am always afraid someone will get hit by the propeller in some similarly stupid way. Paid hangar rent and took off at 14:48 E.S.T. Landed on Mitchel Field at 16:47 E.S.T. Drove to Lloyd Neck. Jon met me with the question: "Have you a turtle for me?" Land had lost his last one. I had none, so my homecoming was largely a failure.

Dwight and Margot were at the house. They are about ready to start with Dr. Samuel Morison[87] on a six-month cruise, following the routes of Columbus. We went for a swim and then had supper on the porch; beautiful evening but too many mosquitoes and other insects for pleasant eating outside. Don't mind them so much beside a campfire, but they don't go well with napkins and silverware.

Monday, August 14

Packed after breakfast, drove to Mitchel Field, and took off for Washington at 10:50 E.S.T. Flew via Annapolis and landed on Bolling Field at 12:10 E.S.T. Army car to apartment. Phoned Dr. Lewis and made an appointment to meet him at 2:30 at the NACA offices. Decided to fly to Dayton to talk to General Brett. Met Lewis at 2:30 and spent half an hour with him, then took taxi to Bolling Field. Lewis told me that appli-

87. Harvard historian and author.

cations are coming in from all over the country for the new NACA laboratories—from Indianapolis, St. Louis, San Antonio, even Dismal Swamp somewhere in the Carolinas.

Took off for Dayton at 15:30 E.S.T. I have a P-36 again; it arrived at Bolling a few days ago—a much better flying plane than the P-35. I was glad to trade for it. Landed at Patterson Field at 17:35 E.S.T. General Brett was waiting for me with his car and asked me to spend the night at his home. We talked over the possibility of locating the new NACA laboratories at Dayton. After supper we drove to the site of the Wright memorial which overlooks both fields. It is still boarded up and no one there had the key. Returned to Brett's home. Colonel Echols[88] and Major [Franklin O.] Carroll came for a conference after dinner. We talked of one- and two-engine pursuit, multiplace fighters, gun caliber, accidents in "hood" flying with pursuit planes, etc.

Tuesday, August 15

One difficulty in keeping a diary is that the more one does the less time there is to write about it, not only because activity removes hours of contemplation, but also because of the difficulty of forcing one's mind from the problems of the day to that completely different attitude required for intelligent writing. I find there is great inertia in my mind. It likes to keep right on doing whatever it has been doing before, especially when it has been working hard. It seems to have all the directive force of a spinning projectile. Once launched, it takes some hard object to make it deviate or stop. This morning I flew into Washington from Dayton, and my mind has been on flying ever since. Several hours have passed since I landed, and I have just completed, forcing myself considerably, that transition period between flying and writing. It is inevitable. I always have to go through it. Too much or too little activity blinds one to true values and to the real beauty of living. To observe, to think, and to write well, one should act only enough to keep his senses sharpened and to avoid that theoretical, impracticable, narrow outlook of the man who never acts at all—the critic who speaks lightly and conceitedly of an art he never knew. But in acting, one must be careful not to dull his senses by overwork, by too great and too prolonged concentration. One must avoid that practical, logical, material, mineral-like outlook of the man who knows nought but action as the answer to everything in life.

88. Colonel Oliver P. Echols became a major general in 1942.

It is impossible, and one would not even desire to always hold a perfect balance between action and contemplation, between earth and sky. It is pleasant to swing into one and back to the other as a pendulum, for one sees only by contrast. One feels only that which is new. Touch deadens after prolonged contact. Beauty is lost in staring. Flowers have no perfume if one lingers too long.

Drove over to Wright Field with General Brett. Went with Major Lyon to look over the specifications for new types of pursuit, bombardment, and observation planes. Some of the designs look excellent at first glance.

Drove back to Patterson and took off at 9:45 E.S.T. Climbed up over the cloud layer and held an altitude of from 14,000 to 18,000 feet most of the way to Bolling Field. Started breathing oxygen after about 12,000 feet. Was gliding down to circle Bolling—about over the Potomac River —when I suddenly saw a Navy plane about 200 yards on my left and headed straight at me. Pulled up quickly, but don't think he saw me at all. I had been watching carefully for planes but did not notice him until he was uncomfortably close. Landed on Bolling at 11:15 E.S.T. Army car to apartment.

Wednesday, August 16

Walked to the Munitions Building for an 11:00 conference with General Arnold in regard to NACA and the location of the new laboratories. We discussed Dayton and Sunnyvale particularly. Dr. Lewis came in at 11:15. Jimmy Doolittle[89] arrived at 12:00 and discussed his latest trip to Europe.

Thursday, August 17

Went to the Munitions Building for a 10:30 meeting with Truman Smith in his office in G-2. We went to Colonel McCabe's[90] office together and

89. James H. Doolittle, aviator, engineer, and winner of numerous air trophies. On April 18, 1942, he led sixteen Army Air Force B-25 bombers from the U.S. aircraft carrier *Hornet* in a spectacular low-level attack against targets in Tokyo. In 1943 he became a major general. He later headed the North African Strategic Air Forces and led the Eighth Air Force in massive attacks on Germany.

90. Colonel Edward R. W. McCabe had been a military attaché in the U.S. embassies in Prague and Rome in the 1920's and early 1930's. He was chief of the

spent half an hour talking over the situation in Europe and America. Then to Colonel [Hamilton] McGuire's office where we discussed the European situation for another twenty minutes. Conference with General Arnold at 11:45. Conference with Dr. Lewis at 2:00 at NACA offices. Talked about methods for grading applications for the new NACA laboratories site. Back to apartment. Packed, put on uniform, and took taxi to Bolling Field. Took off at 16:48 E.S.T. Landed on Mitchel Field at 17:35. Anne was waiting for me in the De Soto. We drove to Lloyd Neck for supper and the night.

Friday, August 18

European crisis becoming extremely tense. Germany is not bluffing and will fight if necessary to gain her ends in the East. Decided to lay plans on the supposition that a European war will start this fall, although I think the chances are slightly against it.

Read Anne's review of *Wind, Sand and Stars* by Saint-Exupéry— beautifully written, as usual.

To Thayers' home for supper with Bob and Virginia. We spent the evening discussing the political situation in this country.

Saturday, August 19

Morning papers announce that Germany has taken over the direction of the Slovakian Army and will institute military measures in Slovakia.

Read [Theodore C.] Blegen's *Building Minnesota* in the evening.

Sunday, August 20

Can't keep mind off war. It is just like the Munich crisis last year except that we are in America this time and do not feel the atmosphere of preparation, apprehension, and depression there was in London a year ago. The German-Russian pact did not surprise me, but I believe it has greater significance than appears on the surface at this moment.

Military Intelligence Division, General Staff, from 1937 to 1940. In 1944 he was recalled to active service and became a brigadier general.

Monday, August 21

Drove to Mitchel Field after lunch. Took off at 15:03 E.S.T. Hazy along route, and sky filled with cumulus clouds. Flew above clouds, via Annapolis. Landed on Bolling at 16:13. Army car to apartment.

Tuesday, August 22

Phoned Colonel Eaker[91] and told him I would prefer to go back and forth between New York and Washington by train or with my own plane unless my trips were in direct connection with Army work. I suggested that the P-36 be used for training flights by the officers at Bolling Field until I needed it again. Eaker replied that the Chief of Air Corps had assigned the plane to me personally and that I could take it to New York whenever I wished to. I thanked him but said I did not feel justified in commuting with an Army plane and felt I would be setting a bad precedent by doing so. Eaker said he would follow my wishes and that he knew of a number of officers who would be very glad of an opportunity to get some flying time on a P-36. I felt better after making this arrangement. I love flying the plane, but I can do so at any time on Army missions, and I now have a greater independence of action than before.

Dinner at home of Colonel and Mrs. McCabe. Drove there with Kay Smith. Colonel [Bernard R.] Peyton was the only other guest. He has been appointed military attaché to Germany and is leaving for Berlin in the near future. Truman Smith came in after dinner. McCabe, an old Virginian, is an exceptionally intelligent officer. I thoroughly enjoyed the evening with him. As usual, the discussion centered around European and internal American conditions. He is very apprehensive about the future of this country. I have been for a long time. I do not like the trends of recent years. And we have this race problem which is bound to cause the most serious type of trouble. The Civil War did not settle the Negro problem by any means.

91. Colonel Ira C. Eaker was with the executive office of the Chief of the Air Corps, 1939–40. He became a lieutenant general in 1943 and commander in chief of the Mediterranean Allied Air Forces in 1944.

Wednesday, August 23

There is talk of war everywhere. The press is full of it. Reminds me of Europe last September.

Spent the afternoon writing and going over papers. Dr. Lewis came at 5:10 for a conference on NACA matters.

Walked to Bill Castle's[92] home at 6:00—about ten minutes from the Anchorage. Fulton Lewis[93] was the only other person there. The three of us had dinner together and discussed the European situation and the action this country should take if war breaks out over there. We are disturbed about the effect of the Jewish influence in our press, radio, and motion pictures. It may become very serious. Lewis told us of one instance where the Jewish advertising firms threatened to remove all their advertising from the Mutual system if a certain feature were permitted to go on the air. The threat was powerful enough to have the feature removed. I do not blame the Jews so much for their attitude, although I think it unwise from their own standpoint.

Thursday, August 24

Breakfast in apartment, then went to the Munitions Building to meet Truman Smith in the G-2 offices. We discussed the European crisis. There seems to be about an even chance of war. I cannot believe that England and France will attack Germany under present conditions. It would be suicide to attack the German "Western Wall," and what else can they do? England can clear the sea of German shipping but that in itself will not win a war. Poland is beyond help under any circumstances. The German Army will close the Corridor within a few days after it attacks, and there is no other way for England and France to get to Poland. They can't go through Rumania or through one of the northern Baltic countries. Of course, there is the question of what Italy will do. But whether she joins Germany in war or stays neutral, the problem is

92. William R. Castle helped with clearances and diplomatic arrangements for Lindbergh's Far Eastern flight in 1931. A former Ambassador to Japan, he had been Undersecretary of State, 1931–33. Assistant to the chairman of the Republican National Committee.

93. Radio commentator and journalist. For many years Lewis spoke every night on national affairs for the Mutual Broadcasting System.

not much simplified as far as France and England are concerned. My guess is still slightly against a general European war this year, but I wish I could feel more certain.

Spent the first part of the evening writing; then packed and took taxi to Union Station. Bought round-trip ticket to New York and boarded train about 11:30.

Friday, August 25

Off train at 7:30. Checked suitcase and went for half hour's walk. There is an entirely different group of people on the streets of New York at this time in the morning.

Took 9:30 train to Huntington. Not recognized or bothered since I left Washington. Have been wearing lensless, horn-rimmed glasses and have been very careful, of course. It is a great relief to be able to move around so freely. Christine met me at the station. Margot was at the house for a short visit with Anne. She and Dwight have been expecting to sail daily, but the *El Capitana* is not quite ready, and the last details have still to be completed. Everyone wanted news of the situation in Europe, and we talked for half an hour about that.

Anne and I went for a swim before supper. These evening swims with her are the most fun of all. There is seldom anyone within sight on the beach, and usually the nearest boat is a mile or two away. And the afternoon light makes the sky, the trees, and the water more beautiful. We spent the evening writing and listening to a radio concert.

Saturday, August 26

We drove to the Blackwells' home for dinner. Looked at first as though it would be a boring evening but became more interesting as time passed. More intelligence than one usually finds at a Long Island party. Enjoyed talking to some of the men there. The Blackwells tell me I stayed in their house for a weekend in 1927, but I can remember it only with extreme vagueness. I did so many things in that year—most of them superficial— that I remember very little detail. After I returned to this country from Paris, most events now merge together in my mind until they become only a general impression of hectic summer months—of extravagant and false values with which I had never had contact before. New York and

Long Island life interested me, but only from the standpoint of seeing into an environment of which I had only read. I never had a desire to live myself as people lived in these places. Even today I would not think of establishing a permanent home in New York City or on Long Island. I do not want to live or to have my children grow up under the set of values which exist in this section.

Sunday, August 27

Jim Newton arrived just as we returned to the house. I went down for a swim again with him. We spent the evening talking and listening to the radio. A commentator gave us an outline of Hitler's letter to Daladier—excited, superficial, and stupid, as most of these radio commentators are. He drew the conclusion from the letter that Hitler was weakening. Later on, we listened to a translation of the letter itself—not a trace of weakness in it. But how much can one depend on what Hitler says? What change of circumstances will justify his mind in breaking new treaties? All of our countries have broken treaties in the past, but Hitler has established a new tempo—a tempo possibly more in keeping with this modern age. It seems that a treaty, to be effective, must be backed by strength, just as a law, to be effective, must be backed by a police force.

Monday, August 28

Phoned Wyckoff and invited him and his wife for dinner. Spent the morning writing and thinking over the war situation. A telegram came from Truman Smith saying, "Yes, 80." That means information has come in that makes him think that the probability of war arising from this crisis is eighty per cent.

Dr. and Mrs. Wyckoff came in time for a swim before dinner. After supper Newton, Wyckoff, and I went down to Anne's study to talk over the effect war would have on our plans. The possibility of organizing an institute for Carrel hinges, probably, on whether or not there is war. We decided that nothing could be done until this crisis has turned one way or the other.

Tuesday, August 29

Morning press reports Russia massing troops on the Polish border.

Newton left for New York after breakfast. Aubrey came out for lunch.

Wednesday, August 30

Phone call from Colonel Eaker. There is to be a special meeting of the Kilner Board at 9:00 tomorrow morning, which they want me to attend. I plan on going down by train tonight.

Constantly thinking about war. Seems impossible to keep it from one's mind or conversation. Have been considering whether anything I could say in a radio address would be of constructive value, even in a minute way. I am afraid events have gone too far on the other side for words to have any effect. Better not to speak at all in that case. Phoned Bill Castle at Hot Springs, Virginia, and Truman Smith in Washington. Smith says there is great activity on the eastern German border.

Aubrey and Constance came out for supper. Aubrey and I left about 10:00 for New York in his car. He let me out at the subway station, and I took the 12:30 train from Pennsylvania Station for Washington.

Thursday, August 31

Off train at 7:30. Spent the entire morning sitting on the Kilner Board. The question that caused the meeting was in regard to specifications for a certain type of bomber. (Secret, so cannot describe here.) Turned out that the general characteristics we laid down during our last meetings were sufficiently comprehensive and that there was really no need for us to have held this meeting. Well, I wanted to come to Washington about this time anyway. But this incident does not add to my respect for Army organization. There is too much form and not enough responsibility.

General Arnold and Truman Smith came for dinner. We talked about the Army, the Air Corps, conditions in America and in Europe. As we were talking, extras were out on the streets, carrying headlines to the effect that Poland had refused Hitler's offer for a peaceful settlement.

Took taxi to Union Station later in the evening and boarded the night train for New York.

Friday, September 1

Off train at 7:40 Daylight. Huge headlines across all papers: GERMAN TROOPS ENTER POLAND. The war has begun! What will England and France do? If they try to break the German Western Wall, I think they will lose unless America enters the war. In that case, if we go in, Europe will be still more prostrated after the war is over. And I don't know what will take place in this country by that time. Why did England and France get themselves into such a hopeless position? What has happened to "democratic" leadership? If they wanted to fight a German eastward movement, why in heaven's name pick this particular set of circumstances to fight over? They are in a hopeless position militarily, and Danzig, Poland, and the Polish Corridor are not banners which will encourage the Allied armies to attack on German soil. And the English talk of stupid *German* diplomacy! It is "The Charge of the Light Brigade" again. Somebody blundered.

Newton was to meet me at the gate to the trains, but there were several gates on two floor levels, and I missed him. Went to the Engineers Club and phoned his secretary; left message for Newton to meet me at the club. He arrived half an hour later. After breakfast we phoned Wyckoff and arranged for him, Dr. Ebeling, and Mr. Bakhmeteff[94] to meet us at 11:00 at the club. It was 10:30 when we finished telephoning, so Newton and I went out for a twenty-minute walk along Fifth Avenue and some of the side streets. There seems to be a somewhat subdued atmosphere. The war news has affected everyone.

We returned to the club a few minutes before 11:00. Wyckoff and Ebeling arrived on time, and Bakhmeteff came in a little later. We discussed the war and how we could be of help to Carrel. Wyckoff suggested that we attempt to arrange for the financing of a small research hospital in France, similar to the one Carrel had during the last war. We decided to send a cable to Carrel, asking how we could best be of assistance to him, and what plans he was making. We agreed among ourselves that Carrel could be of more value in the United States than in France in these times. We also agreed that he would probably insist on staying in France if there was any way in which he could be of assistance in the war.

94. Boris Bakhmeteff, civil engineer and author. He had been Russian Ambassador to the U.S., representing the provisional government of Alexander Kerensky (1917–22), and in 1922 became a consulting engineer to the City of New York.

Drove the De Soto to Lloyd Neck. Anne and I discussed the war situation. Will it be long or short? It is too early to tell. We spent the evening in the parlor, thinking and listening to radio reports. The latter are excited, speculative, and superficial, with few exceptions. The future of the human world hangs in the balance today. This war will change all of our lives.

Saturday, September 2

Spent the morning on routine and thinking, trying to plan for the future, even the near future. What stand should America take in this war? This is now our most pressing issue. We have enough internal problems without confusing them with war. I see trouble ahead even in times of peace. War would leave affairs chaotic—and always the best men lost.

The radio commentators are beginning to ask why England and France have not declared war. Why indeed! They're in no position to fight one. The question is why they ever made this alliance with Poland. There are reports—fairly direct ones—that Chamberlain did not consult his general staff before he made the Polish alliance. I told Anne that England and France seemed hesitant about declaring war in spite of their promises to Poland. "Maybe they've talked to a general," she said.

Sunday, September 3

War declared by England and France! German troops continue their advance into Poland.

Spent the morning writing and making plans. We listened to the King's speech over the radio at 1:00. I read Fisher's *History of Europe* in between thinking about the European situation and what action I should take in this country. It is hard to concentrate on anything but the aspects of war.

Jim Newton arrived in the afternoon with a huge fifty-eight-pound Florida turtle for Jon. It is the biggest turtle I have ever seen outside an aquarium. Jon was in school, so we put it in Land's wading pool temporarily—fresh water but probably better than none. The turtle seemed to enjoy it.

Anne, Jim, and I went swimming. Jon came back soon after we returned to the house. We let him "find" the turtle on the lawn as he went outdoors. It seems to have no tendency to snap, but its mouth is so powerful and sharp that I am worried about Jon and Land playing with it.

Anne and I listened to Roosevelt's address at 10:00. It was a better talk than he usually gives. (I differ from the opinons of most people in regard to the quality of his speeches.) I wish I trusted him more. He warned people to beware of propaganda—pledged himself to an attempt to keep this country neutral.

Monday, September 4

Morning paper reports the Cunard liner *Athenia* torpedoed off the Hebrides with 1,400 passengers on board—uncertain how many lost.

The radio reports that the French have attacked and penetrated the German Western Wall! I do not think it is true, but the conception of those human waves dashing themselves to pieces on that concrete line of fortifications brings the war home to my mind for the first time; it is staggering. I believe, however, as the first shock passes, that it is one more of these damnable radio press reports. The French would never attack the German fortifications without a long preliminary bombardment, and there has not been time for that. But someday, if this war goes on, they must hit that line. And if they do, the heart of France will beat out upon it.

The evening radio report carries the German denial of torpedoing the *Athenia*. The Germans say the ship probably struck a mine. The British maintain it was a torpedo. Most of the passengers were apparently saved. We listened to the short-wave broadcasts from Europe later in the evening. They came in clearly.

Tuesday, September 5

Very little reliable information in the morning papers; no definite reports from the Western front. The German troops seem to be penetrating Poland rapidly.

Anne took Jon to the little public school on Lloyd Neck. Jon was back early today. We let the big turtle go when we went swimming. It was obviously not well—had hardly moved during the night. It was sent up from Florida as a soup turtle and, I think, pretty badly handled on the way. I did not want it to die in Land's wading pool. Also, if there is any hope for it at all, it will be in salt water. Possibly it may get back to a southern climate. I told Jon the turtle was sick and would die if he did not let it go and that if he did, it would be very happy. Jon made the decision immediately to let it go. We took it down to the beach in the Franklin's trunk and let it crawl gratefully into the water and swim away. There was a strong wind, with high waves.

I drove to New York after lunch for a routine appointment with my dentist, Dr. [H. C.] Scobey.

Back to Lloyd Neck in time for a swim with Anne before supper. High waves. Thor does not like to swim in them but feels he has to stay nearby Anne. He swam around her, hoping she would hold onto his tail while he pulled her in to shore. Beautiful sky in the evening—a clear, green-blue light like the Italian backgrounds in paintings. Anne and I spent the evening together in the parlor. She read me some of the poems she has written during the last several years.

Thursday, September 7

The radio reports trains arriving in Paris full of wounded soldiers. (These war reports are very unreliable and are seldom substantiated the next day.) The press reports that English antiaircraft guns fired on their own planes and brought one down.

I have now written one article and two radio talks, but events have moved so rapidly that the first two are already out of date. I do not intend to stand by and see this country pushed into war if it is not absolutely essential to the future welfare of the nation. Much as I dislike taking part in politics and public life, I intend to do so if necessary to stop the trend which is now going on in this country.

Friday, September 8

Anne and I left for New York in the De Soto. I met Dr. Bush at the Century Club for a 12:30 lunch. We spent about three hours discussing NACA matters and the methods which might be used to develop antiaircraft defense.

Sunday, September 10

Phoned Bill Castle and Fulton Lewis. Decided to go on the radio next week.

Monday, September 11

I spent most of the day working on my radio address and an article for *Reader's Digest*. Read a little in the evening: Fisher and [Rainer Maria] Rilke. (Anne has given me a copy of Rilke's *Letters to a Young Poet*.)

Tuesday, September 12

Jim Newton came in the late afternoon and stayed for supper. He and I drove to New York together in his car. He dropped me at Pennsylvania Station, and I boarded the 12:30 train for Washington.

Wednesday, September 13

Spent most of the morning with Lewis, Victory, and Robinson, studying the various applications for the site of the new NACA laboratories. It seems that the choice lies between Los Angeles (Mines Field) and San Francisco (Sunnyvale), with the advantages pretty definitely in favor of Sunnyvale—even though it is 400 miles from the center of the West Coast aeronautical industry.

Phoned Admiral Towers, Mr. Hinckley, and General Arnold's office, and arranged for a meeting of our special committee at 9:00 tomorrow morning. Phoned Mutual Broadcasting Company to check on arrangements for my address Friday night.

Back to Anchorage for an 8:15 meeting with Truman Smith. He brought a map of Europe, and we went over the military developments in detail. Seems obvious that the Polish Army is collapsing and that the French are not attacking with much spirit. Evening papers carry headlines: WARSAW SURROUNDED.

Thursday, September 14

Taxi to Navy Building for 9:00 meeting of special committee in NACA offices. Arnold, Towers, Hinckley, and I spent two hours studying the applications for the site of the new NACA laboratories. After the meeting was over, I went to General Arnold's office to discuss the need of a new engine-research laboratory for NACA. The development of better engines is one of our greatest needs in the United States at this time.

I also talked to Arnold about my intent to speak over the radio tomorrow night. It was the first time I had mentioned this to him, although he knows how I feel about the entire situation. Arnold suggested that it would be advisable for me to discontinue my present status in the Air Corps while I am taking active part in politics. I agreed thoroughly, but did not know I had any status in the Air Corps, since I have received no pay except for my first two weeks of active duty last spring. It seems, however, that I am on an "inactive-active status." It developed later that the official communication appointing me to "inactive-active" status was still in the files and had not been sent to me. The matter was of minor importance, however. My main concern was to avoid causing the Air Corps any embarrassment. Arnold said there would be no difficulty in arranging for me to be relieved (he is a grand fellow) and that it could all be done in about five minutes. Said he did not like to see me go, but fully understood the situation. I told him I would be glad to help him or the Air Corps in any way I could in the future, regardless of my status.

I told Arnold I would be glad to have him read my address and that he could rest assured there was nothing in it of a confidential military nature. I took a taxi to the Anchorage to get a copy for him. After reading it, Arnold agreed that it contained nothing which could in any way be construed as unethical due to my connection with the Air Corps, and that I was fully within my rights as an American citizen.

The question arose as to whether the Secretary of War (Woodring) should be shown the address. I said I preferred not to have him see it, as I had very little confidence in him or in the politics of the Roosevelt Administration of which he is a part. (As a matter of fact, I am far from being sure that Roosevelt would not sacrifice this country in war if it were to his own personal interests; he would persuade himself that it was also to the best interests of the country.) I told Arnold frankly that I had great confidence in him and in General Marshall, but not in Secretary Woodring. During these conversations, I could tell from Arnold's eyes that he was on my side. I like him—think he is the best Chief of Air Corps we have ever had.

Back to the apartment for lunch with William Dolph, head of Mutual Broadcasting Corporation in Washington. Discussed my radio talk with him, also the present situation in Europe and America. In reply to his inquiry I told him I would not give a press interview or talk for the "movietones" in connection with my radio address tomorrow night.

Walked to the Navy Building after lunch and wrote the report for our special committee, recommending that the new NACA laboratories be located at Sunnyvale (Moffett Field). After it was copied by one of the stenographers, I took it to General Arnold's office for signature. He told me he had talked to Secretary Woodring, telling him I was being relieved from my "active-inactive" status in the Air Corps, at my own request. He also told Woodring I was planning on speaking on the radio tomorrow night against the United States entering a European war. Woodring was very much displeased, Arnold said. He asked Arnold if he (Arnold) couldn't find some way of stopping me. Arnold replied that he did not think so. Woodring then said he was very sorry because he had hoped to make use of me in the future, but didn't see how he could do so if I followed out my plans! (There was obviously something behind that statement.)

From Arnold's office, I took the report to Towers for his signature, then left it at the NACA offices and took a taxi back to the Anchorage.

Jim Newton arrived about 6:00. Walked with him to the Mayflower Hotel, where he is staying, then on to the Army & Navy Club for a 7:00 dinner with Hunsaker's committee (NACA) (to select a co-ordinator and define his duties). The committee consists of the following NACA members: Hunsaker (chairman), General Brett, Captain [Sydney M.] Kraus, Ed Warner,[95] and Dr. Lewis. Dr. Bush and General Arnold, although not members, were also there. The discussion centered around the duties of a co-ordinator and his position in the NACA organization.

Jerry Land called during the dinner. NBC had phoned him to try to locate me. They wanted to carry my address tomorrow night. I talked to a Mr. Berkeley of NBC and found that Mutual had not contacted them and that they did not know I was going to speak until they read the press announcement to that effect. My understanding with Fulton Lewis had

95. Edward P. Warner, onetime Assistant Secretary of the Navy for Aeronautics and former professor of aeronautical engineering at M.I.T. (1920–26). Member of CAA and author of many works on aeronautics.

been that Mutual would offer both NBC and Columbia the chance of carrying what I say tomorrow night, if they wished to do so. I phoned Mutual and they phoned Dolph, who had gone to Chicago by plane this afternoon. Finally, after numerous phone calls, we got the matter straightened out. NBC, Mutual and Columbia will all carry my address. That means complete national coverage.

Left the meeting at 10:30 and walked back to apartment. Message there from Truman Smith. Asks me to call him in the morning. Marked "Important." Anne had arrived from New York.

Friday, September 15

The committee meeting began at 10:00, Dr. Bush presiding. The committee unanimously adopted the recommendation of our special committee that the site of the new NACA laboratories be at Moffett Field. There was very little discussion and no opposition. After this was finished, Hunsaker's report came in. No action was taken, as more time seemed desirable.

Hunsaker ended up by saying that he felt the solution would be for me to take the vice-chairmanship of NACA and move to Washington for the winter! He said it was necessary for the NACA to have a very active chairman or vice-chairman in order to avoid a conflict of authority between the director of research and the co-ordinator of research in the organization he proposed. In other words, and bluntly put, his idea was to throw the entire problem over on my shoulders! They all seem to feel that because I have kept myself clear of the obligations (with their rewards) that they have tied their lives up with, I am available to carry on whatever problems they feel need attention and do not desire for themselves. How often this happens in aviation! How little people realize the necessity of keeping free time to think and to live!

I have already declined the suggestion (made unofficially by Bush and Arnold some weeks ago) that I take the chairmanship of the NACA. I wrote Bush that I did not want or feel justified in accepting a reappointment to the NACA (for five years) after my present appointment expires in December (unless an emergency arose, which now seems to be the case). I have frequently said to NACA members, including Hunsaker, that I could not continue to devote my time to NACA matters in the future.

I told the committee (after someone suggested I consider the matter until the next meeting—I have already had the whole summer to think about it) that in fairness to them I thought I should tell them I had considered the question carefully and that it would be impossible for me to devote the time necessary to carrying on the work of a vice-chairman properly. I said I would be glad to help the NACA in any way I could, but that I could do that just as well by remaining an ordinary member of the committee. I said I had no illusions about the amount of work which would be required to carry on the work of vice-chairman properly, that I could not see my way clear to do that work, and that unless I could do it properly I would not want to attempt it at all. I made my refusal as definite as I could with courtesy, but I am afraid I will have to go through it all again. It seems to be a modern American idea "not to take no for an answer," and that makes a courteous reply doubly difficult.

Next, I read the first report of my special committee on the extension of research facilities, etc. It was accepted by the main committee. Next, the routine business and miscellaneous detail was completed. Then we went into a readjustment of the NACA budget. I noticed at once that the "university projects" had been given no consideration. I immediately brought the matter to the committee's attention, and we refused to adopt the budget revision. Instead, we instructed Lewis and Victory to bring forth a new proposal at the next meeting, which would include a provision for the "university projects." We suggested a minimum increase of $50,000 and preferably more.

The meeting continued much longer than usual. It was the most active NACA meeting I have ever attended. It ended at about 2:00 and I took a taxi back to the apartment. Anne and Jim Newton were there waiting for me for lunch. Fulton Lewis phoned, and I asked him to come over, too, making four in all. Truman Smith came in a little later and had coffee with us. (I had phoned him in the morning as he requested, but he could not come over before 10:00, when I had to be at the NACA meeting, although he said he had something very important to talk to me about.)

Truman and I went into the bedroom, where we could talk alone. He told me he had a message which he must deliver, although he knew in advance what my answer would be. He said the Administration was very much worried by my intention of speaking over the radio and opposing actively this country's entry into a European war. Smith said that if I would not do this, a secretaryship of air would be created in the Cabinet and given to me! Truman laughed and said, "So you see, they're worried."

This offer on Roosevelt's part does not surprise me after what I have learned about his Administration. It does surprise me, though, that he still thinks I might be influenced by such an offer. It is a great mistake for him to let the Army know he deals in such a way. Apparently the offer came through Woodring to General Arnold, and through General Arnold to Truman Smith. Smith told me that Arnold, like himself, felt they must pass the message on since it came from the Secretary of War's office. Smith said he asked Arnold if he (Arnold) thought for a minute that I would accept. Arnold replied, "Of course not."

At 6:15 Anne and I took a taxi to the home of Mr. and Mrs. Fulton Lewis for dinner—no other guests. At about 8:30 we drove to the building which contains the Mutual studios—about one block from the Carlton Hotel. Lewis put his car in the basement garage, and he, Mrs. Lewis, Anne, and I walked to the hotel. (I originally planned on broadcasting from the Mutual studios, but NBC and Columbia preferred a neutral location and agreed upon the Carlton Hotel.)

The room where I was to broadcast was filled with radio apparatus and about twenty people. It was a small room, too. There were six microphones on a desk—two from each of the chains. I requested that they be placed in front of the desk and raised so I could talk standing up. A commercial photographer set up his camera and lights and took half a dozen pictures while I stood at the microphones.

The radio people wanted me to read part of my address in advance so that they could adjust their "tone control." However, I did not feel that I could read it twice without losing an intangible something that I wanted to keep. They were very considerate about this and said that they could adjust during the first word or two after I started.

I went on the air at 9:45 E.S.T., after a ten-second introduction. (I had requested that it be short and simple.) I was not well satisfied with my delivery. I think it could have been much better. However, everyone else seemed to feel it was all right. Anne and I left with Fulton Lewis and his wife soon after I finished. We went back to the Lewis home where we listened to a rebroadcast of my talk over one of the other stations. It is strange, listening to your own voice—seems most unnatural. From there Fulton and Mrs. Lewis drove us back to the Anchorage. Anne and I packed and took a taxi to the station, where we boarded the 2:00 A.M. train for New York.

Saturday, September 16

Anne and I left the train at 6:50. We drove to Lloyd Neck for breakfast. About forty telegrams had arrived in regard to my address. Only one was unfavorable. The press reaction seems to be good—talk carried in full by both *Times* and *Tribune*. Slept most of the afternoon. Anne and I drove to Oyster Bay after supper to get the evening papers.

Monday, September 18

Finished the final draft of my article on "Aviation, Geography, and Race" and mailed it to Wallace.[96]

Tuesday, September 19

Wallace phoned in the morning while I was walking on the beach. Left word that he liked the article very much.

Wednesday, September 20

Drove to New York in the De Soto in time for a 1:15 lunch with Roy Howard[97] (Scripps-Howard) at the Cloud Club. Karl Bickel[98] came in for a few minutes after lunch. We discussed the question of neutrality and the arms embargo. Went to the Pan American offices at 3:15 to see C. V. Whitney. We talked about Pan American affairs and the company's internal troubles. Trippe came in while we were talking, and we all discussed future equipment for the transatlantic route. Spent half an hour with Bixby[99] after leaving Whitney's office. Then stopped on the fifty-seventh floor for a five-minute talk with [William] Van Dusen.

96. DeWitt Wallace, founder (1921) and editor of the *Reader's Digest*.

97. President Scripps-Howard newspapers.

98. Editor, and president of United Press, 1923–35; chairman of the board of Scripps-Howard.

99. Harold M. Bixby, banker, president of the St. Louis Chamber of Commerce, and one of the original backers of Lindbergh's *Spirit of St. Louis* flight. From 1932 to 1938 he was Far Eastern representative of Pan American Airways, and later became vice president, director, and member of its executive committee.

Herbert Hoover's office called and asked me to meet Hoover at the Waldorf-Astoria at 11:00 A.M. tomorrow.

The papers from the West arrived this afternoon, and I read the editorials about my radio talk. They are about ninety per cent favorable. This country is at present, at least, definitely opposed to entering a European war.

Thursday, September 21

Left at 9:15 in the De Soto for New York and my appointment with Hoover at 11:00. His secretary, Mr. [Lawrence] Richey, met me at the door and took me into a large parlor. Hoover came in almost immediately. We talked for about forty minutes about the war and the policy of the United States. He is definitely opposed to the United States entering this war, but feels the question of repeal of the arms embargo is not of fundamental importance in keeping the country from war. He feels that Roosevelt definitely desires to get us into this conflict. Hoover feels, as I do, that the British Empire has been on the decline for some time—he says since the last war. He said it was inevitable that Germany would expand either peacefully, or by fighting if necessary. He said he told Halifax[100] some time ago that the only way to avoid a European war was to permit a German economic expansion in Eastern Europe. Hoover suggested that after the embargo controversy was over, an organization should be gotten together to keep this country out of the war—nonpolitical, of course. He suggested that I take part in it. I told him I would be much interested and would like to learn more about it. (Hoover's favorite solution for any problem seems to be the construction of a committee. Personally, I am very skeptical about the effectiveness of most committees.)

Walked to the Engineers Club from the Waldorf-Astoria and read the papers until it was time for my lunch appointment with Juan Trippe. We went up to the Cloud Club for lunch. Discussed internal Pan American troubles and the trouble Trippe was having with his directors.

After lunch, I drove back to Lloyd Neck. The maids were off, so Anne and I cooked supper. Anne read some of her poems to me afterward. She has *great* genius in writing.

Drove to New York in the Franklin after supper. Put the car in a

100. Lord Halifax, 3rd Viscount (Edward Frederick Lindley Wood). British Secretary of State for Foreign Affairs.

garage near Pennsylvania Station, and boarded the midnight train for Washington.

Between activities our minds are always on the war.

Friday, September 22

Off train at 7:30. Taxi to Anchorage. Table piled with packages of letters sent over by broadcasting company. Harry Byrd came for breakfast with me at 8:30. We discussed the war, American neutrality, the question of repealing the embargo act, what requirements to substitute for the act if repealed, Dick Byrd's[101] expedition to the South Pole, etc., etc. We agree practically one hundred per cent on the necessity of keeping the United States out of war, and I believe we also agree on the best way of handling the embargo situation. We are having breakfast together again next Tuesday morning to discuss the matter further. Byrd asked me if I would care to meet some of his friends in the Senate, and I accepted his invitation gladly. He suggested some day next week.

Lunch at 12:45 at the Washington Hotel, with Elmer Irey (head of investigation, Department of Internal Revenue) and Frank Wilson (head of the United States Secret Service). Walked back to the Anchorage after lunch for a 2:45 meeting with Truman Smith. We talked over the European military situation, etc., what the next move is likely to be, whether Germany will use her Air Force in an attempt to cut England off on the sea, or whether the German strategy will be a move against the British Empire, with the help of Russia, Italy, and Japan, and possibly Turkey—a march on the Suez and northern Africa, for instance, possibly in conjunction with a Russian (or Afghan) move on the northwest frontier of India, and Japanese pressure on the British interests in China.

Truman and I opened about fifty of the letters which have come in about my radio address. About ninety-five per cent are favorable, and most of them are from people of a good type.

Packed, walked halfway to the station, took a taxi the rest, and boarded the 2:00 A.M. train for New York.

101. Admiral Richard E. Byrd, aviator and polar explorer. He made the first flight over the North Pole in May, 1926, and the first flight to the South Pole in November, 1929. In subsequent expeditions to the Antarctic (1933, 1935) discoveries of new mountain ranges, islands, etc., were made.

Saturday, September 23

Off train at 7:55. Walked to the garage on Twenty-ninth Street where I had left the Franklin. Drove to Lloyd Neck for a 10:00 breakfast. Phone call from Hoover; he says the press reports have indicated that he and I are working together on some committee related to the "Neutrality Act." Said that he had issued a denial and suggested I do the same. I replied that I had not issued a press statement for many years and did not want to start again now—that I would prefer to arrange to counteract the report indirectly. (Actually, I do not regard press rumors of this type as of any importance and think it unnecessary to do anything at all about them.)

Slept for two or three hours in the afternoon. Jim [Newton] arrived while I was asleep. I invited him to come out to write the Moral Re-Armament article he is planning for *Reader's Digest*. I think he has it in him to do something worth while in this line—something far above the average Oxford Group article. I am hoping that he may become a strong and constructive force in the religious rejuvenation of this country, and it is essential to help him start in the right way.

Monday, September 25

Spent a large part of the morning laying plans for the winter. We must either have heat put in the house where we are staying or move else-where. Long Island has both advantages and disadvantages. It lies in the sea, which I love and which I miss terribly when I am away from it. New York is easily accessible—almost too easily. We live near very wealthy people and are therefore much less conspicuous in our smaller house and simpler ways. These people offer us protection by drawing away attention, but with few exceptions, they are not our people. We get along with them without difficulty, but we do not understand their ways, and they do not understand ours—beyond that border line of superficiality which screens the depths of human character as a shore line screens a continent.

Went for a swim alone before lunch, and lay in the sun for a time afterward. Anne and I left at 4:30 in the De Soto for New York. She is going to Northampton with Constance to see her mother open Smith College as acting president. I left Anne and the De Soto at the Cosmopolitan Club. Walked to the Engineers Club, stamped and mailed the envelope containing Anne's poems to the *Saturday Review*, and then walked to Pennsylvania Station and boarded the midnight train for Washington.

Tuesday, September 26

Breakfast with Harry Byrd at 8:45. He brought the latest draft of the neutrality bill, and we discussed the entire question: what authority Roosevelt could be trusted with (we both agreed that it should be as little as possible), what restrictions on shipping and credit would be advisable, what would be acceptable to the different factions, etc. I brought up the danger to neutral shipping of an air blockade of England—the difficulty of recognizing the nationality of a ship by the bomber in a plane flying in poor weather or at high altitude.

Taxi to Senate Office Building for a 12:50 appointment with Byrd at his office. We walked through the tunnel to the Capitol. We stopped for a moment in Byrd's office, then went on to another room where we had lunch with Senators [Josiah W.] Bailey (North Carolina), [Edward R.] Burke (Nebraska), [Walter] George (Georgia), [Hiram W.] Johnson (California), and [Peter G.] Gerry (Rhode Island)—all Democrats. We spent most of the time discussing the pending neutrality legislation. All except Burke were (apparently) in favor of repeal of the present law with drastic substitutions which would minimize the chances of the United States becoming involved in the war. I believe all of them, except Burke, favored our keeping out of the war regardless of who wins. Burke felt the United States should go to war rather than let England and France lose.

Wednesday, September 27

Wrote and thought for an hour or two, then called Senator Borah's[102] office. He was out but called back about 11:15 and asked me for lunch at 12:30. Taxi to Senate Office Building. On the way through his rooms, his secretary showed me the stacks of mail which had come in about the embargo act. There were two piles, one about eight or nine times larger than the other; it contained the letters in favor of Borah's stand. Borah

102. William E. Borah, Republican Senator from Idaho.

was sitting at his desk when I came in. We sat in his office and talked for quarter of an hour before starting for the Capitol.

Borah is a real character. I liked him instantly—before I knew his political stand. He is a true son of the West, and his face and eyes have strength in every line and glance. Of course, Borah is against repeal of the embargo; the press has blazoned that around the world. But a man's newspaper character is far different from his own (God forbid that it be otherwise); even political character changes with personal acquaintanceship and intimate knowledge. Borah spoke frankly to me. I believe we both gained confidence in each other at first glance. His stand in regard to neutrality and the embargo is tempered with judgment and moderation; it is considerably different from the impression one gains from our newspapers. We took the monorail through the tunnel to the Capitol and had lunch in Senator Borah's office. No one else was present, and we talked freely for about an hour. Borah feels the debate on this embargo act will last in the vicinity of a month. He believes it is essential to demonstrate that there is a strong opposition, even though it may be necessary to compromise eventually.

I left at 8:40 for a 9:00 appointment with Truman Smith. Truman had invited Congressman Tinkham[103] to come over and join us. While we were waiting for him, we talked over the latest European developments and the indications of an Axis thrust at the British Empire in the eastern Mediterranean region. By 9:45 we began to wonder what had happened to Tinkham. Kay tried to get him on the telephone unsuccessfully. We decided to drive to the Arlington Apartments where he stays, as Truman did not have his phone number and thought Tinkham had probably lost the street address where we were to meet. (The Smiths just moved in a few days ago.) But there was no one at the Arlington when we arrived—not even an elevator operator, and the windows of Tinkham's apartment were dark. We drove on to the Anchorage and phoned Truman's home, but Tinkham had not come. The Smiths started out to Walter Reed Hospital, where Truman is still staying. I was just in bed when the phone rang and Kay's sister said Tinkham had just arrived at their house. I dressed and took a taxi out there, arriving about 10:45.

Tinkham was waiting in the parlor. He stood up to greet me as I arrived—a strange-looking man of about sixty years—a high, bald head with a huge hooked nose curving down to a long heavy beard which still showed how black it had once been. It was a face you could never forget

103. George H. Tinkham, Republican Representative from Massachusetts.

—one you would recognize as long as life lay within it, regardless of the molding of intervening years. Tinkham's conversation was as unique as his features. His vanity, which at first was the most obvious thing about his words, was soon subdued by a wisdom in observation and a richness of experience seldom encountered in any man. He told me in length of his travels: twenty-seven trips to Europe, he said, and several of them extending beyond—Africa, China, Japan, scarcely a country in which he had not been. He talked of Europe in the past, in the present, in the future, and the hours of the night merged into this narrative of human life, until midnight came and went without our noticing it pass. In between, we talked of the arms embargo and of the policy America should follow. He is definitely opposed to repeal—feels it would be a great step toward war, which he thinks would be disastrous for this country. At 12:30 we called a taxi and left.

Thursday, September 28

Wrote for a time after breakfast, then walked to the Munitions Building to sign the last Kilner Board report. Captain White[104] came in while I was there, and we went over and discussed Major Vanaman's latest report on German aviation. I also went over the latest reports on French and Italian aviation. General Kilner came in, and we spent half an hour talking over the European situation and the reports by the Germans (denied by the British) that British battleships were successfully bombed in the North Sea. Kilner is to be appointed head of the NAA [National Aeronautical Association] and will, successfully I think, attempt to put some life into that organization.

Walked back to the Anchorage. Truman Smith arrived about 1:25, and Harry Byrd came at 1:45—both for lunch. We discussed the Neutrality Act and the European situation. Will there be peace now that Warsaw has fallen? The lack of fighting on the Western front indicates a reasonable possibility of this.

Walked to Stonley Court for a 7:00 dinner with General and Mrs. Yount[105] in their apartment. They played the new Air Corps song for me

104. Captain Thomas D. White became a general in 1942, and Air Force Chief of Staff in 1957.

105. General Barton K. Yount had been military attaché for air in Paris in 1927. In 1940 he became Assistant Chief of the Air Corps in Washington, and in 1942 Commander of the Third Air Force (Tampa, Fla.)

on their phonograph. I think it is mediocre at best; neither the music nor the words appealed to me. But what could one expect from a song which arose from a prize offer of $1,000 from Bernarr Macfadden (*Liberty, The Graphic, Physical Culture,* etc.)? Great music and great poetry are not likely to come from such a source. We discussed the Air Corps and the days when we were together in Paris in 1927. General Yount was military attaché for air under Ambassador Herrick at that time. He had a great deal to do with my reception and the program I followed during my week in France.

Walked back to the Anchorage, packed, took a taxi to the station, and boarded the midnight train for New York.

Friday, September 29

Boarded 9:30 train for Huntington station, arriving at 10:36. Anne was waiting when I arrived. She had had a successful and very interesting trip to Northampton, and said her mother was extremely happy in the work she was doing. The *Saturday Review* has taken one of Anne's poems—selected by the editors without knowledge that she wrote it (the one named "Security").

Went for a walk on the beach with Anne. After Jon came home from school I took him to some rocks where, the tide being low, we found about three dozen very low-grade oysters. Jon ate three of them raw as I pried them off the rocks. I managed one, but that was all—would have had to miss two or three meals before I could have eaten them raw and fresh with relish.

Saturday, September 30

Our two maids are leaving, very unwillingly, as they promised their previous employer (Mrs. James Roosevelt) to return to her this fall. Nevertheless, we are again confronted with the servant problem.

Calamity! Grapie, the turtle, is lost. Jon, Soeur Lisi, and I looked all over for it but with no luck. Jon is left with only four turtles now: Sleepy, Climby, Sweety, Coldie (Coldie—so named because he was found on one of the days Jon had a cold). No one knows how it got out of the pen. Land is, of course, suspect, but Jon says he thinks the turtle climbed up on top of one of the others and then pulled himself over the top of the

board which forms one of the sides of the pen. Seems quite a performance for a turtle, but then Jon knows much more about them than I do,
even though I used to raise mud turtles myself.

Sunday, October 1

I am working on a new radio address, "Neutrality and War," which I
may or may not give, depending on developments.

Monday, October 2

Herbert Hoover phoned and asked me if I thought he would be safe in
saying that France and England could be successful in a defensive policy
built around the Maginot Line. He said it seemed to him that while airplanes could cause great damage behind that line, they could not win a
war by doing so. He said he thought England could maintain control of
the surface of the sea in spite of German air attacks. He said he planned
on making a statement at this time because he felt there was a wave of
hysteria sweeping the United States—arising from the rather sudden
realization that England and France might lose the war—and that he
regarded it as essential to counteract this hysteria on the grounds that it
would create, and be used to create, the desire for this country to enter
the war. Hoover said he felt Germany could not win the war because of
the Maginot Line and British fleet.

I replied that I agreed the best policy for Britain and France to pursue
would be a defensive one built on the Maginot Line and the British fleet,
but that I thought Hoover should consider the possibility of a German
thrust toward the Suez and North Africa, with the assistance of Italy and
Russia and possibly that of Turkey. I told him I thought it improbable
that the Germans would attempt to cross the Western front. I also told
him I felt he should be careful in saying what the result would be of a
conflict between the British fleet and the German Air Force. I said that
was something we knew very little about—that aviation people tended to
be overenthusiastic and naval people too conservative. Hoover replied
that he did not think a German thrust toward the eastern Mediterranean
would be practicable. He said he did not think the German Air Force
could overcome the great supremacy of the British fleet.

I have been reading some of Anne's writing. She has unique ability to give great depth of feeling with lightness of touch. Her writing carries philosophy with delicacy unparalleled.

Anne and I were discussing the feeling of pressure one often has. We decided that if the work one is doing is of enough importance, there is no feeling of time, no detail too trivial. A feeling of pressure, then, may be a subconscious indication that the work you are doing is not of sufficient importance to justify your effort.

Tuesday, October 3

Wrote for a time after breakfast, then left with Anne in the De Soto for New York. I had an appointment with Harry Davison. When I arrived in the office of the Morgan partners, old Mr. Morgan invited me to have lunch with him in the firm's big dining room. Mr. Morgan is really a fine character. I have liked him ever since I first met him years ago. He is now well on in life—not far from seventy, I suppose; I am not even sure on which side. He is a large, kindly faced man, with an air of pleasant hospitality. His handshake carries a feeling of personal warmth and integrity that persists as long as you are with him.

The office of the Morgan partners is a long, rather dark room, filled with two (or is it two and a half?) rows of desks—there must be fifteen or twenty of them in all—the high type with drawers and cubbyholes—not the usual flat-topped kind. Each desk has a chair at its side for the use of guests. During certain times of the day, all the partners work together in this room. They each have an individual office on the floor above—also very dark. The entire place leaves the impression of mahogany and of oak-paneled walls, of heaviness, conservatism, and integrity—a proper impression for a great banking firm, I suppose, but rather depressing to me. I long for sunlight as soon as I get inside the doors, and feel that the people there mustn't know the wonders of the outdoor world, that they are, in a sense, like a blind man who has either never seen the sky or who has been blind so long that he has become inured to the loss of its beauty. Yet these men do get out to see the sky; they live on Long Island and in other outskirts of New York; they sometimes take long trips through the West. How they can spend most of their lives in that dark oppressive atmosphere of 23 Wall Street, I am unable to understand. I would rather a thousand times over live my life on a farm than in that building, regardless of the amount of money I could make. But then, I like a farm anyway, so living on one would not be much of a sacrifice.

Almost as soon as the lunch began, the talk turned to the war in Europe and the arms embargo. Mr. Morgan asked me if I planned on making any more radio speeches. I told him I was not certain, but that I probably would, and that it would depend largely on developments. During the conversation at the table I expressed the opinion that France and England would lose the war if they tried to attack Germany across the Western front. Tom Lamont[106] (senior partner) said he thought England and France would wait and let Germany attack. I asked him why Germany should attack. He said Germany could not stand a long blockade and, therefore, would have to attack. I told him that if Germany attacked, I did not think it would be in the West, but in the East—except that Germany might attempt an air blockade of England. Lamont said he did not think an attack by Germany in the East (Turkey, Suez, northern Africa) was practicable and that he would bet ten to one Italy would not go into the war on Germany's side.

The talk then turned to the arms embargo. Someone asked me if I had taken a stand in regard to the embargo. I said I had not, but that I doubted the advisability of complete repeal, *either* from Europe's standpoint of our own. That statement started a very warm discussion in which Tom Lamont took the lead. As far as I could tell, I was the only one in the room who was not in favor of unqualified repeal. Obviously, my stand was extremely unpopular. The discussion continued until some of the partners had to leave for meetings. In fact, it took so much time that I missed the talk with Harry Davison for which I had come. He had planned on our having lunch together in a private room and had an early appointment after lunch. We all parted in a courteous (no personal feelings, you know) but tense atmosphere. I walked to the nearest (Wall Street) subway, where I took express to Grand Central Station.

Walked to Abercrombie & Fitch on Madison and Forty-fifth. Bought two leather-bound (blank-sheet) books, made in Italy, for Anne; also several miscellaneous items for myself, including a raincoat and a pair of canvas tennis shoes. (I loaned my previous pair to Antoine de Saint-Exupéry when he, Anne, and I went swimming last summer, and I have not seen them since. I think he probably left them on the beach; he could not possibly have packed them in his suitcase wet.) Buying a new pair makes me wonder where he is. I read a short notice some time ago that he was in the French Air Force—and of course he would be there. That is the tragedy of war (of this one in particular, for it seems so ill-advised

106. Thomas W. Lamont, old family friend. Partner of J. P. Morgan & Co., 1911–40. He became director in 1940 and chairman of the board in 1943.

and unnecessary). Men like Saint-Exupéry are killed, and the world has too few of them anyway.

I met Anne at five o'clock. We drove to Lloyd Neck for supper.

Thursday, October 5

Spent the first part of the morning writing. Tom Morgan[107] phoned in regard to Pan American Airways reorganization—outlined his plan. Started for New York in the De Soto at 11:00.

President Hoover and I had lunch together in one of the rooms in Hoover's suite. We talked at length of the arms-embargo controversy and the practicability of placing a restriction on the sale of destructive armaments. Hoover plans on advocating this policy, both because he believes in it and because he thinks it a compromise that may appeal to both sides as they become more exhausted with their arguments. As a matter of fact, I think it would be an excellent policy for us to adopt in this particular situation, even though I can see the arguments that will be made against it, and they are numerous.

There is no sharp dividing line between offensive and defensive armaments, but there is seldom a *sharp* dividing line in anything. I do not like the idea of this country selling bombs to Europe, and I do not think that either America or Europe would gain by it in the long run. On the other hand, I do not think it practicable (as Hoover apparently does) to legislate internationally against the use of such items as poison gas and bombs. Such legislation, to be successful, presupposes that there will be an international police force strong enough to enforce it and numerous enough to make sure these items are not manufactured secretly. And, after all, it is only a minor war that would bend uncomfortably far in the direction of regulations, regardless of how humane they are. A nation with its back to the wall will use any means whatever that will assist its own survival. It is all very well, and I believe extremely desirable, to make rules for humane warfare and to come to agreements for the limitation of armaments, but these rules and agreements should be based on mutual benefit as much as on idealism; and trust of one's enemy should not pass far beyond one's knowledge of his actions. International agreements should never completely lose sight of the strength that stands behind them and which plays such a large part in their success.

107. Thomas A. Morgan, president of the Sperry Corp. and chairman of the board of Sperry-Gyroscope Co.

Parked the De Soto at the Engineers Club. I had arranged for a room in which to have dinner with Jim Newton and two of this friends—Johnny Roots, whom I met some weeks ago in Washington, and Ken Twitchell, who came with his wife to visit us one afternoon at Long Barn. We discussed the international situation and American neutrality. All three of my guests were Oxford Groupers—all fine fellows and far above average. The Oxford Group certainly attracts a good type, and it brings out an enthusiasm such as I have only seen in the early days of aviation. But for some reason I still have reservations about this movement. There is some atmosphere about it I don't quite like. Trying to put my feelings into words, the best I can do is to say that they are trying to place everybody and everything into the movement, instead of the other way around. I think religion and spirit should be brought into life instead of life being brought to them. Religion is spiritual food. Nothing is gained by trying to immerse someone in it. Left the Engineers Club about 8:30 and drove to Lloyd Neck.

Saturday, October 7

Left at 11:00 in Franklin for New York. Lunch at Harvard Club at 1:00 with Bill Castle, ex-President Hoover, Ackerman,[108] and three or four other Republicans. Of course, I am rapidly being lined up as a Republican, although actually I have no special interest in that party. My primary interest lies in the character of a man, and not in whether he is a Republican or a Democrat. I would as soon vote for one as the other. The issues between them are quite superficial at this time. I think, however, that they will begin to clarify and become more fundamental from now on. Whether or not future issues will choose to follow either of these parties remains to be seen. As far as I am concerned personally, I have but little fear of being classed as a Republican for long. I have too little interest in either politics or popularity. One of the dearest of rights to me is being able to say what I think and act as I wish. I intend to do this, and I know it will cause trouble. As soon as it does, the politicians will disown me quickly enough—and I will be only too willing. I shall have far more interest in my own ideas than in their support. At least I shall hold my self-respect—and possibly that of a number of other people. I have no intention of bending my ideas or my ideals to conform

108. Carl W. Ackerman, journalist and author. Dean of Columbia University Graduate School of Journalism.

to the platform of either party. One must make certain compromises in life—that is a part of living together with other men—but compromise is justified only when the goal to be gained is of greater importance than what is lost in compromising.

We discussed the American and European situation at lunch. Hoover read a speech he proposed making, in regard to the neutrality bill and arms embargo. (The same one from which he read me extracts at our last meeting.) The suggestion was made that some Senator be induced to advance the idea of a partial arms embargo on the floor of the Senate before Hoover spoke—a Democratic Senator if possible. Question arose as to whether a Democratic Senator would do it, etc., etc.

It struck me that there were no particularly brilliant ideas advanced at the lunch. The Republican Party will have to get better leadership than I have yet seen if it is going to solve many of the problems the country is now facing. Nevertheless, Hoover and Castle have a far broader outlook on the European situation than most people I know who have had similar opportunities to judge it. I would feel much safer if they were controlling our foreign policy instead of the group now in Washington.

Castle is a fine fellow, and I like him very much. He has had a long experience in the State Department. I regard his advice as good along certain lines; but he is far too conservative for these times. Also, like all politicians I know, his mind is occupied with issues which are important only in a very stable era—they are relatively superficial in these times. I get a great deal from talking to Castle, however, and he represents an outlook I don't want to lose contact with.

Ackerman (Columbia School of Journalism) is an able man, but I gained the impression that he had a very journalistic sense of values. He suggested, among other things, that I might make a flight to South America in the interest of keeping this country (and South America) out of the war!

All of the men at lunch were interesting and *far* above average, but I do not believe they represent the type that will lead this country to a new life.

Hoover (and many other people I know) thinks Roosevelt wants this country to get into the war eventually. As a matter of fact, I am afraid that may be true. Roosevelt can persuade himself that about anything he desires is to the country's best interest.

Walked to the parking lot on Forty-third and drove back to Lloyd Neck.

Anne and I talked over the possibility of her writing an article in regard to the war—advocating another attempt at settlement before it starts in earnest. We both feel strongly that nothing is to be gained by the war continuing. We also feel that peace in the fairly near future is a reasonable possibility, and that it is essential for people to know the facts of the European situation rather than rely solely on the misinformation and propaganda they are getting from the press.

After supper we walked down to the beach together and lay on the shore, looking up at the stars. The night was very clear, and the Milky Way brushed across the sky directly above us. There was hardly any wind or sound—except from the ripples lapping on the sand. Walking up the road from the shore, Anne told me: "The trouble with me lately is that my heart is beating too fast. The world is too beautiful and too terrible at the same moment."

Monday, October 9

Anne read me parts of the article she is working on in regard to the present crisis. It is, as all of her work, excellent, and I believe it will have great effect at the right moment.

I telephoned Byrd, Smith, and Hoover, and told them I planned on speaking over the radio again next Friday night. I told them I planned on advocating the continuance of an embargo on offensive munitions (supporting Hoover in this item), the restriction of our shipping as far as European belligerents are concerned—but not in this hemisphere, and the refusal of credit to belligerents. They all felt Friday night was an opportune time for the address.

Byrd believes in the complete repeal of the embargo, but agrees with me on the restriction of shipping and credit. Smith would prefer the retention of the embargo, but agrees on shipping and credit. Hoover is in accord with all these points. Personally, I think the embargo has become a symbol that is out of all proportion to its actual importance in this instance. Hoover told me he would release his statement to the press on Wednesday. Smith feels the prospects of peace are fairly high. Byrd says the neutrality bill is not likely to come to a vote in the Senate for another ten days or so.

Tuesday, October 10

Spent the day writing and telephoning the radio stations in Washington. We will have a large phone bill this month. I prefer to contact the stations in Washington rather than in New York because I now know the people there personally. Finished the semifinal typed draft of my address. I decided to take the night train for Washington. Drove the Franklin to a garage and took the 12:50 train from Pennsylvania Station. Again, only an upper berth available. After all, an upper berth is a luxury in comparison to the way I used to travel—sitting up all night to save money.

Wednesday, October 11

Off train at 7:45. Phoned Borah and accepted his invitation for lunch in his office in the Capitol at 1:00. I outlined to Borah the points I planned on making in my address, i.e., an embargo on offensive arms, the unrestricted sale of purely defensive munitions (the Hoover proposal), the refusal of credit to belligerents, and the restriction of American shipping from European belligerent countries and their danger zones. Borah said he felt we could consider ourselves successful if Congress would adopt even an embargo on offensive arms. He said he felt it essential to continue the fight against repeal, however, and intended to do so. He said he felt the program I outlined was good and practically said he would support it if the opportunity arose. (He told me the last time I had lunch with him that he would be willing to make a compromise on his stand against repeal if he felt such a compromise would be successful. Otherwise, he would fight repeal to the end.)

During the lunch Borah and I discussed the coming presidential election and the possible candidates. Neither of us are Roosevelt men, of course. Borah made the startling statement that he thought I might make a good candidate! This idea has been discussed in the press in isolated instances and in a few of the letters that arrive in the mail, but it is the first time anyone in an important political position has mentioned it to me. I have, though, considered the possibility carefully in time past, just as I have given careful consideration to many suggestions in regard to my life in the future. Many years ago—about 1927 or '28—Henry Breckinridge[109] suggested that I lay my course toward the White House. I concluded, however (and I have never regretted it), that my happiness and usefulness lay along other routes. Among other things, I enjoy too

---

109. Lawyer, active in Democratic politics, Assistant Secretary of War (1913–16) under President Woodrow Wilson. For many years Lindbergh's legal adviser and friend.

much the ability to do and say what I wish to ever be a successful candidate for President. I prefer intellectual and personal freedom to the honors and accomplishments of political office—even that of President. I told Borah I felt his suggestion was a great honor but did not believe I was well suited for political office and that I would probably be very unhappy if I ever held one.

After lunch I walked from the Capitol to the Senate Office Building, to Byrd's office, and talked to him about the points I intended to make in my address. Then to Shipstead's[110] office at 3:30 to discuss the possibility of my going to Minneapolis to deliver an Armistice Day address on November 11.

Phoned Anne at Lloyd Neck and suggested she come down tomorrow.

Friday, October 13

Spent the morning working on final draft of address. Anne read it and made several very good suggestions, which I incorporated. This talk is going to create more criticism than the last one. It is more detailed and more controversial. However, I think it is desirable to get people thinking about fundamental problems and to speak clearly on this present issue of "neutrality." The criticism which arises is of very secondary importance.

Taxi to the Mutual studios, arriving at 9:00. Quite a number of people there. Spoke from 9:30 to 9:45. Spent twenty minutes with the guests in the studio, then returned to the Anchorage with Fulton Lewis and his wife.

Saturday, October 14

I took a taxi to the Navy Building for a 9:30 appointment with Dr. Lewis. We discussed research facilities, and Lewis gave me a report he had drafted for our special committee on research facilities. I have made a point of drafting the committee's reports myself, but I thanked Lewis and took his draft. We will go over it at our next meeting and make whatever changes seem desirable. Lewis is a good politician—almost too good at times—but a very valuable man for NACA and one we would have great difficulty in replacing.

110. Henrik Shipstead, Democratic Senator from Minnesota.

Monday, October 16

Met General Arnold in his office at 12:15. He and I took a taxi to the Army & Navy Club, where I had engaged a room for a meeting of our special committee on research facilities. Admiral Towers and Mr. Hinckley arrived a few minutes later. We went over Lewis's suggested draft of our report and decided to adopt only a fraction of the recommendations he had outlined. Our most important decision was to recommend the establishment of a new NACA engine-research laboratory. Our meeting lasted till past 2:00.

Opened some of the letters from a sack of mail that had been sent over from the Mutual studios earlier in the day. There were many intelligent letters and telegrams, and nearly ninety per cent of those opened were favorable. Of course, the people who like what you say are more likely to write than those who don't—at least that is true in the intelligent classes. The unintelligent group is more likely to write when they don't like what you say. A neatly typewritten or handwritten sheet is usually favorable, while you can be almost certain that a dirty, scrawly, penciled sheet, or one written in red ink, is unfavorable. This has been the case with the mail I have received for many years.

In the early evening, Anne and I went to see *Stanley and Livingstone* at a theater on the corner. Excellent films of African wildlife.

Tuesday, October 17

Breakfast in apartment with Anne. Spent most of the morning writing the first draft for our special committee's report—recommending a new engine-research laboratory. Anne worked on the radio address she may give if conditions seem right—a plea for peace. We went for a walk together later in the morning.

Thursday, October 19

Took final draft of special committee's report to Arnold's office for signature. Then to NACA offices for 10:00 meeting of the main committee.

Talked to Orville Wright a few minutes about the possibility of his writing, or co-operating with someone to write, a book on his early flights and experiments. He has talked of doing this for years, but he has never started, as far as anyone knows, and he shows no indication of starting now. It is a tragedy, for Wright is getting well on in years, and no one else is able to tell the story as he can. It seems that Wright does not trust anyone else to tell it properly. The words and phrases people use in telling of the achievements of Orville Wright and his brother are never quite satisfactory and never of sufficiently comprehensive accuracy. Wright tells me that "no one else quite understands the spirit and conditions of those times." What people say about them in articles is never "quite accurate."

Orville Wright tells me that some day he may write a book himself; but then he always adds that he does not like to write and that he has not the ability to do so well. There are many writers who would be glad to do a book in co-operation with him, but the writers do not understand aviation well enough to suit him; he prefers a technical person. But when Ed Warner once offered to take six months off from his work, to do a book with Wright, the offer was never accepted. And I am afraid the book will never be written, although I intend to talk to Orville Wright about it again.

It is strange to look at this quiet, mild, gray-haired man and to realize that he is the one who flew the plane at Kitty Hawk on that December day thirty-six years ago.

Got Towers and Hinckley to sign the report of our special committee as soon as they arrived. I read the report later on in the meeting. Dr. Ames's resignation was read. Dr. Bush was elected chairman in his place, and Dr. Meade was elected vice chairman. Dr. Ames has not been well for a long time. He has served on the committee long and faithfully and well. He now thoroughly deserves all the best that old age can hold for a fine man.

Anne and I decided to take the afternoon train to New York.

I went to see *All Quiet on the Western Front*—the bloodiest film I can ever remember seeing. I wanted to find out what type of war film was being shown these days. It is a terrible play and enough to turn anyone against war, but I think it is not a very constructive type to place before the people of America today. We do not want a nation that is afraid of war if it should become necessary to enter one. And *All Quiet on the Western Front* will turn people against war more through fear than through intellect. It will not add to the courage of our country.

Taxi to station.

Friday, October 20

Off train at 7:45. I drove to Lloyd Neck from the Cosmopolitan Club. Great to be in the country and on the sea again. Anne came back on the late train for an 8:30 supper. We walked down to the beach and lay on the sand later in the evening—the night clear and starry.

Saturday, October 21

How much time we spend on plans! It seems a ceaseless problem for us—where to live—what to concentrate on—how best to fit our unique set of circumstances to this changing world. Sometimes I think it would be simpler if I had ten lives to plan instead of one. I could fill them all to overflowing with action, interests, and desires. But with only one it is necessary to choose so carefully and to balance so many factors. Where can we go to give Jon and Land a normal home and school life? Where will Anne be able to write—and do her best writing? Where can we live away from this deadly life of a modern city, and yet not isolate ourselves from those contacts and associations that make up civilized life?

We want to establish a real and permanent home, and we want two things that cannot be obtained in any one location: the intellectual contacts of the city and the strength of a real agricultural country. It probably means living in two places, and I prefer to make the country place our permanent home—something worth passing on to Jon and Land and to their descendants.

For our country home, aside from practical considerations, I am drawn by the West, by the mountains and by the sea. For Anne (and for myself) I want beauty; for the children I want something that can be self-supporting and which is founded on sound agricultural principles. I am drawn by the West—but I think still more by the sea; I cannot describe adequately what the sea means to me. But to find good agricultural land on the sea is difficult—especially when one loves mountains, too.

Sunday, October 22

Anne and I were waked by the sound of guns everywhere. Must be duck-hunting season, I felt, and I was right. Something about it I did not like—possibly because the shots were so frequent that they made the hunting seem on a sort of mass-production scale and took the wild romance away from it. Long Island is no place to hunt ducks, at least not this part of it. One might as well hunt them in a zoo. It puts hunting in the same class that a Long Island estate puts farming. Somehow, I never have felt at home on Long Island and, much as I am glad to have spent the summer here, I will be glad to leave. Anne, I think, feels about the same way. There is something unstable and lavish and even unhealthy about this area—and Lloyd Neck is far far better than the area closer to New York; Lloyd Neck is just beginning to be spoiled.

Morning papers carry a rather silly article by Harold Nicolson about my radio addresses—reprinted from some English publication. Like so many others (I expected something better from him), he attacks me personally rather than the things I advocate with which he disagrees. Naturally, the English did not like my addresses, but I expected a somewhat more objective criticism from them than from my opponents in the United States. However, the country is at war, and one should be prepared to overlook and excuse many acts from the citizens of a country at war—even the things Nicolson wrote while claiming at the same time to be a friend. Nicolson *is* a friend in a sense; after all, he wrote Mr. Morrow's[111] biography and, in doing so, came into the confidence of the entire family. Also, Anne and I rented Long Barn from Mrs. Nicolson (at a very adequate price), and he and she came over to visit us on two or three occasions during the two years we were living there, and we visited Sissinghurst (their home) two or three times for tea. But I do not feel that we ever really knew either of them, or they us. The parts of Nicolson's article quoted by the American newspapers make me certain of this.

There is one point Nicolson skips over briefly in his article which I want to set down more fully here as a matter of record. It is interesting to show the English attitude at the time, and I prefer to have a record of what took place, both for my own satisfaction and because of Nicolson's article and present attitude.

It was in 1936, not long after I had returned to England from Ger-

111. Dwight W. Morrow, lawyer, banker, and diplomat; partner of J. P. Morgan & Co.; adviser to Allied Maritime Transport Council in World War I; chief civilian aide to General John J. Pershing; trustee of Amherst College. In 1927 President Calvin Coolidge appointed him Ambassador to Mexico. His service there brought about a new spirit of co-operation between Latin America and the U.S. He was elected to the U.S. Senate in 1930 (Republican, New Jersey).

many. I had been greatly impressed with the German development of military aviation, and I thought I could foresee what it was leading to. I felt convinced, from what I had seen in Germany, that the Germans would have complete supremacy of the air within a few months and hold about the same place in European air that England held on European seas. I felt it desirable that Germany regain strength, as I thought (and still think) a strong Germany essential to the welfare of Europe. But I did not like to see England fall so far behind in air strength. I regarded a strong British Empire essential to world stability. I had seen enough of aviation in England to realize what a deplorable condition it was in.

As I turned these thoughts over in my mind, I decided that I should attempt to help the aviation people in England in whatever way I could as an American citizen. I was not well acquainted in England and knew Harold Nicolson better than anyone else who had connections with the government. The fact that he was an M.P. also made him seem the logical man for me to go to as an intermediary. I was not at all anxious to take an active part in aviation in England. In fact, I wanted to spend my time in learning about Europe, traveling and, in extra moments, carrying on some experiments I was interested in (biological and others). However, I felt a duty to do something about the situation I saw coming in the European air.

I telephoned Nicolson and later went to London to talk to him. He was interested in what I told him and arranged for a lunch in the House of Parliament with James Ramsay MacDonald[112] and Sir Thomas Inskip, making four of us in all. Inskip, according to Nicolson, was the man who could exercise the most influence in regard to English aviation. I discussed with them the aviation situation in Europe, and I outlined as much of what I had seen in Germany as I felt that I could ethically. Some of the things the Germans had shown me they asked that I not discuss in other European countries, although they said they had no objection to my giving whatever information I wished to responsible authorities in the United States—in confidence, of course. However, I felt I was able to say enough to give Inskip, MacDonald, and Nicolson an idea of the competition they would have to meet in military aviation. They all seemed impressed and interested (if an American is able to judge and recognize such qualities in Englishmen, which I sometimes doubt). They were, of course, very courteous and polite. I told Inskip that I would be

112. British statesman, one of the founders of the Labour Party, and Prime Minister of England, 1929–35.

glad to help in any way I could which would not meet with the disapproval of the American Embassy. I suggested a higher production rate for airplanes, and improved methods of pilot training which would better fit them for service missions (night bombardment, etc.); also, a number of other items. Inskip said he would get in contact with me again, and the lunch ended.

Some months passed by, during which I gradually forgot about our lunch in the House of Parliament. I took for granted after a time that there was nothing they wanted me to do, and I was learning how difficult it was for a foreigner to contribute anything to English life. If it wasn't British, it simply wasn't "best." Then, one day, I got an invitation to deliver a lecture on navigation at the Flying Cadet College (Royal Air Force) at Cranwell. I learned that it was a development of the lunch with Sir Thomas Inskip. I accepted the invitation and had a very pleasant time at the college—fine group of officers and cadets. That ended the entire matter, and I made no further attempt to revive it. Obviously, the English preferred to carry on in their own way, and, after all, that was their decision to make. It was their right and their responsibility. As a matter of fact, I felt rather relieved to be free of any obligation.

One other time when I was in England, I attempted to make them realize what was happening in European aviation. It was at a dinner in York House to which King Edward VIII had invited Anne and myself. Anne was talking to the King after dinner, and I was talking to Prime Minister Baldwin. I started to discuss the aviation situation in England in relation to the more rapid continental development. However, it was easy to see from Baldwin's actions and looks that he preferred not to talk about the subject, so I changed the topic and made no further attempt to bring up anything about aviation.

I believe the events which have taken place since that time have fully justified my concern about the condition of British aviation.

Tuesday, October 24

Threatening letters are beginning to come in with the problems they always bring for us. Where should we spend the winter, and where will the children be reasonably safe from this sort of thing? This house is a little [too] isolated to make me feel comfortable when I am away. Of course, safety for my family lies in my keeping out of the public eye and the attention of the press. That is hard enough in normal times, but in a period of crisis in which one's country may become involved in war, one must take part in the affairs of his country and exercise his influence in the direction he thinks right. I feel I must do this, even if we have to put an armed guard in the house. But how I dislike the idea of Anne and Jon and Land living under such an environment. It is a fine state of affairs in a country which feels it is civilized: people dislike what you do, so they threaten to kill your children.

We probably can't spend the winter on Lloyd Neck, and we don't want to spend much of it in Englewood. We must think clearly. No one can tell what the next five or ten years will hold. Personally, I think a great change is coming all over the world.

Friday, October 27

Lunch at Next Day Hill—Mrs. Morrow, Anne, Constance, Connie Chilton, Janet Johnson,[113] Aubrey, and myself. After lunch we all went down to see the Little School. Most of the structural work is completed. The heating system is installed and running. The outside of the building is painted (white), and the first coats are going on the inside walls. The linoleum is about to be laid. The outside grading is still to be started. The building is attractive in appearance, and I think well designed as a school.

Sunday, October 29

Anne and I talked over plans again. When the tide was high and the sand covered, we ran over the rocks of the breakwater to the end, scaring the gulls who flew a hundred yards or so out to sea as we approached their favorite rocks at the end of the breakwater. There they stayed, riding the low waves like the feathers that they were, eying us and obviously hoping we would soon leave and let them return, which we did. There were hundreds of ducks on the water, just over gun-shot range offshore. Occasionally, a few of the younger and less experienced birds swam in closer.

The lull in the European war continues. In fact, there has hardly been any war in the West—probably a few hundred casualties at most. The newspaper reports of heavy actions on the French-German border were

113. Constance Chilton and Janet Johnson were co-organizers of and teachers on the staff of the Little School.

as false as usual. The newspapers have made a pretty bad record for themselves in reporting this war, and I believe people are beginning to realize how unreliable they are. Still, the public mind perceives with difficulty and forgets with ease. Most people have probably already forgotten that the Siegfried Line was reported (by our press) broken in five places (by the French Army) during the first day or two after war was declared.

The criticism which arose over my last radio address is beginning to abate. It was about what I expected in amount, although I thought it would be slightly more objective and less personal. It seems that most people do not like to fight on issues but prefer the easier method of personalities.

Anne and I had supper at the home of Mr. and Mrs. Allen Dulles,[114] on the Cold Spring Harbor shore—a quarter hour's drive from our house. Dulles was interesting to talk to, and we have somewhat similar views in a number of instances.

Monday, October 30

The truck arrived from Englewood about 9:00. I helped Anne pack some of the suitcases. The truck was finally loaded and left at 11:00.[115]

I may go to Minnesota to speak on Armistice Day—November 11. It is not decided yet, and I will not be certain until I hear from Senator Shipstead again. However, I am starting to think about the outline of the talk I will give if I go.

Spent the evening with Anne, beside the open fire in the living room, writing and reading. It is our last night in this house.

Tuesday, October 31

Anne left about 4:30 with Soeur Lisi, Jon, Land, Thor, and Skean in the De Soto. I stayed to make final arrangements about leaving the house.

114. Allen W. Dulles, diplomat and lawyer. During World War II he was a member of the Office of Strategic Services, and in 1953 he became director of the Central Intelligence Agency.

115. The Lindberghs were returning to Next Day Hill, Englewood, to live, because their lease for the (Colgate) house at Lloyd Neck had expired and the house was inadequately heated for the winter.

Wednesday, November 1

Went for a last walk on the beach in the morning. Spent the rest of the time packing and making final arrangements for departure. Left for Englewood shortly after lunch. Walked down to the Little School building soon after I arrived at Next Day Hill. The grounds were never more beautiful—the trees all colored, and age mellowing the house and grounds.

Saturday, November 4

This morning I telephoned [Simon] Elwes, the English portrait painter, to ask if he would do a portrait of Mrs. Morrow. We have for a long time been anxious to get Mrs. Morrow to have her portrait painted. She agreed to do so a year or two ago, but could not find an artist that suited her. Elwes told me he would be glad to do the portrait and in reply to my inquiry said that his secretary would write to me about prices.

By coincidence, this was also the day on which I had made an appointment to see the sculptor Paul Fjelde, about the possibility of doing a head of my father for the Minnesota Historical Society. Dr. Nute and I talked about getting a head of my father for the Society many months ago. She suggested Fjelde and at my suggestion wrote to him recently, asking if he would do the work. I am anxious to have it done while I am nearby so I can offer suggestions and criticisms.

I had a 12:00 appointment with Fjelde. He is a man of a little over forty-five years, agreeable, and pleasant. He did not have many samples of his work in the studio. However, there were two or three heads and some plaques, in addition to photographs of other pieces he had done. His work is rather conventional. However, I think he might do a better head of my father than some well-known sculptor who would have little interest in it, especially in view of the fact that it must be done from a small number of not-too-good photographs. I liked Fjelde's appearance and attitude, and I think he might, through desire, interest, and enthusiasm, make this head his best piece. The fact that he is a Scandinavian is also an advantage, for he will understand how to handle the Scandinavian features my father had.

This seems to be a day of art. I stopped at Tiffany's on the way back to Englewood to pick up Despiau's head of Anne,[116] on which they had engraved, at my request, the following inscription:

ANNE MORROW LINDBERGH
By Charles Despiau
Paris, 1939

Tuesday, November 14

Anne and I drove to New York for lunch at the Cosmopolitan Club with Mr. Weeks[117] of the *Atlantic Monthly*. We took a taxi to Harcourt, Brace and Co. afterward and spent ten or fifteen minutes with Mr. Brace.[118] Mr. Harcourt[119] was out. Brace was disappointed that Anne did not have another book ready for publishing. I took back the original drawings I made for *Listen! the Wind* when we left. Harcourt, Brace and Co. has been holding them for me.

Wednesday, November 15

Took the 5:15 for Dayton and the NACA conference, which takes place there tomorrow. I transferred to the special NACA car from Washington at Harrisburg. Supper in the diner with Victory. Discussion with various committee members afterward.

Thursday, November 16

Off the train at 7:00. All of the members had breakfast with Colonel Deeds at his home on the outskirts of the city (Dayton). I sat between Orville Wright and Ed Warner. I talked to Orville Wright again about writing a book, but with no more success than before.

We went from Colonel Deeds's home to Wright Field and made a tour of the field before the NACA meeting. Most of the discussion centered

---

116. Presented to the Museum of Modern Art, New York City.

117. Edward A. Weeks, editor and author.

118. Donald C. Brace, one of the founders of Harcourt, Brace and Co., in 1919, of which he was vice president and treasurer until 1942, and then president.

119. Alfred Harcourt, co-founder of Harcourt, Brace and Co., and president until he retired in 1942.

on the annual report of the committee, its wording, emphasis, etc. The trouble with these committees is that none of the members can give them enough attention. I usually feel I am wasting time on the NACA and that I should either give up my membership or put more time on committee affairs. During the summer I feel I have really done something for the committee, but I have no intention of continuing to devote so much time to it. I want to do other things. Consequently, I have suggested to the chairman that someone who can give more time be appointed in my place when my term expires. I have felt I should resign ever since I went to Europe in 1935, and I wrote to the chairman to that effect several times. I withheld my resignation only because he requested me to do so.

The NACA is an important organization, and if I intended to continue activity in aviation I would want to hold my membership. Aviation, however, is past the stage which held greatest interest for me—that of pioneering and development. Now it is better for men of a different temperament to carry it on into the routine place it will hold in commerce and life in the future. There is still romance in aviation, but of a different type. I shall always be interested in it, probably much as one loves and is interested in a grown child. But I realize, and have for a long time realized, that my mind is turning to a diverging path. Where it will lead I do not yet know.

After the meeting we had lunch together and then made a second and more detailed tour of the field before boarding the 5:00 train back to New York.

Sunday, November 19

Anne and I drove to Long Island for supper at the Blackwells' home. They had invited several other guests, including a Mr. Romano, who was a sort of combination scientist, magician, yogi, artist, conversationalist, and clairvoyant. He looked, and said he was, half French and half Spanish. Said he had traveled all over the world and spent many years in the East—China, Tibet, India, etc. His sleight-of-hand work was the best I have ever seen. He was extremely clever, but left one wondering why he devoted such ability to such triviality. He told me some of the things he did were just fake, and that was not difficult to see. He said some of his work was not fake, but telepathy (or whatever else you want to call it). And on the latter statement I am unable to contradict him by explaining otherwise what I saw him do. His cleverness and handwork leave me wondering, though, if there is not some other explanation. I shall describe some of the things he did.

Romano talked incessantly and threw unsurpassed vanity out with every sentence. He was good, knew he was good, and wanted to tell everybody about it. I wondered if he used this type of conversation purposely as a mild form of hypnosis, but he impressed me as being extremely vain aside from his profession. Romano was of medium height and build with very highly developed muscles bulging through a dark business coat and vest, which looked as though they might be stuffed here and there with something besides muscle. He asked me to feel his arm, and it felt more like wood than flesh when he flexed it. He had dark, rather curly hair with gray vying about evenly with black for eventual supremacy. He looked about fifty-five and claimed to be seventy-six. Thick eyeglasses covered Latin brown eyes.

Romano touched my right hand with his left, clasping my fingers lightly with his own for a moment, then he held the closed but extended fingers of his right hand about ten inches away from the palm of my left hand (held out in a vertical position). I felt a very distinct current of air strike the palm of my hand. It was so distinct that I felt quite certain it came from a rubber tube in his sleeve (although I could see none). Romano repeated this demonstration for one of the women in the room, but after she said she felt the air current, he put a large, book-shaped cigarette box between his extended fingers and her hand, and she said she could still feel the current of air. I asked him to do the same thing for me. The current of air without the box was very distinct and could not be mistaken. When he put the cigarette box between his hand and mine, however, I thought I could feel a slight current, but it was not at all distinct; probably it was only a feeling due to suggestion.

Romano stopped his pulse beating while I held his wrist, and he told me to listen while he made his stomach start digesting. The latter was supposed to be demonstrated by the sound of air passing around in it. I think he simply swallowed some air; at least the sound was the same as when one swallows air.

One of the women in the party said her eyes ached. Romano used a form of hypnosis on her—telling her that when he passed his fingers over her eyes they would be better (looking intently at her while talking). He moved his extended fingers over her closed eyes, with a downward movement. She said she felt better immediately.

Romano showed us some sleight-of-hand work and some beautifully done card tricks. But with his first card tricks, someone in the room had to select a card and touch it in doing so. I am always suspicious of a card trick where someone touches the card they select. It was his later card tricks that interested me and that I do not understand. He did one of them with Anne, and as it was typical of the others, I shall describe it.

Romano took a pack of cards and, while holding them with faces away from him, spread them out in his hands, telling Anne to select a card in her mind. In two or three seconds he asked if she had selected it. Anne replied, "Yes" (no other words passed). Romano then closed the deck while the faces of the cards were still away from him, turned the closed deck around, and spread it open again with faces toward him. In a few seconds he selected a card and extended it toward Anne, face down, asking her to name the card she had selected. Anne said, "King of Diamonds." Romano turned the card over. It was the King of Diamonds!

I was standing watching only a few feet away while this was going on. If Romano had been working with someone else than Anne, I would have thought it collusion. But the fact that he did it with Anne eliminates that possibility. I am unable to give an explanation unless it was actually mind reading in one form or another. Being of a cautious nature in matters of this kind, I would like to see the demonstration repeated and study it carefully before coming to the latter conclusion. I believe there is some form of transmission between minds, but the ease and control Romano demonstrated makes me hesitant to say too quickly that it was actually mental telepathy and not a skillful trick I failed to discover.

I shall not take time to describe much more of the evening. Romano talked of everything under the sun, it seemed, and was certainly wrong in a number of his statements. Nevertheless, he is a remarkable man and, as I have said, the most able I have ever seen in this field. A young New York doctor, whom I met once before at the Blackwells and was much impressed with, told me that Romano was deeply interested in medicine. This doctor said he had given Romano a bad case of arthritis to cure and that Romano had achieved very good results with his treatment.

Monday, November 20

If I remember correctly—I have not the first book here—this is the anniversary, the second anniversary, of this record. While we were living at Long Barn, I decided to start a daily record in earnest. I have written a daily record for short periods in years past, but never for more than a few weeks at a time. Now I feel this one is well begun. How long it will go on I cannot tell. The more active my life is, the more difficult I find this record to keep. And when the quality of material to record is best, the conditions—personal and environmental—for recording seem worst. Good writing necessitates a life of its own, and is prevented, or at least cramped, by most other activities. It is impossible for me to sit down in a quarter hour sandwiched between action and write about the day's incidents, except in a most mediocre way. Then, writing a diary takes away from writing letters and from contact between people, which depends to quite an extent upon letters. I know I wrote more and better letters before I started writing this record, and I think letters may be more worth while. On the other hand, there are things you can put in a diary that you cannot very well put in a letter, and I believe a diary clarifies your thinking even more than letter writing.

Day at Englewood—dictating, writing, and reading. Two trips to school for inspection of work and conferences with Connie Chilton. Have finished second reading of Fisher's third volume and am now re-reading Whitehead's *Adventures of Ideas*.

When I watched Romano stop his pulse, I was under the impression that he had something under his armpit; at least, he held his arm pressed close to his side. Today, I put a rounded piece of soap under my armpit, pressed my arm close to my side, and found that my pulse stopped beating. Later, I found that by holding my arm in the right position I could stop my pulse without having anything under my armpit. Also, I found that the "digesting" noise Romano made in his stomach could be duplicated exactly by simply swallowing air.

Tuesday, November 21

Fifteen ships reported sunk by submarines and mines during the last four days.

Usual trip to school after breakfast. The linoleum laying and painting in the first-floor classrooms are not far from completed, and the halls and office rooms are started. The basement is still to be done. All the workmen are concentrating on the first floor to get it ready for the school to open on November 30. We have decided to open even with workmen still in the building. Otherwise, we would have to postpone the opening until after Christmas vacation. By shifting the Thanksgiving vacation slightly, we are giving the workmen three extra days instead of opening on the twenty-seventh. If necessary, we can put two grades in one room for a few days and let the work go on in the empty rooms.

Much of the planting in front of the building has been completed, and it makes a great difference in appearance. The front walk will certainly not be ready by the thirtieth, but the work road can be used in the beginning.

Drove the Franklin to New York for an 11:30 appointment at Fjelde's studio. I went over the photographs of my father which Dr. Nute sent (duplicates from the Minnesota Historical Society's collection) and discussed them with Fjelde, commenting on their characteristics so he could better understand my father's character and typical features. The bust is only in a roughed-out state at present.

Friday, November 24

Met Mrs. Morrow at Elwes's studio at 3:00 and discussed portrait he is to do of Mrs. Morrow. He had a number of portraits there in all stages of completion. All seemed well painted, but most of them I did not like. I am afraid it was because the subjects had more effect on me than the painting. They were of New York society men and women and made me feel I wanted to take Anne and the children as far away from where those people lived as I could.

I am not convinced that Elwes is a great artist, but I feel he is among the best of contemporary portrait painters and that he handles his paints beautifully. And he is still young. I believe we can get no one better for Mrs. Morrow, except Augustus John, and he is in England and possibly not obtainable even if she could go there.

After Mrs. Morrow left, Elwes and I talked about England and the war. He was objective—as most Englishmen are—but receptive to outside ideas—which most Englishmen are not. I felt there was a continental "give and take" in our conversation. Drove back to Next Day Hill from Elwes's studio.

Sunday, November 26

Elwes came out for lunch with Mrs. Morrow, Anne, Margot, and myself. He spoke to me of Anne's "exceptional violet-colored eyes"—as if I didn't know about them! As a matter of fact, I *would* like to have a painting of Anne by Elwes. I think he might get something about her that Brackman[120] missed—much as I like Brackman's painting of Anne. No artist could get all of Anne in a painting. I think I shall consider getting Elwes to do Anne—but he is high in price ($5,000 for a head and shoulders)—and I hate to bite on his fishhook baited with "violet eyes." Still, he is probably just using subtle English bait in an American pond, and maybe there are so many fish in it that any bait is good enough. I hate to have him think it works that easily, though. If I get him to do Anne, it will be because I like his work—and he will think it is because he spoke of violet eyes—but, after all, there is more amusement than importance in the situation.

Anne finished writing her article, "Prayer for Peace," this afternoon and after discussing it we decided that it should be published. We both feel it is essential to get people in America thinking clearly about Europe and what is taking place there. I dislike Anne getting into the situation at all, but it is better to take part in preventing a catastrophe than to be dragged to the guillotine after it has taken place. There is a time when everyone must act, and I have little sympathy for those who wait for the flood to sweep over them. More than one artist has shouldered a gun to protect his art. And thank God Anne has the courage to do that if it is necessary. I don't believe a woman exists who is her equal—if one ever did.

We decided to try the *Reader's Digest*. We think it by far the best magazine of large circulation in America—but we are afraid it may be too late for the January issue, and I think it would be a great advantage to have "Prayer for Peace" come out at Christmastime. (The *Reader's Digest* is placed on the stands about the twenty-fifth of the preceding month.) I phoned the *Reader's Digest* editor at his home, but no answer. Phoned Jim Newton, and he said he would contact the *Reader's Digest* in the morning.

Monday, November 27

Jim Newton called at 8:30. He had talked to Miss Clark of the *Reader's Digest*. Most of the forms for the January issue have gone to the printers, but she thinks it will still be possible to get Anne's article in. I talked to

120. Robert Brackman, American painter; member of the faculty of the Art Students League in New York.

Miss Clark on the phone, and then to the editor, Mr. [Kenneth] Payne, working out arrangements. Anne spent the morning checking the manuscript, and Christine retyped it in time to give a preliminary copy to the *Reader's Digest* messenger who called for it at 1:00 P.M. The editor (Payne) phoned about 5:00. Said he liked the article very much and would be able to get it in the January issue by taking two others out, which were not important for that issue.

We went to bed early so Anne could have as much time as possible to work on her article. It must be handed to the *Reader's Digest* messenger at 1:30 Tuesday in final form. As I lay in bed, I realized that Christine could not [again] finish typing the article in time for Anne to go over it carefully and make the changes she wishes to, and always does make in a final draft before it goes to the printers (those changes that, like the last strokes of an artist's brush, often make the difference between excellence and genius). Anne would need the article most at the same time Christine would be copying it.

There was only one answer. I told Anne I felt restless and would sleep in another room so that I would not keep her awake with a hard day ahead. (I would not have been successful if she had not been half asleep by that time.) Went up to the room on the third floor which we have been using as an office and retyped the article. Since I use two fingers on a typewriter, I did not finish until 6:00 A.M., but I enjoyed it. I felt I was doing something essential and worth while, and hard work is a real satisfaction when you have that feeling. Fatigue never does catch up with you if the goal you have is great enough, and I felt that Anne's "Prayer for Peace" was great enough. Bed at 6:00.

Tuesday, November 28

The messenger from the *Reader's Digest* arrived at 11:00 with a letter from Payne containing several suggestions in regard to the article, most of which Anne had covered since the preliminary copy was sent to him. He liked the article, and his suggestions were intelligent and constructive. We turned the final manuscript over to the *Reader's Digest* messenger at 1:30. Anne worked on it up to the last minute.

After another telephone talk with Payne, Anne and I went for a long walk through the woods. It was a great relief to both of us to be outdoors again and to have all the details in connection with the article completed. However, I think it was worth the effort, for people will never be more receptive to a plea for peace than at Christmastime. And if there is not peace before spring, God only knows what the summer will bring to Europe—and to all of us, for that matter. I do not see how England and France can survive another major war without their internal conditions becoming chaotic.

Wednesday, November 29

To Little School with Anne after breakfast. The place was in chaos—rooms and corridors filled with teachers, school equipment, workmen, tools, members of Morrow family, small boys running back and forth, and even Thor lying dejectedly in the center of the hall. Fortunately, the teachers are so happy about the new building that they don't mind the mess it is in. The workmen are behind their promised date and feel a little too chagrined to complain about the teachers and the equipment, and the children love the noise and excitement and feel that a sort of circus is going on for their benefit. So it will probably work out all right, and by the time the school gets down to routine the workmen will be gone, or at least gone from the ground floor. I doubt they will be entirely finished with the building and grounds before Christmas.

Phoned Deac Lyman, Jerry Land, and Mr. Hinckley about the possibility of Phil Love[121] being appointed to the CAA. Phil told me he was interested in the appointment, and I want to do everything I can to help him get it for two reasons. First, because I think he is as well or better fitted for the position than anyone else in the country; and second, because he is one of the finest fellows I know.

Jon asked me to get him a lasso a few days ago, and I brought a short "spinning rope" back from Abercrombie & Fitch the last time I was there. Jon said he wanted it to lasso four boys who were enemies of his at school. I told him he better try one at a time, and I talked to him in detail about the desirability of having some of the boys on his own side—preferably at least half of them if he expected the lassoing to be effective. Jon has some of the tendencies and all of the courage of a terrier. He starts a fight regardless of the odds against him and has already had one

---

121. Philip R. Love had been a cadet in Lindbergh's class at Brooks and Kelly fields in Texas, 1924–25. Lindbergh chose him as one of the pilots for the St. Louis–Chicago air-mail route in 1926. Later, he was an officer of the Bureau of Aeronautics, Department of Commerce. He was an Air Force colonel in World War II.

or two unpleasant experiences at school as a result. Fortunately, the fighting at school is not yet beyond the pushing stage.

This afternoon I was standing near the Mexican Room window when I saw four boys about Jon's age coming up the hill from the school. A moment later, Jon came around a corner of the house, swinging his lasso around his head and charging down at all four of them. They stopped, and when Jon got about ten feet from them he stopped, too, swinging the lasso. The four boys began to move forward slowly, two of them moving out to the side to surround Jon. Jon backed up toward the house, facing the two boys downhill, but with the other two behind his back. One of the boys behind started to close in but did not dodge low enough to miss the lasso, and the end of it struck him heavily on the side of the face and put him out of the fight for several minutes. But Jon lost the swing of his lasso, and it dropped to the ground. The other three boys grabbed it and were soon joined by the fourth. Jon hung on to his end but was dragged downhill by the four boys, yelling at them as he went. They tried to tie him to a tree, but Jon was much too quick for that. Then, when they found the tie-to-tree plan would not work, two of them pulled one end of the rope while the other two gathered acorns—large, heavy ones—and threw them at Jon's face as hard as they could and from a distance of about two feet. It obviously hurt, for their aim was good. Jon screamed but would not let go his hold on the rope.

At that moment Thor entered the picture with far more strategy and effectiveness than Jon had displayed in his attack. One of the four boys had a dog, and apparently Thor had just seen it from the hilltop. He emerged suddenly from behind a tree and pounced on the strange dog, fur up and all teeth showing. I shouted at the dogs. My shouts and the snarling of the dogs broke up the fight over the lasso.

After the dogs were straightened out, I got Jon away alone and told him how difficult it was to fight against such odds. I suggested again that he find some way of getting half the boys on his side—possibly by letting those on his side play with the lasso now and then. I explained that it was inadvisable to go into a fight unnecessarily against such odds. Jon agreed and went off to find the boys, who had by that time disappeared in the direction of the schoolhouse.

Later in the day I found (by inquiring discreetly) that he had carried out my suggestions to advantage—getting two of the boys on his side with the lasso, and all having a good time. I like his ability to go back into a bad situation and work it out satisfactorily. I have now seen him do that on a number of occasions.

Saturday, December 2

Went for a long walk through the woods with Anne and Thor. We could not see more than a hundred yards through the fog, which hung heavily in the trees and over the damp ground. We felt shut off from all the tension and nerves of New York. Even the gray, burnt-over drabness of the scraggly woods seemed full of mystery and veiled beauty. How one feels the need for solitude in this artificial modern life!

Friday, December 8

We had dinner with Mr. and Mrs. Harcourt and Carl Sandburg, who recently finished his "War Years" biography of Lincoln. He is interesting, kindly, and mild-mannered—the type of man who gives one renewed confidence that a quiet, unseen vein of character runs through this country still, as it has in past generations. Possibly the times that are coming will bring it to the surface again. Sandburg has an air of infinite patience—and one gains confirmation of this impression in glancing through his books —some million and a quarter carefully chosen words, Harcourt tells me, representing twenty years of study and work.

Saturday, December 9

Anne and I went for a short walk, talking of the winter, and of building a permanent home somewhere in this country—the same old problem we have tried so unsuccessfully to solve all these years—how to obtain safety, normalcy, beauty, and a balance between seclusion for work and contact for inspiration. Of course, we cannot obtain everything we want in a home, but it is essential to weigh every element with the utmost care. Nothing is more important than one's home and all it represents. The satisfaction of living, the effectiveness of thinking and acting, spiritual depth and appreciation, all are intertwined to a large extent with the home one lives in—not that these elements are *impossible* without a home, but they are lacking in balance. One needs roots, and those roots must have real soil to grow in and come back to. We have wanted for years a permanent home that we loved, and now I must find one—but it is difficult to look clearly into the future in these unsettled times.

Stability will be hard to find from now on for an indefinite period. War and social upheavals are likely to upset all plans. But one must try; we may never see stability again in our lifetimes as we have known it in the past. If we cannot build on a home, then we must build on life and the living of it, even though it be from day to day. When there is life, there is adventure for the taking, and the world is filled with beauty if one does not become blinded by convention and routine. Whatever the future holds, it will be well worth living—if the living is done intelligently. One must not hang life entirely on a home, no matter how much it means. One must try as best he can and then be satisfied with what he attains. With a wife like Anne and children like Jon and Land, I probably should not ask for more—but it is really for them I want a home and land to give them the feel of soil and growth and the true elements of life that I found on the farm in Minnesota as a child.

Sunday, December 10

I read some of the writing I have been doing and decided to start it fresh again. It is extremely difficult to convey in words to others what you yourself feel and have in mind. Words are inadequate to convey more than a portion of thought and when written down often give an appearance of being contradictory when the idea behind them is perfectly consistent. For me, this means rewriting again and again.

Told Anne I had arranged with Elwes to paint her—as a trial balloon. I would not think of making a definite agreement without Anne's approval; she knows that, but still is never quite certain whether I am telling her the truth or not under such circumstances. Anne was partly embarrassed, partly angry, and partly pleased. I saw immediately that she could be persuaded to have the portrait done, and I am very anxious to have one of her by Elwes.

Tuesday, December 12

Anne and I drove to New York for her first appointment with Elwes at 2:30 in his studio at 36 Central Park South. After a few minutes, I left her there while I drove to Fjelde's studio to leave the new pictures of Father I had found over the weekend.

Wednesday, December 13

Spent the afternoon writing ("A Conflict of Rights"), going over old papers, and repacking the bedroom closet. Had early supper with the children and then left for New York at 7:00. Arrived at the hospital at 8:00 to see Major Barry. I just learned that he has a hopeless cancer and cannot live more than a few weeks. I have not seen him for years. He used to be secretary and treasurer for Transcontinental Air Transport. A friend of his wrote me that Barry wished to see me, and of course I went to the hospital. He is a fine type of man, and I think no company ever had a more loyal or honest officer. I never knew him really well, but I always liked and respected him. His wife, son, and daughter-in-law were there and told me he did not know the hopelessness of his case. Personally, I would prefer to know if I were going to die. I would not want to be misled. It is impossible to know with certainty how one would feel under the actual test of approaching death, but I do not believe I would fear it, and I would want to know of the meeting in advance. It is the last, and possibly the greatest, adventure of life.

Saturday, December 16

In the evening Anne and I drove to the Harry Davison home [on Long Island] for a Davison family dinner—Harry and Anne, Trubee[122] and Dot, Mrs. Davison,[123] Anne and myself; no other guests. We listened to a radio account from South America about the *Graf Spee* being ready to sail out to enter battle with the British and French warships waiting for her—an extremely dramatic situation. Also listened to Dewey's[124] speech —largely against the Administration, of course. It was well delivered, but seemed very superficial to me. Possibly a political speech has to be superficial to be successful these days. They are all busy dodging the most important and controversial issues.

122. Trubee Davison, Assistant Secretary of War for Aviation (1926–32), a trustee of the Daniel Guggenheim Fund for the Promotion of Aeronautics, and later president of the American Museum of Natural History.

123. Mrs. Henry P. Davison, widow of the J. P. Morgan partner, and active in philanthropic, social, and civil work.

124. Thomas E. Dewey had been elected district attorney for New York County in 1937. He was Governor of New York from 1942 to 1954 and Republican nominee for President in 1944 and 1948.

Sunday, December 17

Evening radio reports the *Spee* blown up by her crew at Montevideo.

Wednesday, December 20

Anne and I drove to New York for a 7:30 dinner with Jim Newton, Mr. and Mrs. Twitchell, and Dr. Frank Buchman.[125] It was the first time we had met Buchman, and I was more impressed by him personally than I had been by the radio speech I listened to several weeks ago. He has a certain magnetism and openness, and I felt that he was sincere and honest in all he was doing—although I would want to know him a little better before coming to a final conclusion. I still cannot understand what it is in his "movement" that brings out such devotion and enthusiasm in his followers. Nevertheless, with all my reservations, I believe it is a constructive movement at this time and under present conditions. Possibly it will develop into something better. If it does not, it will not last.

Friday, December 22

Anne went to the theater with Mrs. Morrow and Margot in the evening. I did not go with them, as I would be sure to be recognized, and there would be the usual unpleasantness and pushing forward of the worst types of people—for autographs, etc. I knew they would have a better time if they went alone and were let alone, so I put on my glasses, blew my nose as I purchased a ticket, and went to see *Gone With the Wind*. I was not recognized and enjoyed the film, although it seemed a bit tedious in places.

It is interesting to see how much effect a pair of glasses has—even the rims without any glass that I usually wear. Of course, when Anne and I go together we are easily recognized even though we wear glasses. But when we are alone, glasses make a tremendous difference, and we are seldom recognized on the street. Stupid people are fooled by the glasses, and those who are more intelligent usually realize—on the few occasions

125. American evangelist, who founded the international movement of Moral Re-Armament in 1938. The movement stressed absolute honesty, purity, love, and unselfishness for personal and national spiritual reconstruction.

they do recognize us—that we wear the glasses because we want to be let alone. Of course, glasses or no glasses, America is much more difficult for us than Europe in this respect.

Monday, December 25

Christmas—Jon and Land's day. The floor of the Mexican Room is covered with toys, unopened packages, paper, string, Christmas cards, etc. Anne and I left the children later in the morning and went for a two-hour walk, arriving home just before lunch. We went through the woods and crossed the "hill" road to the north of the house. Thor went with us, of course. Most of the perfunctory callers had come and gone by the time we returned. Mrs. Morrow, Anne, Constance, Margot, Dwight, Aubrey, René d'Harnoncourt,[126] and I for lunch. Afternoon spent playing with Jon and Land, talking to René, and carrying on routine of various types. René and I talked about the Southwest and the Indians there. He knows them well.

Tuesday, December 26

Anne and I went for a walk through the woods. We decided to rent the Manor House on Lloyd Neck for the months of January through May. Anne phoned Mrs. Wood [127] after we returned to the house, to tell her of our decision, and to make the necessary arrangements.

We plan on leaving for Detroit tomorrow with Jon.

Wednesday, December 27

Early supper at Next Day Hill; then Anne, Jon, and I drove to Grand Central Station. Anne and Jon purchased the tickets while I put the De Soto in a nearby garage. We met again on the train and were not recognized; this is important if we are really to enjoy ourselves with Mother and give her the utmost happiness. The Detroit press can make our visit very unpleasant if they know we are in the city. Jon immediately

126. General manager of the Indian Arts and Crafts Board, U.S. Department of the Interior, 1937–44, d'Harnoncourt became the director of the Museum of Modern Art, New York, in 1949.

127. Mrs. Willis Delano Wood, the owner of the Manor House.

claimed the upper berth. He regards anything high and treelike as his domain.

Thursday, December 28

Off train at 8:45 (slightly late). Mother and B. were waiting for us, and we all had breakfast together. Mother was extremely happy. It is the first time Jon has been in her home and, of course, he can go with us from now on when he does not have to be in school. He is old enough so that the trip is not difficult, and he loves it. It all reminds me very much of my own childhood visits to my grandfather[128] and grandmother in Detroit. Jon is now having the same kind of experience.

Anne and I drove to Henry Ford's home for lunch, picking up Jim Newton at his hotel as we passed through Detroit. We did not like to leave Mother so soon after our arrival; but I was anxious to talk to Ford, and this was the best chance I would have. Also, I knew Mother would like nothing better than to be alone with her grandson.

There were five of us at the table: Mr. and Mrs. Ford, Jim Newton, Anne, and myself. I talked to Ford about the war, the industrial situation in America, about his ideas of decentralization, etc. He is a combination of genius and impracticability, with the genius definitely on top. Ford is a great man and a constructive influence in this country. One cannot talk to him without gaining new ideas and receiving much mental stimulation. His greatness is demonstrated by his vision and his success industrially and by his interests and activities in many other fields. His impracticability is demonstrated by his "Peace Ship" [129] at the time of the last war and by such ideas as his big transport plane (the one that started with Ford's conception of a plane for one hundred passengers and ended with an abortion designed for thirty-six passengers, which taxied across the field at Dearborn but never took the air). The plane was too far ahead of its time, and much too far ahead of the aeronautical engineers in the Ford organization. But even though it was a failure, it showed real vision. Ford simply tried to take too big a step for that period of aviation. I can't give him as much credit for the "Peace Ship" idea. It seems utterly

128. Dr. Charles H. Land, Lindbergh's maternal grandfather, great pioneer in porcelain dentistry. He invented and constructed high-temperature gas furnaces.

129. In December, 1915, Ford chartered the Scandinavian-American liner *Oscar II* and sailed with a privately sponsored peace delegation to the neutral European countries in an attempt to mediate an end to World War I.

silly to me, but possibly I am not well enough acquainted with the circumstances that surrounded the project. It is unfair to judge without more information than I have.

At lunch we were introduced to a new drink—carrot juice. It was very good, I thought. Ford said it was made by crushing carrots and collecting the juice.

After lunch he and Mrs. Ford showed us around the house—their books, rooms, etc. We left about an hour after lunch and drove back to 508 Lakepointe Road. B. had saved some old pamphlets and papers of Grandfather's for me, and I found some of his original patents in other old papers in the basement. One of these related to a "baby jumper"—a device for rocking or swinging babies.

Friday, December 29

We all went for a drive in the morning in Mother's Ford. I think I have never seen her happier. The road went out along Lake St. Clair. All water was covered with ice—most of it broken and rough. The day was quite cold and the ground covered thinly with snow. We passed Selfridge Field on our way, and terminated our journey at an "Indian" store which sold souvenirs from the nearby reservation.

The papers are carrying a rumor that there is a revolt in the Russian Army attacking Finland. I do not know whether I have less confidence in the Russian Army or in the accuracy of newspaper reports!

Saturday, December 30

After breakfast I spent the morning clearing out the basement room. I am anxious to get it done before we leave. Mother will not let B. do it because she is afraid he will throw away some paper or article I want. I want to get it cleared out so she won't worry any more about it. Also, so that if there are any more papers of interest there they won't be destroyed or lost. The bundle of my grandfather's patents was alone worth all of my effort.

In the afternoon Mother, Anne, Jon, and I went to see Aunt Harriet and Uncle John.[130] They are both getting old, and she is so frail that we

130. Brother and sister, they were the children of the first wife of Lindbergh's great-grandfather Dr. Edwin Albert Lodge. "Uncle John," the Honorable John

have not known how she could live through the last decade. They have never seen Jon, and children mean more than anything else to old people, I believe. We must start back to New York tomorrow night, and none of us want to go.

Sunday, December 31

Spent the morning with Mother and B. and finishing in the basement. We all spent the afternoon together and drove to the station—five of us packed in the Ford with the suitcases—in time to board the 7:29 train for New York. We have never had a better visit and look forward to the next.

Monday, January 1

Off train at 8:45. Took taxi to garage and drove to Englewood in the De Soto.

Tuesday, January 2

Dr. Nute, who had been visiting her sister for the holidays, came in the morning and stayed for lunch. After lunch I drove her to Grand Central Station, and then went to Elwes's studio, where Anne had just started a sitting. The painting shows promise, I think, but it has not sufficient strength or depth as yet. I was rather disappointed, but it is a little too early to judge fairly.

Wednesday, January 3

Anne and I had planned on taking a train to Cambridge, Massachusetts, for dinner with Professor and Mrs. A. N. Whitehead[131] tonight. However, when I phoned the reservation office I found that all the drawing rooms and compartments were taken. Since we cannot ride in an open

---

C. Lodge, had been mayor of Detroit in the late 1920's and was for many years alderman and one of the city's great political figures.

131. Alfred North Whitehead, English mathematician and philosopher, who taught philosophy at Harvard.

Pullman car without being recognized and bothered by people, we decided it would be more fun to drive—even though it takes about six or seven hours from Englewood to Boston. We left Next Day Hill in the De Soto at 11:45, bought sandwiches for lunch on the way, and arrived in Cambridge at 6:15.

Professor Whitehead is all one would expect from reading his books. He is the type of Englishman that makes one understand how the greatness of the empire was built. But where are these men in England today? Were they killed under the volunteer system in the last war? Have they gone to the colonies and empire in order to find opportunity in youth? Or have the changing conditions of modern life in England failed to bring them out?

Whitehead has a wonderful mind. It was worth many trips to Boston to talk to him. Mrs. Whitehead is also a remarkable person. It is seldom, indeed, that one finds two such people together.

Whitehead discussed many subjects, and Anne and I were only too glad to have him talk and to listen to him. He spoke of the rise of "gentleness" over the centuries. I asked him if he thought it could exist without the protection of "force." He agreed with me that it could not. I was anxious to get his reaction to this, as I came to that conclusion long ago, and if he felt differently I wanted to learn of his reasons.

We left the Whiteheads after one of the most interesting evenings I have ever spent, and drove back as far as Ford's "Wayside Inn" [132] for the night.

Saturday, January 6

Drove to Fjelde's studio after breakfast. He started doing a bust of me. Several weeks ago he asked if I would sit for him. I was very hesitant about accepting, for several reasons. It was really a bust of Father I wanted, and I did not want to confuse the plan of presenting the Minnesota Historical Society with Father's bust and a project to do one of me at the same time. Also, I had just sat for Jo Davidson in Paris last winter; Anne was done by Despiau about the same time; the year before we both sat for portraits by Brackman; Mrs. Morrow and Anne are at this moment sitting for portraits by Elwes; and Constance, Aubrey, Anne, Mar-

132. An old tavern at Sudbury, Mass., which Henry Ford restored as part of a re-creation of a miniature colonial development, modeled after Greenfield Village in Dearborn, Mich.

got, Dwight, and I are planning on a head of Mr. Morrow by Davidson as a present to Mrs. Morrow (in fact, we have practically completed the arrangements). It seemed the family had sat for enough heads and portraits.

After starting the sitting, I found there was an advantage I had not thought of, and which in itself made the sittings worth while. As I sat, or rather stood, for Fjelde, I placed the bust of my father about six feet in front of me, with one of his photographs just below, or to one side, of it. Every quarter hour or so, I would change the position of the bust, so I could look at it from a new angle. This not only gave me something to look at and to think about, but I found that the constant looking at the head would bring to my attention little details of shape and shadow that permitted Fjelde to make great improvements through the added effect of these small changes that I suggested to him. His patience with and interest in my suggestions made me feel well repaid for agreeing to sit for him.

After leaving the studio I had lunch at the Engineers Club with Jim Newton and John Roots and two of their friends from England—a labor leader and ex-Communist named [William] Rowell and the tennis player [H. W.] "Bunny" Austin. Rowell was an interesting character; he had been a sandhog in his time and, in addition to the multitude of other experiences that always fill the life of such a character, he had been "blown" up through the river he was tunneling under. Newton told me that Rowell had turned Communist when, after being out of a job and short of food in London, his baby had died for lack of proper nourishment. I cannot blame a man for turning to anything that opposes the existing order under such circumstances.

Wednesday, January 10

After lunch, I drove to Elwes's studio to see the progress he had made with Anne's portrait. He was not at all satisfied with it, and I felt, too, it was not very satisfactory. The portrait he had done of Mrs. Morrow, on the other hand, was exceptionally good.

I left the studio after a few minutes to make some purchases we will need on the trip we are planning to Florida. Back to the studio at 4:15 to pick up Anne. Elwes had made progress, and I think he will eventually end with a good portrait.

Anne and I drove back to Next Day Hill and had supper together on the sun porch. We spent the evening in the Mexican Room—Anne playing on the piano and singing. Later we had music from the phonograph and radio—Anne dancing beautifully to it—the Spanish dances she did in Mexico years ago.

Thursday, January 11

Anne went to New York for an 11:00 appointment with Elwes. Lunch alone. Anne called while I was eating to say that Elwes had decided to start an entirely new portrait, as he was dissatisfied with the old one; it had apparently been a bad morning in the studio. I admire Elwes for making the decision, but we will both be badly pressed for time—he is leaving for England soon and we for Florida. We had arranged our departure for Florida to correspond with his finishing date for the portrait.

Friday, January 12

Mr. Payne, editor of *Reader's Digest*, came for lunch, and I talked to him about the possibility of putting the article I am writing in the *Reader's Digest* for March or April. I gave him the manuscript, and he said he would telephone me after reading it. He suggested the possibility of placing the article first in some other magazine, such as the *Atlantic* or *Harper's*.

Saturday, January 13

Payne called on the phone and said he thought the *Reader's Digest* would like to have my article and that he had sent it on to [Edward] Weeks, editor of the *Atlantic*. He suggested going through with the plan of *Atlantic* first and *Reader's Digest* second—the procedure they use with most of their articles.

Anne phoned and said that Elwes was anxious for me to come down to see the new portrait. He had apparently made a good start. I drove in to New York. It was much better, and I think he may do something really good this time. But we must change our plans if he is to finish it; we must postpone our departure date for Florida, and that is complicated, for I have already made most arrangements, including the reservation of a compartment on the train. Still, I think the trouble will be worth while if we obtain a good portrait.

Monday, January 15

Drove to New York for lunch with Juan Trippe at the Cloud Club. We talked of the war, new Pan American equipment, the reorganization of the company, etc. I stopped to see Priester[133] and Gledhill[134] after lunch, and we talked of Pan American's plans for the future—of transoceanic routes and equipment. It seems they have eventually come around to the ideas I have been advocating for so many years in regard to using landplanes for the North Atlantic route! Priester was violently opposed to this policy not so long ago. I have for many years advocated the start of transatlantic routes with flying boats, but changing to landplanes after the pioneering years were passed. I have written many letters and reports to Pan American in regard to this.

I was also interested to find that my old reports in regard to the Azores have turned out to be correct, after much controversy and opposition. I took the stand that the Azores were not suitable for the scheduled year-round operation of flying boats, because they had no harbors of sufficient size. The Pan American expedition to the Azores, on the other hand, reported that it would always be possible to find satisfactory operating conditions on the lee side of one of the islands. I disagreed with this report. Recent operating experience has demonstrated that I was correct in my stand. Returned from the Pan American offices to Next Day Hill.

Tuesday, January 16

Drove to New York for a 12:45 lunch with Mr. Weeks (*Atlantic*) at the Century Club. He liked my article and is going to put it in the March issue of the *Atlantic*. We went over it together, and he made several very good suggestions for improvement.

133. André Priester, vice president and chief engineer, Pan American Airways.
134. Franklin Gledhill, vice president and general purchasing manager of Pan American Airways, from which he retired as a senior vice president. He had been a World War I pilot.

Saturday, January 20

Anne left for Elwes's studio at 10:40, and I drove to Fjelde's. After leaving Fjelde's studio, I drove to that of Elwes. He has Anne's portrait nearly done and it is incomparably better than the first, although I think it is not quite as good as the one he is doing of Mrs. Morrow; there is not enough depth of character in it for Anne.

Constance came to the studio and feels as I do about the portrait. Elwes decided he wanted to work on it during the afternoon also, so Anne, Constance, and I took a taxi to Robert's on Fifty-fifth Street for lunch and rushed through it in order to give him as much good light as possible. We were back at the studio in forty-five minutes, as we had promised to be, but Elwes was, as usual, twenty minutes late. I stayed at his invitation and watched him finish, just as dusk was settling. I am satisfied with the portrait, and glad to have it, but I believe that Elwes could do better if he were not under pressure. He is rushed for time and worried about the war.

Sunday, January 21

First part of morning spent packing and making final arrangements for our departure for Florida.

The train—the Florida West Coast Special—left at 2:05. Anne and I decided to have our meals in the diner, even though it might involve some newspaper difficulty when we arrived in Florida. We were recognized in the diner, of course, but no one bothered us, and the train employees were all very considerate and nice. After we had returned to our compartment from the diner, Anne suddenly called out and pointed at a Pullman car on a siding we were passing. I looked just in time to see the name COLONEL LINDBERGH painted on its side. Strange coincidence; must be a relic of the old Transcontinental Air Transport–Pennsylvania Railroad days.

I spent the rest of the afternoon rereading [H. G.] Wells's *Outline of History*. I read it many years ago, and I think it gives one a general grasp of the sweep of human history better than any other book I know. Of course, Wells leaves much to be desired, but I admire his vision and his courage in these volumes, and I enjoy his opinions and eccentricities— they are both stimulating and provocative. What the volumes lack is much more than made up by what they contain.

Anne is reading *The Medieval Mind* by [H. O.] Taylor. I hope to start it soon.

Monday, January 22

We arrived at Haines City at 2:40—a little late. Jim Newton was waiting for us and drove us to the island of Captiva. It was a long drive through west-central Florida. We stopped for a few minutes in Fort Myers while Anne purchased some warmer clothes. The weather has been exceptionally cold for Florida. We arrived at the ferry to the island about 6:00. It was a half-hour trip across, and the full darkness of night had fallen by the time we reached the other side. The lighthouse was flashing, and the palms on the beach silhouetted dimly against the sky as we approached the dock.

After another half hour spent driving over a shell road that passed between palms and Australian pines, we arrived at the small frame cottage Jim had rented for us and which his mother had stocked with provisions in a manner that grows only with ability and experience. She had sent over one of her servants to take care of us—an old Negress, chock-full of character and that mixture of friendliness and respect that makes the Southern Negro so lovable. There was nothing fawning or antagonistic about her. She was a part of the land and of the life of Florida; she knew neither the problems nor the unhappiness of the Northern Negro.

We had supper, and then Jim, Anne, and I walked for a mile or so along the white sand beach in the moonlight. Thin clouds changed the shading of sea, trees, and sky, leaving the moon now clear and bright, now veiled and dim, but always an eye above watching and guiding us. We went to sleep with the wind blowing softly through the bending boughs and long needles of the Australian pines, and with the odor of semitropical land and sea coming through the window and relaxing all the tension one has gathered through the weeks of a New York winter.

Tuesday, January 23

It was a little warmer in the morning, but with a light rain still falling at intervals. Jim, Anne, and I talked over a trip to the Everglades. In the afternoon we got into Jim's little eighteen-foot centerboard sailboat and spent about two hours in the bay. The wind was just right, and the spray blew pleasantly over our southwesters.

Anne, Jim, and I had supper together and then went for a walk along the beach in the moonlight. The sky has cleared and the moon is nearly full. We held a competition to see who could put a stick in the sand nearest to the heavy surf. We followed each receding wave and, of course, all got wet.

Wednesday, January 24

A cold wind was blowing when we awoke. Anne and I spent the first part of the morning reading and writing by the fireplace. The pitch-pine logs burned furiously. I have never seen such a hot fire from wood. We went for a walk on the beach before lunch, and I went for a swim alone. The water was very cold. I stayed in the surf for about half an hour, letting it break over me. The waves were so close together that, try as I would, I could not get out beyond them. They washed me in faster than I could swim out. I think, however, I did not use quite the right technique. In the afternoon Anne, Jim, and I drove to the end of the island and tried fishing, but without success. We had lots of fun, though, even in the cold, penetrating wind that was still blowing. I practiced casting.

Thursday, January 25

Jim left at 8:15 to make arrangements for a boat to go to the Everglades. Anne and I spent the morning reading and writing, and walking on the beach. The day is a little warmer, and the sun is out part of the time; but the wind is still cold. Jim returned in midafternoon. He had arranged to get a thirty-foot cabin cruiser from one of his friends. It draws only about two and a half feet of water, and we will be able to go far up the rivers of the Everglades with it. Evening by the fireplace. Tomorrow we will leave Captiva and spend the night on Estero Island in a cottage near the wharf where our boat is moored.

Friday, January 26

In the morning Anne and I went for a two- or three-mile walk along the beach. The sun was out but the wind still blew, and the air felt cold against our cheeks. About a mile south of the cottage, we found a long bank of shells—truckloads of them—lying two or three feet deep and in almost perfect condition. There were dozens of different kinds. Anne

309

found one "lion's paw," and I found two. They are supposed to be quite rare, but they are by no means as beautiful as many of the common varieties.

Saturday, January 27

Last night was the coldest since we arrived in Florida. We spent the morning packing the boat and making final arrangements for our departure. A young fellow by the name of Charles Greene is going with us on the trip as guide and boat captain. He knows the boat and its two 70-h.p. engines well and, more important, knows almost every foot of the Everglades. He was game warden for the Audubon Society for five years— about twenty-five, slender and wiry, with a frank and intelligent face. When he saw the diving outfit I put on board, he said he knew where two old cannon were lying in about twenty feet of water in the vicinity of the Keys. So we put a prong shovel on board so we could dig up the bottom around where they were. By noon all was ready and we started out. Within half an hour we were in the Gulf, rolling heavily in the following sea. However, Anne and I were able to keep a pot on one of the two burners of the little stove, and we put together a simple but adequate meal. We stopped at Marco to fill our fuel tanks, as we were not sure where we could get gasoline again. Then we went on to Indian Key, which we reached in darkness and where we anchored for the night.

Sunday, January 28

This morning, we started off soon after 8:00; we were in no rush and had no intention of making daybreak starts. Anne and I cooked breakfast as we cruised south. We stopped at Turkey Key later in the day and found we could get fuel, water, and ice. The old fisherman in charge of the station said everyone was suffering from cold and that they had never experienced anything like it before. (It had dropped almost to freezing during the night.) Turkey Key consists of a few fishermen's shacks. From the appearance of the place I should say the population is a few dozen at most.

From Turkey Key we cruised on to Shark River and turned up toward the headwaters. We passed by a small and cold shark that wiggled stiffly down out of sight after I touched it with a boat hook. We cruised on for miles up the river, twisting with it through the swamps and rows of man-grove trees—over the dark, quiet, glassy water. No one unfamiliar with the Everglades could have found his way, for watercourses turned off at every bend, and one looked identically like the other. All were lined with mangroves, and behind them, when one had a glimpse through some gap in the foliage, was the high dry grass of the swamps. Birds were every-where—ducks, pelicans, ibis, and egret, in addition to many smaller birds. Sometimes a flock of a hundred or more would fly within 200 or 300 feet of the boat.

Only the unusual cold kept us from feeling we were in the heart of a tropical land. A strange, out-of-place northern sky took away the bril-liant light and hot sun one associates with southern Florida. And there were other signs of the cold. While we were coming down the coast we had passed by many dead fish floating on the surface. Then there was that numbed-with-cold shark I poked with the blunt end of the boat hook. Farther up the river there were dead birds—very small ones, not larger than an English sparrow—floating on the water. And there were no alligators or tarpons to be seen anywhere. One of these little birds lighted on the boat rail and was so cold that it could fly no more. I picked it up in my hand and put it in a paper bag which, after putting a few air holes in it, I hung up in the cabin. (It was no use; the bird was exhausted and died during the night.)

We anchored for an hour at the old site of an outlaw's home; he had died years ago, and there was no longer any sign of the buildings he lived in. But the sugar-cane patch was still there—growing wild—and there were banana and lime trees. The bananas were too green, but we cut several stalks of cane and picked up a dozen ripe limes under the trees.

We anchored for the night near the head of Shark River—about twenty-five miles from the mouth. The moon came up an hour or two after nightfall, flooding the river and the mangroves with light. Anne and I took the small boat and rowed for half an hour in the moonlight. The quiet of night was broken only by the calls of birds and the splashing of a water turkey. When we returned, the rails of our boat were covered with frost.

Monday, January 29

We got up late, for the night was cold—the coldest we have yet experi-enced on our trip. The sky was clear, however, and it soon became warm in the sun. We spent most of the day cruising through the Everglades—narrowing, widening, ever opening on ahead. At one place we left the cruiser at anchor and went farther upstream in the little boat we had towed along for that purpose. We kept going until the stream disappeared in the thick swamp grass. The engine would not run, so we poled the boat as far as we could push it into the swamp. There was no way to go farther except by wading. Great flocks of white birds flew low overhead, their wings swishing through the air. We anchored in Tarpon Bay for the night. Jim, Charlie, and I took the little boat and rowed along the shore after supper, searching the banks with our flashlights in the hope of seeing deer. But there was no eye larger than a spider's to reflect the beams. In one place the grass was matted down where several alligators had been sunning themselves.

Tuesday, January 30

We cooked breakfast while we were still at anchor. We cruised out through the mouth of Shark River into the Gulf and turned south. All the large mangrove trees are dead here—killed by the recent hurricane. As far as one can see there is a tangle of dead branches. We anchored again off Middle Cape, near a cold tarpon moving sluggishly at the surface of the water.

Leaving the cruiser at anchor, we walked inland over a strip of hard ground to the edge of the jungle growth, about half a mile from the shore. There were a few low coconut palms (the high ones had been blown over by the hurricane). We cut open some of the dry coconuts and drank the milk and ate the meat. We carried several of them with us back to the boat. Here and there we passed by bits of roof from some house that had collapsed in the hurricane and been washed away by the high water it caused.

From Middle Cape we cruised on down to Marathon, where we took on fuel and ice. Jim went ashore and called his home by phone. A telegram had come to Anne from the *Reader's Digest* saying the British Ministry of Information in England had requested permission to reprint "Prayer for Peace" in a pamphlet and in foreign newspapers. Anne wired back permission provided it would be carried in full. We talked it over together and wondered whether the British Ministry had misunderstood her article, or whether England was gradually and at last realizing what she is up against in this war.

We took the cruiser about a mile from Marathon and anchored for the night beside a sand bar which is submerged at all but low tide. After supper Jim, Charlie, and I went out in the small boat, spearing crayfish on the bar. We had a gasoline lantern on the bow of the boat, and each got several. They are larger than our Maine lobsters but have no claws big enough to eat.

Wednesday, January 31

We cruised out to the Gulf Stream and fished for a time, but no one caught anything. We talked over the possibility of looking for the cannon Charlie spoke about when we started on the trip, but we decided the water was too rough and muddy to let us find them in the first place and that the barracuda were biting too well to make it safe for us to go down even if we could find them. The barracuda had followed up almost every fish we caught in the morning—long, dark shadows in the water, coming within ten feet of the boat sometimes. They cut some of our fish in half before we could land them, and they will eat anything, even another barracuda. We went back to the Keys for lunch and then stopped at Marathon to fill up with fuel and supplies. After that we turned north.

The sunset was exceptionally beautiful, turning the thin broken clouds into bands and layers of brilliant colors while the smooth, glasslike surface of the Gulf turned gold and purple and finally merged into the gunmetal sheen that precedes complete blackness. Anne and I sat on the forward deck and watched the sun go down. We stayed until all the stars were out—Orion above us, with Sirius shining so brilliantly nearby, and Capella with its little triangle almost directly overhead. We followed the North Star to a landfall near East Cape, where we anchored for the night.

Thursday, February 1

Anne, Jim, Charlie, and I went ashore after breakfast and walked along the beach. We were on the edge of the hurricane country, and most of the mangroves and coconut palms had been killed. We walked inland a half mile to a grove of papaw trees, but the fruit was all too small and green to eat. We walked cautiously, for Charlie said there were many rattlesnakes about—but we saw none.

We cruised into Whitewater Bay and anchored for the night near an island bird rookery. There were thousands of birds—in the trees and dotting the surface of the water as far as we could see—pelicans, cormorants, and ducks. The trees of the island were white with their droppings. The pelicans roosted on the lower branches, and the cormorants on those above. The pelicans have great grace and dignity in flight, but lose both when they make a landing.

Anne and I are beginning to love the Everglades—their beauty and quiet, and endlessness, and isolation.

Friday, February 2

We cruised along the coast and put into Turkey Key for fuel. Then we turned up Chatham River into Chevalier Bay. Anne and Jim and I rode on the bow of the boat a large part of the way. The river and bay were shallow and full of oyster bars which made navigating difficult. As we turned into the bay, we saw that the oyster bars near the far end were covered with white pelicans—200 or 300 of them. Far over on the horizon, a huge flock of birds puffed white like a shrapnel burst, and then disappeared as they turned in a different direction. They reflected the sun only as they banked, and then they seemed to turn into the sky itself—exactly as a puff of smoke. We rowed over to one of the oyster bars and gathered enough for supper. Then we went on slowly toward the pelicans. They let us get within about one hundred yards and then flew leisurely away to the next oyster bar. After returning to the cruiser we started back down the river. For the lake—or bay—was so shallow that we might not be able to get out of it at low tide.

We anchored for the night just above the old "Watson place." Its owner, according to the story, used to hire workers for the summer and then kill them when the time came for them to be paid. The story goes on to say that he disposed of thirty or forty people in this way—mostly Negroes. Finally, he was shot by the indignant people of the town where he went to trade.

Anne and I stood on the bow of the boat as night fell, watching another semitropical sunset with its warm red and golden colors giving way quickly to darkness and a star-filled sky.

Saturday, February 3

We started at daybreak, for the tide was going down rapidly. We grazed over oyster bars and dragged over mud flats on the way out—Charlie doing a very skillful bit of navigating. Our next anchorage was Rabbit Key, where we stopped to look for stone crabs. We found none, but it was a beautiful little island.

From Rabbit Key we cruised on to Cape Romano and anchored again just off the shore. We put on bathing suits and walked for a mile and back over the shell-covered beach. The sun was warm and the wind light. We were, as usual, alone. That has been one of the attractive elements of this trip—miles of beach without other human life; all the Everglades, with no trace of man, except a game warden's launch that passed us one day, and the old outlaw camps. When one lives in a city, one wants contact with human life (there is no difficulty in getting that in New York), but when one leaves the city for a vacation, there is an advantage in having real contact with nature for a time; it is a medicine that is irreplaceable, and one which cannot be obtained in the midst of crowds.

After leaving Cape Romano we turned in through Little Marco Pass and, after cruising a few more miles northward, anchored for the night. We are nearing the end of our trip, and how I hate to leave the Everglades behind for a winter near New York.

Sunday, February 4

We started late and cruised out through Gordon Pass and along the coast to a long sandy beach where we anchored, put on bathing suits, and spent an hour or so in the sun. Jim and I went swimming. We cooked lunch while cruising up the coast and anchored again off Big Hickory Island. Anne, Jim, and I went ashore and walked to the end of the island—a mile or so to the north of our anchorage. There were flocks of different kinds of birds on a bar a hundred yards or so from the beach—many different varieties. As they flew away, each kind flocked together; but the flocks did not separate. They reminded me of squadrons of pursuit planes (ducks) and bombers (pelicans) and observation planes (cormorants) all going in the same direction—separate and yet part of the same plan.

We continued cruising northward, and turned in from the Gulf

315

through San Carlos Pass, stopping at the oyster beds in Rocky Bay to get enough oysters for supper. We all spent the last hour of daylight opening them. After supper we moved on to Estero Bay for the night. Charlie Greene left us there and took the little boat to his home.

Monday, February 5

After breakfast we took Jim to the dock at Fort Myers Beach, and then Anne and I returned to Estero Bay with the boat and spent the rest of the morning cleaning it up. Leaving the boat at dock, we drove to the hotel and had lunch with Jim's family. On the way back to the Fort Myers Beach Hotel we stopped at the boat to unload the last of our equipment. After returning to the hotel, Anne and I went for a long walk on the beach at sunset.

Tuesday, February 6

Boarded the Atlantic Coast Line train at 10:45 at Fort Myers. Spent the rest of the day reading—H. G. Wells and various articles in the *Atlantic Monthly*.

Wednesday, February 7

Off train at 3:20. Taxi to garage on Thirty-fourth Street, where I left the De Soto. Then we drove to Next Day Hill. Jon, Land, Thor, and Skean all came running up as we drove into the court.

Thursday, February 8

Phoned Elwes's secretary regarding painting. She said he had landed in England without difficulty en route.

In the afternoon we drove to Jo Davidson's studio to see the head of Mr. Morrow. It was in plaster and was much better than when we last saw it. Jo had made a number of improvements at Mrs. Morrow's suggestion. And, best of all, Mrs. Morrow liked it very much. We were all afraid that the best head any artist could do would be a disappointment to her. She thinks the profile excellent and is well satisfied with the head as a whole—although she says the full face is not as good as the profile.

Saturday, February 10

Anne and I had breakfast with a Mr. Sumner who is visiting Mrs. Morrow in connection with some project they are working on. I came into the dining room a little ahead of Anne and found Jon asking Mr. Sumner what "infinitesimal" was in French! That is one of the words that intrigued me when I was about Jon's age. I mentioned it to him some time ago, and it has apparently caught his imagination as it did mine.

I packed the De Soto with books for Lloyd Neck, and Christine drove it over to make preliminary arrangements for our moving there.

Thursday, February 15

It has been the heaviest overnight snow I have yet seen in Englewood. Of course, the roads are blocked, and no cars can get in or out. Fortunately, I have no engagements in the city today.

I spent the day packing and making final arrangements for moving to Lloyd Neck tomorrow. Went skiing for half an hour in the morning, and again in the afternoon. The snow is so deep that we had to go over it several times before the skiis would slide downhill.

I ordered a two-door Ford car to replace the Franklin. I hate to let the Franklin go, but it is getting old (nine years) and more and more difficult to keep in repair. I have come to have an affection for it, however, just as I do with every piece of machinery I have used constantly over a period of years. I ordered a two-door car so the children would not get their hands caught in the back door—or fall out.

Friday, February 16

Spent the morning and early afternoon packing boxes, suitcases, and trunks. I am sending all our books from Next Day Hill to Lloyd Neck as the first step in assembling Anne's library. Anne has not been well, so moving is taking more time than we expected. Finally, in midafternoon we started off with both cars—Anne, Jon, Thor, Skean, and I in the De Soto, and Christine, Soeur Lisi, and Land following in the Franklin with the rear seat piled full of baggage. We had a slow trip. The streets in New York were jammed with snow. The Long Island roads were better, but the trip took nearly three hours. We arrived at Lloyd Manor after dark. The house was all lighted, and everyone waiting to help us unload. The house seems more attractive than any we have been in since Long Barn, and it reminds one of Long Barn, although the shape is entirely different —high and compact, instead of rambling all over the grounds.

Monday, February 19

Day at Lloyd Manor—unpacking, arranging office, unpacking books, dictating, etc., etc. I saw the estate manager and arranged to have a Franklin stove put in the little playhouse on top of the hill, so Anne will have a place to write undisturbed.

Mrs. Trask[135] came to visit in the evening, but Anne was not well enough to see her. I walked back to her house with her (just across the road) and met her husband. Still more important, I introduced Thor to their dog. It is essential to have friendly relationships between the dogs of neighboring families. The human relationship can come later and is not quite as delicate to establish. In fact, friendship between dogs may have a decided effect on the friendship between their masters. Thor is sometimes a little difficult in this respect. Tonight's visit, however, was very successful from all standpoints.

Thursday, February 29

Went for two walks with Thor—one in the morning and one in the afternoon. Down to the beach each time. There are hundreds of ducks on the water, just offshore—thousands on some days. When they fly off, their wings make a whistling and swishing sound that can be heard for half a mile or more.

After supper I packed and then left for New York in the De Soto at 9:30. Left the car at the service station for a general check. Taxi to station. Boarded the 12:50 train for Washington.

135. Mrs. John Trask, a neighbor and friend at Lloyd Neck, who had gone to school with Anne Morrow Lindbergh.

Friday, March 1

Off train at 7:55. Taxi to Army & Navy Club. Breakfast. Major Black[136] came into the dining room shortly after I sat down, and we had breakfast together. We talked of Germany and the war.

Taxi from Army & Navy Club to Munitions Building for a 9:00 appointment with General Arnold. Was a few minutes early so stopped to see Colonel Eaker. Discussed air developments with Arnold; also possibility of a trip to Italy. He was interested in the trip and said he would like to see me make it—that it would have his support. He suggested I talk to Secretary Woodring, who will not be here till Monday.

Went to see Lewis (NACA) at 11:45 and discussed NACA developments with him—with special reference to the engine situation.

Had the afternoon free, so took a taxi from the Army & Navy Club to the Smithsonian Institution. I have not seen the *Spirit of St. Louis* for several years, and I wanted to know how it is being cared for. It is nearly twelve years now since I last flew in it.

I was anxious to get in the building without being recognized, so after leaving the taxi I walked around the building in the hope of finding a side door open, but there was none. A dozen or so people were sitting on the benches on each side of the front entrance, watching all passers-by. Another dozen, including guards, were inside the door where the plane is hanging. However, by blowing my nose at the right moment, I got by them all. I did not want to have to talk to the guards, be taken to call on the museum officials, and look at my plane with a crowd of people gathered around.

Immediately after entering, I turned right, into the room of Presidents' wives and dresses. I never thought I should have such a close personal debt of gratitude to Martha Washington, but her dress and figure, and the glass case which contained them, were in exactly the right position for me to stand behind and look through into the adjoining room at the *Spirit of St. Louis*. No one took notice of me there, for if they looked at all it was at Martha Washington's dress, and not at me. I felt she and I had something in common as we watched the *Spirit of St. Louis* together. I rather envied her the constant intimacy with the plane that I once had.

How strange it seemed, standing there looking at the plane, and what

136. Major Percy G. Black, assistant military attaché with the U.S. Embassy in Berlin.

319

a chasm of time and circumstances separated us. Yet in another sense how close we still were! I could feel myself in the cockpit again, taking off from the rain-softened runway at Roosevelt Field, skimming low over the waves of mid-Atlantic, or brushing past a high peak of the Rockies. Such a little plane, it seemed to me today; I felt about it as I once felt about the old Wright biplanes. Still, there was a trimness about the *Spirit of St. Louis* that even now gives me a feeling of pride. I felt I could take it down from its cables, carry it to some flying field, and feel perfectly at home in that cockpit again. (I have, in my dreams, flown the old ship several times since that last landing on Bolling Field in 1928, and I have always felt worried, and sorry I had taken it from the museum lest it crash in that post last flight. I was always relieved when I woke and found I had not really violated my decision that the plane should never be flown again.)

People stopped beneath it as I watched, and looked up at the plane and at the articles of equipment in the showcase. The plane is in excellent condition—perfectly cared for. I stood looking at it for nearly an hour, I think, losing all count of time. Finally, I noticed two girls looking at me—they were not certain—in a moment they would ask. It had been the most pleasant visit I had ever made to the museum—the first one on which I could really think about and appreciate my old plane. I did not want to talk to people. I left.

Saturday, March 2

Spent an hour or so reading the papers and writing letters after lunch; then took taxi through the rain to Smiths' home for "tea," arriving at 4:00. Mr. Frederick Libby[137] (president of the Society for the Prevention of Wars—or some such name) was there when I arrived and left a few minutes later. He (Libby) told me his organization had sent out 140,000 copies of my radio speech, "America and European Wars." Libby looked very much like a New England preacher. He is apparently rather a pacifist, but showed unusual understanding and intelligence (if one can apply the latter term to a pacifist). After Libby left, several of Truman's and Kay's friends came in, including one very able officer from the War College. We discussed the war and American and European military aviation.

137. The dean of American pacifists, and executive secretary for the National Council for Prevention of War.

Left the Smiths' home at 6:00 and took taxi to the Wardman Park Hotel for dinner with Dr. Bush. We talked of NACA matters—who should be reappointed in General Kilner's place, etc. We also discussed Orville Wright and how to get him to co-operate in writing a record of his early aviation experiences. In this connection I told Bush a little about the Wright-Smithsonian controversy and the attempts to get the Kitty Hawk plane back to this country from England. Later on, we talked of antiaircraft developments and many other subjects. I left Bush's apartment about 9:15, took a taxi to the station, and boarded the midnight train for New York.

Sunday, March 3

Off train at 7:40. Walked to Engineers Club for breakfast. Then walk and taxi through light rain to De Soto Service, where I picked up the car and drove to American Museum of Natural History. Planned on looking at the *Tingmissartoq* and spending the morning in the museum. But a sign on the door said it did not open until 1:00.

I then spent an hour driving through the streets of New York, studying conditions and watching the faces of the people. I cruised down Third Avenue to the lower East Side, and drove slowly back and forth through its streets. Then around past the Battery and up the West Side elevated highway, past the *Normandie,* the *Queen Mary,* and the *Mauritania,* all lying idly at their docks and already looking like old ships through need of paint. The *Queen Mary* and the *Mauritania* are painted gray and make one feel the atmosphere of war. The peacetime colors of the *Normandie,* however, have not been changed.

Went to Fjelde's studio for a sitting. Left the studio at 4:45, picked up my suitcase at the Engineers Club, and drove through the rain, which has continued all day, to Lloyd Neck.

Monday, March 4

The trees were covered with sleet when we woke this morning, and large branches had split off with its weight during the night. The school bus could not get over the road, so Jon had a holiday. The sleet continued all morning, and by 10:00 both telephone and light wires were down. I took Jon for a walk before lunch, as he was anxious to go out and I was afraid to let him go alone; it was too dangerous. The ground under all of the large trees was covered with branches, some of them weighing several hundred pounds. We climbed up the hill, slipping over bits of ice-covered branches and waiting for a lull in the wind before running past the high trees along our route. Once on top of the hill we left the woods and walked through the fields, where there was no danger of falling branches.

The damage to trees was great on the hill, where there was no shelter from the wind. Every tree had broken branches, and some were so completely stripped that it seems they must die for lack of leaves next summer. Even the blades of grass in the fields where we walked were coated with ice. They formed stalks of ice with a diameter of between half and three quarters of an inch, and sometimes a foot and a half high. They broke like glass as we walked through, the bits of ice scattering about in fragments. Every now and then there would be the crash of another branch falling from a tree—always with the same sound of breaking glass. At less frequent intervals, we could hear the boom of a whole tree falling nearby in the woods.

The smaller trees were bent so their branches touched the ground. If they could not bend that far, the trunks broke off. It is by far the worst sleet storm I have ever seen. Jon, Thor, and I walked as far as the Woods' house and then started back home. On our return trip the wind, which had been at our backs, bit icily on our wet cheeks, and the rain penetrated every opening in our clothing. The damage done by this storm will be great, and the freezing rain still continues.

The damage is increasing. Whenever one listens near the edge of a wood, there is the constant crack of breaking branches. This sleet is as deadly as it is beautiful. One large tree has fallen across the driveway to our house, breaking a telegraph pole in half as it fell. Another has fallen just at the end of the brick wall which forms our garden. The drive is covered with branches of all sizes. As I sit here in the north parlor writing this record, a huge limb has just crashed down into the brick enclosure outside the west windows. I am writing by candlelight.

Tuesday, March 5

Left for Next Day Hill in the Franklin immediately after lunch. The woods on each side of the road are glistening white and beautiful. Broken branches cover the ground everywhere. Lloyd Neck seems to have suffered the worst for some reason; but Englewood has been badly injured, too. Fortunately, comparatively little damage has been done on the Morrow property.

It was my last trip in the Franklin, and I hated to let the old car go. It seemed like throwing down a true friend simply because he has grown old. I have had the Franklin for nine years, and it has served me well always. But it is hard to get repairs now that the Franklin Company has gone out of business, and the cost of upkeep is becoming too high. Unfortunately, one cannot keep old automobiles for the pleasure of past associations—much as I would like to do so.

The Ford we are buying was in the garage when I arrived at Next Day Hill. I went through the formalities of transferring the Franklin to the dealer; and then, feeling I was doing something wrong and indecent, I drove the shining new Ford out of the garage, past the old Franklin, and down to the house. (The Ford Company has apparently gone to a great deal of trouble to see that I got a good car and engine. The dealer tells me that they pulled out two engines they were not satisfied with and that the engine I have is the third they tried. He says they also did a special paint job on the car.)

For the next two hours I packed various articles that Anne and I wanted at Lloyd Neck and stowed the boxes and suitcases away in the back seat and in the luggage compartment of the Ford until it would hold no more. By that time it was nearly 7:00, and I left for Lloyd Neck. The Ford handles beautifully, and I like it very much. But I miss the old Franklin. I arrived at Lloyd Manor at about 8:30 after a slow drive because of the newness of the Ford. The telephone is working again, but light wires are still down, and the company says it may be two to three days before they can get them repaired.

Monday, March 11

Phoned General Arnold this morning. He made an appointment for me at the State Department at 10:00 Wednesday. Said he had talked to Woodring about possibility of my going to Spain and Italy and that Woodring had no objection; suggested I talk directly to State Department.

Tuesday, March 12

Left for New York in the De Soto at 11:00 and arrived at the [Harlan] Millers' apartment at 12:30. Dr. and Mrs. Lin Yutang came a few minutes later. We went to a Chinese restaurant in the lower East Side for lunch as guests of the Lin Yutangs. Our table was in an open and crowded room, but no one bothered us! The food was excellent, and I think there is nothing better than real Chinese food. Of all the countries I have been in, China and Sweden have the best meals. (England is without competitor in having the worst.)

The Lin Yutangs leave on Saturday on their way back to China. They go through Mexico, then a month's ocean voyage, and after that they must go into China through the back door (because of the war). The final stage of their journey is by air from Hong Kong to Chungking. They will live some miles outside of Chungking. (I suggested they live in a house that was like many others in the vicinity, so it would not attract the notice of Japanese bombing planes. Of course, a house in the country is not likely to be bombed, especially if it is not conspicuous.)

Returned to Lloyd Neck after lunch. After supper I packed my bag and left for New York at 10:00. On the way in I passed a wrecked motorcar at the side of the road. It had been badly smashed, and from its appearance I would judge that the people in it had probably been killed.

I left the Ford in a garage on Tenth Avenue, walked to Pennsylvania Station, and boarded the 12:50 train for Washington.

Wednesday, March 13

Peace terms between Russia and Finland have been announced in Moscow and Berlin. In spite of newspaper vagueness and contradictory reports, they appear to be authentic.

Off train at 7:40. Taxi from Army & Navy Club to State Department for conference with Mr. Tom Burke[138] (arranged by General Arnold). Told Burke that I was considering a trip over the Pan American route to Lisbon and that I would like to go on to Spain and Italy before returning. I told him that before making any definite decision I wanted to find out from the State Department what complications might arise from their

138. Thomas Burke, chief of the Division of International Communications, Department of State.

standpoint in my making such a trip. Burke replied that he would take the matter up and would probably be able to give me some reply within twenty-four hours.

Walked to the Munitions Building for a conference with [Truman] Smith and Whitehead.[139] We discussed the apparent heavy weight of American military planes in comparison to European types. Also, we discussed the new types of fighting planes now being built in Germany to take the place of the Messerschmitts 109 and 110.

Thursday, March 14

Walked through the Washington Monument grounds to the art gallery and spent an hour going through its rooms of paintings and Oriental art. In one small alcove stood a Chinese Bodhisattva of the T'ang Dynasty—life size. I thought of the generations of Chinese worshipers who had knelt and bowed before that idol, and how out of place it was there in the center of a modern room in a modern American museum. I probably would not have noticed it as much if the figure had been lined up beside a number of others along the wall of one of the museum rooms. But there, all alone in that alcove, it seemed singularly out of place. I wanted to take it back to the gold and lacquer decorations of an Oriental temple—to the people in whose life and tradition it belonged.

After leaving the museum, I walked to the Natural History Museum and spent fifteen minutes with the mastodon skeletons and petrified wood logs. I met an old friend in one of the mastodon skeletons, for I remember going to see it with Mother many years ago—one of those memories that hides unknown in the back of your mind until some happenstance calls it forth again. The amazing thing is that so vivid a picture can be completely dormant for decades, as vivid as ever except for a little dust of intervening time.

I took a taxi to the Army & Navy Club; then to the Smiths' for tea with Truman, Kay, Ambassador and Mrs. Hugh Wilson, and Lieutenant Colonel and Mrs. Fiske.[140] (Fiske went to Vidonia—the aviation re-

139. Major Ennis Whitehead, Air Intelligence. He became a major general in 1943 and commanded the Fifth Air Force in World War II; he became second in command of air forces in New Guinea.

140. Lieutenant Colonel Norman E. Fiske, military attaché at the U.S. Embassy in Rome, 1940–41. In 1942 he became chairman of the Joint Intelligence Subcommittee of the Combined Chiefs of Staff.

search station—with me when I was in Rome in 1937.) We talked of Europe and the peace terms between Russia and Finland. General Andrews[141] came for dinner. We went over the European picture again and discussed the trends the war may take. Left the Smiths' home at 10:45. Boarded the sleeper for New York.

Friday, March 15

Off train at 7:35. Drove to Lloyd Manor for breakfast—a late one, about 9:30. Anne is able to go outdoors again now, and we walked up to the little house on top of the hill before lunch. It was the first time Anne had seen the house, and she was very much pleased with it. The view from the hilltop is quite beautiful, and the Franklin stove we put in will keep the room plenty warm enough for this time of year.

Saturday, March 16

In the afternoon I marked our flying trips on the big globe of the world. Anne and I started doing this years ago—marking only the flights we have made together. Our first flight was in 1928, in—or rather around— Mexico City. We have decided to stop with our flights of 1938—making ten years in all, since we were married, and eleven years if we include that circle around Mexico City and over Popocatepetl. I have marked down all of our long flights and as many of the short ones as I could without making a smear of black ink. Wherever we have flown twice over the same route I have put in only a single line.

Sunday, March 17

Left for New York in the De Soto for a 2:00 appointment with Fjelde. He has about completed the bust of Father, and we spent the first hour making minor changes and improvements. Then I sat for an hour and three quarters while Fjelde worked on the one he is doing of me. It was the fifteenth sitting, and Fjelde is worried and apologetic about the slowness. I told him I would be glad to come in whenever I could, no matter how many sittings it took. I have grown to like Fjelde very much, and I

141. General Frank M. Andrews, member of the War Department General Staff, 1939–40. In 1943 he became commander of U.S. forces in Europe.

enjoy talking to him. Back to Lloyd Manor for supper. Have finished my first reading of Lao-tze.

Tuesday, March 26

We had an early lunch, and then I left for New York at 1:00 for an appointment with Fjelde. Spent an hour and three quarters with Fjelde, a large portion of it in discussing Father's bust, and the rest sitting for mine. Fjelde expects to cast Father's bust in plaster tomorrow.

From the studio I drove to the Chrysler Building and spent half an hour with [André] Priester, discussing the transatlantic route and future equipment for it. Priester is now completely sold on landplanes for transoceanic flying! I discussed the Azores operation with him, including the possibility of constructing a landing field on the islands.

I put the Ford in a garage on Thirty-fourth Street, walked to Pennsylvania Station, and boarded the train for Washington.

Wednesday, March 27

Off the train at 7:30, after a night punctuated with jerks of starting and stopping. Spent twenty minutes with General Arnold discussing my proposed trip to Europe. He is anxious to know more of the Italian aviation situation—whether or not they are holding their relative position in view of recent expansion and development in other countries; how fully their productive facilities are being used, whether they are building many planes for foreign use, etc., etc. Italy is now in a number of ways the key to the European situation. After leaving Arnold, I spent half an hour with Major Chidlaw[142] and other Air Corps officers discussing technical differences in American and foreign aircraft. Then spent an hour in the G-2 offices studying data connected with the Mediterranean area and discussing the defensive position on the North African borders.

Taxi to the Capitol for lunch with Harry Byrd. I arrived a few minutes early so walked through the grounds where I played as a boy. For the first time I noticed what seems to be neglect and indifference in the care of the grounds. Footpaths were worn across the grass in many places—deep and yellow—giving more the impression of cow paths in a farm

142. Major Benjamin W. Chidlaw, member of GHQ, Air Forces Staff, 1939–42. In 1942 he became a brigadier general.

pasture than I like to see on the lawns of the national Capitol. Almost every tree on the grounds is badly in need of surgery, and there seems to be an unnecessary quantity of bits of paper lying about. People walk freely across the flower beds. (Of course, it is too early for anything to be growing in them, but even the beds have a ragged, trampled, and untidy appearance.) Worst of all, dozens of initials and names now adorn the outer pillars and walls of the Capitol building itself—some in crayon and others actually carved in the stone. I felt depressed by the walk and could not avoid wondering if I was seeing the signs of the beginning of an American decline, and what could be done to stop such a trend. This nation is too young to decline, but there are alarming signs, and sometimes the smaller ones are most significant.

I sent my card in to Byrd on the floor of the Senate and waited for him in one of the Senate halls. Before going to lunch Byrd took me to see Vice-President Garner in the Vice-President's office. We talked for about five minutes, during which time I told Garner of the time in 1924 when I landed an old "Canuck" in the center square of his home town of Uvalde, Texas. I was flying west and had lost my way. Fuel was running low when I reached Uvalde and finally located my position. There was an open square in the center of the town large enough to land in. I got down all right and refueled; but the square was not large enough to take off from, as it was surrounded by buildings. I decided to attempt a take-off from the street that passed along one side of the square. To do this it was necessary to pass between two telephone poles that were only two or three feet farther apart than the wingspread of the plane. The road was rather badly rutted, and I missed by six inches. The plane was whipped around by the pole, and the nose hit the side of a hardware store, knocking down pots and pans that were hanging on the inside wall. Fortunately, neither the plane nor the wall was very badly damaged—a broken propeller and a few smashed boards being the major consequences of the accident. The store owner was not at all unpleasant about it. In fact, he seemed to enjoy the excitement and demonstrated true Texas hospitality rather than the complaint and objection one would expect under such circumstances. I had the plane patched up and flying again within a few days.

Lunch with Harry Byrd in his office in the Capitol Building. I spoke to him about the need of tree surgery on the grounds, and he said he would try to do something about it. We discussed the war in Europe, the American gold policy, dangers of propaganda, and many other subjects. Byrd has no more confidence in Roosevelt than I have and thinks he may easily run for a third term. Byrd said Roosevelt had promised Farley[143] that he would not run. Farley said later that Roosevelt could easily change his mind. Most people who know the President do not seem to regard his promises very highly. After lunch Byrd brought Senator Shipstead to the office. (Shipstead had called on the phone.) Byrd said goodby and left for the floor of the Senate, while Shipstead and I talked for another half hour.

From the Capitol I walked to the Munitions Building and stopped at the G-2 offices long enough to talk to Lieutenant Colonel Fiske about Italy and the military situation in North Africa. We went over various maps together and discussed the fortifications on the Libyan-Tunisian border.

Thursday, March 28

Spent an hour writing, and then walked to the Senate Office Building for an 11:00 appointment with Senator Lundeen.[144] Lundeen knew my father well, and we spent the largest part of the next hour and a half talking about my father and various memories Lundeen had of him. Lundeen is greatly concerned lest we be pushed into this war eventually—drifting imperceptibly closer, as we did in the last war, until it is too late to stop. We discussed this for a time. From Lundeen's office I took a taxi to the Carlton Hotel for lunch with Thomas Burke of the State Department (International Communications). We discussed South American problems—particularly in relation to Pan American Airways. Also, the various political complications of the transatlantic operation.

Midnight train back to New York.

Saturday, March 30

Jon and I hung a number of maps on the walls of his room (he has the southwest room on the top floor). I found the maps in some of the boxes I brought over from Englewood. They cover most of the world; only Asia and Australia are missing. While we were hanging the maps, Jon

143. James A. Farley, U.S. Postmaster General, 1933–40. He successfully managed the first two presidential campaigns of Franklin D. Roosevelt.

144. Ernest Lundeen, Republican Senator from Minnesota.

brought up the subject of money (by asking me to open his "cash-register" bank). It registers nickels, dimes, and quarters, up to $10.00 and cannot be opened until $10.00 has been deposited. (Jon had only $1.25 in it.) I am very anxious for Jon to understand the true value and significance of money, so I spent fifteen minutes telling him how it was earned and the difficulty of obtaining it. I told Jon he was now old enough to begin earning money himself and that in the future I would pay him ten cents an hour for all actual work he did around the house. Since he has worked very hard recently, cutting and carrying wood for the fireplaces, I told him I would allow him twenty hours for the work he has done since we moved to Lloyd Neck. I paid him the $2.00 in change, and he put it in his bank, ringing up a total of $3.25. Jon is to keep and mark down his own time, using an old wrist watch I gave him a week or two ago.

Monday, April 1

Lunch with [Harold] Bixby. We discussed various Pan American affairs. Bixby has done fine work for Pan American and is now at the head of both the Pacific and Atlantic divisions.

Wednesday, April 3

A telegram arrived, informing me of the death of Mrs. Nettie Beauregard. She was a grand old lady, full of courage, kindness, loyalty, and all those characteristics that make one admire the qualities of old age. She always looked on me rather as a son, and nothing I did could be wrong in her eyes. I always looked forward to seeing and talking to her when I passed through St. Louis. She had a way of giving one renewed confidence in human character. She faced life proudly and resolutely, and I know she faced death in the same way. Anne and I ordered a spray of spring flowers sent to the funeral; one can do so little, except perhaps in honoring the memory that lives on. There is in memory a bond with the dead that may grow as a living spirit—a communication, a contact between life and death that spans that gap called time. And after all, there is no wall but time between the living and the dead—a moment, an hour, a century, without dimension or substance, yet more permanent, more formidable than stone.

I phoned Mrs. Wood and arranged to rent this house for the summer. We do not plan on spending the entire summer here—I hope we can spend part of it in Maine—but we must have some place to use as a base until we can establish a permanent home in this country, and Anne and I both like Lloyd Neck and this old house.

Monday, April 8

Cone[145] and Smith[146] (Pan American) came for supper and to discuss company problems along the transatlantic route—Azores, Portugal, etc.

Wednesday, April 10

Left at 11:30 for New York and lunch at 120 Broadway with Harry Guggenheim and Lester Gardner.[147] We discussed Gardner's plan for the development of the archives of the Institute of Aeronautical Sciences.

After lunch I drove to the Chrysler Building for a conference with Juan Trippe at 3:30. We discussed Pan American interests in Spain and France.

Taxi to Rockefeller Center, where I spent an hour with Harry Guggenheim and Lester Gardner, going through the rooms of the Institute of the Aeronautical Sciences. Gardner showed me a number of old papers and documents, including some of the early foreign contracts of the Wright brothers.

Thursday, April 11

The war continues with almost no definite news; even the most important and major events are shrouded in contradiction. One can read almost anything about the fighting, depending upon what newspaper he buys. It is obvious that the press has no idea whatever of what is actually taking

145. Carroll Cone, onetime director of civil air regulations in the Bureau of Air Commerce and adviser to the U.S. on European aviation, 1936–37. In 1939 he became assistant vice president of Pan American Airways.

146. James H. Smith, a lawyer, who became vice president of the Atlantic Division of Pan American World Airways in 1949, and in 1953 Assistant Secretary of the Navy for Air.

147. Executive, aviator, writer, and publisher of aviation periodicals, fellow and former vice president of the Institute of the Aeronautical Sciences.

place. They report at the same moment that the British Navy has control of the Skagerrak and that the Germans continue to land troops in Norway. A great naval battle is reported under way in the Skagerrak. Reading between the lines, however, it seems to me that the Germans are meeting with amazing success in taking over Norway in the face of the British fleet. If so, it is a victory for air power and a turning point in military history. But has the main British fleet actually entered the Skagerrak, or is it another battle built up largely by the newspapers? After all, modern journalism can make a war out of a dogfight. One must remember that the newspapers reported the German "West Wall" penetrated by the French Army in five places during the first forty-eight hours after war was declared last September, and press reports have been consistently inaccurate.

Friday, April 12

The war reports continue to conflict. Our papers give the impression that England and France have control of the sea, but this seems to be more of a wish than a fact, if one can judge by the little information that does seep through. The Germans are carrying on an extremely daring project. It seems they have great confidence in the power of their aviation to cope with the British fleet. If the British do bring their main fleet within reach of the German Air Force, there is the possibility of one of the decisive battles of world history—and a decisive battle could not be won by the fleet under these circumstances. Therefore I doubt that the British would fully expose their main fleet.

Monday, April 15

Drove to the North Beach Airport for an appointment with Carroll Cone. We walked through the shops and inspected the clippers under repair. Also went through the clipper that was to take off for Europe in the afternoon. I talked to a number of Pan American officers and looked over several maps and charts of the Azores. We discussed weather and sea conditions around those islands. The big rollers have been the main problem during the last winter.

Drove to New York for lunch at the Engineers Club; then to 505 Fifth Avenue for a conference with a Mr. Hart,[148] who desires to bring together

148. Merwin K. Hart, lawyer, and president of the New York State Economic Council.

a number of men who are opposed to this country entering the war. (Bill Castle wrote, suggesting I talk to Hart.) I agreed to attend an informal dinner in New York two weeks from today, at which we would discuss how to counteract the war agitation. I believe this country is still solidly against entering the war, but as German success continues (as I believe it will), more and more pressure will be brought upon us by the Allies and their supporters. I would feel less disturbed about this if I had the slightest confidence in Roosevelt.

Tuesday, April 16

Overcast sky this morning—low ceiling and hazy. I had planned on going to Hartford to get the Lambert plane that we put in storage after sailing for Europe in 1935. Phoned North Beach for a weather forecast. They reported contact flying between New York and Hartford, except in the smoke and haze immediately surrounding North Beach Airport, and said that conditions might improve slightly in the afternoon. I left with Richard Holsten[149] in the Ford at 10:00. Instead of improving, the weather became constantly worse until low clouds rested on the hilltops. When we arrived at Rentschler Field, it was obvious that flying to New York without radio would be impossible during the rest of the day. I sent Holsten back with the car and, after talking to Whelan,[150] the airport manager, for a few minutes, drove to the Pratt Whitney factory to see Wilson.[151] I spent the afternoon talking to Wilson and going through the factory. They have put up a new building since my trip to Hartford last summer and have purchased much new machinery—largely because of French and English orders. Spent the night at the Wilsons' home.

Wednesday, April 17

Spent an hour in conference with Wilson and other officers of the Pratt Whitney organization. Then went through the Hamilton Standard Propeller factory with [Frank] Caldwell, Hamilton,[152] and others. Spent half

149. A young Irishman who worked for the Lindberghs.

150. Bernard L. Whelan, head of the airport division of United Aircraft, 1931–43. He later became general manager of the Sikorsky Aircraft Division and a vice president of United Aircraft.

151. Eugene E. ("Gene") Wilson, president of United Aircraft Corp., 1940–43. In 1943 he became a vice chairman of the company.

152. Thomas F. Hamilton, founder of Hamilton Aero Manufacturing Co., which

an hour with Rentschler[153] before lunch, with officers of the company.[154]

After lunch I took off in the Lambert (now NX-211 instead of NR-211—changed to conform to the new rating policy of the CAA). I have not flown the plane since we left it at North Beach Airport when we sailed for Europe in 1935. I spent an hour in making flights around the field and getting acquainted with the plane again. It is one of the most difficult planes to handle I have ever flown. The take-off is slow, the aileron control sluggish, and the landing tricky. In fact, aside from its appearance, which is quite neat for a high-winged monoplane, the Lambert is almost everything an airplane ought not to be.

I bought it in 1934 after we had put the *Tingmissartoq* in the American Museum of Natural History. I had no special flight planned at that time and did not want to go to the expense and trouble of having a plane specially built. We looked over all the standard types of light planes in the country and found nothing that seemed very good. In fact, there was nothing in any size that seemed a very great improvement over the *Tingmissartoq*. In another year or two, however, new and advanced types would probably be available. We decided to buy something temporary, small, and inexpensive, and decided on a "monocoupe" for the following reasons:

I had flown one of the monocoupes, and while it was a high wing, which I did not like, it handled well. Also, the monocoupe was built in St. Louis, and Harry Knight[155] was interested in the company. I liked the idea of having a St. Louis-built plane, and felt I could do Harry a good turn. I feel a debt of gratitude to all those men who took part in the *Spirit of St. Louis* organization, which I will never be able to fully repay.

---

later merged with Standard Steel Propeller Co. to form Hamilton Standard. From 1937 to 1938 he was president of United Aircraft's international unit.

153. Frederick B. Rentschler, founder of United Aircraft Corp. (in 1928) and its chairman of the board until 1956. He had been a captain of the U.S. Army Air Service in World War I and was in charge of aircraft production in New Brunswick, N.J., 1917–18. From 1919 to 1924, he was vice president and later president of Wright Aeronautical Corp. In 1925 he organized Pratt & Whitney Aircraft Corp., of which he was president until 1930.

154. In 1940 United Aircraft consisted of Pratt & Whitney Aircraft at East Hartford, which produced engines; Vought-Sikorsky Aircraft at Stratford, which produced naval aircraft, including fighters and amphibians; Hamilton Standard Propeller at East Hartford, which produced propellers.

155. Member of the brokerage house of Knight, Dysart & Gamble, and president of the St. Louis Flying Club in 1927, Knight was one of the main backers of Lindbergh's 1927 flight.

I arranged with the Lambert Aircraft Corporation, who manufactured the monocoupe, to put in a Warner 145-h.p. engine instead of their standard 90-h.p. Lambert engine. They made a number of additions for me, such as parachute flares, Sperry gyro and horizon, ailerons which could be used as additional flaps in landing, extra gasoline dump valves, etc. My recollection is that I paid them about $4,500 for the completed plane. (Our agreement was that I pay actual factory cost for the completed plane.) The Lambert Company was planning on building a low-wing plane within the next year or two, and we had an understanding that I would trade my high-wing plane for a low-wing type as soon as it was built.

The first thing that went wrong, and probably the element that was responsible for most of the plane's troubles, was when the factory decided to use a new wing curve in place of their old standard. If I remember correctly, they used a Gothingen 23 in place of a Clark Y. The Bureau of Aeronautics had ordered about twenty monocoupes with Gothingen wings, so I took for granted that they had tested the characteristics of this wing thoroughly before placing the order. In this assumption, I was wrong.

But to return to today and Hartford, I spent an hour getting used to the plane again and in practicing landings at Rentschler Field in a wind too gusty to make the flights very enjoyable. Then I set an approximate course for home—it had to be approximate, for the compass card had "sunk" and was useless. I crossed [Long Island] Sound, circled Lloyd Manor at 2,500 feet, and flew on to the Long Island Aviation Country Club field, where I landed. I spent an hour making landings on the L.I.A.C.C. field, then drove to Lloyd Neck with Richard Holsten, who had brought the Ford for me.

I had planned on flying to Washington in the morning, but fog is forecast for tomorrow morning, so I made reservations on the 3:15 train. Drove to New York, put car in garage near Pennsylvania Station, and boarded the train at 11:00.

Thursday, April 18

It was a jerky night, punctuated with stops, starts, and mechanical indecisions. For some reason the 3:15 train seems to be rougher than the earlier schedule. Taxi to Bill Castle's home. We discussed European and American politics for half an hour. Back to the Army & Navy Club for a

1:00 NACA lunch. It is the twenty-fifth anniversary of the committee, and all the living members were invited to attend. After lunch I again talked to Orville Wright about writing a book. He was pleasant and courteous, as usual, but not at all encouraging.

Walked from the Army & Navy Club to the Smiths' home. He and I went to call on Ambassador [Alanson B.] Houghton, who was Ambassador to England when I was there with the *Spirit of St. Louis* in 1927. We discussed the war and trends in America and Europe. Later, Houghton asked me if I had forgiven him for sending me back home on the *Memphis* in 1927. It recalled the time clearly to my mind, and we both laughed. The occasion was in the American Embassy in London. I was staying there during my visit to England. Houghton had asked me to come to his study and had told me that President Coolidge had placed a battleship at my disposal for my return to the United States. I had no wish to leave Europe so soon and had hoped to fly to a number of countries in Europe. I had then been to only three—France, Belgium, and England. I had even considered the possibility of continuing my flights eastward and eventually circling the world. I would much prefer to have flown back to America. But Houghton insisted I return home on a battleship, with the *Spirit of St. Louis* in a crate on board. He eventually won the argument by saying that it was an order from the President of the United States.

Friday, April 19

Phoned General Arnold later in the morning and took a taxi to the Munitions Building for a conference with him in regard to my projected trip to Europe. Arnold called in Major Hodgeson, who has just returned from Italy, and we talked for half an hour about conditions in that country. Afterward, I spoke to Colonel Eaker about flying the new types of pursuit planes and arranged to go to Wright Field next week for this purpose. Spent an hour in conference with Major Chidlaw and various other officers in regard to foreign aircraft developments. We went over a list of the items in which the Air Corps is particularly interested.

Then to Commerce Building for a quarter hour's conference with Hinckley. We talked over Roosevelt's plan for reorganizing the Civil Aeronautics Commission and placing it under the Department of Commerce. Hinckley said he had received no advance notification of this plan. Possibly commercial aviation should be under the Department of

Commerce as long as there is no Department of Transport and Communications, but it seems a singularly unfortunate time to make this change. After all, it was in the Roosevelt Administration that civil aviation was taken away from the Department of Commerce and the Civil Aeronautics Authority created. Now, after the CAA has set up an astounding safety record, it seems an inadvisable moment to change back again.

Lunch alone at the Army & Navy Club. Then to the Navy Building for a 2:30 appointment with Admiral Towers in regard to naval developments. Then to G-2 in the Munitions Building where I talked to Magruder[156] about the code telegrams which are to be sent to the military attachés in Europe in advance of my arrival. Spent quarter hour with Colonel Fiske discussing Italy, and the possibility of her early entry in the war.

Boarded the sleeper for New York at 10:15.

Tuesday, April 23

Left for Fjelde's studio at 9:00 and stayed until 12:30. He is nearly finished, and I will be glad when the head is done. I had no idea it would take so long and thought he could finish within three or four weeks after the start. Fjelde estimated twelve sittings, and I planned on visiting his studio frequently anyway while he was working on the bust of Father. But there have been about twenty sittings now. I enjoy talking to Fjelde and like him as much as ever. I want to give him every possible chance to finish the head as he wishes it—an artist should never be rushed—but I really cannot continue these sittings much longer. There are other things on which I must spend my time. And on these spring Sundays I like to be with Anne and the children in the country.

Wednesday, April 24

Drove to the Long Island Aviation Country Club after breakfast and flew for two hours in the Lambert. Anne, Jon, Land, Christine, and Soeur Lisi came over in the afternoon. I rented a three-place Fairchild and took them all up. (The Lambert has only an experimental license and cannot be flown with passengers, according to CAA regulations.) The

---

· 156. General John Magruder, chief of the Intelligence branch of the War Department, General Staff, 1938–41.

first flight was with Anne and Jon. It is the first time Jon has flown since 1935, when I took him up from the field beside the Morrow house at North Haven. He was too young to care much about flying then, but now he loves it and asked to go up as many times as he could today. The second flight was with Anne and Land. Land was startled at first and soon decided he did not like it—about the same reaction Jon had in 1935. Jon was then about as old as Land is now.

Thursday, April 25

Drove to Mitchel Field after breakfast for my semiyearly physical examination. Passed without difficulty, as usual. There is nothing as important as a sound inheritance. One should be forever grateful to his ancestors for such a gift. Wealth, position, all else in life is negligible in comparison to it.

Friday, April 26

Each morning the papers carry headlines of Allied victories, but each morning the German positions have advanced.

In the evening I got the necessary maps together and laid out my course for Dayton and St. Louis.

Sunday, April 28

Spent the day at Lloyd Neck working on our wills and outdoors playing with Anne, Jon, and Land. It has been a late and cold spring, but today is warm and sunny. We walked to the sheep pasture on top of the hill, and I took Jon inside with the lambs, ewes, and ram. The ram is typical and never misses a chance to butt. Jon has no idea how to handle a situation of this kind, and I am anxious for him to learn. It is essential for a boy to know how to take care of himself in difficult situations—both physical and mental. A butting ram can build either great confidence or great fear in a boy of Jon's age. After a half hour in the pasture, we returned home. It has been a good start.

Monday, April 29

Gave Christine my will for copying, then took Jon to the sheep pasture and showed him how to handle the ram. He was much more confident today and learned rapidly. After fifteen minutes, during which time Jon was gaining confidence and learning technique, I left them both alone in the middle of the pasture while I walked away, climbed the fence into the adjoining field, and hid where neither could see me while I watched. It worked perfectly. The ram got tired of butting, and Jon gained perfect confidence in his own ability to keep from getting hurt. I would regard the day well spent, even if I did nothing else.

Routine work during most of the afternoon; then drove to New York to attend a dinner given by Mr. Hart, president of the New York Economic Council. There were fifteen or twenty men in all—invited by Mr. Hart to discuss the danger of our being drawn into the war, and means of counteracting the present propaganda for that purpose.

Tuesday, April 30

Read first draft of will and mailed it to Henry Breckinridge to put in legal form. Legal terminology always annoys me, but some of it seems essential under the conditions lawyers have let themselves get into. They are so tied by tradition and complication that they have as unique a language as a baby who is just learning to talk and can be understood only by mother and nurse. It is a sort of second childhood for the law, though. Why is it that men with an excellent education—long college training and all that—can't state their ideas and agreements in good English?

Sometimes I divide things done by man in my mind into two groups; those that must conform to natural laws (such as the design of an airplane), and those that are not bound by any more discipline than comes from the ideas and arguments of man himself. Of course, all action— even law—comes eventually within the plan of nature. It is only in the thoughts of man that he really passes beyond nature's bounds.

How interesting and enlightening it is to compare the streamline of an airplane to the awkward, complicated, and conflicting chapters of a law book. The success of one is clearly measured by nature, while the value of the other is estimated by partisan men. How beautiful and simple life really is, and how complicated man tries to make it. He worships God on the one hand; tries to improve upon Him on the other. The fallacy is rarely seen.

Drove to the L.I.A.C.C., and took off for Dayton at 2:30 in the Lambert with all tanks full. I took off cornerwise of the field, with a twenty-mile quartering wind. It became a headwind as soon as I turned west and took up my course—the same one I have followed so often before—Pittsburgh, Columbus, Dayton.

I passed over the Allegheny ridges, and Anne's poem ran through my mind: "You and you and you!" The mountains were covered with purple forests, the valleys with the green fields of early spring. I passed through light rain at times. Everything was moist and springlike—the clouds, the air, the wings of the plane, the streaks of water on the windshield, the darkness of the rocks on the mountains, the swollen creeks and rivers, the shade of green in the fields.

I had just enough gas and just enough daylight to make Dayton, and for the first three or four hours it was a question of whether I should draw on fuel or daylight to save the other. Daylight won; I landed on Patterson Field with not more than twenty minutes of gasoline left in the tanks, but with a full half hour of daylight to spare. Colonel Echols met me soon after I landed, and I spent the night at his house. General Brett was staying there, too. Major Lyon came over after supper, and we discussed various subjects connected with military aviation.

Wednesday, May 1

Breakfast with Colonel and Mrs. Echols and General Brett. Then to Wright Field, where I looked over some of the new planes and the latest pursuit specifications. I was especially interested in the new methods of "leakproofing" fuel tanks. Major [Alden R.] Crawford showed me the different experiments that had been made in this respect. I watched some of the test firing on the "leakproof" gasoline tanks: .30-cal. and .50-cal. and even 20-mm. shells (nonexplosive) were fired through a tank full of gasoline, without causing appreciable leakage except in one instance.

Spent an hour flying a P-36B in the afternoon (Curtiss pursuit). The wind was gusty and the sky overcast at 1,500 to 2,000 feet. I had planned on flying the P-40 (the Air Corps's newest pursuit plane) but wanted to take it to high altitude for maneuvering so put the flight off until tomorrow. I do not want to take a new pursuit plane through a thick cloud layer with a low ceiling below. It is also against regulations. The weather report indicates a broken sky tomorrow.

Thursday, May 2

It was sleeting and cold when I woke this morning. The mist dropped down into the trees on the hilltops. Colonel Echols and I drove to Wright Field after breakfast. There was no possibility of making any test flights, so I spent the first part of the morning looking over new types of planes in the hangars—bombers, trainers, and pursuit. The weather report indicated clearing skies in the midafternoon.

Lunch with Colonel Echols, Major Crawford, and Major Lyon. Afterward, we went to see the effect of firing a .50-cal. bullet through an oxygen cylinder. Reports have come from Europe that oxygen cylinders explode when hit and are extremely dangerous. The tests this afternoon confirmed these reports. The first cylinder—one of the regular aircraft type, with 2,000 pounds pressure—tore itself in half lengthwise and threw one of the halves over fifty yards through the air. The damage done apparently depends upon the caliber of the bullet and the pressure in the cylinder. A .30-cal. bullet striking a 2,000-lb. cylinder will penetrate one wall and cause a great flame of burning gas to spurt out through the opening it makes, but the cylinder does not explode.

The newspapers report the British evacuating southern Norway. I do not understand why they attempted to land there.

Friday, May 3

The sky was still overcast when I awoke this morning, contrary to all reports. Colonel Echols and I drove to Wright Field after breakfast. The weather report gave no hope for improvement during the day. The ceiling at Wright Field was only 1,000 feet, but I decided I could not spend more time at Dayton, so I requested that the P-40 engine be started. I would not be able to take the plane to high altitude, but I could at least find out how it handled taking off and landing and in maneuvers close to the ground. I borrowed parachute, helmet, and goggles from Major Crawford, for I had left all of my own flying equipment in the Lambert at Patterson Field.

I was very pleasantly surprised by the characteristics of the P-40. It is a type that was rushed through design and construction by the Curtiss-Wright Corporation after the Air Corps had suddenly woken up to find European pursuit planes far ahead of ours. This P-40 is really a P-36 with the nose changed sufficiently to incorporate an Allison liquid-cooled, in-line engine in place of the radial, air-cooled type used in the P-36. The wing is the same as the P-36 wing, and the fuselage back of the engine is the same, although the gross weight is about 1,000 pounds heavier. The speed of the P-40 is approximately 370 m.p.h., or a little over 60 m.p.h. faster than the P-36.

Usually when a standard-type plane is changed to incorporate a radically different engine, the handling characteristics suffer. But the P-40 seems to be an exception, for it seemed to take off, control, and land just as well as the P-36. The forward vision is, of course, much better with the inverted, in-line engine. Everything considered, it seems to be an excellent single-engine pursuit plane, and a definite step forward from the P-36. I cannot help wondering, however, what the Germans are bringing out about this time. The P-40 is probably a little better than the Messerschmitt they have had in service during the last few months, but it is about time for them to produce something new, too.

I spent forty-five minutes in the P-40. (The XP-40, to be exact. It is the first one built and preceded the line production by some months.) Even at low altitude, the plane cruised at nearly 300 miles an hour. It gave me the greatest feeling of speed in flying I have yet experienced.

After lunch I drove to Patterson Field and took off for St. Louis in the Lambert. The engine started cutting out on take-off, just as I was about ten feet above the ground and headed for trees at the edge of the field. (One can always trust this plane to do something wrong at the most inopportune moment.) I banked quickly to follow the edge of the field and pulled out the altitude adjustment for a second or two. After the first few coughs the engine ran smoothly again and continued to do so as I climbed and circled the field. I set my course for St. Louis, detouring just enough to avoid the airways. There was a head wind blowing about fifteen or twenty miles an hour. The sky was overcast, with light rain at intervals, but the ceiling never dropped below 800 feet. By the time I passed the Indiana-Illinois line, the sky had cleared and I had unlimited ceiling and visibility.

A few minutes before reaching the Mississippi River I glanced at my map and noticed I was passing over the town of Sorento, where I had barnstormed on more than one occasion in the years preceding 1927. I circled, but could recognize none of the buildings or fields where I used to land. It was typical of the towns where I used to barnstorm when I first started flying, and it brought back old memories. I used to fly there from Lambert Field in the old "Jenny," which belonged to a man named Lingle. The plane did not fly too well, and most of the pilots around the field did not like to take it out on barnstorming trips. It had been somewhat rebuilt, and the original OX-5 engine had been replaced by a more powerful Hispano-Suiza. But the added weight of the engine more than made up for its power. The take-off was slow and the controls loggy. I seldom carried more than one passenger at a time when I flew it. Lingle usually went with me when I took this plane barnstorming, and we got along well together. He loved to fly, although I do not remember whether he ever soloed himself, and never lost an opportunity to go barnstorming with the plane.

We would pick out some small town in Missouri or Illinois and attempt to find a farmer's field, not too far away, where we could land. After my first few months of barnstorming I could tell exactly what a field was like after I had circled it once or twice—whether it was level, how soft the ground was, whether there were any bumps or holes, in fact almost everything I could have learned by walking over it on the ground. As soon as we had landed, Lingle would go to look for the farmer who owned or rented the property to obtain permission for us to carry passengers. Meanwhile, I would walk over the field to confirm the impression I had gained of it from the air and to acquaint myself with the best directions for landing and taking off. By the time Lingle returned there was usually a small crowd gathered around the plane. Our price was standard for those days: $5.00 for a flight of between five and ten minutes. Lingle would stay on the ground and try to persuade people to fly, while I made flights over the nearby countryside. I did not do a great deal of barnstorming with Lingle, but the procedure I have described here was typical of that I used in most places. I barnstormed with a number of planes and with various people during the two or three years I based at Lambert Field.

I circled Sorento again and headed for St. Louis. My course lay nearly over the junction of the Mississippi and Missouri rivers, and I could see for miles along that old familiar route on which I used to carry the mail between St. Louis and Chicago.

I landed on the grass between the runways at Lambert Field. Taxied the Lambert over to the Robertson hangar and drove to the Chase Hotel in St. Louis. Phoned Dr. Lambert, Tom Dysart,[157] and Brandewiede.[158] Brande came to the hotel, and he and I drove to his home for a few minutes' visit with Alice [his wife] and the two children. Then back to the Chase, where Brande and I had supper together while we talked over old times and present developments in St. Louis. Dr. Lambert joined us later in the evening and invited us to go to police headquarters to see the plans he had made for enlarging Lambert–St. Louis Field.

While we were there he showed us the police radio system, and then we all cruised the streets of St. Louis in his car. He really is the life and spirit of the St. Louis police department today. The city has reformed under his leadership until there is not enough crime to make the night patrols interesting any more. Yet not many years ago St. Louis was a city of gangsters. I once saw gunplay between a gangster and the sheriff at the corner of Lambert Field.

"Doc" Lambert may not look like a policeman, but he has probably been the best one St. Louis ever had. His detectives say he tries to lead every major raid, no matter how dangerous it is, and that he enters the door first, if possible, with his little pearl-handled revolver in hand. Their greatest worry is that he will be shot.

Saturday, May 4

Germany reports heavy sinking of British battleships off the Norwegian coast.

After lunch Brande drove me to the waterfront to see the beginning of the new park project. They are just beginning to tear down buildings along the river. From the waterfront we drove to the Jefferson Memorial Building in Forest Park, where I had arranged to meet Reverend and Mrs. Jacobson. Reverend Jacobson is secretary of the Swedish Cultural Society, which presented a painting of my father to the Missouri Historical Society last winter. It is the first time I have seen the painting. It was done from photographs, of course, and resembles my father in many ways, but is so unlike him in others that it seems a different man. Like

157. A partner of Knight, Dysart & Gamble, brokerage house in St. Louis, Mo., 1925–34; president of the St. Louis Chamber of Commerce, 1934–43.

158. Gregory Brandeweide, an officer with the Robertson Aircraft Corp. in St. Louis. He had helped Lindbergh lay out the St. Louis–Chicago air-mail route in 1925–26.

Fjelde's bust, it is a composite of several photographs taken at different times during my father's life. In a sense, it is like him at all times, yet not like him at any single one. I thanked the Reverend and Mrs. Jacobson. Then Miss Douglas,[159] Brande and I went down to the basement to find a place where the Lambert can be stored.

Several years ago, when we were living in Europe, I asked the Missouri Historical Society whether they would like to have the plane. I told them in my letter that it was not a very good airplane and had made no important flights. However, I felt that someday it would be interesting for them to have one of the early planes built in St. Louis. I told them I would not want the plane to be put on exhibition at this time, as I did not think it of sufficient interest, but that it could be stored in the basement of the building and assembled in ten or twenty years when it would probably be interesting from a historical standpoint. One advantage of the Lambert is that it is small and can be suspended in the room of the Jefferson Memorial Building above the showcases. The Society replied that they would like to have the plane, and I told them I would fly it to St. Louis at the first opportunity after we returned to the United States. Now the Lambert has made its last flight, and I am glad, for I have never felt comfortable flying it. We found a satisfactory place for storage and Brande offered to take care of all details of getting the plane from the field to the Jefferson Memorial Building.

Brande then drove me to Lambert Field to see the new Curtiss two-engine transport and the latest intercepter fighter with a 5,000-feet-per-minute rate of climb. Then back to the hotel for a light supper, and on to the station, where Brande bought my ticket so I could board the 6:28 train without being recognized. I am going to stop for a day in Detroit with Mother on my way back east.

Sunday, May 5

Off train at 7:30. Phoned Mother and took taxi to 508 Lakepointe Road in time for a late breakfast. She and B. are both looking exceptionally well. After breakfast we all got into Mother's Ford, and I drove out to Pine and Orchard lakes, where Mother and B. spent many summers as children. Great-grandfather Lodge[160] had a farm on Pine Lake. We

159. Marjory Douglas, curator of manuscripts for the Missouri Historical Society.
160. Dr. Edwin Albert Lodge, physician, editor of medical journals, and Baptist preacher.

drove by the old white frame church where he used to preach. We continued on around the lake to where the farm used to be. Some of the old fruit trees are still standing, and part of the old house is left. Another part of it has been moved down near to the lake shore. On one side of the house is the hill which Mother and B. used to roll down as children.

We returned to 508 Lakepointe for lunch. Afterward, Mother played Ambroise Thomas's *Mignon,* including the overture, which I liked best. I wanted to stay for the night and tomorrow, but I have a passage reserved on the Clipper for the Azores on May 11. Mother and B. drove me to Pennsylvania Station, and I boarded the 5:25 train for New York.

Monday, May 6

Train late. Off at 9:45. Walked to the Pan American offices in the Chrysler Building for a conference with Harold Bixby in regard to my proposed trip. We discussed conditions all along the route and in Europe. I postponed my take-off date from the eleventh to the fifteenth, as that date is more convenient for everyone concerned and will give me sufficient time to be sure that the wills are drawn as we want them.

Lunch at the Engineers Club with André Priester. We discussed new Pan American equipment and the possibility of moving the transatlantic route farther south next winter. We also talked over possible changes in the European terminal in case the war spreads to Spain and Portugal. It may be necessary to have our eastern terminal in Africa in that case—if we can operate at all. We talked of bases as far south as Portuguese Guinea.

I drove to Lloyd Neck. The leaves on the chestnut trees in front of the house are out, and spring is well advanced.

Friday, May 10

The radio reports that German troops are invading Holland and Belgium.

Drove to New York after lunch for a 3:00 appointment with Van Dusen at the Pan American offices. Van was worried about handling the press in connection with my trip to Europe. I told him I thought it best to simply say I was looking over the Pan American route. Van felt the papers would not be satisfied with such a statement and would want more. And we came again to that old conflict between the press and myself that has gone on with more or less intensity for thirteen years. They want to know everything about what I do and think, while I prefer to tell them little or nothing. There seems to be no middle ground, for if you try to co-operate with newspaper reporters, they take whatever you will give them and then try to steal whatever else they can get. I tried co-operation for two or three years after 1927 and found it so unpleasant and unsatisfactory that for over eight years now I have not given an interview.

Spent half an hour with Trippe after I left Van Dusen's office, discussing my trip and Pan American problems.

Sunday, May 12

Drove to New York after lunch for an appointment with Fjelde. The bronze casting of Father's bust had just been finished. I think it is good. It is filled with his characteristics, although it is not like him at any single time in life. It is, and had, of course, to be a composite, but I am very glad to have it and feel the cost and effort worth while. I sat for two hours for Fjelde. It was my last sitting, and I am glad to be finished so I can devote my time to other things. Returned to Lloyd Neck for supper.

The German advance has been rapid—dive bombing, tanks, parachute troops, and all the technique of modern warfare that other nations have scoffed at for years. Nothing seems to hold them. Will they stop with Holland and Belgium and turn to England, or will they try to break the extension of the Maginot Line and drive into France? If they hit the Maginot Line, the losses will be heavy on both sides. To me, the worst part of this war is the hereditary loss to the countries involved. And the best men are killed first in war. The effect of this is shown in England today. The leaders she might have had were killed in the last war.

Monday, May 13

The German advance has been so rapid and the probability of Italy entering the war is so high that I decided to postpone my trip to Europe for the time being. I can do nothing there under these conditions and feel it is essential for me to keep in close contact with developments in this country. There will be greatly increased pressure for us to enter the war.

Wednesday, May 15

Devoted most of the day to writing a radio address, which I will probably title "The Air Defense of America."

The German advance continues furiously. The casualties must be very heavy.

Thursday, May 16

Truman phoned and told me the German advance was extremely rapid and that the short-wave radio announced the Maginot Line broken near Sedan!

Left for New York at 10:00 and put the De Soto in a garage near Pennsylvania Station. Walked to the station and purchased a ticket for Washington. The conductors at the Pullman bench were talking war. One said, "We'll be in it before long." Another said, "No, by God, we won't." The third said, "Well, I went over there once, but never again." The press is hysterical. The newspapers give one the impression that the United States will be invaded next week!

Friday, May 17

Off train at 7:30. Phoned Columbia Broadcasting Corporation and arranged to speak at 9:30 Sunday from their Washington studios.

Saturday, May 18

Antwerp has fallen, and the French armies seem on the verge of collapse. The Germans are reported to be forty miles from Paris.

Drove to Munitions Building with Truman and spent fifteen minutes with General Arnold (alone). We discussed the situation in Europe, and I outlined to Arnold what I intended to cover in my talk tomorrow night. While I was in his office, a young officer came in to mark a new German advance into France. The Maginot Line west of Montmédy has been broken along a wide front. They went through the Maginot Line extension along the Belgian border as though it had been sand instead of concrete and steel. French and British air activity has dropped greatly during the last several days. They have fallen back on night bombardment, while the German Air Force flies freely during the day and German troops march along the roads in Belgium unmolested.

Arnold told me he had seen Secretary of War Woodring and that the Secretary had asked Arnold whether he could get me to include several items in my speech about the percentage of Army appropriations used for maintenance of the services, the percentage left for new equipment, etc., etc. It was obviously a clumsy effort to dull the edge of my talk and turn it to the Administration's advantage. I feel quite certain that Arnold did not wish me to follow Woodring's suggestions, but he passed them on like a good soldier. I did not impose upon him to ask his own opinion. I told Arnold that my speech was too far along to permit incorporating the Secretary of War's suggestions—that to do so would require complete rewriting (and that is true).

Sunday, May 19

The German advance continues.

Miss Gillis of Columbia Broadcasting called and told me the Movietone organizations wanted me to read part of my speech for them. They offered to select one man and one camera to take the picture and to divide it equally among all the newsreel companies. Their offer was so reasonable and considerate that I told Miss Gillis I would think about it and call her back within the hour.

The newsreel companies have treated Anne and I pretty badly in the past. I can never quite get over the times their men tried to sneak up behind us with a microphone hidden under their coats. I do not believe they were ever successful in getting a conversation in this way, but they did succeed in leaving us with a feeling of disgust for newsreels in general. And then there was the time when Anne and I were on the *Mouette* during our honeymoon and anchored in an island bay off the Maine coast. Some motion-picture news photographers came in a speedboat and demanded that we come on deck and have our pictures taken. We made no reply, so for *over* six hours they circled the *Mouette* in the speedboat, just fast enough for the waves to keep our boat rocking unpleasantly from side to side, while they shouted at us loudly. I finally left the harbor and headed out to open ocean. They followed for a time and then turned back—without the pictures they wanted.

Everything considered, my personal feeling toward motion-picture operators is not the best. Still, this present situation concerns the welfare of the country and should not be decided on personal feelings. But what advantages and disadvantages are there in speaking for the sound pictures at this time? The advantage is that additional millions of people will be reached. The disadvantages include the fact that only a small portion of my speech would be carried and that I would not be able to control its setting. The news companies could sandwich my picture and talk between the sack of cities and the mangled bodies of refugees. Once they have such a film, they can cut it and use it in any way they like. I decided against speaking for the sound films, but asked Miss Gillis to thank them very much for their offer.

Hailed a taxi. Got out about three blocks from the Earl Building (Columbia Broadcasting studios). Had no trouble getting into the building and to the studios. Everything had been very considerately arranged by Miss Gillis—even to installing the microphones in a special room without the usual show-glass window. I spoke for just over twelve minutes. After I had finished, the newsreels sent one of their representatives to again request that I let them take a talking picture. I refused as courteously as I could.

New York train at midnight. Twenty-four telegrams had arrived before I left the Columbia studios; twenty-three of them supported my stand.

Thursday, May 23

There have been about 200 telegrams, running about twenty to one in support of my speech. Letters are running about fifteen to one. This is a very encouraging result. The average quality of the letters is high.

Spent most of the afternoon in the little house on the hill, writing. I lit a fire in the stove, as the day has been cold and cloudy with mist drifting by at intervals. The leaves are not yet entirely out.

Saturday, May 25

German troops continue to close in on the surrounded Allied armies of the north.

Spent the morning working on my next radio address. Mr. Richey called and told me that ex-President Hoover is planning on including something about me in a radio address he is making next Monday evening. Richey asked a number of questions concerning the reports I made on European aviation two or three years ago. I suggested that I discuss the matter personally with Hoover, and we made an appointment for 3:00 this afternoon. Drove to New York after lunch for the appointment with Hoover. I outlined to him some of my aviation activities and reports during the time I was in Europe. I spent half an hour with Hoover altogether, during which we discussed the war and the problem of feeding Europe this winter.

Tuesday, May 28

The radio reports that the Belgian Army has surrendered by order of King Leopold.

The papers announce that Carrel has landed. I telephoned his apartment and made an appointment to see him at 3:00. Hart called and asked me to meet Ackerman and himself at the University Club at 5:00. Drove to New York after lunch. Carrel is staying at 56 East Eighty-ninth Street. We talked for nearly an hour, mostly about the war, of course. Mme. Carrel had been at the part of the Maginot Line extension the Germans first broke through (near Montmédy) but had gone to Saint-Gildas just before the attack to arrange for the "Pardon" [161] which takes place once each year on the island. She was on Saint-Gildas when the break-through took place. Carrel is still able to discuss the war objectively and sees the causes clearly. He saw years ago the decay that was taking place in France. On only one major point we talked about do I disagree with him. Carrel feels that if Germany wins, Western civilization will fall. I believe that Germany is as much a part of Western civilization as France or England. Carrel regards Germany in about the same light that I regard Russia, although even he admits that Russia is incomparably worse than Germany.

From Carrel's apartment, I went to the University Club for the meeting with Hart and Ackerman. As usual, *they* have an idea for *me* to carry out. Ackerman wants me to start on a flying tour of the United States, giving statements to the press when I land and take off at the various cities! He said he thought it would please people to think that I was going around asking various well-known men like Henry Ford their opinion about our attitude toward the war!!

161. A religious pilgrimage.

Wednesday, May 29

Spent the morning writing and laying a plan of action. The pressure for war is rising, but I believe it is a minority becoming more vocal rather than increasing greatly in numbers.

Kay Smith phoned from New York, and I could tell from her voice that something had gone wrong. She had been up to see her daughter at school but had to return to Washington immediately, she said. She wanted very much to talk to me, so I left for New York. The situation which has arisen is not at all surprising to me, having seen the Administration in action against the air-mail carriers several years ago. It is, of course, well known in Washington that Truman is a good friend of mine. He is one of the many people who are rumored to have written my radio addresses. (As a matter of fact, he is one of the few people who have even seen those addresses before I delivered them.) The Administration thinks that if they can get him out of the way, it will injure me. Kay says Secretary of the Treasury Morgenthau[162] told General Marshall that he should discharge Truman from the Army! Marshall replied he could not do that because Truman was too valuable to him. Morgenthau then apparently discussed Truman's connection with my activities!

Marshall is sending Truman to Benning for a two-week assignment to give this all a chance to blow over. He told Truman it would be advisable to avoid the appearance of such a close friendship with me for a time. Truman was, of course, very angry and offered Marshall his resignation. Marshall refused it. Kay says the report is around Washington that the Administration is out to "get me." Well, it is not the first time, and it won't be the last.

Thursday, May 30

Drove to New York for lunch with Messrs. Douglas Stewart and Eggleston of *Scribner's Commentator*.[163] (Juan Trippe arranged for our meeting.) We had lunch in an apartment in uptown New York and discussed their plans for the magazine, which they have recently taken over. They claim to be one hundred per cent behind the stand I have taken.

162. Henry Morgenthau, Jr., Secretary of the Treasury.

163. Douglas Stewart was the publisher and George T. Eggleston was the editor of *Scribner's Commentator*.

Then to the Engineers Club for a 4:00 meeting with Carrel and Détroyat. We discussed the war and why governments are so blind to facts. Détroyat is here on a French air mission.

Monday, June 3

Drove to New York in the afternoon for a 5:00 appointment with Hart and Ackerman at 505 Fifth Avenue. They had more ideas for me to carry out! I believe most people in New York think that taking action consists of getting somebody else to do something. Today Ackerman and Hart wanted me to give up everything else I was doing and form a committee of ten prominent men with myself as chairman. This committee was to give out a statement to the press against war. I asked what the committee was to do after that, and they replied that the committee would then do whatever I directed them! This idea of forming committees to get action is one of the greatest of American fallacies. To me, a committee is a limitation of action rather than an asset. It is cumbersome and slow-moving and controversial. One can get good advice without forming a committee. And one can select advice much better if he is not tied to a committee.

I told Hart and Ackerman that I would like to turn the matter over in my mind because it involved many difficulties, and forming a committee of ten of the country's most influential men was not a matter to be undertaken lightly.

Supper at the Engineers Club with O. K. Armstrong of the American Legion. He showed me the Legion mandate, which is an excellent American defense—antiwar policy. We talked over plans for the Legion to take a more active part in opposing our entry into the war. Armstrong is a Missourian, and what a contrast to these Easterners I have been in contact with recently! His ideas concern what he can do and what the Legion can do in this situation. He is full of action and was even a little apologetic when he asked if I would consider speaking at one of the Legion meetings. I told him I would help in any way I could and would be glad to speak. I believe the Legion can be of tremendous value if it becomes active in this situation.

Back to Lloyd Neck for the night. The evening papers are extremely excited and are on a regular "witch hunt" for "fifth columnists," etc. Hysteria is in full swing.

Tuesday, June 4

Spent the first part of the morning on routine and then drove to New York for lunch with Eddie Rickenbacker.[164] He is a Legion man, and I wanted to talk to him about plans for Legion activity. Dinner with Carrel and Bakhmeteff at the latter's apartment. Our conversation was, of course, mostly about the war. Returned to Lloyd Neck for the night.

Wednesday, June 5

The German drive for Paris has begun.

Drove to Oyster Bay after breakfast to talk to Theodore Roosevelt[165] in regard to the American Legion and its activities. We also discussed conditions in the United States and the trend toward war.

Back to Lloyd Neck for lunch. Anne has forgotten a word she thought of while taking her bath this morning, and is still trying to recall it. "It expresses so vividly" what she means. I never knew anyone to have such a feeling for words. That is part of her genius for writing.

I drove to New York to a supper appointment with Guy Vaughan at the Engineers Club. Guy and I discussed the chaos that exists in the aviation industry due to the mismanagement of the Administration. Guy says he wishes he could "resign from the presidency of Curtiss-Wright and write a book about it all." He told me about his recent trip to Washington, when the President called a meeting of the entire aviation industry. He said the Administration had no plan whatever and that the entire meeting seemed to be a publicity arrangement by Administration officials. Guy said the heads of the aircraft industry were forced to listen to several speeches and then spend thirty minutes having their pictures taken.

164. Top U.S. ace in World War I, Rickenbacker became president of Eastern Airlines in 1938. During World War II he carried out special missions for the Secretary of War.

165. Theodore Roosevelt, Jr., son of the twenty-sixth President. He served with great distinction in World War I, and was an organizer of the American Legion in 1919. He was Assistant Secretary of the Navy, 1921–24, Governor General of the Philippines, 1932–35. Since 1935 he had been an editor at Doubleday, Doran & Co. In World War II he returned to active duty with the U.S. Army,

Saturday, June 8

In the afternoon I worked on my address and went for a walk to the duck pond with Jon. On our way through the woods Thor flushed a wild duck from her nest in a hollow stump. Jon and I went over and found twelve eggs in the nest. To make the day perfect, we saw a turtle on top of a tree trunk, which had fallen into the duck pond. Jon tried to crawl out and get it, but the turtle jumped into the water at first sight of him.

An hour or so after supper Mrs. Morrow phoned from Englewood to tell me she had just received a phone call from some unknown person, telling her that her daughter (Anne) was in danger. Again, that same old feeling of unknown danger. I would rather live in the front-line trenches than have the constant worry of safeguarding my family against criminal stealth.

I questioned Mrs. Morrow carefully. Some woman "with a calm and steady voice" had telephoned her at Next Day Hill, saying that she (the woman) was a friend of the Lindleys (old Englewood people), and that she wanted to tell Mrs. Morrow her daughter was in danger.

"Which daughter?"

"The famous one."

The woman had hung up without giving her name, and the Lindleys were not at home when Mrs. Morrow phoned. I came to the conclusion that the woman had probably been trying to worry Mrs. Morrow about her speech, or was insane, or had had a dream, or some such thing. It did not sound serious to me as I listened to Mrs. Morrow's account. I told her to phone the Lindleys in the morning to see if they knew who the woman was.

Nevertheless, it brings back the same uncomfortable feeling we had before going to Europe to live in 1935. We used to get threatening letters every week then. Government officials made more than a dozen arrests because of threatening letters we received during the previous two years. One of the worst parts about these threats is the effect they have on one's home. They create an atmosphere in which it is impossible to bring up a family normally. Anne is wonderful about it, but I realize what is going through her mind when I hear her say, as she did this evening, "I told you to stay upstairs, Thor" (with the children).

---

serving as a colonel commanding the 26th Infantry, 1st Division. He advanced to brigadier general in December, 1941.

Monday, June 10

The German Army is reported thirty-five miles from Paris and advancing rapidly.

Theodore Roosevelt telephoned, and I phoned Senator Clark[166] of Missouri to make an appointment to meet him in Washington Wednesday.

It was announced that Mussolini would speak in Rome at 1:00 E.S.T. We brought the radio down to the dining room to hear him. It was, as we expected, a declaration of war against France and England. Mussolini shouted until it must have been impossible even for an Italian to understand him. Every few words were punctuated by great howls from the crowds—howls for blood. It was like a pack of animals ready for the kill, howling over the division of the body—the already half-dead body, the mortally wounded body of France. I shall never forget that broadcast as long as I live. Mussolini's voice was incapable of the pitch and volume he attempted. But the mob carried on for him, and it was all in keeping —the leader and the pack.

Roosevelt (F. D.) spoke at 7:15, at Charlottesville. His speeches never seem to me to be those of a quite normal man. I seldom listen to him and always trust him less after I do. Tonight, as his voice came over the radio, I felt he would like to declare war, and was held back only by his knowledge that the country would not stand for it. He was dramatic and demagogic as usual.

The evening radio announces that the French government has left Paris for Tours.

Wednesday, June 12

Off [Washington] train at 7:15. I have decided not to see any of my friends in the Air Corps on this trip, as I know that the politicians of this Administration make as much trouble as possible for anyone I have contact with. Since I do not want to make life difficult for my friends, it is best not to see them—except where they are already known opponents of the Administration.

Taxi to the Senate Office Building for a 2:30 appointment with Senator Clark (Missouri). We discussed the war, the Administration, and the

166. Bennett Champ Clark, Democratic Senator from Missouri.

pressure being brought to bear to involve the United States in the war. We both agree that conditions are critical and that the trend toward war must be stopped. We discussed what the American Legion could do in this respect. Congressman Van Zandt[167] came in later, and we considered what action might be taken by the Veterans of Foreign Wars and other ex-service organizations in forming opposition to our involvement in the present war. After a half hour's discussion, Clark, Van Zandt, and I went to the Capitol, where we met with La Follette, Wheeler, Reynolds, and other Senators.[168] We discussed plans for counteracting war agitation and propaganda. Everyone is very much worried about Roosevelt and feels he is leading the country to war as rapidly as he can.

Returned to the hotel after the meeting broke up for a roll call and telephoned the NBC studios to ask for broadcasting time. They told me they would be glad to give me time and would let me know the day and hour tomorrow morning.

Thursday, June 13

The morning newspapers announce that the Germans have taken Paris.

After lunch I took a taxi to Senator Clark's office for a 3:30 appointment. He asked two or three other Senators to come in, and we discussed the war and the best policies for this country to follow in regard to it.

Friday, June 14

Fulton Lewis called and drove me to the Chevy Chase Club for lunch. We discussed politics and the war. He told me that someone had started the rumor that he had taken part in writing my radio addresses and that two of his "sponsorships" in New York City had been canceled as a result. Lewis had been forced to state over the radio that he had nothing whatever to do with writing my addresses. (As a matter of fact, he only

167. James E. Van Zandt, Republican Representative from Pennsylvania; national commander in chief of the American Legion, 1933–35.

168. Robert M. La Follette, Jr., Progressive Republican Senator from Wisconsin, 1925–47; Burton K. Wheeler, Democratic Senator from Montana, 1922–40, who in 1924 was the vice-presidential candidate of the Progressive Party on the ticket with Robert La Follette; Robert R. Reynolds, Democratic Senator from North Carolina.

saw one of them in advance of my broadcast, and that was the one I gave over the Mutual System.)

Spent most of the afternoon typing, and then took a taxi to the House Office Building to see Congressman Van Zandt. He had invited the head of the Veterans of Foreign Wars to come to Washington, and we discussed the possibility of the V.F.W. taking an active stand against our entry into the war.

Dinner with Senator Shipstead at the apartment of one of his friends. They drove me back to the Hay-Adams House later in the evening. As I stepped out of the car, I met Dr. Bush (NACA) on the sidewalk. He was talking to a friend of his about the war and said he did not believe the Germans would be able to invade England because of the British Navy.

The evening papers are beginning to show signs of a public reaction against our involvement in the war.

Saturday, June 15

Carrel phoned from New York and asked me to include in my address some friendly reference to France. I told him I would like to do so, but did not see how I could appropriately include a reference to France in this particular address, since it was primarily an argument against our entry into the war.

Taxi to the NBC studios. Arrived early, so walked over ten minutes before going in. There were a fine group of men in the studios, and they did everything possible to assist with my broadcast. I stayed for half an hour after it was over, talking to a young Yale student who wanted to organize the colleges against our entry into the war.

Shipstead had invited me to meet a friend of his after my broadcast, and I drove to the address he had given me with O. K. Armstrong. We opened the thirty-odd telegrams that had arrived before I left the NBC studios. All but three were in support of my stand. Returned to the Hay-Adams long enough to check out, then drove to the station and boarded the 2:10 train for New York.

Sunday, June 16

Press reports that the French have retreated to a line sixty miles south of Paris. Their retreat has apparently become a rout. The radio announces that the French Cabinet has fallen.

Monday, June 17

The radio announces that France has asked for peace terms.

It is difficult to do more than plan from month to month in these times. New problems arise almost daily. For instance, now that Germany has about conquered the continent of Europe, what will England do? And what will our reaction be in America?

A phone call came from someone connected with the Republican convention arrangements in Philadelphia, asking me if I would attend the convention. I replied that I felt I would have more influence in my stand on the war if I did not go to Philadelphia.

Anne and I drove to the home of Mr. and Mrs. Foster Dulles[169] for dinner. We discussed the war and American policies.

Tuesday, June 18

Spent the morning on routine and a long walk along the beach. The shore is becoming littered with tin cans, bottles, oranges, paper, and other refuse from the myriad boats that appear on Long Island Sound during the summer months. I long for real wilderness with its cleanness and solitude, away from the crowded litter of cities. When this crisis has passed —whenever that may be—Anne and I will go far into the north or into the desert until the space and solitude have washed all this feeling of crowded city life away. One should really go to the wilderness each year long enough to regain the strength that comes only from solitude and distance and starlight nights.

Drove to New York after lunch for a conference with Détroyat at the Engineers Club. He had telephoned and said he was very anxious to see me. Détroyat asked me what I thought he should do: return to France now or try to find a job in America. He does not know, of course, what will be left of France after the German peace terms. Possibly there will be little or no French aviation, and Détroyat's life has been aviation. He knows no other profession. His home near Lille is in German-occupied territory. (It was occupied by the Germans during the last war also.) I suggested that Détroyat wait a few days before deciding—until a little

169. John Foster Dulles, diplomat and lawyer. He became Secretary of State (1953–59) under President Dwight D. Eisenhower.

more is known about the German and Italian terms. I told him that before going back to France he should talk to his friends here to find out what positions might be open to him in American aviation. I also suggested that he inquire about entering this country on the French immigration quota. After he returns to France it may be much more difficult for him to make inquiries and arrangements. In fact, it may be very difficult for him to get out of France again if he returns.

Friday, June 21

I went for a walk after lunch through the woods and along the beach. It seems I spend most of my time these days thinking. My mind is not on the trees and birds and clouded sky as I would wish it to be, but on the war and chaos of these turbulent days. I wish I could be either wholeheartedly in the war and fighting for true beliefs and ideals, or else far enough away from it mentally and physically to be able to see the forest when I walk through it, and to feel the beauty of wind-rippled water without having part of my mind thinking of politics and bombing planes and plans. Here, at this moment, I feel in contact neither with the world of men nor with the world of God. What can be done to bring this country back? What has happened to America? To the character of the pioneer? To the courage of the Revolutionary Army? To the American destiny that we once had?

Spent the evening reading Father's *Why Is Your Country at War?* and Fisher's *History of Europe.*

Saturday, June 22

Senator Clark (Missouri) phoned in regard to my speaking at an antiwar rally in Chicago. I think I will accept, but want to learn a little more about it.

Wrote for a few minutes after lunch, then drove to New York for a 4:30 appointment with Dr. Carrel. He thinks Mme. Carrel is in Brittany, but has not had any word from her. He asks me what I think the Germans will do to France. I reply that I don't know and that we can only hope. I tell him it may not be as bad as people in this country believe. Carrel then asked me what I think best for him to do under the circumstances. I suggested waiting a few days before taking any action and that no intelligent plans could be laid until we had some idea of what was

happening in France. I told him it might be possible for him to work with
the new French government, and that if it did not prove practical for him
to do this, I hoped he would stay in this country and write—articles or a
book.

Sunday, June 23

Anne and I drove to the beach at 11:00, and I went swimming with Jon
and Land. Jon is the best swimmer among the children on the beach and
the only one who is confident of himself in deep water away from shore.
Land paddles gaily along near the shore line. He has no fear whatever of
the water and goes out until it is up to his chin, then turns and paddles in
to shore. I took him on my back out to the raft.

Spent the afternoon planning, reading, and playing with the children.
Anne and I walked to the bluff and along the shore at sunset.

Monday, June 24

Détroyat and one of his friends drove out in the evening for supper with
Anne and me. We talked of France and England and the war. What will
Germany do to France? Détroyat's friend thinks she will divide it up
until France proper is left with no more than 20 million people and that
the same will be done to England. He says nothing can be done for
France until Germany moves out. He doesn't know what to do himself—
whether to go back to France, join the still-existing French armies in
Africa, or to volunteer his services to the English government. Asks me
what I would advise.

Détroyat plans to go back to Europe on the PAA Clipper Saturday. His
friend advised him against going. They again asked me my opinion. I
suggested that Détroyat stay here long enough to see what kind of a job
he could get if he wanted to remain in, or return to, this country (which
he told me he was considering). I suggested he also look up the question
of immigration and quota before going to Europe. I suggested to him,
too, that he let a few more days pass before deciding. We will all know
much more and be calmer in another week. But Détroyat was worried
about his family; they may have lost everything they have, and they may
need help, although his wife and children are in the south of France and
therefore probably safe. I understand his feeling about that and his desire
to go back to be with them.

I have great admiration for the French ability to talk objectively even under conditions of war and defeat. Détroyat and his friend showed more acceptance than hatred, more calmness than hysteria, more courage then despair. Their hearts were heavy, but their heads were high. Tonight they demonstrated qualities of character which we need badly in this country.

Tuesday, June 25

Telephoned Mother that I would be in Detroit tomorrow morning. Packed my suitcase and left for New York at 2:30. Supper alone at Engineers Club. Met Guy Vaughan as I was walking out. He told me the Administration was making it extremely difficult for the aviation industry to contract for government business—too many regulations and not enough co-operation. Guy said he was afraid that many Administration supporters wanted to "nationalize" the industry.

Taxi to Grand Central Station. Boarded the 7:10 train for Detroit.

Wednesday, June 26

Off train at 8:15. Taxi to 508 Lakepointe. Breakfast with Mother and B. Spent the morning with them and telephoning. Asked [Frank] Campsall (Ford's secretary) to inquire about the proposed Chicago meeting. Campsall told me that Jim Newton was in Detroit and gave me his phone number.

B. caught a garter snake in the pile of rocks alongside the drive, and I plan to take it back to Jon—in my suitcase, I suppose.

Telephoned Senator Clark in regard to the Chicago meeting (Senate Office Building, Washington), then phoned Judge Grace,[170] who is organizing the meeting, and agreed to speak.

Thursday, June 27

Up at 6:30. Jim came at 7:00, and we drove to their home near Dearborn for breakfast with Mr. and Mrs. Henry Ford. After breakfast I talked to Mr. Ford about the American Legion and my feeling that it is desirable to give them all possible backing in their campaign against our entry into the war. He agreed completely and called in Mr. Bennett,[171]

170. William J. Grace, chairman of Citizens Keep Out of War Committee, Chicago.

171. Harry Bennett. Employed by Ford since 1918, he was director of personnel, labor relations, and plant security.

who has close contact with the Legion in Detroit, for a conference on the matter. Ford told Bennett that he wanted to assist the Legion in any way he could.

Later in the morning Mr. Ford took Jim and myself on a tour of his decentralized factories along the River Rouge. We went in one of his new Mercury cars, Ford riding in the front seat with the driver and Jim and I behind. As we went along over back country roads at speeds of sixty miles and above, even though they were not paved and far from smooth, Ford turned sidewise, with his arm over the seat, while he carried on a constant conversation with us. We spoke of the efficiency of his decentralized plants, of the future trends of industry, of the boys' camps he is running, of the war, and an infinite variety of subjects.

I have great admiration for this man; he has genius, understanding, fearlessness, optimism, humor, and a simple, open character that seldom survives success, especially great success. He combines firmness with consideration and kindness. Even his extremes of genius are tempered eventually with a practical outlook, and his excursions into the fantastic always leave him in the end with both feet planted firmly upon the earth. Ford is now over seventy, but alert, agile, and overflowing with energy and new ideas. He is, and will always remain, one of the greatest men this country has produced. As we walked through one small factory after another, Ford showed us the products of each, introduced us to the foremen, dropped behind us to talk to the older hands. He had a personal relationship with these men that I have never before seen in a great modern industry.

After inspecting several of the decentralized factories, we drove through Camp Legion,[172] where boys were working the adjoining farms. Then we went to the Ypsilanti plant, where starters and generators were being built in mass production. There were great lines of parts traveling steadily along, suspended from endless overhead chains. After lunch we went to see the Rolls-Royce airplane engine, which Ford is considering building, and to talk to Mr. Sorensen,[173] who has charge of the project. We found Sorensen with Edsel Ford, looking over a torn-down Rolls-Royce engine. Sorensen went over the engine parts with me and showed me the changes he planned in order to make it a mass-production job.

172. A summer camp in Dearborn operated by Henry Ford for the sons of Ford employees and members of the American Legion. The farming projects at Camp Legion provided employment for these young men.

173. Charles Sorensen had been with Ford since 1904 and was vice president (engineering) of the company.

This included reducing the number of parts, casting the crankshaft instead of forging it, etc. He showed me a crankshaft that he had had cast and which was then undergoing test for comparative strength.

Sorensen told me, however, that he was very disappointed with his reception in Washington when he went there to discuss the production of aircraft engines for the government. He said he was asked whether the Ford Company could produce 9,000 Rolls-Royce engines if they were given the order. He replied that they could. Nothing else happened, and he said no one he talked to seemed to have a definite idea of what they wanted. Finally, he returned to Detroit without any request on the part of the government and without any concrete proposition being put to him. He had neither been asked to build engines, nor even to bid on them. Sorensen's description of the whole affair was very much like Guy Vaughan's description of his visit to Washington earlier in the year. Sorensen took me through the engineering division and then through the experimental and test division.

During my conversations with Ford, Edsel Ford, Sorensen, and other Ford officers, the question frequently arose as to the results obtained with different types of military aircraft in the fighting in Europe. I suggested that we ask Détroyat to come through from New York so we could have the benefit of his experience. Détroyat is possibly in closer contact with the flying characteristics of military aircraft than any other man in the world. He has tested most of the French planes, many of the British and American, and some of the German and Italian—over 300 types in all, he told me. He has also been in close and recent contact with the French combat pilots. I phoned Détroyat, and he agreed to come through on the night plane.

Later in the afternoon Jim and I went to the showroom with Bennett and then to Ford's model village,[174] where a guide showed us around. We went through the Edison laboratory, the Wright bicycle shop, and several other places. Jim and I returned to 508 Lakepointe for supper with Mother and B.

174. Greenfield Village, a reproduction of an early American village, established in 1933 by Henry Ford at Dearborn. In addition to the village buildings are Thomas Edison's Menlo Park workshop and Fort Myers laboratory, Noah Webster's birthplace, Stephen Foster's home, and the Wright brothers' cycle shop and home. Nearby is the Henry Ford Museum, which houses a large collection of Americana.

Friday, June 28

I phoned Campsall at 9:00 and found that Détroyat was about to leave the airport hotel for his office. Jim met me at 508, and we drove to Dearborn. We found Détroyat talking to Ford in Bennett's office. We went from there to Sorensen's office and found Edsel Ford and others assembled to hear Détroyat. We discussed planes, engines, performances, and the results of the fighting in France—Détroyat speaking in English at first and then through a translator. The president of the Packard Company was also there, as he too was considering a contract to build airplane engines for the government.

[O. K.] Armstrong arrived in the early afternoon. He, Bennett, and I discussed American Legion affairs, while Sorensen took Détroyat through the automobile factory. Détroyat took the late-afternoon plane back to New York. Jim and I went to the Ford museum and met Ford at the aviation exhibit. There were probably a dozen planes there, including the *Bremen* (first westward crossing of the Atlantic), and both of Byrd's polar planes (North and South Poles).

(I gave Henry Ford his first ride in an airplane. That was in 1927 when I had landed at Detroit on his airport with the *Spirit of St. Louis*. I showed Ford the plane and then asked him if he would like to go up in it. Ford had always refused to go up in his own tri-motored ships, and the *Spirit of St. Louis* had only one engine and one cockpit. But, to my surprise, Ford accepted my invitation. He had to sit crouched up on the arm of my seat in anything but a comfortable position. I took off and flew around the field at Dearborn—probably five or ten minutes in the air. Ford apparently enjoyed the trip greatly. Later on, I took him up in one of his own tri-motored planes together with a number of officers of the company.)

After visiting the museum, I met O. K. Armstrong, and he, Jim, and I drove to 508 Lakepointe, discussing war trends and American Legion projects on the way. Packed my suitcase and said good-by to Mother. B. drove Jim and me to the station, where we boarded the 7:30 train for New York.

Saturday, June 29

Breakfast with Jim on diner, then drove to Lloyd Neck and spent most of the day outdoors.

Judge Grace called from Chicago and said they had been forced to postpone the meeting, as the "Kelly machine" [175] would not give them the use of Soldier Field until a later date. Grace suggested the first week in August as a tentative date.

The [Truman] Smiths came for dinner and the night. We discussed the war and Roosevelt's recent actions. Will he try to take over the French islands in the West Indies? What will his policy be in South America? Does he or does he not wish to draw this country into the war? All life seems to revolve around the war, and I suppose it must revolve around all major wars. But how I wish I could put my mind on other things and that Anne could think of writing again. Her mind is too much on the war to write now, aside from her diary.

Thursday, July 4

Spent the morning and first part of the afternoon on dictation and routine. Then took Jon and the gardener's three children to Huntington to get some fireworks. We stopped at an ice-cream wagon on the way. I had given Jon fifty cents to spend, and sent him into the store with the other children while I waited outside. It was his first trip to a store alone. He came out with a bag of fireworks and five cents left over. The selection he made was surprisingly good. I stopped at another store to purchase some Roman candles and rockets. Then we returned to Lloyd Manor and spent the rest of the afternoon and evening celebrating. I know of nothing that requires more attention than three young boys and several packages of firecrackers. We shot the Roman candles and rockets over the water from the old pier southeast of the house.

175. Named after Chicago mayor Edward J. Kelly. It was alleged that the Kelly-Nash machine, which ruled Chicago, was a combination of politics and crime.

Bronze head of Anne Morrow Lindbergh
by Charles Despiau

Ambassador William C. Bullitt

Edouard Daladier,
Premier of France

Ambassador Joseph P. Kennedy

UPI

Prime Minister Neville Chamberlain
Radio Times Hulton

David Lloyd George

Colonel Lindbergh
in the cockpit
of his P-36 fighter,
1939

St. Louis Post-Dispatch

A meeting of the National Advisory Committee for Aeronautics in Washington. *Left to right in background:* Brigadier General B. K. Yount USA; Dr. L. J. Briggs; Captain S. M. Kraus, USN; Robert H. Hinckley, CAA; Dr. Edward P. Warner; Colonel Charles A. Lindbergh; J. F. Victory, secretary *(standing);* Dr. Orville Wright; Dr. G. W. Lewis; Dr. C. G. Abbot, acting chairman; F. W. Reichelderfer; C. M. Hester; Commander F. W. Penneyer, USN. *In the foreground left to right:* Captain J. H. Towers, USN; Major General H. H. Arnold, Chief of Army Air Corps; Brigadier General G. H. Brett, USA; Rear Admiral A. B. Cook, USN; Edward J. Noble

Orville Wright

Igor Sikorsky piloting his helicopter, the VS-300

Lauren D. Lyman

Juan T. Trippe

Dr. Alexis Carrel

Mme. Alexis Carrel

At the
rocket-launching tower
on Mescalero Ranch
near Roswell,
New Mexico.
Left to right:
Harry F. Guggenheim,
Robert H. Goddard,
Charles A. Lindbergh

Esther C. Goddard

Robert H. Goddard at his control shack on Mescalero Ranch near Roswell, New Mexico, 1940. Rocket-launching tower in the distance

Esther C. G

Anne Morrow Lindbergh

Anne Morrow Lindbergh and Land,
Englewood, New Jersey, 1939

Soeur Lisi and Jon, Lloyd Neck, 1939

In the garden of the Manor House, Lloyd Neck, Long Island, 1940.
Left to right: Land, Colonel Lindbergh, Jon

Anne Morrow Lindbergh and James D. Newton on the *Aldebaran* off the Gulf coast of Florida, 1941

The *Aldebaran* in a channel of the Everglades, 1941

Friday, July 5

The morning papers report a battle between the British and French fleets.

Spent most of the afternoon going over old papers and articles from storage and making plans for a trip to Maine with Anne.

Wednesday, July 10

Anne and I left for Maine in the Ford. We ate a sandwich lunch on the way and arrived at the Wayside Inn about 7:30. They gave us the same room we had on our last trip. A large number of people were visiting the inn—many tourists. We were not bothered during dinner, but found we could not go walking through the grounds afterward. As soon as I stepped out the door, I was met with demands for autographs, and when we tried to walk over to the little church Ford is building, two carloads of people followed us over and shouted at us: "Hey! Lindy! We know ya. Why dontcha say something? Come over and talk to us!" And as we walked back to the inn one of the cars followed less than ten feet behind us, its lights turned on us, and its occupants still excited and shouting.

Thursday, July 11

We started at 10:00 and drove through Concord and Lexington to Portland. After lunch we drove on to Brunswick and spent about two hours driving along the nearby "fjords" to find out what possibility there would be of buying a summer home in that vicinity. We wanted a location on the sea, close enough to Brunswick to send the children to school if we stayed there during the winter, yet far enough away to have solitude for writing and study, and the type of unspoiled natural beauty one needs for inspiration and contemplation. We were not encouraged by the country we drove through. The farms were abandoned in most instances, with falling-down buildings—evidences of poor soil and hard living conditions. A community of abandoned farms is never a happy community. In the places of greatest natural beauty "summer people" had built their garish cottages, entirely out of keeping with Maine and its gray rock coast.

We arrived at Rockland at 8:00 and found Captain Quinn and the

Mouette[176] waiting for us at the dock. (We had telephoned ahead.) We reached North Haven[177] before it was completely dark. Margot met us with the beach wagon, and we had a late supper of warmed-up lobster in the kitchen with Margot and Dwight. The night was cool and misty—typical North Haven weather.

How high the spruces seem after these five years we have been away! Coming back to a place you know well after a long absence gives you a strange feeling of the passage of time. I had it when I went back to the farm in Minnesota and saw the bushes of my childhood changed to full-grown trees. I had this same feeling when I opened the door to the bay tonight and found spruce trees towering above me where there were only shrubs in the picture of my mind. I felt out of gear with time, as though the cogs of life had stripped and meshed again in different timing.

Friday, July 12

Up late; 9:00 breakfast; then went for a walk over the grounds—down through the garden to the rocky shore, and over to the hillside field where we used to land our plane. Everything is the same except for the trees, which have sprung up and hidden many of the old views.

Anne, Margot, Dwight, and I took the *Mouette* out for a trip around Vinalhaven and Isle au Haut. We left Quinn behind, as I wanted to handle the boat again myself. It was great fun navigating through the rocks and narrows and to see the old landmarks again—Leadbetter, the White Islands, Hurricane. We stopped to have our lunch on the "Western Ear" of Isle au Haut, leaving the *Mouette* anchored in the cove formed by the Ear and the island. After lunch Dwight and I walked around the Ear, which is really an island at high tide. It is a rather difficult walk, over rocks and along cliffs. Afterward, I climbed through the thick spruce trees to the top of the island. We left Western Ear midafternoon, continued on around Isle au Haut and through the small islands, back to the "Thoroughfare" and the dock at North Haven. We had supper at home, and then Anne and I walked to the shore to watch the sun set in indescribable colors over the Camden Hills.

176. Captain Quinn operated the small yacht *Mouette* for Mrs. Morrow. This yacht was previously owned and operated by the Lindberghs, who spent their honeymoon on it.

177. The Morrow family summer home.

Sunday, July 14

We decided to spend the day cruising on the *Mouette,* and left the dock in the Thoroughfare at about 10:30 (Anne, Mrs. Morrow, Margot, Dwight, and myself). As before, we left Quinn behind. We set our course through the Thoroughfare, past Swan Island and Long Island to Crow Island, a small uninhabited island just off Frenchboro. We ate our lunch on the shore of Crow Island, where we could see the mountains in the distance and small isles in between them and us. After lunch we continued on around Swan Island and through Eggemoggin Reach, back to North Haven and Deacon Brown's Point.

Tuesday, July 16

Anne and I went for a sail in the *Astrea.* There were waves in the bay, and the wind was gusty but not strong. We were out for an hour or so, tacking up to Mark Island before we turned back. Made the buoy on our first try.

Wednesday, July 17

We decided to start back for New York this afternoon. Packed and boarded the *Mouette* about 4:30. Captain Quinn took us to Rockland, where we put our luggage in the Ford, and with a sandwich supper en route drove to the Wayside Inn, arriving about midnight.

Thursday, July 18

After leaving the inn, we stopped to go through the nearby mill, from which we now buy flour. Ford rebuilt the mill and still grinds the whole grain between stones. The flour is much finer and the food value higher than that of the standard grocery-store product. We arrived at Lloyd Manor about 5:00, after eating a sandwich lunch in the car as we drove. We had driven almost an even 1,000 miles since we left—lacking only a few tenths of a mile.

Friday, July 19

Went for a swim with Jon and Land in the later afternoon. Land is beginning to take a stroke or two by himself. He walks out from shore until the water is up to his chin, then turns and half swims, half walks, back to shallower water. The tide was low and the water warm, though rather dirty. It seemed an excellent day to take Jon to the lighthouse, and he was terribly anxious to go. He swam out without becoming tired, although the tide was somewhat against us and the distance nearly half a mile. Near the lighthouse, however, the tide was stronger, and the water very turbulent. Jon could not do much more than hold his own in the current. I think he would have made the ladder to the lighthouse eventually, but the keeper tied a light rope to a stick, tossed the stick in the water, let it drift down to Jon, and then pulled him up to the ladder.

Jon and I climbed up to meet the lighthouse keeper and his wife—a pleasant and hospitable German couple. The woman gave Jon a towel to dry himself with, and the man took him to the sunny side of the lighthouse for warmth, while he pulled up a box of fish from the water to show Jon. The day was made when the lighthouse keeper took us up to the top of the tower and actually lit the light. On the way down, for good measure, he rang the fog bell. The keeper and his wife asked Jon if he wanted them to take him back in the lighthouse boat, but Jon said he preferred to swim. We went back down the ladder and dove into the water. The swim back was with the tide and much easier.

Saturday, July 20

Day at Lloyd Neck. It was the hottest of the summer—no wind, a thick haze, and fog patches on the bay. For me it was one of those turbulent days in life when one's intuition races far ahead of one's ability to plan. It seems to me that I see chaotic conditions ahead—unrest, depressions, labor troubles, violence—even if we escape the war. What should one do? How best prepare and protect one's family? How can one best contribute to the future of his nation under such circumstances? I have no intention of standing by and letting the flood sweep over us, but there is no clear-cut course to follow, and intelligent plans are difficult to lay.

I spent most of the day walking along wood roads, where I could be alone to think. History is in a period of mutation; life lies ahead, wide and open. What course should one lay for his family and for his nation? I tried to re-evaluate old ideas and to form new ones.

Sunday, July 21

Anne and I talked of the winter and of the future. We discussed the possibility of buying a ranch on the mountainous coast of Oregon. There would be beauty and solitude and the feeling of land and sky and sea. But living there would cut us off from the world, and this is not a time when we should be cut off; too much is happening. If one does not take part in guiding this period, he will be engulfed by it. Nevertheless, I spent several hours studying maps of the Northwest and looking up data on Oregon.

Monday, July 22

Have been trying to get Senator Clark on the phone for several days, unsuccessfully. Something is wrong, and I am not yet sure what it is. Possibly he now thinks the Chicago meeting is dangerous politically. His secretary always says the Senator will be in within an hour or two, but he is never there when I call, and does not call back.

Wednesday, July 24

Deac Lyman phoned in the afternoon to say that a friend of his, a Mr. Taylor,[178] was closely connected with Willkie[179] and wanted to talk to me about a separate Air Force for the United States. I told Lyman I thought the idea of a separate Air Force was in the right direction, but that it should be approached with extreme care, and that a very careful study should be made before arriving at conclusions. I said I had not made such a study and did not feel in a position to enter more than a very general discussion on the subject. I invited Lyman and Taylor for supper, and we spent the evening discussing Willkie's campaign, the war, a separate Air Force, etc.

178. Henry J. Taylor, economist, journalist, author, and prominent Republican.
179. Wendell L. Willkie, Republican presidential candidate in 1940.

Thursday, July 25

Spent most of the day on my address and various telegrams and phone calls. Went for a swim with Jon and his playmates (the gardener's two boys) in the afternoon. Spent the evening reading *The Tempest*.

Friday, July 26

Left for New York at 4:45. I left the Ford at the Cosmopolitan Club for Anne, who will be back this evening, and took a taxi to [Roy] Howard's office in the Grand Central Building. It is a curious room, furnished almost entirely in an Oriental fashion. We met Mrs. Howard a few minutes later and drove to the dock where their yacht was waiting—a large ocean-going diesel cruiser. Karl Bickel and his wife arrived at the same time we did. The five of us had dinner on the boat as we cruised slowly out to Lloyd Neck. Our discussion centered around the war, a unified Air Force, Willkie's candidacy, etc. Howard says his papers are going to come out in support of a unified Air Force. He has already come out in support of Willkie. Howard wants me to write an article or two on a unified Air Force. (He originally suggested an interview, but I told him that if I did anything, I would rather write an article myself.) I told Howard that while I was with his policy in general in regard to a unified Air Force, an article would require careful study, and that in making such a study I would want to discuss the matter with various Army and Navy officers. It would be difficult to do this, I told him, because of the stand I have taken in regard to the country's involvement in war, not from the standpoint of the officers I wished to talk to, but because such conversations might place them in difficulty with the Administration. I cited Truman Smith's experience. Howard replied that the ranking officers of both Army and Navy would oppose the creation of a separate Air Force, and that conversations with them would be of little value. I said the value to me would lie in hearing the best opposition arguments and that without a comprehensive knowledge of those arguments one could not take an intelligent stand. I told Howard I would also want to talk to the younger officers in both services. We decided to discuss the matter again after Howard returns from a trip to the Orient, on which he is leaving in the near future.

Howard and Bickel both believe Willkie will win the election. They were originally supporters of, but are now very much against, Roosevelt.

I had planned on swimming ashore at Lloyd Neck, and had brought bathing trunks and an oilskin in which to wrap my clothes for towing through the water. However, since the yacht carried a dinghy, I went ashore in it instead.

Saturday, July 27

Sherman Fairchild [180] called in the afternoon to say that Guy Vaughan wanted to see me and was on his boat near Lloyd Neck. I invited them to come over later in the afternoon. Vaughan was greatly worried about the Administration's attitude toward the aircraft industry. He said the situation in Washington was chaotic, that no definite program had yet been adopted, and that he was afraid they might even attempt to nationalize the aviation industry (as was done so disastrously in France under the Blum Administration). Guy said the manufacturers were now asked to operate within an eight per cent profit limitation and to guarantee the deliveries of all of the subcontractors. He said they could operate under the eight per cent profit limit but could not possibly give a guarantee for the subcontractors.

Wednesday, July 31

Senator Clark's secretary called to tell me the Senator was in a St. Louis hospital with an infected foot and would not be able to attend the Chicago meeting!

Thursday, August 1

Henry Ford phoned and asked if I could come to Detroit for a conference. I told him I would go up from Chicago and arrive Monday morning. He said he had planned on going to Huron Mountain but would postpone his trip until Tuesday.

180. Chairman of the board of Fairchild Aviation Corp. and inventor of the Fairchild aerial camera.

Friday, August 2

Finished my address this morning—final draft. It will not be popular but, I think, covers subjects which must be brought out and discussed. Made plane reservations for trip to Chicago tomorrow on TWA.

Anne and I went swimming in the late afternoon. In the evening we drove to the north shore of Lloyd Neck and walked for half a mile over the pebbly beach.

Saturday, August 3

Left for New York after breakfast. Boarded one of the new Boeing "stratoliners" and had a smooth flight to Chicago. Colonel McCormick's[181] chauffeur was waiting at the airport and drove me to McCormick's office in the Tribune Building. Colonel McCormick had invited me to stay at his home while I was in Chicago.

I phoned Mr. Brundage[182] (who is in charge of the meeting) and went over to his office to talk to him for half an hour. Grace came in while we were there. We discussed arrangements for the meeting tomorrow; then I returned to Colonel McCormick's office, and we drove to his city home for supper.

Sunday, August 4

Lunch with Colonel McCormick. Then left for the LaSalle Hotel in Chicago—about an hour's drive—where I met Mr. Brundage. We drove to Soldier Field from the hotel, arriving about 2:30. The stands were filling rapidly. The speakers' platform was filled with veterans in uniform, and the flags of the various organizations were in the field in front. The meeting opened with several local speakers, including a veteran of over ninety years. People were constantly coming up to ask me some question, so it was impossible for me to follow what was being said—messages, autographs, requests to speak elsewhere. Everyone meant well, as usual, but chose a rather bad time to talk. It caused quite a commotion

181. Robert R. McCormick, publisher of the Chicago *Tribune*.

182. Avery Brundage, Chicago engineer and builder; president of the American Olympic Association.

on the stand, and, after all, the speakers deserved attention. To add to difficulties, a problem arose in regard to broadcasting Senator McCarran's[183] speech. (McCarran had come to speak in place of Senator Clark.) It seemed the radio company had asked to broadcast my speech, but not McCarran's. When the Senator heard about it, he felt insulted and threatened to leave without speaking. The committee, in desperation, asked me if I could cut down part of my talk so McCarran could get on the air. I told them I could not cut it down appreciably, but that I would change places with McCarran and give him all of my time. They replied that this could not be done, as my talk had already been advertised in the radio programs. I did not feel it would be advisable to cut my address without careful study, and there was no time for that. Fortunately, McCarran decided he would speak anyway, and we went on with the original program.

Brundage introduced me. I spoke for twenty minutes; then Van Zandt spoke for fifteen; then McCarran closed with a talk that lasted nearly an hour, during which probably a third of the crowd left.

I found it much easier to speak to an audience than to microphones alone. The crowd seemed to want to applaud at every opportunity, which is rather disconcerting when one is not used to it. We had an excellent crowd, I felt. The stadium was about half full—the police estimated from 35,000 to 40,000 people. For a hot Sunday afternoon in August, with the sun beating down in an open stadium, this is as much as anyone could ask, and more than I expected. Brundage and Grace were disappointed, however, as they had hoped for a full stadium.

Boarded the night train for Detroit.

Monday, August 5

Off train at 7:55. Mr. Campsall (Ford's secretary) met me at the station and drove me to Mr. Ford's residence (Dearborn).

Breakfast with Mr. and Mrs. Ford. After breakfast Ford asked me if I would consider a trip to Europe if I could assist in bringing the war to an end. I told him I would be glad to (having no idea what I could do to stop the war at this time). Ford said he thought they were getting to a point in Europe when they might be willing to discuss peace terms, and that he thought if anyone could help in bringing peace about, I could! I told him I was afraid England would not be willing to accept any terms

183. Patrick A. McCarran, Democratic Senator from Nevada.

Germany would be willing to offer at this moment. Ford replied that it might be so and that I would have to be my own judge of the best time to go. He said he just wanted me to know that he would be glad to take care of any expenses involved in such a trip! I thanked him and told him that unless the expenses were very high, I would be able to carry them myself. I said I would like nothing better than to take part in ending the war if the opportunity ever arose.

We then discussed the trends in Europe and in America and switched from this subject to aviation engines and Ford's plans for building them. After that, we drove to the engineering building via the "old village." Edsel Ford and Sorensen were there waiting for us. They had a Hispano-Suiza engine torn down, and we all looked over it together. Sorensen told me he liked the basic design better than that of the Rolls-Royce. He said he had not been able to get a JU-211 engine to tear down. While we were in the engineering building, Ford took me to a new Mercury car and said he had selected it for me—in exchange for the old Franklin I am giving him for his museum. I felt very embarrassed and told him there was no need for him to give me anything in exchange—that the Franklin was really of no value and that I wanted him to feel there were some people at least who did not want to obtain anything from him in return for what little they were able to do for him. However, I could see that Ford, Edsel, and Sorensen all wanted me to take the car and that it would be difficult to refuse. Also, a relationship has grown up between us that made me not want to refuse it. I felt greatly pleased that Ford wanted to give it to me.

After lunch, at my request, they assigned a guide to take me through the factory, or at least through that portion of it which could be covered in the brief period of two hours. The steel rolling mill was especially impressive, with the great, glowing bars of metal running backward and forward over the rollers—starting as a huge ingot at one end, and coming out in several long slender bars, almost wirelike in appearance, at the other. In one place I stood for several minutes watching the men on the engine assembly line. One fellow had the job of putting in three studs as the engines passed by. His hands moved with nervous rapidity as he first inserted the studs and then screwed them firm with an electric socket wrench. He was undoubtedly paid well, but it was not the type of activity that builds character in men. He made me feel that I would rather work seventy hours a week on a farm than forty hours in a factory; yet these workers of Ford's are among the best cared for in the country. Going through the big River Rouge plant made me realize again the benefit of the small, decentralized country factory, not from the standpoint of efficiency, but from that of humanity.

Tuesday, August 6

Left Detroit at 9:00 and drove to Cleveland via Toledo. It was a hot, though not unpleasant, morning. Bought a sandwich lunch and continued on toward New York. About an hour after I left Cleveland I picked up an old Spanish War veteran—something I seldom do, but I could see by his face and age that he was harmless. He told me he was on his way from Michigan to a soldiers' home in New York. I carried him for about one hundred miles along his way and bought some sandwiches for him at the next town we came to. I asked his opinion about politics and war. He said he didn't know whether we would get into the war or not, but that he couldn't see any reason to fight for the British Empire. He said he thought "this young fellow Lindbergh" had the right idea. He said, "They call him a 'fifth columnist,' but he ain't no more fifth columnist than I am."

I drove until nearly 1:00 A.M.—540 miles for the day.

Wednesday, August 7

Started at 9:00. Sandwich lunch. Arrived at Englewood in midafternoon. Stopped to talk to [P. D.] MacKenzie, the garage operator, about putting the old Franklin in shape to drive to Detroit. He had towed it up to his garage from High Fields, where it had been in storage since 1933. From Englewood I drove to Lloyd Neck, arriving home about 6:00. Supper with Anne on the porch. We walked to the bluff in time to see the last of the sunset.

Monday, August 12

Press reports the mass air raids continuing over England. Both sides, as usual, claim success.

Phoned Hoover in Colorado Springs to find out what the true facts are in regard to starvation in Europe. I was connected with Willkie's headquarters and cut off several times before I could get through. The place sounded like a madhouse, and the voices answering the phone, as my call was switched first to one place and then to another, seemed out of patience and exhausted. I was finally informed that Hoover had left for Denver. I reached him at the station in Denver in the evening, just before he caught his train for California. He said famine was not immediate and that he did not expect to take strong action before he returned east in the first part of September. He said there were indications that the British might allow food to go through the blockade. He said the countries involved had enough money to buy food if it could be sent through the blockade.

Wednesday, August 14

The German bombing raids on England and English reprisals on Germany continue—with each side still claiming the advantage. It seems probable that the Germans are losing a few more planes than the English, because they are attacking. Also, the English save every man who jumps from his plane over England, while all the Germans who jump are naturally put in concentration camps. However, it seems the losses on both sides must be considerably higher than they admit and lower than the other side claims.

Mr. Eggleston and Mr. Stewart arrived on the 5:39 train. I met them at Huntington station. We went for a short swim before supper and spent the evening discussing conditions in the United States, together with trends and policies.

Thursday, August 15

Left for New York at 11:00. Parked car next Chrysler Building, and spent half an hour with Harold Bixby and Frank Gledhill. We discussed politics and the war. Afterward, Bix and I went to the Engineers Club for lunch. We took a private room so that we could talk without worry of being overheard. Bixby is almost as much concerned about the conditions and trends in this country as I am. We both believe the next few years may bring serious trouble whether or not we go to war; war would bring them sooner and make them practically certain to come. If we can avoid war, it is possible—I would not place the odds too high—that we may find reasonably moderate solutions to our problems. Bixby asked me if I sometimes felt these days that I was sitting on the edge of a live volcano. I told him I did. He said that was the way the country seemed to him.

Saturday, August 17

I become more and more disturbed about the trends and conditions in this country—the superficiality, the cheapness, the lack of understanding of, or interest in, fundamental problems. National debt increases; we involve ourselves unwisely and unnecessarily in the European situation, and we seem to have no understanding of our own limitations.

In the afternoon Anne and I listened to Willkie's acceptance speech. It seemed honest and open, but immature and anything but inspired. It was definitely a political speech—couched primarily for votes. We had hoped for more and felt depressed and disappointed after listening to it. Willkie had not had time to prepare the talk—that was obvious. It was just as obvious that he had listened to too many people before he wrote it. Also, he was tired; his voice showed that. But the nation was waiting for a message it did not receive; it hoped for greatness, and heard mediocrity. One can only hope there is more in the man than this speech showed. We were never more in need of leadership in this country, but it seems to be as lacking as it was in England and France at their time of crisis.

Spent the evening writing, and reading Igor Sikorsky's *Ideas Inspired by The Lord's Prayer*.

Sunday, August 18

Phoned Sikorsky after breakfast, but he was away. I talked to Mrs. Sikorsky instead. She said Sikorsky had flown to Colorado to spend a week alone in the Rocky Mountains, where he could rest and think. Mrs. Sikorsky said she had dreamed of me during the night. It is interesting, because she is a very sensitive person, and I had thought of telephoning Sikorsky yesterday evening but had concluded it was too late. It is years since I have seen her and months since I have seen Sikorsky. There seems to be a strong possibility of telepathy in this instance. Mrs. Sikorsky said she would ask her husband to phone me when he returned.

379

Tuesday, August 20

Took Jon to the Aviation Country Club in the afternoon for fifty minutes' flying, to keep my hand in. I have not done much flying this summer. I let Jon take the stick after we were in the air, and we climbed up to a cumulus cloud at 6,000 feet. After flying through the cloud several times, I gave him some wing overs and two loose loops. He loved them.

Anne and I ate supper on the porch, then walked to the bluff. Thor caught a baby rabbit on the way back, and brought it to us in his mouth —frightened but unharmed! We put it in a box with some grass to show to Jon and Land in the morning.

Friday, August 23

Off [Washington] train at 7:45. Taxi to Hay-Adams. C. B. Allen[184] came at 10:30, and we talked for half an hour. Met Shipstead at the Senate Office Building after lunch. He is very discouraged about the trend toward war. We agree that the public does not want war, but that Roosevelt does and is leading us toward it as rapidly as he can.

Returned to the Hay-Adams from Shipstead's office, and made several phone calls. Then taxi to the House Office Building for a meeting at Congressman Van Zandt's office at 5:00. Senator Nye, Congressman Maas, Congressman Curtiss,[185] Frazier Hunt,[186] and several others were there, or came in later. We discussed the war trends and Roosevelt's attitude. Everyone was very discouraged. Maas predicted that Roosevelt would have us in war within thirty days. I cannot agree with him about that; but we are all agreed that Roosevelt seems determined to get us into the war as soon as he can. At least, he never misses an opportunity to push us closer to involvement.

There is talk of a revolution in Mexico, and we discussed that possibil-

184. Carl B. Allen, friend of Lindbergh. As a New York *World* reporter he covered the 1927 New York–Paris flight. He was later aviation editor for the New York *Herald Tribune*. A pilot and member of the federal Air Safety Board (1939–40), he became in 1953 assistant to the president of the Martin [Aircraft] Co.

185. Gerald P. Nye, Republican Senator from North Dakota, 1925–45; Melvin J. Maas, Republican Representative from Minnesota; Carl T. Curtiss, Republican Representative from Nebraska.

186. Frazier Hunt, newspaper correspondent and author.

ity for a time. The Mexican elections come about the first of September. Most of the people in the room thought Roosevelt would intervene if there were revolution in Mexico, although they said he had sent word to the Mexicans unofficially that he would not interfere. The possibility of trouble in South America was also discussed; and then we talked about the Orient for a time.

It was a discouraged and gloomy meeting. Several of the men there thought the chance of staying out of the war had already passed. I cannot follow them in this, but I am very much concerned by present trends.

Saturday, August 24

Walked from the Hay-Adams to the Senate Office Building for a 3:00 appointment with Senator Clark (Missouri). We discussed the war and Roosevelt. No one I know trusts Roosevelt. Went to Senator Lundeen's office for a 3:45 meeting. Lundeen thinks we are likely to get into the war. He cited the similarity of the present situation to that of 1917. He says Congress is very pro-English, although still antiwar. After an hour with Senator Lundeen, I returned to the Hay-Adams.

Congressman Tinkham came for supper. We ate in my room so we could talk freely. He is an extremely interesting man. He likens Roosevelt's policies to Plato's description of a democracy turning into a dictatorship.

Taxi to the Hay-Adams to pick up my suitcase; then to station where I boarded the 2:10 for New York.

Wednesday, August 28

Stewart and Eggleston came for supper. [They] want me to form and head some sort of organization—nationalist, antiwar, etc. I don't think that is my field or that I am well suited for such work. Try to argue them out of the idea, rather unsuccessfully.

Wednesday, September 4

Off [Washington] train at 7:30. Taxi to Hay-Adams. Phoned Congressman Van Zandt and went to his office for a 10:00 meeting. R. Douglas Stuart[187] from the Chicago "Defend America First Committee" was

187. R. Douglas Stuart, Jr., a leading organizer and later national director of

there. Also Major Fellers,[188] who leaves tomorrow for Spain to be assistant military attaché. We discussed the Chicago organization and plans for an antiwar campaign. I asked Stuart to have lunch with me at the Hay-Adams. He seems a fine type of young fellow. (I met him once before, at the dinner after the Chicago meeting last month.) He has been taking a postgraduate law course at Yale, and together with several other Yale students became interested in, and opposed to, the attempt to draw this country into the war. He was in the Yale group that circulated the antiwar petition that caused such a stir last winter.

After lunch I phoned Mr. Libby (National Council for the Prevention of War), and he came over to the Hay-Adams to see me. He realizes the need for all antiwar groups to work together at this time, regardless of their diverging opinions concerning other matters. We discussed programs and policies for nearly an hour.

My room is on the sixth floor, overlooking Lafayette Park and the White House beyond it. The Washington Monument in the background lines up with the center of the White House porch. The porch, with its large columns, is brightly lighted at night. With field glasses I could probably see much of what is going on in the rooms on this side.

Thursday, September 5

Taxi to Capitol for appointment with Senator Wheeler at his office adjoining the Interstate Commerce Committee Room. We discussed the destroyer sale to Britain and Willkie's apparent uncertainty and inaction. We both feel he must move fast if he is to retrieve the situation. What is Willkie's real personal attitude on the war? No one seems to know. Bill Castle came for lunch in my room at 1:15. He says most of his Republican friends are greatly disappointed in Wilikie's campaign to date and that no one seems to be very sure of where Willkie actually stands.

Harry Byrd came at 6:00. He says he thinks Roosevelt is headed for war if he wins the election; thinks it is important to back Willkie, as "any change will be to the good." Byrd says he will have to vote for Roosevelt, much as he dislikes doing so, because a candidate for the Senate in Virginia must promise to vote for his party's presidential nominee. Byrd

---

America First. He had studied government and international relations at Princeton, graduated in 1937, and entered Yale Law School in 1938.

188. Major Bonner F. Fellers later became a brigadier general, serving with General MacArthur in Pacific areas.

says, however, that he will not work for Roosevelt's re-election and has already come in for much criticism in Virginia for not doing so. Byrd is definitely opposed to our entering the war. He told me that the way he now feels, he would rather resign his seat in the Senate than vote for war. He says Senator Vandenberg[189] has gone West to advise Willkie to take a stronger antiwar stand. Byrd suggested that I talk to Senator Townsend [190] about Willkie's position, and I agreed to stay over until tomorrow to do so. I had originally planned on taking the train to New York tonight.

Had no supper engagement and was not very hungry, so I pulled my hat down, put on a pair of glasses, and ate at the counter of a corner drugstore, without being recognized. It was great fun for a change.

Friday, September 6

Senator Townsend came for breakfast at 7:45. We discussed Willkie's stand on the war. Townsend and I are in quite close agreement on the entire situation, and we both feel it is essential to know more definitely what Willkie's attitude actually is.

After Senator Townsend left, I spent an hour writing, then took a taxi to Earl Findley's[191] apartment and spent an hour visiting with him. He lost his wife recently, and I did not want to go through Washington again without stopping to see him. Findley is a close personal friend of Orville Wright, and I once tried to get him to write Wright's biography. I brought the subject up again today. To my surprise Findley told me that about twenty-five years ago he had written the manuscript for a book about Orville and Wilbur Wright, but that Orville had felt it was too personal, so the book was never published. Findley said he had the manuscript in a box in the adjoining room! He said he had spent six months in the writing at a time when his finances were in a condition which made it very difficult to put the manuscript aside without publication. I could see he had been badly hurt by the whole affair—so badly hurt that it was still somewhat painful to discuss the matter, even after the lapse of a quarter century. I think he was hurt even more by Wright's feeling that the manuscript was unsatisfactory than by the loss of six months' work.

189. Arthur H. Vandenberg, Republican Senator from Michigan, 1928–51.

190. John G. Townsend, Republican Senator from Delaware.

191. Owner and publisher of U.S. Air Services, the oldest aeronautical monthly publication in the U.S.

Yet the friendship between Findley and Wright went on and apparently became even closer as the years passed. I asked Findley if I might talk to Wright about the manuscript when I next saw him. After considerable persuasion, I obtained his acquiescence.

I boarded the midnight train for New York.

Saturday, September 7

Off train at 7:50. Walked to garage and drove to Lloyd Neck for a late breakfast. The galley proofs for *The Wave of the Future*[192] arrived in the morning's mail. I spent most of the morning going over them and talking to Anne about my trip to Washington. We went for a short swim before lunch. After supper Anne, Thor, and I drove to the north shore and walked for a mile or so along the beach. Thin, low clouds drifted slowly overhead under a new moon and star-filled sky. We lay on the pebbles and watched for familiar constellations in the open spaces between the clouds.

Wednesday, September 11

Anne and I drove to New York in the morning for a last conference with Mr. Harcourt in regard to publishing details and to give him the galleys for *The Wave of the Future.*

In the afternoon I drove to Englewood in the Mercury to get the old 1928 Franklin I am giving to Henry Ford for the old-car exhibit in his museum. It is the car that was given to me by the Franklin Company in 1928. They sent me the car with the statement that their sales had increased so greatly because of my flight to Paris they wanted to do something in appreciation. They said they did not want to advertise that I was driving one of their cars and that there were no strings attached to the gift. I had refused many offers of this type because they were connected with advertising. The Franklin Company was so courteous and considerate and seemed to be so earnest in their offer that I accepted the car. Nothing they did afterward made me regret doing so. They never went back on their word about advertising. I asked the Franklin people how they connected my flight to Paris with an increase in their sales. They replied that everyone knew the *Spirit of St. Louis* was equipped with an

192. By Anne Morrow Lindbergh.

air-cooled engine, and that since their car was the only one manufactured in America with an air-cooled engine, they had benefited greatly from my flight. They said their sales curve jumped rapidly after I landed in Paris.

I drove the car from 1928 until 1933. I took Anne out to Falaise in it for our first flight together—in a little Moth biplane which I landed in a nearby field. This was our first flight together in the United States, and the first flight we made alone. It was not actually our first flight together, as I had taken Anne, Elisabeth, Constance, and Dwight, and several other people up over Mexico City in a Ford tri-motored transport plane in 1927.

It was while we were riding in this car over the roads of New Jersey that I asked Anne to marry me. And during the months we were engaged we spent much of our time together driving in it. Once, when we were being chased by reporters, the road I took came to a dead end. Ahead was a vacant lot and on the other side of it, down beyond a terrace, was a sidewalk and paved street. There were no fences or ditches between. The reporters were still out of sight behind us. I drove ahead through the lot to the point where the terrace sloped down to the sidewalk six or eight feet below. The angle at the top was steep—almost too steep for the Franklin. Still—I measured it with my eye as we approached—it seemed probable that we could pass over. I threw the engine into low gear, and we went over the edge. There was a slight bump as the center portion of the car cut through the sod; then we rolled down over the sidewalk, over the curb, and happily away along the street, leaving a very startled man and woman staring after us from the veranda of an adjoining house.

We drove the old Franklin until 1933 and then left it in the garage at High Fields. We did not want to sell it because it had been a gift in the first place. It had very little value by that time, and also we had developed an attachment for it, as one does develop an attachment for mechanical things which have served well during important experiences in one's life.

When I was in Detroit last summer, Henry Ford was taking Jim Newton and I to see several of his decentralized factories along the River Rouge. We were talking about his museum and village, and he told us he was looking for a Franklin car for the automobile exhibit. I told him I had a 1928 model he was welcome to, if he cared to have it. Ford told me that 1928 was about the period he wanted, and I agreed to drive the car through from New York on my next trip west. Since the Franklin had been in the garage at High Fields, unused for seven years, I arranged with MacKenzie, who had been the Franklin dealer in Englewood, to tow the car to his garage and put it in running condition.

I left the Mercury with MacKenzie, with instructions to send it to the parking lot next to the Chrysler Building in New York City, and I started off in the old Franklin. I thought a test drive to Lloyd Neck would be advisable before starting on the 800-mile trip to Detroit.

It seemed strange driving the old car again. It had once seemed so new and modern and powerful; now, all the lines were much too square and upright. I felt I was surrounded by glass windowpanes, like a plant in a greenhouse. The controls and instruments were all a bit out of place, and the steering wheel was not geared to the wheels of the car in the manner I have become used to in recent years. But I soon became used to the car again, and while the acceleration was slow, it cruised along well when once under way.

Thursday, September 12

Dictated several letters and telegrams after breakfast, then left for Detroit in the old Franklin (10:00 A.M. daylight time). The acceleration was slow, but I found I could cruise the car at 60 m.p.h. without difficulty. I crossed the Triborough and Washington bridges, and took Route 6 across the mountains (via Scranton, Cleveland, and Toledo). Bought a sandwich lunch, which I ate as I drove. Stopped twenty minutes for supper at the counter of a small-town restaurant. Drove all night—a little slower than usual, because the lights of the car are no longer very bright.

Friday, September 13

Daybreak came in Ohio a few miles west of Cleveland. I was interested to find out whether daybreak would have the same effect on me while driving a car that it has when I am flying a plane. Whenever I have flown a plane all night long and into daylight, I have found that by far the most difficult time to keep awake was not during the darkness of the night but just as the first streaks of dawn lightened the eastern sky. It is during the dawn that I have always had my greatest struggles with sleep.

All during the night, driving the Franklin, I felt wide awake—not the slightest tendency to sleep as I covered mile after mile of the road. I was alert and fully awake as I passed through Cleveland, with dawn only an hour or so ahead. I thought that for once I might pass through the dawn without experiencing that almost overcoming desire for sleep that is really worse than pain when one must fight it and cannot give way to its demands. But I was wrong. As soon as the faintest sign of approaching day brightened the eastern horizon the desire for sleep came upon me. I could not keep my eyes from closing; I could not keep my mind alert and on the road ahead. No amount of will I could exert, no amount of bouncing up and down in the seat had more than momentary effect. In a plane, one *must* go on; there is no alternative. But in a car, driving along the ground, there *is* an alternative; and one's subconscious mind knows when alternatives exist; it cannot be fooled by any amount of conscious argument. I pulled up to the side of the road and got out of the car. The shore line of Lake Erie lay less than a hundred yards away. I walked over to it through the thin woods that lay between. A fairly strong wind was blowing, and small waves rushed in to the beach. The wind and the coolness of morning, the smell of water and the walk combined to waken and freshen me, and by the time I returned to the car ten minutes later I was ready for the new day. I stopped twenty minutes for breakfast at a roadside restaurant and arrived at the Dearborn Inn for a bath and change of clothes.

I had originally planned on stopping along the route for a few hours' sleep, but the dimness of the old headlights and the extra time required by the detours along my route ate up most of the hours I had hoped to have for rest. The meeting was set for 3:00. (I have come to Detroit to attend a meeting between Ford, General Robert Wood,[193] and R. Douglas Stuart, Jr., in an attempt to interest Ford in the America First Committee, which is being organized in Chicago to combat the increasing war agitation. I would have preferred to come to Detroit by train, but this seemed as good an opportunity as I would ever have to bring the old car.)

I ate a quick lunch at the inn. While I was there, a phone call came from R. D. Stuart. He was at a hotel in Detroit and told me that a misunderstanding had arisen in regard to our meeting (which he had arranged). Apparently Stuart had talked to one of Ford's assistant secretaries, and Ford had not been asked about the engagement before it was

193. Kansas-born West Point graduate and chairman of the board of Sears, Roebuck and Co., General Wood became chairman of the America First Committee.

agreed to. As a result, he had made a previous engagement himself. (Stuart had told me by phone that the meeting was definitely set for 3:00 P.M. Friday, and by the time he learned of the conflict in dates, I had left for Detroit.) Stuart was very much upset about the situation. I told him I would look into it and call back as soon as possible.

After hanging up the phone, I went to see Harry Bennett and asked him to find out what could be done to straighten out the confusion. Bennett got in touch with Ford's residence and found that Ford was sleeping after an exhausting morning. I asked them not to wake him, for he is at an age when rest is essential. He awoke, however, within half an hour of the time Bennett phoned and came over to see us immediately—very much disturbed that there had been a mistake. After talking the situation over, it seemed best to hold the meeting on Monday, as that was the first day we could all arrange to be present. (General Wood had not come to Detroit, and Ford said there was no way for him to break his afternoon appointment even though Wood had come.) So in order to make the best of a bad start, we set the meeting for Monday, and I phoned Stuart to that effect.

Ford looked very tired—I have never seen him that way before—and I felt it was really better that our meeting was not to be this afternoon. Before we left, Ford, Bennett, and I discussed the campaign and Willkie's attitude on the war. Ford and Bennett had both talked to him a few days ago. They said Willkie was definitely opposed to intervention—much more so than his speeches and statements made it appear.

I had planned on taking the night train back to New York, but decided to spend the weekend with Mother.

Sunday, September 15

Mother and I spent most of the afternoon going through the trunk of old records. There were family photographs for generations back, letters of Father's, of Grandmother and Grandfather Land's, of Great-grandfather Lodge's, and many others. I am boxing some of them to be sent to Lloyd Neck to be copied. We had phonograph music in the evening and went to bed early, as Mother must be in school by 8:00 tomorrow morning. I worry about her long hours and the amount of work she does, but she will not hear of any change, and as long as she is happy, it is probably best not to make one.

Monday, September 16

Drove Mother to school, then went on to Bennett's office in the Rouge plant of the Ford Motor Company. I arrived ten minutes early. Bennett came a few minutes later, and Ford arrived promptly at 9:00. Before there was time to say more than good morning, General Wood, and R. D. Stuart came in through the door. We discussed the America First Committee, its policies and organization. Ford was cautious at first and reluctant to become a member—said he would have to look into it very carefully. We did not press him at all. Ford spoke of the Peace Ship he financed during the last war. Said he simply wanted to help, but soon found himself placed in the position of leading the entire enterprise. It was obvious that he wished he had not become involved. As the discussion developed, Ford became more interested and indicated he would probably take an active part on the committee. As we shook hands goodby, Ford told me he had had a hard week—out five nights straight at his grandchildren's parties, he said.

General Robert Wood is an able man and carried on the conversation intelligently and with great discretion. Stuart is alert, enthusiastic, and a hard worker. I drove them both from the Rouge plant to the Detroit airport, where they boarded the plane for Chicago.

Immediately after lunch, Bennett phoned and said that both Mr. and Mrs. Ford were willing to go on the committee and were anxious to help in any possible way. Half an hour later Ford telephoned and said he wanted to do everything possible for us. He asked if a donation would be in order. I told him that accepting membership was the most important aid he could give and that if the committee needed more money they could get in touch with him about that later on. Ford said he and Mrs. Ford had signed a letter for the committee, which they had left at Bennett's office for me. I told him I would get it personally. Phoned General Wood when he landed at the Chicago airport to tell him of Ford's acceptance. Then drove back to the Rouge plant to get Ford's letter, which I mailed to Stuart in Chicago.

Mother was back from school when I returned. I packed, and she and B. drove me to the station, where I boarded the 5:25 for Washington.

Tuesday, September 17

The train arrived at Washington an hour late, and I got off at 9:45. Haircut after breakfast, then phoned Senator Vandenberg and made an 11:30 appointment to see him. Vandenberg has recently returned from a trip west to see Willkie. I asked him what Willkie's real attitude was on the war issue. Vandenberg said Willkie was personally very definitely against our intervening in the war. Willkie felt, according to Vandenberg, that a stronger stand than he had taken against our involvement in the war would endanger eastern votes. Vandenberg is not at all pleased with Willkie's campaign thus far, and apparently told him so in no uncertain terms. Willkie replied that it was unfair to judge before he had started his active campaigning and asked Vandenberg to withhold his opinion until another week or so had passed. Vandenberg says that if Willkie is elected, the Republicans will "certainly have a problem child on their hands." He feels, as I do, that Willkie is inexperienced politically and that he has almost no understanding of foreign affairs.

After spending half an hour with Vandenberg, I walked back to the Army & Navy Club, and took a taxi from there to Bill Castle's residence to have lunch with Castle and Ambassador Cudahy.[194] Castle and I spent half an hour talking before Cudahy arrived. Castle told me that in his opinion Willkie has almost no understanding of the foreign situation. This has seemed obvious to me ever since I started reading Willkie's speeches. As soon as Cudahy came, we went into the dining room for lunch. I am much impressed with Cudahy, although I know very little about him. I like his face and the way he looks at you.

We talked about the food situation in Belgium. Cudahy said the shortage would be felt by October and would increase rapidly in seriousness. He said that when he was in London the British told him they would not permit food for the Continent to pass the blockade. Cudahy told us that in all the time he had been in occupied Belgium he had not seen an atrocity on the part of the Germans, or talked to anybody who had seen one. Cudahy said that while he felt it was essential to get food through to Belgium this winter, he thought nothing could be done until the tension lessens over the Battle of Britain. Cudahy told us that Leopold had no alternative to surrender and that history would eventu-

194. John Cudahy, Ambassador to Belgium. Former Ambassador to Poland, 1933–1937, and Irish Free State, 1937–39.

ally give him credit for what he did. Cudahy agrees with me that the best we can hope for now is a negotiated peace between England and Germany, and that even if an English victory were possible after a long war (which we doubt), it would leave all Europe in a condition of Bolshevism. Castle and Cudahy both feel that Willkie has made a very unfortunate start in his campaign. Cudahy and I left Castle's home at 4:00.

Phoned Truman Smith and took a taxi to his home. He asked Major Whitehead and Lawrence Dennis[195] to come over also. The latter is in Washington to attend a New Deal economic conference. Dennis is a striking man—large, dark-complexioned, strong, and self-assured. It is rather a shock when one sees him for the first time, especially in a room in Washington, for one is so unprepared for his type. He would seem more in place at some frontier trading post along the eastern border of Europe. I tried, as I talked to him, to fathom the nationality of his ancestors. I concluded that some of them might have come from the Near East. I must get to know Dennis better. He has a brilliant and original mind—determined to the point of aggressiveness. I like his strength of character, but I am not yet sure how far I agree with him.

After supper I took a taxi to the station and boarded the 2:10 train for New York.

Thursday, September 19

Stewart and Eggleston came for supper. We discussed plans for coordinating the various antiwar groups in this country. They expect to make a trip west within the next few days—Detroit and Chicago. I will arrange for them to see Stuart in Chicago and Bennett in Detroit.

Saturday, September 21

The morning papers report a new kidnaping case in California. It brings back all the old fears and worry about our children's safety. If this is not solved quickly and punished severely, it will encourage every criminal in the country who ever thought of such a thing.

195. Diplomat and writer. He was in the U.S. diplomatic service from 1920 to 1927, in Haiti, Rumania, Nicaragua, Honduras, and Paris. He resigned to enter banking, and was later editor of *The Weekly Foreign Letter*, 1939–43 and author of *The Dynamics of War and Revolution* (1940) and other books.

Mr. and Mrs. Igor Sikorsky arrived at 5:15 and stayed for supper. They both have very sensitive and exceptional minds—the insight and intuition of the Russian at his best. We talked of America, Europe, Russia, of racial problems, of the Ukraine, of flying boats, of his new helicopter. Sikorsky showed me some motion pictures of his helicopter and asked me to come to Bridgeport to fly it.

Tuesday, September 24

British warships bombard Dakar, and air raids continue over England and Germany.

The first ten copies of *The Wave of the Future* arrived from Harcourt, Brace. They are well turned out and very attractive in appearance.

Mr. Libby came for supper. I met him with the car at Huntington station. In the evening we discussed methods of co-ordinating the various antiwar groups. Libby is a pacifist, and I am not; but we are both on common ground as far as the present war is concerned. He comes from an old Maine family whose first American ancestor landed near Portland in 1637.

Wednesday, September 25

Anne and I drove to New York for lunch with a group of leading Quakers at the Cosmopolitan Club (Mr. Rufus Jones, Clarence Pickett, and John Rich). We talked of the coming famine in Europe and how we could counteract the sentiment which is being whipped up in the United States against sending food to the occupied countries. Anne wishes to give her royalties from *The Wave of the Future* to the Quakers for war relief in Europe. We discussed this with them, and they were very much pleased. We were greatly impressed by these three men. They seem an exceptionally fine type.

After lunch we took the three Quakers to the Waldorf, and then Anne and I drove out to Next Day Hill. The house is full of children—Stephen, Saran,[196] and several refugee children from England.

O. K. Armstrong arrived at 3:30. We talked of the American Legion

196. Stephen Morrow, son of Dwight and Margot Morrow, and Saran Morgan, daughter of Aubrey and Constance Morgan.

convention in Boston and of the change in their neutrality stand. We discussed the possibility of Armstrong working with the America First Committee in Chicago.

Stewart phoned from Detroit. He said that he and Eggleston had a very satisfactory meeting with Bennett.

Saturday, September 28

Drove to Huntington station to meet Stewart and Eggleston on the 5:39 train. We discussed their trip to Chicago and Detroit until 7:00, when O. K. Armstrong arrived. We talked for half an hour in regard to future plans; then I left the three of them together for supper while Anne and I went over to the Trasks'. We had promised to have dinner at the Trasks' several days ago, but I was anxious for Armstrong, Stewart, and Eggleston to meet before Armstrong went to Detroit, and tonight was the only opportunity. Consequently, the rather unique arrangement of leaving them alone for supper at Lloyd Manor.

Sunday, September 29

Spent most of the morning with Anne in the sun, discussing a new poem she is writing. After lunch Jon and I drove to the Long Island Aviation Country Club for an hour and a half's flying in their Fairchild monoplane. We made about sixteen flights in all, as I have done very little flying this summer and am anxious to keep in practice. I find that an hour spent in landing and taking off is worth many hours of cross-country flying as far as skill is concerned. Jon, however, was disgusted with the short flights and wanted to go farther away from the field.

We returned to Lloyd Manor in time for tea with Mr. and Mrs. Allen Dulles and Ambassador and Mrs. Hugh Wilson outside on the porch. We spent most of the time they were here discussing the campaign and Willkie's chances of election. At present, they seem less than even.

Monday, September 30

After an early lunch Anne and I drove to Englewood to register, so we will be eligible to vote in November. We returned to New York for a 4:00 meeting with Dr. Carrel in his apartment. He says that French people now feel more bitterly toward the English than toward the Germans.

Tuesday, October 1

In the afternoon I drove to New York for a conference with Hart, Stewart, and Eggleston. I took the original bronze head Despiau did of Anne to the Modern Museum. I hate to let it go, but we have a copy—the first copy—and I do not want to take any chance of the original being damaged. If we had a permanent home, I would keep it; but with the present uncertainty of conditions in general, and of our own lives in particular, I think it is best for the head to be in a museum. I believe it is one of the best pieces of work Despiau ever did.

Returned to Lloyd Neck for supper. Stuart phoned and I told him it was essential to avoid friction between antiwar groups. I told him I thought they should all be able to look to his committee in Chicago for leadership. He agreed, finally, to come to New York for Hart's meeting on Thursday. Stuart says he is having trouble buying radio time for the America First Committee! Some of the radio stations have taken the stand that the committee has to do with a "controversial issue" and therefore comes under the code they have formed against selling time for controversial issues. It is a fine state of affairs if the question of war and peace cannot be debated before the American people because it is a "controversial issue"! Stuart says a final decision has not yet been made and that there is still a chance they will be able to buy the time they want.

Wednesday, October 2

Anne woke at 2:00. We phoned Dr. [Everett M.] Hawks, packed, and left in the Mercury for Doctors Hospital at 3:15. We arrived about 4:30 and were taken to Room 1109. Dr. Hawks arrived a few minutes later. Then Miss Johnson [the nurse], Dr. [Edward H.] Dennen, and Dr. Flagg[197] arrived. I thought Anne might have a few hours' sleep, but events moved too fast. Hawks and Dennen predicted the baby would be born between 12:00 and 1:00. I told them that judging from the speed of Land's birth, it would be long before that. Anne began having strong

197. Dr. Paluel J. Flagg arranged and took part in the first meeting between Lindbergh and Dr. Alexis Carrel at the Rockefeller Institute in 1929.

pains about 9:20. Up to that time she refused to take gas—said it was better to wait as long as she could stand the pain. I have never seen anyone show greater courage. At 9:20 I could see it would not be much longer and went to tell Hawks and Dennen, who were waiting in a nearby room. They thought I was overestimating the progress when I told them I thought the baby would be born within forty-five minutes. Flagg left immediately to give Anne a little gas, but had to administer it on the way to the operating room. I put on a cap, mask, and gown, and went in with the doctors and nurses. I have been present at the birth of all of our children. Hawks had to hold the baby in while they made the last details ready and to prevent too rapid a birth, he told me. They were caught almost as unprepared as the doctor in England when Land was born. (In England, the anesthetist did not arrive in time, and Dr. [Eardley] Holland, the obstetrician, had to administer the anesthetic himself in addition to doing everything else.) Land was partially born on the way to the operating table.

The baby came at 9:45—a girl—just what we had hoped for, and apparently in perfect condition. I stayed with Anne until she was back in her room and ready for a rest, then went to the Engineers Club for a 10:45 breakfast.

Phoned Christine to find out if she were having any trouble with newspapers. She said a car with two men and a woman, from Hearst's *Journal-American,* was parked on the road in front of the house and that they had come to the door several times, demanding information about Anne. I told Christine to call the police if she had any trouble with them.

Went for a two-mile walk in the early afternoon, along West Side streets near the Engineers Club. Then went into one of the newsreel theaters. I was impressed by the silence of the crowd when pictures were shown of American National Guard units entraining for camp. There was no cheering whatever. There was slightly more clapping for Willkie than for Roosevelt. But I wish Willkie would stop this big, honest, arms-outstretched, simple-fellow attitude.

Phoned Miss Johnson at the hospital. She said Anne was awake, so I went over. Anne looked very well and happy. Mrs. Morrow came for a short visit while I was there. (The hospital has been having trouble with the newspapers. One reporter even got up to the maternity floor! I told the superintendent to refuse all information and not to put any calls through to Anne's room.) Stayed with Anne until it was time for her to rest again; then drove out to Lloyd Manor for the night.

Thursday, October 3

Left for New York at 9:00. Met Stuart (Chicago) at Engineers Club at 10:00. We discussed the America First Committee and the advertisement they have in this morning's *Times*. I think it is very good, but a little confused in layout. After talking over America First Committee plans and its relationship to eastern antiwar groups, we went to Chester Bowles's[198] office for a half hour's discussion about the committee. Bowles is one of its members, and he took a major part in laying out the advertising campaign.

Hart had called a meeting of fifteen or twenty men for 2:00 at the University Club. All entered into the discussion, but nothing in the form of a definite organization emerged from the meeting. Hart appointed a committee of three to formulate plans (Ackerman and me, in addition to himself), but I do not think much will come of this, either. Hart has the eastern idea that one need only appoint a committee to accomplish results. We don't need a committee; what we need is a man of ability to take over and direct an eastern organization, as General Wood is directing the America First Committee in Chicago. In lieu of such a man, the best thing for us to do is to throw our support behind the Chicago group. I think I can bring this about, but it will take a little time. Spent twenty minutes talking to Hart after the meeting, then went to the Waldorf for a half hour's discussion with Castle and Stuart (in ex-President Hoover's suite). Mr. Hoover came in and spent fifteen minutes with us while we discussed the war and the Far Eastern situation.

Supper with Anne in her room at the hospital. She is very well and happy.

Friday, October 4

To the Waldorf-Astoria for a fifteen-minute conference with ex-President Hoover. I asked his advice about men who might take part in an eastern antiwar organization. It is obvious that they will be difficult to find in New York City. Hoover suggested I talk to [Jeremiah] Milbank among others.

198. Co-founder with William Benton of Benton & Bowles advertising agency in 1929, Bowles later served in the administrations of Presidents Roosevelt, Truman, Eisenhower, Kennedy, and Johnson. From 1943 to 1946 he was national administrator of the Office of Price Administration; later Ambassador to India, 1951–53.

Arrived at Doctors Hospital at 5:55. Anne was nursing. The baby is deliberate and quiet in its movements. We have decided to name the baby Anne Spencer after its mother. Supper with Anne, then left for Lloyd Neck at 8:00.

Sunday, October 6

Afternoon on writing and routine until 4:15; then left for New York to see Anne. She read my address, which I plan on entitling "A Plea for American Independence," and made several suggestions—all of them good, as usual. Anne and I discussed the possibility of her talking over the radio in support of selling food to Europe to prevent famine this winter. If we do not send food, conditions there will be terrific. Left the hospital at 8:00, and returned to Lloyd Neck.

Monday, October 7

Drove to New York for a 9:45 meeting with Jerry Milbank in Stewart's apartment. We discussed the Willkie campaign, and I showed him the manuscript for my address. Then to Hart's office with Stewart. We discussed methods of setting up an eastern antiwar organization. It will not be possible to do unless we can find someone of energy and ability, who can devote most of his time to the work. There is no use continuing these conferences on the present basis. It takes too much time without producing any results. I suggested that we give our support to the America First Committee in Chicago unless and until we get something started in the East. Hart and Stewart were rather reluctant, but could suggest nothing else, except that we postpone making a decision for a day or two.

Drove to the hospital for lunch with Anne, and then out to Lloyd Neck. After supper I decided to go to the World's Fair, as it is closing this month and I have not yet been inside the gates—although I drive past it on the parkway every time I go to Englewood or to uptown New York. I put on an overcoat so I would be less easily recognized, parked the Mercury outside the grounds, bought a ticket for twenty-five cents, and walked in. I decided that I would spend most of my time walking through the grounds instead of going into the first buildings I came to. I did, however, go into the "Perisphere," as it is the symbol of the fair and seemed to be one of the main exhibits. It contained a model "city of the future," which one viewed from above as he rode slowly around it on a revolving ring platform. Lights changed from day to night, and a phonograph voice described the "utopia" of the dwellers. Finally, columns of singing and marching citizens were thrown from motion-picture projectors onto the dome above—all converging toward the center as they marched. The whole affair was tinted with extremely subtle Communistic propaganda.

Most people were in the amusement area of the fairgrounds, and most of them were gathered in front of the nude-girl exhibits. In this respect the New York World's Fair is similar to the Chicago World's Fair, which Anne and I went to see in 1934 or '35 (I have forgotten which year). As an attraction for crowds, science does not seem to be able to compete with an undressed woman.

Tuesday, October 8

Reports from Washington say people there are resigned to our getting into the war. I gather this does not by any means include the House and Senate, however, and the rumors and society gossip that run around Washington are of relatively little importance. Nevertheless, the war atmosphere is increasing in this country.

Dictated a few letters after lunch and then drove to the Long Island Aviation Country Club for an hour's flying in the Stinson—about fifteen flights around the field in the rain and mist. From the L.I.A.C.C. I drove to New York for supper with Anne.

Phoned Fulton Lewis to make arrangements to give my address over the Mutual Broadcasting System. Apparently there is still no difficulty in getting time on the air. I don't know how much longer I will be able to do this, for there are many people who would like to see me stopped. I plan on speaking from Washington to avoid drawing attention to our home in New York. The threatening letters I receive about my own safety don't worry me; but the threats about the children do. If I speak from a studio in New York, it is bound to draw attention to the fact that we are making our home on Long Island.

Wednesday, October 9

Left for Bridgeport at 8:00. Stopped at Port Washington for Deac Lyman, who is going with me to visit the Sikorsky factory and to see Igor

Sikorsky fly his helicopter. We arrived at Sikorsky's office a little before 11:00. He took us directly to the flying field and gave an extremely interesting demonstration of his helicopter. The morning was gusty, with wind velocities approaching twenty-five or thirty miles at times. Sikorsky said it was the gustiest weather he had yet flown in with the helicopter. He flew it beautifully and seemed to have plenty of control.

It was like the old days of aviation again; we were off, rather secretly, in a corner of the flying field. The helicopter was built not for appearance but to carry on an experiment as cheaply as possible. Its tubular steel framework was not even covered with fabric. The engine was connected to the rotors by belts instead of shafting. Sikorsky flew in a business suit without helmet or goggles. Except for the fact that we were looking at a helicopter instead of some old biplane, the setting was identical to that of an experimental flight a quarter century ago.

After the flights Sikorsky took several of us to lunch at a small inn on the outskirts of Bridgeport—six or eight in all: Sikorsky, Lyman, some of the officers and engineers of the company, and myself. While we were eating, Willkie drove by in an open car with a large motorcycle police escort. I caught a quick glimpse of him as he flashed by the window. It takes my mind back to 1927 and '28. He is more than welcome to it all.

After lunch we walked through the Vought-Sikorsky factory. They have a large number of Navy planes on production—hope to reach a rate of eighteen per week this winter, they said. Sikorsky showed me the jigs that are being set up for his new transatlantic flying boats and the preliminary drawings for a six-engine flying boat and for his next helicopter.

After leaving the factory Sikorsky took me to his home, several miles away on the road back to New York. Mrs. Sikorsky was there, and three of their boys. Sikorsky, Mrs. Sikorsky, and I spent an hour talking about America, Europe, and Russia. They understand the problems of Europe well, both by experience and by intuition. They have a grasp of life that is known by few people today.

From the Sikorskys' home I drove to New York, for dinner with Carrel and Bakhmeteff at the latter's apartment. We discussed conditions in America and Europe, and, surprisingly enough, we now agree on almost all details. We are all greatly concerned about the war trends in this country.

Stopped for a half hour with Anne on the way out to Lloyd Neck.

Thursday, October 10

I have been reading the copies I am having made of my old diaries, and this morning I read several that were written in 1939, in the months preceding the war. It is extremely interesting to see how events have turned out and to compare what has taken place with what one thought would take place—to compare history with prophecy, fact with intuition. One can do this with a diary; it is one of the great advantages of a written record as opposed to memory. As I read through my daily entries in 1939, I am struck by the fact that I applied a little too much logic to the peoples and the politicians in Europe. It is not that I thought people were logical; I cannot remember ever entertaining such a fallacy; I do not even believe it is desirable for people to be completely logical in their viewpoint. Logic must be based on knowledge; and since knowledge is limited in man, so must be his logic. I never trust logical conclusions unless they combine with an inner intuitive feeling, which I find to be really much more reliable. Unless I have this feeling I know with almost complete certainty that my logical reasoning is wrong.

But to get back to Europe, the war, and the outlook I had during the preceding months: until war was actually declared by England and France, I felt, although without much confidence, that a major European conflict would not take place in 1939. It is true that I laid my plans on the basis that a war *would* start in that year; but until the movement of armies began, I kept hoping for a peaceful settlement, or at least a postponement of hostilities. I had seen the strength of Germany, and I knew the weakness of England and France. I felt certain that Germany would expand eastward, even at the cost of a major war, but I did not believe she wished to throw herself against England and France—at least at that time. As far as England and France were concerned, I could not believe that in their weakened and unprepared condition they would throw their forces against the German Western Wall, or that they would open their cities to the attack of the vastly superior German Air Force.

Everything considered, I felt—probably I should say I reasoned—that a major European war in 1939 was improbable, and 1940 was another year. One had sufficient difficulty looking ahead a few weeks or months without attempting the impossible and planning on what would happen the next year. But the war started in 1939; Germany moved her armies into Poland; that I expected. Poland resisted; that did not surprise me in view of the encouragement given by England and France. England and France declared war on Germany; this did surprise me, for it was obvious they could not help Poland, and just as obvious that they could not invade Germany through the Western Wall and against the German Air Force. Russia entered the Polish war on the German side; nothing that Russia did would surprise me, for that country is completely unpredictable.

As I read through my diaries, I realize that the element I foresaw least clearly was the vacillation of the "democracies" and their complete inability to follow a consistent policy. I could not believe that the nations which let Germany rearm, march into the Rhineland, take over Austria, build the Western Wall, and disarm the Czechoslovakian Army, would declare war over Poland under conditions which made it impossible to give her effective aid. France and England committed themselves to a policy of inaction when they permitted Germany to build her Western Wall; after that, their only hope lay in letting Germany do as she would in Eastern Europe and contenting themselves with their empires in Africa and elsewhere. I felt the French-English policy should be to divide Europe by the Western Wall–Maginot Lines and to build up their own military strength until the cost of a westward attack by Germany would be too great to warrant the attempt. I felt Germany would have enough to occupy her attention in Eastern Europe and in her relationship with Russia.

I felt the welfare of our Western civilization necessitated a strong Germany as a buffer to Asia, just as it necessitated a strong British Empire. I felt that peace in Europe, and throughout the world, for that matter, could be maintained only by co-operation between England and Germany. In view of my "reasoning" I thought up to the last days that 1939 might pass without a major European war, and here my judgment was probably somewhat affected by my hope. I had seen war avoided at the time of "Munich," and there seemed even more reason to avoid it at the time of "Poland."

But the fact is that war *was* declared (although in a sense the real war was not fought until the following year). France moved her armies up to the Western Wall, and there they stopped. England chased all German commerce from the oceans and then could do no more. The United States became ineffectively hysterical about the whole situation. Meanwhile, Germany defeated Poland and divided it with Russia. She bombed the British fleet out of the North Sea, torpedoed British shipping, overran

Denmark, conquered Norway, took over Holland and Belgium, routed the British expeditionary force in Flanders, broke the Maginot Line, and defeated the French Army. Now she is bombing England relentlessly and continuing to sink merchantmen in ever-increasing numbers (now over 3,000,000 tons).

All the logic I used in concluding that war would probably not come before 1940 turned out to be correct. I thought Germany would expand eastward—she did. I thought the French Army could not break through the West Wall—they failed. I felt there was no way to give effective aid to Poland—none was given. France has been defeated, and England is on the defensive, fighting desperately for her life. I knew the German Air Force was vastly superior to all other air forces in Europe combined—that is now a well-established fact. In every technical estimate I was right; in fact, my estimates turned out to be conservative. Nevertheless, war was declared—declared by the weak and not the strong, by those who would lose, not by those who would win. The declaration was brought about by something that lies completely outside of logic—by emotion, by blindness, by vanity, by courage, by indifference, by pride, by many and infinitely complicated elements, by elements which are intangible, unpredictable, and unforeseen.

I say that "in every technical estimate I was right"; but to be accurate this needs one qualification, which is very important, even though it does not change my general conclusion. I did not realize the weakness of the Maginot Line along the Belgian border. I did not expect the Germans to break that line during the early stages of the war. I expected Germany to strike at France and England by air bombing, and by submarine blockade. I thought both sides would take up their positions in the Maginot–Western Wall lines and remain in them until at least a partial decision had been reached in Eastern Europe. I expected action in the Balkans, coupled with a movement on Egypt and the Suez Canal, to take place before any major movement on the Western front.

The German invasion of Norway did not surprise me; neither did their invasion of Holland. But I did not foresee the ease with which the German armies would march through Belgium, break the Maginot Line, rout the British expeditionary force in Flanders, and defeat France. I know of no one who accurately estimated either the weakness of the Maginot Line extension west of Sedan, or the irresistible strength of the German mechanized divisions. Our military estimates were wrong in each of these instances—more wrong about the Maginot Line than about the

German strength. But between the overestimate on one hand and under-estimate on the other, the breaking of the Maginot Line was a shock to everyone; I think the ease with which it was done must have been something of a shock to the Germans themselves.

There was one element, however, I do not forgive myself entirely for overestimating. That was the strength and morale of the French Army. I knew that France was in a weakened condition, that her politics were corrupt, her financial situation serious, her people divided, her workmen dissatisfied. This had been the case for some years. Looking back now, it seems obvious that a country with such internal conditions could not have a large, efficient, and well-disciplined army. In this modern, mechanized age the condition of an army can be closely estimated from the condition of the country in which it is raised. A prosperous country *may not* have a good army, but a demoralized country *cannot* have a good army today.

Everyone I met in the months prior to the war, including American and British and even German officers, spoke of the French Army with great respect and praise. As a result, I allowed myself to gain the same impression, where more careful and objective consideration would have warned me that France was too weak in her body to be strong in her arms.

But notwithstanding these false estimates, the general trend of the war has been as I expected. The Germany Army and Air Force was a little stronger than I thought; the French Army was considerably weaker than I realized; the British have bungled about as much as I expected them to; Germany has been successful in most of her actions and seems to be in a better position than ever to win the war.

Now, here in America, I am again trying to see into the future, to apply logic to plans for my own action and for the welfare of my family. Will America enter the war? It seems to me that logical reasoning says she should not. Our interference will do no good in Europe; we should have acted five years ago if we intended to fight; we are not prepared for a foreign war; it seems improbable that we could win a war in Europe under present circumstances (we would have to land and maintain an expeditionary force on the continent of Europe against the opposition of the German Army, Navy, and Air Force); polls of the country show over eighty per cent of our people opposed to entering the war; before we could take an effective part the chances are that England will be defeated; in which case we would have to attack Europe unaided to be successful; Japan is in a position to cause trouble in the Pacific if we turn all of our effort toward Europe.

These and many other reasons indicate the inadvisability of our entering this war. But here again I am using logic at an emotional and illogical time. Will we in America allow ourselves to be enticed into war, as were the people of England and France, under conditions that make success impossible, even though by some miracle we were able to defeat the armies of the Axis? Will our vanity, our blindness, and our airy idealism throw us, too, into the conflict, heedless of the future? Must we fly moth-like into the flame of a war that burns an entire ocean away? I am not sure. I know what we should do, but no one knows what we will do. Our thinking is confused; our direction is undecided; our leadership uncertain. I shall work against war, but lay plans for one.

Saturday, October 12

Left for New York at 4:30 for supper with Anne. Both she and the baby are very well. Anne and I talked about the food situation in Europe. She read the outline of an article she is writing in an attempt to make Americans see that nothing will be gained by starving the people of the defeated countries of Europe—that it will eventually turn them to Germany and against us. Anne is very anxious to help the Quakers with their work in European relief. She is hardly strong and fresh enough yet for much writing, and the hospital is not a very good place in which to write —especially with a baby to nurse every four hours in addition to the other routine.

Monday, October 14

Off [Washington] train at 7:50. Lunch with Fulton Lewis at the Chevy Chase Club. He had also invited Senator Clark, Congressman Cox,[199] William Dolph (Mutual Broadcasting Company). After lunch I drove with Lewis to the Mutual studios to arrange details in connection with my broadcast tonight. The newsreels again requested that I read part of my address for them after I had broadcast. In the past I have refused their requests; first, because of the difficulty they have often caused for me; second, and much more important, because of the Jewish influence

199. Edward E. Cox, Democratic Representative from Georgia.

in the newsreels and the antagonism I know exists toward me. To speak for the newsreels on a political subject is dangerous, because one has no control over the way they cut the picture or over the setting in which they place it. They can pick either the best or the worst sentences from your talk, as they wish; and they can control the emotional attitude of the audience to a large extent by the type of picture they place before yours. By speaking for the newsreels, I take the chance that they will cut my talk badly and sandwich it in between scenes of homeless refugees and bombed cathedrals. However, this is a critical period, and I think it is worth the chance.

The Mutual Broadcasting Company headquarters in New York had telephoned Dolph to ask me to remove the sentences at the end of my address which referred directly to the election. Dolph said it would be a great favor to him if I could do this, but that if I felt I could not do so, he would not insist. Copies of my address had already gone to the papers, but Dolph said that made no difference as long as I made the change in reading it over the radio. The changes he asked for were unimportant from my standpoint, so I gladly made them. (It seems the broadcasting companies have agreed on a code which requires them to prevent "political speeches" from being made over their system unless the speeches are paid for at the regular commercial rates. Since my radio time is not paid for, I come under this code. Although it is not strictly enforced, the broadcasting companies are expected to make a reasonable effort toward its enforcement.)

Drove to the Mutual studios in time to broadcast at 8:45. Then spent about an hour reading portions of it for the newsreels in an adjoining room—very bright and hot lights. After finishing with the newsreels, I drove back to the Lewis home with Dolph. None of the guests had left when we arrived.

Tuesday, October 15

Made a number of phone calls, including one to Kay Smith. Kay called for me a few minutes later with her car, and we drove over the bridge to Arlington while we discussed the situation in Washington. Both she and I think it is inadvisable for me to see Truman on this trip, so that he can say we did not meet. Since I attacked the Administration in my address last night, they might make life very difficult for Truman if they thought he had any part in it. The Smiths think their telephone may be tapped and their house watched. I think this is doubtful, but telephones *have* been tapped in Washington. There is nothing I do that I fear to have known, but I do not want my actions to be a source of any embarrassment to my friends. The freedom of action and speech that we used to know in this country seems to be rapidly disappearing.

I took a taxi to Mrs. Lundeen's home. It was the first I have seen her since the Senator's death.[200] Her daughter was there also. It is a tragic situation. There had not been an accident on the airlines for about a year and a half prior to the crash of Lundeen's plane. And he had difficulty in getting a place on that plane; finally, the airline officers found that a girl who had passage was willing to trade it for a seat on the following schedule. Mrs. Lundeen spoke about her husband's files and papers. I suggested that she give them to the Minnesota Historical Society. Boarded the 2:10 train for New York.

Wednesday, October 16

Off train at 7:30. It is the day of registration for men from twenty-one to thirty-five. The morning papers carry instructions for those registering, and there are placards in a number of the windows along the street. Made several phone calls, then got the Mercury from the garage where I had left it and drove to Doctors Hospital for half an hour with Anne. Lunch at Lloyd Manor.

WOR, the Bamberger station in New York, did not carry my address, although it is the New York member of the Mutual System. I do not know the background of what has taken place here; but there seems to have been confusion about the radio program, which was not accidental. Dolph told me WOR would carry the address. People who telephoned WOR got conflicting information. Mayor La Guardia[201] spoke over WOR at the time I spoke in Washington Monday night—but it seems that his broadcast was originally scheduled for Tuesday night. I shall be interested to find out exactly what took place.

Thursday, October 17

Left for New York at 3:00 for an hour's conference with Carrel at his apartment on Eighty-ninth Street. He had had two letters from Mme.

200. On August 31, 1940, Senator Lundeen and twenty-four others were killed in an airplane crash near Lovettsville, Va.

201. Fiorello La Guardia, mayor of New York City from 1933 to 1945.

Carrel; one written on September 9, and the other on September 15. One of the Carrels' friends carried the letters to unoccupied France, and they were mailed from there. Carrel says that communication with occupied France is very difficult. Mme. Carrel was on Saint-Gildas when the letters were written. She said she had enough food but very little coal. The Germans have taken the Carrels' two cars and their small motorboat. They have been out to Saint-Gildas, but have been very courteous, according to Mme. Carrel. She says they have occupied Illiec. Carrel says the British won't let his hospital unit pass through the blockade. In fact, the British won't even allow medical supplies to go to France! After leaving Carrel's apartment, I spent two hours with Anne at Doctors Hospital, then drove back to Lloyd Neck. Anne will leave the hospital Saturday.

Saturday, October 19

Sunny, clear, and cold. Left for New York at 9:00. Stopped to cash a check. Then to Doctors Hospital, where I arranged for the bill and tips. Anne, Miss Johnson [the nurse], and I left at 11:30, stopped at a nearby apartment for Miss Johnson's suitcase, and arrived at Lloyd Manor at 1:00. Jon, Land, and Soeur Lisi rushed out to meet us. Jon and Land were very interested and excited. They kept saying, "How small she is!" "What small hands she has!"

Sunday, October 20

The intensive bombing of England continues.

It is another cold day. I drove to Port Washington for an hour's visit with Deac Lyman. I spoke to him about the trip to Europe I am considering and asked his opinion about the possibility of my writing several articles for one of the news syndicates.

I am anxious to regain firsthand contact with the situation in Europe. I have not been there for over a year and a half now, and I believe a trip would be of the utmost interest and value. It is only by direct contact that one can judge with accuracy and comprehension. But I cannot go to Europe in these times without having some obvious reason for going—a reason that is obvious enough to obtain passports and visas in belligerent countries. I might go as a military observer, but that would restrict both my movements and my expression. I might go for the purpose of writing several articles for a news syndicate. There would be both advantages and disadvantages to that. But in these times one must act quickly and do things he would not consider under other circumstances.

Drove to New York after supper and boarded the midnight train for Washington.

Monday, October 21

Off train at 7:45. Breakfast with Armstrong, Stewart, and Eggleston. We discussed plans for the meeting which Armstrong has called, and which opened today at the Lafayette Hotel. After Armstrong, Stewart, and Eggleston left for the meeting, I went out for a half hour's walk. Armstrong, Stewart, and Eggleston returned in the afternoon. Armstrong has agreed to let the press come to the dinner tonight! That brings real complications, for there was to have been an informal discussion; but I certainly cannot take part in an informal discussion with reporters present. In the first place, it would do away with my precedent of never talking for publication except from a written manuscript. In the second place, some well-meaning peace leader would probably suggest a wild scheme involving my actions, which would make excellent and disadvantageous press copy, no matter how firmly I turned it down.

Armstrong had previously told me the meetings would be held in private. However, he has done good work, and I want to back him up in every way that I can. I suggested to him that I arrive just as people were sitting down at the table and leave as soon as the speaker of the evening, Mr. Thorpe,[202] had finished his address; and that later in the evening we meet somewhere else with the delegates and without the press. It seemed this plan would satisfy everyone, so it was arranged that Eggleston would appear to give me a message just as Thorpe sat down; that I would leave the table with him and not come back. The delegates would then reassemble at Mr. Libby's apartment, and I would come over later.

The dinner worked out as planned. There were about twenty-five people at the table. I sat between Mrs. Libby and Douglas Stewart. When the meal was over, I spoke for about two minutes (at Armstrong's request), and then remained until Thorpe finished. He took long enough —the best part of an hour, I believe—but his talk was interesting, and a good balance for the preponderance of "peace group" delegates. It was

202. Merle Thorpe, editor and publisher of *The Nation's Business.*

amusing to watch the reaction to his talk, for most of the delegates were well to the left of center politically, and Thorpe's address was far to the right. Armstrong presided exceptionally well.

I left with Eggleston as soon as Thorpe finished. We went to the Hay-Adams for half an hour and then to Libby's apartment. All the delegates sat in a semicircle and asked me questions during most of the evening—about Europe and the war. I asked them to keep what I said in confidence and then spoke fairly freely, taking the chance that someone would violate my request. I gave them rather a military lecture, and they all seemed to enjoy it!

Tuesday, October 22

Lunch with Bill Castle and R. D. Stuart, Jr., at the former's home. Stuart says the response to the activities of the America First Committee has been excellent, and that they are having a hard time to keep up with the growth of the organization. He asked me if I could arrange to speak before a student gathering at Yale University in the near future. I replied that I would let him know tomorrow.

Met O. K. Armstrong at the Army & Navy Club later in the afternoon. Then to the Hay-Adams for a conference with Stewart, Eggleston, and Armstrong. Jim Newton was in Washington, and I asked him to come up to the room where we were talking. The four of us had dinner there together.

After dinner Jim and I went to a Trans-Lux newsreel theater to see the film of my last radio address. As I expected, it was not well cut. Even the sequence of my address was reversed. As they threw my picture on the screen, they started with the words "The fact is today that we are divided." A number of people in the theater began to hiss and continued to do so as long as my picture was on. But at the end of the picture a still larger number clapped! If I have support in Washington, there must be still more support in other sections of the country, for there is probably more war hysteria in this city than almost anywhere else. The news pictures and comments were on the average very pro-English. After the theater Jim and I took a taxi to the station and boarded the 2:10 train for New York.

Thursday, October 24

Phoned Kingman Brewster[203] at New Haven and agreed to speak there on October 30.

Left for New York at 2:00. Miss Johnson is leaving today, and I took her back to her apartment on Sixty-third Street. Then downtown to 23 Wall Street for a conference with Mr. [George C.] Henckel about the best method of transferring the royalties from *The Wave of the Future* to the Quakers.

Sunday, October 27

When I got up this morning, I found Skean lying outside the door to the baby's room. He had apparently climbed the stairs during the night to take his old place near the new baby. Skean has been with all of our babies. From the time he was a puppy with Charles, Jr., he seemed to prefer staying nearby them. He would sleep in the baby's room at night and lie under the carriage during the day. No matter how roughly they played with him as they grew up, he never snapped; at most, if they molested him too much, he would walk slowly away. (We bought Skean when he was just old enough to leave his mother. He was a little too large a Scottie to be a show dog, and there were always a few white hairs in among the long black curly ones—although one had to look carefully to find them. But whatever he may have looked like from a fancier's standpoint, he more than made up in loyalty and disposition.)

But Skean is showing the signs of age. He is much too fat and simply will not go on a diet. If we cut down on his food, he picks up crumbs, gets into the garbage pail, begs from everyone at mealtimes, goes to the neighbors, and will even eat mice if he can catch any—and he can still move like lightning after a mouse, old and fat as he is. In the last two or three years Skean has been climbing the stairs less and less, and previous to this morning, I have not seen him upstairs for some months. Almost all of his time recently has been spent in the kitchen and dining room. The smell of the baby, however, seemed to bring out all of his old loyalty and affection, and somehow he managed to get up those stairs again last night. Anne is the fourth baby to whom he has attached himself; old and gray, he still tries to carry on as he did when he crawled in and out of our first baby's playpen in the farmhouse near Princeton.

203. Kingman Brewster, Jr., became president of Yale University in 1963.

Wednesday, October 30

Spent the morning working on my address and going for a half hour's walk in the rain along the bluff road. I left at 3:00 for New Haven, via the Whitestone Bridge. Arrived at Timothy Dwight College at 6:00. Kingman Brewster, Jr. (Yale *News*), and several others were there waiting for me. They all seemed to be fine, clean-cut young fellows of an unusually high type.

We drove to Professor Griswold's[204] home for supper—a pleasant and informal affair, with six in all at the table. (Professor and Mrs. Griswold, Kingman Brewster, Jr., Richard Bissell, Kent Chandler, and myself.) Richard ("Dickie") Bissell is an old friend of Dwight's. I first met him in Mexico City in 1927, when he was visiting with Dwight at the embassy. He is now a professor in economics at Yale, where he has already established an excellent reputation for his ability.

After supper, we all drove to Woolsey Hall together. Every seat was taken, and people were standing along the walls. (The seating capacity is about 3,000, I was told.) We met with an enthusiastic reception and with even more enthusiasm after the speaking was completed. Brewster opened the meeting with a good and tactfully short address—four or five minutes at most. He outlined the general purpose of the meeting and explained the principles of the America First Committee, under whose auspices it was called. Bissell then spoke for about five minutes, introducing me and explaining a little more about the purpose of the meeting—that it was part of a movement in opposition to the attempt to involve this country in the war. I spoke for about thirty minutes (being the main speaker of the evening). It was the longest address I have yet made. I expected considerable opposition and probably some heckling from the audience, but none took place. They listened attentively during the entire half hour, and it seemed everyone in the hall was clapping after I finished! Although it was not large, it was by far the most successful and satisfying meeting of this kind in which I have ever taken part.

We returned to the Griswolds' home after it was over. Then, after another hour spent talking and visiting, I started the trip back to Lloyd Neck—arriving about 1:15.

204. A. Whitney Griswold, assistant professor of government and international relations, Yale University; he became president of Yale in 1950.

Saturday, November 2

I am very much worried about Skean. He is limping badly, and a large lump is developing on the side of his neck just above his right shoulder. The veterinary I want to take him to is away and will not be back until Monday.

Sunday, November 3

Took the day off and spent most of it trying to paint a portrait of Anne I started a year ago.

Jim Newton, John Roots, Aubrey, Constance, Elizabeth Baird Murray,[205] and John Wheeler-Bennett[206] came for dinner. I asked Jim to come out when I spoke to him on the phone this morning. He told me that Roots was arriving on the afternoon plane from California, so I asked them both. Then, in midafternoon, Aubrey phoned and said he and Wheeler-Bennett wanted to talk to me about a conference that is to be held in December on Pacific relations. He said there was to be one group of men from England, another from Canada, another from Australia, a fourth from New Zealand, and that they wanted me to be present in the group from the United States! I asked them to come out for dinner, and to bring Con and Elizabeth Murray, who were with them at the time.

After dinner Aubrey, Wheeler-Bennett, and I went off to a separate room for half an hour's discussion. I told them I felt the action that could be taken in the Orient depended almost entirely on the outcome of the war in Europe, that successful action in the Orient necessitated an understanding between the United States and Europe. I told them frankly that I did not see how England could win the war in Europe unless Germany collapsed internally. They agreed that there is no indication of a German internal collapse at this time. They also agreed that an invasion of the European continent by England was out of the question under anything approaching present conditions.

It is obvious that Englishmen are gradually beginning to understand the seriousness of their country's position. (If only enough of them real-

205. Friend of Aubrey and Constance Morgan, who came from England with three children to live at Next Day Hill for the duration of the war.

206. Historian, scholar, and author of *The Wooden Titan, Munich, Nemesis of Power*, Sir John Wheeler-Bennett was an old family friend. He later wrote the authorized biography of King George VI. He was a member of the British Information Services, New York, 1939–41.

ize it in time to accept peace terms before the empire is completely broken and England completely prostrated.) But even if the war ended tomorrow, it seems to me England faces the most difficult problems of modern times. What is she to do with her 50 million population based on a system of industry and empire that is past?

We discussed all of these matters frankly. I told Wheeler-Bennett I did not know what I could contribute to the proposed meeting on Pacific affairs, but that if I was in the East at the time, I would be glad to attend if they wished me to. (It is to be private and without publicity—if that is possible.)

Roots says the Communists in California are working for Willkie on the theory that his election will bring on a social revolution! Whether or not that is true, we all look for difficult times ahead. Personally, I am inclined to believe that bad times would come more quickly under Roosevelt than under Willkie.

Tuesday, November 5

Anne and I left for Englewood at 11:30 and arrived at Next Day Hill at 1:00. We drove past the polling place, but it was crowded, so we decided to have lunch before voting.[207] Mrs. Morrow, Anne, and I were the only ones at the lunch table. We discussed the election and Willkie's chances. It seems to me he has at best an even chance to win, but there is no way for one to judge accurately. The Democrats I know are very worried. The Republicans, on the other hand, are overconfident, and some even think Willkie will win by a large majority. At the time Willkie made his acceptance speech I had the feeling that he had lost the election, but he has certainly been gaining rapidly in popularity during the last several weeks. I do not believe he is a great leader, and I doubt that he has much understanding of the problems in Europe, but regardless of these failings, I think he would be far preferable to Roosevelt. I hope Willkie wins, and it now seems he at least has a chance.

I drove to the poll as soon as lunch was over. The line was not long, and I only had to wait about ten minutes before entering the booth. I voted the straight Republican ticket except for governor, when I turned the lever opposite Edison's[208] name. Anne and I decided to vote for him.

207. It was Election Day, 1940.

208. Charles Edison, son of the inventor, Thomas A., was Secretary of the Navy, 1939–40, and running for governor of New Jersey. He won the election and held that position from 1941 to 1944.

We have not seen Edison for some years, but he impressed us as being an honest and able man. Also, I have so little confidence in either party that I do not like to vote a completely straight ticket, and I have not yet done so in any election. I wish that someday I could vote for a President in whose leadership I had real confidence.

We left for Lloyd Neck at 4:00. The traffic was fairly heavy, and we arrived home just in time for me to turn around and start back for New York City and a dinner engagement with Carrel, Jim Newton, and Boris Bakhmeteff, at the latter's apartment. After dinner we discussed the campaign, the war, and the future of America and Europe.

Our meeting broke up about 11:00, and I started back to Lloyd Neck. The early election returns were coming in over the radio. They showed a decided margin in favor of Roosevelt and the third term. (Carrel felt Roosevelt would win. Bakhmeteff thought Willkie had a little better than an even chance. Jim and I felt that Willkie had at best an even chance.) I listened to the returns all during the drive home. Shortly after midnight Flynn[209] (speaking from Democratic headquarters) made what seemed a somewhat premature speech, claiming victory for his party. But only a few minutes later the New York *Times* (which had been supporting Willkie) conceded the election to Roosevelt. And so it looks as though we will have Roosevelt for a third term as President.

Wednesday, November 6

I sent Skean to the veterinary today to see if an operation would be of any help to him. He is limping on his right forefoot, and I thought it might be caused by the lump on his neck. The veterinary's report is bad —as bad as it could be. Skean has a malignant disease, and nothing can be done to help him. All we can do is to let him be happy as long as he can. I gave orders that his food be limited only enough to keep him from being ill through overeating.

Monday, November 11

Armistice Day, and strangely enough still observed as a holiday. Many business establishments are closed and there is no school; but there will

209. Edward J. Flynn, chairman of the National Democratic Committee and Roosevelt's campaign manager in 1940.

be very little celebrating this year. I drove to New York for supper with Bakhmeteff, Carrel, and Jim Newton at Bakhmeteff's apartment.

Ambassador Kennedy has given a long and rather unusual press interview, in which he takes the stand that it is essential for us to keep out of the war. I think he must be planning on resigning his post, for I do not see how he can go back to England after this.

Thursday, November 14

Press reports heavy damage inflicted on Italian Navy by British bombers and torpedo planes. A release from London claims that three battleships were hit and a number of smaller vessels sunk.

Drove to New York in the afternoon for a 6:30 dinner at the University Club with Hart, Stewart, Eggleston, Payson (co-owner with Stewart of *Scribner's Commentator*), Sherman (editor of Hartford *Courant*), Cless, and Verne Marshall (editor Cedar Rapids, Iowa *Gazette*).[210] We devoted most of the evening to discussing the war, American politics, and plans for building opposition to intervention propaganda. There was a good deal of speechmaking, but not very much was accomplished. Hart wanted to form another committee to continue the discussion—"a board of strategy," he called it—but thank God we avoided that; we have had more than enough of committees already. We need leaders, not committees. We need someone with executive ability to create and run an eastern antiwar organization, and we need enough financial support for a nationwide operation.

I think Hart feels that I should take over the direction of both organizing and finding funds, but that would mean giving up the type of work I am now doing, which I feel is more important—and certainly more tangible at this time. I feel someone else should come in and help carry the load. What I need is more assistance, not more obligations.

Drove back to Lloyd Manor for the night.

210. Charles S. Payson, publisher and managing editor of *Scribner's Commentator;* Clifton L. Sherman had been managing editor of the Hartford *Courant* from 1904 to 1919, when he joined the Hartford *Times;* George H. Cless, Jr., author and lecturer; Verne Marshall had been editor of the *Gazette* since 1914.

Friday, November 15

Spent the morning until 11:15 on routine. Then drove to New York for a 1:00 lunch appointment with Roy Howard and his son at the Waldorf-Astoria. I wanted to talk to Howard about the possibility of my making a trip to Europe and writing several articles for Scripps-Howard and the UP. I am anxious to see at first hand what is happening in Europe, and one must have an obvious cause to go there these days. I can think of nothing that would give me more freedom of action than a connection with one of the large American news associations. I chose Howard and the UP because I know him well, and he is taking a decided stand with his papers against American intervention. I would plan on doing a few general articles but would, of course, make no attempt at "spot news" reporting. Howard was decidedly interested in the plan I outlined. Our discussion was on a very tentative basis, and I told him that before I decided definitely to take the trip I would want to study all details and complications with great care, including the relationship I would have with his organization.

The press reports that the Germans have raided Coventry and practically demolished the city. It is said to be the worst raid of the war.

Sunday, November 17

Skean refused to eat today—the first time in his life. He does not seem to be in pain, but I am afraid he will not live much longer. I carried him into the parlor with us in the evening and placed him on a rug in front of the fireplace. At night, when we went to bed, we left him in his favorite place beside the kitchen stove.

Monday, November 18

Southampton reported heavily raided.

Skean is weaker this morning, still refuses to eat, and walks with difficulty. Thor and I went out after breakfast and spent half an hour in the strong and cold northwest wind. We walked over to the bluff. The bay was covered with whitecaps and the foam streaks of wind. One could tell from the water alone that winter was at hand.

I carried Skean in on his quilt, and put him in front of the open fire. At one time he got up and staggered closer to the table where I was writing. I held his head in my hands for a long time.

Drove to New York for dinner with Stewart, Eggleston, Payson, and Armstrong at Stewart's apartment. We discussed the war trends and Armstrong's plan for an antiwar organization. I believe this meeting may lead to something definite. Returned to Lloyd Neck for the night.

When I entered the kitchen, I found Skean lying stretched out on the floor. He did not even lift his head when I came in, and his breathing was shallow and rapid. I lifted him onto his quilt at his favorite place next to the stove and gave him some water. He still knows me. I can tell that by the way he moves his eye and lifts his ear when I touch or speak to him; but he is almost past interest in, or communication with, this world. I am afraid he will not live until morning.

Tuesday, November 19

Greeks claim more successes, including capture of Korytsa. British suggest that we give them one hundred more destroyers and armed convoys!

Skean is dead. I went down to the kitchen early and found him on his quilt by the stove in the same position I had left him last night. I dug a grave and buried him in the northwest corner of the walled garden. It took an hour of hard work, but I felt much better doing it myself. It seemed an obligation that I, personally, must fulfill, and in which I could not let anyone else take part.

Skean has helped to raise all of our children. We bought him from a breeder in New Jersey in 1931, a small, black, curly puppy. He grew through puppyhood with Charles, Jr., running in and out through the bars of the playpen. After that he always stayed with our children, leaving them only for food or when we called him for a walk. His usual place was in the nursery at night and under the baby carriage during the day. He has always played with, but has never bitten one of the children—no matter how roughly they treated him. His temper he reserved entirely for Thor and for any strange dogs that came in the vicinity of his home. There has never been any question about which dog ran the house. It was always Skean. Although only a small fraction of Thor's size, Skean never feared him in the least and never hesitated to bite if Thor annoyed him. Thor liked Skean from the first and always gave in rather than bite him.

Skean brightened up the whole household with his scamper and his grin. (I taught him to grin when he was a puppy—whenever I clapped my hands after making him sit up.) His weakness was food, and as he grew older he became excessively fat. But up to the last few days before his death, he could move like a streak of lightning in the presence of a mouse or rat. Everyone in the house will miss him. No better Scottie ever lived.

Wednesday, November 20

Press reports Birmingham heavily bombed. Congress votes against adjournment.

The third anniversary of this diary!

First part of morning on routine. Then left for Hopewell and High Fields in the Mercury at 11:00. Arrived at High Fields at 2:40. It has changed very little during these last nine years. The house needs a new coat of paint, and the small trees surrounding it have grown appreciably; otherwise it is the same. The day was warm and beautiful. A representative of the Mathews Construction Company was waiting for me, and Mr. Lyons, the caretaker, met me at the door. We went over the house carefully and discussed what work should be done before it is turned over to the State of New Jersey next month (for child-welfare projects). We offered the property to the state some months ago, and Governor Moore[211] accepted. It now remains only for his acceptance to be ratified by the Legislature. It has already been ratified by the Senate. We decided to paint all the outside, make a few minor repairs in the masonry, and paint the woodwork on the stairs and in the nursery (to remove some of the marks left by the police in 1932).

Left at 3:30 and drove to Weber's dog-training home near Princeton. (We bought Thor from Weber in 1932.) He was away, so after talking to his daughter for a few minutes, I started the drive back to Long Island. I wanted to talk to Weber about getting another dog.

211. Arthur Harry Moore, Governor of New Jersey three times (1926–28, 1932–1935, 1938–41), and elected U.S. Senator in 1935.

Sunday, November 24

Rumania joins Axis. Negotiations with Turkey continue.

Spent most of the morning working on an inventory I want to place in our safe-deposit box. I want to leave this, together with a letter of instructions, for Anne, in case I should meet with an accident. One should prepare for every contingency in times such as these.

The Wave of the Future is now top best seller. It is reported by fifty book stores in the *Tribune* book-review section.

The Sikorskys came for tea and supper. He brought some flowers for Anne, and she gave us a cherry pie she had baked for the children. "Something beautiful, and something sweet." Mrs. Sikorsky said it was the Russian custom to make such a gift to one's friends on the first visit after the birth of a child.

Wednesday, November 27

Bristol raided again. Stories that filter through British censorship indicate that conditions in England are becoming increasingly serious, due to air raids and shipping losses. War agitation here is rising. Repeal of Johnson Act is demanded. Assassinations reported in Rumania. British increase pressure on United States for aid—admit desperate situation.

Spent the evening writing. I am trying to write an account of the organization and flights of the *Spirit of St. Louis*. I started this work in Paris more than a year ago, but have been able to devote very little time to it since then.

Friday, November 29

Papers report naval battle off Sardinia. British and Italian claims conflict. Germans bomb London and Liverpool.

Roy Howard called—says I can have UP and Scripps-Howard backing for trip abroad if I decide to go. Says he has just talked to Ambassador Kennedy and that conditions in England are desperate. Howard suggested that I telephone Kennedy direct. (He is staying in the Waldorf Tower.) I saw Kennedy frequently in Europe and worked very closely with him at the time of the Munich crisis. But I have not communicated with him since I returned to the United States, as I thought the antiwar stand I have taken might make contact between us embarrassing for him —at least as long as he was Ambassador to England. I mentioned this situation to Howard, who said he would phone Kennedy and discreetly ask his feeling in the matter. Howard called me again a few minutes later and said Kennedy wanted to see me, and requested that I phone so we could arrange for a meeting. Phoned Kennedy and made a 3:30 appointment. He invited Anne to come, too.

We arrived at the Waldorf at 3:30. Kennedy kept us there talking until nearly 5:00, telling us about conditions in England and on the Continent. He feels, as we do, that the British position is hopeless and that the best possible thing for them would be a negotiated peace in the near future. He said the damage done by bombs was far greater than had been admitted and that the British could not continue for long to stand the present rate of shipping loss. He said that war would stop if it were not for Churchill and the hope in England that America will come in. Kennedy said that weeks before the Germans invaded Norway, Churchill had inquired of Roosevelt, through him (Kennedy), whether the United States would stand for a *British* invasion of Norway.

Kennedy said that at the time he left practically every major port in England had been either closed or seriously damaged, except Bristol, Liverpool, and Glasgow. (Bristol and Liverpool have both been heavily bombed since he departed.) He estimated that England had about two months' food supply if all shipping were cut off.

He said the reports of the Polish Ambassador, which were captured and published by the Germans some months ago, were almost entirely correct as far as the parts which concerned him were concerned. He laughed, and said he didn't know about what Bill Bullitt said (but I gathered he felt that was pretty accurate, too). Kennedy said the Polish Ambassador had made "one or two" understandable errors in his report. For instance, Kennedy had told him that he was sending his son back to lectures (in the United States). The Polish Ambassador thought, and put in his report, that the American Ambassador was sending his son back to lecture in the United States.

Kennedy said Roosevelt carried on most of his negotiations with the British Ambassador (Lothian) in Washington and very few through the

American Embassy in London. Kennedy says he intends to fight to the limit American entry into the war, that he thinks our entry would be unsuccessful and do nothing but damage in the end.

Saturday, November 30

Civil war in Rumania continues.

Wrote for a time after breakfast; then Anne and I drove to New York for lunch with ex-President Hoover in his suite at the Waldorf-Astoria. During lunch we discussed the war, the question of food relief for Europe, and the attitude toward both here in America.

After leaving Hoover, I went to Douglas Stewart's apartment for a conference with Stewart, Eggleston, and Armstrong. Among other items, we discussed the No Foreign War Campaign and the possibility of getting Hanford MacNider[212] to head it. We also discussed plans for a rally in St. Louis next month. Armstrong will stop in St. Louis to make arrangements. I told him to get in contact with Tom Dysart (president, St. Louis Chamber of Commerce) and Dr. Lambert (police commissioner). Armstrong agreed to communicate with me before making any promises about my speaking at the rally. Armstrong is a little impetuous at times, so I tried to impress him with the necessity of telephoning me before making any promises concerning my personal action. I am not sure he realizes the complications that could arise in St. Louis if the situation is not carefully handled.

Sunday, December 1

Greek advance continues in Albania. Revolt reported in Bessarabia. Southampton bombed. More United States loans for China.

Drove to New York for a 10:00 meeting with MacNider, Stewart, and Eggleston at the Hotel Astor. We talked to MacNider about the possibility of his taking the chairmanship of the No Foreign War Campaign. He was not at all enthusiastic about the chairmanship, although very definitely with us in our stand against war. MacNider said he had promised General Wood to help him with the America First Committee in Chicago and that he could not consider the chairmanship of the No

212. Iowa manufacturer and former national commander of the American Legion.

Foreign War Campaign unless, among other reservations, General Wood released him from his promise.

We left after about an hour, and MacNider said he would think the matter over and talk to us again at a later date. Lunch at the Engineers Club with Stewart, Eggleston, and Armstrong. Then drove back to Lloyd Neck.

Brandeweide (St. Louis) and Mr. and Mrs. Ralph Damon[213] came for supper. (Damon is an ardent interventionist.) I again suggested to Brande that he write a book about the old barnstorming days in Missouri. If he could write about his experiences as well as he describes them in conversation, the book should be extremely interesting, and it would cover a period in aviation of which there is now a very inadequate record.

Saturday, December 7

Left the house at 7:30 and drove to New York. Stopped at Aubrey's apartment long enough to pick up him and Wheeler-Bennett, and then went on to Princeton, arriving at the Princeton Inn just before 11:00. Wheeler-Bennett had invited (in fact requested) me to attend the conference on Pacific relations, which is now being held in Princeton. There are representatives from England, Canada, Australia, New Zealand, and the United States. I felt I would be rather out of place among these groups but decided that the conference would be of sufficient interest to compensate for any embarrassment and effort involved.

The morning meeting opened shortly after we arrived. The discussion centered around the relationship of the United States and Great Britain in the Pacific—where there could be joint action and what the attitude of each would be in the event of various military and economic developments. During many of the conversations it was taken for granted that the most desirable course of action for this country was that which would be of greatest aid to England, whether or not it involved us in war! In other words, the prime concern of the conference seemed to be the future welfare of England rather than of the United States!

One of the discussions involved the question of whether we (the

213. Ralph Damon, aviation executive. In 1933 he developed the Curtiss-Wright Condor commercial transport. Vice president of American Airlines, he later was president, 1945–49. In 1949 he became president and director of Trans World Airlines.

United States) would aid Great Britain more by going to war with Japan or by avoiding a war in the Pacific. Upon this there was considerable division of opinion. One group took the stand that if we entered a war with Japan, we would decrease our aid to Britain in order to equip our own military forces more quickly, that our fleet would be occupied in the Pacific for an indefinite period, and that the result would, on the whole, be disadvantageous to Great Britain. (What would be most advantageous to America was not discussed. The attitude was that whatever was best for Britain was also best for America!) The other group took the stand that our people are not yet sufficiently interested in the war and that we will not exert our maximum national effort until we get into it ourselves. They therefore concluded that by declaring war on Japan we would increase our national effort and productivity so rapidly we would be able to *increase* our aid to Britain, in addition to waging war ourselves. As to our fleet, this group took the stand that a large part of it would have to stay in the Pacific anyway, and that it might as well be fighting the Japs.

At one time a discussion took place in regard to what steps "short of war" would involve this country in war most quickly. It was generally agreed that the American people would not at this time support an actual declaration of war. But it was also agreed that the people *would at this time* support steps "short of war" that would inevitably lead to war eventually.

I took no part in these discussions, for there was no suitable opportunity. Later, I took part in a discussion about Greenland and answered a few questions about aviation fuel and the effect of high-octane gasoline. I felt constantly out of place, although everyone there was courteous and friendly. I kept wanting to remind them that we were in *America* and *not* in England—that our *primary* concern was the future of *America,* and not that of the British Empire. I decided that two sessions were enough so left the Princeton Inn at 5:00 en route home. Arrived at Lloyd Manor about 8:45.

Sunday, December 8

$3 billion asked by Navy for "air defenses"!

Stuart phoned and said he would have $50,000 in the bank tomorrow with which to start the No Foreign War Campaign. Armstrong came for lunch. We discussed plans for the campaign. Mr. [W. H.] Auden (English poet) came for the afternoon and evening.

Monday, December 9

London heavily bombed. German merchantman sunk off Cuba. Greek advance continues.

Mr. and Mrs. Weber came for lunch. Weber is one of the best dog trainers in the United States. Weber told me Thor was one of the best dogs he had ever seen, provided he was properly handled. I liked Thor the first time I saw him and purchased him for $250.00. We were living in our house near Hopewell, New Jersey, at the time. It was necessary for Weber to go in the car with me when I took Thor home, for Thor was attached to him and would not go with me alone.

When we arrived at our house, we put Thor in the garage, and then Weber left to return to his kennels. I had planned on feeding Thor in the garage for several days, until we became better acquainted with each other. But Weber's car had no sooner passed out of sight than Thor appeared, racing around the side of the house, looking for him! It had taken the dog less than ten minutes to learn how to open the garage door—by lifting the latch with his nose. We had a very difficult time getting him back in the house. I do not recall exactly how we did it, but it seems to me we had to telephone for Weber to come back.

Then began the effort to make friends with Thor. He had a tendency to bare his teeth and growl when anyone approached him. But within a day or two he adopted Anne—entirely through his own initiative, for I was with him possibly more than she. From that time to this—over eight years now—he never left her side when she was at home, except for short inspection trips through the house and around the grounds, and he is never happy when she is away. I always have been Thor's second love. When Anne is away, he stays with me, and he is completely satisfied only when we are both together.

Thor was about half trained when we bought him, and I instructed him in most of the rest of what he now knows. I taught him to open and close doors on command (it had been only by his own desire previously), to pick Anne up by the wrist and lead her to the kitchen to get him some milk, to take Skean out walking on a leash, to take messages to Anne for me and vice versa, to find the baby, wherever it was, and guard it, to pick up his own tail and bring it to me (at which he was always rather disgusted—moving around in circles as he came), to bring newspapers, magazines, etc., and many other things. He had already been trained for protection by Weber, and in addition would jump over objects several feet high, go back over a trail and find a dropped object, retrieve practically anything, sit up, lie down, salute with one paw, say "hello" in two syllables, stay in any position you told him to, etc., etc. I finally trained him to take all of his commands in a whisper. And when Anne went swimming, Thor would always go with her, hoping she would hold on to his tail while he pulled her back to shore. Thor's character and intelligence is as close to human as a dog's can be—more so than I realized was possible before he came with us.

Weber had not seen Thor for nearly eight years and was very pleased at his condition and retention of training. Thor showed off beautifully. I was proud of him. But Thor is getting old now, and slightly deaf. I talked to Weber about getting another dog to replace Skean (not that you ever can replace a dog you have loved) and to help Thor in guarding the house. Weber said we were spoiled and that it would be practically impossible to get another dog like Thor. He said it was difficult to even get a good puppy here in America, that almost all puppies were raised in kennels and that that spoiled a dog. He said he used to get all of his German shepherd puppies from Europe, where they were raised in the house with the family. He suggested that we wait until the war was over before getting another dog!

Tuesday, December 10

British advance in Egypt; claim 1,000 prisoners.

Drove to New York in the afternoon for a 3:30 appointment with Mr. Harcourt to discuss *The Wave of the Future*. It is selling well—over 50,000 sold to date, and 67,000 printed. The reaction, on the whole, is good. Of course, there is considerable controversy over the book. One book-store owner in Connecticut asked to return the ten copies he had ordered from Harcourt, Brace, but decided not to after Harcourt wrote to him and he had cooled down a bit. (He had written Harcourt that he thought Anne and I both should be put behind barbed wires!) *The Wave of the Future* is still top best seller on the *Herald Tribune* list (national survey of book-store sales).

From the Engineers Club to the New Weston Hotel for dinner with Carrel, Bakhmeteff, Newton, and Harris[214] in a private room. We discussed general conditions in this country and abroad. Carrel has had a letter from Mme. Carrel—sent through a friend and mailed in unoccupied France. She says she has enough food but gave almost no other details about conditions in Brittany. (She is at Saint-Gildas.)

After leaving the New Weston, I stopped at the Biltmore for a half hour's conference with George Eggleston and his uncle, Mr. Chamberlin. We discussed the question of a chairman for the No Foreign War Campaign. The only choice seems to be between MacNider and [Verne] Marshall. Most people concerned would prefer MacNider, but it seems doubtful that he would accept the position. He has a business to run in Iowa. Also, I do not believe he is at all enthusiastic about taking the chairmanship.

Marshall has apparently said that if MacNider will not be chairman, he will. As far as I can find out, Marshall is the man who has obtained the financial support for the organization. Since Marshall has been the most active man, he might make the best chairman.

Thursday, December 12

British take Sidi Barrâni. British convoy problem becomes increasingly serious.

Drove to New York for a 3:00 appointment with General Robert Wood (America First) at the Waldorf-Astoria. We discussed the war and methods of organizing against our involvement. Wood is an exceptionally fine and able type of man and anxious to co-operate in every way. Everyone likes him. After I had been talking to Wood for about fifteen minutes, Bob Stuart and Hanford MacNider came in. A few minutes later John T. Flynn,[215] Bruce Barton,[216] Charles Payson, and Verne Marshall arrived. The gist of the discussion was whether there should be a single

214. Hayden B. Harris, Chicago businessman.

215. Author, journalist, columnist for *The New Republic,* and lecturer in economics at New York's New School for Social Research. Flynn was the leader of the liberal wing of America First.

216. Former New York Republican Representative, 1937–39, author of the best-selling *The Man Nobody Knows* (1925) and other books, and president of Batten, Barton, Durstine & Osborne, advertising agency.

national antiwar organization under America First or two separate organizations, one (America First) in Chicago, and the other (the No Foreign War Campaign) in New York. The tendency at present seems to be to combine under America First. Marshall asked MacNider to take the national chairmanship, but MacNider seemed reluctant and said he could not give a definite answer before returning to Iowa. (General Wood says his work with Sears, Roebuck and Company prevents him from devoting sufficient time to America First. He is willing to continue in a less active position, however.)

After the meeting I went to the Biltmore Hotel for supper with MacNider and Stuart. MacNider told me in confidence that he will probably be involved most of the summer in a personal lawsuit in Iowa and would be unable to devote sufficient time to an antiwar organization to justify his taking the chairmanship. MacNider and Stuart left immediately after supper to catch the Eastern Airlines plane for Florida, where they are to see Ambassador Kennedy.

Phone call from Marshall at midnight. He had talked to MacNider at the airport and told him we could not "wait a week" for his decision. Marshall said MacNider had given him authority to do whatever he thought best in the selection of a chairman. "What do you think we should do?" I had been expecting this, as it seemed obvious to me during the afternoon's conference that Marshall wanted the chairmanship himself, even though he asked MacNider to take it. So I had discussed the matter with Jerry Milbank on the phone. I told Milbank of my concern about Marshall's nervous condition, but Milbank said he was a nervous type, and that he had demonstrated his ability in running the Cedar Rapids *Gazette*. Milbank felt he would make an excellent chairman and cited his drive and enthusiasm and initiative. Anyway, there seemed no alternative, and in many ways Marshall has an ideal background for chairman—good war record, editor of a Middle Western newspaper, etc. He is an excellent counterpart for William Allen White.[217]

I suggested to Marshall that we decide definitely on two organizations —one eastern and one Middle Western—and that he take the chairmanship of the eastern organization. "That's just what I hoped you'd say," he replied! I like Marshall personally, but there is something about his attitude on life that disturbs me. Still, I think he will be an active and

217. Newspaperman and author, White had been proprietor and editor of the Emporia (Kansas) daily and weekly *Gazette* since 1895. He was national chairman of the Committee to Defend America by Aiding the Allies.

aggressive chairman, and we need activity greatly. The people who stand against our involvement in the war are badly organized at this time, and I believe we are rapidly approaching a crisis.

Friday, December 13

The press reports that the British have captured 20,000 prisoners in Egypt.

Lord Lothian died yesterday at the British Embassy in Washington. He was a great Englishman, and I think his death is a decided loss to America as well as to England. When a great man dies, even his enemies are in a sense poorer. When peace comes, as come it must eventually, and regardless of how the fortunes of this war turn, Lothian would have been a constructive influence. The last time I saw him was in London, when he and I went to the theater together one evening. I have not seen him over here, for I felt that, in view of the stand I have taken, a call from me would be embarrassing to him in his capacity as Ambassador from Great Britain.

Drove to New York for a 12:30 appointment with Stewart, Eggleston, Armstrong, and Marshall. We had lunch in Marshall's room while we discussed plans for organizing the No Foreign War Campaign. After lunch Eggleston and I went to the Biltmore for a conference with his uncle, Mr. Chamberlin, about Marshall and the organization. Mr. Chamberlin is a retired lawyer from Iowa and a very old friend of Marshall's. He is leaving for California today, but will be back in January and says he will help with the organization. I talked to him again about Marshall, and he told me he thought Marshall would handle the chairmanship well —has great confidence in him.

Marshall called while I was with Chamberlin, and asked me to come to the Waldorf for a meeting with General Wood. When I arrived at General Wood's apartment, there were present, in addition to the general, Verne Marshall and the Richardson brothers (Vick Chemical).[218] The Richardsons are firmly opposed to our entry into the war and are anxious to help us in every way possible—both with men and finance. They are, I believe, unusually able men, with the type of sincerity and determination that is of inestimable value to the success of any enter-

218. H. Smith Richardson, chairman of the executive committee of Vick Chemical Co., and Lundsford Richardson, chairman of the board of Vick Chemical Co.

prise. Meeting them made me feel that we are at last getting the right kind of men on our side of the war issue. Up to the present time there has been too large a percentage of cranks and people with strange ideas.

Returned to Engineers Club for supper. I had invited C. B. Allen, Wesley Stout, and Martin Sommers (latter two from *Saturday Evening Post*). We had dinner in a private room so we could talk freely and discuss the war and conditions in America and Europe. I told Stout I thought his editorials excellent. He replied that the *Saturday Evening Post* intended to continue its stand against America's participation in the war, but that it looked "like a losing fight."

I do not agree with this. I believe conditions are very serious and that we have been traveling rapidly along the road to war, but I think there is still a good fighting chance to keep out—if enough of us are willing to fight and say what we believe, regardless of consequences. Also, I think it quite possible that the war will be over in Europe before this country can really get into it.

During our conversations about Europe and the war, Stout told me the *Saturday Evening Post* representative in Europe had flown over a large portion of Germany and had seen very little damage from bombing. In the past I have estimated that the Germans are inflicting from three to ten times the amount of damage on the English by bombing that the English are inflicting on the Germans. Stout says that from his representative's report he thinks the ratio may be more than ten to one against England.

Returned to Lloyd Neck after the dinner, arriving just in time to help Anne with the baby.

Sunday, December 15

Laval dropped from French government. Flandin named to succeed him.

George Eggleston phoned—very discouraged. Marshall has been temperamental and irritable. Eggleston was up with him and doing things for him most of the night. I phoned Marshall and left for New York immediately. Believe I got matters straightened out after talking to Marshall for half an hour, but I am not sure how long the calm will last. He is quick to form impressions and has a violent temper. He needs a rest badly.

Conference with Marshall, Armstrong, Stewart, and Eggleston. We discussed plans for the organization—officers, finance, press releases, etc., etc. After the meeting was over Armstrong and I went to the Engineers Club for lunch. We discussed names for a sponsoring committee, etc. After lunch we all met again in Marshall's room in the Waldorf. The problem arose as to what position O. K. Armstrong should hold. He is merging his peace and religious organizations with Marshall's committee, and the committee is taking over the name of "No Foreign War" from Armstrong's groups. Instead of being the "No Foreign War Campaign," directed by Armstrong, in the future it will be the "No Foreign War Committee," directed by Marshall. I suggested that Armstrong be appointed "director" in the new committee, in charge of field organization primarily. Everyone agreed to this. We discussed opening an office in New York and another in Washington. Plans were laid, tentatively, for radio programs, advertisements, rallies, etc., etc. The question arose as to my connection with the committee. I told them I felt I could be of most value and assistance by working independently. They agreed to this.

Monday, December 16

British forces have entered Libya.

To the Waldorf-Astoria for a meeting with Marshall at 3:00. He is working on a press release for tomorrow. Soon after I arrived Stewart, Eggleston, Armstrong, and Flynn came in. Several changes in the release were suggested, and Flynn did considerable editing at Marshall's request. After reading the release I realize that Marshall is anything but cautious in what he says. Still, he is hard hitting, and we need some hard hitting at the moment.

Later in the afternoon Armstrong and I went to see Libby, who is in New York for a day or two. I like him more as I know him better—much as I disagree with his ideas on pacifism. We met in the hotel manager's room at the Woodstock. Libby said it was obvious that his peace organizations could not work under Marshall's direction and suggested a plan of co-operation, which he called "parallel action." Armstrong and I both agreed to the wisdom of this. (At least, Armstrong gave the impression that he agreed.)

While I was at the Woodstock Marshall called, and I went back to the Waldorf to see him. Eggleston and I went over the final draft of the release he is giving out tonight for tomorrow's papers. It is not what I would write; but after all, Marshall is chairman and has the right to word his own release. It is not bad; but I think it could be better, and I don't quite like the tone.

Tuesday, December 17

Pressure starting here for more aid to England.

Eggleston called and told me that Armstrong was very much disturbed by the way Marshall has been handling press relationships. (I am too.) Marshall apparently went to see a number of newspaper editors at 3:00 this morning! I am afraid Marshall intends to run a one-man show. Armstrong arrived at 1:42, and we continued the discussion for a time. Then I took a taxi to the new No Foreign War Committee's headquarters at the Lexington Hotel.

The friction between Marshall and Armstrong is increasing, and it is having a very bad effect on morale. The causes seem trivial to me, but the effect is extremely important. I talked to Marshall alone in his office, trying to find some way to straighten out this latest difficulty. The conversation was enlightening and disturbing.

Wednesday, December 18

The press notices about the No Foreign War Committee are good. The *Herald Tribune* surprised me by giving it front page.

Drove to New York in the afternoon for a conference with Marshall. The No Foreign War offices at the Lexington Hotel were full of people. I stopped to talk to several of them as I went through.

The Quakers have asked Anne to make a radio broadcast on Christmas Eve on the need for sending food relief from this country to Europe.

Friday, December 20

German troops are reported flying to Italy. Churchill warns again of possible invasion. War hysteria in America is increasing.

Drove to New York and arrived at the Lexington Hotel at 4:45. The organization workers have had very little sleep and show signs of great tension. One girl—Marshall's secretary—has averaged three hours' sleep per night for the last three nights, and unnecessarily.

Marshall has written an advertisement today and plans on running it, full page, in newspapers all over the country. He apparently has $100,-000 to spend (I thought he was going to use it to run the No Foreign War campaign for the next several months), and he says he is "going to shoot the works" on this ad. When the final check was made, it was found that the cost of the ad would be only $34,000.

Monday, December 23

Wide R.A.F. raids reported over the Continent—"from Norway to Italy."

Roy Howard called in the afternoon. Said William Allen White had just telegraphed a statement to him, which he had printed in full in the *Telegram*. He read it to me over the phone. I was amazed as I listened. White says, among other things, that we should stay out of this war, that we should not carry contraband into the war zones, that we should not repeal the Johnson Act,[219] or use our Navy to convoy. He says that if he were making a motto for the use of his committee (the Committee to Defend America by Aiding the Allies), it would be "The Yanks Are Not Coming." Howard asked me if I would consider making a statement about White's statement. I told him I hadn't made a press statement for years, but that I would certainly consider breaking my precedent in this case and I would call him back within an hour or two.

I sent to Huntington for a copy of the *Telegram* and read White's statement carefully. Why did he give it? Has there been a division in his committee? Does he feel some of its members are advocating too many steps that may not be "short of war"? Is it the effect of his Middle Western environment? I am inclined to believe he is sincere in what he says and that he has become alarmed by the belligerent attitude of some of his eastern committee members. In any case, it seems to me advisable to accept his statement at its face value and to welcome him to the camp of the "isolationists."

I called Howard and told him I would write a statement and telephone it to him in time for tomorrow's edition of the *World-Telegram*. The antiwar sentiment seems to be gaining, at least momentarily, in this country. Telephoned my statement to Howard's office after supper.

219. Passed in 1934, the Johnson Act prohibited loans to countries that had defaulted in their payments to the U.S. on war loans.

Tuesday, December 24

British advance continues in Libya. Greeks advance in Albania. Germans bomb Manchester.

Spent most of the morning helping Anne with her manuscript—reading, marking for timing, etc. Drove Anne to New York in time for tea with the Vaillants.[220] Sent her manuscript to the NBC studios by a postal telegraph messenger. Anne and Sue Vaillant left for the studios early, by taxi. Phoned Mother in Detroit and told her time of Anne's broadcast. (This is the first time Anne has spoken over the radio since 1931, when she gave an address on flood relief in China.) Anne spoke beautifully. Her voice was vibrant with feeling, and the whole talk was perfectly delivered. She is an exceptional radio speaker. I believe her address will have great effect on most people who heard it.

Wednesday, December 25

German troops are reported entering Rumania.

Anne's address has been played down in the newspapers. There is very little notice of it in any of them. This is probably partly due to the fact that the Quakers are not experienced in handling such things. It is somewhat due to inadequate advertising on NBC's part.

It is strange, our desire in this instance for newspaper attention. For many years we have tried to avoid the attention of the press. For years we refused to speak over the radio, to give statements or interviews, to take part in political meetings. Now, this morning, we are disappointed because Anne's address last night is not carried in the papers on our breakfast table. How can we justify this attitude, this seeming inconsistency? It is not that we enjoy seeing our names in the paper or having attention drawn to us any more than before. That is as unpleasant as ever, and it adds to our difficulties of life; we cannot go to theaters or restaurants, or walk together on the streets without being stared at, or run after, or annoyed in some other way. As I analyze it, I think our apparent change

---

220. George and Sue Vaillant, old family friends. George Vaillant, author and archaeologist, was assistant curator of Mexican archaeology at the American Museum of Natural History.

in attitude is due to the intensity of our feeling about the causes we support. In the past, the publicity and attention was focused on us, like a brilliant, burning, hardened spotlight. Now, the light is thrown upon an approaching danger—upon war, famine, disease, and revolution. And our attention is focused upon the problems it illuminates. They are so important that the few diverging rays that still fall upon us we hardly notice. We are no longer the objects upon which the light is thrown; we ourselves are behind and beside it, trying to guide it, that we and others may see the better and act the more intelligently in this crisis.

Anne and I spent the morning with the children—Jon, Land, and even Anne, downstairs in her mother's arms—beside the Christmas tree in the parlor. It seemed we spent hours opening all the presents. There were too many of them, really, although we had hidden a few away, and will let others disappear during the next few days. People should not deluge children with presents on Christmas. It dulls appreciation, not only of the presents, but of the day itself.

It seems to me that Christmas has deviated as much from the birth of Christ as Christianity has from his teachings. The keynote at the birth of Christ was simplicity. The keynote of Christmas today is luxury. The birth and life of Christ were surrounded with things mystical. Christmas and Christianity today are surrounded with things material. Sometime I would like to have a Christmas in our home that conforms to the true spirit and significance of that day 2,000 years ago—a Christmas unadorned by tinsel, uncluttered by gewgaws and ribboned boxes, unstuffed by roast turkey and sweet potatoes; a Christmas pure in its simplicity, akin to the sky and stars, of the mind rather than the body. It should be almost the reverse of a modern Christmas. One should eat too little rather than too much, see no one rather than everyone, spend it in silence rather than in communication. Christmas should be a day that brings one closer to God and to the philosophy of Christ.

Thursday, December 26

The antiwar forces seem to be rallying again. The country—or is it the newspapers?—blows hot and cold on the war. People do not understand either the issues or the conditions which now exist.

Went for an hour's walk with Thor after breakfast. As we passed the duck pond the ————— and some of their guests started shooting ducks from a blind at one end. Their procedure seems to be to scare the ducks from the pond and then shoot at them when they come back to alight on the water again. Since the ducks are tamed by feeding during most of the year, they return rather quickly.

I stood watching these people, dressed in the latest shooting-clothes style, banging away at the startled ducks, fifty or seventy-five feet above them. Usually, they missed completely, and then the ducks would go right ahead and land on the pond; they were too tame and inexperienced to fly off to a safer location. But there were hundreds of ducks, and after every fifth or sixth shot, one of them would be hit—fluttering down heavily through the tree branches.

What pleasure, I kept wondering, do people get from this sport? I do not mind shooting a bird to eat occasionally, especially if I am on an expedition of some sort, and I thoroughly enjoy target shooting with rifle or shotgun. But this pleasure in seeing something happy and beautiful fall maimed and fluttering, I do not understand.

The Paramount Newsreel Company called up to ask Anne to read part of her Christmas Eve address to the talking pictures. After talking it over, she decided to do it. It will be the first time. We phoned [John] Rich (Quakers) in Philadelphia to make the necessary arrangements and stipulated that Paramount must give the film to the other newsreel companies, as they did with my Washington address. Anne spent most of the day selecting the paragraphs from her address that she will read. Then we went to the woods along the north shore for a two-hour walk. Spent the rest of the afternoon listening to Anne practice her talk. She reads and speaks much better than I do. I should be the one who practices reading my addresses; but I hate to read something I write more than once. I seem to lose spirit and feeling in the second reading.

Friday, December 27

Anne and I drove to New York. Anne's appointment with the newsreels was between 2:30 and 3:30 at the NBC studios. She phoned as soon as she had finished, and I met her at the Vaillants'. We drove to Lloyd Neck together.

Monday, December 30

Roosevelt demands more aid for Britain. Says Axis will lose war. London is reported in flames. German armies are on the Bulgarian border.

Lunch at Stewart's apartment, with Stewart, Eggleston, and [Richard K.] Hines. Hines is [H. Smith] Richardson's lawyer.

Wednesday, January 1

Spent the first part of the morning on routine and a walk with Thor. Then drove to New York. After lunch I went to see Anne's picture in a Trans-Lux theater. She was thrown on the screen immediately after a picture of Roosevelt. The caption was "Shall We Feed Hitler's Europe?"! They never miss a chance to do something like that. The picture itself was excellent, although not well cut. Anne's delivery could not have been better. The audience showed no reaction whatever. In fact, during the entire newsreel the only time they cheered was when Roosevelt said the Axis would not win the war. And the only time they booed was when a picture of Mussolini was thrown on the screen. They almost snarled at Mussolini—reminded me more of animals than of people. To my surprise, there was not the slightest attempt at cheering when films of soldiers going to training camps were shown.

Saturday, January 4

British assault Bardia. Roosevelt announces large ship-building program. German raids over England continue. R.A.F. raids Bremen.

Spent most of the morning working on my article for the *Saturday Evening Post*. Went for a short walk with Jon, and later with Anne and Thor. While Jon and I were walking, he asked me about vaccinations. I had to explain in detail—even going into the difference between vaccination for smallpox and inoculation for typhoid.

Armstrong came for supper and the evening. We talked of the No Foreign War Committee and the impossibility of his continuing to serve under Verne Marshall. We discussed the possibility of Armstrong forming another antiwar group and organizing mass meetings throughout the country.

Monday, January 6

Bardia falls. Twenty-five thousand Italian troops reported captured.

The pall of the war seems to hang over us today. More and more people are simply giving in to it. Many say we are as good as in already. The attitude of the country wavers back and forth. First, it seems the antiwar forces are gaining, and then there is a swing in the other direction—and one must always try to separate the headlines in the newspapers from the factual attitude of the country. But, on the whole, I think we who are against American intervention have been slowly losing ground, at least from a relative standpoint. Our greatest hope lies in the fact that eighty-five per cent of the people in the United States (according to the latest polls) are against intervention. On the other hand, about sixty-five per cent want to "aid Great Britain, even at the risk of war." In other words, we seem to want to have Britain win without being willing to pay the price of war. We are indulging in a type of wishful thinking that must lead us, sooner or later, to an impossible position.

Tuesday, January 7

Balkan situation tense.

Roosevelt has asked for "all-out aid" to the democracies, but his message is not specific—as usual. Roosevelt seems to be holding back somewhat on the war. Is he afraid it is too late for us to enter it successfully? I have tried to analyze his thinking, but it is extremely difficult, for the man is so unstable. I think he has the ability to persuade himself that whatever he wants himself is also to the best interests of the country. I feel sure he would, consciously or unconsciously, like to take the center of the world stage away from Hitler. I think he would lead this country to war in a moment if he felt he could accomplish this object. But in war he is faced with reality. If a war is lost, the reality is too stark and too obvious to be hidden in propaganda or sheets of figures, or fireside chats. If Roosevelt took this country into war and won, he might be one of the great figures of all history. But if we lost, he would be damned forever. The cards are now stacked against us, and I think that is why he is wavering—temptation balanced against discretion. And Roosevelt is clever, even though I do not give him credit for being very wise.

Wednesday, January 8

Admiral Towers testifies before a congressional committee that the Navy had 2,145 planes on January 1, 1940, 2,590 planes on January 1, 1941, and expects to have 6,270 planes on January 1, 1942. He said many of those on hand were trainers, and that very few were of a modern combat type.

Day at Lloyd Neck—most of it spent working on "A Letter to Americans." Phoned Carrel. He has talked to a man who has just arrived from France and who talked to Mme. Carrel while he was in Brittany recently. She is well and has enough food. She sends us word that Illiec is no longer occupied by the Germans, but that everything movable has been taken from the house.

Thursday, January 9

British advance in Libya. Roosevelt 1942 budget set at $17.5 billion with possible increase.

Went down to the duck pond for an hour's play on the ice with the children in the afternoon. There is a small area of free water near the center of the pond, and as one approaches it, most of the ducks fly off. A few that have been wounded limp toward the woods at the side of the pond—the leftovers from the season's sport!

Armstrong came out for supper and to discuss his plans for a new antiwar campaign. He expects to resign from the No Foreign War Committee within the next few days, which I think is wise.

Saturday, January 11

A bill has been introduced in Congress to give Roosevelt almost unlimited war powers. R.A.F. bombs Calais and the Ruhr.

The No Foreign War Committee difficulties continue. I have adopted a policy of "isolation."

Monday, January 13

Willkie comes out in support of Roosevelt's requested powers!

Drove to New York in time for lunch with Stewart.

Drove back to Lloyd Neck in time to take Anne to supper at the Ames[221] home—near Fort Hill. They had a Mr. Webster[222] for their only other guest. He is a partner in one of the brokerage houses in New York and plans on giving up his business for several months in order to take part in organizing against American intervention in the war. He is the type of man who will carry this country through this crisis—if it is to get through. I have often felt that the greatest hope and strength the United States has lies in the men and women who have quietly devoted their lives to business and their own affairs, but who will step forward to leadership when times become so chaotic that they can no longer continue to absorb themselves in their businesses and their affairs. I am certain that leadership lies dormant in this country—if only it comes out before too much time has passed. If we drop too far, the return will bring great suffering.

Tuesday, January 14

The No Foreign War Committee is going through a spasm of reorganization. They asked me if I would join the policy committee if ex-Senator Reed [223] or Senator Holt[224] would take the chairmanship of the committee. I told them that, while I was anxious to help, I did not want any connection with the No Foreign War Committee under present circumstances.

221. Amyas Ames, partner in Kidder, Peabody & Co., later became governor of the New York Stock Exchange, 1949–55.

222. Edwin S. Webster, Jr., New York investment banker, partner in Kidder, Peabody & Co.

223. James A. Reed, Democratic Senator from Missouri for three terms (1911–29). In 1941 he was practicing law in Kansas City.

224. Rush Dew Holt, Democratic Senator from West Virginia.

Wednesday, January 15

England admits three warships hit last week by German dive bombers in the Mediterranean.

A telegram has come from Hamilton Fish,[225] asking me to appear before the House Foreign Relations Committee in regard to the Lease-Lend bill.[226]

Anne and I went skating with the children in the afternoon. I bought a pair of hockey skates—the first time I have had a pair of ice skates on since I was an engineering student at the University of Wisconsin (and I had them on only once or twice then). However, my roller-skating experience as a schoolboy in Washington came to my rescue, and I soon found I could move about fairly well. Read *Treasure Island* to Jon in the evening.

Thursday, January 16

Hull asks for utmost aid to Britain. Congress votes $3 billion for anti-aircraft equipment for the Navy!

Gave statement to the press services this morning to the effect that I have no connection with the No Foreign War Committee, and that I found myself unable to support its methods and policies. I disliked doing this, but could not continue to stand for Marshall's references to me in his interviews.

225. Republican Representative from New York.

226. Lend-Lease bill. In January, 1941, President Roosevelt submitted to Congress a program designed to circumvent existing limitations of the neutrality legislation and make American war materials immediately available to the Allies. This was to become the Lend-Lease Act, which authorized the President to "sell, transfer, exchange, lease, lend" any defense articles "to the government of any country whose defense the President deems vital to the defense of the United States" and make available to such countries the facilities of American shipyards. This touched off a bitter and prolonged debate in Congress. The bill was passed March 11, 1941, and it made, Roosevelt said, the U.S. the "arsenal of democracy." Under its provisions the U.S. provided $50 billion worth of arms, foodstuffs, and services.

Friday, January 17

Phoned Congressman Fish in Washington. He says the House Foreign Relations Committee wants me to testify next week between Wednesday and Friday.[227]

Saturday, January 18

Churchill demands more ships and planes from United States. French sink two Siamese warships.

Anne and I drove to Colonel and Mrs. Theodore Roosevelt's home for dinner.

Sunday, January 19

Washington claims that 800 "military" planes were constructed in this country in December.

Telegram arrived from Sol Bloom, chairman of the House Foreign Relations Committee, asking me to appear before the committee Thursday morning.

Monday, January 20

Spent most of the day working on the statement I expect to make before the House Foreign Relations Committee. Refused all phone calls through the day so I could concentrate on my statement.

Wednesday, January 22

Rioting reported in Rumania. United States ends plane embargo against Russia.

Off [Washington] train at 7:50. Phoned the Hay-Adams and the Anchorage from the station, but no rooms available. Hotel clerk says Washington is crowded with people interested in defense contracts. Finally got

227. In regard to trends toward war and danger of involvement.

a room at the Carlton Hotel. To the Munitions Building for a fifteen-minute conference with General Arnold. Met a number of old friends while I was there. Walked back to the Army & Navy Club; then taxi to the Carlton Hotel, where I had lunch in my room with Major [Ennis] Whitehead (Air Intelligence). Walk and taxi to the Smiths' home, and he and I drove to Congressman Fish's home for supper. Congressman and Mrs. Fish, their daughter, Congressman Maas (Minnesota), Congressman Stewart,[228] and one or two others made up the table. Hanford MacNider came in for a few minutes afterward. We discussed the war, trends in this country, the committee hearings, etc., etc.

Thursday, January 23

Tobruk taken by Australians. Civil war continues in Rumania.

Breakfast in room. Then walked part way and took taxi rest of way to House Office Building. Arrived early, so walked around the Capitol grounds and the Congressional Library. Went in through the front door to the new House Office Building and arrived at the Ways and Means Committee Room at 9:55, as scheduled. There was a large crowd, and people were lined up outside of the doors, trying to get in. Bloom, who made every effort to be considerate, took me into an adjoining room until the committee was ready for my appearance. Then we followed the police officers into the committee room. It was jammed; probably 1,000 people were inside. The room was flooded with brilliant lights for the motion-picture cameras, and there were two or three dozen still photographers gathered around the table where I was to sit—almost all the things I dislike and which represent to me the worst of American life in this period. Up above me, extending in a curve to either side of the room, sat the committeemen; there must have been twenty or more of them.

I read my statement and then attempted to reply to the questions of the committeemen until about 12:30, when an adjournment was made for lunch. I had expected to encounter great antagonism, but found relatively little of it, to my surprise. In fact, on the whole, they were extremely courteous. One or two of the Congressmen were a little unpleasant, but not for long. And to my amazement, I found that the crowd was with me. They clapped on several occasions!

Spent another two hours testifying in the afternoon. After I finished I

228. John G. Stewart, Republican Representative from Delaware.

remained to hear General Hugh Johnson[229] testify. Then left the building through a side entrance and walked for half an hour—alone. One seems to gain strength when one is alone, even though it is in the midst of a city. Stopped for a half hour's visit with Jerry and Betty Land; then walked to the Carlton, packed, took a taxi to the station, and boarded the train for New York.

Sunday, January 26

Germans report another dive-bomber attack on the British fleet in the Mediterranean.

Went for a walk with Jim Newton in the morning; then spent most of the day correcting my testimony before the House Foreign Affairs Committee. The manuscript arrived special delivery this morning. Bloom telegraphed me it was coming, and I sent a car to the post office to get it.

Monday, January 27

Left for New York at 5:45 (snowing and icy roads) for dinner with Mr. Webster and a number of young New York businessmen who have formed an organization called College Men Against War, or some such name. There were about fifteen for supper, and as many more came in afterward—a high type. We discussed the war and plans for organizing against this country's involvement. Back to Lloyd Neck at midnight.

Wednesday, January 29

Jim Newton phoned to say that he had bought the sailboat we wanted, for $850. It is a centerboard yawl—about thirty-two feet, with a four-bunk cabin. The boat is old but in excellent condition and probably better built than many of the new ones.

229. Administrator of the National Recovery Administration (NRA), 1933–34. Since 1934 he had been an editorial commentator for Scripps-Howard and other newspapers, as well as radio.

Thursday, January 30

Wrote a letter to Mme. Carrel in the evening. Dr. Carrel is leaving for France Saturday, and Anne and I both want to send letters with him.

Friday, January 31

Hitler announces that if American ships are sent to aid Britain, they will be torpedoed! He says a decision with Britain will be forced in the spring.

Anne and I drove to New York for a 2:00 appointment with Dr. Carrel at the Rockefeller Institute. We gave Carrel the letters for Mme. Carrel, then stayed for a few minutes talking to him. He is leaving for Portugal on a small American steamer. He has just returned from Washington, where he visited the French Embassy. He says the French military and air attachés agree one hundred per cent with the stand I have taken about the war! They say that Germany now has 70,000 airplanes of all types.

I believe Dr. Carrel can be of great value to France at this time, if only the people in power can be made to realize his abilities. Carrel makes enemies easily and makes little attempt to "sell himself." I admire him for this, but I am afraid it may result in wasting the powers he could otherwise contribute to a reconstruction of France. He antagonizes so many of the people he comes in contact with, and few of them are able to see beneath his surface shell to the great mind it contains. Carrel has it in him to be one of the great men of France in these times. If only he is able to make the right contacts and uses a little care in his approach.

Saturday, February 1

Sent a telegram to Senator George in reply to his invitation to appear before the Senate Committee on Foreign Affairs, telling him that I covered practically all I had to say when I testified before the House committee, but that I would be glad to appear before the Senate committee also if he felt it desirable for me to do so. As a matter of fact, I would much prefer not to go.

Sunday, February 2

Anne is feeling ill and had lunch in bed; says she has chicken pox and is much annoyed because I don't agree. Spent most of the afternoon working on the statement I will read before the Senate Committee on Foreign Affairs if I am asked to appear before it, as I am afraid I will be. The Archie Roosevelts[230] and the Marquands[231] came for supper. Anne was not well enough to come down. Maybe she *has* got chicken pox!

Monday, February 3

Riots in Johannesburg.

Anne definitely *has* chicken pox. I moved the bed over to the window so she would have a better light to read by during the days she will have to be in the room.

Made several phone calls to Washington—Senators George, La Follette, Clark. It seems the Administration Senators *don't* want me to appear before the Foreign Affairs Committee, while the "isolationist" Senators do. In that case, I will go.

Tuesday, February 4

Negotiations continue between France and Germany. There are indications in Washington that the Lease-Lend bill may be modified.

Spent the afternoon finishing my statement. Gave it to Christine to type. Packed, and left for New York in time for a 7:30 dinner appointment at the Miyako with George Eggleston and a professor from Cleveland. [He] is what Anne calls one of those "hidden-hand people." He sees a secret organization behind most moves and coincidence or happenstance behind very few. He sees great plots everywhere and is suspicious of

230. Archibald B. Roosevelt, investment broker, and son of President Theodore Roosevelt. A veteran of World War I, he served as a major with the 3rd Infantry Battalion in New Guinea in World War II.

231. John Marquand, novelist and winner of the Pulitzer prize for *The Late George Apley* (1937). Mrs. Marquand was the former Adelaide Hooker, friend of Anne Morrow Lindbergh.

everything, especially of the Jews. I am beginning to feel the world is divided into two groups of people (how easy it is to divide problems into two for the convenience of your momentary argument): those who are inherently suspicious of everything and those who are not. In my experience it seems that Latin blood (and Asiatic) tends to suspicion, while Nordic blood tends away from it. Personally, I prefer to be with people who are not suspicious about everything in life. And, as a matter of fact, I think the "suspicious" people are wrong more of the time than their opposites.

After we finished dinner I phoned Lloyd Manor to find out whether Senator Clark had phoned from Washington to confirm the Foreign Affairs Committee's desire for me to appear before them. He had not called, so I started back to Lloyd Neck. By the time I had covered half the distance home, I began to have the feeling that I should go to Washington anyway, even though I had not heard from Clark. I turned back at the first crossroads and took the midnight train from Pennsylvania Station.

Wednesday, February 5

Laval demands the power of Premier. R.A.F. raids Düsseldorf and Channel coast.

Off train at 7:45. Phoned Hay-Adams and Anchorage; both full. Finally got a room at the Carlton as before. Phoned Senator Clark, and met him at his office at 10:00. He phoned La Follette and Wheeler, who arrived a few minutes later. We discussed the question of whether or not it was advisable for me to appear before the Senate Foreign Affairs Committee, and decided in the affirmative.

After leaving the Senate Office Building, I walked past the new Mellon museum. It is a beautiful building. I enjoy just walking by and looking at it. Stopped at the Smithsonian Institution to see the *Spirit of St. Louis,* but remained only a minute or two because of the crowd.

Phoned Earl Findley (United States Air Services) and asked him to come for lunch. I wanted to talk to him about the manuscript (unpublished) he wrote about the Wright brothers many years ago. Also, I think he is very much in need of friendship since his wife died. They were very close to each other, and he depended on her tremendously. When Findley arrived, he was much concerned about a sentence he had placed in the editorial page of the last issue of his magazine in opposition to my stand on the war—not that he had changed his opinion, but he was afraid it would hurt my feelings. I told him not to worry about that, and that disagreement about politics and the war should not affect our personal relationship.

I talked to Findley at length about the Wright manuscript. I think I have mentioned it before in this record, but, briefly, fifteen or twenty years ago—possibly more—Findley wrote the manuscript for a book on the Wright brothers. Due to his own honesty, and a disagreement with Orville Wright, the manuscript was never published. I had not read it, so cannot pass upon it, but I know Findley held Orville Wright's confidence and that he was well acquainted with the early days of flying (although from a reporter's standpoint). The manuscript should be extremely valuable and should not be lost, even though Findley will not consider publishing it. I suggested to Findley that he place the manuscript, sealed, in some library with instructions that it not be opened for twenty-five or fifty years, or for whatever time he thought advisable. I don't know how much impression I made on him, but he said he would consider it. The subject is so sensitive to him that I think I shall not try to press it farther. He says the manuscript is now in a box beside his bed in his Washington apartment.

Went for a long walk along the city streets in the afternoon; then spent an hour studying the Lease-Lend bill and its recent modifications.

Thursday, February 6

Checked out of the hotel about 9:15. Left my suitcase at the Army & Navy Club and took a taxi to the Capitol grounds. Walked around the grounds for fifteen minutes and then to Senator Clark's office, arriving at 10:30. Clark's secretary took me to a room adjoining the committee room where the testimony was taking place. Colonel McCormick (Chicago *Tribune*) was on the stand ahead of me. He finished testifying about 11:00, and I started immediately afterward.

The Senate hearing was, on the whole, conducted with more dignity than the House hearing on the Lend-Lease bill. Senator [Claude] Pepper of Florida took up almost half of the time I was on the stand and got himself into several rather amusing situations. He and two or three other Administration Senators were definitely antagonistic, but only during their questioning. When the committee adjourned for lunch, they were courteous and friendly. I have often noticed this in Washington: Congressmen and Senators will curse each other in debate and be, apparently at least, on the most friendly terms after it is over. Pepper has called me everything from a fifth columnist on down, but he was smiling and good-natured during the lunch hour. In a sense, it demonstrates a dangerous irresponsibility in the speech of public men. I think that more care about the accuracy and dignity of what is said would create a better and more stable government. The afternoon session started at 2:00. I finished testifying about 4:30. Walked from the Senate Office Building to the Army & Navy Club, past the Mellon museum (which always gives me a feeling of renewed strength and confidence in life). Spent fifteen minutes telephoning; then talked to O. K. Armstrong for half an hour in regard to his plans for a series of antiwar rallies.

Taxi to Senator Shipstead's home for dinner with Senator and Mrs. Shipstead and Eva and George Christie.[232]

Friday, February 7

Off [New York] train at 7:25. Drove to Lloyd Neck for a late breakfast. The day is warm, and the snow is melting rapidly. Anne was much better when I arrived, but she is covered with pox scabs, and it will probably take a week or more before they disappear.

Sunday, February 9

House passes Lease-Lend bill—260–165.

Spent most of the day working on "A Letter to Americans."

Wednesday, February 12

Worked until noon correcting the Senate Committee testimony. Finished it and sent it to the post office in Huntington.

Anne, Jr., has chicken pox.

Drove to the Long Island Aviation Country Club in the afternoon for an hour and ten minutes' flying in their little Stinson monoplane (eight

232. Eva Christie, Lindbergh's half-sister, daughter of C. A. Lindbergh, Sr., by his first wife, Mary La Fond. George Christie, her husband, was a newspaper owner and editor.

flights). The field was frozen, and there was considerable traffic in the air. One must watch for approaching planes with extreme care. These high-wing monoplanes are dangerously blind. In a bank you cannot see what you are turning into unless you lift the down wing back above the horizon.

Returned to Lloyd Manor, then drove to Huntington station to meet Mr. [J.] McEvoy from the *Reader's Digest*. [DeWitt] Wallace asked me to talk to him about an article he is writing concerning my stand on the war issue. I dislike these personal articles, but they have a constructive value at this time. McEvoy is interesting and far more perceptive and sensitive than most magazine writers one meets.

Thursday, February 13

Spent the first part of the morning on routine, then drove to New York for a 12:15 lunch with Wallace and McEvoy in Wallace's room in the St. Regis. Spent most of two hours discussing the war, its outcome in Europe, its effect on America, and the *Reader's Digest* policy concerning it. Dinner at 7:00 at Stewart's apartment. Have a fever and feel rotten, so I left at 9:30 and returned to Lloyd Manor. Chicken pox?

Friday, February 14

Chicken pox!!!

Saturday, February 15

Chicken pox. Can't even read comfortably.

Monday, February 24

Strikes increase in United States.

Went for an hour's walk with Thor after breakfast. I went to the bluff, but I could not see the lighthouse or the bay. They made an impression on my eyes but not within my mind and feeling. I could not see the trees, or the stones along the path, or the last year's leaves, or the frost crystals on the shady side of the banks. All these things were there, but only as flat, physical facts. Life and spark were gone from them, for my mind is on the war, on politics, on the things spread over the front pages of the morning newspapers. I can no longer see, and it is time for me to go far away until I learn to see again. There is a danger to not seeing and feeling, for then one relies too greatly on reasoning, and life cannot be guided successfully and happily by reason alone. Something else must be combined with it.

It is that something which is so lacking today in modern American life. It does not live long in great cities, or factories, or newspapers. To have it, one must have in life a certain amount of solitude. Some say real solitude can be found in the midst of cities—in an empty room, or on a park bench, or along a darkened street in the hours past midnight. I think there *is* an element of solitude in these places—a ray that passes through a hole in deep clouds—but to me solitude means beauty and distance and uninhabited places. I feel a city around me, even though no one knows where I am within it. There seems to be an atmosphere of people and unhappiness and the uninspired drabness of everyday life. I feel it as I feel the smoke in my lungs and the concrete under my feet. I sometimes think I can feel the tension and turmoil of a city as I fly over it 5,000 feet in the air.

Tuesday, February 25

[Wesley] Stout (*Saturday Evening Post*) phoned in the afternoon. He told me the *Post* had decided not to take my article. He said that while he "agreed with practically every word of it," he felt it was "a little too late." I gathered that he referred to the speed with which the Lend-Lease bill seems to be going through Congress. I cannot help wondering whether it is not more a case of the article being a little too "hot" than a little too "late" for the *Post*. Spent the afternoon on routine and plans to place my article elsewhere. *Collier's*? A book? *Scribner's Commentator*? A newspaper syndicate? Decided to try *Collier's* first.

Wednesday, February 26

Contacted *Collier's* through Deac Lyman and sent the manuscript of my article to a Mr. Chaplin of that organization.

Anne and I drove to New York for a 7:30 dinner with ex-President and Mrs. Hoover in their apartment at the Waldorf Tower. Herbert Hoover, Jr., and his wife were also there. We discussed the war, food relief, the future for America, and many other subjects. Hoover told us a little about the problems he is encountering in connection with sending food to the occupied countries in Europe. His latest plan has apparently been accepted practically in its entirety by the Germans, but the British have not even replied to it as yet. Among other items, as I remember the figures, Hoover said he had stipulated that Germany send 25,000 tons of wheat and similar foodstuffs to Belgium per month, provided the British permit certain meats and fats to pass through their blockade.

Hoover said he had demanded more of Germany than it would have been possible for her to take from Belgium. (The charge has been made that Germany has already taken far more from Belgium than she would be willing to return.) The Germans replied that they would send immediately not 25,000 but 80,000 tons of breadstuffs to Belgium, while, as I have said, the British have as yet not replied at all. Hoover felt that, even from their own standpoint, the British were being extremely stupid and shortsighted in their attitude toward the impending famine in the occupied areas. He said that Belgium would be struck by famine first, and that occupied France had sufficient food to last until the next harvest. In fact, Hoover said, occupied France had food to export to unoccupied France. He said this situation was being used by the Germans as a trading point with which to gain military concessions.

Thursday, February 27

Left for New York at 3:30. Haircut at the Engineers Club; then drove to 35 Beekman Place to meet [Edwin] Webster at 6:00. We discussed the America First organization and the possibility of holding a rally in Washington next week. While we were talking, Mrs. Wheeler[233] (America First chapter, Washington) phoned to say that opposition to the Lend-Lease bill was rising and that she felt it very important to hold a Washington rally as soon as possible. Webster said he felt America First should send people to a Washington rally from all of its chapters. He and Mrs. Wheeler asked if I would speak at such a meeting. I told them it would mean canceling all of our plans for a vacation in Florida, but that if they

233. Mrs. Burton K. Wheeler, wife of the Senator, was active on the national committee of America First.

felt a Washington rally would be effective at this time, and if America First would fully back such a rally, I would arrange to speak there. (I hate to cancel the Florida trip. Anne and I have looked forward to it for months. We bought the little sailboat for this trip, and Jim is now outfitting it at Fort Myers Beach. Also, Anne really needs a vacation, and I want to get far enough away from this New York–Washington–Atlantic Coast atmosphere to view conditions and the war situation from the objectivity of distance and relative solitude.)

Met Anne at the Cosmopolitan Club at 7:15, and we walked the three or four blocks to Roy Howard's home for supper. The table consisted of Roy and Mrs. Howard, Mrs. Howard's sister, Colonel and Mrs. Theodore Roosevelt, and a Mr. Parker[234] of the *World-Telegram*. We spent most of the evening discussing the war and its accompanying trends and policies. Howard is a quick, able, and cautious man, with an exceptional knack for illustrating his conversation with typically American expressions. Howard's general policy seems to be to stay close enough to center so he will not be caught out, whichever way events turn. In this way he has the double advantage of safety and great influence over the mass of people who stay close to center in thought and action.

I think his policy is wise, but personally I prefer the adventure and freedom of going as far from center as my thoughts, ideals, and convictions lead me. I do not like to be held back by the question of influencing the mass of people or by the desire for the utmost security. I must admit, and I have no apology to make for the fact, that I prefer adventure to security, freedom to popularity, and conviction to influence. I like to be in contact with the "center," and to use it as a base from which to organize, so to speak, but I prefer to spend most of my life and thought on the frontier—or occasionally somewhat beyond. There is need for both types of people, I believe, and one complements the other in life. Not that Howard never makes excursions out from "center," but they are "excursions"; he does not belong on the outskirts and want to live there, come what may, whereas I do. He is not happy too far out, while I am not happy too far in. It was both an interesting and an amusing evening. We stayed late and did not arrive back at Lloyd Neck until 1:30—Anne driving ahead with the Mercury and I following with the Ford.

234. George B. Parker, editor in chief of twenty-one Scripps-Howard newspapers.

Friday, February 28

Eastern Airlines plane crashed near Atlanta last night. Seven killed; nine injured. Eddie Rickenbacker was on board and is reported seriously injured.

Land has chicken pox and is very much pleased with himself.

Phoned Senator Byrd to talk to him about the Lend-Lease bill. I asked what he thought Roosevelt actually had in mind in regard to our participation in the war. Byrd replied that he did not think Roosevelt wanted to get the country into the war, at least at this time, and that he himself (Byrd) felt it would be disastrous for us to intervene, but that the trouble was no one could tell when the President would change his mind. Byrd said Senator George (Chairman, Senate Foreign Relations Committee) was definitely opposed to intervention, but that Roosevelt had persuaded him that he actually intended to keep this country out of the war, and that he wished the Lend-Lease bill passed in order to help England negotiate a better peace than she could otherwise obtain—"a sixty per cent peace instead of a forty per cent peace," according to what Byrd said George said Roosevelt told him. Byrd told me in confidence that the Senate Foreign Relations Committee had agreed to modification of the bill to the effect that Roosevelt will have to inform Congress of what part of each appropriation asked for will be "leased or loaned" abroad. He said there would be an attempt to insert terms which would prohibit convoying or sending troops abroad.

Saturday, March 1

Bulgaria reported joining the Axis. The movement of German troops toward the Balkans is reported. Germans continue to claim heavy British shipping losses.

Phone call from Mrs. [Bennett Champ] Clark in the evening. They have decided not to hold the Washington rally. So we will have our trip to Florida after all.

Monday, March 3

Phoned Jim Newton at Fort Myers Beach and arranged to meet him at Haines City Thursday afternoon. To Pennsylvania Station to purchase our tickets. Bought them to Tampa instead of Haines City in order to throw off reporters and photographers. Word always gets ahead in one way or another, and if they expect us at Tampa, they won't be waiting for us at Haines City. It costs a little more but is worth it. Returned to Lloyd Neck and went for a short walk in the dusk before supper.

Rube Fleet phoned from San Diego. He wants me to take charge of a research organization he plans on setting up in connection with his company. Offered me first $25,000 per year, and then $50,000, plus an interest in profits. He says he will soon have 35,000 men employed in his factory and that his government contracts are approaching the half-billion mark. He has always wanted to have a research organization connected with his factory and now has enough money to establish one. He said he would build it in California or in Arizona, or any place that I wanted it; said I could write my own ticket.

It was almost impossible to explain to Fleet why I could not do this, and we talked for over forty minutes long distance. I told him it was a most generous offer and that I felt the work would be extremely interesting, that I greatly enjoyed research work, etc., but that it was not a question of money. (This was when he raised his salary offer from $25,000 to $50,000.) I told Fleet that aeronautical research simply did not fit into the plans I had made for my life and that I could not take the position much as I appreciated his offer. Fleet asked me what my plans were. I told him I could not describe the objective, but that I knew the course. Fleet could not seem to understand this and kept repeating that I could write my own ticket. He finally asked if I would consider the proposition if he could get Douglas and Ford to go into it with him.

It was an exceptionally fine offer, made in real friendship and confidence, and it was a compliment I thoroughly appreciate. But in 1927 I decided that as long as I could earn a living in any other way I would never do anything primarily for money. I decided then that money must always be a secondary consideration—even in the business enterprises I took part in. In other words, I decided I would do nothing *because of* money that I did not want to do *regardless* of it. I have never regretted that decision, and it has simplified many decisions for me—such as the one tonight. I left commercial aviation many years ago to concentrate my attention on other things, and I do not intend to go back into it now. Fleet asked me to think his proposition over before coming to a final decision, but I told him I had already decided and that it would only be misleading to tell him I would consider it further—that it was only fair to tell him now I could not accept, so he could look for someone else to fill the place.

Spent the rest of the evening working on my article for *Collier's*.

Wednesday, March 5

German troops continue to pour into Bulgaria. Britain severs diplomatic relations. South Wales bombed again. Jap forces reported moving toward French Indo-China.

Finished packing and final details. Thor has been dejected since we first brought out the suitcases. He lies sunk into the carpet and will hardly raise his head when we pass by. He has accepted our departure and will now wait watchfully and sadly for our return. He will even be happier after we are gone, I believe, for he can then hope each day for our return. Now he thinks only of our leaving, and there is not the slightest sign of hope or happiness in his eyes.

Anne and I left for New York at 10:00. Take taxi to Pennsylvania Station after lunch. I get out two blocks away and walk so Anne can go in alone with the suitcases. In this way—going in separately—there is less chance of recognition and bother. The train started at 2:05. We have a compartment. Spent the evening reading *The Brothers Karamazov* by Dostoevsky.

Thursday, March 6

Off at Haines City, twenty minutes late. Jim Newton waiting for us. Drove us to Fort Myers. Then to Mrs. Edison's[235] home for a tea-supper. There were several other guests, including some of Jim's friends who had helped outfit the boat. After leaving the Edison home, we drove to Fort Myers Beach, stopping to see the boat as we passed the small shipyard where it is moored. It is larger than I expected and seems sturdy and well

235. Mrs. Thomas Edison, widow of the inventor.

designed. It was dark, so we did not stay long. Then to small cottage on the canal, where we are to spend the night.

There is very little "foreign" news in the local paper. Negotiations continue between Yugoslavia and the Axis. Strong opposition to the Lend-Lease bill is reported in Washington.

Friday, March 7

Spent the morning on final details and sorting out our equipment for the boat. Went with Jim to get the boat from the shipyard. Took it, by engine, to the Powers' dock—less than a quarter mile away. Late start. Head wind. Storm warnings are out. We used the engine and reached Big Hickory Pass just before dark. Jim knew the pass and the way into it— between two shoals, fifty yards apart, parallel to the beach and with breakers over each of them. I sounded the depth of water with the boat hook.

At times we had less than six inches to spare, but we got through the pass without difficulty. We anchored just inside the pass and began to prepare supper. There is a two-burner kerosene stove at the side of the passageway leading to the small, four-berth cabin. I cannot stand upright to cook, except by leaving the hatch above the steps open; then, by keeping one foot on the lower step and by stretching a little, I can reach the pans on both burners and still stand erect.

The boat is built for a combination of speed and seaworthiness. Luxury in cabin accommodations was obviously a secondary consideration in the designer's mind. The cabin is low, and the two forward bunks are tucked up into the bow, so one has to slide into them feet first. The cabin is well arranged, however, and everything about the boat is very much as we would want it if we had it built according to our own specifications.

Saturday, March 8

Woke late, cooked breakfast, weighed anchor, and started out through the pass. The wind was higher, there was more sea, and apparently the tide was slightly lower than when we came in last night, for we ran aground about 200 feet from the beach. There was not enough power in the engine to back off, and we could not get the bow turned around as the wind and rollers carried us, bumping, closer to shore. Finally, we all jumped in the water and attempted to push the bow around, but it was no use; the waves were too strong for us. They carried the boat along broadside, foot by foot closer to the shore, pounding slightly on the sand bottom as it rose and fell. Jim tossed the anchor overboard, and I carried it out a hundred feet from the boat, but it, too, was carried along, dragging slowly through the sand. Since there was nothing more we could do, I told Jim to take the dinghy and go for help.

As soon as he left, Anne and I began unloading the most valuable articles from the boat. It was now less than a hundred feet from the shore, and pounding rather heavily. Each wave threw it far over on its beam, and some of them broke over the gunnel into the cockpit. Anne brought things up from the cabin, and I carried them to shore and piled them above the tide line. Soon, the boat was rocking so violently that it was difficult to stay aboard without clinging to some object with both hands. When one unusually large wave hit us, there was a crack of wood, and I thought the bottom was going. The only way to get on and off was to synchronize one's movements with the rocking of the boat. As it keeled over with a wave, I would jump off with the object I was carrying ashore; and on my return for the next load I would climb on board while the boat was in the same position, letting it lift and slide me into the cockpit on the backward rock. How Anne managed to work in the cabin I don't know.

For a long time I thought we would lose the boat. But after what must actually have been not over half an hour, Jim came back with two boats. One was a small, open fisherman's boat with an automobile engine for its power plant. The other was about a thirty-foot launch. The fisherman's boat arrived first but was somewhat handicapped by the fact that its crew consisted only of the fisherman and his small son. I finally cut the rope from one anchor, tied it to the chain of the other, and got the end out to their boat. But the first tug pulled a board out of their old boat, and they had to turn the rope over to the larger launch, which was by that time on the scene, skillfully maneuvering in the shallow waters another fifty yards offshore. As soon as the rope was fast, Jim, who had come back on the launch, jumped into the water and waded over to help us push on our boat. The fisherman from the first rescue boat came also, making four of us in the water with our shoulders to the hull.

Fortunately, the tide was coming in, and inch by inch we moved the bow around until it pointed out toward the sea. Then, slowly, with each large wave, our boat moved off the bar. As it floated free Jim and Anne climbed aboard, while I stayed to watch the articles on the beach. Before wading ashore, however, I waded and swam between the bars to find where the channel lay. I found that we had been in the deepest part when we went aground and that it was simply a case of the waves being too high and the tide too low for our boat to get out. We drew three feet of water, and it was about six inches too much. After examining the bars thoroughly, I waded back to shore and waited until the fisherman came to get me in his boat. He and his small son helped carry the articles I had piled on the beach across the key to where they had left their boat on the lee shore.

Upon careful inquiry we found that the main channel had shifted completely and now lies straight out from the pass instead of parallel to the shore. But Jim inquired of some fishermen this morning and was told it was in the same place as last year!

We anchored inside the pass for the afternoon and night—a quarter mile farther in than before. The boat needed a careful inspection, and our equipment had to be gone over and restowed. There was considerable water in the bilge, and it kept coming in slowly. At first, we thought the pounding of the surf had opened a seam, but it turned out that the water was coming in along the propeller shaft where the packing nut had come loose. The launch captain asked only $15.00 for his help. We gave him $30.00, for he had probably saved us much more. After supper Anne and I took the dinghy and outboard engine to the fisherman's shack. We left $15.00 with the fisherman for his help and returned to our boat. Bed at midnight.

Sunday, March 9

Local paper reports that Lease-Lend bill passed the Senate 60 to 31. London heavily raided.

Quick breakfast; then Jim dove under the boat to cut the dinghy rope, which had become wound around the propeller shaft. He found the rudder slightly bent and the propeller shaft loose. We fixed the shaft with the help of the captain of the launch. After that was done the captain offered to lead us out through the pass. We followed behind him, but as he approached the breakers he turned back, saying they were too large for his boat. However, he pointed the channel out to us. Since he had navigated that channel for years, and since our boat drew nearly as much water as his, we decided the breakers were too high for us, too. We anchored back of Big Hickory Island and took the dinghy ashore for a walk along the beach—the same walk we took last year, scaring up what seemed to be the same flocks of birds.

Lunch in boat. Later in the afternoon Jim went to drag for the anchor. (He had thrown it overboard, not realizing I had cut off the rope to use as a tow line.) Anne and I went to the island (Big Hickory). I waded and swam out through the "new" channel to make sure we would know where it was when the wind died sufficiently to let us get out to sea again. In places there were less than five feet of water—plenty on a calm day, but dangerous in breakers. The tide turned as I was wading back and forth, and I had to return to shore before exploring the channel as thoroughly as I would like to have. (The current becomes too strong to swim against soon after the tide starts to come out.) In the evening I pitched our small bugproof tent among the trees on Big Hickory, and after supper Anne and I took the dinghy and went ashore for the night. Jim stayed on the boat.

Monday, March 10

Half an hour before high tide we weighed anchor and started out. The launch met us and guided us out through the channel. Even with the lowered wind we had to pass through breakers about three feet high. After leaving Big Hickory, we sailed most of the way to Gordon Pass— making slow time, as the wind was light and the sea choppy. We arrived at the pass just before sunset. But there was nothing but white water and heavy breakers between us and the pass. Several flags bobbed up and down on buoys, but there was no way of telling what they meant, or whether the channel had shifted since they were put in place. Our chart was no help; it showed no markers at all. We decided not to try Gordon Pass and to go on to Big Marco or Caxambus, even though we would have to make the trip at night. The wind dropped soon after sunset, and we started the engine. It was a beautiful, clear night—the moon almost full. When we arrived at Caxambus, we throttled the engine and sounded our way through the channel with the fish spear—Jim at the tiller, Anne and I taking soundings. We anchored about midnight, a half mile from the town.

Tuesday, March 11

Jim took the dinghy to Caxambus and returned with extra provisions. We had intended to take the boat out of water to look the bottom over, but Caxambus was not equipped for boats of our size—only for small fishing boats—so we decided to go on to Cape Romano where we had anchored for a few hours last year. When we arrived at Cape Romano, there were two other boats at the usual anchorage, so we continued on around the Cape and dropped anchor at the mouth of one of the numerous passages through the glades. We took the dinghy through this passage, winding in and out through the mangroves, until we came to Morgan Pass.

There were hundreds of birds. They seldom flew away until we approached within a few yards. We decided to move on to Indian Key by moonlight. Took turns at the tiller and throttled the engine down to two or three knots until we had passed through the bars and shallow water between Cape Romano and Indian Key. As soon as we reached deeper water—as soon as the flashing beacon on our left crossed the north star —we opened the engine and set a direct course for Indian Key. We arrived about 2:00 in the morning and dropped anchor behind the key at about the same spot where we spent our first night out last year.

Wednesday, March 12

We decided that Anne and I would camp on Indian Key while Jim took the boat to Everglades—about five miles or so inland—to have the hull looked over and the rudder inspected. The rudder does not seem to work as freely as it should, and we suspect it was damaged in the pounding it got at Big Hickory Pass. If Anne and I went to Everglades, there would just be a lot of fuss and annoyance from the season's tourists, and Jim will be able to get all the help he needs at the shipyards. If it were not fishing season, we would go, for it would be interesting, and local people never bother us. But as it is, the town will be full of tourists, and they always cause trouble.

We put all our camping equipment in the dinghy and, after helping Jim haul up the anchor, we headed for Indian Key, and he started for Everglades. Just as we were about to beach, the propeller of our outboard engine struck a coral rock and sheared the pin.

Most of Indian Key seems to be swamp, covered with mangrove roots. But there is a small gravel beach where we landed, and a few yards inland we found a sheltered spot on dry ground for the tent. We pitched it under a sea-grape tree. The mosquitoes are terrible—the worst I have ever seen south of Labrador. The only relief from them is in the tent; and they are not as bad on the beach near the water. Cold supper from cans: bread and crackers on the beach near our tent (tomatoes, condensed milk, crackers, and wheat bread).

We lit a driftwood fire to help keep the mosquitoes away. It was partially successful. The moon was full and shone down on us through the masts and rigging of an old fishing wreck, which had been grounded just off the beach where we were sitting. The name, *Theodore Roosevelt,* was still visible in faded black paint on the bow. After supper we returned to our tent, crawled in quickly through the net door, and zipped it shut as soon as possible after we were inside. Even so, we spent the next five or ten minutes killing the mosquitoes that had come in with us. We spent an hour writing by our electric torch, and then climbed into the sleeping bag. Thank God we have no newspapers to read and no radio to listen to.

Thursday, March 13

Breakfast on the beach, walking up and down in the sun to avoid mosquitoes. (One can condensed milk—sucked from hole punched in can—crackers, wheat bread, and oranges.) After breakfast we went out in the dinghy to get away from the mosquitoes. We tried fishing with a spoon hook, but no luck. Decided to take the dinghy over to a nearby island where there seemed to be a clearing and a small shack. When we arrived we found that no one was living there. To our surprise there were relatively few mosquitoes on this key, and there was good high ground for our tent, exposed to the sea breeze. We decided to move the tent over from Indian Key if Jim did not return in the early afternoon. He thought he would be back last night, or this morning at the latest, but he may have found more to do on the boat than we expected.

We decided to go for a swim before lunch, in spite of a large sea turtle that had been blowing a few yards off our beach. I could not see its body, but its head seemed about the size of a seal's. However, the natives in Florida say they don't bother anyone. No need to bother about suits here, and swimming is much pleasanter. Lunch of corned beef, corn, wheat bread, crackers, and grapefruit. We are cutting down slightly, as there is no way of knowing when Jim will return. With care, we have enough food to last through tomorrow.

In the late afternoon there was still no sign of Jim, so we pitched our tent in a small clump of trees near the beach. There are relatively few mosquitoes, even under the trees. Made a driftwood fire on the beach and ate supper beside it (one slice wheat bread each, crackers, beans, and cherries). The moon rose as we were sitting by the fire, and thin, low clouds drifted swiftly across the sky—a Florida night at its best.

Friday, March 14

We lit a fire for breakfast, and finished the rest of our left-over corned beef, padded out with a slice of bread, crackers, and a half grapefruit each. Just as we were finishing, Anne heard Jim blowing the boat's fog-horn—the signal we had agreed upon. We ran out, climbed up on an old abandoned pier and waved. We thought Jim saw us as he dropped anchor in the channel on the near side of Indian Key. But we learned later that he had not seen us and had anchored in that position to obtain shelter from the wind. We struck camp and pulled the dinghy over 200 feet of coral beach, as the tide was low. The water between the keys was choppy and our small dinghy was packed full; but we made the boat without shipping water. As soon as we had stowed our equipment we hoisted sail and with a following wind set our course for Shark River. We arrived after dark and anchored near a fisherman's lighter about a half mile up the river.

Saturday, March 15

We cruised through the end of Tarpon Bay and up Shark River—part of the time by sail alone. With the motor off we could approach very close to the birds before they flew away. At sunset we found ourselves at the edge of a large savanna, where we decided to spend the night.

Sunday, March 16

We all went swimming before breakfast, then decided to take the dinghy on ahead to see whether there was any object in cutting our way farther through the branches. (They looked thicker ahead.) We found that the stream we were following ran into a larger river a mile or so beyond our anchorage. There would be a great deal of cutting to do before we could get through with the big boat; but it would be fun, and we decided to try it. Spent most of the afternoon cutting branches—some as much as eight inches in diameter. We could cut most of them from the boat, but in some places Jim or I had to climb the trees. We hacked away with the hatchet tied to our wrist by a cord, as it was the only one we had on the boat.

Monday and Tuesday, March 17 and 18

We went swimming and then lay in the sun for a time after breakfast. Later, we weighed anchor, hoisted sail, and drifted along toward the Gulf in a light wind. As noon approached the wind died, and we had to start the engine. We took up a course to Dry Tortugas, cruising with the engine, as there was not enough wind to sail. We decided to run two-hour watches until midnight; then I would take the 12:00 to 4:00 and Anne the 4:00 to 8:00. That would give her the daybreak watch, which I was very anxious for her to have. The daybreak watch is the most difficult, but it is also the most romantic, and in some ways the most beautiful.

Navigating a boat or flying a plane into the dawn and sunrise is worth all the cold, cramped, and wearisome hours that lead up to it. One cannot appreciate the dawn without those hours, without fatigue, without feeling and seeing the night pass. One cannot "get up in time to see the sunrise." Such a sunrise is an artificial thing—only a step better than a sunrise reproduced in a motion-picture theater. To *see* the sun rise, or the dawn, one must experience it as a part of one's day or night—not as a single and special objective in itself. When you get up "to see the sunrise," you stare at it without fully seeing or appreciating. When the sunrise comes as a real part of your day and your work, you seem hardly to look at it, and yet it is only under these circumstances that you feel and fully appreciate what it means.

We cooked dinner as well as we could; then I took the tiller at 8:00 to relieve Anne. The wind rose during my shift, so we hoisted sail and shut off the engine. It was following and puffy and made steering difficult. At first, I held my course by the stars, checking occasionally with the compass, but low, thin clouds began to drift past overhead, becoming more and more numerous until at times the sky was completely overcast. Then it was necessary to use the compass alone; and that was difficult because we had no compass light. A flashlight held in the hand is a poor substitute.

Jim took the 10:00 to 12:00 shift, and then I went back on at 12:00. The wind had freshened and was very puffy, but the sky had cleared, with only a few clouds remaining. I started out with Aldebaran on the starboard bow. Then Bellatrix, Betelgeuse, the pointers of Orion, Rigel, and Procyon slowly crossed over as the night passed. But by the third hour of my watch the sky was again overcast. It had clouded up gradually until not a star showed through.

The continuing wind had thrown up a choppy sea, and it was very difficult to hold the ship on course. To make matters worse, the wind had shifted to a point where the sails were ready to jibe at any instant. The lack of a compass light just topped things off. It seemed that every time I pressed the flashlight button I was ten degrees off course. Then another wave would hit us, and the compass card would swing twenty degrees in the opposite direction. I was blinded for a time after I turned the flashlight off, so I could not see the sails in the darkness. But if I left the light on, it was almost certain the battery would not last until morning. It was a case of making the best possible compromise with a ship inadequately equipped for night sailing. The accuracy of my course suffered considerably as a result.

I turned the tiller over to Anne at 4:00, wondering whether four hours under those conditions would not be too much of a strain for her. But she wanted to take the full watch. I made her a cup of hot coffee and turned in. The ship rolled so much that I had to wedge myself in the bunk to keep from sliding off. Sleep was almost impossible. Jim took over at 8:00. The wind had dropped, so he started the engine again.

When we had logged one hundred miles (statute; our log, for some reason, is set for statute miles), we picked up a lighthouse about ten miles off our port beam. We took it for Isaac Light and continued on course. But after an hour's sailing, Dry Tortugas Light did not show up. Obviously something was wrong with our navigation, so we turned back and set course for the lighthouse we had passed. It turned out to be Dry Tortugas and not Isaac. We were fully ten miles off course and twenty miles ahead of our log reading.

Pretty poor navigation, but, considering all circumstances, it was not surprising. We had swung the compass roughly by the North Star one night in the Everglades (the deviation was 28° on a 90° magnetic course, and we had only swung on four points); the accuracy of our course through the night was doubtful, and our log had never been calibrated. We were told it read in statute miles, but that seemed strange at the time. If it reads in nautical miles, it is not so far off. The fact is that when one starts out with a strange ship and without adequate preparation for navigation, one cannot expect to steer an accurate course. We were in a hurry to start our trip, and now we are paying for our carelessness. Still, what difference does a few miles off course make on a vacation (except to one's pride)? There is nothing to hit, and one cannot very well get lost with the keys to the south and coast of Florida to turn back to.

As we approached the keys of Dry Tortugas the engine began to "pink" and smoke. We turned it off and hoisted sail. The wind was strong and the sea choppy. Jim took the tiller, and Anne and I handled the sails. We got thoroughly soaked and put on rather an amateur exhibition, jibing up to an anchorage in front of Fort Jefferson an hour or two before sunset. However, we were glad to be in a sheltered harbor and not on one of the numerous coral reefs surrounding it. One soon learns that the proper handling of a sailboat requires both experience and skill.

Wednesday, March 19

Breakfast of fried eggs, bacon, coffee, bread, butter, and jam. When we had finished, Jim took the dinghy to shore to get the "lay of the land," while Anne and I cleaned up the dishes and boat. After an hour he came back with fifty pounds of ice from a fishing yawl which had come in to avoid the wind and high seas.

Jim told us of his conversation with the superintendent of the Park Service at Fort Jefferson—a Mr. [James] Felton. It seems the old fort is now being restored as a W.P.A. project. Anne and I had never heard of Fort Jefferson before we arrived at Dry Tortugas. It is a huge, red-brick structure, rising abruptly out of the sea. The sand and coral island on which it is built cannot be seen until one has approached within a few miles. Until the streak of yellow beach shows up it seems that the fortress rises out of the sea itself—like a mirage rising from open ocean. The fort, it seems, was started in 1847 as a deterrent to British men-of-war, who might otherwise have had interests along the Gulf Coast. American warships and raiders could be anchored safely under the guns of the fort.

But politics, inefficiency, and bad luck seem to have dogged the project from its conception. Although the construction of the fort was begun in 1847, its guns were not adequately mounted when the Civil War broke out. According to the superintendent's story, a single Confederate warship sailed up to Dry Tortugas and demanded that the Union garrison surrender. Not a gun was in place at the time, but the Union commander sent word that he would blow the Confederate ship out of the water if she did not depart at once, and won through his bluff. (Personally, I would want to check this report pretty carefully before accepting it, although the superintendent is an able man and obviously has quite a detailed knowledge of the fort's history.)

After the Civil War Dr. Mudd,[236] who treated Booth after Lincoln's assassination, was imprisoned in Fort Jefferson. While he was there, a yellow-fever epidemic broke out, affecting about half of the garrison of 1,500, and ending fatally for about fifteen per cent of those affected. During this epidemic the theory was advanced that the "miasma" of yellow fever could be blown away if openings were made in the walls of the fort, through which the wind could enter. As a result, great holes were knocked through the brick walls around the cannon ports in the second tier—adding to the abandoned and dilapidated appearance of the structure.

About the end of the nineteenth century the Army decided that enough money had been spent on Dry Tortugas—somewhere around $40 million, it is said—and the Navy took over the key, fort, and harbor. But it was not long before the Navy, too, abandoned the place. Then a salvage company destroyed the interior buildings—barracks and officers' quarters in the parade grounds enclosed by the walls of the fort. Then an Army officer was sent to finish demolishing the interior buildings. He used both dynamite and fire, but left the place in far worse condition than before he arrived—cracked walls and sagging roofs.

From that time on, the place was left to yachting parties and vandals until, one day early in his Administration, President Roosevelt arrived at Dry Tortugas on a warship fishing party. He saw Fort Jefferson and decided to make it part of his "Park Project" program. Now, more money is being poured into the place to restore it as a "historical monument" of

236. Dr. Samuel A. Mudd, who lived near Bryantown, Md., had set John Wilkes Booth's broken leg and harbored him in his home for several hours during Booth's flight from Washington after the assassination of Lincoln. Dr. Mudd was brought to trial with seven other defendants in May, 1865, on charges of conspiring to assassinate the President. He was found guilty and sentenced to imprisonment in the military prison at Dry Tortugas, Fla. In 1869 Dr. Mudd was pardoned.

the United States. (It seems to me a singularly befitting monument to the "New Deal.")

After lunch I started working on the engine. It was hard to get at, and I had to work in a cramped and inefficient position. I found the overheating had been caused by a small hole rusted through the exhaust-manifold water jacket. I plugged it up with a piece of pine wood, cut to shape, and hope it will last for our trip home.

The wind shifted in the afternoon, so we moved our anchorage to the lee of Bush Key. By that time it was too late to visit the fort before dark, so Jim, Anne, and I went for a half hour's walk on Bush Key instead. We saw two or three old wrecks of fishing boats and a large sea turtle that waddled down into the water as we approached.

Thursday, March 20

The wind shifted during the night, and our boat rolled heavily. It was difficult to sleep, as one's body tended to roll to the low side of the bunk, and a conscious effort was necessary in order to stay put. We shifted anchorage to the lee side of Bush Key before we started breakfast. Afterward, we all went ashore for a walk along the key. It is still too rough for diving. (We have a helmet, pump, and forty feet of hose.)

In the afternoon we took the dinghy to Garden Key. Mr. Felton went with us on a tour of Fort Jefferson. The place depresses me more than ever. It seems to exude failure and desperation. It also reminds me of the qualities I dislike most in contemporary American life—emphasis on size, number of guns, and formidable appearance. It was a tremendous project, but apparently never very effective. It is like a house much too big for the family that built it and never lived in properly by anybody else. Now it is to be a government monument. A monument to what? Political red tape and military failure? Or to just the quality of bigness? My idea of a monument implies the connection with something accomplished—something one wishes to honor and to remember.

Friday, March 21

It was sunny and clear when we woke, and the wind had dropped. We ate a quick breakfast, then cruised out to Hospital Key, where we dropped anchor on the lee side in about fifteen feet of water. The water was still a little riled from the waves of the last several days, but we could see bottom quite clearly. We got out the diving outfit, and Jim and I matched for first one down. Neither of us had done any diving before. Jim won. Anne pumped, and I lowered the helmet on over his head as he hung on to the gunnel. He lowered himself down on the anchor rope until his feet touched bottom, then walked slowly away from the boat as I played out the rope and hose. Jim made several dives, and then Anne went next. On her second dive she went out to the end of the forty-foot hose. I had to jerk on it to bring her back. She finally came up holding a small piece of coral in one hand.

I was last down. The helmet did not seem heavy once I was under water, and it was not difficult to breath, although it seemed I had the tendency to breath more deeply and with less frequency. The great difficulty was in walking, for the helmet made it impossible to see where I was stepping unless I bent over to look down. And when I bent over, a big bubble of air would escape from the helmet and the water level in it would rise unpleasantly high. On a level bottom walking would have been simple enough, but with sharp coral growths all around and numerous sea porcupines underfoot, it was necessary to be careful. At times I tried squatting down so I could get a better view of the seaweed and coral. There were many small and brilliantly colored fish. My presence did not seem to bother them at all. I pulled up a small piece of coral to take back to the boat. I found that one has to develop a new sense of distance under water. Things are not where they seem to be at first when you reach for them.

I went down twice—about ten minutes the first time and fifteen minutes the second. Then we moved the boat to a new location, and Jim went down again. He reported the bottom not as interesting as at our previous anchorage; so we gave up diving for the day and cruised around the fort to Bird Key Bay, where we anchored and took the dinghy out to hunt for crawfish. We located some big round coral heads in about four feet of water with "feelers" sticking out from under them. Jim and I jumped overboard with the spear and got several medium-sized crawfish. Then Anne and Jim went off in the dinghy to look for more coral heads. I kept the spear and waded through the shallower water near the reefs. Some places the bottom was sandy, and some places it was covered with a coral growth several inches high—sharp and crunchy.

I found a three-foot shark under one head in about four feet of water. He swam off leisurely after I touched him with the end of the spear pole.

A little later I noticed a barracuda just out of spear range ahead of me. It was about as long as the shark but of course very slender. Suddenly it was gone, leaving no sign but a swirl on the surface of the water where it had been. I would have paid little attention to the barracuda had it not reappeared several times on different sides and about the same distance from me. I would see it motionless in the water for an instant, and then it would be gone. Suddenly I realized that it was circling round and round like a wolf, with me as its object of interest. It gave me an uncomfortable feeling, although I recalled that the "natives" in these parts say barracuda are curious and will come near you when you are in swimming, but that they "never bother anyone." Nevertheless, it seems to me that I have read reports that show pretty clearly that barracuda have bothered people on occasion.

I was in water up to my chest at the time. My first thought was to spear the barracuda, but he stayed too far away and was much too quick. The only thing to do was to wade nonchalantly toward shore, and this I did without delaying longer. I could see the barracuda plainly as the water became shallower, and since I was fully 200 yards from shore when I first noticed him, I had plenty of time to observe carefully. He circled swiftly, round and round, always fifteen or twenty feet away—just out of spear range. He stayed with me until the water was not more than knee deep.

Before long Anne and Jim came back with the dinghy. They had located more coral heads, with a number of large crawfish beside and beneath them. They had returned for the spear. We got one huge crawfish. He must have weighed four or five pounds. He was at the side of a big coral head, and there were many more underneath it. We could tell that from the "feelers" sticking out on every side.

Before cooking supper, we moved the yawl back to our usual anchorage near the fort. On the way we passed a dozen or more large fish, three to three and a half feet long. We might have speared one of them easily, but we already had enough for supper.

Saturday, March 22

Overcast and light rain. Breakfast of coffee and grits. We are getting short of food: no eggs; last end of ham spoiled; only one can of meat left, etc., etc. With care, however, we can get along comfortably for several more days, and by that time we must be on our way home. Jim to

Fort Jefferson in the evening. Anne and I stayed on the boat to experiment with white-flour pancakes. They turned out well and add one more item to our rather short menu. We are getting a bit tired of crab tails.

Monday and Tuesday, March 24 and 25

After breakfast we cleaned up the boat and started home. Light wind and partly overcast sky. We used both sails and engine. Jim caught a mackerel as we passed over the shoals of Dry Tortugas—just large enough for a light lunch. We started watches at 8:00 (Anne 8:00–12:00; Jim 12:00–4:00; I 4:00–8:00). The wind rose early in the evening, and we shut off the engine. Sea became choppy. Hard to sleep, due to rolling about in bunk. Nearly fell out once. The sky was completely overcast by the time my watch started. Had to steer entirely by compass, but it was not difficult, as I had rigged up a compass light during the previous afternoon.

Wednesday, March 26

State police clash with pickets at Bethlehem, Pennsylvania. Yugoslavia signs pact with Germany and Italy at Vienna. Unrest reported in Yugoslavia. United States freezes Yugoslavian credits.

Cruised through inland waters to Gordon Pass. Canal lined with mangrove and hundreds of birds. Stopped at Gordon Pass to inquire about position of channel going out. The buoys were out of place at Gordon Pass also, and one marker flag had blown over. We had to be careful, as there were only five and a half feet of water in the channel, and the breakers gave little or no indication of where it lay.

Sail and engine to Fort Myers Beach. Arrived just before sunset. To Fort Myers Beach Hotel after supper for a visit with the Newtons. We had planned on staying over tomorrow; but Mrs. Newton has inquired about reservations, and was informed that the only Pullman room we could get between now and Saturday was on the 10:00 A.M. train tomorrow, and that was available only because an extra car had been added at the last minute. We decided to leave in the morning. We cannot ride in an open car without being bothered for autographs, introductions, etc., etc., until it spoils any pleasure in a trip; and we really must get home before Sunday.

Thursday, March 27

Jim drove us to Fort Myers, and we boarded the train for New York.

Friday, March 28

Press reports pro-Axis regime overthrown in Yugoslavia. Peter now in power. C.I.O. strikes continue.

Arrived New York about 2:30. Taxi to garage where I had left the Mercury. One of the men there recognized me and came up to say he had read my "Letter to Americans" in *Collier's* and thoroughly agreed with my stand. Said a lot of other men around there did also. Met Anne at Cosmopolitan Club and drove out to Lloyd Neck. Jon and Land met us at the door. I gave each of them a coconut—the present Jon said he wanted most when we left for Florida. Anne gave them the shells she brought back. Little Anne has changed a great deal. We do not realize how fast she is growing when we are with her every day.

Sunday, March 30

British claim heavy damage to Italian fleet in Mediterranean. British success in Ethiopia continues. Bristol raided. Tension increases between Yugoslavia and Berlin.

Ed Webster came for lunch. He wants me to take the national chairmanship of America First. Says I will receive a letter from General Wood shortly, asking me to do this. I told Webster I would gladly work with America First and assist the committee in any way possible, but that I felt it would be a mistake for me to take the national chairmanship at this time, if at all. I told him that if I took the national chairmanship, I would have to give up the type of work I am now doing, that I could not write and make addresses on the war and at the same time carry on the executive duties that would be required. After I outlined my reasons Webster agreed and suggested I take the honorary chairmanship or some other office. I told him I would consider that, but I felt it would probably be enough for me to join the national committee—that I could do as much in that capacity as in any other.

Monday, March 31

United States seizes thirty-five Danish, twenty-eight Italian, and two German ships. French shore batteries fire on British warships. British claim three Italian cruisers and two destroyers sunk in Mediterranean.

Letter arrived from General Wood, asking me to take the national chairmanship of the America First Committee.

Tuesday, April 1

Germany and Italy protest seizure of ships and arrest of crews.

Spent first part of morning on dictation and other routine; then drove to New York for lunch with Mr. [William L.] Chenery and two other officers of *Collier's* at the University Club. They suggested that I write another article for *Collier's*—on the air-training program in this country. But I have not time. They said the mail they received in regard to my "Letter to Americans" was possibly the largest they had ever received concerning a *Collier's* article. The mail addressed to *Collier's* was, they said, about two to one in support of their publishing the article; while the mail addressed directly to me was nearly twenty to one in support of the article itself.

Wednesday, April 2

Strikes continue. Serious trouble at Ford plant. Strikers battle police at Allis-Chalmers plant. War expected between Germany and Yugoslavia. British admit 59,000-ton shipping loss for week ending March 23; Germans claim 397,000-ton British shipping loss for that week. New York Herald Tribune comes out for policy of "war if necessary."

Drove to New York for 5:00 meeting with General Wood at the Waldorf-Astoria. We discussed America First and his letter asking me to replace him as chairman. I told him I thought it would weaken the organization greatly if he resigned as chairman, and I outlined my objections to taking the chairmanship myself. We talked until 5:30; then I phoned Bob Stuart, who had come to New York with General Wood, and asked him and several of his friends for dinner at the Miyako. We discussed America First plans during the dinner. Then I took Stuart to the Engineers Club for a half hour's conference with him alone. Wanted to talk to him about America First and also to get to know him a little better personally.

Monday, April 7

German armies advance into Yugoslavia. Belgrade bombed. British capture Addis Ababa.

Webster came for supper and the evening to discuss America First problems—internal friction in committees, etc., etc. It is essential not to have the announcement of my membership in the committee coincide with the outbreak of internal trouble. Our opposition would be only too quick to make use of such a situation. I decided to feel my way slowly in regard to the America First connection—to burn no bridges unnecessarily.

Spent the evening reading and going through some boxes of old papers. Found an envelope containing a lavender and gold handkerchief Anne dropped one night when we were sitting together in the embassy parlor at Mexico City before we were married. I picked it up when she left and never returned it to her.

Thursday, April 10

German drive nears Albania. German and Italian forces claim recapture of Tobruk. Heavy air raids over England. Churchill asks for United States convoys.

Bob Stuart called from Chicago in regard to an America First Committee meeting in Chicago on April 17. I agreed to go there to speak. William S. Thomas (son of Norman Thomas[237]) came for dinner and to discuss his plans for the Oyster Bay chapter of the America First Committee.

237. American Socialist leader, reformer, and author. After 1928 he was repeatedly the Socialist Party candidate for President, polling his highest vote (800,000) in 1932.

Friday, April 11

United States takes over the "protection" of Greenland. German advance continues in Yugoslavia and Greece—claim capture of many prisoners. Germans and Italians claim capture of British force in Libya, including commanding general. R.A.F. claims heavy raid on Berlin.

A huge, blood-red moon rose in the evening. It made me think of Europe and bombed cities. Whenever I see the moon now, I think of the bombing that is going on over there. As the moon rises here, it is high over Europe, and bombs are almost certainly falling on English and German cities.

Wednesday, April 16

Hitler and Mussolini recognize "independent" state of Croatia. Yugoslavian armies are reported collapsing. German advance continues in Greece and Egypt. Italian troops in Ethiopia ask terms of surrender.

Off [Washington] train at 7:45. Worked on address for an hour. Then to Harry Byrd's office for a half hour's conference. We discussed the war and trends in this country. Byrd thinks the trend is away from intervention; says the people are at last seeing the futility of our entering the war.

To Senator Tobey's[238] office for half hour's conference. Discussed his anticonvoy bill and other plans for blocking intervention.

Boarded 5:45 train for Chicago.

Thursday, April 17

London heavily bombed—"worst raid of the war." Germans continue to advance in Greece. British sink Axis troop convoy in Mediterranean.

Off train about 8:30. Taxi to Chicago Club, where I met Bob Stuart. We went over arrangements and plans for the dinner this evening. Conferences with various people until 4:00. General Wood arrived at 4:00 to

238. Charles William Tobey, Republican Senator from New Hampshire.

discuss the schedule for tonight. Dinner at 6:30 with about thirty America First supporters.

Arrived at auditorium at 8:00. Songs. Then General Wood introduced Mr. Pettingill,[239] who made a forceful but slightly too long extemporaneous speech. General Hammond [240] spoke next. Then General Wood introduced me, and I spoke for about twenty-five minutes. Well received; enthusiastic crowd. Had expected considerable opposition, but there was practically none. (In fact, I had thought there might be some fighting and was surprised by the orderliness of the crowd. Was also surprised by the amount of anti-British feeling in Chicago.) The hall was jammed— crowd estimated at 10,000 to 11,000 inside and about 4,000 outside. After the meeting I drove with General Wood and his daughter, Anne, to his home on the lake for the night.

Friday, April 18

Yugoslavian armies capitulate.

Conference with Judge Grace at 10:15. Discussed the friction between his organization and America First and means of improving the situation. It has been caused by a lack of tact and time. Stuart and Pettingill for lunch in room. Discussed America First plans and problems and methods of co-operating with other antiwar organizations. Conferences until 3:00. Then to America First offices with Stuart. Met personnel. Stuart and I to President Hutchins' [241] home for dinner with President and Mrs. Hutchins. Very informal; trays on lap in parlor.

Boarded night train to Detroit.

Saturday, April 19

Off train at 7:50. Taxi to 508 Lakepointe for breakfast with Mother and B. Spent most of morning and afternoon working on New York address. Evening in parlor with Mother and B.—listening to phonograph music

239. Samuel B. Pettengill, former Democratic Representative from Indiana.

240. General Thomas S. Hammond, manufacturer, and leader of the Chicago chapter of America First.

241. Robert M. Hutchins, president and chancellor of the University of Chicago, 1929–51.

and going over Great-grandfather Lodge's old diary (1843). It covers very briefly his trip to this country from England and skips through many years of his life—very finely written—seldom more than a single line in a day, and many gaps in the record.

Sunday, April 20

Germans take Mount Olympus and Larissa.

Spent part of day on address and the rest with Mother and B. The address did not go well. I could not seem to get the right start—probably too soon after the last one to have a fresh mind. Early supper; then Mother and B. drove me to the station, and I boarded the 7:00 train for New York. Worked on address until 11:30. Then read Dostoevsky for fifteen minutes before going to sleep.

Wednesday, April 23

Germans reach Thermopylae. British warships shell Tripoli.

Spent morning on routine—phoning about arrangements for the meeting tonight, putting final touches on address, etc.

Anne and I drove to New York in time for a 6:00 dinner at Ed Webster's home at Beekman Place. After dinner we all took taxis to Manhattan Center, arriving just before 8:00. The street in front was jammed. We went to the back entrance, but found a crowd of over a hundred people around it, too. [John] Flynn went ahead to arrange with one of the police officers to let us in. He had considerable difficulty persuading the officer that he was the chairman of the meeting and that he had all of the speakers with him, but finally convinced the officer that he was not just one more man trying to bluff his way in. Even with police assistance we had a hard time wedging our way through the crowd.

The hall was jammed when we arrived; a second hall upstairs in the building was nearly full, and several thousand people were in the street outside. The police estimated 5,500 in the main hall, 2,000 in the upper hall, and 15,000 to 20,000 in Thirty-fourth Street. The hall was decorated with American flags everywhere. Mrs. Marquand opened the meeting. Flynn presided. Senator George spoke for forty minutes, Mrs.

Norris[242] for fifteen minutes, and I spoke for twenty-five minutes. The crowd seemed one hundred per cent with us. It was courteous and good-humored and, I think, represented an unusually good cross section of New York. As in Chicago, there was considerable anti-British feeling. I think it is due to pent-up emotion and a feeling of frustration—a feeling that we are being pushed into war regardless of how the people feel about it, and that England is largely responsible for the mess we are being dragged into. It results from resentment against British interference with American life and affairs.

Thursday, April 24

Greek government moves to Crete. German Army nears Athens. Unrest in Australia and New Zealand.

Anne and I to New York for 7:30 cocktails at the Marquands' apartment. Dinner at the home of Mrs. Marquand's mother, Mrs. [Elon Huntington] Hooker (mother of Anne's old Chapin School friend Helen Hooker), at 620 Park Avenue. The dinner was in honor of General [Frank] Aiken, Irish Minister of War. There were present: Mrs. Hooker, General Aiken, Mr. and Mrs. Marquand, the Archibald Roosevelts, the John Rockefellers,[243] the John T. Flynns, and ourselves.

I had very little chance to talk to Aiken—always too many people around—but we had a few minutes together just as people were leaving. Also, he discussed the Irish position fairly freely at the dinner table. He says Ireland is fearful of an invasion by either England or Germany and that he is not sure which one is most likely to try it first. He is over here in an attempt to get arms and food for Ireland and has met with little success. I told Aiken it seemed to me a German invasion of Ireland would be extremely difficult because of her geographical position. He thought it might be done by planes or by fast boat in order to attack England on two sides. When we were alone, Aiken told me he was very much in accord with the stand I have taken on the war. Among other things, he told me that the loss of British shipping was much higher than

242. Kathleen Norris, author and novelist.

243. Grandson of John D. Rockefeller, active in business and philanthropic interests. Trustee of the Rockefeller Institute for Medical Research, former trustee and chairman of the Rockefeller Foundation, later president of the Rockefeller Brothers' Fund. Mrs. Rockefeller was the former Blanchette Hooker, friend of Anne Morrow Lindbergh.

admitted, and that most of it was occurring quite close to the British Isles. He said aircraft were responsible for a constantly increasing percentage of total losses.

Friday, April 25

Knox says the war "is our fight." Hull says we must get full aid to Britain now.

The pressure for convoys is rising. The Gallup Poll carries strange contradictions. More than eighty per cent of the people, it appears, are opposed to our entering the war; but seventy-one per cent are for convoys, if Britain would otherwise lose. Yet the poll published only three days ago indicated that a majority of Americans are against sending any part of our Army, Navy, or Air Corps to aid Britain. Either people are confused, or the questions of the poll confuse them, or both.

Deac Lyman phoned in the late afternoon to tell me that Roosevelt had attacked me personally in his press conference. A few minutes later Webster phoned and said that, among other things, Roosevelt had implied treason in connection with my name.

I sent for the afternoon papers. The President's attack was more than just a political attack, for he did so in connection with my commission in the Army. If it had been only a political attack, without any connection with my commission, I would pay little attention to it. As it is, a point of honor is at stake, and it may be necessary to tender my resignation. But I don't like to resign, for my commission in the Air Corps has always meant a great deal to me, and I would prefer to hold it.

What luck it is to find myself opposing my country's entrance into a war I *don't* believe in, when I would so much rather be fighting for my country in a war I *do* believe in. Here I am stumping the country with pacifists and considering resigning as a colonel in the Army Air Corps, when there is no philosophy I disagree with more than that of the pacifist, and nothing I would rather be doing than flying in the Air Corps.

If only the United States could be on the *right* side of an intelligent war! There *are* wars worth fighting, but if we get in this one, we will bring disaster to the country and possibly to our entire civilization. If we get into this war and really fight, nothing but chaos will result. If we enter this war, it won't be like the last, and God knows what will happen here before we finish it—race riots, revolution, destruction; America is not immune to any of these. But for some reason—ignorance, vanity, blindness, or whatever it may be—we seem to think we *are* immune to these things.

Sometimes I feel like saying, "Well, let's get into the war if you are so anxious to. Then the responsibility will be yours." In comparison to the work I am now doing the fighting would be fun. But my mind tells me that we better face our problems and let Europe face hers without getting messed up in this war. I have an interest in Western civilization, and I have an interest in my race, or culture, or whatever you want to call it, and I have an interest in the type of world my children are going to live in. That is why I will probably stay on the stump with the pacifists and why I will resign my commission if necessary and never regret my action in doing so. This war is a mistake; we will only bring disaster if we enter it; we will do no good either to Europe or ourselves, and therefore I am going to put everything I have behind staying out.

No one, not even Germany, was more responsible for the conditions which caused this war than England and France. They declared the war without consulting us. If it were possible to help them win, the result would probably be Versailles all over again. Europe must straighten out her own family affairs. Our interference would simply cause another postponement, as the last war did. Europe faces adjustments that must be made, and only she can work out what they are going to be.

I decided to go to Washington to discuss the question of resigning with several of my Army friends there. Drove to New York and boarded the 12:50 train for Washington.

Saturday, April 26

British are evacuating Greece. Fall of Athens expected soon. Roosevelt announces extension of "neutrality patrol."

Off train at 7:15. Breakfast with Truman and Kay. Truman at first definitely against my resignation. Later, he saw some of the points I raised, but when I left he was still opposed to my resignation, although less so. He agreed that a point of honor was involved, but did not think it necessitated resigning.

To Senate Office Building for a quarter hour's conference with Senator Clark of Missouri. He is just back from a speaking tour through the Southwest. Says sentiment is rising against war, but "no one knows what Roosevelt will do next." Boarded 6:00 train to New York.

Sunday, April 27

Roosevelt to extend American "neutrality patrol" and to take additional transport planes from our airlines for British use. British forces are evacuating Greece. Large portion of civilian population is being evacuated from Plymouth.

Have decided to resign. After studying carefully what the President said, I feel it is the only honorable course to take. If I did not tender my resignation, I would lose something in my own character that means even more to me than my commission in the Air Corps. No one else might know it, but I would. And if I take this insult from Roosevelt, more, and worse, will probably be forthcoming. Spent most of the day drafting my letter of resignation and working on manuscript. (One letter to Roosevelt and one to Stimson.[244])

Monday, April 28

German Army enters Athens.

Mailed letters of resignation this morning. Spent rest of day on routine, working on St. Louis address, another reading of Anne's manuscript, phone calls, etc.

Wednesday, April 30

Roosevelt implies that the "neutrality patrol" has been further extended. Long-range guns bombard Dover.

Read Dostoevsky in the evening. Certainly the Russian has a viewpoint on life far different from that of the Central and Western European. Possibly one should consider the Russian as midway between the European and the Oriental. We do not expect to understand the outlook of the Oriental, but the Russian is sufficiently European to mislead us. We always expect to understand him better than we do.

244. Henry L. Stimson, Secretary of State (1929–33) under President Herbert Hoover; Secretary of War, 1940–45.

Thursday, May 1

The pressure for war is high and mounting. The people are opposed to it, but the Administration seems to have "the bit in its teeth" and hell-bent on its way to war. Most of the Jewish interests in the country are behind war, and they control a huge part of our press and radio and most of our motion pictures. There are also the "intellectuals," and the "Anglophiles," and the British agents who are allowed free rein, the international financial interests, and many others.

Friday, May 2

Jim and I left for New York at 12:45 after an early lunch. He dropped me at Pennsylvania Station, where I boarded the 2:45 train for St. Louis. Ate a sandwich supper to avoid going to the diner, and the bother it usually involves.

Saturday, May 3

Fighting starts in Iraq. Cabinet shake-up reported in England. Hamburg, Liverpool, and other cities heavily bombed. American Legion backs convoys.

Off train at 8:40 C.S.T. Taxi to Park Plaza Hotel. Dinner at 6:00 with about fifty men and women interested in America First.

The Arena, our meeting place, was full except for about 1,500 seats at the far end. There were about 15,000 people present, although the meeting had not been well advertised. Senator Clark spoke first. Then General Wood introduced me. I had not timed my speech for a radio broadcast and spoke four minutes overtime—the first time I have ever done it. Must be more careful in the future. We had a fine and enthusiastic crowd.

Back to the hotel for a "buffet supper." Hundreds of people—all types. Shook hands until train time. There are few things I dislike more than shaking hands with an endless line of people. Your hand gets sore, and everybody says silly things because there isn't time to speak sensibly. You get hot and packed in with people who are also hot and tired. There is something clean and sharp and right about addressing a meeting. But one of these "buffet suppers" or "cocktail parties" seems to me a kind of prostitution of human effort, no matter how nice the people taking part may be. A meeting, such as we had at the Arena, at least gives birth to thought, and expression to enthusiasm. But I don't know what the value of the "buffet supper" was. Possibly it will bring money and support to the St. Louis America First chapter; if so, it was probably worth while attending. But if it weren't for the intensity of my feeling about this war, no amount of money, or persuasion, or anything else, could get me to attend such things.

Boarded the 12:05 train for Chicago with General Wood and Bob Stuart.

Sunday, May 4

Twenty-six American freighters loaded with war supplies are reported at Suez.

Off train at 7:00. Then drove with General Wood to his home on the shore of Lake Michigan. We went for a half hour's walk along the beach, while we discussed the war and plans for America First. In the afternoon I drove with Bob and Barbara Stuart to Stuart, Sr.'s[245] farm weekend home in the country. Mr. and Mrs. Stuart, Sr., and three daughters were there when we arrived. Family supper. Then all the Stuarts left, and I was alone for the night. (I asked Bob Stuart to find me a quiet place where I could write my address for Minneapolis on the tenth. From all appearances this will be ideal.)

Monday, May 5

Cologne, Liverpool, Belfast, and other cities bombed.

Spent the day working on my address, and several walks through the fields. One sees much more walking alone. On my first walk this morning I suddenly realized that the fields had a very familiar appearance. And then I remembered that these were the fields, or rather just like the fields outside of Detroit, that my grandfather took me to on Sundays when I

245. R. Douglas Stuart, first vice president of Quaker Oats Co., Chicago.

was a child. It all came back so clearly it seemed he was there beside me, that if I turned my head he would be there, walking along with his paper bag for mushrooms in one hand and a bunch of wild flowers in the other. I imagined for a moment it was really thirty years ago and that all that had happened in between was just a dream. And it seemed I saw through childish eyes again. We were among the fields of Seven Mile Road (it is all built up now) on a Sunday morning, walking on the spring-green grass. Now we were passing through an open gate and into a tree-filled pasture. There were patches of wake-robins and dandelions, and here and there a few jack-in-the-pulpits. The roots of the oaks were lost in violets. Two wild ducks flew up from one of the pools left over from a recent rain. My feet sank into the damp dead leaves and mold as I crossed its edge. A turtle slipped into the water from a fallen branch, and a frightened rabbit hopped away into the wood.

Tuesday, May 6

British claim bomb hits on Scharnhorst *and* Gneisenau *at Brest. British forces gain in Iraq. Heavy Axis air activity reported over Crete. Roosevelt orders increase in aircraft production, especially bombers.*

Spent the day working on my address. Several walks through the fields between showers. Mr. Stuart, Sr., came for a half hour's visit after supper. We spent most of the time discussing the war. He is by no means in agreement with his son's outlook, and is apparently not too happy about Bob's position in America First.

Wednesday, May 7

Stimson urges the use of American warships for convoys to Britain.

Spent the day on my address and several walks through the woods and fields.

Thursday, May 8

German Air Force raids Liverpool for seventh consecutive night. House passes "ship seizure bill" 266 to 120.

Drove to Chicago for a conference with Stuart and Bill Benton[246] at the America First offices.

Friday, May 9

Heavy air raids over England. British claim thirty-nine German planes brought down.

To Chicago in the afternoon for a conference with Colonel McCormick and Bob Stuart at the Tribune Building. We discussed America First and war trends. Colonel McCormick has given us excellent backing with his paper.

Saturday, May 10

Berlin, Hamburg, Bremen, and other German cities heavily raided. Germans retaliate on Liverpool, Hull, and other English cities. British government announces April shipping loss at 488,124 tons. "Alien raids" continue in the United States. British gaining in Iraq.

Spent most of morning on phone calls: Lewis, Landon, Taft,[247] and others. Then to the airport, where Bob Stuart, Dick Moore,[248] and I boarded the North West Airlines plane for Minneapolis. Except for a slight haze near Chicago and a few scattered clouds en route, the weather was clear. It is strange to me, this flying as a passenger in a modern transport—nothing to do and rather unpleasantly screened from the outside air and the ground below. It has none of the "feel" of flying that I have always loved so much. I can't help thinking of the preface I wrote in England for *Listen! the Wind.* Today I felt what I then foresaw. In the cabin of these transports one is insulated from the elements. And it is the very contact it used to have with the elements that made flying in those early planes such an attraction for me. Riding in a modern transport

246. William Benton, co-founder of Benton & Bowles, advertising agency, and vice president of the University of Chicago, 1937–45; Assistant Secretary of State, 1945–47; Democratic Senator from Connecticut, 1949–53. In 1943 he became chairman and publisher of the Encyclopaedia Britannica.

247. Robert A. Taft, Republican Senator from Ohio, 1939–53, an expert in financial affairs. In 1952 he was a leading contender for the Republican presidential nomination.

248. Richard A. Moore, assistant national director of America First.

plane is strangely like riding the train in a subway. In an aisle seat you see and feel about as much in the one as in the other.

We were met at the Minneapolis airport by various members of the local America First Committee and driven to the La Salle Hotel, where I was given the "Nordic Suite"! What a press story that could make! But "Nordic" out here doesn't mean what it does in the east. In Minnesota the word "Nordic" has no anti-Semitic tint. And the situation is probably saved because, as I learned soon after arrival, Lord Halifax and his party stayed in this same suite and left only yesterday.

Afternoon spent on conferences and phone calls and plans for this evening's meeting. Dinner at a nearby club with fifty or more Minneapolis people interested in America First. Mrs. [Charles] Weyerhaeuser and Mrs. Musser (old Little Falls friends of Mother) were there. I remember driving from the farm to the Weyerhaeuser house for tea with Mother when I was five or six years old.

After supper we drove to the meeting hall a few blocks away. It was already jammed with about 10,000 people when we arrived, and there were several thousand more in the streets outside soon after the meeting started. Senator Shipstead spoke first; then Hanford MacNider introduced me. This time I kept well within my half hour. The crowd came up onto the stage after the meeting and made it rather difficult for us to get our party together and into the cars. The people seemed to be one hundred per cent behind our stand on the war, and they averaged a very high type of American.

As I go around to these meetings I feel that, without question, if this country is run by people, we will not enter this war. I always feel this way after one of our meetings is over; but I know that tomorrow, or the day after, as I read the misinformation and propaganda in our newspapers, I will begin to wonder whether people can withstand such a barrage indefinitely. And even if they can withstand it, will popular opinion be enough to keep us out of the war? Which is stronger, the money and power and propaganda pushing us into war, or the will of the people to stay out?

After the meeting I returned to the club for a short conference. Then went on to the hotel, where many people were waiting to see me. In addition to the others, there was a delegation from Little Falls—old friends of my father came down to Minneapolis to wish me well. Martin Engstrom and Carl Bolander[249] were among them. I think the greatest

249. Real-estate dealer in Little Falls, Minn., and at one time partner of C. A. Lindbergh, Sr.

satisfaction I have had at any of these meetings lay in the applause I received when I spoke of my father tonight. People are beginning to appreciate his vision and his courage.

Sunday, May 11

London, Berlin, and other areas heavily bombed.

Breakfast with a number of newspaper editors in my rooms. J. D. Holt-zermann[250] asked me to talk to them and arranged for this "off-record" meeting.

We had a lunch of about fifty leading men and women of Minneapolis, who are interested in our America First activities. Mayor [George E.] Leach and his wife attended, although, as J. D. Holtzermann told me later, they "were not with us"—or at best neutral. I am not sure which. Anyway, it was very decent of them to come. I spoke for about ten minutes extemporaneously, much as I dislike doing so.

If and when this war ends, I hope I never have to make speeches again. I thought I was through with them years ago, and here I am at it again. Speaking is not my life or my mission in life. I am convinced of that. I like best a mixture of activity and thought and, possibly, writing, but *not* speaking. I would not mind speaking so much if I could take plenty of time to prepare an address—so that I prepared it as much for myself as for my audience—and then give it from a platform, without any elaborate ceremony, and say good night, and go away with a few interesting people with whom I could discuss the meeting.

What I dislike most are these conferences before the meeting, and the people who have world-saving economic plans, or world-revolutionizing inventions, and the press photographers who want your picture in the hotel room, and the numberless people who want to shake hands, "and that's all." It makes me feel as I would if I had to go through library shelves, taking off each book, opening it at random, reading one sentence on the page I happened to turn to, and closing the book before I had time to read the sentence before or after. I want to pick out a book and read as much as I am interested in, and then close it and pick out another— and sometimes not read anything at all for a little while.

250. A Minneapolis newspaperman, Holtzermann had been Thomas E. Dewey's campaign manager in Minnesota in 1940.

After the lunch was over Mr. Appel [251] took me over to a corner of the room and told me he hoped I would consider moving back to Minnesota and run for Senator! I tried to tell him I was not cut out to be a politician, that I was not suited for political work by training, experience, or inclination, and that I was appearing on public platforms now only because we were in a wartime emergency and because I felt so strongly we should not enter the war that I could not in justice to my own conscience remain inactive. But I could make no impression in the few minutes we had without interruption. Mr. Appel thought I was giving him nothing but a clever political "front"! He replied that I was taking exactly the right attitude at this time and that it would be inadvisable to let people know I had my eye on political office until a later date!!

Returned to the hotel, packed, and boarded the afternoon plane for Chicago. Bob Stuart took the same plane. We landed shortly after dark and were met by Bob's wife and sister. To the Stuart home for the night.

Monday, May 12

London heavily bombed; House of Commons, British Museum, Westminster Abbey all hit. Hamburg and other German cities bombed by R.A.F.

Boarded 12:05 American Airlines plane for Detroit. Found that Caperton[252] was the pilot. He was pilot of the last plane to turn back from following the *Spirit of St. Louis* after I took off from Roosevelt Field for Paris in 1927. He was carrying a press photographer in a Curtiss Oriole and flew alongside me until I passed over the shore of Long Island and out over the Sound.

It was a clear day, and I could see many miles into Canada as we approached Detroit. The country looked the same—the same fields and woods and farmhouses. It was hard to realize that the people on one side of the river were at war, while those on the other side were at peace.

A Ford car and driver met me at the airport and took me to Harry Bennett's office. Talked to Bennett for half an hour, outlining America First plans and our hope that Ford might be willing to assist us.

Then to the Ford residence, where I spent an hour with Mr. and Mrs.

251. Monte Appel, lawyer, and chairman of the America First chapter in Minnesota.

252. Arthur L. Caperton, flight captain for American Airlines.

Ford, talking to them about war trends and America First activities. I told Ford I never wanted to ask him to do anything that would be embarrassing to him, or against his interests, but that I knew how strongly he opposed our getting into the war and that he could be of great assistance in preventing this in many ways. I told him America First was badly in need of money for an advertising campaign, and that I hoped he might be able to assist in this respect. I told him we felt it necessary to exert our utmost effort against war during the next few weeks, as there will be a decided attempt to involve us. Ford told me he was very much interested and that he and Mrs. Ford had been wanting to do something to help us and had previously discussed what they might do. Ford seems to have great confidence in his wife and obviously relies greatly on her advice and judgment. Both Mr. and Mrs. Ford are firmly opposed to intervention. Ford suggested that I meet him at Harry Bennett's office at 9:00 tomorrow morning to work out plans for his assistance in the America First program.

One of the Ford drivers took me to 508 Lakepointe, where Mother and I had supper together. Soon after I arrived, it was announced over the radio that Roosevelt had canceled the radio broadcast he had announced for next Wednesday. This may be of great significance, as we had expected a very belligerent talk—possibly one that would be equivalent to a declaration of war. What is the cancellation due to? Public opposition to war? Developments in Europe? The health of the President? It is most unexpected and most welcome from the standpoint of those of us who oppose intervention.

Mother and I spent the evening together, talking and listening to several of her phonograph records—European folk songs.

Tuesday, May 13

Hess landed in Scotland by parachute after what is reported as an unauthorized flight from Germany. All sorts of wild rumors have started: that he fled from a purge in Germany, that he came to England with peace terms from Hitler, that he is insane, etc., etc.

Arrived at Bennett's office at 9:00. Ford came about 9:15. He told Bennett that he and Mrs. Ford had talked the situation over and wanted to help in every way possible to prevent intervention by the United States. He told Bennett to work out plans with me. Bennett suggested I meet a Mr. [Lou] Maxon, who handled the advertising of Ford's Lincoln and Mercury cars. He said he thought Maxon would be the best man to take charge of a national advertising campaign for America First, which Ford would back financially.

We found that Maxon was driving up to his summer home in the northern part of the state and would not arrive until after noon. Decided to fly up to see Maxon in afternoon. Bennett borrowed a three-place Fairchild plane for me. Took off from the Ford airport with Harry Wismer, one of Maxon's partners. Clear day. Landed at Onaway after a flight of two hours and twenty minutes. I backed the Fairchild as far as it would go into the hangar, which left all of the wing outside, arranged for a guard, and started for the Maxon property in the car he had sent for me.

Maxon met me on arrival—a virile, aggressive, heavy-set man in his early forties; a good host. Maxon showed me over the place; then we had dinner in a dining room in the main cabin. After supper we discussed an advertising program for America First. Maxon said Bennett had implied over the phone that there was practically no limit to the backing Ford would give to it. Maxon suggested a tentative program of $250,000 for the first month! His idea was to take a quarter page twice a week in from 100 to 200 newspapers.

Maxon phoned his office to send up their four best ad writers on the night train. I phoned Bob Stuart and arranged for him to come up by plane in the morning to discuss the program from the America First Committee's standpoint. Phoned Anne that I could not be back at Lloyd Neck for supper. I had planned on being back tonight.

Wednesday, May 14

Breakfast at 8:00 with the ad writers who came up on last night's train. Short walk along lake shore alone while preliminary advertising layouts were being made. Conference with Maxon and writers before lunch. Stuart arrived about 12:45. Spent most of afternoon in conferences.

Thursday, May 15

Rumors about Hess flight continue—thought to be peace mission, but without official backing. So far, it has simply added to confusion.

Drove to the flying field immediately after breakfast; refueled and took off for Dearborn with Bob Stuart and Harry Wismer as passengers. Conference with Bennett in regard to the advertising campaign. He felt $250,000 a reasonable program *as a start* and said Mr. Ford wanted to give us all possible backing, and that there was almost no limit to what he would do in opposing American intervention in the war. Bennett phoned Maxon at Onaway and told him to go ahead with the advertising program as we had planned it, starting as soon as possible. The extent of the program is to be limited by its effectiveness rather than by its cost, according to what Bennett says Mr. Ford told him.

Bennett is certainly a colorful character. Ford seems to surround himself with such men. But I sometimes wonder whether Bennett does not try to handle the Ford workmen with a little too much of the mailed fist. Left Bennett's home about midnight, drove to Detroit, and boarded the New York Central train for the east.

Friday, May 16

Spent the morning writing and reading Ouspensky's *A New Model of the Universe*. Arrived at New York City one hour late. Drove directly to Lloyd Neck. Evening with Anne, discussing developments while away.

Webster sent a telegram to Senator Tobey while I was away signing my name to it! Apparently the telegram asked Tobey to withdraw his anticonvoy amendment, and Tobey did withdraw it! I think the amendment should have been withdrawn, as it would almost certainly have been defeated, and the Administration would then have claimed that its defeat was an implied authorization for convoys. But I cannot afford to let anyone sign my name to telegrams, or anything else, for that matter. There is nothing in life I feel more strongly about. I must stop Webster from doing this again without hurting him too much. He is a good and loyal friend and has made a great personal sacrifice to take over the business and financial management of the New York chapter of America First. He sent the telegram under high pressure, and believing he was doing the right thing. After it was sent and he had time to think it over, Anne tells me, he was greatly worried about what my reaction would be. Phoned Tobey and explained to him what had happened—without using Webster's name.

Saturday, May 17

Spent most of the day working on my address. Phone calls to General Johnson, Norman Thomas, Landon, and others. I asked Landon if he would consider joining the National America First Committee. He was very courteous, but refused. Landon was very discouraged about the war trend. Thinks we will probably be pushed into it.

Webster came for supper and the evening. He is encouraged; thinks trend now away from war.

Deac Lyman phoned, also encouraged; thinks Hoover's speech, and mine, stopped the Administration's plan for convoys, at least for the present. Lyman quoted the conversation at a dinner of Administration supporters that he attended in Washington, to the effect that the rising opposition to war was slowing up plans for intervention and having a definite political effect.

Sunday, May 18

German planes bomb Iraq. British planes bomb Syria.

Anne and I discussed sending Jon to camp this summer. He is now old enough, and it would be an excellent experience for him—away from home, and with other boys in an outdoor life. It would teach him self-reliance and how to get along under new and changing conditions. Also, our plans for the summer are uncertain. I must spend most of my time in opposing the war agitation. It is impossible for us to lay any definite plans until this crisis is over and we are either in the war or out of it, or at least walking the fence more skillfully. Some people say that the present state of emergency will continue indefinitely. But, after all, an emergency that extends long enough eventually becomes normalcy.

Neither Anne nor I like this semipolitical life, and we want to get away from it as soon as conditions and our consciences permit us to do so. The longer I stay in it, the more difficult it will be to get out. Some of my friends are already saying I must enter politics permanently and eventually run for office. But I have no intention of doing that. They say I cannot avoid it, that I will find myself pushed into it. But I *can* avoid it, and I can do it by making one address, or by writing one article in which I discuss truthfully and openly the fundamental issues which face this country today. One need only face the fundamental issues squarely and write and speak what he actually believes, and in these times he need have little fear of being pushed into politics—even by his friends. Possibly the greatest divergence I have with the people who want me to enter politics is that they think a political life is the greatest achievement and contribution a man can make, and I do not. I think some men are naturally adapted to politics, and that they are the ones who should enter it and who can contribute the most to it. But, thank God, all the world and all life is not made up of politics, and there is work of at least as great importance to be done in other fields.

Tuesday, May 20

The entire advertising plan I worked out with Ford, Bennett, and Maxon has collapsed. I received a telegram to the effect that Ford had decided not to carry it through! I phoned Bennett, who told me Ford had decided that if he were going to put so much money into advertising, he would prefer to do it over his own name instead of through the America First Committee. Bennett implied that Ford did not trust some of the people on the America First Committee, but did not name them. But none of the reasons Bennett gave were clear-cut. It was obvious that he was trying to find excuses for Ford's action, possibly not knowing the real reasons himself.

What is it really due to? Eccentricity and advancing years? Actual suspicion of the America First Committee? The desire to completely control everything in which he invests heavily? Or is it government pressure in the form of "defense" contracts and the growing penetration of government influence into business? Possibly the C.I.O. troubles have diverted Ford's attention; possibly Edsel Ford or officers of the Ford Company have discouraged him on the war issue. Whatever the cause may be, the plan has collapsed, and collapsed flatly.

Friday, May 23

R.A.F. withdraws from Crete. Germans claim several British warships sunk.

Anne and I drove to New York. I went directly to the Engineers Club to meet a Mr. Brown, of the Guaranty Trust, who recently arrived from

France, and who told Miss Crutcher[253] he had a message for me from Dr. Carrel.

Mr. Brown told me he had seen Dr. and Mme. Carrel in Paris during the first week of this month and that they were both looking well. He confirmed my belief that the story of Dr. Carrel's detention in France was false. According to Mr. Brown, Dr. Carrel was about to go to Belgium to study famine conditions in that country, and the Germans were assisting him, even to the extent of waiving the usual visa requirements. Brown said the German occupation had, on the whole, been orderly.

The message that Mr. Brown was carrying to me was to the effect that Mme. Carrel had managed to remove our Lang Madonna[254] from Illiec and that she now had it safely in her possession at Saint-Gildas! I remembered that several months ago Dr. Carrel and I were discussing the report that Illiec had been looted by the Germans and everything movable taken away. I had remarked that the only thing we cared greatly about was the carved wooden madonna. Carrel apparently told Mme. Carrel about this when he arrived in occupied France, and she, according to Mr. Brown, had put on her black Brittany cloak one dark night, ridden muleback to Illiec when the tide was out, found the madonna, which had not been taken by the Germans, and returned with it to Saint-Gildas. Mr. Brown said she had been shot at by a German sentry on her way back! How like Mme. Carrel! Her entire life has been punctuated with such experiences.

Mr. Brown said the German soldiers had at first ordered Mme. Carrel to leave Saint-Gildas, saying that all the islands along the north coast must be evacuated. Mme. Carrel refused to go, apparently so resolutely that she won the respect of the German officers and was allowed to stay on the island.

Brown tells another story about Mme. Carrel. One day when she was walking over Saint-Gildas, she came upon a number of Germans in swimming—nude. An argument ensued, in which one of the men fell back upon his authority as an officer in the German Army. Mme. Carrel looked straight at him and replied, "I see no stripes." The officer later appeared at Mme. Carrel's house in full uniform to show that he actually held the rank he had claimed.

Walked to the Waldorf in time for an early dinner given by John T.

253. Katherine G. Crutcher, Dr. Carrel's secretary at the Rockefeller Institute.

254. Carved by the famous Lang family, German potters and wood carvers of Oberammergau, Bavaria.

Flynn. The guests were Senator and Mrs. Wheeler, Mr. and Mrs. Norman Thomas, Mrs. Longworth,[255] Mrs. Marquand, and several others.

After dinner we drove to Madison Square Garden. It was jammed when we arrived (holds over 20,000, I am told), and there were from 10,000 to 20,000 more people in the streets outside. We always have loudspeakers installed outside of our meeting places. We were ahead of time and went to a room outside the main hall to talk over final arrangements and let a little time pass. While we were there, someone told Flynn that Joe McWilliams[256] was in one of the front rows and surrounded by press photographers. Flynn flew into a rage and said he was going to denounce McWilliams from the platform. I told him I felt it advisable to disclaim any connection between America First and McWilliams, but that it should be done with dignity and moderation.

The crowd was above average and enthusiastically behind us. Flynn held the McWilliams incident under control, but I am inclined to think it would have been better not to have mentioned McWilliams by name. That simply added to his apparent importance and gave him the press publicity he desired. By the time Flynn finished, the crowd was about ready to tear McWilliams apart. Uniformed police and detectives began to surround him, and Flynn had some difficulty in getting people seated and quiet again. Mrs. Marquand spoke after Flynn, then Norman Thomas, then Mrs. Norris; then I spoke for about twenty-five minutes; then Wheeler finished the meeting with one of the best addresses he has yet made.

Saturday, May 24

Battle of Crete continues. Germany lands more troops by air. Claims sinking of more British cruisers and destroyers.

Drove to New York with Bob Stuart for an hour's conference with Senator Wheeler and Dick Moore at the Waldorf. We discussed the possibility of demanding a national referendum on the war issue, what Roosevelt would probably cover in his speech next Tuesday, plans for new America First activities, etc.

255. Mrs. Nicholas Longworth (Alice Roosevelt), daughter of President Theodore Roosevelt.
256. Joseph E. McWilliams, leader of the American Destiny Party, alleged to be a Nazi-oriented organization.

Mrs. Marquand and General Aiken came for supper. They arrived early, and Aiken and I walked to the bluff overlooking Cold Spring Harbor. He told me about his trip to Washington and his recent conference with Roosevelt. Aiken said that as soon as he arrived in Washington it became obvious that our government would not give the Irish anything in the way of munitions and ships unless there was closer "co-operation" with England. Aiken said Roosevelt talked incessantly during the short conference he was able to obtain, and that he finally "had to break in" in order to get down to the subject he came to talk about.

Aiken said he asked Roosevelt for a message to take back to the Irish people. Roosevelt replied that he could tell the Irish people that he (Roosevelt) supported them in their resistance to German aggression. Aiken thanked him, and said, "Can I also tell my people that you support them in their resistance to British aggression?" To which Roosevelt replied, "There's no such thing as British aggression."

Later, when Aiken found he would be able to obtain practically nothing from this country and that the Administration was blocking his every move, he suggested to the State Department that all facts in regard to the Irish-British-American relationship be given out to the press. Shortly afterward, he read in the papers that Ireland would be allowed to obtain two ships, and $500,000. (The money to be used for refugees in Ireland!) "I'd hate like hell to think our nuisance value was only a half million dollars," Aiken said.

We spent most of the evening discussing the war. Aiken fears that if the Germans don't try to invade Ireland, the English will. In this respect he fears the English more than the Germans.

Sunday, May 25

Battleship Hood *sunk by the* Bismarck *in North Atlantic. Battle for Crete continues. Strikes continue in United States.*

Everyone was out in the evening except Anne and I and the children. Anne wanted to be on the bluff for the sunset, so I stayed in the house with the children while she went to the bluff with Thor. I don't like to have her out alone on the wood roads at night; but it means everything to her, and she has no fear. Sometimes one loses more of life by not taking a chance than by taking one. I think it is very safe here on Lloyd Neck, but there are many fanatics in the world—political and otherwise.

Monday, May 26

Spent the day on routine and working on my next address. Had the usual difficulty getting started. When I sit down to write, it seems that I have already used up all the arguments against getting into the war. There are plenty of subjects I want to write about, of course, but they won't do for an America First meeting; and this is not the time to bring them out, anyway. Now, we must concentrate our attention and our efforts on staying out of this war. The more fundamental issues would simply confuse people, and they are confused enough already.

I sit down and write a paragraph and then get up and walk about and think. First, what I write seems good; then, when I reread it, it seems unimportant and dull and poorly put together. I cross it out and start over again; and after several tries and several days an address gradually takes form that I am reasonably satisfied with.

Tuesday, May 27

We listened to Roosevelt's fireside chat in the evening. His address was confusing and clever, as usual. He seemed somewhat held back—and, to me, he always sounds vindictive—but he ended by proclaiming a "full national emergency." What does a "full national emergency" mean? What effect will it have on free speech and our America First meetings? I must find out exactly what is involved in this proclamation—and that requires specialized legal advice.

Wednesday, May 28

Bismarck *sunk by British air and naval units. Roosevelt declares a full national emergency.*

It seems that Roosevelt's "full national emergency" need not have much effect on our plans and meetings. I have talked to Phil La Follette, Amos Pinchot,[257] and various other people who are well versed in the legal technicalities of the situation. Roosevelt's proclamation, as I thought,

257. Philip F. La Follette, Governor of Wisconsin, 1931–33 and 1935–39; Amos Pinchot, lawyer and publicist, member of the New York executive committee of America First.

does not in any way limit our freedom of speech or our right to hold meetings. Of course, the interventionist groups will try to make people think it is unpatriotic for us to continue our opposition to war now that the President has said a full national emergency exists—and in view of the criticism he directed toward us in his speech. They will try to use this speech to silence us, while the prowar groups increase their propaganda with the encouragement of the Administration.

The next few days, during the formation of public attitude, will be critical for us. We must fight hard and intelligently. Much will depend on the reaction to my Philadelphia address, as it will be our first major America First meeting after Roosevelt's "chat." Much also depends on the reaction in Congress. Roosevelt seems hell-bent for war. If the country backs him in all of his "steps" toward it, we may be shooting before many more weeks pass. If people have the courage to hold back, we may still be able to keep out. One of my greatest hopes is that the American public is slowly beginning to realize that a Roosevelt promise is not to be relied upon, and that what he says one month is often the reverse of what he says the next.

Thursday, May 29

Germans capture Canea. British bomb port in French Tunisia. Roosevelt says in press conference that he does not contemplate the use of convoys, or any immediate change in the neutrality law.

Anne and I left for New York after an early lunch. Stopped at Bankers Trust for money and boarded the 3:00 train for Philadelphia. Arrived about 4:30.

Mr. [Isaac A.] Pennypacker, America First chairman in Philadelphia, came in soon after we arrived. He brought several friends and America First officers and supporters. Among them was an old man who had come to this country from Germany nearly sixty years ago. He was a contractor by trade, and told me he had already lost a number of contracts because of his nationality.

Dinner at 6:00. About sixty people present—members and potential members of America First. Then to meeting hall. It was full when we arrived, and a crowd estimated at between 4,000 and 7,000 was standing in front of the loudspeakers outside. (The hall held about 8,000, I was told, and several hundred people were standing around the edges.)

Mrs. Norris spoke first. Then I followed (9:30 to 10:00), and Senator Walsh's[258] speech ended the meeting (10:00 to 10:55). In some ways the audience was the most enthusiastic we have yet had. They seemed to be one hundred per cent with us all of the time. I think it was partly a reaction to Roosevelt's address. This country is not ready for war, and the people who are against it do not intend to be intimidated into silence. Our meeting gave them the chance to express their attitude, and they took it.

Friday, May 30

British forces evacuating Crete. Italians land.

Anne and I took the 11:00 train to New York and drove to Lloyd Neck. Made an appointment with Hoover for 10:00 tomorrow morning.

Saturday, May 31

Spent half an hour with Hoover in his apartment at the Waldorf Tower. Hoover thinks England may be considering a negotiated peace and that the terms may be under discussion at this moment. There are strong rumors, according to Hoover, that Churchill will tell Roosevelt that either the United States enters the war in the near future or England will negotiate.

At one time during our conversation we discussed the possibility of Roosevelt being impeached before his term expires. We both feel it is possible but not probable.

Hoover says many children in Belgium are now dying from starvation and that a great many more will be permanently stunted and weakened from lack of food. He feels Belgium is the worst area at the moment.

Hoover said this morning that the British "cannot win" the war! That seemed obvious to me before they declared it. But why has it taken Hoover so long to come around to that conclusion? It is partly due to his underestimation of air power. But in addition to that, I do not believe he recognized the decadence in England or the virility in Germany. Hoover, like most other Americans—though in a much lesser degree—had never carefully analyzed the claim to greatness of the present generation of

258. David I. Walsh, Democratic Senator from Massachusetts.

Englishmen. It was an inherited claim, and, like most things inherited, it had never stood the test of conflict. A great tradition can be inherited, but greatness itself must be won.

Hoover says that the battle of Crete shows that a coast with properly installed air bases is impregnable to naval attack. Good God! As though that hasn't been shown before—in the North Sea, in the Skagerrak, off the coast of Norway, and at Sicily. Why does it take so long for people to see these things? The first two or three examples should convince them, it seems. And most people don't understand yet what aviation has done to navies. But Hoover is far ahead of most in his thinking. I sometimes wonder if the whole British Navy must be sunk before the average person understands the changes that aviation brings to Europe and to the world.

But I am probably giving a wrong impression of Hoover's ability. He has opposed our entry into the war from the beginning, and his influence and effort in this respect has been of the utmost value. His last two addresses particularly have had great effect. Hoover has a great fund of knowledge, and his judgment is far ahead of that of most men in political office today.

Hoover is looking better than I have ever seen him before. He has stability and, I think, integrity. But he lacks a certain spark; he lacks that intangible quality that makes men willing to follow a great leader even to death itself.

My primary object in going to see Hoover was to ask if he would consider making another antiwar address in the near future. He told me he was planning such an address and that he would probably speak in about a week—depending on when the time seemed opportune. He thinks it would be inadvisable for him to speak sooner—to which I agree.

Returned to Lloyd Manor in time for a late lunch. Truman and Kay Smith arrived at 5:45. (They drove up from Washington.) We discussed the war and trends in America and Europe. I phoned Hoover, as he had told me he wanted to see Truman if a meeting could be arranged without embarrassing Truman. (Hoover was afraid that the Administration would cause additional trouble for Truman if they knew he talked to Hoover while in New York. Truman said he wanted to talk to Hoover whether or not it caused trouble.)

Sunday, June 1

Germans complete occupation of Crete. Claim British Navy suffered heavy losses before withdrawal.

Truman, Kay, and I left Lloyd Manor at 8:00. We arrived at the Waldorf at 9:30 and spent an hour and a quarter with Hoover. Hoover was at his best and questioned Truman brilliantly in regard to military developments in Europe. After leaving Hoover's apartment, the Smiths started back to Washington, and I returned to Lloyd Neck.

Monday, June 2

Tried to catch up a bit with mail, but I am weeks behind. So many people write about subjects that have little or no relationship to the work I am doing, and others write long letters about unimportant details—and it seems that they all want to see me personally to talk over their ideas. Everyone feels that his particular interest involves the most important project of all.

Bob and Barbara Stuart arrived on the 6:14 train to spend the night. We went over various America First plans and discussed the developments of the war.

Tuesday, June 3

Drove to New York, arriving at 10:15; then went on to the America First offices. Webster and Flynn were there, and introduced us to the staff—probably thirty-five or forty people in all. Over half of these people are volunteers. They carry on their work enthusiastically in overcrowded and poorly lighted rooms—hot and without enough ventilation. Flynn and Webster have a small office together, with no outside windows. The thing I like most about this work is the loyalty and spirit I find in these America First organizations and at our meetings.

Flynn and Webster are doing a great job together; and they are typical of the extremes of viewpoint that the war has brought together—at least for the moment. Flynn has been what might be called a "left liberal," while Webster has been a "conservative"—possibly even a "right-wing conservative." Flynn has written articles and books taking many of the "capitalists" and much of their system to pieces. Webster gave up, at least temporarily, his partnership in a New York brokerage firm in order to devote his time to America First activities. And in spite of all the difference in their viewpoints, they somehow manage to get along together and run the New York chapter of America First. Whether this relationship can last permanently, I am not sure. The war, and the practical problems they have encountered in running the New York America First chapter, have caused Flynn to move more toward the "right" and Webster more toward the "left." But each has remained definitely on his own side of center. This is an ideal situation from the standpoint of the America First organization, if friction does not arise. But the brilliant and more theoretical mind of the liberal is apt to collide with the steadier and more practical mind of the conservative. The liberal should lead the van, while the conservative should command the main body of troops. In this way, the conservative can follow up and consolidate the successes of the liberal, while the liberal can fall back on the conservative's position to reorganize after his failures. Each needs the other for success, and possibly even for survival. The trouble is that neither is likely to recognize his own limitations or his partner's assets. Flynn and Webster come as close to forming the ideal relationship in this respect as I have ever seen two men come.

Lunch with Bob Stuart at the Engineers Club. We discussed America First and war developments. I agreed to speak in San Francisco about the fourteenth.

Monday, June 9

After breakfast Anne and I discussed the possibility of moving west later this summer. She decided to go to San Francisco with me when I make my address, so that she can investigate the possibility of renting a house in the country, either in northern California or in Oregon.

Tuesday, June 10

Stuart phoned shortly after breakfast; said the hall at San Francisco would not be available until the latter part of this month, and that only a ball park could be rented before that time. He suggested we postpone the

San Francisco meeting and that I speak at Louisville, Kentucky, instead; then at the Hollywood Bowl in Los Angeles, or vice versa. I told him I would turn the problem over in my mind and let him know within the next day or two.

Drove to New York for a 6:00 meeting with General Wood. I wrote to him a few days ago, outlining my reasons for not wanting to accept the national chairmanship of the America First Committee. To my relief, the General agreed and consented to continue as acting chairman himself. We spent an hour discussing war trends and America First plans.

Wednesday, June 11

Anne and I drove to New York for a 6:00 dinner with General Wood at the Waldorf-Astoria. Spent most of the time discussing war trends and America First plans. General Wood said Senator Wheeler had been told by an emissary from Roosevelt that the President would like to have a little more antiwar activity! The inference apparently being that Roosevelt is being pushed by the interventionists faster than he wants to go. Wheeler says he is not at all sure the President wants to get into a shooting war under the conditions which now prevail in Europe. Roosevelt may be using the war to build up his powers here and keeping himself— as he has so often done in the past—in a position where he can jump either way according to which he thinks will be the most advantageous.

Telegraphed Stuart an O.K. for the Hollywood and San Francisco meetings.

Sunday, June 15

Tension between Germany and Russia is reported increasing. Roosevelt issues order "freezing" Axis funds in United States. Naval action reported between British and French fleets in Mediterranean. R.A.F. raids on Continent continue, with German retaliation.

Spent part of the afternoon writing, part shooting with Jon and the [gardener's] boys, and part reading Anne's 1935 diary. I did not realize the depth of her depression that year, although it was one of the main reasons that led me to take her and Jon to Europe. I could see she was very unhappy and that Jon was feeling the abnormal environment under which we were living—Englewood, press, guards, police, etc. I knew that pressure would increase during the appeal. Anne had passed through a terrific ordeal as it was, and I felt she should not be subjected to more. We had done everything the police and federal authorities had asked, and there was nothing else for us to do in connection with the trial or the appeal. I knew we would be hounded by the newspapers wherever we were in America and that we would have to keep an armed guard around our home. I therefore decided to take my family abroad, and to stay abroad until the time came when we could maintain a normal home in this country. But as I read Anne's diary for that year, I feel I should have taken her abroad before I did—although I do not know how we could have gotten away much earlier.

Wednesday, June 18

Anne and I left for the airport at 8:00. Boarded 9:30 TWA Douglas (DC-3) for Los Angeles. This is the first time I have flown over the line as a passenger—always before as pilot.

Dick Moore (America First) met our plane at the Chicago airport. We discussed arrangements for the Los Angeles meeting while the plane was refueling. Frye and Collings (TWA)[259] met us at Kansas City. Half hour with them at airport. Clear and smooth flight from Albuquerque to Los Angeles. Arrived 12:00 P.C.T. Could dimly see a large number of camouflaged Lockheed bombers staked out along one side of the field. There must have been in the vicinity of fifty of them, ready for delivery to England. The present delay in the delivery of aircraft to England seems to be in transportation fully as much as in manufacture. I understand that the docks in Canada are piled high with aviation supplies. Earl Jeffrey (America First organizer) and Senator Clark[260] (Idaho) met us at the airport. To the Biltmore Hotel for the night.

Thursday, June 19

"Friendship" treaty between Germany and Turkey signed. Air raids continue. Tension between Germany and Russia increases.

259. Jack Frye, president of Transcontinental & Western Air (later Trans World Airlines), 1934–47; John Ayers Collings, early Ford tri-motor pilot; superintendent of system operations for Transcontinental & Western Air, 1939–42.
260. D. Worth Clark, Democratic Senator from Idaho.

Spent the first part of the morning reading (*Adventures of Ideas*) and marking my address for emphasis and timing. Several conferences with local America First officers: John Wheeler (Senator's son) and others.

Friday, June 20

Germany and Italy close United States consulates.

Breakfast; then half hour on my address before turning it over to Jeffrey for release. Spent the rest of the morning writing and reading—except for a visit from Douglas Corrigan,[261] which lasted for one and a half hours. Corrigan talked a blue streak, telling me all about his flight to Ireland, his preparation for it, his reception in Europe, his trip back, his reception and tour here, his present activities and thoughts, etc., etc. He is a good-natured, well-meaning Irishman. He did a very good job with very mediocre equipment, and his explanation of "following the compass backward," and "going in the wrong direction from New York" is so well done that one would practically have to lay the course out on a chart to refute it.

Lunch in the Biltmore with about fifty men invited by the local America First Committee. Was promised I would not be asked to speak; but the chairman asked me to rise, so I talked for about fifteen minutes. I don't like to speak extemporaneously, but I would rather speak than simply rise and stand like a fool while everybody looks and claps. I talked about America First and war developments.

Made final check of my address after lunch. Then various conferences until we left for the Hollywood Bowl at 7:00.

Heavy traffic. We arrived at 8:00. The Bowl was already jammed, and there were several thousand people on the hills and standing outside the doors. It is the most beautiful and inspiring meeting place I have ever seen—open sky and stars above, and hills dimly outlined in the background, so that the rows of people merge into the hills themselves. Kathleen Norris spoke first, then Senator Worth Clark, then Lillian Gish.[262] I

261. Corrigan helped build the *Spirit of St. Louis* in the Ryan factory in 1927. In 1938 he made his famous flight across the Atlantic in a nine-year-old Curtiss Robin and landed in Ireland. Since certain federal regulations were broken, he said he made the flight "by accident," having intended to fly west instead of east. For his feat he became known as "Wrong-Way" Corrigan.

262. Film and stage actress. Her films include *Birth of a Nation; Broken Blossoms; Orphans of the Storm.*

was the last speaker. The crowd was enthusiastic, good-natured, and attentive—fine type of people.

Saturday, June 21

Finland mobilizes. United States Submarine 0-9 sinks near Isles of Shoals. Ford signs C.I.O. contract.

Breakfast with Phil Love, who is in Los Angeles on his way back from an inspection trip in Alaska. We discussed war developments and conditions in the Army. Love says the present training in the Air Corps leaves much to be desired and that our new soldiers are "soft."

Phoned Hearst and arranged to meet him at his northern California ranch tomorrow.

Out for dinner with Mr. and Mrs. Wheeler[263] at a restaurant overlooking the Pacific. When I looked out the window, I thought the curve of the lights on the shore had a vaguely familiar appearance. The Wheelers told us that the city in the distance was Redondo Beach (where I once went to high school.) Our restaurant was on the bluff overlooking the beach, where Mother and I used to go for serpentines (green agatelike stones, which looked like the waves of the sea when polished). As I remember the bluff, it was covered with sage, and there were no buildings on it at all in 1917.

The location brought back to my mind memories of a quarter century ago, memories of an afternoon when Mother and I had taken the long walk from Redondo, along the beach to the serpentine bluffs. We had collected a heavy bagful of stones and were both very tired. The bag of stones was too much to carry home, and we did not want to leave it behind. Also, I felt the walk back to Redondo would be too much for Mother, even without the stones. So I left her on the beach with the serpentines, and walked and ran back to Redondo for our car—an old Saxon Six.

By the time I got to the garage where we kept the car, it was dark. Something had gone wrong with the headlights, and I had to make the trip back to the bluffs with the single spotlight I had installed on the windshield. On the way, I was arrested for driving with one light—the only time I have ever been arrested in my life! I persuaded the policeman to let me go on to pick up Mother, but he gave me a ticket to appear in

263. John L. Wheeler, head of the America First committee in Los Angeles.

court the next day. And worse luck, they found out I was underage to be driving under the California laws, although I had been driving a car for four years and had been in entire charge of the car all the way out to California from Minnesota. Mother did not drive at all at that time.

It is interesting to find how some coincidence will draw forgotten memories from some corner file in your mind and make them live again as vividly as ever.

Jeffrey says we broke all records for attendance at the Hollywood Bowl and are officially credited with having done so. Jeffrey claims there were about 80,000 people there—but I am sure that figure is too high. However, the Bowl was jammed, and there were many thousands sitting on the hills and standing outside.

Sunday, June 22

Germany invades Russia. British take Damascus. United States orders Italian consulates closed. Air raids continue.

Final arrangements and phone calls. Then Anne and I boarded a United Douglas for San Francisco. The day was clear except for the usual clouds drifting in from the Pacific. Rube Fleet was on the plane with his two sons. He spent the entire time it took us to fly from Los Angeles to San Francisco trying to persuade me to join his organization in one capacity or another. He told me about the progress his company was making, about the orders he had on his books, and about the profits he expected to take in. He said he was ready to invest several million dollars in a research organization, that he would put it anywhere in the southwest that I wanted it, and give me a salary of $100,000 per year (up $50,000 per year over the offer he made to me over the phone some time ago). I thanked Fleet and told him again I did not plan on going back into aviation as a business. He asked me what I *did* intend to do. I told him that I didn't know what the future held.

It was hard to explain my feeling and my decision. Fleet will never understand why I turned down his offer. I couldn't explain it because I am not sure that I fully understand why myself. I can seldom, if ever, put my deepest feelings into words. But the things I am surest of are the things that I feel, that I know, deep down inside. Reason, I have found, is far less reliable. If I don't feel that what I reason out is right, I try not to act on it. On the other hand, if I can't put my feelings into logic, I can't help being suspicious of them. But when feeling and reason combine, then I have no hesitation in acting. And under these circumstances, I cannot remember ever having made a mistake.

Why I feel so definitely that I will not re-enter commercial aviation I am not sure. I love flying, and I love research. Aviation was my life for many years, and it made a very happy one. I look back on those years with tremendous satisfaction. I could easily give myself over to that same kind of life in the future; and it might be of more importance than anything else I could do—that, only the future can tell. I have nothing definite that I can say is my objective. There is nothing that I greatly want in life. Yes, there is an intangible something, but I don't know what it is; I can't describe it, and I can't visualize it; it's more a direction than an objective; and what it will lead to I don't know. It isn't power, or money, or fame. But whatever it is, it's the reason why I turned Fleet down and why I am not actively engaged in some form of aviation activity today. It isn't just my opposition to the war, either, although that would be enough to make me refuse Fleet's offer for the time being. But if there were no war, and if I wasn't engaged in opposing American intervention, I would still feel the same way.

Fleet told me of an order he had been given by the British before the Lease-Lend bill was passed. He said the British had not confirmed the order in writing until they could transfer their original order to a Lease-Lend appropriation. Fleet says they now want everything to be Lease-Lend.

We landed at San Francisco and at Oakland; then took off for Medford, Oregon. Met at airport by one of the Hearst drivers. Two-and-a-half-hour trip to Wyntoon, the Hearst ranch at the foot of Mount Shasta. Hearst has built a number of Bavarian cottages—two small villages of them—on the edge of the McCloud River. The one we were assigned to had a balcony built out over the river, so you could fish from it. The opposite bank of the river rose up steeply for some hundreds of feet, covered with great redwoods and pines. The villages were really in a narrow valley between mountains. Rushing water, huge trees, mountains, and mist—Oregon. The cottages were painted in front with murals of fairy tales, by Pogany.[264] They looked quite a bit like a movie set but were elaborately and substantially built. Ours was "Cinderella House."

Mr. Hearst met us at the door and took us inside. The rooms were full

264. Willy Pogany, Hungarian-born artist. Illustrator of more than 150 books, mural painter, and art director of motion pictures.

of old art pieces and reproductions. Marion Davies[265] arrived a few minutes later and showed us our bedrooms—heated by old Dutch-tile stoves.

We drove to the other "village," about a half mile downstream, for supper at 9:00. (They told us breakfast would be at 11:00 and dinner at 4:00!) There were probably a dozen people present: Mr. Hearst, Marion Davies, her sister, her niece, Mr. Conan Doyle (English lecturer), Mrs. Conan Doyle, Mr. and Mrs. Swinnerton,[266] and several others. After supper I talked to Hearst for a few minutes about the war and his editorial policy. Then we all drove up a winding road to a castlelike building to see a motion picture—a very stupid one, I thought. Bed at 1:30. (They said it was very early!) Rushing water outside the windows.

Monday, June 23

Broken clouds and sunshine when we woke, and the sound of water. It is very beautiful here; but for some reason there is no feeling of solitude, and it is the kind of place where there *should* be solitude. There is too much of Hollywood, too much efficiency, too much organization. People come to a place like this to get away from the city, to get something they subconsciously feel is missing in the city, something they find when they go to the location in the country where they eventually build. And then they take so much of the city along with them that they lose what they went after.

City and country are different qualities of human life, and each is essential to it. But they are like sugar and salt, not to be taken together in the same spoon. You should go from one to the other, and even change your clothing on the way. You see and appreciate the city most when you have just come from the country. You appreciate and see the country most when you have just come from the city. Difference of background allows you to see more clearly. After you have lived in one place a long time you may gain in complacency, but you lose that quality of appreciation that comes from sharp contrast.

It is like the odor of the sea when you first come to it after months in an interior country. After you have lived on the sea for a few days, it is gone. (That is why I often say that if one is going to write a book about a foreign country, it should be written either after a few weeks of travel or

265. Film actress, who began as a dancer in the Ziegfeld Follies. Among her films were *When Knighthood Was in Flower; Peg O' My Heart; Ever Since Eve.*
266. James Swinnerton, cartoonist and artist for the Hearst newspapers.

after many years of residence. If it is written immediately, it is justified by contrast. If it is written after long residence, it is justified by experience. It seems to me the worst time to write is after you have lost contrast and before you have gained experience.)

Wrote for a time after getting up; then Anne and I walked the half mile to the "lodge" in the lower "village," arriving at 10:45 for breakfast. No one else was there, so we sat down alone at the long table. Two more guests arrived at 11:00. Then gradually the others assembled. Back to Cinderella House and spent an hour or two working on my address for San Francisco.

Lunch at 2:30. Marion Davies, without saying anything about it, had asked seventy schoolchildren to come to the lodge to meet us. We were completely unprepared, and there is nothing worse than being confronted with a group of children if you have made no plans for their entertainment. I am not one of those politicians who can go out and pat their heads and talk about what fine-looking boys and girls they are. I remember how I felt about such things when I was a child, and I have too much respect for them and for myself to do it. Fortunately, Marion Davies had provided ice cream.

Anne and I returned to Cinderella House by way of a trail on the far side of the river. On the way we saw several deer and a medium-sized brown bear. The bear was fifty feet up the hillside. It ambled off as I climbed toward it.

I worked on my address during what was left of the afternoon. Then Anne and I climbed up the mountainside across the river from Cinderella House. We intended to go to the top when we started, but after climbing several hundred feet it was obvious that night would fall while we were still on the mountain unless we started back immediately—and the mountain seemed to extend on indefinitely.

Supper at 9:00 with a dozen other guests. Moving picture afterward—an insane affair.

Tuesday, June 24

Germans take Brest Litovsk. R.A.F. raids Channel coast. Germans bombard British coast with long-range guns.

Raining. Wrote for a time. Then a car called to take us to the lodge for breakfast. Spent several hours on address. Lunch at 2:30. Rest of afternoon on address, and a walk with Anne. Sky still overcast, but only a sprinkle of rain now and then. Saw another deer at a bend in the road. Supper at 9:00. Said good-by and left for the station at 10:00. Boarded the 11:00 train for San Francisco.

Wednesday, June 25

Roosevelt promises aid to Russia. Russian planes bomb Warsaw. Turks mass troops on Syrian border. German advance into Russia continues.

Off train at Oakland about 8:30. Taxi to the Sir Francis Drake Hotel. Conference with Jeffrey after breakfast. Spent rest of day on address. I find it difficult to get under way; feel written out on addresses.

Thursday, June 26

Reports from Russia and Germany confused and conflicting. Russian planes bomb Finnish cities, and Finland is apparently entering the war on the German side.

Anne and I went to the apartment of Colonel and Mrs. Clarence Young for dinner. (He was the C.O. of my squadron at Richards Field, Kansas, in 1925. Later, Assistant Secretary of Commerce for Air. Now head of Pan American's Pacific division.) Young says the government has taken three of Pan American's new Boeings to give to the British and that the company now has practically no reserve for its transoceanic schedules. In other words, if a plane is damaged, a schedule will have to be curtailed. The domestic lines are also being stripped of their reserves.

Friday, June 27

German advance on Moscow continues. Local paper carries the follow- ing bulletin: "Heavy defeat was inflicted on German Panzer and mecha- nized forces before they drove Red forces out of most of Lithuania and back upon Minsk, Moscow radio claimed." German mechanized units reported within fifty miles of Minsk. Finland announces it has entered the war against Russia. R.A.F. bombs Kiel and Bremen. American news- papers minimize reports of German air raids over England. German communiqué claims heavy British shipping losses and night air raids on south coast of England. British and German reports of planes lost and damage done always conflict.

First part of morning on address. Then Anne and I packed and left for the Norris ranch to accept Kathleen Norris's invitation for a several days' visit. The ranch is in the coast range of mountains, about fifty miles from San Francisco and a few miles west of Saratoga.

Mr. and Mrs. Norris and various members of their family were there when we arrived. They assigned us to a hillside cabin overlooking a wooded valley, with mountains in the distance. It is an exceptionally beautiful location: mountains, redwoods, sloping fields, and bits of clouds breaking over the ridge that separated our valley from the Pacific. A barbecue lunch under the redwoods. Then Mrs. Norris, her sister, her niece, Anne, and I climbed to the top of a nearby mountain, cutting the trail wider as we went along.

More Norris family arrived after supper: nieces and nephews and their children. Found that among them were four members of the Communist Party—two men and two women. The two men had fought for Loyalist Spain! The family represented all shades of political opinion. How they all manage to get on together I don't know. As Anne says, it must be due to the character of Mrs. Norris. There were all of the elements of revolution in the parlor that night. It was like a curtain lifting for a moment to give one a glimpse into the future—the future that I fear this nation must pass through. It is an interesting future, but not one that is pleasant to look forward to.

Saturday, June 28

German advance into Russia continues. R.A.F. intensifies raids on Continent.

American press accounts of the war are so prejudiced and confused that it is almost impossible to obtain a balanced picture. Reports from Russia are headlined while those from Germany are played down, although the latter are certainly the most accurate. Results of R.A.F. raids over the Continent are exaggerated, while results of German raids over England are minimized. The result is that the impression given by our newspapers is far more favorable to the British cause than is warranted by the facts.

Watched family games in the afternoon. We carried on a cautious conversation all day, avoiding political subjects almost entirely. But the tension that existed last night was gone. Case of a divided family held together by Mrs. Norris. Wonderful woman—real character—reminds us a little of Mme. Carrel.

Monday, June 30

Germans claim they have surrounded two Red armies and captured or destroyed 4,000 planes, 2,000 tanks, 1,000 armored cars, 600 heavy guns, and many prisoners. Russian denials and conflicting claims continue. Hoover made an excellent antiwar speech. German mechanized units have apparently passed Minsk. Moscow reports deny everything and are completely unreliable. Roosevelt authorizes the induction of 900,000 more men into the Army.

Left at 9:45 and drove to San Francisco with Mrs. Norris's son. Rest of day spent in conferences and on my address for tomorrow night.

The San Francisco chapter of America First does not appear to be well organized. There is an unusual amount of friction between the various factions. (Seems to be Irish trouble as much as anything else.)

Tuesday, July 1

We arrived at the Civic Auditorium at 8:00. It was soon jammed, and by the time the meeting was over the crowd outside in the street was estimated by different people at from 10,000 to 30,000. I spoke from 8:30 to 9:00. Then Mrs. Norris, Miss [Lillian] Gish, and Senator [D. Worth] Clark, in the order named. I think the meeting was a little too long, but the crowd was responsive and apparently ninety per cent or more behind us, if one can judge by the demonstration.

Wednesday, July 2

German armies capture Riga. British transfer General Wavell to India.

Phoned General Wood in Chicago and arranged to meet him tomorrow morning at the airport. Boarded 6:45 United Airlines Douglas sleeper to Chicago.

Thursday, July 3

German advance into Russia continues. Claim 160,000 prisoners. Russians deny.

The newspapers continue to misquote my address and to remove sentences from their context. Sometimes what they carry between quotation marks is completely made up and does not even approximate what I have said, or even what I believe.

Breakfast on plane before landing at Chicago at 8:15 C.S.T. General Wood was at the airport to meet us. Lunch in General Wood's suite in the Chicago Club: General Wood, General Dawes,[267] Colonel McCormick, Senator Vandenberg, Stuart, Moore, and myself.

Vandenberg says he has had letters from most of the officers and men of several Michigan companies, asking him to oppose the extension of their service beyond one year and saying that "they have not been learning anything, have had enough of it, and want to go home." It is a case of bad leadership, inefficient organization, lack of equipment, and various other factors. Army morale is low all over the country. As nearly as I can judge, the Army is at least three quarters opposed to entering this war.

Friday, July 4

Germany reports Russians retreating along entire front. Russians claim most of their lines holding. British claim R.A.F. maintaining heavy air raids over Continent. Germans claim British losses heavy and little damage done.

Breakfast at 9:00 with General Wood. Then half hour's walk along the beach of Lake Michigan while we discussed probable war developments and America First plans. Boarded 3:05 TWA plane for New York. The weather report indicated that we might not get through, but the expected fog held off, and we landed at La Guardia field, New York, at 8:20 E.S.T. Drove to Lloyd Manor for the night.

267. General Charles Gate Dawes, Vice-President of the U.S., 1925–29, and old Morrow family friend. In 1925 he was awarded the Nobel Prize for Peace jointly with Sir Austen Chamberlain, British Foreign Secretary.

Saturday, July 5

Germans claim Russian forces routed. Russians say their troops are withdrawing to the "Stalin line." General Wavell says an A.E.F. will be needed if Germany is to be defeated.

Anne, Jr., seems much larger. You never realize how fast a child grows until you are away from it for several weeks. Land has changed, too. His conversation is much clearer and more interesting. We all miss Jon, but he seems to be getting along very well at camp.

Sunday, July 6

Germans claim they have reached the Dnieper. Russians say they have slowed down the German drive. British claim heavy air raids over Continent continue. (The Russian reports are obviously the most unreliable of all. The British are probably exaggerating the extent of and damage done by their air raids in order to encourage Russian resistance and increase their prestige in America.)

Spent most of day on routine and reading over my old radio addresses with the idea of possibly publishing them in book form. They hold water quite well, I think, but the quality drops when I make them too close together. Personally, I prefer to speak less often and with more careful preparation. Most of my friends want me to speak more often and with less careful preparation.

Monday, July 7

Anne and I spent some time checking and glancing through diary copies. This project is now nearing completion. During the last year I have often wondered whether we would get it done before the start of war, and I have been anxious to finish the project before the start of war; first, because it would be a tragedy if Anne's diaries were lost; and second, because I want some accurate record of my own activities during these war years. This diary cannot cover everything, but it will show the falsity of at least some of the stories told.

Captain Smith (America First) came at 3:30. He had phoned to say he had an urgent message that he must deliver personally. The message is that the F.B.I. began tapping our telephone last Saturday and have a constant watch on it. The men in the F.B.I. are, according to Smith, on the whole, friendly; they are simply following out orders. Smith says the America First telephones are also tapped. I told him to tell everyone in America First that there was nothing we wished to hide and that if our phones were tapped we should speak more plainly, rather than less plainly in the future. I told him to tell his friends on the F.B.I. that if there was anything they didn't understand in my own phone conversations, I would be glad to give them additional information. Captain Smith says he is certain the phones are tapped and that the information came from friends of his on the F.B.I., who are also friendly to me. Personally, I think it is probable that they are tapped, but I still have some question. It really makes very little difference as far as I am concerned. My main interest lies in knowing whether or not these tactics are being used by the Administration.

Tuesday, July 8

American naval forces land in Iceland.

The morning papers announce that American forces have occupied Iceland. This is, I think, the most serious step we have yet taken. It may mean war. Iceland is in the German war zone, and, in my opinion, it is definitely a European island. Its political connections have been primarily with Europe—Denmark—and I believe it is also a European island from a military standpoint. (It is more accessible to European naval and air bases than to American.) Since Iceland is politically, racially, and militarily European, it seems to me a doubtful asset and a great hazard for the United States. The trouble is that our people think of Greenland and Iceland as two similar islands, lying up around the Arctic Ocean. Since we have already occupied Greenland, they see no reason why we should not occupy Iceland. And since Iceland lies closer to Greenland than to Norway or Scotland, it seems logical to them to claim Iceland as a part of the Western Hemisphere. They know nothing about the Arctic climate of Greenland's eastern coast, and whether or not we are in a position to hold Iceland in a major interhemispherical war is something they have never considered.

Roosevelt has persuaded the American people that Iceland *should* be occupied; he has not told them the danger involved, and they have never seriously considered for themselves what the results may be. National polls show that the great majority of Americans (seventy-five per cent or more) are opposed to entering the war. Yet a majority are behind Roosevelt in practically every step he takes toward war. They want to stay out of war; but they want to occupy Iceland and convoy ships through the war zone so Great Britain may win the war, without our having to do any of the fighting. If this policy is carried on much longer, it will probably lead to our getting into the war *without* Britain winning it.

One of the things that worries me most about America is the attitude of those people—and there are many of them—who say that this is "our war," but that we should not fight it—the "send guns, not sons" attitude. If I believed this was our war, I would be for putting everything we had into it. Too many Americans of this generation want to live without working and win without fighting. Will Germany pick up the gauntlet we have thrown down? We have now entered her declared war zone for the avowed purpose of getting war supplies to England. It is now Hitler's move—or will he pass?

In one sense, the most serious part about this occupation of Iceland lies in Roosevelt's making such a move without consulting Congress. I am not sure which is worse—the danger of being thrown into the war or the internal implications of such dictatorial procedure.

Thursday, July 10

French ask armistice in Syria.

Anne and I walked to the bluff in the morning, discussing the seriousness of the war situation. Drove to New York in the afternoon. Conference with John T. Flynn later in the afternoon in regard to war developments and America First plans. We both agree that the occupation of Iceland creates an extremely serious situation. The question is will Hitler order his submarines to torpedo our ships, and if so, what will Roosevelt do? The President has very cleverly maneuvered us into a position where he can create incidents of war and then claim we have been attacked. The country is now half democracy and half dictatorship, and neither system is functioning efficiently.

Friday, July 11

Drove to New York for a 3:00 conference with Richardson and Flynn at the former's room in the Commodore Hotel. We discussed the possibility of a congressional investigation of the groups agitating for war in this country. We feel it important to bring the names of the war makers out into the open—both as individuals and as groups. Flynn will go to Washington next week to look into the possibilities of an investigation. Richardson will assist in assembling facts and data.

Saturday, July 12

New York Times *first-page headline:* NAVY NOT ATTACKING NAZIS, KNOX SAYS, BUT DEPTH BOMB AS WARNING IS INDICATED; BRITISH SAY AMERICAN TECHNICIANS ARE WORKING ON BASES IN IRELAND; ROOSEVELT SENDS MESSAGE OF SYMPATHY TO KALININ.

Took Jon to the Aviation Country Club for an hour's flying in the Fairchild.

Sunday, July 13

German forces advance beyond the Stalin line. Truce in Syria. R.A.F. raids over Continent continue.

Spent part of the afternoon redrafting the inventory I have made of our possessions and interests. I am trying to create a simple and complete list, including suggestions for Anne in case I should meet with accident or death.

Mr. and Mrs. Norman Thomas and their son from Princeton came for supper. We discussed the war and plans for opposition to American intervention.

Tuesday, July 15

Germans claim Russian armies on verge of collapse. Russians, of course, deny. The Administration postpones its attempt to get Congress to authorize the President to send draftees overseas at his discretion.

Wednesday, July 16

Russian government reported moving from Moscow to Kazan.

Day on routine and drafting a letter to the President. Secretary of the Interior Ickes[268] has been attacking me and spreading misinformation about me for months in the cheapest and most inexcusable sort of way. My policy has been to say nothing in reply and to let him have all the rope he wants on the theory that he will eventually hang himself. In his latest utterances, however, I believe he has put both himself and the President in a position where I can attack with dignity and effectiveness.

I intend to address a letter directly to the President, basing it on his responsibility for the actions of his Cabinet officers. In this way I think I can counteract Roosevelt's tactics, which are to put his Cabinet members out in front while he "carries the ball." Thus he lures his opposition into attacking his Cabinet officers instead of himself. I am trying to reverse that procedure and to strike through Roosevelt's interference by holding him personally responsible for his appointees. Nothing is to be gained by my entering a controversy with a man of Ickes's type. But if I can pin Ickes's actions on Roosevelt, it will have the utmost effect.

Friday, July 18

Germans take Smolensk. General Marshall asks Congress to proclaim state of national emergency.

Drove to New York in the afternoon for a conference with Roy Howard and Jack Howard. I talked very frankly about my viewpoint on the war and American intervention, but I don't think they understood very well. I doubt they have any conception of what "prostration" in Europe really means, and that is the only alternative I see to a German victory or a negotiated peace. I believe they think of prostration as something approximating our 1929 depression. Also, these people are not used to *open* discussion. They are always looking for something underneath what you say, something behind your motives. During our discussion I told Howard there was still nothing I would rather do than go to Europe and study the war conditions over there at firsthand. But, I told him, I

268. Harold L. Ickes, Secretary of the Interior, 1933–46.

could see no practical way of accomplishing this at the present time. On this point at least we agreed. Back to Lloyd Manor for the night.

Saturday, July 19

Spent the morning checking over diaries and other records and writing a letter to [Bernhard] Knollenberg (Yale librarian). Anne and I have decided to turn our old files and records over to the Yale Library for safekeeping. These files and records contain material which should not be lost and some of which will be of interest in the future. We are making a provision that the boxes we send are not to be opened during our lifetimes without our authorization. We have considered various alternate dispositions that we might make of our files. In normal times I think we might keep them in the vaults and warehouses where they are at present. But in times such as we are now going through, when war may start next month and life itself is uncertain from one year to the next, I prefer to have our records in the safest possible location. I want them available in the future, both for ourselves and for our children.

There are portions of everyone's life that could be improved if they could be lived again in the light of later experience; but Anne and I are not ashamed of the way we have lived our lives, and there is nothing in our records that we fear to have known. I wonder how many of our accusers would be willing to turn their complete files and records over for study in the future. Our only hesitation in doing this lies in our feeling that certain portions of life are, and should be, one's private possession and are not meant for public gaze. But since these files will not be opened until after we are dead, time will clothe the nakedness of their contents.

Sunday, July 20

United States to transfer one hundred more tankers to Britain. Rationing of gasoline and fifty per cent cut in motorcar production is being discussed.

Too many people pass through New York and call up as they are passing through. It takes a tremendous amount of time just when you want to concentrate on writing, or dictating, or some other work. And, worse still, many of them are not satisfied with a phone call but want to see you personally. Either they are old acquaintances, or they have an idea they want to talk to you about, or they have something else in mind that can't be discussed over the phone.

New York is probably the worst place in the world for this type of thing. Almost everyone we know passes through New York at least once a year, and they usually call up and want to see us. Of course, we often do the same thing ourselves when we are in other cities, just "passing through." It isn't that we don't want to see our old friends; quite the contrary; but if we saw them all, we would have to give up our other interests and enter that deadly social life that is so typical of Long Island. Lloyd Neck is too close to New York now that everyone knows we are living here. If we were farther away, people would not call up just because they were "passing through"; and if we were nearer to the city, the effort involved in meeting would not be so great.

Tuesday, July 22

Germans claim advance. Russians claim lines holding.

Anne left for New York in the evening. She is going to Martha's Vineyard to see the house that is for rent. If it meets our needs, we may go there next month.

Wednesday, July 23

Japanese tension growing.

First part of morning on routine. Then Land and I went swimming. I offered him two pieces of candy to sit down on the edge of the float and jump into the water without my help. Land finally found enough courage to make the jump (about one and a half feet), and I took him back to the ladder on my back. He went right back to the edge of the raft and jumped off again. After several jumps sitting, I offered him two more candies to jump off standing, and he did—feet first, of course. By that time he was swimming around to the ladder by himself—about ten feet. Then he jumped off the diving board. And a few minutes later, without saying a word of warning, he jumped off the float and started swimming for shore—a distance of about seventy-five feet. And he made it!

When I saw what Land was doing, I planned on staying well behind him in order not to distract him and so that help would not be *too* easily available. But the usual thing happened when older people are around children. Mrs. [Willis Delano] Wood was on the float and thought the swim would be too much for Land. She started out to "rescue" him, and I had to swim in between them. She wanted to help Land with misdirected kindness and, of course, made the situation much more difficult for him. Most people are so "kind" to children these days that they make it almost impossible for them to grow up to be men and women of character and resourcefulness.

In this instance, for example, I felt it best to let Land carry through the responsibility he had taken on his shoulders when he jumped off the float. I intended to stay close enough to him to help if he started to go under, but otherwise I intended to leave him alone. If he made shore, he deserved the satisfaction and the feeling of independence that accomplishment would give him. If he started to go down, he would at least gain a sense of caution that might even save his life sometime in the future. In any case, the experience would give him a measurement of his own ability. He wanted to try his wings, and I felt my mission was to guard but not to hinder. Mrs. Wood, on the other hand, with all the best instincts of a good, kindly woman, and a Long Island grandmother, wanted to meet Land halfway to shore and help him whether he wanted to be helped or not. Fortunately, Land was able to make shore alone, and I was able to ward Mrs. Wood off without creating an unpleasant situation. She really is a very nice person.

Spent the first part of the afternoon on routine. Then Anne arrived back from Martha's Vineyard with a glowing account of the country there. The house for rent is a little small; but we can fit into it, and possibly rent another place nearby for an office. The house will be available after the eighth of August. We decided to take it.

Anne and I met Phil La Follette on the 4:11 train at Huntington station. We had early supper on the garden porch at Lloyd Manor: then drove him to Richmond Hill, where he is to speak at an America First meeting. Phil La Follette is brilliant and extremely interesting. I would like to have talked to him for a longer time. I feel we did not have enough time together for either of us to understand the other more than superficially. He has a large fund of knowledge, definite opinions, is informal, and pleasant.

Sunday, July 27

I went to Port Washington for a short visit with Deac Lyman. (Lyman had phoned to say he had some information for me that he did not want to give over the phone.)

After a few minutes in the parlor with the Lyman family, Deac and I went out into the garden to talk. Deac said he had received word from a friend in Washington to the effect that the members of Roosevelt's Cabinet were going to "gang up" in an attack on me which was to start in about eight or ten days. Deac said he was going to Washington soon, and would try to get more detailed information. I told Deac that if there were to be an attack on me, I knew of nothing to be done about it and that I thought the best policy would be to let them attack if they wished. If there is nothing to be done, why worry? Much as I dislike the fact, I am in political life, of a type, today; and when one is in politics, he must expect opposition.

Back to Lloyd Manor through very heavy Sunday traffic; late for lunch. Anne and I drove down to the beach at 3:00 to meet the Howards' yacht. They sent a small boat in for us and took us on a three-hour cruise in the Sound. In addition to Roy and Mrs. Howard, his doctor and secretary were on board. We discussed the war, the attitude of the press, etc.

Monday, July 28

Spent the day on routine, and plans for our move to Martha's Vineyard.

I had the phone number changed this morning, from Huntington 3256 to Huntington 3788. The old number was unlisted, as is the new, but so many people knew it that it might almost as well have been in the directory. The phone was ringing all day, and it was almost impossible to concentrate on anything.

Anne, Land, and I went for a swim in the afternoon. The story is going around Lloyd Neck that "it's no wonder the Lindbergh children swim well. Their father throws them in the water!" It all started because an English nanny saw me push Land off the float several days ago. And the mothers whose children *don't* swim just love it!!

Wednesday, July 30

Churchill says United States "is advancing . . . to the very verge of war."

Day on routine and packing and writing an address I will probably give at an America First meeting at Baltimore.

I had the veterinary look over Thor to see if anything could be done about the stiffness which has been slowly developing in his back legs. The vet said it was simply age and that nothing could be done. He gave me some "conditioning" pills, but said they would have little effect on the stiffness. Thor is now eleven.

Thursday, July 31

Roosevelt warns of inflation; asks additional powers in price fixing.

Day on routine—mail, dictation, packing, etc. I find that my own personal equipment is quite simple and easy to pack. It gives me a feeling of satisfaction, for I hate to be tied down to elaborate possessions. I am inclined to think that, within reason, the less one possesses, the richer the life he leads.

Friday, August 1

Webster phoned from Senator Wheeler's office in Washington. They say that Baltimore is not the best place for an America First meeting at this time—local chapter not well enough organized, etc.—and advise 1) Boston, 2) Pittsburgh, 3) Cleveland.

Tuesday, August 5

"Full United States aid" pledged to Russia. House passes $3 billion tax bill. Japan cancels all direct sailings to United States.

Wednesday, August 6

Strong rumors that Roosevelt and Churchill are to meet "somewhere in the Atlantic."

Spent most of the day working on my address. It is to be given at Cleveland Saturday evening.

Friday, August 8

Anne and I drove to New York after lunch. I dropped her at Fifty-seventh and Lexington and went on to the Engineers Club for a conference with John T. Flynn. Flynn says the investigation he has been carrying on is "bringing amazing results," and that he thinks he will be able to show clearly that a strong undercover movement for war exists. He says it is most obvious in the motion-picture industry. Flynn says the Administration has made direct requests that the motion-picture producers run a certain percentage of "war films." Flynn feels certain that this situation can be exposed in a congressional investigation.

Anne and I boarded the 5:10 United plane for Cleveland. Landed Cleveland at 7:55.

Saturday, August 9

Spent most of the day on conferences and arrangements for the meeting. The police here have taken exceptional precautions—more, I think, than circumstances warrant. They have gone over my apartment with a fine-tooth comb; say they have even "X-rayed" the furniture. They have assigned a detective to every door at our meeting hall and have guards in the rooms beneath the speakers' stand! All this in addition to the motorcycle escort and uniformed police.

The hall (12,500 seats) was only half full when we arrived, probably because all arrangements have been made in five days. The America First chapter at Cleveland was not notified that a meeting was to be held until last Tuesday. But people were standing by the time the meeting was over, and only a few seats in the balcony at the far end of the hall were left unfilled. As nearly as I could judge, there were more people standing on the main floor than there were empty seats in the balcony.

Senator [D. Worth] Clark spoke first (an improved version of the same address he had given at the Los Angeles and San Francisco meetings; he warned us of this in advance with a great deal of humor; said he had not found time to write a completely fresh address, but that since his Los Angeles and San Francisco addresses had not been nationally broadcast, he hoped to get by with the same one at Cleveland). My address ended the meeting (broadcast over NBC red network) and we returned to the hotel, where a number of people had gathered in our rooms.

It was an excellent meeting—enthusiastic crowd which, as usual, seemed to be eighty per cent or more with us. No sensible person can attend these meetings without realizing that public opinion is *not* ready for war.

I remained in Cleveland for the night in order to take the morning plane to Washington.

Sunday, August 10

Boarded 7:00 Penn Central plane for Washington. Clear day and a good flight.

Lunch with Truman and Kay. Then to Senator Nye's apartment. Senator and Mrs. Nye were there when I arrived. Senator and Mrs. Wheeler and Senator D. Worth Clark came in later. We discussed the war, and trends in this country. They believe the draft extension bill can't be passed in the House at the present moment, but they think Roosevelt may be able to swing a number of members to his side before it comes up for vote. Wheeler says he is still doubtful that Roosevelt wants to get into a shooting war under present circumstances.

Boarded the night plane for New York. Bus from La Guardia field to the city. Got car from garage and drove to Lloyd Neck, arriving about 1:30.

Monday, August 11

Germans advance in Ukraine. Roosevelt curbs installment credit. Japan placed on war economic basis.

Anne, Land, Anne, Jr., and Soeur Lisi left Lloyd Manor at 4:00 en route to Martha's Vineyard via the night boat.

Drove to Huntington station to meet [Larry] Kelly (Hearst, Chicago) on the 6:14 train. I had agreed when we were in Cleveland to give him a story provided that I could check the direct quotes and that there not be too many of them. I went over the manuscript. It contained a great deal of direct quotation, fairly accurate in meaning but not at all accurate in words or shading or balance. Kelly does not understand my values and standards too well, but I think he did the best he could, and on Hearst standards of journalism it was not a bad piece of work. I straightened out the manuscript as well as I could, and discussed with Kelly the additional portions he intends to write.

I thoroughly dislike press interviews. What you say is invariably twisted, no matter how friendly and able the reporter. It would not be as bad if they would write in the third person: "he said," etc. But they never remember your exact wording, and when they use direct quotes, which they invariably do, they make you seem like a different person than you are or want to be. I have kept away from interviews for many years. I gave Kelly this story only because I felt it would have a constructive effect on the present war issue and because the Hearst press has given us such good support in this issue. The Hearst press has done things to me in the past which I cannot forgive from a personal standpoint; but the issue of war or peace for America at this time is far above personal issues. Hearst has been assisting us, and I intend to assist him as far as this war issue is concerned. I cannot forget the past, but I have put it in the background, at least for the time being.

I would feel better about the situation if I had any trust in the consistency of Hearst's attitude. Experience warns me that the principles his papers follow may be only as stable as the popularity of his stand and the circulation figure which results. The latest polls show that the country is eighty-three per cent opposed to entering the war. What will the attitude of the Hearst papers be if that percentage drops?

I like to have men on my side on whom I can count to the last shot. There are few of them at present, but that is probably to be expected in an opposition movement such as we are carrying on. It is a heterogeneous mass of Americans who have banded together in this antiwar movement. We would break up in an instant on almost any other issue. But at the moment I believe the most important thing for this country is to keep out of the war. For the issues that follow, our ranks will re-form. Then one must be more careful about who is shooting on his side. If we can stay out of war, I believe America has at least a chance to work out its internal problems with moderation. But if we get into this war in our present condition, God knows what the future holds for us.

Friday, August 15

Rumored meeting between Roosevelt and Churchill is confirmed. Eight "peace aims" announced. Germany reports Odessa surrounded and Ukrainian armies in a "state of collapse."

Arrived Seven Gates Farm in time for lunch with Anne and the children. It is a very beautiful place. Reminds me of Illiec, although there are many differences, of course. There are all kinds of trees on Martha's Vineyard, and the change of tide has but little effect on the appearance of the island. But there is the sea, and there are rocks and islands in the distance.

In the afternoon, Anne and I walked over the grounds and looked for a site where we can pitch our tent. There are more different kinds of berries on this island than I have ever seen before in one place—blueberry trees six feet high (several within a hundred yards of our house), huckleberry bushes everywhere, blackberries, beach plums, elderberries, wild grapes, and a large number of berries which are probably not edible and the names of which I do not know—and with the berries there are numberless birds.

Saturday, August 16

Churchill and Roosevelt propose conference with Stalin. German advance in Ukraine continues. Relationship with Japan continues tense.

Misty and raining; too wet to set up tent.

Sunday, August 17

Roosevelt lands at Rockland, Maine, returning from Churchill conference. Usual vague and evasive statements. Reports from German-Russian front conflict.

Spent first part of afternoon writing. This is an excellent place to work—quiet, stimulating, inspiring. Walk with Anne and Thor at sunset. Thor still enjoys life and loves to go with us on walks. But instead of running on ahead and investigating everything on each side of our path, he now spends most of his time following closely at Anne's heels.

Monday, August 18

Two men came to set up the tent house at 9:00. I showed them where to place it: on the side of a hill overlooking the sea, in a slight hollow where it will be protected from the wind as much as possible and still have a view both ways along the coast.

General Wood phoned from Chicago. I agreed to speak at America First meetings at Des Moines, Oklahoma City, and Washington, D.C.

Tuesday, August 19

Germans advance on Leningrad.

Anne, Thor, and I went for a long walk in the late afternoon—along the coast and through the woods. This is an island of great contrasts—a little like Illiec, a little like Maine and Labrador and Monterey. It has the sea, lakes, streams, hills, trees, a rocky coast, and a northern twilight; some of the trees have almost a tropical appearance.

Monday, August 25

Churchill warns Japan of joint British-American action. Russians claim counterattacks.

I took the 1:05 train to New York. Had to pay two fares for a drawing room! Would much prefer a coach, but know I would soon be recognized and given very little chance to make a final reading of my address. I want to turn a copy of it over to the New York chapter for advance release. What wouldn't I give to be able to ride on trains and go to theaters and restaurants as an ordinary person. Phoned Webster as soon as I arrived in New York.

Tuesday, August 26

British and Russian troops invade Persia. Germans advance on Leningrad. New York Times *headline:* BRITAIN AND SOVIET ASSURE TEHRAN OF PEACEFUL AIMS.

Suddenly found I had set my watch on standard instead of daylight time at the Boston station and that I was late for an appointment with Webster at the America First offices. (Now I know why I woke so early this morning.)

Captain Smith was waiting for me with a car and drove me to the America First headquarters at 515 Madison Avenue. Spent twenty minutes there, then drove with Webster to the Wall Street branch. Several people saw me go in, and a small crowd assembled outside the plateglass window—a very friendly crowd. Twenty or thirty came into the building, and I believe several of them joined up. Webster and I were to have lunch with Mr. Potter[269] at the Guaranty Trust Company across the street. We had planned on walking across from the America First offices; but due to the crowd, we got into our car and drove around several blocks before returning to the door to the Guaranty Building. By that time the people had disbanded, and we were not recognized again as we walked in the door. Lunch in a private room with Potter and several of the vice presidents of the bank. He and two or three of the others have a viewpoint of the war quite similar to Webster's and my own. But like so many businessmen they say, "What can be done about it?" They are all ready to admit that the country is headed toward chaos, but few of them are willing to expose their own position enough to take part in opposing that which they believe is wrong.

To John T. Flynn's office at 3:00. Spent an hour discussing war trends and America First plans. While I was there the Chicago headquarters phoned to say the contract for our meeting hall at Oklahoma City had been canceled! I replied that if we could not rent a hall we could hold our meeting in a cow pasture.

To Waldorf-Astoria at 5:30 for a conference with Hoover. We discussed developments of the war, internal conditions here, etc.

Taxi to Engineers Club. Met Guy Vaughan in the club and talked to him for half an hour. He is very depressed about the labor situation in

269. William C. Potter, banker and chairman of the Guaranty Trust Co.

the aviation industry and the lack of leadership in Washington. Boarded the 8:15 train for St. Louis.

Wednesday, August 27

Britain advances in Persia. Germany advances in Russia, claims capture of Dnepropetrovsk. Japan reported to have told Moscow that American supplies for Russia would not be permitted via the Pacific.

Arrived St. Louis 4:45. As I left the car, the conductor stopped me to say he wanted me to know that he was "very much with me." Taxi to Jefferson Memorial Building. Miss [Marjory] Douglas and Miss [Esther] Mueller were there when I arrived. I looked over the cases and some of the records. They are taking excellent care of the collection. Back to Chase.

Jeffrey called from Oklahoma City. Said they had obtained a sand lot for our meeting place, and that the situation there is tense—threats of breaking up meeting, shooting, etc.

Thursday, August 28

Laval wounded in shooting at Versailles. Germans claim to have crossed lower Dnieper. Tension rising between United States and Japan.

Up at 6:30. Worked on address for an hour. Phoned Major Lambert, Bill Robertson, Brandewiede, Tom Dysart. Bill Robertson drove me out to the airport and took me through his school for aviation mechanics. Saw Brandewiede for a few minutes at the passenger terminal. Then boarded the 10:36 American Airlines plane for Oklahoma City.

On landing at Oklahoma City I was met by Jeffrey, Mr. [Arthur H.] Geisller (America Minister to Guatemala when I landed there in 1928 and '29), Mr. [Herbert K.] Hyde (America First chairman), and several others. Drove from airport to Skirvin Tower, where rooms had been reserved for us. We had an escort of ten motorcycle police, with guns very much in evidence.

Jeffrey told me he had encountered considerable trouble in this city—the most anywhere to date. There have been threats of shooting, of cutting light and telephone (radio) wires, eggs, stones, etc. The situation is tense, he says, but showing signs of calming down a little. Pressure is being brought to bear from Washington to cause as much difficulty for us as possible. All of the papers here are unfriendly. After our lease on the auditorium was canceled, Jeffrey obtained a lease on a ball park—but he is not sure that lease will not be canceled, too.

Conferences with various people in rooms. Then to see the Governor, who seems to be quite friendly. He takes the stand that there should be free expression of opinion in Oklahoma. His attitude will help us considerably—and, I think, will help him considerably at the next elections. He offered us the Capitol steps for our meeting in case we could obtain no more satisfactory place. The issue here is developing into one of free speech rather than one of intervention. Feeling is running high on both sides. People are driving in from all parts of the state, and even from adjoining states, to attend the meeting. Governor Murray ("Alfalfa Bill")[270] is coming down from Broken Bow to introduce me.

Friday, August 29

Conference between Roosevelt and Japanese Ambassador. Russians claim to have blown up the Dnieper Dam. New Persian government issues order to cease fire.

Most of morning spent in conferences. Ex-Governor Murray arrived— amazing character—old, deaf, partly blind, but a keen mind and full of life. He is tall and thin, and was wearing an unpressed dark suit, and an incredibly dirty and out-of-shape straw hat. We talked of his term as governor, of present conditions in the state, and of the books he has written (one of which is just coming out). I gather that his newest book covers such items as punctuation, grammar, civilization, governorship, and many other subjects! Conversation was difficult because of his deafness.

Returned to room after lunch. The mayor, the chief of police, and the city manager were there waiting for me, having arrived before the lunch table broke up. The mayor seemed a fine type of man. It was obvious from his talk and actions that he felt ashamed of his part in refusing the auditorium for our meeting tonight. He made several rather lame excuses, and I felt so embarrassed for him that for some reason I found

270. William H. Murray, former Democratic Representative from Oklahoma, 1913–17, and Governor of that state from 1931 to 1935.

myself trying to help him out. The city manager was harder to size up. He did not leave me with added confidence in humanity. They left after a half hour's conference which included various details about arrangements for our meeting in the ball park. People came in all afternoon from all parts of Oklahoma and from nearby states. Farmers drove in 100 and 200 miles, bringing their families with them. There has been a great popular reaction against the people who were responsible for refusing us the hall. Several priests came in to tell me of their support. Senator Wheeler arrived about 5:30. Early supper with America First workers.

Then drove to ball park behind the ever-present police escort. Road to park jammed with cars; also crossroads. There were about 8,000 people in the ball park when we arrived, and lines were filing in through all the entrances. Planks had been laid on bundles of shingles for seats. We took our places on the platform at 7:40. There was singing and an informal address by Mr. Hyde, who is an able extemporaneous speaker. Crowd started good-humored but skeptical. Hyde was heckled once and made the error of inviting the heckler to come up on the platform and have his say. The man accepted—turned out to have recently served several months in a National Guard unit. Said a few words about having an honorable discharge and being ready to go back; then left platform. Incident turned out well enough, but could have caused considerable difficulty under the tension that existed. Governor Murray spoke for fifteen minutes introducing me. (He had previously told me it might be his last speech—he is an aged man.)

There were about 15,000 people in the park by that time. I spoke from 9:00 to 9:30. Then Wheeler ended the meeting with an extemporaneous address. By the time it was over, it seemed that at least eighty per cent of the crowd was with us, cheering and applauding. I find great encouragement in these meetings. Contrary to press reports, we draw a high type of people—better than a cross section of the community. As I travel around the country, I am more than ever convinced that American citizens are definitely opposed to intervention. But what has Roosevelt in his mind, and how far will he be able to take us? How close can we skate to the edge of war without falling in? It was a very successful meeting. None of the predicted trouble arose. The crowd was orderly at all times. Threats had been so numerous and pointed, however, that we had double-wired the light and radio circuits and even had a battery radio transmitter available for emergency.

Saturday, August 30

Germans capture Tallin. Executions continue in France.

Boarded 9:53 Braniff plane to Chicago. Considerable bother from press at Kansas City. General Wood met me at the Chicago airport. Press there, too, and very unpleasant when we refused to be interviewed. The general took me to his home in the country (Forest Hills). We spent the evening discussing plans for America First.

Sunday, August 31

Russians claim counterattacks. British evacuating nationals from Japan. Roosevelt warns that peace "isn't all in our keeping."

I boarded the night train for Detroit.

Monday, September 1

Rumors of peace between Russia and Finland.

Taxi from station to 508 Lakepointe. Breakfast with Mother and B. The yard is full of fruit and birds, and I think Mother is very happy here. I suggested a drive in the country, but Mother felt [there was] too much traffic. She looks a little tired, and I am worried about her working so hard—but she prefers teaching to doing anything else and will not consider letting anyone come to the house to help her in the kitchen and cleaning up. Says she would much rather do it herself than be bothered with servants.

Tuesday, September 2

Drove to Dearborn in the afternoon for an hour's conference with Mr. and Mrs. Henry Ford. We discussed the war situation and the America First Committee. Ford did not speak of the advertising plans that blew up, and neither did I. Ford showed me some photos he had of the Dagenham factory in England [271] after it had been bombed by the Germans.

271. The Ford Motor Co., Ltd., of England at Dagenham was the center for manufacture, sales, and service activities throughout Europe.

The damage seemed heavy, but he said they had it running again in a few days. Drove Ford to Bennett's office for a half hour's conference, primarily about the labor situation and the war.

Every time I see Ford I am impressed both by his eccentricity and his genius. How such genius succeeded is easy to understand, but how it carried such eccentricity along with it is more of a problem. But I always come away refreshed and encouraged after a meeting with Ford. I only wish this country had more men like him. (More—but not too many more.)

Supper with Mother and B. at 508. We played a number of Russian, German, and French records, including *Mignon*. They drove me to the station for the 8:00 New York Central train to New York.

Wednesday, September 3

United States to make loan to Mexico for "anti-Axis aid."

Off train at 8:30. Lunch with Bill Benton at Engineers Club. Discussed war polls, America First plans, etc. Thought I would see a motion picture in the afternoon, but could find none that seemed worth the time. Went to a newsreel theater and left after the "news." The other films bore me. They are as bad as cheap novels and sex magazines. I always leave them feeling discouraged and wondering where such a sense of values is leading us as a nation.

Supper with Ed Webster at his home. He and I attended an America First street-corner meeting in the evening. Young America First speaker was standing on a stepladder and addressing a small crowd of about twenty people. There was no heckling; but one of the America First members, who recognized Webster, told us that someone, apparently drunk, had just tried to tear down the flag and push over the ladder. He had left with police escort a few moments before we arrived.

Boarded 11:30 train for Woods Hole.

Thursday, September 4

Konoye warns Japan that she faces the gravest emergency in her history. Berlin bombed.

Off train at 7:10. Boat to Oak Bluffs. Swim with Anne, Jon, and Land before lunch. Believe the camp this summer has been very good for Jon, but I am glad to have him back. Two months away is enough the first time.

Saturday, September 6

Senate passes $3.5 billion tax bill. Assassinations continue in France.

Took Jon and Land to the middle of Hallock's Pond in the boat and let them swim to shore through the weeds, to be sure they could do it. Both are very good swimmers, considering their ages, and had no difficulty. Afterward, I told Jon he could take Land fishing with him provided he kept the boat close to shore. Land has been wanting to go alone with Jon for a long time. I realize it is taking a certain chance, but I would rather let a child take some chances than to have the kind of child that is never allowed to come into contact with danger of any kind. Carrel once said that some contact with danger was essential to the building of character in children, and I believe he is correct. Life can be made so precious that it is not worth living.

Tuesday, September 9

British forces occupy Spitsbergen. Berlin heavily raided.

Walk with Anne and Thor in the afternoon. Thor seems happier up here. He likes the wildness and freedom, but not enough to make him leave Anne's side for a moment.

Boarded the night sleeper for New York at Woods Hole.

Wednesday, September 10

Russians claim advance toward Smolensk. Morgenthau warns of inflation.

Off train at 7:30. Boarded 9:15 TWA plane for Chicago. Took bus from Chicago airport to Blackstone Hotel. Met Bob Stuart at the Chicago Club. We had early supper while we discussed plans for America First. A meeting in Washington, D.C., on the twenty-seventh now seems of doubtful advisability. We talked of shifting it to some other location— Fort Wayne, Seattle, Portland, Boston, or elsewhere. Reports from the capital indicate that the government is in such a strong position there that the success of our meeting would be doubtful. Opinion conflicts about this, but we cannot afford to hold an unsuccessful meeting in the nation's capital.

Boarded United plane for Des Moines. There was a crowd waiting for me on the airport at Moline; wanted me to give a radio address while the plane waited! Found it very difficult to persuade the people there that it was neither possible nor advisable.

Jeffrey, his wife and son, and several officers of the local America First Committee met me at the airport. We drove to Hotel Fort Des Moines.

Thursday, September 11

Lunch with about twenty-five Des Moines citizens representing both sides of the war controversy. Interesting and pleasant; no formal speeches, but we discussed war trends and conditions here and abroad.

Afternoon spent reading over my address, and in conferences. I decided to hold the release of my address until the President has given his out. All sorts of people came in during the afternoon. One, a preacher, said a prayer as he left. Another had a religious prophecy he wanted to tell me about. One man had a new economic plan. A fourth wanted to show me his collection of magazine and newspaper records of "undercover British dealings." Several "old friends" came to call, most of whom I had apparently met *once* many years ago at a time when I was meeting thousands of people every week. They recalled the circumstances surrounding our meeting "fourteen years ago," and expected me to then remember all details connected with it. The unfortunate part is that the real friends you would like to see stay away because they are afraid of intruding when you are busy, and you are left surrounded by people who push themselves forward claiming to be friends. Then, the wildest and most absurd newspaper stories appear about you, told by "an old friend," who probably bases his lifetime acquaintanceship on two meetings, more than ten years apart, of less than half an hour each, and with several other people in the room at the time.

Supper with several members of the America First Committee at a nearby club. Then back to hotel, where our party assembled, and from there to the meeting hall behind the usual police escort. I always ask the police to avoid using sirens if possible. I think people dislike them when their use is not essential. I know I do. We drove into the car entrance to the meeting hall and sat behind the curtain until the President finished his address.

We had a unique and difficult situation to meet here at Des Moines. After we had arranged and announced the date of our meeting, President Roosevelt's mother died, and the President postponed the speech he was to have given several days ago until this evening. Jeffrey decided that the President's speech should be broadcast in our meeting place before we opened our meeting. The timing was such that we began immediately after the President finished. I felt very doubtful about this arrangement; but it had already been announced when I learned of it, and there was nothing to do but back Jeffrey up in his decision. The question then arose as to whether we should sit on the stage while the President spoke, or come onto the stage immediately afterward. The latter course was decided upon.

Since the President is an able speaker, and since he has the ability to arouse crowds, it gave us about as bad a setting as we could have had for our meeting. I say the President is an able speaker. I refer to his national popularity and not to my own impression. From the standpoint of popular appeal, Roosevelt is possibly the greatest speaker of our time. Personally, I decided, after listening to two of his radio addresses in 1932, that I did not trust the man who gave them and that I did not want to see him President of the United States. As a result, I voted for Hoover. I felt Hoover had ability and integrity, but that he lacked the spark of leadership so greatly needed for our nation in these times.

Roosevelt attacked the Nazis, spoke of the sinking of ships, and ended by saying he had ordered the American Navy to clear the sea of enemy warships wherever it was necessary for American interests. Within a minute of the time he finished, the curtain went up and we filed onto the platform. We were met by a mixture of applause and boos—it was the most unfriendly crowd of any meeting to date, by far. Also, the opposition had been organized and there were groups of hecklers in the galleries strategically located to be effective for the microphones. We learned after the meeting that these groups contained paid "shouters." Confusion was increased by the improper functioning of the loudspeakers during the first several minutes.

Mrs. Fairbank[272] was the first speaker. She did a very good job under very difficult conditions. Before long we began to win over the crowd,

272. Janet Ayer Fairbank, Chicago author and novelist, active in causes of women's suffrage and in politics. She was on the national executive committee of America First.

and the clapping and cheering of our supporters overcame the cries of our opposition. [Hanford] MacNider made a strong address and was well received. (It was interesting to note that the least popular portion of his address consisted of a quotation from President Hoover.) I spoke for twenty-five minutes. It seemed that over eighty per cent of the crowd was with us by the time I finished; but the ice had been well broken before I started, by the previous speakers. When I mentioned the three major groups agitating for war—the British, the Jewish, and the Roosevelt Administration—the entire audience seemed to stand and cheer. At that moment whatever opposition existed was completely drowned out by our support.

Dozens of people came to our hotel rooms after the meeting—America First members and supporters and advisers, local officials, newspapermen, etc. Some were solid, stable citizens; some erratic; some intelligent; some stupid; all types are present at these meetings, but on the whole we have a much better than average cross section of the communities where we meet. Our opposition press, of course, picks out and emphasizes the radical and fanatical types who attend. They had more success at doing this, however, before the Communists threw their support to the interventionist cause after war started between Germany and Russia. We were thankful to be rid of the Communist support which we never wanted and always tried to avoid.

Friday, September 12

Roosevelt orders Navy to shoot on sight German or Italian warships entering waters "the protection of which is necessary for American defense."

Boarded the Broadway Limited for New York.

Saturday, September 13

Off train at 9:45. Breakfast at Engineers Club. New York *Times* carries bitter attacks on my address from Jewish and other organizations and from the White House.

Went to see the motion picture *Sergeant York*. Thought the acting much above average. It was, of course, good propaganda for war—glorification of war, etc. However, I do not think a picture of this type is at all objectionable and dangerous.

Went for an hour's walk through the streets, then boarded the 11:30 train for Boston. Porter put me in right berth number, but on the wrong car. A drunk, who had the ticket for the berth I was in, came aboard late and refused to trade cars. I had to dress again and change over.

Sunday, September 14

Off train at 7:00. Boarded 7:35 train for Woods Hole. Arrived home just in time for lunch. After supper Anne and I pitched our small bug-proof tent in a hollow in the hills west of the house. It was a clear and cool night, and we could leave the top of the tent open over our heads.

Monday, September 15

My Des Moines address has caused so much controversy that General Wood has decided to hold a meeting of the America First National Committee in Chicago. I must, of course, attend. I felt I had worded my Des Moines address carefully and moderately. It seems that almost anything can be discussed today in America except the Jewish problem. The very mention of the word "Jew" is cause for a storm. Personally, I feel that the only hope for a moderate solution lies in an open and frank discussion.

Tuesday, September 16

Packed and boarded 4:30 boat en route for Chicago. Was recognized by everyone, of course, as I left the island. It was not so bad on the boat, but on the train people wanted autographs. They never understand when I say no, but I know what happens if I sign one. The only thing to do, unless you want to spend your life signing your name wherever you go, is to establish a reputation for never signing in public places. If you sign once, it brings ten more requests. If you refuse the first request, the word quickly gets around.

When the train arrived at the Boston station, a friendly drunk insisted on walking off the platform with me! I tried to get supper at the station, but word that I was there quickly got around, and I had to leave halfway through to avoid a crowd gathering. Spent half an hour walking through the streets, then slipped back into the station through a side entrance, bought some fruit for the rest of supper, and boarded the night train for New York.

Wednesday, September 17

Germans claim rout of eighteen Russian divisions on Leningrad front. Navy announces 2,831 ships ordered since July 1, 1940.

Off train at 7:30. Taxi to Webster's home. He says Flynn much upset about my Des Moines address, but that majority of America First members are in accord with what I said.

Walked back to Engineers Club, spent an hour writing, ate lunch at a standing counter at Grand Central Station, took the bus to airport, and boarded the 1:05 TWA plane to Chicago. Bob Stuart and Page Hufty were waiting for me at the airport. We drove to the Chicago Club. General Wood and Dick Moore were there. We ate supper while we discussed tomorrow's meeting. General Wood suggested the possibility of adjourning the America First Committee! His plan would be to state that since the President had already involved us seriously in war, the committee saw nothing gained by continuing its activities at this time and would adjourn until the congressional elections next year.

General Wood had to leave for an engagement, and Stuart, Moore, Page Hufty, and I continued the discussion. We all felt the committee should continue its activities unless and until Congress declares war, or unless it becomes obvious that we are no longer being effective—which is far from the case today. Stuart showed me the telegrams that have come in from America First chapters in regard to my Des Moines address. Ninety per cent or more of them are in accord with what I said. Apparently the only strong opposition comes from one portion of the New York City chapter.

After the conference ended Stuart and Page Hufty drove me to General Wood's home for the night. Half hour's conference with the general before bed. I suggest that the American First Committee continue for the present and until the war situation shows more definitely its trend. Much is unforeseen, and I prefer to go down fighting for what we believe in, if we must go down at all.

Thursday, September 18

Up at 6:30 for breakfast and discussion with General Wood. I told him
1) that I felt it was not the time for the committee to adjourn; and 2)
that while I was not willing to repudiate or modify any portion of my
Des Moines address, I would, if the committee wished, issue a statement
to the effect that the address represented my personal opinion and not
the policy of the committee. I told General Wood that the latter course
seemed to me inadvisable.

To the Chicago Club for an hour's conference with Archbishop Beckman.[273] We discussed the need of obtaining more support from the Catholic Church.

John Flynn came at 11:00, and we talked the situation over for an
hour. Flynn says he does not question the truth of what I said at Des
Moines, but feels it was inadvisable to mention the Jewish problem. It is
difficult for me to understand Flynn's attitude. He feels as strongly as I
do that the Jews are among the major influences pushing this country
toward war. He has said so frequently, and he says so now. He is perfectly willing to talk about it among a small group of people in private.
But apparently he would rather see us get into the war than mention in
public what the Jews are doing, no matter how tolerantly and moderately
it is done.

Lunch alone at the Chicago Club. I thought it best not to attend the
meeting of the committee, since the discussion will center largely around
my Des Moines address. Stuart phoned at 2:15 and asked if I could
come over. The meeting was at Mrs. Fairbank's home. When I arrived,
General Wood, Amos Pinchot, Mrs. Fairbank, Ed Webster, John Flynn,
Page Hufty, Dick Moore, Bob Stuart, and several others were there. I
found that the majority of the committee wanted to issue a statement
backing up my Des Moines address, but that Flynn had objected so
strongly it was decided to issue a statement that really took no stand at
all.

When I arrived, the discussion centered about the question of whether
or not it would be advisable for me to issue the statement I had suggested
to General Wood this morning. I reaffirmed my willingness to do this,
and at the same time said I thought it would be a mistake. A vote was
taken, and everyone was against it except Flynn. Flynn said afterward

273. Francis J. Beckman, Archbishop of Dubuque, Iowa.

that certain rules should be laid down for America First speakers. I told him that the committee could lay down rules if it wanted to, but that such rules would have to be stated at the time invitations were issued to prospective speakers. It would then, I said, be up to the speaker to decide whether or not he wished to accept the invitation. I knew this type of situation would arise in connection with America First, and it was among my reasons for refusing to accept the national chairmanship when it was offered to me last spring.

Friday, September 19

Roosevelt asks $5,985,000,000 additional for Lease-Lend program. German armies continue to advance in Russia. Government seizes freighters tied up by strikers.

Up at 7:00. Took the 8:10 airport bus and boarded the TWA plane for Pittsburgh via Fort Wayne and Columbus. (All places taken on the through schedules.) Changed to Penn Central plane at Pittsburgh. There is heavy traffic on the airlines. The government has taken all reserve planes and much personnel. Bombers in their war paint are beginning to be noticeable on all airports—like Europe in 1938.

Boarded the 10:00 P.M. train for Boston.

Wednesday, October 1

Germans execute fifty-eight Czechs. German Air Force bombs town in northeast England.

Anne and I took the 4:30 boat from Vineyard Haven and boarded the Boston train at Woods Hole. We had no trouble on the train; but soon after we went to a hotel in Boston for supper newspaper reporters and photographers arrived. We missed them by going out a different entrance than we came in (with the help of the hotel manager and detective, both of whom took the opportunity to tell me in a low tone of voice that they were with me in my war stand). We took a taxi to the station and boarded the night train to New York. Many soldiers in uniform in the station.

Thursday, October 2

Army lands troops in Iceland. British bomb Hamburg and Stettin. Germans bomb Newcastle. Chinese claim Japanese troops routed in Changsha area. Siege of Leningrad continues.

Off train at 7:15. Taxi to Webster's home at Beekman Place. Breakfast with Webster while we talked over America First problems and plans. The friction between Webster and Flynn continues to develop. Webster is too far "right" for Flynn, and Flynn is too far "left" for Webster. I tried to explain to Webster that America First could never be a powerful organization if it alienated the liberal groups represented by such men as John T. Flynn. I told Webster that an organization which went too far to the right would lose the spark and incentive of the liberal mind, while one which went too far to the left would lose stability and direction.

My experience has been that the people on the "right" of center are the best organizers, while those on the "left" of center have the most brilliant minds. But, after all, how can a mind be brilliant if it is always concentrated on organization? And how can a mind which soars through clouds and space and life be weighed down with the details of organization?

Webster is broad enough to agree that we must keep Flynn in America First. And I realize how difficult Flynn's inability to decentralize often makes life for Webster. Flynn is one of those men who want to keep their fingers on every detail. But there is something to be said on Flynn's side in this; America First is too heterogeneous an organization, and one made up of too many divergent viewpoints to make decentralization an easy matter.

Took the bus to La Guardia field. Boarded the 1:00 P.M. TWA Douglas for Pittsburgh. Changed to local plane, and went on to Fort Wayne. We seem to have an exceptionally good chapter here in Fort Wayne—largely due to the activities of a young woman by name of Vera Sessler (secretary of the chapter) and to the fact that one of the local papers has been giving us its support. We have become so accustomed to an opposition press that it is a strange and pleasant experience to pick up a local paper which carries friendly headlines and editorials.

Friday, October 3

The opposition paper here is carrying a large advertisement in which statements are attributed to me which I never made. As far as the "war party" is concerned, what I actually say seems to be of little importance. They quote me as saying what they *wish* or *think* that I said. They do not bother to refer to my addresses, which are all available; at best, they refer to some garbled newspaper account. The result is that I am often quoted as saying things which I not only never said, but which I never believed.

We arrived at the Gospel Temple at 7:55. The mayor says that with the extra seats they have put in it holds 8,000 people. We started the meeting at 8:00. The crowd was with us from the beginning. There was no opposition during the entire meeting. (As a matter of fact, I think some opposition is a good thing.) Mrs. Fairbank spoke first. Then Mayor [Harry] Baals introduced me. He is a man of conviction and courage—one of the few local politicians I have met who is not afraid to stand on the platform with us. I spoke from 8:30 to 9:00. Then Father O'Brien[274] spoke for another half hour.

We returned to the hotel after the meeting. People kept coming up to the room until 12:30. Father O'Brien showed me a telegram he had just received, to the effect that a poll of the Catholic hierarchy showed that ninety per cent were opposed to entering the war.

Saturday, October 4

Had accepted an invitation to have lunch with General Wood in Chicago, but my plane had been held down by weather during the night and was three hours late leaving Fort Wayne. Since I was hours too late for my lunch appointment, I took a taxi directly to the Blackstone Hotel for a conference with Bob Stuart, Page Hufty, Dick Moore, and Ed Webster concerning America First plans and organization.

Then to General Wood's home for an hour's conference with the general. We discussed, among other matters, the possibility of adjourning the America First Committee until the congressional campaigns begin in 1942. I took the stand that an adjournment at this time would not be understood by our members, that they would feel we were showing

274. Reverend John A. O'Brien of Notre Dame University.

weakness at the very moment we should be fighting the hardest. The noninterventionist forces in this country have placed their confidence in us and their support behind us. We have accepted their confidence and support—in fact, we have asked for it. Now, we cannot let these people down at the very moment they have a right to expect us to stand firm. Wood agrees, but thinks our action in regard to adjournment should probably be decided by the result of the action Congress takes on the Neutrality bill. I reserve judgment about this until later.

General Wood has given a tremendous amount of his time and effort to the America First Committee. He is working much too hard for a man of his age and looks tired. He sees the country being led closer and closer to war in spite of anything we do. Our strength and influence is growing rapidly, but the power of our opposition is great. The amazing thing is not that we are so close to war but that we have been able to hold the war forces back as long as we have. Their ranks include the American government, the British government, the Jews, and the major portion of the press, radio, and motion-picture facilities of the country. We have on our side the mass of the people, but it is a question of how long the people can withstand the flood of propaganda with which the country is being covered. They have no accurate source of information to which to turn. Also, regardless of the attitude of our people, it is a question as to whether the President will force us into war by actions and incidents which will make it unavoidable. He is in a position where he can force war on us whether we want it or not.

General Wood and I both see this situation and are in quite close agreement in regard to the dangers involved. Both of us would prefer to be devoting our time to other affairs, but both of us feel the work of the America First Committee is worth any personal sacrifice we can make at the present time. Wood says he must soon choose between giving up his work with Sears, Roebuck and giving up such active participation in the affairs of the America First Committee. He says it is impossible for him to continue to carry on both.

I have a different decision to make, and one which is not quite so pressing. I am very anxious to do some writing which will require more concentration than I can give and still be very active in America First work. Also, this semipolitical activity connected with America First is not leading to the type of life I wish to live. I have now spent the larger part of my time for over two years on this and similar work, to say nothing of the months I spent in the Air Corps in 1939 and the survey I made of European aviation before that. Since I have no intention of going into politics permanently, I feel it is time for me to begin building toward the future of a different type of life.

I would like to do some writing on aviation and other subjects, carry on some of the biological-research projects I discontinued when the war clouds began to gather, and build a permanent home for my family somewhere in the country—possibly in northern California or Oregon. (It is long past time for us to plant the roots of a real home. It is all very well to travel, and I love it as much as I ever did, but one should have a home he owns and loves to return to. I want one; Anne deserves one; and the children need one.) But if we get into the type of war Roosevelt is headed for, there probably won't be any opportunity for writing or research or a permanent home for years at best. So, no matter what sacrifice it involves, I feel my time is well spent in opposing our participation in this war. And even aside from a personal standpoint, I simply could not stand idly by and watch my country follow a leadership I think is so dishonest, so incompetent, and so wrong.

Sunday, October 5

Russians claim successful counterattacks.

Off [Detroit] train at 7:25. Taxi to 508 Lakepointe. Breakfast with Mother and B. The garden is full of pheasants and other birds and various kinds of fruit. The new radio-phonograph I bought for Mother has arrived and seems to have an excellent tone. Early supper. Then to station and boarded the 7:00 train to New York.

Monday, October 6

Russians claim German losses 3,000,000. Put own at 1,128,000.

Stopped at Hoover's apartment at 11:00 for a short conference. He felt that whether or not we intervene in the war now depends far more upon the speed of military developments in Europe than upon opposition that can be exerted in this country. Hoover told me he felt my Des Moines address was a mistake (the mention of the Jews in connection with the war-agitating groups). I told him I felt my statements had been both moderate and true. He replied that when you had been in politics long enough you learned not to say things just because they are true. (But, after all, I am not a politician—and that is one of the reasons why I don't wish to be one. I would rather say what I believe when I want to say it than to measure every statement I make by its probable popularity.)

Lunch with Harold Bixby in my room in the Waldorf. He is discouraged about the general situation in the country. We discussed the general inefficiency in Washington. Bix says the British are trading as hard as ever and were very hesitant about letting Pan American ferry military planes across Africa lest the company take the opportunity to try for a commercial concession on that route! Much as they may need the planes for their fighting forces, the British can still take time out to make a good trade. But, after all, they have got to live *after* the war as well as *through* it; and that is not as simple a problem for them as it is for us (not that it looks so very simple for us at this time).

Wednesday, October 8

German armies continue to advance into Russia. United States brings pressure on Finland to make terms with Russia. British sink additional Italian shipping. China claims success in war against Japan—recapture of Ichang.

Anne and I decided to leave for Martha's Vineyard on the night train.

Lunch with Truman Smith and Paul Palmer[275] in the latter's apartment at the Volney Hotel. We discussed war trends and the Russian situation. The reports that come through indicate that the Russian armies are in a state of collapse. Palmer says one of the reasons why the papers give such an erroneous impression about the war is that the editors have discovered that their newsstand circulation drops whenever they headline Axis successes. As a result, they try to find some Allied success to headline, no matter how insignificant it may be.

Boarded the Boston train at 10:30.

275. Editor with *Reader's Digest*.

Thursday, October 9

Germany reports collapse of Russian armies in Ukraine; take Orel.

Off train at 7:00. Anne and I left separately to avoid recognition. Breakfast standing at a station counter. Then went for a half hour's walk through the narrow and winding streets. Boarded the 8:20 train for Woods Hole. The conductor was very considerate to us, and no one on the car bothered us during the trip. People who live in the country and in small towns seem to invariably be more considerate than those who come from large cities. Arrived home just before lunch. Everyone well.

Friday, October 10

Conflicting reports from Germany and Russia. The Germans claim a great victory. The Russians claim the German Army has been checked. Roosevelt asks Congress to revise the Neutrality Act and for authority to arm United States merchant ships.

Anne and I spent most of the afternoon on plans for the winter. Soeur Lisi is leaving for Switzerland this month. Christine is leaving in December. We are moving to a heated house (about a mile away) about November.

Saturday, October 11

House passes second $6 billion Lend-Lease bill 328 to 67. Conflicting claims from Germany and Russia continue.

Anne, Jon, Land, and I drove to Gay Head. There was a strong wind, and the seas were high. Jon and I found a barrel that had been washed up on the beach. He got inside, and I rolled him down the slope to the edge of the breakers. Then we carried the barrel to the top of the bluff, and Jon, Land, and I pushed it over the edge.

Monday, October 13

German armies nearing Moscow.

Tuesday, October 14

The question has arisen as to whether I should make my next address in Boston or New York. Personally, I would prefer Boston, as I have already spoken twice in New York this year. But Flynn and Webster have engaged Madison Square Garden for the thirtieth and are extremely anxious that I be one of the speakers. Of course, the America First headquarters in Chicago wants me to speak at *both* Boston and New York (Boston on the twenty-fifth). But I feel "written out" and think it would be a mistake to give a poorly prepared address in either place.

If you ask thousands of people to come to listen to you, you owe it to them to say something worth listening to, and that takes time to prepare. I think I will decide on New York. If we had unlimited time in which to organize, Boston would be a more effective place for our next meeting. But conditions are so critical that we must lay our plans for each meeting as though it were our last meeting. A meeting at Madison Square Garden in New York will have more immediate effect than one in Boston.

Friday, October 17

Soviet Cabinet reported fleeing Moscow. Japanese Cabinet resigns. Morgenthau says debt limit must be raised above $65 billion.

Saturday, October 18

United States destroyer Kearny *torpedoed off Iceland. House votes arming of merchant ships 259–138. Navy orders United States ships in Pacific to friendly ports. Defense heads draft plan for $100 billion for arms.*

Soeur Lisi left this morning for Switzerland. She was an excellent nurse and wonderful with the children. We all shall miss her. Spent part of the day working on my address, part chopping wood with Jon, and part on routine. Evening reading by the fireplace.

Monday, October 20

German armies reported forty miles from Rostov. Dies lists 1,124 names of government employees alleged to be Communists or affiliates.

Most of the day on address and routine. Spent an hour outdoors in the afternoon, chopping wood with Jon. He is cutting down the nearby dead trees and chopping them into lengths for the fireplace.

Saturday, October 25

Germans advance in Ukraine. Russians claim to be holding on Moscow front. German reports stress snow and cold in northern Russia. Roosevelt says Army tank program to be doubled. Executions in occupied France continue.

Most of the day on address. Spent an hour cutting trees with Jon in the afternoon.

Tuesday, October 28

Strikes continue. Russia reports clash with Japanese patrol on Siberian border. Roosevelt says "shooting has started."

Wednesday, October 29

Russians claim German drive on Moscow stopped. German dispatches continue to stress weather. Strikes in United States continue.

Left in the Mercury after breakfast and crossed on the 9:15 boat to Woods Hole. Drove to the Long Island Aviation Country Club for the night.

Thursday, October 30

German armies enter Crimea. Russians holding on Moscow front.

Took off in Fairchild at 9:00. Spent half an hour in short practice flights around the field. Averaged about one flight every three minutes. Lunch at club. Then drove to New York. Left suitcase at Webster's home.

Webster and I walked to the Marquands' home for dinner. About fifty people there—most of them America First members and supporters. Among those I recall quickly were: Mr. and Mrs. Marquand, Norman Thomas, John Flynn, Amos Pinchot, Mr. Pennypacker (Philadelphia), Truman and Kay Smith, Oswald Garrison Villard,[276] Senator Clark (Idaho), Senator Nye, and Ambassador Cudahy.

We drove to Madison Square Garden behind the usual and apparently unavoidable police escort. The place was jammed when we arrived— every seat filled and a large crowd in the street outside. (The final police estimate placed the crowd outside at between 20,000 and 30,000, making a total attendance of more than 40,000 people, more than 50,000 if there were 30,000 outside the building.) John Flynn was chairman and Cudahy the first speaker. I followed Cudahy, and Wheeler ended the meeting, finishing his address shortly before 11:00.

This was in many ways the most successful meeting we have yet held. The only ones that would compare to it in size are the first meeting we held at Madison Square Garden last May and the meeting we held at the Hollywood Bowl in June. And we have never before had quite such enthusiasm at so large a meeting. I was unable to start speaking for six minutes after I was introduced! There is no better indication of how people feel about this war.

All of us who spoke took turns in going outside to speak briefly to the people who were not able to get inside the building. A small wooden stand had been built for this purpose on the sidewalk, and loudspeakers had been installed. The entire block in front of Madison Square Garden was jammed with people—both street and sidewalks. And the next block west was jammed as far as I could see!

The amazing thing was that we had the same reception from the people in the street as from those in the Garden. I had expected strong vocal opposition outside. There was *none*. It seemed as though every man and woman in the crowd was behind us! During the entire meeting there were only two instances of individuals trying to cause trouble, and they occurred at the time Flynn was opening the meeting. First, someone shouted out something I could not hear. A little later a man shouted, "Hang Roosevelt." The latter was almost certainly an opposition "plant." They will say that there were demands to hang the President at our meeting. But with over 40,000 people present those were the only two incidents that took place within my sight or hearing.

276. Author, journalist, and former editor of *The Nation*, 1932–35.

The thing that I think pleased me most about the meeting was the quality of the people who attended. I studied their faces carefully while I was sitting on the platform, and they were *far* above the average of New York. Those people are worth fighting for.

The meeting broke up at 11:00. I went to Webster's home afterward to attend a reception he was having for America First members and sympathizers. There seemed to be hundreds of people there. I stayed for two hours shaking hands and trying to carry on discussions with constant interruptions. It was far more work than the meeting itself. It was impossible to talk to anyone for more than ten or fifteen seconds before someone else broke in.

Saturday, November 1

United States destroyer Reuben James *sunk west of Iceland. Germans advance in Moscow area.*

Raining. We moved to the "Webb house" today. (Also on Seven Gates Farm.) Spent most of the morning helping to move. Went for a short walk in the rain before lunch. Got soaking wet, but enjoyed it. There is something unnatural about walking in the rain without getting wet at all. Spent the afternoon writing. I have started the second draft of an account of the flight from New York to Paris in the *Spirit of St. Louis*. This draft will be an expansion of the first draft. I want to write down all the details of the flight so they will not escape my memory. I will not try for the correct balance, shading, sequence, and accuracy until the third draft.

Thursday, November 6

Tension high between United States and Japan. Special envoy (Saburo Kurusu) en route to this country. German submarines reported in the vicinity of Newfoundland.

Raining. Spent most of the day writing. Half hour's walk in the afternoon.

Friday, November 7

Roosevelt pledges Stalin $1 billion in Lease-Lend aid. Conflicting reports from Germany and Russia continue.

Monday, November 10

British claim eleven Axis ships sunk in Mediterranean. Russians claim successful counterattacks in Moscow area. Germans claim success in Ukraine.

Anne and I left for New York at 8:30 in the Mercury. Crossed to Woods Hole on the 9:00 boat. Stopped at the Knollenbergs' home in New Haven for tea at 4:00. Anne decided to spend the night with them. After an hour's stop I drove on to New York. Boarded the 10:40 New York Central train for Detroit.

Tuesday, November 11

Off at Detroit at 12:30. Walked toward the nearest phone booth; but just before I reached it, I heard someone calling my name and found that Mr. [Frank] Campsall of the Ford Motor Company had come to meet me. He had been standing outside the New York Pullman but had not recognized me at first, as I was wearing glasses (without glass) and had my hat pulled down in front. He said Mrs. Roosevelt was on the same train, which explained the group of photographers and reporters I had just passed by.

Campsall left me at the Fords' home in Dearborn for lunch with Henry Ford. There was no one else there. We discussed the war and the trends in this country. After lunch we picked up Mr. Sorensen and drove out to the new bomber plant.[277] It is a huge building, with a large flying field in front of it, still in the process of construction. According to present plans, they expect to go into production on four-engine bombers.

277. Construction of the bomber plant at Willow Run began in 1941 for the purpose of manufacturing the Liberator B-24, a four-engine bomber designed and originally produced by Consolidated Vultee Aircraft. The plant was a mile long and a quarter mile wide and cost $165 million to build. Seventy assembly lines were set up, and the estimated number of aircraft workers needed was 100,000. It began production in 1942.

I cannot help wondering what all this military construction is leading to. It is, of course, much more than we need for defense. As a matter of fact, what we need most for defense is an intelligent plan rather than great quantities of military equipment. It is not enough to simply build arms. We must have some idea of *how* and *where* we are going to use them. When we build planes, we must, at the same time train the personnel to go with them, construct airports from which they are to be operated, etc., etc. In other words, it must be part of a balanced program if it is to be successful. I don't see much balance as I travel about the country, and most of the people I talk to in the aviation industry say that their greatest problems lie in their relationship with the government. Washington, they say, is in great confusion.

I am certain of one thing, however; if we continue to follow our present leadership and our present trends, all life in this country is going to go through a revolutionary change of the first magnitude. And it is not going to result in spreading "the four freedoms" all over the world, or even all over our own country. What has happened to Europe is now happening to us. Unless I am greatly mistaken, this country is about to face the greatest test in its history. The early indications are not encouraging, but I am convinced that under the surface there is still real character in our people. We have in our nation both the worst and the best. The question is, can we find a way to bring the best forward? If we can do that, we have a great destiny. But if we must depend upon a complete mixture, if we must depend upon averaging together all the elements of which we are composed, if we continue to follow our present trends, then I am doubtful of the future.

From the bomber plant, we drove back to Bennett's office, where Ford, Bennett, and I spent half an hour in conference. Bennett and Ford are now optimistic about the labor situation. Bennett feels we should attempt to get the labor groups to take a stronger stand against entering the war.

Dinner with Mr. and Mrs. Ford at their residence. We discussed many subjects, including the early days of the Ford organization. Ford told me that both he and his wife had been born within seven miles of where they are now living. Night at the Ford home.

Wednesday, November 12

British claim seven more ships sunk, five damaged in Mediterranean.

Breakfast with Henry and Mrs. Ford at 9:00. Afterward, Ford took me aside and said he and Mrs. Ford wanted to do something to help oppose American intervention. He asked me to talk to Bennett about what could be done. In view of the collapse of the plan we had worked out for an advertising campaign some months ago, I had not planned on asking Ford for help again. I do not want my friends to feel I am always trying to get something from them. Ford could be a great factor in opposing this war, but I have talked the situation over with him before, and my feeling has been that if he wanted to do anything, it was his turn to make the first move this time.

Ford is greatly interested in creating a "Parliament of Man, Federation of the World." I don't discourage him, but it seems to me that there are an awful lot of intermediate steps that require our attention at this time.

Drove to Campsall's office for a quarter hour's conference. Then went with Sorensen to see the design of the new Army tank the Ford Company is building. Later, we went through the aircraft-engine factory. Then we looked over the Sperry antiaircraft sight, which the Ford people expect to put on mass production.

Conference and lunch with Bennett. We discussed what Ford might do to help the noninterventionist cause. I suggested that he start by contributing an amount of money to America First each month. Bennett asked if I thought $5,000 or $10,000 would be about right. I told him I thought that would be too much and out of proportion to the amounts given by other contributors. I suggested $2,000. Bennett and I agreed that we must protect Ford from too much adverse criticism in whatever part he took. Ford may be too old to see the reaction that will come after this war is over, and we do not want him to be the victim of war hysteria during the last years of his life. Bennett suggested that Ford give the $2,000 directly to me each month. I said I thought it would be much better for him to give it directly to General Wood. We spent some time discussing John L. Lewis[278] and labor's attitude on the war.

From Bennett's office I drove to 508 Lakepointe to spend the rest of

278. President of the United Mine Workers, and organizer of the C.I.O. in 1935.

the afternoon and have supper with Mother and B. We spent the evening playing records on the new phonograph. Then I took a taxi to the station and boarded the 12:30 train to Chicago.

Thursday, November 13

Off train at 7:20. Taxi to Chicago Club. Breakfast with General Wood and Truman Smith. Then to Wood's rooms in the club, where we discussed the developments of the war in Europe. Truman gave a brilliant outline of the situation.

Lunch with General Wood, Truman Smith, and Colonel McCormick at the Chicago Club. Earl Jeffrey came for a short visit after lunch. I went to the headquarters of the Illinois America First Committee to see Mrs. Fairbank. We drove to Mrs. Fairbank's home to discuss America First plans in light of the news we have just received that the Neutrality Act revision has passed the House 212 to 194.

To Chicago Club after supper, where Truman outlined war developments on a map of Europe to General Wood and myself. He really makes a map become alive.

Friday, November 14

House passes Neutrality bill amendment. Germans advance in Crimea. Russians claim successful counterattacks in Moscow area. Labor troubles in United States continue.

Taxi to Sears, Roebuck offices to attend a conference between General Wood and Mr. [Arthur S.] Hatch, manager of the Chicago branch of the Ford Motor Company. We discussed the support Henry Ford has promised to give us. Returned to Chicago Club for a conference with Bob Stuart and Truman Smith at 11:15. Bob is just back from Washington, where he has been working against the revision of the Neutrality Act. Lunch at 1:00 with General Wood, Bob Hutchins (University of Chicago), and Bill Benton (also University of Chicago).

Hutchins asked me whether I thought it was time to bring out a peace plan. Said he had been studying the possibility of doing so. I told him I doubted that the American people were well enough acquainted with conditions in Europe to be willing to accept at this time any plan that would be practical. I told him I was afraid we would find ourselves in the position of guaranteeing a peace that could not possibly last.

Saturday, November 15

Roosevelt refuses to order "closed shop." British announce sinking of Ark Royal near Gibraltar. Marines ordered to leave posts in China. Reports from Germany and Russia conflict.

Breakfast with General Wood at 7:45. I advocated that America First take part in the 1942 elections as a nonpartisan organization.

I took the 2:30 train for New York.

Sunday, November 16

Russians claim gains at Leningrad and in Donets Basin. German reports continue to stress weather and now mention "fierce Russian resistance."

Off train at 8:20. I drove to Woods Hole. Boat almost on time. Home for dinner.

Wednesday, November 19

Conflicting reports from Germany and Russia. Strikes continue in United States. Japanese situation tense.

Spent the morning working on my *Spirit of St. Louis* manuscript.

Mail and papers arrive. Udet killed "testing a new type of gun." I can't help thinking of his mother and the evening we all spent together at Udet's apartment in Berlin.

Thursday, November 27

Japan sends additional troops to Indo-China.

Went through some of the old letters and papers Mother gave me. Letters from Mother to me. Letters I wrote when I was going to school, when I was barnstorming, when I was a flying cadet at the time of Father's death. They all bring back old memories and leave me with thoughts of how much was left unsaid. One only writes down a small portion of life, and what one writes gives a warped and imperfect picture. You write about the unusual rather than the usual, the abnormal rather than the normal. The normal in life is the most difficult to see. Someone else can perceive it better than you can. You don't see life clearly because you live too close to it. The records of life are mostly of the *strange* events that pass through it, and, consequently, records give a very distorted picture of life. Records are more apt to be of illness than of health, of controversy rather than of happiness, of arguments rather than of agreements.

Friday, November 28

British advance in Africa. Germans advance in Moscow area. United States Marines leave Shanghai.

Stuart phoned from Chicago to tell me about the meeting of the national committee. (I had told him not to announce that I would speak at Boston until after the national committee had met.) I told him it was all right to go ahead with plans and to announce the Boston meeting whenever he thought advisable.

Saturday, November 29

Japanese situation critical. Press of both countries talking of war. President Quezon says Philippines unprepared for war. Blames United States.

Morning and first part of afternoon on dictation and routine. Rest of afternoon helping Jon and Land build a tree house.

Sunday, November 30

Russians claim successful counterattacks in Rostov area.

Anne left in the Mercury for New York this morning to look for a new nurse. Spent first part of morning helping Jon and Land with their tree house. Land has become a monkey and climbs about on the tree with an eight-foot rope tied behind him for a tail. I finished the framework for the floor and installed a "drawbridge," consisting of a plank from the framework to the hillside. When down, it can be crawled over on hands and knees. It is lifted by a rope and pulley arrangement; and when up, it makes the tree house quite impregnable. Left Jon and Land to hammer in some extra nails and spent the rest of the morning finishing the first draft of my address for Boston.

All the ships passing by the island are now in dark "war paint."

Monday, December 1

Relationship between United States and Japan becoming more critical. Roosevelt cuts vacation and returns to Washington. Russia claims recapture of Rostov and route of German armies in that area.

Spent the morning in Anne's tent working on my Boston address. Anne leaves her character stamped on everything she touches. She has made even this tent beautiful and inspiring, and she does all this with the utmost simplicity. She has put blue print curtains on the windows (the same ones she used in the little house on the hill at Lloyd Neck). And she has tacked up pictures of Chartres saints and angels on plywood boards around the walls—two or three of them, not enough to interfere with the uncrowded simplicity of the others. In front of the unvarnished wood table are three Botticelli post-card reproductions and one Renoir. On the table are two very old, small brass elephants from Siam. Beside the elephants are a stone, a feather, and a shell. The tent is a wonderful place to work, secluded—a view to islands beyond the sea—and wild-cherry branches hanging over the window. It is very easy to keep warm, too, and putting an occasional stick of wood in the little airtight stove breaks up the monotony of too constant writing.

Thor has been at my side ever since Anne left this morning. In some way, he knows when she goes on a long trip. When Anne takes the children to school, Thor lies outside the porch, or goes a hundred feet down the road and waits for her to come back. But after she left this morning, he came directly to me and seemed to have given up hope of her returning today. He knows that suitcases mean a long trip, and I think he can also tell the difference in the clothes Anne wears. Some clothes mean a walk in the woods; others mean a trip to school; and he may associate still others with a longer absence. He is more intuitive than many people.

Saturday, December 6

British declare war on Hungary, Rumania, and Finland. Russians claim continued advance in Rostov area. Germans claim Russian drive stopped.

First part of afternoon on writing and routine. Then spent an hour with Jon and Land at the tree house, shooting at targets with Jon's .22 rifle. Evening on writing, reading, and a phone call to Anne. She has engaged an old Breton nurse.

Sunday, December 7

Roosevelt appeals to Hirohito. Russians claim Germans trapped at Taganrog.

The radio is announcing that Japan has attacked the Philippines and the Hawaiian Islands and that Pearl Harbor has been bombed! An attack in the Philippines was to be expected, although I did not think it would come quite so soon. But Pearl Harbor! How did the Japs get close enough, and where is our Navy? Or is it just a hit-and-run raid of a few planes, exaggerated by radio commentators into a major attack? The Japanese can, of course, raid the Hawaiian Islands, or even the West Coast, with aircraft carriers. But the cost in carriers and planes lost is going to be awfully high unless our Navy is asleep—or in the Atlantic. The question in my mind is, how much of it has been sent to the Atlantic to aid Britain?

Monday, December 8

Japan declares war on United States and Britain. Hawaii and Philippines attacked. Guam bombed.

I find it impossible to keep my mind off the war or to concentrate on writing. How did our Air Force and Navy let the Japanese get to Hawaii so easily? What have the Japanese losses been? And ours? I am not surprised that the Japs attacked. We have been prodding them into war for weeks. They have simply beaten us to the gun. But the radio reports indicate that the attack on Hawaii was a heavy one. Have we sent so many of our planes and so much of our Navy to the Atlantic that the Japs feel they are able to get away with an attack on Pearl Harbor?

Phoned Bob Stuart in Chicago and told him I felt the Boston meeting should be canceled. Phoned General Wood in Boston. His first words were, "Well, he got us in through the back door."

Wrote a statement for the press and sent it to the America First headquarters in Chicago. Went for a walk along the beach with Anne while we discussed the new war developments.

The President spoke at 12:00. Asked for a declaration of war. Senate passed a declaration of war unanimously. Only one "no" in House.[279] What else was there to do? We have been asking for war for months. If the President had asked for a declaration of war before, I think Congress would have turned him down with a big majority. But now we have been attacked, and attacked in home waters. We have brought it on our own shoulders; but I can see nothing to do under these circumstances except to fight. If I had been in Congress, I certainly would have voted for a declaration of war.

279. Miss Jeanette Rankin, Republican Representative from Montana, registered the sole vote in Congress against President Roosevelt's resolution to declare war on Japan. In 1917 she had voted against war with Germany.

United States
Wartime

United States declares war on Japan. Japanese forces reported landing in Philippines. Navy reports serious losses at Pearl Harbor. Fifteen hundred killed in Hawaii. Thailand surrenders. Britain declares war on Japan. Germans say Moscow drive will be halted for winter.

Morning on writing and routine. Walk along beach before lunch. High wind and spray. To Vineyard Haven in the afternoon for poison-ivy injection (Anne and I). The town had just had an air-raid alarm! (Not practice—actual.) The doctor said it was so genuine that Mitchel Field sent up several squadrons of fighting planes. Everyone was excited. People here actually expect to see enemy planes flying overhead, and they believe there is grave danger of the town being bombed.

Evening until 10:00 writing and reading. Then listened to the President's broadcast. "All news bad," he says. Apparently we have had heavy losses in the Pacific. I had the impression that Roosevelt was forceing himself to speak with more conviction than he felt.

Thursday, December 11

British confirm loss of Prince of Wales *and* Repulse. *Japanese advance in Malaya. British lift Tobruk siege.*

Germany and Italy have declared war on the United States. Now, all that I feared would happen has happened. We are at war all over the world, and we are unprepared for it from either a spiritual or a material standpoint. Fortunately, in spite of all that has been said, the oceans are still difficult to cross; and we have the time to adjust and prepare, which France lacked and which England has had only in part since aviation has spanned the barrier of her Channel. We can, of course, be raided; but unless we let ourselves go completely to pieces internally, we cannot be invaded successfully.

But this is only one part of the picture. We are in a war which requires us to attack if we are to win it. We must attack in Asia and in Europe, in fact, all over the world. That means raising and equipping an army of many millions and building shipping, which we have not now got. And after that, if we are to carry through our present war aims, it probably means the bloodiest and most devastating war of all history.

And then what? We haven't even a clear idea of what we are fighting to attain. We talk about spreading democracy and freedom all over the world, but they are to us words rather than conditions. We haven't even got them here in America, and the farther we get into this war the farther we get away from democracy and freedom. Where is it leading us to, and when will it end? The war might stop this winter, but that is improbable. It may go on for fifty years or more. That also is improbable. The elements are too conflicting and confused to form any accurate judgment of its length. There may be a series of wars, one after another, going on indefinitely.

Possibly the world will come to its senses sooner than I expect. But, as I have often said, the environment of human life has changed more rapidly and more extensively in recent years than it has ever changed before. When environment changes, there must be a corresponding change in life. That change must be so great that it is not likely to be completed in a decade or in a generation. Periods of great change bring advantages to some nations and disadvantages to others. They affect the possessions and the "rights" of men, as the coming of the white man to America affected the possessions and "rights" of the Indian. I think the best attitude to take is that we are entering such a period of change and must adjust our outlook and our action accordingly.

Spent the evening reading.

Friday, December 12

Germany and Italy declare war on United States. We declare war on them. Japanese reported checked on all "land fronts."

Now that we are at war I want to contribute as best I can to my country's war effort. It is vital for us to carry on this war as intelligently, as constructively, and as successfully as we can, and I want to do my part.

My first inclination was to write directly to the President, offering my services, and telling him that while I had opposed him in the past and had not changed my convictions, I was ready in time of war to submerge my personal viewpoint in the general welfare and unity of the country. But the trouble is that I have no confidence in President Roosevelt. When I think of the President of the United States, I have one reaction; but when I think of Franklin Roosevelt, I have another.

It is not only my own experience and judgment, but I do not know a single man who has known Roosevelt, friend or enemy, who trusts what he says from one week to the next. And the President has the reputation, even among his friends, for being a vindictive man. If I wrote to him at this time, he would probably make what use he could of my offer from a standpoint of politics and publicity and assign me to some position where I would be completely ineffective and out of the way.

Then what is the best move to make? Should I write to General Arnold and offer my services to the Air Corps? I trust Arnold, but of course he would have to take my offer up with the President. Still, that may be the best plan. On the other hand, I might turn back to the aviation industry and make my contribution through it, through some organization such as United Aircraft, or Curtiss-Wright, or Pan American. But I have the feeling that where I really belong and where I really want to be in time of war is in the Air Corps. I sometimes wish, for a moment, that I had not resigned my commission; but whenever I turn the circumstances over in my mind, I feel I took the right action. There was, I think, no honorable alternative.

If it were not for the war, I would like nothing better than to spend a year or two thinking and reading and writing. But I simply cannot remain idle while my country is at war. I *must* take some part in it, whatever that may be.

Monday, December 15

Four Japanese transports sunk off Luzon. Russians claim Germans cut off in retreat in Orel area. Claim advances along entire front.

Packed suitcase after lunch, arranged various details, and left for New York in the Mercury. Boat to Woods Hole nearly an hour late.

Tuesday, December 16

Heavy fighting reported in Malaya. Japanese land in Borneo. Russians report new advances.

Went for an hour's walk through the [New York] streets, and then to Ed Webster's home for a dinner he was giving for his fiancée, to which the America First street speakers from the Greater New York area had been invited—about forty in all. Webster is to be married next month to a girl he met in the America First organization. Some of the more radical groups were represented at the dinner, and some of them were not at all in sympathy with the decision to dissolve the America First Committee after the Japanese attack and the declaration of war by all the Axis powers. I tried to explain to them that it was really to the best interests of the country, and that no matter what we did or advocated or stood for, we would have been viciously and bitterly attacked if we had continued our activities after the start of war.

Wednesday, December 17

Japanese shell Maui and Johnston islands. Attack on Hong Kong continues. Lull in the Philippines. Russian Army recaptures Kalinin.

An antiaircraft searchlight has been installed in the park outside my window [Engineers Club]. Sentries are pacing up and down beside it. It is obviously more for appearance than for use, and there is no sign of the crew except their duffel bags thrown into a pile near one of the trucks. Of course, New York might be raided, and the city certainly should be prepared. I am inclined to think, however, that the Germans have enough on their hands for the time being without organizing transatlantic bombing expeditions. Of course, if they could catch us as much asleep again as the Japanese did at Pearl Harbor, it might be worth while.

Transoceanic raids, either by carrier or long-range bomber, are perfectly possible. The question is whether or not they are worth while, and that depends on many elements which are not predictable. It depends on the psychology of the attacker, the preparedness of the attacked, the momentary trends and policies of the war, etc. The attack on Pearl Harbor was certainly worth while for the Japs. But whether they would have found it worth while if we had been on the alert is another question.

Spent first part of morning on phone calls. Then drove out to the Long Island Aviation Country Club for lunch. I had planned on flying in the afternoon, but found that all pilots' licenses had been canceled and that to get my license reinstated would require a trip to an inspector's office, photographs, fingerprinting, birth certificate, etc., etc.

Returned to New York and spent two hours at the Engineers Club, writing. There was to have been a test of air-raid sirens this afternoon, but something apparently went wrong again. There was no sound. The city has been having considerable difficulty in installing a satisfactory air-raid warning system.

Thursday, December 18

Army, Navy, and Air Force commanders replaced in Hawaii. House passes bill extending military service to all men between twenty-one and forty-four. Military situation in Philippines reported "improved." Japanese pressure on Singapore increases. Russians claim the German armies are "in confused retreat."

Phoned Major Beebe[1] regarding an appointment with General Arnold— he will reply by wire. Phoned Dr. [Vannevar] Bush—appointment for Saturday morning.

Friday, December 19

Senate votes for draft age of nineteen. Russians claim continued advance. British claim additional successes in Libya. Reports about our submarine activity in the Pacific conflict.

The newspapers are rapidly winning the war for us. I wish our military forces could keep up to them. From now on it will be extremely difficult to find out what is really happening in the war. I mark down only what the papers carry each day. Much of it I feel is wrong or distorted, but I seldom have any way of checking.

Phoned Harry Davison, but he was away. Wanted to talk to him about purchasing defense bonds. Bob Stuart came at 11:00 to discuss his plans for the future. He is uncertain whether he should volunteer or return to law school long enough to get his degree. He left Yale Law School to or-

1. Major Eugene Beebe, aide to General Arnold; later a brigadier general.

ganize America First and needs one more year to finish his course. He thinks he might be able to get his degree in six months, however, by working overtime. He wanted my advice. I told him I could only discuss the various conditions he would encounter in each course, and that I would not attempt to say he should take the one or the other, because I felt that was a matter he only could decide. I told him that people with differing viewpoints would quite properly make different decisions under the same set of circumstances.

Boarded the night train for Washington.

Saturday, December 20

Japanese enter Hong Kong. British advance in Africa continues. Russians continue to advance. British evacuate Penang. Congress passes bill to draft men twenty to forty-four.

Off train at 7:30. To Carnegie Institution to meet Dr. Bush at 9:30. I told him I was trying to find the way in which I could contribute most effectively to the country's war effort and that before coming to any definite decision I wanted to discuss the situation with him. (Bush is in close contact with a great number of activities, both in and out of aviation.) We discussed various research projects in connection with the war, and among other suggestions Bush said he thought I should look into the possibility of making a connection with Colonel Donovan's[2] organization. He said they were in need of someone who had a general knowledge of aviation. Bush says he has given up thinking of the past and the future for the time being and is devoting his mind entirely to the present.

Walked for half an hour, and then took a taxi to the station to buy my return ticket. There are many uniforms on the streets. Went to a news film in the late afternoon. The clapping for the war pictures was sporadic and forced—not at all as I remember it in the last war. The most clapping came for a picture of the President, but even that showed little enthusiasm.

Returned to the Carlton and wrote a personal letter to General Arnold, offering my services to the Air Corps. I wrote it in such a way that he

2. Colonel William J. Donovan, a veteran of World War I. An attorney, Donovan became co-ordinator of information in the U.S. government in 1941. In 1942 he was appointed director of the Office of Strategic Services, and later became a major general.

could take action or not, as he felt most advisable. Night train to New York.

Sunday, December 21

Heavy fighting reported at Davao, Mindanao. Our submarines sink another Jap transport. Admiral King appointed Commander-in-Chief of the United States fleet. Axis submarines reported off both American coasts.

Off train at 7:45. Sent for Mercury and left for Vineyard Haven at 8:15. Delayed half an hour by a "war" parade at Fall River. Bands and "Legionnaire" girl band leaders with short skirts and very red legs. (It is one of the coldest days of the winter.) Behind them marched crowds of citizens carrying small flags. I could not help feeling that the American spirit was there but that it was without direction or leadership. Those people wanted to do their part. Most of them would probably be willing to make any sacrifice their country called on them to make. They were giving play to their spirit in that parade, working off some of their desire to take their part in the war. In a few minutes it would be over, and they would return to their homes and shops and offices, back in the routine of their old lives. This energy, this spirit in America must be directed intelligently if we are to wage this war with any degree of success. Up to the present time that direction has been lacking. These people must be given something more important to do than collect tinfoil and scraps of paper, and bundles for Britain, and organize New England villages against transatlantic air raids. They must be given a real, an active, an effective part in their country's destiny.

Crossed to Martha's Vineyard on the 5:30 boat. Home for supper. The house is full of holly that Anne and the children have cut from the trees on the place.

Wednesday, December 24

Pétain reported resigning. Japanese land on Wake Island. British continue to advance in Libya.

Anne, Jon, Land, and I cut a Christmas tree from a clump of overcrowded pines a few hundred feet from the house. It is about twelve feet high! Most of afternoon with Anne and the children, setting up the tree. We trimmed it after the children's supper.

Thursday, December 25, Christmas

Japanese land at additional points in Philippines. Now hold seven beachheads. Washington announces loss of Wake Island. American freighter torpedoed off the California coast.

Spent most of the day with Anne and the children—opening presents, flying gliders, etc. Went for several walks through the woods and along the shore. It has been a happy family Christmas, but overhung by war.

It is definite now. Anne is bearing her fifth child.

Friday, December 26

Hong Kong surrenders. Japanese advance in Philippines. British take Bengasi. United States protests occupation of Saint Pierre and Miquelon by "Free French."

Spent most of morning walking through the woods and along the shore, trying to lay plans. What part am I to take in the war in view of the obvious antagonism of the Administration? Decide to make another trip to New York and Washington next week to try to find what I can best do and to sound out the attitude of the President.

Tuesday, December 30

Japanese advance in Malaya.

An announcement has come over the radio that I have volunteered for the Air Corps. Apparently General Arnold has given out the substance of the letter I wrote him. Is it an indication that my offer will be accepted? And if so, will it be as a civilian or as an officer?

Saturday, January 3

Japanese capture Manila. Heavy fighting reported in Malaya. British capture Bardia.

Letter came from Jerry Land. He has talked to Colonel Donovan. Suggests I see him. I am hesitant about joining Donovan's organization. I understand that it is full of politics, ballyhoo, and controversy. But nothing can be lost by discussing the situation with Colonel Donovan.

Monday, January 5

Chinese claim total of 52,000 enemy casualties in Changsha campaign. Japan claims capture of city. Russia claims new advances, including capture of Borovsk. Rioting in occupied France.

Phoned Jerry Land at 11:00 and arranged to meet him in Washington Thursday. Rest of day putting affairs in order. I am trying to arrange everything, so that if I should be called away it will leave the least possible burden on Anne.

Wednesday, January 7

Boat on time. Not many passengers on board—mostly local people. Bought coffee and sandwiches at the lunch counter and talked to several of the island men while I was eating. A young soldier came up and introduced himself, then introduced me to a Captain P. W. Gray, who has been ferrying planes to England. Normally he (Gray) devotes his time to managing the Mayflower Airlines. His home is on Nantucket. Gray told me he has made fourteen ferry trips to England—some landplane and some flying boat, some via Newfoundland and some via Bermuda. Was attacked by German fighters south of Ireland on one of his flying-boat trips, and several members of his crew were hit. He gets $500.00 per ferry flight; guaranteed at least two flights a month. We sat together on the train to Boston, and discussed transatlantic flying and the war.

Boarded the 11:00 train for Washington.

Thursday, January 8

Roosevelt submits budget for $59 billion to Congress; asks $9 billion in new taxes. Japanese continue to advance on Singapore. Russians claim new gains.

Train late. Off at 8:30. Took a taxi to the Hay-Adams instead of to the Carlton (where I had reserved a room) to confuse the press. Breakfast and haircut; then went to the Carlton. Rooms are almost impossible to get in Washington these days and must be reserved well in advance. Phoned Jerry Land, and made an appointment to see Colonel Donovan at Jerry's office at 12:00. I arrived ten minutes early to talk to Jerry. I told him my feeling of hesitancy about making a connection with Donovan's organization. He agreed with most of my points.

Jerry had to leave for an engagement soon after Colonel Donovan arrived. Colonel Donovan and I discussed the situation for about fifteen minutes. I told him I was trying to find the best way in which I could take my part in the war effort and that it had been suggested I might make some connection with his organization. He said he would be glad to have me take part in his organization (provided, of course, that it would be satisfactory to the President!), but that he was not sure where I would fit into the work they were doing. Apparently the study of international air transportation that Dr. Bush thought Donovan was carrying on is actually being done by the Army and Navy. Donovan said he thought I should be working with the Air Corps. I told him I agreed but doubted that Roosevelt would permit it. Donovan thought he would. We left it that I would contact Donovan again after I had seen General Arnold and talked to him about the possibility of working with the Air Corps, either as an officer or a civilian. Donovan was very pleasant, but my conversation with him did not leave me with a feeling of enthusiasm for joining his organization.

Phoned Earl Findley (he had telegraphed two or three days ago asking me to get in touch with him). Made a 4:30 appointment. Findley came to ask what policy I thought he should follow in regard to the war in the Pacific.[3] I told him that I thought the Pacific was the most important area from our standpoint in America and that I felt it would be a tragic error to follow the people who advocated that we turn our back to the Pacific in order to concentrate on the war in Europe. I pointed out to him that if the Japanese gained control of Singapore, they would be a major threat to most of the British Empire and possibly cause the Allies to abandon their war in North Africa because of the difficulty of convoying supplies through the Indian Ocean.

3. In his capacity as editor of *U.S. Air Services.*

Friday, January 9

Japs continue advance on Singapore. Russians claim siege of Sevastopol lifted. Latest reports say seven Japanese warships lost in taking Wake Island.

Harold Bixby came for a half hour's visit before lunch. We discussed Pan American and the war, and I spoke to him about the possibility of my returning to active work with Pan American if political opposition prevents my returning to the Air Corps.

Dinner with Senator and Mrs. Shipstead and Mrs. (Cissy) Patterson[4] at the Shipsteads' home on East Capitol. We discussed the war and Minnesota and my father. Shipstead talked about my father's campaign in 1918. During the campaign it seems that a regulation was made, largely for political purposes, Shipstead says, that no public meetings could be held in Minnesota because of an influenza epidemic. A farmer, who was a strong supporter of my father at Dunnell, invited a large number of his friends and neighbors to his farm for a picnic. His plan was to have my father address them informally. Apparently no official objection was made to the people assembling for a picnic; but when my father began to talk to them, he was arrested by the sheriff. The farmer, a Mr. Olson, objected, and called upon his guests to preserve the right of free speech and to throw the sheriff out. Thereupon, he too was arrested. Charges were dropped against my father, but Olson was prosecuted.

Saturday, January 10

Japanese advance in Malaya. Russians report siege of Leningrad lifted.

A "blackout squad" arrived to put blackout strips around the edges of the [hotel] windows. It is, of course, quite possible that Washington will be raided, and it is wise to be fully prepared. Unless we permit an enemy base to be established on this side of the ocean, raids on American cities cannot be very heavy in comparison to the raids on European cities; but raids on a smaller scale could be made either by transoceanic bombers or by carrier-based aircraft.

4. Eleanor Medill Patterson, publisher and owner of the Washington (D.C.) *Times-Herald.*

Phoned Major Beebe at 10:00 and asked if it would be possible for me to see General Arnold over the weekend. Beebe asked me what I wanted to see Arnold about. I told him I wanted to find out from the general whether or not I could be of any assistance to the Air Corps. Beebe advised me to go directly to the Secretary of War. He said: "I am sure the Secretary of War will see you if you call his office and ask for an appointment." Sometimes you can tell more from the tone of a man's voice than you can from the actual words he says, especially if you know that man. It was obvious that everything had been arranged for me to see Secretary Stimson.

I phoned the Secretary of War's office. Stimson was away for the weekend but would be back Monday. His appointment secretary suggested I phone Monday morning at 10:00. Everyone I talked to was extremely courteous. They seemed to be expecting my call. What is in the wind? Reappointment to the Air Corps? Political intrigue? I wish I had more confidence in the members of the Roosevelt Administration.

To the new House Office Building for a 4:00 appointment with Congressman Knutson[5] (from my father's old district, the sixth of Minnesota). There are machine guns on the roofs of the House and Senate Office Buildings and sentries walking up and down in front of the Capitol. Spent half an hour with Knutson. At first, we discussed the developments of the war. Then he told me he thought I should run for the Senate in Minnesota, that I could be elected with no difficulty at all! I told Knutson I did not feel I was suited to political office and that I did not think I would make a good Senator. He was very insistent and kept on talking about it and trying to persuade me to take up residence in Minnesota.

It seems impossible for me to explain to most people my feeling about running for a political office. When I say I do not feel suited to such a position, they usually think I mean that I simply lack the necessary experience and training; but it is far deeper than that. It is the red tape, the indoor life, the handshaking, the compromising, the trivial details, the conventions, and a thousand similar elements that make me unsuited to political life. Also, the rewards do not appeal to me. I have no desire to be a Senator, or even a President if that were possible, simply for the satisfaction of having held such a high office. To be in politics would cut me off from the things in life I value most—freedom to move and think

5. Harold Knutson, Republican Representative from Minnesota, 1917–49. He was Republican "whip" in the House and chairman of the Ways and Means Committee.

and act as I think best; and it would remove all opportunity for solitude and all it represents. There is nothing I dread more in life than being bound by the opinions of other people and being tied to a permanent routine.

"But you have a duty to your country," says Knutson. Yes, I have a duty to my country, and I have tried to follow it; but duty to his country does not mean that every man should allow himself to be run for political office regardless of whether or not he feels suited to it. Harry Guggenheim once said, "The trouble with Cuba is that there are 6,000,000 Cubans and only one President." The welfare of a country requires, I think, that some of its people remain outside of politics. If a man feels he can contribute more out of political life than in it, then it is his duty to stay out.

Dinner at the home of Senator and Mrs. D. Worth Clark. Senator and Mrs. La Follette were also guests. We spent most of the evening discussing developments of the war.

The opinion of the House and Senate is that the truth of Pearl Harbor has not been told. The story that is told almost everywhere is that four battleships were sunk and three damaged, that at least twenty-seven warships were sunk or damaged, and that the docks were badly damaged. If these reports are true, Pearl Harbor was one of the great naval disasters of history and may change the future of the entire world.

Sunday, January 11

Japs claim capture of Kuala Lumpur. Russians claim new advances.

Harold Bixby came for lunch in my room. We spent most of the time discussing war conditions in China and Burma. Bixby suggested the possibility of my going to China to take part in directing military aviation operations against Japan. He said Japanese shipping lanes could be effectively harassed from Chinese airfields. He also suggested the possibility of upsetting the Japanese financial system by having a large amount of Japanese paper money printed and then dropping it over Japan from planes at night. Of course, there is nothing I would rather do than take charge of a project of this kind.

Dinner with Senator Shipstead at his home. We discussed many subjects, including the last war, my father, and his campaigns in Minnesota.[6]

6. During his political career C. A. Lindbergh, Sr., campaigned for election to the

Shipstead said he was running for the state Legislature at the same time my father was running for the Senate in 1916. He told me Father was responsible for breaking up the Non-Partisan League[7] when he discovered that corrupt practices were being carried on by officers of the organization.

Monday, January 12

Japanese land in Dutch Indies.

The morning papers carry a story with a Boston date line, saying I told "a friend" that I was going to Washington at the request of President Roosevelt! Of course it is an unmitigated lie. The press seldom misses a chance to add to the difficulties.

Phoned Secretary Stimson's office at 10:30. Received an appointment to see Stimson at 3:30. Stimson's secretary phoned to change my appointment from 3:30 to 4:30. I had to phone Senator Taft to change an appointment I had with him at 5:00. He said he would come at 3:00 instead.

Senator Taft arrived at 3:15 and stayed for half an hour. We discussed the war and the future. Taft says he hopes the country will take a more reasonable attitude on war aims after the contact with reality the next year or two is bound to bring. (My God! Will it take *a year or two?*)

Taxi to Munitions Building. Sentries all around, and a pass necessary to get in. Taken to Stimson's office after about a ten-minute wait. Stimson was seated at his desk. Greeted me courteously and spoke of the time I did him a favor in connection with Grandi's[8] visit to this country.

---

national House of Representatives, the national Senate, and the governorship of Minnesota.

7. Founded by Arthur C. Townley in 1915 in North Dakota, the Non-Partisan League supported state supervision of grain inspection and state-owned terminal elevators, flour mills, packing and storage plants, and also emphasized farmer-labor co-operation in politics. It became a powerful political force in North Dakota and in 1918 began to gather support among farmers, miners, and factory workers in Minnesota. It endorsed Charles A. Lindbergh, Sr.'s gubernatorial campaign in 1918, in which he was defeated in the primary.

8. Dino Grandi (Count di Mordano), Italian Ambassador to Great Britain. After World War I he had led the Fascist movement in the north of Italy. He came to the U.S. while Minister of Foreign Affairs, 1929-32.

(It was in 1930, as I recall. I was flying a Lockheed Vega to Miami. When I landed at Savannah, Georgia, I was told the State Department was trying to get me on the phone. It seemed that Grandi was to land at New York the following day. An anti-Fascist demonstration had been planned by Communists and antagonists of Mussolini. The Secretary of State [Mr. Stimson] was very anxious to avoid the demonstration and at the same time avoid the publicity which would attend the use of a large police force. The State Department wanted me to return to New York and meet Grandi in the harbor with a Sikorsky S-42 flying boat and fly him to Washington. The demonstration would thus be avoided without incidents.

The request involved complications, for I was scheduled to pilot the first one-day passenger flight to South America in the new Pan American S-42. Thirty-three passengers were in Miami, booked for the trip. If I turned back north to meet Grandi, the flight to South America would have to be postponed for at least two days. After phone calls to both Pan American Airways and the State Department, I agreed to meet Grandi and flew back to Washington. This was the "favor" Secretary Stimson spoke of. A heavy fog prevented my meeting Grandi, but the announcement of the plan to meet him by flying boat so confused the "demonstrators" that they were not on hand to demonstrate.)

I told Secretary Stimson that since my country was at war I naturally wanted to take my part in its war effort and that I was trying to find the way in which I could make the greatest personal contribution. I told him I had been considering the possibility of taking some position in the aviation industry, but that before doing anything else I wanted to see if there was any way in which I could be of assistance to the Air Corps. I told him that in time of war I would rather be in the Air Corps than anywhere else and that I had come to offer my services. Stimson then went through a rather long dissertation which began and ran on along these lines: "As I said to the press, I will welcome any advice or suggestions that will help us in carrying on the war. No matter who or where they come from they will be given consideration," etc. (The wording is not exact, but this was the gist of his statement.) I replied that I had not come with advice or suggestions, but rather to see if there were any place where I could fit into the picture to help.

Stimson said he would speak with complete frankness, that he would be extremely hesitant to put me into any position of command because of the views I had expressed about the war. He said he did not think anyone who had held such views should be in a position of command in this war because he did not believe such a person could carry on the war with sufficient aggressiveness! Stimson said he doubted very much that I had changed my views. I replied that I had not changed them and that I felt it had been a mistake for this country to get into the war, but that now we were in the war my stand was behind my country, as I had always said it would be, and that I wanted to help in whatever way I could be most effective.

Stimson then referred to my speeches and showed that either his memory or his information was very confused in regard to what I had said. He spoke about my advocating an *alliance* with Germany and about my *antagonism* to China! I told him I had not advocated an alliance with Germany and that I certainly felt no antagonism to China; but that I had said, and still thought, that the greatest danger to this country lay in Russia and Japan. (In the case of Russia I am thinking of their system rather than of their military danger.)

But there was not time to go into all I have said and all I feel. I had not intended to go into such matters at all and would not have done so if Stimson had not forced them upon me. Stimson said that of course I had a right to say what I did in my addresses, but that I must realize it made him very hesitant to put me in any position of command. He kept stressing *"position of command."*

I told Secretary Stimson I was extremely sorry that my political viewpoint left him with any doubt as to my loyalty to my country. (Stimson had mentioned the question of loyalty somewhere in our discussion.) He hedged at this, saying it wasn't exactly a case of doubting loyalty, but that he doubted that with my views I would have the feeling, "the aggressiveness," for a position of command. I replied that, everything considered, it seemed it would be best for me to turn to the aviation industry and try to make my contribution to the war through some industrial project.

Stimson then said that there might be positions "not of command" in which I could help the government. He asked me if I had any suggestions along this line. I told him I thought I was best fitted by training and experience to work on special projects rather than in a routine executive position, that I would like to be in a place where my general knowledge of aviation and my experience in surveying airlines in various parts of the world could be put to use.

Stimson then said he would call in General Arnold; but Arnold was in

conference with some British staff officers. He then called Assistant Secretary Lovett[9] and outlined the situation to him. I must say I did not
enjoy sitting quietly by while Stimson spoke to Lovett of my "political
views" and consequent "lack of aggressiveness" and the inadvisability of
placing me in a position of command—not that I particularly want to be
in a position of command, but I didn't like his saying it. (After all, we're
supposed to be fighting for democracy and one's right to express his own
political views, aren't we?)

Lovett said he would arrange for a conference with General Arnold in
the morning. Then, turning to me, he said that of course if they found they
could not use to the best advantage my *"highly specialized"* and *"very
unusual"* knowledge in the Air Corps, it would be better to let me know
at once so I could turn elsewhere where they could be better used. I told
him that was exactly what I wanted him to do. Lovett was courteous and
did not seem to be unfriendly. He said he would arrange for an appointment with General Arnold in the morning, and asked me to phone Major
Beebe at 10:00.

Tuesday, January 13

*Jap attack repulsed in Philippines "with heavy losses." Russians report
recapture of Orel. British recapture Sollum. Japanese advance in Malaya
continues.*

Phoned Beebe at 10:00. Appointment with General Arnold at 12:00.

Wrote for an hour; then walked to the Munitions Building. General
Arnold was delayed in conference. While I was waiting for him I spent
the time talking to an Air Corps colonel, who told me of a bricklayers'
union somewhere out west that wanted to give a $1,000 prize to the first
pilot to bomb Tokyo. As I was listening to his story, another officer
passed by. "He'll write a good speech for you on any subject," the colonel said as he nodded to him. Speeches are on mass production these
days, too. It's no wonder the public is so confused. Everything is routine,
quantity, superficial; leaders seldom write their own public addresses.
People go to listen to a prominent man but hear a speech written by

9. Robert A. Lovett, special assistant to the Secretary of War, 1940–41. He became Assistant Secretary of War for Air, 1941–45, Undersecretary of State,
1947–49, Deputy Secretary of Defense, 1950–51, and Secretary of Defense,
1951–53.

some friend, secretary, or ghost writer, the primary object of which is 1) to avoid bringing any criticism to the speaker, and 2) to win as much applause as possible from the audience.

I met General Arnold in Lovett's office. I told them both what I had told Stimson, i.e., that now we are at war I want to take the most effective part I can in our war effort and that before turning elsewhere I wanted to see whether I could be of assistance to the Air Corps and to the government.

Arnold and Lovett said there were many ways in which I could be of assistance to the Air Corps, *but* they were not sure what the public and press reaction would be to my taking an important position in the Air Corps at this time. They asked me what, in my opinion, the reaction would be. I said that reaction would obviously be divided—some for, some against, but that I had no way of telling what the percentage would be. They said that before I returned to the Air Corps they thought it would be necessary for me to find some way of clearing up this "doubt" in the public mind—possibly by issuing some kind of a statement.

I told them that I had issued a public statement the day after the Japanese attacked us, but that if they wished I would be glad to issue another. Lovett said the statement I had issued was not enough, that it would be necessary to say more. I replied that any statement I made would have to be based on the fact that I had not changed my beliefs, but that now we were at war my stand was behind my country. I told Lovett and Arnold I was not willing to retract anything I had said that I still believed in, and that I still believed pretty thoroughly in what I had said. They asked me if I thought that on that basis I could issue a statement that would satisfy the people and the papers who were objecting to my return to the Air Corps. I said I doubted it greatly, because most of those people and papers wanted a retraction from me and that I would not retract what I still believed in.

Lovett then said that prior to the war I had attacked the President very strongly and that, after all, the President was Commander-in-Chief of the Army. Could I, he asked, serve loyally (!) under a President I had so recently attacked? Before I had a chance to answer Arnold said, "What are your convictions now? Would you have confidence in the President as your Commander-in-Chief?" Lovett then added that he felt sure I was sincere and believed fully everything I had said about the President in my addresses and that since I said I still believed in what I had said he did not see how I could serve loyally under a man I felt that way about.

I replied that as far as my convictions were concerned, they were the same as they had been before the war started. I said I thought the questions they asked would always confront a democracy in time of war, that political opposition was inherent to a democratic system and that there would always be the problem of how to handle, after a war began, those who had opposed it before it started. I said that as far as my personal attitude was concerned, I could best answer their questions in the following way: that as a citizen I had very little confidence in the President, that I would like to see the present Administration changed, and that I intended to vote against it at the first opportunity; but that if I returned to the Air Corps, then, as a soldier, I would follow the President of the United States as Commander-in-Chief of the Army.

"But," said Arnold, "in view of your past stand, would your associates in the Air Corps have confidence in you?"

I replied that I did not know, but that if I would not have the confidence both of my associates and of my superior officers, I would not want to return to the Air Corps.

The discussion lasted for about half an hour in all. Finally, I told Arnold and Lovett that in view of the feeling which existed it seemed to me it would be a mistake for me to return to the Air Corps at the present time and that I thought it would be better for me to try to make my contribution to the war through the aviation industry. I told them I was not sure that the situation which worried them could be straightened out satisfactorily, because I was not willing to retract what I had said in my addresses. I said that the passage of a little time was often the best way to solve problems of this type and that a few weeks or months spent in the industry would not preclude my return to the Air Corps later on, if that seemed desirable.

They seemed to be taken aback at first by this suggestion. Apparently, it was unexpected. I think they were possibly prepared to give me some position if I pushed hard enough and especially if I agreed to issue a statement even bordering on retraction. However, after a moment's consideration, they both agreed it was the best course to follow and seemed to be relieved that some, at least temporary, solution had been found.

Before leaving, I told Lovett that obviously a political situation was involved, and I asked him whether he thought there would be any objection on the part of the Administration to my taking an active part in the work of some commercial company, such as Pan American Airways, Curtiss-Wright, or United Aircraft. Lovett said he didn't think so and that as far as the War Department was concerned he thought they would support such a move on my part.

Arnold's parting words were: "I think you *can* find some way to straighten all this out." Both Arnold and Lovett seemed friendly personally, but I constantly had the impression that they were thinking of orders from higher up. They were both in a difficult position—particularly Arnold, with whom I worked very closely during the months I served in the Air Corps in 1939, and who, I feel sure, is far from being in complete agreement with the policies the President has followed. (In fact I believe that most Army officers have not been in agreement with the President's foreign policy.) Arnold and Lovett both knew the situation was loaded with political dynamite and handled themselves accordingly.

It goes against my grain to be out of the Air Corps in time of war, but I am convinced it would be inadvisable for me to push my way back into it. The next few weeks will bring many developments, and the general attitude of the country is likely to go through great changes. I am convinced that the stand I took on the war was right, and I believe this will be realized eventually.

Thursday, January 15

Army goal of 3,600,000 men for 1942 announced by Stimson. Air Corps to add 2,000,000.

I have begun to go through a fifteen-minute period of calisthenics in my bedroom after getting up in the morning. I thoroughly dislike calisthenics, but I feel the lack of outdoor exercise.

Lunch with Eddie Rickenbacker in his apartment at the Carlton. (Happened to meet him as I walked out of the door this morning.) He says the Administration is making things as difficult as possible for him due to his past stand in opposition to their war policies. He says that airline operation is, of course, completely upset by the war. He looks much better than I expected after his crash. He still feels the effects, though, and one leg is a little stiff. It was one of the worst crashes that any man has lived to tell about.

Bixby came for supper. We talked of the war in China and C.N.A.C. [China National Aviation Corporation] and the experiences of the pilots at Hong Kong and elsewhere. I discussed with Bixby the possibility of my becoming actively associated again with Pan American. He says there are many places where I could help. The next move is, of course, to contact Juan Trippe. Bix says Trippe will be in Washington in the morning.

Rumors are circulating in Washington to the effect that courts-martial and executions will result from the fiasco of Pearl Harbor.

Friday, January 16

United States submarine sinks 17,000-ton Japanese liner.

Spent the morning writing and trying to contact Juan Trippe. Afternoon till 2:30 writing. Then to Capitol to see Senator Wheeler. Spent a half hour with Wheeler discussing developments of the war.

There were reporters and photographers waiting at the door as I left the room. I shook hands with them and said there was nothing to tell them. The reporters wanted to know about my "new job." Apparently the War Department announced that I am working on a "project" which is of "vital interest to the government," with their full approval! These War Department statements are amazing and confusing. What does it mean? Does it mean that whatever work I select in the aviation industry will be the "project" of "vital interest to the government" which I "carry on with their full approval"?

Taxi back to Carlton. Trippe phoned. Appointment with him Monday at 3:00 at Pan American offices, New York. Phoned Anne at Martha's Vineyard. She says the ferry service to the island was halted because of the submarine menace—going again now, though she doesn't know how regularly. Went for a walk in the evening. The White House is completely blacked out.

Saturday, January 17

Navy reports five more Japanese ships sunk; confirms sinking of second ship off Long Island. British say Japanese checked in Malaya.

Spent first part of morning writing, then took taxi to station to purchase ticket. Temporary war buildings seem to be springing up like toadstools all over the city.

The Capitol Building is completely blacked out, but most other buildings are lighted, and the streetlights are, of course, left burning. Boarded the 2:10 A.M. train for New York.

Sunday, January 18

British capture Halfaya Pass. Japanese continue to advance on Singapore. United States Navy announces more Jap shipping sunk.

Went to see *Fantasia* in the afternoon. It has interesting possibilities, but most of it is simply sensational and cheap. Stayed for only three quarters of an hour. Went to see a newsreel later. There was almost no clapping of the war pictures. It is clear that the American people are *without enthusiasm for the war.*

New York seems strange on a Sunday night now. Most of the show windows are dark, and only a few windows are lighted in the buildings. The streets remind me of London; much of the bustle is gone. As a matter of fact, I think I prefer New York this way. At last it has learned enough to go to bed at night, as a respectable city should.

The papers carry an announcement from Germany of General von Reichenau's[10] death. I think of that evening at his apartment in Munich and of the Chinese painting on the wall—the king who was defeated.

Monday, January 19

Steps taken to merge C.I.O. and A.F. of L.

First part of morning on phone calls. Then taxi to La Guardia Airport to get pilot's license reinstated. Harwood[11] was very helpful, but there is getting to be more and more red tape and confusion. They were unable to keep up with regulations, he told me. I had to have fingerprints taken of both hands—some of them twice. If we are not careful in this country, it will soon take so many people to carry out regulations that there won't be enough left over to regulate.

Phoned Harry Davison and told him Anne and I wanted to purchase

10. Walther von Reichenau, German field marshal. He commanded the German army that captured Warsaw in 1939, and in 1941 an army group on the southern sector of the Russian front.

11. O. P. Harwood, senior aeronautical inspector of the CAA at La Guardia field.

our share of government war bonds and left to his judgment how much that should be.

To Chrysler Building to see Trippe at 3:00. I told him about my discussions with Stimson, Lovett, and Arnold at the War Department and told him that since it seemed best for me to make my contribution to the war through the aviation industry, my first choice would be Pan American. I told Trippe, however, that before any definite action was taken I thought it advisable for him to find out whether or not the President would have any objection. Trippe said there were many things I could do for Pan American and that he thought he would have a chance to talk to the President later this week. He asked me whether I thought he should talk to [Lord] Halifax, too. I told him by all means to do so, if he had the opportunity. (Pan American is, of course, ferrying planes across the ocean for the British and must work very closely with them.)

Flynn phoned, apparently much disturbed about the dinner I attended at Webster's home last month. He says some of the radical elements were represented there. Apparently, the opposition press played the meeting up as a formal postwar America First gathering and, of course, quoted me as saying things I neither said nor believe.

Boarded the midnight train for Boston.

Tuesday, January 20

Fourth American ship torpedoed off Atlantic coast.

Off train at 7:40. Boarded 8:20 train for Woods Hole and arrived home in time for lunch. Anne is much better. She is up and outside for short periods in the morning. Children all well. Jon, Land, and I went for an hour-and-a-half walk along the beach to the ruins of an old farmhouse a mile or so to the west. I thought it would be too far for Land and did not want to take him at first. (Also, Jon advised strongly against it.) But Land insisted on accompanying us. "I won't get tired, Father. You will see." He straggled slightly on the way back, but whenever I asked him if he was getting tired, he resolutely shook his head. Land enjoyed the walk but was very disappointed because he missed his cookie for tea.

Monday, January 26

Navy sinks five Japanese transports. Norwegian tanker torpedoed thirty-five miles off New Jersey coast. American forces counterattack on Bataan Peninsula. Russian reports of breakthroughs continue.

Juan Trippe phoned in the evening. He said that "obstacles had been put in the way" of my taking on active work with Pan American. Obviously that means obstacles have been put in the way by the White House. I could see that Juan did not want to talk about it over the phone, so I agreed to meet him in New York next week. I would prefer to talk to him sooner, but his plans make an earlier engagement difficult.

Tuesday, January 27

American Expeditionary Force lands in north Ireland. Navy torpedoes Japanese aircraft carrier. Japanese advance in Malaya. British retreat in Libya.

Our cook, Helen, literally can't soft-boil an egg! The one sent up to Anne tonight was hard-boiled again. I took it down and told Helen to *soft*-boil an egg for Anne. I explained that to *soft*-boil an egg you got the water boiling, put a raw egg in, waited for two and a half minutes *by the clock,* and then took the egg out! When the second egg came up it was almost raw! I took it back down and asked Helen to tell me *exactly* how she had cooked the first egg, and then to tell me *exactly* how she had cooked the second egg. The first egg, she said, had been boiled for two and a half minutes; but since the rest of the supper was not ready, she had left the pot of water with the egg in it on the back of the stove for a few minutes more to keep the egg warm! The second egg, she said, she had boiled for a little less than one and a half minutes, because Mrs. Lindbergh had once told her that she did not want her eggs boiled for more than one and a half minutes! (Anne was trying to find some way of keeping them from being constantly hard-boiled.) I cooked the third egg myself.

Finished second draft of *Spirit of St. Louis* manuscript. But I am not at all satisfied with it. The manuscript will have to go through at least two more drafts. If I only had six free months, I feel sure I could finish it as I want to. Of course, what I would like to do is to wait six months, write the third draft with a fresh mind, and then wait a year and write the final draft.

Sunday, February 1

British retire to island of Singapore. Japanese take Moulmein.

Packed. Breakfast. Then left in Mercury for New York. Crossed on 9:45 boat. Arrived New Haven at 4:40. Hour's visit with Mr. and Mrs. Knollenberg. Then to Hartford for dinner with Gene Wilson at his home. We discussed war developments and the possibility of my working with United Aircraft. Wilson outlined various projects he thought I could be of help in carrying on—particularly in a study of comparative aircraft performances he wants to have made. I told him about the discussions I had at the War Department and about Trippe's statement over the phone to the effect that obstacles had been put in the way of my working with Pan American Airways. I told Wilson I thought the President might not object to my taking on work with a manufacturing company. I suggested, however, that it would be advisable to find out definitely. Wilson said he thought he could do this through Deac Lyman. He outlined various company projects and policies to me. As I get to know him better I have more than ever the impression that he is an exceptionally able and far-sighted man. I will enjoy working with him—*provided the President has no objection!* (And, as a country, we are supposed to be fighting for the principles of democracy and free speech and *against* dictators!) Drove to the Long Island Aviation Country Club for the night.

Monday, February 2

Navy attacks Japanese bases in Marshall and Gilbert islands. Japanese begin bombardment of Singapore. Russians claim German rout in Ukraine. Axis forces advance additional sixty miles in Libya.

Spent one and a half hours flying in the Fairchild—about fifteen landings. It is now necessary to get a clearance from the interceptor command before taking off. Then, unless the clearance is for a cross-country flight, a pilot must stay within ten miles of the flying field.

Jim Newton came for lunch. We planned on an hour's flying afterward, but it has been one of the coldest days of winter, and the Fairchild would not start. Finally, I took a Stinson in its place, but we had only thirty minutes left for flying before Jim had to leave for New York. I gave him several landings and some air work.

Tuesday, February 3

Japanese attacks repulsed on Bataan Peninsula. Japs continue to make general advance in the Indies. Axis forces advance in Libya. Russians claim more successes.

To Pan American offices to see Juan Trippe at 10:00. He said he had talked to the War Department and that "they" were entirely willing that I take an active part in Pan American projects. *But,* he said, when he talked to the White House, "they" were very angry with him for even bringing up the subject and told him "they" did not want me to be connected with Pan American in any capacity. He said the feeling at the White House toward me was extremely bitter. Juan seemed very much chagrined about the entire situation. He agreed with me that it would be inadvisable for me to make any active connection with the company at present but suggested that the door be left open because attitudes and conditions might change later on.

Lunch with Deac Lyman at Engineers Club. Discussed the possibility of making a connection with United Aircraft. He is going to Washington and will inquire about what the attitude of the President would be.

Wednesday, February 4

Japanese bombers raid Java and southern New Guinea. British evacuate Derna. Foreign Affairs Committee approves Roosevelt's request for a half-billion loan to China.

Subway to 23 Wall Street for a conference with Harry Davison in regard to purchasing government war bonds for Anne and for myself. I told him we wanted to carry our share. Mr. Morgan came over and shook hands jovially, and joked about the war cutting off his grouse shooting in England. But it is easy to see that beneath the surface everyone at 23 Wall

Street is tremendously concerned about the war and about the expenditures and actions of the Administration.

Phoned Miss Crutcher. She has had no recent word from Carrel but has no reason to believe he or Mme. Carrel are in any difficulty. He had cabled her to the effect that he would accept a speaking engagement in the west in June, but the cablegram was sent before we entered the war.

Decided to go see a motion picture—Douglas Fairbanks, Jr., in *The Corsican Brothers*. He is not as good an actor as his father. A long government propaganda film came after the main feature. It seemed to me incredibly cheap. Cheapness and ridicule, I think, are not elements that lead to victory. Yes, humor is necessary in time of war as well as in time of peace, but it should be mixed with seriousness and stirred with dignity.

Thursday, February 5

Breakfast at club. Then drove to Next Day Hill. Conference with Mrs. Morrow in regard to the Little School. Spent rest of afternoon sorting and packing articles in attic and in bedroom closet. I want to send as much as possible to storage to get it out of Mrs. Morrow's way. She has never complained in the least, but it is unfair to clutter her house up unnecessarily. We haven't had a great deal there in recent years, but most of what is there can just as well be sent to our room in Quirk's Storage Warehouse.

Back to Engineers Club for dinner with Boris Bakhmeteff in my room. We discussed war trends and developments all over the world. Bakhmeteff told me about a dinner he had attended recently. Most of the guests were members of interventionist groups such as the Committee to Defend America by Aiding the Allies. They were discussing what should be done with Germany after the war was over. The first suggestion made to these defenders of civilization was that every German male between the ages of ten and sixty be killed! After discussing this, they decided they couldn't very well do that, so the idea was advanced that instead of killing them they simply be sterilized. And, said Bakhmeteff, the discussion continued along these lines during a large portion of the evening. Finally, he said, he was asked to state his opinion. He replied that he felt there was a preliminary problem, the problem of winning the war, that had to be decided first. And, he said, several of the people there surprised him by agreeing with him. He and I both felt that showed some progress in interventionist thought!

Saturday, February 7

Torpedoing of American ships continues. Shipping situation reported critical.

Drove to Port Washington for lunch with Deac Lyman, his wife, and three of his daughters. I talked to Deac again about working on a project for United Aircraft. He phoned Lovett at the War Department in Washington to arrange an appointment. Lovett told him the War Department would support such a connection and might even go so far as to "hold an umbrella" over United!

Deac and Mrs. Lyman took me to see a Port Washington family which specializes in wood carving. Reminded me of Europe. The father and all of his sons do the work—each one responsible for his own field—and they have a real pride of craftsmanship. They were having a sort of family party when we arrived. One of the sons is being drafted, and it will be the first time the group has been broken up.

Monday, February 9

British claim Axis halted in Libya. Torpedoing of ships continues along Atlantic coast.

Was reading *The Progressive,* January 31 issue, and found an article so typical of the irresponsibility of modern columnists that I am going to enter it here, in part. Under a Boston date line the writer says he learned from some "source" that I went to Washington a short time ago at the invitation of President Roosevelt, that I admire the La Follettes, dislike politicians like [Calvin] Coolidge, wrote all my own speeches, don't want political office, am concerned for the safety of my children, and believe that "now we are in the war there is only one thing to do—win it." The article is a jumble of truth and lies and certainly came from no source that is close to me.

But the statements made by this columnist have been spread all over the country and even picked up by papers which don't carry his column.

In the future the beliefs he attributes to me will undoubtedly be used in other columns and news articles as though I had written his column myself. This has happened time and time again in the past. Some reporter writes an article in which he makes statements which are not true and which he has not even tried to verify. He must write something to hold his job, so he just sits down and writes it. Some editor reads his story and writes an editorial about it. Then the whole thing goes into the files of the nation's newspapers for future use in other articles.

But why should this columnist say I was going to Washington at the invitation of the President? There was not the slightest foundation for that statement. Any "source" close to me would know it wasn't true. It does no harm to say that I admire the La Follettes, although such a statement implies a closer agreement with their policies than facts justify. But why go out of the way to slur a President who is dead, especially when the slur is a lie? I always liked Coolidge, and I admired him in many ways. He may not have been a great leader, but I think he was an excellent President for the period in which he held office, and I respected him as a man. The next two statements are true. I did write my own speeches, and I don't want to hold political office. As to the safety of my children, I have been concerned about that ever since 1932, so that is true, too, but I don't make a practice of talking about it.

The last statement is only partly true. I don't think it is reasonably possible for us to win the war on the basis of any war aims we have yet stated, or on the basis on which England declared it. I do believe, however, that now we are in the war we should carry it on as intelligently, constructively, and successfully as possible. That we will be able to win an unconditional victory is, I think, improbable. We will only harm our cause by blinding ourselves to that fact. This war is almost certain to end in negotiation. But how favorable or unfavorable that negotiation is to our side is still within our power to influence.

Tuesday, February 10

Japanese establish bridgehead on Singapore island. Batavia raided. Normandie burns at dock and overturns. Tension between Vichy and United States increases.

Deac Lyman phoned. Said he had seen Lovett and that the War Department said they would be "glad" to have me make a connection with

United. And he said he had gotten word from [Stephen] Early that the President would have no objection to such a connection! Early said he thought I should be in the Air Corps, but that "some of the other people around the White House" thought differently. *But* a new complication has arisen. Some Senator has started an attack on United Aircraft for having sold aviation equipment to Japan and Germany during the years before war started. Of course, I had no connection whatever with this, but [Eugene] Wilson feels it would be inadvisable for me to make a connection with the company under these circumstances, and I agree with him. The war is going badly for us, and people will be looking for a scapegoat. United will come under heavy criticism for having sold equipment abroad that our enemies are using against us. Many people are still bitter about the stand I took against this country being involved in the war, even though the developments of the war are proving that what I said was true. For me to make a connection with United under these circumstances would simply be giving fuel to the enemies of both of us.

I think my next move will be to talk to Guy Vaughan about a connection with Curtiss-Wright. (Curtiss-Wright sold equipment to Russia, but that is now considered all right.)

Thursday, February 12

Packed after lunch and left for New York in the Mercury at 3:45. Drove past the overturned *Normandie* before going to the Engineers Club.

Friday, February 13

German fleet sails through English Channel. United States Navy announces total of sixteen Japanese ships destroyed during Marshall and Gilbert island raids on January 31. Japanese troops on outskirts of Singapore City. Japan claims capture of Bandjarmasin and Makassar. Russians continue to claim successes. Stimson orders entire Army vaccinated against yellow fever.

Drove to Long Island Aviation Country Club for lunch and two hours' flying in the Fairchild in a very strong and gusty wind—over forty miles per hour in gusts. Spent most of the time practicing landings.

Back to Engineers Club for supper with Guy Vaughan. I talked to him about a Curtiss-Wright connection and outlined my discussions at the War Department and with Juan Trippe and Gene Wilson. Guy said he would like me to make a critical study of their prototype aircraft, and that there were many other things I could do in connection with Curtiss-Wright activities. He agreed with me that it would be advisable to make sure the President had no objection before we took any definite action. He will try to sound out the White House attitude next week. We spent the rest of the evening discussing the war, American aviation, and the confusion in Washington.

Monday, February 16

Singapore surrenders. Japanese land in southern Sumatra, advance in Burma.

Off [Washington] train at 7:00. Taxi to Carlton Hotel. To old National Guard Armory at Sixth and Pennsylvania at 10:00 to register. It was not very crowded when I arrived, and I was registered at once. Everyone there was considerate. Several people, including two or three of those doing the registering, came up to tell me quietly that "we're right back of you in all that you do."

Lunch with Harry Byrd at his committee room in the Capitol Building. He is gloomy about the outlook for the future; has no more confidence in Roosevelt than I have. Harry has three sons of military age, two of them already in service. Byrd told me the story of Senator Walsh's meeting with President Roosevelt after Pearl Harbor. It seems that as soon as Senator Walsh heard of the Pearl Harbor attack he went to Admiral Stark[12] and asked what damage had been done. Since Walsh was chairman of the Naval Affairs Committee, Stark gave him the exact details. Walsh immediately called a meeting of the Naval Affairs Committee, at which Byrd and several other members advised Walsh to go directly to the President and "ask him to tell the truth to the American people."

Walsh agreed that the truth should be told, but was hesitant at first to be the one to go to the President with such a request. After further urging, however, he agreed to do so. In his account of his interview with the President, Walsh said that Roosevelt flew into a rage when he asked him

12. Admiral Harold R. Stark became Chief of Naval Operations in 1939, and commanded U.S. naval forces in Europe from 1942 to 1945.

to tell the American people the truth about Pearl Harbor. Roosevelt demanded that Walsh divulge the source of his information. Walsh replied that it came directly from the Navy and Admiral Stark, to whom he had gone as chairman of the Naval Affairs Committee. Roosevelt said that Stark should never have given out the facts about Pearl Harbor (even to the chairman of the Senate Committee on Naval Affairs). Then, according to Walsh, Roosevelt said, "Why in hell should we admit that they're sunk? They're resting in only a couple of feet of water; we'll raise 'em!" (Referring to the battleships sunk by the Japanese attack.)

It is generally accepted by Congressmen and Senators that seven battleships were either sunk or damaged at Pearl Harbor. Some say three were sunk and four were damaged. Others say four were sunk and three damaged. The figures for the total number of warships hit vary between twenty-seven and thirty-four.

Taxi from Capitol to Commerce Building for a fifteen-minute conference with Jerry Land. Told him of the developments connected with my attempt to find a position in the aviation industry. Jerry is almost as gloomy as I am about the war outlook. Boarded the 2:10 train for New York.

Wednesday, February 18

House passes $32 billion war appropriation. Japan renames Singapore "Shonan." Senators Walsh and Johnson demand adequate defenses for our coasts.

Burnelli[13] phoned about 9:30. Was just starting breakfast. I went down to talk to him while he ate. We discussed his newest planes for a time—the performance characteristics and structural qualities of his designs, etc. Burnelli said the P-38 (Lockheed twin-engine pursuit) had developed "boom wabble" and had been placarded for a maximum speed of 287 m.p.h. (That would make it unsuitable for service use unless a remedy can be found.) He said that 500 P-38's had been built at a cost of about $50 million. He said that the Martin B-26 bomber was also causing serious difficulty because of its high landing speed. A number of crews have already been killed, according to Burnelli.

13. Vincent J. Burnelli, inventor and engineer. He designed lifting-body, flying-wing, and other types of airplanes.

Wednesday, February 25

Japs advance in Burma. Russians claim German Sixteenth Army sur-
rounded southwest of Leningrad. Japanese submarine shells California
oil refinery.

Phoned Guy Vaughan [from Martha's Vineyard]. Says he has talked to
his Curtiss-Wright officers and will sound out Roosevelt at the first opportunity. He says the more he thinks of it the more he thinks the
situation is "loaded with dynamite." Guy is playing golf with Jerry Land
on Saturday, he says, and will talk to Jerry about the best method of
contacting the President. Obviously, Guy and his officers are afraid of
the vindictiveness of the White House, and they have good reason to be.
I told him I would under no circumstances want to be a part of any
action that would injure Curtiss-Wright.

I am beginning to wonder whether I will be blocked in every attempt I
make to take part in this war. I have always stood for what I thought
would be to the best interest of this country, and now we are at war I
want to take my part in fighting for it, foolish and disastrous as I think
the war will prove to be. Our decision has been made, and now we must
fight to preserve our national honor and our national future. I have always believed in the past that every American citizen had the right and the
duty to state his opinion in peace and to fight for his country in war. But
the Roosevelt Administration seems to think otherwise.

Monday, March 2

Japanese advance in Java. Heavy naval losses claimed on both sides.
German submarine activity in Atlantic continues.

A letter arrived from England in the afternoon mail containing one of
those newspaper articles that both anger and depress me. Newspaper
articles usually don't bother me much. I have grown accustomed to the
inaccuracies and the bombast of the press. As a matter of fact, most of
the favorable articles are usually so sickly sweet and false in tone and
shading that on the whole I think I almost prefer those that are antagonistic. But this article from England is of the worst, the most annoying,
and the most dangerous type of all—the type that twists what you your-

self say and which often quotes you as saying what you have neither said nor even believed. It is always cleverly done—just enough fact mixed in with the lies to make the whole seem plausible—just enough of what you have said in it to tie the story to you, and more than enough of what you didn't say to damn you even in the eyes of the people who actually agree with you. Then, editorials are written about what an awful person you are to believe what you actually don't believe at all! I don't mind how much the papers curse me or disagree with me, as long as they do it on a basis of what I have said and what I stand for. As long as a fight is over true issues I rather enjoy it; but when issues are purposely made false, that is a type of fighting I don't understand and in which I have no desire to gain skill.

This article starts out by saying that I "arose at a banquet in New York the other evening" and that I said that "Britain and Germany should have combined to beat the yellow race." The article refers to the dinner Webster gave to his fiancée last December at his home, 35 Beekman Place. I did not know Webster was giving the dinner until I phoned him that morning. He told me he was giving the dinner and that he had asked the America First street speakers to come. It was to be a combination engagement and farewell dinner, he told me. Webster was anxious for me to come, and I accepted on his promise that I would not have to speak. The dinner was in no sense an America First organization meeting, aside from the fact that it was a sort of last get-together and farewell party.

Under pressure, I finally spoke for about five, possibly ten, minutes. I said nothing about England and Germany getting together and nothing about the "yellow race:" I remember very clearly what I said that evening. I said: 1) that since we had been attacked there was nothing for us to do but fight; 2) that I felt the America First national committee had been correct in its decision to dissolve, although I personally had advocated adjournment instead of dissolution. (It turned out that the committee was about evenly divided on this issue. In view of this fact, I think dissolution was advisable, and I would have voted for it had I been present at the meeting in Chicago. My telegram advocating adjournment was sent before Germany and Italy declared war—or rather a few hours before I knew they had declared war); 3) that I thought the developments of the war had already shown the wisdom of the America First policy of concentrating on strong defenses for America; 4) that all of our attention should be devoted to carrying the war on as intelligently, constructively, and successfully as possible.

However, I have often said in private conversation and in magazine articles that I feel it is a tragic error for the Western nations to turn their backs on Russia and Japan to carry on a prostrating war among themselves. I have said, and I believe, that the longer this war in Europe goes on, the more Russia and Japan will be the gainers. I base this on the belief that Japan's conquests were made possible by, and that Russia's survival depends upon, the continuation of the war in Western Europe. Western nations have everything to lose by a long war (in Europe), while Eastern nations have everything to gain. Our greatest hope is that the war in Europe ends before all Western nations are too worn out to resist the nations of the East. If we in America were not fighting Germany, Japan would not have met with such success in the Pacific. As it is, Japan has defeated us in the Pacific, and if we *are* successful in crushing Germany we automatically create a victory for Russia. A Russian-dominated Europe would, in my belief, be far worse than a German-dominated Europe. England and the United States have managed to get into a war where *if they win, they lose.* If we win, we will have created worse conditions than those we went to war against. I think we are in one of the most confused situations history ever recorded.

But to get back to the dinner and the article, I mentioned none of these things when I spoke that evening. I did not mention them for the reason that we were in the war, and I felt it was an inopportune time to talk about why we shouldn't have gotten in. The press article accused me of doing exactly what I refrained from doing. If it had said that I believed in the solidarity of Western nations, that would be true. But when it says that I advocated Britain and Germany getting together "to beat the yellow race," that is false. It goes on to say that by the time the war is over I will probably be advocating the lynching of Negroes!

Well, I suppose I should pay no more attention to this type of article than I do to the others, but somehow it bothers me to have it said that I stand for and believe in things that I don't. It is the difference between a knife in front of you and a knife behind you.

As I reread this day's entry I find some uncertainty in my mind. I am sure I said nothing about the "yellow race." I am sure I said nothing about England and Germany getting together (although I have always felt they should have done so). I certainly said nothing about "beating the yellow race"—my ideas of Western solidarity do not involve a conquest of the Orient, although they do involve the prevention of the type of conquest by an Oriental nation that Japan is now carrying on. However, it is possible (and if so, I have no apology to make) that I said it was a tragedy for us to fight among ourselves while we gave Japan a free hand in the Orient.

Friday, March 6

Japanese armies thirteen miles from Batavia.

Guy Vaughan phoned from New York. He said his inquiries in Washington indicated that the White House would look unfavorably on my working on any Curtiss-Wright project—said he thought the situation was "loaded with dynamite"!

Sunday, March 8

Packed, arranged final details, and left for New York at 9:00 in Ford. While I was on the ferry a young Coast Guardsman asked me to give him and his buddy a ride as far as Fall River. The "buddy," a native of Little Rock, Arkansas, recognized me almost as soon as he got in the car. I had to be cautious of conversation and steer it away from dangerous subjects such as the war and politics. I would have enjoyed talking freely, but I know the almost inevitable result of doing so. The people I talk to under these circumstances usually repeat what I say, and since they cannot remember the exact phraseology, they make up what they can't remember, giving their story whatever tone they personally prefer it to have. Finally, some newspaper reporter gets hold of it and puts it in direct quotes as though he had taken the words down in shorthand as they were spoken. I am constantly confronted with this problem. Safety lies in not speaking at all to strangers. But if one follows a policy of absolute safety, one becomes separated from life.

Purchased lunch at a delicatessen and stopped at the roadside to eat. Supper at Long Island Aviation Club. Night at club.

Monday, March 9

Japanese land at Salamaua and Lae, New Guinea, claim capture of Rangoon, report surrender of Dutch Army in Java. MacArthur's forces are holding on Bataan. R.A.F. again bombs Paris area. Russians claim new advances.

Drove to Engineers Club in New York. Lunch at club. Drove to the Englewood Ford agency in afternoon to arrange for trading in our Ford on a newer model. I selected a 1941 Ford which has run less than 8,000 miles (our old one has run nearly 34,000). Only people on the priority list can purchase 1942 models. It is not exactly what I want—wrong color, etc., but it is in good condition, and one's choice is limited these days. Night at Engineers Club.

Tuesday, March 10

Netherlands government in London denies Japanese claims of Java surrender. United States Navy lists more Japanese warships sunk by submarines. British confirm withdrawal from Rangoon.

Fifteen-minute walk. Breakfast in club. Harold Bixby came for lunch. He says the government may take over Pan American Airways. If they do, it will certainly reduce the efficiency of the organization, and I do not see what would be gained. The company is doing everything the government requests, as it is, and a commercial organization cannot be turned into a military organization overnight.

Drove to Long Island Aviation Country Club for the night.

Wednesday, March 11

Mrs. Lyman arrived at 9:00 with three of her daughters. I had told Deac I would take them up if they would come over to the field—their first flight for the little girls. Took them up for about fifteen minutes each. Mrs. Lyman would not fly. Then spent an hour and a half in landings and air work, getting in part of the ten hours necessary for my license renewal.

Drove to Engineers Club. Supper at club. Went to a motion-picture theater afterward—very cheap film—hotel bedroom scene, frame-up, etc., poor acting. I believe motion pictures have had a great deal to do with the decline in character that is obvious in this country today. Cheapness and immorality do not go hand in hand with strength.

Thursday, March 12

Strong rumors of an Allied invasion of Norway in near future. German battleship Tirpitz *"loose in Atlantic."*

Breakfast with Rube Fleet at his room in Waldorf-Astoria at 9:00. He again proposed that I take charge of a research and development program for Consolidated. He also had a development project for a postwar product that he wanted me to take part in. I told Fleet that whatever I did would have to be connected with the war and that the only reason I was looking for a job was so I could take my part in the war effort the country is making. I said I would be glad to consider a connection with Consolidated, but that before coming to any definite decision I would want to look the situation over to see where I would fit into their picture.

Fleet asked me what salary I would accept. (He offered me $100,000 per year less than a year ago to take charge of the company's research program.) I told him I did not want to make money out of the war and that if I worked for Consolidated I would not want to take more than $10,000 per year during the war. I told him I would rather work on a retainer basis than as an officer of the company and that I thought such an arrangement would be advantageous from all standpoints. I told him about the situation I have encountered in Washington and suggested that he investigate the Administration's attitude toward the connection with Consolidated he proposed.

There is another problem. Fleet recently sold out his entire interest in Consolidated and therefore no longer controls the company. He must take the matter up with its present officers and directors, and they may feel differently about it than he.

I arrived at Fleet's room at 9:00, had breakfast and lunch, and left at *4:20!* We spent considerable time discussing the war. Fleet sees the picture about as I do and is, I think, no more optimistic. Fleet told me he might run for governor in California. I believe he is well fitted for political office—successful businessman, quite well known, loves to talk, enjoys being with people, and most important of all, he has vision and judgment.

Saturday, March 14

Japanese fleet reported off Solomon Islands. R.A.F. bombs points in Western Europe. Submarine activity continues.

It has been raining all day, and the grass court west of the library is already green—my window on the fifth floor [of the Engineers Club in New York] overlooks it—the view ending against the wall of buildings on Forty-second Street. The tops of the high buildings are in clouds.

Sunday, March 15

Off [Detroit] train at 8:15. Taxi to 508 Lakepointe. Breakfast with Mother and B. Drove them out to Orchard Lake past Great-grandfather Lodge's old farm and the little country church where he used to preach.

I am worried about Mother. She is working much too hard and needs more rest. One of her hands shakes excessively. But she will not think of stopping teaching or of letting someone come to help her with the housework, or of seeing a doctor. Somehow I must get her to consult a doctor, but I can see it is going to be difficult to arrange.

Monday, March 16

Drove to Dearborn for lunch with Harry Bennett. After lunch we visited the Ford Naval Training School, where 2,000 young men are being trained.

Outlined to Bennett the experience I have had in attempting to make a connection with Pan American, United Aircraft, and Curtiss-Wright, and discussed the possibility of a connection with Ford. (Henry Ford is in Georgia.)

Bennett recently returned from the West Coast. He tells me the "Japanese air raid" over Los Angeles, recently reported in the newspapers, was caused by a number of our own Air Corps bombers from March Field.

Boarded 12:30 train for Chicago.

Tuesday, March 17

General MacArthur flies to Australia to command forces in that area. Draft lottery for men in third registration (twenty to forty-four) takes place today.

Off train at 7:15. Breakfast with General Wood. We discussed war developments and probable trends. General Wood is one of the keenest and ablest men I have ever met—a fine mind and wonderful character. It is inexcusable that the Administration is not making better use of his talent. At present we are losing the war about as rapidly as we can, and still the President is unable to rise above petty politics.

Taxi to B. & O. station to buy ticket and Pullman to Washington. Half hour's walk to Tribune Building for a meeting with Colonel McCormick. Colonel Patterson[14] of the New York *News* was also there. Patterson told me of his trip to Hawaii and his view of Pearl Harbor. He said he saw six *battleships* in the harbor either sunk or seriously damaged, in addition to other sunk and damaged warships. He said the officers in Hawaii are still worried about the possibility of another Japanese attack and do not feel we have yet sent enough men and equipment to make the islands safe. I told McCormick and Patterson about the incidents I have encountered in trying to make a connection with the aviation industry.

Spent nearly an hour in the Chicago Art Institute after lunch. Then taxi to B. & O. station and boarded the 3:50 Capital Limited for Washington.

Wednesday, March 18

Germany closes Norwegian ports. Four more ships reported sunk off Atlantic coast.

Off train at 8:40. Phoned Carlton Hotel. No rooms available. Room clerk promised to have one for me later in the day. Taxi to Hay-Adams for breakfast. To Senate Office Building to see Vandenberg at 11:00. He is very depressed about war and conditions in this country. Said indications were that war failures were making Roosevelt more vindictive rather than less. Prophesied a large Republican gain at this year's elections.

To Union Station to purchase ticket and Pullman to New York. Then

14. Joseph M. Patterson, founder of the New York *Daily News*.

to Mellon art museum—the first time I have been inside. It is beautifully designed and so filled with old masters that one can only get a general impression in the first visit. It is strange, but as I entered I felt disappointed that the center of the dome was artificially lighted instead of being open to the sky. Without thinking about it, I gained the impression from the outside of the building that the dome would be open, as in Rome. I was also disappointed at the number of guards. Every room seemed to have its own guard watching every move you made. Of course it is necessary, but it takes away some of the enjoyment and lack of pressure that I associate with an art museum. But the paintings and sculpture and architecture more than made up for these trivialities. Still, I have the desire to tear the glass and plaster out and open that dome to the sky.

Planned on walking for an hour after leaving the museum, but a heavy rain sent me to a newsreel theater instead. The war pictures brought *no clapping or cheering whatever.* People were silent, even where the film was designed to bring applause. There is apparently even less enthusiasm for the war now than a month ago! Something is happening to people in this country; they are silent, suspicious, confused. Where it is all leading to God only knows.

To Senate Office Building for half hour's conference with Bob La Follette. He is greatly concerned about the attempt to make labor "the goat for the Administration's failures in the war." We spent some time discussing the war and probable developments during the summer. To Shipstead's office for a few minutes. Then through the subway to Senator Walsh's office in the Capitol. Twenty minutes with Walsh discussing war and internal conditions, then back to Senator Shipstead's office. Senator Wheeler came in for a few minutes.

Boarded 2:10 train to New York.

Thursday, March 19

Navy announces twenty-three Japanese ships, including twelve warships, sunk or damaged at New Guinea bases. Japanese advance in Burma. Russian claims continue. Two more merchant ships sunk off Atlantic coast. Rationing of gasoline begins again in Atlantic states.

Off train at 7:30. Phone calls: Trippe, Flynn, Lyman, Springer, Miss Crutcher, Harwood, Wood, Bennett, Newton, and others. Could only reach about half of them.

Bennett told me he had word "from two reliable sources in Washington" that I would soon be recommissioned in the Air Corps and that the "Army is one hundred per cent in favor of my return." The Administration, however, "is holding off for an opportune moment"! Bennett's sources of information are usually pretty good. But I have learned to mistrust practically everything the Administration does. What is their object? Is pressure becoming too high in view of war reverses? Or do they want to get me out of the way for the elections? I wish I thought some higher motive were involved.

Mr. E. Burke Wilford[15] phoned. He is staying at the club, and I have met him on two or three occasions in years past; wanted to talk to me about some new aviation developments. I went down to his room for fifteen minutes and discussed beryllium, gyro planes, and Burnelli designs, all of which he is interested in. Wilford told me he was going to see Willkie at 10:30 and suggested that Willkie would be "the man" to straighten out the situation I was encountering with the Administration. (I don't know where he heard about that, as I did not mention it to him.) I avoided the issue by telling him there were enough political complications already and that I felt it would be inadvisable for Willkie to take any action at all in the matter.

Friday, March 20

Up at 7:00. Breakfast with Wilford in the club buffet. He wanted to discuss a tank-carrying plane and other ideas; said nothing more about Willkie.

Left the club at 8:10 and began the drive to Martha's Vineyard. Fuel rationing has begun, but I had no difficulty getting gasoline along the route. Traffic is noticeably lighter. Crossed on 5:30 ferry from Woods Hole. Arrived home in time for supper with Anne. She is feeling much better, and the children are all well.

15. Director of Burnelli Aircraft, 1928–50; chief consultant of the Stout division of Convair, 1941–42.

Saturday, March 21

Japanese advance to Toungoo, Burma.

Harry Bennett phoned from Detroit. Says Ford wants to talk to me about assisting him with the bomber factory. I agreed to meet him in Detroit Tuesday morning.

Monday, March 23

Up at 4:30. Took the Ford and crossed on the 5:45 ferry. A clear and brilliant sunrise. Stopped in Plymouth long enough to see Plymouth Rock. The coastal road I was following passed within a few feet of it. The rock in its present setting is as unnatural as a stuffed animal. A pillared temple stands around it, and the rock itself is in a sort of well, which keeps it from being covered by the earth which has been filled in on two sides to make a park. However, someone had enough taste to leave the sea side of the well open so the water still touches the rock at high tide, passing in through upright iron bars which prevent tourists from getting in the same way. The rock itself now lies on a concrete foundation. On top of it "1620" has been carved in large numbers. I had a little the feeling I had when I went into Lenin's tomb: I wanted to cover it up with earth and sod and let imagination take the place of this futile attempt to frustrate time. Such artificial preservation cheapens history and creates a false sense of values.

Before this morning, when I read of Plymouth Rock, I had a picture in my mind of a small boatload of pilgrims debarking on a wild and lovely New England coast. From now on this picture will be mixed with one of a rather longish, rounded rock lying in concrete on a small patch of sand beach in the bottom of a temple-covered well at the edge of a signboard-lined auto highway. I understand that doubt exists as to whether this really is the rock upon which the Pilgrim Fathers first set foot. I think— that I hope it isn't.

Drove on to Boston, parked car in garage, purchased ticket to Detroit, and walked to a motion-picture theater to pass time until train departure. For the first time in months I saw a combination of good acting and good writing in *How Green Was My Valley*. Unfortunately, the film was nearing its end when I entered, and a poor slapstick comic took up so much time that I had to leave for my train before I could see the first part of the feature. Bought some black bread, fruit, and cheese for supper and boarded the 7:00 train for Detroit.

Tuesday, March 24

Swedish Army mobilizes.

Off train at 12:30. A Ford driver was waiting for me and took me to Bennett's office. Lunch with Henry Ford, Bennett, Cameron,[16] and other officers of the Ford Company. After lunch we stopped at the Motor Building for Sorensen and drove to the bomber plant at Willow Run— Ford, Bennett, Sorensen, and I in one car and the others following. The plant has progressed greatly since I was last there—runways all in, most of the building finished, much of the machinery installed. We drove first over the field and then through the factory. Sorensen and I got out in one place to look over some of the machines and jigs. The Ford workmen are being moved into the factory as fast as the contractor's workmen are being moved out.

After leaving the bomber factory we drove back to the Rouge plant. On the way Ford and Sorensen asked me if I would come out to Detroit and help them with their aviation program. I replied that I would like to very much but that I thought it would be advisable for them, and for me, to take the matter up with the War Department before reaching a final decision. Ford was at first opposed to asking the War Department anything about it; but I reminded him that we would have to have much contact with them in the future and that a good start would be of great advantage. Ford agreed. It annoys him to think he has to ask anyone about what he wants to do in his own factory. (And, as a matter of fact, it annoys me to have to ask the government's permission to make a connection with a commercial company; it's too damn much like Russia!)

I told Ford and Sorensen that if the Administration did not put any serious obstacles in the way, I thought it would be best for me to come to Detroit and "live" with the bomber project for a time before deciding exactly what my connection would be. I suggested that I come out in the morning and meet some of the officers of the project. Sorensen said he would arrange this. One of the Ford drivers took me to 508 Lakepointe, where I had supper with Mother and B. and spent the night.

16. W. J. Cameron, personal assistant to Henry Ford.

Wednesday, March 25

American Volunteer Group fliers destroy forty Japanese planes on airport at Chiengmai, Thailand. Japanese raid Corregidor with fifty-four bombers. Navy announces two more destroyers lost near Java—Pillsbury and Edsall.

Borrowed Mother's car and drove to the motor building in the Rouge plant for a conference with Sorensen, Roscoe Smith,[17] and other Ford officers. Phoned Lovett at his office in the War Department and made an appointment to see him in Washington Thursday.

Drove to the bomber plant and spent rest of morning going over designs, procurement programs and through the factory building with Roscoe Smith. The Ford schedule calls for the first bomber to be produced in May. From the appearance of the factory it seems to me it will be very difficult to meet this program. However, Ford uses production methods I am not well acquainted with, and I must reserve judgment until I know more. Of course, if I go with the company and if the program is behind, I will get a large portion of the blame whether or not I have had anything to do with it. But this is the latter part of March, and much of the machinery is yet to be installed; it will be little short of a miracle if the actual production of four-engine bombers is under way in April. However, the Ford Company has the *parts* for two bombers, brought from the Consolidated factory in San Diego. These could probably be assembled by May—or even in April—and in a sense the first plane could be produced on time in that way, but that would certainly be cutting corners. (These unassembled planes were brought through to assist in laying out machine designs and assembly methods.)

I boarded the 5:45 B. & O. train for Washington.

Thursday, March 26

Japan captures Andaman Islands. Jap forces advance in Burma.

Off train at 8:20. Breakfast with Sorensen and the head of the Washington Ford branch at Wardman Park Hotel. To Carlton to make several phone calls. Have had no exercise for several days, so spent rest of the morning walking along Rock Creek and through the zoo. The zoo always

17. Factory manager for Ford at Willow Run.

depresses me—such a difference between wild animals and caged animals. The thing that changes most about a caged animal is in its eyes. When it first arrives, they are wild and clear and piercing; then they slowly dull and deaden—and die.

Walked to Munitions Building for 2:15 appointment with Lovett. He said he thought a connection with Ford would be excellent! Lovett was very friendly and pleasant. I gather that the War Department has not been at all responsible for the difficulties placed in the way of my getting back into the aviation industry. These obstructions have apparently come entirely from the White House. (The internal confusion at home and the war reverses abroad have made Roosevelt no less vindictive, but they apparently *have* made him a little more discreet.) Lovett told me he had no question about the Ford Company's ability to produce aircraft in quantity, but that there *was* question as to their ability to produce aircraft of high quality. He said he doubted the company would be able to meet their program, which calls for the start of production in May. Lovett also said that the rest of the industry was very much opposed to the Ford Company entering aviation and hoped the production program would *not* be met.

To a newsreel theater later in the evening. No clapping whatever for war pictures except mild applause when General MacArthur's picture was thrown on the screen. Boarded the 11:00 P.M. train for Boston.

Friday, March 27

Japanese continue advance in Burma, bomb Corregidor. R.A.F. raids Ruhr. Churchill says "battle of Atlantic" has turned "momentarily" in favor of Axis.

Train forty minutes late; off at 8:50. Had hoped to make the morning ferry to Martha's Vineyard, but it would have meant fast driving even if the train had been on time. Pulled into an unused wood road and parked in a sunny patch of ground between pine trees. The morning is warm and clear, with a light wind rustling the last year's oak leaves and sighing through the tops of pines. I can hear roosters crowing in some nearby farmyard, and bees and bugs are flying past the car windows. It is the first day of real spring. Spent the rest of the morning and the first part of the afternoon writing and walking in the sun. Crossed on 5:30 ferry and arrived in time for supper with Anne.

Monday, March 30

India is offered dominion status "after the war" if she co-operates with England now. Renewed Japanese attacks on Bataan Peninsula are unsuccessful.

Spent day packing, closing up final details, laying plans with Anne, playing with the children, and walking through the woods and along the beach. I shall miss the freedom and solitude of this island.

We are undecided about whether to move the children to Detroit later this spring. Will Anne be able to write if we move to Detroit, or will the "social pressure" be too high? I am extremely anxious for her to be in an environment where she *can* write; but we don't want to be too far apart, and I want to be in close contact with the children. It is an exceptionally difficult problem to solve. If she could move to Detroit quietly, it would be simple enough; she would concentrate on writing while I concentrated on bomber production, and we could be together at night at least. But I know what would happen if she moved out with me; the newspapers would carry a story about it, and then invitations and requests would begin to file in to an extent that would be so distracting and take up so much time that concentration on writing would be impossible.

Anne needs solitude and peace, and she would have neither; she would not even have my excuse of war work as a shield. If people ask me to go to a dinner or sponsor some function, I can say quite truthfully that all my time must be devoted to factory problems and the war, and they will understand and call it "patriotic"; but if Anne were to say that she had to devote her time to her writing, the same people would say writing was unimportant in wartime, and that she should be rolling bandages for the Red Cross or sponsoring some garden-party benefit.

Tuesday, March 31

German naval forces attack British convoy off North Cape. Japanese continue to advance in Burma. Russian claims of success continue. "Pacific Council" set up in Washington. Cripps presses India for answer to British terms.

Went for a last short walk along the beaches and wood roads. Spent an hour playing with the children in the evening. Finished last packing and clearing up about 10:00. Played several Bach records with Anne. Bed at 11:00.

Wednesday and Thursday, April 1 and 2

Japanese forces land at Akyab, seventy-five miles from Indian border. R.A.F. raids objectives in Germany, Belgium, and France.

Up at 4:30. Left in Mercury at 5:00. Crossed on 5:45 ferry. Took U.S. Route 6 through Providence and Hartford, and crossed the Hudson via Bear Mountain Bridge. Stopped only for gasoline and sandwiches, which I ate, driving, during the day. Took half an hour for hot supper at a small-town restaurant in the evening. It was crowded, and I think I was recognized by a girl at the counter, even though I was wearing glasses and a pulled-down hat. Left before finishing to avoid the inevitable questions and stares and newspaper story.

I would give almost anything to be able to travel as I used to years ago, freely, as one man among many other men, without questions or stares, or the necessity of guarded conversation. Being well known separates one from life. To live and know life one must be the observer rather than the observed; one should be able to alternate solitude and contemplation with friendship and discussion. This is not impossible when one is well known, but it is many times more difficult.

Day broke soon after I passed through Cleveland. During the night I had little difficulty staying awake, but at dawn the almost irrepressible desire for sleep, which I have always experienced at that time, came again. I stopped the car at frequent intervals and got out and walked briskly for several minutes away from it; then I would run back as fast as I could, hoping to wake myself completely and permanently. I always felt refreshed and wide awake when I got back into the car, but within ten or fifteen minutes I would find myself falling asleep again and have to go through the whole procedure once more.

Stopped for breakfast soon after daybreak and had no subsequent trouble with sleep. Arrived at Dearborn Inn at 9:30—968 miles from Seven Gates Farm. Engaged room, bathed, and phoned Bennett's office. He was away for the day. Drove to Willow Run factory and spent most of the day with Roscoe Smith, looking over production and procurement figures and meeting personnel. Told Smith I felt the weak places in production would lie in outside purchases and final detailed assembly— failure of subcontractors to meet their delivery dates, etc. He felt confident that all these matters are well in hand; but if they are, the Ford Company will have performed the miracle in aircraft production.

The Willow Run factory is a stupendous thing—acres upon acres of machinery and jigs and tarred wood floors and busy workmen. It is a sort of Grand Canyon of a mechanized world. One cannot absorb it suddenly.

Went for an hour's test flight in a bomber—a B-24C [18]—in the late afternoon. This is a plane built at the Consolidated factory in San Diego; the Willow Run plant will not be in production for several more weeks. The bombers now being built at the Consolidated factory are called B-24C's; those which will be built at the Ford Willow Run factory will be called B-24E's. They will both be of Consolidated design, and similar aerodynamically. The planes built at Willow Run will differ somewhat structurally because of the changes incorporated for mass production.

I am not overly impressed with the qualities of this bomber. Its design seems unnecessarily awkward, and the details of construction could certainly be improved upon. When I flew it for a few minutes in the air, I found the controls to be the stiffest and heaviest I have ever handled. Also, I think the gun installations are inadequate and the armor plate poorly installed. I would certainly hate to be in a bomber of this type if a few pursuit planes caught up with it. There are many improvements which can and should be made before American fliers are sent out to fight in these ships.

Supper alone in room at Dearborn Inn. I planned on going to bed early, but Henry Ford phoned and asked me to come over to his home for a short time. He and Mrs. Ford and several guests were there. I stayed until 11:00, discussing military aircraft and the Willow Run plant. Night at the Dearborn Inn.

Friday, April 3

British continue to retire in Burma. R.A.F. bombs occupied France. Race riot between white and Negro troops at Fort Dix; three killed. Chinese troops attack in Burma. Cripps given free hand in India negotiations.

18. The Liberator bomber, originally built by the Consolidated Vultee Aircraft Corp., was a four-engine, high-wing monoplane, accommodating a crew of seven to ten. Its maximum speed at altitude was about 300 m.p.h.; its service ceiling about 28,000 feet.

Spent day between Willow Run and Rouge plants—studying production and procurement data, drawings of plane assembly, going through the plane itself, and in general getting to know the Ford organization and its methods. One never knows an organization until he knows its troubles and jealousies and frictions; and that often takes some time. I will not get over the feeling of being a stranger until I find where these elements exist—and I will not feel I have contributed my share to this organization until I have found a way of lessening them. So far, I am greatly impressed by this lack, and that is a high compliment to Mr. Ford.

Soon after I arrived at the Willow Run plant this morning, Bennett told me that reporters from all the Detroit papers were at his office in the Rouge plant and wanted to see me. He asked me how we should handle them. I told him I felt it essential to treat them courteously, but that an interview would almost certainly cause trouble. I suggested that I drive in and meet them, but with the advance understanding that it be "off the record," and that I not be quoted in anything I said. He agreed to this, and we drove in together.

The meeting took place fairly smoothly—possibly because I agreed to two sentences of what seemed to me rather banal "quotes." Henry Ford came in a little later and we had a photograph taken together. That helped, too, as far as the reporters were concerned. I feel a little differently about a press relationship where I am taking part in a project of definite public concern. There are certain things people have a right to know—things they are really told too little about. It is in a sense of values that I clash with the press. They want stories of personal life that I regard as private, while I feel they fail to keep people informed of developments they must understand if our government and our system of life is to survive.

Saturday, April 4

Navy announces loss of aircraft tender Langley, *destroyer* Peary, *and tanker* Pecos. *The* Langley *was sunk on February 27. United States bombers raid Japanese fleet in Bay of Bengal; hits on cruiser and three troop ships claimed. Seven more Allied ships announced sunk in Atlantic and Caribbean.*

The war news is so censored, and frequently so delayed, that it is useless to attempt to make these entries objective. Rather than being factual and objective they represent the news emphasized in the daily press. Our successes are headlined; our enemies' successes are hidden. I try to make some selection—to leave out trivialities, etc., but since much news is obviously not even printed, intelligent selection is impossible. Probably I could do better if I had time to study the back pages more carefully each day. I find that items hidden in back pages are often the most important of all.

Drove to bomber plant with Henning.[19] Spent first part of morning checking procurement figures and studying drawings of plant and plane. Then to Henning's office where I studied specifications, performances, and operating instructions for the bomber.

Monday, April 6

British shoot down fifty-seven Japanese planes raiding Ceylon. Japanese continue attack on Bataan. Russians claim high German losses in men and equipment. Japanese raid India.

Breakfast with Henning at the inn. Then to Stinson factory. They are getting the jigs ready for the manufacture of liaison planes for the Air Corps and, like most other companies, have all the orders they can handle. Was shown through the Ford paper mill after lunch, both the new and the old processes. Spent an hour with Van Ranst[20] going over the New Ford liquid-cooled engine—twelve cylinders, about 1,800 h.p., integral supercharger, fuel injection, etc.

Tuesday, April 7

Chungking, China, announces that units of the United States Air Force are fighting in Burma. Japanese launch heavy attack on Bataan. British fleet in Bay of Bengal.

Breakfast at inn with Henning. Then to Willow Run factory and spent rest of morning going through the factory, getting to understand the layout and operating plans of the various departments. I am greatly im-

19. Hal P. Henning, chief test pilot at Willow Run and head of the flight-test department.

20. Cornelius Van Ranst, Ford engineer.

pressed with the elaboration of tooling and jigs. Since this has been done to a large extent on theory, we must expect many unforeseen problems in getting actual production under way. But when it is under way, the output of this plant will be tremendous.

I started at the receiving platforms, where freight cars are run into the building to unload, and walked through almost all of the various departments. Some of them are already in operation; there are over 9,000 workmen now employed. (About 60,000 will be required for capacity production.) The building is 3,500 feet long and 1,200 feet in maximum width. Much machinery is still being installed, and concrete is still being poured at the final assembly end. It now looks as though the first bomber will be ready to roll out before the floors are finished. At one end of the plant machinery is going full blast, while at the other end the contractors are still erecting steel. Bomber parts follow the contractors as water follows a canal dredge. The first planes will be largely hand assembed—the first one will be simply a Consolidated-built plane reassembled. Then more and more mass-production methods will be used until capacity production is reached—405 per month (knock-down and built-up) on present plans. The knock-down planes will be shipped to Consolidated, Douglas, and North American. The built-up will, of course, be assembled at the Willow Run plant.

To the administration building (Dearborn) for lunch with Bennett, [William B.] Taylor (C.I.O.), [Richard T.] Frankensteen (C.I.O.), Commander [Alexander D.] Douglas (Naval Intelligence), and several others. We spent much time discussing air-raid and sabotage protection for the Willow Run plant. I took the stand that while air raids would be extremely costly and light in comparison to those England has experienced, they were technically possible and therefore should be prepared for. At the present moment there are no precautions whatever at the Willow Run plant for either air raids or sabotage (outside of the usual plant guards). The workmen are not even instructed what to do in case bombs started falling. There is no warning net in this area, no antiaircraft guns around the factory, and no pursuit units in readiness to even hinder a hostile attack.

I boarded the 5:45 Ambassador for Washington.

Wednesday, April 8

General Marshall and Harry Hopkins arrive in London on "wartime mission." Axis forces advance in Libya, raid Malta and Alexandria.

Japanese advance in Bataan; siutation critical. Gasoline ration in east and northwest to be cut again. Russian forces cross upper Dnieper to attack German "Moscow salient." Loss of Allied shipping continues heavy. R.A.F. and Germans exchange air raids.

Off train at 8:20. To Wardman Park, where I made several phone calls and arranged my schedule for the day. Taxi to Social Security Building to see Mr. Meigs[21] (Aviation Department of the War Production Board). Arrived early, so spent ten minutes walking. It is difficult to get enough exercise while leading this type of life. I miss the woods and beaches of Martha's Vineyard already.

Meigs had been called away for some conference, so I spent an hour talking to his officers and going over plans for large-bomber construction. The present plans call for a production of 1,300 four-engine bombers per month in 1943. However, the availability of material will probably cause delay in the production schedule. There is already a serious shortage in nickel, steel, copper, and various other essentials. Also, there has been great confusion in the allocation of such materials (a part of the general confusion which exists in Washington).

One of the officers in Meigs's department told me the nickel-steel available for aircraft production had been reduced nearly fifty per cent (through priority allocation), and that information was not available with which this fifty per cent reduction could be intelligently allocated within the aviation industry. He said it was finally decided to go through the lists of contracts they had available in their office and to assign nickel-steel only to those projects they knew could not make use of some substitute. But they found the lists inadequate and the numbering within the lists confused. In one instance, he said, they found a large quantity of nickel-steel allotted to a designation number which, when they looked it up on their lists, called for ink!

Arrived at Room 2000, Munitions Building at 3:00 and was introduced to the three Air Corps pilots who have just returned from the Pacific war zone: Captains Wheless, Green, and Smelser. (I had asked the War Department to arrange for a conference with pilots who had been in combat in four-engine bombers.) These men have seen service in the Philippines, in Java, and in Australia. Captain Wheless had most of his crew hit in one engagement, and returned with some 1,100 bullet holes in his B-17 bomber, according to the major who introduced him.

21. Merrill Church Meigs, director of the aircraft section of the War Production Board, 1940–42, and from 1942 to 1944 senior consultant on aviation.

I asked them a number of questions, which I shall list in more or less detail, telling them I thought it essential for the manufacturer of aircraft to keep in the closest possible contact with the operators of those aircraft. They seemed exceptionally fine young men, and I gained a great deal of information from our discussion.

I asked them whether the interplane system of telephonic communication had proven satisfactory in actual combat. They replied that they had found it satisfactory up to an altitude of about 25,000 feet, but that above 25,000 feet they had experienced difficulty in speaking through the face masks they had to wear because of the low pressure. In other words, conversation was not clear enough when they spoke through a face mask. They told me they did not like the throat type of microphone.

I asked how they felt about the four-engine bomber v. the two-engine bomber during an enemy attack. They said they preferred a two-engine bomber because of its greater maneuverability.

In reply to my questions about the value and best locations of armor plate, they said it was of vital importance but disagreed somewhat as to where it should be located. One officer wanted it in front of the pilot and co-pilot, while the other two felt it was best located in its present position in the rear. They all wanted more of it, especially for the members of their crew. Many men had been killed and wounded, they said, because of the lack of sufficient armor plate—particularly the tail and waist machine gunners.

As I questioned them more closely, however, I found that their attitude on armor-plate position was largely based on the firepower and gun position of the bombers they had been flying. For instance, the officer who wanted armor plate in front had been flying a B-17 with only one .30-cal. machine gun in the nose. The Japanese pilots had discovered, from the tracer bullets, that the tail of his plane was well protected. Therefore they attacked head on and naturally gave him some very uncomfortable moments. When I asked how he would feel about armor plate if he had two .50-cal. machine guns in the nose, he said in that case he thought he would prefer it in the rear. This shows how carefully one must look into the reasons for pilots' recommendations concerning structural changes.

All three officers told me they had no use whatever for periscope sights for their machine guns. One said his bottom turret had been equipped with a periscope sight and that his crew had tied the guns loosely in a position pointing back under the tail—so they could wabble about a bit—and simply pulled the trigger without aiming whenever a Japanese plane flew in that general area. They said the Japanese had a very great respect for tracer bullets, and that while they were good and courageous fliers, they showed none of the suicidal tendencies attributed to them by American newspapers. They said the Japs were using mostly Zero fighters—a highly maneuverable low-wing type of pursuit, with a high speed below our best types but sufficient to be effective against bombers. These pursuit planes were usually equipped with two 20-mm. cannon and six .27-cal. machine guns.

I asked how often weather conditions had prevented bombing from high altitude. They replied that they were frequently forced down to low altitude because of clouds, and that the Jap pursuit planes made it "very hot" for them when they were low. They said in that case their greatest protection lay in getting into the clouds. I asked them what their chances were when they were caught by a pursuit squadron. They said they felt their chances were good, even when there were no clouds for protection. But I found they were basing this statement largely on the low penetrating power of the Japanese guns. They said the .27-cal. bullets left only a "pin prick" on five-eighths-inch armor plate, and that the 20-mm. cannon or .60-cal. guns, as they called them, left no mark at all because of their low velocity. They said that if the Jap pursuit planes had been equipped with guns similar to our .50-cal. it would have been a different story.

The officers were divided in their opinion about the tricycle landing gear. Two of them looked on it with disfavor, while the third said he thought their attitude might be due to the fact that they had not flown tricycle gears enough to get used to them. One objection, which was legitimate enough, was that they had seen bomber nose wheels fold back when landing on a soft field. I suggested that this trouble could be avoided by stronger construction, and they agreed.

A more novel and debatable objection was that a tricycle gear would not ground-loop. (After all, the tricycle gear was designed to prevent ground-looping.) The two officers who advanced this objection said they often had to operate out of fields which were both small and wet and that the best protection from overshooting lay in ground-looping. They said that jamming the brakes on had little effect on a wet clay-surface field, that the smooth tires simply skidded along and helped very little in slowing up the plane. I suggested the use of tires with deep treads, and they thought it might be a great help.

They said they had had considerable trouble with control cables being cut by bullets and that all control cables should be doubled and also the oxygen lines.

They said the escape hatches were not adequate in the bombers they had been flying and that a parachute jump was therefore so difficult they had formed the practice of putting their parachutes in *convenient* rather than in accessible places.

They did not use their bombsight to fly the plane over the target, they said—did not want to fly straight and level long enough to get the bombsight into automatic operation; said they could get into position and away quicker flying the plane by hand.

They want the bomber to be able to get to the bomb bay without too much difficulty, and feel that any man should be able to get to any other while the plane is in flight, so wounded may be cared for, etc.

They prefer a single-rudder design for combat—say twin rudders get in the way of the top guns.

They say that ice has more effect on a Davis wing than on a Clark Y.

In judging the recommendations of pilots it is necessary to remember that the majority of them are, though they would deny it hotly, a pretty conservative group as far as developments in aircraft are concerned. It is not safe to put too much confidence in a pilot's report on any device he has not used long enough to become thoroughly accustomed to it. I always remember the slowness of the pilots of the Transcontinental Mail to change from the DH-4 to the Douglas, although the Douglas was a far safer and better-performing plane. For a time each pilot insisted on two planes—a Douglas for *good* weather and a DH for *bad* weather.

Then, when we tried to introduce the low-wing type for mail and passenger flying in 1930–31, we met strong opposition from the pilots. Some of them took the stand that flying a low-wing ship was like flying upside down, that it was unnatural and just wouldn't work. But while one must be careful in accepting too quickly formed judgment, one must always be open-minded and receptive to the ideas of service pilots. And these fellows who have been flying under fire have earned the right to have their recommendations considered with the utmost care.

Spent half an hour discussing endocrine-gland-secretion levels in the blood stream with an Army major; then took a taxi to the Wardman Park for my bag, and on to the station to catch the 5:50 train for Detroit.

Thursday, April 9

Bataan falls.

Train in at 8:20. Talked to Sorensen about the desirability of building up our own aircraft engineering department. He feels, as I do, that it should be done; and, to my surprise, he agreed that the best procedure might be to start with the design of a pursuit plane around the new Ford liquid-cooled engine. Spent rest of morning with Sorensen. We went to see the mock-up of the new engine, then to see the experimental engine. After that we spent half an hour with the experimental tanks the Ford Company is constructing, while Sorensen conferred with several of his engineers on methods of construction. The Ford design of tank is closer to the ground than the Chrysler tank, but neither is as low as the similar German model. I called Sorensen's attention to this fact.

Sorensen spoke to me about salary. When I accepted the invitation of Mr. Ford and himself to come to work with the company, I told them I did not want to accept a large salary during the war. (Sorensen had told me that he would have to find some way of paying me more than Administration officials would want me to be paid.) He said he had spoken to Lovett when he was in Washington, and that Lovett had said that no question could be raised if I were to receive $666.66 per month. Sorensen was rather apologetic about this figure. I told him I did not want to take more than I would have received if I had gone into the Air Corps as a colonel.

Lunch with Mr. Ford, Sorensen, Cameron, and several other officers of the Ford Company. Henry Ford is amazingly active and keen and highly respected by his men. It interests me greatly to listen to him and to watch the reaction of the men he talks to—their interest when his genius asserts itself, their silence when he outlines some obviously impractical idea. But I find that his genius penetrates even his impractical ideas. There is usually some element in them worth studying no matter how wild they seem to be at first glance.

To the Willow Run plant after lunch. Spent half an hour with Henning, discussing the recommendations of the three Air Corps officers I talked to yesterday afternoon. To Dearborn, to pack and make final arrangements for flying to San Diego. Just as I was about finished, the American Airlines office called to say the flight had been canceled on account of weather, and that unless I had war priority, no passage to California was available until April 15. This brings up the whole question of priority in travel. It goes against my grain to use priority to push someone else off the plane I want to take. But this is war work, and it is essential for me to get to San Diego soon.

Friday, April 10

Washington announces that 36,000 American and Filipino troops were on Bataan, say 3,500 have reached Corregidor. Japanese sink two heavy British cruisers and aircraft carrier Hermes *in Indian Ocean. Allied planes score "near misses" on Jap aircraft carrier. Italian cruiser and several supply ships sunk by British submarines in Mediterranean. British proposals to India rejected.*

Drove to bomber plant. Spent hour discussing engineering problems with Ed Scott, who is in charge of the engineering organization at Willow Run. He has been with the Ford organization for many years, but has had little aviation experience. However, he recognizes this fact and has engaged aeronautical engineers to help and advise him. If he has the ability to select his engineers well and sufficient broad-mindedness to do so, his lack of personal experience in aeronautical engineering may be little or no disadvantage.

Scott gave me a much clearer picture than I have had before of the relationship that exists between Ford and Consolidated. It seems that every change in design made by the Ford Company, no matter how slight, must be checked and authorized by Consolidated engineers. Ford can suggest changes for purposes of mass production, etc., but these changes must be okayed by Consolidated. Contrary to a number of Ford officers, Scott said that with minor exceptions the Consolidated Company had given good co-operation. He said that the Ford engineers had found it necessary to make a complete set of drawings for the B-24 because the Consolidated drawings were inaccurate and inadequate. Apparently a lot of Consolidated design exists only in the heads of the shop foreman. Over a period of years many changes have been made that were not incorporated in the design drawings. Scott said that the Consolidated templates, loft boards, and drawings frequently would not match at all.

Phoned about passage to San Diego. It seems there is no alternative to

America First Committee rally at the Chicago Arena, 1941. *Left to right:*
Colonel Lindbergh, General Robert E. Wood, Mrs. Janet Ayer Fairbank

Colonel Lindbergh speaking at an America First Committee rally at Fort
Wayne, Indiana, October, 1941

Wide World

America First Committee rally at Madison Square Garden, New York, 1941.
Left to right: Senator Burton K. Wheeler, Colonel Lindbergh, Mrs. Kathleen
Norris, Norman Thomas

Colonel Lindbergh testifies at a congressional hearing on the Lend-Lease bill,
January, 1941

Senator Harry F. Byrd of Virginia

Ex-President Herbert Hoover speaking against United States
participation in war

Courtesy of Henry Ford Museum

Igor Sikorsky presenting his helicopter, the VS-300, to Henry Ford for the Henry Ford Museum at Dearborn. *Left to right:* Henry Ford II; Colonel Lindbergh; Leslie Morris, Sikorsky helicopter pilot; Henry Ford; Igor Sikorsky

Charles E. Sorensen and Russell Gnau

Courtesy of Henry Ford Museum

Admiral Emory Scott Land   Harry Bennett

Final assembly line of B-24 Liberator bombers, Willow Run

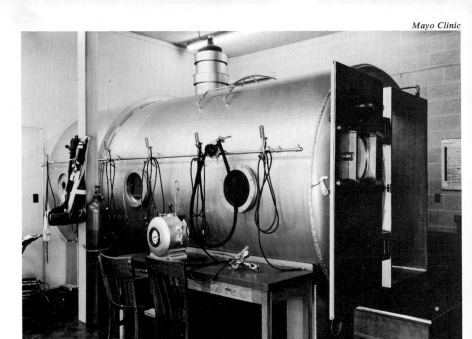

Altitude chamber of the Aeromedical Unit for Research in Aviation Medicine, Mayo Clinic, Rochester, Minnesota

Anne Morrow Lindbergh and her children at Bloomfield Hills, Michigan, 1943. *Left to right:* Anne, Scott, Jon (standing), Land

General Robert B. McClure and Colonel Lindbergh in the Solomons, 1944

Major Joseph J. Foss
and Colonel Lindbergh
on Emirau Island,
1944

Harris & Ewing

475th Fighter Group (Satan's Angels) camp area at Hollandia,
New Guinea, 1944

Campsite of the 432nd Fighter Squadron, 475th Group, on Biak Island, 1944

taking priority, much as I hate to do it. Either I take priority or I take the train, and I haven't time to do that and be in Albuquerque by the fifteenth.

Packed and wrote a short letter to Anne in the few minutes I had before departure time. One of the things I like least about this type of life is the lack of time to think and write. I would never go back into it except for the war. Still, this change is probably good for me, and there are elements that I enjoy—getting to know the inside of a great industrial organization, for instance.

Left the inn at 6:30 with a Ford Company car and driver and arrived at the airport ten minutes ahead of plane departure. Off the field at 7:30.

Saturday, April 11

Japanese forces land on Philippine island of Cebu. Britain admits collapse of India negotiations. Cripps states that the proposal he brought to India has been withdrawn. Roosevelt acts to check inflation—is expected to place ceiling on prices and wages.

Slept fairly well during the night, waking only during the rapid changes in altitude before and after we landed for fuel and passengers at Omaha and Cheyenne. There was considerable military activity on the Salt Lake field; frame buildings going up, sentries pacing up and down, warplanes lined up along the edges, sandbagged enclosures for planes and bombs in case of an enemy raid. Landed at Long Beach. Field there also covered with pursuit planes and bombers.

Reuben Fleet met me on the field at San Diego and, after driving me around the field, past rows of four-engine bombers and twin-engine flying boats, he took me to his new offices in the administration building. Fleet is now a consultant for the company. Night at the Fleets' home—in their guest house—on Point Loma.

Sunday, April 12

The Fleets have a large, white, castlelike house on Point Loma, overlooking San Diego Bay. The grounds are rather formal and planted with a semitropical foliage. Directly across the entrance of the bay is the North Island Naval Station with its hangars and buildings and warplanes staked out at intervals all over the field. (There are no more lines of planes left out to be destroyed by another Pearl Harbor attack.) To the left, beyond some Navy transports, is the city of San Diego, a white, southern city, outlined against low mountains in the background. A little farther to the left is the civil airport and the Consolidated factory buildings. It is a beautiful location but a rather noisy one, with this flying activity of wartime.

To airport for an hour and a quarter flying in a B-24. First flight with Colonel Bryant and Doug Kelly. Then I took the controls while Kelly showed me the operating technique of the bomber. Made two flights—about an hour in all. This is the first four-engine plane I have flown since I was in Germany in 1938, and the first one I have landed since the Pan American S-42 was tested in 1935. Also, it was my first experience with a tricycle landing gear on a large plane. I spent some time getting the feel of the plane in the air before trying the first landing; but I found that landing the B-24 is very simple, due largely to the tricycle-type gear and its long oleo travel. It is the mechanical complication, rather than the flying characteristics, of these large planes that one must spend time in mastering. Kelly was a great help, both because of his ability and because of our old friendship—dating back to 1927. I met him at San Diego when I was waiting for the *Spirit of St. Louis* to be built. As I recall, he was flying for Ryan Airlines at the time.

Monday, April 13

Heavy R.A.F. raids on German and Italian arms factories. Churchill says strong Japanese battle fleet operating in Bay of Bengal. Tension rising between Russia and Japan. Bombing attacks on Corregidor continue. Russians claim additional success.

Phoned the factory and arranged to meet Doug Kelly at 9:00. Walked around the grounds, wrote for half an hour, and drove to the airport in Major Fleet's car. Met Kelly and spent the better part of an hour with him discussing the B-24 and the development of four-engine bombers.

Spent half an hour with Laddon[22] talking about aviation developments and relationships between the Ford and Consolidated companies. (Con-

22. Isaac M. Laddon, aeronautical engineer for Consolidated Vultee Aircraft Corp., 1927–41; later executive vice president, general manager, and chairman of the board.

siderable friction has developed at times, and the article in this month's *Fortune* magazine has not helped the situation at all. The article shows Sorensen as a production genius showing the old aviation manufacturer, Consolidated, how to build aircraft.)

Mr. Leonard, Ford engineer, called for me about 3:30 and drove me to the Ford offices in San Diego while we discussed the problems he is encountering: briefly, most Consolidated men think the co-operation between Ford and Consolidated is good; most Ford men think it is poor.

Wednesday, April 15

Tension increasing between United States and France. Germany strengthens fortifications along Channel coast. Heavy R.A.F. raids over Continent. Japanese forces near Burma oil fields. Russians claim breakthrough of German lines near Vyazma.

To the airport for the 11:30 Western Air plane to Los Angeles. Arrived at the terminal early and found the plane was twenty minutes late. Spent the extra half hour walking in the sun along the sidewalks of San Diego —along walks I must have passed over in 1927 while the *Spirit of St. Louis* was being built; but the city, and especially the waterfront, has changed so much I cannot recognize old landmarks. About the only place I have seen on this trip that has not changed much is the bare, gray, sand-mud field, now called Speer Airport, where the *Spirit of St. Louis* was assembled, and where I made the first test flights.

This ability to walk freely along the streets of a city is a great joy to me. It is one of the few advantages I have found coming out of the war—a trivial, personal advantage to be sure, but since it involves no sacrifice on anyone's part, my conscience does not prevent me from enjoying it. The fact is that the newspapers are so busy with the direct and indirect developments of the war they haven't as much time to devote to harassing individuals. And since the papers concentrate public attention on the war, people are less interested in individuals and the trivialities of peacetime life—not that trivialities have been left behind; they are with us as much as ever, but like everything else, they have become associated with the war; they have become wartime trivialities.

Plane took off at 11:55. Clear sky except for scattered cumulus clouds. Landed [Los Angeles] at 1:00. My TWA plane, scheduled to take off at 1:00, was still loading. I hurried to the ticket office, but the plane took off while I was turning in my ticket! The next schedule to Albuquerque leaves at 5:45. I decided to spend the time walking in the sun. Bought lunch at a roadside restaurant; then walked for about two hours along the country roads. I write this entry sitting in the grass a mile or so from the airport. Boarded the 5:45 TWA plane for Albuquerque. Clear skies and a good flight. Taxi to Hilton Hotel for the night.

Thursday, April 16

United States bombers make long-distance raid on Philippines. Japanese advance continues in Burma. United States and Vichy break reported near. General Hugh Johnson died yesterday.

Breakfast with Colonel [C. D.] McAllister at 7:30. (I received a note of invitation from him when I arrived at the hotel last night.) McAllister and I collided with our SE-5's while we were attacking an observation plane during training maneuvers at Kelly Field in 1925. We both had to jump but landed without injury. McAllister, who was a student officer at the time, was a bit stuffy about it and claimed I ran into him. I didn't think so and was under the impression that he was out of place in the three-ship formation we were flying. However, it hadn't occurred to me to question who was at fault. We had been doing a dangerous type of flying, our C.O. and instructors took it as a matter of course—a part of training—and as far as I was concerned, I was happy to be alive and rather proud of the distinction of being a member of the "Caterpillar Club." (Anyone who saved his life by a parachute jump automatically became a member of a rather mythical organization called the Caterpillar Club. Parachutes were just coming into general use in 1925—ours was the first class of cadets to be equipped with them—and McAllister and I became members number twelve and thirteen.)

Since I was a cadet in 1925 and McAllister an officer, I had no opportunity of getting to know him well. But this morning I found him to be a pleasant and interesting friend. If he ever held any resentment toward me, as I was told was the case, there was certainly no trace of it remaining. And all during the day he went out of his way to be as considerate and helpful as possible, even to the extent of telling me he had been in almost complete agreement with the stand I took in opposing this country's entering the war.

Colonel [Frank D.] Hackett (C.O. of the air base) called for me at

8:00, and he, McAllister, and I drove out to the training station. We spent the morning looking over the field and planes, visiting the civil staff of instructors, and discussing improvements that might be incorporated in the B-24 bomber—strengthening the nose wheel, removing the shimmy, simplifying the hydraulic system, improving pilot's vision for night landings, etc., etc.

There are about fifteen to twenty Consolidated bombers of the B-24 type in use at the school. Army pilots, some of them with little over 200 hours' previous experience, are trained to handle four-engine equipment. It is no wonder we are having so many crashes these days. The training of pilots is being pushed too fast for safety, and I think too fast even for the maximum effectiveness in war. I cannot help feeling sorry for the crews of these planes. If a pilot crashes, he has at least had his life in his own hands; but these crew members have to go up with any pilot who is authorized to fly the plane, no matter how good or bad he may be. And they grow to know very well when a pilot is inexperienced and handles his plane poorly. I heard a general say, "None of these 200-hour pilots for me." But the members of a crew say nothing; they simply go when they are called.

Went up in a B-24 with Colonel McAllister for an hour after lunch. A forty-five-mile wind was blowing clouds of dust across the field, but the ship seemed to handle well in the rough air.

Boarded the 10:52 TWA sleeper for Chicago.

Friday, April 17

Disorder reported in France as Laval assumes power. British destroy oil wells in Burma. Japanese advance continues. New Allied shipping losses reported.

Transferred to an American Airlines plane at Chicago. Landed [Detroit] about 9:45. Stopped at the inn long enough to wash and make several phone calls; then drove out to the bomber plant. Rest of morning going over mail and writing a report on the future of large bombers.

Harry Bennett tells me that several Communist workers in one of the divisions of the Ford Company have been trying to cause trouble for me among the workmen—ineffectively, he says.

Ford and Sorensen came out after lunch. Spent most of the afternoon going through the plant with them. Work is progressing rapidly, but the first plane will not be out by the eighteenth of April by any means. It is now clear that the Ford people have been a little overconfident of the speed with which the factory could be built and machinery installed. Also, as has been feared, they are having trouble in obtaining G.F.E. (government-furnished equipment) and outside purchased parts. As a matter of fact, the speed of construction has been amazing. It was unfortunate and needless that someone estimated that the first bomber would be out in March.

Anne may come out here next weekend and bring Jon. The children, she says, are all well.

Saturday, April 18

United States bombers raid Tokyo, Yokohama, Kobe, and Nagoya, according to a Japanese announcement. Laval sets up new Cabinet in France. Japanese capture Cebu, Philippines. Russians claim new advance in Smolensk area. Relationship between United States and France reported critical.

Invited [Cornelius] Van Ranst to lunch at the inn (engineer in charge of development of the new Ford liquid-cooled aircraft engine). I wanted an opportunity to talk to him alone and in a quiet atmosphere. I find I can get a much better grasp of a situation and much more accomplished in this way. An office conference is usually too formal and too tense for fundamental and comprehensive discussions. People don't seem to talk as freely or think as well.

Stopped to see Bill Mayo[23] at his house at 1457 Seminole. He looks better than when I last saw him, but says he has been through a bad year as far as his health is concerned. We discussed the Willow Run plant and the Ford Motor Company's background in aviation. Everyone has wondered why Henry Ford decided to get out of aviation some years ago, after building the best transport plane of the time—the old Ford Tri-Motor. And almost everyone who knows anything about it gives different reasons as the cause of his decision. I thought Mayo would be in a position to know, since he was in charge of Ford's aviation department at that time; but he seems as uncertain as the others.

Mayo told me that about 1930 he went to Ford with a plan for the

23. William B. Mayo, builder of the Ford Tri-Motor monoplane. Ford's chief aviation engineer from 1925 to 1933.

development of a new and advanced type of transport to replace the old Tri-Motor. He told Ford that Boeing was coming out with a transport plane that would put the Ford Company out of the aviation business unless they built something to compete with it. Ford said to wait a year. Mayo replied that in a year it would be too late. Ford said that Mayo and his engineers had enough brains to build a plane good enough to take the business from Boeing even after giving Boeing a year's start. And there the matter ended.

Mayo told me he had at one time arranged with the air-transport lines flying into Detroit to use the Ford airport at Dearborn as a terminal. But one Sunday a large number of airplanes flew over the Ford house. Mrs. Ford told her husband she thought those planes oughtn't to be flying on the Sabbath. The next day Henry Ford told Mayo to stop all flying from the airport on Sundays! Mayo replied it would be impossible for the airlines to operate on that basis; but it made no difference and flying was stopped. Of course, that ended all possibility of the Ford airport being used as a terminal for the airlines.

Ford has never been an aviation enthusiast, Mayo says, citing, among other things, the fact that Ford made his first, and so far his last, flights with me, in 1927. I took him up once in the *Spirit of St. Louis* and once in one of his Tri-Motors, and he has never flown since. But there are other considerations that probably influenced Ford to discontinue his aviation activities. Two of his pilots were killed flying planes he had built—[James W.] Brooks and Manning—and those who were near him say he felt their loss deeply. Then there was the fiasco of the "one-hundred-passenger plane" he built; it turned out to be about one-third that size and was so poorly designed it never left the ground. And about that time it was the practice for airlines and manufacturers to merge. It looked as though a manufacturer of aircraft would have to operate his own airlines in order to find a market for his equipment. All these things and probably many more entered into Ford's decision. How much any single one influenced him, probably he himself does not know.

For a time Mayo and I discussed Ford's personality and the rise of one of the greatest industries in the world under his leadership. I asked Mayo how he accounted for the success of a man of Ford's eccentricity and genius. I told Mayo I knew of no other man with these characteristics who had made a success in business, to say nothing of such an outstanding success. Mayo has come to the same conclusions I have in this respect. He said he attributed Ford's success to his ability to make such sound fundamental decisions in a sufficient number of instances that his more superficial eccentricities became unimportant in comparison.

As I get to know Henry Ford better and learn more about him, it seems to me that in describing him one could say his heights of genius so overpower his shadows of eccentricity that the shadows serve to accentuate the heights.

Tuesday, April 21

Hour's conference with Sorensen in morning. We discussed the progress at Willow Run, the need for building up an independent engineering organization (in which he agrees), the progress of the Ford liquid-cooled engine, etc.

Phoned Major [William S.] McDuffee about the possibility of getting a B-26 assigned to the Ford Company for running tests on the Pratt & Whitney 2800 engines. But *all* the B-26's (two-engine Martin bombers) are grounded, so that's out for the time being at least. Possibly we can get a B-34 instead. The B-26's have an extremely high landing speed—said to be due to interference between fuselage and engine nacelles—and have been killing too many crews, especially in night landings.

All the B-26's grounded! And boom flutter in the P-38's! And the Allison engines not functioning properly in the P-40's! And God knows what else has gone wrong. The way this country is going into war reminds me of an inexperienced man going into a fight with a trained boxer, mad, excited, arms swinging. The trouble is that the men who will do the paying and the dying are not those who make the blunders and who are responsible for it all.

I tried my best, in 1938 and '39, to get this government to concentrate on aircraft design and research. But I was only partially successful and was criticized severely for suggesting that it was more important to develop the right types of military aircraft than to begin mass production at that time.

Wednesday, April 22

Roosevelt reported planning on limiting pay, profits, and total income. British Commandos raid French coast.

Lunch with Henry Ford and other officers of the company. Much of the lunch period was spent discussing the shortage of scrap material (iron, copper, etc.). Sorensen says, in regard to the Willow Run bomber plant, that it is the first time in his life he ever built a factory without knowing where the raw material was coming from to run it with. The Ford officers, like the officers of most other companies I know, feel the government is hindering rather than aiding the war program.

After lunch Ford, Sorensen, and I went to look at the experimental opposed-piston engine which is being secretly developed for use in motorcars. The present model is small, clean, and develops about 35 h.p. Ford says that is plenty large enough for the cars they will be building in the future and that cars will be smaller from now on. He has apparently changed his opinion in this respect since I talked to him a year or so ago.

Thursday, April 23

Russian offensive reported along entire 2,000-mile front. Axis air attacks on Malta continue "with heavy losses."

We are having trouble with the generators for the B-24. None of them last for more than a few hours of flight. Of the three companies building these generators, two have had to shut down because of the inferiority of their product. The third, General Electric, has a new design, incorporating an air-scoop cooler, which recent tests indicate will prove satisfactory. Meanwhile, there are not enough generators available to equip the B-24's. (The old General Electric type, which was the best of the three, would seldom last for more than ten hours of flight.)

Sunday, April 26

Morning and lunch at 508 Lakepointe. Then Anne and I left Jon with Mother and drove to the Dearborn Inn. Afternoon discussing plans and going over Anne's review of [Aldous] Huxley's *Grey Eminence*. Anne will probably move the household to Detroit sometime in June. The next baby is due late in August; whether she will have it in Detroit or return to Dr. [Everett M.] Hawks's care in New York, we will decide later. I want her to have at least two weeks free on Martha's Vineyard, to be outdoors, rest, write, and enjoy the days of spring.

Monday, April 27

Heavy R.A.F. raids over Germany continue—Pilsen, Rostock and other cities. German Air Force raids Bath and other English cities. Japanese advance in Burma and continue bombing of Corregidor. Registration of all male citizens between forty-five and sixty-five to be completed today.

Anne has not had very much luck looking for houses—either too large, too small, or in the wrong location; and few of any kind available.

Tuesday, April 28

Russian armies attack Finns in north. Japanese within sixty-seven miles of Lashio. Roosevelt asks limit on prices, wages, and war profit; advocates increased rationing.

Went with Anne in afternoon to look at a medium-sized house about seven miles from the Willow Run factory and four miles from Ann Arbor. The grounds are wooded, rolling, and attractive, cut through by a small stream. The house is not very attractive, but would do very well for us if it only had two more bedrooms. As it is, I don't see how we can fit in. The furnishing is not by any means what we would like, but we cannot expect to find that in a rented house. Long Barn was probably the closest we will ever come.

Drove back to the inn. Anne packed her bag, and we drove to 508 Lakepointe for supper with Mother, B., and Jon. Jon has caught twenty snakes since he arrived! I don't think he ever had a better time, and it has done Mother a great deal of good, too. Left at 6:15 and drove Anne and Jon to the station. It seems only yesterday that they arrived.

Thursday, April 30

Heavy bombing raids over England. Japanese forces reach Lashio. Russians report new gains. German peace offers rumored.

Spent an hour in the B-24C familiarizing myself with instruments, controls, and other installations.

Lunch at the Dearborn "round table" with Mr. Ford and other officers of the company. The "round table" is, as the name implies, a large round table where Mr. Ford frequently has lunch with his department heads and guests. There were three generations of Fords there today—Henry Ford, Edsel, and one grandson. The room is located in a corner of the garage building, behind the engineering building. It is well filled by the table—just comfortable room for the waiters to pass when the chairs are filled. The wood-paneled walls are hung with pictures taken of Mr. Ford and visiting celebrities.

To the Ford airport after lunch to see the opposed-piston, four-propeller experimental aircraft engine Mr. Ford is so much interested in. He wanted to show it to his guests. Then to see the opposed-piston car engine running on the test stand (second time in two days).

My radio-equipped company car was turned over to me this afternoon —a 1942 Mercury. Tested out the high-frequency transmitter and receiver on the way in to Dearborn. It worked effectively up to a distance of ten miles from the factory.

Friday, May 1

Van Ranst came at 11:45 to discuss the setting up of a design organization to lay out a pursuit plane around the new liquid-cooled engine. We decided the best procedure would be to make several pursuit layouts before selecting the type to produce.

Saturday, May 2

Packed briefcase and to 508 Lakepointe for supper and the evening with Mother and B. I have never seen the house looking so beautiful— the lilac hedge in full bloom, the spring-green grass in the yard covered with pure white apple-blossom petals, as though a light snow had fallen, the branches above still white with blossoms, new green leaves screening off the yard from surrounding houses, more purple lilacs in the corners, and iris flowering here and there around the edges of the irregular lawn. Under one of the trees was a bed of blue violets. Everything well enough, but not *too* well cared for. And the branches and lawn and flower beds filled with birds come for their supper of bread crusts and cracked corn— pheasants, grackles, sparrows, robins, redbirds, and thrushes. And everything covered with the light of a cool, clear spring evening.

Sunday, May 3

Breakfast with Mother and B. at 7:30. Rather a cold, raw day with rain clouds on the horizon, but a welcome contrast to the excessive heat we have had recently. We decided to spend the day at home instead of going for our usual weekend drive in the country.

With Mother's help I cleared out one of the basement storerooms and carried a number of in-the-way articles to the attic—old unused china, a dressmaking form that Grandmother used, several picture frames, an old fishing rod of Grandfather's, etc., etc.—things no one will ever use but that somehow you just don't want to throw away. It turned out to be a full day's job. Among other items, I sorted and carried out to the garage about 700 lbs. of old magazines—magazines Mother has been saving for years—some of them dated as far back as 1900. I picked out about five per cent of the most interesting and the others will be given to some war organization for waste paper.

At mealtime we sit with the double dining-room doors open on to the yard and watch the pheasants and other birds come for the cracked corn B. throws out over the grass. Now and then a rabbit comes in to eat a little. After lunch and dinner we have half an hour's music from the rather large library of records Mother has accumulated.

Left at 7:45 and drove back to the inn. A "blackout" is scheduled for 10:00, so I must turn in early.

Monday, May 4

R.A.F. raids France and northern Europe; Copenhagen bombed. Japanese advance in Burma continues—now thirty miles from Chinese border. Issue of sugar-ration books begins.

Inspected sound laboratory with [Carl J.] Lund (assistant flight superintendent). Then spent half an hour watching Link-trainer instruction. Then to Willow Run flight hangars to look over the new .50-cal.-gun installation in the nose of the B-24C. It is so badly done that it is practically useless. The angle of movement is so slight that the gun could not be used unless an enemy plane just happened to fly within its limited field of fire.

Conference with Henning, Roscoe Smith, Ed Scott, and others in regard to setting up a design organization for making improvements in the B-24. Conference with Henning and Sorensen at the engineering building, Rouge plant, at 3:00, in regard to design organization. Made affirmative decision and decided to begin with redesign of B-24 nose to permit adequate machine-gun installation.

Tuesday, May 5

British forces attack Madagascar. R.A.F. raids over Continent continue. Germans claim naval victory in "Arctic waters"—one British cruiser and six freighters.

Flew to Ford airport, Dearborn, in Grumman amphibian (G-21) with Henning (pilot) and [William J.] Hadden (flight engineer). We picked up Van Ranst and flew on to Buffalo (via the direct route over Canada), arriving at the Municipal Airport about noon. Lunch at Curtiss factory. Afternoon with Curtiss engineers discussing specifications of the new Ford engine and the new Curtiss P-60 pursuit plane in which they plan to install one as soon as it is ready. The Curtiss engineers seem to be greatly impressed with the performances of the engine, which Van Ranst outlined to them.

During the discussion we went over to the airport to look at a Rolls-Royce installation in a P-60. The Rolls-Royce is underpowered for the plane. Looked over the new Curtiss Army transport while we were there.

Frank Caldwell (Hamilton Propeller Division of United Aircraft) was visiting the Curtiss factory, and we spent a few minutes discussing high-altitude propellers and the future altitude trends for bombers and pursuit planes. Has the pendulum swung too far, and will cloud layers and haze keep bombing planes even lower than the altitudes they can now attain, or will high-speed bombers, flying at altitudes of 40,000 feet and above, be too fast for pursuit planes to climb and catch?

Ever since I can remember there has been this competition between bombers and pursuit planes. At one time it is thought that the pursuit plane will shoot the bomber out of the sky; at another, the bomber enthusiasts say that the bomber is too fast and too well armored for pursuit to cope with. A change in design, a new engine, or a shift in military policy will let one surge ahead of the other for a time; but it has never been for long, and there is no indication of any permanent trend yet taking place.

Caldwell and I discussed the latest idea advanced by the bomber adherents—an idea that justifies very careful thought, i.e., that the speed of high-altitude bombers which will be constructed in the near future will be so close to the velocity of sound (and the rapidly mounting resistance at that velocity) that pursuit planes cannot be designed to go enough *faster* to cope with them—that there will not be sufficient margin between the speed of the bombers and velocity of sound to give the pursuit plane enough additional speed over the bomber, unless some means is found to let the pursuit plane operate within speed ranges which now seem impractical due to the tremendous resistances encountered.

Left Buffalo about 5:30.

Wednesday, May 6

Washington announces the fall of Corregidor. Japanese forces take Akyab airfield 300 miles from Calcutta. French and British forces continue battle on Madagascar. London reports unrest among generals of German Army.

Conference with Bennett and other officers in regard to apparent inefficiency in factory at this stage of construction and possible need for certain changes in personnel.

Evening spent studying for examination for radiotelephone operators license I am scheduled to take at 9:00 A.M. tomorrow. I took the radiotelegrapher's examination in 1931 and didn't need a license to operate the radiotelephones in the Army planes I flew in 1939; but now, in order to operate the phones in commercial planes (and no cross-country flight can be made without radiotelephone equipment since war started), I must take the examination. However, it is not very complicated and should not take long.

Thursday, May 7

Gas ration for private cars in eastern states set at two to six gallons per week. British forces advance in Madagascar. Russians continue to report successes. Sinking of Allied shipping continues.

Up at 6:00. Hour's final study for examination (reminds me of my flying cadet days at Brooks and Kelly fields). Drove to Detroit, arriving at the

Federal Building at 9:05. The Mr. Lee who is in charge here was one of
the men who gave me my radiotelegrapher's license test at New York in
1931. Had to have both hands fingerprinted—second time in two days!
The examination, fingerprinting, and filling in of forms took about one
and a half hours. Lee told me I passed with a high grade, but that there
was a regulation against telling anyone his exact grade! (In 1931 I made
about ninety-six per cent, as I remember—the regulations have changed
since that time—probably often if the F.C.C. is anything like other government agencies.)

Lunch with Ed Scott to discuss problems connected with the redesign
of the nose and machine-gun mount on the B-24.

Friday, May 8

*Major "five-day-old naval battle" reported now going on in South Pacific,
northeast of the Australian coast. Allies claim thirteen Japanese ships
sunk or put out of action. Japanese claim five ships, including sinking of
U.S.S. California (battleship) and the United States carriers Saratoga and
Yorktown. Gasoline ration for Eastern Seaboard to be three gallons per
week for nonessential driving. Japanese forces reported to have crossed
Indian border. British capture naval base of Diego-Suarez on Madagascar. Japanese claim surrender of all American forces in Philippines.
Russians claim advance in Leningrad sector. R.A.F. bombs Stuttgart.*

Arrived bomber plant at 8:20. First part of morning on routine. Then
drove to motor building, Rouge plant, for a conference with Sorensen in regard to pursuit-plane designs and the problem of obtaining aeronautical engineers. Sorensen had sketched out several possible engine
installations for pursuit planes—offset shaft-driven propellers in each instance.

Sorensen is a man of exceptionally strong character but with a number
of the weaknesses that often accompany strong character and obvious
success. Along with great ability he has great vanity. His confidence in
his own ideas leaves him without much interest in the ideas of others. His
heart is so filled with his love of the machine that it has somewhat
crowded out his love of the man who must run it. Sorensen has the reputation of being the best production engineer in the United States, of im-
posing and "bulling through" sweeping ideas quickly formed, of being
ruthless in his dealings with men. "Cast-Iron Charlie," they call him;

men's eyes drop to their work as he passes along the aisles of the shops; no man wishes to cross him, and no man can cross him and hold his job.

The story is told among Ford workers—whether it is true or not I do not know—that many years ago Charlie Sorensen was walking through one of the factory buildings and saw a workman sitting on an empty box, cleaning the end of an insulated wire with his knife, leisurely, and in an indifferent sort of way. Sorensen, who is a large, well-built man, walked up and kicked the box out from under him. The workman picked himself up cursing. Sorensen told him he was fired.

"Hell," said the man, "you can't fire me!"

"Why not?" demanded Sorensen.

"Because I don't work for Mr. Ford. I work for the Bell Telephone Company!"

The story goes on to say that now only Ford men work on Ford telephones and that no telephone-company men are allowed to enter the Ford factory grounds. Whether or not the story is true, it gives a pretty accurate picture of Cast-Iron Charlie Sorensen and his relation to his men.

But notwithstanding all this, there is much in Sorensen I like and much I want to get to know better. His average is, I believe, well on the constructive side of the ledger, and he is certainly one of the men who has built this nation into whatever it is today.

Back to Willow Run for an early lunch before taking off for Dayton in the B-24 with Henning, Major McDuffee, Mr. [E. A.] Dunton, and several others. I acted as co-pilot on the flight. I am taking every possible opportunity to familiarize myself with the B-24 and its operation. The actual flying of the ship is simple enough, but the secondary controls, instruments, switches, radio, hydraulic system, electrical system, etc., etc., remind me of a pipe organ. In fact, I think the instrument board of a modern bomber *is* more complicated than the keyboard of a pipe organ. I find the best way to get to know a new airplane is to spend as much time in it as possible—both on the ground and in the air, and to combine with this a study of design, performance specifications, and operating instructions. But no amount of theory, important as it is, will make up for the experience of preparing a plane, and handling it in flight.

We landed at the Dayton Municipal Airport after a fifty-minute flight from Willow Run, long enough to drop one of the Army officers who rode down with us. Then, a ten-minute hop over to Wright Field. Spent an hour in conference with [Lieutenant] Colonel [Reginald C.] Harmon and other officers concerning the redesign of the B-24 nose to permit a better machine-gun installation. The Ford Company was authorized to proceed with the design and construction of an experimental nose section.

Fifty-five-minute flight back to Willow Run.

Saturday, May 9

Headlines, JAP FLEET BEATEN, *seem to be based on a communication from United States headquarters in Australia couched in milder language: "Naval battle off northeastern Australia has temporarily ceased, and the enemy have been repulsed." Washington reports seventeen Japanese vessels sunk or badly damaged; Japanese claim victory, too.*

Workmen are being rushed to get the first plane completed by May 15. They will not be able to make the date, but I think it may be possible to have all but a few details completed by that time. Personally, I think we would gain time by not rushing quite so much. The primary value of this first ship is to train the workmen and not to show how fast it can be put out. There is too much tendency in this country to overemphasize the "showing" and to underemphasize the final and less spectacular results —too much interest in apparent rather than actual accomplishment.

Sunday, May 10

United States losses in South Pacific naval battle reported "comparatively light." One hundred thousand tons of Japanese warships estimated lost. United States fleet and air forces reported in pursuit of Japanese fleet "remnants." Japanese forces advance toward Calcutta. Chinese cut Jap supply line in Burma. R.A.F. continues to raid German cities. Russians report Germans using poison gas.

Spent afternoon flying the B-24. One flight as co-pilot with Henning. Two flights as pilot with Henning co-pilot. One flight as pilot with Skocdopole[24] co-pilot. Two flights as co-pilot, with Skocdopole pilot. I find the plane easy to land for a four-engine ship, but heavy on the controls and rather lacking in stability.

24. Erwin F. Skocdopole, senior pilot with the Ford Co.

Monday, May 11

Allied pursuit of Japanese fleet in Coral Sea continues. Chinese claim Japanese routed on Burma Road. R.A.F. raids over Europe continue. Tension growing between United States and France.

Arrived Willow Run at 8:15. Sorensen and Bricker[25] arrived about 10:00. Rest of morning spent with them, Roscoe Smith, and other officers, laying plans for a design department in connection with the B-24 nose modification.

Lunch with Roscoe Smith and Logan Miller[26] at company dining room, discussing the fact that the Willow Run factory will be a month or more behind its production schedule. I advised Smith, who is flying to Wright Field for a conference with General Wolfe[27] tomorrow, to state the facts openly, and to overestimate rather than underestimate the time required to get the first ship through our production lines. The Ford Company has a habit of setting a production date ahead of their actual production estimate in order to get their workmen to push harder. There may be advantages to this system but there are also serious disadvantages —especially in dealing with the Army Air Corps.

Another clipping arrived in the mail in regard to a completely fictitious incident in which I was supposed to be hissed and booed by workers at the Willow Run factory as I walked through the aisles. I have walked through the factory every day and have never met with anything other than courtesy on the part of any individual or group, either at Willow Run, the Rouge, or anywhere else. The average worker here is very friendly and usually nods a greeting as I pass. Whether they agree with my political views, I do not know and do not ask. Probably some do and some don't and others don't know or don't care—but I have yet to see the slightest sign of antagonism. But someone, apparently some organized group, is trying to cause trouble, and making up whatever stories they desire in their attempt; and whoever they are, are clever enough to know what kind of rumor makes a good press story. It is difficult to

25. Mead L. Bricker succeeded Roscoe Smith as factory manager at Willow Run.
26. Ford Co. inspector at Willow Run.
27. General Kenneth B. Wolfe later headed the 20th Bomber Command, the first B-29 organization to strike Japan; in 1945 he became commanding general of the Fifth Air Force.

know how to combat the absolute lie that is picked up by the newspapers and spread over the country as fact. These lies have nothing to do with one's actions; they are started, in cases like the above, with intent; a denial is almost always ineffective and often serves only to emphasize the original fictitious story.

Drove to Detroit in the late afternoon to attend a meeting of the automotive engineers to which I was invited—reception, dinner, and lectures afterward. For years I have made a practice of not accepting these invitations; but since I am working with the Ford organization and since this was an engineering and technical meeting (and since I was not asked to speak), I felt it advisable to attend.

At dinner I sat between Mr. Avery and Mr. Fisher (Fisher Body Company).[28] The most interesting event of the evening was the last—an R.A.F. film of a bomb raid over Germany. It was well filmed and acted out by an R.A.F. squadron. I felt it was the best film I had seen in many months.

Tuesday, May 12

German spring offensive reported opening in Crimea. Crisis reported in France. Malta claims 101 Axis planes destroyed or damaged in seventy-two-hour period. Chinese armies claim successes on Burma frontier; heavy battle reported in progress.

Lunch with Van Ranst at the administration building discussing engine developments and the urgent need of additional engineers. After lunch he took me to see the new equipment for making centrifugal aluminum castings. After that, we watched the breakdown test of a centrifugally cast turbosupercharger rotor (steel). It flew to pieces at just over 37,000 r.p.m.

Back to Willow Run. Found that no break cord or sea anchor is attached to the B-24 life rafts. When the emergency life-raft release is pulled, the carbon-dioxide inflation bottle is turned on and the raft catapulted away from the fuselage. The slightest wind would blow it over the water faster than the crew could swim after it; and since there is almost always a wind at sea, it is not likely the crew would ever reach their life

28. Clarence W. Avery had been chief developmental engineer at Ford, 1912–27; in 1942 he was president and chairman of the board of Murray Corp. of America; Frederick J. Fisher, chairman of the board of Fisher & Co.

rafts after they were catapulted. The idea of the catapult is that the B-24 bomber would sink so fast after landing on water that the only hope of getting to a life raft would be to catapult it away from the ship *immediately* upon striking the water. I wrote a letter to Major [Bradley] Saunders (Air Corps representative attached to Willow Run) advising the installation of a sea anchor or a break cord or both.

Wednesday, May 13

Germans claim decision in Crimea. Russians claim to be holding. U-boat sinks freighter in St. Lawrence River. Japanese fleet reported massing north of Australia for new attempt at invasion. Churchill warns of possible air invasion of England.

Made my first attempt at "flying" a Link trainer this morning. I have never been in one before. They came into use long after my time of flying the air mail. It is a strange sensation—none of the "feel" of flying, and I find it hard to follow the instruments mechanically and without any regard to pressure or gravity or centrifugal force. However, it is excellent training, and I intend to take the full course if I have time. The trainer is much more sensitive and tricky than a plane. Spent forty minutes in the Link; then watched one of the Willow Run pilots execute a flight problem in it.

Thursday, May 14

Battles going on along entire Russian front. Russians claim breakthrough of German lines near Kharkov. Japanese forces advance into China along Burma Road. French warships at Martinique being immobilized.

Spent forty-five minutes in the Link trainer—spun in twice!

Took off for Tulsa at 3:00 in B-24 (co-pilot—Henning pilot). First portion of flight clear and unlimited except for occasional electrical storms. Ceiling and visibility lowered after St. Louis. Had difficulty getting in to Tulsa—clouds dropping down to cover the hills in places and less than 500 feet over the airport. Static was so bad we could not understand the Tulsa tower until we were almost over it. We came in the last few miles on ground contact, and the B-24 is no airplane to be playing around in close to the ground under haze and low-ceiling conditions. Put the plane in one end of the new Douglas B-24 assembly factory (over 4,000 feet long) and were driven to the Mayo Hotel for supper and the night.

Friday, May 15

Germans claim Russian armies defeated in Crimea. Russians claim important advance in Kharkov sector. U-boat sinks merchantman off mouth of Mississippi River. France reported ready to scuttle ships at Martinique rather than turn them over to United States. Germans claim American cruiser and destroyer sunk between North Cape and Spitzbergen.

Arrived at the Douglas B-24 assembly plant about 8:45. Spent rest of morning going through plant and inspecting the fuselage sections sent down here by the Ford Company. One of the reasons I came on this flight was to look over these fuselage sections, as the workmanship on them was reported extremely bad, although they were passed both by the Ford Company inspectors and by Army inspectors. When the Ford parts arrived at Tulsa, the Douglas Company inspector and the Army inspectors attached to the Douglas Company refused to accept them. I found the workmanship to be fully as bad as reported by the inspectors here at Tulsa. In fact, I feel the officers and inspectors here have been reasonable in their criticism. Their attitude was fair and friendly.

This situation pierces deeply into the Ford organization and brings up vital questions of policy. As soon as it became known that the Ford Company would engage in the construction of military aircraft, the members of the aviation industry cocked a weather eye toward the future and wondered how Ford competition would affect them, not only during the war but *after the war.*

Almost as soon as Ford Company personnel reached San Diego to work out arrangements with the Consolidated Company for the manufacture of Consolidated's B-24 at Willow Run, friction arose. Consolidated personnel took the attitude that the Ford Company was entering a field it knew very little about and that the Ford men were out in California to *learn* from Consolidated men how to build aircraft (which, as a matter of fact, was true, though the Consolidated men stressed the fact with unnecessary frequency).

The Ford organization has never been run on tact; its officers and workmen have long been impressed with the power and prestige of their company, and Charlie Sorensen has set an example of hard dealing and straight talking. In short, if the Consolidated men were carrying a chip on one shoulder, the Ford men arrived with a chip on each shoulder. Instead of taking the attitude that they had come to San Diego to learn how to build Consolidated bombers from the company that had developed those bombers, they took the attitude that they were there only as a preliminary to showing Consolidated how to build Consolidated bombers better and on mass production. The inevitable result was a deep-rooted antagonism which still exists.

Since Consolidated has been producing aircraft for many years, and since the Ford Company has *not* been producing aircraft for many years, the Ford personnel fell into the fatal error of boasting not how good they were (Consolidated personnel had that advantage) but how good they were *going to be.* Promises were made of delivery dates that were impossible of fulfillment. Ford workmanship was going to be not only as good but considerably better than Consolidated workmanship. (This in reply to the charge that motor-car manufacturers might know *mass* production but that they couldn't compete with aircraft manufacturers in *quality* production.) From Mr. Sorensen down through executives, engineers, and mechanics, Ford personnel put themselves in a place where almost everyone in the aviation industry was expecting and hoping they wouldn't make good on their claim.

Now, after talking big for many months, we are in the position of having to deliver in the concentrated spotlight of watching expert eyes. And the first article we have delivered is not only as bad but considerably worse than the aviation people said it would be—rivets missing, rivets badly put in, rivet holes started and forgotten, whole lines of rivets left entirely out, wrong-sized rivets, lopsided rivets, badly formed skin, corner cuts improperly made, cracks *already* started, soft metal used where hard metal is essential, control holes left out, pilot's escape hatch incredibly badly constructed, rubber de-icers installed on an angle and with an inch-high wrinkle where they should be smooth, frame tab to stringer flanges broken off and not replaced, grommets left out of flippers and inspection hole forgotten, wrong name plates on oil tanks and other parts, metal edges bitten rather than cut out, round-head rivets in bomb-door tracks where flush rivets *must* be used, sharp and protruding corners on skin plates, etc., etc., etc.

As the Douglas inspectors showed me the various items that were wrong, there was nothing to do but agree. It was the worst piece of metal aircraft construction I have ever seen; yet it was passed by both the Ford Company and the Army inspectors at Willow Run. All I could do was recall to the Douglas officers' minds the fact that they had asked the Ford Company for plane parts in a rush in order to start the training program in the new Douglas assembly plant at Tulsa. But, as they said, they asked for a full set of completed parts, and had a right to expect reasonably good workmanship. (The inspector said they were short 4,751 parts for a complete B-24.)

My personal opinion is that the Ford Company should send a truck and trailer to Tulsa and take back all parts on which the workmanship is poor, and hold at Willow Run the center wing section that is about to be shipped to Tulsa. (The workmanship on it, I am told, is no better than on the fuselage sections.) This ship was built practically entirely on Consolidated loft boards and specifications for the primary purpose of training Ford engineers and workmen. Possibly the best plan would be to salvage it and charge the loss to the training program. I doubt that the ship, if assembled, would be worth equipping with good engines, guns, instruments, etc.

I intend to make this recommendation to Sorensen and Smith when I return to Willow Run. Will they see the advisability of it? I am not sure, but I am inclined to think they will if I can put it to them clearly enough. It will be an important decision, as the whole question of quality and quantity is involved, and the Ford Company's primary interest has always been quantity production.

Lunch at the Douglas plant with various officers of the organization. Went on a demonstration flight (of the Sperry A-5 automatic pilot) in the afternoon, during which we landed the B-24 at the Air Corps training field at Enid, Oklahoma, and at Wichita, Kansas. From Wichita we returned to Tulsa to pick up our regular crew, and then flew on to Fort Worth, Texas, for the night.

The entire day has been clear and cloudless—typical Texas summer weather except for the heat. It takes me back many years to the time I used to fly regularly over Texas and the Southwest. The country and the people are the same—the only change is in the number of uniforms one sees in the streets and in the Army fields and training barracks that have sprung up everywhere like mushrooms after a rain. (This, in turn, reminds me of Germany in 1937.)

We taxied the B-24 into one of the huge hangars of the Consolidated Company's Fort Worth branch factory and drove into town for supper and the night at the Worth Hotel.

After supper I called a conference between Henning, Mr. [Logan] Miller (Ford Company inspector at Willow Run), Captain Rooney (Army inspector at Willow Run), and myself, to discuss the situation we found at the Douglas branch factory in Tulsa. What has happened is clear enough: under pressure, and encouraged by the desire to get production under way at Willow Run, and more than a little due to lack of experience, both Army and Ford inspection passed material that should have been rejected (and which was rejected by the more experienced and impartial inspectors at Tulsa).

Saturday, May 16

Germans claim capture of Kerch. Laval refuses United States proposals on Martinique. Roosevelt commutes sentence of Earl Browder. Mexico reported on verge of war with Axis. Russians claim advance in vicinity of Kharkov.

Spent most of morning at the Consolidated factory, discussing plans with the officers and inspecting the assembly line. The factory is getting well under way—there were forty B-24's being assembled (from parts shipped through from the main Consolidated factory in San Diego).

Major McDuffee called for us about 7:30 to take us to dinner with one of his friends (his home was in Dallas until a few months ago, and he seems to know about everyone who passes by). It was one of those drinking parties where everyone talks a great deal and drinks enough to feel rotten for the next day or two and kids himself into believing he is having a good time. Talk is trivial and actions cheap. The only reason I know for going is to avoid separation from one's flight companions and to keep in at least remote contact with what is a large portion of American life at this period.

I don't find any embarrassment from not drinking; people don't seem to mind that if you are both positive and matter of fact about it. But I get terribly bored with the conversation—men and women you never met before trying to get "chummy" and getting to call you *obviously* by your first name when their friends are within hearing; drunken arguments about politics; the difficulty of avoiding sensitive issues; the attempt to say something about anything when it would be much better to say nothing at all; conversation lagging as the hour becomes late; people hanging around, seemingly unable to make up their minds to go home, etc., etc. Finally, about midnight, it was decided to go to Fort Worth to dance. I slipped off at my hotel on the way. They were all fine people but it seemed to me they had lost a true direction for their lives. Yet this is what we call civilization and a high standard of living.

Sunday, May 17

War Production Board "spokesman" states that "virtually all" contracts for war plants that cannot be "completed and in production by mid-1943" will be canceled; press estimates that two-thirds of war-plant building will be stopped. Russians claim continued advance in Kharkov area.

Checked out from hotel. Taxi to airport with Henning and crew. Weather overcast at 1,000 feet and four miles' visibility. We took off and climbed to 7,000 feet at 500 feet per minute (Henning piloting, I co-piloting) and leveled off on course, still in the clouds. There is a rather poor radio installation in the B-24. The rain static was so bad we could not complete our ground contacts. Finally we got authority to climb to 9,000 feet and broke out into clear sky. After that, our radio contacts were reasonably good. The weather forced us to fly home by way of Nashville and Louisville—about 1,100 miles. The clouds broke soon after we left Texas, but we held a 9,000-foot altitude until we began our descent for Willow Run. The trip took an even five hours, take-off to landing.

I left the airport immediately, as I had telegraphed for reservations on the night train to Washington. But when I received these reservations on arriving at the Dearborn Inn, I found the train was leaving in less than five minutes. Since I had been given a telegram when we landed at Willow Run to the effect that Secretary Lovett, whom I was going to Washington to see, had been instructed to go to Canada and consequently had to cancel the appointment he had made, I phoned the station and postponed my reservations for twenty-four hours.

Phoned Anne at Martha's Vineyard. I miss Anne and the children terribly, but I want her to have a few quiet weeks on Martha's Vineyard; also, we have not yet located a satisfactory place to live near Willow Run.

Monday, May 18

Russian armies advance on Kharkov. Heavy air battles between R.A.F. and German Air Force reported over occupied France. Germans claim capture of 68,000 Russian troops on Kerch Peninsula. Chinese claim Japanese retreat on Burma Road.

Conference with Sorensen about 10:00. I told him of the conditions I found at Tulsa and that I believed it would be advisable for the Ford Company to take back to Willow Run the fuselage sections that had been sent to the Douglas Tulsa factory. Sorensen was open-minded to the suggestion and made no attempt to brush it aside hastily, as I have seen him do so often in other instances. I outlined the situation as clearly as I could and was much impressed by the way he took what must have been rather a hard blow to his personal pride. I saw in him this morning some of the qualities that have taken him to his present position, and I found myself drawn to him as I have not been at any time before. I told Sorensen I would like authority to remove the fuselage sections from Tulsa. He said I had his authority to do so, if that seemed the best procedure to follow.

Before leaving, I brought another matter to Sorensen's attention. Some days ago I found that Henning, who is in charge of the entire flight division at Willow Run, was still punching a time clock. He had started doing so when he was first employed by the Ford Company, and apparently no one had ever stopped him. I spoke of this fact to Sorensen, who immediately called Henning and told him to stop at once. At the same time, Sorensen called for Henning's salary figures. I imagine a raise is likely to be forthcoming, and Henning certainly deserves one both from the standpoint of loyalty and ability.

Roscoe Smith is factory manager at Willow Run. Previously, he was factory manager at the Ford generator plant at Ypsilanti. Henry Ford selected him for the Willow Run project. Smith is about forty, slender, and as a disciple of Charlie Sorensen, he has a definite tendency to sweeping decisions, to blunt and tactless conversation, and to driving his organization beyond the point of pride in workmanship.

When he speaks of Smith, Henry Ford makes a point of telling you that he is a descendent of Abraham Lincoln—and as a matter of fact there is a striking resemblance in build and features.

Spent an hour or so on routine; then a phone call came from Smith's office asking me to come up to attend a conference that was going on. When I arrived, I found Smith, Henning, Miller, Saunders, Dunton, Rooney, and one or two other Ford officers seated around the long oak conference table. They were discussing the Tulsa situation. I said I felt it would be best to take back the fuselage sections and wait until we had something with good workmanship on it before making another shipment to the Douglas plant there. Major Saunders and Mr. Henning were of the same opinion, and Mr. Miller confirmed the fact that the workmanship was poor and in some instances dangerous. Roscoe Smith seemed open-minded at first and then became rather stubborn about the matter, saying the Douglas people had asked for something in a hurry, that it was up to them to fix it up, that they shouldn't expect good workmanship on the first pieces, etc.

I stated that in my opinion it would be to the best interests of the Ford Company and the war effort to take the fuselage sections back to Willow Run, and either fix them up ourselves or salvage them and charge them up to training. I said I favored the latter course. The argument continued around the table until lunchtime.

Tuesday, May 19

Large A.E.F. lands in Northern Ireland; reported ready for continental invasion. Russians claim continued advance in Kharkov area.

Spent first part of morning at the power building on the Ford airport, learning the technique of operating a Link trainer—fifty-five minutes "under the hood." I am getting more accustomed to the instruments, controls, and lack of "feel" in comparison to an actual airplane.

Left with a Lincoln car and one of the Ford drivers to meet Colonel Patterson (New York *News*) and his daughter (Mrs. Reeves) at the commercial airport. Patterson [has], in general, taken a courageous and intelligent stand on the war, and is a member of the most powerful anti-administration group of papers that exists at the present time. I can never forget what the *News* did and printed in 1932, but the entire future of this country is at stake today, and the issues are so great that they must of necessity overshadow issues of the past, no matter how deeply the latter cut at the time. Also, I don't know how closely Patterson was connected personally with the policy and actions of his paper in 1932, and I shall not inquire, for the memory is still too painful and too much scarred within me.

Colonel Patterson and his daughter arrived on the 11:35 American Airlines plane from Chicago. We drove in two cars to Harry Bennett's office in the administration building. Henry Ford came for a half hour's visit before lunch. Party arrived at Willow Run about 3:00. I took Colonel Patterson and Mrs. Reeves through the factory. After that, I arranged for them to be shown through the Ford–Pratt Whitney engine factory at the Rouge, and left at 4:15 for the B. & O. station on Fort Street. Boarded the Ambassador for Washington.

Rest of day [on train] writing and studying instrument- and radio-flying technique. Methods of airline operation have changed greatly in recent years, and I want to have a thorough understanding of present practices. The rapid development of radio has caused the greatest change, and better instruments and aircraft have also made their contribution. But the great difference between flying the airlines now and flying the airlines when I was an air-mail pilot lies in the fact that now we know by radio the weather that lies ahead and the weather that lies below, and then we did not.

Wednesday, May 20

Nationwide gasoline rationing set for July 1. R.A.F. bombs Mannheim. Russian and German claims conflict on Eastern front.

Off train at 8:15. It is already getting unpleasantly hot here in Washington, a forerunner of the sweltering summer that is coming and that always comes to the nation's capital. One of the most noticeable things about this city is the percentage of young women on the streets. They come from all over the country to get jobs and to take part in the excitement and turmoil of Washington.

Met Colonel [Eugene] Beebe at 9:00 and then went to General [Oliver] Echols' office, where I discussed with him the problem of how to get experienced aviation engineers for the Ford projects. General Echols is extremely anxious to increase the output of large bombers as rapidly as possible—says he realizes our need for engineers and will try to help find some, but that good aeronautical engineers are "scarce as hens' teeth."

Echols says he thinks our present bomber speeds are high enough for the near future. (In reply to my statement that I felt we would soon need faster bombers.)

After forty minutes with General Echols, I spent quarter of an hour with General Arnold. I told him that the automobile manufacturers would have saved many weeks—possibly many months—if they had been able to salt their untrained workmen with a reasonable percentage of experienced aviation personnel. Arnold told me he was in great need of more large bombers. The production is now only about 130 per month, and twenty per cent per month replacements are required in combat areas.

Although I feel I know Arnold fairly well because of my close contact with him in 1939 while I was on active duty, attached to his office, I make a point of never discussing politics with him, or asking his opinion about the progress of the war.

The Munitions Building is jammed with uniformed officers, stenographers, and secretaries. Offices full of desks and tables, and the overflow lined up along the corridor walk. One gets an impression of confusion rather than of military orderliness.

Hour's walk in Rock Creek Park before returning to my hotel. Went as far as the first cage of the zoo—a net-wire enclosure containing a ragged white wolf, his eyes deadened by the heat and hopelessness of captivity.

Truman [Smith] called and asked me to come to his apartment at 4:00 to meet a Colonel Clear, who went through most of the fighting on Bataan and much of the bombing on Corregidor. Colonel Clear has a keen, alert, and penetrating mind. His description of the defense of Bataan and the bombing of Corregidor was an account of courage, politics, and incompetence, and about as contrary to the popular impression of what took place as anything could be.

With eight hours of warning (after Pearl Harbor), he said, our American planes on the Philippines were still in line and perfect targets when the Japanese bombers arrived. Colonel Clear said we lost the Philippines in that first air raid of the Japs. The first wave of bombers passed over at high altitude, he said, at 15,000 or 20,000 feet, and hit their targets with amazing accuracy. Then the Zero fighters came and while some engaged our P-40 pursuit planes, others dove down and machinegunned our big bombers lined up on the field. And just after the Zero fighters left, and while our P-40's were on the ground refueling and reloading, a second wave of Japanese bombers came over, this time at lower altitude, and destroyed many of our pursuit planes on the ground.

Colonel Clear said two or three of the Zero fighters dove directly into our barracks, and that most of our planes were destroyed and many of our pilots killed in that first day of raiding. He said the Japs dropped a note in a rice bag, saying they would return the next day to bomb the radio (power?) station that was located next to the hospital, and advising evacuation of the hospital. The hospital was evacuated and the station bombed. Of course the dropping of the warning note was left out of the accounts of bombing the hospital which were carried in our papers; at least nothing was said about this in any of the accounts I read.

I asked Clear about the stories concerning Japanese atrocities. He said he had seen Philippine soldiers bayoneted by Japs after they had raised their arms in surrender, and that in the heat of battle little quarter could be expected. He said experience showed, on the other hand, that reasonable consideration could be expected from Japanese forces when a surrender was negotiated in advance.

Colonel Clear said the soldiers on Bataan ran out of food and quinine, and that most of them were suffering from fever and dysentery long before they finally surrendered. He said that, man for man, he felt the American soldier was the superior of the Japanese, and that our equipment was better but much more costly. Clear says the officers on Bataan believed a large part of their normal supply of quinine had been sent to the British forces at Singapore or elsewhere in the East before our war with Japan began. He said the general impression was that other essential supplies had been sent along with the quinine, leaving our Philippine forces short of their normal provisions.

Colonel Clear was on Corregidor during a number of bombing attacks. He said there was not sufficient shelter for the soldiers there and that many of the vital installations on the island were not protected against air attack—cold-storage plant exposed, water tanks exposed, even the big guns exposed. Colonel Clear was finally evacuated in a submarine because of his long experience in and detailed knowledge of the Orient and his value to our Army because of that.

I asked Clear how the morale of our men had stood up. At first it was very good, he said, and then, when the expected reinforcements and supplies did not arrive, it began to lower. He said the lowest point in morale came when the men listened to a short-wave broadcast by President Roosevelt, in which the President told of the troops and supplies he was sending to North Ireland and to India and to Australia and to almost every place but Bataan. After the broadcast, he said, a big Army sergeant picked up his rifle with fixed bayonet and hurled it eight or ten feet into a tree trunk. "Who do you think you're throwing that at?" an officer asked him. "Who the hell do you think I'm throwing it at?" he replied!

Clear said the American regulars and the old Philippine troops fought extremely well and courageously. He said the newer "MacArthur division" of Filipinos did not make a very good showing.

Walked to the Lands' apartment for dinner with Jerry and Betty. Jerry is under fire because he is unable to meet the impossible shipping program forced upon him by the President. Jerry says the production program for this country was never co-ordinated with the shipping available, and that even if it were possible to meet the program the President demands, there would still not be enough shipping to move the material which will be produced on the existing production program. Jerry is also depressed—as far as he ever allows himself to be—by the fact that we are now losing ships faster than we can build them.

Left for the station at 5:00 and boarded the 5:55 B. & O. train for Detroit.

Friday, May 22

Tension rising between Germany and Mexico. Opposition starts to plan for nationwide gasoline ration. Russians issue more claims of success.

Phoned Sorensen after breakfast and outlined to him the conversations I had had with Generals Arnold and Echols. Sorensen had already received a letter from Echols in regard to engineers, and I believe my trip was worth while from this standpoint alone.

After lunch I went to see the Houston house and property—a very large house on a now unused farm, between Ann Arbor and Ypsilanti. The house was rather heavily papered and furnished, not the kind of rooms I like to bring Anne to, and she has already spent too much of her time fixing up the many houses we have rented in our nomadic existence. I would give almost anything to find a nice one for her at this time. Anne has books to write, children to take care of, a baby to bear, a move to make. To refurnish a house now is just too much.

Saturday, May 23

Opposition to gasoline ration continues to rise. Discussion in Washington in regard to seizing private autos for war purposes.

Breakfast at inn. Arrived at bomber plant at 8:45. First part of morning on routine. Then an hour-and-a-half inspection trip through the factory with Gus Miller, chief inspector at Willow Run. I asked him to show me the *worst* workmanship he could find on the B-24's now in the jigs. (I had previously examined the wing and fuselage sections myself, and found many places where riveting, fitting, and finishing were far from satisfactory. In fact, it is perfectly clear that the first dozen or two ships that go through the Willow Run factory are not going to establish a reputation of high-class workmanship for the Ford Company. I hope the quality of workmanship on the later ships will be good enough to make up for that on these early ones.) After going through the plant, Miller and I discussed ways and means for improving both workmanship and inspection.

Monday, May 25

Russians report new advance on Kharkov. Germans report advance south of Kharkov. Activity increasing on Libyan desert.

Breakfast at inn with Henning; then to the power building at the Ford airport for an appointment to spend another forty-five minutes in the Link trainer. I am beginning to feel much more at ease in the contraption and now have it reasonably well under control most of the time.

Mr. Edsel Ford and Mr. Sorensen came out with Senator Clyde Herring of Iowa. Accompanied them on a half-hour trip through the factory.

Drove to Dearborn Inn for a lunch appointment with Earl Jeffrey and Clay Pough (America First organizers up to the time the committee was dissolved). On the way from Willow Run to the inn, I received a radio call from the Dearborn station, asking me if I could stop at Harry Bennett's office to meet a party from out of town. I radioed an O.K. and changed my course to the administration building. Harry Bennett had General Short[29] with him (Pearl Harbor). The general told us a little about the circumstances that existed prior to and at the time of the Japanese attack. Of course, they differ materially from the impression created by the Administration through press and radio reports.

Arrived at the inn ten minutes late, but had sent word ahead for

29. General Walter C. Short was in command at the time of the Japanese attack on Pearl Harbor, December, 1941. In 1942 he headed the traffic department of the Ford Motor Co. in Dallas, Texas.

Jeffrey and Pough to be taken to my rooms. We discussed war developments and trends. Both Jeffrey and Pough want to take part in some kind of war work, but have found it impossible to get into anything because of their previous connection with the America First Committee.

Back to Willow Run to see a film on the physiological effects of high-altitude flying.

Tuesday, May 26

German advance south of Kharkov continues. Heavy fighting reported in China.

Spent fifty-five minutes in the Link after breakfast. Then drove to Willow Run. Half hour's conference with Bennett, Bricker, and Roscoe Smith in regard to the poor workmanship on the planes now going through the factory. Roscoe Smith finally phoned Mr. Williams at the Douglas factory in Tulsa and offered to take back the fuselage sections that were sent down there by the Ford Company. Williams replied that after the amount of work they had put on repairing these sections they would prefer to keep them. It was agreed, on Smith's suggestion, that No. 2 center wing be sent to Tulsa instead of No. 1. No. 2 center wing is far better than No. 1, although the workmanship on it is by no means good.

The unfortunate part about all this is that Smith feels I have been unduly critical. Most of the men have had so little experience in aviation they actually don't know the difference between good workmanship and bad workmanship. Almost the only men at Willow Run who are thoroughly experienced in aviation are in the flight department under Henning. Our greatest danger in this project lies in overconfidence, lack of experience, and the stressing of production above quality—above even *reasonably good* quality.

Wednesday, May 27

Territory negotiations continue between Italy and France. Russians claim to have halted German offensive south of Kharkov. Germans claim to have surrounded the Russian armies. German forces advance in Libya.

Had planned on flying to the Mayo Clinic at Rochester, Minnesota, to see a demonstration of their high-altitude chamber; but the weather conditions would have necessitated an "instrument flight" practically all the way, with doubtful trends, so we canceled.

Spent first part of morning dictating, then accompanied Mr. Sorensen, Roscoe Smith, Mr. DeGroat,[30] and Mr. Ed Scott to the new engineering development department.

Lunch with Scott and DeGroat. The chef sent in an individual piece of chocolate cake for dessert, with *Spirit of St. Louis* written on it in white frosting script. Poor man, he said he knew the day (twenty-seventh) was right but he wasn't sure of the month. I explained as tactfully as I could that the month *was* right but the day a little off.[31] I went out to the kitchen after lunch to thank him, and I think everything ended well in spite of his embarrassment about the date. (I could have passed over that if he hadn't asked the direct question.) I was very grateful to him for not bringing in some huge cake to be cut and divided, or an airplane modeled in ice and lighted with searchlight batteries.

Harry Bennett arrived at 4:00. I had invited him for a flight over the factory and his home, which happens to lie in our flight area No. 3. (For purposes of local training, wartime regulations assign certain flight areas to each airport. Special clearances are required for flights outside of these areas.) I took him up in one of the Stinson 10-A's and after circling over his home gave him the controls. Bennett said it was the first time he had ever had the controls of a plane, but he handled it exceptionally well for a first-timer. After about fifteen minutes he turned the plane back to me, and we flew over the country around his home and above the houses of some of his friends.

We were about 1,200 feet above the ground when Bennett asked me how slow the ship would fly. I headed into the wind, throttled back, put the flaps down, and pulled the nose up until the air speed dropped to fifty-five miles an hour. Then, just as I was calling Bennett's attention to the air-speed indicator, the engine stopped dead—the propeller in a trim, exactly horizontal position! We were below 1,000 feet by the time that happened. I nosed the plane down into a dive, pulling up the flaps at the same time. The propeller turned over once or twice jerkily, but the engine refused to start. We were too close to the ground to dive more steeply.

I picked out a sod field on a hillside, banked steeply into position, came in between two trees, with a little excess speed, banked 45° to the

30. Wilson F. DeGroat, head of developmental engineering at Willow Run.
31. The date was May 21, 1927.

right, dropped the flaps and landed uphill and into the ten-mile wind that was blowing.

The field was good, and there was plenty of room to take off. Bennett and I got out and walked over it in take-off direction to make sure there were no holes, ditches, or ridges. "Jesus," he said, as we walked along, "I didn't know you could land 'em after that propeller was stopped!" I explained that it was not difficult, if one was fortunate enough to have a good field below. Silence for two or three minutes. Then, "Jesus, you know when you're shot at it's over with quick!" (Bennett has twice been shot in clashes with strikers and gangsters.)

We had to take off uphill in order to head into the wind and take advantage of an adjoining oats field that was not separated by a fence or ditch. The wheels were not off the ground when we hit the oats, and we ran through fifty or seventy-five yards of it before finally stalling into the air. We still had plenty of room ahead before there were any fences or trees, but Bennett told me afterward he didn't think we were going to get off the ground. All in all, he got quite a kick out of the flight.

We landed back at Willow Run an hour and ten minutes after our departure. The mechanics and pilots eyed the grass on our landing gear and tail wheel as we taxied in to the line and cut the engine.

"Are ya going to say anything about it?" Bennett asked. " 'Cause if ya are, I'm going to tell the old man [Henry Ford] that we did it on purpose." (Mr. Ford does not like his officers to fly, and the knowledge that we had a forced landing might result in the demand that Bennett stop flying entirely.) I said I thought it would be best to make a note of it on the flight report (this is required by the wartime regulations), but that I didn't think it would go any farther. (By some miracle, no one saw us make the landing—at least no one came up to the plane while we were on the farm field.)

Thursday, May 28

United States orders war workers "frozen" to present jobs. Axis forces advance in Libya. Congressmen protest gasoline ration. Quintuplets bob their hair! (Also front-page news.)

To Rouge administration building for a 12:00 conference with Mr. [I. A.] Capizzi (Ford Company lawyer) in regard to my position and financial arrangement with the Ford Company. I told him that after full consideration of the situation I thought it would be best all the way around for me to work on a retainer basis rather than on a salary. I outlined some of the reasons which had brought me to this conclusion—greater flexibility, need for some time to put on my own affairs, problems of legal residence, uncertainty of the future, etc. I told Mr. Capizzi that the amount of the retainer was of secondary importance, and that my reason for coming here was to help in the war effort, not to make money. I told him I would be satisfied with an amount that would cover my added expenses in coming here.

Friday, May 29

Nazi official purge reported in Germany. Bridges ordered deported from United States.

Mr. Snyder (Birmingham Real Estate) came at 11:15, and we discussed lease terms for the house at Bloomfield Hills—one-year lease with renewal option, emergency cancellation clause, $300.00 per month, etc.

General Jimmy Doolittle landed on the airport (Willow Run) shortly after noon. Lunch with him and various Ford and Army officers after a quick inspection trip through the factory. Jimmy arrived in a Martin twin-engine bomber—testing out its qualities in comparison to the North American bomber of similar type. He is looking somewhat tired.

Saturday, May 30

Germans shoot hostages in Czechoslovakia. British claim Axis advance halted in Libya. Germans claim great victory in Kharkov battle—Russian armies surrounded and wiped out. Chinese continue to win battles; Japanese continue to advance.

Drove to bomber plant, arriving 7:45. A long, eight-page Selective Service questionnaire has arrived from the Englewood draft board. It seems to me I finished filling out one just about like it only two or three weeks ago.

Spent rest of morning trying to hurry up the work on the nose-gun mock-up and on a trip through the wing-assembly sections with Gus Miller. I finally got a bombsight mock-up started by staying with Mr. Scott until he got the blueprints and took them to the pattern shop himself. (He told me he would have the bombsight mock-up under way nearly two days ago—but he, too, is ordered to concentrate on too many projects all at once.)

The trip with Gus Miller (chief inspector) brought out more inadequate workmanship. Miller tells me, however, that the action I have taken recently has resulted in a decided improvement in both workmanship and interest in good workmanship throughout the plant. (I think I can see some improvement myself; but the statements I made about riveting, skin fitting, etc., have certainly not increased my popularity with some of the officers and foremen in the factory. When one criticizes workmanship and methods in an organization of this kind, it is almost impossible to do so without making enemies.) Miller told me, after showing me the salvage department, that he estimated we had been forced to reject enough material (because of errors of planning and workmanship) to build sixteen B-24 bombers!

Supper with Mother and B. The yard is still full of iris. Robins and other birds search the lawn for bits of cracked corn.

Sunday, May 31

A storm during the night cleared off the air. The morning was cool, sunny, and pleasant. Mother and I spent a large part of it in the garden. I talked to her about making this her last year of school, and I think I can get her to agree. Mother was sixty-six last Friday and for the first time is beginning to realize that the work she is carrying on is a little too much. (Full courses in chemistry, commuting by car or bus to downtown Detroit each day, taking care of the house—she still refuses to consider a servant.) I have been more concerned about her health this year than ever before; she is showing the effect of too long hours and too little rest. I have not pressed too hard against her teaching in the past because I knew how much it meant to her; but now I know it is time for her to stop.

There is so little I have been able to do for Mother in recent years, and I have been with her such a small portion of the time, that I am grateful for this time in Detroit. It seems providential that in time of war we should be brought together again and that her grandchildren will live not far away from her in Detroit. I have wanted her to see more of the children, and now it seems that will be possible. I think nothing on earth can mean so much to the old as the possession of their grandchildren. I could tell how much it meant to Mother by the tone of her voice when she asked me if and when the children would come.

Monday, June 1

Cologne raided by 1,250 planes. Heavy damage and fires reported. British report Axis forces thrown back in Libya. Food riots in Paris.

Arrived at bomber plant at 9:00. Stopped to check progress on nose-gun installation. Hour's conference with Captain Rooney in regard to Army inspection.

Drove to Ford Hospital to talk to Dr. [J. P.] Pratt about Mother and the trembling of her hand. He agrees that she needs more rest and quiet, but says he thinks there is little else that can be done. He wants to see her, of course, but it will be extremely difficult to persuade Mother to put herself in a doctor's care. However, I must find some way of doing this. How deep it strikes to see someone you love grow old.

Lunch at "the round table" with Henry, Edsel, and Benson Ford, and various officers of the organization. To Willow Run after lunch. Spent an hour with DeGroat and Henning on the nose-gun installation. Rest of afternoon on routine. Supper and evening at the inn.

Tuesday, June 2

German Air Force bombs Canterbury. R.A.F. bombs Essen. German and English reports on Libyan front conflict. Heavy Allied shipping losses continue. Japanese advance in China. Conflicting reports from Russian front.

I cannot keep my mind off Europe: the British bomb Cologne; the Germans bomb Canterbury. I think of those cathedrals and those people and wonder what possible gain will come, and what it all will lead to.

Wednesday, June 3

British claim German drive "shattered" in Libya. Essen reported in flames. Japanese forces continue advance in China. Russians report "protective attacks" on northwest front. United States and British convoy arrives at Murmansk after heavy battering—report six ships lost; Germans claim eighteen. Roosevelt asks Congress to declare war on Bulgaria, Hungary, and Rumania. Assassinations continue in Paris. Hostilities between French and British flare up in Madagascar. Riots reported in Nassau. Malta bombed again.

Forty minutes in the Link trainer. Made a perfect U pattern!!

Gus Miller phoned after lunch; asked me if I had time to meet him in the salvage department. I went out for a few minutes while he showed me Duralumin stampings that had been run through in quantity before the first one was checked, and all wrong and useless. He also showed me a list of the riveters who had worked on the center-wing skin that had to be rejected a few days ago—eleven of them. Only the foreman and one man had gone through the riveting school. Several of the others had started but not completed the course, while some of the men had had *no training at all!*

Drove to the flight department for an hour and ten minutes in the Grumman amphibian, practicing landings, single-engine performance, etc. It is a good ship, the best amphibian I have flown, but it has an exceptionally steep gliding angle with flaps down.

Norman Smith[32] was waiting at the hangar as we taxied up—Harry Bennett was trying to get me on the phone. He said he had been talking to Mr. Ford and Mr. Sorensen about the general situation at Willow Run. I told Bennett I had written a letter to Sorensen. Bennett said Sorensen was "low," that Mr. Ford had "jumped on him" for one thing or another, and that Sorensen was disturbed because I was disturbed about various things at the bomber plant.

There is obviously quite a little rivalry between Bennett and Sorensen. Well, I said I would not feel that I knew this organization until I learned its internal frictions and jealousies. Now, I am in the midst of them. It is an extremely interesting, if not always pleasant, study. I told Bennett that as far as I was concerned there was nothing that could not be straightened out. I told him the only immediate problem I was confronted with lay in the fact that I was unwilling to accept full responsibility for the design of a successful nose-gun installation unless I had engineers to work with in whom I had confidence. I told him I would straighten that matter out with Sorensen and there was no need for him or for Mr. Ford to worry about it.

A few minutes after Bennett hung up, Sorensen phoned, saying he had

32. Assistant to Harry Bennett.

received my letter and wanted to talk to me about it. We agreed to meet at his office at 9:15 in the morning.

Then a phone call from Bennett's office, asking me to call car No. 9 by radio (Harry Bennett's car). We arranged to meet on Michigan Avenue. I got in my car and met car 9 about one mile east of the factory. (These radio-equipped cars are very convenient at times.) Bennett told me of his discussion with Ford and Sorensen as he drove with me to his farm. Bennett has been a great help, but at the same time he has been building his own fences. These personal relationships between the officers of the Ford Company are becoming of great interest to me. Every one of these men has a strong character, and loyalties and conflicts weave in and out through every move they make.

Bennett showed me the white-faced buffalo and the Rocky Mountain ram he keeps on his farm. The two of them fight at regular intervals, and the buffalo has a swollen eye to show for the last battle.

Thursday, June 4

Japanese bombers raid Dutch Harbor. R.A.F. raids Ruhr. German planes bomb English cities. Russia claims advance in north. Germans attack in Libya.

To Rouge motor building for 9:15 appointment with Sorensen to discuss the letter I wrote him yesterday. He was very cordial and agreed to the suggestions I made in my letter concerning my relationship with the Ford Company. (I said that the methods, etc., of the Ford organization were so completely different than those I had followed in the past that I found myself more in the position of a student than an adviser, and that for the time being I would prefer to accept no compensation whatever from the Ford Company—that we could consider the question of compensation at a later date, and that meanwhile I would continue to devote a large part, but not all, of my time to Ford Company affairs. I could see I would have great difficulty in working with Sorensen, and knew that I would have a much more independent position if he did not feel I was accepting a salary from him—even though it be a small one.)

Sorensen said he was sorry I did not want to do things the way he wanted me to, as he could "push me ahead faster" that way. Said it would take longer my way. He brought up Mr. Bricker (factory manager) as an example of the relationship he preferred, saying, "I can go out and kick him in the head, and he'll come right back; and he can do the same to me."

Drove to the Highland Park plant with Sorensen to see the first thirty-ton tank come off the line. Then to see tank engine building. Then to Sperry antiaircraft-director building.

Friday, June 5

Japanese bomb Midway. Allied submarine sinks Japanese troop ship. R.A.F. raids on occupied France continue. New Allied shipping losses announced. Senate approves declaration of war on Hungary, Bulgaria, and Rumania. Senate votes for payments to all dependents of men in armed services.

Signed lease for the house at Bloomfield Hills and forwarded to real-estate company.

Conference with Henry Ford, Edsel Ford, and Harry Bennett. Henry Ford spoke of the need for unity in the organization. (Apparently there has been some friction recently between Bennett and Sorensen.) He told us about his experiences at the time the N.R.A. [National Recovery Administration] was being organized.

The workmen at Willow Run went out on a strike at noon. (Strikes seem to be taken rather as a matter of course out here.) Strike over at 2:00.

Trip to hangar with Jovanovich, a new engineer, to show him the gun turrets on the B-24. He is to work on an improved turret design.

Saturday, June 6

Japanese fleet reported bound for Hawaii after battle at Midway. R.A.F. sends 1,000 planes over "invasion coast." Allied reinforcements sent to India. Japanese attack in China. Skirmishes on African front. Revolt rises in Congress against gasoline ration.

Drove to airport to meet Mr. Donald Nelson[33] and party. Conference with Bennett. To rotunda for lunch with Henry and Edsel Ford, various officers of the Ford Company, and the Nelson party (Donald M. Nelson,

33. Chairman of the War Production Board, 1942–44.

Oliver Lyttelton,[34] W. Averell Harriman,[35] W. S. Robinson, and others). Drove to Fort Street station.

Monday, June 8

Japanese fleet reported withdrawing from Midway area with heavy losses. Japanese drive ahead in China. Tank battle reported raging in Libya. Germans continue siege of Sevastopol. R.A.F. raids over Continent continue.

Off [New York] train at 7:30. Reserved tickets on night train for Boston. Lunch at club. To Abercrombie & Fitch to get some fishing equipment for Jon.

Supper with Fred Ayre, a young engineer, friend of Henning's, who is interested in the possibility of coming to work for the Ford Company. It is difficult to talk to these men, as I can make them no offer as long as they are connected with another organization. Business ethics require that they be free before we make them a direct offer. No aviation company I know about was built by following any such ethics; but the government is extremely anxious to avoid "piracy" at this time, and the Ford Company is making every effort to co-operate. Boarded Boston train at 10:30.

Tuesday, June 9

British warn French to evacuate coastal areas. R.A.F. bombs Bruges and other areas. Executions continue in Czechoslovakia.

Off train at 7:45. Anne has employed a Mr. and Mrs. [William] Miller to work for us, replacing Mr. and Mrs. Dewart. Mr. Miller was at the dock to meet me with the Ford car. Land came with him. There was a little less traffic on the road to Seven Gates Farm than when I was last here. People are feeling the gasoline ration (three gallons per week for

34. President of the British Board of Trade, 1940–41; Minister of State and member of the War Cabinet.

35. After serving as an administrative officer of the N.R.A., 1934–35, and as an official in the Department of Commerce, 1937–40, Harriman became chief overseas administrator of Lend-Lease in 1941. He was appointed Ambassador to Russia in 1943.

"A" cards). Stopped at a crossroads store long enough for Land to run in and buy an ice-cream cone. I gave him a dime, and he came back with the cone and five cents—his first purchase, I think.

Home in time for lunch with Anne and the children. It is the nurse's day off and Anne is taking care of them. Anne, Jr., looked at me a bit timidly at first, but soon came over with as much confidence as ever. Thor is getting very old and stiff. He is as glad to see me as ever but cannot run around and jump as he used to when Anne or I came back from a trip. Spent afternoon with Anne and the children. Anne read me a poem she has just written. Gave Jon the fishing tackle I bought for him. The new household seems to be working smoothly.

Wednesday, June 10

United States and Britain to pool production and food resources. Japanese advances continue in China. Chinese still claim to hold Chuhsien. British claim sinking of four Axis merchantmen and one destroyer in Mediterranean. Italians claim sinking of two Allied submarines in Mediterranean. R.A.F. raids over Continent continue.

Morning on routine—arrangements for packing, etc. Anne spent most of the morning in the tent writing. The tent arrangement has been very much worth while; she does most of her writing there. Croquet with Jon in the evening. Walk over the hills to the beach with Anne after supper. How we will miss the sea this summer! When will we find it again?

Thursday, June 11

Naval action reported in Aleutian area. Germans attack in Kharkov area. Japanese claim occupation of western Aleutians. Washington "partially denies." Japanese acknowledge loss of one aircraft carrier, severe damage to a second, and damage to a cruiser at the Battle of Midway; claim to have sunk two United States carriers and one large transport, and to have wrecked 134 United States planes. Admiral Nimitz claims that Japanese fleet at Midway consisted of more than thirty warships, and that "perhaps half of them" had been sunk or damaged. Prague Radio announces that Germans have completely wiped out the village of Lidice, killing all men and sending women and children to concentration camps. The village was charged with harboring the assassins of Heydrich.

665

Most of morning packing and making arrangements and plans for leaving. Half hour's walk with Anne before lunch. Thor is too stiff to go with us any longer. We try to leave the house without his knowing we are gone.

Saturday, June 13

Spent most of the afternoon with Anne. Drove over to Harlock's Pond to say good-by to Jon. He was at one end of the pond, about one hundred feet offshore, with one of his new plugs caught on a snag! A ten-mile wind was drifting his boat away from the snag and forcing him to alternate rapidly between fish pole and oars. He managed to shout out "good-by" and tell me he had already caught three fish; and since there was no time to help, I left him at the pond and drove back home for my suitcase.

Boat on time! No bother either on boat or train, although I was recognized by several people. Went to see a poor motion picture in Boston. The streets are dimmed out and dark—just light enough to see to walk— and crowded with soldiers and sailors and their girls. Boarded the midnight train for New York.

Sunday, June 14

Several United States bombers forced down in Turkey; crews interned. New United States convoy debarks troops in Ireland. Axis advances in Libya. Chinese claim to have checked Japanese drive. "Silence shrouding fight in Aleutians."

It is very close and hot, even for New York, and my train does not leave until this evening. There were no boats between Martha's Vineyard and Woods Hole early enough Saturday afternoon to catch the Detroit train in Boston and no boats on Sunday that would have gotten me to New York in time to catch the train here this evening. Spent most of the day writing—not a breath of air. Boarded 4:45 train for Detroit.

Monday, June 15

Rommel's forces advance on Tobruk. "Citizens' army, including women and children, takes part in defense of Sevastopol." Japanese forces have landed in western Aleutians.

Off train at 8:15. Car and Ford driver waiting for me at station. Drove to Willow Run. Conference with DeGroat in regard to the new nose-gun mock-up. There has been definite progress, but how slow! Spent fifteen minutes talking to [Henry] Ford. Then short conference with Ford and Bennett regarding conditions and developments in the factory.

Wednesday, June 17

Allies claim forced retirement of Italian fleet in Mediterranean, with one heavy cruiser sunk, two battleships damaged, and six other warships destroyed or damaged. Russian forces counterattack in Kharkov area. Allied shipping losses continue. British surrounded at Tobruk.

Lunch at Dearborn Inn in my rooms with Frank Buchman and Kenneth Twitchell. Buchman sees what is happening to the country more clearly than most people. He realizes that something is seriously lacking in our character and spirit and is trying to do something about it. But his movement has always seemed to me to lack a tangible philosophy and strength, and most of the people in it have a dismaying immaturity and softness.

To Willow Run for conference with Bennett. He has just had the picket fences torn down that Sorensen ordered erected through the factory to keep the workmen from straying from one department to another. Some of the men started a strike, saying they were not animals to be fenced in. I think Bennett was right, but it will not help his standing with Sorensen.

Friday, June 19

Churchill in United States, reportedly to discuss second front. British retreat in Libya. Tobruk again under siege. House passes $8.5-billion naval construction bill.

Flew the Grumman for an hour in the afternoon. Went up for a forty-minute flight with Henning in the B-26 later. The B-26 has an extremely long take-off run and lands at about 120 m.p.h., although I think it might be brought in more slowly with care and practice. It is known to the services as "a dangerous ship" and has already killed a number of crews in training. It flies beautifully in the air, however.

Henning test flew "O-1" today. This is the bomber that [was to have been] completed by May 1 at the latest. It was finally rushed out of the factory, far from complete, on May 15. The engines were started and the plane taxied over to the flight department. The newspapers carried headlines to the effect that the production of bombers by the great Willow Run plant had begun. Now, more than a month later, the ship is test flown, and the test flight shows that much is still to be done before it will be in condition to turn over to the Army. As a matter of fact, "O-1" is really not a Ford-built ship. It is a Ford-assembled ship, assembled largely of parts produced by the Consolidated Company in San Diego and used by the Ford Company to check blueprints, jigs, tools, etc., during the last several months. This is why the plane is called "O-1." Plane No. 1 is now just beginning final assembly in the Willow Run factory and will not be ready for test for many weeks.

Monday, June 22

Tobruk surrenders. Japanese land on Kiska Island in Aleutians. Russians claim 100,000 German soldiers lost in siege of Sevastopol. R.A.F. raids over Continent continue.

Attended 9:00-to-10:30 lecture on altitude flying by Dr. Clark in the flight department at Willow Run. Lunch with Dr. Clark in Room "C." He showed me through the Willow Run hospital afterward.

Tuesday, June 23

Two Sevastopol forts fall. Japanese submarine bombards point on Oregon coast. Axis tanks advance into Egypt.

Arrived Willow Run airport at 6:40. Took off in Grumman G-21 with Henning and Storment[36] at 7:40 en route to Washington. Army and Navy planes in war paint scattered all over fields at Bolling and Anacostia. Landed on the Washington airport at 10:05. Henning and I drove to the Weather Bureau for a conference with Dr. Reichelderfer[37] in regard

---

36. Albert C. Storment, Ford pilot.

37. Francis W. Reichelderfer, chief of the U.S. Weather Bureau. He directed expansion of meteorological service for aviation, specializing in weather forecasts for aeronautics. A member of NACA.

to obtaining better weather service at Willow Run. Weather information is now under very strict censorship, and we are unable to obtain all we will need for safe and efficient operation this winter.

Taxi to Senate Office Building. Taxi drivers are beginning to grumble about the rubber ration. Sentry with rifle and bayonet guarding the door. Quarter hour with Senator Shipstead. Drove with him to his home and spent half an hour there before leaving for the airport—discussing the war and old times in Minnesota.

Took off at 6:02. Landed at Willow Run at dusk.

Friday, June 26

Germans advance in Kharkov area. Axis forces advance over one hundred miles beyond Egyptian border. Germans reported destroying second Czech village.

Morning on routine at Willow Run. Lunch with Major Saunders and several Army and Navy representatives who are on gun-turret committee. All to see nose-gun mock-up after lunch. Phoned Anne in regard to final arrangements for coming out here. She leaves Martha's Vineyard tomorrow.

Wednesday, July 1

Axis forces eighty miles from Alexandria. R.A.F. drops 4,000,000 lbs. of bombs on Bremen in five nights.

Colonel McDuffee phoned to tell me of a party scheduled to go through Willow Run. I thought he said, "King is coming." Knowing that a visit from Admiral King[38] has been expected for some time, I said, "I know him; tell him I'd like to see him." "Sure I will," says McDuffee. And then, after McDuffee had hung up, I learned it was not Admiral King but the King of Yugoslavia who was coming! And by that time McDuffee had left his office! I finally caught him by radio and got the situation straightened out.

Bennett and I discussed the Buchman movement after lunch and the possibility of assistance from the Ford Company. How effective is the movement? We are not sure.

Then, conference in Bennett's office between Henry Ford, Sorensen,

38. Admiral Ernest J. King, commander in chief of the U.S. Atlantic fleet.

669

Bennett, Campsall, and Hannagan[39] in regard to company policy toward "group piecework" and the award of service buttons to old-time Ford employees. Henry Ford doesn't like the idea of "piecework." Bennett and Sorensen rather favor "group piecework." Sorensen is for giving service buttons to employees who have been with the company for twenty-five years. Bennett favors service buttons for five to ten years. Hannagan, the new publicity director, wants to give them for two weeks of service!

Henry Ford still holds tight to the reins of his company. At seventy-eight, his opinions are definite and his mind clear. His eccentricity is largely balanced by the combination of Bennett, Sorensen, and Campsall.

Drove to the Rouge motor building with Sorensen after lunch to draft a letter to Wright Field in regard to obtaining a Lockheed Ventura (B-34) for test flights in connection with the Ford–Pratt Whitney engine.

To naval barracks at 7:30 to see a presentation of Buchman's play *You Can Defend America*. Mr. and Mrs. Henry Ford were there, and the playhouse seats were filled *by order of* the commanding officer of the station. The play seemed to me to be too long, and rather "sickly sweet." Whoever wrote it certainly had "a tenacious grasp of the obvious." I always want to say to these people that it is all very well to believe in "bigger and better babies," but one has to do more than that to become a good obstetrician. It is not enough to believe in *good* and to advocate *good*; one must develop a philosophy that I believe the Buchman movement is lacking. Still, these people are definitely on the constructive side of life and deserve encouragement, at least until something better is brought forward. As Whitehead says, "Life consists of a choice of alternatives—the better or the worse," and the people in the Buchman movement are undoubtedly one of "the better." They are sincere amateurs, giving their time and money, often at great personal sacrifice.

Met most of the cast and a number of the Navy men after the show. Drove Buchman to his house back of the Dearborn Inn, where he and part of his cast are staying at Henry Ford's invitation. Half hour's conversation. Buchman is constantly talking about raising funds and what various people have done for him on his birthday. "My birthday" punctuates his conversation with a rather amazing regularity.

39. Steve Hannagan, public-relations officer with Ford.

Thursday, July 2

Germans claim fall of Sevastopol. Russians deny. Crucial battle reported sixty miles west of Alexandria. Churchill attacked in Parliament. Japanese advance in China.

Met Henry Ford at Campsall's office. Half hour's conference. He then took me through Greenfield Village and showed me the interior of several of the old houses. We ended up looking at his first automobile and the machinery and tools in the shop where it was constructed. (Like the other buildings, this has been transported in detail from its original location to the Village.) Ford spent nearly half an hour telling me about the car and shop and how certain parts were built and how they functioned. Then he got into my car and I drove him to one of his farms near Willow Run. Ford wants me to arrange a meeting between himself, Bennett, Campsall, and Buchman this afternoon.

Lunch at the "round table" with Henry Ford, Sorensen, McCarroll,[40] Cameron, and other officers.

To Greenfield Village with Ford again after lunch, Henry Ford going with me in my car. We stopped to see the "Carver House," now nearing completion. From Greenfield Village I drove him to the Ford airport, where he suggested we drive around the test track! I took him around at about fifty-five miles an hour. I suspect he felt it was pretty tame driving, although he didn't say so. At any rate, after we made the first round he wanted to go again. On the second round he asked me to drive over the rough portion of the track—the portion that is made of large stones and concrete bumps and that breaks the best of cars down in a hurry. He enjoyed every bit of it! Then we went over to the synthetic-wool laboratory; and then down to the Rouge, where I drove him in and out between machinery and great factory buildings and railroad tracks. He showed me through one of the machine shops and the main powerhouse. On our way back from the Rouge we saw a number of Army Douglas transports landing on the Ford airport. They were parachute planes to be used for the exhibition tomorrow. Ford wanted to go right in after them.

A group of mechanics were gathered around a crap game in front of the nearest transport when we arrived. Ford asked me to drive over and stop near them. He jumped out of the car and walked over to them. "I'm

40. Hudson McCarroll, engineer and metallurgist.

Henry Ford," he said, extending his hand to the nearest man. They all got up, slipping the dice and stakes into unionall pockets, and stood looking at him in a half-pleased, half-embarrassed way. A rather excited colonel came running up a few minutes later to tell Mr. Ford that "the officers" were "at the other end of the line of planes." We got back in the car and drove down there. But Mr. Ford had no more than been introduced to the officers when he was off to talk to another group of mechanics; and this time they *could not* pull him away.

Some of the pilots invited me to look through one of the "paratroop" planes. While we were talking, one of the younger officers pointed out that the planes carried no armor plate and no gun turrets. "We may be able to sneak in and drop the parachuters," he said, "but they'll sure catch up with us on the way out."

"We can probably slip into the objective at low altitude," another officer said, "but how are we going to get back?"

"The answer is that *we won't get* back," replied the first.

The only protection these planes have is from the "tommy guns" of the paratroops. Each window in the cabin has an opening in the center to accommodate a gun barrel. But above and below, ahead and behind, the plane is completely unprotected. And on the way back from a mission, there won't even be any paratroops with "tommy guns."

Finally Mr. Ford suggested that we go to the engineering laboratory to see Mr. Cameron. On the way he talked about the Buchman movement, factories, machinery, methods of construction, the employment of labor, etc. I felt he was tired, but it seemed impossible to get him to take any sort of a rest. After arriving at the engineering laboratories, however, with the aid of Frank Campsall, we persuaded him to call it a day.

Saturday, July 4

Russians admit loss of Sevastopol; claim victory in Kursk area. Germans claim to be within twenty miles of Alexandria; British deny.

The Army is becoming dissatisfied with the progress here. We are far behind schedule, and the Ford Company officers continue to make promises of deliveries that they themselves must realize they can't meet. Of course, the Army and the Administration have constantly encouraged such promises, and even threatened to withhold machinery from the Willow Run plant if they were not forthcoming.

British advance in Libya. Germans claim to have reached Don River on broad front.

Half hour with [Major] Saunders on relationship between Ford Company and the Army, etc. Hour with Bill Smith on air-raid precautions and factory organization. I don't think a raid at this time is likely, but it is technically possible, so we should be prepared for one. I think the Germans have too much on their hands in Europe this summer to go to the added effort of organizing transoceanic air raids. The returns would not justify the cost—unless they caught us asleep again as the Japs did at Pearl Harbor.

If the war continues long enough, there will probably be transoceanic raiding, but I think it is improbable this summer, especially so far inland as Detroit. Still, we went to the expense of raiding Tokyo at high cost and with doubtful results. (It is rumored that every plane on the raid was lost, except one which landed in Siberia. Apparently the planes [B-25's] reached China at night and, due to some slip-up in organization, the fields where they were to have landed thought they were Japanese bombers and did not light up. All crews apparently had to jump from their planes, but only a few lives were lost during the raid. There is another rumor that the aircraft carrier from which the planes took off was forced to turn back nearly 1,000 miles farther from Japan than Doolittle had planned.)

To developmental engineering department after lunch to look over the nose-gun mock-up with a group of visiting Englishmen. They say the tendency in England is to install 20-mm. cannon rather than .50-cal. machine guns in aircraft.

Wednesday, July 8

Germans claim capture of Voronezh. Desert battle continues in Libya. Berlin claims sinking of United States heavy cruiser and twenty-eight out of thirty-eight ships in convoy to Russia. General Spaatz appointed commander of United States air forces in European area. Roosevelt warns that all car tires may be seized.

First part of morning on routine and a conference with Bricker—told him that I doubted we would get No. 1 bomber out of the factory before

August, and possibly not before September! (It was originally scheduled to be out in May.) Half hour's flying with Henning in the B-26. It is a dangerous plane if not handled with extreme care and caution—high take-off, landing, and stalling speeds; unreliable propellers, and tricky single-engine performance. I must find more time to spend flying and studying planes of this type.

Thursday, July 9

Tirpitz reported torpedoed by Russian submarine in Arctic. Germans capture Oskol.

Henry Ford and Frank Campsall walked into my office. Ford, who has turned part of the Dearborn Inn over to Buchman's M.R.A. group, now feels that they want to leave him "holding the bag." Says he is not going to do "another damn thing for them." Says they asked him to come to their party at the Dearborn Inn for "two or three minutes" the other evening, and that he "didn't get away till 2:00 or 3:00 in the morning!" I tried to tell him of the value as well as of the weakness of the Buchman group, but I must say I feel very much the way Ford does a great deal of the time.

Drove to Bloomfield Hills to see the house again. It looks very attractive as one drives in the gate and much smaller than it actually is—a characteristic I like about a house. Of course, it is overdone inside, with colors and furniture not well chosen, and the grounds are a little too formal for our taste, but we are fortunate to get anything as good around Detroit. I liked it better than the first time I saw the place—possibly because I was alone—except for the Scotch gardener. The flowers and trees and three acres of ground seem exceptionally attractive after three months of living on the second floor of the Dearborn Inn.

Friday, July 10

Germans advance in Russia, cross Don. Desert battle continues in Libya.

Trip with Henry Ford and Harry Bennett to the Army camp beside the small lake, west of the factory, to inspect the student mechanics. They were all standing at attention in front of the tents when we arrived—

dressed in their mechanics' coveralls which they wear during their instruction in the various departments. Ford was embarrassed by the formality. Seeing this, Bennett suggested that they be placed "at ease." The command was given, and Ford walked along the lines shaking hands with each man—fifty or sixty of them.

Saturday, July 11

German armies advance on Caucasus, capture Rossosh. Battle rages in Libya. Three ships rumored sunk in St. Lawrence.

To New York Central Station to meet Anne on the 8:15 train. As I stood at one of the gates, waiting, Colonel McDuffee came up to talk to me. As he did, Anne slipped through another gate, about seventy-five feet away and I missed her! After waiting a quarter hour, I drove to 508 Lakepointe, where Anne and I had arranged to meet if anything went wrong at the station. After that, Anne and I drove to our new home in Bloomfield Hills. William and Anna Miller were already there, having driven through from the east a day earlier than we expected them. Anne feels as I do about the house. We wish many things were different, but it is the best we have seen around Detroit, and we are fortunate to get it.

Sunday, July 12

Spent most of the afternoon making plans for the house. Half hour outdoors in the sun. The garden is full of birds, and in one corner there is a raspberry patch with exceptionally large and well-flavored berries. The local air-raid warden called and left forms to be filled out—whether there was a shovel and bucket of sand in the attic, where the gas shut-off valves were located, what basement room we would use in case of a raid, how the room was equipped, etc., etc.!

Mrs. Morrow phoned to ask if she could take Anne, Jr., and Land to North Haven for a week. We decided it would be very good for both of them in addition to making Mrs. Morrow happy.

Monday, July 13

Ed Moore came for supper and the evening. He is still trying to organize Carrel's "Institute of Man"—thinks it should be easier to raise money now than before the war because of the effect of high wartime taxes on estates.

Tuesday, July 14

First part of morning on routine. Then an inspection trip through the factory with Gus Miller. Discussed means of improving workmanship, which is still pretty poor—due largely to inexperience.

Drove back to Bloomfield Hills via a new route—Telegraph Road—which is a little shorter than Southfield. One now sees cars with punctured or blown tires drawn up at the roadside. The rubber shortage is beginning to tell, but it is still not very noticeable.

Thursday, July 16

Afternoon, until 5:00, on routine, studying operating data, etc. Then to flight department for a parachute-harness fitting and an hour in the Grumman with Henning. Made several landings on Belleville Lake, southeast of Willow Run.

Friday, July 17

Germans renew attack in Egypt. Tension grows between United States and Vichy France and Finland. German armies advance in Russia; Moscow claims high casualties—claim German losses 900,000 between May 15 and June 15; Red Army losses placed at 399,000 during same period. British House of Commons discusses shipping losses in secret session. China claims recapture of Tsingtien.

Supper on porch with Anne. We discussed the possibility of buying a car trailer for use as a sort of studio—a place where we can write and work, which would be secluded and also mobile. Michigan winters are too cold to use the type of tent we had on Martha's Vineyard, and for the uncertain life that lies ahead a trailer might have many advantages.

Saturday, July 18

Tank battle continues in Egypt. German advance continues toward Stalingrad; claim capture of Voroshilovgrad. Pressure for second front

grows in England. Fighting reported in Yugoslavia near Fiume. United
States planes bomb Japanese positions in Aleutians.

Spent part of morning in conference with Boyer[41]—in regard to the delay
in production being caused by improper die design and the necessity of
changing a large percentage of the 11,000-odd dies which are required to
build the B-24 on Ford methods. One difficulty, and one of the major
causes of delay, lies in the fact that the Consolidated Company was unable to furnish a complete set of up-to-date blueprints for the B-24.

Sunday, July 19

German armies advance in lower Don region. Russians advance in vicinity
of Voronezh. R.A.F. attacks Ruhr. Battle continues in Egypt. Japanese
attack on Siberia rumored.

We brought the dogs home from the kennel today. Thor is alarmingly thin
and weak. I ordered more meat and milk and left word in the kitchen to
give him anything he wanted to eat. I am sorry we did not bring him
from the kennel sooner, but there was no place in the house to keep
him—all rooms full of cloth-covered furniture, floors covered with tinted
carpets, etc. We finally fixed a sheltered place for his mattress on the
screened porch. Thor does not belong on a place like this. He belongs on
Vineyard Haven, or in Maine—in a wilder country. But he could never
be happy away from Anne.

Monday, July 20

Moscow admits fall of Voroshilovgrad. Claims German drive on Stalin-
grad checked. R.A.F. bombing of Continent continues. Chinese armies
claim successes.

Reached Willow Run about noon. Afternoon on routine and a trip
through the factory. Many of the men are loafing on their jobs. At first
glance, they may appear to be working; but as one looks closer, they are
only in the positions that make it look as though they were doing something—and sometimes, if they think they are being watched, going
through motions with their hands. They are, in some instances, indiffer-

41. Raymond Boyer, a general foreman with the Ford Co.

ent; but I think this condition is caused primarily by improper organization and a lack of understanding by the workmen of what they are expected to do.

Tuesday, July 21

Germans advance on Rostov. Russians take bridgeheads near Voronezh. Air raids continue. House passes $6.27-billion tax bill; votes ninety per cent profits tax.

Arrived Willow Run at 8:40. Almost as soon as I stepped in my office a radio call came in from Harry Bennett asking me to meet him on Michigan Avenue to look at some trailers that were for sale. He directed me to his location by radio and we went through one of the trailers.

Then back to Willow Run for a conference with Bennett and Henry Ford. There is considerable internal friction in the company between Henry Ford and Harry Bennett on the one side, and Edsel Ford and Charlie Sorensen on the other, in regard to the labor check-off system. All agree that it is coming and can't be avoided; but Sorensen and Edsel Ford are in favor of the company accepting it gracefully for this reason, while Bennett and Henry Ford are for making the government force the issue. Bennett believes the check-off system will prove very unpopular among the workers, and that the responsibility for its acceptance should be clearly the government's and not the Ford Company's.

After some minutes of discussion Ford turned the conversation to other matters, among which the subject of the old Ironton Railroad [42] and its sale came up. Ford told in detail the circumstances surrounding the transaction. It seems that the antitrust laws forced the Ford Company to sell. Ford said he thought they (the company) might have beaten the case in the courts, but decided not to try it. A group of eastern capitalists desired to buy the railroad and asked the Ford Company to state the price that would be acceptable. Mr. Ford asked Edsel what the railroad had cost the company to date. After going over the records, Edsel figured the cost at about $21 million. "Don't take a cent less than $36 million," his father told him, "and in cash!" The eastern group refused to buy at that price.

42. The Detroit, Toledo & Ironton Railroad (renamed the Detroit & Ironton Railroad) was purchased in 1921 by the Ford Motor Co. for $7,500,000 to facilitate the shipping of automobiles from the River Rouge plant.

Weeks passed by until one day Mr. Ford was showing the president of the New York Central Railroad through the museum at Dearborn. "I just happened to be showing him around," Mr. Ford said. "It didn't have anything at all to do with buying the railroad." But someone connected with the eastern interests heard about Ford and the New York Central president being together, and apparently thought the New York Central was trying to purchase the Ironton. The result was that Mr. Ford had an immediate offer at $36 million for his railroad, which he accepted on the condition that it be in *cash!* And he stuck to it—made the purchasers' representative bring $36 million in bills to Detroit! There were two suitcases full of the money. After it was turned over and receipted, the Ford Company's treasurer didn't want to go to the expense and trouble of hiring an armored car for transportation, so Harry Bennett and one of his assistants carried it personally to the bank.

Henry Ford asked me to meet him in the afternoon at one of the Ford laboratories, where Dr. Carver,[43] the Negro scientist, is giving a demonstration of the grasses and weeds he uses for medicine and food.

To Rouge administration for lunch with Harry Bennett. Then to the plant laboratory to meet Ford and Dr. Carver. A few minutes later, after Dr. Carver had gone to the back of the building to look after the preparation of his weed sandwiches, I was introduced to him. He is very old, and was much more interested in the green spinachy substances on the stove than in meeting people. He had a kindly and intelligent face.

Met Harry Bennett soon afterward at the Dearborn garage to see a trailer Ford bought several years ago, and which he has been keeping in the Edison Institute Museum. Ford wants to give it to us, Bennett says! It is exactly the right size and really just what we want. I told Bennett we would rather buy it; but he said Mr. Ford would not hear of it, and that it had about passed its usefulness for the museum, as trailers were now so common. I don't like to take things this way but, after all, I am working at Willow Run for no pay—and I think Ford really wants to give the trailer to us.

43. George Washington Carver, American Negro agricultural chemist. He joined the staff of Tuskegee Institute in 1894, and in 1896 became director of the Department of Agricultural Research, remaining in this post the rest of his life. He worked to improve the economy of the South, teaching soil improvement and diversification of crops, and discovered hundreds of uses for the peanut, sweet potato, and soybean.

Thursday, July 23

British advance in Egypt. Germans drive wedge between Rostov and Stalingrad. Three hundred R.A.F. bombers raid Continent; drop fifty two-ton bombs on Duisburg. Guerrilla armies reported active in Yugoslavia. Shipment of rubber from Japan reported to have arrived in Germany. Roosevelt asks more power to stabilize wages and prices. Meat shortage in eastern cities.

Sorensen phoned and, point-blank, asked me what I would think of building a plane with a 1,000-foot wing span! Said, "You know the Ford Company could do something like that." (He had been reading the newspaper articles about the Kaiser air-transport publicity.)[44] Now Sorensen hasn't the slightest idea what a 1,000-foot wing span involves, and he has apparently completely forgotten the fiasco the company made of its attempt to build a model larger than the old Ford Tri-Motor. (After spending some hundreds of thousands of dollars on the plane, the design turned out to be so poor that it was junked after being taxied across the field.) Also, Sorensen is completely overlooking the fact that we have no competent aeronautical engineering organization today and that engineers are not available with which to build one.

I tried to outline the desirability of taking reasonable steps in increasing the size of aircraft, and the necessity of building up an engineering organization before we even considered starting a project of the magnitude he had in mind. But Sorensen said, "Well, talk to DeGroat about it. Of course, he isn't such a good fellow to talk to, because he blocks everything I have in mind. I'll call him up first, and then you talk to him."

I suggested to Sorensen that if he called DeGroat he limit himself to suggesting a 500-foot wing span. "But I want to knock 'em over with the idea," says Sorensen. "What's the matter with a 2,000-foot wing?" I told him I thought he would knock them over sufficiently by suggesting 500 feet, and we hung up.

Lunch with Boyer (dies). Afterward, we drove to the Rouge where he showed me the methods of constructing and repairing hard dies. Most of the dies for the B-24 were improperly designed and have had to be changed. The aviation industry warned Ford against the use of hard dies,

44. The Kaiser organization planned to mass-produce huge wood-construction flying boats for the transportation of military personnel and cargo.

but the Ford Company still believes the eventual efficiency of the hard steel die will justify the cost and time required for installation.

Friday, July 24

German armies at outskirts of Rostov. British "advance slowly" in Egypt. High pressure in England for second front. German Air Force raids British Isles. Prime Minister of Australia warns of "grave threat" from Japanese. Secretary Hull sets limits on "freedoms" after the war.

Spent twenty minutes in the Link. Then lunch with a group of visiting engineers. Phoned the Henry Ford Hospital and arranged for Anne to see Dr. [J. P.] Pratt Monday morning. Interview with a Mr. Gardner, who is applying for an engineering and management position with the Ford Company at Willow Run. He used to be factory manager for the old Fokker Company.

Sunday, July 26

German armies advance in Caucasus near Stalingrad. R.A.F. bombs Mannheim and Frankfurt. Navy announces five Japanese ships sunk by United States submarines.

Anne and I drove to 508 Lakepointe for lunch with Mother and B. I spent most of the afternoon clearing out the basement and going over old papers with Mother. B. and I found dozens of old tools from Grandfather's laboratory. I remember many of them very clearly, even to the feel of their handles. They still "feel" as they used to in my hand, although I have not touched them for more than twenty years.

Monday, July 27

Germans claim crossing of Don southeast of Rostov. Axis troop movements into Bulgaria reported. R.A.F. again bombs Duisburg.

When I took our Mercury to the Ford garage at the Rouge to have the trailer-towing attachment installed, Bennett insisted I turn it in for a 1942 car. I foresaw complications; but he would not listen to my arguments and said Mr. Ford would want us to have the latest-model car along with the trailer and that the trailer installation could be made more easily on a 1942 Mercury because of the heavier rear springs. He was just as nice about it as could be; but I felt we were already taking enough from Mr. Ford by taking the trailer, and, also, I was concerned about the government's restriction on the sale or transfer of new cars. This morning a man arrived with car-purchase papers for me to sign, which included a statement to the effect that the car being purchased was to be used in connection with war work. Since I have a company radio car for my personal use, this was not true, and I was unable to sign the papers. I phoned Bennett and laid the situation before him. After more phone calls and considerable discussion, we decided it would be better to keep the old car after all.

Henry Ford came out. I went with him to see General Knudsen,[45] who landed on the Willow Run airport this morning. We found him in the developmental engineering department talking to Edsel Ford, Sorensen, Bennett, and Campsall.

Tuesday, July 28

Russians retreat in Caucasus, evacuate Rostov. Six hundred R.A.F. bombers raid Hamburg and other continental cities.

Conference with Colonel Saunders in regard to the B-24 board, which meets Monday. The Ford Company is planning on sending Dunton and Houston. Saunders thinks Sorensen and Bricker or Smith should go. He thinks the Consolidated Company is going to bring the Ford failure to meet schedule to a head; says they are talking about sending men to Willow Run to show the Ford Company how to operate an aircraft factory!

As a matter of fact, there are many things the Ford Company could be shown about operating an aircraft factory. Unfortunately, Sorensen is typical of many Ford officers who *don't want to be shown.* Lunch with Bennett, General Short, and General Powell. Continued conference in regard to B-24 production schedules after lunch. Colonel McDuffee arrived

45. William S. Knudsen had once worked for the Ford Motor Co., supervising the building of assembly plants. In 1937 he became president of General Motors Corp. During the war he became a lieutenant general in the U.S. Army and directed production for the War Department.

with data concerning the delivery schedules Sorensen has promised the Air Corps.

After conference ended I drove to the garage back of the engineering laboratory to get the trailer. Drove it home at 40 m.p.h. Strange feeling to have anything so large tied behind your car. Managed to get it in place in the woods back of the house without disconnecting the car. Anne and I looked all through it before supper—closets, drawers, stove, ice box, and cubbyholes. After supper I took the wheels off and put wood blocks under the frames. Put the wheels in the basement; can't take any chance on tires these days.

Wednesday, July 29

Heavy German forces cross Don. German Air Force bombs Birmingham and Midlands.

Conference with Colonel Saunders regarding B-24 schedule, factory progress, and Ford-Army relationships. Conference with Henry Ford, Bennett, and Bricker regarding B-24 production schedule.

General [Samuel M.] Connell and other Air Corps officers arrived in a B-24 to look over the airport with a view toward bringing several B-24 squadrons here for training. Accompanied him on a tour of the area.

Thursday, July 30

Conference with DeGroat in regard to Sorensen's idea of a cargo plane with a 1,000-foot wing span. DeGroat discouraged and rather humiliated at Sorensen's putting such a wild idea up to him at this time, while he is already desperately short-handed and in the midst of serious B-24 production problems. He talks of leaving the Ford Company.

DeGroat has worked out the approximate dimensions for a 500,000-lb. flying boat. (The largest boat we now have, the Martin "Mars," grosses slightly over 150,000 lbs.) He says it would have a wing span of about 340 feet and require about 33,000 h.p. And Sorensen wants, not a 340-foot, but a 1,000-foot, wing span!

Hannagan's office called from the Rouge to tell me that press dispatch says I have been subpoenaed by the defense for Pelley[46] at Indianapolis!

46. William D. Pelley, organizer of the Silver Shirt storm troopers in 1933 and

I first think this a press story, as I have never seen or had any contact with Pelley or his organization; but as I inquire further, it looks as though a subpoena has actually been issued.

Phone call from Bennett's office in the afternoon asking me to come over. Capizzi (Ford lawyer) was there. We discussed the Pelley-trial subpoena. Bennett first suggested that I avoid receiving it; but I told him I felt that would be a mistake and that it would be best to accept it immediately—to which Capizzi agreed. Capizzi said the defense in a criminal trial could subpoena anyone they pleased, regardless of whether he had any knowledge of or contact with the accused. I gave Hannagan a short statement for the press, which I felt advisable in this instance, and returned to Willow Run.

Supper with Anne on porch. Thor has not eaten all day; would touch nothing and seems to have lost all interest in life except when Anne or I come over to pet and rub him.

The children arrive tomorrow.

Friday, July 31

Up at 6:15. Thor could not get up by himself. His hind legs simply won't follow what he wants them to do any more. I had to lift him up. After that he could walk. But he ate his breakfast. I left him sleeping on his mat and started for Willow Run.

Got a bottle of chloroform from Dr. Clark, in case Thor gets much worse. But how I hate to think about using it. I don't believe one should interfere with death. But how much suffering should one let a dog go through? I decide not to use it unless Thor is really in pain—never as long as I think life is bearable for him or as long as he shows such joy when Anne goes over to him.

To Willow Run airport to meet General Arnold and party. Thinking I might be embarrassing to Arnold politically, I remained in the background when he landed. But he came over and introduced me to the various American and foreign officers who were with him. Lunch with Arnold and party at Willow Run. Arnold brought up the question of whether it was better to ship entire engines, or simply repair parts, to combat zones. He cited the difficulty of getting inexperienced crews to

_____

publisher of numerous political pamphlets. He was one of twenty-eight defendants brought to trial by the Justice Department in Indianapolis.

make repairs with parts as against the cost and difficulty in transportation of complete engines. He says the effects of sand and combat usage have cut down the average life of an aircraft engine in the combat zone to fifty flying hours! Prior to the war the Air Corps had estimated they would get an average of 300 hours from an engine in the United States and an average of 200 hours from an engine abroad.

Accompanied the party on a trip through the factory after lunch. Had planned on spending the afternoon at Willow Run, but Arnold asked me to accompany him on his trip through the rest of the Ford factories and demonstrations. From the bomber plant we went to the tank-testing grounds to watch a demonstration of Ford-built tanks, jeeps, and armored trucks. Then to the Rouge aircraft engine building, where Ford is building the Pratt-Whitney-designed 2,000-h.p. radial engine (the R-2800). While we were going through the building, Arnold asked me if I would look into the cylinder-head situation for him and let him know what Ford would be able to turn out in the near future. (Cylinder heads have become a critical item.) Sorensen told Arnold that the new foundry building they are putting up in the Rouge will be completed in ninety days. Arnold is skeptical about it.

Home at 5:00. Anne, Jr., and Land have arrived, and the house has suddenly come to life. Anne is walking well, and both seem to have grown a great deal. I helped set up a canvas wading pool we bought recently, and we played with the lawn sprinkler system—Land running into and away from the sprays, Anne, having been caught once, watching with cautious enjoyment well out of reach. Thor ate some meat and drank a pint of milk; but he is very weak and sleeps most of the time.

Saturday, August 1

I had to lift Thor up again this morning, and I could not persuade him to eat anything. He loses strength each day. When I think he is getting better, it turns out to be only temporary. His only interest in life now is to be with Anne. He struggles pitifully to get up and follow her whenever she goes by, and sometimes he is able to get to his feet and walk along behind her—dragging his rear legs stiffly over the grass—but with an expression of great joy in his eyes at being near her. When he is lying down, his eyes follow her as long as she is in sight.

Signs along the roadside on the way to Willow Run: SLAP THE JAP SAVE THE SCRAP; AMERICA NEVER LOST A WAR; REMEMBER PEARL HAR-

BOR; EAT HOLLYWOOD DIET BREAD. And innumerable billboards advertising cigarettes (picture of man and girl in uniform; HIS CIGARETTE AND MINE), service stations "for defense," etc., etc. All of them sensational, gaudy, and depressingly superficial.

Sunday, August 2

Germans reach Salsk, one hundred miles southeast of Rostov. R.A.F. bombs Düsseldorf. Roosevelt warns of fuel-oil shortage this winter.

Thor was lying on his mattress, very stiff. I lifted him out onto the grass where he could stand firmly enough with his forelegs but uncertainly with his rear. But he shows no sign of pain, and I think he still enjoys living. When I see him look at Anne, I know that he does. When I am with him, I feel that after ten years of such faithfulness, he deserves all our attention and that we should be constantly with him until he dies. But that is impossible, especially in this time of war; and fortunately he sleeps almost constantly when we are away—most contented when he is on the grass, under the shade of a tree. He would eat nothing this morning, but last night he took a little meat and milk.

Mother and B. arrived about 11:15. Land rushed out to meet the car; Anne, Jr., following behind him, more cautiously. Both of them ran up and hugged Mother. There is some essential element lacking in life where there is no contact between the very old and the very young; and what the one gives to the other is beyond measure. When Mother and B. came around to the back of the house, Thor woke, raised his head, and barked. He still feels a responsibility for guarding our home. He cannot inspect every caller as he used to in years past, but he warns us that someone new has arrived of whose rights and intentions he is not quite sure. Then he lowered his head and closed his eyes, leaving the responsibility to us.

Bennett phoned to tell me the judge for the Pelley trial wants to talk to me personally before I testify. Says the judge is friendly and was a "pre-Pearl Harbor isolationist." He is reputedly a fair and able jurist and has sent word that he would try to get me on and off the stand the same day I am called. In other words, if I go on the stand Tuesday, I should be able to start home Tuesday afternoon or evening.

Thor took some food, but he is sinking rapidly. I must leave for Indianapolis tomorrow, and am afraid he may die before I can return. Anne and I picked a spot on the hillside in the woods southwest of the house, and I dug a grave for Thor. The ground was hard, and I did not finish until half past ten at night. I hate to dig his grave before he dies. It seems to make it such a certainty. But I don't want anyone else to do it while I am away.

Monday, August 3

German Air Force bombs southeast England. Russians claim German advance slowed in Caucasus and checked northwest of Stalingrad. New York motorists ordered to use only parking lights or "dimmed-out" headlights. Riots reported in Paris.

I carried Thor out into the morning sun on the lawn. He drank a little water but would not eat. He cannot even stand alone now; but he likes attention and can still hold his head high, ears up, when he sees or hears you coming. His breathing is fast and shallow.

I phoned [John] Thompson in Indianapolis (Ford public-relations officer, who once lived there and who has gone home for a visit—at Harry Bennett's suggestion, I suspect). He said the judge would like to see me this afternoon or evening. I told him I had a reservation on the 5:06 plane.

To Bennett's "island" on the Huron River to talk to him about Arnold's request that I give him a confidential report on the cylinder-head production prospects at the Rouge plant. I told Bennett I would not want to give such a report without Ford's knowledge and authorization. Bennett said to give General Arnold any information he wanted to have, that Mr. Ford would not want to hold anything from him, and that he, Bennett, would tell Mr. Ford what I was doing and arrange for Ford officers and employees to furnish all the co-operation and data I called for.

Back to Bloomfield Hills to get suitcase and say good-by to Anne and Thor. Thor seemed somewhat better this afternoon and showed that he thoroughly enjoyed the massaging I gave his legs and back.

American Airlines plane to Chicago. Eastern Airlines plane to Indianapolis. Pilot asked me to come forward to cockpit. Said he had been a member of America First. Now about to go on active duty with the Marines. Taxi from Indianapolis airport to Marott Hotel. Discussed general situation with John Thompson (Ford), and, through him, refused to pose for press photographs or give an interview. Told him to simply say I thought it inappropriate under the circumstances. Read some of the recent press accounts of the Pelley trial to get some idea of what it is all about. The defense attorney phoned and wanted to talk to me before I testified. I refused, saying that I preferred to go on the stand without previously talking either to the prosecution or the defense.

Tuesday, August 4

Germans reported strengthening defenses along "invasion coasts."

We drove to the courthouse at 9:00. Reporters and photographers at entrance. Met by United States marshal, who escorted us to the library to wait until court opened. The court convened shortly after 9:00. I was called as the first witness. The defense seemed extremely incompetent; asked questions which had no relationship to the trial, and just as I thought they were about to start, they excused me from the stand. The prosecution, wisely, I think, did not even bother to cross-examine. I was on the stand for a total of twelve minutes. Then the court adjourned because none of the other defense witnesses had turned up! I have always been under the impression that a subpoena was something to be answered, both from a standpoint of honor and of law; but the others who were subpoenaed at the same time I was apparently feel differently, including the government officials. Ideas of law and honor are rapidly changing in this country.

Spent half an hour with the judge in his chambers. (I got in too late to see him last night.) I told him I hoped the verdict would be clear cut and leave the American people with no question in their minds about whether or not Pelley was guilty, that I believed a conviction on uncertain evidence would do great damage at this time. I draw the impression that the judge is a fair and honest man.

While I was in the judge's chambers a number of court and state officials came in and shook hands. All of them were friendly and many of them told me that they had been "one hundred per cent" behind me in my stand against entering the war.

From courthouse back to hotel. Phone message in my room from Phil Love. He has landed on the Indianapolis airport with an Army transport. Told him to come right to hotel if he could. Unfortunately, I had invited (through Thompson) a number of local newspaper editors and owners for lunch. Warned Phil, and asked him to come for lunch also. I felt the circumstances of the Pelley trial and the action of the defense in subpoenaing me made it advisable to have some personal contact with the newspapers here in Indianapolis.

There were seven newspapermen in all, plus Love and Thompson. We discussed the war and the Pelley trial—both with caution. I told them I thought they had a great responsibility in regard to the trial—that I knew nothing about Pelley but that it was important for him to be clearly guilty of sedition in the public mind if convicted, and that from the newspaper accounts I had read I did not think he had either been clearly proven guilty or treated in an impartial manner. I tried to show them the future danger to the press itself if the right of expression is improperly restricted under the pressure and hysteria of war. But I am afraid it was over their heads. They apparently see no connection between the trial of Pelley and possible future restrictions of the freedom of the press itself. I am afraid they see far more of the superficial than of the fundamental elements involved.

[Phil Love] is a full colonel now and has avoided the opportunity of being appointed a brigadier general. He says he does not want the responsibility for taking untrained squadrons into combat, and he feels that the training being given at present is disgracefully inadequate for units about to be sent to the battle area. Early supper with Love in my rooms at the hotel. Then he drove me to the Municipal Airport. Boarded the 7:00 P.M. Eastern Airlines plane for Chicago, where I transferred to American Airlines and arrived at the Detroit City airport at 11:50 E.W.T.

Thor is dead. He died this morning under the hickory tree on the lawn. Anne buried him in the grave I dug the night before I left. He had no pain, and I think he died as the old should die, not lingering so long that all joy is gone from living. I think Thor found something worth while in life to the very day he died, and yet I think he was ready and willing to go. But now, for us, there is a great empty, lonely feeling in the places he used to be. Anne is very tired, and I am concerned about her and the strain she has gone through.

Thursday, August 6

All-India Congress threatens disobedience campaign unless independence granted by Britain. German armies threaten Stalingrad, continue advance in Caucasus. Pelley convicted of sedition.

Arrived at Willow Run at 9:00. Hour on routine. Then DeGroat called up and asked if he could come in for a few minutes. Sorensen has ordered him to make a model of two B-24's put together as a biplane! DeGroat is extremely depressed. Says he doesn't know how to do it, that he can't afford to have his reputation involved in such an absurd project. He speaks again of leaving the company and finally said, "What's the use of my being here? They don't seem to want engineering experience."

Conference with Colonel McDuffee in regard to the general situation at Willow Run and cylinder-head production at the Rouge. Drove with him to Gate 4 of the Rouge plant, where I met Rausch,[47] who took me on an inspection trip through the aluminum foundry and other buildings—hot, crowded workshops full of fumes and sweating workmen, both Negro and white. Rausch thinks the cylinder-head building will be up by November 1. But is this another optimistic estimate on the part of a Ford officer? I have learned to be skeptical of all estimates since coming here. However, Rausch has been relatively accurate in the estimates he has given me in the past and, as a result, I have considerable confidence in what he says now.

Half hour's conference with Sorensen at his office in the Rouge motor building. I tried to dissuade him from his idea of putting two B-24's together to make a biplane, but he said that DeGroat was constantly trying to block him in everything new he suggested, implied that I was doing the same thing in this instance, and spent most of the time talking about his accomplishments and how pleased General Arnold had been with his visit to Willow Run. Sorensen took literally what General Arnold said to be courteous and polite.

Hour on routine after lunch; then went with Colonel McDuffee to see Major Rogers and officers of the B-24 squadron, which is to train on the airport here for the next three weeks. The south half of the flight building (four hangars) is already filled with long rows of Army cots. Major Rogers is a young man in his early thirties—alert, able, active, with a somewhat Southern voice. He has had great difficulty in training his squadron, has much still to do, and is scheduled to be sent overseas in the next few weeks. Many of his pilots have been out of school for less than six months. The last field where he was sent for training had uncompleted runways—cement still being poured. And his gunners have been given no machine-gun ammunition with which to train. (I learned

47. Ray Rausch was in charge of production at the Rouge plant.

from one of the other officers that the last bomber [B-24] squadron to be sent overseas had been given only twenty-five rounds per gunner for training before they left.)

In order to train his gunners Major Rogers had removed a top Martin turret from one of his bombers, removed the .50-cal. machine guns, and installed a twelve-gauge shotgun in place of the right-hand machine gun. With this arrangement his gunners shoot clay pigeons for practice. And they break up to twenty out of twenty-five birds when experienced! Rogers said he ran into great opposition from his higher officers when he applied for permission to mount a shotgun in a turret and finally had to go ahead on his own authority at the risk of being court-martialed. He is now trying to put a tail turret in the nose of the B-24 and again being discouraged and told it is no use.

The officers of this squadron are not B-24 enthusiasts. They say the Bendix bottom turret is no good, the nose gun no good, the armor plate inadequate, the take-off run too long, and that it is impossible to fly a close formation at altitude. The morale is extremely low, and both officers and men tired out. They have experienced even more than the usual amount of red tape. One afternoon they were ordered to be ready to move to Willow Run the next morning. They worked all through the night, crating and packing their trucks and planes. Early the next morning they received a telegram ordering them to stay where they were and to get at least six hours' flying practice in that day, per plane. They unpacked and got the six hours in. In the evening they received orders to leave the next morning. Now, most of them have had little or no sleep for forty-eight hours, and show it. I told Major Rogers I would try to get some help for him on the turret. He has been revising the tail turret from one of his planes; but has had to do the work somewhere it would not be noticed by his higher-ranking officers, who say that such things should be done at experimental stations. (They should, but they aren't—at least in time.)

Friday, August 7

Germans advance in Caucasus. Russians claim success in Don bend northwest of Stalingrad. R.A.F. raids Continent. German Air Force raids England. Tension rises between Britain and India. Washington announces sinking of merchant ship with 406 on board; twenty-five lives reported lost.

Conference with Colonel Saunders in regard to his trip to Tulsa and the complaints of the Douglas Company concerning Ford workmanship. Conference with DeGroat in regard to helping Major Rogers and Major [Marion D.] Unruh with their nose-turret project. Took DeGroat over to see them and their mock-up and to discuss the tail failure on one of their B-24's, which occurred shortly before they came to Willow Run. We all went over to see the clay-pigeon shooting with the Martin turret: amazing accuracy.

Saturday, August 8

German armies advance to point within sixty miles of Maikop oil fields. (Berlin claims troops only thirty miles away.) R.A.F. raids Duisburg. United States bombers raid Tobruk. Office of War Information reports United States production behind schedule in planes, tanks, and artillery and that sinking of merchantmen in first half of 1942 had considerably exceeded construction. Britain's First Lord of Admiralty claims "heavy toll of U-boats." United States planes raid Japanese bases in China. Gandhi calls for civil disobedience in India.

Land comes into our room and crawls into our bed at 7:00: "I'm awake!"

Arrived Willow Run at 9:00. First part of morning on routine—phone calls, studying data, etc. Trip to flight department and inspection of troop quarters with Colonel Saunders. Arrived home at 3:00. Took Land to 508 Lakepointe to spend the rest of the afternoon and the night with Mother and B. More birds than ever before in the yard: thirteen pheasants (mostly young ones), about 150 sparrows, several doves, robins, and thrushes, and one rat! We played Mozart in the evening.

Sunday, August 9

United States Navy attacks in Solomons and Aleutians. British arrest Gandhi and other Congress Party leaders. Germans continue to advance in Russia. Six Nazi saboteurs executed in Washington. O.P.A. opens drive to punish price violators.

Up at 7:00. Left Land with Mother and B., and spent first part of morning in basement—shoveling coal to one end of the bin in order to make room for more. (B. has built a bin large enough to hold about three tons of coal—an emergency reserve in case they cannot get sufficient oil for the furnace this winter.) Rest of morning spent cleaning, oiling, and putting away some of Grandfather's old tools, and trimming trees and bushes to let more sunlight into the yard and dining-room windows. Anne, the children, and I arrived home in Bloomfield Hills shortly after 6:00: it is about an even hour's drive.

Monday, August 10

Battle continues in Solomon Islands. Heavy naval losses rumored on both sides. Rioting reported in India. Germans claim capture of Maikop. Growing pressure for second front in United States.

Anne had a restless and painful night; very little sleep. The baby is due almost any time now, but Anne thinks not for another week or ten days.

Phoned Sorensen to get his O.K. on assigning man to help Major Rogers with his B-24 nose-turret mock-up. It is exactly the type of thing Sorensen likes—the short-circuiting of red tape, engineering, and sequence of authority. "Give 'em all the help they want," he said. "Those boys know how to get things done." (And in this instance I think he is right.) I told Sorensen I had already cleared the project unofficially with Colonel McDuffee and Major Saunders. Sorensen said, "To hell with Army authorization! Go ahead anyway."

Lunch with Colonel Acheson, Lieutenant Colonel Mussett, Major Rogers, and Major Unruh. Completed preliminary details in regard to turret mock-up. DeGroat came up to join our conference after lunch. We arranged for the mock-up to be removed from the squadron's quarters in the flight department and set up in the developmental engineering department in the factory building. Left Willow Run at 4:15 and boarded the 5:45 B. & O. Ambassador for Washington.

Tuesday, August 11

United States troops land in Solomons. Rioting increases in India; deaths reported in several areas. Russians destroying Maikop oil fields. Germans report capture of town 150 miles southeast of Maikop. London reports 200-plane raid on Osnabrück.

Taxi to Munitions Building. Spent twenty minutes with General Arnold discussing Ford production (especially cylinder-head situation), defects of the B-24, lack of armament, etc. Arnold says the combat squadrons greatly prefer the B-17 (Boeing four-engine bomber), because "when we send the 17's out on a mission, most of them return. But when we send the 24's out, a good many of them don't." Arnold says the B-17's "can take terrific punishment," and often land "full of bullet holes"—members of crew dead, wounded, etc., but still they get back. He says the Japanese Zeros are not well armored, but that they close in regardless of losses. He says a good burst from a pair of .50-cal. guns will knock a Zero to pieces and that we are shooting down a large number of them. General Wood is in the city and stopped for a half hour's visit. Boarded the 2:10 train for New York.

Wednesday, August 12

Fighting in Solomons continues. Germans continue advance in Caucasus. Troops used to suppress rioting in Bombay and New Delhi. Laval announces German plan to exchange prisoners for French war workers. United States Navy attacks in Aleutians, bombards Kiska. "Isolationists" lead in New York primaries.

Off train at 7:20. Walked to Engineers Club. New York seems much quieter. There are fewer cars on the streets, the red and green lights are blocked out to small crosses, the store windows are filled with cheaper and less well-displayed articles, and people walking give the impression of more seriousness. There is a definite atmosphere of war, although not the feeling of bombs falling in the streets tomorrow that existed in London at the time of the Munich crisis. Here there is no mass issuing of gas masks or digging of trenches in the squares and parks. Took a room for the day at the Engineers Club. Breakfast at club. *Then*—a phone call from Anne in Bloomfield Hills. She has packed her suitcase and is leaving for the hospital at once! Canceled all appointments and plans and by good fortune obtained a reservation on the 1:00 P.M. American Airlines plane to Detroit. Landed Detroit 4:55 Eastern War Time. William met me at the airport with the Mercury, and I drove directly to the Henry Ford Hospital. Found Anne resting comfortably in Room 108.

Arrived home in time to see Anne, Jr., and Land for ten minutes before supper. Land is very anxious to hear about his mother and is impatient for his new baby (brother? sister?) to be born. Anne stared at me as though I had been gone for a month and refused to say hello until instructed to by Land!

Thursday, August 13

United States Marines are holding positions on three "key" Solomon Islands. London India Office reports rioting "well in hand." Conflicting reports from Germany and Russia. Berlin claims capture of more than 1,000,000 Russian prisoners since start of offensive last spring. R.A.F. raids Mainz, Koblenz, Havre, and other continental objectives. British Admiralty confirms sinking of aircraft carrier Eagle *in Mediterranean. Grenades dropped into group of German aviators at Bouin Stadium, Paris, kill twenty-two, injure eighteen.*

The phone rang at 3:00. I had left the door open so that I could hear it. A doctor's voice from the Henry Ford Hospital: "Your wife asked me to phone to say she has been in labor for about an hour." Up and dressed quickly. Why did they wait an hour before calling? I told them Anne's last two babies had been born quickly!

I put the little wooden madonna and the glasses case in my brief bag and left in the Mercury for the hospital at 3:20. The madonna and the glasses case have taken part in the birth of Land and Anne, Jr., and I know they will help again this time—the madonna, a beautifully carved one, on the table beside the hospital bed, and the glasses case in Anne's hand. (It is oval-shaped and just large enough for her to grip tightly when she is in pain.) Arrived at the hospital at 3:50. Anne was already in the operating room. (They may have called me an hour late, but I find they are taking no chances on getting caught themselves!) Dr. Pratt came up to meet me, and I went down to the operating room with him. Put on cap and gown and extra-thick mask, as I have a cold and didn't want to take any chance of giving it to Anne.

Anne's pains were fairly strong and frequent when I first saw her. I told the doctors I thought the baby would be born in not less than thirty minutes and not over two hours. Anne had a postal-card photograph of a deer's head propped up on the table beside her—a beautifully fashioned head with mystical shell eyes inserted in the carved wood—discovered in Florida by some archaeologist and representing an artistry I did not know the American Indian had attained. It represented pain, acceptance,

695

understanding, and much else that helped Anne to pass through the long minutes of waiting.

She always had something of the kind around her. It may be a seashell, a feather, a painting, or just a post-card photograph of a centuries-old sculptured head of a deer. The intrinsic value of the object itself is unimportant, but it always holds something that is beyond life and beyond this world in a sense, just as Anne holds that same element herself. She uses it as a bridge, and on it crosses into a world beyond our own—a world to which she belongs more than anyone I have ever known. Anne always seems to me to stand on life and, at the same time, touch something beyond it. Yet her ability to touch beyond does not cause her to relinquish life any more than her ability to live restricts the unlimited travels of her spirit. She uses life to strengthen spirit and spirit to strengthen life. I placed the oval glasses case in her hand, which closed firmly around it.

Dr. Pratt was greatly interested in the deer's head and talked to me about it, saying he had never seen a woman bear the pains of childbirth as Anne was doing, and speculating on the psychological effect of the deer's head at which she was looking. I wanted to tell him that the scientifically logical word "psychology" was inadequate to describe what the deer's head did for Anne and that elements were at play far deeper than those of which he was then thinking. He had the responsibility for the physical birth of a child in accordance with the best practices of modern medicine. Anne had the physical birth to pass through; but in addition to that, something far greater, something beyond the science of psychology, something he vaguely recognized but did not understand, something I can only vaguely indicate with the words I write in this description. Anne refused to take any anesthetic until the actual birth of the baby, and then she was under its full influence only for a few minutes.

Dr. Pratt showed himself to be a highly skillful obstetrician, with an extremely efficient staff. He uses his hands with great dexterity and creates confidence in anyone who watches him work.

The baby was born at 5:12 A.M.—boy, strong and sound—seven and a half pounds.[48] It was the least difficult time Anne has had with any of her children. (Not that childbirth is ever easy.) I stayed with her until her bed was wheeled back into her room and she was ready to sleep. Then returned to Bloomfield Hills, arriving shortly after 6:00. Bed for an hour; then phoned Mother and Mrs. Morrow. Breakfast, including

48. The boy was named Scott.

coffee for my cold. (Find that coffee, if you do not use it regularly, acts somewhat as aspirin does for a cold.) I drove to Willow Run with the radio car.

Half hour in office on mail and routine. Then to development engineering department to see what progress had been made on the B-24 nose-turret mock-up. When I arrived, I found one of the engineers in the nose-gun mock-up, puttering around in an attempt to find some way of following out the last order that has come through, demanding the installation of three .50-cal. pivot guns in the nose. (A "four-star general" is reported to have given the order, so—good or bad—it must be carried out.) He was terribly discouraged when I talked to him; said the two side guns would spoil the effectiveness of the nose-gun installation we have about completed and so crowd the bomber's compartment that it would interfere with bombing while the guns themselves would get so much in each other's way they would be practically useless. Just one more impractical and little-thought-about idea, he felt, and more valuable time lost.

Phone call from Bennett. He told me he and Mr. (Henry) Ford are greatly worried about Edsel, who has been ill again. Bennett informed me, in confidence, that Edsel Ford has cancer of the stomach and that the doctors have given him only a year or two to live! Edsel's son, Henry, is in the Navy, and Benson is the only grandson available "to take over." Benson wants to enlist in the Air Corps—is chafing more and more at his civilian status.

Rest of afternoon on routine and a conference with DeGroat in regard to Hunsaker's offer to send an NACA research engineer to Willow Run to help us improve the cowling design for B-24 engines. (They are running hot at altitude.) We decided that Willow Run is too short of engineers to take on a major redesign project at present and that it would be best to advise Hunsaker to work with the Consolidated Company in San Diego in this respect. They have a large engineering organization and are in a far better position to carry on research and improvement projects than the Ford Company is at present. I hate to take this stand, but we are even now desperately short of engineers and literally have none to spare for anything new. After all, the original agreement between Ford and Consolidated called for Consolidated to take care of all redesign on the B-24 so Ford could concentrate on mass production. Before leaving my office, DeGroat told me of his last conference with Sorensen, in which the method of weighing the B-24's came up. Sorensen said that the system of floor scales being installed at Willow Run was no good and that to be weighed properly an airplane should be suspended from the ceiling!

To Henry Ford Hospital for half an hour with Anne. She is recovering rapidly and very happy.

Friday, August 14

Marines advance in Solomons. United States Army fliers continue raids on Japanese bases in China. Germans within 140 miles of Grozny oil fields in Caucasus. Germans claim to be less than 200 miles from Astrakhan, and the high command claims sinking or damage of twenty warships and merchantmen, including aircraft carriers Wasp *and* Furious *from a convoy in western Mediterranean. British call claim "inaccurate." American Army bombers hit three Italian cruisers in eastern Mediterranean. United States and R.A.F. bombers continue raids on continental objectives. Allied shipping losses reported lower for July and U-boat sinkings higher.*

Up at 6:15. Drove to New York Central Station to meet Miss [Amy] Waddington, whom I am bringing through from New York to take care of Anne and the baby for the next few weeks. She was so competent and helpful when Anne, Jr., was born that we are anxious to have her again for this baby. William took her to the Henry Ford Hospital, and I drove to Willow Run.

Monday, August 17

Moscow acknowledges loss of Maikop and new withdrawals in Caucasus. New hostages reported seized by Germans in Holland. Mohammed Ali Jinnah warns Britain against concessions to All-India Congress. United States planes participate in raids over France.

Conference with Colonel Saunders in regard to the recent change in production plans. We will now assemble the first fifteen B-24's at Willow Run instead of sending part of them in "knock-down" condition to Fort Worth and Tulsa. The Army is to bring in a number of aviation experts as inspectors.

Conference with Major Unruh in regard to the nose turret and about the B-24 which crashed Friday night near Battle Creek with the loss of the entire crew of nine men. I found the pilot had been out of flying school for only a few months and had less than 500 hours' total flying time; yet he was captain of a four-engine bomber and sent out through a stormy night to carry on a practice mission! What possible good can come from pushing men so fast? First, this B-24 squadron is organized of young and inexperienced officers; then it is sent for training to a field with the concrete runways uncompleted; then it is ordered to be ready for the combat zone "in one month," untrained, unequipped, and without having had a single round of .50-cal. ammunition which which to train its gunners.

Wrote telegrams to Wright Field for Sorensen to sign, requesting a B-34 (Lockheed Ventura) and a P-47 (Republic Thunderbolt) for use in our high-altitude ignition test program.

Interviewed, at Sorensen's request, a young engineer from Texas. He has a small model of a flying wing he wants to build and says that back in Texas he has a twenty-four-foot flying model nearly completed—showed me photographs of it; workmanship seemed good. He works for Pan American Airways at Brownsville. I size him up as energetic and intelligent, but he has no engineering training or experience except what he has been able to get from studying after work hours in Brownsville. He is obviously impetuous. He is the type of fellow I would have no hesitation in taking into an organization, but to back him in a flying-wing project that would probably involve the best part of $1,000,000 for development is another story.

Sorensen simply received a telegram from an unknown man in Texas several weeks ago, saying that the sender had a flying-wing project he wanted to show the Ford Motor Company. Sorensen wired back telling him to come along and show it! (The Ford Company gets thousands of such telegrams each year, has a department to answer them; but this particular one, for some reason, happened to get through to Sorensen.) There was nothing new or unusual about the model; but Sorensen was quite enthusiastic about it—possibly because [the engineer] made the ridiculous claim that if the Ford Company would back him, he could have a one-hundred-foot-span flying wing in the air in three months!

I phoned Sorensen after the conference and told him I thought [the young engineer] a good man but without the experience necessary to carry through a project of the size he had in mind. Sorensen took rather the same attitude that he takes with DeGroat, i.e., that someone is always blocking his ideas, but that somehow he will force them through in spite of hell and high water.

Tuesday, August 18

Navy announces United States position in Solomons now "well established." Berlin claims occupation of entire Don bend. United States and R.A.F. planes continue raids on Continent. Heavy Allied shipping losses continue. United States warned of meatless days and food rationing this winter.

Sorensen wants to make a trip to Europe and wants me to go with him! England, Africa, Russia, etc. I told him I thought it would be politically inadvisable for me to go. Sorensen thinks the war will be over and that we will win within a year.

Started to drive to the Rouge for a conference with Sorensen in regard to a "flying-wing" transport plane. Radio call from Bennett—the Governor of Michigan was en route to Willow Run, and Bennett wanted me to return to meet him and the party he was bringing. I had not yet passed the gate so returned to Flight and phoned Sorensen, who insisted that the conference was more important! Since I had made the arrangement with Sorensen first, I decided to leave for the Rouge and left word for Bennett that I would return as soon as possible.

I looked over [the flying-wing] model again. It was fairly well constructed but rather roughly finished. [The young engineer] told us he had graduated from Chanute Field about 1935 and had studied engineering in his spare hours since that time. He is now working as head of the structures department of Pan American Airways at Brownsville for a little over $1.00 per hour. Sorensen first asked him a number of direct questions and then offered him $100.00 per week and a "couple of draftsmen" to help him! He of course accepted.

Back to Willow Run. Met the Governor and his party at the final assembly line; about fifty men in all—state officials, Army officers, etc.

To Henry Ford Hospital at 6:00 for an hour with Anne. She and the baby are in excellent condition—fine report from the doctors on the baby's physical examination.

Sunday, August 23

Brazil declares war on Axis. United States submarines active against Jap shipping. Renewed rioting in India. Donald Nelson reports United States war production up sixteen per cent in July but still behind goal.

Phoned Anne at 8:15. She has had a bad night—cramps—possible appendix. I phoned the doctor; he felt she was much better and that danger of appendicitis was past. To the hospital to see Anne at 4:15. She is feeling much better, but still weak after an exceptionally painful night. Anne makes so little fuss when she is in pain that the doctors don't realize how bad it is at first. They waited too long before giving her anything to counteract the pain; then, when her growing weakness showed them how bad it really was, they decided she might be in the danger stage of appendicitis and hastened to take blood counts, temperature, etc.

Monday, August 24

Up at 6:30. Cooked breakfast, and arrived at Willow Run at 8:45. Trip to developmental engineering to inspect progress of nose-gun turret. Back to office for various conferences. Half hour at flight department. Then to Dearborn Inn for haircut. The barber talked incessantly about the war. Said he thought it would be over by next summer and that "some people think it will be over by January. Boy! When we really start dropping pineapples on those German cities, they won't last long!"

To Henry Ford Hospital for lunch with Dr. [Roy P.] McClure. Stopped to see Anne for ten minutes en route to his office. Dr. Johnson was in her room when I arrived. Dr. McClure's office is on the fourth floor of the hospital. During lunch we talked of Carrel and Europe and the war and experimental work of various kinds. It was like being back at the Rockefeller Institute for a day. Then he took me through the hospital —laboratories, nurses' home, operating rooms, wards, etc. The war is taking many of their best men, Dr. McClure told me. Rest of afternoon with Anne. She is feeling quite well again. Baby in to nurse at 6:00— healthy and active.

Wednesday, August 26

Japan launches counteroffensive in Solomons. Navy Department claims hits on many Japanese warships. Twenty-one enemy aircraft shot down during attacks on American positions on Guadalcanal Island. Chinese armies claim new advances. R.A.F. planes bomb Frankfurt and Wiesbaden. Duke of Kent killed in air crash. London reports new Gestapo executions on Continent. Roosevelt discusses plan to stabilize wages and farm prices.

Arrived Willow Run at 8:30. To motor building at the Rouge for a 10:00 appointment with Sorensen and [the flying-wing engineer]. Sorensen has given the latter a corner in Van Ranst's office, in which a drafting board has been screened off, and Van Ranst has loaned him a set of drawing tools, as he had none of his own. I told Sorensen (when he inquired what the first step should be) that I would advise making a wind-tunnel model of the flying wing and having it tested out in the University of Michigan tunnel. Sorensen agreed to this, and I got [the engineer] in touch with McCarroll (Ford executive), who is a University of Michigan engineering graduate and who will arrange for the wind-tunnel tests.

Thursday, August 27

Russians announce offensive northwest of Moscow; claim 45,000 Germans killed in fifteen days. Germans continue advance in Caucasus and on Stalingrad. Cairo announces rout of Italian division on Egyptian front. United States Navy announces sinking and damage of more Japanese warships and merchantmen and more planes shot down. Vichy orders roundup of all Jews who have entered France since 1936.

To Henry Ford Hospital at 6:00 for half an hour with Anne. I am coming to take her home in the morning. Then to 410 University Place for an 8:00 appointment with Dr. Barker, who has been taking care of Mother —as far as she will let anybody take care of her. Dr. Barker feels as definitely as I do that Mother must not try to teach school again this winter and that it is important for us to reduce all surrounding tension for her. He believes that the trembling of her hand can be reduced in this way. Says Mother's trouble is more common with men than with women and that it is closely related to nervous tension. He is on the whole encouraging, although he regards a complete cure as doubtful.

Mother is an extremely difficult problem for any doctor, as she has definite ideas of her own as to what she should do, even in respect to taking medicine, and not too much confidence in a doctor's advice. Mother's independence of medical advice often worries me, and yet I respect her for that very independence.

Dr. Barker is greatly interested in archaeology and has taken part in expeditions in the southwestern states, central America, and many other places. He knows most of the Carnegie archaeologists, has been in the De Chelly del Muerto, in many of the Mayan sites, etc. Our trails have crossed more than once in these places but at different times. He showed me his archaeological library and a number of the photographs he has taken on his trips.

Friday, August 28

Japanese Navy retires in Solomons area. Chinese advances continue. Russians claim success in counteroffensive in north but continue retreat in Caucasus. United States and R.A.F. planes raid Continent. London reports fresh uprisings in occupied areas on Continent.

Land and I drove to the hospital to get Anne, the baby, and Miss Waddington. Back home at 12:00. First part of afternoon on routine. Then to Ford airport to give Bennett an hour's instruction in Ray Dahlinger's[49] Fairchild. It is equipped with "stick" control, and Bennett flies it better than the Stinson type, which is equipped with "wheel." The Fairchild stalls and drops a wing somewhat more easily than the Stinson, but is on the whole a much better plane.

Monday, August 31

Japanese forces defeated at Milne Bay in New Guinea. Chungking claims Chinese troops fighting in outskirts of Nanchang. Moscow claims Soviet bombers start fires in Berlin. Dim-out regulations to be enforced in New York City.

49. Ray Dahlinger had charge of a variety of projects for Henry Ford, including the management of the Ford farms.

Arrived at Willow Run at 8:45. Morning on routine. Lunch at flight department with Gerding,[50] Heffley, and Dr. Clark. Trip to developmental engineering department with Colonel Rogers and other officers. Then through the factory with Mr. Gardner. The workmanship is still poor, and inexperience shows everywhere. But there is a gradual improvement, and bombers are beginning to flow up the final assembly line. Conference with Major Kirby at 4:30. He has the impression that aviation people are not very welcome here. Unfortunately, he is right.

To Flight for half an hour in the bomber (O-1) with Gerding as co-pilot—five landings. I am beginning to feel at home in the plane, although I will never grow to like the multiengine ships as well as the smaller ones.

Tuesday, September 1

Rommel's forces attack in Egypt.

Hour in bomber (O-1) with Gerding as co-pilot. I tried three engine take-offs with first the right and then the left outboard engines cut. On one of the take-offs, after we were a hundred feet or so off the runway, I shifted both feet to the left rudder, as the pressure required to hold the ship straight was very great and my leg was getting tired. A few seconds after taking this position, I shifted my heel slightly and without realizing what I did kicked over the rudder-adjustment lever. The rudder shot forward with a bang, and the ship veered sharply to the right. I thought something had gone wrong with the controls and attempted to hold the ship straight with the throttles until we gained enough altitude to look around in reasonable safety to see what had happened. There were a few tense seconds, both for me and for Gerding. Then, [William] Hadden, who was riding as flight engineer and who had been standing on the walk between us, told me what had happened. He had seen it at the time I kicked the adjustment lever, but thought I knew what I had done until, as he said, "I saw the worried expression on your face!" It was certainly a great relief when I found that I could control the plane with the engines and a still greater relief when Hadden explained what had happened. We were not over 200 feet at the time, and a B-24 out of control at 200 feet is about the last thing I want to be in. But there is no time for fear of death under such circumstances. Your mind and body are too busy thinking and acting to save the situation you find yourself in.

50. Stanley Gerding, flight superintendent at Willow Run.

Friday, September 4

Japanese land reinforcements in the Solomons. British claim successful counterattack on Egyptian front. German forces advance in Russia. R.A.F. bombs Karlsruhe. United States submarines sink five Japanese ships. Japanese continue to claim high American naval losses.

Arrived Willow Run at 8:45. Mr. Ford opened the door to my office and walked in about 9:30—no advance notice, as usual. Harry Bennett arrived about ten minutes later. Half hour with them discussing the war, labor problems, etc. Then all to airport, Bennett driving. Looked over turntable for swinging B-24 compasses. Then picked up Sorensen, and the four of us drove around the area east of Willow Run airport to select a location for a permanent Army base and consider the possibility of lengthening the runways. Then, Bennett still driving, we went on to the engineering laboratory at Dearborn.

Sorensen brought up the question of our production schedule and the quality of workmanship at Willow Run—said we were ahead of schedule and that our workmanship was just as good as that of other companies. He tried to get me to agree with him and put me in a corner where I had to say bluntly that we were *not* making schedule and that the workmanship on the first bombers that went through Willow Run was the worst I had ever seen. Sorensen is not used to having anyone oppose him, and I have seen him bluff his way through a difficult situation time and time again. He tries to get a man to agree with him either out of fear or courtesy, and then constantly reminds him of the fact that he once agreed. The only way to handle Sorensen is to say exactly what you believe when he asks a question, and I did. Henry Ford listened quietly and apparently enjoyed the situation very much! We went into the electrical department to see the reversible spark ignition developed by Emil Zoerlin.[51]

Saturday, September 5

Russians claim Stalingrad drive checked. Germans claim they have reached city's suburbs. British claim advance in Egyptian battle. Budapest bombed. United States planes bomb Japanese bases in China. Germans announce retaliation executions in Czechoslovakia. United States

51. Ford electrical engineer.

State Department protests deportation of Jews from unoccupied France.
United States government to regulate wholesale and retail inventories.
War Manpower Commission takes steps to increase number of women
in industry.

Arrived at Willow Run at 9:15. Note on my desk to call Heffley at the flight department. He told me that the CAA inspector was coming over to give one of the Ford pilots (Hurlburt)[52] his rating test on the B-24 and asked if I would like to take mine at the same time. I had not expected to take my rating test so soon. I have not been flying multiengine ships for a number of years and had planned on studying the B-24 in much more detail and putting in several more hours in the air before taking the rating test. When I last flew multiengine equipment, there were no ratings for different horsepowers as there are today. If a man held a "C" license, he could fly anything he desired, regardless of horsepower or the number of engines it carried.

I decided to take the test, as long as the inspector was coming anyway. It turned out to be easy, and I passed without difficulty. We were up an hour and forty minutes in all. Hurlburt took the test first (I got him to do this so I could watch the procedure he followed; he has been studying for the test for months), and I took mine second.

In a sense, I am learning to fly all over again here at Willow Run. The procedures used are very different from those I have used in the past, in that they are based largely upon radio control and precisely laid-down rules and regulations that depend on constant contact with the ground and knowledge of what lies beneath, behind, and ahead, regardless of whether the ground is covered with fog or not. Here, one's safety depends upon ground facilities.

In most of the flying I have done, safety depended upon *independence* of ground facilities. To have counted on any assistance from the ground after I once started on a flight would sooner or later have been fatal for me. During my early flights radio was so unreliable that I did not carry it at all; and during the later ones I used it as an added safety and convenience but never counted on it greatly in planning my flights.

Once, off the Japanese island of Ketoi, radio saved our plane when Anne brought the *Shinshiru Maru* to our assistance after we had been forced down in open ocean by fog. Many times her radio contacts permitted us to start or complete a flight we would not otherwise have

52. Theodore Hurlburt, senior pilot at Ford.

started or from which we would have turned back. But in no instance was our flight begun unless we felt we could complete it or land en route or return safely, even if our radio failed entirely. Radios, airways procedure, clearances, meteorological reports, all such matters were of quite secondary importance to us in comparison to the position they hold in the flying that is being carried on in the United States today.

Here, and now, a flight is based primarily on radio and telephonic contact between plane and ground. Elaborate and quite accurate weather data are gathered before a flight is begun. Changes in weather are transmitted to the pilot in the air. He is dependent on radio beams and signals and instruments which permit him to descend to a landing through layers of cloud and fog. And since there are usually many planes flying back and forth over his route, he must follow the rules of airways procedure with extreme precision to avoid collision. Most of this is new to me and involves a technique so different that, as I say, it is like learning to fly all over again.

Flying was at first more an art than a science. Now it is more a science than an art. It has passed from the era of the pioneer to the era of the routine operator, from the time when a "good pilot" forgot his instruments in an emergency to the time when a "good pilot" turns to his instruments in an emergency.

Anne and I carried radio on our flights largely as a safeguard *in case something went wrong*. Radio is carried in planes today almost entirely *to keep anything from going wrong*. Anne's radio contacts brought our plane into Point Barrow when we might otherwise have turned back or landed in one of the desolate north Alaskan lakes; they warned us of fog ahead in the Chishimas; they guided us to Lauge Koch's[53] base on the east coast of Greenland; they found the *Westphalen*[54] and told us of clear weather on the Brazilian coast when we crossed the South Atlantic; they were of inestimable value on both our flights to the Orient and our flight around the North Atlantic; but even though they saved our plane at least once and permitted us to fly when we would otherwise have been on the ground, we considered them an added safeguard rather than a basic necessity.

53. Danish geologist and explorer engaged in scientific and cartographic activities in Greenland. During his expedition to North Greenland from 1920 to 1923 he completed the mapping of the coast of Greenland and did extensive geological surveys of North Greenland.

54. A ship used by the Germans in connection with their flying-boat service between Africa and South America.

I had planned on learning the new techniques in detail before taking my rating test in the B-24, for while I had no concern about my ability to fly the ship, I was by no means certain that I could fly the ship according to the ideas of the inspector whose entire life is wound around regulations and conventional airways procedure.

Sunday, September 6

Russians again claim Stalingrad drive checked. Germans say their forces have crossed the Kerch Strait. Heavy air raids on Havre, Bremen, and other objectives. Russian planes raid Vienna, Breslau, and Koenigsberg. British claim Rommel slowly retiring in Egypt. London reports roundup of Jews in France for deportation to Eastern Europe and forced labor of Czechs and Serbs in Norway.

Left with Anne, Jr., Jon, and Land at 9:30 for 508 Lakepointe Road. Morning with Mother, B., and the children in the garden. It is the first time I have had all three children at Mother's home together. Anne was considerate to let us go, as I know she was lonely; but she encouraged the visit, and it means so much to Mother that I felt justified in going. With the war and internal conditions that exist today and with Mother's age and the uncertainty of life, I do not know how many more such visits there can be. I sometimes feel that they are like an Indian summer, of which I do not want to miss a day.

Monday, September 7

Germans claim capture of Novorossisk on Black Sea. Russians claim successes north of Stalingrad. United States bombers raid Crete.

Cooked breakfast and arrived at Willow Run at 8:30. To flight department with intention of spending some time "under the hood" in one of the Stinsons, but the ceiling and visibility were too low (too much danger of striking other planes in this crowded area).

The P-47 has arrived! It was standing in the hangar as I passed through on my way to operations—a fast, powerful-looking plane. I have not flown pursuit since the spring of 1940 and can hardly wait to get into it. Spent rest of morning studying the P-47 (Republic Thunderbolt) and operating data. It has a ceiling of over 40,000 feet and a speed of more than 400 miles an hour—almost an even hundred miles an hour faster than the P-36 I was flying in 1939.

Lunch with Henning and Major (now Lieutenant Colonel) Rogers in the flight restaurant. Rogers says his B-24 squadron is under orders to leave for the Eastern war area as soon as the weather clears. They will, of course, fly across the Pacific to the combat zone.

Spent the afternoon on routine and studying the T.O.'s [technical orders] for the P-47. Home at 6:00. Read to Anne, Jr., for twenty minutes—or, rather, let her turn the pages of a child's picture book and point to the object she knew. Spent half an hour pulling wood splinters out of Land's feet. (He tried to slide down a toboggan barefoot!)

Wednesday, September 9

Churchill promises aid to Russia. Says British lost 80,000 men in this year's African campaign. Rommel withdraws farther in Egypt. United States bombers raid Crete. R.A.F. raids Havre and Cherbourg. German Air Force raids English "southwest coastal town." Japanese forces drive on mountain passes en route to Port Moresby. Henderson warns against inflation.

Arrived Willow Run at 8:45. Stopped at flight department to check weather: low overcast, breaking. The B-24 squadron leaves for the Pacific today.

Henry Ford drove into the administration building as I arrived. Hour or so on routine. Then radio call from Bennett asking me to meet him at the Rouge administration building. Bennett wanted to talk to me about Ford's desire to improve the armor-plate installation in the B-24. It is obviously inadequate, and pilots returning from the combat zones report the situation as serious. (General Arnold: "When we send the B-17's out on a mission, they come back. When we send the B-24's out, a lot of them don't.") Ford wants to set up an experimental department on the Ford airport at Dearborn, bring an entire B-24 fuselage there from Willow Run, and turn the problem of armor plate over to me.

I told Bennett that if we were to put adequate armor plate on the B-24, the first thing we would need would be close Army co-operation, that we would have to have data on where enemy bullets were hitting, what their penetrating power was, how much weight we could devote to armor

plate, etc., etc.—data that only the Army could furnish. One of the difficulties in working with the Ford organization is that once they get an
idea, they want to start in right now and get action tomorrow, if not
today. Their policy is to *act* first and *plan* afterward, usually overlooking
completely essential details. Result: a tremendous increase of cost and
effort unnecessarily.

"Don't forget," Sorensen once told me, "when you want to do something, the most important thing is to get it started. And don't let the
engineers keep it on the drafting board; they'll keep on drawing lines as
long as you'll let 'em." My own policy has been almost the direct opposite of this. I believe that "when you want to do something, the most
important thing is to get it started," but I believe the best start lies in
careful planning and that no time is saved by rushing a project off the
drafting board too quickly. The result of the Ford-Sorensen policy is that
the lower-ranking officers of the company have learned that the best way
to keep their jobs and stay out of trouble is to "start" any project suggested by Ford or Sorensen right now and show a large amount of action,
regardless of whether it has direction behind it or not.

For instance, if Henry Ford wants armor plate on the B-24, the Ford
organization will rush about hanging armor plate all over it, regardless of
how much weight is added, or whether it is in the right place or of the
proper gauge. Their objective will be to show Mr. Ford armor plate on
the B-24 this afternoon, if possible, and if it can't be done this afternoon,
tomorrow. Then, after much unplanned effort has been expended, and as
they slowly, through trial, error, mistakes, and "lucky breaks" begin to
learn more about what they're doing, their effort begins to take on a
more intelligent form; and if, after their objective is reached, they are
able to spread the excessively high developmental cost over the sale of a
sufficient number of units, as the Ford Company is usually able to do,
the project is considered a great success and an example of "Ford
methods."

But for every project that reaches "successful completion" in this
manner, several are dropped (like Sorensen's idea of putting two B-24's
together to make a large cargo-transport biplane). In these cases, after
the flourishing start is made, practical problems present themselves
which are so obviously difficult, if not impossible of solution, that everyone concerned realizes the impracticability of continuing. This is always
realized first by the men who are actually working on the project. Then,
if they are old-time and experienced Ford employees, they find ways of

letting "the boss" see that the project he ordered carried on is better dropped than continued.

Mr. Ford is much more reasonable than Mr. Sorensen in this respect, although not easily turned aside from any idea he starts developing. When Sorensen realizes that one of his pet projects is impractical, admission of that fact is the last thing in his mind. It is always: "Those fellows don't know how to go about it." Then he pays less and less attention to that particular project (on which he concentrated his attention in the early stages) until he overlooks and eventually forgets it entirely. The old Ford men know this sequence well, help it along, find excuses for "the boss," which they finally half believe themselves, and at last go on their way as before it all started, well satisfied to be still holding their jobs and to have kept out of serious trouble. I have no intention of starting a project in this fashion, or of starting it at all without a careful study.

Harry Bennett and I drove to Ford airport to look over the various hangars and buildings in which this work could be carried on and in which a B-24 fuselage could be placed. While we were there, we inspected the glider the Ford Company is building for the Army. It is nearly completed and will be ready for test in a few days. Then to Willow Run. The low overcast had broken enough to take up the P-47, and I took off on a thirty-five-minute flight. It has a good take-off and excellent control, and the cockpit is, on the whole, well arranged, but it is very blind in taxiing, and I feel there is not enough visibility in the air. Also, you don't see the runway ahead when you come in for a landing unless you sideslip the plane. Made only one flight, as the tail-wheel tire was in poor condition and had a long tear in its side which had materially increased in length when I got out to look at it.

Thursday, September 10

United States transport Wakefield (*former liner* Manhattan) *burned at sea while returning from Europe. Australian troops holding Japanese in New Guinea. Russian bombers raid Budapest.*

Arrived at Willow Run at 10:00. Conference with Bennett. Henry Ford came in a few minutes after we started talking. We phoned for Sorensen and Henning, and all spent some time discussing armor plate for the B-24. After the conference was over, and Ford and Sorensen had left, Bennett, Henning, and I discussed my proposal to take the Willow Run pilots off time clocks. I have for a long time felt that time-clock punching for pilots was a mistake and bad for morale. It is probably more distasteful to them than anything else they are called upon to do here, and it is not required by other bomber manufacturers such as Consolidated or Lockheed. Also, the fact that their hours are irregular and that they are frequently away on extended flights makes the punching of a time clock seem to them absurd and annoying. We all agreed that time-clock punching for pilots should be discontinued and left the exact date and incidental arrangements in Henning's hands.

Saunders, Henning, Gerding, Heffley, and I flew over to Wayne County airport in the afternoon to look over the armor plate and gun installations in a new B-17F that has just arrived from Seattle.

Left for home at 5:30. Spent quarter of an hour reading the "paddle book" to Anne, Jr. The reading consists of finding a canoe which is somewhere on almost every picture page, sometimes very large, sometimes very small. As soon as I arrive home, Anne waits patiently, "paddle book" under her arm, until I sit down to read to her. If I seem to take *too* long, she will come up and say, "Book? Book?" After we start, Land usually comes out and takes part in the search; but we have an agreement that Anne gets first chance to find the canoe. Finally, Jon comes and stands behind and watches—a little too old to take part; a little too young to stay away.

Friday, September 11

Russians retreat in Stalingrad area. British forces attack Madagascar. Churchill bars compromise in India.

Henry Ford walked into my office about 10:00—alone. Ford talked about the war and the Roosevelt Administration. "People like that always get what's coming to them"; about food and knowing how to eat (he is very particular about his diet and has definite ideas about what foods are good for you and what are not); about production at Willow Run; about putting armor plate in the bomber; about his feeling that the Du Ponts are responsible for most of the country's troubles, and the control they have on politics; about his belief in "a Federation of Man and Parliament of the World—it was Tennyson said that, you know."

Saturday, September 12

Arrived Willow Run 8:45. Stopped at flight department. Then half hour in office on routine. Back to flight department to take the P-47 up for an hour and a quarter. Spent the last half hour with a number of other planes from Willow Run and Wayne County airport, circling over Willow Run to "greet" Assistant Secretary Patterson.[55] Lunch with Patterson party. (Governor Wagoner[56] had invited me to meet the party in the morning and attend the dedication of the Willow Run roadways and the speeches involved, but I found it possible to compromise by attending only the lunch.) Hour in office on routine. Then conference with Dr. Clark in regard to pilot problems, pay, etc. We also discussed oxygen technique in relation to high-altitude flying.

Monday, September 14

To Willow Run (without breakfast!) for basal metabolism test and pilot's physical examination (Dr. Clark, flight surgeon). Phone call from Norman Smith when about two-thirds finished. Says Mr. Henry Ford is arriving at Willow Run about 10:30 and wants to see me. Breakfast with Dr. Clark in Flight restaurant. Then to Bennett's office for conference with Henry Ford, Bennett, Saunders, and two Secret Service men. President Roosevelt is to visit Willow Run on Friday, and no advance announcement of the visit is to be made!

Senator and Mrs. Nye came out for lunch. They had phoned from Detroit and wanted to see Willow Run. Took them through the factory afterward. Finished the last installment of my physical examination later in the afternoon.

Tuesday, September 15

Russians holding at Stalingrad. Germans advance in Caucasus. R.A.F. raids Bremen. Soviet planes raid Rumanian oil fields, Ploesti, Bucharest, and Koenigsberg. Heavy Allied shipping losses continue. (Germans

55. Robert P. Patterson, Undersecretary of War, 1940–45; Secretary of War, 1945–47.
56. Murray D. van Wagoner, Governor of Michigan, 1941–42.

claim 122,000 tons of merchant shipping, two destroyers, and one corvette from a single Allied convoy.) United States federal workers put on draft basis.

Conference at 8:00 with Henning, Dr. Clark, and several of the Willow Run pilots—Gerding, Johnson, Loomis and others—in regard to the altitude test program we are laying out for the P-47. The attitude toward doing this type of flying was varied. Some of the pilots were eager to take it on. Some were skeptical about the practicability of flying at 40,000 feet without pressure suits or cabins. Some were averse to taking any part in high-altitude experiments.

Took the B-24 to Wright Field, leaving Willow Run at 10:00. I went to Wright Field to discuss problems of armor plating the B-24. The chief armament officer is Frank Wolfe, who was a classmate of mine at Brooks and Kelly—now a full colonel. Spent half an hour with Wolfe; then went over to the new armament laboratory for a conference with Captains [Robert G.] Evans and [Thayer E.] Bartlett and a number of other armament officers. In addition to discussing armor plate for the B-24, we looked over a British Lancaster which is on Wright Field and then went to see some armor plate from a shot-down Junkers 88.

Wright Field is in a chaotic state. One gains the impression of immaturity, sloppiness, and indifference, with here and there an efficient officer or department as a sort of an island with waves of disorganization lapping around the shores. There are rooms full of commissioned officers in uniform slouching about in shirt sleeves on desks and chairs, hands full of papers from the piles of papers overflowing the file boxes in front of them. Smoke from cigarettes, cigars, and pipes is everywhere. Young stenographers in bright and varicolored dresses move tiredly about in the narrow spaces between desks and chairs. Now and then a fluttering, cardboard-bound report goes sailing through the air from one stretched-out officer to another, who gathers his feet together long enough to catch it and toss it on top of a pile of similar-looking reports. The corridors are full of people moving back and forth, from generals to messenger girls. At every intersection there is a conspicuous Coca-Cola stand where a bottle, ice cold, comes out in return for a coin placed in the slot.

I spent about an hour in conference with the armament officers. Told them, to start with, that Mr. Ford wanted to improve the armor plate on the B-24 and that the facilities of the Rouge plant and the Ford engineering organization would be available for this purpose. The officers seemed uninterested. They were, of course, courteous, but kept emphasizing their feeling that it would be inadvisable for the Ford Company to do anything about armor plating the B-24 except in the closest co-operation with the Wright Field armament division. I told them that I had come to Wright Field because we desired just the type of co-operation they suggested.

I then asked what they thought we should start on. They had no suggestion to offer except to say again that whatever we did should be "in close co-operation" with the armament division. I asked if they could furnish us any data in regard to the penetrating power of enemy bullets or the direction from which most hits came. They said the data they had was not in a form that would be of value to us. One of the officers said that there were too many different ideas about armor plate anyway. I could see what I have seen so often before at Wright Field and at Army stations—that their primary desire was to be left alone to carry on their own experiments and work out their own solutions, and that outside assistance was really unwanted. I thanked them all, told them to let us know if we could be of any help in the future, and left.

Phoned General [Arthur] Vanaman. He was away on a flight to the East Coast, but I spoke to Mrs. Vanaman, who invited me to stay with them on my next trip to Wright Field. I have purposely kept away from the Vanamans in the past in order to avoid embarrassing them in any way because of the bitter antagonism of the Roosevelt Administration and the political attempts to "smear" even my friends because of the stand I have taken. However, conditions have changed enough now so that a casual visit is not likely to cause trouble for my hosts—especially out here in the Middle West.

Rode back to Willow Run as co-pilot for Gerding in the B-24.

Wednesday, September 16

Japanese renew attack in Solomons and in New Guinea. Russians claim lines holding at Stalingrad. Germans claim to have taken city's main railroad station. R.A.F. raids Wilhelmshaven, Cherbourg, and other points.

Flight in B-17 with Colonel Brandt[57] and Henning. I think I like the flying characteristics better than the B-24, although this may be due to

57. Colonel Carl Brandt, military liaison officer with Consolidated.

the fact that the B-17 has been in service longer and had its details of control, throttle position, instrument location, etc., worked out much more to the pilot's liking than is the case with the present B-24. Burst a brake expander on landing.

Drove Bennett and two Secret Service operators to the Ford airport, where I gave Bennett an hour's instruction in the Fairchild. Bennett had promised to throw the opening ball for a game this afternoon between two Ford teams. When we got to the airport, I found that he intended to drop it from the plane! I flew low over the ball park, parallel to the crowd, and managed to hit the diamond. One of the players caught the ball on the first bounce. Bennett was as pleased as a small boy. I will feel better about it if no complaint arrives from the CAA within the next few days. Dropping baseballs to start games used to be all right in the early days of aviation, but for some years past it has been strictly against regulations.

Thursday, September 17

German armies reach Stalingrad. Navy announces that the carrier Yorktown *was sunk in the Battle of Midway last June.*

Hour on routine. Then to Flight for one hour and forty minutes in the Grumman amphibian, practicing water landings on Belleville Lake, preparatory to taking the water-rating test.

President Roosevelt's bulletproof Lincoln car has arrived at the administration building garage, and everything is being prepared for his visit tomorrow; a roadway is being cleared right through the factory building. The car is to enter at the receiving department, drive in between the close-packed rows of big presses, along the subassembly lines, out through final assembly, and last of all, through the hangars of the flight department where an exhibit of Ford military products is being set up. The visit is supposed to be a secret, but people at Willow Run are already saying that the Ford Company wouldn't go to so much trouble "for anybody but the President."

I am undecided whether to be here or not tomorrow; but between the politics and the journalism that will be involved, my inclination is to find business somewhere else.

Friday, September 18

Met Sorensen, Bennett, and other Ford officers at the flight department to inspect the lineup of Ford military products which are being arranged in a semicircle for the President to drive past—tanks, armored cars, jeeps, engines, etc., etc. Sorensen got me to one side and told me he planned on showing the President a blueprint of the flying wing. "Just to show the President that *we're* thinking of big airplanes, too." (Sorensen was referring to the recent Kaiser publicity.) I advised against showing the blueprints and told Sorensen again that I was afraid [the young engineer] did not have the experience to carry on such a project, and that it would be wise not to say too much about this flying-wing design until we at least saw the results of the wind-tunnel tests. Sorensen took the attitude of being "blocked by everybody" and seemed far from convinced. I could see that he wanted to show Roosevelt *something* in the line of plans for big future aircraft and that my arguments against this particular project were not having much effect. So I suggested that if he mentioned the design at all, he speak of it as *one* of the Ford Company's design projects.

I decided it was best to be away from Willow Run when the Roosevelt party arrived, so left at 2:45 and drove to Bloomfield Hills.

Saturday, September 19

One hundred and sixteen people executed by Germans in Paris.

Drove with Mr. McCarroll to the University of Michigan College of Engineering at Ann Arbor to discuss the flying wing with the men who have been running the wind-tunnel tests. Their conclusion is what I expected: nothing in the design to justify an expensive developmental program, and a number of dangerous characteristics such as controls blanketing out in a stall. Asked them to send the Ford Company a written report and returned to Willow Run.

Monday, September 21

Phone call from Sorensen. McCarroll told him of our conference at the University of Michigan Engineering College, and Sorensen seems convinced, at last, that the flying wing does not justify the expenditure of great time and effort by the Ford Company. Apparently he has decided to drop the project as quickly as he decided to take it up.

Tuesday, September 22

Packed suitcase and drove to Willow Run. Had planned on taking off for Rochester, Minnesota, at 9:00, but a faulty inverter in the B-24 held us up until 11:20. Gerding was pilot, Hammond co-pilot; Dr. Clark, Smith, and I rode in the tail; Johnson, Loomis, and several other men rode on the flight deck and in the nose. We were all going to Rochester to obtain experience in the Mayo altitude chamber.

Just before we started across Lake Michigan gasoline began pouring down into the tail section of the fuselage from the center wing—gallons of it. I was sitting on my parachute, writing, and Dr. Clark was standing nearby. Smith, who was closest to the wing, was the first to give the alarm. It was an extremely dangerous situation, for a single spark might have blown up the entire tail end of the plane. I gave orders to attach parachutes (most of us were equipped with the detachable chest-type packs), and I swung on my back-type as quickly as possible. I then went forward to see where the fuel was coming from. By that time Smith had signaled the man on the flight deck of our difficulty, and the flight engineer was already crawling over the top surface of the center wing toward the fuel-transfer valves, which proved to be the source of trouble.

It was all over in two or three minutes, and we got the gasoline vapor out of the fuselage by opening the bomb bay. But the incident made me think of those unexplained reports that are so disturbing to fliers and which are talked about for years afterward wherever pilots gather: "Apparently exploded in air; the tail was found over a mile away from where the plane crashed." (Was it structural failure, hit by lightning, freak turbulence in a storm, or possibly sabotage? Or might the same thing have happened that could so easily have happened to us today: a gas leak, a spark, an explosion?)

Landed at Rochester at 1:20 C.W.T. Dr. Boothby[58] and several other men from the Mayo Foundation were waiting to meet us and take us to lunch at the Kahler Hotel.

58. Dr. Walter M. Boothby, chairman of the Aeromedical Unit for Research in Aviation Medicine, Mayo Clinic. In 1938 he was one of the recipients of the Collier Trophy for his contributions to aviation medicine in general, and pilot fatigue in particular.

We all went over to the experimental laboratories at the Mayo Aeromedical Unit in the afternoon. Several of us made a flight in the altitude chamber to a simulated altitude of over 40,000 feet. The altitude chamber is primarily a large steel tank, laid in a horizontal position and attached to a motor-driven vacuum pump. Entrance is gained through a heavy steel door at one end. This chamber we went up in today has two compartments: one, the main chamber where the altitude tests are made, and, two, an air lock which permits entrance and exit without changing the pressure of the main chamber. In other words, when someone is in the main chamber at a simulated altitude of, say, 35,000 feet, it is possible for attendants to go in and out through the air lock without affecting the experiment.

Dr. Boothby was at the controls when we made our ascent. The simulated rate of climb was much faster than that of a plane and, consequently, there was a more noticeable change in pressure. I had on a "demand" type of oxygen mask, which causes a slight negative pressure in the lungs when one is inhaling. However, it had a "constant flow" attachment which, when turned on, removes the negative pressure at the expense of a higher oxygen consumption. I found the constant flow much preferable at high altitude. We had microphones attached to our oxygen masks, and although it was a decided additional effort, we could communicate well even at 40,000 feet.

Attended cocktails at the home of Dr. Charles Mayo[59] later in the afternoon. A number of the Mayo Foundation people were there as well as our own crew from Willow Run. Dr. and Mrs. Mayo invited Dr. Clark and myself to stay for supper and the night. Dr. and Mrs. Mayo are among the exceptional people one meets in life. I wish Anne were here to talk to them.

Wednesday, September 23

Up at 6:30. Breakfast with Mayo family: Dr. and Mrs. Mayo, three boys, one girl, and the nurse. They have eight children, including three of Dr. Mayo's brother's children whom they have adopted.[60]

Dr. Clark and I drove to St. Mary's Hospital with Dr. Mayo and spent

59. Son of Charles Horace Mayo, founder of the Mayo Clinic. Surgeon and associate professor of surgery at the Mayo Foundation Graduate School, University of Minnesota. He became a consulting surgeon to the armed forces in the Western Pacific during World War II.

60. Dr. Mayo reared as wards two of the children of his deceased brother, Dr. Joseph Graham Mayo.

most of the morning watching him operate. He removed a cyst from one woman's breast, and an intestinal tumor from the abdomen of another. The latter operation required over an hour. I was tremendously impressed with the certainty and precision with which Dr. Mayo worked. His fingers never seemed to make a false move, and at one time he had his entire forearm inside the woman's abdomen, feeling for adhesions of the liver.

After the operations were over Dr. Mayo took us through the hospital. Then I went to the Aeromedical Unit and, without stopping to denitrogenize, went into the altitude chamber through the air lock. The chamber was at 40,000 feet when I went in and soon was raised to 44,200. Altogether, I was above 40,000 feet for about half an hour.

Lunch with the Willow Run pilots and Mayo Aeromedical personnel at the Kahler. Back to the Aeromedical Unit in the afternoon to watch some tests on the "G" (gravity) machine—a sort of human centrifuge on which a man can be given an acceleration similar to that obtained in a plane coming out of a dive. A test pilot by name of Kelly from Bell Aircraft was the first subject. He reached an acceleration of 9.7 G but passed out at the peak of the test. The first time I got in I went up to 4.5 G, and the second time to 5.8 G. I then stopped due to a slight headache, probably caused by my ascent in the altitude chamber this morning without going through the oxygen desaturation program.

Next, attended a group conference with Dr. Boothby. Asked him about the altitude where blood vapor pressure becomes dangerous and the effect of frequent and prolonged anoxia on brain tissue. There is controversy about both of these points, and I believe much research is still to be done in regard to them. Armstrong[61] describes vapor forming in the blood stream of animals at 55,000 feet. Boothby disagrees with this. The commonly accepted altitude of blood vapor formation is 63,-000 feet. But it is all too vague, and it seems to me there is too little interest in this subject. After all, we are going to 45,000 feet in the chamber now, and while the difference between 45,000 and 55,000 feet is two miles of air, it is an awfully small distance on the mercury column of the chamber monometer. A little inattention or inaccuracy on the part of the operator and one could easily reach it. Then, when I was working in the Rockefeller Institute with Carrel and running experiments in the circulating tissue-culture flasks I invented, I found that either too much

61. Dr. Harry G. Armstrong, author of *Principles and Practice of Aviation Medicine* (1939).

or too little oxygen had a decided effect on certain cells over a period of two or three days. Have we run accurate enough controls on the effect of altitude and oxygen on the brain?

Thursday, September 24

To Aeromedical laboratory at 8:45. Dr. Robins (Grumman Aircraft) and I desaturated for half an hour. (The desaturation program consists of riding an exercise bicycle, or walking on a treadmill, for thirty minutes while breathing pure oxygen through a rubber face mask. This washes most of the nitrogen out of the body and prevents the formation of nitrogen bubbles under decreased pressure.) After desaturation we entered the chamber and, together with Miss [Lucille] Cronin, the technician, ascended to 40,000 feet in seven minutes. We remained at 40,000 feet or above for one hour, nine minutes, and at one time reached 42,000 feet, where we remained for five minutes. During this time I walked about the chamber and took my oral temperature at intervals. I found that moderate exercise was not difficult or unduly fatiguing. My temperature fell 1° F. at the end of the hour. I noticed that I felt somewhat less alert after about forty-five minutes had passed (after returning from the ascent to 42,000 feet).

At the end of an hour I prepared to make a simulated parachute jump from 40,000 feet, using standard Army equipment (consisting of rubber mouth mask attached to a parachute O_2 bottle). At a given signal I removed my oxygen mask, placed the rubber mouth mask between my teeth, turned on the oxygen jump bottle, and began exercise—simulating that necessary to open a jammed cockpit hatch. Meanwhile, the pressure in the chamber was dropped at a rate simulating a parachute descent. I intended to continue exercising for one minute, but I noticed a serious lack of oxygen almost immediately. I pinched off the rebreathing tube (Dautrebande) with one hand to determine if the oxygen flow from the jump bottle was sufficient. When I attempted to inhale, I found that the flow was a small fraction of that which would be necessary to avoid the partial inhalation of air.

I realized that I was approaching a state of unconsciousness, gave the signal for a rapid descent, and sat down. I remember nothing more until consciousness returned at about 25,000 feet. I came to quickly, as I have come to in time past after taking an anesthetic before having my shoulder set, and noticed no ill effects whatever from the experience. I found that Miss Cronin had fastened on my oxygen mask a few seconds after I became unconscious, and that the chamber had been dropped from 40,000 feet to 25,000 feet in less than a minute. I suggested reascending, but Dr. Boothby felt it would be inadvisable until later. I experienced no headache or aftereffects.

Dr. Clark, several of the Willow Run pilots, and I had lunch with Dr. Mayo and several of his friends at the Kahler. After lunch we attended a lecture by a Dr. Joseph McSpanon, a missionary who had been twenty-five years in Japan at the time of Pearl Harbor, and who has only recently returned to the United States after spending several months in prison in Japan. It was a Rotary Club lecture, and I expected it to be a great bore. But Dr. McSpanon was both frank and perceptive and told more about Japan and her attitude on the war in thirty minutes than the newspapers tell in six months. He warned of American overconfidence in the Pacific and said that Japan was prepared to fight long and bitterly. But I am afraid that his lecture was far over the heads of most of the men who attended. They clapped for him, of course, when he finished—in a restrained and perfunctory manner. His was not a "pep talk," and Rotary Club members are trained to expect pep talks. Still, if it had an effect on just a few men there it was worth while.

Returned to the Aeromedical laboratory in the afternoon. A group of engineers from the Minneapolis Honeywell Company had arrived to go up in the chamber, and since all of Dr. Boothby's technicians were tired out from the effect of too frequent high-altitude ascents, I went with them as "technician" (after another half hour of nitrogen desaturation). We stopped at 35,000 feet, as one man had bad gas pains and another had sinus trouble. One man pulled off his lifeline, and I had to replace it for him. Another looked so ill that I was greatly concerned about him during the entire time.

To Dr. [Donald C.] Balfour's home for supper—about fifty people there; some from the Mayo Foundation, some just passing through the city, some come for treatment at the clinic. Louis Johnson (ex-Assistant Secretary of War) and several of the Roosevelt Administration politicians were among them. One of the members of Johnson's party, a Colonel Harrington, made a half hour's informal talk on the trip Louis Johnson and he made to India some months ago. After Harrington finished, Johnson went on for another fifteen minutes. They were very doubtful of Britain's ability to hold India and very critical of the British and British policy in regard to the war. In fact, they were *very anti-British* in practically everything they said.

Among Johnson's statements was the following: "But you *see* the Administration's wisdom in withholding the situation from the American people; because if they *knew,* it would make them anti-British." It was interesting to sit there and hear these Administration ex-officials make far stronger statements about British intrigue in the war than they criticized me for making only a little more than a year ago. And it was also interesting to hear these supposed supporters of the principles of democracy and freedom advocate withholding the truth from the American people, because that truth would influence the people's viewpoint. This is, as Igor Sikorsky says, "the era of the Great Lie"; and it crusades under such masks as "the Four Freedoms."

Friday, September 25

Accepted Dr. [H. Corwin] Hinshaw's invitation to visit the animal research building. Went through each of the labs and met the various doctors working there. Some of the experiments parallel work I carried on at the Rockefeller Institute, and I think some of the developments I made would be of value here. It made me want to get back into medical research again long enough to find out.

To Aeromedical lab in the afternoon. Desaturated for half an hour and then went up to 40,000 feet in the altitude chamber for another simulated parachute jump. Several of the Ford pilots went with me. The ascent took ten minutes. I remained at 40,000 feet for seven minutes, walking about and exercising mildly. I had a different emergency oxygen arrangement this time. For one thing, I had an oxygen jump bottle with a higher rate of flow. For another, I had the jump bottle connected directly to my regular oxygen mask, so that the transfer from regular mask to jump mask was eliminated.

At a given signal, I turned off the chamber oxygen line and turned on the jump bottle. I then went through thirty seconds of exercise approximating that required to open a jammed hatch. After this I sat down, and Dr. [Louis B.] Wilson began increasing the pressure in the chamber at a rate approximating that of parachute descent (3,000 feet per minute for first two minutes; then 2,000 feet per minute). I found the oxygen supply to be sufficient at all times. (Dr. Boothby is much more concerned about the danger of becoming unconscious from anoxia than I am. In running experiments on animals under low air pressure some years ago, I found that they would regain consciousness quickly, after passing out, when the air pressure was increased sufficiently—even though they had reached a state of violent convulsions. I found this to be true in the case of mice, guinea pigs, rabbits, and monkeys.)

The chamber descended to 4,000 feet, where I waited, breathing oxygen, for twenty minutes while a new Army standard type of oxygen jump bottle was filled and brought in through the air lock. This bottle had a higher rate of flow than the one I had been using and was fitted with an old-type wood mouthpiece. We reascended to 35,000 feet, where I turned on the jump bottle, removed my oxygen mask entirely, and inserted the wood mouthpiece between my teeth. I went through thirty seconds of exercise and then sat down while the chamber descended at parachute rate. The flow from the jump bottle was too high for satisfactory breathing, and the drying effect in my mouth and throat caused a tendency to cough. I decreased the flow by partially closing the jump-bottle valve, but the adjustment was too coarse to allow accurate regulation. Had plenty of oxygen at all times. Removed the mouthpiece at 25,000 feet, and continued to ground level without oxygen. (We continued the descent from 25,000 feet at parachute rate and I noticed a slight lack of oxygen at 23,000. Felt all right again at 20,000 feet.)

Saturday, September 26

Arrived at Aeromedical lab at 8:45. Denitrogenized, entered chamber with Willow Run pilots, and ascended to 40,000 feet in seven minutes. Remained at 40,000 feet for ten minutes, exercising mildly during part of time. (Today's experiment was to try out new standard jump bottle and wood mouthpiece in simulated parachute descent from 40,000 feet.) Then turned on jump bottle, removed face mask, inserted wood mouthpiece between teeth, carried on thirty seconds of heavy exercise (simulating effort required to get out of plane), and sat down. Noticed a serious lack of oxygen within a few seconds. Turned on oxygen from chamber line in order to avoid unconsciousness. (As a precaution, I had connected the chamber oxygen line to the wood mouthpiece through a T tube in the jump-bottle line.)

This test indicated pretty definitely that the standard type of Army parachute equipment is inadequate for jumps at altitudes in the vicinity of 40,000 feet. We descended to 25,000 feet where I rested for a time, breathing pure oxygen. Then reascended to 35,000 feet, at which pressure the chamber remained for eight minutes while I exercised mildly at intervals. Then I turned on the jump-bottle valve (this jump bottle had a lower rate of flow than the one I used at 35,000 feet yesterday and at 40,000 feet today on the previous ascent), removed my oxygen mask, placed the wood mouthpiece between my teeth, carried on thirty seconds of heavy exercise on the jump-bottle flow alone, and sat down.

The chamber then began descending at parachute rate. I felt the need of additional oxygen for some seconds and thought at first I would have to turn on the chamber line which, as on the last experiment, I had connected to the mouthpiece, through a T tube and shut-off value. However, I was able to retain consciousness and continue the descent without resorting to additional oxygen, and soon began to feel better. Removed mouthpiece at 23,000 feet. Continued descent to 20,000 without oxygen.

At 20,000 feet we brought a fresh jump bottle in through the air lock and reascended to 35,000 feet, so that Hadden (one of the Willow Run pilots) could attempt a simulated jump from 35,000 feet (with the new type, high-flow-rate bottle). Hadden went through fifteen seconds of exercise, and sat down. The chamber was then dropped at parachute rate. He had sufficient oxygen at all times. During this last descent, I took my oxygen mask off at 27,000 feet and left it off until we reached ground pressure.

Sunday, September 27

To Aeromedical Unit later in the morning for a conference with Dr. Boothby and his staff concerning plans for the day. Then desaturated for half an hour and went up in the chamber with Hadden and Miss Cronin. Gave two alveolar air samples at 35,000 feet, and two more at 40,000. Hadden made a jump from 40,000 feet, using the wood mouthpiece and high-flow-rate oxygen bottle—had to take emergency oxygen on the way down.

We stopped the descent at 30,000 feet and after holding at this altitude for seven minutes reascended to 40,000 feet, so I could try out the effect of breathing air at this altitude. I found that after taking four normal breaths, or three deep breaths, I noticed a serious lack of oxygen and came within a few seconds of unconsciousness. Possibly if I had not been in the chamber so long prior to the test I could have taken one or two breaths more—but I think that is all. I noticed the maximum effect of anoxia fifteen or twenty seconds *after replacing my oxygen mask* (due to time lag in circulation of blood from lungs to brain).

Desaturated again after lunch and ascended to 35,000 feet with [Bill]

Pongratz and one of Dr. Boothby's technicians. I wanted to try a simulated jump under conditions approximating as closely as possible an actual jump from high altitude. After remaining at 35,000 feet for thirteen minutes, during which time I carried on mild exercise at intervals, I turned off the chamber oxygen line and turned on the jump bottle, which was attached to my face mask; then exercised for one minute (lifting steel cylinder from floor to overhead); then removed mask entirely and breathed air in chamber for fifteen seconds (chamber started descending at parachute rate when I removed mask); then inserted wood mouthpiece from jump bottle between teeth and began breathing oxygen from jump bottle.

After several seconds I noticed a lack of oxygen, but normal feeling returned within a minute. Removed wood mouthpiece at 22,500 feet and discontinued using oxygen (still at parachute-descent rate) until chamber reached 15,000 feet, at which altitude I put the oxygen mask on again in order to avoid a "hangover."

Chamber rate of descent:

MINUTE	FEET PER MINUTE
first	3,000
second	2,500
third	2,000
fourth	2,000
thereafter	1,000 to 1,500

To Dr. Boothby's home for cocktails. Back to Aeromedical lab later with Dr. Wilson to set up an emergency-oxygen arrangement I have designed—where pulling the parachute rip cord automatically turns on the oxygen jump bottle, which is connected directly to the regular oxygen mask. In this arrangement a pilot leaving his plane in an emergency does not have to think of his oxygen at all.

Monday, September 28

Up at 7:00. Spent a few minutes writing reports. Then to Aeromedical lab. Spent the morning taking alveolar samples and attaching the new oxygen apparatus to my back-pack-type parachute—with the aid of Dr. Boothby, Dr. Wilson, and other members of the staff.

The bomber has landed on the Rochester airport to take us back to

Willow Run. I have decided to stay over for another day or two and go back alone by train.

Back to Aeromedical Unit after lunch. Desaturated for thirty minutes. Then entered chamber and ascended to 40,000 feet in seven minutes. (Went up to test the new type of equipment we have constructed.) Remained at 40,000 feet for ten minutes. Then carried on thirty seconds of exercise (lifting steel cylinder). Then broke the connection attaching my mask to the chamber line. (At this moment the chamber started descending at parachute rate.) Remained without any oxygen for ten seconds (simulating time required after leaving plane to pull parachute rip cord). Then pulled the rip cord, thereby opening the jump-bottle valve and starting flow of oxygen from jump bottle to mask. The chamber continued to descend to 20,000 feet at parachute rate, during which time I noticed no serious lack of oxygen. At 20,000 feet we stopped the descent, and I reconnected my mask to the chamber oxygen line to prepare for the next experiment.

Reascended to 35,000 feet and remained at this altitude for five and a half minutes. Then carried on exercise for thirty seconds (still on the chamber oxygen line). Then broke connection attaching mask to chamber oxygen line and removed face mask. Chamber started descending at parachute rate. I had intended to remain without oxygen, breathing the air in the chamber, for fifteen seconds; but an error in timing increased this period to thirty-five seconds before I was given the time signal.

On receiving the time signal, I pulled the parachute rip cord, which should have opened the jump-bottle valve; but the valve (which we had improvised) was excessively tight and did not open. I failed to notice that the value had stuck, and attempted to breathe oxygen through the emergency mouthpiece. Within a few seconds I realized that unconsciousness was approaching and held the chamber emergency-oxygen mask to my face. (We kept a mask with a high oxygen flow close at hand for just such emergencies.) I signaled for the chamber to be dropped rapidly, but still reached the verge of unconsciousness. Then, as oxygen entered the circulation sufficiently, my senses returned to normal very rapidly. We dropped the chamber to 20,000 feet and held it at that altitude for ten minutes in preparation for another attempt.

Reascended to 35,000 feet and remained at that altitude for five and a half minutes. (I felt the effect of the previous two flights and was not in top condition for this test.) Then carried on thirty seconds of exercise, at the end of which I broke the connection attaching my mask to the chamber oxygen line. Then I removed my mask entirely (simulating the mask being blown off during a jump). The chamber started descending at parachute rate. I remained without oxygen for fifteen seconds; then pulled the parachute rip cord, thereby opening the jump-bottle valve. I detached the emergency mouthpiece from its fitting and breathed oxygen from the jump bottle through the Dautrebande tube connected to it (an improvement added by Dr. Boothby). I noticed a lack of oxygen during the descent, but was able to continue at parachute rate and felt better rapidly as the altitude decreased. I removed the mouthpiece entirely at 25,000 feet and discontinued breathing oxygen until we reached 15,000 feet; then replaced my oxygen mask in order to avoid a hangover.

Back to lab after supper and spent two or three hours working on the improvement of the emergency equipment.

Tuesday, September 29

Up at 7:00. Breakfast in room. Then to Aeromedical lab. Spent the morning taking alveolar air samples with new type mask Dr. Boothby has constructed, and in an ascent to 35,000 feet in the chamber to test out the Dautrebande jump feature which is incorporated in the mask. I had an adequate supply of oxygen at all times and believe the system and the equipment we have developed is a great improvement on that previously used. With this equipment, properly used, it is possible to leave a plane at 40,000 feet under service conditions and have a fully adequate supply of oxygen at all times, both during the time required to get out of the plane and during the descent. With the present Army service equipment and technique, a man jumping at 40,000 feet, especially if he has undergone much exertion in getting out of his plane, is almost certain to become unconscious and have convulsions during his descent—unless he does a delayed-opening jump to lower altitude. But to do a delayed-opening jump a man should be in full possession of his senses, and that necessitates a sufficient supply of oxygen.

The result of these tests we have been making indicates that the emergency-oxygen equipment the Army is now using should be either redesigned or replaced for flights above 35,000 feet, and there is doubt that it is adequate even at that altitude. Spent the afternoon writing reports, conclusions, and recommendations on the various experiments we have made. Hour with Dr. Boothby later in the evening, discussing the joint report we plan on making to Wright Field.

Wednesday, September 30

To Aeromedical lab at 8:15. Morning spent with Drs. Boothby, Clark, and Wilson, writing report and arranging for drawings and photographs of equipment. To Aeromedical lab in evening. Dr. Balfour was there with Dr. Boothby. I showed him the equipment we have developed. Then spent an hour with the doctors, working on report. There have been too many people working on it. Dr. Boothby has changed the last draft considerably, and it is now in a rather confused condition. Time will probably be saved by starting at the beginning and writing it over again.

Thursday, October 1

Churchill announces loss of nearly fifty per cent in Dieppe raid.

Spent an hour going over the draft of the report I wrote last night. Then to Aeromedical lab to go over report with Dr. Boothby. Then desaturated for half an hour and went up in the small one-man altitude chamber to find out what effect altitude had on body temperature and to try out a system of pulsating breathing I have developed. Dr. Wilson was at the controls outside the chamber. I stayed above 36,000 feet for about three and a half hours, and at one time reached an altitude of 42,000 feet. We had some difficulty with the vacuum pumps, which had a tendency to overheat.

Found that the [body] temperature decreased a degree or two after remaining at high altitude a sufficient length of time. Then it increased to slightly above normal. The pulsating breathing seemed to have a beneficial effect, but I had no adequate control, and consequently cannot be certain.

When we were living in England, I made a number of experiments on guinea pigs and mice at low air pressures and was able to reduce their body temperatures by 10° C.—sometimes more. I tried to repeat these experiments on a monkey at the Rockefeller Institute in New York but could not get a temperature reduction of more than 2° or 3°. Then the temperature would rise again. The monkey's temperature reaction was similar to mine in the chamber today. However, the experiments should be run over a considerably longer period of time.

Friday, October 2

Spent first part of morning working on report. Rest of morning preparing for chamber ascent in afternoon and studying altitudes where vaporization of blood begins. Decided not to go above 45,000 feet until I had learned more about vaporization.

Back to Aeromedical lab in the afternoon. Denitrogenized and ascended to 40,000 feet in the chamber. Took alveolar air samples and tried effect of pulsating breathing. As far as we could measure, it had no advantage over normal breathing. (In "pulsating breathing" I hold my breath with lungs full and pulsate my lungs three times to each breath, thereby creating a higher than normal pressure during a portion of each pulsation.)

We decided to try a rapid descent from 40,000 feet and dropped from that altitude to ground pressure in one minute, twelve seconds. Noticed no ill effects as a result. Spent rest of afternoon working on our report. It is in bad shape. Will have to completely rewrite it.

Saturday, October 3

Congress passes anti-inflation bill. Wages and prices to be fixed by Roosevelt.

Up at 7:00. The trees in front of the hotel are full of grackles—tens of thousands of them—all singing and making a great noise. They have been there every morning since we arrived. Half hour reading draft of report I wrote last night. Then to Aeromedical lab. I had planned on working on the report, but Dr. Boothby was anxious to try out a pressure-breathing apparatus at 45,000 feet. Miss Cronin was to make the test, and he wanted someone to be in the chamber with her in case anything went wrong. All of his other assistants were tired out and showed the effect of too much time in the chamber, so I offered to go. Denitrogenized for thirty minutes and ascended to 40,000 feet with Miss Cronin. From 40,000 feet we made two ascents to 45,000 feet for between three and five minutes each time. One feels a tremendous difference in going from 40,000 to 45,000 feet. We decided to try another rapid descent from 40,000 feet and stationed someone at every air valve in the chamber. At a given signal we opened all the valves and descended from 40,000 feet to ground-level pressure in thirty-six seconds. The previous record for this chamber was one minute, eighteen seconds.

Back to laboratory in the afternoon and finished writing the report. Dr. Boothby thought it O.K. (I had expected him to make all kinds of changes), and we signed it as a joint report by Drs. Boothby, Wilson, Clark, and myself. Boarded 8:30 North Western train for Chicago.

Sunday, October 4

Off train at 8:00. Phoned airport. No seat available to Detroit until 11:55. Spent the time walking through the streets of Chicago. War is now apparent everywhere—in the store windows; in the numerous uniforms; in the hotels on Michigan Avenue turned over to military-training purposes.

Lunch on American Airlines plane. We flew above an overcast sky most of the way to Detroit, but it was clear when we landed. William met me with the car, with a note from Anne saying that Jon was at Mother's. Drove to 508 Lakepointe and let William take the car back. I found Jon in the basement, bending glass tubing over one of Grandfather's old bunsen burners. Stayed till 5:00.

Supper in parlor with Anne. She read me her last poem ("Christopher").

Monday, October 5

Up at 6:30. Then to Willow Run via the Rouge administration building. Part of morning in office (conference with Henry Ford, Harry Bennett, and Bricker), part at flight department, and part spent making inspection trip through factory with Colonel McDuffee. Lunch with pilots and flight personnel. Find that the friction between the pilots and the flight superintendent is increasing and becoming rather serious.

Supper and evening with Anne by the fireplace in the parlor. Anne has rearranged the room, and it seems much more homelike and pleasant —couch in front of fireplace as in most of the other places where we have lived. Anne has the ability to make a home out of almost anything—a few pieces of cloth, a little rearranging, and a room takes on a quality that she, and she only, can give it.

Home for half an hour's play with the children before bedtime. Found Land brushing his teeth with "just a little" chocolate cake in his mouth.

Thursday, October 8

Roosevelt announces intention of punishing "war criminals."

To Borg-Warner Company to see the new "all-position" gun turret they have developed. It is a roomy, typically English type of design, electric-hydraulic operation. It has too large a cross section for proper installation in the nose or tail of the B-24, but might be reduced in size and looks interesting in many ways.

Friday, October 9

Morning at flight department on conferences and one hour, fifteen minutes in the Link. Got a bad start and did a very poor problem in the trainer. I started out today without enough respect for the Link.

The pilots are restless in regard to the time-clock situation. For some reason Henning has not yet authorized them to stop punching it. I must talk to him about it and see if we can't get the matter straightened out. Otherwise there are liable to be some quits among our best pilots.

To Rouge administration building for lunch with Bennett, Lieutenant Governor [Frank] Murphy, Rausch, Gnau,[62] and others. Murphy says six Negro soldiers were found hung to trees at the Sault a few weeks ago in reprisal for attacks on white women. (A Negro regiment has been sent up there to guard the locks.) Of course, we have seen nothing about it in the papers. If it was printed at all, it must have been on the back pages.

Monday, October 12

Quarter hour's conference with Henry Ford and Harry Bennett; then walked through the factory with them to inspect progress. The final assembly line is beginning to fill up, and the plant is now really on production—not large production yet, but it will increase rapidly from now on, and workmanship is improving constantly. (In fact, production began last month when the first Willow Run–built bomber was delivered to and tested by the flight department.)

62. Russell Gnau, assistant to Charles Sorensen.

While we were walking along the rows of machines and jigs, Ford turned to me and expressed the opinion that Willow Run would produce more in airplanes than the Ford Company has ever produced in automobiles, that "all freight that *is* carried in the future will be carried by air," and that there won't be so much freight in the future as at present because industry will be decentralized.

Ford is always the optimist. To him, whatever happens, no matter how bad or discouraging, is for the eventual good and has its purpose. For Henry Ford the future is always bright, regardless of the present. And his spirit is contagious. Almost everyone who *really* knows him likes him. He is the one man in the Ford organization who seems to be above its petty jealousies and conflicts. I have never heard anyone here speak disrespectfully of Henry Ford, and to many of the men he is a sort of god. This is all the more remarkable because he has strong and definite—and sometimes quite unreasonable—ideas. But the things his officers like about him so greatly overweigh the things they don't that the latter serve as a sort of setting for the former and are told and retold in exaggerated form to give a human touch to Ford's genius and fabulous industrial accomplishments. Ford is a unique character who has surrounded himself with other unique characters to form one of the greatest industrial establishments the world has ever known—an establishment with methods, policies, and relationships differing greatly from any other I have seen.

Early lunch in Flight restaurant. Then forty-five minutes in the Link trainer. Then went up for an hour's flight in the P-47. The flaps were out of synchronization, and the landing gear refused to retract—one wheel stuck ten inches down. Made the last landing without using the flaps.

Conference with Henning in regard to pilots' pay, which is too low and all tangled up in red tape.

Tuesday, October 13

Roosevelt advises draft of eighteen- and nineteen-year-old boys.

To Willow Run. Arranged a conference between Bennett and Graham[63] in regard to flying instruction. Bennett is about ready for solo, and solo flights are supposed to be made only under the supervision of a licensed instructor. This regulation was established years after I instructed my

63. Lyle Graham, instrument-flight instructor.

last student (Anne), and I have never applied for a license. (It requires considerable time to get and involves the nuisance of regular renewal.) Graham is a licensed instructor, and Henning thought him the best man to take charge of getting Bennett ready for his license tests.

Spent rest of morning on routine at office and in flight department—a large part of it in following through a rumor that ten P-47's had cracked up in Florida and killed ten pilots, due to engine failure on take-off. It turned out that the only pilots lost had been on patrol duty over the ocean and that the P-47's make good belly landings in emergency.

Up for a forty-five-minute flight in the P-47. Find that the plane handles well; but it developed a bad hydraulic leak. Half hour in Link trainer, working out an orientation problem without compass or directional gyro. Then drove to Ford airport to test out the spinning characteristics of the Fairchild before taking Bennett up for spins. Found the plane to spin fast and come out quickly, both left and right. Took Bennett up to 4,000 feet and gave him several spins in each direction. After the first two he turned to me and said, "Say, do ya have to do this to get a license? Because if ya do, I'm not going to get one." But before we came down he had learned to recover from a spin without any assistance from me. No one who knows Bennett can justly accuse him of lacking courage.

Saturday, October 17

"Victory tax" voted by Congress.

Drove Jon, Land, and Anne, Jr., to 508 Lakepointe after lunch. Mother is looking much better and now realizes that the long hours of teaching school would have been too much this winter. It has been a godsend for her to have her grandchildren for regular weekly visits at the very time she had to give up her teaching.

Monday, October 19

Spent the morning at the flight department—thirty-five minutes of it in the Link trainer, and the rest preparing for an altitude flight in the P-47. Spent first part of afternoon making final preparations for the flight. Then denitrogenized for half an hour and took off. Climbed to 10,000 feet and took first set of readings. Found that there would be insufficient fuel and oxygen to take readings at 5,000-foot steps all the way up, so climbed directly from 10,000 feet to 36,000 feet to try out general characteristics of plane and equipment at altitude. Was up for a total of one hour and twenty minutes. Purpose of flight was to test out ignition system on the Ford-built 2,000-h.p. Pratt & Whitney engine.

Wednesday, October 21

Congress votes $9-billion tax bill.

Henry Ford arrived with Dr. McClure and Jim Newton, who is on his way back from the M.R.A. headquarters in northern Michigan. Took them all through the factory at Henry Ford's request.

Took off for an hour's landing practice in the P-47 and made a number of simulated dead-stick landings. Found that the P-47 can be brought in satisfactorily with flaps down and without engine at a gliding speed of 135 m.p.h.

Thursday, October 22

Part of day spent in office and part at flight department. Dictation and studying various data; hour in Link trainer; conference with Smith and Skocdopole regarding salaries, poor inspection of planes, etc. Harry Bennett phoned to tell me that "Washington is out to get Sorensen" and that government officials there are claiming that Sorensen is "blocking production" at Willow Run.

Friday, October 23

Stopped at Flight to make preliminary arrangements for an altitude flight in the P-47. After lunch the sky, which had been clear all morning, became overcast with thin broken clouds. I decided to try for altitude anyway, although in this ignition-test work it is desirable to see the field at all times in case a complete engine failure should necessitate a dead-stick landing. (The P-47 is a dangerous ship for a dead-stick landing at best, and in this broken country it would probably be advisable to jump from the plane if one did not have a large airport in sight to land on.) Made final preparations for the flight, including denitrogenization for half an hour. Then took off and started climb; but the left landing gear would not retract. (Stuck sequence valve, causing wheel streamline to close before the wheel.) Landed and remained in cockpit, breathing oxygen, while the sequence valve was knocked free, the plane refueled, and the oxygen supply replenished, all of which took a full hour. Then taxied out and took off again; but left landing gear stuck as before. Turned back and landed second time. Too late for a third try. Gave orders to remove wheel streamliners entirely until new sequence valves could be obtained.

Saturday, October 24

Arranged clearances and details for an altitude flight. Denitrogenized for half an hour. Took off in P-47 at 11:55, and climbed directly to 35,000 feet. At that altitude the cockpit began to fill with smoke until the instrument board became hazy. Reduced turbo r.p.m. and dropped down to 30,000 feet, at which altitude the smoke cleared—probably oil on the turbo stacks. Made a run at 30,000 feet (at 43.5 inches manifold pressure and 2,550 r.p.m.), where I took a complete set of readings (magneto and distributor head temperatures, cylinder-head pressures, etc.). Then climbed back to 35,000 feet and made another run at that altitude. Then climbed to 39,000 feet and made a flash run there.

The engine missed and vibrated badly with magneto and distributor heads in ambient condition above 35,000 feet. Thirty-nine thousand feet is close to the ceiling of the plane. I was too busy with the readings and watching my oxygen supply to look out very much; but I could see for many miles in every direction. There were great banks of clouds to the northwest and southeast. Below me it was clear, and the airport of Willow Run, with its long concrete runways, made an excellent landmark. (Excellent as long as long-range enemy bombers don't come this way.) There was a high wind from the north. Radio contact was poor above 30,000 feet. I tried to notify the Willow Run tower of the smoke in the cockpit, but they could not understand. Landed after one hour and twenty-five minutes, with less than forty gallons of fuel left in the tanks (310-gal. capacity).

Spent rest of afternoon making out reports of the flight and in a conference discussing the poor workmanship on the B-24's now being produced and methods of improving.

Sunday, October 25

Allies advance in North Africa. Russians still holding Stalingrad; British bomb Genoa and other Italian cities.

Left for 508 Lakepointe at 10:15 with Anne, Jr. She loves these week-end trips to see Mother and stands about impatiently, little suitcase in hand, if I am not ready to start as soon as she is. Anne, Jr., is an *exceptionally* attractive little girl, if I do say so myself!

Monday, October 26

Spent the morning at a conference between Henry Ford, Edsel Ford, Harry Bennett, C. E. Sorensen, [Mead] Bricker, Roscoe Smith, Arnold Miller,[64] Logan Miller, and several other Ford officers, in Bricker's office. The discussion centered around the question of employing more men, the housing problem, the fact that we are behind schedule, the quality of workmanship on the B-24's, etc.

Edsel Ford took the stand that we should employ more men at once. Bricker felt that we would progress faster if we refrained from employing more until our present personnel is better trained. (We have more than 30,000 employees at Willow Run now, and less than 400 of them had experience in aircraft manufacture before they came here.) I sided mostly with Bricker and told Edsel Ford that the quality of the planes now being put out is poor, and that Ford is getting a reputation in the industry for turning out poor quality of workmanship. I mentioned the B-24 that Skocdopole refused to fly until the fuselage tail section had been strengthened, and other instances. I said that if we took on too many additional untrained men now, the poor quality of workmanship would continue.

I told Mr. Ford (Edsel) that on the other hand our quality would improve rapidly if we gave our men the chance to learn their jobs thoroughly, and that after our present personnel had gained experience it would then be possible to expand quickly. I outlined to him the difficulty of producing so complicated a plane as the B-24 without a highly trained nucleus to build around and the handicap we started with in comparison to the aviation companies, who had such a nucleus at the time their war-

64. Ford personnel director.

expansion program began. I said I felt the government had made a great mistake originally in not dividing the experienced aviation workers up among the various concerns who were given war contracts for aviation products. Edsel Ford countered with the statement that nevertheless we were just up against it and would fall still farther behind on our schedule unless we took on many thousand more workers. I replied that it was a question of balance between production and quality, both at the moment and in the future.

Bricker brought out the fact that some of the assemblies we recently sent to the Consolidated plant at Fort Worth have been turned down and sent back because of unsatisfactory quality. (I saw that coming months ago and warned Sorensen, Bricker, and Smith that such a situation was inevitable unless we changed our policy.)

Sorensen said—about the company's failure to meet production— "We knew it was a tough problem, but we didn't know it was quite so tough."

Edsel Ford replied, "But a lot of people told us it was." (Reminding Sorensen of the fact that he made all kinds of production promises for months and listened to none of the warnings the aviation engineers and executives gave him.)

Bricker reported that Consolidated Aircraft Corporation in San Diego is now turning out B-24's in less than 30,000 man-hours per ship. (We have over 30,000 workmen here at Willow Run, and, as yet, our production is nowhere near a ship per day.)

Henry Ford said very little during the meeting. He simply sat and listened. The meeting broke up at noon.

Tuesday, October 27

Conference at 10:30 with Captain Moonert, Lieutenant [William P.] Jones, Henning, and others in regard to various defects found on inspection of the B-24's which have been turned over to the flight department by the factory. In one instance, a turnbuckle was found in the aileron-control system of a ship which had already been flown, with seven threads showing. We are faced with inexperience, indifference, and resentment at interference on the part of the workmen. However, there is encouragement to be found in the fact that morale is better than it was a few weeks ago, and that the bombers now on the final assembly line are much superior to those which have been delivered to Flight.

Spent first part of afternoon on routine and studying B-26 operating data. Then took the B-26 up for an hour's flight with Lyle Graham as co-pilot and Bill Pongratz as flight engineer. The B-26 is a dangerous airplane in a number of ways, but also has some exceptionally fine characteristics. The take-off is long and the landing fast. A motor failure on take-off would be extremely serious. But once in the air the B-26 is the best handling multiengined plane I have ever flown, and it cruises along at about 230 miles an hour. There are many things about it I like; but one must watch it every minute.

As I was leaving the flight department, a young Army mechanic came up to me and asked, "How long do you think this war will last, sir?" There was both hope and resignation in the tone of his voice, and it was clear that he wished it would not be long. He was one of the men who are being trained as flight mechanics to accompany the B-24's being built at Willow Run. I replied that there was no way of telling and that his guess would be as good as mine. One can no longer discuss the war, except among closest friends, with any degree of objectivity.

Wednesday, October 28

To Willow Run. Morning in office on routine. Lunch early. Intended to fly the P-47 at noon, but Bennett phoned and asked me to meet Admiral Read [65] (NC4) and his party, who were arriving at the airport at 1:00. Made trip through factory with Bennett, Read, and party. Then returned to Flight and was just making out a clearance for the P-47 when a radio call came from Sorensen asking me to meet him at final assembly. Took half an hour to locate him. He was with some English lord I had met in London in 1927! Spent an hour with them; then back to flight department. Finally took off in the P-47 at 4:45. Hour in the air, including three simulated forced landings.

Half hour's discussion with Gerding in regard to pilots' salaries.

Thursday, October 29

Conference with Bennett in regard to the poor quality of workmanship on the B-24's. He says again that I am a perfectionist!

---

65. Rear Admiral Albert Cushing Read, who commanded the Navy NC4 flying boat on its flight from Rockaway, N.Y., to Plymouth, England (via Newfoundland, the Azores, and Portugal) in May, 1919. This was the first airplane flight across the Atlantic Ocean.

Lunch at administration building restaurant with Colonel [Carlyle L.] Nelson and Captain [Silas A.] Morehouse in regard to the possibility of the Ford Company developing a laminar-flow propeller one of Nelson's friends is interested in. The performance and test figures look good, but Sorensen has taken the position that the company is now developing so many new projects that it is inadvisable to take on anything more, regardless of its merit. I believe Sorensen is right in this instance, and I outlined the situation to Nelson and Morehouse as well as I could. They seemed to understand at once and did not press the matter further. I suggested that they take the project to United Aircraft or Curtiss-Wright, both of which companies are in the propeller business. Took them through the factory after lunch.

Saturday, October 31

Japanese fleet defeated in Solomons battle.

Was planning on an altitude flight today, but the sky was overcast when I got up and showed no sign of clearing. So decided to spend day at home. George Vaillant[66] had gone to Ann Arbor.

George returned for late lunch. Took him through Greenfield Village and the Edison Institute in the afternoon. Then we drove through Ford airport and then to the Rouge. Arrived at the blast furnaces just as a pour was to be made. We remained to watch the 200 tons of metal run through the open trenches and into the crucible cars on the tracks at the side of the building. Three cars were filled, each one holding about seventy-five tons of metal. The foreman took us through the building and showed us the various procedures involved. We had not taken a guide, as we thought it would be more interesting to explore around for ourselves. After leaving the furnaces, we drove around the grounds of the Rouge, stopping long enough to go through the rolling mill—where it seemed that we walked for miles between lines of machinery and rollers, cooling racks, etc. The huge, red-hot steel bars would come shooting along a few feet to one side of the walkways, almost burning our faces with their radiated heat as they passed, and roaring like great animals as they entered the quenching sprays.

66. George Vaillant was visiting the Lindberghs for the weekend.

Sunday, November 1

I decided to try for an altitude flight with the P-47. George Vaillant asked to go with me to see the procedure involved. We arrived at Willow Run at noon. I arranged for George to get lunch while I was flying. Then made out clearances, checked plane, denitrogenized for half an hour, and took off. Just as I reached 3,500 feet the forward center strip of the left emergency-hatch exit blew off. Fortunately, the glass panel was held in place by the rainproofing cement, and I was able to land without losing it. The panel came loose on the top, bottom, and rear edges, and I had to push on it slightly to keep it from fluttering in the air stream; but the cement on the front edge held on like a hinge. I had checked the emergency-release safety wire before taking off. Later, we found that the emergency release had been tripped by catching on a slight projection as I closed the hatch after passing out the oxygen carrier bottle. The same thing had happened to Gerding on take-off several weeks ago, but we were unable to find the cause at that time.

I showed George through the Willow Run factory, and then drove him to Pennsylvania Station for his train.

Spent most of the evening typing. Halfway through, the phone rang: C. E. Sorensen calling! He had just been reading *Listen! the Wind* and was enthusiastic about it. Wanted me to tell Anne how much he liked it. It was Sorensen at his best—the side of him that I like.

Monday, November 2

Stopped at Flight to give orders for a temporary repair to be made on the P-47 hatch. Then to office for a half hour's conference with Ford, Bennett, and Bricker. I outlined to them the danger of pushing the bombers through flight inspection too fast, as now seems to be the tendency. They all agreed, and I think a somewhat different attitude will result.

Tuesday, November 3

Spent the morning on routine and an hour's conference with Henry Ford and Harry Bennett. Walter Lippmann[67] arrived while we were talking—

67. American essayist, author, and editor, known for his syndicated columns.

here to see Willow Run. Spent a few minutes talking to him; then back to office to complete various routine details before lunch. Had an invitation to attend the company lunch for Lippmann and Prince Bernhard of The Netherlands, but was able to beg off.

Wednesday, November 4

Dewey elected Governor of New York. Republicans gain in Congress. Allied advance in Egypt.

Radioed the tower to have the P-47 ready for altitude at 10:00. Drove directly to Flight. Checked plane, made out clearances, denitrogenized, and took off at 11:01 after some delay due to trouble with the battery cart. Climbed directly to 30,000 feet, where I took the first set of readings. On the way up to 35,000 feet the engine missed and jumped once. When I ran the initial 35,000-foot magneto check, both mags were O.K. But when I made the valve check readings at the end of the 35,000-foot run, the left mag was out completely.

I had planned on climbing to 40,000 feet today, but throttled down— or, rather, pulled the turbo down—when I found the mag was out and started to descend at once. On the way down the right mag became slightly rough, so I called Detroit radio for authority to descend directly over Willow Run instead of by way of area No. 2. I wanted to keep within gliding distance of the airport in case of complete ignition failure. Finally got an O.K. after much calling and circling at 20,000 feet. I made a simulated dead-stick approach, but the right mag functioned well enough all the way down.

Friday, November 6

To Wayne County airport for lunch with Colonel Nelson, Captain Morehouse, and other officers of the Ferry Command.[68] We discussed methods of jumping from pursuit planes at low and high speeds and under what circumstances it would be better to jump than to stay in during a forced landing. They advised not attempting a dead-stick landing with a modern pursuit plane off an airport and were skeptical about attempting one *on* an airport. Their general philosophy was to jump if

68. The branch of the Air Force charged with ferrying aircraft from one station to another.

the motor failed, regardless of what lay below. I do not agree in this—believe a dead-stick landing on a large airport to be perfectly practical, and that one could be made in many places off an airport when there are open fields and nothing more than fences in between—provided, of course, that the pilot is in proper training.

Monday, November 9

Pétain severs relations with the United States.

Bennett came into my office shortly after I arrived, and Captain Moonert came in a moment later. We discussed the invasion of Africa, production problems at Willow Run, and the inadvisability of the attempt some Ford officers are making to get the Army to accept the first B-24's without the incorporation of safety changes.

Conference in Bricker's office with Henry Ford, Bennett, Bricker, Roscoe Smith, Logan Miller, and Captain Moonert. Then we all drove over to the airport to see the Consolidated B-24 which has just landed and which has been modified for the transport of passengers. Drove back to the Administration Building with Bricker and Captain Moonert.

Tuesday, November 10

Giraud commands French pro-Allied forces in Africa. United States troops pass Oran. British land at Algiers.

Drove to the Rouge to go through the supercharger factory with Major Forbes. The Ford Company is now building forged turbos. Although Sorensen has been claiming for months that cast turbos are superior and cheaper, the Army breakdown tests have not backed him up so far.

There are many women working in this factory. They seem to be of a higher type than the men—and are doing better work, according to Forbes.

Wednesday, November 11

Picked up a message from Car 10 (Henry Ford's car) on the way to the factory. He was on the way to Willow Run, too, and arriving in twenty minutes—wanted me to wait for him at the office.

The door opened, and Henry Ford walked into the room soon after I was at my desk. We spent the next half hour talking about Willow Run, war, and politics. Ford spoke again, as he so often does, of "a Federation of the World," [and] his confidence in the ultimate future. He brought up Jim Newton's visit, and reiterated his confidence in Jim and lack of confidence in Buchman and his M.R.A. movement. He told me that Mrs. Ford was coming out to Willow Run with a party of women a little later and asked me to take them up onto a platform where I had once taken him and where a good overhead view of the sub- and final assemblies could be obtained.

I had an appointment with a Captain [Robert E.] McIntyre, of the Transitional School at Wayne County airport, for lunch. He wanted to fly the P-47 and was bringing over a Mustang (P-51) for me to fly in return. I phoned and postponed our lunch from 12:30 until 1:00.

Took Mrs. Ford's party through the factory—they in a big Lincoln car, and I riding about with Mr. [William] Simonds in a small, radio-equipped Ford. We drove along the corridors of machinery and jigs, and I took them up onto the balcony which had impressed Mr. Ford so much. Then to Flight for lunch with Captain McIntyre.

Showed Captain McIntyre the working of the P-47 cockpit after lunch, and he showed me the cockpit of the P-51 (North American Mustang—single-place fighter; metal; low wing; Allison in-line engine). I flew the Mustang for one hour and thirty-five minutes in all, and made several landings and take-offs. It is the best-handling pursuit plane I have ever flown (with the exception of the engine, which is somewhat rough and underpowered). There is very little change of trim in a dive. The visibility is excellent. The plane takes off quickly and lands slowly, and there is very good control at all times. Its appearance is much like the Messerschmitt I flew in Germany several years ago, but the Mustang has better control and performance—and a much better cockpit, of course. The air speed indicated 270 m.p.h. at 3,000 feet, 30 inches, and 2,280 r.p.m. It will slow-roll as long as the fuel lasts. Obviously, it is an excellent low-altitude fighter.

Home at 7:10 for supper with Anne. After supper we went to Carl Milles's[69] home at the Cranbrook Foundation to spend the rest of the

69. Swedish-American sculptor, who taught at Cranbrook Academy in Michigan. He is represented in the U.S. by statues in Rockefeller Center, New York, St. Paul, Minn. (the Peace Monument), St. Louis, Mo. (the Fountain of the Meeting of the Waters), and other cities.

evening. Mrs. Milles was ill, but he showed us his Greek sculpture and Swedish paintings and gave us good Swedish coffee and some cookies made by Mrs. Milles. We spent the time talking of art, Sweden, and Europe. It was, as Anne said, another world—especially after flying 400-mile-an-hour fighting planes a few hours before.

Friday, November 13

Most of morning in conference with Harry Bennett and Sorensen in regard to Willow Run, the war, and Washington. It is extremely interesting to watch these two men and their relationships. Both of them grew up in the hard competition of industrial life; both of them are strong characters; together, with the guidance of Henry Ford and his son, they run one of the world's greatest industrial empires. They are constantly fighting between themselves, yet either one will stand up for the other against an outside attack. Bennett is interested more in the man than in his product. Sorensen is interested more in his product than in the man. Today they were discussing one of the engineers at Willow Run.

Bennett said, "You better watch—————. He can be bought for money. He fought for Red Spain, and he's a member of the Comintern."

Sorensen replied, "He's a good engineer, though."

Later on in the conversation, while we were talking about foreign and domestic policy, Sorensen made the following statement: "If those birds [the Administration] will just let us alone, we'll keep everybody in the country busy [after the war]. Why there's enough market in Russia to give us more business than we can handle."

To which Bennett replied: "I think we could get along pretty well with South America [alone] if we had to."

Sorensen: "Why, when I went to Russia, everybody here was telling me what to say and do—and they told me again when I got to England. But I just kept an open mind and came back with $32 million worth of business." The response to this put Sorensen somewhat on the defensive, and he demanded, "What damage can it do to show backward countries how to do things our way?" I replied that, after all, the crisis we found ourselves in in the Pacific was the result, to a large extent, of showing Japan how to do things our way.

Sorensen's entire mind seems devoted to production and to finding new ideas to produce. "Why, I don't even like to drive my own car any more! I spend almost every minute I'm awake thinking and making sketches." Sorensen, about Willow Run: "And we've done all this our-selves—hardly taken in anyone from the outside."

Saturday, November 14

Stopped at Flight to check the weather and see if Loomis was ready for his first altitude run. He is going up to get acquainted with high-altitude flying conditions and will make no attempt to take any readings the first time. I found him watching the sky out of one of the west windows. There was a high cloud layer, but it was thin, and broken in places. I felt that sky conditions were satisfactory for him to go up, especially as he was not going to turn off the magneto and distributor-head supercharg-ing, which has been the cause of ignition failure in the past. But Loomis told me he had been ordered to fly only so long as he could see the airport at all times, and that he had no confidence in the "management," anyway, and felt he would get no protection if he took off while there was "a cloud in the sky" and anything should go wrong. I told him that if he wanted to go under the existing weather conditions, I would take the responsibility for clearing him, and that I thought he would be safe enough as long as he had openings here and there in the cloud layer and a good ceiling and visibility underneath. I told him to use his judgment on the weather, but that if he decided to go up today and got down in time, I would follow him with a second flight.

Phone call from Dr. Clark at 11:45. Loomis had just taken off. I left at once for Flight to get an early lunch and be ready when he landed. Made all preliminary arrangements: notified medical department to have oxygen ready, got equipment from parachute room, etc. Then waited in the tower control room until Loomis landed and reported the plane O.K. Denitrogenized, took off, and climbed directly to 30,000 feet. Made the first run parallel to the edge of a layer of alto-stratus clouds that hung over the airport. I stayed within sight and gliding angle of Willow Run at all times, which the position of the clouds fortunately allowed me to do. Ran out of gas on the auxiliary tank midway through the first run, but found no difficulty in transferring to main tank (although some had been reported in the operating instructions for the plane). Then climbed to 35,000 feet and made a run. The left mag cut out completely while I was taking the ambient readings. Pulled the turbo back to twenty inches and began descent at once. My radio was cutting out rather badly, but I got enough of a message through to have the field cleared for my landing.

The right mag was rough and seemed to be getting worse, so I kept the plane in a position where I could make a dead-stick landing at any time in case of complete ignition failure.

Conference with Loomis while taking off my equipment. He told me he had been unable to attain more than 34,000 feet and asked what I thought the trouble was. After going over the details of his flying procedure, it seemed probable that he had misread his turbo tachometer and been turning the turbo 8,000 r.p.m. instead of 18,000 r.p.m.

Stopped at Operations long enough to turn in weather code and clearance. Then to office to make out report on flight.

Supper with Anne by the fireplace. After supper we decided to drive over to the Rouge to see the blast-furnace pour. We arrived just in time. The men were extremely considerate and showed us everything. First time for Anne. Drove her around the Rouge afterward to give her some idea of the magnitude of the place. It is certainly the home of Faustian man in his highest state of development.

Monday, November 16

Warm and sunny. Day at home, packing and making final arrangements for trip east. Half hour's walk with Anne before lunch—through grounds of the Cranbrook Foundation. We talked about the possibility of Anne spending a month on Captiva [Florida] this winter. She needs a rest after nursing, and it would give her a good chance to write. Possibly I could go down and spend the last week with her. We had lunch together, outdoors on the porch. To station for 5:45 B. & O. Ambassador to Washington.

Tuesday, November 17

Japanese fleet defeated in naval battle in Solomons. Heavy fighting reported in Tunisia.

Off train about 8:00. Clear, sunny, and warm. Crowd waiting for taxis at station; had to walk several blocks to get one. To Hay-Adams House for breakfast and phone calls.

To Commerce Building to see Jerry Land at 12:00. A pass is now required to get in through the doors of the building. Jerry shows signs of overwork and is under heavy fire from the C.I.O. because of a recent speech he made. He says the various Communist groups are making a strong attempt to "get" him and flooding the White House with letters against him. Like most Roosevelt appointees, he is not sure how long the President will back him up if pressure gets high.

Had some extra time after leaving Jerry's office before an appointment I had made with Senator Shipstead. So decided to walk to the Senate Office Building and stop at the Mellon museum en route instead of going somewhere for lunch. Spent half an hour in the galleries. Then walked through the Capitol grounds to the Senate Office Building and Shipstead's office. He had not arrived yet. I phoned a number of Senators while I was waiting—Byrd, Wheeler, Clark (Missouri), Clark (Idaho), Taft, Vandenberg, and others. Most of them were on the Senate floor.

Spent half an hour talking to Shipstead—about the recent elections, the results in Minnesota, the developments of the war, etc. Then to Bob La Follette's office for a quarter hour with him. He told me of a conference he and other "isolationist" Senators had attended with Foster Dulles, who had recently returned from England. Dulles told them that he had talked "with almost all the officials of the government up to Churchill" and that he was very concerned, "because England obviously intends to pursue an imperialistic policy after the war and has no idea of a world organization for peace [such as Dulles believes in]," etc.

Walked over to station from Senate Office Building to get reservations for New York. Taxi to 2200 S Street, N.W., to see Mrs. Castle for a few minutes. (Bill Castle is in New York.) Then to Washington Hotel to see Justice Murphy,[70] who had asked me to call on him when I was next in Washington. He is an interesting, somewhat eccentric, somewhat mystical, outspoken and politically liberal Irishman—one of those New Deal appointees who has become, after the passage of time, a strong critic of the New Deal. We discussed the Philippines, war in the Orient, war in Europe, political trends here and abroad, etc., etc. Murphy thinks the New Deal will be heavily defeated in 1944. Murphy also stressed his belief that Frankfurter[71] has tremendous power with Roosevelt and is responsible for many of the President's moves.

Boarded B. & O. train for New York.

There are strong rumors in Washington to the effect that the invasion

70. Frank Murphy, justice of the U.S. Supreme Court and former mayor of Detroit (1930–33).

71. Felix Frankfurter, associate justice of the Supreme Court, 1939–62.

of North Africa was scheduled to begin two days before the election and that it misfired because of weather and high seas. According to these reports, the idea was to have the attack begin just in time to turn the election toward the Administration, yet close enough to election day so that any bad news would not be carried in the papers or on the radio until the voting was over.

Wednesday, November 18

Gasoline ration cut to three gallons for eastern states.

Off train at Jersey City at 7:15. Took train bus to Forty-second and Lexington. Walked to Engineers Club and engaged room. Lunch in room at club with George Bakeland, a friend of Truman Smith's, and president of the Bakelite Company. He is interested in plywood and plastic material for planes and the improvement of glues for plywood structures. He wanted me to go to Toronto, Canada, to see a plane being built of plywood and plastic materials, and suggested that if I could not do that, we might go to Grand Rapids together to see the work being done there by the Haskelite Corporation along these lines.

To Pan American offices at 2:30 to see André Priester, Hugo Leuteritz, and Evan Young. All the other officers I know are either in Washington or out on the lines.

Back to club. Paul Palmer came for supper at 7:30. He is now one of the *Reader's Digest* editors and has a considerable voice in deciding their policies. Palmer told me of an evening he spent with Vice-President [Henry] Wallace and a Mr. Marsh in Washington. Wallace and Marsh were discussing the war and agreed that it was "necessary for it to continue" until the "social reforms" the Administration is attempting are closer to completion. The question arose as to what would be a good date for the war to terminate. One said that January 1, 1944, would be a "good date"; the other thought "reforms" would be sufficiently far along by October 1, '43!

The streets and buildings are dark—all lights "dimmed out." New York seems more like a European city without its bright lights. Some of the store windows have screens hanging just inside the glass. One can see fairly well when looking straight through them, but from an angle they shut off the inside light completely. The street stop signals are now nothing more than small crosses of green and red. As I walked along, I suddenly realized that I was seeing the stars and the outlines of the high buildings against them. New York seemed more attractive than ever before.

For a period of slightly over a year Colonel Lindbergh discontinued making entries in his journal. They begin again in December, 1943. During intervening months Lindbergh, in addition to his activities with the Ford Motor Company, had entered a consulting relationship with the United Aircraft Corporation, headquartered at East Hartford, Connecticut. In this capacity he devoted his primary attention to improving the Navy Marine Corsair (F4U) fighter and to plans for a still more advanced fighter to supersede the Corsair.

His trip to Pacific Ocean areas in 1944 was for the purpose of studying the Corsair under combat conditions and to discuss with personnel of active combat squadrons the characteristics desired in the next generation of fighting aircraft.

Monday, December 6

To Willow Run. Most of morning in conference with Henry Ford, Bennett, Ray Dahlinger, and others. Lunch at flight department with pilots. Half hour in Link after lunch. Then to Dearborn airport to check over list of items which may be taken out of the company's Grumman amphibian to save weight. I find that most flights with the plane have been made in an excessively overloaded condition. Recommend that it either be stripped of several hundred pounds of weight, including its automatic pilot, or exchanged for a landplane with better performance. Very difficult to explain problems of safety and overload to Ford officers. Henry Ford likes an amphibian, because he thinks it safer in a lake country like Michigan in case of a forced landing. But he wants to get rid of it at once when I tell him it has low single-engine ceiling and has been flying illegally overloaded. He and Bennett ask what I think is best plane for them to get. I tell them it depends on purpose they want to use it for, but can get no satisfactory answer to that.

Tuesday, December 7

Morning preparing for altitude flight in the Thunderbolt. Then up to maximum altitude of 42,760 feet in afternoon—the highest I have been able to attain as yet. Above 42,000 feet the cylinder-head temperatures pass safe operating limits. Also, the altitude is approaching the limit a pilot can stand without pressure, even with pure oxygen. Willow Run had clouded over during the flight, so I descended over Selfridge, which was clear. There is often an open area in the vicinity of Detroit when the skies everywhere else are overcast. Drove down at highest possible speed to stay below the "compressibility" limit.

Friday, December 10

Morning in conferences and preparing for altitude flight in Thunderbolt. Early lunch, then up for hour-and-forty-minute flight to maximum altitude of 38,000 feet, where I made a series of tests in an attempt to find out what causes engine surging at low r.p.m. at high altitude. Opinion is divided as to whether it is due to the ignition system or to the turbo-regulator. Willow Run clouded over during flight, but Canada remained clear. Descended at just below compressibility speed, east of the Detroit River.

Saturday, December 11

Morning at flight department in conferences. Hawley[72] has had a voice recorder installed in the Thunderbolt at a weight cost of seventy-five pounds. I think it a poor idea, as a pilot is unable to talk much at high altitude regardless of the efficiency of the machine. Also, written readings are satisfactory for the work we are now doing. However, my main objection is that he neither got permission to have the installation made nor arranged to have the new C.G. [center of gravity] properly checked before flying. All this has caused needless delay and has tied the plane up for installations when it might otherwise have been flying. Talked the matter over with [Ed] Bond, Hawley, and [Ed] Scott and believe we will avoid similar occurrence in the future.

72. Murray Hawley, Ford senior pilot.

Took a bomber up for its initial flight in the afternoon (B-24, H-2343). Turned out to be an exceptionally clean ship, so extended flight plan by radio and ran the Army acceptance test also. Beautiful sunset—the clearest colors I have ever seen, I think. Landed after dark.

Tuesday, December 14

Day at home on dictation, income tax matters, and working on my *Spirit of St. Louis* manuscript in the trailer. (Anne at sculpture class at Cranbrook.) The trailer is comfortable, even on these cold days, after it has had two or three hours to warm up, and the solitude it affords out away from the house is a great help in writing or studying.

Thursday, December 16

Sky began to clear so drove to Willow Run and took the Thunderbolt up for an altitude flight lasting an hour and forty-five minutes. Maximum altitude 41,000 feet. Above 35,000 feet for an hour and six minutes. Got into a "compressibility" dive at about 33,000 feet at an indicated air speed of about 330 m.p.h. The nose began to get very heavy, and when I attempted to pull it up, the "compressibility" shudder commenced. I held the angle of dive constant, opened the throttle, and rolled back the elevator tab slightly. The shuddering ended as soon as I stopped trying to pull the nose up, and I had full control of the plane again before I passed the 25,000-foot level. Willow Run had clouded over, so I descended over Grosse Isle on the Canadian side of the river and flew back under the clouds. Landed with about twenty-five gallons of gas left in the tanks.

Friday, December 17

Anne, Jr., and Land are in bed with flu.

Conference with Bricker about need of sending another pilot to Mayo Clinic for altitude training. Conference with Dr. Clark and Hawley on general policy of pilot selection. Phoned General Wood in evening. Arranged to meet him in Chicago next Tuesday.

Monday, December 20

Conference with Bennett and Bricker during most of morning. Phone calls in regard to B-24 nose-turret controversy. To Michigan Central Station and boarded 12:30 train for Chicago.

Tuesday, December 21

Off train at 7:20 Most of morning at club in conference with General Wood about political and war trends, the possible [presidential] candidacy of [General] MacArthur, etc. Lunch with Wood, Clay Judson, Colonel McCormick, Sterling Morton,[73] and others at Chicago Club. Short visit with Senator Nye at his room in Morrison Hotel in afternoon. Supper with General and Mrs. Wood at their daughter's home in Forest Hills. Back to Chicago in time to board the 11:50 train for Detroit.

Friday, December 24

About fifteen quail and several pheasants came into the yard this morning to get the grain we scatter around the trailer.

To Willow Run. Lunch with pilots, and informal conferences following. Afternoon in office.

Home at 5:00 for Christmas Eve with children and Anne. Anne has made a very simple and beautiful little crèche in the library, and we had music and reading in front of it, with all children taking part, except Scott, who is in bed with a fever. It was the best Christmas Eve we have ever had.

Saturday, December 25

Breakfast with Anne and the children. Extra ration of grain for the birds. More are coming into the yard each day. Most of morning with the children and their presents. Scott was well enough to come down, and Jon built a fire in the large fireplace to keep the room warm. Hour's walk

73. Clay Judson, Chicago lawyer and member of the executive committee of America First; Sterling Morton, secretary and director of the Morton Salt Co., later chairman of the board.

through the fields with Jon before late lunch. Afternoon divided between playing with the children and working on my *Spirit of St. Louis* manuscript. Evening with Anne in library—music and reading.

Sunday, December 26

Anne, Anne, Jr., Jon, Land, and I drove over to spend the day with Mother and B.—a second Christmas for the children—with a roast-goose dinner. I spent half an hour working on my *Spirit of St. Louis* manuscript in the afternoon. Then gave Land a few lessons in shooting a .22 rifle, and spent the rest of the time playing in whatever happened to be going on. Found Jon and Land quarreling savagely over Jon's right to run Land's boat when Land didn't want him to! Hope I made enough impression to decrease the frequency of such problems in the future. But it was a good day, and I am constantly more thankful for this time I have had with Mother and the children here in Detroit.

Tuesday, December 28

Delivered a bomber to Romulus Field, and spent an hour or two with the officers there. Conference with Colonel [Leroy] De Arcey in regard to Ford–Ferry Command relationships. They have improved greatly during last several months. The Ferry Command is anxious to use Willow Run for transitional training, and to take delivery of B-24's there instead of at Romulus.

Wednesday, December 29

Short conference with Henry Ford, Bennett, Bricker, and Campsall. Then took the P-47 up for an altitude flight. Ground haze but unusually clear beyond the Detroit area. From 30,000 feet I could see far south of Toledo, all of Saginaw Bay, a large part of Lake Huron, up into the northern part of lower Michigan, many miles into Canada, half of Lake Erie, and, vaguely, westward to the shore of Lake Michigan. Made my top altitude today—43,020 feet. Previous maximum was 42,760 feet. Descended from 43,000 feet to 15,000 feet in just over two minutes.

Friday, December 31

Planned on an altitude flight in the Thunderbolt, but conference developed with Bennett and Bricker, which took all morning. Most of these conferences, which start out to be about business, are taken up with reminiscences of old times and accounts of personal experiences. Finally rode into the Rouge with Bennett to get in the questions I wanted answered: 1) concerning Ford Company's relationship with the Army Ferry Command, and the latter's desire to take delivery of B-24's at Willow Run instead of Romulus; 2) the possibility of Ford financing Harry Elmer Barnes[74] to write a history on the origins of the present war. Bennett insists I stay for lunch, to which he has invited one of the notorious Detroit gangsters!

Tuesday, January 4

Spread grain for the birds; the quail were back yesterday. Breakfast and to Willow Run. First part of afternoon packing and making final arrangements before leaving for east. Anne and I to Rouge administration building garage to pick up driver, and then on to Pennsylvania Station. Boarded 5:30 Ambassador for Washington.

Wednesday, January 5

Off train about 9:00. I took taxi to 2200 S Street for half hour's conference with Bill Castle in regard to war developments and the political situation. Apparently the old Hoover crowd are tending away from Bricker[75] and toward Dewey at present. To Navy Building at 2:00 for conference with Brigadier General [Louis E.] Wood (Marines) concerning possibility of my going to the South Pacific for a survey of Corsair operating bases in the combat zone. He would favor such a trip and will take matter up with higher naval officers. But will they feel they have

74. American historian, sociologist, and teacher, author of *History of Western Civilization* (1935) and *An Intellectual and Cultural History of the Western World* (1937).

75. John W. Bricker, Governor of Ohio, 1939–45, and Republican candidate for Vice-President in 1944.

to bring the matter to Roosevelt's attention? If not, there is probably a good chance of obtaining authority to go.

Thursday, January 6

Phoned General Wood at 11:00. He said arrangements could be made for my going to the South Pacific, but that whether or not I could obtain a Corsair to cover the combat-zone fields would depend on the local commanders. In reply to my inquiry, he said he (unofficially) felt that would be simple in some cases and difficult in others. Phoned Gene Wilson, who said he felt trip might not be worth while unless a Corsair could be made available. He will contact Admiral Towers. Lunch at Commerce Building with Jerry Land. He says shipping losses now relatively light. Boarded New York train about 11:00.

Friday, January 7

Morning on phone calls and short walk. Lunch with Guy Vaughan—discussed Curtiss-Wright, war, and politics.

Sunday, January 9

Anne and I to 10 Gracie Square for dinner with Juan and Betty Trippe at their apartment. Juan and I discussed Pan American—present and future—the war, domestic politics, the question of "freedom of the air," etc.

Monday, January 10

Boarded 9:10 White Mountain express for Hartford. Conferences with Frank Caldwell and Gene Wilson. Lunch with company officers. Afternoon in office and on conferences.

Tuesday, January 11

Boarded 8:55 train for Bridgeport—drawing room with Frank Caldwell and others. Taxi to Chance Vought factory. Conference and lunch with

Paul Baker.[76] Discussed new designs for fighters—single-engine, twin-engine, jet propulsion, etc. Went over preliminary designs and specifications. Afternoon at airport. Took one of the Corsairs up for an hour's acceptance flight.

Wednesday, January 12

First part of morning on phone calls and writing. Then to Chance Vought. Conference with Rex Beisel.[77] Lunch with company officers. To Sikorsky factory in afternoon. Through factory with Sikorsky and Mike Gluhareff.[78] To Sikorsky's home in the country for supper and evening. Mrs. Sikorsky and three of the boys there. We discussed the manuscript of the book he has written, *The Mysterious Encounter*. Sikorsky showed lantern slides of the Mexican volcano he recently visited. Night at the Sikorsky home.

Thursday, January 13

Breakfast with Igor and Mrs. Sikorsky. To Sikorsky factory with Igor. We spent most of the morning watching test flights of the XR5—the largest helicopter they have yet built (about 5,000 lbs. gross). Lunch with Sikorsky and first part of afternoon at the factory. Took 7:50 train to New York. Subway to Medical Center and bus to Englewood—jammed until there was no more standing room left. Got off at foot of Palisades and walked to Next Day Hill. Mrs. Morrow, Anne, and Wheeler-Bennett there when I arrived.

Friday, January 14

Walk through woods and conference with Arthur Springer about Little School and family affairs. Phone call from Gene Wilson. He has learned through Russell Vought[79] that major military movements are expected in

76. Test pilot, chief of aerodynamics and flight test, engineering manager of Chance Vought Aircraft Division, United Aircraft, 1930–52.

77. Acting general manager of Chance Vought Aircraft Division of United Aircraft; in 1943 he became general manager. From 1946 to 1948 he was vice president of United Aircraft.

78. Michael E. Gluhareff, chief engineer of Sikorsky Aircraft Division, United Aircraft.

79. Vice president of United Aircraft Service Corp., 1941–58.

the South Pacific in the near future, which make it advisable for me to postpone my projected trip.

Saturday, January 15

Phoned Bridgeport to arrange for transportation to Eglin Field, where a fighting-plane conference and demonstration is being held. Difficult to arrange for Navy plane on such short notice, so will probably go by train.

Sunday, January 16

Left for city at 5:00 with Anne, Mrs. Morrow, and Wheeler-Bennett. Dropped Anne at Con's apartment; she took 7:00 train for Detroit. To Pennsylvania Station to get ticket. Supper with Aubrey and Con at their apartment. Boarded 10:00 train for Montgomery, Alabama, en route Eglin Field.

Monday, January 17

Train full of soldiers. Many more on platform, some with wives and mothers come to say good-by. Sad faces—no enthusiasm apparent anywhere.

Reached Montgomery, Alabama, about 12:30 A.M. Boarded train for Pensacola.

Tuesday, January 18

Up at 6:30. Boarded train for Crestview—about an hour's trip. Eglin Field officer invited me to ride to the field in his car. Spent day inspecting new Army and Navy fighters and in discussions concerning fighter requirements. We drove to one of the testing grounds in the afternoon to watch firing of bombs, shells, and rockets. Two 1,000-lb. bombs were dropped by a low-flying P-38 on a dugout similar to those the Japanese are using in the South Pacific islands. Direct hit but ricocheted and did no damage (delayed-action type). A B-25 two-engine bomber made several passes at a nearby target using 75-mm. shells. A dive bomber dropped one bomb on a target about a mile from our position. A Mustang (P-51) fired six rockets at a target only one hundred yards to one side—fair accuracy. And a Mustang put on a 37-mm.-cannon demonstration.

To officers club for supper with officers and company representatives who are taking part in this conference—one hundred or more in all. Night with United officers at Bacon's Lodge on the beach. Wish Anne were here and we could spend a week together in the Everglades. How I miss those vacations we had before the war!

Wednesday, January 19

To field, and up for an hour's test flight in the P60-E (low-wing, single-seat fighter; R-2800 engine; 2,000 h.p.). Lost radio mast in a dive at about 380 m.p.h. indicated. An interesting plane with many good characteristics, but still experimental. Took P51-B7 up next (low-wing; single-seat fighter; Packard-Merlin engine). Excellent plane—among best in world today. About an hour's flight—dives up to 485 m.p.h. indicated, stalls, aerobatics, etc.

Afternoon in conferences and watching film on air combat in Europe. Attended lecture which followed—deflection vision requirements and gun sighting.

Thursday, January 20

To Eglin Field and up for an hour's flight in the Bell P63-A1 (low-wing fighter with submerged Allison engine; tricycle gear; single seater). Excellent plane: high rate of climb, good speed, and other characteristics. Took P40-N (Curtiss low-wing, single-seat fighter; Allison engine) up next. Obsolete type. Has seen much use in war but no longer of great interest. Attended general fighter discussion in afternoon—engine and plane requirements.

Friday, January 21

To Eglin Field and up for forty-five minutes' flight in the Mosquito bomber (two Rolls-Royce engines; wooden; two-place monoplane). Very awkward and complicated cockpit; no check-off list, and mechanic in charge, who was only one there who knew anything about the plane, was uncertain about several of the switches and levers. Good take-off, climb, and high speed. Ailerons unstable near stall. Excellent slow roll, etc. Kept plane up for only forty-five minutes, as many pilots anxious to fly it.

Up for an hour's flight in the Republic P47-K (metal; low-wing Army fighter; single seater; R-2800 engine; bubble canopy). Excellent vision except ahead. Excessive rudder forces in dive. Ailerons became unstable at 450 m.p.h. indicated at 8,000 feet.

Attended conference on fighters during first part of afternoon. Up for an hour's flight in Boeing B-29 later in afternoon (as passenger, except for about fifteen minutes at controls). Was invited by young first lieutenant who has plane here for tests. Smooth and quiet cockpit. Gives impression of well-engineered plane. However, first impressions are dangerous.

Short walk along beach at sunset—clear sky and deep Florida colors. Almost too beautiful to look at. (There are such things at times.) I think of the Everglades and Anne and the years before the war. At night, when I stand on the beach and look at the stars, I wonder why man describes as progress the science which screens such beauty from his life. In our search for knowledge we lose appreciation and trade God's great gifts for man-made baubles.

Saturday, January 22

To Eglin Field for 8:15 fighter conference during which the Navy types were discussed. Ended at 11:30. Lunch with Bell Aircraft officers. Discussed fighter types, including jet-propulsion types, with their engineer, Salisbury. Up for a forty-five-minute flight in the latest P-63 in afternoon. Back to inn about 5:00.

Sunday, January 23

Arrived at field at 9:00. United Lodestar delayed by low fog. Finally off for Washington at 11:25 as passenger. Full plane (fourteen passengers), mostly United officers. Landed at Washington and New York. Then on to East Hartford at night.

Tuesday, January 25

Drove to United offices with [Gene] Wilson and McCarthy.[80] Morning on trip through wind tunnel with John Lee,[81] routine and conferences. Conference with Lee and engineers concerning future fighter designs. Conference in [Frederick] Rentschler's office on general United development for Pratt & Whitney engines. Afternoon on routine and conferences. Conference with Wilson and McCarthy in regard to future transport designs; with McCarthy and John Lee concerning this and also the choice between turbo and two-stage supercharging for the 4360 engine to go in the B-29.

Supper and night at Hartford Club. Worked on manuscript, and went for a walk through Hartford later in the evening.

Wednesday, January 26

To Bridgeport with Gene Wilson in Boeing 247. Lunch with Chance Vought officers. Several Congressmen here on visit, including Maas of Minnesota. Warm political welcome from them as I entered the dining room! Most of afternoon in conference with Paul Baker in regard to fighter designs and the possibility that jet propulsion may take over the pursuit field entirely. Wilson took part in the last half hour of discussion.

Friday, January 28

Taxi to Chance Vought factory. Morning in conferences. Early afternoon at factory and airport—conferences and a half hour in Link. Train to New York to meet [Harold] Bixby at Grand Central. Out to his home in Bronxville for supper and evening. Mrs. Bixby and two of his daughters were there, and a young Mr. Zimmerman, who had been in China about the same time as the Bixbys. He has just completed training as a parachutist to be dropped in China to organize resistance against the Japanese. Like so many other ventures these days, the whole idea collapsed—just as he was about to finish the course. He is now with Pan

80. Charles J. McCarthy, vice president of United Aircraft, 1942–54.

81. Assistant director of research at United Aircraft; from 1955 to 1964 director of research.

American Airways, and Bix is planning to send him to India to attempt the salvage of vital parts from planes which have crashed in the mountains on the air route to China.

Spent most of the evening with Bixby in an upstairs room, discussing the incidents which preceded the construction and flights of the *Spirit of St. Louis*. I want this data for use in the first part of my manuscript.

Back to Bridgeport for the night.

Saturday, January 29

To airport and took a Corsair up for initial shakedown flight—1:35. The quality of the planes is excellent now—very few and unimportant "crabs."

Monday, January 31

First part of morning in room working on manuscript. Then taxi to Chance Vought factory for conference with engineers concerning designs for future fighters. We discussed three types: a single-engine fighter around the new wasp Major 4360 engine; a twin-engine type around R-2800 engines; and a jet-propelled type—all single seaters with a radius of action (combat) of 750 miles and a landing speed of between eighty-five and ninety m.p.h. Preference was for the twin-engine plane as against the single-engine; but the speed, compactness, and other advantages of the jet type made us question the advisability of building any more fighters around conventional power plants. But we haven't sufficient information about the jet to decide intelligently, and decided to try to obtain comprehensive data from the Army or Navy before coming to any conclusions.

Took late afternoon train to New York to meet Harry Elmer Barnes at the Engineers Club for dinner. We discussed his intention of writing a history of the causes of the present war and the possibility of Ford financing the project. I outlined the general situation to him, and suggested that I try to arrange a meeting with Bennett in Detroit next week.

Tuesday, February 1

Boarded the 7:28 train for Hartford. Taxi to United offices, East Hartford. Conference at 11:30 in Fred Rentschler's office concerning result of Eglin Field tests, future fighter designs, and the impact of jet propulsion on military aircraft. (United has been carrying on its own experiments in this field.)

Late afternoon train back to New York. Took room at Engineers Club. Started in to dining room and saw Donald Hall, who is east on patent business for Consolidated. He was with Burnelli. We all had dinner together. Evening with Hall and Burnelli. After the latter left, Hall and I discussed the concept and construction of the *Spirit of St. Louis* in San Diego—material I want to use in my manuscript.

Wednesday, February 2

To Harcourt, Brace and Company to look at new cover design for *The Steep Ascent*.[82] It is very good, although not exactly what we wanted. The book should be out about March 16, Brace says. Walked to station and boarded the Detroiter.

Thursday, February 3

Taxi to Rouge administration building garage. Picked up my radio car and drove to Willow Run. Late breakfast at flight department restaurant while I talked to Murray Hawley. Frictions and troubles still continue in flight department, but with much less intensity under Ed Bond—who seems to be doing an excellent job as head of the department. Conference in Logan Miller's office in regard to the possibilities of steam-turbine engines in aircraft.

Friday, February 4

Talked to Bennett about Harry Elmer Barnes and his desire to write a book on the causes of the present war. Bennett suggested a meeting with Barnes Monday or Tuesday.

Saturday, February 5

Few minutes in office; then through the plant with members of British party visiting Willow Run: Sir Andrew Rae Duncan (British Minister of

82. By Anne Morrow Lindbergh.

Supply); General Sir Walter K. Venning (Director General, British Supply Mission); Sir Charles Hambro,[83] Mr. George Briggs, and others.

Up with Dr. Clark for first oxygen flight in the new Willow Run altitude chamber—to 42,000 feet. It is probably the best altitude chamber in the country—set up under the direction of Emil Zoerlin.

Monday, February 7

Took Dr. Barnes through Willow Run during first part of morning. After that, we drove through the streets of Willow Lodge and then in to the Rouge administration building. As usual, Bennett had a number of other guests for lunch. After it was over we (Bennett, Barnes, and I) discussed Barnes's desire to write a book on the causes of the present war.

Thursday, February 10

Drove home via Detroit and picked up William Henry Chamberlin[84] at the Book Cadillac. He, Anne, and I spent the evening discussing the war, domestic politics, future trends, etc. Much speculation about Russia. No one knows much about what is actually happening on the Eastern front, yet it is the key to the European war.

Friday, February 11

Dropped Chamberlin at the Book Cadillac en route to Willow Run. Then to flight department for conference with Dr. Clark and Emil Zoerlin about experiments to be run in the new altitude chamber. Made an ascent in the chamber to 48,000 feet and another to 49,000 feet. In making this ascent, Clark, Duffy, and I went up together to 35,000 feet. I remained there for ten minutes. Then Clark and Duffy went into the air lock and remained at 35,000 feet, while I continued to ascend in the main chamber. The idea was to have assistance quickly available if I passed out during the experiment. However, as I was ascending above 40,000 feet, Clark got the "chokes" and had to be lowered in the lock. I found it impossible to go higher than 48,000 feet and gave the signal to

83. Head of British Raw Materials Mission, Washington, 1943–44.

84. Writer, Moscow correspondent for the *Christian Science Monitor,* 1922–34, and author of numerous books on Russia.

descend when I realized I would become unconscious if I remained longer at that altitude.

I was dropped quickly to about 30,000 by Zoerlin, who was at the controls outside the chamber and noticed that the outer door to the air lock was open. As soon as it was found that Clark was all right, Duffy reascended in the lock and remained at 35,000 while I tried another ascent. Made 49,000 the second time, possibly because the rate of climb was higher. Then descended to 35,000 to pick up Duffy, and we both reascended to 40,000, and tried a rapid descent to field elevation—getting down and the chamber door open in about one and a half minutes. Since I have been flying as high as 43,000 feet in the P-47, I was anxious to find out how much higher I could go without getting too close to the edge of consciousness. Forty-three thousand feet is obviously close to the maximum altitude where one can remain for long without a pressure mask.

Sunday, February 13

Anne and I drove to Orchard Lake to attend service at "the Church of the Wildwood," where Great-grandfather Lodge used to preach. Drove to 508 Lakepointe for rest of afternoon with Mother and B. Back home with Jon and Land about 6:00. I let them take turns sitting next to me and running the car with the accelerator.

Friday, February 18

Karl Scott came to my office almost as soon as I arrived. He was much disturbed over the Ford Company's apparent lack of interest in building up an aeronautical engineering organization. It is the old story. The Ford officers are not sure what they want to do in aviation after the war and consequently have no definite policy about research. On the one hand, they want to keep themselves in the position where they can manufacture aircraft if they desire to. On the other, they do not want to be committed too far. The result is a series of statements and press articles which indicate the company is going to build postwar aircraft while little or no actual preparation along these lines is being made. Henry Ford says he wants to build large transport planes, but neither he nor his officers seem to face the fact that a large transport plane must be preceded by a large engineering organization and several years of design and construction. Many of the men at Willow Run are undecided whether to stay with the company and take a chance on its postwar aviation activity or start looking now for a job with a company which is more certain of staying in the business. A number of men here are so dissatisfied that they would have left some time ago except for the wartime restrictions and the fact that they could not get a release. Some of the engineers have obtained "medical releases," and others are attempting to get them. There is a general atmosphere of uncertainty that is quite bad for morale.

There is a column in one of the Detroit papers to the effect that I persuaded Henry Ford to allow smoking in the lunchrooms at Willow Run as a courtesy to visiting officers and dignitaries to improve company and government relationships, etc. Fact is that when I first came here I found Army officers and personnel smoking at the same tables with Ford officers and personnel—who did not dare keep them company because of the strictly enforced company rules against smoking on or around Ford property. I suggested to Harry Bennett that this situation was embarrassing for the Ford men and would inevitably cause a lowering of morale. He fully agreed, spoke to Henry Ford about it, and arranged for the rule to be rescinded. My action was in behalf of the Ford men, not of the visitors.

Thursday, February, 24

Spent most of day testing bombers. Took No. 94982 up for its initial flight. Unable to accept it because of nonfunctioning propeller governor on No. 4 engine. Landed and had governor repaired while crew getting lunch. Let my co-pilot take the ship for its second flight while I co-piloted for him. All O.K. on this flight, and I accepted the plane. Took No. 4822 up for its Army acceptance flight just before sunset. Plane O.K.—accepted. Landed after dark.

Thursday, March 2

Talked to Bricker about fuel situation at Romulus Air Base—an excellent example of government red tape. There is a shortage of 100-octane gasoline in the country. The factory tests on the B-24's are run with 100-octane. But because of the general shortage of this grade of fuel, the

Ford Company has been ordered to put only 1,400 gallons in the tanks at the time the bombers leave Willow Run. The bombers are flown by company pilots to the Romulus Air Base of the Ferry Command—a distance of about ten miles. From there the Ferry Command pilots take these planes to the modification depot at Birmingham, Alabama. But an additional 200 gallons of fuel have to be put in at Romulus in order to have a safe margin for the trip to Birmingham. Because of the 100-octane shortage there is a regulation requiring Romulus Air Base to put 91-octane gasoline in the bombers for ferry flights, although they have 100-octane gasoline available on the field.

At Birmingham, the airport where the bombers land has rather short runways and is located in a hollow between hills (according to reports—I have not been there). Consequently, there is a regulation which requires that the bombers must have 100-octane gasoline in the tanks for take-off. Regulations require that the octane rating of fuel in an airplane be considered that of lowest grade of fuel placed in the tanks since they were last drained. Therefore, all the gasoline in the tanks of the bombers landing at Birmingham from Romulus is treated as 91-octane fuel and must be drained and replaced with 100-octane before the bombers can take off again. The amount drained averages 600 or 700 gallons. In other words, we save 200 gallons of 100-octane gasoline at Willow Run and thereby lose 600 to 700 gallons at Birmingham. If we were permitted to put 1,600 gallons instead of 1,400 gallons in the tanks before the bombers leave here, it would be unnecessary to add any fuel at Romulus, and all the fuel in the tanks when the planes land at Birmingham would be suitable for operation from the airport there. I am trying to arrange for authority for the Ford Company to do this. All company officers are in favor of the move, and it only remains for us to get an O.K. through official government channels. At 450 gallons per plane the net saving in 100-octane fuel would be about 125,000 gallons per month on our present production at Willow Run, to say nothing of the red tape and labor involved.

Friday, March 3

Phoned Paul Baker in regard to the Corsair the Vought Company is getting ready to send to the Pacific area. The plane was to contain all the latest improvements, and I was considering going with it at least as far as Hawaii and possibly to Australia and the combat areas. Baker told me the plane had crashed and that its pilot, Boothby,[85] had been killed. Details were not yet available. Boothby had radioed that the plane was on fire and apparently made several radio contacts with the ground station. He reported the fire out but the engine dead over territory where there was no satisfactory place to land. He said, or implied, that he was about to jump. He did jump, but his body was found badly broken. Eyewitness accounts, which are always of doubtful reliability, reported the chute only partly open during his descent.

Always, after I hear of the death of a pilot I have known, I see him for a time with exceptional clarity—more clearly than if I had just left him to step into another room. In fact, I see him with my mind almost more clearly than if I were looking at him with my eyes at the moment. Death gives a background to life as night to the stars. I did not know Boothby well, but I saw him almost every time I was on the airport at Bridgeport —a young pilot, probably about twenty-two or twenty-three years old but looking much younger—slender build—large, friendly eyes, his lips always seeming about to smile. He was one of the most skillful test pilots on the field.

Saturday, March 4

The newspapers today carry headlines FORD FIRES SORENSEN three inches high and all across the front page. It has been coming for a long time, but seems an unnecessarily crude way to handle such a situation. There was no need to have such headlines. Still, it is true to the character of the Ford organization, and there is a certain justice in them. Sorensen has shown little or no consideration for the men under him, and he has fired many a workman in a flash of temper and for no reasonable cause.

Sorensen was born for another era, an era which is rapidly passing even in the industries of Detroit. His production genius lay to a large extent in this driving ability exercised in a day when engineering was less important in industry than it is at present—when the success of new designs was not so dependent on the drafting board. Probably it is unfair to judge this man on the standards of the present generation. He was raised in different times and under different customs and ethics. He lived in the "two-gun" days of American industry and "shot it out with the best of them." He was a hard-boiled, hard-fisted fighter and probably would prefer to be known as such.

85. Willard B. Boothby, test pilot for Vought.

Sunday, March 5

Anne and I went for an hour's walk along the country roads to the south and west. Then I drove to Mother's, where Jon and Land had spent the night. Jon found his way there alone by bus from Detroit, and was extremely proud of the accomplishment. Spent the afternoon with Mother and B. and the children. Both Jon and Land do a great deal of shooting in the little rifle range in the basement. Land now enjoys it very much, and Jon is getting to be an expert shot.

Monday, March 6

Conference with Bricker in regard to Ford taking over all B-24 engineering. Lunch with Bricker, [Detroit] Mayor [Edward] Jeffries, and other Ford officers. Jeffries came to Willow Run to give a "pep talk" on war production. Home early and rest of day spent on preparations for trip I hope to make into the South Pacific area.

Wednesday, March 8

Anne and I drove to the station in time to board the 7:00 train (Detroiter) for New York.

Thursday, March 9

Anne to Cosmopolitan Club. I to Engineers Club. Bakhmeteff came over for lunch. We discussed the war, Russia, and political trends in this country. Supper with Con and Aubrey at their apartment. Anne and I to Hotel Chatham for the night.

Friday, March 10

Train to Bridgeport. Lunch with Vought officers. Conference with Rex Beisel in regard to my prospective trip into the Pacific area. He phoned Admiral Richardson[86] in Washington. Richardson was cautiously in favor of my going but replied that it was a "delicate problem."

86. Admiral Lawrence B. Richardson, Assistant Chief, Bureau of Aeronautics, Navy Department.

Most of afternoon in conference with Paul Baker and the engineering troop in regard to the design of a twin-engine Corsair fighter. Enthusiasm was low. There have been too many projects and too little definite action. Also, the high theoretical performance of the jet-propelled fighter, backed by increasing practical experience, leaves much doubt about the value of a new fighter built around conventional engines. Spent most of evening working on my *Spirit of St. Louis* manuscript.

Saturday, March 11

Morning in conference with engineers. Lunch with Beisel and Baker in regard to fighter designs. Late afternoon train to New York. Met Anne at Chatham Hotel. Dinner together in a French restaurant. To Carlton House to see Agnes Herrick afterward. French maid; French furnishings. The years have brought no change. Here, Paris of 1927 lives today.

Sunday, March 12

Up late. Most of morning discussing plans with Anne. Hour's walk along the streets. Another hour in the Engineers Club's library working on my manuscript. Lunch at Grand Central station. Met Anne at Aubrey and Con's apartment at 4:00. Hour visiting. Walked back to Engineers Club. Worked for a time on manuscript. Train to Bridgeport.

Tuesday, March 14

Taxi to United offices in East Hartford. Conference with John Lee concerning fighter designs and results of research on jet performances. Afternoon in office studying research data, etc. Night at Hartford Club.

Wednesday, March 15

To United offices. Phoned Brigadier General Wood in Washington. Conference with Frank Caldwell and John Lee in regard to fighter designs. Train to New York. Went to see a news picture. Night at Engineers Club.

Thursday, March 16

Anne's book is out today. The reviews are reasonably good, everything considered, but only one or two of them get more than the superficial points.

Went for a walk in the afternoon. Kenneth Boedecker[87] came over from Paterson to have supper with me. Guy Vaughan joined us for a short time. Spent most of the evening talking about 1927 and the days at Curtiss Field before I took off for Paris. I was anxious to clarify my memory about a number of items in connection with the manuscript I am writing.

Saturday, March 18

Edward Moore came for lunch with me. We discussed Carrel, the war, and Moore's desire to carry out Carrel's plans for an "Institute of Man" in this country. Anne's book is beginning to show up in the bookstore windows—in three out of four that I passed today.

Boarded the 12:55 Pennsylvania train for Washington. *The Steep Ascent* has good reviews in the *Times* and *Tribune* book sections.

Sunday, March 19

Taxi to Carlton Hotel. First part of morning working on manuscript. Bought second Sunday papers and found three reviews of Anne's book— all good except one syndicated from the New York *Post*—political, untrue, and unfair.

Monday, March 20

Tom Lanphier[88] came over for lunch (now full colonel—head of G-2 aviation). We talked about air developments, the war, and his sons—

87. Assistant director of sales and service, and engineer at Wright Aero Division, Curtiss-Wright Corp. He assisted Lindbergh at Curtiss Field, Long Island, in 1927, in readying the *Spirit of St. Louis* for the flight to Paris.

88. Thomas Lanphier, old friend of Lindbergh and World War I pilot, had been the commanding officer of the 1st Pursuit Group at Selfridge Field, Mich. He resigned in 1928 to become an officer of Transcontinental Air Transport (a predecessor of Trans World Airlines). In April, 1943 his son, Colonel Thomas Lanphier, Jr., shot down Admiral Isoroku Yamamoto in one of the most extraordinary interceptions of the Pacific war.

one in civil life because of health, one a prisoner of the Japanese (shot down during an air raid), and one back in this country after an exceptionally fine record in the Pacific area. (The latter two are fighter pilots.)

To Navy Building at 2:00 to see Rear Admiral Ramsey[89] in regard to my going into the Pacific area. He said he thought it could be arranged and told me I would have his personal support. I find a very friendly reception wherever I come in contact with service personnel—Army, Navy, or Marine. He suggested starting from California about April 15. Had planned on returning to New York tonight and to Bridgeport in morning, but have changed my plans and am taking tomorrow afternoon train to Detroit.

Friday, March 24

Took a bomber up for initial shakedown flight in late afternoon. Plane in excellent condition so ran Army acceptance flight also. Gave my co-pilot two landings and take-offs while we were passing time. (A bomber must have at least two and a half hours in the air before the Army will accept it.)

Monday, March 27

To Willow Run. Conference with Bennett and Bricker. Bennett is just back from a month at his ranch near Palm Springs, California. Most of the discussion was about Sorensen. Conference with Henry Ford, Henry Ford II, Bennett, and Bricker. Ford explained his recent statement to the press, to the effect that the war would be over in two months, by saying he thought Russia would be out of it by that time, and that that would mean the war was over. We discussed some of the problems involved in the construction of postwar aircraft. We have been ahead of schedule for several months now, and produced over 400 B-24's in February (including the knock-downs shipped to Douglas, Consolidated, and North American).

89. Rear Admiral DeWitt C. Ramsey, Assistant Chief of the Bureau of Aeronautics, 1941–42; wartime commander of aircraft carrier and task forces.

Tuesday, March 28

Morning at home putting affairs in order. Family lunch. To Ford airport, Dearborn, in afternoon. Stopped at Edison Institute en route to leave a photograph of Grandfather and his old iron mortar, to be placed in the showcase with his gas furnace.[90]

Wednesday, March 29

Phone call from Jack Horner.[91] Authorization for my trip to the South Pacific has been received from Admiral Ramsey. I plan to leave here tomorrow night. First part of the morning spent on plans and putting affairs in shape. To Willow Run for a short conference with Bricker. Lunch with Bennett at the Rouge administration building. Henry Ford and Henry Ford II came in afterward to say good-by and wish me good luck on my trip. Home early and rest of afternoon putting affairs in order for leaving. Hour with the children before their bedtime. Supper in the library with Anne and Jon.

Thursday, March 30

Letter came from Donald Brace saying that a 23,000 second edition of *The Steep Ascent* was being printed. Anne and I went for a half hour's walk before lunch—to the apple orchard hill and back. Finished packing in the afternoon and completed a number of odd jobs such as jacking up one side of the trailer where it had sunk into the ground during last week's warm spell. Kept the last half hour free for Anne and the children. Drove to Rouge to pick up driver to take my car back. Then to Michigan Central Station and boarded the 7:00 Detroiter for New York.

90. Lindbergh's maternal grandfather, Dr. Charles H. Land, held a number of patents on high-temperature gas furnaces. The Edison Institute has a model of one of these furnaces. The old iron mortar was used by Dr. Land to break down and grind into powder form various materials for his experiments and dental techniques.

91. H. M. Horner, president of United Aircraft, 1943–56, when he became chairman of the board.

Friday, March 31

Train on time. Boarded 10:30 train for Hartford. Taxi to the United offices in East Hartford. Lunch with officers: Jack Horner, Luke Hobbs, Walsh,[92] and McCarthy. Spent afternoon making arrangements for my trip: letter to draft board, letter to Admiral Ramsey, phone calls, etc. Hour's walk through the streets of Hartford before supper.

Saturday, April 1

Nine o'clock appointment at hospital for inoculations. The nurse came in with *six* large syringes laid out on a tray! "Is someone else taking this, too?" I asked. "No, these are all for you." Schick test, typhoid, typhus, cholera, tetanus, and smallpox. She told me to sit down. I replied that I preferred to take them standing. She said they often had men pass out during the procedure! As a matter of fact, it was not so bad, and apart from one slightly sore arm and one very sore one, I noticed no effects. Spent a few minutes talking to the doctors, and then returned to my office to complete final details for the trip. Lunch with Frank Caldwell and John Lee. We discussed pursuit designs, jet propulsion, etc. To Hartford Club. Packed and took the 3:15 train to New York.

Sunday, April 2

First part of afternoon working on manuscript. Then subway to American Museum to see the *Tingmissartoq*. It is now ten years that it has been hanging silently in the Hall of Ocean Life, still trim and sleek and beautiful, a plane that was years ahead of its time. I stood looking at it, thinking of the places it had taken Anne and me, of the weather and the skies it had flown through, of the Arctic and the tropic bays where it had landed, of the nights we had slept together in that slender fuselage— through the typhoon off the island of Ketoi, away from the disease and

92. Leonard S. Hobbs had been with Pratt & Whitney Aircraft since 1927; he became vice president in 1934. From 1935 to 1944 he was engineering manager of United Aircraft. In 1944 he became vice president of engineering and later vice chairman and a member of the executive committee. Raycroft Walsh, general manager of United Aircraft's Hamilton Standard Division. In 1940 he became vice president and in 1943 vice chairman.

dust and dirt of the Cape Verdes, on the Rio Minho between Portugal and Spain. The equipment from our flights is still in the showcases down below, and there are still men, women, and children filing past them just as ten years ago. I stood on the balcony and watched for a time and then went down and looked at the showcases myself.

Spent over an hour walking through the halls and rooms of the museum; stopped for a last look at the plane and returned to the club for another hour's work on my manuscript.

Monday, April 3

To Brooks Brothers to buy uniforms and equipment for trip. Uniforms must be worn in combat areas. I go on a "technician status." Therefore, on leaving this country, I must wear a naval officer's uniform without insignia of rank. Bought a waterproof flashlight at Abercrombie & Fitch. Purchased a small New Testament at Brentano's. Since I can carry only one book—and a very small one—that is my choice. It would not have been a decade ago; but the more I learn and the more I read, the less competition it has.

Subway and taxi to Marine Hospital at 67 Hudson Street to get my inoculation for yellow fever. I found Dr. W. G. Nelson to be in charge; he was attached to the embassy in Moscow when Anne and I were there in 1938. Hour on manuscript in afternoon. Phoned Aubrey and Con to ask them out for dinner, but they were giving a dinner for Wheeler-Bennett and several of his friends at their apartment. Phoned Harold Bixby. Out for dinner with him. Hour working on manuscript after returning to club.

Tuesday, April 4

Subway to 23 Wall Street to get $250.00 in cash and $1,500 in American Express checks. Afternoon train to Bridgeport. The Associated Press has been trying to contact me through United Aircraft in Hartford. I left word to say I could not be reached. Apparently the AP learned that I got a yellow-fever inoculation in New York Monday.

Wednesday, April 5

United States Navy attacks Palau and Yap. Japanese advance in India. Bucharest bombed.

Taxi to Vought factory. Spent most of day in conferences and assembling data to take with me. Snowing, and ceilings too low to run test flight on my plane. Divided evening between studying Corsair data and working on my manuscript—fifth draft—Newfoundland chapter.

Thursday, April 6

Russians advance near Odessa. Japanese advance in India. Willkie withdraws candidacy as a result of his failure in the Wisconsin election.

Took my plane up for a test hop. Had planned on several landings to test new landing-gear arrangement, but smelled something burning as I circled the field. Sent the plane into the hangar for inspection. Trouble turned out to be in one of the radio transmitters. Lunch with Paul Baker and several of the Vought engineers. Took my plane up again in the afternoon. Six landings this time; they have made a great improvement in the gear. Rest of afternoon in conferences and assembling data to take on my trip. Drove in to Bridgeport with Baker.

Friday, April 7

Baker stopped for me at 8:00, and we drove to the factory. Short conference with Baker and engineers. Then to airport and packed up my Corsair. (The space I used for baggage on previous flights is now largely taken up with high-frequency radio equipment, so I had to divide my equipment up into four portions—part back of the radio, part in front of me between the rudder pedals, and part in one wing.)

Took off at 11:46. Airways to Raleigh. Direct to the Marine base at Cherry Point [North Carolina]. Conference with Colonel C. F. Schilt, Lieutenant Colonel [C. J.] Schlapkohl, Colonel [Edward A.] Montgomery, and other Marine officers in regard to fighters in general and the Corsair in particular.

Saturday, April 8

To operations office with Colonel Schlapkohl. Short conference on Corsair dive tests (radio control). Then took off for the training field at Oak Grove—a fifteen-minute flight. Talked to the officers there about their experience with the Corsair and their ideas for improvements.

Sunday, April 9

Took off for Jacksonville at 09:32. Direct to Charleston. Airways from Charleston to Jacksonville. Landed Naval Air Station at 11:42. Short conference with Commander [John S.] Thach. Then to BOQ for lunch. Slept for an hour in the afternoon. Then with Lieutenant [C. H.] Seymour to the skeet range to watch the shooting and for a buffet supper. Shot a few rounds myself.

Monday, April 10

To the administration building for a 9:00 conference with Lieutenant Commander Thach in regard to fighter design. He is much interested in the development of a single-seater, all-purpose carrier plane—one that is primarily a fighter, but also a dive bomber and torpedo carrier. This is along the lines we have been studying at Bridgeport.

To the dispensary to get my second set of inoculations. Captain Smith showed me through the building and explained their procedures for high-altitude indoctrination. They have two chambers—one for low temperature. Both were in operation. To the airport in the afternoon for a conference with Lieutenant Colonel Dobbin in regard to his Corsair squadrons and the results they have had with the new oleo modification. The reports are excellent. To the operations building to see a motion picture of experimental Corsair landings.

I had planned on flying to Eglin Field this afternoon but decided to spend another night at Jacksonville. Attended a birthday party at the home of Lieutenant Commander and Mrs. ————. Many officers and their wives present as well as several Jacksonville people. Heavy drinking and nearly everyone drunk. On and on into the night. Ended with more drinking, singing, and dirty stories, and they all seemed to think they were having a good time. For a few minutes I was sitting in a chair with a view of the bay and the rising moon. Everything was so beautiful outside, and none of these people had the slightest realization of what was there just beyond their windows. I would have given anything to go out alone just for a quarter hour, but convention prevented that. Everyone was considerate—didn't seem to mind my not drinking or smoking at all. But the talk was dull and the evening long. I cannot understand what people get out of these parties. There is so much worth while that could be done instead.

Tuesday, April 11

To skeet range with Lieutenant C. H. Seymour. Made three rounds (75 shots). To my surprise, I broke seventeen the first time and nineteen the second, and got several doubles. Dropped down on the third round, to fifteen, I think.

Wednesday, April 12

Took off for Eglin Field at 4:17. Good flight. Landed at 17:57. Found a large delegation of newspapermen here for a demonstration. Too late for conferences. Supper early with Captain Smith at officers club to avoid reporters. But several came in and asked for interview, which of course I refused. Spent evening making rounds of the post with Captain Smith (Provost Marshal).

Thursday, April 13

Took off for Galveston at 10:08 E.W.T. Airways to Beaumont. Direct to Galveston. Planned on landing at Navy field at Hitchcock, but found a large grass fire burning on the windward side of the field, and smoke covering most of the landing area. Hitchcock Navy radio informed me that they had no 100-octane gasoline, so, after circling, landed at the Army field at Galveston instead (12:52 E.W.T.). Took off again at 14:03. Airways to Austin. Direct to El Paso. Clear weather, but head winds. Found a sandstorm covering the field at El Paso. A B-24 had cracked up and was lying at the side of the runway on Biggs Field. I landed at the municipal airport, refueled, checked weather, cleared, and took off again at 18:13—after waiting at the end of the runway for about ten minutes until an exceptionally heavy blow was over and I could see a few hundred feet ahead. Airways to El Centro. Clear weather, but head winds. Landed at the Marine base at 20:42 E.W.T.

Friday, April 14

Morning and first part of afternoon in conferences with Marine officers in regard to the Corsair and fighter characteristics in general. Gave a short talk (Corsair and compressibility characteristics, etc.) to some of the younger officers and let two of the squadron commanders fly my plane. Took off for Palm Springs at 15:19 P.W.T. Flew over the town to let Russell Vought know I was there, and landed on the Army field at 15:55. Vought drove out to pick me up. Conference at his home. Then he and I and one of his guests went for an hour's walk through the desert—to the base of the nearest mountain and back.

Saturday, April 15

A cracked-up Grumman F6F (Hellcat) was being hauled away from the Army field when we arrived. A ferry pilot was taking it off and encountered an excessive vibration as he left the ground, apparently from a blown tire; no one seemed sure of the details. He cut the gun, landed with wheels down, at the side of the runway, and turned over. Injured, but not seriously.

Took off for Mojave at 12:00. Landed at 12:40. Conference with Marine officers regarding their Corsair operations. Took off for Santa Barbara at 16:11. Landed at the Marine Air Base at 16:45.

Sunday, April 16

Breakfast at officers club. To hangars at 8:00 to meet some of the Marine officers. Arranged for several of them to fly my plane to test out the new oleo system. Went up to the tower to watch the landings.

I had planned on leaving this afternoon, but a bad oil leak developed in my Corsair. Since several hours of work were involved in making repairs, I decided to accept Colonel [Chauncey V.] Burnette's invitation to spend the night at his home in Santa Barbara. Drove out to the field to see Congressman Maas, who had just arrived in a Navy plane. Drove with Colonel and Mrs. Burnette to a country club for supper. Many women reserve officers present. Night at Burnette's home.

There was a bad and unusual Corsair accident here a few days ago. One of the pilots of a formation radioed to his partner that his parachute life raft was starting to inflate. His partner advised him to puncture it with a knife. He replied that he had no knife. That was the end of the radio conversation. A few seconds later the plane went suddenly into a dive and the pilot was catapulted from his cockpit *without* a parachute! In trying to get rid of the life raft, he had apparently removed his parachute harness, and the expanding raft probably forced the stick forward quickly—throwing the plane into a dive and catapulting the pilot out through the cockpit. He had already opened the hood—probably with the intent of pushing the raft out through it. Orders have now been issued to carry a knife in the cockpit whenever parachute rafts are used.

Monday, April 17

Spent most of morning talking to Marine officers about the Corsair. As I was about to take off, a sergeant came up to report what had looked to him like a spinning plane in the distance. He said it had flashed regularly in the sun and disappeared behind a hill in the direction of Santa Barbara. And as we looked along his pointed finger, there was a cloud of black smoke rising from some point behind that hill. It was a plane. I flew over it on my way to El Toro—still burning, at the edge of a clump of trees. No parachutes were reported. Advance training fields in this area are reporting one fatality for every 3,000 to 3,500 hours of flying.

Landed at El Toro at 12:45. Spent the afternoon in conference with various Marine officers. During the last conference, word came that a Corsair was circling the field with one wheel stuck down and the other stuck partway down. After much radio communication and many unsuccessful attempts to get the second wheel down, the pilot was given his choice of bailing out or landing. He chose the latter and came down on the runway in front of the tower where I was watching—made a normal, tail-low landing with the landing gear lever in *up* position so the unlocked wheel would retract on contact with the runway. The plane took it well—didn't even ground-loop badly and had no tendency to turn over.

Took off for North Island at 17:40. Landed at 18:20. Night at Hotel del Coronado.

Tuesday, April 18

Russians reach outskirts of Sevastopol. TWA Constellation crosses continent in six hours, fifty-eight minutes.

First part of morning spent on phone calls and laying plans for trip farther west. Then to Naval Air Station to fill out logbooks and turn my Corsair over to the Navy. Lunch with Admiral [Eliott] Buckmaster, Lieutenant Colonel [Valentine] Gephart, Congressman Maas, and several other officers from North Island. Conference with Colonel Gephart and ABG-2 officers in the afternoon in regard to the Corsair (maintenance, modifications, etc.). Later conference with Commander [James H.] Flatley and some of his officers.

I am trying to get a plane to ferry to the South Pacific area rather than ride as passenger on Pan American. The chances of doing so seem to be about even. The main difficulty is that crews for the larger planes are usually trained together. I have offered to take anything from a P-38 to a flying boat.

The traffic at North Island is so heavy that planes frequently come in over the hotel at fifteen-second intervals. And that does not include the small ones which land on another portion of the field.

Wednesday, April 19

Two thousand Allied planes raid Berlin.

Breakfast with Lieutenants Bliss and Jimmy Smith, who are staying at the hotel. (Bliss is Neil and Zaidee Bliss's son.[93] I checked Smith out for his first solo flight at Harry Guggenheim's request about 1928 or '29 on Long Island.) Colonel Gephart stopped for me at 8:00, and we drove to the Naval Air Station together. Conference with Commander Campbell in regard to getting a plane to ferry. Conference with Captain [William] Sinton. Stopped to see Admiral Sherman.[94]

93. Cornelius ("Neil") Bliss, director of Banker's Trust Co., Milbank Memorial Fund, and trustee of the Metropolitan Museum of Art.

94. Admiral Forrest P. Sherman, with the office of Chief of Naval Operations. In 1943 he became assistant chief of staff, Commander in Chief, Pacific Ocean areas.

Thursday, April 20

Heavy Allied raids over Germany.

Breakfast at 7:15 with Lieutenant Bliss. Phone call from Jack Hospers[95] when I got back to my room. He returned last night from two days on a carrier, during which the new Corsair landing-gear arrangement was tested out with excellent results. Phoned Paul Baker in Bridgeport to discuss plans and various items concerning the Corsair.

Decided to go up to the Marine Air Base at El Toro while I am waiting for transportation to Hawaii, to study the Corsair operations there. Various phone calls in connection with this. Lunch with Jack Hospers and Frank Geltz of United Aircraft. Discussed company problems and my coming trip into the South Pacific.

Packed, checked out, and drove with Hospers and Geltz to El Toro, where they dropped me on their way to Los Angeles. Night at the Laguna Beach Hotel.

Friday, April 21

Naval planes raid Sumatra. Turkey halts export of chrome to Germany.

Left for El Toro Marine Base at 7:00 with Captain Richards. Conference with squadron officers. Up for six-plane (Corsair) gunnery flight with Major [Kenneth J.] Kirk and four other officers. Tow plane at 8,000 feet. Fired about fifty rounds from the inboard guns (.50-cal. banner target). Target lost.

Lunch with Major Kirk at Field officers mess. Conference with squadron officers. Up for oxygen gunnery flight in afternoon in six-plane (Corsair) formation with Captain [Stanley T.] Synar leading. Tow plane at 18,000 feet. Fired forty-seven rounds. Made five hits (banner target—horizontal)—high sides, low sides, and roundhouses. Feel pleased with target, as I had the highest percentage of hits of anyone in the flight and have not fired machine guns from a plane since I was a cadet nineteen years ago. Also, planes and tactics have changed tremendously since then.

95. John J. Hospers, sales manager of the Chance Vought Division of United Aircraft.

Saturday, April 22

Cologne heavily bombed. Japanese advance in China; retreat in India.

Major Kirk picked me up at 7:50, and we drove to the El Toro base—a beautiful road through hills and canyons. First part of morning spent in conference with Marine officers, phone calls to Paul Baker in Bridgeport, Jack Hospers in Los Angeles, etc. Then up in a two-plane unit (Corsair) with Major Kirk for a series of simulated strafing runs and two dogfights (from 10,000 feet down to about 4,000).

The trip to El Toro was very much worth while. In addition to learning a great deal about combat tactics with the Corsair, I was able to help considerably with several of their problems. The company is sending a man down next week to arrange for the new landing-gear arrangement to be installed on all planes.

Lieutenant Colonel Gephart sent a Martin JM-1 up to get me in the afternoon. Co-piloted back to North Island.

Sunday, April 23

Spent morning in room assembling data, making final plans for trip, and working on manuscript. Finished the fifth draft of another short chapter ("The Thunderhead"). Went for a swim in the surf in the afternoon and lay in the sun for an hour. There are no cameras here; there has been no publicity, and nobody bothers. It is wonderful—about the only advantage I know from the war. Message under my door to call Consolidated when I returned. They are ferrying an R4D to Oahu tomorrow afternoon and want to know if I would like to go along. I said I would let them know in the morning after I had contacted the Navy.

Pacific Wartime

Monday, April 24

United States forces land at Aitape and Hollandia in New Guinea.

Decided to go on the R4D (the Navy designation for the commercial Douglas DC-3 or the Army C-47). Rest of morning spent writing a letter to Paul Baker in regard to the Corsair, phone calls, and packing. Early lunch. To North Island to attend a 2:00 briefing of the plane's crew. Charles Lorber is the captain. He was my co-pilot on several of the flights I made laying out the Pan American routes in the Caribbean in 1929 and 1930. (We were using Sikorsky amphibians at that time—S-38's.) He is now one of the most experienced of the transoceanic pilots.

Early supper at hotel. Checked out and drove to North Island with the navigator for the flight—R. A. Bryant. Took off at 21:38 P.W.T. The plane was in the air quickly, although loaded to nearly 30,000 lbs. gross, and we had a quartering tail wind of about ten knots (to avoid the runway pointing toward Point Loma). A new moon and clear night except for scattered clouds at about 3,000 feet. We took turns flying. There was no heat in the plane, and as the outside temperature was close to freezing and the tail end rather drafty, we spent most of the time forward, even though it meant standing up for two men. (The captain and co-pilot, who wore heavy, fur-lined flying suits, were able to get some sleep, stretched out behind the fuselage gas tanks, while I relieved them at the controls.)

We flew at 8,000 feet during the night, with scattered to overcast clouds rising as high as 6,500 feet. The sky was clear at all times. Food at intervals from boxes and cans—and lukewarm black coffee—good only for keeping awake. Everyone was able to get a little sleep except the navigator who was too busy taking star sights, laying out the course, and filling in reports. Lorber got an hour or two; Richards (co-pilot) got several hours; Romag (radio operator) could sleep for half an hour at a

time between his contacts; and I got a total of about an hour in catnaps
in either the pilot's or co-pilot's seat while the other man was flying. I
flew for the last two or three hours of night and through the dawn. The
clouds thickened to a solid layer after sunrise but broke again as we
approached the islands. We had to follow a coded wartime procedure in
radio contacts and route—approaching through definite channels, following certain shore lines, making certain turns, etc.

Landed at the naval field at Kaneohe [Oahu, Hawaii] after a flight of
fifteen hours, seven minutes. Lieutenant Roosevelt (T.R., Jr.'s son)
[was] at Operations to meet us. After saying good-by to the crew, I went
to clean up. Bob Douglass (now a brigadier general) phoned from
Hickam Field and asked me to come over for lunch with himself and
General Richardson[1]—said he would pick me up in an hour. (We went
through training together at Brooks and Kelly, and both graduated in
pursuit in 1925—he a student officer and I a cadet.) Stopped at headquarters to see Admiral John D. Price.

General Douglass came in a C-47, piloting himself. We flew from
Kaneohe to Hickam Field (fifteen minutes). Lunch with General
Richardson, General [Willis H.] Hale, and General Douglass. Then to
Ford Island to see Admiral [Charles A.] Pownall. Another R4D waiting
to take me from Ford Island to the Marine Air Base at Ewa. Stopped to
see General [Ross E.] Rowell. General [Walter G.] Farrell arranged
quarters for me next to his own. (Small single room, screened-in hut—
white—rough board—comfortable.)

Wednesday, April 26

Morning with squadron officers and inspecting maintenance facilities. Up
for gunnery flight in four-plane Corsair formation in afternoon. Tow
plane at 8,000 feet. Banner target. Got high score again! Nineteen hits
out of 200 rounds—inboard guns (overheads and high sides). Rest of
afternoon in conferences.

I have had no chance to see anything of the island as yet—except
from the air. The surf looks wonderfully inviting, and I would like to get
up into the mountains on foot. There are very few trees on the mountains, but they are green everywhere, even on the faces of the precipices.
No surface seems to be too steep for this growth to cling to, whatever it

1. General Robert C. Richardson, appointed commander Hawaiian Department
and military governor of Hawaii, June, 1943.

may be. There are airfields everywhere along the coast, it seems, and all day the air has been full of planes—bombers, fighters, transports—Army, Navy, and Marine.

Thursday, April 27

A cool and pleasant night. A clear sky above. Cloud-covered mountains through my window in the distance. Breakfast with Marine officers at 7:00—all veterans of the early air battles of the Pacific war. Conference with General Farrell. Conference with Bill MacPhail (Pratt & Whitney representative) in regard to Pratt & Whitney engines in this area. All reports on United products here are good.

Drove to Pearl Harbor for lunch with Admiral Towers and his aides. Discussed the war and future fighter requirements for the Pacific. Back to Ewa after lunch (driving the car the Marine Corps has placed at my disposal). Conference with Lieutenant Colonels J. L. Smith and F. H. Wirsig. Then to my hut to work on reports and study data accumulated. It is a hot, sunny afternoon, but with a pleasant wind blowing through the open screen walls of the room. The base here is simple but comfortable. Attended supper party at officers club—General Rowell and staff there. Also several men and women who live on the island. Conversation broken up at intervals by antiaircraft practice. One of the battery locations is nearby.

Friday, April 28

Heavy Allied bombing raids over occupied Europe continue.

To Post Exchange to get ties, shoe polish, and chocolate bars, which I keep on hand for use when I miss meals. Drove to Hickam Field for lunch with General Douglass and other Army officers. Inspection trip through underground fighter control center afterward. Talked to a group of about fifty squadron commanders for an hour. Then flight around the island with General Douglass in an Army Lodestar—over all the various airfields on Oahu.

Supper with Army officers (General Douglass, General Hale, General Frank, General [William J.] Flood, General Walter Reed, Colonel Munn, Colonel Musset, Colonel Eskridge, Colonel Moore, Colonel Carr, Major Grum, Lieutenant Stecher, and other officers).

There was rather a bad Corsair accident here today. One of the Marine pilots was coming in to land, let his air speed drop a little low, and stalled down pretty hard. The plane bounced high and out of control. He made the mistake of opening the throttle quickly, which threw the plane over on its side and into two dive bombers parked nearby. A fire started, but a sergeant, who had been standing a few yards away, ran in and pulled the pilot out of the cockpit. Both were badly burned but will live. The planes had to be stricken.

Saturday, April 29

Had planned on going on a dive-bombing flight with Colonels Wirsig and Smith but decided to accompany General Farrell on his flight to Midway in a Marine Commando. Ten minutes to pack. Off at 08:15 (Oahu time). I rode in the fuselage most of the time with a number of officers and Marines. Flew the plane for about half an hour from co-pilot's side. Detoured slightly south to pass over the landing strip at French Frigate. West of the main group of islands there is very little land—mostly reefs and shoals. The islands themselves contain only a few acres of land. Some are low lying with sand beaches surrounded by coral reefs. Some are the tips of mountain peaks, extending abruptly upward from the sea. (One can imagine the whole range submerged down there beneath the surface.)

Since there was nothing to see between the islands—just the clouds and the Pacific extending endlessly in every direction—I spent most of my time working on "The Moon" chapter of my manuscript. The Marines, in most instances, carried a book or magazine with them. Several slept, stretched out on the mail-sack cargo or leaning against some corner of the cabin. There was the usual signing of "short snorters," [2] but not a great deal of conversation because of the engine noise.

I noticed that while the cargo we were carrying was well lashed down, there were suitcases, tool boxes, and other heavy articles piled loosely in the tail of the fuselage. When I called one officer's attention to the hazard this created in case of a forced landing, he replied that their policy was to throw everything out before landing on the water. I then learned that the Commandos from Ewa are making the flight to Midway with a rather low fuel reserve and without much single-engine ceiling.

2. A dollar bill, or one of larger denomination, on which autographs were collected.

On two flights recently it was found necessary to jettison every loose object aside from emergency equipment. On one of these flights an engine failed, and although everything possible was thrown out, the plane is reported to have sunk down to about one hundred feet above the water before it finally reached the emergency landing field at French Frigate. Everyone on board expected a landing at sea. On the other flight they simply ran short of fuel after bucking head winds most of the way. When their wheels finally touched the runway at Midway, the gauges showed zero, and actual measurement showed that they had only fifteen minutes of fuel left on board. In this instance, too, cargo and personal effects were thrown overboard.

We landed at Sand Island, Midway, at 15:22, amid more birds than I have ever seen at one time before. The ground was dotted with them, and they actually gave a shading to the air, like mosquitoes in Labrador in summer. The officers of the island were on hand to meet us, and since it is two and a half hours earlier there than at Oahu, the afternoon was just starting. I accompanied Commodore [Giles E.] Short and General Farrell on a short tour of the island—a small body of land, crisscrossed from one shore to the other by runways—mostly coral and sand except for a grove of trees planted by the Cable Company thirty or forty years ago (Australian pine and others).

The gooney birds are the distinctive feature of the island and take one's attention from everything else, even the overpowering atmosphere of the military. They are a form of albatross—graceful in the air, awkward on the ground, stupid and yet crammed with character. As far as one can see, the presence of Marines, motor trucks, and airplanes has not disturbed them in the least. They make their nests at the sides of the runways, and within a yard of roads and foot paths; and they act like farm cattle when you approach them—the older ones moving out of the way slowly, and the younger ones not moving at all, but pecking at you if you come within reach. The goonies are slow to get out of the way of a car, and many of them are killed by planes landing and taking off; there are always a dozen or more dead birds on the runways.

Although the goonies steal the show, there are many other varieties of birds—terns by, literally, the hundreds of thousands; bosun birds, which fly backwards at times and are unable to walk at all; canaries; golden plover which are said to fly here nonstop from Alaska; Japanese lovebirds, etc. The striking thing is that all this wild island life goes on as though the airplanes and the Marines were not there at all. Killing a bird intentionally is a court-martial offense. As a result of this and of the character of the birds themselves there has been no retreat of wildlife from "civilization"—as there was from our westward-moving frontiers during the last century in the United States.

Conference with squadron officers after our tour of the island. General Farrell outlined some of his plans to them and inquired about their local problems. I talked to them about the Corsair, fighter design, their experiences in combat, etc. Then to officers quarters of VMF-113,[3] where Major [Theodore] Olsen insisted on my using his room. Conference with squadron officers and inspection trip around their dispersal area and through their shops with Major [Joe] McGlothlin. Supper at officers mess—mostly canned food, but good. Back to squadron quarters in evening for another conference.

I am invited to go on the dawn patrol tomorrow—the island is always guarded at dawn and dusk by fighters carrying a full war load and ready for instant combat. To bed early. A clear and beautiful night outside with the sound of birds in the background like the breaking of waves on a distant beach.

Sunday, April 30

General MacArthur says he would not accept nomination for presidency.

Up at 3:45. Dressed and to ready room with Major McGlothlin. Cup of coffee while pilots were assembling and the flight being briefed. (There is a stove in the ready room, and coffee is kept hot at all hours.) Major McGlothlin decided to take two flights on an interception problem, rendezvousing at Kure Island, fifty miles or so west of Midway, instead of taking the dawn patrol as we planned last night. I took his wing, and Major Olsen led the second unit of our flight (of four Corsairs). The other flight of four fighters took a more southward course.

The sky was about eight-tenths overcast. We flew above the cloud layer—twenty-five minutes on first course, then fifteen minutes on the second. At the end of that time, the little island and its shoals appeared through a hole in the clouds. On our return flight to Midway, all eight planes wove in and out as though convoying bombers. We landed amid goonies and terns after a flight of one hour, twenty minutes. Turned in equipment (parachute, life raft, sea pack, and rubber vest).

3. Marine Fighter Squadron.

Attended services for Secretary of Navy, Frank Knox. Tour of the island and conferences with officers during rest of morning.

Had planned on going up on a gunnery flight this afternoon, but word came that one of the Corsair tow planes had radioed in that it was lost. So I accompanied Major McGlothlin to the Command Post to listen to the radio and watch the procedure of bringing the lost plane in by radar. Everyone was slightly tense, as the radar was not working as well as usual and the lost Corsair was getting low on fuel. I stayed until the pilot reported sighting the island and asked for permission to drop his tow target. He had hung onto his target even though there were only twenty gallons of gasoline left in his tanks when he landed!

Major McGlothlin drove me over to a nearby beach, and I went in swimming for a quarter hour—a strong wind and tide. Several goonies—turned magically into beautiful albatrosses in the air—soared low over the waves to see what I was—so close that I splashed water over them with one hand as they passed.

Monday, May 1

Heavy air offensives over Europe continue for fourteenth day.

We drove to the runway to see the general off for the return trip to Ewa at 7:00. I had planned on going back with him in the Commando but found that by taking the NATS [Naval Air Transport Service] flying boat this afternoon, I would be able to get in a gunnery run with VMF-113 in the morning. Flew in a seven-plane flight with Captain McDonald leading. We fired on a vertical banner target towed at about 8,000 feet. I spent most of the hour and twenty minutes of the flight learning the technique of low side approaches. Fired 200 rounds from the inboard guns, and got no hits!

Down just in time to say good-by to the squadron officers and drive over to Commodore Short's residence for lunch. Practically all driving on the island is in jeeps; an ordinary motorcar would get stuck the moment it got into the sand at the roadside, and in a number of places there are no roads at all where it is necessary to have transportation. One simply throws all four wheels of the jeep into low gear and bumps over pretty near anything.

Commodore Short took me on a drive through a corner of the island I had not seen before. Hidden among the Australian pines is a clearing which has been filled with tropical and semitropical plants and cared for just as a garden would be back home. And adjoining it is a small farm with a bull and half a dozen cows and heifers—and a hundred or so chickens. The hospital, and sometimes the commanding officer, have fresh milk and eggs.

On arriving at the ramp just before 2:00, we found the flying boat, a large Martin PBM, was having trouble with its port engine (ignition). Made another tour of the island in a jeep with Lieutenant Colonel [Roy] Kline. The military details, both land and sea, were elaborate and interesting, but of course cannot be set down in a journal, especially one which is going into the South Pacific combat zone.

Finally off at 4:20 Midway time. The plane carried a crew of eight, and about a dozen passengers. I found an empty freight compartment and was writing in my journal when the plane's captain, Lieutenant Commander L. S. Drill came aft and asked me if I would like to "work" my passage. I told him I would like nothing better, and we arranged to take one-hour shifts at the controls through the remainder of the afternoon and night. He told me with a smile that he had been the chairman of the Miami chapter of the America First Committee. During the remainder of the flight, I stayed forward with the crew and had early supper with them in the plane's galley. It seems very strange to me—all this elaborate equipment in an airplane: three regular pilots, a navigator, a radio operator and hundreds of pounds of radio, a cabin aft, full of passengers, baggage and freight in the tail, and even a cook and a ship's galley with stove, icebox, and table for four. The change has been so great since I first started flying that I cannot quite get used to it.

I took two one-hour shifts at the controls—instrument flying when I started the first one, but the clouds gave way to a clear night later on. We landed at the NATS base, Oahu, at 23:49 (starting time) after a flight of seven hours and twenty-nine minutes. A Navy station wagon took me out to the Marine base at Ewa, arriving about 03:30.

I found my hut cleaned out—bed gone, dresser with my clothes in it gone—only a bar of soap and some articles I had hung up in the closet remained. I thought they had probably moved me to another hut, but could not find it. They were either locked, empty, or had a bed full of Marine officer. Fortunately, the night was fairly warm, so I slept comfortably on the floor with my raincoat and the shower curtain for covers and my traveling bag for a pillow. The boards were clean, and my clothes needed laundry anyway.

Tuesday, May 2

The "slicked-up" Corsair had arrived while I was at Midway, so I drove to the Service Squadron, where it was parked, to look it over and talk to the Vought representative, Harry Fleming, and the Pratt Whitney representative, Paul Hagan. They were having some difficulty with the shotgun starter; otherwise everything was going well.

Drove to naval housing project at Pearl Harbor for supper and evening with (Captain) Tommy Tomlinson. We talked about the war, military aviation, conditions at home, and old times. Tommy is now head of NATS.

Left early and back to MAB, Ewa, for the night. I have another hut now. It turned out that my first one was to be "renovated." Orders had been issued to take all furniture out of the row it was in. So—typical of all military establishments—the Marines who got the orders simply carried my bed and dresser out without bothering to look inside the latter and put them in the post's storehouse. The dresser was brought back the same way (after I inquired the whereabouts of my belongings). Two husky Marines carried it into my new hut and carried it out again after I had removed the contents of the drawers.

Wednesday, May 3

Navy strikes Caroline Islands.

Up for a dive-bombing flight with Lieutenant Colonel [James] Mueller at 1:00 in two Corsairs. We started a formation take-off, but he used such low power that I pulled on ahead of him at the end of the runway to avoid the possibility of stalling my plane. We flew to the bomb range on the island of Molokai. Started dive bombing from 6,000 feet with our practice bombs but had to turn to masthead bombing when clouds drifted in over the target. After two or three masthead runs[4] the sky cleared again, and we returned to dive bombing. We spent over an hour on the range, simulating bomb runs after we ran out of bombs. Then returned and landed on the Marine field at Ewa.

Message waiting for me to phone General Farrell. He invited me to go spear fishing with him; said there was just time before our dinner engage-

4. Low-level runs.

ment with General Rowell if we left right away. Drove to my hut to get trunks. We left in a Marine truck loaded with equipment—spears, rubber foot-fins, gloves, a special rubber mattress, etc. There were six of us in all: General Farrell, Lieutenant Colonel Mueller, two lieutenants, a corporal, and myself.

We drove to the nearest shore—about fifteen minutes away. There was a light swell and a surf breaking on coral and lava rocks. The rocks and surf looked pretty formidable to me, but the general said it was all right for our purpose, so we put on our trunks and started in. I watched the general and others go through the surf, then began to follow as best I could. One of the first breakers bumped me against a sharp rock, and I was bracing myself for the next when I heard Farrell call out to put my head under the water so I could see. (I was wearing a glass face mask like the rest of them.)

The difference was amazing. The whole bottom became visible for yards around. It was like suddenly entering a new world, one which turned from enemy to friend the instant you entered it. The rocks I had been bumping against were clearly visible and became hand- and footholds in the breaking surf. I wondered how I had been so clumsy before. It was only necessary to stick my head above the surface to get a breath now and then, hold on when the waves passed by, and crawl and swim out into deep water in between.

It was much more fun and more interesting than going down with the diving helmet, as Anne, Jim, and I did two or three years ago near Dry Tortugas. You can see more, and you move about like a fish instead of being weighted down like a diver. You feel a real part of the water you are in—at home in it for a few seconds as though it were your own environment. I forgot all about spearing—there were no big fish around, anyway—and simply floated about on the surface outside the breakers, face down, watching the ocean bottom and its life—the clumps of coral, the ledges and pits, the brilliantly colored and marked small fish which passed by apparently undisturbed by my presence. The general dove down among them as though he were one of them—searching holes and crevices in the coral for whatever he might find.

We had only a half hour in the water, and it passed much too quickly. I would like to have stayed in the rest of the afternoon. However, we had to start back for our dinner engagement with General Rowell. We gathered at General Rowell's quarters at 6:00 and started supper soon afterward—probably twenty officers in all. The general asked whether I would be ready to leave for the South Pacific by Friday morning, as an

R4D is taking off then—a ferry flight (Marine). I replied that I was ready to go at any time and that Friday would be excellent. We then discussed the various places I might visit and the sequence which would be desirable. General Rowell was most considerate and anxious to do everything possible to assist with my trip.

Later, we watched several motion-picture reels of the war—both European and Pacific areas. There was considerable propaganda, of course, but much of interest in between. The officers present watched in silence and at times obvious skepticism. But the only spoken criticism came when a picture of a company of Negro engineers was shown at one of the South Pacific islands where several of the men present had been engaged. One of the generals present said that there had been no Negro troops on that island for at least a month after the fighting was over. Another grunted out that it looked to him like New Deal propaganda (which it obviously was).

Thursday, May 4

Drove to other side of field and took off in a Corsair for a gunnery flight with Lieutenant Colonel John Smith in an F6F he is testing. Tow plane at about 8,000 feet—vertical banner target. We stayed up for about an hour, making mostly side and low side runs. I fired 152 rounds and got seven hits. I am trying for technique and position rather than for score.

Phoned Admiral Pownall and made 3:00 engagement. Drove my Marine car to Ford Island. Conference with Admiral Pownall in regard to my trip through the South Pacific areas. We talked for a few minutes about single-seater fighters and the importance of pursuit planes in dive bombing. The admiral told me he had written to some of his friends in the South Pacific telling them to expect me down there in the near future. He was a great help in every way.

Back to MAB, Ewa. Packed as much as possible and spent the rest of the afternoon writing and on phone calls. Supper with officers at General Farrell's mess. The general was not present this evening. Word came in that another bad crash took place this afternoon. During the working out of a simulated combat problem, an attacking Corsair dove into a formation of dive bombers, striking two of the planes. There was an explosion which threw debris into other planes of the formation. The Corsair and the two dive bombers crashed into the ocean about twenty miles off-shore. Two parachutes were seen to open. Two survivors have been picked up—slightly injured. Five men were in the three planes which crashed. A parachute was reported seen stringing out from the Corsair—apparently ripped. A search of the area is being made and will be continued all day tomorrow.

Evening on phone calls and final arrangements for leaving tomorrow.

Friday, May 5

Up at 6:15. Finished packing. (I am carrying one flexible canvas bag on this trip—weight about forty pounds.) Said good-by and drove to the field. General Farrell came to see us off and gave me one of his face masks for underwater swimming. (I was asking yesterday where I could buy one, and he heard about it.)

Off at 09:24 Hawaiian. Flew at 8,000 feet during entire flight. Few minutes of instrument flying as we let down for Palmyra—an island-studded atoll with one long wide strip for landing, one shorter narrower one, angling off from it, and water facilities for seaplanes. Many of the islands of the atoll are covered or partially covered with palm trees.

Landed at 16:19 Palmyra. Made courtesy phone call to commanding officer, Commander [Liles W.] Creighton. He drove over a few minutes later and took me on a tour of the atoll. A fairly good road runs around most of it. Like Midway this is also a bird island, although they are not as much in evidence except in certain parts. The terns have selected a point of land some distance from the buildings and are now nesting by the hundreds of thousands. Almost every square foot of ground is covered with their eggs—laid without any attempt at making a nest. In another portion of the atoll, the booby birds are nesting. They build nests in the trees—some high, some low—and refuse to leave unless you practically push them off their nests. With them are a number of white Japanese lovebirds, or Japanese terns, which lay their eggs on the branches of trees without any nest at all. We found one of the young just hatched out. God only knows why they don't fall off the branch when they hatch.

The atoll is surrounded by barbed-wire entanglements placed out in the water, partially spoiling the view of the beautiful surf breaking over the reefs. We saw a frigate bird caught in this wire at one point, and I waded out and untangled him. He had apparently been there a long time and was very weak, but no bones were broken, and his spirit began to pick up as soon as I placed him on the shore—pecking at me and apparently blaming me for all his troubles. Since the wire was put there by men, maybe he was right.

Supper at the BOQ with Commander Creighton and other officers of the post. Watched the booby birds fly in from their day's fishing in the evening—some high, some low, trying to avoid the attack of frigates (which attack until the boobies disgorge the fish they have caught, then dive down and catch the fish for themselves before it reaches the water).

Saturday, May 6

Of at 7:34 Palmyra time. Usual Pacific weather for this area—broken sky and mixture of cloud types. Started out cruising at 8,000, but soon climbed to 10,000 feet to clear cloud tops—pleasantly cool at this altitude. At the moment we are at 10,000 over a clear blue ocean—scattered clouds below—broken alto-stratus and cirro-stratus layers above. We have just crossed the equator, and members of the crew are taking turns for lunch.

Landed at Funafuti at 2:45 P.M. Funafuti time. Colonel [Curtis W.] LeGette (C.O.) and other officers came down to meet us. After the planes were parked we drove to the colonel's quarters through a hot sun and equatorial climate. The colonel suggested that we take one of the Navy landing barges to a nearby island of the atoll to see a native village and watch one of their dances, which he said he could easily arrange. He gave me three strips of colored cloth to present to the chief.

It was only a fifteen-minute trip across. Several members of our crew and officers of the post went with us under the guidance of a Marine gunner who was credited with having the best understanding of the natives. To me, the visit was both interesting and disappointing. This village has been in too close contact with the whites. There were a dozen or more sailors and Marines there when we arrived, and the appearance of the natives shows only too plainly that the first white men to find the atoll came many years ago. There are all kinds of mixtures, from European to Oriental and African, and in most cases, the result has not been good.

The huts were full of such items as issue pillows and mattresses, obviously traded in for baskets, mats, etc. There were flies and dirt everywhere, and evidences of disease such as head scabs and elephantiasis— one bad case of the latter. I am told that many of the natives proudly trace their ancestry back to one O'Brien, an Irishman who landed here sometime in the last century. A number of them have very light skins and a red tinge to their hair.

The dance was a sort of tom-tom affair with good rhythm and at times very graceful gestures—the men and older women in the background beating the drum and singing while five or six girls did the dancing—mostly rhythm of hands and body, with little or no foot movement except at the end of each dance when all the dancers stepped forward toward the audience. The last dance called for partners from among the onlookers, and each dancer came forward to make her selection. I pleaded an injured leg and agreed to make the speech of thanks if the Marines with me would do the dancing—a bargain that seemed to be welcome from all standpoints.

The chief seemed well chosen—the best combination of physique and intelligence I saw on the island. He made a short speech of welcome, and I replied by telling how we flew for thousands of miles over water with only islands such as these now and then to break our flight, that we often looked down on them from far above and saw a few native huts and villages. I picked up a pebble and said that the huts and sometimes even the villages looked smaller to us than the pebble I was holding in my hand, and that we often wondered what kind of people lived in them and what kind of life they led. I ended by thanking the chief and his people for giving us the chance of finding out, of meeting the people and seeing how they lived, etc. Then I presented him with the three strips of cloth. It took a long time through a native interpreter, but seemed to go over well. We received shell bracelets in return and started back for the main island.

I accompanied the colonel to the outdoor picture theater in the evening—the Marines standing at attention when we arrived, and a dogfight going on right in front of the colonel's seat. It was an old film—gangster story—not too well acted, and the sound device kept cutting out. I kept looking up at the full moon through the coconut palms and thought how incongruous it was to be watching a gangster film and listening to the blare of canned music in such a setting. There was something very wrong about it—such cheapness in the wild solitude of a tropical island of the South Seas.

Sunday, May 7 and Monday, May 8

The runway is lined with revetments, but there is little sign left of the Japanese bomb raids which took place as late as December of last year —the fuselages and wings of a few planes pushed over to the side of the runway. Everything else has been repaired, and this is now regarded as a quiet area. (The native church in the palm grove is still in ruins—only the walls standing.)

Took off at 8:20 Funafuti. Good weather and typical mixture of clouds for this time of year over the Pacific—scattered to broken cumulus and a few stratus. One of the crew members thought he sighted the bilge pumpings from a submarine, and we circled several times overhead. Personally, I think it was only the foam which often gathers where ocean currents come together. However, both the pilot and navigator feel certain they saw two submarines which crash-dived as our plane came over the top of a cloud bank. They estimate the submarines to have been about five miles away. We were flying at about 8,000 feet. Japanese submarines are reported to be operating regularly in these waters.

Landed at the Army base on Espiritu Santo at 02:25 G.C.T. (1:25 P.M., May 8, Espiritu Santo). A strong cross wind was blowing over the runway. General [William J.] Wallace had sent his aide with a car to meet us, and we drove to the Marine station about thirteen miles distant. Colonel [William G.] Manley was in command, and I found Lieutenant Colonel [John S.] Holberg, whom I met at El Centro last year, to be his executive officer. I am to share quarters with the engineering officer, Major [Leslie] T. Bryan, Jr.—a single-room, screened-in shack in a beautiful location, under palm trees and only a few feet from the shore line and looking toward small islands and tropical foliage in the distance. I had just started to unpack when the major arrived. We went swimming and lay in the sun for a few minutes while we talked over Corsair operation and maintenance at this station. Later, he took me through the shops, where I talked to the mechanics and test pilots about some of the problems they are encountering with the plane. There is much trouble with corrosion of the water-injection system. But on the whole they are well satisfied and pleased with the Corsair's performance. Maintenance problems are reported to be not excessive.

Tuesday, May 9

Up at 5:30. Went for a half hour's swim alone in the dawn—the full moon about to set, the sun about to rise, the sky clear, the water alternately warm and cool as I swam across to the opposite shore, coconuts floating slowly along with the tide. Breakfast at the field officers mess—the sound of airplane engines constantly overhead and being tested in the background. First part of the morning in hut, writing, looking out over the water, islands, and low hills in the distance—small lizards running over the screens (both inside and out), pictures of pin-up girls all around the walls. Then with Major Bryan to the Service Squadron for a conference with officers and personnel.

To Service Squadron 11 in the afternoon to fly one of the Corsairs they have been having trouble with and to check the report that the wing fuel tanks can't be used for half an hour or more after purging with CO_2. Kept the plane up for two hours, running tests at varying altitudes up to 20,000 feet. Found manifold pressures to be badly off—unable to obtain either military or war-emergency power. Took fifteen minutes to get the wing tanks feeding again after I purged them. Carburetor-air-temperature warning light came on much too soon, etc.

Wednesday, May 10

To Service Squadron 11 to run tests on wing-purging CO_2 bottle. The only reason I could think of to explain the time lag after purging (before the tanks could be used again) was that the bottle must keep on expelling gas into the fuel lines. (It is connected to the wing tanks through the fuel feed lines.) This proved to be the case; the bottle kept expelling gas for over half an hour. We ordered a shut-off valve installed in the line, and I will flight-check it tomorrow.

Drove with Major Bryan and [Walter] Darracott [Vought representative] to Luganville, where I held an hour's informal discussion with the pilots and officers of VMO-251.[5] They recently encountered difficulty with compressibility at high diving speeds (above 20,000 feet) with the Corsair. Then to the Air Center where we had lunch with Commander [Leonard] Kirby. Captain [Nicholas] Drain (COMAIRSOUTH) was in from Guadalcanal, and I talked to him about methods of improving communication between field representatives and their companies back in the States. It is poor at the present time, and much inefficiency results.

Drove from the Air Center to Pallikula, where the New Zealanders have their Corsairs. They are having an unusual amount of trouble with vibration in some of their planes; about one out of six is reported excessively rough. After a conference with their officers and an inspection trip through their shops, I took one of their worst planes up for a twenty-minute flight. It was the roughest Corsair I have ever flown. Possibly the propeller—they have found several out of balance—possibly ignition.

5. Marine Observation Squadron.

All the New Zealand planes have Bosch mags, and they have been a great source of trouble. I promised to return tomorrow with the Pratt Whitney and Hamilton Standard service men.

Thursday, May 11

Russian Army captures Sevastopol.

Twenty-minute swim before sunrise. Breakfast at staff officers mess. Half hour working on notes. Then to Service Squadron for conferences and to lay plans for the day. The representatives of Vought, Pratt Whitney and Hamilton Standard were there. We discussed MAG-12[6] problems and agreed to meet at Pallikula this afternoon to see what we could do to help the New Zealanders with their vibration problems.

One of those situations has arisen which are so frequent in the military services. The squadrons now going north plan on doing considerable dive bombing. But there are no bomb racks on hand, and they have no information about the angles of dive from which bombs can be released without danger of falling into the propeller. The result is that they are building their own racks and setting up their own tests. I am trying to get the proper information for them and find out where the Corsair bomb racks, which were built months ago back in the States, are now stored. We were under the impression that they were sent out to the combat squadrons immediately, but like as not they will turn up in some warehouse covered with rust. (Much of the material received in this area is in bad condition due to improper packing and corrosion.)

To field in afternoon and took No. 265 (Corsair) over to Pallikula and the New Zealanders. Flew two more of their Corsairs—both rough. (They were picked from the planes which had been reported unsatisfactory.) Discussions in regard to procedure for running down cause of roughness.

Friday, May 12

Forrestal appointed Secretary of Navy.

The Service Squadron here (SS-11) has presented me with a waterproof wrist watch on a steel bracelet made by one of the Marines and engraved

6. Marine Air Group.

803

by a Seabee. The craftsmanship is good, and it is excellent for this climate. Have set Monday tentatively for my departure for Guadalcanal.

Saturday, May 13

Heavy Allied bombing raids over Europe continue.

To Service Squadron 11 to take one of the Corsairs up for a routine shakedown flight. Had difficulty starting. Then difficulty with radio and had to stop engine again. The crew stayed with the plane without lunch, so I did, too. Finally off the strip at 13:10 (Espiritu Santo time). Ran tests from sea level up to 30,000 feet. Found oxygen mask leaking badly at 30,000 so turned on the emergency valve slightly to give a constant flow. Level flight runs at 10,000 feet, 20,000 feet, and 30,000 feet. Water injection runs at 16,900 feet, 12,400 feet, and 700 feet. Stall tests at 10,000 feet. A good day, with plenty of open spaces between the clouds.

Landed at 15:00. Made out my report on the plane. Then took Corsair No. 56265 up for water-injection and wing-tank purging tests. Purging valve worked perfectly again; could turn on the wing tanks immediately after the valve was closed. But the plane failed its water-injection runs again—something wrong with the blowers, apparently. Landed at 17:10 (after an even hour's flight).

One of the Corsair test pilots reported overdue—but only by four minutes, so I thought nothing of it. An invitation arrived from Colonel Manley to come to his hut and meet some friends. Found General [Claude A.] Larkin there. All had supper together at staff officers mess. Saw an antiaircraft searchlight pointing into the sky when we came out. The Corsair pilot is still missing. Eight TBF's have been sent out to search for him in the hope that he landed or parachuted into the sea. All fighter pilots carry parachute rafts and a back pack equipped with flares. If he is afloat, they should be able to find him easily on a clear night and be able to guide a boat to him, but it is an off chance. He had only a total of about thirty hours in Corsairs and was sent out to run tests up to 30,000 feet—probably with little training in the use of oxygen equipment.

Sunday, May 14

Allied armies attack in Italy.

TBF's have been taking off since dawn to search for the missing Corsair pilot. I am told that only a week ago the squadron lost another Corsair and pilot during an altitude-test run. The plane was seen at about 8,000 feet by one of the coast watchers, in a vertical dive which it continued straight into the sea. Nothing was found by the searching party except a part of the pilot's head rest.

Met Colonel Manley at 3:05. He, Major Bryan, one of the enlisted men, and I drove to a portion of the plantation where cocoa trees are planted and went pigeon hunting. Very rough roads. Had to put the jeep in four-wheel drive and low gear. The colonel got seven birds, the major none. I became so interested in the various birds and plants that I slipped off into the jungle alone and did no shooting. Supper at the plantation house—an impromptu but rather elaborate meal—soup, salad, fish, chicken, steak, and pineapple desert (each a separate course and all very well cooked). The plantation is short-handed, as most of the workers have been shipped home, their term of indenture completed, and replacements are hard to get these days.

The plantation owner lives his life as he wishes and makes no bones about it—typically French in demeanor, rather fat, pleasant, obviously a good trader, in his late forties. He took us to his bedroom to wash before supper. Most of the room is taken up by a bed fourteen feet in width. He has a "Tonck" mistress, and I am told that three others finished their period of indenture (of five years) a short time ago and returned home. At any rate, I gather that the bed accommodated five people in its time— and from the appearance of the owner may do so again. The present mistress is a slight girl, probably in her late twenties, Chinese in appearance and costume, less than five feet in height, weighs probably eighty-five pounds—a midget beside the Frenchman. She is treated openly and obviously as his mistress—a position more important than a servant but less important than a wife—present for brief moments but not introduced to the guests; giving orders to the servants with much show of authority; lowering her eyes to the Frenchman with the demure attitude of the mistress. We spent most of the evening after supper sitting in a beach house made of bamboo.

Monday, May 15

Had planned on leaving today for Guadalcanal, but word came that the plane I was going on won't come through until Wednesday. To the Service Squadron with Major Bryan. Two red flares were seen last night—one about 4:00, and one about 6:00—apparently coming from the jungle about one and a half miles southwest of the field. Was someone out experimenting with a pistol, or were they fired by the missing pilot? Possibly he had engine failure during his landing circle and crashed in the jungle without anyone seeing his plane go down. If so, he might be alive, close to the field, and injured too badly to walk. Each pilot flying fighter planes in this area has six red flares and a projector in his backpack jungle kit. Two SNJ's went out this morning to search the area—circled over it for an hour and a half without seeing anything. The men who saw the flares and most of the Service Squadron personnel still feel unsatisfied about the matter.

I suggested that we organize a searching party to go into the jungle on foot. The necessary permission was easy to obtain. We met at noon—a gun, canteen, and compass for each man, several machetes, a first-aid kit and some emergency rations—about a dozen of us. Two or three of the men lacked compasses. We divided into groups of two—at least one compass to each group—and fanned out into the jungle. Every ten minutes group No. 1 was to blow a whistle once, group No. 2 twice, and so on in order to keep proper interval and contact. I took one man—a young second lieutenant—with me to form group No. 1.

To start with, the jungle was extremely dense, and we had to climb up a vine-tangled and matted hillside, often on our hands and knees and cutting our way where we could not go otherwise. The first ten-minute contact worked well; we heard even the whistles of group No. 4. On the next contact we heard Nos. 2 and 3. On the third contact, group No. 2. The fourth time we whistled there was no answer. We were apparently well ahead of the other groups and had reached a clearer portion of the jungle. Keeping together was obviously going to make slow progress.

I decided to go on as rapidly as we could, regardless of contact. As we got farther into the jungle, our rate of progress increased to probably two miles an hour. Frequently we would find wild cow and pig trails leading in the direction we wanted to go (220° magnetic). The place must be full of both of these animals, for there were fresh tracks everywhere, but we neither saw nor heard any. There were many doves and other jungle birds—one type which answered whenever we blew our whistle and which often sounded disturbingly like a whistle in return. After traveling for about an hour and a half, dodging the ferns and hanging vines, and following the wild-pig trails, we came to a human trail—definite although not well traveled. As it led almost exactly in the direction of 220°, we followed it for nearly another mile toward the interior of the island. Cuttings along the trail indicated that someone had passed along it within the last four or five days.

When we reached a point we estimated to be three to four miles airline from the Turtle Bay airstrip, we decided to turn back and re-cover the area closer to the field. Since there was not time prior to nightfall to return all the way through the jungle itself, we decided to retrace our steps along the trail for about a mile, then turn at right angles to our course for about a quarter mile through the jungle, and then parallel our outbound track back to the field. Before we had backtracked a half mile, we heard an answering whistle and met groups four and five following the same trail we were on. They, too, had lost contact with the others. We divided again and started combing the jungle backward to the base. At one point, I came onto a big wallow—moist, fresh tracks all around it.

We came out on the bank of a stream near the field, almost exactly a quarter mile from where we started out. Our clothes were soaking wet from exertion and the heat of the jungle. Stripped and swam in the cool, spring-fed stream for a quarter hour. Then back to the jeep in which we had driven to the edge of the jungle. Two groups were still out. We left one jeep for them and returned to the base.

Tuesday, May 16

Allies continue to advance in Italy.

Took a Corsair up for shakedown and water-injection tests. Weather overcast with several cloud layers and light rain squalls. Found that the plane's receiver did not cover the radio-beam frequency and that the ZB[7] was not working. Therefore no way of orienting myself above the clouds. However, typical of island cloud formations, there were breaks here and

7. A frequency converter in the airplane homing system (used to locate a carrier on returning from a mission).

there in the layers—although not many. Using the breaks and setting my course from one to another, I had no difficulty in running the low-altitude tests—up to 15,000 feet—and by compass, timing, and several coinciding breaks in the clouds I managed to get the 20,000- and 30,000-foot runs in also.

Down too late for lunch so went with several Marine officers to a nearby volcanic crater for a swim. The crater is surrounded by jungle and filled with clear, deep water which forms the source of a small brook. The bottom can be seen through more than fifty feet of water.

The wreckage of a Corsair has been located on a mountaintop near the end of this island. There have been many planes lost here since the military operations started, and it is always necessary to make sure that one has not simply refound an old wreck. However, new burning is reported in this instance and it does not take many days for the jungle to grow. An expedition will be sent out, but the point of crash will be hard to reach.

Wednesday, May 17

Colonel Manley and I left at 11:45 in a Marine speedboat to visit Admiral [Van H.] Ragsdale on one of the carriers which recently came in from the north—a converted tanker. Lunch with the admiral and his officers. Afterward, they took us on an inspection trip through the ship. Returned to MAG-11 in midafternoon. Hour or two writing; another chapter of my manuscript almost finished.

Evening playing Ping-pong with Colonel Manley. Among other subjects, we discussed the situation which is building up in Australia as a result of the presence of so many American soldiers, sailors and Marines. American pay is much higher than Australian, and Americans spend freely. Morals in Australia are considered low (by all the officers I have talked to who have been there). The result is a thriving black market, loose women, and a rising resentment toward Americans, mixed in with gratitude for our protection against Japan.

Most of our men go to some place like Sydney for their vacation, if possible, trade cigarettes for gasoline and liquor when they cannot buy it with money, and expect to sleep with about any girl they can get to go out with them. The Japanese are using this situation as a part of their propaganda, dropping leaflets with verses and cartoons to remind the Australians of what is going on at home. "Thinking you diggers will never come back alive, the blacks and the Yanks are raping your wives, your daughters, your sweethearts. . . . They're helpless without your protection," etc.

Thursday, May 18

Strikes in Detroit—over 50,000 out.

To Service Squadron with Major Bryan. There were a number of Corsairs waiting to be tested and a shortage of test pilots. So I phoned Operations and upon learning that General [James T.] Moore's plane was still unreported, I took one of the planes for its shakedown and water-injection tests. A beautiful day for flying—the sky broken by all types of cloud formations with large clear areas in between—so that the tests could all be run with the shore line and the landing strips in view. From 30,000 feet I could see several of the islands and far beyond into the open Pacific. Some twenty or thirty miles away the top of a volcano stuck up through the surface of the sea. Was unable to make the water-injection runs because someone had used steel wire instead of copper as a throttle stop, and it was too strong for me to break to get into the water-injection range of the quadrant. Landed at 11:17 after a flight of two hours, fifteen minutes.

Borrowed Colonel Manley's fish spear and went swimming after lunch —Major Bryan trolling from a rubber raft, and I paddling along face down on the surface, using the face mask General Farrell gave me. Not much to see at first, but as I rounded the end of one of the islands, a school of fairly large fish came by leisurely and almost within range of my spear. I followed them for several minutes but only once got close enough to use the spear, and I wasted that opportunity getting a breath of air and trying to place myself in a slightly better position.

Found some ledges and coral growths farther on around the island —shallow water next to deep. There were many small and brilliantly colored fish moving in and out of the coral branches—some bright blue, some yellow, some mixed. In the deeper water, I could see the outlines of larger fish; but I could never get near them. At one place I found part of the fuselage of a plane; then, a few feet farther on, the wing of a Corsair; then the tail section; and then the forward portion of the fuselage—at depths varying from ten to twenty feet. At first, I thought it might be part of a plane which crashed into the water near the field several weeks ago and which was never found. However, more careful examination showed that a rope was tied around the fuselage, and that the wreckage had simply been dumped there by some boat or barge.

Colonel Manley phoned soon after we returned to our hut. General Moore has arrived on the island. Landed at Bomber 2 and has just driven through the gate at MAG-11.

Friday, May 19

Up at 5:45. Finished packing and cleaning up. Said good-by and took Marine station wagon to Bomber 2, where I found General Moore's Douglas already warming up, the general in the co-pilot's seat. A few minutes later a truck arrived with a large wooden box which was lashed in place in the plane. We took off at 7:51, the general, the crew, a half-dozen sailors en route to Guadalcanal, and myself.

I am always concerned about the loose items carried in these transports. The only article lashed down was the large box. Loose in the tail are heavy boxes of tools, mail sacks, baggage, two large sacks of potatoes, and miscellaneous smaller items. A minor accident could send them all hurtling forward like so many cannon balls.

It is a clear day except for the usual broken clouds in this area. We cut across the island, while I studied the jungle below and watched for native villages—unsuccessfully except for smoke columns here and there in the distance—and then headed out over the Pacific toward Guadalcanal.

We came in through broken cumulus clouds, across the island of Guadalcanal, skimming over the green, jungle-covered mountaintops and foothills. It seemed much more settled than Espiritu Santo. There were native clearings and huts on many of the mountainsides, and it was seldom that there was not at least one thatch roof somewhere in sight. Landed at Koli Field at 11:40. Tropical heat. Colonel [Herbert P.] Becker was waiting with a car to take us to the Marine base—a heavy, four-wheel-drive affair, weighing some 7,000 lbs. I am again assigned to a hut on the water's edge, this time with the outfit's doctor, a young captain.

Lunch at officers mess, with General Moore, Colonel Becker, and others. General Moore has invited me to go to Emirau with him tomorrow. I think I will accept, and stop at Guadalcanal on the way back, but will not decide definitely until after I have seen Admiral [Ernest L.] Gunther.

Flew to Henderson Field with General Moore in midafternoon; he to see General [Ralph J.] Mitchell, I to see Admiral Gunther. Admiral Gunther was about to go swimming, so I stayed only long enough to talk briefly about fighter development and outline my plans for continuing north with General Moore. It was agreed that I go north tomorrow and stop at Guadalcanal on my way back. Then back to Koli Field with General Moore. Dusty roads everywhere. It was a ten-minute drive from the field to the Marine quarters where we are staying—through a great deal of military activity—tanks, trucks, etc., kicking up clouds of dust. Short swim before supper. An excellent meal, including steak, boiled potatoes, green beans, biscuits, bread, butter, jam, and ice cream— plenty of everything. Life, on the whole, seems to be comfortable except for the heat and dust. There is no blackout, and ships offshore carry masthead lights. The air has cooled off considerably since nightfall.

Saturday, May 20

Allied armies take Cassino.

Sound of the ocean all night long. Up at dawn. We drove to the field through clouds of dust kicked up by trucks carrying troops to the shore for embarkation. The plane was being filled with cargo when we arrived —a heavy load and very poorly lashed down as usual. Off the field at 8:45 (Guadalcanal time) en route to Bougainville. We flew over many of the smaller islands of the Solomon group—some mountainous, some almost level with the sea—all jungle-covered except for occasional coconut palm plantations and military camps and airstrips. Landed at Bougainville at 11:32—on the third attempt, after being cut off by fighters on the first two approaches. Military activity and vehicles everywhere.

Driven to General [Field] Harris's headquarters. Lunch at officers mess with Brigadier General Harris, General Moore, and other officers. Found that all the Corsair squadrons have left the island, except a New Zealand outfit, which has only recently been equipped with these planes. Could hear artillery fire in the distance while we were eating lunch. Since General Moore is remaining here for the night, I asked General Harris if it would be possible for me to get up to the front lines. He said he thought it could be arranged and phoned General [William H.] Arnold (Army), who is now in command on the island. General Arnold said he would take me around himself.

To Army headquarters. We started out in a jeep, the general, a driver, and myself. The beachhead which has been established here is just large enough to protect the airfields and camp from artillery fire. There has been no attempt to clear the entire island of Japanese forces. The Japanese have lost heavily in recent assaults on the beachhead, and they have been quite effectively cut off from supplies; but there are still large numbers of enemy troops on this island—and some artillery.

We followed a road which has been constructed just behind the front lines and from which the forward pillboxes and communications trenches can often be seen. General Arnold directed the driver to the hill where the Japanese attacked our positions on March 10. Prior to that date it was jungle-covered, like the other hills on the island. Now, artillery and machine-gun fire have cleared the thick growth until one can see most of the battlefield from the hilltop. The Jap troops attacked up a steep hillside, starting about two hours before daybreak. They captured the hilltop where we were standing and a small portion of the ridge, forcing our men to counterattack. When the battle was over, the Japanese had retreated back into the jungle, leaving 1,700 dead on the field. Our losses were eighty killed and several hundred wounded.

General Arnold took me along the trenches and pointed out the key positions. Japanese skulls, bones, and articles of equipment were still hanging in the barbed-wire entanglements. Most of the bodies had been buried in the shallow trenches and foxholes the Japanese had scooped out during their attack—as was only too evident where they were not well covered up. But our men had not dared to enter the entanglements to remove the bodies, as they are heavily mined and spotted with booby traps. The general pointed out a hand-grenade booby trap as we passed on our way to one of the outpost pillboxes.

The hillside was littered with Japanese boots, canteens, trench spades, clothing, knapsacks, etc. A half-buried, stockinged foot stuck out from the earth at the side of the path we were following. The Japanese attack had been made with great courage and little strategy, the general said. Few of the attackers lived to retreat—probably none from the forward positions. They stuck to their shallow foxholes until they died. Many were burned to death by flame throwers.

We next drove to the point the Japanese attacked on March 14 and where they penetrated our lines for a considerable distance before we threw them back by the aid of tanks. They would attack by night, the general said, and then dig in and lie in their little foxholes all day long—often within fifty or one hundred feet of our lines.

A tropical storm came up, and we got thoroughly drenched while we were going over this area. I asked General Arnold if he was not concerned about the possibility of snipers operating from the hills outside the lines (which were within easy range of us at times). He replied that our patrols went out regularly and that he did not think there was a Jap within ten or fifteen miles. After leaving this position, we drove out through the lines to a forward howitzer post. Then to see a hill where the Japanese had been forming their ranks in the jungle and which we had bombed rather heavily. Then out along a newly made road toward the most advanced outpost.

When we were about three miles from the outpost, the general ordered the driver to turn back and later informed me that Japanese lookouts might be along the side of the road and that while they would be unlikely to give away their position by shooting at an ordinary car or truck, the sight of a general's star (which was in plain sight on our jeep) might be too great a temptation for them. (That same idea had been occupying my own mind for some time.)

There is no blackout here—a few miles from the Japanese lines. Lights are not shaded in the tents, and the stage of the outdoor theater is just as bright and open to the sky as it would be back at home in peacetime. Yet there are still a few enemy seaplanes somewhere on the island, probably hidden under branches up the rivers. No one seems to worry about them, and they apparently confine their activities to going after PT boats at night.

Sunday, May 21

United States forces capture airstrip and most of Wakde Island. Allies continue advance in Italy.

Conference with Generals Harris and Moore in regard to the radius of action of the Corsair and methods of increasing it. Attended an Intelligence summary of yesterday's activities in this area. Japanese installations on this island were bombarded by the Navy and bombed from the air. It is thought that at least one antiaircraft installation was knocked out.

General Arnold came with a jeep to take me over to see General [Robert B.] McClure. Another tour of the beachhead with General McClure, this time to see the coast positions. There are nothing but tree trunks standing in places along the shore where the original Japanese lines were heavily shelled. The Army engineers are putting in a road through this area—still in rough condition but passable for our jeep with all four wheels pushing. Several places along it, Japanese skulls had been set up on posts, and there was the extremely disagreeable odor of decaying bodies where the bulldozers had reopened the shallow and unmarked graves where they had been buried following the battle.

Left at 1:15 with General Moore for Piva U strip. Took off at 13:30 for Green Island—turning far enough out to sea to avoid possible Japanese antiaircraft fire before we left the beachhead. Low broken clouds and local squalls. Spent most of the trip writing. Landed at Green Island at 14:35—a jungle-covered atoll except for the camps and flying strips, with a steep and cliff-lined shore in places. Met by Marine officers and driven to our huts in jeeps. Inspection trip through Service Squadron (14) area with Captain Johnson. They were salvaging several Corsairs which had recently crashed and repairing others. One of the planes had been rather badly hit by flak this morning.

Half hour at officers club, where I met, much to my surprise, a Marine who had been an active and leading member on the Illinois America First Committee, and who said openly in front of the others present that he had not changed his views in the least. First part of evening spent talking to VMF officers. I asked to go on one of the patrols tomorrow and received an immediate invitation to take part in the 09:00 to 11:00 patrol over Rabaul. There will be four Corsairs in all. If we encounter nothing in the air, we will make a ground-strafing run before returning to Green Island.

Monday, May 22

Six thousand Allied planes hit Europe—drop 8,000 tons of bombs.

A hot tropical morning—no wind—broken skies. Up at daybreak. Washed at the side of the hut—rough board stand—water brought each day in cans—steel helmet for a basin. Breakfast with General Moore and other officers. Told the general I would like to remain two or three days at Green Island before going on to Emirau. Accompanied him to his plane to say good-by.

To pilots' ready room to get my equipment and listen to the briefing of the patrol I am to go on. Drew a .45 automatic and a leg knife in addition to the regular parachute, life raft, and jungle-kit back pack. Off the

Major Thomas B. McGuire and Colonel Lindbergh on Biak Island, 1944

P-38 Lockheed Lightnings over New Guinea

Light bombers en route to target, New Guinea, 1944

A B-24 Liberator bomber attack in the Pacific

Barge strafing along the New Guinea coast

Japanese air base in New Guinea following an American attack

Above: Colonel Charles H. MacDonald, Commanding Officer of the 475th Fighter Group

At left: Colonel Lindbergh and General George C. Kenney in Brisbane, 1944

F4U Vought Corsair

Colonel Lindbergh and General Ennis Whitehead

General Douglas MacArthur inspecting battle damage in the South Pacific

Brown Brothers

General Carl A. Spaatz, Colonel Lindbergh,
General James H. Doolittle (*at right*)

Antoine de Saint-Exupéry in the cockpit of his P-38

Refugees in Germany at the end of World War II

Munich after the war

Ruins in a German city at the end of World War II

The Russian occupation of Berlin, 1945

strip at 8:40. I am flying wing on Major [Alan J.] Armstrong. Our route to Rabaul lay over New Ireland. We cruised a little faster than usual to make up for the late start, clearing our guns over the water about halfway to New Ireland. Each plane carries about 1,600 rounds. Our radio call was Onyx 12. I used the code name of Jones.

Rabaul lies on the edge of a beautiful volcanic harbor. The city does not show the effects of bombardment from a distance, and it is hard to realize that a place of such natural beauty is the scene of such destruction and death. As one first approaches it looks tranquil and harmless.

We circle overhead for a time—at 10,000 feet. A "strike" is scheduled for this morning, and before long a formation of TBF's appears, coming in from the west. At a higher altitude, and coming in from the north, we see a formation of P-40's, and still a third formation in the distance—too far away to recognize the type of plane. All converging for the attack on Rabaul.

The TBF's begin their dive. Black puffs of ack-ack appear below them. One of our Corsairs reports a bogey[8] at 7:00 at 2,000 feet. I stop watching the bombers, arm all my guns, and we dive down to meet it—a two-engine plane, probably friendly. It is—American insignia standing out clearly on each wing. We climb up again, spiraling.

Message over the radio; a life raft is reported on the water. Fighters are already circling over to protect it and a dumbo[9] has been directed in for the rescue. The smoke and fires from magnesium clusters spring up from a grove of coconut palms below us. The TBF formation has broken up, and planes are everywhere amid the ack-ack—the blue silhouettes of TBF's, the black bursts of the antiaircraft—all against a background of jungle green. Several planes have accomplished their mission and are making their getaway low over the water. Great splashes of water follow them far out from shore. The Japanese antiaircraft gunners at Rabaul are considered the most accurate in the South Pacific. They should be; they have had constant practice.

Another bogey. We go down. Only a P-39 strayed from the flock. The higher formations are already out of sight, returning home. The TBF's are re-forming, low over the water, out of range of the shore batteries. One of them is smoking badly—a long trail of white, like sky-writing, trailing out behind. Several Army P-38's are above us. There is no more ack-ack. The strike is over, the sky clearing of aircraft.

Small fires have been started on the ground. The radio is busy with

8. An unidentified airplane that might prove to be an enemy plane (a "bandit").
9. A flying boat assigned to rescue operations.

directions for rescuing the downed pilot. We are back at 10,000 feet again and circling directly over Rabaul. There are wrecks of ships in the harbor—victims of previous raids. All is quiet; no sign of life below on the streets or roads. Yet we know there are thousands of Japanese: hundreds of eyes looking at us, range finders keeping us in view, someone figuring out whether it is worth while to shoot at pursuit planes flying at our altitude. The Japanese are cut off from most of their shipping. Ammunition must be running low. Pursuit planes are difficult targets. Probably it is not worth while.

We circle over the airstrips. There are several of them around the harbor. Most are pock-marked with bomb craters. Three or four are serviceable. I see a number of planes in revetments along the side of one field—probably unserviceable, or they would be better camouflaged. There has been no sign of air opposition during the last several strikes. We sweep over the harbor again. It is almost 11:00 and the end of our patrol. Four more fighters will be out to relieve us. We fly over the objectives we are to strafe before we start back to Green Island—two oblong buildings near the shore and surrounded by coconut palms. Gunfire was seen coming from them on one of the previous raids. I am to take the one nearest the beach, Major Armstrong the one a hundred yards inland. I reach down and purge my wing tanks and set controls for the dive.

We swing around into position. Major Armstrong noses down. Five seconds later I follow. The building is squarely in my sight; but Armstrong's plane is in the way—don't want to shoot so close to him. His tracers are striking his target and ricocheting back up off the ground. I am at 2,000 feet now, but he is still in the way. I keep the building in my sight and hold fire—roof, palm trees, and ground rushing up at me. No sign of life. Armstrong pulls up. I press the trigger. Long streams of tracers bury themselves in the roof and wall. Everything is still lifeless.

The ground is close. I level out over the tree tops. It was a short burst, but most of the bullets went home. I hope there was no one in that building except soldiers—no women, no children. I will never know. There is no time to think about it. Tree tops are twenty feet below, passing at 400 miles an hour. Armstrong is ahead, firing at some huts. I get another in my sight and give it a short burst—a dozen rounds; we are moving too fast for more. Still no sign of life on the ground. An airfield lies ahead. It is probably well defended with machine guns. We bank out toward the sea. The shore line flashes past. I hold low over the water.

We are to rendezvous over a small island off the coast. Here we are met by the other two planes of our patrol. They had been assigned a different target: similar buildings, two or three miles away. Everyone has ammunition left. We fly over to the Duke of York, an enemy-held island northeast of Rabaul containing a Japanese airstrip—apparently abandoned. Orders are to strafe everything in sight. We fly low over the palms and fire on huts and villages. The native inhabitants are reported to have gone to the hills in the interior long ago, and Japanese troops have been using their dwellings.

I get a line of a dozen huts in my sights and rake them from one end to the other—dust and fragments flying into the air—tracers bouncing up into the sky. I bank left, low along the coast, and then head in toward shore. I see the other Corsairs diving down on their targets. There is a hut much larger than the rest directly ahead of me. I rake it with fire as I approach. The tracers disappear inside. I keep shooting until within one hundred yards and pull up steeply to miss the hill and trees of the shore line, banking as I climb.

Another row of huts along the shore, but there is time only for a short burst. They were well hidden among the trees, and I was too close before I saw them. I circle back toward the airstrip. There is a larger building at ideal range ahead. I bank steeply and get it centered in the sight rings. I am about to pull the trigger when I see a steeple rising through the palms. I hold fire. Yes, a church. I flash thirty feet above it. Thank God I saw what it was in time. It is difficult to identify buildings when one is flying at tree-top level, and one is too good a target for machine guns at a higher altitude. In wartime one must be either very low or very high for safety. I find another group of huts and rake them with fire. My ammunition boxes are almost empty—only one gun still shooting. (I learned later in the day that even churches are fired on in this area; the Japanese are said to use them for their troops. However, I will leave churches for someone else to shoot at unless I see gunfire coming from their windows. I suppose our enemies say the same about our churches. It seems that both sides can find an excuse to shoot at anything in war.)

The patrol planes are rendezvousing off the coast. I join them, and we start back to Green Island. A radio message comes to sweep St. Georges Channel for a rubber boat. Apparently some plane is unaccounted for. We spread out 1,000 yards apart and fly 500 feet above the water, keeping a sharp lookout. We find nothing. Back into tight formation as we approach Green Island—in right echelon for landing breakup. On the ground at 12:20. Turn in equipment. Report what we saw during the patrol, and off to lunch. Other planes are getting ready to take off for a strike as we drive away.

Neither Major Armstrong nor I saw any antiaircraft fire near our planes. However, one of the pilots of the second unit reported that we were shot at over Rabaul—the burst being high and behind.

Met Lieutenant Colonel [Roger T.] Carleson, the C.O. of MAG-14, as I was walking along the path to my hut. He had been informed that I was going up on a patrol over Green Island, not the one over Rabaul. Nothing ever happens over Green Island. There hasn't been an enemy raid for weeks. He was much concerned when he learned that I was over Rabaul—one of the Marine officers told me that as we were driving from the airstrip to our quarters in the jeep. "It's so very irregular," the officer said. "You're on civilian status. If you'd had to land and the Japs caught you, you would have been shot." I replied that I didn't see it made much difference what status you were on if you were forced down on Jap territory, because according to reports they shot you anyway. (The Marine camps are full of stories about the torture and beheading of American pilots captured by the Japanese.)

"You didn't fire your guns, did you?" Colonel Carleson asked. I told him that I had fired my guns. "But you should never have done that. The Japs would shoot you if they caught you." The discussion continued while we went off for lunch together at the officers mess. "You have a right to observe combat as a technician, but not to fire guns."

"Of course, it would be all right for him to engage in target practice on the way home," another Marine officer put in. The tenseness began to ease up.

"Yes, he has a right to observe combat—and there's no reason he shouldn't observe it from an F4U any more than from a TBF or an SBD. We've had civilians observing from them, you know."

"Yes, he can observe from an F4U, and he can engage in target practice on the way home if he wants to; there's nothing wrong with that."

"Let's wait a day or so and see if anybody kicks up a fuss."

The more I see of the Marines the more I like them.

Stopped to talk to the maintenance crews of both Corsair squadrons. Then to see some of the Navy B-24's which are under repair. One of the B-24's exploded on take-off a few days ago—cause unknown. It crashed into the water not far from the end of the runway. No one is certain whether the explosion took place before or after the crash. All of the crew lost.

Have arranged to go out to the native village with Captain [C. W.] Buckley (the Catholic father) tomorrow afternoon.

Tuesday, May 23

Took Colonel Carleson's jeep, picked up Father Buckley, Markey (Chance Vought), and Major Williams (New Zealand), and started out for the native village. There is only one village on the island now, and less than 150 natives—all men. The women and many of the men—over 1,000 natives in all—were evacuated to Guadalcanal soon after our forces captured Green Island—partly for medical treatment, partly because the natives were not entirely trusted. They are to be returned later.

We followed a good military road for the first several miles; then turned off onto a newly cut and extremely rough road through the jungle. It could hardly be called a road; the trees had simply been cut close to the ground and the tops knocked off the higher humps of coral. There were not even ruts in most places, and I don't think that even a jeep had traveled it more than half a dozen times previously. I threw in the four-wheel drive, and we bumped along in low gear at about five miles an hour.

The village, fortunately, was not much more than a mile in the interior. An Australian administrative officer came out to meet us. He lives with and supervises the natives. We were introduced to the higher tribesmen and gave them presents of tobacco and candy, which was accepted with reserve and dignity. The remaining natives seem to be in most instances in fairly good condition. A few have skin troubles, but the worst cases, I am told, were evacuated to Guadalcanal. They played a little on the huge, hollow log drums (at the administrator's request), grinning rather sheepishly as they did so, and apparently not enjoying the demonstration at all.

The huts were dirty, and there was a disappointing lack of native art. (It reminded me of Calcutta.) The natives have lost their natural habits and resourcefulness without gaining enough from Western civilization to make up. Their wild, barbaric freedom has been taken away from them and replaced with a form of civilized slavery which leaves neither them nor us better off. The white man has brought them a religion they do not understand, diseases they are unable to combat, standards of life which leave them poverty stricken, a war which has devastated their homes and taken their families away; and they are still supposed to be grateful to us for giving them the benefits of Christianity and civilization. We ate some of the native fruit and nuts with the administrator and started back over the rough road to camp.

Supper with Father Buckley and others at the MAG-14 mess. A nurse is on the island—great excitement—the first white woman since it was recaptured from the Japs. She is with one of the SCAT [South Pacific Combat Air Transport Command] transports and is held here overnight by weather. I met her sitting on the porch at the officers club: young, rather good-looking, surrounded by officers. The enlisted men haven't got a chance. Poor girl; she is stared at constantly by the men around her. However, she seems to have the situation fairly well in hand. Conversation overheard as I leave: "Well, then I'll be a mother to you."

"Oh, but that would be a step in the wrong direction."

Wednesday, May 24

Arranged to go on a reconnaissance and strafing mission this afternoon along the northeast coast of New Ireland. To Intelligence hut for briefing at 1:00. There are to be four planes—no restrictions on targets. But weather is moving in toward the coast of New Ireland; possibly the ceiling will be too low. We are to take off and go on or turn back according to the conditions we encounter.

I get my chute and equipment, check code and radio signals, and start my plane—first cartridge this time. We are off at 13:55 and join up as we circle the field. Charge our guns and take up combat formation as soon as we are over the water. The New Ireland coast is clear—not enough low clouds to bother. The center of the storm is still north of us.

We fly along the coast at 2,000 or 3,000 feet at first, looking for signs of new Japanese activity. Then down 200 or 300 feet above the jungle, zooming up mountainsides, clearing the trees on top by less than our wing span, diving steeply down into the valley beyond, always just over the tree tops, watching for targets ahead or the telltale streaks of tracers from the ground.

We cut inland to avoid a Japanese airstrip where strong antiaircraft positions have been reported. "There are no targets in that vicinity worth the risk." There is a bridge below—bombed a few days back—hit squarely by a 500-pounder from a Corsair. A great gap shows in one end of the structure. Several Japanese are working on a scaffolding in an attempt to make repairs. We come on them too suddenly to shoot and are past like a flash. "We'll get them on the way back" (over the radio).

More miles over the tree tops, zooming up now and then for a few seconds to get a better look around, and then down again before there is time for someone to train a gun on us. Out to the coast line—four Corsairs abreast, racing over the water—I am the closest one to land. The trees pass, a streak of green; the beach a band of yellow on my left. Is it a post a mile ahead in the water, or a man standing? It moves toward shore. It is a man.

All Japanese or unfriendly natives on New Ireland—everything is a target—no restrictions—shoot whatever you see. I line up my sight. A mile takes ten seconds at our speed. At 1,000 yards my .50-calibers are deadly. I know just where they strike. I cannot miss.

Now he is out of the water, but he does not run. The beach is wide. He cannot make the cover of the trees. He is centered in my sight. My finger tightens on the trigger. A touch, and he will crumple on the coral sand.

But he disdains to run. He strides across the beach. Each step carries dignity and courage in its timing. He is not an ordinary man. The shot is too easy. His bearing, his stride, his dignity—there is something in them that has formed a bond between us. His life is worth more than the pressure of a trigger. I do not want to see him crumple on the beach. I release the trigger.

I ease back on the stick. He reaches the tree line, merges with the streak of green on my left. I am glad I have not killed him. I would never have forgotten him writhing on the beach. I will always remember his figure striding over the sand, the fearless dignity of his steps. I had his life balanced on a muscle's twitch. I gave it back to him, and thank God that I did so. I shall never know who he was—Jap or native. But I realize that the life of this unknown stranger—probably an enemy—is worth a thousand times more to me than his death. I should never quite have forgiven myself if I had shot him—naked, courageous, defenseless, yet so unmistakably man.

There is no more time to think about it. We turn inland again, skimming the palms of a coconut plantation, up and down more mountain sides. There is an antiaircraft position on our right—out of range; they do not shoot. We are over hills and jungle. There will be no antiaircraft here—too wild. We climb for altitude—to 4,000 feet. We have reached the limit of our patrol.

We circle and turn back. We are to strafe on the way home. The first dive is started. I switch on my gunsight—bright orange circles on the glass in front of me. A plantation is the target. Tracers from the plane on my right. The range is too long. I pick out a thatch roof among the palms. Time now. I press the trigger. A stream of yellow dots leaves my plane. Red balls of fire ricochet up from the ground around the hut. The air around it was clear. Now it is a cloud of dust; the burst went home. I give it another hundred rounds—splinters flying. Time to pull up.

I hope that there are no natives in that hut. "Shoot anyway. The natives on New Ireland are unfriendly. All the plantations have been taken over by the Japanese." That's the trouble with this air war. You don't know what you're shooting at. The hut may be empty. It may be full of Japanese soldiers. It may be a cover for machine guns. It may hold a mother and a child. "The area is unlimited. Everything is a target. All the natives are unfriendly. Japanese have taken over the plantations."

You press the trigger and death leaps forth—4,200 projectiles a minute. Tracers bury themselves in walls and roof. Dust springs up from yard and garden. Inside may be emptiness or writhing agony. You never know. Holes in a dirt floor; a machine gun out of action; a family wiped out; you go on as you were before. Below, all is silence again. Death has passed. It is in your cockpit. You carried it in your hands. You hurled it down into those peaceful palm tops. You wiped out a squad of enemy troops, surprised by the suddenness of your attack. You endangered your life and your plane to attack an empty and worthless native hut. You left children wounded and dying behind you.

The beach is on my left—another plantation ahead. We are strung out abreast, all four of us. We zoom up to get a better view of our target. It will be a converging attack—must keep the other planes in sight—just the kind of place where collisions occur.

I throttle back slightly to let my partner gain the lead. In range; I am in line with a row of huts. No sign of life on the ground. Never is around these villages. They have been strafed before—probably take cover as soon as they hear the sound of an airplane engine. I sight on the nearest hut, let my fire rake the entire row as I pull the stick back slowly. My tracers cross with those of the other planes. The village is a cloud of dust. My partner is too close to my line of fire, 300 yards ahead. I stop shooting. He crosses over and pulls up. I have time for a short burst—pick a building beyond the village. I am well clear of the other two Corsairs—no danger of hitting them. Dust—splinters—just time to pull up over the palm tops—must be careful not to hold the dive too long.

We skim up a mountainside and push over the top of the ridge. Heavy antiaircraft positions lie on the point ahead according to Intelligence reports. We hoped to surprise some target on the far side of the mountain but find none. We turn toward the sea before reaching the antiaircraft emplacements. Our second section has dropped behind. One of the pilots reports his carburetor air-temperature warning light on. We throttle down and circle around until his engine cools—too far at sea for the shore batteries.

Back over the jungle; up a few hundred feet for observation. Down low to close in on some plantation. A group of buildings ahead along the shore. Two planes are already pouring tracers into them. I am pointed at an angle. I bank quickly to get my sight lined up. There is no time to straighten out again. I find myself firing from a nearly vertical position—forgetting my plane—tracers streaming to their mark. There is no need to be upright in the air—it is the sight that matters. Soon one forgets the plane; it follows the mind's desire as unconsciously as the hand.

The low wing almost cuts the palm leaves as I pull the stick back to recover. Another group of buildings ahead. I take two on my side and pour a burst into each of them. Tracers from the other planes are streaming on my right. Over the jungle—turning—low—up a hillside, angling toward the summit. The second section reports that one of my buildings is on fire—an incendiary went home. I glance back—too low—too far away—I see nothing.

A dozen black dots streak past my wing. Antiaircraft? No, of course not, ridiculous; only small birds at 300 miles an hour. What must they think of our intrusion of their jungle, these roaring monsters brushing over their tree tops. I am within twenty feet of the leaves, but I cannot see them. They pass too fast.

We are at the end of New Ireland. We set our course eastward toward Green Island, sixty miles away—a fifteen-minute flight at cruising speed. The island is in sight. We safety our guns and switches. Close in for a parade formation over the landing strip—ten feet, wing tip to wing tip—echelon to the right. The leader peels off. I wait three seconds and follow. Then the Corsairs of the second section.

We are in the landing circle. Throttle down to fifteen inches. Air speed 170 miles an hour. The leading plane drops its gear. I push my lever forward. Roll the tabs back as the nose drops. Propeller to 2,300 r.p.m. Air speed 140 miles an hour. The plane ahead of me is on its final. I bank over and open up the hatch; 130 miles an hour—slow enough to drop the flaps. I put them down all the way.

The plane ahead is rather close. I overturn the strip to gain distance.

Propeller up to 2,500 r.p.m. in case I get a wave-off. Manifold pressure up to twenty inches (take no chance of the engine loading up; the runway drops off abruptly at its end, and undershooting would probably be fatal). The plane ahead has landed, is rolling rapidly ahead. I bank right for final line-up. Over the end now. Throttle closed. Stick back.

I am on the ground. Is there a plane close behind me? I am strapped in so tightly that I cannot turn my head enough to see back. How close am I to the plane ahead? Suppose he blew a tire and ground-looped? How would I see him in time to stop? I am going slow enough now to swing the nose over—no, the runway is clear ahead—and behind.

Cowl flaps open—propeller, high r.p.m. Oil and intercooler flaps open. I move all the levers into their proper position. Here is the runway end. I unlock the tail wheel and turn off onto the taxi strip. In and out past revetments with their planes—torpedo planes, dive bombers, fighters—a long taxi. There is my revetment ahead. The crew chief stands out in front, both hands in the air, waving me on. Into the revetment. Blow the tail around into position. Mixture—idle cutoff. Fuel off. The propeller slows down and stops. Switches off. Radio off. Gyros caged. Reset the tabs for the next pilot. Yes, the plane's in fine shape. No, I didn't purge the wing tanks. Yes, the guns were fired. I unsnap my safety belt and sign the report sheet on the plane. The crew swarms over it. In half an hour it will be ready for another flight.

I leave for Emirau Island in the morning. Colonel Carleson has offered me his F6F for the trip, and I will fly with the fighter escort for the SCAT transports. We leave at 6:15—at daybreak. Colonel Carleson comes to tell me that his F6F carries only 250 gallons of fuel, which is considered insufficient for the flight to Emirau (in case a storm over the island forced us to turn back to Green). Therefore I am to take a Service Squadron Corsair instead. I feel that there was enough fuel, but am glad to make the change.

A beautiful night. I walk out under the stars. They are new here, and those I know are upside down. The Southern Cross is high, and the North Star is below the opposite horizon. I wonder what Anne is doing, and the children. Asleep, of course. It is not yet dawn at home.

Thursday, May 25

Coffee and toast at the SCAT hut at 5:45. The pilots and crews move about sleepily. It is still night. Got my plane started after numerous attempts at 6:20. But some of the transports had trouble getting started, too, so I am at the end of the runway in plenty of time, waiting for them to take off. Dawn has broken, but outlines are not too clear in the distance, and wing lights are still burning. Off the strip at 0644—palm trees on each wing until I rise above them. The SCAT planes have circled and are forming to the north—seven R4D's. We cut across to join them—our three Corsairs.

The day is clear—visibility unlimited—scattered clouds, through a blue sky. We detour north of a direct line to Emirau, to keep well away from Japanese-held islands. Five of the transports keep in good formation. There are two stragglers. We weave back and forth above them with the Corsairs, sweeping the entire sky as we turn, watching for ships or other aircraft.

We land at Emirau at 0925 on a long coral strip between green walls of jungle. This is one of the outposts of our advance against Japan. There are supposed to be about 100,000 Japanese troops between us and the main American bases. But we control the air and the sky. I taxi up to the line, turn my plane over to a crew chief, and go to the operations office to check in. VMF-115 is stationed on the island. I inquire about Foss[10] and [Captain William B.] Freeman. They are not in. One of their pilots was killed yesterday on a test flight in a Corsair. Engine cut on take-off, and he hooked a wing trying to turn a little more toward shore, too close to the water. They are attending the funeral.

I ride over to General Moore's quarters and am assigned to a tent nearby. Admiral Halsey[11] is expected to arrive about noon on a farewell tour of the area. Preparations are being made for his welcome. Joe Foss comes in, and other officers assemble. The admiral's plane is late. He has delayed to watch a "strike" on one of the Japanese positions down the line. Finally, his plane is reported a quarter hour out. We all drive to the landing strip to meet him. There is a crowd—Marines, sailors, Seabees. It is raining lightly, one of the numerous tropical squalls—small but soaking and sticky.

The admiral lands in a B-24. General Mitchell is with him. We drive back to "generals' country" for lunch. The squall has passed, but it is still

10. Major Joseph J. Foss, the leading Marine ace in World War II, with 26 victories. He was awarded the Congressional Medal of Honor. In 1955 he was elected Governor of South Dakota.

11. Admiral William F. Halsey, Jr., commander of the U.S. fleet in the South Pacific.

hot. The lunch is informal, as everything is in the combat zone. No one wears ties. Few uniforms are pressed. But there are white cloths on the table, and the admiral makes a short farewell address after it is over.

I ride over to the strip with Foss to see the admiral off. The troops of the island are assembled in formation. A loudspeaker has been hoisted up on a crane. A band is playing. The admiral makes another address. Planes take off in his honor. He takes off. The formations wilt. The planes start landing.

Foss and I drive over to his squadron. Freeman and other officers are there, whom I met last year in Santa Barbara. We talk about the Corsairs and their operating problems. I am much pleased with their reports on the plane. Most of the troubles encountered a year ago have been worked out.

Friday, May 26

General Moore is leaving the island this morning for a new station. Drove over to the airstrip to see him off. More troops in formation, planes taking off for escort, the band playing, and a farewell address. Drove to VMF-115 in the jeep which has been assigned to me during my stay on Emirau Island. Then back to the ready room to assemble equipment I will need to go on the noon patrol over Kavieng—parachute, life raft, life belt, belt containing a canteen, first-aid kit, .45 pistol, etc. Down to the Intelligence hut to get "briefed" for the flight. (Information about new antiaircraft emplacements, shipping in the area, recognition signals, weather, etc.)

Off the strip at 12:40. There were to be three of us, but one man could not get his engine started, so Captain Freeman and I take off without him. If he can get under way in time, he will meet us over New Ireland. We charge our guns and fire a trial burst as soon as we are over the water. The mountains of New Hanover are already visible between the clouds. We see a wrecked Japanese ship on one of the reefs as we skirt the coast toward New Ireland and Kavieng.

The bombed city of Kavieng lies at the tip of a peninsula and is sheltered by two islands and their reefs. We approach at 10,000 feet and pass at a respectful distance—about a mile offshore—changing course constantly to prevent the larger antiaircraft guns from lining up on us. Bomb pocks are everywhere around the city and its airfields—hundreds of them. Many buildings are destroyed, but others have remained intact despite the bombs of aircraft and the shells of battleships. There are several sunken ships in the harbor. Small circles show where some of the antiaircraft guns are placed.

"The most accurate antiaircraft gunners in the South Pacific are at Rabaul and Kavieng."

"They ought to be. They have had the most practice."

"There was a time when between Rabaul and Kavieng we lost an average of a plane a day."

"We still lose them pretty frequently."

Everything is quiet below: no sign of life; no sign of danger. We are just a little too far away to draw fire from those hidden guns. We pass on to the southwest coast of New Ireland. Freeman knows where a Japanese barge is located. Orders are to stay above 10,000 feet except when a barge is sighted. This one has been sunk but is still repairable. We dive down on it—point-blank range. Spurts of water and flying splinters as our tracers bury themselves in the wooden sides. We make three passes in all, firing several hundred rounds. Most of the bullets find their mark. We leave the barge in an unrepairable condition. Now it will lie on that shore for decades, until wind and water slowly rot the wood away. A war barge yesterday; a wreck today; beams bleaching in the sun tomorrow.

We are on a two-hour patrol. We fly back and forth over the northwestern end of New Ireland—around the city, back over the mountains, around to the city again. I wonder what kind of life the Japanese must lead with enemy planes overhead all through the day and night—never knowing when a bombing raid will start, never knowing when a fighter will dive down and strafe them—their aircraft shot out of the air, their surface craft sunk—too far from Japan for effective assistance. Their only outside contact must be by submarine and possibly an occasional plane at night which slips in below our radars. Still, fairly small number of Japanese are keeping large Allied forces occupied, and our cost in equipment and effort has been high. These islands are distant outposts of Japan. Her strength lies closer to the center.

We land back at Emirau at 1530, turn our planes over to the ground crew, turn in the reports on our flight, and drive over to the pilots' camp where I am assigned a tent in the VMF-115 line. It is a beautiful location —on a high bluff overlooking the sea and the shore of the island.

Saturday, May 27

Anne and I were married fifteen years ago today—the wisest thing I ever did. The most important decision in a man's life is made when he selects the woman he marries. All else is secondary. I wake with the distant sound of breakers in my ears, birds and crickets singing outside, and dawn faintly lighting the sky. I get up quickly, wash, and dress. I am to fly on the morning Kavieng patrol.

Briefed and off the strip at 8:40. We follow the route of yesterday to Kavieng. The wrecked ship on the New Hanover reefs has become a marker. We dive down and strafe Kavieng as we pass. I am flying a single plane, second section.

We alternate between low strafing and high patrol. [Lieutenant Rolfe F.] Blanchard reports antiaircraft fire on one of our strafing runs— machine guns in a roofless building down below. I pass directly over them and do not see the fire. There are no holes in our planes. We go on. The wake of a submarine is reported in the channel between Kavieng and New Hanover. We fly over, dive down, and sweep back and forth across the area—a few hundred feet off the water. We sight nothing, radio a negative report to "Fido," the Emirau radio station which guards us. We have been out two and a quarter hours. Our patrol is over. We take up a course for Emirau. Land at 11:15.

Captain Freeman and I are to go on a PT-boat patrol tonight along the southwest coast of New Ireland. We leave camp at 3:00 in my jeep to be at the naval base in time to hear the briefing. We arrive early. There is a long wait—fifty men in a hot, sweaty room. The briefing does not take long. The PT boats are to go out in pairs. Each pair is assigned to an area along the New Ireland coast. We have the southwest coast, about midway along the island. Also, we are to make a landing in the morning, on the island of Tingwan, off the west coast of New Hanover. A briefing of air reports follows. It is badly garbled. They have our flight of this morning reporting the wake of a submarine! Just the opposite of our actual report that we saw no sign of one. I inform the Intelligence officer of this fact, but we must leave. There is no time to straighten it out. It will have no effect on the night's mission anyway.

We walk down to the dock where the boats are moored—low-lying, powerful, warted with guns, torpedoes, and depth charges. The engines are already running. In a few minutes we are under way, gliding swiftly through the clear water of the channel. I lean over a torpedo and watch the bottom pass by, fifteen or twenty feet below. It shows almost as plainly as though there were no water in between. As soon as we leave the channel, we speed up to twenty-six knots—spray flying up behind like a fountain, the white wake extending hundreds of yards behind, the ship skimming the top of the water like a giant surfboard. There is no pounding. The ocean is calm and almost glassy. The swells are far apart. We ride over them with little motion.

Lieutenant [Leonard R.] Hardy brings out his carbine for target practice on flying fish—the wake of our boat scares one of them out of the water every few minutes. He hits two in the air with his carbine. I manage to get one with my .45 automatic. It is excellent practice—quick shooting—and one can see exactly where his bullet lands.

A beautiful sunset—deep reds and greens and grays, and the blue of water. The mountains of New Hanover are out of gun range on our left. The PT boats have divided and set course for their patrol areas. All the others are out of sight. We are only two now, heading into the night and a hostile coast. We take turns going below for "chow."

It is quite dark, and the stars are out when I return on deck. There is not a light in view—everything blacked out along the distant shore. Everything blacked out aboard ship. There are only silhouettes—the ridge of the mountains, the mast of the radar, the barrels of guns, the second PT boat astern. I brace myself against a depth charge and study the stars in the South Sea sky.

We have turned southeast, paralleling the coast, still well offshore. We will not be on location until 10:30 and expect no action before midnight. All the crew not on duty are curled up in corners, sleeping. I stretch out on deck between a torpedo tube and the bridge. There is just room enough to lie in comfort. The night is cooling. A strong wind, caused only by our speed, sweeps over the deck. I look upward to the stars and doze off for minutes at a time. Raindrops wake me from a light sleep. Everyone is taking cover. I jump up and make my way to the bridge, where there is enough shelter from the wind to put on the waterproof suit Captain Freeman brought for me.

We turn our backs to the wind until the squall passes. Then I find my place on the deck and lie down again. But before I fall asleep, the engines slow, and we swing in toward the dark band of coast on our left— barely perceptible in the light of a quarter moon. We are almost on location, and the last five miles toward shore will be covered with engines idling to avoid the phosphorescent wakes the PT boats kick up at high speed. By creeping in toward shore, we will prevent the Japs from spotting us until we are very close, if at all.

The PT boats are built for stealth and striking power. They are so low and small that they leave very little silhouette. They are painted in grays and blacks to blend into the night. They can leap forward in an instant, throwing a smoke screen behind them to baffle enemy fire, and when a flash is seen on shore, they can spit back death from seven guns—one 37-mm. cannon, two 20-mm. cannon, four .50-cal. machine guns. For more formidable targets they carry four large torpedoes and two depth charges.

Every man is on deck, except those who have duties below. All eyes are on the shore watching for a glow of light. All guns are manned and pointing toward the land. I have borrowed a carbine and several clips of ammunition. Possibly, if we get close enough, I will be able to shoot, too. The mountains grow higher and clearer in the moonlight. It appears a formidable and hostile shore. Now, the radar shows us to be a half mile off. There is a reef between us and the shore. We turn northwest and parallel the coast, guns ready for instant action. Sometimes the Japanese batteries open up on the PT's. Then they depend on smoke and speed and return fire.

Our mission is to prevent barges from moving along the coast. Somewhere ahead of us is a cove where aerial photographs show a road to end. It is a possible unloading point for barges. We are to locate it and bombard any construction that is there. It is well hidden and will be difficult to find at night.

We locate the approximate position by dead reckoning and radio the Black Cat (a Navy flying boat on patrol) to drop a string of flares. Meanwhile, we drift offshore. Within fifteen minutes there is the sound of engines overhead. The Black Cat has located us by radar. It circles and drops three parachute flares along the coast. They illuminate the shore for us as they float slowly down. They also illuminate us for any Japanese batteries that may happen to be there. Everyone is tense. The gunners crouch in position. The flares drift down one after another and show nothing but jungle. We have missed our location and an off chance to find an enemy barge. The last flare goes out among the trees. We begin to cruise slowly along the coast again. At midnight we turn out a mile to sea and drift while we have sandwiches and coffee.

Sunday, May 28

After a half hour's midnight meal of sandwiches, coffee, and doughnuts we take up our patrol again. We are to bombard a plantation where Japanese activity has been reported. We reach the position by dead reckoning shortly after 2:00. The reef lies closer in shore here, so we creep cautiously to within a quarter mile of the beach. Both boats turn broadside to bring all their guns to play.

We fire a flare from our mortar. It curves skyward and brilliantly illuminates the coast. There are palm trees along the shore but no sign of buildings. The flare dies out. We move a half mile along the coast and drop another. We are so close that I can use my carbine if there is anything to shoot at. I am crouched behind the starboard torpedo, between the .50-cal.-machine-gun turrets. All of us are wearing steel helmets. But the flare illuminates nothing but the jungle of a cliff and mountainside. If there were more time, we would ask the Black Cat to come back and help us find the plantation. But we must be at the island of Tingwan at daybreak to make our landing.

The engines are opened wide. The boats leap forward. The white wake appears behind. I stand forward on the deck for a time, cooling off in the wind, then lie down again beside the torpedo. There is more room farther forward, but no railing and nothing to keep one from rolling off into the sea.

I get half an hour's sleep. Then a rain squall sends everyone to shelter. There is no overhead cover, no shelter from the rain, but there are places on board which break the wind, and where we can put on our waterproofs. It is too hot and sticky to leave them on after the squall passes, so we are constantly getting caught as the frequency of storm clouds increases. I manage to get another half hour's sleep, and then day has broken.

The island of Tingwan lies five miles ahead, low, green, and jungle-covered. We approach full speed to its reef, then throttle down and swing around its coast line while we sweep the shore with our glasses. "If the natives come out on the beach, it is a sign that no Japs are on the island. If there are Japs, the natives won't come out."

The plantation house comes in view as we round a point of land. In front of it is a beach, and on it are *no natives*. We turn broadside to the coast and drift a quarter mile offshore—the guns of both boats covering the plantation. "No natives. That's bad." There is no movement, no sign of life on shore. There is a Japanese lifeboat a half mile away on the beach. Someone recalls that it has been reported before—came from some wrecked Japanese ship. I look over to another island in the distance. Is something moving on the beach? I reach for the glasses. It looks red. Yes, it is a native with a red cloth wound around his middle. There are a number of them on the beach. They are pushing canoes into the water.

We move over to meet them. They paddle out to a reef which lies between us and the island. There are four canoes—dugouts with outriggers. There are several natives in each. All are very black. They get out, pull the dugouts across the reef and paddle closer. Two chiefs are squatting on the nearest canoe, feet on the gunnels. I marvel that they stay afloat at all. If the waves were four inches higher, they would wash over the edges. Several natives are paddling. One is bailing out the water that leaks in. Each chief wears a visored cap. The one with the white band around his cap is the chief of the entire group of islands. The one with the red band around his cap is the chief of the particular island from which the canoes have come.

We have an Australian aboard, a Lieutenant Bell, who speaks the native tongue. Also, we have brought two natives from Emirau and a Chinaman who has lived in this area for many years. The Australian goes forward to speak to the chiefs. The other canoes gather around. A rope net is let down over the side of our boat, and a number of natives climb on board, following the two chiefs. They are naked except for a pair of trunks or a piece of cloth. Their black bodies shine with sweat. Only the two chiefs have headgear. The others have nothing but their thick, curly hair to ward off the rays of the sun. The natural hair of the natives is very black; but on many the use of lime to cure lice and scabs has left the hair with a distinct reddish tinge on top.

The conference is over. Some of the natives climb back down into the canoes. Several others, including the two chiefs, stay on board. We move back over to Tingwan, and approach to within a hundred yards of shore. The natives say there are no Japanese on the island. They would hardly go with us if they were lying—especially the chiefs. They say there are guns and ammunition and fuel barrels at the plantation house left by the Japs. Lieutenant Bell, three natives, and one Marine go ashore in the first boatload; it will only carry six. Captain Freeman and I go ashore on the second trip.

The shore is lined with fuel drums from a Japanese ship which was sunk nearby. The plantation buildings are in a dilapidated condition. Under the house and in one of the outbuildings we find the guns and ammunition reported by the natives. We move about cautiously; the Japs may have left booby traps behind. There are two American .50-cal. machine guns, a case and a half of shells, and two extra barrels for the guns. Also half a dozen Australian rifles and one German rifle—apparently loot captured in some Japanese raid during the earlier stages of the war.

These items were in the outbuilding, a sort of shed beside the plantation house. The main cache was under the house itself—a Japanese mortar, a homemade cannon (apparently for throwing smoke shells), several shells for the cannon, and probably 200 high-explosive bombs for the mortar (in excellent condition). Further search of the buildings and grounds brought out only odds and ends and a few sheets of paper containing Japanese writing, which we gathered up for translation by Intelligence.

After going through the buildings I separated from the party and made a one-man excursion along the beach. About 200 yards away from the house I found a tumbled-down machine-gun nest, set back just far enough in the jungle for concealment. A few feet away was a pile of Japanese postal cards—dozens of them—which I gathered up for the crew. ("Bring us back something from the island.") On my way back I shot holes through all the fuel barrels on the beach and set them on fire behind me. Another party set fire to those which had drifted in the opposite direction. There were forty or fifty barrels in all, each spilling fire out onto the land and sending columns of black smoke into the air.

The men who remained at the plantation had rolled drums of gasoline under the house, placing them next to the ammunition pile for the mortar and cannon. The American machine guns and samples of the Japanese equipment were taken on board our boat. After the last man was off the island we bombarded the plantation with the 37-mm. and 20-mm. cannon, setting fire to the gasoline almost immediately. The dry timbers of the house caught quickly, and as we backed farther away the mortar shells began to explode with loud reports, throwing fragments well out into the water.

We stood by, watching the fire for a time, and then took the natives back to the island where we found them. The dugout canoes came out to meet us. This time there were several women in them in addition to older men and boys. Two of the children were half-white. The young babies were carried on their mothers' backs in cloths wound around both bodies—heads covered—only the feet sticking out, one on each side of the mother. They brought bananas and tropical fruits as presents for us. They were given candy, cigarettes, and chewing tobacco in return. The chiefs and other natives climbed down into the canoes, waved good-by, and we were off for our return to Emirau Island.

Took my face mask and found a coral reef full of tropical fish and sea growths—an entirely different world. Some of the coral is in bloom—purples, blues, and yellows. Fish of all descriptions and colors swim in and out of the crevices and cavities, paying little attention to me, dodging out of the way if I come too near. I can see for at least a hundred yards through the water. With one of these masks one can be part of the wave motion like the fish, swim right up to the breakers, and with slight movement of his arms and legs keep from banging into the coral. There are moments when one actually feels that the sea is his environment.

Monday, May 29

Mother's birthday. To Intelligence at 8:00 for briefing. This morning I am to drop a 500-lb. high-explosive bomb on Kavieng. There will be three Corsairs in the flight, trying out the bomb racks. We are delayed getting under way. Start and shut our engines off twice—first time, weather; second time, red tape. Finally off the strip at 0945; Major [Marion] Carl leading, Lieutenant Blanchard his wingman. I have a single plane, second section (my favorite position). We fly direct to Kavieng, circle, and dive down on the city with the sun at our backs.

Major Carl and Lieutenant Blanchard aim at the airstrip. I aim for an area in the city where we know there is Jap military activity. I release at 5,500 feet (orders are to stay high over Kavieng and to aim at the area rather than a pin-point target). I pull out of the dive and bank out toward sea, changing direction regularly to keep the guns from lining up on me. I have seen no antiaircraft fire, but the Japs are reported to have stopped using tracers recently. Several of our pilots have reported that they did not know they were being shot at until their planes were hit. My bomb overshoots its mark, but lands in a strip of buildings along the beach where antiaircraft guns have been reported—possibly a better target than I aimed at. It dropped in an area where it may have been effective. How much damage was actually done we will never know.

I don't like this bombing and machine-gunning of unknown targets.

You press a button and death flies down. One second the bomb is hanging harmlessly in your racks, completely under your control. The next it is hurtling down through the air, and nothing in your power can revoke what you have done. The cards are dealt. If there is life where that bomb will hit, you have taken it. Yet it is still living, still breathing; the bomb is still falling; there are still seconds before it will hit. The plane drills on. The sky has not changed above. The ground is quiet below. Only a dot in the air between—getting smaller—so much smaller that it has disappeared from sight.

You bank your plane over a bit to see better. A column of black smoke and debris rises from the ground below—small—insignificant, like the houses. The world is the same. The sky is the same. Only that column of smoke, settling now, dissipating. How can there be death down there? How can there be writhing, mangled bodies? How can this air around you be filled with unseen projectiles? It is like listening to a radio account of a battle on the other side of the earth. It is too far away, too separated to hold reality.

Our mission is over. We head back for the fighter strip on Emirau Island.

Tuesday, May 30

American troops land on Biak Island, New Guinea.

Took off at 12:55 on the Kavieng patrol. Three Corsairs in all. We fly direct to Kavieng, pass over the city at 10,000 feet, and continue on to the southwest coast. We are to drop two bombs on the Lakafarange plantation and plan to arrive over it unexpectedly by coming in over the mountains from the southeast. We climb to 12,000 feet and turn back, skirting a high cumulus cloud bank. We are almost over the plantation. We spread out to 500-yard intervals, and each dives from different angles.

I have selected a red-roofed building, which is a camouflaged antiaircraft gun, according to Intelligence reports. I nose over steeply and open fire with my guns. The tracers stream forward to their mark. I continue firing down to 6,000 feet before I drop my bomb—a 500-lb. high explosive. I turn out toward the sea, following an irregular course to frustrate fire from the ground.

I watch the bomb dropping down until it passes out of sight. A column of smoke and earth rises up from the jungle—Lieutenant [Stephen G.] Warren's bomb—it is an over. A second column. Mine is an over, too. Our dive angle was not steep enough, and we released too late. Anyway, the .50-calibers went home.

We climb and re-form out at sea. Then follow the coast to Kavieng. We dive down on the airfield and the gun emplacements, sprinkling them with bursts from our guns.

Our mission is to harass the enemy and patrol the general area of Kavieng. We will fire irregularly from high altitude, first in this area, then in that, never giving them warning in advance. All through the day patrols will keep up harassing fire. All through the night the coasts will be raided by PT boats. All enemy shipping, all enemy aircraft must be cut off from New Ireland. We fly over to the southwest coast again, then turn back behind a cloud bank. Freeman and Warren find a hole in the clouds through which to fire on the city. I am too far over to the side and miss my run. We join up again over the water and continue our patrol.

Back over Kavieng. Another dive. I get in a burst this time, but not a good one. The clouds are in the way. We join up over the water. The patrol is almost over. We are to make one more run on Kavieng. I get in a good burst this time, but still have many rounds left for my guns. The other planes are going on to rendezvous over the water. I turn back, climb, and make a run down the side of a cloud. There is no way for the antiaircraft guns to see me until I am in just the right position for my burst. I pull up into the cloud again before they have time to sight and fire.

Freeman is calling for my position. I reply that I do not have the other planes in sight and ask for their position. The situation is ideal for attack. I cannot leave with so much ammunition for my guns. I make another run—a long burst this time. Back into the clouds. Freeman is calling again. I see the two planes circling high over the channel. "Roger, Roger, I have you in sight." I make a last run on Kavieng.

"Did you make a run just then?" They have seen my diving plane against the whiteness of the cloud. I am caught.

"Roger."

There is no use trying to deny it, even by silence. They have done such things themselves. They will smile and wink after we land and say that my altimeter must have been in error (we are supposed to stay above 10,000 feet on the Kavieng patrol). I climb and join up, and we head back for Emirau Island. Landed 1530.

Took up Corsair No. 56407 to test for high-speed aileron grab. The right aileron has been changed since I last flew it. Captain Freeman flew on my wing with a Corsair he was testing for engine temperatures. The aileron change eliminated grab in a right turn, but there is still a bad grab in a left turn, starting at about 280 knots indicated. After completing the grab dives, we did some Immelmanns and slow rolls, and then returned to base—an even hour's flight.

Three dive bombers were lost during the strike on Kavieng today. The Japanese opened up with all their guns while the dive-bomber formation was approaching at high altitude, at 16,000 feet, the pilots say, and continued firing until they were out of range over the water. One bomber was seen to crash on the shore. Two managed to get out over the water before they landed. Six men went down. Three have been saved. Two were undoubtedly killed when they hit the ground. One is missing. The costs were far out of proportion to any objective which could have been accomplished at Kavieng in its present condition.

I listen to the dive-bomber pilots talking over the strike at supper in the mess hall. "Who did they pick up?"

"Who was killed?"

"R. was killed. He was in the plane that crashed on the beach."

"You mean R. was killed?"

Someone stops eating. There is silence.

"S. and L. landed in the water. The dumbo picked them up."

There is a mixture of conversation and silence. Supper continues.

Thursday, June 1

The officers of VMF-115 leave today, their combat tour completed, for a week's vacation in Sydney. I drive over to where the SCAT planes are warming up. Being two-engine and fully equipped with instruments and radio, they will take off in spite of the weather. The VMF-115 pilots are standing under a wing glumly in a light rain while the SCAT planes are loaded and the engines started. SCAT has a bad reputation among the combat pilots. There have been too many accidents, too many passengers lost. The SCAT pilots are often inexperienced and insist on trying to handle their Douglas transports as though they were pursuit planes. As a result, the operation has come to be known in this section as "Murder Incorporated." The 115 pilots do not relish the idea of riding as passengers with a SCAT crew under the best of conditions, to say nothing of taking off into a low overcast with a front ahead. The engines are started. I wish them luck, tell them they will need it—remarks are exchanged lightly to hide genuine concern. We wave good-by as they climb into the sweltering cabin, and they are off.

Friday, June 2

Took off at 12:40 on the noon Kavieng patrol. Three Corsairs from VMF-222. We dropped our bombs on Kavieng at irregular intervals, circled over the area, and nosed down to machine-gun some positions every few minutes without warning. The patrol planes are constantly overhead, and we make it a point to keep the Japs from knowing where we are going to strike.

I was last to drop my bomb. There were broken clouds over Kavieng. My target was the area of the Japanese officers club—located through Intelligence reports. I maneuvered around at 12,000 feet until I found the club through a hole in the clouds—a rather large, red-roofed building. Dropped dive brakes, did a wing over, and lined my sight up on the building in a 60° dive, spattering the area with my machine guns. Pressed the bomb-release button with my thumb, began my pull-out, and raised the dive brakes to increase my getaway speed. Clouds immediately covered my target, and none of us saw the bomb hit.

I took advantage of the cloud cover to make a number of strafing runs—on the antiaircraft area, on the barracks area, and on several areas where Japanese activity has been reported. By using the clouds carefully I could get my bursts in before the ground guns had time to line up on my plane. For the first time today I got close enough to the airstrip to get a good look at the revetments and the Japanese planes—most or all of them out of commission. One is going too fast to see much detail in a place as heavily defended with antiaircraft guns as Kavieng.

At the end of our patrol we made a long, low sweep over the area, starting on the southwest coast and flying close to the ground. We passed over a sort of meadow in the middle of which a Japanese bomber had crashed and burned. The Jap red-sun insignia still showed up clearly on the wing tips. The wreckage looked more as though the bomber had a forced landing than a crash. We flew low over Balgai Bay, just out of range of the Jap gun installations on each side of us, and took up our homeward course for Emirau. Land at 3:15.

Off the strip at 7:00. Three Corsairs. Direct to Kavieng, but we pass over without bombing. Might as well keep the Japs uncertain about when they will be hit. We fly all around our patrol area at 10,000 feet; then return to Kavieng, and Lieutenant Gillespie drops one bomb. I dive down and strafe with my guns while it is being dropped—to divide the attention of the ground gunners. I see no antiaircraft fire. Either they are not using tracers or they are short of ammunition and holding what they have for better targets than pursuit planes. We fly around for another twenty minutes. Then I go in for my drop.

Climb to 12,000 feet and circle around over the city and airstrip, always making irregular turns to throw off the aim of the larger antiaircraft guns. Finally get my target lined up, drop my dive brakes, do a wing over, and line my sight up on the group of long, narrow buildings I have selected—Japanese supply houses.

It is a screaming dive—over 60°. I open up with my machine guns— the ground rushes up—mustn't get too low—the Kavieng gunners are deadly—three SBD's on the last strike. I stop firing—line up for the bomb—press the button—start the pull-out—lift the dive brakes—altimeter shows 5,000 feet.

I am blacking out—ease the stick forward slightly—the sky is clear again—I turn out over water—reverse turn—there are antiaircraft on the island below—I reverse again—and again. The island is behind—out of range. Where did the bomb hit? I look back at my target. There is a thin column of smoke on the ground. Is that all that 500 lbs. of high explosive does? It must be. Time passes, and there is no other mark to indicate a bomb hit. Then I overshot—still, it is among the buildings. I will know better how to aim next time.

I am back at 10,000 feet. I turn over the city. Even at this altitude I can see some Jap planes in revetments around the airstrip. How they must feel down there! They have not had a plane in the air for weeks, unless it is at night, and that is doubtful. We circle wherever we wish above them with no opposition except when we come within range of the ground guns. I spot some long buildings hidden among trees below not far from the airstrip. There are no bomb pits around them. Our pilots appear to have overlooked them in favor of more obvious objectives.

I dive down—almost vertical—and watch my tracers sink into the roofs. My recovery takes me over guns along the coast. I weave back and forth until I am far out over the water.

I climb again and dive on another objective. My guns must be almost empty—they hold only 400 rounds apiece—2,400 altogether. I must hold some for an emergency. We are not yet home. I join the planes of the first section. They have been circling at 10,000 feet. We finish our two-hour patrol and head back for Emirau.

Monday, June 5

Up at 4:45. Washed, packed, breakfast, and to the VMF-222 ready room for the dawn Kavieng patrol. I will have time to go on the patrol and still take off with the fighter escort back to Green Island. SCAT will not be in before 9:30, and it will take them at least an hour to unload and get started again.

Off the strip at 0635. Three Corsairs. I have a single plane, second section. I have the only bomb this morning—a 500-lb. high explosive. For some reason, the dawn patrol is not ordered to carry bombs; but one was slipped onto my plane unofficially. After I drop it we are to put on oxygen masks and climb to 30,000 feet as part of a training schedule for the squadron. Many of the pilots have done no high-altitude work.

We take off in the dawn and watch the sun rise as we fly along the New Hanover coast. At first, the clouds in the west are as red and brilliant as those in the east, as though there were two suns rising, in opposite directions. Then, for a moment, the sun itself shows blindingly through a crevice in the clouds. On the reef on our right is the hulk of the wrecked Japanese ship. We are climbing slowly in combat formation. I am on my right wing tank, with the mixture control in auto lean.

We arrive over Kavieng, and I go in for my drop, climbing to 14,000 feet, and banking first one way and then the other as I get over the guns. I have selected for my target the same group of supply buildings that I bombed yesterday. They are extremely difficult to see in the early morning light. Finally, I get into position, drop my brakes, and wing over into my dive. But there is a film of dust and oil on my windshield and bulletproof glass. The sun strikes it at such an angle that I cannot see the buildings at all. There is no use releasing the bomb. I sweep the entire area with my machine guns and then pull up. I am down within range of the 20-millimeters so I pull out hard—past the gray-out—riding the edge of the blackout. In three more seconds I won't be able to see anything. I ease forward slightly on the stick. Gradually sight returns. There are guns along the coast under me. I drop a wing and bank as I head out to sea.

I will have to select another target. I climb back to 14,000 feet over the water and wobble in over Kavieng. The best target is the coral runway of the airfield. I can see that, regardless of the light. I line up with it, drop my brakes again, and start the dive, banking slightly to get the runway exactly in line. Several bursts from my machine guns to divert attention on the ground. I am in perfect position. I release the bomb at a little higher altitude this time, and pull out with fewer G,[12] banking first toward the sea and then back so I can watch the runway.

A white column of coral shoots skyward—a direct hit—directly in the center of the usable portion of the runway. It could not have been better placed by a blasting crew on the ground. The column thins out as the solid fragments fall back down. The white dust remains a column, drifting slowly away. The bomb crater is deep and clearly visible, points of whiter coral raying out from the center like a star. The runway is definitely out of commission. It will be useless until the Japs can get in with repairs.

I join the other two Corsairs, waiting for me at 10,000 feet and out of range of the ground guns. We adjust our oxygen masks and start for altitude, climbing slowly. But Lieutenant Vaughan soon drops behind and we are unable to get any reply from him by radio. At 19,000 we lose sight of him in a turn and I dive back down to get his silhouette against the sky and make sure he is not in serious trouble. I find him quickly, but he gives no response to our radio calls, so we decide to give up our climb for altitude. Later, it developed that his difficulty was the result of insufficient training in the handling of plane and equipment in altitude flying.

We drop to 10,000 feet and fly over the northeast New Ireland coast toward Kavieng. [Captain John] Downs radios that he is about to strafe a plantation below. He and Vaughan go down.

There is a point below me where the PT boats have reported new gun emplacements installed. (They drew fire on one of their night patrols.) I dive down and machine-gun the area and buildings. Back up again. Radio from Downs, suggesting that we rendezvous over the northeast point of New Hanover. I strafe Kavieng again on the way—get too close to my target before I start my wing over and find myself shooting from

12. Not as many times the normal effect of gravity (G).

an almost vertical position and slightly upside down. I do not think about the plane's position; that is taken care of subconsciously. All my conscious attention is concentrated on the sight. The tracers are going home; that's all that matters. I am in a screaming dive—must start the pull-out—everything gray—black—stick forward slightly—gray again—the nose is on the horizon—stick forward again—sight returns—bank slightly to confuse the ground guns—I am over the bay and out of range.

I cruise along to the tip of New Hanover. Radio from Downs—not very clear—all I get is that he is orbiting at 3,000 feet. I arrive at the appointed position and drop down to 3,000. No planes in sight. Radio very garbled. Finally get message from Downs suggesting that we proceed to base independently. It takes several minutes to get my "Roger" through so that he can understand it. I pull my r.p.m. down to 1,700, drop down to within one hundred feet of the water, and take up a course for Emirau.

On the strip at 0925. Turn in report and drive over to SCAT operations. The transports are starting back as soon as they can unload. Off the strip again at 1105 with the fighter escort for SCAT—four Corsairs. We fly in two plane sections. Land at Green Island at 1335. Turn my plane over to the squadron, etc. Late lunch at officers mess. Very hungry as I had only a cup of tomato juice for breakfast—no time to wait for the cakes and bacon.

Tuesday, June 6

Invasion of France begun. Rome captured by Allied forces.

Heavy tropical rain and wind during the night—blew in through the screen sides of the tent, and dripped down through the roof. I covered my belongings with a blanket and moved my cot around until I found a reasonably dry corner.

First part of afternoon writing, then to VMF-218 ready room for a patrol over Rabaul. We took off at 2:00. Four Corsairs. We flew across New Ireland directly to Rabaul and circled the area around the city and its volcanoes. Dropped down to 3,000 feet along the north coast and made one strafing run. Then over to the Duke of York for several strafing runs, all ending within one hundred feet of the tree tops.

Major [Ian] McNab and the other pilots sight a group of boats on the water "almost as big as barges." McNab orders a line abreast strafing run. I have not seen any boats but pull up to my place in line. Around a cloud and dive down toward the middle of the bay. There are fish nets in the middle of the bay that look a little like boats. A burst from McNab's guns, bullets spatter in the water a hundred yards short. The next burst is on target. I fire a burst, wondering what it is all about. I drop down to within fifty feet of the water. Yes, they are fish nets. We have made a strafing run on fish nets!!! We join formation again, climb, and fly along the west coast of New Ireland for a quarter hour. Then our patrol is over. Four more Corsairs arrive to relieve us, and we head back toward Green Island at 4:40.

A message comes over the radio that the invasion of Europe has started; the Allies have landed on the north coast of France! The news spreads over the island like wildfire. I go out into the night and look up at the sky and stars and moon. The invasion of Europe! It is impossible to realize it on this island in the South Seas. I cannot project myself halfway around the world and realize what is happening on that "north coast of France." The destiny of the world is being shaped in the battle which is now raging—all hell broken loose along the English Channel. Millions of men attacking—defending—dying. And it is so peaceful here tonight—palm trees silhouetted against the moon—white clouds and stars sharing the rest of the sky—the evening cool for the tropics—the camp quiet.

Wednesday, June 7

Up at dawn. I think of the battles on the coast of France. It is nightfall in Europe—the end of the first day's fighting. But it won't stop. It will go on at night almost as fiercely as during the day. How many men are already dead? How many more will die? And what great gain is coming from it all?

Tidy up, make bed, sweep out hut, and to mess hall. There is no one there yet. I return to my hut and wait a quarter hour. I cannot work on anything. I look out across the lagoon to the islands on the far side and then down at the rough-sawn teak and mahogany boards on the floor, and think of Europe and the fighting.

At 7:30, I walk to the mess hall. Gradually, the others come in and take their seats on the bench at the table. The doctor, who sits on my right, is greatly pleased that the invasion has started, and thinks that now the war in Europe may be won and over by October. The two Marine lieutenant colonels on my left are more reserved with their opinions. There is, however, a general air of optimism, and the wish is frequently voiced that the Marines could be "in it, over there."

I had planned on spending the morning writing a report on the Corsair and fighter design for the Pacific area. But before I got under way, a messenger arrived from Fighter Command with an invitation to join the 9:00 Rabaul patrol. I had just time to get my equipment together and drive over to the line.

Off the strip at 0900. Four Corsairs. We flew direct to Rabaul, over New Ireland and the Duke of York. The second section had to turn back to Green Island because of motor trouble in one of its planes. Captain [Fred] Gutt and I dropped down to 7,500 feet and wove over Rabaul and its airstrips, turning and climbing and diving rapidly and irregularly. We saw no fire from the ground, although we passed over some of the most heavily defended positions. Possibly the Japs were shooting and not using tracers. Possibly they are short of ammunition and thought we offered too poor a target.

One of the airstrips was in quite good condition and clearly showed signs of recent work. Do the Japs expect to get some planes into Rabaul, or are they keeping the strip up simply on the hope? There were a number of pursuit planes and bombers in the revetments, but they have been there for a long time, and most or all of them are thought to be out of commission.

We turned out over the water, climbed up to 9,000 feet, and flew over to the north coast of New Britain west of Rabaul. There are clouds all around and at different levels, with heavy storm squalls in the distance. But most of the coast is clear. We turn back east, drop to 2,500 feet, and weave back and forth, trying to locate a target on the ground worth diving on. Most of the plantation buildings are already burned down. We find one near the coast that looks suspicious—dive and riddle the buildings with bullets. I bank and watch for ground fire after I have finished my run. The Japs have a habit of hiding machine guns around such places. I see none.

We climb high again to cross the coast, then weave down to 3,000 feet in the area southwest of Rabaul. Captain Gutt spots some trucks moving on a narrow road below—several of them—brown military transports. We circle, get into position, and start our run.

We converge on the trucks. I am 1,000 feet behind and to the left of Captain Gutt. He fires first. The burst is short. Again. It is on target. His tracers spatter the area. I start firing as he pulls up; first, spattering the area to discourage return fire from the ground, and then concentrating on the largest truck. It bursts into flames. I turn to the next—keep firing until I am within one hundred yards.

I miss the tree tops by less than thirty feet and bank away over the jungle. Captain Gutt has spotted another road with two or three trucks along it. We divide, and I go back for another run on our first target. The truck is covered with flames and sending a column of smoke high into the air. But the other two are not burning. I make my run from a different angle this time. The trucks are on a hill—pulled quickly over to the side of the road and under some branches when their drivers heard us coming.

This time, I am in line with the road. I can get down lower in the valley. I can see them all better. I spatter the area with bullets from a distance, then concentrate on the farthest truck—just beyond the one in flames. I watch my tracers sink into it while a cloud of dust rises from the ground beneath. This time, I almost touch the tree branches as I pull up and bank for a third run. I take the nearest truck this time. First, spatter the area again; then concentrate fire on the truck. I give it a long burst and pull up. The plane jerks! Did the engine miss or did something hit it? There is another jerk. It does not feel like the engine. Antiaircraft? There are no holes in the wings, and I have seen no sign of ground fire.

I head toward the water. Whatever is wrong, I better get over water as soon as I can. A pilot landing at sea is fairly safe. A dumbo will pick him up if he is not too close to shore and enemy guns. I radio to Captain Gutt that something is wrong and I am heading for the water. He gives me his location—at "Angels four" (4,000 feet) over a bay to the west. But my engine is running smoothly and all the gauges show normal readings.

We rendezvous north of Watom Island, at 5,000 feet. There is only twenty minutes left before we will be relieved by the next patrol, so we take up a heading for Green Island. I radio that everything seems to be all right and that we can do a little strafing on the way. We drop down over the Duke of York group to look for barges but see none. We strafe some of the buildings on our way out. I see the church again that I almost fired on on my first flight to Rabaul.

There are storm clouds over the New Ireland mountains. We fly over them. A heavy squall is approaching Green Island. "Flying conditions very bad," Lagoon tower radios. "A thirty-mile cross wind at 90° from port." It is very gusty. I start down for a full-flap landing, but the air is so rough that I decide to go around again and come in with 30°. Captain Gutt lands ahead of me—O.K. The wind catches my wing just before I hit the ground—can't hold it with aileron—a one-wheel landing. I dump the flaps and the plane rolls straight along the runway.

There are no holes in the plane. We look it over carefully. It must have been the engine, but why just at that moment? Just as I had passed over an enemy target? Well, it is due for its sixty-hour check before the next flight. I note the trouble on the "crab" sheet.[13]

A pilot was lost from the patrol which relieved ours this morning— shot down by the Japs during a strafing run on some trucks. The trucks were on one of the coastal roads near Rabaul, not many miles from where we strafed ours this morning. There were three of them, put there as a booby trap, camouflaged just enough to keep them from looking too suspicious, and surrounded by machine guns. Another Corsair was shot down in this same location several weeks ago, and the pilots have all been briefed about the trap and its exact position. But the patrol forgot or for some reason made the run anyway.

Friday, June 9

A message has just arrived from COMAIRSOUTH, asking me to "investigate failure Corsair wing folding mechanism" at MAG-11 before I leave the South Pacific area. That will take me back to Espiritu Santo. I will probably start tomorrow.

I have completed everything I wanted to do at Green Island except for a flight over Rabaul at night with an F4U. The Japs work a great deal at night, according to our "night hecklers." Except in bad weather, one of our light bombers flies over Rabaul every night to drop a few bombs at irregular intervals. The Japs are always trying to get this bomber in their searchlight beams and shoot it down. Whenever the bomber starts for one of the searchlights, the Japs naturally put the light out before it can get overhead to drop a bomb. I would like to take a Corsair over with the bomber and shoot out the lights. But I haven't been able to get to first base with the idea. Neither Colonel Carleson nor Colonel [Alexander] Bunker are in favor of it. "Too risky!" As a matter of fact, it would be much safer than a lot of flying we do by day. "There are regulations against sending single-engine fighters out at night in this area," etc., etc. The fact is that night flying with fighters has been sadly neglected, a complex against it developed, and much opportunity to strike the

13. A form on which a plane's operational defects are listed.

enemy has been lost as a result. The average fighter pilot simply hasn't got adequate instrument and night-flying training.

To the VMF-212 ready room at 8:15. Off the strip at 0845 for the Rabaul patrol and to cover the strike which is to be made this morning. Four Corsairs. We set our course for Rabaul and begin a slow and steady climb. A scattered cloud layer at 2,000 feet. We are above them. I charge my guns and nose down for a short test burst.

At 6,000 feet we can see over the mountains of New Ireland to the volcanic harbor of Rabaul far in the distance. Clouds float all around—above, below, beside us. To the north there is a squall. All shades of gray and blue and green and white—pale blue sky over Rabaul; patches of deep blue above us; gray, misty clouds on the horizon; dazzling white clouds on our left where the rays of the sun pierce through; the blue water of the South Pacific; the green jungle-covered mountains of New Ireland; the purple volcanoes of faraway Rabaul. And through the limitless space of that sky, above the ocean and the mountains, surrounded by unbroken loneliness, piercing the beauty of land, sea, and air, our four Corsairs float like hawks, the only sign of man or life.

Below us, above us, all around us, there is peace and beauty. We are life; we are death. At the foot of those mountains of New Ireland, hidden in the greenness of the jungle, are our enemies, their guns already pointing upward. At Rabaul, on New Britain, on New Ireland, on Buka and Bougainville behind us, there are thousands of Japanese troops. Amidst all this peace and beauty we are, in our own element, like the animals of the jungle, constantly in the presence of death. We live to pounce upon our enemies and to be pounced upon by them. Death lies hidden all around us, so subtly that we cannot realize it is there. Like rabbits playing in a clearing, like ducks winging through the sky, we are unaware of the circling hawk until it swoops; we do not see the hunter's gun until it speaks.

We see only the loneliness of the sky, the joy and beauty of the earth. We feel only the companionship of each other, four Corsairs hanging gracefully in the air, moving ever so slightly in relation to each other, too high above it to be much concerned about the earth below or to be aware of the speed with which we are hurtling toward the Japanese positions on Rabaul.

We arrive over Rabaul at 9:15 and cruise along the north New Britain coast. I see a column of water rise from the sea, a hundred yards off the point of land below—a wide miss. There is the blue outline of a twin-engine plane making its getaway along the shore. The PV's are carrying out their bombing missions. A little coastal village farther on seems to disintegrate into dust and debris as another low-flying PV scores a direct hit with a thousand-pounder. We circle. I see a high column of smoke rising from the side of a mountain farther west. It looks like the smoke which rises from a crashed plane. I notify the patrol, and Section Two peels off to investigate. Meanwhile, Captain [Franklin] McHugh and I circle back over Rabaul and its airstrips.

At 10:00 the SBD's and TBF's come in with their bombs. We circle overhead and watch them dive and drop their bombs. Jap antiaircraft guns fire on them as they make their getaway out over the water—great splashes in the sea nearby. The second section joins us again. The column of smoke on the mountainside came from a burning house one of the PV's had used for a target.

At 10:20, the P-38's and 39's come in for their strike—the 39's down low, the 38's starting their dive from about 10,000 feet. I watch the bombs explode among the palm trees of a plantation. It is supposed to be a Japanese supply area, but no fires are started and apparently little damage has been done. A flight of B-25's comes over at 10:40 to drop their bombs from an altitude of 10,000 feet. We are on a level with them when they drop. There are black bursts of antiaircraft in the sky—nearer to us than to them, and far enough away from both to cause no bother. The PBJ's arrive to bomb at 11:00, and then the strike is over. We drop down over the Duke of York on our way home, but find no targets worth a strafing run. We land on the fighter strip at 12:15.

Saturday, June 10

Up at dawn. Breakfast with officers. Good-bys. Took off at 0944 in rear seat of dive bomber (SBD-4). Landed Piva U airstrip, Bougainville, at 10:45. Lunch with General Moore and officers. To Torokina strip in the afternoon to talk to the New Zealand squadrons about their experience with the Corsair. Rest of afternoon writing report on Corsair and future fighter requirements for the Pacific area.

Sunday, June 11

Off the airstrip at 8:25 in TBF bound for Guadalcanal. We fly out past the Japanese-held point, keeping out of gun range offshore, and set course for American-held Treasury Island. Cloudiness and squalls increase as we approach Guadalcanal. Land at Henderson Field at 10:40.

To ARU to see the wing-hinge pin from the Corsair which crashed at Espiritu Santo; wing folded on take-off; pilot killed; plane burned. Pin and fitting appeared to be in excellent condition. Conference with officers in regard to preventive action. Lunch with Admiral Gunther and staff.

To the New Zealand squadrons in the afternoon with Commander [Jack J.] Tomamichel. They have had high operational losses—nine recent fatalities in Corsairs—another again today. Most appear due to lack of pilot training. One or two may be due to engine failure. They have a long list of wheels-up landings, collisions in air, running inexplicably out of fuel on not very long flights, etc. A great contrast to the report of the New Zealand squadron at Bougainville.

Hope to arrange for a trip to New Guinea to see [Ennis] Whitehead —now a major general.

Tuesday, June 13

Took off Henderson Field at 8:01 in a JRF-3 (twin-engine Grumman amphibian) and set course for Rennell Island. Landed on the island lake at Rennell Island at 0932. There are several native villages on the island—no white men. An outrigger canoe came out to meet us, help moor, and take us ashore. (There were six in our party, including crew.)

On shore, with the natives gathered around us, Captain Drain made a speech to the chief, who understands a little English, telling him that we were friendly and would protect his people, that we had come to trade but would first give him presents. (The presents consisted of parts of red-and-white silk tow targets, packages of cigarettes, pencils, matches, a pair of scissors, etc.) Captain Drain then showed the chief a magazine photo of President Roosevelt, and after much explanation suggested that the chief might like to send "our big, big chief" a present. The chief nodded his head and sent for two large and decorated war clubs. Captain Drain then suggested that the chief write a letter, presenting the clubs to President Roosevelt through himself (Captain Drain)! This also was agreed to.

After the speech and presents trading began. We had all brought various odds and ends, of which the cloth from shiny red-and-white silk tow targets was most conspicuous. Commander [Carrol S.] Graves had given me some old clothes, spools of thread, matches, etc., and I had borrowed three cartons of cigarettes. I became so interested in watching the natives, however, that I did not start "trading" until later. They are by far the healthiest group I have seen on the trip so far—well fed, clear faces, mostly clear skins. Of the sixty people in the village, one man was ill with a foot infection, one baby had a fever, and three or four had skin troubles of the less severe type. The rest appeared to be in first-class condition, although I am told that there are a number of cases of yaws in the village.

For the most part, their dress consisted of a yard or two of cloth wrapped around the hips—no clothing above for either men or women. The chief wore a pair of khaki shorts, his wife a faded khaki dress. Wherever they could obtain it, the men wore cast-off service clothing. The rest of the men and most of the women simply wore a strip of cloth wound loosely around their hips—usually white or red tow-target silk. I saw only one girl with a native dress—yellow-stained and made from the bark of a tree. These people are known as "shrewd traders." The faces are intelligent, and several of them speak a few words of English—enough for trading purposes.

Trading was carried on in one of the oblong huts—bamboo floor raised three or four feet off the ground, thatch roof, woven and partly open sides. For barter the natives had war clubs, woven bags, and a few tooth-and-shell necklaces. Although very few planes have landed on the island, prices have already skyrocketed as the natives are far better traders than the whites. A package of cigarettes will no longer buy much. I paid two packages (against four asked) for each woven bag. One piece of tow-target silk would buy only the poorer war clubs, and a well-worn pair of shorts given me by Commander Graves would bring nothing at all. However, a new pair of navy-blue work slacks brought two good war clubs with no effort to trade for a higher price.

I came away with three clubs, several woven bags, and a pair of "cat's eyes," [14] which Commander Graves had asked me to get for his wife. Wives are for sale, too, at the standard price of $16.50. A few months ago the price was $3.00, so there has apparently been some demand. We took none home with us!

Took off on return flight at 1304. Headed for Cape Hunter and fol-

14. The operculum of a turban shell found in the Pacific, externally convex, with a lustrous brightly colored central area surrounded by zones of white, ivory, and brown.

lowed the coast of Guadalcanal around to Henderson Field. In places, the coast is lined with sunk Japanese shipping—transport ships run ashore in sinking condition, dozens of wrecked barges, two midget submarines, all brown with rust—monuments to the Japanese occupation. Landed Henderson Field 1439.

Wednesday, June 14

Breakfast with Admiral Gunther and staff. Good-bys, and to Henderson Field for a 10:16 take-off in a NATS C-54A (four-engine Douglas transport) for New Guinea. I flew the plane for thirty minutes—good stability—excellent cockpit. Landed [Gurney airstrip] at 1340, after being cut off several times by Army planes apparently out of contact with the tower.

Drove to naval headquarters. Commander Arthur H. Graubert invited me to spend the night with him. Tour of the naval establishment during the afternoon. Supper with Commander Graubert and several naval officers. Discussion of the operations now going on in western New Guinea. Back to his quarters with Commander Graubert. We discussed the war in Europe. He was naval attaché in Berlin at the time the war started.

Thursday, June 15

To Gurney airstrip. Took off as passenger on the Australian line, D.A.T., at 6:13. Landed Finschhafen [New Guinea] at 0950, the Australian pilot, like so many of our American pilots on these combat-zone lines, trying to show off by landing from a rather steep bank—and making a poor job of it. Was waiting for the regular courier plane to Nadzab [New Guinea] when a young Army pilot invited me to go with him in his Stinson L-5 (small, single-engine liaison plane).

Off the Finschhafen strip at 11:39. Over the hills and jungles, and landed at the Army air base, Nadzab, Strip 5, at 12:22. Phoned General Whitehead's headquarters. He is at the front in western New Guinea, but Colonel [Merian C.] Cooper asked me to have lunch with him at headquarters. Conference with Colonel [James O.] Guthrie and other officers in the afternoon.

Friday, June 16

To airstrip with Colonel [Robert L.] Morrissey in afternoon for an hour's flight in a Lockheed P-38. I am anxious to get a comparison of twin-engine and single-engine pursuit planes. Plane swerved to right on take-off, but I caught it by throttling port engine momentarily—an excessively long take-off. Flew formation with Colonel Morrissey and tried plane out for about an hour. Then came in to land. Brake was frozen—apparently dragging all during the take-off. Tire blew on contact. Plane swerved to right. I jammed on left brake and managed to hold on runway until almost stopped. Ended up about twenty feet off right side. No damage aside from tire.

Sunday, June 18

Marines land on Saipan. B-29's bomb Japan.

We discuss Russian roulette at breakfast. I first heard of this game from the Marines in the Solomons but thought it was just one of the yarns that are built up and circulated among troops. Apparently there is more to it than that. Russian roulette, as the name implies, is supposed to have been originated by the Soviets and is regarded by those who play it as a game of courage. Large amounts of money are said to be staked on the outcome. Briefly, the soldier playing the game takes a service revolver, puts one shell in the chamber, twirls it rapidly, holds the muzzle to his head, and pulls the trigger! Obviously, he has five chances out of six to live. The "game" is usually played after heavy drinking. An actual instance occurred recently among the troops of this area. Seven soldiers decided to pass the gun around, but the game ended when luck ran against the first one—he blew his brains out when he pulled the trigger. The incident has been hushed up officially and recorded as an accidental discharge.

Phone call from General Whitehead when I returned to fighter head-quarters; he got back this afternoon from the front. Dinner with him at ADVON [Advanced Echelon]. Evening together discussing the war and conditions at home, mutual friends, etc. We go over the latest maps and reports. He has done an exceptionally fine piece of work here in New Guinea.

Tuesday, June 20

French forces land on Elba. Rocket-plane bombing of England continues.

Drove to Topline strip with General [Paul B.] Wurtsmith and brought his jeep back to Fighter Command after he took off, through the long lines of planes parked in revetments. The cheapness of the emblems and names painted on the bombers and fighters nauseates me at times—mostly naked women or "Donald Ducks"—names such as "Fertile Myrtle" under a large and badly painted figure of a reclining nude.

To Strip 4 in General Wurtsmith's jeep for a flight with the 35th Squadron, 8th Group. Four Lightnings. Up for an hour and twenty minutes. At one time we were in the vicinity of Lae and apparently got too close to shipping in the harbor. Several antiaircraft shells burst a few hundred feet to one side of us and at almost our exact altitude. We were apparently fired on by our own Navy! Army pilots say the gunners on board ship get very jittery in forward areas. We circled the puffs from the shells and turned back inland.

Wednesday, June 21

United States troops cut off Cherbourg. Rocket bombs continue.

General's account of killing a Japanese soldier: A technical sergeant in an advanced area some weeks ago complained that he had been with combat forces in the Pacific for over two years and never had a chance to do any fighting himself—that he would like the chance to kill at least one Jap before he went home. He was invited to go out on a patrol into enemy territory.

The sergeant saw no Jap to shoot, but members of the patrol took a prisoner. The Jap prisoner was brought to the sergeant with the statement that here was his opportunity to kill a Jap.

"But I can't kill that man! He's a prisoner. He's defenseless."

"Hell, this is war. We'll show you how to kill the son of a bitch."

One of the patrol members offered the Jap a cigarette and a light, and as he started to smoke an arm was thrown around his head and his throat "slit from ear to ear."

The entire procedure was thoroughly approved by the general giving the account. I was regarded with an attitude of tolerant scorn and pity when I objected to the method and said that if we had to kill a prisoner I thought we ought to do it in a decent and civilized way. "The sons of bitches do it to us. It's the only way to handle them."

Spent the morning assembling a parachute, life raft, and jungle kit to take with me when I leave for the advanced areas.

To Topline strip in afternoon for an hour-and-twenty-minute flight in a P-61 (Northrop twin-engine night fighter). An exceptionally fine plane.

Saturday, June 24

Accepted an invitation from John Myers (Northrop test pilot) to fly with him to Mount Hagen in a P-61. Mount Hagen is a landing strip on the edge of a valley among the mountains in the interior of New Guinea and in the midst of native territory.

We took off at 11:16—Myers, pilot. I navigated. We climbed above the clouds and set a direct course for Mount Hagen. No radio facilities at Mount Hagen; inadequate maps of the interior of New Guinea, and no way to check the wind drift except by cloud shadows on the jungle when I could see down through an occasional hole in the clouds. I checked my navigation by valleys and mountain ranges. Some of the mountain peaks rose to over 14,000 feet, and every few minutes there would be a hole in the clouds through which I could get a fairly good view of the ground below.

We found Mount Hagen near the foot of a mountain range—a sod airstrip, rather short for fast planes, 5,500 feet above sea level. We circled the village and had no trouble in landing—Myers doing a skillful job. But the P-61 which accompanied us, with a young and rather irresponsible Army pilot and crew, came in so fast behind us that it nearly overshot the field. Paying no attention to his instructions, the pilot landed before we were clear of the runway—so fast and so badly that except for Myers' quick thinking, a serious accident would undoubtedly have taken place. Myers kept our plane rolling rapidly along the strip until he had a chance to swing off to the side. The ground was soft and the wheels sank in, but he kept our plane rolling until the Army crew passed by, and then swung the plane back onto the more solid surface of the runway. If we had not been clear of the runway, the Army pilot would either have crashed into us or have had to ground-loop his plane off the side at high speed. He was going too fast to stop before hitting us no matter how hard he applied the brakes.

There were hundreds of black, almost naked savages on one side of the field. They were gesticulating, laughing, and running along beside our plane as we taxied along the strip. Although many planes have been here before, the natives always act the same way whenever a new one arrives, the ANGAU[15] told us. Some of them gathered about us as we climbed out of the plane, friendly, and deeply interested in every move we made. Others inspected the plane, peering in through openings, feeling the fuselage and tires, and crouching in the grass nearby.

There were no women in sight when we first arrived, but a few minutes later they appeared, as naked as the men, bringing their children with them, and almost all pregnant again. The women wore only a grass cord around their hips from which a few long black, woven grass cords in center front and rear hung down to form their clothing. Some of the men wore feather headgear. Most had stuffed a dozen or two green leaves under a sort of belt, front and rear, as their contribution toward advancing ideas of modesty. They looked like oversized roosters with green tails and white headfeathers as they ran along the edge of the runway.

We had tea with the ANGAU, a young Irishman, and several American medical officers. Then, a several-mile jeep drive along a narrow and beautiful country dirt road, lined with plants and flowers by the natives, who apparently take great pride in the appearance of their huts and roads. There were nine of us in the jeep. I sat on the engine hood with one of the crew members of the second P-61. We stopped at two of the villages and to take pictures of some natives we passed on the road.

We loaded up with green corn and tomatoes and took off on the return trip at 1712. The usual building up of clouds in this area forced us to detour north into the next valley. Landed on Strip 3, Nadzab, at 1819, just before nightfall.

Monday, June 26

Took off [in a P-38] Strip 3 at 0838 and set a direct course for Hollandia over the New Guinea jungles. Good weather; broken clouds over the valleys and on the mountains. Passed one peak over 15,000 feet high. My course took me well inside the Japanese-held coast. First, mountains and valleys, then swamp, then a coastal range. Then Hollandia. I passed several Army transports (C-47's) along the route. Wreckage of the

15. The head of an Australia–New Guinea administrative unit.

Japanese Air Force was strewn in between the revetments around Hollandia airstrip—shoved out of the way by bulldozers to make room for our own fighters and bombers and transports. Broken fuselages, engines, and wings everywhere, most of them marked with the red-ball insigne of the Japanese rising sun.

Landed at 10:05, parked my plane, filled out arrival report, and phoned General Hutchison. To his quarters for a conference and lunch with the general. Drove to the 475th Fighter Group[16] quarters for a conference with Colonel [Charles H.] MacDonald and several of his officers. Arranged to go on a mission with them tomorrow morning. Had planned on spending the night with General Hutchison, but Colonel MacDonald came to tell me that we are leaving at daybreak for a reconnaissance and strafing mission in northwestern New Guinea. To simplify the transportation problem I accepted the colonel's invitation to spend the night at his quarters. A group of officers were there when we arrived, and we spent the evening until after midnight discussing fighter characteristics and the war in this area.

There were three silk Japanese flags hanging on one wall of the hut we were in, taken from the bodies of Japanese soldiers. The souvenir value of one of these flags was about £10, one of the officers told me ($33.00 American). Someone who has a Japanese officer's sword is asking £250 for it. The talk drifted to prisoners of war and the small percentage of Japanese soldiers taken prisoner. "Oh, we could take more if we wanted to," one of the officers replied. "But our boys don't like to take prisoners."

"We had a couple of thousand down at ———, but only a hundred or two were turned in. They had an accident with the rest. It doesn't encourage the rest to surrender when they hear of their buddies being marched out on the flying field and machine guns turned loose on them."

"Or after a couple of them get shot with their hands up in the air," another officer chimed in.

"Well, take the ———th. They found one of their men pretty badly mutilated. After that, you can bet they didn't capture very many Japs."

16. The 475th Fighter Group (known as Satan's Angels) of the Fifth Air Force consisted of a headquarters and three combat squadrons, the 431st (Hades), the 432nd (Clover), and the 433rd (Possum). The Group was equipped with twin-engine Lockheed P-38's (Lightnings). In 1944 it was commanded by Colonel Charles H. MacDonald, who emerged from World War II as third-ranking ace in the Pacific area with official credit for 27 planes shot down. When World War II ended, the 475th Fighter Group was credited with shooting down 545 enemy aircraft.

The talk drifted to air combats and parachute jumps. All of the pilots insisted it was proper to shoot enemy airmen coming down in their parachutes. However, several said that they themselves would not do it. "The Japs started it. If they want to play that way, we can, too." Accounts were given of American airmen shot down hanging from their parachutes by the Japanese.

Tuesday, June 27

Up at 5:30. Raining—a typical New Guinea mountainside drizzle. Finally off the strip at 10:28—four Lightnings, all with full tanks and belly tanks (Colonel MacDonald, Major Meryl M. Smith, Major T. B. McGuire,[17] and myself). We set a direct course across the jungle and Geelvink Bay to Salawati Island and the Japanese bases of Jefman and Samate. We flew a combat formation, above the overcast, and passing close to some of the mountain ranges.

I looked down on a mountain stream cascading through the jungle—a raveled white thread on a cloth of green—the heart of the New Guinea jungle, not even charted on the map until this war started, an area known only to natives and explorers, the objective of long, hazardous, and carefully organized expeditions. Now we were flying over it as a matter of course, oblivious to the hardships and the romance, the solitude and the beauty of those jungle-covered mountains—four Lightnings cruising swiftly toward the enemy bases of Jefman and Samate—carrying violent death through the sky on the opposite side of the world from home.

We struck the northwestern peninsula of New Guinea south of Mawi Bay and continued on course for about one more hour until we reached the coast of Kaiboes Bay, south of Jefman. Then north, and within a few minutes the Japanese airstrips lay in view. We had hoped to catch a few Jap planes in the air, but had no luck. Circled the strips at about 9,000 feet, weaving constantly to confuse ground fire. The Jap antiaircraft was quite accurate, however. Many of the black bursts were at almost our exact altitude and a little too close for comfort. We circled once, checking for ships in the harbor and planes on the field. Then turned northeast along the coast to hunt for barges.

We found the first one run up on the beach only a few miles away,

17. Major Thomas B. McGuire, Jr., second leading ace of World War II, with 38 victories, holder of the Medal of Honor. McGuire died January 7, 1945, while leading a flight of four P-38's in an attack on an enemy airstrip on Negros Island in the Philippines.

camouflaged with leaves and branches. Entered strafing circle and each made two runs on it with machine guns and cannon. My gunsight was so far off that I had to hold the top of the 50-mm. ring where the "pipper" ought to be. My first burst was, consequently, wild; the second close; and the third, home.

We found two barges around the next point on the coast, both camouflaged with leaves and branches, and anchored or run aground about 200 feet offshore. They were cleverly placed in a scallop in the mountainous coast, so that you either had to shoot at them from a bank or chandelle up a steep mountainside after making your pass. Any error in judgment would leave you crashed on a mountain. I curved in over the top of one ridge at an indicated speed of 250 m.p.h., missing the trees by not over ten feet, partially straightened out while I was shooting, and pulled up the mountainside beyond in a steep left turn which left me headed out to sea and in position in the strafing circle.

The nearest boat, which we first concentrated on, was too large for an ordinary barge—probably a "lugger." On my second pass I opened fire with both machine guns and cannon, striking just above the waterline, aft of midships. I saw a burst of flame, continued firing for another second, and passed thirty feet above the masts just as the fuel tanks exploded. We made two more runs on the second barge but had difficulty shooting accurately through the clouds of smoke pouring from the first one. Since the second did not catch fire, we left it and continued on along the coast.

There seemed to be enemy barges every few miles. Barge traffic is their only means of supplying their eastern positions, as they do not dare send larger ships. We found two more around the next bend, but three of my .50-cal. guns jammed after my second run, and the fourth was shooting so erratically that the tracers were doing barrel rolls in air. I used up my cannon ammunition and then circled overhead while the other planes completed their runs. One of the pilots set a second barge on fire.

We started home, leaving the barge I got in flames, a second on fire, two others smoking slightly, and two or three more well strafed. Returned via Ransiki airstrip, where we encountered light and inaccurate antiaircraft fire. Landed at 1652 after a flight of six hours, twenty-four minutes. Turned in report of flight to Intelligence, and off to mess hall for supper. Evening with officers and writing.

Wednesday, June 28

Russians advance—surround German force in Vitebsk.

No mission today, so decided to go out into the jungle. No one else wanted to go, so I took a compass, my canteen, a .45 automatic, and a bar of tropical chocolate, and started up into the mountains, following an old and very poor trail along a rushing stream of clear water. "You'd better take a .45. There might be a few Japs out there. Once in a while a couple of them come into the camp to try to steal food. But they haven't got any guns. They rust too fast in the jungle."

The walking was rough in places. About a half mile upstream I came on the ruins of an old Dutch mill. After that, all traces of the military occupation were gone—only the jungle and the fresh, clear water tumbling into pools and over rapids. I pushed on up the creek bed for about two miles, and then sat for a time on a large rock on the edge of the rapids, watching currents and eddies of the rapids, and wondering why the clamor of war had to be brought to such a spot. On my way back to camp, I passed through a Jap bivouac area—all the shelters burned down by orders of an American general.

Supper and evening with 475th officers. Talk again turned to war, prisoners, and souvenirs. I am shocked at the attitude of our American troops. They have no respect for death, the courage of an enemy soldier, or many of the ordinary decencies of life. They think nothing whatever of robbing the body of a dead Jap and call him a "son of a bitch" while they do so. I said during a discussion that regardless of what the Japs did, I did not see how we could gain anything or claim that we represented a civilized state if we killed them by torture. "Well, some of our boys do kick their teeth in, but they usually kill them first," one of the officers said in half apology.

Later in the evening, as I was getting ready for bed, another officer showed me his souvenirs. Several Japanese soldiers had walked into the camp at about two hours after midnight. (There was argument among the officers as to whether the Japs had come to steal food or to surrender.) The officer who was showing me the souvenirs woke, saw the Japanese, grabbed his .45, and shot two of them. Another officer accounted for a third.

I don't blame them for what they did. After all, one can hardly afford to ask questions when he sees Japanese soldiers in camp during the darkest hours of morning. What I do blame them for is the attitude with which they kill and their complete lack of respect for the dignity of death. The souvenirs consisted of a silk Japanese flag containing the usual characters, a number of Japanese bills, including invasion money, a name stamp, a postal savings book, a number of postal cards already written and addressed, several other articles, and a photograph of several Japanese soldiers, including the one from whose body the "souvenirs" were taken—a young boy of about fifteen to seventeen years of age.

Thursday, June 29

Wrote for an hour after lunch. Then took my canteen, .45, and compass, and started out on the same jungle trail I followed yesterday. Went about a mile farther up the mountain today, but the trail still continued. It was probably a Jap escape route to the coast. There were no fresh footprints along it. Returned to a pool in the stream formed by a small waterfall eating out a pocket in the bed—small and shallow, but crystal-clear water and a sand bottom. I stripped, placed my gun on a rock at the edge of the pool, and jumped in—cool—just the right temperature after an hour's climbing of a jungle trail. A hundred feet away was a lean-to made of saplings and the leaves of ferns, apparently used by Japanese troops during their retreat across the mountains. A few old coconut shells scattered around indicated that they must have been short of rations. I stayed in the water for about half an hour. Then returned to camp.

Friday, June 30

Allied advance in Normandy continues.

To briefing hut at 10:00 for instructions on the bombing mission to Noemfoor Island. Off the Hollandia strip at 11:25—seventeen Lightnings. We each carry one 1,000-lb. bomb with a ten-second delay action. Broken clouds. We follow the coast until it turns southwest and then set a direct course for Noemfoor Island. The A-20's are just finishing their runs as we arrive. The entire revetment area along one side of the strip seems to rise in the air as the bombs hit. We circle until they are finished, then begin our runs.

Our bombing is very poor. It is the first time any of us have dropped bombs from a P-38. I begin my dive from the edge of a rain squall and release at about 2,500 feet. I pull up steeply and watch the ground for the burst, but it does not come. Another plane starts its run. The bomb overshoots and lands in the water a hundred yards offshore. I see three bombs land in the target area, two in the jungle, and three in the ocean.

There is considerable confusion rendezvousing after all bombs are dropped—seventeen planes following each other in a big circle, everyone trying to find his own flight position. We finally get organized and start back to Hollandia. Landed at 1610.

Saturday, July 1

Dewey and Bricker nominated by Republicans. Russians take Mogilev.

Up at sunrise. Breakfast in Colonel MacDonald's hut. Message arrives to the effect that thirteen bogies staged at Jefman and are going on to Moari (on the west coast of Geelvink Bay). Apparently a Jap message has been intercepted, and they intend to raid Biak or Wakde or one of the other American bases. We had planned on flying to the Kai Islands today, but changed our plans, in view of the intercept, and cleared for a mission through northwestern New Guinea.

Off the strip at 10:18—four Lightnings. Colonel MacDonald led the first section. I led the second. We set a direct course over the mountains and jungle to a point about midway along the southeast coast of Geelvink Bay. Our flight today goes under the radio code name of "Possum Special." Being leader of the second section, I am "Possum Special Three."

We follow the Geelvink Bay coast down to a point several miles northeast of the Japanese airstrip at Nabire. Then turn inland, flying low through the valleys to avoid detection by the Japanese radar, skimming twenty or thirty feet over the tree tops of the ridges we had to cross. Flashed across the Nabire strip so suddenly from the mountains that the Japs did not have time to man their guns before we were out of range above the tree tops. There were no planes on the strip except a few old wrecks.

From Nabire we again turned inland and followed the valleys through a mountainous terrain until we struck the large swamp on the south coast of McCluer Gulf. At times, my wingman and I flew within ten feet of the tree tops, dropping down below them over a river which paralleled our course, zooming up above the bank at the end of the bend. We turned northwest and crossed the first Sagan airstrip at tree-top height, turned southwest and flashed across the end of the second Sagan strip. There were several planes lined up along one edge. We banked around over the Otawiri strip, strafing as we passed. I held my guns on a hut on one edge until I had to pull up to keep from striking the ground—not over fifteen feet above it.

The Japs were ready for us when we crossed the Sagan strip the second time. My wingman picked up two bullets in his plane—no serious damage done. The planes on the side of the strip turned out to be nothing but wooden framework dummies. We turned northeast, passing close enough to the Babo strip to make sure there were no serviceable planes in its revetments. Then cut across Bintunei Bay and followed the mountain passes to a point a few miles south of Ransiki. Just before reaching the Ransiki strip, we banked out to sea, picking up light and inaccurate fire from the shore—both large and small guns. We saw the spray of machine-gun bullets and the splash of the heavier calibers hundreds of yards inland from us.

From Ransiki we followed the coast past Moari, looking for barges without success. Then across the point of land at Manokwari and west along the north coast. Still seeing no barges, we made a sweep out to sea to the northward, thinking they might be holding out of sight offshore. But although we flew north for twenty miles or more, we sighted nothing. We cut back across the point of Manokwari and took up a course for home, passing a few miles north of Japen Island.

Landed on the Hollandia strip at 1708 after a six-hour-and-fifty-minute flight. All during the day, I had been holding my engine down to get a check on minimum fuel consumption. Landed with 210 gallons in my tanks.

Supper at officers mess. The P-38 squadron which followed us back from Noemfoor Island yesterday has a pilot still missing.

Sunday, July 2

This is "D day" for Noemfoor Island. Drove to the 433rd Squadron ready hut for briefing at 11:30. The squadron is furnishing fighter cover this afternoon for the Noemfoor landing. I am to lead the "White Flight" of four Lightnings. Off the strip at 12:05. Paralleled the coast to the point where it bends south into Geelvink Bay. Then took a direct course to Noemfoor Island. There was a large cumulo-nimbus over Noemfoor when we arrived, which drifted slowly off the island, giving us a good view of the ships and landing barges of our task force.

The landing had been made at one of the Japanese airstrips which lay along the coast. Apparently there had not been much opposition, for our tanks and piles of supplies already dotted one end of the airstrip. Barges were churning back and forth between the ships and shore. A small convoy of transports, which had already unloaded, was steaming back eastward. A single cruiser, moving leisurely along a mile or two off the coast, was firing an occasional shot inland. Otherwise, all seemed quiet on the ground.

We had hoped that the Japs would set up some air opposition to the landing, as they often have before. Once, a low-flying bogey was reported by the ground control, but it turned out to be simply a friendly plane. Our patrol was scheduled for two hours over the island, but our relief arrived twenty minutes early, and we turned back to Hollandia. Return trip uneventful. Landed at 1725.

Monday, July 3

United States breaks diplomatic relations with Finland.

Drove to Hollandia strip for a 6:30 briefing. The group is giving fighter cover to the heavy bombers which are to strike Jefman this morning. Off the strip at 0725. I again led the "White Flight" of four Lightnings. Landed at Wakde at 0805 for rebriefing. Off again at 0838. Maximum auto lean cruising speed to False Cape, the rendezvous point with the bombers on the north coast of northwestern New Guinea. There were sixteen of them in all—four flights of four B-24's each. Our "Hades" flight of twelve Lightnings wove back and forth above them the rest of the way to the Japanese base at Jefman.

The bombers closed formation as they flew some 10,000 feet above the airstrip. I brought my flight into position to see the drop. A single column of black smoke rose from the center of the strip below, and then the entire runway seemed to rise into air, the delay-action bombs flashing like distant lightning amid the smoke and debris. It was a perfect hit. Hardly a bomb missed its mark. We circled overhead and followed the bombers back for a distance; then turned out to the coast for strafing.

Colonel MacDonald led the flight to the Waigeo Islands and in and out in line formation through the intricacies of their channels. The islands are mountainous with unusually steep and pointed hills, on many of which low clouds were lying, forcing us to fly close to the water at times—through clear channels of air which burrowed through clouds and between the hillsides. We found only two barges in these islands— one in the interior channels and one on the outer coast. The first looked to me like a native boat, so I did not strafe it. With twelve planes in line we made only one pass each at the second and almost certainly left it in a useless condition.

From the Waigeo Islands we crossed Dornpier Strait to the north coast and again found good hunting in the same vicinity where we encountered barges on our previous flight through the area. We first encountered a single barge on the beach, camouflaged as usual with green leaves. We formed a strafing circle and within a few minutes left it in flames. Around the next point, cleverly placed in a scallop in the mountainous coast, we found a large "lugger," a loaded barge, and several very small barges pulled up under foliage along the shore.

The lugger and loaded barge drew too much water for the Japs to get them closer than a hundred feet or so to the beach. But even at that distance the mountainsides were so steep and the scallop in the coast so small and deep that it was necessary to make the first part of our strafing run in a bank, straightening out just in time to get in a good burst before it was necessary to pull up to keep from crashing into the mountain on the other side of the scallop. We did not bother with the small barges on the shore, set the loaded barge on fire, and filled the lugger so full of 20- mm. and .50-cal. holes that it will probably be useless to the Japs.

On my runs I opened fire at about 350 yards and held it to within twenty feet of the water. My guns are now perfectly boresighted, and the first bullets find their mark—the 20-millimeters flashing as they explode on target, and the red tracers ricocheting up into air. The speed of the modern fighter is so great that you actually fly through the ricocheting tracers as you pass over the target.

One of the pilots reported low on fuel and was ordered to return home. Two or three minutes later a second reported his fuel tanks low and was sent back. Then a third. After that, Colonel MacDonald started back with the entire squadron. I had plenty of fuel in my tanks, having nursed the engine at minimum r.p.m. and auto lean, and continued along the coast with my wingman. We found a barge up on the beach and made two runs on it. At first appearance it looked like a wreck; but as I flew thirty feet above it I could see that it was loaded and simply cleverly camouflaged. I then found two very small and empty barges nosed up on the shore and made two strafing runs on them.

Around the next point, in a large scallop in the mountains, I saw two barges about 1,000 yards apart. The sea bottom fell off so sharply from the shore and the barges were so close to the high-tide line that some of the tree branches overhung them. It was necessary to come in along the coast in a bank, and there was no possibility of straightening out long enough to make a run. However, I found that by sideslipping I could get in a good burst and that the barges were far enough apart to make two runs on each circle.

After my second run, however, I noticed that my wingman was simply circling overhead. In reply to my radio query he replied that he, too, was low on fuel. I asked him how much was remaining in his tanks. He replied, "About 175 gallons." It was more than enough. I told him to pull his engine r.p.m. down to 1,600, to put his mixture control in auto lean, and to open his throttle wide enough to stay in loose formation with me. I then set course for Owi Island at an altitude of 1,000 feet above the water and an indicated air speed of 185 m.p.h. When we landed at Owi, he had seventy gallons left, a full hour's flight throttled down. I had 260 gallons in my tanks, although we both had exactly the same amount of fuel when we took off from Wakde Island in the morning.

The trouble is that the newer pilots, and many of the old ones, cruise their engines at too high an r.p.m. and often leave their mixture controls in auto rich during an entire flight. They have never tried low-r.p.m. cruising and cannot believe that it will not injure their engines—or make such a difference in fuel consumption.

Refueled and took off from Owi Island at 15:27. Landed on Hollandia strip at 1702. We called all pilots for a meeting in the evening. I talked to them for half an hour on maximum range and fuel economy.

Tuesday, July 4

Up at 5:00. Pancake breakfast at mess hall. Drove Colonel MacDonald's jeep to the strip for briefing at the 433rd Squadron ready room for the day's heavy-bomber strike on Jefman. Off Hollandia strip at 0655; Captain [John] Parkansky led the flight. I had the White section of four

Lightnings. Landed at Wakde Island for rebriefing. Rendezvoused with the bombers at 10,000 feet over False Cape and escorted them to Jefman. No sign of Japanese air resistance. The bombs were dropped on the island strip—effective but not as accurate as yesterday.

We stayed with the bombers for a quarter hour and then turned out to the coast for barge strafing. Heavy storms on the coastal mountains; but we found a hole through the clouds leading to the ocean, where there was plenty of ceiling. Found and strafed three barges. Then started back for Hollandia due to Captain Parkansky's plane developing hydraulic trouble. I led the flight on the last half of the return trip, each plane forming behind me in a large V. Landed on Hollandia strip at 1517. Lowest man reported 160 gallons of fuel in his tanks after the six-hour-and-forty-minute flight, making me feel that the talk last night was worth while.

Wednesday, July 5

My plane is undergoing a routine check. Colonel MacDonald and I decided to visit one of the native lake villages we fly over so often. Drove to the Dutch headquarters in his jeep. The lieutenant in charge spoke English well. He himself found no interest in native villages, he said; but if we would return at 4:00, he would take us to a village on the shore of the lake nearby. We could drive most of the way there in our jeep. He could not leave before then, he said, because he had to deal with twelve native chieftains who had arrived that morning. (The yard was full of almost naked natives who had probably spent days walking in from their villages.)

We drove to Hollandia strip to check on the overhauling of our Lightnings, passing a wrecked Jap plane every few hundred feet. In places, there were piles of these planes, pushed together by bulldozers in order to clear the area. From the strip we drove up on the hill to General Hutchison's headquarters to talk to the general about the possibility of taking four Lightnings along on the next daylight bomber raid on Palau.

We have been able to find no Japanese aircraft in New Guinea and know that a number of fighters are on the strips at Palau—seventy-three, according to our latest Intelligence reports. Our bombing raids have met fighter resistance at Palau in addition to heavy ack-ack fire. It would be inadvisable to take our entire squadron because of the distance from Biak Island (the nearest American airstrip) and because of the weather along the route (three equatorial fronts are usually encountered and must be passed through both going and coming). However, four planes with experienced pilots should be able to get through without difficulty. Unfortunately, General Hutchison told us that no more daylight raids are contemplated in the near future.

Back to the Dutch headquarters to pick up the lieutenant (Lieutenant Emeys). Then we started out for the native village. I started asking the lieutenant questions about his dealings with the natives. He looked directly at me with flashing, humorous blue eyes, and said, "You see, I'm really a slave trader. We are at war. We must have labor for the camps. Of course we pay them, but still they don't like to work. It's like a tax. I have to see that the chiefs send in enough men. When they don't, we send out and get them. I have some patrols out now."

We passed several naked natives on the trail. They all faced us and saluted. "The Japs taught them to do that. If they didn't salute a Jap soldier, they were beaten."

We came to a broken-down bridge and had to park our jeep and walk the rest of the way along a winding and, at one point, very steep foot path. All the village huts were built on stilts out over the water. On the shore were a number of dugouts they had constructed for protection when our forces were bombing some Jap antiaircraft emplacements located nearby. We walked out along a lightly constructed and rickety walkway over the water to the chapel and school maintained by the Dutch government, where the intelligent and rather Chinese-appearing preacher and teacher lived with his rather beautiful and still more Chinese-appearing wife. They asked us to stay for coffee and some fried bananas. The hut, larger than the rest, was very clean. The Dutch lieutenant told us that the food and water was safe and that he was "sure of these people." We accepted and while the food was being cooked went to see one of the native huts.

The interior was dark, with the lighter water of the lake showing through wide chinks in the split-wood flooring. In one corner lay the ashes of a fire which was used for cooking and apparently burned without any consideration of how the smoke would get outside. In the end of the hut next the door were two semiprivate rooms, screened off somewhat by a sort of split-board fence. Scattered around the main portion of the dwelling were a number of natives, lying on the floor and squatting, both young and old. Near the center was a hunchback imbecile, and a few feet beyond him, a young man lay moaning with fever. An extremely unpleasant odor permeated the whole place. We remained only for two or three minutes and were glad to get out into the air again.

The bananas were delicious—a kind I have never tasted before. I gave a tropical chocolate bar to each of the couple's three small children. I carry them in my canteen pouch for emergency rations.

We dropped the lieutenant at his headquarters, and returned to the 475th Fighter Group too late for supper. I cooked a meal in Colonel MacDonald's hut from one of the "ten-in-one" ration boxes—roast beef, bacon, lima beans, jam, biscuits, and coffee for those who wanted it.

Just as we had finished supper Colonel Morrissey phoned me from General Hutchison's headquarters. Said he had bad news for me; that a message had come in "from the south" (meaning Australian Army headquarters) saying a rumor was circulating to the effect that I was flying combat in New Guinea, and that, if true, there should be no more of it. Morrissey had been sent up from Nadzab to deliver the message to me. I borrowed Colonel MacDonald's jeep and drove over to General Hutchison's quarters. But Morrissey had no details. Decided to fly to Nadzab tomorrow and find out what happened; looks like politics.

Thursday, July 6

Russian Army captures Minsk.

Spent morning saying good-by, packing, and writing. Off Hollandia strip at 1400. Two Lightnings—Colonel Morrissey and I. Detoured along the coast because of weather reported inland. Flew over Jap territory south of Wewak. It is difficult to realize, looking down on the green foliage, that the jungle is infested with Japanese troops—like looking at the surface of the ocean and trying to visualize the fish that swim beneath.

Encountered storms along the coast southeast of Madang. Forced down until we were flying within ten feet of the water. Almost reached Finschhafen, hoping to get back to Nadzab through the valley, but met a solid wall of storm within five miles of the cape. Turned back to Madang and found an opening in the clouds through which we reached the valley in which Nadzab lies. But eastward the valley was blocked by one of the blackest storms I have ever seen, which forced us to return to the coast and land at Saidor.

Friday, July 7

Cleared and off at 7:30. We skimmed the peaks to Nadzab, set our props at 3,000 r.p.m. to make the greatest possible noise, dove down over Fighter Command, and landed at 7:55.

To ADVON to see General Whitehead. He is leaving for the south this morning. Apparently the situation is not as bad as I feared. The message from Australian headquarters simply inquired about my orders, saying they had no record of them in their files. I gave a copy to Colonel Cooper when I arrived at Nadzab, but he apparently either misplaced or forgot about them. There seems to be a good chance that I will be able to go back into the advanced area and do a little more combat flying.

Saturday, July 8

Lieutenant Colonel Archie Roosevelt phoned in the evening and came over to Fighter Command for a visit. He is at the hospital here, recovering from a shrapnel wound received at Biak, and from a generally run-down condition—forty pounds underweight. At fifty-three, he is a battalion commander in the 41st, with a wonderful record—four campaigns, including some of the toughest fighting in New Guinea. He brought over a copy of *The Steep Ascent* for me to sign—just received it from his wife. We talked over the war and politics back home, the now obvious hypocrisy of the prewar idealists. We laughed about the fact that the war records of those of us who opposed getting into it are far better than the records of those who demanded intervention, the record of the America First National Committee being among the best—General [Robert E.] Wood, General [Thomas S.] Hammond, General [Hanford] MacNider, Captain [R. Douglas] Stuart. All of us have served to the best ability we had, and as far as we were permitted.

Sunday, July 9

Spent most of day writing letters to Paul Baker in regard to my observations in this area concerning fighters and fighter design.

Monday, July 10

B-29's bomb Japan again.

Breakfast at Fighter Command. To Strip 1 at 9:30 to fly my plane back to Strip 3. The Service Squadron has just finished putting a new cloth strip on the entering edge of the wings. Spent most of afternoon working on manuscript and writing a letter to Gene Wilson. Supper and evening with officers. To bed early.

About midnight Colonel Guthrie woke me. A message had just arrived from Brisbane requesting me to come down, signed "MacArthur." Guthrie said a B-25 was leaving for Australia at 0630 and that passage had been arranged for me.

Tuesday, July 11

To Strip 3 at 6:30. Had a hard time finding the B-25 and arrived twenty minutes late. But the plane was held up for another half hour by various delays, including oil-gauge trouble. Finally off at 0754. I rode as passenger. Direct course for Townsville [Australia] across the New Guinea mountains and ocean. Clear to scattered clouds at start, merging into a solid overcast as we approached Australia. Caught glimpses of the Great Barrier Reef through an occasional hole. Had to climb to 11,000 feet to top the clouds. Quite cold, as we were dressed in tropical cotton clothing. The clouds broke just before we reached Townsville. Landed at 11:51.

Brisbane was reporting 600 feet and rain, with a front about paralleling our route and conditions probably deteriorating. We decided to spend the night in Townsville. Drove to the city. Stopped to get a haircut, and then drove through the city streets to look at the people and stores. There seems to be much less racial mixture here than in most American cities—mostly British stock.

Wednesday, July 12

British take Caen.

Took off at 0851. Landed at Brisbane at 1219. To American Army headquarters to see General Kenney.[18] Kenney told me that a situation

18. General George C. Kenney commanded the Allied Air Forces and the U.S.

had arisen which caused some of the officers at headquarters much concern: that somehow I had managed to get into the forward areas in New Guinea without their knowing about it; that rumors had filtered back to the effect that I was flying combat with the Army squadrons; and that, of course, flying combat as a civilian was against all the regulations there were.

He went on to tell me that if I were caught by the Japs, I would have my head chopped off immediately if they found out I was flying combat as a civilian. Kenney then made some quite uncomplimentary remarks about the Navy and their giving me orders to come into this area without consulting General MacArthur's headquarters, which, he said, they had no right whatever to do.

I explained to him that the Navy had simply given me orders to go to New Guinea, at my request, to see General Whitehead, that I had turned a copy of those orders over to Colonel Cooper when I arrived at Nadzab, and had been under the impression that all formalities had been satisfactorily met. I told him that the last thing I wanted to do was cause anyone embarrassment at headquarters. Kenney was very decent about it all, and said that he would get my papers legalized for this area, but that he would have to ask me not to fly combat any more.

I told him that if he gave such an order, I would naturally follow it, but that I didn't want to go back up to New Guinea and sit on the ground while the other pilots were flying combat. Kenney spoke again about Army regulations, the "reaction back home" if I were shot down, etc. I asked him if there wasn't some way to get around the regulations. He became thoughtful and his eyes twinkled. (The ice was broken.) "Well, it might be possible to put you on observer's status, but, of course, that would not make it legal for you to do any shooting. But if you are on observer's status, no one back in the States will know whether you use your guns or not." I replied that I didn't care what status I went back on as long as I could go back and carry on as I did before.

"Well, how well do you know General Sutherland?" [19]

"I have met him, but I don't know him very well."

"He's the man you'll have to see to straighten this out."

Kenney picked up the phone on his desk, and called for Sutherland. In another moment, to my amazement, I was listening to him argue my

---

Fifth Air Force in the Southwest Pacific from 1942 to 1944, and the Allied Air Forces and Far East Air Forces until 1945.

19. General Richard K. Sutherland, chief of staff for General Douglas MacArthur.

case with General Sutherland. After that, the wheels ran smoothly. We went upstairs to see General Sutherland. General Kenney had to leave for a conference he had scheduled, leaving me alone with Sutherland. Sutherland asked me when I had last seen Truman Smith (one of his old friends).

"A few weeks before I left the States. He was about to leave on a vacation in Santa Fe, New Mexico, with Kay."

"How was he?"

"He looked rather tired. He goes up and down quickly. After a few days of hard work, he looks badly. After a few days of rest, he looks much better again."

"Yes, he retired once, but General Marshall called him back to active duty after the war started. He told me there's no one he relies on more for analysis of the European theater."

I told Sutherland about Marshall sending Truman's report on prewar German aviation (which I helped him to prepare) to President Roosevelt as an example of outstanding military intelligence. We discussed what a tragedy it was to have Truman afflicted with diabetes at a time when he could have rendered such a great service to his country. General Marshall wanted to take Truman to Europe with him, but the Surgeon General refused to let him go—said it would probably be fatal.

I outlined to General Sutherland the work I am doing and my reason for being in this area, i.e., studying pursuit operations in connection with the design of future fighters, with special interest in the relative merits of single and multiengine fighters. Sutherland said that he would arrange the necessary papers for me for this area, putting me on observer status and that that would put me in a position to do about anything I wanted to.

We then discussed the situation in New Guinea and some of the missions I had been on, and the subject of fighter range came up. I said that none of the squadrons I had made contact with understood the subject of fuel economy, that they were wasting a large percentage of their gasoline by cruising their engines at too high an r.p.m. and too low a manifold pressure, and that I thought a combat radius of 700 miles could be obtained with the P-38's after the pilots were properly instructed and trained. I told him that I believed the more experienced pilots could get a 750-mile combat radius from their planes and still have a safe landing reserve, i.e., a full hour.

Sutherland said that if a 700-mile radius could be obtained, it would be of the utmost importance to their plans in this area. I told him that my experience with the 475th Fighter Group made me feel sure that such a range was entirely practical and that I would be glad to work with all of the fighter groups in the area and show them how to obtain maximum range on their combat missions. Sutherland then suggested that we go in and talk to General MacArthur.

MacArthur was much younger-looking than I expected. He was alone in the room when we stopped in, greeted me warmly, and spoke of the last time we had met, years ago, when he was Chief of Staff in Washington. He then turned immediately to the subject of combat radius for fighters, saying that General Sutherland had told him that I said the P-38's were capable of 700 miles. Did I mean that would be possible with the planes just as they were, without any modifications, he asked.

I repeated what I had told Sutherland, i.e., that I thought the average P-38 squadron, after a little instruction and training, could fly a 700-mile combat radius without much difficulty and with just as much fuel reserve as they are now coming back with from their present missions.

MacArthur said it would be a gift from heaven if that could be done and asked me if I were in a position to go back up to New Guinea to instruct the squadrons in the methods of fuel economy which would make such a radius possible. I told him there was nothing I would rather do and that I could go back at once. He said I could have any plane and do any kind of flying I wanted to, and that an increased fighter radius would be of very great importance to his plans. He then took me over to a map of the South Pacific and showed me his general plan of action— immediate steps, future steps, etc., and the limitations which were imposed by present fighter combat radii.

I then spoke of the general's wife, Jean Marie, and asked him if I might call on her that evening. He said, of course, and that he would arrange it before I left, and that his wife had often spoken to him about her trip on the boat with my mother. (Jean Marie and Mother met on board ship in 1929 when Mother was returning to the United States from Turkey. They formed a friendship which was cemented when the newspapers—the ship was in mid-Atlantic—announced the engagement of Mother to the captain—caused by the improper transmission and translation of an Italian message. Mother was much upset, and Jean Marie was a great help to her. Of course, when the boat docked at New York, it was met by dozens of reporters and photographers demanding a confirmation, a denial, pictures, any kind of an interview, etc. Mother very wisely remained in her stateroom. When I went on board, harassed as usual by the pressmen, Jean Marie, whom I had never seen or heard of, met me at the head of the gangplank, and with great dignity and firmness said, "Charles, will you come with me. Your mother is waiting for you in my stateroom." I was very cautious about attractive young ladies at the time because of several attempted frame-ups by the New York press; but there was something about her face and attitude which convinced me, and I followed.)

After leaving General MacArthur's office, I stopped to see General Kenney. MacArthur had seen him first. He greeted me with a smile and said, "Well, you're all set." He told me he was going north in the morning and asked me if I would like to go along. I thanked him and said I would like to hold over in Brisbane for one day. I asked if there might not be a plane I could ferry north the following day.

Kenney said he could let me have a P-47 any time I wanted it. But, he said, "I wish you'd be satisfied to fly around in a bomber instead of a fighter after you get there." I told him I wasn't any bomber pilot even though I had tested some of them. He laughed and said he liked fighters better himself, but they had sort of clipped his wings lately. "But," he said, "you could see just as much from a bomber, and I wouldn't have to worry as much about you." I told him I didn't like to get shot at unless I could shoot back, and that I wasn't a turret gunner.

Back to Lennon's Hotel ten minutes late for my appointment with Jean Marie. We talked of Mother and of the boat trip they were on together. She told me how her acquaintance with my mother had resulted, indirectly, in her meeting General MacArthur. She asked me about Phil Love's death. She had met him through Mother.

Thursday, July 13

Roosevelt says he will accept fourth-term nomination.

Breakfast at 8:00 with General Fellers. Rest of morning spent walking alone along the streets and through the stores of Brisbane, studying the people, their faces, their products, etc. Purchased a few unimportant items—spool of strong thread, shaving stick, can of shoe polish, etc. There has been nothing in the Australian papers about my being here; consequently, no one recognizes me, and I am able to move about with complete freedom.

General Fellers loaned me his car and driver in the afternoon. Drove out to the park to see the koala bear, the wallabies, and the kangaroos. The keeper had a police dog which reminded me very much of Thor, and who followed him around carrying a small bear on his back, clinging tightly to his fur. The dog followed his master's instructions obediently, but with the same bored and disgusted expression that Thor assumed when I used to make him lie down on the floor while Skean jumped back and forth over him.

Supper with Phil La Follette. Phil cooked supper. We discussed the war, old times, and the political situation back home. At one point, the conversation turned to the atrocities committed by the Japanese and by our own men. It was freely admitted that some of our soldiers tortured Jap prisoners and were as cruel and barbaric at times as the Japs themselves. Our men think nothing of shooting a Japanese prisoner or a soldier attempting to surrender. They treat the Jap with less respect than they would give to an animal, and these acts are condoned by almost everyone. We claim to be fighting for civilization, but the more I see of this war in the Pacific the less right I think we have to claim to be civilized. In fact, I am not sure that our record in this respect stands so very much higher than the Japs'.

Friday, July 14

To Eagle Farms Airport in Army car. Laid out course on maps and filled out clearance for Horn Island just off the south tip of Australia. Army operations did not want to clear me nonstop to Horn Island, the captain in charge saying that a P-47 was not capable of making the flight from Brisbane to Horn Island without refueling, and that he knew because he had gone up there several times in P-47's. I asked him what his fuel consumption had been. "About eighty gallons an hour." I told him that the R-2800 engine in the P-47 should be capable of cruising in the vicinity of fifty gallons an hour. He said he could hardly believe that and that he had never been able to approach such a low figure. However, he was very pleasant and considerate and cleared me direct to Horn Island as I requested. I told him that if my fuel ran low, I would land at one of the intermediate fields in southern Australia.

Checked my plane, and off the strip at 0845. Set a direct course for Horn Island, which took me inland a considerable distance from the coast. Dropped down to 200 feet above the ground over the valleys of northeastern Australia in the hope of seeing some wild kangaroos or wallabies, but sighted only cattle and an occasional small ranch building.

Had the r.p.m. down to 1,450 during the latter portion of the flight and arrived over Horn Island with enough fuel to reach Nadzab with almost a two-hour reserve. Tried to contact Horn Island by radio to extend my flight plan to Nadzab, but without success. Landed at Horn Island at 1511.

Supper and evening with the Australian officers—pleasant and hospitable. The Australian camps are much simpler than the American. The Australian officer still thinks of cost, while the American officer has no regard for it whatever. The main exhibit at the officers club here is a "tire" from the first Zero shot down over Australia. Found a centipede over eight inches long crawling under my bed! Went for a half hour's walk along one of the camp footpaths in the evening. Slept in a screened-in hut with two or three of the "Aussies."

Saturday, July 15

Took off the strip at 0830. Almost dropped my external fuel tanks on take-off, as the runway was short for a P-47 and the wind direction forced me to take off over hills. Cleared the hilltops with a slight margin to spare. Set my course to the nearest New Guinea coast to cut down the distance over water on the direct route to Nadzab. Passed over numerous islands and reefs. Landed on Strip 3 at 10:35. Checked in at Operations and took a jeep to Fighter Command. General Wurtsmith and Colonel Morrissey have gone to Owi Island, where advanced fighter headquarters are being established.

Sunday, July 16

Off the strip at 0957 with the same P-47 I brought up from Brisbane. One of the P-47 pilots from Wakde Island was going back this morning, so we took off together. Followed the valley to a point a few miles southeast of the Japanese base at Wewak. Then out to sea, following the coast just out of gun range off the shore. We separated at Wakde, and I continued on to Owi Island alone, landing on the strip at 1349. Jeep trip over extremely rough and muddy roads to Bomber Command, where General Wurtsmith is staying until Fighter Command campsite is completed.

The rather large hut where I am staying is on a coral bluff about fifty feet from shore. Went swimming in the afternoon, using my face mask.

Tuesday, July 18

There is much concern about the typhus cases on this island. Thirty new cases today, bringing the total to about 150. There has been too much rain to burn the brush and dead wood around the camp areas. The typhus tick abounds in rotting wood, and there are plenty of rats on the island to carry it.

Wednesday, July 19

Had planned on flying with the 8th Group this morning, giving cover to the heavy bombers on a strike over Samate. The strike had to be canceled because of weather. However, if tomorrow is clear, we plan a four-plane (P-38) mission to Ceram and the Japanese base at Ambon on the island of Amboina. There is a good chance that we will find enemy planes in the air. Intelligence reports Japanese air strength in that area to be thirty-six single-seater fighters, twenty-five twin-engine fighters, nine light bombers, thirty-six medium bombers, and six planes of other classes.

Out fishing in the afternoon with General Wurtsmith, Colonel Hutchison, Colonel Morrissey, and several other officers in a small and rather slow launch. Saw a shark on the surface behind some of the troop ships—about fifteen feet in length. Cruised up slowly and one of the men put a carbine bullet through his back. Trolled partway around the island without success. Then pulled up to the edge of the coral reef and General Wurtsmith tossed in a stick of dynamite. Several of us took turns diving for the stunned fish with my face mask. All of the fish we got were rather small and most were brilliantly colored.

Got a bucket full of fish from two charges, but did not know which were good and which might be poisonous. Passed some natives on the road back to camp. Stopped the jeep and asked them if the fish were good to eat—using gestures, pointing to our mouths, etc. We gave one of the natives a brilliantly colored fish. He smiled, pointed to his mouth, patted his belly, and slipped it into a sack he was carrying. The same with the next and the next. The more poisonous the fish looked, the more joyfully the natives seemed to accept it, laughing and smacking their lips to indicate those they considered to be the tastiest morsels. Apparently all the fish we caught are edible. We kept only a few of the more conservative-looking ones for ourselves, and I think I shall let someone else eat them—some of the officers who are more enthusiastic than I about unknown tropical fish.

Thursday, July 20

Morrissey and I to the strip at 9:00. Started and checked our engines and taxied to end of strip to wait for MacDonald and [Major Meryl M.] Smith. They "buzzed" the strip at 10:00 sharp, and we were off. Set a direct course for Amboina Island, throttling down for fuel economy. Clear sky with only scattered clouds as far as McCluer Gulf. Then cumuli began building up until we ran into a heavy storm area about thirty miles southwest of Pisang Island. Tried to climb above the clouds but they were too high. Tried to fly around the storm, first to the south and then to the north, without success. Obviously, we were confronted by a tropical front, black with rain close to the water, and rising probably about 30,000 feet.

We turned back to the Pisang Islands, where I broke off from the formation and scouted the coast lines for barges. There were none to be found. Then we turned southeast to Cape Fatagar and searched the coast to Fakfak. Several of the larger buildings on the hillside were plastered with large red crosses. I flew quite close to the shore line, but picked up no antiaircraft fire. Then along the coast of Pandjang Island, where we caught a number of small canoes offshore. The men in them were paddling like mad for the nearest land. We flew low over them but could not tell whether they were natives or Japs. No one fired on them. We continued on along the coast, but were turned back by another storm.

Retraced our steps to the Pisang Islands and tried to get through to Ceram by detouring far to the northward. We got far enough to see the coast vaguely through rain. The island seemed to be covered by a solid wall of storm. Turned back past the Pisang Islands to Cape Sabra. Then down to the Sarigan Islands, where we found some new Japanese construction work under way on the easternmost island. MacDonald and Smith went in close to the village of Sagan to strafe a barge. They received some light but quite accurate antiaircraft fire from hitherto unreported shore batteries. Morrissey and I were coming in behind them but saw the flashes of ground guns and the black puffs in the air in time to turn off. MacDonald radioed that he thought he had been hit in the tail. (No holes were found after landing.)

We circled around the Sagan airstrips at tree-top height to make sure no enemy planes had come in. All the Japs had taken cover, and we saw no antiaircraft fire. Then across Bintunei Bay and low over the mountains to Moari airstrip, passing low, out of gun range off the west end. There were no planes on that strip either. It seems to be impossible to find a Japanese plane in the air anywhere in New Guinea. Back to Owi Island, where we landed at 1528.

Friday, July 21

The Japanese stronghold on the cliffs of Biak is to be attacked again in the morning. Several hundred Japs are still holding out in caves and crevices in an area about 300 yards wide and 1,000 yards long. So far, they have thrown back all of our attacks, and inflicted nearly one hundred casualties on our infantrymen. They have as perfect a natural defensive position as could be devised—sharp coral ridges overlooking and paralleling the coast, filled with deep and interlocking caves and screened from our artillery fire by coral ledges. This area is clearly visible from the top of the coral cliff, ten feet from the back door of the officers quarters where I am staying—a brown ridge surrounded by green jungle on the coast of Biak about three miles across the water from Owi Island.

The intense artillery fire has stripped the trees of leaves and branches so that the outline of the coral ridge itself can be seen silhouetted against the sky. Since I have been on Owi Island, at irregular intervals through the night and day, the sound of our artillery bombarding this Japanese stronghold has floated in across the water. This afternoon, I stood on the cliff outside our quarters (not daring to sit on the ground because of the danger of typhus) and watched the shells bursting on the ridge. For weeks that handful of Japanese soldiers, variously estimated at between 250 and 700 men, has been holding out against overwhelming odds and the heaviest bombardment our well-supplied guns can give them.

If positions were reversed and our troops held out so courageously and well, their defense would be recorded as one of the most glorious examples of tenacity, bravery, and sacrifice in the history of our nation. But, sitting in the security and relative luxury of our quarters, I listen to American Army officers refer to these Japanese soldiers as "yellow sons of bitches." Their desire is to exterminate the Jap ruthlessly, even cruelly. I have not heard a word of respect or compassion spoken of our enemy since I came here.

It is not the willingness to kill on the part of our soldiers which most concerns me. That is an inherent part of war. It is our lack of respect for even the admirable characteristics of our enemy—for courage, for suffering, for death, for his willingness to die for his beliefs, for his companies and squadrons which go forth, one after another, to annihilation against our superior training and equipment. What is courage for us is fanaticism for him. We hold his examples of atrocity screamingly to the heavens while we cover up our own and condone them as just retribution for his acts.

A Japanese soldier who cuts off an American soldier's head is an Oriental barbarian, "lower than a rat." An American soldier who slits a Japanese throat "did it only because he knew the Japs had done it to his buddies." I do not question that Oriental atrocities are often worse than ours. But, after all, we are constantly telling ourselves, and everyone else who will listen to us, that we are the upholders of all that is "good" and "right" and civilized.

I stand looking at the patch of scorched jungle, at the dark spots in the cliffs which mark the caves where the Japanese troops have taken cover. In that burned area, hidden under the surface of the ground, is the utmost suffering—hunger, despair, men dead and dying of wounds, carrying on for a country they love and for a cause in which they believe, not daring to surrender even if they wished to, because they know only too well that our soldiers would shoot them on sight even if they came out with their hands above their heads.

We must bomb them out, those Jap soldiers, because this is war, and if we do not kill them, they will kill us now that we have removed the possibility of surrender. But I would have more respect for the character of our people if we could give them a decent burial instead of kicking in the teeth of their corpses, and pushing their bodies into hollows in the ground, scooped out and covered up by bulldozers. After that, we will leave their graves unmarked and say, "That's the only way to handle the yellow sons of bitches."

Over to the 35th Fighter Squadron in the evening to give a half hour's talk to the pilots on fuel economy and the P-38.

Saturday, July 22

Japanese Cabinet resigns.

Stood out on the cliff at 9:00 to watch the heavies strike the Jap positions. The B-24's—eight planes in all—hit on the minute; first two bombers, then two more flights of three ships each—spread at sufficient intervals to allow the smoke from one flight to drift aside before the next was in position to release its bombs. Since there was no enemy antiaircraft opposition, the bombers came over at the ideal altitude of about 6,000 feet. The bombs were perfectly placed, covering the entire length of the ridge. I could see them released with my naked eye—specks curving gracefully through the air—irretrievable death in flight. Then the flashing concussion waves as they hit, and the great column of smoke shooting skyward. In six minutes it was all over, the smoke drifting slowly away to show the torn trees and battered coral ridge. Then the ground artillery began its bombardment, covering the ridge with smaller puffs. This afternoon, our infantry will attack.

A report came in on the area bombed this morning. The infantry moved in following the artillery bombardment after the bombing. They occupied the area "without firing a shot"—found about forty dead Japs in one cave and "parts of quite a few more" scattered about. The few who were living were sitting and lying around in a dazed condition and made no move as they saw our soldiers. One prisoner was taken, according to the first report; but an infantry colonel told me later that no prisoners were taken at all. "Our boys just don't take prisoners."

Typhus cases now number about 200 on the island. For some reason there are very few on Biak, only three miles away. However, the number of new cases per day is decreasing. I have started rubbing my body twice daily with anti-bug oil.

Monday, July 24

Roosevelt and Truman nominated by Democrats. United States forces land on Guam. Attempt to assassinate Hitler fails.

Was going over to Biak in a B-25, but we could find no trace of the plane in the revetments. Started to go over in a C-47, but it was called back from the runway to take on some two and a half tons of high-explosive shells. Finally in the air, after a long take-off run, with the shell cases rather inadequately lashed down. Landed on Mokmer strip, Biak, ten minutes later. We are to strike the Halmaheras in the morning, and I am flying with the 475th.

Major [Claude] Stubbs, several other officers, and I drove a jeep over to the Mokmer west caves in the afternoon. Here the Japs made one of their most stubborn stands against our troops. A rough military road has been cut into the area, so we were able to approach within a few hundred feet of the caves before we got out of the jeep. The road passed a number of Japanese supply dumps, stinking with the smell of souring rice and unburied rotting bodies.

We climbed up a steep hill which had been heavily bombed and shelled, stumbling over fallen trees and the rough coral ground. Few trees were left standing, and Japanese equipment littered the ground. The side and top of the hill were covered with shallow foxholes with coral rocks piled up for eight or ten inches around the edges. Many of the foxholes had been covered with a framework of branches topped with leaves, and most of them contained bits of discarded Jap equipment—a shoe, a canteen, a rice cup, a steel helmet, a leather belt container, a bit of uniform, etc. Alongside the Jap equipment were American K-ration boxes, American shells, rain-soaked American magazines, etc.

Going down the hill, we came to a pass with the bodies of a Japanese officer and ten or twelve soldiers lying sprawled about in the gruesome positions which only mangled bodies can take. They had gone down fighting in defense of the pass and been left lying there unburied. Since the battle took place several weeks ago, the heat and ants of the tropics had done their work, and little flesh was left to cover the skeletons. In some places there would be a body with two heads lying together. In others there would be a body with no head at all. Some of the bodies had been so badly torn apart that there were only fragments left. And as one of the officers with me said, "I see that the infantry have been up to their favorite occupation," i.e., knocking out all the teeth that contain gold fillings for souvenirs.

We had to cross a road and climb another hill to get to the caves themselves. At the side of the road we passed the edge of a bomb crater. In its bottom were lying the bodies of five or six Jap soldiers, partly covered with a truckload of garbage our troops had dumped on top of them. I have never felt more ashamed of my people. To kill, I understand; that is an essential part of war. Whatever method of killing your enemy is most effective is, I believe, justified. But for our people to kill by torture and to descend to throwing the bodies of our enemies into a bomb crater and dumping garbage on top of them nauseates me. On the way up the hill we had to step over the bodies of more Japanese, apparently Marines, for their blue and white uniforms were scattered everywhere. We had to progress cautiously, for there were numerous booby traps on the ground, apparently all disarmed by the infantry, but we took no chances.

The west caves were down in a hollow beyond the hilltop. Here, too, the hillside was covered with shallow foxholes and small natural holes in the coral. The latter were in a number of instances filled with the bodies of dead Japanese soldiers, dumped on top of one another by our infantry. In the bottom of the hollow was a great pit in the coral, probably fifty feet wide, one hundred feet long, and thirty feet deep. A ladder, obviously of Japanese construction (poles lashed together), led to the bottom. At each end of this pit were the entrances to the west caves.

We climbed down the ladder past the bodies of more soldiers and picked our way over to the entrance of one of the caves. The interior was dark and wet. We could hear water dripping down off the roof onto the floor. I threw my flashlight into the interior. The cave was large, with a number of side passages. The floor, some twenty feet below the entrance, was littered with boxes of ammunition, cases of food, sacks of souring rice and soybeans, and miscellaneous articles of clothing and equipment all soaked by the water dripping down off the roof.

I climbed down a ladder roughly made of poles. The rungs were wet and slippery with mud. Inside the cave the stench was terrific—decaying food and decaying bodies. I stayed only long enough to sweep the place with my flashlight. The Japs had built small huts inside the cave in which to live: framework of poles; floor of plank and poles; roof of leaves. Most of them had been tumbled down and partly burned by our grenades and flame throwers.

The cave at the other end of the pit was larger and a little deeper. A path ran steeply down into it over boulders and debris. Charred skulls and bodies marked the work of the flame throwers. The inside of the cave was a mire of mud and filth, with the bodies of Japanese soldiers scattered everywhere. On the higher and somewhat less wet positions were stacked boxes of ammunition and food. At the center and far end of the cave the Japs had set up huts similar to those in the first cave we entered, but in better condition, since they were far enough in to escape the flame thrower. One of them had apparently been used for a hospital. One of the bodies on the floor was still lying, partially covered, on a stretcher. This is the cave where the Japs reportedly tried to surrender and were told by our troops to "get the hell back in and fight it out." The far end of the cave opened into a second pit, also littered with dead bodies. We could stand it no longer and turned back to our jeep. Drove to the shore and bathed in the cool and clear water of a small spring, which the Japs in those caves had probably used only a few weeks previously.

I learned that Colonel [Archibald] Roosevelt is back with his regiment—the 41st. Major [Claude] Stubbs and I drove over to see him later in the afternoon. He told me that his brother, Theodore Roosevelt, had written shortly before his death to the effect that he was completely exhausted from taking part in the fighting in the European area and that he could not seem to get back his strength.

Supper at the mess of the 475th's new quarters. Then we drove back to the temporary quarters near Mokmer strip. Colonel MacDonald was back from Owi Island with orders from Colonel Cooper at Nadzab not to let me fly on the Halmahera strike in the morning! Colonel Morrissey had brought the word. What has happened? After all, I cleared with General MacArthur, General Sutherland, General Kenney, and General Whitehead. Has Colonel Cooper not been so informed, or has something gone wrong higher up? I phoned General Wurtsmith at Owi, and he promised to get a radio message out at once—said he would get word back to me tonight. But it is now nearing midnight and the phone has not rung, and the fighters take off soon after daybreak in the morning.

Tuesday, July 25

Russian advance continues. Purge reported in Germany.

Up at 6:00. No phone call from General Wurtsmith. We can hear the drone of the engines already warming up. I dress and go down to the mess hall with the pilots on the off-chance that authorization will still come through. Just as we finish eating, a phone call comes from Colonel Morrissey; authorization has come through, and I am clear to go on the strike. Back to the tent to get my equipment. We drive to the alert tent on the strip. Word comes that strike is postponed one hour on account of weather. Then two hours. Then it is canceled altogether.

First part of evening writing. A red alert was called about 8:30—siren screaming, antiaircraft firing, men shouting, lights going out. I picked up my helmet, turned out the tent light, and sat on the side of the sand-bagged pit a few yards west of our tent. There was a new moon dimly lighting the ground. Red antiaircraft tracers were spurting up into the sky. Searchlights were playing about trying to locate the intruder, constantly baffled by thin cloud layers in the partly broken sky. Several soldiers walked rapidly by, looking for a slit trench. A terrified voice called after them, "Wait for me, wait for me," and a man came running through the darkness, stumbling over coral and brush stubble.

The pit where I was sitting was also a scene of contrasts: two men crouched down on the floor; others standing up watching the ack-ack; several of us perched on coral sandbags around the rim. A few feet away, Colonel MacDonald and several other officers stood watching the sky. The ack-ack stopped for a few seconds. Searchlights blinked on and off. The ack-ack guns to the east of us began firing heavily, the shells flashing in air thousands of feet above. We hear the explosion of bombs somewhere in the vicinity of Owi Island. Then all is quiet. I return to my tent and lie down on my bunk. In another quarter hour an antiaircraft gun fires a single shot; the siren blows once; the camp lights go on; and the normal life of evening is resumed.

Wednesday, July 26

After supper Major McGuire and I drove to the base of a nearby cliff where one of the Japanese caves is located—a large opening about two-thirds of the way up the cliff, with shell marks in the coral all around it. We climbed up a steep trail past a Jap supply dump, dozens of shells, and what was apparently the hose from an American flame thrower. All trees in the vicinity were splintered and denuded of branches. At the mouth of the cave were several battered Japanese machine guns, cases of ammunition, and scraps of clothing. Just inside of the entrance, we came on the body of a Jap soldier, bound and roped [to a post] in an upright position.

The main portion of the cave contained boxes and bags of food, mud-covered articles of clothing, a huge supply of ammunition for both cannon and machine guns, and platforms and huts similar to the west caves. There were several side passages, in which more ammunition was stacked. When we were about twenty-five yards inside the entrance, I could see the reflection of daylight at the opposite end. However, the sun had already set and we were half a mile from the nearest American troops, with none at all between us and Japanese-occupied territory. Since there were only two of us, armed with pistols, we felt it advisable to postpone further exploration, and returned to camp.

Thursday, July 27

Up at 5:30. To the strip and off on the Halmahera strike at 0745, with the 433rd Squadron. We fly above an overcast along the north New Guinea coast to the rendezvous point at the Ajoe Islands. We arrived four or five minutes before the strafers and were circling when they arrived. Took up a direct course for Cape Lelai in the Halmaheras—about forty twin-engine B-25's, escorted by several squadrons of P-38 fighters.

Intelligence reports the Halmahera Japanese strength to be in the vicinity of 150 planes, of which between seventy-five and one hundred are single- and twin-engine fighters. Uncertainty exists as to whether enemy air strength in the Halmaheras has been increased or decreased during the last several days. There are reports of new fighter squadrons coming in, and others of fighter squadrons being sent from the Halmaheras to Ceram and Palau.

Weather begins to clear as we approach the islands. We fly close to the water to avoid radar detection as long as possible. The coast rises slowly above the horizon, purple and hazy in the distance. We pass the cape, cross the bay, and fly low over the mountain pass to the Japanese base at Galela. High cover climbs as we reach the coast. We enter string formation and weave back and forth over the strafers.

We flash over the strip at about 1,000 feet through moderate and fairly accurate ack-ack fire. We see a number of Jap planes in the revetments below us, most of them apparently in flyable condition. There is no sign of an enemy plane moving on the strip or in the air. The parafrags from the strafers began bursting all over the area. An oil fire is started on the edge of the runway—from what, I cannot see. (There is an active volcano near the strip, covering the area around it with a dense cloud of dust.) We turn inland, circle, fly back across the strip and along one side of it. The first wave of strafers has gone, so the antiaircraft fire concentrates on us. Still, we see no enemy aircraft.

We catch up with the strafers over the bay and continue giving them cover. There is a medium-sized freighter and several barges down below, all churning madly toward the nearest shore or harbor. But our mission is to cover the strafers; we cannot go after them. Cut down our r.p.m. and air speed, and begin our cruise back toward home. A heavy storm covered the strips at Biak and Owi islands when we arrived. After trying unsuccessfully to get underneath, we turned back and landed on the newly completed Kamiri strip on Noemfoor Island at 1445.

Reports are still a little vague, but apparently several enemy planes were found and shot down. One of our own P-38's had engine trouble and landed in the water. The pilot was rescued by the Catalina flying boat sent along for the purpose. We took off from Noemfoor at 1625 and landed on Mokmer drome at 1655.

Friday, July 28

Up at 5:30. Breakfast with pilots, and to the strip at dawn. Off at 0740, flying Blue 3. Squalls and high cumuli begin building up as we parallel the north New Guinea coast. We keep climbing. I put on my oxygen mask at 15,000 feet. Major [Warren] Lewis starts down through a hole in the clouds with Red Flight. Colonel MacDonald continues climbing with Blue. We reach 18,000 feet. Long discussion between fighters, rescue planes, and strafers about whether to turn back or try to make the target. Reconnaissance plane ahead reports weather fairly good in vicinity of target. We decide to go on.

We pass over the Pisang Islands, our point of rendezvous. Weather improves constantly but still large areas of overcast covering the sea and Ceram Island. We pass over the Boela strips without any sign of ack-ack fire or air interception, although the Japs reportedly have fairly strong fighter forces in the area. The interior of Ceram is covered with a solid cloud layer. We fly above it at 10,000 feet. Twenty miles or so on our right two high peaks project through the clouds. On each side strings of fighters, sleek and powerful, bore their way to the target—the Japanese airstrips on the south coast of Ceram.

The clouds break as we approach the strips. We push our air speed up to 250 miles an hour indicated; there may be enemy fighters out of sight above us. We fall into string formation and weave over the strip at Amahai. No sign of enemy aircraft, even on the ground. We are too high to see what the revetments on the dispersal taxiways hold, but the strip itself is clear. We cross Elpaputih Bay. The airstrips on its west coast are clear also. We turn southwest to Haroekoe Island; no sign of Japanese activity in the air; none at Haroekoe strip, nor at Lianga, nor at Ambon. Apparently the enemy has no intention of opposing us by air.

We circle northward and start back toward the east when the radio, which has been filled with mostly idle chatter, suddenly springs to life. "Captive" Squadron of the 8th Fighter Group has made contact with enemy aircraft and gone to the attack. We listen to the messages of the pilots making their passes. Apparently they are in contact with no more than a few enemy planes. We try to get the location, but everyone is too busy to answer or to hear.

"There he is now! Go in and get him."

"Can't somebody shoot him down?"

"God-damn! I'm out of ammunition."

"I'm out of ammunition, too!"

"Somebody get him who's got some ammunition."

"The son of a bitch is making monkeys out of us."

"Who's got some ammunition?"

Another calmer voice breaks in, annoyed at not being able to get the location, and at "Captive" cluttering the air with conversation.

"What's the matter, Captive, having trouble?"

Meanwhile, we have been weaving in and out around the clouds, trying to spot the Captive fighters. We finally locate them over Elpaputih Bay. The air above Amahai strip is black with antiaircraft bursts of the heavy calibers. Down below we see two enemy planes. A P-38 has just completed an unsuccessful attack on one of them.

We jettison our drop tanks, switch on our guns, and nose down to the attack. One Jap plane banks sharply toward the airstrip and the protection of the antiaircraft guns. The second heads off into the haze and clouds. Colonel MacDonald gets a full deflection shot on the first, starts him smoking, and forces him to reverse his bank.

We are spaced 1,000 feet apart. Captain [Danforth] Miller gets in a short deflection burst with no noticeable effect. I start firing as the plane is completing its turn in my direction. I see the tracers and the 20's [20-mm. cannon] find their mark, a hail of shells directly on the target. But he straightens out and flies directly toward me.

I hold the trigger down and my sight on his engine as we approach head on. My tracers and my 20's spatter on his plane. We are close—too close—hurtling at each other at more than 500 miles an hour. I pull back on the controls. His plane zooms suddenly upward with extraordinary sharpness.

I pull back with all the strength I have. Will we hit? His plane, before a slender toy in my sight, looms huge in size. A second passes—two—three—I can see the finning on his engine cylinders. There is a rough jolt of air as he shoots past behind me.

By how much did we miss? Ten feet? Probably less than that. There is no time to consider or feel afraid. I am climbing steeply. I bank to the left. No, that will take me into the ack-ack fire above Amahai strip. I reverse to the right. It all has taken seconds.

My eyes sweep the sky for aircraft. Those are only P-38's and the plane I have just shot down. He is starting down in a wing over—out of control. The nose goes down. The plane turns slightly as it picks up speed—down—down—down toward the sea. A fountain of spray—white foam on the water—waves circling outward as from a stone tossed in a pool—the waves merge into those of the sea—the foam disappears—the surface is as it was before.

My wingman is with me, but I have broken from my flight. There are six P-38's circling the area where the enemy plane went down. But all six planes turn out to be from another squadron. I call "Possum 1," and get a reply which I think says they are above the cloud layer. It is thin, and I climb up through on instruments. But there are no planes in sight, and I have lost my wingman. I dive back down but all planes below have disappeared, too. Radio reception is so poor that I can get no further contact. I climb back into the clouds and take up course for home, cutting through the tops and keeping a sharp lookout for enemy planes above. Finally make radio contact with "Possum" flight and tell them I will join them over our original rendezvous point (the Pisang Islands).

The heavies are bombing as I sight the Boela strips; I turn in that direction to get a better view. They have started a large fire in the oil-well area of Boela—a great column of black smoke rising higher and higher in the air. The bombers are out of range, so the ack-ack concentrates on me—black puffs of smoke all around, but none nearby. I weave out of range and take up course for the Pisang Islands again. I arrive about five minutes ahead of my flight. We join and take up course for Biak Island. Landed at Mokmer strip at 1555.

(Lieutenant Miller, my wingman, reported seeing the tracers of the Jap plane shooting at me. I was so concentrated on my own firing that I did not see the flashes of his guns. Miller said the plane rolled over out of control right after he passed me. Apparently my bullets had either severed the controls or killed the pilot.)

Saturday, July 29

Another air raid this evening, an hour or two after dark. Sky clear except for a thin cloud layer in places, and the moon approaching full. There is exceptionally heavy ack-ack fire in the vicinity of Mokmer strip and Owi Island—both heavy and small-caliber—and the dull boom of bursting bombs rolls clearly in.

Tuesday, August 1

Up half an hour before dawn. Colonel MacDonald and I cook breakfast and drive to the strip. The weather is bad over Ceram, and the heavy strike is canceled. We check weather in all enemy directions and find it unusually good in the direction of Palau. We decide to run a four-plane fighter sweep over the islands. Latest Intelligence reports place enemy fighter strength at Palau at about 150 planes, so we will have to be cautious in our approach.

We take off Mokmer strip at 0927 and set a direct course for the Jap airstrip of Babelthuap. The plane I have been flying recently is laid up for a fifty-hour check, and I have borrowed a P-38 from the 31st Squadron. As we reach the north coast of Biak Island, I dive down and check the boresighting of my guns on the reef. It is perfect; the bullets splash in the water exactly where I hold the sight. We climb slowly to 8,000 feet and throttle down to maximum cruising efficiency. A front has been reported along our line of flight "lying east and west, one degree north of the equator." Clouds bunch and rise as we approach it, and storm squalls appear ahead. The front is a solid wall of storm—dark-gray streaks of rain extending between clouds and water.

We angle southward and climb up through a hole in the clouds, toward the blue sky above. Channels open up between the cumulus heads. We follow them and pass through the worst of the front within a quarter hour. The clouds continue to break as we fly northward. Colonel MacDonald does an excellent bit of navigation, and we are directly on course when we sight the southern island at 12:05. We climb to 15,000 feet, and parallel the southeast coast about five miles offshore. Half of the sky is covered with bunched cumulus cloud masses, but there is an opening through which Babelthuap strip appears. From our altitude and distance we can see no enemy air activity.

North of Babelthuap we angle inland and cross to the west side of the islands, weaving in and out between clouds. We push our air speed up to 250 miles an hour and keep a sharp lookout for enemy aircraft. After rounding the northern tip of the main island, we turn south along the west coast, dropping down to the deck to search for low-flying enemy aircraft. We cross the lagoon in the center of the island about fifty feet above the water, skipping over the top of a medium-sized sailing yacht to the obvious amazement and concern of its occupants. Off the east coast we find a Japanese patrol ship of probably 300-400 tons steaming north. We strafe as we pass. I see the shattered cabin as I pull up—not fifty feet below me. I look back over my shoulder. The ship is circling to the left, apparently out of control, with a thickening column of smoke rising skyward.

We continue south, paralleling the coral reef. There is another ship ahead. MacDonald banks toward it. We will strafe again—no, he banks left—the drop tanks tumble off both first-element planes—they nose down and streak forward. Then they have sighted the enemy! I press my drop-tank release—feel them bump against the wing as they slip off the racks. Mixture auto rich—r.p.m. 2,600—forty-five inches manifold pressure. I brighten the gun sight, throw on the combat switch, and search the sky ahead for enemy planes. There is only one in sight—a seaplane ahead to our right, low over the water.

We circle right, string formation. I spot a second seaplane to our left, but we must hold formation. The enemy strength at Palau is too high to take a chance—150 fighters. MacDonald slips in behind the seaplane. It banks frantically left—straightens out—the P-38 is in position—a streak of tracers—a sheet of flame trails out behind the enemy—his plane becomes a comet of fire—rolls over—crashes into the sea—the surface of the ocean flames where it has disappeared. It has been only a matter of seconds.

The second seaplane is still is sight. MacDonald and Miller turn back in our direction. I bank left and radio that I am going in for the attack. MacDonald replies that he will follow. I am in position for the dive. The enemy is banking left. I nose down—in five more seconds . . . There is another plane turning in from the left—it is a landplane—fast—an enemy fighter. I give up the seaplane and bank into it—still too far off—but I give it a burst—in a second now—but it has twin booms—it is a P-38! It's Smith! But he's supposed to be on my wing guarding my tail—he was on my wing a moment ago. Thank God it was a long shot—that I didn't hit him.

The temptation was too much. He just couldn't resist slipping ahead to get that float plane. He must have turned off while I was still following MacDonald; otherwise he couldn't have come in from that direction. I watch him close in on the float plane. Streaks through the air from his tracers. The Jap pilot noses down and flies his plane into the water, apparently attempting to land. A white splash from his pontoon. He bounces fifty feet into the air. Smith is closer. Another streak of tracers. The enemy plane bursts into flames and crashes into the sea.

MacDonald radios that he is attacking again. I turn back in time to see him pulling up behind another enemy plane. He is firing. The plane bursts into flames—dives down toward the sea—a parachute—one of the crew has jumped. We are close to the airstrip. No telling how many fighters have taken off, and we are in a bad position to be attacked—far too low for safety. We bank left toward the open sea. MacDonald and Miller are a mile ahead of us, also headed out to sea.

I glance up into the mirror. An enemy fighter is above us, at six o'clock, diving on us. I give the alarm. MacDonald and Miller turn back. The Zero is swinging around onto Smith's tail. I turn back. Smith is heading for a cloud. The Zero shifts his attack to me. I have turned too soon. He is too far above for me to climb into him. I would be in a stall by the time I reached his altitude, and that is fatal with a Zero.

I bank right to give MacDonald and Miller a better chance to cut in toward me. I push the r.p.m. full forward and the throttles to the fire wall. The propellers surge up past 3,000. The manifold reaches sixty inches. But he has altitude advantage. He is closing in on my tail—almost within gun range now.

I am not high enough to dive. It is useless to try to outturn a Zero. I must depend on speed and armor plate and the other members of my flight. I nose down a little and keep on turning to avoid giving him a no-deflection shot. He must have his guns on me now—in perfect position on my tail.

I hunch down in front of the armor plate and wait for the bullets to hit. I think of Anne—of the children. My body is braced and tense. There is an eternity of time. The world was never clearer. But there is no sputtering of an engine, no fragments flying off a wing, no shattering of glass on the instrument board in front of me.

The Zero is climbing away. MacDonald has forced him off with a long deflection shot. Smith gets in a second burst as he flashes past. Miller comes in on one wing and starts the Zero smoking. We last see it zooming skyward toward the nearest cloud.

We turn eastward to re-form our flight. There is another fighter above us. But he does not see us. He is apparently coming in from patrol. We are getting short of fuel. At any moment an entire Zero squadron may come

swooping down. We start a high-speed climb and keep on heading eastward.

We are out of sight of the islands, flying in between the clouds. We
turn south, throttle down, and take up the course for home. I look over
my plane. There are no holes in sight. The engine readings are all
normal. As far as we can see, none of us has been hit.

We land on Mokmer strip at 1600.

A phone call from Fighter Command, Owi Island, comes this evening
—Colonel Morrissey calling Colonel MacDonald. Apparently news of
our Palau mission has caused considerable stir and not been at all well
received by Fighter Command. It seems that the bombers have been requesting fighter cover on their Palau raids for some time past and that
they have been turned down by Fighter Command on the grounds that
the distance was too great and the weather too bad. Since our flight somewhat refutes this claim, Fighter Command feels that it has placed them
in an embarrassing position, which they do not at all appreciate.

General Wurtsmith has ordered Colonel MacDonald to report to
Fighter Command headquarters tomorrow morning. I am fully as much
to blame for the flight as he; but unfortunately he must carry the responsibility, as he commands the group. I may be able to do something to
straighten the matter out later on. Knowing General Wurtsmith, I am not
much worried about the eventual outcome.

Wednesday, August 2

Another air raid over Owi Island last night—sky full of small-caliber
tracers and heavy ack-ack bursts. Apparently some damage was done.
Spent day writing and with officers. Colonel MacDonald back this evening—reprimanded but not grounded or fined. I am inclined to think that
after his first flash of anger General Wurtsmith was rather pleased with
the flight to Palau.

Thursday, August 3

Phone call from Morrissey, Fighter Command, this morning. He first tells
MacDonald that he has been grounded for sixty days; then tells him that
he has been given leave for a two-month trip to the United States to see
his family. (MacDonald has never seen his baby son.) Much rejoicing.

[Major Meryl] Smith will take temporary command of the group. Mac-Donald will leave almost immediately.

Friday, August 4

Allied advance in Normandy continues.

Another red alert last night. The Japs are making full use of the moon but fortunately haven't much equipment to do it with. We are up at 5:45, cook breakfast, and start for the strip. MacDonald leaves for Nadzab this morning. I am flying Blue 3 on a strike on Liang airstrip, Amboina Island. Off the strip at 0917 with the 431st Squadron. Captain [William] O'Brien leading Red Flight; Major Smith leading Blue Flight; Lieutenant [James] Barnes, Smith's wingman; Lieutenant [Horace] Reeves my wingman. About one hundred miles out, Smith and Barnes turn back. I radio Smith, asking if the flight is returning to base and get a "Roger." I turn back with my wingman to join them. Then one plane turns back on course. No radio contact. I circle, then fly back to check the numbers on the two returning planes. Neither is Smith's. He has apparently changed his mind and gone on with the mission. Two planes are enough to get home in safety. I turn back on course.

All planes are out of sight ahead. I set my engines for maximum auto lean cruise and take up course for the Pisang Islands, our rendezvous point with the bombers. I catch up with the fighters about halfway between the Pisang Islands and Ceram. But I am unable to locate the 431st Squadron. As we approach the target I tack on to a three-plane flight as No. 4, approaching cautiously so they will know I am not an enemy fighter.

The sky is almost completely overcast in the target area—stratus and high-bunched cumulus clouds. Suddenly, a phosphorus bomb explodes ahead—white streamers shooting out and falling down in graceful arcs. At almost the same moment I see two enemy planes on our right, climbing rapidly and silhouetted against the side of a great pillar of cloud. I give the alarm.

We jettison tanks, and the attack begins. The enemy planes dive for cloud cover. At least a dozen P-38's are after them. There is a general milling about. We are over a mile away from the fight, diving toward it. Suddenly, there is a great flame in the sky. Out of the corner of my eye, I think I have seen two planes collide head on—two P-38's? One of our planes crashing with the enemy? The flame dies out, leaving a cloud of thin black smoke in its place. Small fragments are falling earthward; not one of them as big as a tail surface. The faster falling dots must be the engines.

A flash of fire—two lives wiped out. We fly on to catch the bombers. There is nothing else we can do. They are unable to drop on their primary target—sky completely overcast. They turn east toward the secondary target. We follow them, weaving back and forth overhead. There is no more interception. Down below, close to the water, I see a single P-38 headed homeward. He has lost one engine—I hear his radio conversation back and forth with his flight. But why is he alone? Why are no other fighters down there guarding him?

We fly with the bombers for a few more miles. Then one of the squadron leaders radios that his flight is getting short of gas and must leave. (They have been cruising their engines too fast.) The bomber leader thanks him and says good-by. Then all fighters take the homeward course. I have plenty of fuel and drop down through the clouds to look for the crippled plane. But it is hazy, and I cannot find him. I climb back up and start for home. I land at Mokmer strip at 1512.

The crippled plane is trying to land as I park my plane. I throttled down so far that he came in ahead of me. He is having landing-gear trouble—can't get one of his wheels down. He is circling for his third attempt to land. The tower has the strip clear for him. This time the wheels are down. He gets down all right and pulls over to the side of the runway while he still has speed. (A P-38 won't taxi on one engine.) Major Smith and I drive over to meet him. There is a jagged hole through the spinner cap of his left engine. Since there was no ack-ack, he was apparently hit by a fragment of the phosphorus bomb. He said he was fairly near to the explosion.

We drive to the 431st Squadron's ready tent. A group of pilots and mechanics are standing outside, sweeping the horizon with their eyes and field glasses. All planes are now accounted for except Captain O'Brien's. Several other pilots saw the explosion above Piroe Bay. All are under the impression that two planes ran together, but none sure. Finally, two pilots come over from the 9th. They saw the actual collision and are able to give details. Captain O'Brien was diving on a Zero. The enemy plane looped, and while it was upside down on top of the loop, the two planes crashed head on.

Both pilots say they looked back after passing the scene of the explosion, and saw a parachute, probably 2,500 feet below. It seems impossible that anyone could have lived through either the crash or the explosion. But such miracles have happened before. Was O'Brien or the Jap pilot blown clear and left sufficiently conscious and uninjured to pull their rip cord after falling 2,000 feet or so? Or was the parachute from another Jap fighter that was shot down in the same vicinity a minute or two before?

I drive out to the new campsite with Major Smith for supper and to pack my belongings. I am moving back to the old camp at the east end of Mokmer strip. With Colonel MacDonald gone, it will be easier to get to the squadron ready tents from there for early-morning take-offs. My new quarters will be with Major McGuire—C.O. of the 431st Squadron.

Gave a talk to the 9th Squadron later in the evening on long-range and fuel economy.

We plan a search mission to Ceram to look for O'Brien tomorrow.

Saturday, August 5

Another air raid last night, or rather in the early hours of the morning. The siren began screaming the red alert. I dressed, lay down on my bunk, and went back to sleep. I was awakened by loud and rapid explosions. The first thing that entered my mind was that the Japs had dropped a string of "daisy cutters" [20] along the Mokmer strip (such as the fragmentation bombs that killed several men at Owi Island the other night). I was through the mosquito net and flat on the ground in an instant, not even bothering to throw my blanket off. Major McGuire was only a few seconds behind me. I could feel the detonation waves in my chest and body. But it was only the firing of a nearby 90-mm. antiaircraft gun.

We got up and walked outside the tent. The sky is full of flashes and the red balls of tracers. Streams of tracers are going up from the west end of the strip like hoses of fire. One of the searchlights has found the enemy plane. It is a dive bomber, coming down on the revetment area. The streams of tracers converge. The heavy-caliber bursts follow a quarter mile behind the plane. Flashes from the bombs. He gets away. The firing stops. We go back to bed. In ten minutes the "all clear" sounds.

Off the strip at 0935 to search for Captain O'Brien. Major McGuire is leading the squadron. I am leading White Flight. We climb slowly and

20. Fragmentation bombs set to explode close to, but above, ground level.

throttle down to 1,600 to conserve fuel. We set our course for the north coast of Ceram, giving Ambon a wide berth to avoid alerting the enemy. We are ten planes in all. Six of us will sweep the area for signs of a signal from O'Brien. Four will stay at 5,000 feet to cover us against enemy attack. A flying boat with fighter cover will be at Seleman Bay in case we should find O'Brien on the water.

We arrive at Seleman Bay at 11:30. A number of B-25 strafers are flying east along the coast, leaving smoke and fires behind them. They have hit a fuel dump on a small island off Cape Namaa. A column of smoke rises 5,000 feet into the air. The clouds build up over the west end of Ceram and Piroe Bay—a front, with heavy storms. We try to get over, around, under, unsuccessfully. We have to turn back. There is no sign of enemy interception. We strafe shipping along the coast as we fly eastward. Land on Mokmer strip at 1519.

Sunday, August 6

Overcast skies, and no air raid last night. Up at 6:00. Breakfast with the pilots at squadron mess hall. Then to the 432nd ready tent. The take-off is postponed for a half hour because of weather. I take my equipment out to the ship I am to fly and get it ready. Then back to the alert tent to wait. Several pilots are lounging about on rickety chairs, benches, and boxes. The coral humps still protrude through the dirt floor—no attempt has been made to smooth it off. Conversation is mostly about leave in Australia—Sydney and its liquor and women. In the center of the tent is a bulletin board with notices and Intelligence maps spread across it. At the far end is a blackboard with lists of pilots available, ships in commission, flight orders, etc. At the bottom of the blackboard, a naked reclining girl has been outlined in chalk. At the top, a shining, white Japanese skull is hung.

The missions are canceled completely. I return to my tent and spend the rest of the morning writing. Lunch in mess hall with pilots. Afternoon writing and with officers. Evening with Major McGuire.

Monday, August 7

United States troops take Rennes. Rocket-plane bombing of London continues.

Another red alert last night. Lasted only five minutes. Possibly just a friendly plane with its IFF turned off.

Up an hour before dawn. Breakfast, and to the 431st Squadron ready tent. Off the strip at 0854. I am leading White Flight of the 431st Squadron. Our mission is to cover the B-25 strafers on a shipping strike on the Halmaheras. But we are turned back by a tropical front and heavy storms. Land on Mokmer strip at 10:15.

Early lunch. Letter to Anne in afternoon. Early supper; then organized a small fishing expedition—two one-man rubber rafts and several officers. Got 187 fish from one charge of TNT—about fifty pounds in all. Divided them among group officers and cooked them this evening as they will not keep overnight in this climate without refrigeration.

Wednesday, August 9

Up at 5:30. Breakfast with pilots, and to 433rd alert hut at 7:00. Off the strip at 0847. Major Lewis is leading the squadron. I am leading White Flight. We are covering the 90th Bomb Group on a strike on the Japanese airstrip of Haroekoe, Haroekoe Island, south of Ceram. We rendezvous with the bombers over the Pisang Islands at 10:18 and fly above a solid cloud layer to the target. The clouds break slightly in the vicinity of Haroekoe Island, but not enough to permit the heavies to drop their bombs. They turn back to the oil fields (their secondary target).

Our squadron divides. Eight fighters—Possum Blue and Green—accompany the bombers to guard against the improbability of a Jap air attack. Eight fighters—Possum Red and White—drop down through the overcast to scout the ground below for enemy aircraft and surface activity. We spiral down through a hole in the clouds in combat loose formation. We find ourselves over Piroe Bay, just off the north coast of Amboina Island. At close intervals along the shore are large fish nets, one of the important sources of enemy food supply. We cut southward through a pass in the mountains to Amboina and the Japanese airstrip.

We break out over the strip and bay suddenly and are surrounded by antiaircraft bursts almost at once—the air dotted by the deadly black puffs. We start weaving and changing altitude, and the Japs are unable to calculate our position far enough ahead to fire with precision. But they fill the air in front of us and force us to fly through the bursts, hoping that by chance a fighter will collide with one of them. (I think of an old lesson in molecular physics; so many molecules of one gas in a container with so many molecules of another, each hurtling erratically at tremendous speed through space. The molecules are of such and such a size; there is so much space around them; what are the probabilities of collision? Eight P-38's, weaving erratically at 300 miles an hour. A hundred cannon projectiles bursting into fragments in a rectangular block of air a half mile long, a half mile wide, and 1,000 feet in depth. We must fly for fifteen seconds before we are out of range. What are the probabilities of collision?) But our ships are seldom hit by ack-ack; why, I do not understand.

We check on the shipping in the harbor (twenty or thirty boats of varying sizes), on enemy air activity (there is none is sight), on planes in the revetments (a dozen or two twin-engine bombers in plain sight)—and constantly new ack-ack bursts to distract attention. The small-caliber guns must be firing on us, too, for we are well within their range, but we see no tracers. Possibly they are using none here, as at Rabaul.

We are out of range. The ack-ack stops. We re-form and swing northward across the mountains, back over Piroe Bay. We drop down to 1,000 feet above the water and turn east along the coast. Apparently the Japs have no intention of intercepting us, but we keep our eyes peeled for black dots against the clouds.

As we come within sight of Liang strip, we see a large sailing ship in the center of Haroekoe Strait. At almost the same instant there is a string of splashes in the water, starting from Liang strip and pointing a half mile out toward sea in our direction. Some new type of Jap antiaircraft gun? Just trying to scare us off? No; there are explosions in the revetment area; some of our bombers have found an opening in the clouds, and one of them has missed the land entirely. We form a strafing circle and come in to attack the ship. Lewis is already diving down on the target.

A ship with sails full set heeled over gracefully on the sea; a patch of clear blue sky above; freshening rain squalls in the distance. Mottling of sunlight. Rippling of wind. The jeweled setting of tropical land and sea. Those eternal seconds of stabbing clarity between life, peace, beauty, and the certainty of death. Spouts of foam rise up from the water. Splinters fly off the deck. A cloud of smoke veils the ship. Flashes mark where the 20-millimeters burst. Red 1 has made his pass and Red 2 is now in range.

The ship is wounded. The straight wake bends. The sails begin to flutter. There is no one there to steer or trim. The ship is the center of another cloud of smoke. The wind haphazardly catches the sails, and it heels to the right again. It takes on the personality of a living, dying thing, as though it were made of flesh and blood instead of cloth and wood. It seems to be writhing in its agony like a wounded animal still trying to escape.

Red 2 has finished his pass and is firing on a barge a mile or two ahead. Red 3 and 4 come in. My flight will follow them in attack. There can be nothing left alive on deck. The ship is filled with dead and wounded men. Those who jumped overboard are swimming in the water a quarter mile behind. Probably a few of the crew are still unhit, crouching behind cargo and bulkheads in the hold.

Red 4 is on his pull-up. I am nosing down. I glance in the mirror. White 2, 3, and 4 are in the circle behind me. I sweep the sky a last time for enemy aircraft. One thousand yards; 250 miles an hour. I lift the sight ten millimeters above the target and fire a sighting burst. The 20-millimeters flash on the hull just above the water line. Six hundred yards. I hold the sight on the center of the deck and clamp the trigger down. Flashes of the cannon bursts. Long streaks of tracers. Red balls of fire ricocheting off the hull. Bits of debris flying up into the air. All covered with a haze of smoke.

Time to pull up. I stop firing. Skim over the target. Littered decks; shattered portholes; a fallen sail. Like a derelict abandoned in a storm. Lewis continues circling with Red Flight. There is a lugger heading for the farther shore. I follow with White Flight. All eight fighters strafe it. Red Flight banks left. I continue on with White Flight to strafe a camouflaged barge churning madly toward the shore. We bank sharply left to re-form with Red Flight. I look back over my shoulder. The barge and lugger are circling out of control.

We look once again for enemy aircraft; then climb up through the cloud layer into the tranquil beauty of the upper sky. Here all is peaceful —no sign of conflict—only the graceful lines of the fighters boring through the crystal sky. The rolling white cloud layer has drawn together like a stage curtain. What happened underneath it now seems like a dream. We cannot fully realize how close we ourselves have brushed to death, that our guns have left ships sinking, on fire, with men dead and terribly wounded on their decks, with others drowning in the water, with rescue boats not daring to set out from shore. We throttle down our engines and take up our course for home, nearly 500 miles over enemy territory; but we feel as safe as though we were already there. A few years ago, in peacetime, such a flight would have been considered hazardous. Now, in war, we think nothing of it at all. We cross the sea, and the northwest neck of New Guinea, and land on Mokmer strip at 1427.

Supper with officers—new potatoes from Australia. I never realized how good they could taste.

Friday, August 11

No flying today; all but the patrol planes are laid up for inspection. It is overcast and raining anyway when we wake. We organize a dynamite-fishing expedition for the high tide of the morning—several of the pilots and myself. Very few fish with the first two charges, and most of them in deep water. I bring up several from over thirty feet. The third charge is a dud. Then I find a coral sand pocket in the reef with bottom at just the right depth for diving. It is fairly well filled with fish.

I toss in a charge, but just as the fuse lights, my rubber raft turns sidewise and I dislocate my shoulder as I throw—the shoulder I injured at St. Louis years ago, when I jumped from a spinning plane and had to collapse my parachute close to the ground to keep from drifting into high-tension wires. I tell two of the pilots to stay and get the fish. A third pulls me in to shore in the second raft. I try to set my shoulder over the back of a chair, as I have done twice before, but it is twelve or thirteen years since the last time, and I can't seem to do it again. One of the officers drives me to the hospital in his jeep, and the surgeon very skillfully pulls it into place.

We drive back to get the rest of our party and the fish—about thirty pounds in all. We give the small and brightly colored ones to the natives, who seem glad to take any kind of fish we catch, and take a good mess of fairly large ones back to camp. We are hours late for lunch, so we cook our fish in mess kits and eat them with coffee, bread, and tropical butter.

Evening writing and with officers. We talk of many subjects: of the war, Jap aviation, Australian women in Sydney, prisoners of war, atrocities on both sides. We speculate on where and when the Japs will set up strong opposition again, on why they have bombers in the revetments on Ambon strip unless they intend to use them on night raids against us. We discuss the promiscuousness of "Aussie" women and compare conditions there to those at home. Some officers are of the opinion that morals in Australia have always been relatively low. Others say it is due to the war and that conditions are now just as bad—or good—at home. A major says that American soldiers never meet the higher type of Australian girl because our men have carried on in such a manner that to be seen with an American uniform in Sydney practically identifies a girl as a whore.

Several days ago I saw a band of nineteen Japanese prisoners brought in by Biak natives in their war canoes. One—a young boy, proud, erect, and in good physical condition—was said to be an officer. Most had unintelligent faces. Several appeared to be reasonably well fed and in good health. Several were covered with sores, dejected, and limping. Two looked as though they were ready to die from starvation—limbs hardly larger than the bones beneath—and had to be half carried by the natives since they could not stand upright by themselves. These, I realized, were the same men who had lived and fought in the damp and stinking caves in the coral and whose companions' bodies now lie rotting where they fell. Our troops gather around them curiously while they are jammed into the truck with natives all around them armed with rifles.

Sitting on boxes and the edge of bunks in the rather poorly lighted tent, we discuss the question of Japanese prisoners. I said I felt it was a mistake not to accept surrender whenever it could be obtained; that by doing so, our advance would be more rapid and many American lives would be saved. If the Japanese think they will be killed anyway when they surrender, they, naturally, are going to hold on and fight to the last—and kill American troops they capture whenever they get the chance. Most of the officers agree (not very enthusiastically) but say that our infantry [doesn't] look on it that way.

"Take the 41st, for example; they just don't take prisoners. The men boast about it."

"The officers wanted some prisoners to question but couldn't get any until they offered two weeks' leave in Sydney for each one turned in. Then they got more than they could handle."

"But when they cut out giving leave, the prisoners stopped coming in. The boys just said they couldn't catch any."

"The Aussies are still worse. You remember the time they had to take those prisoners south by plane? One of the pilots told me they just pushed them out over the mountains and reported that the Japs committed hara-kiri on the way."

"Well, you remember when our troops captured that Jap hospital? There wasn't anyone alive in it when they got through."

"The Nips did it to us, though."

"You can't blame the Aussies too much. They found some of their men castrated; and they found some with steaks cut out of them."

"They captured one place where the Japs were actually cooking the meat." (Only yesterday a notice was posted on the squadron bulletin board telling where several Japs had been captured on Biak while they were cooking the flesh of one of their own people.)

The fact is fairly well established that little mercy is shown and numerous atrocities committed by our troops during the early stages of a campaign. Later, as positions are well established, some Japanese troops find it possible to surrender without being killed in the act. But barbaric as our men are at times, the Orientals appear to be worse.

Saturday, August 12

Another air raid last night in spite of the waning moon, lasting from about 0330 until almost daybreak. The sirens and shots sounding the red alert gave us about ten minutes' warning. The bombing was directed entirely at Owi Island, although some of the enemy planes came within range of our antiaircraft guns here on Biak. I stood outside my tent watching the sky. The night was clear, the stars bright; every light on earth was out. Several falling stars streaked through the upper atmosphere, leaving a white vapor trail behind them.

At first, there was no sign or sound of war. Then, the unsynchronized droning of engines—the Japanese bombers. Soon the sky is filled with the streaming red balls of the 37-millimeters and the brilliant flashes of the heavy guns. The droning comes closer. The streams of tracers converge over Owi Island. There is the boom of bombs exploding. The sky over the island becomes red. A column of black smoke rises. Flames jump above the trees. It is a gasoline fire. Planes? A fuel dump? The ack-ack stops. The bombers are out of range.

Minutes pass; but they do not go away; we can still hear their engines in the distance. More ack-ack. Again the boom of bombs. The noise of the engines recedes. The firing ceases. Then a streak of red tracers from another angle through the sky, apparently originating from black space —one of our night fighters has made contact. There is the scream of a plane in a dive; a flame miles away on the water; some pilot's plane has crashed. There is a long period of silence.

We go back to bed. Almost immediately, the shooting starts again. We get up and stand near the slit trenches, and go back to bed and get up again. The Japs have no intention of letting us sleep. They stay until the nearness of daylight forces them away.

The day's mission is postponed for two hours because of the bombing at Owi Island. We catch up a little on our sleep. To the strip and off at 0934 with the 433rd Squadron, to cover the heavies on a strike on Amboina Island. But the target is covered with clouds again—a solid layer extending as far as we can see. We turn back toward the Jap base at Babo—our secondary target. My left engine becomes suddenly rough a few miles off the northeast coast of Ceram. I throttle it down, but within five minutes the coolant temperature has hit the peg. I feather the propeller and cut the switch. The generator is on the left engine, so I must turn all unessential electrical apparatus off.

I try to get radio contact with the other members of my flight, but someone has his microphone button down, and B channel is jammed. I rock my wings and shift to A. The other fighters shift also. I report the engine out and otherwise O.K. My wingman will stay with me. The rest of the flight circles and goes on. I climb up and fly formation with the bombers. Have to throttle down to stay with them, even with one engine out—cruising at 155 m.p.h. indicated. After we reach McCluer Gulf, the B-24's angle southward toward Babo. My wingman and I continue on course for Biak. I buzz the strip, get a green light, start up the dead engine as I circle the field (in case someone cuts me off), and land at 1605.

I begin to lay plans for starting back toward home. There is no sign of increasing Japanese resistance in the Halmaheras or Ceram. From now on each flight will probably become duller until the Philippines are reached, and I cannot stay out here long enough for that. We would like to take another four-ship mission to Palau, but the generals will not even consider it. I think I will go to Owi Island tomorrow, and probably on eastward from there.

Sunday, August 13

Major Smith came over to our tent to tell me that General Kenney landed at Biak yesterday and left orders that I am to do no more combat flying! Well, I am about to start home anyway, so this time it won't matter so much. I begin packing and saying good-by to the various officers. Someone comes to the tent to report a column of smoke from the strip. We step outside. The column has already reached 1,000 feet or more—black, oily smoke. No doubt about it; a plane is burning. Someone has crashed. I finish packing and we drive to the strip.

We pass a recently crashed C-47 at one end. On the other side of the strip is the wreckage of a B-24 which crashed a few days ago and has not yet been hauled away to the "graveyard." Midway along the strip, and a little off one side, we see the twin booms of a P-38, still burning. The pilot's nacelle has melted down completely. An ambulance and the flight surgeon are standing alongside. The pilot has been taken to the hospital —"rather badly burned; but he'll come through all right if he didn't inhale flames." A tire blew on take-off and threw his ship out of control.

I fly over to Owi Island as passenger in one of the L-5's. Joe Foss and Major Carl have flown over from Emirau Island in a Marine B-25. I meet them at the far end of the strip, talking to General Wurtsmith, Colonel Morrissey, and several other Air Force officers. Foss tells me his squadron has been doing considerable dive bombing with the Corsairs and that they have attained very satisfactory accuracy, but that his losses have been fairly high—three planes in three days recently at Rabaul.

Bob Morrissey arrives after lunch and tells me that General Wurtsmith is anxious for me to go over to Noemfoor Island and talk to the 35th Fighter Group (P-47's) about fuel economy. I tell him I will be glad to go and that I can start this afternoon. Morrissey wants to go to Noemfoor also, so we plan on taking a P-61.

Morrissey and I drove to the 8th Bomber Wing to see Colonel Guthrie, who has come up from Nadzab but not yet moved to the new Fighter Command quarters. I argue that I can accomplish much more with the 35th if I can go out on combat missions with them. Guthrie and Morrissey agree, but say that General Kenney's orders were very definite and that he also grounded both of them from combat flying. General Kenney is not on Owi Island, so there is nothing more to be done at present.

Morrissey and I take off in the P-61 at 1700. We land on Noemfoor at 1730. Colonel [Edwin A.] Doss, C.O. of the 35th Group, sends a jeep to take me to his quarters—a tent in a recently made clearing—a coral floor on top of the red mud soil. Supper with Colonel Doss. Evening discussing fuel economy with him and some of his officers. I work out a long-range chart for the P-47.

Monday, August 14

Breakfast, and to the strip with Colonel Doss, to look over the P-47's and the newly constructed revetments. Two night fighters collided on the strip last night—one landing, one taxiing. The wing of one cut off the cockpit of the other and decapitated the pilot. Both ships badly damaged. We watch a number of P-47's take off and then drive back to camp.

Afternoon spent talking to officers and writing. I inquire about the fighting which is still going on on Noemfoor. There are several pockets of Japanese left, one of them about two and a half miles from the camp. I suggest the possibility of going over to visit the infantry in that location but meet with no enthusiasm in response. The officers tell me that some of the Fighter Control personnel go out on patrols of their own quite regularly and that they have killed a number of "Nips." They have a half-breed Cherokee Indian in their organization who leads them. "They often bring back the thigh bones from the Japs they kill and make pen holders and paper knives and such things out of them." All of the group officers here are bemoaning the fact that there is no Japanese air resistance within range of their P-47's.

Conference and discussion of fuel economy with group officers in the evening.

Tuesday, August 15

To the strip and off at 0901 in a C-45. Co-piloted to Owi, landing at 0940. Colonel Doss came with me. Men were at work on the side of the strip removing a crashed B-24 as we rolled by. Parked plane in transient area and drove to 5th Bomber Wing headquarters. Then to Fighter Command with Colonel Russell in his jeep. He tells me the value of a bottle of gin on the way: "More effective than the signatures of all the stars [generals] on the island. We couldn't get a bulldozer when we needed it—none available for two weeks—but we got one immediately for a bottle of gin. There wasn't a foot of lumber to be had anywhere; but one bottle of gin brought 4,000 feet at once. The same way with cement and some cloth that we needed. It's a disgusting situation, but you can't get anywhere at all on this island without a bottle of gin—and with one you can buy about anything."

Conference with General Wurtsmith in early afternoon. He wants me to talk to the fighter squadrons on Wakde Island and at Saidor about long-range cruising procedures.

Radio Tokyo has inferred that Owi Island is to be subjected to a gas attack. There is a general overhauling of gas masks and other equipment.

To headquarters building in the afternoon to see General Whitehead.

He asks me to stop in Brisbane to see General Kenney before I start my return trip to the States.

Wednesday, August 16

Breakfast at mess hall. To headquarters to see General Whitehead. We go out onto the porch and look out over the water as we talk: old friends; conditions here in the Pacific, at home, in Europe; the trends of the time and indications of the future. At the end of an hour I see a group of officers waiting for a conference already overdue, and say good-by. Whitehead is, I believe, one of the ablest officers our Army has ever produced.

I stop to say good-by to the officers of Bomber Command. Then back to Fighter Command and pack. Morrissey calls to say a P-61 will be waiting to take me to Wakde Island, at 1:00.

Off the strip at 1319. I look back on the islands as we head eastward. The gashes modern man has cut in the jungle—how long will they show? In another ten years will those long coral strips be covered with green again? Will Owi Island be left alone with its typhus? (Even the natives wouldn't live there before we came.) Will some future archaeologist find Jap bones and ammunition in Biak's coral caves? As we rise higher the marks of war seem but pin scratches in the great areas of jungle.

It is hard to realize that hundreds of bombers and fighters are based on those miniature strips, or that several hundred Japanese are still fighting for their country and their lives in the wilder areas of jungle. Will a few of them turn native and survive the war? Will some of them surrender now that our military order is becoming better established and prisoners being accepted again? Will most of them fight to the death, as their fellow soldiers in the caves, and be left in the mire to rot? Here in the lonely beauty of the sky one seems cleansed of the stench and bedlam of war, free of the suffering, the degradation, and the filth of surface armies. Here, even death is clean, like a steel dagger, swift, surrounded by the dignity of clouds and sky.

The coast line angles in ahead of us. Japanese-held territory again. But there is no sign of war below; only jungle, unbroken except for an occasional native garden and its thatch-roofed hut. Streams curve between overhanging vines and branches. Foothills roll up to unnamed mountains. There is a native village built out upon a lake. How little I know this country for all the weeks I have lived in it, for all the thousands of miles I have flown over it. The military areas where I have landed are scorched areas—one just like another. New Guinea's life goes on outside of them. It has drawn back from the war. All the interior of the country, even the coast line away from the military beachheads, is unchanged. While I am here I wish I could walk over the jungle footpaths to some isolated savage village. When I think of New Guinea in the future, I would like to be able to visualize it as it really is and not as it appears to a foreign soldier during war.

We land at Wakde Island at 1419. Then to Major Moore's quarters on the small and almost adjoining island. The major was out swimming somewhere, so, since his tent is only a few feet from the beach, I stripped, and after a half hour's sun bath, I waded out to the edge of the reef and swam along watching the fish. The sea life is slightly different at every island where I have been—the starfish more purple here, and the "sea cucumbers" have different colored spines.

Major Moore was in when I returned. We discussed fuel economy and range in relation to the P-47 fighters of this group. I will talk to the squadrons in the morning.

Fresh milk for supper—just arrived in the "Fat Cat" [21] from Australia —the first I have seen in New Guinea. Conference with flight commanders and squadron officers in regard to fuel range in the evening.

Thursday, August 17

Forty-minute talk on fuel economy and combat radius with each of the squadrons of the 348th Fighter Group. Finished about 1330. Off the strip at 1450 in a borrowed P-47. The usual number of wrecked planes lined the sides of the runway. Light rain, haze, and low ceiling at start of flight, clearing beyond Hollandia. Followed the coast about five miles offshore except where I cut across points of land. (Since I am flying alone, I left word at Wakde that if I were forced down, I would be found about five miles off the coast.) Most of the flight was paralleling Japanese-occupied territory. Ran low-r.p.m. fuel-economy tests during the flight. Landed on Saidor strip at 1756. Late supper in the mess hall with Colonel [Gwen] Atkinson, C.O. of the 58th Fighter Group. Conference with group officers in evening.

21. A plane arriving with fresh food.

Friday, August 18

Allied forces land on south coast of France.

Spent the morning talking to officers and pilots of the 58th Group (three lectures: long-range and fuel economy). One lecture in afternoon. Then out fishing with officers. We trolled along the coast until dusk.

Saturday, August 19

To the strip at 8:00 to take an A-20 (attack bomber) up for an hour's flight. Off the strip in my P-47 at 1321. Landed on Strip 3, Nadzab at 1422. To Fighter Command.

Had planned on going to Brisbane with General Wurtsmith, but he left this morning, so I have arranged to go on one of the DAT C-47's tomorrow. Three letters from Anne.

Sunday, August 20

Up at 5:30. Take-off delayed by weather. Breakfast at Transport Service mess hall. Back to strip and off at 0815 as passenger in a C-47. Have taken charge of fifteen mail sacks as "courier," which means I can't leave them until they are turned over to an authorized courier officer. One is supposed to meet the plane at Townsville.

Solid overcast when we took off. Went on instruments almost immediately and flew a compass course through the valley between the mountains to Lae. Broke out into the clear near Dobodura and flew above the clouds most of the way from there to Townsville. I piloted the plane for an hour and landed it on the Townsville strip at 1319.

Turned the mail over to a courier officer and off again at 1440 with a new crew. Spent most of my time working on my *Spirit of St. Louis* manuscript, sitting on the floor in the crew's compartment. Dusk an hour out of Brisbane. Numerous grass fires burning down below. Landed at Amberley Field at 1850. Turned mail over to courier officer. (I was given a new batch to bring down from Townsville.)

Spent some time clearing Immigration since I had no passport. "Very irregular," but the officer was good-humored and winked through the papers. Stopped for a moment to see the C.O. of the field. Then to Brisbane in a bus full of soldiers, which I had unavoidably kept waiting for the last half hour—but no sign of grumbling on their part. Talked to several of the soldiers on the rather long trip in to Brisbane. It was their first leave in many months. They had been stationed in New Guinea.

Got off the bus at Lennon's Hotel. They found a room for me and arranged for a late supper. Fresh food never tasted better. To post office to send a cable to Anne.

Monday, August 21

General Wurtsmith came to my room for breakfast at 8:15. We discussed the progress of the war and future air activities in this area. To American headquarters later in the morning, to see General Kenney. Talked to him about fighter range and various conditions I encountered with the New Guinea squadrons. Stayed to see a technical film on latest aircraft rocket developments. Lunch with General Kenney in his apartment.

Kenney: "If you got shot down and the Japs caught you, they would hold a public execution!" (In regard to flying combat on civilian status.)

C.A.L.: "They say you get your head chopped off if the Japs catch you, regardless of your status."

Kenney: "It would raise a hell of a hullabaloo back home."

C.A.L.: "You could say I was shot down while flying as observer."

Kenney: "We couldn't get by with that," etc., etc.

Invited Phil La Follette and General Fellers for supper. They want me to take a colonel's commission and come back to the Pacific to serve with MacArthur. I tell them I think best to complete my present work and go back to the States before deciding definitely. There are political complications, and I am hesitant to accept a commission under Roosevelt, even if I could obtain one.

Tuesday, August 22

United States tanks reach Paris.

To local store to get a pair of shoes. My only pair is almost worn out after five months of constant use. Hour's walk through streets of Brisbane in afternoon. Not very attractive. The people seem in many respects to be about midway between the inhabitants of the British Isles and the United States. Speech and features are more British; hospitality more American.

To AMP Building at 6:40 to see General MacArthur. He was in conference when I arrived, so I spent a quarter hour talking to General Sutherland. We talked about using the increase in fighter combat radius which we have attained through the proper engine settings. I told him I thought we could now count on from fifty to one hundred miles more radius than previously with the same fuel for combat and the same landing reserve. That would be equivalent to increasing the range one hundred to two hundred miles—the difference between efficient and inefficient engine settings and at a cost of lowering the cruising speed considerably.

We went over a chart of the Philippines and islands to the south. We discussed the morale of the troops in New Guinea. I mentioned the great differences in the cooking at various squadron mess halls and suggested the possibility of giving some of the cooks better training. A good cook can make even the dehydrated food attractive. A poor cook often ruins fresh food on the infrequent occasions when it is obtainable and makes such a mess of the dehydrated food that it can hardly be eaten at all. We discussed the speed of advance along the New Guinea coast, etc.

General MacArthur was alone when I went in to see him. He asked at once how much range he could count on for the P-38 squadrons. I told him I felt they were ready for a combat radius of 650 miles, that with a little more training, and subject to reasonable weather conditions, the squadrons, leaving out their newest pilots, should be able to undertake combat missions with a radius of 700 miles, and that selected pilots should be able to operate on combat missions of 750-mile radius. I said that on the latter two missions (700 miles for squadrons, 750 miles for experts) my figure was based on the use of low cruising speeds to and from the target and the ability to break off combat immediately when fuel allowed for combat had been used up. Where the danger of enemy interception was high, I said, making it necessary to hold a high air speed, a corresponding reduction in radius would have to be made. (The maximum combat radius on which the P-38 squadrons were sent when I first went to New Guinea was 570 miles.) (All above figures in statute miles.)

MacArthur asked me about our flight to Palau. I told him exactly what had happened and outlined the dangers of the tropical fronts which usually lie between New Guinea and the Palau Islands. I told him that pilots making such a flight should be well experienced in flying through weather. He asked me how many Japanese planes I had shot down. I told him, "One."

"Where was it?"

"Off the south coast of Ceram."

"Good, I'm glad you got one."

MacArthur told me of his trip to Pearl Harbor to see President Roosevelt. He said he asked Roosevelt whether he thought he would defeat Dewey as easily as he defeated Willkie. Roosevelt replied to the effect that Dewey was a nice little man. By his tone and attitude, MacArthur said, he obviously had no fear of Dewey as an opponent. What interested me most was MacArthur's account of Roosevelt's next observation. It was to the effect that he would have no chance whatever of being elected if the war should end before November. MacArthur said he is informed that Barney Baruch[22] has offered $100,000 at three-to-one odds that Roosevelt will be re-elected.

MacArthur stated that it looked to him as though Roosevelt would be re-elected without much question unless the people learned of his actual state of health. The President never got out of his chair at Pearl Harbor, he said. MacArthur said he had not seen Roosevelt for some time and that he was amazed at his appearance and ill-health. He said he did not think the President would make a public appearance before election but would conduct his campaign by radio. MacArthur said Roosevelt's mind is keen and his voice as good as ever.

Wednesday, August 23

Spent most of the day on writing, packing, and preparations for leaving for Guadalcanal in the morning. Two long walks through the streets of Brisbane. Dinner with General Fellers and Phil La Follette. Have passage booked on the Pan American flying boat which takes off at daybreak tomorrow. Have purchased four boomerangs for the children. Put them in with a bundle of clothes I am sending back to the States.

22. Bernard Baruch, financier, statesman, and government adviser on economics. Chairman of the War Industries Board in World War I. In World War II he was special adviser to the director of economic stabilization, and wrote the report on postwar conversion.

Thursday, August 24

Left hotel in Navy car at 5:00. Checked in baggage and boarded plane. The captain invited me to ride forward with him. We were about to start the engines when a bad gasoline leak was found coming from the right wing. The flight had to be canceled. Back to Lennon's Hotel to get my room for another night.

Friday, August 25

Left hotel at 5:00. Off the Brisbane River at 0717 in a Pan American PB2Y-3R, after some difficulty in starting the engines. A six-and-a-half-hour flight to Espiritu Santo through two fronts and mostly above a solid overcast. Landed in a rain squall. Found upon inquiry that Colonel Manley had left for the States and that MAG-11 has moved forward. Very little Corsair activity here at present.

Saturday, August 26

Phoned Air Transport Command. They said the Guadalcanal plane would leave about 10:30. Stopped at Pallikula strip to see how the New Zealanders were getting along with their Corsairs. Plane delayed. Finally arrived at 10:40 full of wounded from Saipan. Off for Guadalcanal at 11:49 with a number of naval and Marine officers and enlisted men and two stretcher cases on their way back to the United States. Landed Guadalcanal at 1545. Drove to COMAIRSOPAC headquarters. Admiral Gunther invited me to stay at his quarters. He told me circumstances about my tour in New Guinea which I did not know before. It seems that Army headquarters did not wait for me to arrive in Brisbane after they first requested me to come down. They sent a rather abrupt message to the Navy, saying that it had come to their attention that "a Mr. C. A. Lindbergh" was traveling in New Guinea on Navy orders and demanding to know what right the Navy had to send anyone into Army territory without first getting permission. Of course, all this arose because of the old Army-Navy friction and the fact that Colonel Cooper forgot to send the copy of my orders on to headquarters in Brisbane. It is all cleared up now, but it seems to have been an unnecessary teapot tempest.

Supper and evening with Admiral Gunther and his staff.

Sunday, August 27

Allied forces take Paris and Marseilles.

I have decided to stop at Guam on the way home. Several Corsair squadrons are based there.

Tuesday, August 29

Breakfast with Admiral Gunther and staff. Attended Intelligence summary at 9:00. Rest of morning writing. Lunch at staff mess. First part of afternoon arranging transportation papers and writing. Swimming with Admiral Gunther, Lieutenant Colonel Wagner, and other officers at 4:00. Supper at officers mess. Evening writing. Bed early.

Wednesday, August 30

Breakfast with Admiral Gunther and staff. To NATS station at 8:30 to leave my bag and make final transportation arrangements. Back to Intelligence hut for the daily summary of war developments. Said good-by to Admiral Gunther and other officers. Off the strip at 10:18 in a Douglas C-54 (four-engine landplane). Rode forward with the crew. We detoured about one hundred miles to the eastward to avoid the Japanese bases at Nauru and Banaba islands. Landed at Tarawa at 1624. Tarawa is an amazingly small island to have been the scene of so much bloodshed; not much more than enough room for the airstrip.

After supper one of the officers took me around the island in his jeep. In most portions it shows very little sign of the fighting. But some of the Jap emplacements have been patched up and are being used by our own organizations. And at each end of the island the Japanese emplacements have been left about as they were after the battle. There are a number of badly battered naval gun emplacements. The ground is covered with pillboxes, and American graves are everywhere, some marked by long, regular lines of white crosses—row upon row making up a cemetery—some scattered individually among the pillboxes, outlined by coconut logs and marked by a white wood cross with the Marine's steel helmet resting on the ground in front of it. The Japanese graves—several thousand of them

—are unmarked. The bodies were thrown into a pit scraped out by a bulldozer and then covered with coral pushed over them by the same bulldozer. Since the island was small, even the enemy bodies had to be buried!

The officer I was with, who came in soon after the first landing, told me that our Marines seldom accepted surrender of the Japanese troops on the island. It had been a bitter fight; our men had lost heavily; the general desire was to kill and not take prisoners. Even when prisoners were taken, the naval officer said, they were lined up and asked which ones could speak English. Those who were able to speak English were taken for questioning. The others "simply weren't taken."

Spent most of the evening writing. Hour's walk along beach and through destroyed Japanese gun emplacements at end of island. Half-sunken American landing barges, the long barrels of Japanese naval guns, and bomb-broken blocks of reinforced concrete were silhouetted in the moonlight.

Thursday, August 31

Borrowed a jeep and drove to the end of the island to look over the Japanese fortifications in daylight. They were heavily bombed and shelled before the landing, but the Japs were so well entrenched that the losses our Marines sustained were still extremely high.

Off the strip at 0850. Landed at Kwajalein at 12:32. Took ferry across to Ebeye Island to arrange for further orders and clearances. Found Captain [John B.] Pearson there. Captain Pearson said Corsair squadrons at Guam have had no air combat. The Navy carrier planes wiped out all Japanese aviation. On his advice I decided to spend several days with Marine Corsair squadrons in the Marshalls instead of going on to Guam and Saipan. Admiral [Alva D.] Bernhard invited me to spend the night with him. He had asked General Wood and several other officers for supper.

Friday, September 1

Arranged to visit the Marine squadrons at Roi Island. Navy boat to Kwajalein Island. Off in a Navy JRB-4 at 0944. Co-piloted to Roi Island. Landed at 10:05. To MAG-31 headquarters. Colonel Freeman invited me to stay with him while I am on the island. Spent most of the afternoon with squadron officers, discussing the Corsair and fighter characteristics. Have arranged to go on a dive-bombing mission with one of the squadrons tomorrow.

Saturday, September 2

Took off with squadron at 12:58, carrying a 1,000-lb. bomb in place of the belly tank. I was flying as the twentieth plane so I could watch the squadron maneuvering. Climbed to 8,000 feet and flew to Taroa Island, Maloelap Atoll, via Wotje Atoll. Taroa Island is, like most of these atoll islands, not over a few hundred yards in length and width. You wonder how the Japanese troops are still able to live there, for the entire island is pocked with bomb craters until there is hardly a tree left standing. Aside from several reinforced-concrete-block houses all of the buildings have been leveled, and only the outlines can be seen.

There were supposed to be several thousand Japanese on the island when we first attacked it. Reports coming through natives indicate that only a few hundred are now left, and these hard pressed for food. It is thought that few, if any, have been evacuated. No enemy surface shipping whatever reaches the atoll, and it is thought that no submarine has been there for some months.

Our target was a personnel area located by Intelligence from recent low-altitude photographs. We started our dive at 8,000 feet and released at 3,000; angle about 60°; no dive brakes. Most of our bombs landed in or near the area, starting one fuel fire. We encountered moderate and accurate small-arms fire from the ground. The Japanese gunners are still bringing down our planes occasionally. Landed at Roi Island at 1558.

Sunday, September 3

Off the strip at 0535, carrying three 1,000-lb. bombs. (First time three have been carried on an F4U in this area.) Plane took off easily. Took off ahead of squadrons and cruised at maximum economy to Wotje Atoll. Rendezvoused with squadrons a few minutes after I arrived. I made one run for each of the three bombs, starting at 8,000 and releasing at 3,000 feet. Target: Japanese naval gun positions on shore of Wotje Island. Direct course back to Roi Island. Landed at 0813.

Supper and evening with Colonel Freeman and staff officers. They told me some of the incidents surrounding the capture of this island. We started with a terrific sea and air bombardment. The Japanese, as usual, fought stubbornly. The Marines, as usual, seldom accepted surrender.

Monday, September 4

United States forces reach Belgium. British capture Arras.

To the line with Colonel Freeman to look into the possibility of installing a 2,000-lb. bomb on the F4U, which I suggested as a result of my test flight with three 1,000-lb. bombs yesterday morning. I am working with a young lieutenant by the name of Clark, and we plan to build a special belly rack for the larger bomb.

Took F4U-1 (No. 263) up for a test flight to check the rigging. Made diving tests up to 400 knots indicated at 50° with a 3-G pull-out. Also aerobatics. Plane carries 5° left aileron at 7° right rudder. Otherwise O.K. I suggested bending down the fairing strip forward of the left aileron on the bottom wing surface.

One of the doctors on the island tells me that some of the Marines dug up Japanese bodies to get gold-filled teeth for souvenirs.

Wednesday, September 6

Americans in Lyon.

Tested 2,000-lb.-bomb installation today. The rack took a permanent set as the bomb was lifted into place. It will have to be reinforced.

Colonel Freeman and I to Commander [Linfield L.] Hunt's quarters, at his phoned invitation, in the evening to meet Jack Benny, Carol Landis, and troop. They are completing a two-month tour of the Pacific areas and had just finished giving their play for the servicemen on the island. The play started at 8:00, and some of the men in the front rows had been sitting there since 3:00, through a half hour heavy rain and wind. Why? To get a good look at the girls on the stage. The men out here don't see a white woman for months at a time, and when they do see one, many simply stand and stare. In some places, such as Nadzab, where the hospital has women nurses, there were several instances of attack. Finally, an order was issued that no woman could go out at night unless accompanied by an officer and that any officer taking a woman out at night must go armed. Negro troops have been the worst offenders.

Neither Colonel Freeman nor I attended the show, but since he is the highest-ranking officer on the island, and I his guest, we could hardly refuse Commander Hunt's invitation. All the actors looked tired, and I feel sure they would have preferred going to bed as much as we.

Friday, September 8

Russia declares war on Bulgaria.

Spent most of morning inspecting installation and making arrangements for the 2,000-lb.-bomb dive test. All checks O.K. Off the strip at 1301. Slight cross wind. Take-off normal. Good climb and control. Started ten minutes ahead of the squadron making the day's strike. Direct course to Wotje Island. Element of surprise important as nearby Jap gun installation is accurate and has brought down two Corsairs in recent weeks.

Started dive downwind from 8,000 feet—shallower than usual—to be sure 2,000-lb. bomb would miss the propeller. Released at 3,000 and pulled up quickly, as I was directly over the antiaircraft installations. Bomb hit about 100 yards southeast of building, wiping out several small structures and throwing a huge column of smoke and debris into the air. So far as we know, this is the first time a 2,000-lb. bomb has been dropped by a fighter.

Remained over the island for half an hour, watching the squadron bomb a newly discovered ammunition dump on the north shore. (One direct hit and several nearby hits.) Then followed last planes of squadron back to Roi Island. Landed at 1600. Bomb rack showed no sign of strain except that a front supporting pin was slightly bent. Gave orders for the hole to be drilled larger and for the pin to be replaced with a bolt.

Saturday, September 9

British forces enter Holland. Brussels and Antwerp captured.

Up shortly after sunrise. Natives very friendly. Each one says "good morning" as he passes the screen sides of our hut and expects a "good morning" in reply. Since there are dozens of them passing, we take turns at the game—one of us nodding and saying "good morning" while the other two dress.

Breakfast with Lieutenant [Kenneth] Collyer, Captain McCall, and other officers. The talk drifts to the original attack and occupation of Roi Island. Most of our American losses were caused by an ammunition dump exploding, one of the officers told me. He had landed on D plus 3. The American casualties were buried in individual graves, he said, but the Japanese bodies were loaded in trucks and dumped into a big hollow scooped in the ground by a bulldozer. The natives did much of the handling of the Jap bodies and located many of them by "smelling for them."

Before the bodies in the hollow were "bulldozed over," the officer said, a number of our Marines went in among them, searching through their pockets and prodding around in their mouths for gold-filled teeth. Some of the Marines, he said, had a little sack in which they collected teeth with gold fillings. The officer said he had seen a number of Japanese bodies from which an ear or a nose had been cut off. "Our boys cut them off to show their friends in fun, or to dry and take back to the States when they go. We found one Marine with a Japanese head. He was trying to get the ants to clean the flesh off the skull, but the odor got so bad we had to take it away from him." It is the same story everywhere I go.

We passed under a number of terns as we walked to our boat. It made me realize what an absence of birds there is on the occupied islands. War is like a flame. Where it sweeps, life disappears, the birds and the trees with the Japanese. We come with bulldozers and scrape over the surface until it is as barren as a gold-dredged area. One of these occupied places of ours is like another all over the world—the same barrenness, the same tents, the same men, the same wreckage. When you have seen one such place, you have seen them all. Here it may be hot, there it may be cold, but the camp is the same. Only when you get beyond its borders, to the ocean beach, to the outlying island, into the adjoining jungle, do you realize that each portion of the world has a character of its own and that life as it used to be still exists hidden away from war and waiting for a chance to bloom again.

Sunday, September 10

To the line at 8:00 to check on today's target and the bomb installations on my plane. Off the strip at 0952, taking up a direct course for Wotje Island. Over target at 11:00. It is impossible to realize as one flies over

that Japanese troops crouch hidden in dugouts and concrete houses waiting for the rain of death we are about to drop from the sky. It is difficult
to realize that the sting of death lies coiled in belts of machine-gun bullets in those little, harmless-looking circles on the ground. One cannot
realize that when he presses the little red button on the stick he releases a
bomb that may carry death and agony to a hundred men.

One is as separated from the surface of that island as though he were
viewing it on a motion-picture screen in a theater on the other side of the
world. A plane in the sky, an island in the water; there is no thread of
realization, of understanding, of human feeling that connects the two. In
modern war one kills at a distance, and in doing so does not realize that
he is killing.

Tuesday, September 12

We strike Wotje Island at 1:45 this afternoon. I am carrying one 2,000-
lb. bomb and two 1,000-lb. bombs—the heaviest bombload ever attached to an F4U.

To the strip at 11:45 to be ready for a 12:30 take-off. Found a cross
wind blowing, with gusts up to fourteen knots. Ordered one of the 1,000-
lb. bombs taken off, leaving one 2,000-lb. and one 1,000-lb. bomb attached. Heavy rain squall blew over. Took off immediately afterward.
In the air at 12:25. (Made a curving take-off because of the cross wind
—heading toward a point halfway along and on the windward side of
the runway. No trouble getting off, but I apparently had a group of
Marines on the windward side of the runway much concerned. They had
come out to watch me take off with a 3,000-lb. load in the cross wind.)
Captain Clark took off behind me, and we set a direct course for Wotje,
flying ahead of the striking squadron.

Rendezvoused over the lagoon formed by Wotje Atoll. Waited until
the squadron completed bombing runs (which were unusually accurate).
Then maneuvered into position, rolled over at 8,000 feet, and dove on
the radio station at an angle of about 60°. Released the bombs at about
1,800 feet, holding gun sight about twenty-five mils over the target. Was
still "grayed out" when the bombs exploded. Almost a direct hit. A great
column of debris rose in the air, obscuring one end of the radio station.
As the debris settled and the smoke drifted away, I could see the bomb
crater, larger than the others and just touching one corner of the building. The internal damage must have been considerable. Anything but
reinforced-concrete walls would have collapsed. Waited for Captain

Clark to make his run with the photo plane. Then took up course for home. Landed at 1440.

Wednesday, September 13

To the line at 7:30 to inspect bomb installation on my plane. I am taking off with one 2,000-lb. bomb and two 1,000-lb. bombs—a total bomb-load of 4,000 lbs.—which is probably the highest bombload ever carried by a single-engine fighter.

To Operations for briefing, and off the strip at 0823. Circled the island once while Captain Clark joined me with the photographic plane (F4U). Then took a direct course for Wotje Atoll, climbing at military power to get above a thick layer of broken clouds. Two fighter squadrons were to dive-bomb Wotje Island today. Both squadron leaders radioed to us, asking for a report on the weather ahead. We were in sight of Wotje Atoll at the time and replied that the target was clear. A few minutes later one of the squadrons turned back due to storms.

I flew upwind over my target (a small, concrete-block house) at 8,000 feet, rolled over, and started my dive. I was pointed downward at an angle of about 65°, the steepest I have used with a heavy bombload. I trimmed the plane quickly as the ground approached and then got my fingers around the manual releases for the two 1,000-lb. bombs. But I had not rolled the elevator tab far enough forward, and the plane became so tail heavy that I no longer had the strength in my right arm to hold the sight on the target. I was almost down to 2,000 feet. There was not time to retrim the elevator tab and get my fingers threaded through the bomb-release levers again. The present F4U-1D has manual release controls for the two pylon bombs, while we have installed an electrical release for the 2,000-lb. center bomb. Therefore, in order to release all three bombs in salvo, it is necessary to pull the two pylon bomb levers with the left hand at the same moment the center-bomb release button is pressed with the right thumb.

With a lighter load I could have pulled out and made another dive, but it seemed inadvisable with 4,000 lbs. of bombs. Fortunately, the area between the block house and the shore was full of Japanese activity and contained several excellent targets. In spite of all the force I could maintain on the stick, the gun sight was creeping rapidly forward toward the shore line. There was just time. I tripped the bomb releases and pulled up steeply.

When the period of grayout was over, I looked back to see the black column of debris rising above the main naval-gun installation in that area of the island—a large, reinforced-concrete structure jutting out slightly from the shore line. I could not have selected a better target even if it had been intentional, with plenty of time to consider. My bombs had completely wiped out the southern portion of the gun position and probably dislocated the gun itself.

We circled around the island while the squadron which got through made its runs. Then Captain Clark dove down to get his strip of photographs of the bombed area. After that, we rendezvoused over the lagoon and took up course for home. The cloud layer had thickened and the thunderheads were building up. The flight back home was like threading a needle at times—heading for a narrow tunnel of light between towering columns and then finding another farther on. The landing strip finally appeared under my left wing through a break in the cloud bank. We dove steeply down through the hole, Captain Clark flying an excellent formation. Landed on the strip at 10:43.

The take-off and drop with 4,000 lbs. of bombs completes the test program I laid out several days ago. Colonel Freeman is flying to Kwajalein Island this afternoon. I decided to go with him. Landed Kwajalein strip at 1553 after a flight across the center of the atoll. We passed over the wreck of a Japanese submarine on one reef and two sunken freighters on another.

I stopped at Marine Wing headquarters for a short conference with General Wood in regard to the bomb tests at Roi Island, etc., then took the ferry to Ebeye Island (a twenty-minute boat trip). Supper with Admiral Bernhard. Conference with Captain Pearson in the evening.

Thursday, September 14

Navy strikes Mindanao. Japanese losses heavy in shipping and planes.

To Captain Pearson's office to discuss the Corsair, dive bombing, future fighter requirements, etc., and to arrange for my transportation to the Hawaiian Islands. Captain Pearson told me that the Corsair is going back on Navy carriers and that it may replace the Hellcat as the standard carrier plane in the future. We spent some time discussing the possibility of towing fighters behind bombers—a subject he is much interested in.

Lunch with Captain Pearson and other naval officers. Took the 1:00 ferry to Kwajalein Island to discuss the towing idea with General Wood and Colonel Freeman. We agree that it is worth further study. Four o'clock ferry back to Ebeye Island. Packed, said my good-bys, and drove to the NATS station at 1800. Off the water at 1839 (0739 G.C.T.) in a PB2Y-3 (Consolidated four-engine flying boat) as passenger. A night take-off. I selected the last seat in the tail, reclined it as much as possible, and went to sleep.

Thursday, September 14

Woke at sunrise, above broken cumulus clouds. Landed at Johnston Island at 1802 G.C.T. Boat in to the island for breakfast—a small patch of coral in mid-Pacific; barely long enough to hold a strip for the land transports. Stopped to see the commanding officer, who took me back to the plane in his speedboat. Off again at 1939. Flew the plane for an hour en route to Oahu. Landed at 0028.

Colonel [John S. E.] Young and several Marine officers happened to be at the NATS station when I arrived. He invited me to spend the night with him at Ewa. Cleared customs and we drove out to the base. (The customs officer asked me if I had any bones in my baggage. He said they had to ask everyone that question because they had found a large number of men taking Japanese bones home for souvenirs. He said he had found one man with two "green" Jap skulls in his baggage.)

Friday, September 15

To Ford Island as co-pilot with Colonel Young in a JRB-3, arriving about 0830. Spent the morning arranging transportation to San Francisco and talking to the United Aircraft representatives at this post. Drove to Honolulu at noon. Spent first part of afternoon walking through the streets, studying faces and looking in shop windows. There are all types of mixtures here—American, Oriental, European, native—submerged in a sea of military uniforms. The peacetime character of a place like this is lost in the influx of soldiers and sailors and the easy money and loose living that goes with it. Supper at the NATS station.

Off the water in a NATS PB2Y-3 at 0653 G.C.T. as passenger. One of the passengers was a sailor who had been on the *Arizona* when she was sunk at Pearl Harbor. The top of his head still showed the marks from burning oil through which he swam to safety. He told me he

923

couldn't understand why we had been caught so completely unprepared at Pearl Harbor because our ships had been dropping depth bombs on enemy submarines several days prior to the Jap attack and that we had been ordered to be on the alert for torpedo wakes. Several naval officers have also told me that we dropped depth charges on a Jap submarine prior to the Pearl Harbor attack.

Saturday, September 16

United States forces land at Palau and in Halmaheras.

Above a solid overcast at sunrise, breaking as we approached San Francisco. Landed in the bay at 2200 G.C.T. Naval car to Oakland airport. Took off in a United Airlines DC-3 at 1642 E.W.T. Landed San Diego, via San Francisco and Los Angeles, at 2015. Taxi to Hotel Del Coronado, where the manager found me a room for the night.

Sunday, September 17

Phoned Anne and Mother. Anne is just moving into a new house she has rented in Connecticut. The furniture from Detroit has not yet arrived. I will go from here to the East Coast for a few days at home and to get my work with United under way, and then out to Detroit to see Mother and B.

Phoned Russell Vought. Lunch at hotel with Colonel Gephart, who drove over at my invitation. To General Mitchell's home in afternoon with Colonel Gephart to discuss the bomb tests I ran at Roi Island. Colonel Gephart wants to start production on 2,000-lb. racks at once, and General Mitchell feels that 2,000-lb. bombs would be of great usefulness in operations which are coming within the next three months and in which the Corsairs will be involved.

To the North Island Naval Air Station later in the afternoon, where Colonel Gephart showed me the three "slicked-up" Corsairs which will be used in an attempt to break the transcontinental record, landing once en route. They are now "waiting only on weather," and hope for a break about Wednesday. They think they can make the crossing in less than six hours.

Monday, September 18

United States Air Army lands in Holland behind German lines.

People are showing me the press articles which have been printed since I left the States last April—as irresponsible and inaccurate as usual. There was the *Time* article saying that I was doing high-altitude flying in the Gilbert Islands. At the time it came out I had never been in the Gilbert Islands, and I have done no high-altitude flying on this trip, unless the test runs of the F4U's up to 30,000 feet at Espiritu Santo can be called high-altitude flying. Several weeks after the article was printed I spent one night in the Gilbert Islands en route to Kwajalein Atoll.

Then there is the story to the effect that President Roosevelt refused to accede to "a formal request" made by the Navy that my commission be restored. This is news to me, and I doubt that the Navy would make any such move without speaking to me about it first. The article goes on to say that "although still on Henry Ford's payroll as an adviser, he is now serving as a civilian member of Admiral Chester W. Nimitz's staff." The article goes on with a lot more silly statements, including one to the effect that I have "demonstrated that bombers can be flown as high as 60,000 feet without affecting adversely accuracy of fire on targets." The article is favorable enough, but it would be difficult to make it more inaccurate.

There was another story, printed about a week ago, as far as I can gather, to the effect that I had already returned to the States. And another saying that we had bought a house in Connecticut.

Supper with the Voughts at their home. They drove me to the airport in time to board TWA Flight 40 for New York. Off the airport at 2205 P.W.T. This is a local schedule—stops at Las Vegas, Winslow, Albuquerque, Amarillo, etc. The plane is, of course, full.

Tuesday, September 19

Amarillo just after daybreak—nearly two hours late. Same plane out of Kansas City. L. J. Smith was pilot. I flew the ship for an hour en route to Chicago. Lunch at 1445 after leaving Chicago, still over two hours late. An excellent meal is served on all these domestic airlines. Under the handicap of wartime conditions the lines are operating with extraordinary efficiency and are setting a record of which they can be justly proud.

Landed at Pittsburgh at 1740 C.W.T. Clear skies overhead, but flight canceled because of weather in New York. Night train to New York.

Wednesday, September 20

A group of photographers and reporters met me on the platform—about a dozen or fifteen of them. When I first saw them, they were gathered around the opposite end of the Pullman car, and I thought they were there to meet the "Bricker for Vice-President party," which I saw at the Pittsburgh station last night, apparently about to board the train to New York. I have had so little trouble with press in recent months that I have been thrown off guard. I started to walk past with the other passengers, but someone recognized me, and I heard that old, familiar, and annoying cry: "There he is."

I had been wearing eyeglass rims without the glass and took them off immediately to avoid being photographed with them on. The escalator was so near that I managed to get on it before any of the pressmen, but they crowded right up behind me.

"What can you say about your trip, Colonel Lindbergh?"

"I'd rather not say anything."

"But won't you just tell us. . . ."

"No, I'm sorry, I have nothing to say."

"But . . ."

I reached the top of the escalator, picked up my bag, and started for the taxi stand, which was across the entire main floor of the station. The reporters walked alongside, asking questions. The photographers rushed ahead like so many monkeys, crouching down, jumping about, and snapping their flashlights. Everyone in the station seemed to stop and stare. I finally reached the cab stand and jumped into the first car. One of the drivers had pulled out in front when he saw the commotion. The last stunt of the photographers was to pull the car door open so they could get one more picture as I leaned out to shut it. Fortunately, none of them attempted to follow.

One of the things that annoys me most about the press is that you can do nothing effective to fight back—at least at the moment. The law prevents you from hitting them or taking other appropriate methods of preventing their annoyance—methods which would be effective in a lawless country. Theoretically, the law protects you from annoyance by others. The average individual would be arrested in a few minutes if he created a fraction of the disturbance caused by pressmen. But police and politicians both fear the press and desire its favors, and a newspaperman would have to go far indeed before any law-enforcing agency would interfere with him—as past experience has only too well shown.

Got off the cab at the airlines terminal on Forty-second Street to throw off the papers if they attempted to follow me through the driver. Stopped only long enough to get a timetable, then walked to the Engineers Club for breakfast. Phoned Anne at Next Day Hill. The children are all there. Everyone is well. The house near Fairfield is almost ready to move into. We can stay there tonight and bring the children on Friday.

I take the next train to Hartford. Gene Wilson's driver meets me at the station. C. J. McCarthy is with him, back from England only a day or two ago. He tells me of the British satisfaction with their Corsair fighters, of his stay in London, of the German rocket bombs, etc., as we drive to the company offices in East Hartford.

Lunch with company officers. Invitation from Eugene Wilson by phone from Washington to have dinner with him this evening. Decline, of course, and tell him I have not yet seen my family, which he thoroughly understands. Conference with Frank Caldwell concerning recent research and fighter projects. Then train to Westport and taxi to our new house—the "Tompkins House" on Long Lots Road. We had to inquire twice to find it.

Anne at the door—the house set back out of sight of the road, surrounded by trees, quite attractively designed, a little larger than I would like it to be, but with about the right number of rooms. We go through it together and then out around the grounds—oak, poplar, birch, maple, cedar, spruce, and pine—an unused field—an old wooden fence—a brook at one end of the property—a much better home than I dared hope we could find for the winter. Anne looks very well, although a little tired from the moving. Rest of afternoon, supper, and evening with Anne.

Thursday, September 21

German forces surround United States air troops in Holland. Russians advance in Estonia.

First part of morning at home with Anne, helping to get moved in. Train to Hartford, arriving in time for lunch with Gene Wilson and other United officers. Conference with Wilson in the afternoon. He brought me up to date on company problems and affairs, while I told him of various incidents and observations on my trip. Conference with Frank Caldwell and John Lee on fighter design.

Late afternoon and evening with Anne, laying plans and helping get the house in order.

Friday, September 22

United States aircraft carriers strike Philippines. Destroy 205 enemy planes and thirty-seven ships.

Taxi to Chance Vought factory at Stratford. Conference with Rex Beisel. Afternoon conference with Paul Baker and engineers: Corsair and fighter design; new jet project; fuel range; climb; speed; firepower, etc. I question the advisability of the present small fuel capacity.

The attempt to break the transcontinental record by the three Corsairs from San Diego failed because of weather east of the Alleghenies. One of them was over Floyd Bennett ahead of schedule but with poorly functioning radio. He was forced to turn back until he found a hole in the clouds and landed almost out of fuel in some small and out-of-the-way airport. All three were fortunate to get down without crashing.

The children were at home when I got back from the factory—the house full of life. Rest of afternoon with them, going through the house and grounds and eating grapes from an old vineyard on the path to the brook.

Saturday, September 23

Russians enter Tallin.

The spare minutes I usually devote to this record have gone to Anne and the children, and the pure joy of being with them again. Went to the Vought factory to complete some business details. Rest of day at home, helping set the house in order, talking with Anne, and playing with the children.

Sunday, September 24

Jon has grown to be a great help and is a hard and excellent worker for his age. Raised his pay to forty cents an hour. Land gets twenty cents an hour. Phoned Mother in the afternoon. All the children except Scott talked to her. I am going to Detroit in about a week.

Wednesday, September 27

Most of day at factory. Late afternoon getting the trailer into position for the winter and cleaning out its heater, which had clogged. Anne will have a view across an old field toward high trees in the distance. I throw some grain out behind the trailer to start the birds and animals coming. The blue grapes are almost all gone from the vineyard. The children eat them at intervals all through the day.

Sunday, October 1

Day at home with Anne, playing with children, and helping get the house in order. Clear and sunny. Mr. and Mrs. Sikorsky and their son "Nicky" came for dinner and the evening. We discussed the war and the increasing influence of Russia.

Monday, October 2

Phoned General [Robert E.] Wood, who has just returned from his flight around the world. Arranged to meet him in Chicago Friday morning. Phoned Gene Wilson, Deac Lyman, and others. To the factory for lunch. Conference with Rex Beisel and Paul Baker. Ran a half hour's test flight in the Corsair with the soft-rubber motor-mount installation. Vibration is reduced but still excessive in the 1,950-2,100 range.

Home for Anne, Jr.'s birthday supper.

Intensive activity after his return from Pacific areas caused another break in Charles Lindbergh's journal. Entries start again in May, 1945, as he is about to leave on a Naval Technical Mission expedition to Europe immediately following Germany's surrender. The purpose of this trip, made as a United Aircraft representative, was to study Germany's wartime developments in aircraft and missiles.

Europe Postwar

Train on time. Station at Washington full of uniforms—Army, Navy, WACS, WAVES, officers, enlisted men. To State Department to get final passport clearance. (They had issued me a dummy to save time.) To Navy Building at 2:00 to get final naval clearances and medical record (inoculations). Half hour's conference with Admiral Ramsey—in regard to trip, Japanese air developments, etc. To Gravelly Point Airport —NATS station—to get my priority, weigh in baggage (total of thirty-eight pounds), etc. (Baggage allowance for flights abroad is fifty-five pounds. They said I could have more if I wanted it! Anne and I used to travel for months at a time with sixteen pounds each.)

A twenty-minute flight to Patuxent. To Captain [Paul H.] Ramsey's home for a sandwich supper and an hour's visit. Changed into uniform while there. Boarded plane at 2313 E.W.T., an R5D. Flew for an hour and a half at the captain's invitation—most of it by instrument. Got a little sleep on a blanket laid on floor of cabin. Woken by crew for past-midnight supper. New system—plate of frozen food heated in electric oven. Not very good. Too much like dehydrated food in New Guinea!

Slept on the floor for another hour or so before landing at Stephenville, Newfoundland at 0514 E.W.T. Off again with fresh crew at 0641 for the flight to the Azores. Twelve passengers, all in uniform—Army, Navy, technicians. Saw very little of Newfoundland—an area of scraggly pines, swamps, barren rocks. Then we were in the cloud layer which did not break until we were well out over the Atlantic. Flew plane for forty-five minutes—at 9,000 feet. A few icebergs on the surface, through breaks in the clouds, great rollers dashing spray against their windward side.

Slept for two or three hours on the cabin floor, letting my lower jaw sag slightly to keep my teeth from vibrating together. The cabin is well heated—too hot at times. One might as well sleep, for the modern military plane is usually uninteresting from the passengers' standpoint—high above the earth—often above the clouds, so that no details can be seen (even if bucket seats and badly placed windows didn't make it so difficult to see anyway). Every year, transport planes seem to get more like subway trains.

Landed at Lagens Airport, Terceira, Azores, at 1546 E.W.T. Neat white villages and small farms. Supper with passengers and NATS officers. Off again with third crew at 2117 G.M.T.—dusk. Talk with passengers and crew. Everyone wonders what the end of the war with Germany[1] will mean to their personal future. Some will go to the Pacific, some back to homes and businesses; some have no job in sight, especially the young military pilots.

Sunday, May 13

Woke suddenly to shouts and foot jolts on the cabin floor. Jumped up and pressed my head against the nearest porthole. There, 7,000 feet below, in the soft morning light, a gem in its setting, lay Mont-Saint-Michel. Behind it was the curving coast of France—the lush green of spring crops, the deeper green of patches of forest, the brown of lately worked fields. It was the coast of Brittany! The great tidal flats stretched out for miles.

If only I had woken sooner, I might have seen Illiec and Saint-Gildas! No, on second thought, we were too far south to have seen them. What wouldn't I give to spend a day on Illiec and watch and listen to its tides! Carrel is dead; Mme. Carrel is not there; but just the associations, just the memories, just the beauty that they also loved would be enough, since I cannot have them, too. Illiec, a half hour's flight away, six years away, a war away, and God knows how much more.

There was not a sign of the war in that first sight of France. Mont-Saint-Michel was just as it had been when I last saw it—as though Anne and I were simply on one of our flights in the Mohawk from Illiec to Paris. After we crossed the coast, where it turns north toward Cherbourg, there were signs of the fighting which took place less than a year ago—burned-over areas in fields and forest; bomb craters and zigzag trenches around strategic hills; the smaller and more numerous pock-

1. Unconditional surrender was signed May 7, 1945.

marks of shell holes; here and there a collapsed or roofless house. I was looking out through a porthole on the south side of the plane. Except for a heavily bombed airport, the war appeared to have left very little damage. But the men looking out through the north portholes reported two villages almost completely destroyed.

Orly, the Paris airport where we landed, had been quite heavily bombed: open craters around the edges and in unused areas; light-colored, round splotches near the runways, where the craters had been filled in; wrecks of hangars; tangled rolls of steel matting; collapsed nearby houses, where some bomb had missed, damaged German and Allied planes here and there; serviceable transports standing erect beside them.

We landed at 0745 Paris time. An old French taxi was provided to take me to Naval Force France headquarters in the city. All other passengers had business on the field. The driver could speak no English, and I know only a few words of French; but we managed to get ideas back and forth without too much difficulty. Yes, it's a long time since I brought the *Spirit of St. Louis* to Paris. Look at those French prisoners of war (a truckload just back from Germany): old uniforms; insignia removed; covered with dust of travel; rather drawn and, for the French, expressionless faces, apparently still dazed from years of imprisonment. They were faces that showed a mental rather than physical starvation.

The streets in the suburbs were almost empty. The sunlight filtered down through spring-green leaves. Windows were shuttered. Market stalls were almost empty. What little traffic we passed was almost entirely military. How much was due to Sunday morning? How much to war? Toward the central portion of the city there was more life. A few cartloads of vegetables had arrived and were being piled on the market shelves, accentuating the remaining emptiness. Little lines of people were already forming to buy them. Wherever there was food, men and women were standing in line, bags and baskets in hand, to buy it.

Preparations for a parade caused us to detour several blocks through the awakening life in this shell of a city—for it is a shell, as though these present inhabitants had taken it over from its real builders somewhat as the present-day Italian has taken over Rome. The Arc de Triomphe reminded me of some of those columns of old Rome as we approached, although from a distance it appeared entirely undamaged by the war. Nearby, however, one could see the pockmarks of rifle and machine-gun fire.

There were very few officers at Naval Force France headquarters when I arrived—Sunday morning after a weekend celebrating the victory over Germany. After waiting for a time and walking up and down several flights of stairs—the elevator was out of order—I finally contacted Lieutenant [George C.] Seybolt, who was able to take over my orders and make arrangements for my stay in Paris. Checked in with medical department. Am, of course, up to date with my shots, although they now give a typhus booster if you have not had one within thirty days (that is, if you are going into Germany, for typhus is starting to show up there in the prison camps).

Stopped to see Commodore [Henry A.] Schade. Then to Hôtel Royal Monceau for a bath and clean clothes. Lunch with Commodore Schade in his room at the hotel. Met Commander [Henry A.] Seiller later. (In command of the Navy Technical Mission).

Get Mr. Robinson[2] (Coudert Frères) on the phone after considerable difficulty. (There was no phone directory in my room. I called the operator, who said that there was a directory—the one that had been printed before the war. Yes, she would look up Mr. Robinson for me. No, the only Mr. Robinson listed had the wrong initials. I went downstairs and got a directory from the porter. There were several Robinsons listed, the right one among them. I turned the pages to C. Carrel was listed, too: "Alexis Carrel, 5 rue Geo. Delavenne—Invalides 73.05."

I stood looking at it—the name, the number, as it had been before the war. I wanted to pick up the phone and call, to hear his voice at the other end, the precise French accent, the dignity, the warmth of welcome. But he is dead, killed by the unfairness of war, by the false accusations of men who never made a fraction of the sacrifice he did for his country. Possibly Mme. Carrel was there. But I did not dare to call her. With the extreme political antagonisms that exist in France, I must inquire about her situation before I phone. It is possible that a call from me might cause her great trouble.

I returned to my room and gave the operator the number for Robinson's apartment.

"I will call you back," she said.

Ten minutes later I asked for the number again.

"I will call you back."

But this time, in a few seconds the phone rang. A man's voice (strong French accent): "Yes, this is Mr. Robinson's apartment, but he doesn't live here any more. He has let me come to live in it."

2. John B. Robinson, friend of Dr. Carrel.

"Do you know where I can reach Mr. Robinson?"

"Maybe you can reach him at the Travelers Club."

I phone the hotel operator. "Will you please give me the number for the Travelers Club?"

"The Travelers Club? I never heard of the Travelers Club" (also strong French accent). A minute passes while she apparently looks in the directory. "No, there is no Travelers Club."

I hang up the phone, go downstairs to the desk and get the directory again from the porter. There is no "Travelers Club," but there is a "Travelers." I go back to my room and give the operator the number.

"I will call you, sir." Ten minutes later: "The line is still busy, sir."

Finally, I get through.

"Mr. Robinson? No, Mr. Robinson is not here. Who is calling him? Just a minute—hold the phone."

Mr. Robinson was there after all. Would I come down to see him? Yes. It was only a twenty-minute walk.

The seats and benches along the Champs-Élysées were filled with people: civilians and soldiers drinking in the afternoon sunlight; brown-faced men in the uniforms of different countries; white-faced families of Paris. It seemed to me like a great hospital with all the inmates recuperating from the illness of war, like those wheelchair cases you see lined up in the sun in front of a real hospital.

I spent half an hour with Robinson, talking to him of Carrel, France, and the war. He said that Mme. Carrel's apartment was no longer on rue Georges Delavenne. He thought Mme. Carrel had left for the States two or three weeks ago. I suggested that we inquire to make sure. He did not have the number with him, and no one was at his office on Sunday. We phoned Information. The Carrel number was unlisted. She could not give it to us. Robinson said he would send one of the club employees to the address on his bicycle when the club closed and would phone me later at my hotel.

Since I had no other engagements, I decided to walk on to the Place de la Concorde. The fountains were going again; the wind, blowing their spray out onto the sidewalk, sent several French girls scurrying out of the way, laughing and screaming. For an instant it was like prewar France. For that instant one forgot the military traffic on the streets, the foreign uniforms, and the old clothes of the civilians.

Yes, almost everyone in Paris is wearing old clothing—men, women, and children—everyone except the soldiers who have not been prisoners of war. At times it reminds me of the cities of Soviet Russia. But the French will never be like the Russians. There is style and color in the Frenchwoman's dress despite her rags. She makes the most of them, takes pride in them. She is still the woman whom men should look at and admire. In contrast, I often wonder why it is that the Frenchman carries himself so badly. Even their soldiers slouch along the streets, making our own soldiers, who are bad enough in this respect at times, seem highly military by comparison.

Like the Arc de Triomphe the Place de la Concorde seemed untouched by the war when I first saw it. And like the Arc on closer approach one saw that it was pockmarked with machine-gun and rifle fire. A cannon shell from a tank had knocked down an entire column from the Hôtel Crillon; another had knocked a hole in the wall of a building farther on along the street. But even here there was nothing that could not be easily repaired. The city of Paris seems to have escaped the war almost unharmed.

Walked back to the Arc de Triomphe. A crowd was assembling around the Unknown Soldier's tomb, held back by several dozen police. Near the other end of the Champs-Élysées, a parade was getting under way. There have been several parades a day in Paris since the German defeat, I am told. I waited with the crowd for a time but had to leave before the marchers arrived, to keep my supper engagement with Commander Seiller at the Royal Monceau. He is a young man of probably thirty years from the mountains of Tennessee—capable, honest, religious —the type that gives you hope for the future. We went for a walk through the streets and one of the Paris parks in the evening.

Letter to Anne after returning to my hotel. Walked to the Arc de Triomphe for a breath of air a little before midnight. There was an informal celebration going on, a game in which the Frenchmen, girls, and foreign soldiers took part, dozens of people joining hands and marching around in a great ring, breaking at times to take in a nearby part of the crowd. A girl who was thus surrounded was permitted to get out through the ring only by selecting some man from it and allowing him to kiss her. But it was forced, unlike the French, as though they were trying to get back to prewar times by going through the motions, as though they were saying to themselves that maybe if they made the gestures, the spirit would follow in time.

Mr. Robinson phoned. Mme. Carrel left for America *this morning*. Six years away, and I miss her by a few hours!

Monday, May 14

Walked to Naval Force France building—about four blocks. Hour studying Intelligence data—secret documents, etc. Short conference with Admiral Kirk.[3] Rest of morning studying Intelligence data and drawing my field equipment. The Technical Mission office where I work overlooks the Arc de Triomphe. Every few minutes an American plane comes down to buzz it, often barely missing the top. None has hit it yet. P-38's, B-26's, P-47's, L-5's, all come diving down as though the war were not over for that particular pilot until he had made his pass over the Arc. A WAC parade goes by—long lines and columns of American girls in their khaki uniforms. Marching well done.

To lunch with Admiral Kirk at his quarters in a private house. We talk of France, the devastation of her harbors, difficulty of getting the country reorganized, the danger of France going Communist, etc. Back to Naval Force building with the admiral. Most of afternoon studying Intelligence data. Walked to Place de la Concorde for a 5:00 appointment with Ambassador Caffery.[4] We talked of France and the war, the danger of mounting Soviet influence, need for American assistance, attitude at home, etc. Stopped for a few minutes to see Douglas MacArthur II. Walked to Arc de Triomphe and back through still darkened streets before bed. The Arc itself is *brilliantly* lighted.

A high naval officer today: "It did me good to see the way the Italians treated Mussolini. It was just the right thing, to string him up with his mistress. They ought to do the same thing to more of them." And the other officers there agreed.

Tuesday, May 15

First part of morning studying Intelligence reports on German fighters and tactics. Navy taxi to Saint-Germain for lunch with General Spaatz and officers of staff. Talked to him about getting in contact with combat pilots who have met the German jet fighters. It turned out that practically all of them are based in England. Listened to a conversation be-

3. Admiral Alan G. Kirk was with the U.S. Naval Task Forces in the invasion of Normandy, 1944; after the war he was appointed Ambassador to Belgium and, later, Russia.

4. Jefferson Caffery, U.S. Ambassador to France, 1944–49.

tween General Spaatz and others about proper conduct in interviewing German officers. The fact that Goering was treated courteously when he surrendered has been so greatly criticized by our press at home that our officers are much concerned. The fact is that our Army today, like our politician, is afraid of the newspaper. Spaatz took the stand that the salute of a German officer should be returned by an American officer "in accordance with military tradition."

Most of afternoon spent on Intelligence reports and planning trip to Germany.

Wednesday, May 16

Captain Smith phoned the Duchess de Chaulnes, who was with Dr. Carrel frequently during the last days of his life. I arrange to meet her at her apartment at 2:15.

Lunch with Technical Mission officers at Royal Monceau. To Avenue d'Orsay in Captain Smith's car. The Duchess's son, Le duc de Chaulnes, met me at the door and showed me to the parlor—a rather bare room showing the effects of war—once obviously rather luxuriously furnished. The Duchess is an intense woman, who spends much of the day running one of the Paris canteens (the Stage Door Canteen). She was with Carrel and Mme. Carrel right up to the day of his death, she told me, and helped arrange to get Mme. Carrel passage back to the United States—a very difficult proceeding these days. She told me of the false (and seemingly trivial) accusations made against Carrel which, she felt, affected him so greatly that they were the actual cause of his death: that he had co-operated with the Germans during the occupation "even to the extent of attending a party at their embassy"; that he had visited the German Embassy on several occasions, accepted favors from them, etc., etc.

The Duchess went on to explain that Carrel had gone to the German Embassy only to argue against the closing of his institute, which the Germans at one time were going to do, and to negotiate with them concerning problems of operating his institute, etc., that Carrel had even refused to accept wood offered by the Germans, that he and Mme. Carrel preferred to be cold, that Carrel had constantly refused to accept favors from the Germans, that once, when he and Mme. Carrel had been asked to come to the German Embassy, they found a party in progress, of which they had not been informed, that they stayed as short a time as they felt they could, etc., that the accusations of some of the members of the Resistance against Carrel had been unfair and false, etc., etc.

As far as I could see, the accusations themselves were not of great importance except when viewed from the bitterness and hysteria of war. What could Carrel do but co-operate with the government of occupation? What possible advantage would it have been to France if he had refused to co-operate with the Germans and had his institute closed? Carrel was never a pro-Nazi, but he thought the Communists were worse. That, I think, is what caused most of his trouble. Leftist influence is now in control, and Carrel was antileft. I have heard him say many times that if he had to choose between Fascism and Communism, he would take Fascism without hesitation. I have just as frequently heard him vent his disgust with the Germans as only a Frenchman can.

Carrel had a heart attack, the Duchess said, at Saint-Gildas about a year ago, after overexerting himself rowing. The attack from which he died came as a result of the accusations made against him and his feeling that he had been turned on by people whom he had regarded as his friends. He lost weight. It was difficult to obtain the right foods for him. He grew constantly weaker, but his mind was clear to the time he died. Mme. Carrel, not well herself, was with him day and night.

The unfairness of it all is exemplified by the fact that Carrel came back to France by his own desire. He could have stayed in America, respected and well pensioned by the Rockefeller Institute. But while so many other Frenchmen were fleeing France, Carrel said that when his country was in trouble, his place was in it. He left security in the United States and devoted his skill to improving the nutrition of children in his native land under all the difficulties of the German occupation. Then he organized an institute under Vichy, an institute devoted to the welfare of Frenchmen. The leadership he gave is shown by the devotion of the young doctors of that institute, who, the Duchess said, were loyal to him to the end.

There are leading members of the Resistance, according to the Duchess, who are angry and disgusted with the treatment Carrel received. But after the Germans were driven out a different group of people came to take political control of the resistance movement, people who were less obvious in the more dangerous and difficult times. It was those people, the Duchess said, who caused most of the trouble for Carrel, not the real leaders of the Resistance at the time it was an underground movement in occupied France.

As I was leaving I asked about my friend Michel Détroyat.

"Oh, that is a very bad situation. He was supposed to be very friendly to the Germans."

I told the Duchess and her son of some of the things I knew Détroyat had done for France.

"Of course, the Resistance can be wrong. They have been wrong before."

"Do you know anything about what happened to Saint-Exupéry?" I asked.

"There are many reports. He took off somewhere in a plane and never came back."

Taxi to Saint-Germain to see Colonels McCoy and Bradley (the latter just back from Germany). We discussed jet and rocket "targets" (word used for enemy objective to be investigated). Bradley says that the American doughboys are destroying most of what they find—shooting up the German planes for no reason at all, towing them around the field with trucks while they take turns in the cockpit, etc.

Thursday, May 17

Truck to Villacoublay. Took off in C-47 at 11:05: several Technical Mission officers, a jeep, a trailer, and our equipment. We are dressed as "G.I.'s," so that when we are in German territory we will be as inconspicuous as possible. Some sniping is reported in places, and, of course, there are the stories of German "werewolf" activities,[5] which have not as yet materialized. We wear heavy field boots, khaki wool slacks and shirt, medium heavy jacket, and overseas cap. Instead of the usual .45 automatic side arm, I carry a .38 automatic in a shoulder holster under my jacket. In our duffel bags are such items as steel helmets, extra clothing, etc. We wear field belts with canteen, first-aid kit, etc.

Two or three men ride in the jeep, trying to sleep. I am wedged in between the trailer and the wall of the fuselage, sitting on my sleeping bag, looking out through one of the dust-covered windows. At the moment there is not much sign of the war below, but back at Villacoublay the field and its buildings had been heavily bombed. Craters everywhere, some filled, some open; the hangars tangled piles of twisted steel and shattered concrete. What had once been streamlined aircraft were now masses of torn and crumpled metal, and everywhere the black scars of smoke and fire.

Aside from a wrecked railway terminal and the collapsed buildings nearby, the section of Paris we flew over was almost intact, and for a

5. Resistance after surrender, involving sabotage and killing.

time there was no sign whatever of the war on the country beyond it. Then we began to see the zigzag lines of trenches here and there, increasing in number as we approached the German border. A few villages were badly damaged, but most of the fighting had taken place in open country. A hilltop below had been heavily bombed and shelled. Dozens of yellow tracks through the green crop of a field marked a spread-out tank advance on some enemy position. Farther away two big bombers had crashed within a mile of one another.

As we crossed into Germany damage became much heavier—terrific where our forces had hit portions of the Siegfried Line. Railroad tracks were broken every hundred yards or so by deep craters, where German demolition troops had done their work. Portions of a city we passed over seemed to be almost completely leveled and destroyed. But most of the villages were untouched, and most of the fields and farmhouses looked exactly as they had before the war. When you looked at the cities, you felt it would take a century for the Germans to rebuild and reorganize. When you looked at the farms and villages, you felt it would not take long. It is interesting to contemplate the fact that the city, which has produced these devices of sciences and warfare, has reaped the whirlwind they caused. In the country lie the seeds of new strength and the soil for new growth.

We circled Mannheim and landed at 1300 to let off an English flight lieutenant we were carrying with us. The city has been terribly hit—filled with ruined walls and rubble, hardly any sign of life on the streets, surrounded by blasted factories with silent machines and smokeless chimneys. From the ground it reminded me of a Dali painting, which in its feel of hellish death so typifies the excessive abnormality of our age— death without dignity, creation without God.

There were great gaping holes in the concrete hangars that were still standing, shell holes through the walls of buildings, bomb holes through their roofs, German signs painted on the concrete, American signs stuck up on cardboard and shingle. An American mechanic was riding a captured German motorcycle over the field. American Army jeeps and trucks were passing by on the road beyond the hangars. Occasionally, a German on a bicycle would pass by with them.

There were a number of American planes on the field, and two or three German planes over in a corner. A Focke-Wulf 190 fighter stood in one of the hangars. The pilot flew it through from Czechoslovakia a few days ago, preferring to be captured by the Americans rather than by

the Russians. He had flown all the way at an altitude of fifty feet, he said.
to escape machine-gun fire. The plane was in poor condition—excessive
play in ailerons, bent cowlings, covered with mud and dirt.

We took off from Mannheim at 1458. The outskirts of the city were
badly damaged with the exception of a few areas. The nearby countryside was dotted with small shacks, each with a plot of garden around it.
The shacks looked as though they had been built out of salvaged boards
from the rubble of the city. Apparently the inhabitants fled to these places
from the bombing.

There were long distances between Mannheim and Munich where
there was no sign of war whatever: farmers working their fields; houses
and villages, all as peaceful as though there had never been a war nearby.
But there was more than the usual amount of cutting in the forests—
great trees and logs waiting for transportation to start the rebuilding of
Germany.

The center of Munich seemed a mass of rubble from the air—shells of
buildings; oblong walls with no roofs on top of them; high piles of debris
along the streets; some of the side streets entirely blocked.

We landed on one of the airports at 1606, taxied over the round
gravel splotches which marked filled-up bomb holes, and parked next to
a gravel-filled crater in the concrete apron. The terminal building was not
badly damaged—only chips off the walls and broken windows. American
troops were occupying the building—steel helmets, rifles, and khaki uniforms in the vestibule, jeeps and trucks parked all around outside. A
dozen or two American and British planes stood scattered on the field. In
a distant corner were probably fifty German planes of all types, parked
haphazardly in an oval mass, looking as though they were in extremely
poor condition. A hangar near them had been bombed, but a huge gas
tank a little farther on had not been touched.

Our jeep and trailer were unloaded. A storm had come up with light
rain. All of Munich seemed damaged. We drove along streets lined with
piles of rubble pushed to the side to let traffic pass—covering the sidewalks and rising in most places high above our jeep. Near the center of
the city everything seemed destroyed. For block after block there was no
building in which we could live—fallen walls, gutted interiors, cracked
and bulging walls, collapsed ceilings. The few buildings with apparently
undamaged fronts were filled with a pile of rubble when one looked into
them, where floors and roof had fallen into the basement. It is a city
destroyed, and I am told that others have been still harder hit.

The people of Munich, with few exceptions, do not seem to have hatred in their eyes; nor have they the cowed, cringing look which has been described in some of our newspaper articles back home. Since the sidewalks are under piles of rubble, the people must walk in the streets and pass close by your car. Some ride bicycles; most are walking with a market bag in one hand. Now and then a citizen looks purposefully away when a soldier catches his eyes, but most act as people would in any peacetime city. I am told that it was different during the first few days of occupation. Then, many of the citizens remained indoors or looked at you with obvious anger or with sullen, surly faces. But there was much looting during those first days, even by our American troops, who reportedly conduct themselves much better than the French or Russians.

I talked to an American technician who had been to Stuttgart a few days after it was occupied by the French. He said that the French troops themselves had indulged in loot, rape, and murder, but that the black troops, operating as part of the French Army, had been incredibly worse. He had seen one woman in a hospital who had been raped seventeen times. "Practically every woman between six and sixty in Stuttgart had been raped," he said. His statement was partially confirmed by an Army officer who told me later that there were over 6,000 cases of rape reported in Stuttgart and that the Germans were crying for the Americans to come in and replace the French.

Where these people on the Munich streets live, where they come from, and where they are going, I cannot make out. There does not seem to be work of any kind under way—not even the clearing up of rubble. Someone suggested that they are surveying the wreckage of their city and trying to locate friends and acquaintances of whom they lost track during the bombings.

We stopped at the Military Government headquarters in the Grosse Deutsche Kunstmuseum, which has by some miracle been left relatively undamaged, although the row of buildings directly across the street are cracked and blasted. The museum is still draped with camouflage. It has been chipped by bomb fragments and flying debris. Almost all the glass panes in the roof have been broken, and the roof was largely made of glass. Some of the subceilings are falling down. There are cracks in the plaster of the walls. The floors of the exhibition rooms are covered with a quarter inch of water from the rain. But the basic structure of the building is apparently sound, and there seems to be no damage which cannot be repaired.

There are rifle-armed sentries at the museum's door. As one turns left from the entrance into a corridor lined with offices, there is a bulletin board for American troops. On the upper portion a map of Europe is thumbtacked. Across it is a white paper strip with the words in large letters: IT'S ALL OURS. The museum offices are now being used by various Army departments.

From the museum we drove to the BMW [Bavarian Motor Works] factory. Barred gate, quickly opened for our jeep and American uniforms. Outside the gate, looking in through the bars, were a man, a woman, and a boy of about ten, all looking as though they had been hungry for months—white, thin faces and sunken eyes. None of the American soldiers inside appeared to be aware of them. A sergeant, sitting on a railing, was munching slowly on a candy bar.

We went to a corner of the factory where a number of engines, portions of engines, and accessories had been assembled on a shipping platform by Technical Mission representatives. A young British lieutenant was there with them. (The British seem to be everywhere when there is any scientific or industrial information to be gleaned.) Commander Seiller selected several items to take back to Paris in the C-47. (He is returning tonight.) Slight argument with the British about taking *anything anywhere* except to England. Settled by rolling up an American Army truck and loading in the items desired.

Back to flying field, where we left Seiller. After that to our billet quarters on outskirts of Munich—a small house in an area where few bombs had fallen. Then back through ruins of the city to get trailer and our personal equipment. Mile after mile of bombed and ruined buildings, high piles of rubble where God knows how many people died or how many bodies still lie buried. Rest of evening spent studying data on captured material, etc.

Friday, May 18

Off in jeep with Colonel [George] Gifford for the German Air Force headquarters at Zell-am-See, Austria. All along the roadside were the crushed and wrecked bodies of German cars and trucks. Some of them had been strafed by low-flying aircraft. Some had broken down and been pushed to one side by the Germans themselves. But most had simply been bulldozed off the road as the Allied columns advanced. Most were not repairable; many had burned; none that I saw were without serious damage. We passed hundreds of these wrecked vehicles.

After we left the suburbs of Munich there was little or no war damage aside from these wrecked vehicles and wrecked bridges along the autobahn. Colonel Gifford suggested that we stop at an inn or private house for lunch, as he was under the impression that food was plentiful in the area south of Munich. (I had suggested that the Germans might be extremely short.) We pulled up at the door of an inn. No sign of life inside or out. Finally, after much ringing, an old man came to the door. He spoke very badly a few words of English. "No beer. No schnapps. No food." His wife had broken her leg and was away at the hospital (the latter information partly by gestures).

We drove up to the door of a small "castle" a hundred yards from the inn. A woman and several children were moving about inside the archway. A young man in Bavarian green coat and leather breeches came out to meet us. He spoke English well. "Food? We have almost nothing." The children stole glances at us as they passed in and out—apparently busy with some chore—actually to see what these foreign soldiers were like. "The Polish and the Russians—even the Americans—have taken almost everything we have." One gained the impression that there was a little food left, that the family would have produced some if we had demanded it, that the family had resigned itself to being looted by any armed men who passed. His mother was an American, the man said, and he himself had once spent some years in our country.

We said good-by and backed our jeep around. He started into the castle, then turned toward us. "One question, please. I would like to ask you. Some American soldiers came here yesterday. They took our cameras and our field glasses from us. Is it allowed?" The fact is that our American soldiers are out for loot wherever they can get it. There is, I understand, an order that cameras must be turned in. Even that seems rather indefinite, and I have been unable to obtain confirmation. But our soldiers have learned that if they walk up to a German house with rifle over shoulder and demand cameras and field glasses, they are quite likely to get some. To destroy and loot is considered entirely proper and the right thing to do as far as the G.I. is concerned. However, our soldiers conduct themselves on a more civilized basis than either the Russians or the French in this respect.

We stopped for lunch at an American field hospital set up in tents south of the autobahn we were following. Since the road to Zell-am-See passed within a few miles of Berchtesgaden, we decided to detour to see Hitler's mountain headquarters. White flags were hanging out of windows in villages we passed on the way, just as they had been hanging out of many of the windows in Munich. At one point we stopped to ask directions from a group of young German soldiers—in uniform but disarmed and apparently plodding along on their way home—a half-dozen young men, courteous, giving us directions as best they could, showing no trace of hatred or resentment, or of being whipped in battle. They looked like farmers' sons.

We were on the wrong road. We turned around, and I dropped a package of cigarettes as we passed them by. Regulations forbid our giving rides to Germans. There is to be "no fraternization." One is not supposed even to shake hands with them or give a bit of food or candy to the children. I feel it is a mistaken attitude and that it will do more harm than good. As a matter of fact, I doubt if it will be possible to enforce these regulations. Unless I am much mistaken, the American soldier will talk to a pretty girl and pat a child on the head, regardless of what instructions are issued against it. Also, I don't think that is the way to make out of the Germans the kind of people we want them to be. It is, I think, the best possible way to sow seeds for future war.

A small village where we turned onto the road for Berchtesgaden had been heavily bombed—an apparent attempt to knock out the railway terminal, which had taken most of the houses, too. The Bavarian Alps rose up all around us. The winding, stone-paved road up the mountainside to Hitler's headquarters was filled with American military vehicles —jeeps and trucks filled with soldiers, WACS, and Army nurses, apparently bent on seeing where der Führer had lived and operated.

Hitler's quarters and the surrounding buildings had been heavily bombed—gutted, roofs fallen, in ruins. Craters from misses dotted the nearby hillsides. The pine forest around the buildings was stripped of limbs—trunks broken off, split, shattered. About two dozen German soldiers in uniform had begun work clearing up the wreckage. There was still rubble on the rather narrow road leading to the building where Hitler lived and worked and held many of his conferences; but it was passable for our jeep. The German soldiers stepped aside for us and closed in behind to carry on with their cleanup.

We parked our jeep at the side of the building and climbed up over rubble to a gaping doorway. A few yards up the road I watched a German officer (in charge of the soldiers cleaning up) salute an American officer who passed nearby, bowing his head slightly as he did so. The American officer sauntered by, obviously taking no notice whatever, although the German held the salute until he had passed. I shall never forget the expressions of those two men.

Most of the walls of the building, being thickly built of stone, were standing firmly. Inside, rubble covered the floors, and part of the wooden furnishings had burned. We made our way over the debris on the floor of the room said to be Hitler's office to the great oblong gap which was once filled with a plate-glass window. It framed almost perfectly a high Alpine range—sharp gray crags, white fields of snow, sawtooth peaks against a blue sky, sunlight on the boulders, a storm forming up the valley. It was one of the most beautiful mountain locations I have ever seen. As one steps closer to the window, the eyes travel down the mountainside with the ledge—snow fields and bare rocks to deep green forests to steeply sloping fields to the well-kept fields and groups of farm buildings in the valley. To the left the valley disappears amid Alpine mountain peaks, a breeding ground for storms like the one now forming. To the right, through a gap in the mountains, one sees level Bavarian plains extending to the horizon.

It was in this setting, I realize, that the man Hitler, now the myth Hitler, contemplated and laid his plans—the man who in a few years threw the human world into the greatest convulsion it has ever known and from which it will be recuperating for generations. A few weeks ago he was here where I am standing, looking through that window, realizing the collapse of his dreams, still struggling desperately against overwhelming odds. This scene, this valley, these mountains entered into the contemplation, the plans which brought such disaster to the world. Hitler, a man who controlled such power, who might have turned it to human good, who used it to such resulting evil: the best youth of his country dead; the cities destroyed; the population homeless and hungry; Germany overrun by the forces he feared most, the forces of Bolshevism, the armies of Soviet Russia; much of his country, like his own room and quarters, rubble—flame-blacked ruins. I think of the strength of prewar Germany.

We made our way back into the rear chamber. A polished granite column contrasted strangely with the rubble at its base. There was the stench of the dead—bodies somewhere only partly buried. We climbed up the mortar-strewn stairs, the end open to the sky where the roof had been blown off. Down again and to the kitchen, edging past a line of doughboys coming in, rifles over shoulders. The floor was covered with twisted utensils and broken dishes; the stoves, with rubble thrown up by the bombs and fallen down from the ceiling. Not a piece of the china was whole, but the fragments were large enough to carry the flower designs and maker's trademark.

As we approached Zell-am-See we entered territory still ruled by the German Army. Officers and soldiers were still armed and still directing what little traffic passed over the roads. Groups of soldiers stared at us as we passed but made no gesture. I could detect neither friendship nor hostility. In every instance where we asked directions, they responded with courtesy. The two of us in an American jeep drove through divisions of the Germany Army as though there had been no war.

On arriving at Zell-am-See in the late afternoon, we stopped at the newly installed local American Army headquarters to arrange for billets for the night. Several German officers were there arranging for the disposition of surrendered troops and arms. We were assigned a room in a nearby house which had been occupied by a German doctor. The family had been given notice to evacuate only a few hours before. (When our Army moves into an occupied village, the most desirable houses are selected and the occupants ordered out. They are permitted to take their clothing and certain household utensils and furniture—not essential furniture or beds. Where they go for food or shelter is considered none of the conquering army's concern. One of our officers told me that the G.I.'s in his organization simply threw out of the windows any articles they didn't want to keep in the rooms they were occupying.)

As I carried my barracks bag in through the door I met a young German woman carrying her belongings out. There was no hostility in her eyes as they met mine, simply sadness and acceptance. Behind her were three children, two little girls and a little boy, all less than ten years old. They stole glances at me, angry and a little frightened, like children who had been unfairly punished. Their arms were full of childhood belongings or light articles they were carrying out to help their mother.

The room assigned to us was upstairs—a largish bedroom with two single beds, freshly made, with a clean white sheet underneath and a "Danish quilt" for a cover, one of those quilts Anne and I first discovered in Greenland and which reach up to my chest if I cover my feet, or down to my ankles if I cover my shoulders. A large bathroom adjoined it. The furniture was a little too modern and shiny to suit my taste.

We drove around the lake to the headquarters of an airborne unit of the 101st Division—the 506th Parachute Infantry—to talk to the commanding officer, Colonel [R. F.] Sink, about nearby personnel and establishments of the German Air Force. The colonel invited us to stay for dinner with his officers and go for a boat ride on the lake afterward.

"Why are you over on this side of the lake?" asked Colonel Gifford. "Why, god-dammit, the buildings we were supposed to occupy are full of German wounded and evacuated children. We ought to kick 'em all out, but we don't do it!" Here was a soldier who represented what I believe in in America—a real fighter. He had to be to command the 506th Parachute Infantry, yet a man who had not been warped by the hatreds of war. I wish to God we had more like him.

We were out on the lake in a "liberated" motorboat at sunset—the soft colors on the mountain peaks, the darkening sky, the valley filling with night.

Back to the house on the lake used for headquarters. Considerable drinking—"Goering's wine." "You know we captured him near here. His Frau is still living down the road apiece. We've got some German soldiers guarding her and some American soldiers guarding the Germans." He laughed. "Goering's private train's down there, too. You ought to see the way it's fixed up. Why, the highest rank in the German Army's all around here—more generals than you ever saw before in one place." He poured glasses full again from a bottle of Rhine wine. I tasted some of it—an exceptionally fine flavor, although I am no judge.

The colonel had sent for General Oberst Martini[6] (four-star) to attend a 9:00 conference. He was interviewed by Major Van Daum, APWIU [American Prisoner of War Information Unit]—the major sitting at the desk, the general on a small, straight-backed chair in front of it. General Martini said that the German officers who had been in charge of the jet and rocket squadrons (the ones I am most interested in) are "in the north."

Our route to Zell-am-See from Munich took up past Chiemsee, where Anne and I landed in our Mohawk in 1938. I tried to see Hohen Aschau, where we stayed, but it is apparently not visible from the road, although I am quite sure I located the mountain ranges between which it lies. Baron and Baroness [von] Cramer-Klett—are they still living? And their daughter who danced with the peasant boys in 1938—what has become of her?

6. General Wolfgang Martini, former head of German Air Force communication and electronic information.

Saturday, May 19

Discuss plans with Colonel Gifford. We spent the morning arranging to get one of the German Storch liaison planes from the local airfield for use by Colonel Gifford's organization. Stop at German Air Force headquarters on way out to the airfield—German officers in uniform, still carrying arms. Major Van Daum is interviewing several at a table. Two British officers also present.

A number of German planes of different types are lined up along the edges of the airport, mostly liaison and transport. We drive through the guarded gate, past probably a hundred German trucks, fully manned as though waiting for a command to take the road, to a line of Storch planes. Examination shows them all to be in rather poor condition and badly in need of maintenance. In fact, all the planes on the field have the appearance of being in poor condition—and the trucks—and the buildings. Everything there has a sort of worn-out appearance—the last remnants of a hard-fought, hard-lost war.

An American sentry is standing beside one of the Storches. He points out for Colonel Gifford the plane he thinks is best. A German mechanic, at Colonel Gifford's request, selects another. A young German Air Force officer comes up, in full uniform covered with decorations—a dive-bomber pilot of some 300 missions, as far as I could make out, in his early twenties, blue-eyed, erect, courteous. "Who do these airplanes belong to? At the moment they are the property of the German Air Force." His words were precise, his spirit not broken. But the war was over; he was carrying on his duty as an officer who had surrendered. He pointed out the Storch he thought was best—a different one from that selected by either the American sergeant or the German mechanic.

We start out for Munich. Decide to go back by way of Innsbruck. Stop to fill up jeep and two "Jerry cans" with gas. The officer in charge of the station gave me a pair of German Air Force blue-gray dress gloves. They came from Goering's stock, he said. They "had lots of 'em."

Drive through the mountains; sunlight on rocks and snow. Green, fertile valleys, farmers working their fields; roads lined with people walking, people on bicycles, people pushing and pulling carts piled high with bundles of their possessions—mostly small carts, children's carts. One wondered how the toylike wheels stood up under such a load.

A storm drifted down from the mountain peaks on our left. Heavy wind and rain. We stopped under a tree to put the top up—not that it does much good. The water leaks down through the top, and blows in through the open sides. We already have our raincoats on. Many of the people walking have no raincoats. They plod on, apparently taking no notice of the rain. It is cold. Most of them are thinly dressed. We drive past old castles built partway up the mountainsides. One of them is built among older ruins—a reminder of other wars. A small church is built high above the valley—probably centuries old—on the edge of a bouldered canyon overlooking the valley, mountains behind. There is no road leading up to it—a place of real solitude. A cross has been planted on some of the mountaintops.

We drive in to one of the Innsbruck airfields. The rain has stopped. The field is occupied by American troops—long lines of trucks, jeeps, and equipment. Farther out in the field are more lines of German trucks and equipment. A Messerschmitt 262 is at one side. We drive up to it. The G.I.'s have been at work. It is completely ruined: holes and rips where they used it for a rifle target; cowlings torn off where they wanted to see inside; instruments gone for souvenirs; bulletproof glass cracked in a dozen places where someone hit with a hammer to see if it would break. We drive to another 262 a hundred yards farther on. It is in the same condition. We drive past the line of German vehicles; they, too, have been looted and smashed. We do not see a single one in running condition.

We drive through the city to another airfield. More Me-262's here; but in same condition—looted and damaged beyond repair. We drive on toward Garmisch. There are Me-262's parked all along the road—dozens of them—in the same condition. Some burned, many with landing gear collapsed.

We stopped at Garmisch for supper with the officers and technicians at the station there. They discuss the equipment they have "liberated," both personally and officially. The word "liberate" is used in an entirely different sense over here than back at home. At home our papers carry articles about how we "liberate" oppressed countries and peoples. Here, our soldiers use the term "liberate" to describe the method of obtaining loot. Anything taken from an enemy home or person is "liberated" in the language of the G.I. Leica cameras are "liberated" (probably the most desired item); guns, food, art. Anything taken without being paid for is "liberated." A soldier who rapes a German woman has "liberated" her.

In the evening we drove on to Oberammergau, where one of Colonel

Gifford's units has just "liberated" a hotel for their headquarters—and a quantity of beer. While we were there, two officers of the Messerschmitt organization were brought in. One of them recognized me. We had met on one of my trips to Germany before the war—in Augsburg in 1938, he told me later. I spent a quarter hour talking to them about the Me-262's and 163's.

We drove back to our Munich quarters at night through storms and rain, stopped every two or three miles by sentries who always demanded to see our travel orders, and with one exception never noticed that the paper we gave them was made out for a different trip and dated nearly a month before. (Colonel Gifford had not bothered to make out a new set of orders for this trip.) Rolled out my sleeping bag for another night on the floor.

Sunday, May 20

Hour working on notes. Then out with Flight Lieutenant Lee, an English technical officer, for a tour of the Munich airfields. We went in Dr. [Ernst] Heinkel's private car, which Lee had "liberated" for his own use—a modern, highly streamlined design—engine in rear, a fin sticking up over it like the tail on an airplane, apparently to increase stability at high speed. (Or just a selling device?) The car had been sprayed an army brown and painted with the Royal Air Force insigne.

There were dozens of German Air Force planes of all types lined up along the autobahn south of Munich—Heinkel bombers, Messerschmitt jets, Junkers dive bombers, Dornier bombers, and others. They are tailed into revetments cut in the pine woods—branches laid over fuselage and wings for camouflage. They are lined up along the road for miles on both sides. Probably half of these planes have been burned. All those remaining have been destroyed and looted by our soldiers—torn apart, shot full of holes, instruments liberated. We stopped to look at a twin-engine Dornier with the heavy barrel of an unusually large cannon sticking out through the nose. Then we drove into an adjoining airfield. There were more planes tailed into the woods all around it—machine guns mounted on tree stumps nearby. We stopped to go through one of the big four-engine transport planes, the nose of which had been burned.

Drove on to another field where we stopped for lunch with one of the American units. A Hungarian Army band played while we ate. Then to a third airfield. Tremendous damage: terminal and hangars (all brick and concrete buildings) ruined, planes wrecked and burned, runways and sod pitted with bomb craters, no sign of life anywhere around.

To still another airfield, where we found an Arado 234 converted to a four-jet installation—a special job, which had been described to us before we started out, and the approximate location given. This plane, unlike most, was out in the open, shot up by our soldiers, but not very badly. We removed some unique navigating instruments to be sent to England, and I took out the altimeter, which was in perfect condition. The four jet engines had already been taken.

Returned to quarters. Hour or so on notes. Talk to a young medical officer in the evening. We discuss German developments in high-altitude flying, etc. He tells me how our people have been making the Germans talk when they at first refuse to do so—solitary confinement on bread and water; and, if that doesn't work, solitary confinement with no bread and water. Our people had become alarmed at the condition of some of their prisoners, and he had been called in to examine them.

Monday, May 21

Off for Oberammergau after lunch with Colonel Gifford in his jeep. Our first objective was to locate Professor [Willy] Messerschmitt. We found his country home—a large house with a view of hills and valleys—occupied by American troops. The house actually belonged to an American Jew, we were told. Messerschmitt had moved into a small house somewhere nearby. Just where, no one seemed to know; but it was thought that he had gone in to Oberammergau for the day. We drove in to the Technical Mission headquarters at Oberammergau. Messerschmitt had not been there.

Supper with officers of unit. The captain beside me withdrew the last cigarette from the package in his pocket and lit it with a sigh. I gave him a new package from my last week's ration; they are issued, a package a day when available, whether or not you smoke. The unit here had run out of rations a week or two ago. It is amazing to me to see how dependent people become on such things. That alone, I think, would be reason enough for me not to smoke—even if I enjoyed it otherwise.

After supper we set out to find Messerschmitt. In a barn in the country, not far from the Messerschmitt house, we found his sister. She, too, had been evacuated by our troops. She spoke a little English. Professor Messerschmitt was living in a little shack on a nearby hill, she said. She went with us in the jeep to find him. It was a very small place. A young man opened the door as we knocked. Behind him was a German girl with a few-months-old baby. They were getting supper. No, Professor Messerschmitt was not there, but he was expected back shortly. Where had he gone? "Probably in that direction."

We found him with two or three people standing in front of a neighbor's barn, long wisps of hair blowing in the wind. We were invited into a medium-size house across the road, belonging to a young woman whose husband was an officer in an artillery unit somewhere in Germany— where, she didn't know. She had just moved back into the house which had been occupied by American troops. (She had been evacuated twice, she said. The first time she had been given twenty minutes' notice and had time to gather together only a few items of food and clothing. As a result, two of her three young children, including a six-week-old baby, are in a hospital. The second evacuation was not so bad, she said; she had been given four hours.) We talked for a few minutes. Then, since it was suppertime, we drove Messerschmitt and his sister to their homes— if they could be called homes—telling them that we would return for them in half an hour.

Messerschmitt's sister asked me to step inside the door for a moment to see how they were living. Their bed consisted of a few inches of straw thrown on the barn floor, with the few belongings they had been permitted to take with them scattered about. Here, she, her husband, and their children slept and lived. They still had enough food—just enough.

Colonel Gifford and I drove to the headquarters of the American troops which had just moved in to occupy the area. Their commanding officer, a young colonel, had established himself in a house on the bank of a long and narrow lake. A heavy storm comes up as we sit talking to him—trees bending, high waves.

Back to get Messerschmitt, his sister, and her husband, who speaks English and understands technical terms. We drive back to the house where we were before supper and begin a technical discussion centered on jet and rocket aircraft. Messerschmitt feels that the pure rocket type of plane has a great future for both military and commercial use. He prophesies speeds and ranges far greater than those our designers and engineers are considering at home—supersonic cruising speeds with passengers—Europe to America in one to two hours, etc. He says that the Me-262 (twin jet) was ready in 1938, but that "the government" was not interested. "Udet believed that the jet fighter was important, but not Milch."

I asked Messerschmitt when he first began to feel that Germany would be defeated. He said he had been much concerned in 1941 when he saw the American estimates for aircraft production, because he thought we could meet them, although most people in Germany did not. In reply to another question, he said he did not know whether the Me-262's had been used on the Russian front, but that he didn't think so, because their conventional fighter had enough performance to meet anything the Russians had been able to produce. Messerschmitt regarded the Mustang (P-51) as the best Allied fighter. The P-47 Thunderbolt was "not so good." The Me-262 was not built for dive bombing, and the pilots were not properly trained for such work, he said. However, he felt that the 262 would make a reasonably good dive bomber if properly handled. Messerschmitt said he thought the Germans were ready to invade England in the early stages of the war, but concluded that the Russians would attack them in the east as soon as they started the invasion, and therefore they attacked Russia.

Messerschmitt asked me what Munich was like. I told him it had been terribly bombed. He said that, according to German reports, Dresden had suffered more from bombing than any other city; estimates placed the dead at 180,000. The city had been full of refugees, he said, and the bombing unexpected.

Messerschmitt had recently returned from a trip to England, where he had been taken as a prisoner of war. He had been asked by both the British and French to act as technical adviser. I asked him whether he would be interested in working in America if the opportunity arose. He said that would, of course, depend on the conditions.

We drove Messerschmitt, his sister, and his brother-in-law back to their homes, taking them to their doors, as the military curfew requires that they be indoors by 9:00 P.M. except by special authorization. Colonel Gifford and I took turns driving the jeep back to Munich.

A Me-262 is reported to have been built with two 003 turbojet engines and rockets to assist in climb. It is said to have climbed to 11,000 meters in three minutes. Top altitude: 17,000 meters.

Tuesday, May 22

Breakfast at officers mess. Then off in jeep to pick up Dr. [Helmut] Schelp (head of German jet and rocket development under Baeumker). We find Schelp living in a small one-story house. An American "half-track" with loaded machine guns stands in front, the crew crouched under a tarpaulin for protection from the rain. Lieutenant Robinson tells me he ordered it to come out as a precaution, because a number of Russians had moved in next door to Schelp, and there are indications that the Soviet government is trying to get him into their territory because of his scientific and technical experience. (Few people over here trust the Russians. They are feared by the Germans, and many Americans think it is simply a question of time before we will be fighting them ourselves.)

Schelp is a young man for the position he held, probably in his late thirties. He met us at the door. Inside were two other Germans, one of whom was the baroness who owned the lands upon which they were living. She was acting as Schelp's secretary and typing a manuscript on the history of jet and rocket development, which Lieutenant Robinson had requested Schelp to write. The man, obviously well-educated, was working at an old-fashioned spinning wheel. They were short of socks and other articles of clothing, they said in answer to my question, and they had no other way to keep clothed. The American troops had taken much of what they had. Using all his spare time, he could make about one pound of yarn a week, the man said.

On our way to the Bavarian Motor Works factory I talked to Schelp about the German jet program. He told me that many German scientists had moved to the Munich area to escape the Russians. Most of them had their families with them, he said. He himself had been unlucky; his wife and six-month-old child were in Dresden. "No one thought the Russians would come that far west." Schelp was afraid that when they found out his family was in their territory the Russians would tell him that if he wanted to see his wife and child again he would have to come and work for them.

I asked Dr. Schelp whether he thought we would be able to make use of atomic energy for power in aircraft. "I think it will probably come eventually, but not in my lifetime or in yours." (He speaks English well.)

We spent an hour at the BMW factory, while Lieutenant Robinson discussed arrangements for the assembling of a number of their latest jet engines for shipment to the United States for tests. The manager had been my guide during the trip I made through the factory in 1938. While we were talking, a man came up to Lieutenant Robinson, a little white and shaky, to tell him that before the invading troops arrived, he had been given the drawings for one of the jet engines with orders to destroy them. (The BMW officers had said some days ago that their drawings had been destroyed.) However, he had disobeyed orders and buried the drawings in some land belonging to a friend of his. Would we like to have them? He would show us where they were. The location was about a two-and-a-half-hour bicycle ride away.

After the discussion with the BMW officers was over and arrangements for building the jet engines completed, we tied his bicycle on the front of our jeep and drove to the property where the drawings were buried. We had to walk the last hundred yards or so through a pine wood with bits of radar-deceiving tinsel scattered in with the pine needles on the ground. Our guide finally stopped beneath a large pine tree and began feeling about on the ground and lining up marks which he probably made a note of at the time of burial.

I studied the ground carefully where he started digging, but could see no unusual marks of any kind. The earth had obviously been replaced with the utmost care, tramped down, needles scattered over the top, and the surplus carried away. Soon, the spade struck the top of a metal box. It turned out to be about the size of a file box and was hermetically sealed by welding. There was another box buried a few feet away; also a long cylinder which contained the larger drawings. We loaded all three into our jeep; then stopped to have tea with the owner of the property. He had been in New York in 1927, he told me, at the time I returned from the flight to Paris.

We took Dr. Schelp back to his house, gave him three cans of food to make up for the meal he had missed (I had found, while talking to him, that he had eaten very little since morning, and not much then), and stopped at the nearby American camp to arrange for the "half-track" to guard him during the night.

The German Air Ministry decided to develop a new form of propulsion for speeds of over 480 m.p.h. Therefore, Dr. Schelp, in 1938, asked all the engine manufacturers to attend a conference for the purpose of discussing jet-engine development. It was decided to develop the four classes of jet engines outlined below.

CLASS THRUST	PRESSURE RATIO	TURBO STAGES
Up to 1,000 k.g. (static S.L.)	1–3.5	1
1,300–1,700 k.g. " "	1–5	2
2,700–3,200 k.g. " "	1–6	2
3,700–4,200 k.g. " "	1–6.5 1–7	3

They expected to modify Classes 2, 3, and 4 to propeller drives. Then add one more turbo stage to 2 and 3.

Wednesday, May 23

Packed, good-bys and checkout at Munich headquarters. We took the autobahn toward Ulm. We pass collapsed buildings, bomb craters open, bomb craters filled, heaps of rubble, American trucks and jeeps, disarmed German soldiers in uniform, displaced persons walking with carts and bundles along the roadside—a father pulling a small cart uphill, the six-year-old daughter pushing against bundles piled high above her head; a half-dozen men with a larger cart, four harnessed in ropes pulling it, four walking at its side, leaning their weight against it; people on bicycles; people carrying small flags—French, Polish, Russian, Czech.

We talk of Stuttgart and the French occupation. At least there have been few charges of rape against our American troops. But the French with their Sengalese: "There were over 3,000 cases of rape *in the hospital.*" Not in the hospital for abortion, but because of injury. And minor injuries aren't accepted in hospitals in Germany these days.

We see a Red Cross stand ahead and stop for doughnuts and coffee. It is set up in a slightly damaged and completely abandoned gasoline station at the side of the autobahn. A little highly made up, neat, and tired-looking Red Cross girls in Red Cross uniform are passing out the food. Several German children, obviously hungry, stand about watching for bits of uneaten doughnuts. (It is against regulations to give them food.) I leave a doughnut where I have been sitting as we walk off. I look back a few seconds later; it is gone. Two small German boys are standing quietly nearby.

We stop at a factory outside Ulm to arrange for some parts needed for the jet engines which are to be built by BMW at Munich. Then drive on to Esslingen to another factory. Then through the outskirts of Stuttgart. There are many detours for bridges out along the road. Stuttgart has been heavily bombed. There are French sentries and soldiers walking along the streets. We start out on the autobahn for Heilbronn. It is cold and overcast. The bridge over the Neckar is out. We have to detour. Supper at Besigheim with a unit of the 100th Division.

German children look in through the window. We have more food than we need, but regulations prevent giving it to them. It is difficult to look at them. I feel ashamed, of myself, of my people, as I eat and watch those children. They are not to blame for the war. They are hungry children. What right have we to stuff ourselves while they look on—well-fed men eating, leaving unwanted food on plates, while hungry children look on. What right have we to damn the Nazi and the Jap while we carry on with such callousness and hatred in our hearts. But they are not yet really hungry. They still have enough food to live. "Wait until the winter!!" Yes, I know; Hitler and the Nazis are the cause. But we in America are supposed to stand for different things.

We drive cross-country over dirt roads and a pontoon bridge to Heilbronn. The city has been heavily bombed and shelled—worse than Munich. In some blocks there are almost no standing walls, just rubble. Only a few buildings in the central portion of the city can be lived in. We signed in at Military Government and were billeted in the underground German hospital—a basementlike affair lying under rubble piles. German nurses assigned us to a room with about twenty-five cots—no one else in it. I go out for a short walk before going to bed. There is no danger; almost no one lives in the city; there is no place for them to live. The moon lights up the piles of rubble, silhouettes the few standing walls —gaps of windows, twisted girders, bomb craters, the stillness of death. "Our troops had heavy losses crossing the river at Heilbronn."

Thursday, May 24

Breakfast at Military Government building. Russian waitresses. Two American officers are talking about a German who has some information one of them feels will be useful in the future. "What I want is to get him out of that camp. He's seventy-eight years old. I'm afraid he'll die if we leave him there." It seems that there is not enough shelter for all the German prisoners in the American concentration camp here. One of the officers (American) tells me that prisoners are in the open day and night, rain or shine, and with very little food. "God-dammit, they've got it coming to them. Look at the way they treated their prisoners."

A Russian captain is having breakfast. We are introduced to him. I don't think he recognizes my name, but am not sure. He is going north on official business to Berlin; got on the wrong train and ended up at Heilbronn. Could we take him as far as Heidelberg? I don't like his face, but we agree to take him. It's easy to see that Military Government at Heilbronn is anxious to get him out of the way. I decide to ride in the back seat.

We pack our jeep and stop for the Russian captain. He turns up with a young blonde! *"Mein Frau."* He has some baggage—four or five pieces. Fortunately, we have a trailer. While I am not looking, the Russian climbs into the back seat and won't get out. "Sleepy," leaning his head on his outspread hand to emphasize the only word of English we have heard him speak. *"Très fatigué,"* says the girl, pointing to him. But it is our jeep, and I hold out—force him into the front seat. I don't like the way things are going at all—two Russians in the back seat of a jeep— and I don't like the way he looks at me. I make the girl sit on my left so that I can get at my pistol easily with my right hand. (Have already slipped a bullet into the chamber.)

We start out. I study the girl, size her up as not being dangerous and, of course, not being his wife. The Russian, I think, looks capable of anything. I keep my right hand under my coat and on my gun— ostensibly for warmth. Before long, the officer's head falls to one side— asleep?—jerks up again. The movement looks natural enough. Probably he is *très fatigué*. Nevertheless, I keep my right hand on my gun and hold on to his shoulder strap with my left. The road is so rough that I am afraid he may lean toward the outside of the jeep in his sleep and fall over- board. So I have my right hand on my gun to shoot him with and my left hand on his shoulder strap to keep him from falling out and getting killed! A truly Russian situation.

We stop at a salt mine some miles out of Heilbronn. It contains "about 30,000 cases" of art, documents, and other articles of high value, according to one of our American officers at Heilbronn, stored there for safety. Lieutenant Robinson has record of some twenty cases of draw- ings and documents relating to the latest German aircraft developments. But we cannot get down. The mine is 180 meters down, and an Ameri- can artillery shell put the elevator out of commission. Repairs are esti- mated to require another ten days. The only other access is by ladder, and the ventilating system is out.

We drive on to Heidelberg, past more lines of people walking and bicycling along the roadside, mostly women and children and old men. The "Russian Frau" is cold. I give her my raincoat to break the wind. She speaks a few words of English.

"Where do you live in Russia?" I ask her.

She looks confused.

"Do you live in Kiev?"

She grabs the bait, relieved. "Yes, Kiev." She nods and smiles and stops talking.

At Heidelberg we have some trouble getting rid of the Russians. The Military Government doesn't want them, but they direct us to "the Russian liaison officer" only a few blocks away. We drive over and unload the baggage at the curb. I wait with the girl beside it while Lieutenant Robinson takes the captain in to the "Russian liaison officer." A minute or two later Lieutenant Robinson comes out. "Let's go." We drive off. "I introduced him to the major [the liaison officer] and left him explaining why he was there. The major didn't know that he had some baggage and a Frau outside."

I drove from Heidelberg to the Naval Technical headquarters near Bad Schwalbach (near Wiesbaden). The mission is occupying the old Adolphus Busch[7] estate. Prior to the American occupation the buildings were used as hospitals for pregnant women (mostly girls from fifteen to seventeen, a naval officer told me). "The Germans used it for a sort of baby factory."

Friday, May 25

Phoned Colonel Warburg at Wiesbaden. They have some German jet pilots in custody, but they are taking off in a plane for Paris at 10:00. Walk alone through the estate grounds and out through a nearby forest. Still no word of the C-47 which was supposed to arrive at Wiesbaden before noon.

Word comes that the plane arrived unreported from Paris. The ferry pilot (Army) did not bother to phone Navy headquarters. He said he had a date in Paris tonight, so took off with an empty plane in order to make it, leaving 3,000 lbs. of priority documents on the Wiesbaden airport in addition to the passengers who had been waiting for him. This is typical of the Army ferry-service attitude—poor discipline and irresponsibility. Probably the pilot will not even be reprimanded for his action.

I drove to the airport on the chance of arranging for a special plane to take documents and passengers through this evening. No plane was available. We drove back to Villa Lily. In the office is a photograph of Hitler, hung upside down. Go for a walk alone through the woods. The call of the cuckoo, full and clear, reminds me of Long Barn and England. Talk to a naval officer about Villa Lily. He says that our troops found it full of pregnant women—gave them one hour to evacuate. He didn't know where they went.

7. Former president of Anheuser-Busch Brewing Association, St. Louis, Mo.

Saturday, May 26

Lieutenant Robinson and I decide to drive to the Wiesbaden airport and try to get passage on one of the planes for Paris. (There are a number each day, and they usually have room for another passenger or two. The weather is good, so the chance taken in flying with unknown pilots is not great.)

At the airfield everything seemed to be in a state of disorganization. We couldn't find anyone who knew when planes would arrive or depart. Two C-47's were supposed to come in for the use of Navy Tech, but it was uncertain whether they had left Paris. Just as we were about to return to Navy headquarters, a sergeant came running up to tell us that a mail plane was about to leave for Paris and that the pilot would be glad to take us along.

Took off in a C-47, cabin piled with mail sacks, at 10:18. As usual, most of the villages we passed over had received little or no damage, although one on the bank of a river was completely wiped out. We passed over a heavily bombed factory a little farther on—completely destroyed. A tremendous number of bombs had been dropped, and there was a large percentage of misses, some of them more than a mile from the target.

Landed at Villacoublay at 12:19.

Sunday, May 27

Breakfast with naval officers. Then decided to walk to the Bois and try to find the paths we used to follow while we were living on Avenue Maréchal-Maunoury. Walked along Avenue Victor-Hugo to Avenue H.-Martin. There is more life on the streets than two Sundays ago—families with children dressed in the best clothes they have left, going to church. There is more in the store windows, too; but they are still pretty empty. Some of the apartment buildings near the Bois are covered with camouflage paint—shades of green, black, and brown. And there are concrete sentry or observation posts placed on many of the corners. Tangled barbed wire is pushed out of the way along the streets and around the buildings. French soldiers are still living in some of the quarters.

At first, I wasn't sure which apartment house we lived in. Then, I saw the white silk curtains through wide-open windows—Maréchal-Maunoury 11 bis. They were still there after all these years of war.

The Bois was almost empty; only a few people in sight; bushes growing up; the paths where Jon and Land used to play deserted. A woman was filling a big basket with green leaves. It was so changed and overgrown that I couldn't find our old route through the woods. However, there is little damage; all it needs is work and care.

Walked to American Embassy for lunch with Ambassador and Mrs. Caffery. General Clark[8] was there, and two or three other guests. General Clark discussed the situation in Italy: extremely delicate, although he thought the chances were it would not explode; had 70,000 Yugoslav troops in the rear of his positions. He had recently been informed by a Tito general that he (the Yugoslav) would attack that night if the Allied forces were not withdrawn! Instead of withdrawing, Allied reinforcements were sent, and the attack was not made. General Clark said that the Russians were, of course, behind the Tito troops and that a dozen Red Lend-Lease tanks had recently paraded through one of the towns our troops held.

Monday, May 28

Talked to Admiral Kirk about trip to England.[9] He will phone Admiral Stark and let me know what the situation is. We also spent a few minutes discussing the situation in Germany and Russia.

Lunch with officers at Royal Monceau. Then walked along the Champs-Élysées and through the Place de la Concorde to the Place Vendôme. Stopped at Morgan Cie for a few minutes with Dean Jay[10] and to inquire about our account and monthly payments to the caretaker at Illiec. Found that we had about 6,000 francs left. Exchange is bad, and transfer of funds from America complicated, so I simply deposited $150.00 to cover payment of storage charges to Pitt & Scott and leave enough in our account to make the Illiec payments for the next several months. Exchange is slightly under fifty francs to the dollar.

Walked through the Tuileries gardens and past the Louvre (closed doors). Across the river all the bookstores were shut. I walked on past the little stalls (about half of them open) to Notre Dame. Nearby buildings were slightly scarred by machine-gun fire, but the cathedral itself was

8. General Mark Clark, who commanded the 15th Army Group (the U.S. 5th, the British 8th) in Italy.

9. Lindbergh was considering a trip to England to interrogate German Luftwaffe officers who were prisoners of war.

10. President and later chairman of the board of Morgan & Cie, Inc.

hardly touched. French guides were escorting groups of soldiers through the doors. I walked around the cathedral and sat for a time in the garden behind—flying arches against the sky. Went inside for a short time before starting back. No ceremony; a few people praying; lines of sightseeing soldiers with guides explaining in highly accented English. I left the coins in my pocket in the box at the foot of a statue of Jeanne d'Arc.

Walked from Notre Dame to the Royal Monceau. It is extraordinary how the statues in the Jardin des Tuileries have escaped serious damage. There was considerable rifle fire in that area, as is shown by the bullet marks and chips on the bases of the statues; but the statues themselves have been hit relatively little. Most of the gunfire seems to have been low, apparently at soldiers using the bases for cover.

Tuesday, May 29

Supper with Clark Millikan and other members of the Technical Mission. We talk of the stacks of documents taken from Germany, literally tons of them. Army, Navy, British, French, Americans, all competing for the loot of Germany—the spoils in German scientific and industrial progress.

Thursday, May 31

Most of day at Navy building, arranging for next trip to Germany. Walked along Avenue Foch to Parc Monceau in later afternoon. Half hour in church of Saint-François-de-Sales. Ceremony going on; people standing; parade through aisles; robes and chanting.

Friday, June 1

Dressed in G.I. uniform—field jacket and heavy, cuffed field boots. Scheduled to leave hotel at 9:00 but delayed by confusion about trucks and drivers. Delayed again at airport—more confusion. Finally took off from Villacoublay at 11:25 with Clark Millikan and other technical representatives. Lieutenant [E. H.] Uellendahl is along as my interpreter. Low flight under an overcast and a very good view of the ground and battlefields. Newly scarred ground, the Second World War; grass-covered scars, the First World War. The marks will last for centuries—on the earth—on the people.

Landed Wiesbaden at 1305. Jeep to Navy headquarters near Bad Schwalbach. Lieutenant Uellendahl and I drove to Wiesbaden to get the necessary orders for our trip. Started for Heidelberg, I driving. Bridge out. We detour, get lost. Drive through Frankenthal and Mannheim, the latter terribly bombed, a ghost city; nothing but piles of rubble and gutted buildings in the central portion. We drive on through Ludwigshafen to Heidelberg and get billets.

Lieutenant Uellendahl and I walk through the city and climb the hill to Heidelberg Castle in the evening. The castle was closed, but I gave the watchman's wife a package of cigarettes and his daughter a bar of candy, and the gates were opened for us. The watchman showed us through the grounds and described the castle: ruined and rebuilt; ruined and rebuilt again. Centuries of ancient wars unfold. Whatever the destruction, man continues to rebuild. The castle has not been touched by this war, or the city, except for a blasted central portion of the ancient bridge and, possibly, damage from a few stray bombs. It is said that the English and Germans had an agreement that if the one did not bomb Eton (or was it Cambridge?), the other would not bomb Heidelberg.

It is nearly night when we leave and walk back through darkened streets to our hotel. The feeling of security is such that the sentries do not challenge.

Saturday, June 2

Signed out, and off in our jeep at 8:10. Autobahn to Karlsruhe (badly bombed, as usual). Then on to Stuttgart. Our engineers have repaired many of the German-destroyed bridges, but we had to make frequent detours for those not yet repaired. We passed some of the French Senegalese troops on the way into Stuttgart. "They are paid little or nothing by the French, but they are permitted to loot and rape at will; that is part of the agreement."

Some days before, I had been told that in French-occupied territory it was required that a list of the occupants of every building, together with their ages, be posted outside, on the door, and that both the Senegalese and the French soldiers, drunk at night, would go from door to door until they found girls' names listed of any age they wished to rape. As we drove through Stuttgart we saw that each main door of the habitable buildings contained such a list—white sheets of paper tacked onto the panel—a column of names, a column of birth dates. And most of the women of Stuttgart show in their faces that they have gone through hell. The city has been terribly bombed.

We ate a K-ration lunch while driving. Stopped at the Messerschmitt factory at Augsburg—badly damaged. Drove on to the airport at Lechfeld, where a number of Me-262 jet fighters are being assembled for flight to England. Stopped long enough to examine the planes: several service-type fighters, several reconnaissance types, one fighter with a 50-mm. cannon mounted in the nose (all Me-262's). The Lechfeld airport has been bombed, but less heavily than most we have seen; usual collapsed buildings and wrecked aircraft on the field. The standard Me-262 cockpit does not impress me as being well designed; instruments and controls could be better placed.

From Lechfeld we drove on to Munich via Landsberg. Stopped at the art museum to register in. Then drove out to Technical Section quarters. Noticed a disturbance on a street corner ahead shortly after leaving the museum. Turned out to be a man, shabbily dressed in civilian clothes, trying to take a bicycle away from a woman. He was apparently a D.P. A small group of Germans had assembled. The woman's face had a terrified expression, and she was crying. An American M.P. came up and returned the bicycle to her, motioning the D.P. to be off. He (the M.P.) then made a motion as though to wash his hands of the whole affair and walked away.

We are given billets at house No. 3. Lieutenant Uellendahl and I drive in to Munich in the evening. He once attended the University of Munich. We find the house where he lived, the shell still standing but the inside a pile of rubble, no rooms, no floors. He points out the gaping window of the second-story corner where he lived.

We continue to drive around the city—past a house where lived a girl Lieutenant Uellendahl used to call on. It, too, is gutted. The cathedral is cracked and gutted, the university the same. The museum is gutted. The columns and statues where Hitler started his *Putsch* are damaged. But the bronze statue of Ludwig I on horseback is to all appearances intact.

Farther on along the streets, past the scarred and damaged theater building, we come to the columned memorial to the sixteen "fallen heroes" of the 1932 *Putsch*—sixteen bronze coffins lying side by side in rows in two sunken pits, which caused one's head to bow to look down upon them. There had been no bomb damage here. At the top of each coffin were the words, in German, "The Last Call"; near the bottom was the name of the man whose body it contained; and last of all, the word "Here."

We stopped at the station building, heavily hit, partly repaired, hit again. Tracks were torn and twisted, cars blasted. But over to one side, a few hundred feet away, trains were moving. On a pile of rubble on the center of one of the platforms a child's rag doll was lying, sprawled and headless.

Returned to our billets for the night.

Sunday, June 3

We left in our jeep at 8:30 for Wörthsee to try to find Adolf Baeumker, who was the head of D.V.L.[11] when I was last in Germany before the war. He was reported as living in a house in the country on the southwest bank of the Wörthsee.

We locate Baeumker in a small house between the road and the lake, set back from each. Frau Baeumker is with him, and two little girls they have adopted—one about six months, the other about five years. We spent the morning discussing German aviation and research. Baeumker has not been well during the last year or two, and apparently was not in too good standing with the Nazi government. He had disagreements with Milch. Says the government did not back up fundamental research sufficiently but made use of basic research facilities for service improvements. Says that developments like the V-2 rocket bomb were emphasized out of all proportion to their value, to the great detriment of the German war effort. Such things made a great appeal to Hitler, Baeumker says. Hitler was always interested in such radical developments, things that were bigger, faster, more powerful, etc.

Baeumker was obviously glad to see us and was extremely co-operative in every way, suggesting names of German scientists and engineers in whom he thought I would be interested and directing us to their location. He talked at length on methods of organizing aeronautical research and discussed a book he has written on the subject, published after the start of the war. He thinks there has been too much mixing of specialized and fundamental research, that specialized research should be carried on by industry and fundamental research by laboratories devoted to the subject.

Toward noon the discussion turned to eastern Germany and the Russians. "Russian propaganda is very clever," Baeumker said. "Their radio is going all day long. They tell how establishments in their territory are

11. Deutsche Versuchsanstalt für Luftfahrt (German Experimental Institute for Aviation).

being opened up again. They say how well German scientists and workers are being treated—so much coffee, so much tea, so much food. For me, I wish to work with the Americans," Baeumker said, "but some of the younger men are already talking about crossing over into Russian territory when they get the chance."

"Terrible times are ahead for Europe and for Germany," Baeumker said. "Our position is now as that of Poland used to be." He told me that several days ago an American and a Russian officer had called on him, armed, threatening, demanding his papers, accusing him of not telling all he knew. He also was concerned about possible S.S. retaliation; there might be S.S. hiding in the woods at that moment, for all he knew. The S.S. men were "very bad."

He drew me back, as Lieutenant Uellendahl walked ahead, to tell me of the execution by the Nazis of people he had known. This man had disappeared; another had been hung, "by Hitler." He himself had been in a dangerous position, because he was a cousin of Bruening's.[12] I gave two cigars and a can of fruit juice to Baeumker, two packages of cigarettes to Frau Baeumker, and a candy bar to the little girl—all from my Paris weekly ration. Then, about 1330, we left.

From the Wörthsee we drove to Allach to look for Dr. Neugebauer,[13] head of the Munich research center near Hohenbrunn, which never reached completion. Baeumker said he was one of the best men in Germany to give a comparison of the development and uses of their various types of engines. We found him living with his family in a small frame house not far from the Allach railroad station. He had one more week's work to close the research institute, he said. Then, since he had eleven people to support, including five children, he would apply for work in a locomotive factory.

Neugebauer is primarily interested in the development of a diesel turbine to be connected to a free-piston reciprocating engine, for use in long-

12. Heinrich Bruening, leader of the Catholic Center Party in Germany, 1924–33. In 1930 he was appointed Chancellor of the Reich to put German finances in order, but his drastic measures proved unpopular. In 1932 he was abruptly dismissed by President Paul von Hindenburg and succeeded by Franz von Papen. Bruening left Germany in 1934 and came to the U.S.

13. Dr. Franz Josef Neugebauer, engineer specializing in thermal systems for aircraft nuclear propulsion. He had been chief of initial development at the Junkers factory at Dessau, 1924–38; technical and plant manager at the Junkers factory in Munich, 1938–43; manager at the Luftfahrtforschungsanstalt in Munich, 1943–45. In 1945 he came to the U.S. and was a consulting engineer at headquarters, Air Materiel Command, Wright Field.

range aircraft cruising at speeds of 500 to 550 kilometers per hour. This type of engine would be for the immediate future, Neugebauer thinks. The turbine engine will come later when we learn how to use higher temperatures. The sequence of engines used in aviation in the future will be: 1) diesel; 2) turbine with propeller; 3) turbojet, according to Neugebauer. He thinks the Lorin jet will be used for speeds above 1,000 kilometers per hour. He says that a single-cylinder engine for his diesel development was almost finished.

I gave Dr. Neugebauer the rest of the candy I had with me for his children, and we started back to our billets.

Monday, June 4

We drive to Freising, where the Third Army (American) maintains a "cage," or detention camp. I had hoped to find some German jet-fighter combat pilots there, but was disappointed. Went through the list of Germans who were in the "cage" and picked three who had been engaged in work which might put them in possession of interesting information. Two had no knowledge of importance. The third, one Ottokar Dietrich, had worked on plans for long-range rocket turbines for transatlantic use.

The Russians were much interested in the rocket development, he said, and are trying to get Germans with rocket experience into their territory; but he does not want to work for the Russians. He said the Russian radio broadcasts were having a decided effect on the German people—promises of food and better conditions for those who are in the zone of Russian occupation. I asked him about the food he was getting from us. "Barely enough to live on," he replied. Coffee and bread for breakfast, nothing else (no jams, etc.); soup only for dinner and supper; no bread. "It is not so bad for me, but the manager of our company is not well. He has diabetes. I am afraid he cannot live on such food. We came voluntarily, too; we did not come as prisoners."

We had lunch with the American lieutenant colonel in charge of the detention camp, a man who gave the impression of cold, harsh ruthlessness. I asked him how the German prisoners were fed. "We give them whatever the Germans bring in—throw it into a pot, whatever it is. They'll get no American food and no American medicine. I can tell you that. They won't get any sympathy in the way we treat them."

I mentioned the man who was suffering from diabetes.

"What would you do?" he asked coldly.

"Well, I don't think I'd let him die. After all, he came of his own free will."

"No, we don't want him to die on our hands. We'd better get rid of him before he dies."

Drove to the partly completed research laboratories southeast of Munich. No one there but guards and troops. We walked through some of the buildings and then went on to Prien. Lieutenant Uellendahl and I take turns at the wheel of the jeep during a day's driving. We found General Ward [14] of the 20th Armored Division in charge of the area. He was my instructor in pistol shooting at the University of Wisconsin when I was a field artillery cadet in 1920–21–22. (We used Colt .45 automatics. I made the first team.) He feels much as I do about our treatment of people in Germany—disgusted with it.

Tuesday, June 5

To the Prien airport to see Dr. [Felix] Kracht at 7:30. Discussed altitude rocket glider with him and went to see a model of a flying wing some of his associates are working on. Kracht is head of D.F.S.[15] Institute S (Sailplanes). They have been working on the construction of rocket gliders for experimental flying at extremely high altitudes (twenty-five to thirty-five kilometers). They expect to obtain flight data at supersonic speeds, data on control and aerodynamic characteristics in reaching such speeds, meteorological data, etc. Their plan is to tow the rocket glider to an altitude of ten to twelve kilometers, then to climb under rocket power to twenty-five kilometers. They estimate that the climb from twelve kilometers to twenty-five kilometers will require four minutes. There will be rocket fuel for eight minutes. Rocket flights at these altitudes have not yet been made, as the project was unfinished at the time our American troops arrived. Kracht expected to obtain Mach numbers up to 2.6 at thirty-five kilometers, using two rocket units of 4,000 k.g. total thrust. Highly swept-back wings, of course.

The pilot's cabin would be held at a pressure of about 8,000 meters and would be so well sealed that the oxygen exhaled by the pilot, who wears a regular oxygen mask, would be sufficient to make up for any

14. General Orlando Ward, commanding general of the 20th Armored Division, 1944–45.

15. Deutsche Forschungsanstalt für Segeflug (German Research Institute for Glider Flight).

leakage. This cabin is attached to the fuselage by explosive bolts. In case of trouble at altitude the pilot would press a button which would cause the bolts to explode, and the cabin, still under pressure, to separate from the rest of the fuselage and wings. A small parachute, automatically opened, would stabilize the cabin in its descent to about 8,000 meters, where the pilot would be automatically ejected and his own chute opened. (The pilot is to fly in a prone position, very much like that in the XF5U designed by Zimmerman.)[16]

Kracht has also been working on a twin-fuselage glider which would use the wing section between the fuselages (about four meters in span) as a test section, so that various airfoils could be tried out at high Mach numbers. This development is being carried on at Ainring near Salzburg.

Kracht thinks the rocket plane is so limited in endurance and range that "transoceanic travel would be impossible." It is obvious, however, that he is not well acquainted with German plans and developments along these lines. He thinks the Lorin, or ram jet, may be used for long-range, high-speed flying—transatlantic, for instance—with track launching.

D.F.S. has carried on some interesting experimental work with soaring at high altitudes under certain weather conditions. Kracht says that vertical currents capable of sustaining a glider can be obtained at altitudes of eighteen to twenty-two kilometers. The Heinemann flying-wing development, which was being carried on at D.F.S., was designed to use coal for fuel. (Because of oil shortage. "Would have preferred to use gasoline.") With this they hoped to obtain 1,200-1,300 kilometers per hour with a ram jet. Piggyback launching.

Stopped, after conferences with Kracht and his associates, to look over the German planes lined up on the field (the same field where Anne and I landed with our Mohawk in 1938, when I flew to Munich to attend the Lilienthal conference).[17] They were not in good condition, but less looted and damaged than in most places—trainers, fighters, transports. Looked over an Me-109, an FW-189 (reconnaissance), and a Bucker 181 low-wing primary trainer (100 h.p.; Hirth four-cylinder engine; standard trainer for German Air Force).

From the airfield we drove to Kracht's home to look over some drawings and models he had there. On the way I asked about Major and Frau

16. Charles H. Zimmerman, aeronautical engineer with Vought-Sikorsky Aircraft and later Chance Vought Aircraft, 1937–48.

17. An aeronautical conference attended by representatives from various countries.

Braun with whom Anne and I spent many hours during our visit to Prien in 1938. "Major Braun? He killed himself not long ago. Why? We do not know. There are many rumors, but we do not know." I asked about the Baron and Baroness Cramer-Klett. It was thought that they were both still alive. She had been living in a house near the castle not long ago. About him they were not sure. The daughter—the young girl who had danced with the peasant boys in 1938—they were not sure about. The castle Hohen Ashau had been bought by the German government and was now a Marine hospital. Udet's death they thought caused by an accident; they did not know.

From Kracht's home we returned to our quarters.

We drove to the airfield at Ainring, near Salzburg, in the afternoon (Lieutenant Uellendahl, Dr. Kracht, his secretary, Sergeant Walker). We took two jeeps. Since Walker was translating, I suggested to Lieutenant Uellendahl that he take the extra jeep and drive to Berchtesgaden, which he was anxious to see.

En route to the airfield we stopped to pick up one of Dr. Kracht's associates. We found the D.F.S. institute to be in rather bad condition, and the looting still going on, even though American troops are occupying the field; drawers upset on the floor, precision tools gone, drawings scattered about, etc. Still worse, we found that the glider and the pressure cabin we had come to see had been loaded onto a truck yesterday and carted away by one of the Army technical missions—where to, no one knew. The Germans were much discouraged. One American officer had told them to carry on with their experiments. A few days later another American officer carried the glider they were working on away. Meanwhile, they were not allowed to come onto the airfield (at Ainring) to salvage what was left of their tools and equipment, stop continued looting, and put their institute in order.

We drove Kracht's associate back to his home. While I was talking to Kracht, I noticed something a little unusual in a discussion taking place between Kracht's associate and Sergeant Walker, the former looking even more dejected than before, the latter speaking with more emphasis than usual. I moved closer and saw that Sergeant Walker was showing the German some snapshots he had taken at one of the German prison camps—a pit containing dead and starved bodies thrown one upon the other. After we started back Walker said, "He still thought the German government was all right. I told him he'd better stop thinking so, or he might find himself behind bars."

Wednesday, June 6

From Prien we followed the autobahn westward for some miles and then cut across country over winding, narrow roads, toward Oberammergau. It was my turn at the wheel today. A jeep is not comfortable riding, but it stands a terrific banging about—service that would tear an ordinary car to pieces. Our practice is to cover the roads about as fast as we can in reasonable safety.

A bridge was out, which forced us to make a long and beautiful detour through a mountain pass. On our way up the horseshoe turns we passed dozens of horse-drawn German Army vehicles. The soldiers and drivers stared at us curiously. There was no mark of war aside from these returning troops—remnants of a defeated army—and an occasional overturned car or truck bulldozed to the roadside—peaceful villages and farms as far out over the valley as one could see.

We ate a late lunch at the Air Force–operated inn beneath the sheer rock tower of Kofel. Then drove to the Messerschmitt factory on the lower slopes of the mountain on the opposite side of the town. The buildings of the factory are camouflaged to look like Bavarian inns or barracks. The officers of the company were there, led in the professor's absence by a blond young German of obvious engineering ability named [Waldemar] Voigt (in charge of future projects and other departments).

An improved 163, the 163C, has been built by Junkers at Dessau and, Voigt thinks, already tested. The Messerschmitt Company felt that the 163 (rocket) was not a practical fighter because of its short endurance. They concentrated their attention on the improvement of the 262 (turbojet) and had developed the 262 into a night fighter, a two-seat trainer, and a cannon fighter carrying a 50-mm. gun. They were also developing a higher-speed fighter around the HE-001 turbojet engine. Voigt prefers flying-wing type (163) for long range and high angles of attack, but not for high speed and low angles of attack. However, calculations regarding tailless types for high speeds are still under way. While Voigt tends away from tailless type for fighter, Messerschmitt is uncertain.

The 262, Voigt says, lands at about 182 kilometers per hour. They once tried bulging the top surface of the wings, between engine and fuselage, to hold extra fuel tanks. Found gain in speed resulted. The 262 was designed for six 30-mm. cannon, therefore balances well with one 50-

mm. cannon in nose. One 262 was built with a 50-mm. cannon in the nose "at the special desire of Hitler"—carried twenty-eight rounds. Was flown in combat, but made no hits. In the 262, designed for six 30-mm. cannon, space is provided for eighty rounds each. The 262 is armor-plated, forward, against 12 mm. In the first planes produced, armor plate in the rear was made optional. In the later planes it was part of standard equipment.

Voigt says that two men left the Messerschmitt factory for Japan in September or October with drawings, etc., for the 262 and 163. He knows nothing beyond that except that their submarine was damaged and delayed in Norway. Voigt kept emphasizing his feeling that Germany lacked leaders in industrial management—men who could manage the entire enterprise—the entire industry.

After the meeting in the factory, Voigt took us through the tunnels in the mountain, where the new underground factory was being set up. They were unlighted, and our flashlights poor. We stumbled over the debris left by looters and bumped into benches and partially installed machines. The air was damp, and everything covered with moisture.

Supper at the hotel. Afterward, Lieutenant Uellendahl and I started out to climb Kofel. We passed through, at its base, a field in which probably a hundred cattle were grazing, each one with a large bell hanging from a strap around its neck. The path zigzags upward at a fairly steep and constant angle, first to the right and then to the left of a slide of rock, covered by branches until it reaches the base of the precipice which forms one side of the towered peak of Kofel. The last hundred or two hundred feet is a climb over barren rock, worn smooth in places by the feet of pilgrims making their way to the large wooden cross which is planted on the summit. We arrived just in time for the sunset, about an hour and a half after starting from the hotel. View of valley, river and villages—Oberammergau below, a pebble's throw away—higher Alps in opposite direction. We watch the sunset, sign the book on the Cross, and start down. Arrived back at hotel about dark (long summer twilight).

Conference with Colonel Lovelace[18] in evening. He invites me to go see a medical research institute near Garmisch, where he will be tomorrow morning; says very interesting experiments are being carried on there.

18. Dr. William R. Lovelace, active in aviation medicine since 1938. He was a surgeon at the Mayo Clinic from 1939 to 1946 and collaborated in devising the Boothby-Lovelace-Bulbulian oxygen mask. He was a medical consultant to Trans World Airlines, American Airlines, and Convair, and became a member of the special committee on space technology for NACA.

Thursday, June 7

Conference with Voigt. He tells me that Professor Messerschmitt was taken from his home a few days ago by our troops and that he is probably now in prison. Voigt says he understands that an S.S. uniform was found in one of Messerschmitt's vaults and that he thinks this was one of the causes for the professor's arrest. Voigt says Professor Messerschmitt was not a politician, but that he may have been an "honorary member" of the S.S. Voigt also mentioned the Russian propaganda; says it is having a decided effect on the Germans (promises of food, work, etc.).

From Oberammergau Lieutenant Uellendahl and I drove to Garmisch-Partenkirchen to see the Medical Research Institute operated by Dr. [Ulrich] Henschke, located on the slope of a mountain—a small institute, simply built and simply but very intelligently run. Dr. Henschke, a man in his mid thirties, turned out to be a great admirer of Dr. Carrel—had studied *Man the Unknown* with care and understood it as no one else I have talked to. He had a copy of *The Culture of Organs* on his shelves, and the Swiss edition of *Listen! the Wind*. He says his greatest ambition is to have an institute such as Carrel wrote of.

We discuss a number of Dr. Henschke's projects: gunnery sights, artificial limbs, hearing for the blind, cellular emanations, etc. He shows us through his laboratories—small buildings like mountain cabins—views of Alps and valleys through the windows—ideal places for creative work. In one he is testing new methods of controlling guns in aircraft. "It is best to use only one group of muscles." He has a stick (pilot's) with a bar on top which acts as a rudder, "so it is not necessary to use the feet at all in aiming a fighter." I protest, saying that I think we are getting too far away from monkeys anyhow, and that I do not see why we should not also use our feet. He asks me to try it out for myself—a rather crude affair made quickly out of plank and wire. I get down in the seat while the apparatus is adjusted.

At one end of the room is a rotating stick, at the end of which a photoelectric cell is fastened. A spotlight is fastened to the stick, and one is supposed to keep the light beam on the photoelectric cell. As long as the beam covers half or more of the cell, a counter, set to the rate of fire of a machine gun, is in operation. When the beam covers less than half the cell, the counter stops operating. By means of a stop watch the number of hits per minute are counted.

I found that I made a much better score when using the stick alone, which I have never done before, than when the spotlight was hooked up to the rudder and stick as in a normal fighter. The difference was several hundred per cent in favor of the former method! However, in fairness, it must be said that the rudder hookup was cramped and jerky. But this is not enough to account for the great difference in the number of hits I made. I tried removing my heavy G.I. boots and doubled my previous score with the conventional controls—one has a much better "feel" with his shoes off. But the advantage of controlling everything with the arms, "one group of muscles alone," was still apparently great.

At another small building Dr. Henschke showed us where he was developing artificial limbs which would be actuated by the nerves and muscles of the stump. He demonstrated with two German soldiers, one of whom had lost an arm and the other a leg.

From the medical institute Lieutenant Uellendahl and I drove to Munich, where we stopped at the T Section for supper with Colonel Gifford. Half hour's conference. Then off for Nürnberg. Back roads at first. Heavy crops; overturned trucks; walking German soldiers—singly—in pairs—in groups—green uniforms—blue-gray uniforms—white bands of surrender on their sleeves—clear sky, and the long June twilight.

We speed up to 50 m.p.h. after we strike the autobahn. American units at intervals along the roads. Most bridges are out, and we have to follow the detours. At Paris there was talk of sniping and "werewolf" activity in the Nürnberg area—wires strung across the road to cut the heads off jeep riders. But it is always somewhere else: in Germany when one is in France; in the Harz Mountains when one is in Munich; in Nürnberg before one gets there; always a hundred miles ahead or a hundred miles behind; never where one is at the moment. The fact is that after the Germans surrendered there has been remarkably little trouble. Possibly resistance will increase as time passes. Some of our officers think so.

It is nearly night when we arrive at Nürnberg—only a wash of light left in the western sky. It is a dead city: heavily bombed; piles of rubble; gutted buildings; ruined walls; a few lights here and there where a livable room is left. We drive for blocks without seeing a sign of life; not a single person, German or American. We stop in front of a big building on the right side of the street. There are lighted windows, and two American trucks are lined up at the curb. The building has been cracked by bombs, and the windows have been blown out; but the floors have not collapsed.

We go inside to ask about billets for the night. It turns out to be the

telephone exchange and post office. A handful of our troops are there to
guard it and carry on the routine duties of the night. An officer welcomes
us. Yes, there is a room we can use; they keep one specially for tran-
sients who may wish to spend the night, but it is rather littered. If we
don't mind that, we are welcome.

We set up our cots. Then I go over to the window. Most of it has been
bricked up; only a small opening left, and all the glass blown out of that.
Across the street a great pile of rubble is all that remains of what was
once a large building: chunks of brick walls, twisted pipes and girders.
On each side of this rubble pile—probably the result of a direct
hit from a "blockbuster"—are gutted buildings; walls standing, but
roofs blown off and floors collapsed. The sky and the last faint light of
evening show through the higher gaps of windows. Down below, as far as
I can see in each direction, the far sidewalk is covered with high piles of
rubble. On our side of the street it has been cleared away for the distance
of several buildings. Pushing my head farther out, I can see one spire of
the cathedral, gutted, but still beautiful, dimly silhouetted in the night.
Above, there are broken clouds, and the stars are coming out. I feel
surrounded by death. Only in the sky is there hope; only in that which
man has never touched and which God forbid he ever will.

Friday, June 8

The clear light of day shows a devastated city—even worse than it
seemed last night. "None of our outfits are quartered here. There's no
place for them to stay. The city's unlivable for troops. We only keep
enough to man the switchboard." The telephone exchange is the most
intact building we can see, and it would be considered a wreck in any city
back home: holes in the roof; blown-out windows; cracks in the walls.

We start out at 8:15, through the ruins and past the cathedral. I see a
carving of Christ still standing on a shelf on one of the inner columns,
looking down on the rubble which covers the benches where people once
came to worship. We stop and go back and look again at the figure,
apparently untouched.

As I walked to our jeep, a boy and girl ran across the street and
paused to look at us. They were probably between six and nine years old,
thin, not very well dressed, and, I judged, quite hungry. I had a taffy bar
in my pocket, and tore it in half, giving part to each child. *"Danke-
schön; Danke-schön"*; they snatched the candy and began eating it at once,

not as children who want a candy bar, but as children who are hungry.

On the way out of Nürnberg, we stopped at the Nazi stadium. It had been only lightly bombed and little damaged. The central columned structure was camouflaged with nets covering the top and loose bricks covering the marble steps and benches. The figure which had adorned the top had fallen down and crashed onto the stage below.

The dais from which Hitler used to speak to his legions—empty, littered with fragments of brick and marble—reminded me of one of the Mayan temples in Yucatan. Here, too, there was no sign of the people who had built the structure—not a person anywhere within the enclosure —only an American Negro M.P. directing traffic along an adjoining road, visible through one of the great gateways. There were a few yellowish blotches on the field—filled-in bomb craters. The seats and walkways of the smaller galleries were covered with sod for camouflage, and the grass had grown quite high, which, combined with the white oblongish architecture of the structure, made it seem all the more like an excavated Mayan temple.

The interior of the main building had been used as a refuge—probably by people who had lost their homes in the bombing, and by D.P.'s after the surrender. The floors, once so carefully scrubbed and polished, were covered with inches of torn paper, rags, and broken furniture. The glass panes of the phone booths were smashed. Every room I entered had been used as a latrine. I have seldom before seen such filth where people lived. It smelled like a box in which mice have raised their young—only worse.

We took the autobahn toward Leipzig. There were more people walking at the roadside as we went north—a woman, barefoot; a man trudging along with a shoe on one foot and the other bare—the usual baby carriages, bicycles, and small hand-drawn carts—a shining team of horses, probably liberated from some German farmer, hauling what looked like two or three Polish families with their bundled-up belongings. We pass an artillery train going in the opposite direction—American trucks, caterpillars, and guns. "China bound," they say.

We soon meet a sign ordering all traffic to detour off the autobahn. Stop at a battalion ordnance station in a small village for an extra tire. Lunch with the local officers. They talk of the S.S. troops they have in their "cage."

"The last time I saw them, they were sweeping up the streets with their hands," said one of the officers.

"Do you mean literally or figuratively?" I asked.

"Literally. They damn well deserved it—some of their own medicine —just what they ought to get."

The officers seemed to hate Germans in general, and the S.S. above all else. "We rotate being in charge of the cage," a young lieutenant told me. "The fellows try to outdo each other in handling the S.S."

"For instance?" I asked.

"Oh, one of the best is to make them stretch out their arms and lean against a wall. They start falling down after about half an hour. Then we say, 'S.S. goot?' And if they answer, 'S.S. goot,' we make them do it again."

We alternate driving, through a heavy rain the afternoon. Put the jeep top up and raincoats on. But it still blew in and seeped through the canvas. The sky began to clear, however, before we reached Leipzig. This city is not as badly bombed as Munich, although there are parts which are completely ruined. We stopped at the M.P. headquarters to try to find a cousin of Lieutenant Uellendahl, who is in that organization. He was out somewhere around the grounds and could not be located. He left a note, and we started off for Dessau and the Junkers factory.

The Junkers factory and the adjoining airport have been badly bombed, and most of the buildings are destroyed. The field and taxiways are covered with dozens of burned planes of various types, set on fire by the Germans: wing panels and tail lying in position on the ground; central portion burned and melted; lumps of engines sticking up through the debris. Showing through the collapsed roofs of the factories and lined up in rows outside are dozens—no, hundreds—of turbojet engines (JU-004).

We drive along the rubble-lined streets and stop in front of one of the factories, while I climb inside and over the debris to look at some of the machinery. Farther on we find two Me-163 rocket-plane fuselages, used for static test and lacking much equipment. Then along one of the taxiways, past burned piggyback JU-88's—the remains of their FW-190's lying with them. At the far end of the field we found the armament hangar and gun range. In the hangar was the fuselage of an Me-163 which had been subjected to fore and aft gun fire. It was the most intact we have seen, the rocket engine still installed.

To Dr. [August] Lichte's home on Immelmannstrasse for a conference with the doctor. We found Lichte at his supper—black bread, jam, and coffee. He welcomed us courteously, and we asked him to go on eating while we talked.

Junkers did not want to build the 163 rocket plane, he said, but were ordered to by Speer. The Messerschmitt people had been able to get out of doing it because all of their facilities had been devoted to building 162's, he said, but the Junkers JU-88 program was being cut down at the time and was to be stopped on the first of March. Therefore, Junkers had factory facilities available and were ordered to build the 163. Dr. Heinz Schmitt had been in charge of the Junkers jet development, Lichte told us. Would we not like to talk to Dr. Schmitt in the morning? We arranged for the conference and left.

Commander Marchand, who was at the Junkers plant when we arrived, offered to arrange billets for us at a house where he had stayed on one of his previous trips to Dessau. Also, he wanted to talk to me about a plan he had to take ten of the Junkers technical men, together with their families, into the American zone. (Dessau is to be occupied by the Russians.) Marchand says it would serve two purposes to do this. First, it would make the experience of these people available to us. Second, it would keep Russia from getting one of the best groups of engine builders in the world. He suggests that he and I go to the Military Government in Dessau and try to sell them on the plan. I reply that I think the idea excellent, that the only improvement I can suggest is to try to get one hundred of them into our area instead of ten, but that I think it would be unwise for me to go with him to the Military Government because of the political situation. I say that I am willing to "stick my neck out" if I can be effective, but that I think it would be ineffective in this instance. I suggest that he try alone first, and after that, if he thinks I can help, I will go with him. He agrees.

Dr. Lichte has already gone to notify his co-workers and to pack and make arrangements for his own family to start if authorization can be obtained. Russian propaganda about food and work is having little effect here where the Germans are faced with actual Russian occupation. Too many stories are seeping back across the border—stories of murder, rape, and loot. The Germans are terrified. Most of them would give anything they have to get into an American or British—or even a French—occupation zone.

As we are about to start for our billets, I look in through the open doors of the building opposite where our jeep is parked. It has a familiar look. I walk up the steps and in through the doors. Yes, it is the Junkers museum. There is the nose section of one of Professor Junkers' early planes—the corrugated construction that was used in those days. Beside it, on a large table, are parts of a wing of the same period. There are lines of stands for showcases and photographs on the walls showing the early history of flight. Everything is covered with white dust and fallen plaster.

I go outside and then, seeing another open door, down into the basement. It was evidently used for the museum's files and is in terrible shape —films, prints, and documents scattered all over the floor, torn and stepped on, and those near the knocked-out windows ruined by water. I pick up one of the films. It is of an old Junkers seaplane taking off. Another shows a Junkers plane on some northern expedition. There are thousands of them, most of the file drawers being simply dumped on the floor by the looters.

We are billeted at the home of a middle-aged German couple; a frame house rather overfurnished and containing strange odds and ends such as a stuffed monkey in the parlor-bedroom to which we were shown. Located on the outskirts of Dessau, the house has been uninjured by the bombing, although a few hundred yards away several rows of homes have been completely wiped out.

The woman—frail and sad—speaks a little English. The man is almost deaf and dumb; but with great effort can speak and hear a little. We traded three packages of K rations for a few slices of black bread. Then I set my canvas cot up on a small screened-in porch and rolled my sleeping bag out on it. A clear sky—stars—reminded me of the porch on our farm in Minnesota.

Saturday, June 9

Gave Frau ————a cake of white soap (there was only a small bit of dark brown laundry soap in the bathroom) and a can of meat and vegetable hash. She cries a little. They have been eating only once a day, she tells me. They have had no meat for weeks. For twelve years they "have been betrayed by Hitler." No one could speak against what was going on, she said. If anyone tried to, they were taken away. "And now the Russians will come. We will be on the street." She told Lieutenant Uellendahl that the Nazis had wanted to sterilize her husband because of his being partially deaf and dumb.

We drive out to the Junkers factory. Many of the Junkers officers are there. We sit around a table in a room and building which have escaped the bombing.

The Junkers Company didn't want to build the 163 rocket plane because they felt its endurance was too short to make it a practical fighter. However, they were ordered to build it by the Air Ministry. They were also ordered to improve the 163, and had brought out an advanced prototype, which they called the 263. The Junkers people felt that the endurance was still not sufficient to make the 263 a practical fighter. They had built three 263's, they said, but none of them had been flown under rocket power. However, test flights had been made with 263's towed behind an Me-110. The Japanese did not have plans for the 263, they said. They were supposed to send the plans to Japan but hadn't gotten around to it. However, the Japanese "might have plans for the 163." They had, under orders, sent plans for the latest 163 to the Messerschmitt people in December, 1944, and June, 1945, but don't think they were sent on to Japan.

The Junkers officers were doubtful about the rocket plane for long-range flying in the future. However, they think the long-range turbojet is practical, although they have not studied its use on transoceanic lines. Junkers built only ten 162 turbojet fighters. The officers think that not over fifty were built in all of Germany. (It seems that most company officers knew very little about what other companies were doing, or else they are simply covering up what information they have.)

The Junkers people prefer "two turbojet planes for performance; four turbojet planes for safety." They had been studying a project to put four turbojets in a 287.

The JU-287 is a twin turbojet plane with highly swept *forward* wings, built around a 177 fuselage. A prototype was built (destroyed before the surrender, I understand), and partially tested. It has been flown only up to a maximum speed of 600 kilometers per hour, they said. Up to that point no trouble had been experienced with stability or flutter. They expected it to make 870 kilometers per hour at an altitude of six kilometers. (In reply to my question they said the 262 has made 950 kilometers per hour in a dive, at which point difficulty was experienced with the ailerons.) They think the Mach number obtainable with swept-forward wings is about the same as that obtainable with swept-back wings. They felt that swept-forward wings had a decided advantage at high angles of attack, also had "a better place for landing gear in fuselage, leaving more room in the wings." However, they had a "swept-back project" under way from which they expected to obtain a top speed of 950 kilometers at an altitude of six kilometers and 880 kilometers at sea level (turbojet).

The Daimler-Benz Company had developed a "double engine," liquid-cooled, the take-off horsepower of which was 3,000. This was called the DB-610, and was used in the HE-177. (This information in reply to my question about the double engine I had seen in one of the collapsed hangars on the airport.) No, the company had no turbine-supersonic propeller project under way. (This also in reply to my question.)

I asked about the piggyback FW-190–JU-88's—of which there were a number on the field, destroyed. "I should think using a bomber for a bomb would be too expensive to be practical," I said. They had many old JU-88's, they replied, "too old for combat." The Air Ministry had said, "Find some way to use them," since they would otherwise have to be destroyed. The piggyback JU-88 could carry between 3,500 and 4,000 k.g. of explosive, since there was no need for armament, armor plate, or crew, or fuel to return with. The pilot, riding in the FW-190, controlled the JU-88 electrically and released it from a shallow glide about three kilometers from the target. It was not radio-controlled, but continued on its aimed course under the guidance of the automatic pilot.

The Junkers people said that it cost almost as much to convert an 88 for piggyback use as it would to build a new one. However, in spite of the cost, they felt that a piggyback, if properly designed, would be practical—a larger plane, of the V-1 type, to carry the explosive and a turbojet fighter for the pilot.

The Junkers officers said they obtained very little information from the Russian-occupied area on the other side of the Mulde River. But what comes through "is not good." "The Russians are very hard on Germans, especially when they are drunk. They take all a man's clothes except one outfit. If he has good shoes, they take them and give him their poor ones."

"If the Russians come here, I think we will not stay."

"Can you leave?"

"No, we cannot leave, but we will go anyway."

The conference is about to end. I ask about the museum. "Who looted it?"

"It was gone through by American troops. But before they came it was looted by Russian prisoners. It was the Russians who did the greatest damage."

Talk to Commander Marchand before he takes off in his C-47. He tells me he has arranged with the Military Government to get eight of the Junkers men and their familes into the American-occupied zone. They will be given passes and can furnish their own transportation. Apparently many of the Germans learned only in the last three or four days that the Dessau area is to be occupied by the Russians. Before that, they thought they were to be in American territory.

Lieutenant Uellendahl and I drive back to the tank unit for lunch. I study the faces of the people on the streets—drawn, sober. There is no smiling. I realize that those men on the corner know that in another week they may be shot or starving in a Russian concentration camp. At least they will be hungrier than they are today, and they are all hungry. That young girl riding by on her bicycle—she must know that on the day the Russians come she will probably be raped by a dozen soldiers. When do they come? In days? In weeks? That, we have not told the Germans. She has a good face—nicely dressed in old but clean and brightly colored garments—like the daughter of a middle-class American family. I realize that we Americans are holding her at Dessau. She cannot flee to safety. We will not let her pass our sentries on the roads. We are turning her and thousands of others like her over to Soviet soldiers for their sport. I feel ashamed. What responsibility has this child had for Hitler and the Nazis? What right have we to call Germans and Japs barbarians when we treat women thus? It is true, in a sense, that the Germans brought it on their own shoulders, but that is too facile an excuse.

Conference with Schmitt and Lichte in the afternoon. Schmitt said that the Junkers Company has built about 6,000 turbojet engines, of which about 5,250 had been shipped to the Air Ministry before the war ended. He thinks that between 200 and 300 Me-262 fighters were in combat squadrons during the latter stages of the war. Only the Junkers 004 turbojet engine was used in the 262, he said. The first of these 004 engines, except prototypes, was built by Junkers in July and August, 1944. The first shipment of production engines was made to the Air Ministry "about September." The first flight in a 262 was made in June, 1942, Schmitt said, using a JU-004A trial engine. The first mass-production-type engine, an 004 B-1, flew in October, 1943. The 004 B-4 turbojet was used in the later 262's. Its overhaul time was fixed by the combat squadrons at twenty-five hours. Mass production of a still later type, the 004 D-4, was to begin in May.

The low overhaul time of twenty-five hours for the turbojet engines was partly due to the poor quality of available material and the substitutes which had to be used, Schmitt said. He thinks turbojet engines will eventually operate for a longer time between overhauls than reciprocating engines. He also brought out the fact that the overhaul of the turbojet engine is very easy.

Schmitt feels that the project for using a permanent rocket nozzle in combination with a turbojet for assisted take-off was impractical and that it is useless to carry experiments further along that line. Too much weight; too many different tanks; controls, etc. The arrangement tried was a BMW rocket combined with a Junkers jet.

The largest Junkers jet engine being built at the end of the war was the 012, Schmitt said. This was never tested. It would have been completed about May, 1945. Schmitt was uncertain about the value of the super-sonic propeller versus the pure jet in regard to speed, range, etc. He said that Messerschmitt had a four- or six-jet plane planned for a ten-hour flight at 800 kilometers per hour at an altitude of eight kilometers (without payload), using the Junkers 004 D-4 turbojet, which gives 1,000 k.g. static thrust. He said that the horsepower of the present turbojet engines can be increased about twenty-five per cent by "after-burning." The Lorin, or "ram jet," he felt, would be useful only at very high speeds— "1,500 kilometers per hour up, probably."

Dr. Schmitt said that the Junkers Jumo-213 water-cooled engine, developing 1,750 h.p., had been installed in the Focke-Wulf fighter, in a model called the FW190-D9, and that 2,000 to 3,000 of these planes had been built. The Jumo-213 engine added forty kilometers per hour to the speed of the 190, he said. The combat squadrons had fixed the overhaul time on the engine at 150 hours.

Dr. Lichte then described a diesel engine in which he was much interested. The first castings were in the foundry when the surrender came, he said. It was designated as the "Jumo-224."

Dr. Lichte said that in 1939 a JU-86 equipped with Jumo-205 engines had made a fifty-two-hour nonstop flight over Germany in preparation for a nonstop flight to South America.

The interpreter told us that his bicycle had been taken away from him yesterday by six Russian "slaves." [19] Two others had been taken from his family previously.

Before leaving Dessau, Lieutenant Uellendahl and I drove to the bridge across the Mulde which separates the American and Russian armies. The streets and sidewalks near the bridge were crowded with displaced persons. As soon as we got near them we encountered that inevitable mousery smell—men, women, and children, with their carts and bundles, standing around waiting for their turn to cross the river. Long columns of Poles, apparently ex-German prisoners of war, dressed in American uniforms (without insignia, of course), were marching toward

19. Prisoners, displaced persons, and others forced to work in Germany industry.

the river. I studied their faces—most of them young, many of them hardly more than boys. They were expressionless faces. Certainly there was no sign of joy at their return toward their homeland. Was there fear? If so, I could not definitely detect it. The faces were set, even grim. They swung along in step toward the narrow pontoon bridge which replaced the one blown up.

A young man in one of the columns starts to sing—in Russian. Or in Polish? It is forced—he shouts louder. Two or three others take it up. No, the attempt is a failure. They stop all together and march on quietly.

I reach the bridge. Several American soldiers, helmeted and carrying carbines, are on guard. A yard or two beyond them is a jagged concrete ledge where the explosion had torn off the bridge from the street which fed it. There is a gap of probably sixty feet (the river is not wide here); then, another jagged ledge and a single Russian soldier patrolling it, helmeted and submachine gun slung over his shoulder.

Farther on along the bank is a seemingly endless column of D.P.'s, if it can be called a column. Orderless and jammed together as a flock of sheep, it might better be described as an endless mass of humanity. Those people across the Mulde look, and I feel sure smell the same as the crowd on our side of the river—clothing as drab, bundles as large, pushing the same baby carriages and pulling the same carts. At the side of these D.P.'s is a real column of soldiers, appearing identical, at a distance, to those marching past me. They, too, seemed to be clothed in American khaki uniforms. They were too far away for me to guess at their nationality.

I turn again to the men marching past me. Another soldier tries to start a song, and fails. The column bends upstream from where I am standing, to follow the road to the pontoon bridge, which is offset a few yards from the old one which has been blown up. On the far side of the bridge is a crudely made arch, wrapped with red cloth and with the hammer and sickle on its crosspiece. The last column of soldiers marches past toward the river; a flock of D.P.'s presses forward, held in check by guards.

We drive around to the point where the soldiers from the Russian side are to be loaded into trucks. (We meet them with trucks, drive them part way, and fly them the rest of the way to their home countries, an American officer tells us.) They turn out to be French or Belgian soldiers who were captured by the Germans and sent to camps in eastern Germany. They are smiling all over, waving, and obviously overjoyed as they clamber into the American Army trucks waiting for them. A soldier throws the cane he has been carrying down at the roadside as he leaves the bridge—a final gesture to his captivity. Two or three more follow. Soon, there is a small pile of canes. There is no comparison between the attitude of these men and that of the soldiers going in the opposite direction. Still, there is a great difference between the French and the Poles in normal times—but not that much.

All of the ex-prisoners of war seemed to me surprisingly well fed—both those going into and these coming from the Russian area. Faces showed the signs of years of captivity; there was no doubt about that. But I did not see the signs of starvation that I expected after reading the accounts of the way these people have been treated.

We turn back from the bridge and start for Braunschweig—it is mid-afternoon—through the rubble-lined streets of Dessau. The city has been heavily bombed. We have to detour via Bernburg to reach Magdeburg, in order to avoid Russian territory. Bomb plotches on road at intervals. Usual detours for bridges. Women working the fields. A horse and a milk cow harnessed together to draw a wagon. A horse drawing alone a wagon which was made for a team.

A mile or so away on our left we see what appears to be the undamaged hangars of a large airfield. We drive over and find an open gate. A handful of American soldiers are guarding the place, but our passes let us in. There are many planes on the taxiways, all damaged or destroyed, some by fire, some by axe and hammer. We inspect one of the piggyback JU-88's, which has the FW-190 still attached on top. Both units have been damaged beyond repair by some sharp instrument—skin slashed, spars cut into, parts of the engine broken. A third wheel has been attached in the center of the normal JU-88 landing gear to compensate for the added load.

There are a number of HE-162 jet fighters in the hangars—single turbojet engine above the fuselage—much smaller than the Me-262. I examine the general design with its catapult-seat cockpit. It is a strange-looking plane with its low fuselage, high engine nacelle, and sharply drooped wing tips. The field has been bombed, but not heavily.

We start on for Braunschweig. Pass through Magdeburg. It has been badly bombed, too, but there are many buildings which are livable.

Stop at "Target Headquarters" at Braunschweig for the night. We are in time for a second supper—of chicken. There is an abundance of food in the American Army, and few men seem to care how hungry the German children are outside the door. It reminds me of the indifference of the Chinese officials at Nanking [during the Yangtze flood of 1931] to the starving, dying thousands outside the city's walls.

Sunday, June 10

To the D.F.L., Hermann Goering Institute. It is located in the forest outside Braunschweig, buildings well separated to minimize the effects of bombing. There were no guides available, so we borrowed a blueprint of the grounds and organized our own tour of inspection. There were very few people about, none in most of the buildings. We simply went around until we found a door open or with the glass knocked out, and then from room to room, wherever interest took us.

This institute has not been greatly damaged, by comparison at least. We saw no sign of bombing, and while "slaves" had looted the buildings (drawers emptied onto the floor in search of precision tools and other small items of value), most of the equipment was reasonably intact. We went through the eight-meter tunnel, the "high-speed tunnel," two supersonic tunnels, the armament laboratory and workshop, the evacuated tunnel for studying the trajectory of projectiles at high altitude, etc.

It is an immense establishment. Lord only knows how much it cost to build and run. The evacuated projectile range alone was a tremendous undertaking, to say nothing of the several wind tunnels. As in almost every other place I have been, pictures of Hitler and Goering were mutilated almost beyond recognition. It was strange to see these pictures, which were so prominently and proudly displayed when I was last in Germany before the war, now lying torn and trampled underfoot with the rubbish on the floor.

In a drafting room in one of the buildings, lying on top of a pile of rubbish, I found a photograph of a beautifully carved madonna, from southern Germany, I think. It was startling to see it there so clean and undamaged amidst the filth. I "liberated" it for Anne, wondering who had been its former possessor. Who was the draftsman who carried such a photograph on his—or her—desk?

Went through the engine experimental laboratories in the afternoon. Then, on the way back to Braunschweig, stopped to see Professor [Hermann] Blenk at his home (director of the institute and head of the aerodynamics department). Dr. [Theodor] Zobel, who lived nearby, was also present. They said that the institute had been much handicapped in its work because shortage of electrical current (obtained from brown coal) prevented them from using the large wind tunnels except at night.

Zobel thinks the 163 type of fighter will eventually use a rocket only for take-off and to reach a speed of between 400 and 500 kilometers per hour. Cruising power, he believes, should be obtained from a ram jet. He feels that the ram may be the best power plant for supersonic speeds.

After leaving Professor Blenk's house, we stopped to see Professor [Adolf] Busemann (head of the Gas Dynamic Institute). Then to Target Headquarters where we had supper, packed, and checked out. Portions of Braunschweig along our route were badly bombed. Other portions were intact. It was my turn to drive again. We planned on spending the night in Nordhausen. Our route took us through the Harz Mountains and through several towns full of German Army hospitals. Much of the area we passed through showed no signs of the war. Most of the people in the hospital towns looked at us with unfriendly eyes as we passed. The wounded soldiers simply stared at our jeep with expressionless faces, limping, legless, armless, crippled, probably worse inside the buildings.

We had received several reports to the effect that the Harz Mountains area was dangerous to drive through—still full of hiding S.S. troops. It was the usual story: the closer we got the less danger there seemed to be, and the officers in the Harz area, of whom we inquired, said they had heard of no recent "incidents." However, there were places where foxholes along the road seemed quite recently dug. Gun emplacements, burned trucks, and blasted tanks showed where fighting had taken place not many weeks ago; and at one point we passed a meadow with ten or eleven freshly covered graves lined up with German wooden crosses at their heads.

On a hillside, not far from Nordhausen, we stopped to look at a bough-covered sniper's position a few yards off the roadside. Near it lay a German hand grenade. The forest was thick. There were several Harz Mountains canaries in the boughs of trees. We stayed only a few minutes—it is wiser not to pause too long in such an area—and then drove on to Nordhausen. Since it was still daylight we decided to go to the underground factory before looking for our billets. After getting directions from a German passer-by, we had no trouble in finding it. To reach the entrance we had to drive through Camp Dora, an ex-German prison camp from which a large percentage of the factory's workers were obtained. ("They were told when they went into the tunnels that the only way they would ever come out was in smoke.")

The camp's barracks were full of displaced persons, and as soon as we got near the buildings, we were surrounded by the smell of mousery again. The inmates seemed to be of all the nationalities of Eastern Europe. Their clothing was dirty but seemed adequate for the season. From their bodies and faces one would judge that they were not too badly fed. The odor, or at least part of it, could be ascribed to the practice of the men urinating in the open and of the women dumping garbage not far outside the kitchen door. Some of the men were armed and standing at the gate. Apparently the camp maintained a police organization of its own.

There were hundreds of parts for the great V-2 rocket lying on the ground and on flatcars standing on the siding—nose sections, central sections, tails. Surrounded by these strange devices I felt as though I had woken in another planet, so different were they from anything I had seen before. Dozens of the tail sections were being used by the D.P.'s for houses—laid flat on the ground, fins sticking out behind, shiny metal all over, a shelf to sleep on built across the interior like a floor.

The guard at the tunnel entrance said we would have to have a local pass, so we drove several kilometers to his unit's headquarters to get one. Then, since the tunnel went all the way through the mountain and since the headquarters were nearer the other end, we drove up and inside with our jeep from the opposite direction. A full-size railroad track runs all the way through the tunnel. We drove over it for several hundred yards, past side tunnels filled with machinery and engine and rocket parts—a tremendous place, fully lighted as though waiting only for a change in shift before starting operation again. We couldn't drive beyond the center because of a boxcar blocking the way, left there by British troops who are removing some of the V-2 rockets. Since it was fairly late, none of them were at work. In fact, as far as we could tell, there was no one else in the entire system of tunnels.

We left our jeep and followed one of the side tunnels. It contained a production line for V-2 rocket engines—dozens of them in the process of construction. After following this tunnel for several hundred feet, we came to a second main tunnel paralleling the first. Here we found an entire V-2 rocket set up and hacked crudely but effectively into cross section, apparently by Allied experts. Back and forth through the cross tunnels. There were miles of them, some producing V-2 parts, some producing parts for Junkers engines.

As we worked our way toward the entrance, we again encountered the "mouse smell" and knew that we were close to a place where D.P.'s had been living recently. Soon, the litter we came to proved we were correct. They had been living in what must once have been a combination office and hospital tunnel not far from the outer entrance. Here there were many small wooden rooms, two tiers of them. For a time we went from one to the other. Then we separated, and Lieutenant Uellendahl investigated the lower tier while I looked into the rooms of the upper.

One of the rooms contained the identification cards of the workmen—thousands of them—scattered in files over the floor like almost everything else that could be dumped out. Each card contained an identification photograph and a brief description of the worker.

Drove from the underground factory to the Town Major at Nordhausen to get billets for the night—from a man in American uniform who spoke broken English with a strong Dutch accent. He billeted us in a large house near the center of the city—run by a young housemother who speaks a little English.

We found her in a house across the street—answering our ring dressed in a not-too-heavy nightgown. Thus dressed, she escorted us to our home for the night and showed us to a large bedroom containing two big single beds with white sheets and clean thick quilts. Then she showed us where to park our jeep and complained, not too convincingly, as the lights of another jeep driving up practically removed the effect of the nightgown she was wearing.

Monday, June 11

Found two locked jeeps parked behind ours this morning, so had to walk to breakfast. While we were eating, we talked of the underground factory and of Camp Dora. "That's where the Germans had furnaces that were too small to take a whole body, so they used to cut the arms and legs off and stuff 'em in that way."

"The prisoners were so badly starved that hundreds of them were beyond saving when the Americans came. They're still dying."

Back to our billets to pack—a five-minute operation. Our young housemother came in, laughing, to give us each a strawberry from the garden. She was dressed in a German woman's uniform. "What is that uniform?" I asked.

"German blitz girl," she answered, still laughing.

"Were you a blitz girl in the war?"

993

"Me? No, I am half Jewish. I had no clothes. This was given to me as a present—as a joke—after the war ended." She laughed again.

"Do you always laugh?" Lieutenant Uellendahl inquired. (Last night, this morning, whenever we saw her, she was gay and her face was smiling.)

"Yes, every day. Because for ten years I have been afraid."

I gave her a package of cigarettes—now almost unobtainable in Germany. She ran into the dining room and brought back a dish full of strawberries. We took only a small one each, for we know how short of food these people are. Her father was sent to Buchenwald ten years ago, she told us. There had been no word from him since. And over ten years —it would not be possible to find records over such a time. She never expected to hear of him again. Her mother was dead. Her husband had been shot because he married her, a half-Jewess, against orders. (He had applied for permission to marry her and been refused.)

She had traveled much during the war, she said, moving from one city to another every few months to escape "branding" because of her Jewish blood. The German government had become bogged down with records, she told us, and each change of residence gave her a new respite of as much as several months before she would be ordered to report for "branding." And by that time she would have moved again.

We had planned on exploring the opposite end of the underground factory this morning, but decided to drive through Camp Dora first. Some of the barracks—long, low wooden buildings—were occupied by Poles, some by Russians, some by Czechs, some by nationalities we could not place.

On the mountainside above the camp we saw a low, small, factory-like building with a brick smokestack of very large diameter for its height. We could find no road leading to it, so threw the jeep into four-wheel drive and climbed directly up the steep hillside, weaving in and out between the tree trunks. At one end of the building were stacked probably two dozen stretchers, dirty and stained with blood—one of them showing the dark red outline of a human body which had lain upon it.

The doors of the building were open. We stepped in. On our left, through another open doorway, lay a black, peasant-type coffin, a white cross painted on top. Beside it on the concrete floor, covered carelessly with canvas, lay what was undoubtedly a human body; and beside that, another coffin. We moved on into the main room of the building. It contained two large cremating furnaces, side by side, the steel stretchers for holding the bodies sticking out through the open doors. The fact that two furnaces were required added to the depressing mass-production horror of the place.

The statement that arms and legs had to be cut off to get the bodies in was, of course, a myth, for the doors were large and the stretchers long. But what difference did it make? Here was a place where men and life and death had reached the lowest form of degradation. How could any reward in national progress even faintly justify the establishment and operation of such a place? When the value of life and the dignity of death are removed, what is left for man?

A figure steps in through the door—a man in prison costume. No, a boy; he is hardly old enough to call a man. The prison suit bags around him, oversize, pulled in at waist and hanging loosely over shoulders. He moves out of the brighter light so that I can see his face more clearly. He is like a walking skeleton; starved; hardly any flesh covering the bones; arms so thin that it seems only the skin is left to cover them.

He speaks in German to Lieutenant Uellendahl, pointing toward the furnaces. "Twenty-five thousand in a year and a half." He is Polish, he says in answer to our questioning, seventeen years old. He motions us to follow him and walks into the room we first saw. Stooping, he lifts the canvas from the form lying beside the coffins. It covered an ex-prisoner like himself, only thinner, lying, also in prison dress, half curled up on an Army stretcher.

It is hard to realize that the one is dead, the other living, they look so much alike. A few days' growth of dark hair bristling from the head, hunger-chiseled features, burning dark eyes, for the eyes of the dead man are open. The most striking contrast between them lay in the expression on the dead man's face. Never, I think, have I seen such tranquillity; as though at last, after living through hell on earth, peace had been found. Looking at that face, I realized that in death the spirit had triumphed over the man-built inferno we were in, that even a Nazi prison camp could not remove all the dignity from life and death.

"It was terrible. Three years of it." The face of the young Pole is screwed up in grief and anguish of his memories. He points to the body —"he was my friend, and he is *fat!*"—and re-covers it with the canvas.

We walk outside. I do not notice where the boy is taking us. We have stopped near one corner of the building. I am staring off into the distance, my mind still dwelling on those furnaces, on that body, on the people and the system which let such things arise. Suddenly I realize that

Lieutenant Uellendahl is translating. "Twenty-five thousand in a year and a half. And from each one there is only so much." The boy has cupped his hands to demonstrate the measure. He is looking down. I follow his glance. We are standing in front of what was once a large oblong pit, probably eight feet long and six feet wide and, one might guess, six feet deep. It is filled to overflowing with ashes from the furnaces—small chips of human bones—nothing else.

A trail of these ashes runs over the side of the filled-up pit where we are standing. They were dumped in carelessly, as we would dump the ashes from coal into a pit at home. And the pit was dug as a man would dig a pit for coal ashes if he cared nothing for the appearance of the grounds around his home—not very far from the furnaces and where the ground appeared easy to dig. Nearby were two oblong mounds which may have marked other pits. The boy picks up a knee joint which had not been left in the furnace long enough and holds it out to us.

Of course, I knew these things were going on; but it is one thing to have the intellectual knowledge, even to look at photographs someone else has taken, and quite another to stand on the scene yourself, seeing, hearing, feeling with your own senses. A strange sort of disturbance entered my mind. Where was it I had felt like that before? The South Pacific? Yes; those rotting Japanese bodies in the Biak caves; the load of garbage dumped on dead soldiers in a bomb crater; the green skulls set up to decorate ready room and tents.

It seemed impossible that men—civilized men—could degenerate to such a level. Yet they had. Here at Camp Dora in Germany; there in the coral caves of Biak. But there, it was we, Americans, who had done such things, we who claimed to stand for something different. We, who claimed that the German was defiling humanity in his treatment of the Jew, were doing the same thing in our treatment of the Jap. "They really are lower than beasts. Every one of 'em ought to be exterminated." How many times had I heard that statement made by American officers in the Pacific! "And why beholdest thou the mote that is in thy brother's eye but considerest not the beam that is in thine own eye?"

I looked at the young Pole. Where had I seen starvation like that before? It was on Biak Island, too. The picture of a native war canoe came up in memory—paddling slowly toward the shore near our camp, the Japanese prisoners escorted from it by armed, half-naked natives, at the end of the line several so starved that they could not stand to walk, thinner even than this Pole. Oh, we had not starved them in a prison camp like the Germans. We had been too "civilized," too clever for that. We had let them starve themselves in the jungle (their own fault) by simply not accepting their surrender. It was simple, and one was not bothered by burning eyes of famine or danger of disease. A few miles of jungle hid and smothered all of that. It was only necessary to shoot a few men advancing to surrender with their hands in the air. ("You can't trust a Jap to surrender. He'll throw a grenade at you. The only way is to kill him right now.") Or one could be more blunt about it and shout to an enemy emissary, as our infantry officers boasted of doing at the west caves, "Get back in there and fight it out, you sons of bitches."

A long line of such incidents parades before my mind: the story of our Marines firing on unarmed Japanese survivors who swam ashore on the beach at Midway; the accounts of our machine-gunning prisoners on a Hollandia airstrip; of the Australians pushing captured Japanese soldiers out of the transport planes which were taking them south over the New Guinea mountains ("the Aussies reported them as committing hara-kiri or 'resisting' "); of the shinbones cut, for letter openers and pen trays, from newly killed Japanese bodies on Noemfoor; of the young pilot who was "going to cream that Jap hospital one of these days"; of American soldiers poking through the mouths of Japanese corpses for gold-filled teeth ("the infantry's favorite occupation"); of Jap heads buried in ant-hills "to get them clean for souvenirs"; of bodies bulldozed to the road-side and dumped by the hundreds into shallow, unmarked graves ("where they're so close we can't stand 'em, we have to bury 'em"); of pictures of Mussolini and his mistress hung by the feet in an Italian city, to the approval of thousands of Americans who claim to stand for high, civilized ideals. As far back as one can go in history, these atrocities have been going on, not only in Germany with its Dachaus and its Buchenwalds and its Camp Doras, but in Russia, in the Pacific, in the riotings and lynchings at home, in the less-publicized uprisings in Central and South America, the cruelties of China, a few years ago in Spain, in pogroms of the past, the burning of witches in New England, tearing people apart on the English racks, burnings at the stake for the benefit of Christ and God.

I look down at the pit of ashes ("twenty-five thousand in a year and a half"). This, I realize, is not a thing confined to any nation or to any people. What the German has done to the Jew in Europe, we are doing to the Jap in the Pacific. As Germans have defiled themselves by dumping the ashes of human beings into this pit, we have defiled ourselves by bulldozing bodies into shallow, unmarked tropical graves. What is barbaric on one side of the earth is still barbaric on the other. "Judge not that ye be not judged." It is not the Germans alone, or the Japs, but the men of all nations to whom this war has brought shame and degradation.

We drive back down the hillside, past the open, barbed-wire gate, through Camp Dora, and into the underground tunnels of the factory. The walls of the tunnel are simply the rough uneven rock left from the blasting, whitewashed to reflect light. There is even more machinery at this end than there was at the other; and at this end, the V-1's and V-2's were being built, hundreds of them on assembly lines. We spent two or three hours walking through the tunnels and inspecting machinery and parts.

Started for Bad Schwalbach in the afternoon, taking turns at the wheel. Arrived in time for supper with naval officers and technicians. A heaping meal: large pork chop, potatoes, gravy, corn, beets, soup, bread and butter, jam, coffee, cream and sugar, pineapple dessert, Rhine wine—passed twice. I cannot keep my mind from those starved prisoners at Nordhausen and the hungry German children in the city's streets.

I "liberated" the book of *Niederdeutsche Madonnen* for Anne this evening. The naval officers at Villa Lily gave it to me. I had been trying to find someone from whom I could buy it, but "it belonged to the German government. There is no one who can sell it to you—except Hitler. You can pay him if you can find him."

The speedometer reading on our jeep shows that we covered 1,740 miles since we left here on June 1.

Wednesday, June 13

Drove to airport in the afternoon past a garbage dump, where probably two dozen Germans were picking over the filth, looking for food. Communication with Paris is poor. No one knows when our plane is due in, or even whether it has left Paris. We wait. There is the usual confusion and uncertainty. Finally we get on board a C-47 and off the field at 1618 with twenty-one other passengers. Landed Villacoublay at 1828. No transportation available on field. Long wait for Navy truck sent out from Paris.

Thursday, June 14

To Navy building for conferences and to turn in equipment. Conference with Captain Hoffman and others in regard to trip. To Hôtel Monceau for lunch with Captain Hoffman.

Back to Navy building in the afternoon. Commander Marchand told me that on one of his trips he had managed to get about fifteen miles across the lines into Russian-occupied territory (using various methods, one of which included getting a Russian officer drunk). There were many Germans walking eastward along the roads, he said, probably for use as "slave" labor in Russia. These Germans were apparently supposed to stay on one side of the road, Marchand felt, because at one point he saw a German officer walk across to the other side, whereupon a Russian guard walked up to him and, without saying a word, struck the German in the face with the butt of his rifle. When Marchand last saw him, the German officer was lying where he fell, face covered with blood, and apparently unconscious.

Marchand said the Russians shoot anyone they see trying to cross the river into American-held territory—except with proper papers and at authorized crossing points. Numerous bodies are lying on the riverbanks, he said. He had seen in one place the machine-gunned body of a little girl of about seven years.

There are crowds of people around the Arc de Triomphe and along the Champs-Élysées—waiting for the Eisenhower parade. It has been difficult—impossible at times—to get back and forth between the Navy building and the Monceau. Naval Technical Mission Europe offices overlook the Arc across the lower buildings in between. Uniformed French police with rifles stand on the rooftops to keep snipers from shooting at some hated high official down below.

Short walk along the Champs-Élysées in the later afternoon. Attended a rather hectic cocktail party at Commander MacDonald's[20] invitation later, and then had supper with him and several French people who were his guests. I asked one of the French aviation officers about Saint-Exupéry. He replied that Saint-Exupéry had taken off from Corsica in a Lockheed Lightning (P-38) for a 30,000-foot photo-reconnaissance mission over the French-Italian border. From this mission he never returned.

20. Commander Donald J. MacDonald, brother of Colonel Charles H. MacDonald of the 475th Fighter Group, with which Lindbergh flew in the Pacific.

The officer thought that he possibly ran out of fuel on his way back to Corsica.

At the cocktail party there was much outspoken bitterness toward the Germans and the frequently expressed desire to make them pay and suffer for their crimes. Against the French bitterness Commander Mac-Donald was always bringing arguments for tolerance and saying that our own skirts were far from clean. His war record and his decorations prevented those present from giving him the condemnation that most people expressing his viewpoint would have received.

Friday, June 15

Walked to American Embassy at 2:00 for a short conference with Ambassador Caffery in regard to the effect of Russian radio propaganda on German scientists and engineers, and steps which might be taken to combat it. Rest of afternoon on arrangements for trip home.

ACKNOWLEDGMENTS

I am deeply grateful to my wife, Anne Morrow Lindbergh, and to my friend William Jovanovich for invaluable advice and assistance in cutting my journal manuscript to readable quality and size; also to Ethel Cunningham, associate editor of Harcourt Brace Jovanovich, Inc., for her extraordinary perception and months of dedicated effort in the editing and research required to bring the original manuscript through its various intervening stages to final form. I am greatly indebted to Roberta Leighton, managing editor, and Helen Mills, art director, of the Harcourt Brace Jovanovich Trade Department, for skillful editorial assistance and advice.

Additionally, I want to record my appreciation for data and information supplied by the following organizations and individuals:

American Institute of Aeronautics and Astronautics, Inc.; Czechoslovakia News Agency; Department of State, Historical Studies Division; Ford Motor Company, News Department; French Embassy, Information Division; General Services Administration, National Archives and Records Division; Institut für Zeitgeschichte, Munich; Lufthansa German Airlines, Public Relations Department; Mayo Clinic; McGuire Air Force Base; Minnesota Historical Society; Missouri Historical Society; National Aeronautics and Space Administration, Marshall Space Flight Center; Naval Historical Foundation; Pan American World Airways; Secretary of the Air Force, Office of Information, New York; Trans World Airlines; United Aircraft Corporation; United States Marine Corps, Information Office, New York; Wright-Patterson Air Force Base, Air Force Museum; Yale University, Sterling Memorial Library; John G. Borger; George R. Brooks; Lieut. M. J. Collet; Edwin S. Costrell; Karol Dlouhy; Father Joseph T. Durkin, S.J.; C.M.Sgt. Francis C. Fini; Royal D. Frey; Russell Fridley; Esther Goddard; Grace M. Grant; Sanford B. Kauffman; Admiral Emory S. Land; Capt. W. Waldo Lynch; Josiah Macy, Jr.; Erich W. Neubert; Judith A. Schiff; Col. Richard S. Stark; T.Sgt. Douglas W. Stephens.

ACKNOWLEDGMENTS

The journal entries in this book are exactly as they are in my original handwritten pages, except that spelling has been corrected, punctuation revised in places, and the daily date headings standardized in form. In cutting the journals down to single-volume size no rewriting has been done.

CHARLES A. LINDBERGH

GLOSSARY

Technical Terms

AFTERBURNING   The burning of additional fuel in the gases of a jet engine after they have passed through the regular combustion chamber, thereby increasing thrust.

AILERON   A hinged or pivoted control surface, usually forming an outer portion of a wing and including the trailing edge. Used to raise or lower a wing in relation to the longitudinal axis of the aircraft, as in banking.

AIRFOIL   Any surface of an aircraft, such as a wing, stabilizer, or rudder, designed to produce a reaction from the air stream.

AIR-SCOOP COOLER   A cooling device involving a scoop that takes air from the air stream for transmission past the heat-radiating surfaces.

ALTITUDE ROCKET GLIDER   A rocket-propelled glider designed for operation at high altitude.

AMBIENT READINGS (MAGNETO)   Readings of related instruments taken when the magneto is not pressurized.

AMMETER   An instrument that measures electric current in amperes.

ARMOR PLATE   Plate or plates, usually of hard steel, installed to protect personnel and vital parts of a military aircraft from enemy fire.

AUTOMATIC PILOT   A mechanism involving gyroscopes that is automatically able to keep an aircraft in a set flight condition, i.e., on a set course at a set altitude.

BANK   To tilt and turn a plane.

BARREL ROLL   A fast roll executed by quick movements of the controls, also called a snap roll. The stick is pulled back sharply while full rudder is applied in the direction in which the roll is desired. The plane makes a complete revolution about its longitudinal axis without changing its course.

BENDIX BOTTOM TURRET   A gun turret at the bottom of the fuselage, built by Bendix.

BLOW THE TAIL AROUND   To use the propellor air blast while manipulating the rudder and elevators in order to turn an airplane into the desired direction while on the ground.

BOMB BAY   A bomb-carrying area in the fuselage.

BOOM FLUTTER   A shaking of the booms in flight, involving resonance.

BOOMS, TWIN   Two similar spars or outriggers supporting the tail surfaces of an airplane, such as the P-38.

BOSCH MAGS   Magnetos built by Bosch. A magneto is a device containing a rotating element that generates high-voltage alternating current to provide the ignition spark in many piston engines.

BOUNDARY-LAYER CONTROL   The control of a thin layer of air next to and passing over an airfoil, with the object of improving aerodynamic effects.

BUILT-UP (B-24)   A completely assembled airplane.

CAGE   To lock (i.e., a gyroscope) in a fixed position.

CARBON DIOXIDE INFLATION BOTTLE   A small steel cylinder for holding carbon dioxide (CO_2) under pressure. Used for inflating life rafts, escape chutes, etc.

CENTER WING   The central section of a complete wing.

CHECK PILOT   A pilot whose mission is to ride in the cockpit with, and observe and comment on the proficiency of, the pilot flying the plane.

COMBAT SWITCH   An electric switch used to ready a combat system (i.e., machine guns and sights) for instant action.

COMPRESSIBILITY DIVE   A dive in which the air stream exceeds the speed of sound relative to a passing surface, thereby causing the compressibility phenomenon with abnormal pressure changes on the surfaces of an airplane designed for subsonic flight.

COMPRESSIBILITY LIMIT   Air speed beyond which compressibility phenomena take place.

COMPRESSIBILITY SHUDDER   A shaking of the plane caused by compressibility effects, as in a dive approaching the speed of sound.

CONTROL CABLES   Metal cables leading from control levers (or actuating mechanism) to control surfaces, or interconnecting control surfaces.

CONTROLLABLE PITCH PROPELLER   A propeller so constructed that the pitch of its blades can be changed during rotation.

COWLING   A covering (metal, wood, plastic, etc.) placed around an engine or other component, usually to streamline and reduce drag.

DEAD-STICK LANDING   A landing made by an airplane after its propeller, or propellers, have been stationary or have not exerted thrust during descent.

DIRECTIONAL GYRO   A flight instrument containing a gyroscope that holds and indicates a set direction measured in degrees, clockwise from north.

DRAGGING THE FIELD   Flying over a field at very low altitude in order to study the surface and observe any factors of importance, usually prior to landing.

DROP-TANKS   Fuel tanks, so attached below the wings or fuselage that they can be dropped during flight. Used to increase range. They are dropped when additional performance is required, as in entering combat.

DURALUMIN STAMPINGS   Shaped parts, as in a wing or engine, made by stamping Duralumin (an alloy of aluminum).

ELEVATOR TAB   A small control surface that is part of or attached to an elevator.

ENGINE SURGING   A rhythmic increase and decrease of r.p.m. and power.

FAIRING STRIP (AILERON)   A narrow strip of sheet metal covering the gap between the wing and aileron, to reduce drag.

FEATHER   To change the pitch of a propeller so that a line through the leading and trailing edge of each blade is approximately parallel to the line of flight. When one engine of a multiengine plane is shut down in flight, its propeller is usually feathered to minimize air resistance and to keep the engine from turning.

FINS (ENGINE)   Metal flanges that protrude outwardly from air-cooled engine cylinders. They conduct heat from cylinder walls and transmit it to the passing air.

FIREWALL   A wall of fire-resistant material used to separate an engine compartment from the rest of the aircraft. Its purpose is to keep any engine fire confined. The term "to the firewall" (originating from flying early single-engine tractor airplanes) is sometimes used to mean full forward, or wide open, such as "pushing the throttle to the firewall."

FIRST-ELEMENT PLANES   Planes of the leading group (element).

FLAP   A hinged or extendable surface at the rear of an airfoil such as a wing. Extended flaps increase lift and decrease speed. Also applied to hinged surfaces of various usage.

FLASH RUN   A short and incomplete test under prescribed conditions, usually made to obtain indicative information for application to future testing.

FLETTNER SYSTEM   A system of trim tabs or servo tabs, originating from the name of the German engineer Anton Flettner.

FLIPPERS   A colloquial term for elevators—horizontal control surfaces at the tail of a plane.

FLOAT PLANE   An airplane equipped with one or more pontoons for operation from water.

1004

FLYING WING   A monoplane without a conventional fuselage, which carries passengers and/or cargo within the wing itself.

FUEL INJECTION   The forced introduction of fuel into an engine, usually in liquid state.

GLIDING ANGLE   The angle between the glide path and the horizontal. The angle below the horizontal at which a plane can travel the maximum distance through the air without using engine thrust.

GRAB DIVE   A dive to test ailerons for grabbing (the tendency to increase deflection and put reverse forces on the pilot's stick).

GROMMET   A ring (metal, plastic, cord, etc.) used to reinforce a fabric where it is to be attached to something, such as a rope.

GROUND LOOP   An uncontrollable swerve, or turn, of an airplane moving on the ground, usually during the landing roll.

GYRO   Contraction for gyroscope. A wheel, disc, or other form that can be rotated at high speed around its axis, thereby resisting any angular displacement of the axis and, through proper gimbaling, making available a stable reference direction.

HIGH SIDE   A diving attack or simulated attack on the side of an aerial target.

HOOK (A WING)   To strike some object, such as the ground or another plane, with a wing tip.

HORIZON (GYROSCOPIC)   An instrument containing a gyroscope connected to an indicator that informs the pilot of the position of his plane in relation to the natural horizon, thereby making reference to the natural horizon unnecessary.

HYDRAULIC SYSTEM   A system actuated by liquid under pressure, i.e., brakes, landing gear, flaps, control surfaces.

IFF   A radar beacon used in identifying an aircraft. "Identification, friend or foe."

IMMELMANN   A half loop followed by a half roll, reversing the direction of flight and gaining altitude.

IN-LINE ENGINE   An engine having its cylinders arranged in one or more straight rows.

INTERCOOLER FLAPS   Flaps controlling the flow of air through an intercooler radiator.

INVERTER   A device for converting direct current into alternating current.

JUMP BOTTLE   A small steel cylinder containing oxygen under pressure. Used to supply oxygen for breathing during a parachute descent at high altitude.

KNOCK-DOWN (B-24)   Subassemblies, including nose section, center section, tail section, wing sections, etc., to be trucked elsewhere for final assembly into the complete airplane.

LANDING BREAKUP   The breakup of a formation of aircraft prior to landing.

LANDING-GEAR STRUTS   Structural members of wood or metal that support the fuselage, wings, etc., above the wheel, pontoon, or ski assembly.

LINK TRAINER   An airplane simulator built by Link Aviation, Inc. Used in training pilots, for instrument flying especially.

LOOP   A controlled maneuver in which an airplane describes an approximate circle in a vertical plane. In a normal loop, the airplane successively climbs, flies upside down, dives, and returns to normal flight in the original direction.

LORIN RAM JET   A type of ram-jet engine named after René Lorin, French military engineer. A ram jet is basically an open tube without a compressor or turbine. Air is rammed into the tube (engine) by the forward movement of the plane it powers. Fuel is injected into the compressed air, and burning is continuous.

LOW SIDE   A climbing attack or simulated attack on the side of an aerial target.

MAGNESIUM CLUSTERS   Clusters of magnesium bombs used (often together with high explosives) to cause fires in the target area.

MONOSPAR WING   A wing with only one spar, or beam, to support the remaining wing structure, surface, and attachments.

NACELLE   A streamlined enclosure, i.e., for housing an engine and accessories.

OFFSET SHAFT-DRIVEN PROPELLER   A propeller with its shaft not in line with the shaft of the engine turning it, and connected to the engine through shafting.

OLEO TRAVEL   Distance of movement between the two elements of an oleo shock-absorbing system.

OPEN-TYPE SIGHT   A notched rear gunsight.

OVERTURN (AN AIRSTRIP)   To extend an approaching airplane's turn (as from base leg) beyond the line-up with the airstrip, either through pilot error or in order to gain time before touching down. Often done to increase the interval between the plane overturning and a plane ahead in the landing pattern.

OXYGEN CYLINDER   A steel cylinder for containing oxygen under pressure.

PAYLOAD   The load an aircraft can, is licensed to, or does carry in addition to fuel, crew, and other basic items required for a stipulated flight. The revenue producing load. Passengers, freight, bombs, etc., are payload.

PEEL OFF   To bank away suddenly from a formation of aircraft.

PIGGYBACK LAUNCHING   The launching of an airplane that has been rigidly attached above or below another airplane.

PIPPER   Slang for a gunsight.

PITCH (PROPELLER)   The angle a propeller blade forms at a designated point with the plane of rotation.

PROPELLER GOVERNOR   A device that automatically controls the revolutions per minute of a propeller (by changing the pitch).

RADIAL ENGINE   An engine with stationary cylinders arranged like the spokes of a wheel around a common crankshaft.

RADIO-BEAM (FLYING)   Following a radio beam that is formed by two narrow, overlapping bands of directional radio signals. In the area of overlap the pilot hears only a low monotone. If he leaves the overlap area, a characteristic change of sound—an "a" (dot-dash) or an "n" (dash-dot)—tells him which way he is deviating from the beam.

RED ALERT   Designation of the warning issued to be, or the condition of being, ready for immediate enemy attack.

ROLL   A maneuver in which an airplane makes a complete revolution around its longitudinal axis, ending without change of the original direction of flight.

ROUNDHOUSE   A diving tail attack, begun from a half roll after a head-on approach from higher altitude.

RUDDER FORCE   The force exerted by the air stream on the rudder and, therefore, on the pilot's rudder pedal.

SEQUENCE VALVE   A valve that automatically opens or shuts in relation to a preceding condition.

SEXTANT   An instrument for measuring the angle above the natural horizon of a celestial body in relation to the observer's position.

SHAKEDOWN FLIGHT   A flight of a new or overhauled aircraft for the purpose of either establishing its satisfactory condition or discovering (and later rectifying) any malfunctioning elements and/or unsatisfactory characteristics.

SHIMMY   Abnormal vibration involving resonance.

SHOTGUN STARTER   A device in which a shotgunlike shell is fired to create expanding gases that turn the engine over.

SIDESLIP   A sideward and downward movement of an airplane, achieved (in controlled flight) by using rudder opposite to aileron and to the bank.

SINGLE-ENGINE CEILING   The maximum altitude a multiengine plane can maintain while using only one engine (absolute ceiling) and still be capable of a stipulated rate of climb (service ceiling).

SKIN   The outside covering of a wing, fuselage, etc., i.e., treated cloth, plywood, Duralumin, steel.

SLICKED-UP PLANE   An airplane with unusual refinements added to improve performance and/or appearance.

SLOW ROLL   A roll around the longitudinal axis, executed by action of the ailerons. The rudder and elevators are used only to maintain direction. Also called AILERON ROLL.

SPAR   A main, generally lateral, structural member of a wing, stabilizer, etc.

SPERRY A-5 AUTOMATIC PILOT   A device, manufactured by the Sperry Gyroscope Company, involving a gyroscope or gyroscopes capable of indirectly activating the controls of an aircraft to maintain a set condition of flight without assistance from the pilot.

SPIN IN   To crash into the ground while in a tailspin.

SPINNER CAP   A conical or rounded fairing fitted over the hub of a propeller and rotating with the propeller. Also called SPINNER.

STALL   The condition of an airplane when its wings lose lift and sometimes controllability because of insufficient air speed.

STATIC THRUST   The thrust exerted by an engine, by means of a propeller or jet, when stationary.

STICK CONTROL   The control of elevators and ailerons through a sticklike lever (operated by the pilot) in the cockpit.

STRINGER FLANGE   The bent-over edge of a stringer (a secondary member in aircraft structure, often used to reinforce the skin of a fuselage or wing).

STRING FORMATION   A highly flexible formation of aircraft flying one behind the other, usually at wide intervals to allow maneuverability.

SUPERCHARGER   A compressor for forcing additional air or fuel mixture into an engine. Essential for operation at high altitude.

TACHOMETER   An instrument that indicates the revolutions per minute of a turning shaft, such as the crankshaft of an engine.

TOW PLANE   An airplane used to tow a glider or a target.

TOW TARGET   A tubular cloth sleeve, or a flat banner, towed by an airplane and used as a target for the guns of another plane, or for ground guns.

TRACER BULLET   A bullet that emits smoke or flame to make its path visible and permit correction of aim.

TRACK LAUNCHING   The launching of an aircraft from a carriage moving along a track, such as a railroad track.

TRICYCLE LANDING GEAR   A three-wheel (or wheel assembly) landing gear in which the minor wheel (or assembly) is forward and the two major wheels (or assemblies) are aft of the plane's center of gravity.

TRIM   To adjust the surfaces or auxiliary surfaces of an aircraft (or the tensions applied to them) in order to improve balance in flight.

TURBO, CAST   A turbosupercharger with a cast rotor.

TURBO, FORGED   A turbosupercharger with a forged rotor.

TURBOSUPERCHARGER   A supercharger in which the turbine is actuated by engine-exhaust gases.

TURNBUCKLE   A device used to adjust the length of rods or cables. A form frequently used consists of a metal sleeve with a right-hand thread at one end and a left-hand thread at the other, working on rods appropriately threaded.

TWO-PLACE PLANE   An airplane having seats for two people.

TWO-POINT LANDING   A landing during which the two main wheels, wheel assemblies, or skis touch the landing surface well in advance of the tail wheel or skid; therefore, a relatively fast landing. (Non-tricycle-type aircraft.)

TWO-STAGE SUPERCHARGING   Increasing the supply of air or fuel mixture to an engine in two stages, often by a turbosupercharger forcing air through the carburetor and an internal supercharger forcing the already compressed fuel mixture into the cylinders.

UNDER THE HOOD FLYING   Piloting an airplane when a hood or other device prevents any outside visual reference, forcing the pilot to depend entirely on his instruments. Flying under the hood is a method of training in instrument-flying technique.

VOLTMETER   An instrument for measuring and indicating differences of potential of an electric circuit.

WATER-INJECTION SYSTEM   A system for injecting water into the fuel mixture of an engine. Used to obtain greater power for take-off or during a critical condition in combat.

WAVE OFF   To signal a pilot approaching for a landing not to land on that approach.

WHEEL CONTROL   The control of elevators and ailerons through a wheel or semi-wheel (capable of fore-and-aft as well as laterally circular motion, and operated by the pilot) in the cockpit.

WHEEL STREAMLINE   A reinforced sheetlike section that (i.e., in the P-47) closes after the wheel has reached its retracted position, thereafter forming part of the bottom surface of the wing.

WING OVER   A maneuver in which the plane reverses direction after a steep climbing turn near the end of which the nose drops into a dive.

Aircraft

A-20, AIR FORCE ATTACK BOMBER   Twin-engine, mid-wing monoplane. Crew of two to three. Maximum speed at altitude: about 325 m.p.h. Service ceiling: about 25,000 feet (1944). Douglas Aircraft Company.

AIRACUDA, AIR FORCE XFM-I EXPERIMENTAL   Twin-engine, low-wing monoplane. Accommodation for a crew of five (1939). Bell Aircraft Corporation.

AMIOT, BOMBER (FRANCE)   Twin-engine, high-wing monoplane. Crew of four. Maximum speed at altitude: about 300 m.p.h. Service ceiling: about 30,000 feet (1939). Avions Amiot (Société d'Emboutissage et de Constructions Méchaniques).

AR-234, LUFTWAFFE BOMBER   Twin-jet, high-wing monoplane. Crew of one. Maximum speed at altitude: about 470 m.p.h. Service ceiling: about 37,000 feet (1944). Arado Flugzeugwerke G.m.b.h.

B-17, FLYING FORTRESS, BOMBER   Four-engine, mid-wing monoplane. Crew of six to ten. Maximum speed at altitude: about 300 m.p.h. Service ceiling: about 35,000 feet (1944). Boeing Aircraft Company.

B-24, LIBERATOR, BOMBER   Four-engine, high-wing monoplane. Crew of seven to ten. Maximum speed at altitude: about 300 m.p.h. Service ceiling: about 28,000 feet (1944). Consolidated Vultee Aircraft Corporation; also Ford Motor Company.

B-25, MITCHELL, AIR FORCE BOMBER   Twin-engine, mid-wing monoplane. Crew of four to six. Maximum speed at altitude: about 290 m.p.h. Service ceiling: about 24,000 feet (1944). North American Aviation, Inc.

B-26, MARAUDER, AIR FORCE BOMBER   Twin-engine, high-wing monoplane. Crew of seven. Maximum speed: about 290 m.p.h. Service ceiling: about 20,000 feet (1944). Glenn L. Martin Company.

B-34, VENTURA, AIR FORCE PATROL BOMBER   Twin-engine, mid-wing monoplane. Crew of four. Maximum speed: about 300 m.p.h. Service ceiling: about 25,000 feet (1944). Lockheed Aircraft Corporation.

BLENHEIM, R.A.F. BOMBER   Twin-engine, mid-wing monoplane. Crew of three. Maximum speed at altitude: about 275 m.p.h. Service ceiling: about 27,000 feet (1939). Bristol Aeroplane Company.

BRÉGUET 690, BOMBER (FRANCE)   Twin-engine, mid-wing monoplane. Crew of three. Maximum speed at altitude: about 300 m.p.h. (1939). Société Anonyme des Ateliers d'Aviation Louis Bréguet.

C-47, DAKOTA, AIR FORCE TRANSPORT (NAVY R4D; COMMERCIAL DC-3)   Twin-engine, low-wing monoplane. Cockpit crew of two. Maximum speed: about 210 m.p.h. (1944). Service ceiling: about 22,000 feet. Douglas Aircraft Company, Inc.

C-54, AIR FORCE TRANSPORT (COMMERCIAL DC-4; NAVY R5D) Four-engine, low-wing monoplane. Cockpit crew of three. Maximum speed: about 280 m.p.h. Service ceiling: about 25,000 feet (1944). Douglas Aircraft Company, Inc.

CANUCK A Canadian training plane, a modification of the Curtiss JN4 (Jenny), with lighter construction and somewhat higher performance.

DC-5, COMMERCIAL TRANSPORT Twin-engine, high-wing monoplane. Cockpit crew of three. Accommodations for sixteen to twenty-two passengers. Maximum speed: about 230 m.p.h. Service ceiling: about 23,000 feet. Douglas Aircraft Company, Inc.

DH-4, DE HAVILAND, U.S. ARMY OBSERVATION PLANE Single-engine biplane. Crew of two. Maximum speed: about 120 m.p.h. Also converted to an airmail transport with a crew of one (1925).

DO-17, LUFTWAFFE BOMBER Twin-engine, mid-wing monoplane. Crew of three to four. Maximum speed at altitude: about 270 m.p.h. Service ceiling: about 28,000 feet (1939). Dornier-Werke G.m.b.h.

F4U, CORSAIR, NAVY FIGHTER AND DIVE BOMBER Single-engine, low-gull-wing monoplane. Crew of one. Maximum speed at altitude: about 420 m.p.h. Service ceiling: about 40,000 feet (1944). Chance Vought Aircraft Division of United Aircraft Corporation.

F6F, HELLCAT, NAVY FIGHTER Single-engine, mid-wing monoplane. Crew of one. Maximum speed at altitude: about 400 m.p.h. Service ceiling: about 38,000 feet (1944). Grumman Aircraft Engineering Corporation.

FORD TRI-MOTOR, COMMERCIAL TRANSPORT Three-engine, high-wing, all-metal monoplane. Cockpit crew of two. Twelve to fifteen passengers. Maximum speed: about 130 m.p.h. Service ceiling: about 18,000 feet (1930). Stout Metal Airplane Division of the Ford Motor Company.

FW-189, LUFTWAFFE, RECONNAISSANCE OR GROUND ATTACK Twin-engine, low-wing monoplane. Crew of three. Maximum speed at altitude: about 220 m.p.h. Service ceiling: about 27,000 feet (1940). Focke-Wulf Flugzeugbau G.m.b.h.

FW-190, LUFTWAFFE FIGHTER Single-engine, low-wing monoplane. Crew of one. Maximum speed at altitude: about 400 m.p.h. Service ceiling: about 35,000 feet (1944). Focke-Wulf Flugzeugbau G.m.b.h.

FW-200, CONDOR, TRANSPORT Four-engine, low-wing monoplane. Cockpit crew of three. Twenty-six passengers. Cruising speed: about 200 m.p.h. Service ceiling: about 20,000 feet (1939). Focke-Wulf Flugzeugbau G.m.b.h.

GRUMMAN AMPHIBIAN (COMMERCIAL VERSION OF NAVY JRF) Twin-engine, high-wing monoplane. Cockpit crew of two. Maximum speed: about 200 m.p.h. Service ceiling: about 20,000 feet. Grumman Aircraft Engineering Corporation.

HE-111, LUFTWAFFE BOMBER Twin-engine, low-wing monoplane. Crew of four. Maximum speed at altitude: about 275 m.p.h. Service ceiling: about 24,000 feet (1939). Ernst Heinkel Flugzeugwerke G.m.b.h.

HE-162, VOLKSJÄGER, LUFTWAFFE INTERCEPTOR FIGHTER Sometimes referred to as the Ju-162. Single-jet, high-wing monoplane. Crew of one. Maximum speed at altitude: about 510 m.p.h. Service ceiling: about 40,000 feet (1944). Ernst Heinkel A.G.

HENLEY, R.A.F. BOMBER Single-engine, low-wing monoplane. Crew of two. Maximum speed at altitude: about 272 m.p.h. Service ceiling: about 27,000 feet (1939). Hawker Aircraft, Ltd.

HURRICANE, R.A.F. FIGHTER Single-engine, low-wing monoplane, pilot only. Maximum speed at altitude: about 335 m.p.h. Service ceiling: about 34,000 feet (1939). Hawker Aircraft, Ltd.

JM-1, NAVY TOW-TARGET AND GENERAL UTILITY PLANE Stripped version of the Air Force B-26 (1944). Glenn L. Martin Company.

JN4-D, JENNY, ARMY TRAINER Single-engine biplane. Crew of two. Maximum speed: about 75 m.p.h. (1923). Curtiss Aeroplane and Motors Corporation.

JRB, EXPEDITOR, NAVY TRANSPORT   Twin-engine, low-wing monoplane. Cockpit crew of two. Six passengers. Maximum speed: about 220 m.p.h. Service ceiling: about 25,000 feet (1944). Beech Aircraft Corporation.

JRF, GOOSE, NAVY AMPHIBIAN   Twin-engine, high-wing monoplane. Cockpit crew of two. Maximum speed: about 200 m.p.h. Service ceiling: about 20,000 feet (1944). Grumman Aircraft Engineering Corporation.

JRM-I, MARS, NAVY TRANSPORT (FLYING BOAT)   Four-engine, high-wing monoplane. Normal crew of eleven. Maximum speed: about 210 m.p.h. (1944). Glenn L. Martin Company.

JU-52, TRANSPORT   Three-engine, low-wing monoplane. Cockpit crew of two. Sixteen passengers. Cruising speed: about 150 m.p.h. (1939). Junkers Flugzeug und Motorenwerke, A.-G.

JU-86, LUFTWAFFE BOMBER   Twin-engine, low-wing monoplane. Crew of four. Maximum speed: about 225 m.p.h. (1939). Junkers Flugzeug und Motorenwerke, A.-G.

JU-87, STUKA, LUFTWAFFE DIVE BOMBER   Single-engine, low-wing monoplane. Crew of two. Maximum speed: about 240 m.p.h. Service ceiling: about 23,000 feet (1939). Junkers Flugzeug und Motorenwerke, A.-G.

JU-88, LUFTWAFFE BOMBER   Twin-engine, low-wing monoplane. Crew of four. Maximum speed at altitude: about 300 m.p.h. (1944). Junkers Flugzeug und Motorenwerke, A.-G.

JU-263, LUFTWAFFE INTERCEPTOR FIGHTER   Single liquid-rocket (with auxiliary combustion chamber), mid-wing monoplane. Crew of one. Maximum speed at altitude: about 590 m.p.h. (1945). Junkers Flugzeug und Motorenwerke, A.-G.

L-5, SENTINEL, AIR FORCE OBSERVATION AND LIAISON PLANE   Single-engine, high-wing monoplane. Crew of two. Maximum speed: about 130 m.p.h. Service ceiling: about 15,000 feet (1944). Stinson Aircraft Division of Consolidated Vultee Aircraft Corporation.

LANCASTER, R.A.F. BOMBER   Four-engine, mid-wing monoplane. Crew of seven. Maximum speed: about 270 m.p.h. (1944). A. V. Roe & Company, Ltd.

LINCOLN STANDARD TOURABOUT   A rebuilt World War I tractor-biplane training plane, with open tandem cockpits and a Hispano-Suiza engine of about 150 h.p. The pilot flew in the rear cockpit. The front cockpit could accommodate two passengers. Top speed about 90 m.p.h. Landing speed about 45 m.p.h. Nebraska Aircraft Corporation.

ME-109, LUFTWAFFE FIGHTER   Single-engine, low-wing monoplane. Crew of one. Maximum speed at altitude: about 350 m.p.h. Service ceiling: about 35,000 feet (1939). Maximum speed at altitude: about 420 m.p.h. (1944). Messerschmitt A.G.

ME-110, LUFTWAFFE FIGHTER   Twin-engine, low-wing monoplane. Crew of two. Maximum speed at altitude: about 360 m.p.h. (1940). Messerschmitt A.G.

ME-163, LUFTWAFFE INTERCEPTOR-FIGHTER   Sometimes referred to as the Ju-163. Single liquid-rocket, mid-wing monoplane. Crew of one. Maximum speed at altitude: about 550 m.p.h. (1945). Messerschmitt A.G.

ME-262, LUFTWAFFE FIGHTER   Twin-jet, low-wing monoplane. Crew of one. Maximum speed at altitude: about 525 m.p.h. Service ceiling: about 40,000 feet (1944). Messerschmitt A.G.

MOHAWK   Designed to Colonel Lindbergh's specifications. Single-engine, low-wing monoplane. Crew of two. Maximum speed: about 190 m.p.h. Landing speed: about 45 m.p.h. (1937). Phillips & Powis Aircraft, Ltd.

MONARCH   Single-engine, low-wing monoplane. Pilot and two passengers. Maximum speed: about 145 m.p.h. Absolute ceiling: about 20,000 feet (1938). Phillips & Powis Aircraft, Ltd.

MORANE, FRENCH FIGHTER   Single-engine, low-wing monoplane. Crew of one. Maximum speed: about 310 m.p.h. (1939). Aeroplanes Morane-Saulnier.

NC-4, NAVY FLYING BOAT   Three-engine biplane. Crew of six (for transatlantic flight). Maximum speed: about 85 m.p.h. (1919). Curtiss.

P-35, AIR FORCE FIGHTER   Single-engine, low-wing monoplane. Crew of one. Maximum speed at altitude: about 310 m.p.h. Service ceiling: about 30,000 feet (1939). Republic Aviation Corporation.

P-36, AIR FORCE FIGHTER   Single-engine, low-wing monoplane. Crew of one. Maximum speed at altitude: about 310 m.p.h. Service ceiling: about 31,000 feet (1939). Curtiss-Wright Corporation.

P-38, LIGHTNING, AIR FORCE FIGHTER   Twin-engine, mid-wing monoplane. Crew of one. Maximum speed: about 410 m.p.h. Service ceiling: about 36,000 feet (1944). Lockheed Aircraft Corporation.

P-39, AIRACOBRA, AIR FORCE FIGHTER   Single-engine, low-wing monoplane. Crew of one. Maximum speed at altitude: about 380 m.p.h. Service ceiling: about 35,000 feet (1944). Bell Aircraft Corporation.

P-40, WARHAWK, AIR FORCE FIGHTER   Single-engine, low-wing monoplane. Crew of one. Maximum speed at altitude: about 360 m.p.h. Service ceiling: about 33,000 feet (1944). Curtiss-Wright Corporation.

P-47, THUNDERBOLT, AIR FORCE FIGHTER   Single-engine, low-wing monoplane. Crew of one. Maximum speed at altitude: about 430 m.p.h. Service ceiling: about 40,000 feet (1944). Republic Aviation Corporation.

P-51, MUSTANG, AIR FORCE FIGHTER   Single-engine, low-wing monoplane. Crew of one. Maximum speed at altitude: about 450 m.p.h. Service ceiling: about 42,000 feet (1945). North American Aviation, Inc.

P-60 (XP-60), AIR FORCE FIGHTER   Experimental single-engine, low-wing monoplane. Curtiss-Wright Corporation.

P-61, BLACK WIDOW, AIR FORCE NIGHT FIGHTER   Twin-engine, high-wing monoplane. Crew of three. Maximum speed at altitude: about 370 m.p.h. Service ceiling: about 33,000 feet (1944). Northrop Aircraft, Inc.

PB2Y-3R, CORONADO, NAVY PATROL OR TRANSPORT FLYING BOAT   Four-engine, high-wing monoplane. Accommodates crew of ten. Maximum speed: about 190 m.p.h. (1944). Consolidated Vultee Aircraft Corporation.

PBJ, NAVY BOMBER   Navy designation for the Mitchell (Air Force B-25). North American Aviation, Inc.

PBM, MARINER, NAVY PATROL BOMBER OR TRANSPORT (FLYING BOAT)   Twin-engine, high-wing monoplane. Accommodates crew of seven. Maximum speed: about 200 m.p.h. (1944). Glenn L. Martin Company.

R4D, NAVY TRANSPORT (COMMERCIAL DC-3; AIR FORCE C-47; R.A.F. DAKOTA)   Twin-engine, low-wing monoplane. Cockpit crew of two. Maximum speed: about 210 m.p.h. Service ceiling: about 22,000 feet (1944). The Douglas Aircraft Company, Inc.

S-42, COMMERCIAL FLYING BOAT   Four-engine, high-wing monoplane. Cockpit crew of four. Thirty-two passengers. Maximum speed: about 190 m.p.h. Service ceiling: about 15,000 feet (1939). Sikorsky Aircraft Division of United Aircraft Corporation.

SE-5, ARMY FIGHTER   Single-engine biplane. Crew of one. Maximum speed: about 115 m.p.h. (1925).

SNJ, NAVY TRAINER (AIR FORCE AT-6 TRAINER)   Single-engine, low-wing monoplane. Crew of two. Maximum speed: about 200 m.p.h. Service ceiling: about 20,000 feet (1944). North American Aviation, Inc.

SPITFIRE, R.A.F. FIGHTER   Single-engine, low-wing monoplane, pilot only. Maximum speed at altitude: about 360 m.p.h. (1939). Maximum speed at altitude: about 420 m.p.h. (1944). Service ceiling: about 40,000 feet. Vickers-Armstrong, Ltd.

STORCH, LUFTWAFFE LIAISON PLANE   Three-place, single-engine, high-wing monoplane. Maximum speed: about 110 m.p.h. Landing speed: about 30 m.p.h. Service ceiling: about 17,000 feet (1939). Gerhard Fieseler Werke G.m.b.h.

TBF, AVENGER, NAVY TORPEDO BOMBER   Single-engine, mid-wing monoplane. Crew of three. Maximum speed: about 280 m.p.h. Service ceiling: about 22,000 feet (1944). Grumman Aircraft Engineering Corporation.

V-I, FLYING BOMB   Single pulse-jet, mid-wing monoplane. Crewless. Maximum speed: about 400 m.p.h. Ceiling: about 10,000 feet (1945).

V-2, ROCKET (EXPLOSIVE WARHEAD)   Crewless. Maximum speed: about 3,500 m.p.h. Maximum range: about 220 miles (1945).

VERVILLE-SPERRY RACER   Single-engine, low-wing monoplane. Crew of one. Maximum speed: about 190 m.p.h. (1923). Lawrence Sperry Aircraft Company.

VS-300, HELICOPTER (EXPERIMENTAL)   Single-engine, three-blade main rotor. Crew of one (1940). Chance Vought and Sikorsky Aircraft Division of United Aircraft Corporation.

WELLESLEY, R.A.F. BOMBER   Single-engine, low-wing monoplane. Crew of two. Maximum speed at altitude: about 230 m.p.h. Service ceiling: about 33,000 feet (1939). Vickers-Armstrong, Ltd.

WELLINGTON, R.A.F. BOMBER   Twin-engine, mid-wing monoplane. Crew of five. Maximum speed at altitude: about 270 m.p.h. Service ceiling: about 26,000 feet (1939). Vickers-Armstrong, Ltd.

XF5U   Experimental, twin-engine, circular (flying-wing) type monoplane. Maximum speed: about 420 m.p.h. Landing speed: about 30 m.p.h. Chance Vought Aircraft Division of United Aircraft Corporation.

ZERO, ANY JAPANESE FIGHTER (ZEKE, HAMP, TONY)   Single-engine, low-wing monoplane. Crew of one. Maximum speed at altitude: about 330 m.p.h. Service ceiling: about 35,000 feet (1944). Mitsubishi Jukogyo Kabushiki Kaisha (Zeke and Hamp).

INDEX

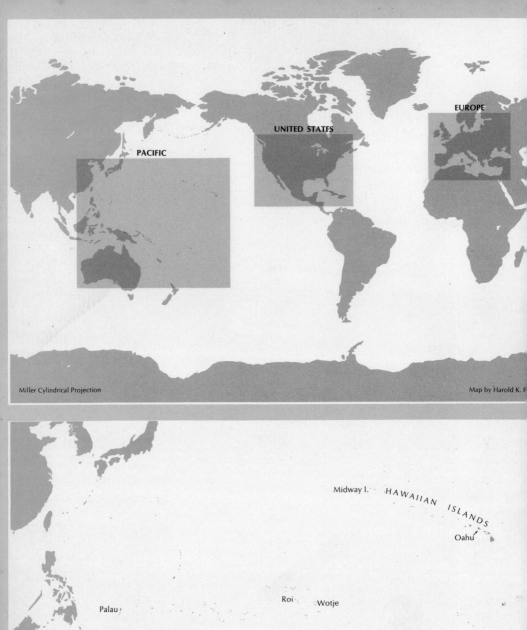

PACIFIC

UNITED STATFS

EUROPE

Miller Cylindrical Projection

Map by Harold K. F

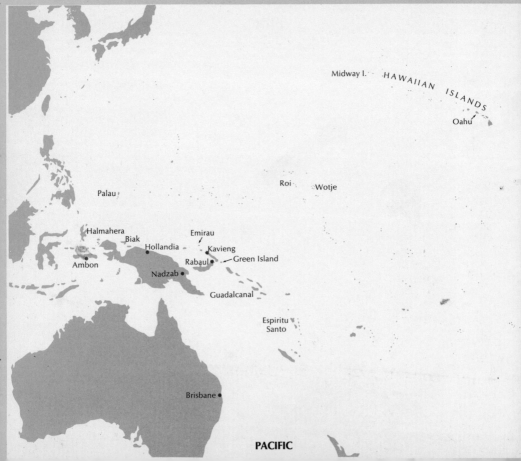

Midway I.

HAWAIIAN ISLANDS

Oahu

Roi

Wotje

Palau

Halmahera

Biak

Emirau

Hollandia

Kavieng

Ambon

Rabaul

Green Island

Nadzab

Guadalcanal

Espiritu
Santo

Brisbane

PACIFIC